D0516151

299

Cooking Light

five ★ star
recipes

Oxmoor
House®

Autumn Apple and Spinach
Salad, page 235

Cooking Light
five ★ star recipes

compiled and edited by

Heather Averett

Oxmoor House®

©2008 by Oxmoor House, Inc.
Book Division of Southern Progress Corporation
P.O. Box 2262, Birmingham, Alabama 35201-2262

All rights reserved. No part of this book may be reproduced in any form or by any means without the prior written permission of the publisher, excepting brief quotations in connection with reviews written specifically for inclusion in magazines or newspapers, or limited excerpts strictly for personal use.

ISBN-13: 978-0-8487-3242-4
ISBN-10: 0-8487-3242-1
Library of Congress Control Number: 2007941805

Printed in the United States of America
First printing 2008

Be sure to check with your health-care provider before making any changes in your diet.

Oxmoor House, Inc.
Editor in Chief: Nancy Fitzpatrick Wyatt
Executive Editor: Katherine M. Eakin
Art Director: Keith McPherson
Managing Editor: Allison Long Lowery

Cooking Light® Five Star Recipes
Editor: Heather Averett
Digital Production Editor: Julie Boston
Copy Chief: L. Amanda Owens
Copy Editor: Jacqueline Giovanelli
Editorial Assistant: Vanessa Rusch Thomas
Director, Test Kitchens: Elizabeth Tyler Austin
Assistant Director, Test Kitchens: Julie Christopher
Test Kitchens Professionals: Jane Chambliss;
    Kathleen Royal Phillips; Catherine Crowell Steele;
    Ashley T. Strickland; Kate M. Wheeler, R.D.
Photography Director: Jim Bathie
Senior Photo Stylist: Kay E. Clarke
Associate Photo Stylist: Katherine G. Eckert
Director of Production: Laura Lockhart
Senior Production Manager: Greg A. Amason
Production Manager: Terri Beste-Farley
Production Assistant: Faye Porter Bonner

Contributors
Designer: Carol Damsky
Copy Editor: Dolores Hydock
Indexer: Mary Ann Laurens
Editorial Assistants: Cory L. Bordonaro, Laura K. Womble
Interns: Tracey Apperson; Jill Baughman; Amy Edgerton;
    Amelia Heying; Ashley Leath; Erin Loudy; Caroline Markunas;
    Mary Katherine Pappas; Rachel Quinlivan, R.D.;
    Mary Catherine Shamblin; Lucas Whittington
Food Stylists: Ana Price Kelly, Debby Maugans
Photographers: Mark Gooch, Beau Gustafson, Lee Harrelson
Photo Stylists: Melanie J. Clarke, Lydia DeGaris-Pursell

To order additional publications, call 1-800-765-6400.

For more books to enrich your life, visit
oxmoorhouse.com

To search, savor, and share thousands of recipes, visit
myrecipes.com

Cover: *Fresh Lime Chiffon Cake* (page 386)
Back Cover (clockwise from top): *Chicken Scallopini* (page 196),
    Grilled Porterhouse Steak (page 132), *Jamaican Margaritas* (page 28),
    Watercress Salad with Blue Cheese and Praline (page 235),
    Flatbread with Pancetta and Asparagus (page 52)

Cooking Light®
Editor in Chief: Mary Kay Culpepper
Executive Editor: Billy R. Sims
Creative Director: Susan Waldrip Dendy
Managing Editor: Maelynn Cheung
Senior Food Editor: Alison Mann Ashton
Senior Editor: Phillip Rhodes
Projects Editor: Mary Simpson Creel, M.S., R.D.
Food Editor: Ann Taylor Pittman
Associate Food Editors: Timothy Q. Cebula;
    Kathy Kitchens Downie, R.D.; Julianna Grimes
Associate Editor: Cindy Hatcher
Assistant Editor: Brandy Rushing
Test Kitchens Director: Vanessa Taylor Johnson
Senior Food Stylist: Kellie Gerber Kelley
Food Stylist: M. Kathleen Kanen
Test Kitchens Professionals: Mary Drennen Ankar, SaBrina Bone,
    Kathryn Conrad, Eunice Mun, Tiffany Vickers, Mike Wilson
Assistant Art Director: Maya Metz Logue
Senior Designers: Fernande Bondarenko, J. Shay McNamee
Designer: Brigette Mayer
Senior Photographer: Randy Mayor
Senior Photo Stylist: Cindy Barr
Photo Stylists: Jan Gautro, Leigh Ann Ross
Studio Assistant: Hayden Patton
Copy Chief: Maria Parker Hopkins
Senior Copy Editor: Susan Roberts
Copy Editor: Johannah Gilman Paiva
Research Assistant: Michelle Gibson Daniels
Production Manager: Liz Rhoades
Production Editor: Hazel R. Eddins
Production Assistant: Lauri Short
Cookinglight.com Editor: Kim Cross
Administrative Coordinator: Carol D. Johnson
Office Manager: Rita A. Jackson
Editorial Assistant: Jason Horn
Interns: Heather Goff, Katy McNulty, Krysta Parsons

4

contents

welcome

When you consider that *Cooking Light* magazine has tested and published more than 15,000 recipes during the past 20 years, you can appreciate what a daunting task it has been to identify our five-star recipes. Compiling a list of only the best, most flavorful dishes worthy of a five-star rating was the easy part—narrowing it down to the top 500 required a little more effort.

Mary Kay Culpepper
Editor in Chief, *Cooking Light*

Ultimately it was only the most essential recipes proven tried-and-true time and time again by our food experts that made the cut. They're the recipes that our staff makes at home for their own families, and the ones that we simply couldn't live without. And with that in mind, you can cook with confidence. Our editors and test kitchens professionals are busy, creative, smart—in short, a lot like you, our readers. Also like you, they believe making something delicious and healthful for yourself and the people you care about is one of the most important things that you can do every day.

Each chapter in *Cooking Light Five Star Recipes* offers incredibly simple, fabulously delicious recipes, complete with our trademark nutritional analyses that will help ensure your meals are healthful. After all, eating smart, being fit, and living well are of the highest priority.

So whether you want to prepare a meal to entertain a crowd or just cook for your family, rest assure that whatever recipe you choose from this cookbook collection is worthy of five stars. Here's wishing you many five-star meals.

Mary Kay Culpepper

Staff Favorites

Memorable. That's the word that best describes the *Cooking Light* staff's favorite recipes. They're the recipes our readers keep calling and writing about, and the ones our staff whip up for their own family and friends. They're not always the ones that rated the highest, but they're the dishes that are definitely the most memorable. Here are just a few of our staff's best-of-the-best five-star recipes.

Oven-Roasted Tomatoes with Goat Cheese (page 10): The concentrated flavor of the tomatoes blends beautifully with aged balsamic vinegar and crumbled goat cheese.

Warm Asparagus Salad (page 250): Twice-baked garlicky breadcrumbs tossed in browned butter add a pleasant nuttiness that complements the garden-fresh flavor of the asparagus.

Spicy Shrimp Cakes with Corn and Avocado Salsa (page 21): Experiment with nontraditional party fare by serving these delightful starters. We promise your guests will love the spicy flavors and a change from the norm.

Asiago and Balsamic Caramelized Onion Focaccia (page 56): The combination of richly nutty Asiago cheese, pungently sweet balsamic vinegar, and delicately caramelized onions yields a perfect Italian bread.

Staff Favorites *(continued)*

Roasted Garlic, Poblano, and Red Pepper Guacamole (page 12): This must-try guacamole is both flavorful and unique, and just as perfect for enchilada night as for your next cookout.

Chocolate Soufflés with Pistachios (page 399): The delicate crunch of pistachios makes every bite of these rich chocolate soufflés even better than traditional chocolate soufflé.

Pappardelle with Tomatoes, Arugula, and Parmesan (page 265): Sweet tomatoes, peppery arugula, and sharp cheese are coated with a light dressing of lemon juice, garlic slivers, and olive oil.

Sautéed Scallops with Parsley and Garlic (page 93): The secret to perfectly browned scallops is a hot skillet and patience. Serve these simply seasoned scallops with gourmet greens.

Fudgy Mocha-Toffee Brownies (page 407): These bars are as yummy as anything you'll find in a bakery. They're welcome in a lunch box, as a weeknight dessert, or any time you need a sweet treat.

Chicken Tetrazzini (page 171): Making this family favorite is a great way to use leftover chicken or turkey. The recipe makes two casseroles, so you can feed a crowd or freeze one for a supereasy supper.

appetizers and beverages

Open-Faced Panini with Goat Cheese, Roasted
Peppers, and Spicy Olive Topping, page 17

Glazed Honey Nuts

Serve these nuts as a snack, or toss them into your favorite salad. Spreading the nuts on a baking sheet before they're completely cooled keeps them from clumping together.

  1 teaspoon salt
  ¼ teaspoon curry powder
  ¼ teaspoon ground red pepper
Cooking spray
  1 cup unsalted pecan halves
  1 cup unsalted walnut halves
  2 tablespoons honey

1. Combine first 3 ingredients.
2. Heat a large nonstick skillet over medium-high heat. Coat pan with cooking spray. Add pecans, walnuts, and honey. Cook 4 minutes or until nuts are toasted, stirring constantly. Sprinkle nuts evenly with spice mixture, tossing well to coat.
3. Spread nut mixture on a baking sheet coated with cooking spray. Cool completely. Store in an airtight container. Yield: 16 servings (serving size: 2 tablespoons).

CALORIES 96 (83% from fat); FAT 8.9g (sat 0.8g, mono 3.3g, poly 4.4g); PROTEIN 1.6g; CARB 4g; FIBER 1.1g; CHOL 0mg; IRON 0.4mg; SODIUM 146mg; CALC 11mg

Cinnamon-Sugar Popcorn

This simple snack can be made several hours ahead. Store in an airtight container to keep it fresh.

  8 cups popcorn (popped without salt or fat)
Cooking spray
  2 tablespoons sugar
  1 teaspoon ground cinnamon
  ½ teaspoon salt
1½ tablespoons butter, melted

1. Place popcorn in a large bowl. Lightly coat popcorn with cooking spray; toss well. Recoat popcorn with cooking spray; toss well.
2. Combine sugar, cinnamon, and salt in a small bowl. Drizzle popcorn with melted butter; toss well. Sprinkle with sugar mixture; toss well to coat. Yield: 16 servings (serving size: ½ cup).

CALORIES 31 (38% from fat); FAT 1.3g (sat 0.7g, mono 0.3g, poly 0.1g); PROTEIN 0.5g; CARB 4.8g; FIBER 0.7g; CHOL 3mg; IRON 0.2mg; SODIUM 81mg; CALC 2mg

Minted Prosciutto and Melon

Transparently thin slices of salty prosciutto wrapped gingerly around a juicy chunk of cubed orange-hued melon is a modern antipasto indulgence. Its roots, however, date back to the Roman custom in classical times of pairing melon or figs with prosciutto di Parma.

  ½ cup sweet Italian sparkling white wine (such as Asti Spumante) or sparkling white grape juice
  1 tablespoon minced fresh mint
  1 tablespoon honey
 24 (1½-inch) cubes ripe cantaloupe
  6 very thin slices prosciutto (about 3 ounces), cut in half crosswise, then lengthwise

1. Combine first 4 ingredients in a large bowl, tossing gently to coat. Cover and chill 30 minutes.
2. Remove cantaloupe, reserving wine syrup. Wrap cantaloupe pieces with prosciutto; secure with a wooden pick. Serve with wine syrup for dipping. Yield: 6 servings (serving size: 4 pieces cantaloupe and 4 teaspoons wine syrup).

CALORIES 101 (16% from fat); FAT 1.8g (sat 0.6g, mono 0g, poly 0.1g); PROTEIN 5.3g; CARB 14.8g; FIBER 0.1g; CHOL 8mg; IRON 0.7mg; SODIUM 276mg; CALC 16mg

Oven-Roasted Tomatoes with Goat Cheese

  6 medium tomatoes, halved (about 1¼ pounds)
  2 tablespoons extravirgin olive oil, divided
  1 tablespoon balsamic vinegar
  ½ teaspoon kosher salt
  ¼ teaspoon freshly ground black pepper
  2 tablespoons crumbled goat cheese
 12 rosemary sprigs

1. Preheat oven to 200°.
2. Place a wire rack over a baking sheet.
3. Combine tomatoes, 1 tablespoon oil, and vinegar; toss gently. Place tomatoes, cut sides up, on rack. Sprinkle with salt and pepper.
4. Bake at 200° for 6 hours or until tender and slightly syrupy (do not overbake or tomatoes will be tough and chewy). Remove from oven; cool completely. Place ½ teaspoon cheese onto each tomato half. Fold slightly; secure each tomato half with 1 rosemary sprig. Place on a serving platter; drizzle with remaining 1 tablespoon oil. Yield: 6 servings (serving size: 2 tomato halves).

CALORIES 88 (65% from fat); FAT 6.4g (sat 1.7g, mono 4g, poly 0.6g); PROTEIN 2.4g; CARB 6.5g; FIBER 1.9g; CHOL 4mg; IRON 0.5mg; SODIUM 189mg; CALC 31mg

Marinated Olives

Cheesy Spinach-Artichoke Dip with Toasted Pita Chips

11 (6-inch) pitas
⅓ cup chopped sun-dried tomatoes, packed without oil
1 cup boiling water
1 (14-ounce) can quartered artichoke hearts, drained and coarsely chopped
1 (10-ounce) package frozen chopped spinach, thawed, drained, and squeezed dry
1 (8-ounce) tub light cream cheese, softened
1 (8-ounce) carton reduced-fat sour cream
¾ cup grated Parmesan cheese
¾ cup fat-free milk
½ cup (2 ounces) crumbled reduced-fat feta cheese
½ cup diced onion
½ cup fat-free mayonnaise
1 tablespoon red wine vinegar
¼ teaspoon freshly ground black pepper
2 garlic cloves, crushed

1. Preheat oven to 350°.
2. Split each pita in half horizontally; cut each half into 6 wedges. Place pita wedges in a single layer on baking sheets; bake at 350° for 10 minutes or until toasted.
3. Combine sun-dried tomatoes and boiling water in a bowl; let stand 1 hour or until soft.

4. Place artichokes and next 11 ingredients in a 3-quart electric slow cooker; stir well. Cover and cook on LOW 1 hour. Drain tomatoes, and stir into dip. Cover and cook 1 hour. Serve warm with toasted pita wedges. Yield: 6 servings (serving size: ¼ cup dip and 6 pita wedges).

CALORIES 162 (25% from fat); FAT 4.5g (sat 2.8g, mono 0.3g, poly 0.1g); PROTEIN 8.1g; CARB 22.3g; FIBER 1.3g; CHOL 15mg; IRON 2mg; SODIUM 329mg; CALC 126mg

Marinated Olives

24 large unpitted Spanish olives
2 tablespoons sherry vinegar
1 tablespoon extravirgin olive oil
2 teaspoons coriander seeds, crushed
1 teaspoon dried thyme
1 teaspoon dried rosemary, crushed
½ teaspoon crushed red pepper
2 garlic cloves, thinly sliced
Rosemary sprigs (optional)

1. Combine first 8 ingredients in a bowl. Cover and marinate in refrigerator at least 8 hours, stirring occasionally. Serve at room temperature. Garnish with rosemary sprigs, if desired. Yield: 6 servings (serving size: 4 olives).

CALORIES 49 (66% from fat); FAT 3.6g (sat 0.1g, mono 2g, poly 1.4g); PROTEIN 0.2g; CARB 3.1g; FIBER 0.2g; CHOL 0mg; IRON 0.4mg; SODIUM 322mg; CALC 13mg

Avocado-Tomatillo Dip with Cumin Pita Chips

Tart tomatillos lend the dip a bright green color and prevent the avocado from discoloring, even after a day or two in the refrigerator. Look for fresh tomatillos in the produce section of most large supermarkets.

CHIPS:
    3 (6-inch) pitas, split in half horizontally
Cooking spray
    1 teaspoon cumin seeds, crushed
    1 teaspoon dried oregano
    ½ teaspoon kosher salt
DIP:
    ½ pound tomatillos (about 5 large)
    2 ripe avocados
    ½ cup chopped onion
    2 tablespoons chopped fresh cilantro
    1 teaspoon finely chopped seeded jalapeño
       pepper
    ½ teaspoon salt
    ⅓ cup fat-free sour cream

1. Preheat oven to 375°.
2. To prepare chips, coat rough side of each pita half with cooking spray; sprinkle pita halves evenly with cumin seeds, oregano, and ½ teaspoon kosher salt. Cut each pita half into 8 wedges; arrange wedges in a single layer on baking sheets. Bake at 375° for 15 minutes or until golden brown.
3. To prepare dip, discard husks and stems from tomatillos. Place tomatillos in a small saucepan; cover with water. Bring to a boil; cook 5 minutes or until tender. Cool to room temperature.
4. Peel, seed, and coarsely chop avocados; set aside. Place tomatillos, chopped onion, cilantro, jalapeño, and ½ teaspoon salt in a blender or food processor; process until smooth. Add avocado and sour cream; process until smooth. Serve with pita chips. Yield: 12 servings (serving size: about 2½ tablespoons dip and 4 pita chips).

CALORIES 106 (42% from fat); FAT 5g (sat 0.7g, mono 2.9g, poly 0.8g); PROTEIN 2.6g; CARB 13.9g; FIBER 2.8g; CHOL 1mg; IRON 0.9mg; SODIUM 266mg; CALC 33mg

Roasted Garlic, Poblano, and Red Pepper Guacamole

When storing the guacamole, press plastic wrap against its surface to help keep it from oxidizing and turning brown. You can use it to liven up a turkey sandwich or as a condiment in a vegetable wrap.

GUACAMOLE:
    6 garlic cloves, unpeeled
    1 medium red bell pepper
    1 medium poblano pepper
    1 ripe avocado
    ¼ cup finely chopped green onions
    2 tablespoons chopped fresh cilantro
    2 teaspoons fresh lime juice
    ¼ teaspoon kosher salt
CHIPS:
    6 (6-inch) corn tortillas, each cut into 8 wedges
    2 teaspoons fresh lime juice
    ¼ teaspoon kosher salt
Cooking spray

1. Preheat oven to 450°.
2. To prepare guacamole, wrap garlic cloves in foil, and bake at 450° for 15 minutes or until soft. Cool slightly; remove skins. Place garlic in a medium bowl; mash with a fork.
3. Preheat broiler.
4. Cut peppers in half lengthwise; discard seeds and membranes. Place pepper halves, skin sides up, on a foil-lined baking sheet; flatten with hand. Broil 15 minutes or until blackened, turning frequently. Place in a zip-top plastic bag, and seal. Let stand for 10 minutes. Peel and finely chop peppers.
5. Peel, seed, and coarsely mash avocado. Add chopped peppers, avocado, onions, cilantro, juice, and ¼ teaspoon salt to garlic in bowl; stir well.
6. Reduce heat to 425°.
7. To prepare chips, combine corn tortilla wedges, 2 teaspoons juice, and ¼ teaspoon salt in a large bowl, tossing to coat. Arrange tortillas in a single layer on a baking sheet coated with cooking spray. Bake at 425° for 10 minutes or until crisp and lightly browned, turning once. Cool 5 minutes. Serve with guacamole. Yield: 8 servings (serving size: 2½ tablespoons guacamole and 6 chips).

CALORIES 87 (38% from fat); FAT 3.7g (sat 1g, mono 1.9g, poly 0.8g); PROTEIN 2.1g; CARB 13.2g; FIBER 3.1g; CHOL 0mg; IRON 0.4mg; SODIUM 151mg; CALC 40mg

Eggplant Caponata

The late James Beard, considered to be the godfather of American cuisine, once said, "Nothing but the best is good enough for friends." If that's your motto, then Eggplant Caponata is a sure-serve for your next cocktail party. Caponata (kap-oh-NAH-tah) is an eggplant-based dish that can be served as an antipasto or a condiment, or along-side chicken, pork, or fish.

    6 cups diced peeled eggplant (about 1 pound)
 1½ teaspoons salt
   ¼ cup golden raisins
    4 teaspoons olive oil, divided
    1 cup chopped onion
    2 garlic cloves, minced
    1 cup diced seeded plum tomato
   ¼ cup sugar
   ¼ cup red wine vinegar
   ¼ cup chopped pitted kalamata olives
    2 teaspoons capers
   ⅓ cup chopped fresh parsley

1. Place eggplant in a colander; sprinkle with salt. Toss well. Drain 1 hour. Rinse well; pat dry with paper towels.

2. Place raisins in a small bowl; cover with hot water. Let stand 15 minutes; drain. Set aside.

3. Heat 1 tablespoon oil in a large nonstick skillet over medium-high heat. Add eggplant; sauté 9 minutes or until well browned. Spoon eggplant into a large bowl; set aside.

4. Heat 1 teaspoon oil in pan over medium-high heat. Add onion; sauté 3 minutes or until golden. Add garlic; sauté 1 minute. Add tomato; sauté 2 minutes. Add tomato mixture to eggplant, tossing gently to combine.

5. Return pan to heat. Add sugar and vinegar, stirring until sugar dissolves. Stir in raisins, olives, and capers. Add eggplant mixture, stirring to combine. Remove from heat; stir in parsley. Serve warm or at room temperature. Yield: 12 servings (serving size: ¼ cup).

NOTE: Caponata will keep in the refrigerator up to five days; bring it to room temperature before serving.

CALORIES 59 (31% from fat); FAT 2g (sat 0.3g, mono 1.4g, poly 0.2g); PROTEIN 0.8g; CARB 10.8g; FIBER 1.5g; CHOL 0mg; IRON 0.5mg; SODIUM 141mg; CALC 14mg

Hot Crab Dip

Serve with melba toast or pita chips.

  1 cup fat-free cottage cheese
  ½ teaspoon grated lemon rind
  2 tablespoons lemon juice
  1 tablespoon Dijon mustard
1½ teaspoons Worcestershire sauce
  1 teaspoon hot sauce
  ½ teaspoon salt
  ⅛ teaspoon freshly ground black pepper
  1 garlic clove, minced
  1 (8-ounce) block ⅓-less-fat cream cheese, softened
  2 tablespoons chopped green onions
  1 pound lump crabmeat, shell pieces removed
Cooking spray
  2 tablespoons grated fresh Parmesan cheese
  ¼ cup dry breadcrumbs

1. Preheat oven to 375°.
2. Place first 9 ingredients in a food processor; process until smooth.
3. Combine cottage cheese mixture, cream cheese, and onions in a large bowl; gently fold in crab. Place crab mixture in an 11 x 7–inch baking dish coated with cooking spray. Bake at 375° for 30 minutes. Sprinkle with Parmesan and breadcrumbs. Bake at 375° for 15 minutes or until golden. Yield: 20 servings (serving size: about 3 tablespoons).

CALORIES 63 (53% from fat); FAT 3.1g (sat 1.8g, mono 0.1g, poly 0g); PROTEIN 6.8g; CARB 1.9g; FIBER 0.1g; CHOL 30mg; IRON 0.3mg; SODIUM 264mg; CALC 29mg

Roasted Butternut Squash Dip

Terrific with toasted baguette slices or pita chips, this creamy, sweet-savory dip can be prepared up to three days in advance. Refrigerate in a microwave-safe container, then reheat in a microwave on HIGH 1 to 2 minutes or just until warmed.

  1 (2-pound) butternut squash
  1 small Walla Walla or other sweet onion, trimmed and quartered
  4 garlic cloves, unpeeled
1½ teaspoons olive oil
  2 tablespoons crème fraîche or whole sour cream
  ¾ teaspoon salt
  ⅛ teaspoon ground red pepper
  ⅛ teaspoon ground nutmeg
  ⅛ teaspoon freshly ground black pepper

1. Preheat oven to 350°.
2. Cut squash in half lengthwise; discard seeds and membrane. Brush cut sides of squash halves, cut sides of onion quarters, and garlic cloves with oil. Arrange squash halves, cut sides down, on a jelly-roll pan; arrange onion quarters and garlic cloves on pan. Bake at 350° for 45 minutes or until tender. Cool slightly. Peel squash. Squeeze garlic cloves to extract pulp.
3. Place squash, onion, and garlic pulp in a food processor; process until smooth. Add crème fraîche and remaining ingredients; process to combine. Serve warm. Yield: 16 servings (serving size: ¼ cup).

CALORIES 35 (28% from fat); FAT 1.1g (sat 0.5g, mono 0.5g, poly 0.1g); PROTEIN 0.6g; CARB 6.3g; FIBER 1.7g; CHOL 1mg; IRON 0.4mg; SODIUM 113mg; CALC 29mg

About Butternut Squash

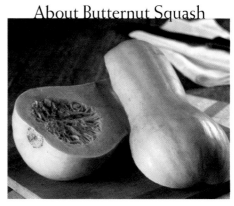

Butternut squash has a firm texture, making it difficult to cut. The secret is to microwave it whole on HIGH 1 to 2 minutes. This step helps soften the winter squash for slicing. After microwaving, cut the squash in half lengthwise; remove and discard seeds.

Beef Tenderloin Bruschetta with Brown Butter

Use sound to judge when the mustard seeds are ready. Much like microwave popcorn, when a second of time passes between pops, the seeds are done. Garnish with fresh cilantro.

½ cup diced peeled mango
2 tablespoons chopped fresh cilantro
2 tablespoons lime juice
2 teaspoons finely chopped serrano chile
½ teaspoon sugar
¼ teaspoon salt
⅛ teaspoon ground turmeric
1½ teaspoons canola oil
½ teaspoon yellow mustard seeds, divided
1½ teaspoons butter, melted
Cooking spray
1 (4-ounce) beef tenderloin steak, trimmed (1 inch thick)
⅛ teaspoon salt
⅛ teaspoon freshly ground black pepper
16 (½-inch-thick) slices diagonally cut French bread baguette, toasted

1. Combine first 7 ingredients in a small bowl; cover and let stand at room temperature 15 minutes.
2. Heat canola oil in a small nonstick skillet over medium-high heat. Add 1 mustard seed to pan; cook until seed pops (about 90 seconds). Add remaining seeds; stir to coat with oil. Cover and cook seeds 30 seconds or until they begin to pop, gently shaking pan. Stir in butter; cover pan. Cook until 1 second passes between pops, shaking pan constantly (about 30 seconds). Remove pan from heat. Scrape mustard seed mixture into mango mixture; stir gently. Let stand 5 minutes.
3. Heat pan over medium-high heat. Coat pan with cooking spray. Sprinkle beef with ⅛ teaspoon salt and black pepper. Add beef to pan; cook 3 minutes on each side or until desired degree of doneness. Let rest 5 minutes. Slice beef across grain into very thin slices.
4. Divide beef slices evenly among toasted baguette slices. Top each bruschetta with about 1½ teaspoons mango mixture. Serve immediately. Yield: 8 servings (serving size: 2 bruschetta).

CALORIES 88 (29% from fat); FAT 2.8g (sat 1g, mono 1.2g, poly 0.4g); PROTEIN 4.4g; CARB 12.1g; FIBER 0.6g; CHOL 11mg; IRON 0.9mg; SODIUM 216mg; CALC 5mg

Bruschetta Gorgonzola and Apples

For this traditional Italian appetizer, we suggest Gorgonzola for its sweet creaminess, but any quality blue cheese will do. A slice of tart apple is a nice foil to the garlic and cheese. If you plan to grill steak or chicken, cook this appetizer first for your guests to enjoy while they're waiting.

$1/3$ cup (about $1\frac{1}{2}$ ounces) crumbled Gorgonzola cheese
2 tablespoons butter, softened
1 tablespoon brandy or cognac
$1/8$ teaspoon freshly ground black pepper
12 (1-ounce) slices diagonally cut French bread (about 1 inch thick)
Cooking spray
6 garlic cloves, halved
3 Granny Smith apples, each cut into 8 wedges (about 18 ounces)

1. Prepare grill.
2. Combine first 4 ingredients in a small bowl, stirring until blended.
3. Place bread slices on grill rack coated with cooking spray; cook 4 minutes on each side or until lightly browned. Remove from grill. Rub cut sides of garlic over one side of each bread slice. Discard garlic. Spread 2 teaspoons cheese mixture over each bread slice. Serve with apple wedges. Yield: 12 servings (serving size: 1 bruschetta and 2 apple wedges).

CALORIES 148 (30% from fat); FAT 5g (sat 2.7g, mono 0.9g, poly 0.3g); PROTEIN 4.1g; CARB 21.4g; FIBER 1.7g; CHOL 13mg; IRON 0.9mg; SODIUM 263mg; CALC 68mg

Cheese Crostini with Prosciutto

This fast appetizer complements pastas, soups, and salads. You can grate the cheese in advance.

6 (1-ounce) slices ciabatta bread
2 garlic cloves, halved
$1/4$ cup (1 ounce) grated fresh Parmesan cheese
2 ounces thinly sliced prosciutto
$1/2$ teaspoon freshly ground black pepper

1. Preheat broiler.
2. Place bread on a baking sheet. Broil 1 minute or until lightly browned. Rub cut sides of garlic over one side of each bread slice. Discard garlic. Sprinkle cheese evenly over bread. Broil 1 minute or until cheese melts. Arrange prosciutto evenly over bread. Sprinkle evenly with pepper. Yield: 6 servings (serving size: 1 crostino).

CALORIES 127 (25% from fat); FAT 3.5g (sat 1.4g, mono 1.2g, poly 0.4g); PROTEIN 7.2g; CARB 16.6g; FIBER 1g; CHOL 13mg; IRON 1mg; SODIUM 442mg; CALC 78mg

About Prosciutto

The best prosciutto (proh-SHOO-toh) sold in the United States comes from the Parma area of Italy; it's made from larger pork legs than American prosciutto and is aged longer. It also isn't smoked like American ham; rather, it's air-cured with salt and seasonings pressed into a densely-textured meat. It's typically sliced thin and eaten raw or lightly cooked. Domestic prosciutto is fine for flavoring sauces, soups, and stews, but when you're really spotlighting the ham, go for prosciutto di Parma. In Italy, it's considered the ultimate indulgence.

Open-Faced Panini with Goat Cheese, Roasted Peppers, and Spicy Olive Topping

(pictured on page 9)

For the best flavor, look for high-quality imported olives, available at gourmet markets or large supermarkets.

  2   red bell peppers
⅛   teaspoon salt
  6   (1-inch-thick) slices Italian bread
¼   cup minced pitted ripe olives (about 6)
  2   tablespoons minced pitted green olives (about 8)
  1   tablespoon minced fresh basil
  2   teaspoons grated lemon rind
  2   teaspoons fresh lemon juice
⅛   teaspoon ground red pepper
  1   small garlic clove, minced
  3   tablespoons crumbled goat cheese

1. Preheat broiler.
2. Cut bell peppers in half lengthwise; discard seeds and membranes. Place pepper halves, skin sides up, on a foil-lined baking sheet; flatten with hand. Broil 15 minutes or until blackened. Place in a zip-top plastic bag; seal. Let stand 10 minutes. Peel and cut into strips. Combine peppers and salt in a medium bowl; set aside.
3. Place bread on a baking sheet; broil 1 minute on each side or until toasted.
4. Combine ripe olives and next 6 ingredients in a small bowl. Spoon about 1 tablespoon olive mixture onto each toast slice; top evenly with bell pepper strips, and sprinkle each serving with 1½ teaspoons crumbled goat cheese. Cut each panino in half. Serve immediately. Yield: 6 servings (serving size: 2 panini).

CALORIES 126 (31% from fat); FAT 4.4g (sat 1.1g, mono 1.5g, poly 0.8g); PROTEIN 4g; CARB 18.1g; FIBER 1.8g; CHOL 4mg; IRON 1.1mg; SODIUM 420mg; CALC 60mg

Corn and Sun-Dried Tomato Quesadilla with Smoked Mozzarella

We liked this quesadilla cold, but you can warm it in a toaster oven or microwave. Serve with a tossed salad for a light meal.

¼   teaspoon olive oil
  2   (6-inch) corn tortillas
Cooking spray
⅓   cup fresh or frozen, thawed, corn kernels
  1   tablespoon chopped red onion
1½   teaspoons sun-dried tomato sprinkles
⅛   teaspoon salt
⅛   teaspoon freshly ground black pepper
¼   cup (1 ounce) shredded smoked mozzarella cheese

1. Pour oil onto one side of a tortilla. Place second tortilla over oiled side of first tortilla, and rub tortillas together to spread oil over both tortillas.
2. Heat a large nonstick skillet over medium-high heat. Coat pan with cooking spray. Add corn; cook 4 minutes or until lightly browned, stirring occasionally. Place corn in a bowl. Add onion, sun-dried tomato, salt, and pepper to pan; sauté 1 minute. Add to corn mixture.
3. Wipe pan with paper towels. Heat pan over medium-high heat. Coat pan with cooking spray. Place one tortilla, oiled side down, in pan. Sprinkle 2 tablespoons cheese over tortilla; top with corn mixture. Sprinkle with 2 tablespoons cheese; top with remaining tortilla, oiled side up. Cook 2 minutes on each side or until cheese melts and tortilla is crisp. Cut into 4 wedges. Yield: 4 servings (serving size: 1 wedge).

CALORIES 64 (32% from fat); FAT 2.3g (sat 1g, mono 0.8g, poly 0.3g); PROTEIN 2.6g; CARB 9.2g; FIBER 1.2g; CHOL 6mg; IRON 0.3mg; SODIUM 131mg; CALC 61mg

Grilled Eggplant with Caramelized Onion and Fennel

To prepare the eggplant rounds indoors, broil until they're browned, then continue the recipe as instructed. White balsamic vinegar offers the sweetness of regular balsamic but won't discolor the salad. You can use regular balsamic vinegar if white isn't available.

1 (1¼-pound) eggplant (about 4-inch diameter), peeled
Cooking spray
¼ teaspoon salt, divided
¼ teaspoon freshly ground black pepper, divided
2¾ cups chopped fennel bulb (about 1 large bulb)
2 cups finely chopped yellow onion
2 cups trimmed arugula
1 teaspoon white balsamic vinegar
1 teaspoon extravirgin olive oil
1 cup quartered cherry tomatoes
½ cup (2 ounces) crumbled goat cheese
2 tablespoons chopped fresh basil
1 tablespoon chopped fresh thyme

1. Prepare grill.
2. Cut peeled eggplant crosswise into 8 (½-inch-thick) slices. Lightly coat both sides of slices with cooking spray; sprinkle with ⅛ teaspoon salt and ⅛ teaspoon pepper. Place on grill rack coated with cooking spray; grill 7 minutes on each side or until browned. Set eggplant slices aside.
3. Heat a large nonstick skillet over medium-high heat. Coat pan with cooking spray. Add fennel and onion; sauté 8 minutes or until vegetables are tender and lightly browned.
4. Combine ⅛ teaspoon salt, ⅛ teaspoon pepper, arugula, vinegar, and oil in a medium bowl; toss gently to coat. Divide arugula mixture evenly among 8 appetizer plates, and top each serving with 1 eggplant slice. Arrange about ⅓ cup fennel mixture on each eggplant slice, and top with 2 tablespoons tomatoes and 1 tablespoon cheese. Sprinkle basil and thyme evenly over cheese. Yield: 8 servings.

CALORIES 73 (30% from fat); FAT 2.4g (sat 1.2g, mono 0.8g, poly 0.2g); PROTEIN 3.2g; CARB 11.3g; FIBER 3.8g; CHOL 3mg; IRON 0.9mg; SODIUM 122mg; CALC 49mg

Fresh Corn Blinis with Smoked Salmon and Chive Cream

Classic blinis are nutty pancakes made with buckwheat flour topped with sour cream and caviar. Our version showcases silver-dollar-sized sweet corn pancakes crowned with cold-smoked salmon.

  ½ cup reduced-fat sour cream
  1 tablespoon minced fresh chives
  1 ear shucked corn
  ⅓ cup all-purpose flour (about 1½ ounces)
  2 tablespoons fine-ground yellow cornmeal
  ½ cup 1% low-fat milk
  1 large egg yolk
  ¼ teaspoon salt
  ¼ teaspoon freshly ground black pepper
  1 large egg white
Cooking spray
  4 ounces cold-smoked salmon, cut into 24 (2-inch) strips

1. Combine sour cream and chives in a small bowl. Cover and refrigerate.

2. Cut kernels from ear of corn; place in a bowl. Scrape remaining pulp from cob using dull side of a knife blade into bowl. Discard cob. Set corn and pulp aside.

3. Lightly spoon flour into a dry measuring cup; level with a knife. Combine flour and cornmeal in a medium bowl; make a well in center of mixture. Combine milk and egg yolk in a small bowl; stir well with a whisk. Add milk mixture to flour mixture, and stir with a whisk just until moist. Stir in corn, salt, and pepper.

4. Place egg white in a bowl; beat with a mixer at high speed until foamy. Gently fold egg white mixture into corn mixture.

5. Heat a large nonstick skillet over medium heat. Coat pan with cooking spray. Spoon about 1 tablespoon batter per blini into pan, spreading to about 2-inch diameter. Cook 2 minutes or until tops are covered with bubbles and edges begin to set. Carefully turn blinis over; cook 1 minute. Transfer blinis to a serving platter, and arrange in a single layer; keep warm. Repeat procedure with remaining batter. Top each blini with 1 piece salmon and 1 teaspoon sour cream mixture. Yield: 8 servings (serving size: 3 topped blinis).

CALORIES 102 (33% from fat); FAT 3.7g (sat 1.7g, mono 1.2g, poly 0.4g); PROTEIN 6.2g; CARB 11.2g; FIBER 0.7g; CHOL 35mg; IRON 0.7mg; SODIUM 386mg; CALC 45mg

Smoked Trout with Apple-Horseradish Cream on Potato Pancakes

For convenience, make the pancakes up to a day ahead and reheat them in the oven before serving.

  ½ cup all-purpose flour (about 2¼ ounces)
  4¾ cups shredded peeled baking potato (about 2 pounds)
  ½ cup grated fresh onion
  1 teaspoon salt
  ½ teaspoon freshly ground black pepper
  2 large egg whites, lightly beaten
  3 tablespoons olive oil, divided
Cooking spray
  ¼ cup reduced-fat mayonnaise
  3 tablespoons finely chopped Granny Smith apple
  2 tablespoons plain fat-free yogurt
  4 teaspoons prepared horseradish
  4 ounces smoked rainbow trout (bones removed), broken into 48 pieces
  3 tablespoons chopped fresh chives

1. Preheat oven to 400°.

2. Lightly spoon flour into a dry measuring cup; level with a knife. Combine flour and next 5 ingredients in a large bowl, stirring until blended. Divide mixture into 48 level tablespoon-sized pancakes, squeezing each to remove excess moisture.

3. Heat 1 tablespoon oil in a nonstick skillet over medium-high heat. Add 16 pancakes; cook 3 minutes on each side or until browned. Arrange on two baking sheets coated with cooking spray. Repeat procedure twice with remaining oil and pancakes. Bake at 400° for 5 minutes or until thoroughly heated.

4. Combine mayonnaise, apple, yogurt, and horseradish in a small bowl; place ½ teaspoon mayonnaise mixture on each pancake. Top each with a trout piece; sprinkle with chives. Yield: 12 servings (serving size: 4 pancakes).

CALORIES 149 (28% from fat); FAT 4.6g (sat 0.7g, mono 2.7g, poly 0.6g); PROTEIN 5.4g; CARB 22g; FIBER 1.7g; CHOL 8mg; IRON 0.6mg; SODIUM 260mg; CALC 12mg

Spicy Shrimp Cakes with Corn
and Avocado Salsa

Spicy Shrimp Cakes with Corn and Avocado Salsa

You can prepare the shrimp cakes up to a day in advance, and refrigerate. Garnish with lime wedges, if desired.

CAKES:
1 pound medium shrimp, peeled and deveined
Cooking spray
1 cup finely chopped red bell pepper
1 garlic clove, minced
¼ cup thinly sliced green onions
3 tablespoons reduced-fat mayonnaise
1 tablespoon fresh lime juice
1½ teaspoons hot sauce
½ teaspoon sugar
¼ teaspoon salt
1 large egg
¼ cup finely chopped fresh cilantro
¾ cup panko (Japanese breadcrumbs), divided

SALSA:
1 cup frozen white corn, thawed
¾ cup diced peeled avocado
¼ cup chopped fresh cilantro
3 tablespoons finely chopped red onion
2 tablespoons finely chopped seeded poblano pepper
1 tablespoon fresh lime juice
¼ teaspoon salt

1. To prepare cakes, place shrimp in a food processor; pulse 10 times or until finely chopped. Set aside.
2. Heat a large nonstick skillet over medium heat. Coat pan with cooking spray. Add bell pepper to pan; sauté 3 minutes. Add garlic to pan; sauté 1 minute. Remove from heat. Place bell pepper mixture in a large bowl. Add shrimp, green onions, and next 6 ingredients, stirring well. Stir in cilantro and ¼ cup panko.
3. Divide shrimp mixture into 10 equal portions, shaping each portion into a ½-inch-thick patty. Dredge both sides of patties in remaining ½ cup panko. Chill at least 1 hour.
4. Heat pan over medium-high heat. Coat pan with cooking spray. Add 5 cakes to pan; cook 4 minutes on each side or until browned. Remove from pan; cover and keep warm. Repeat procedure with remaining cakes.
5. To prepare salsa, combine corn and remaining ingredients; stir gently. Serve salsa immediately with shrimp cakes. Yield: 10 servings (serving size: 1 shrimp cake and about 3 tablespoons salsa).

CALORIES 121 (29% from fat); FAT 3.9g (sat 0.8g, mono 1.4g, poly 0.7g); PROTEIN 11.5g; CARB 10.6g; FIBER 1.6g; CHOL 90mg; IRON 1.5mg; SODIUM 252mg; CALC 34mg

Honey-Ginger Chicken Bites

⅔ cup honey
2 tablespoons minced peeled fresh ginger
2 tablespoons fresh lemon juice
2 tablespoons cider vinegar
2 tablespoons low-sodium soy sauce
2 teaspoons dark sesame oil
1 teaspoon grated orange rind
1 teaspoon Worcestershire sauce
4 garlic cloves, minced
1¼ pounds skinless, boneless chicken thighs, cut into bite-sized pieces (about 16 pieces)
Cooking spray
1 teaspoon salt
¼ teaspoon freshly ground black pepper
2 teaspoons cornstarch
2 teaspoons water
2 teaspoons sesame seeds, toasted (optional)

1. Combine first 9 ingredients in a large zip-top plastic bag; seal and shake well. Add chicken; seal and toss to coat. Refrigerate at least 2 hours or overnight, turning occasionally.
2. Preheat oven to 425°.
3. Remove chicken from bag, reserving marinade. Arrange chicken in a single layer on rack of a broiler pan coated with cooking spray. Sprinkle chicken with salt and pepper. Bake at 425° for 20 minutes, stirring once.
4. While chicken is cooking, strain marinade through a sieve into a bowl; discard solids. Place marinade in a saucepan; bring to a boil. Cook 3 minutes; skim solids from surface. Combine cornstarch and water in a small bowl; stir with a whisk. Add cornstarch mixture to pan, stirring with a whisk; cook 1 minute. Remove from heat; pour glaze into a large bowl.
5. Preheat broiler.
6. Add chicken to glaze; toss well to coat. Place chicken mixture on a jelly-roll pan; broil 5 minutes or until browned, stirring twice. Sprinkle with sesame seeds, if desired. Yield: 12 servings (serving size: about 1½ ounces).

CALORIES 179 (22% from fat); FAT 4.4g (sat 1g, mono 1.4g, poly 1.2g); PROTEIN 18.2g; CARB 18.2g; FIBER 0.1g; CHOL 76mg; IRON 1.1mg; SODIUM 430mg; CALC 14mg

Peppermint Stick Hot Chocolate

Vanilla-Scented Mulled Cider

Loose spices permeate the cider more than those wrapped in cheesecloth.

  8 cups apple cider
 12 black peppercorns, crushed
  8 whole allspice
  2 bay leaves
  1 (3-inch) piece vanilla bean, split lengthwise and scraped
  1 (2 x ½-inch) strip lemon rind

1. Combine all ingredients in a large saucepan; bring to a simmer. Cook 20 minutes, stirring occasionally. Strain cider through a sieve, and discard solids. Yield: 8 servings (serving size: ¾ cup).

CALORIES 140 (0% from fat); FAT 0g; PROTEIN 1g; CARB 35g; FIBER 0g; CHOL 0mg; IRON 0mg; SODIUM 0mg; CALC 0mg

Peppermint Stick Hot Chocolate

For an adults-only party, consider spiking this drink with mint liqueur, such as peppermint schnapps or crème de menthe.

  8 cups 2% reduced-fat milk
 ¾ cup packed dark brown sugar
 ⅓ cup unsweetened cocoa
  1 teaspoon vanilla extract
 ⅛ teaspoon ground nutmeg
  3 ounces semisweet chocolate, finely chopped
 12 candy canes
 ¾ cup miniature marshmallows
Grated whole nutmeg (optional)

1. Combine first 6 ingredients in a large saucepan over medium-low heat. Cook 25 minutes or until chocolate melts and mixture is smooth, stirring occasionally. Serve with candy canes and marshmallows. Garnish with grated whole nutmeg, if desired. Yield: 12 servings (serving size: ¾ cup hot chocolate, 1 candy cane, and 1 tablespoon marshmallows).

CALORIES 194 (18% from fat); FAT 3.9g (sat 2.3g, mono 0g, poly 0g); PROTEIN 7g; CARB 34g; FIBER 0.8g; CHOL 10mg; IRON 0.6mg; SODIUM 96mg; CALC 32mg

Lemon and Mint Iced Tea

This twist on sweet Southern iced tea is refreshingly tart. Serve well chilled.

    8   cups cold water, divided
    3   family-sized tea bags
    1   fresh mint sprig (about ¼ cup leaves)
    ¾   cup sugar
    ¼   cup fresh lemon juice
    8   lemon slices (optional)
    8   mint sprigs (optional)

1. Bring 4 cups water to a boil in a medium saucepan. Add tea bags and 1 mint sprig to pan; steep 10 minutes. Remove and discard tea bags and mint sprig.

2. Combine sugar and juice in a glass measuring cup. Add ½ cup hot tea mixture; stir until sugar dissolves. Pour sugar mixture into a 2-quart pitcher. Pour remaining hot tea mixture into pitcher. Add 4 cups cold water; stir. Serve over ice. Garnish with lemon slices and mint sprigs, if desired. Yield: 8 servings (serving size: 1 cup).

CALORIES 75 (0% from fat); FAT 0g; PROTEIN 0g; CARB 19.4g; FIBER 0g; CHOL 0mg; IRON 0mg; SODIUM 5mg; CALC 5mg

Basil-Infused Watermelon Lemonade

Basil and watermelon provide bright sweetness in this refreshing beverage. Serve well chilled or over ice.

    1   cup water
    ¾   cup sugar
    1   cup thinly sliced fresh basil
    8   cups cubed seeded watermelon
    ½   cup fresh lemon juice (about 3 lemons)

1. Combine 1 cup water and sugar in a small saucepan; bring to a boil. Reduce heat, and simmer 5 minutes or until sugar dissolves. Remove from heat. Stir in basil; chill 1 hour. Strain sugar mixture through a sieve into a bowl, and discard basil.

2. Place watermelon in a blender; process until smooth. Strain watermelon puree through a fine sieve into a large bowl, reserving liquid; discard solids. Combine watermelon liquid, sugar mixture, and juice in a pitcher; chill. Yield: 5 servings (serving size: 1 cup).

CALORIES 197 (2% from fat); FAT 0.4g (sat 0g, mono 0.1g, poly 0.2g); PROTEIN 1.8g; CARB 50.8g; FIBER 1.4g; CHOL 0mg; IRON 0.9mg; SODIUM 4mg; CALC 33mg

Ginger Lemonade

    6   cups water, divided
    1¼   cups sugar
    ¼   cup grated peeled fresh ginger
    1¼   cups fresh lemon juice (about 7 large lemons)
    ¼   cup fresh lime juice
    Lemon slices (optional)
    Lime slices (optional)

1. Combine 1 cup water, sugar, and ginger in a small saucepan; bring to a boil, and cook 1 minute or until sugar dissolves, stirring occasionally. Remove from heat; cool.

2. Strain ginger mixture through a sieve into a pitcher, and discard solids. Add 5 cups water and juices, and stir well. Serve over ice, and garnish with lemon and lime slices, if desired. Yield: 8 servings (serving size: 1 cup).

CALORIES 133 (0% from fat); FAT 0g; PROTEIN 0.2g; CARB 35.2g; FIBER 0g; CHOL 0mg; IRON 0mg; SODIUM 1mg; CALC 4mg

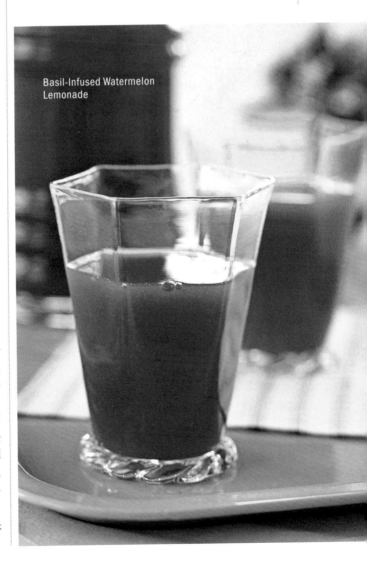

Basil-Infused Watermelon Lemonade

Blackberry Limeade

This summer cooler is great to bring along on a picnic or to serve at a backyard party.

    6 cups water, divided
    3 cups fresh blackberries
    1 cup sugar
   ⅔ cup fresh lime juice (about 4 limes)
    8 thin lime slices
 Fresh blackberries (optional)

1. Place 1 cup water and 3 cups blackberries in a blender, and process until smooth. Press blackberry puree through a sieve into a large pitcher; discard seeds. Add 5 cups water, sugar, and juice to pitcher; stir until sugar dissolves. Place 1 lime slice and a few blackberries, if desired, into each of 8 glasses, and pour about 1 cup limeade over each serving. Yield: 8 servings.

CALORIES 125 (2% from fat); FAT 0.3g (sat 0g, mono 0g, poly 0.2g); PROTEIN 0.8g; CARB 31.9g; FIBER 0.7g; CHOL 0mg; IRON 0.4mg; SODIUM 5mg; CALC 22mg

Sparkling Citrus Punch

You may combine the fruit juices a day in advance. Then add sparkling water or champagne just before serving.

   ¾ cup apricot nectar, chilled
   ¾ cup pink grapefruit juice cocktail, chilled
    1 (12-ounce) can orange-tangerine juice
        concentrate, thawed and undiluted
    3 cups sparkling water or champagne, chilled

1. Combine first 3 ingredients in a pitcher; chill. Add sparkling water; serve immediately over ice. Yield: 2 quarts (serving size: ¾ cup).

CALORIES 114 (0% from fat); FAT 0g; PROTEIN 0.3g; CARB 26.5g; FIBER 0.2g; CHOL 0mg; IRON 0.1mg; SODIUM 4mg; CALC 264mg

Mint Limeade

Mint's fresh coolness is a welcome addition to this warm-weather drink. Try serving it with spicy Asian food.

    6 cups water, divided
  1¾ cups sugar
   ⅓ cup coarsely chopped fresh mint
    1 cup fresh lime juice (about 12 limes)
    8 mint sprigs (optional)
    8 lime slices (optional)

1. Combine 2 cups water, sugar, and chopped mint in a small saucepan; bring to a boil. Cook until sugar dissolves, stirring frequently. Remove from heat; let stand 10 minutes. Strain through a sieve into a bowl; discard solids.
2. Combine 4 cups water, sugar syrup, and lime juice in a large pitcher, stirring well. Serve over ice; garnish with mint sprigs and lime slices, if desired. Yield: 8 cups (serving size: about ¾ cup).

CALORIES 142 (0% from fat); FAT 0g; PROTEIN 0.1g; CARB 37.2g; FIBER 0.1g; CHOL 0mg; IRON 0mg; SODIUM 0mg; CALC 3mg

About Mint

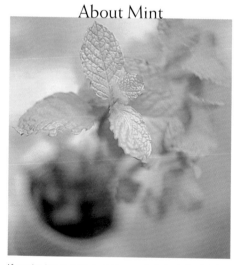

If you're buying mint at the market, look for bright green, crisp leaves with no signs of wilting. Place the stems in a glass containing a couple of inches of water, and cover the leaves loosely with plastic wrap or a zip-top plastic bag (do not seal the bag). Refrigerate up to one week, changing the water every other day. Fresh mint can also be frozen for later use. Simply rinse the leaves, pat them dry, and freeze them in a zip-top plastic bag (the leaves will darken once they're frozen, but that won't affect the flavor). Later, pull out what you need, and return the rest to the freezer.

Pumpkin Pie Shake

If you're seeking an all-American taste in a beverage, this is the perfect idea.

- 2 cups vanilla reduced-fat ice cream (such as Healthy Choice), softened
- 1 cup fat-free milk
- ⅔ cup canned pumpkin
- ¼ cup packed brown sugar
- ¾ teaspoon pumpkin-pie spice
- 3 tablespoons frozen fat-free whipped topping, thawed
- Pumpkin-pie spice (optional)

1. Place first 5 ingredients in a blender; process until smooth. Pour ¾ cup ice cream mixture into each of 4 glasses. Top each with about 2 teaspoons whipped topping; sprinkle with additional pumpkin-pie spice, if desired. Yield: 4 servings.

CALORIES 198 (13% from fat); FAT 2.8g (sat 1.8g, mono 0.6g, poly 0.1g); PROTEIN 6.1g; CARB 38g; FIBER 1.4g; CHOL 18mg; IRON 1.3mg; SODIUM 180mg; CALC 157mg

Blackberry-Peach Smoothie with Walnuts

This smoothie is rich in antioxidants and fiber from berries, potassium from peaches, omega-3 fatty acids from walnuts, vitamin C from orange juice, and soy isoflavones from tofu. Use calcium-fortified orange juice for added nutrition.

- 2 cups frozen sliced peaches
- 1 cup blackberries
- 1 cup orange juice
- ¾ cup chopped soft silken tofu (about 4 ounces)
- ¼ cup honey
- 2 tablespoons fresh lemon juice
- 2 tablespoons chopped walnuts

1. Place first 6 ingredients in a blender, and process until smooth. Top with chopped walnuts. Yield: 3 servings (serving size: 1 cup smoothie and 2 teaspoons walnuts).

CALORIES 237 (18% from fat); FAT 4.7g (sat 0.5g, mono 0.7g, poly 3.1g); PROTEIN 4.4g; CARB 47.1g; FIBER 4.5g; CHOL 0mg; IRON 1mg; SODIUM 7mg; CALC 43mg

Mocha-Almond Latte Freeze

Any coffee will work here, but a darker French roast coffee has a rich, strong flavor that pairs nicely with chocolate. The recipe makes more double-strength coffee than you need; freeze leftover coffee in ice cube trays for iced coffee drinks. Once frozen, coffee ice cubes can be stored in zip-top plastic bags for up to three months.

- 3 cups water
- 1 cup freshly ground French roast coffee
- ¼ cup fat-free milk
- ¼ cup ice cubes
- 1 teaspoon unsweetened cocoa
- ½ cup vanilla low-fat frozen yogurt
- ½ teaspoon grated semisweet chocolate
- 1 tablespoon canned refrigerated light whipped cream (such as Reddi-wip)
- ½ teaspoon chocolate syrup
- 1 teaspoon sliced almonds, toasted

1. Brew water and coffee in a coffee maker according to manufacturer's directions. Cover and chill. Reserve ¼ cup chilled coffee (reserve remaining coffee for another use).

2. Place ¼ cup chilled coffee, milk, ice cubes, and cocoa in a blender; process until smooth. Add yogurt and grated chocolate; process until smooth. Pour mixture into a tall glass; top with whipped cream. Drizzle with chocolate syrup, and sprinkle with almonds. Serve immediately. Yield: 1 serving (serving size: about 1¼ cups).

CALORIES 168 (23% from fat); FAT 4.2g (sat 2g, mono 1.6g, poly 0.4g); PROTEIN 7.6g; CARB 26.8g; FIBER 1g; CHOL 9mg; IRON 0.9mg; SODIUM 94mg; CALC 222mg

Classic Mint Juleps

Mint Juleps are lightly sweetened concoctions that have been enjoyed throughout the South since long before the first Kentucky Derby. This rendition won our Test Kitchens' top score.

  1 cup sugar
  1 cup water
 16 mint sprigs, lightly crushed
  8 cups finely crushed ice
  1 cup bourbon
Mint sprigs (optional)

1. Bring sugar and 1 cup water to a boil in a small saucepan. Cook 4 minutes or until sugar dissolves. Remove sugar syrup from heat; cool completely. Place 2 crushed mint sprigs in bottom of each of 8 glasses. Add 1 cup crushed ice, 2 tablespoons sugar syrup, and 2 tablespoons bourbon to each glass.

Garnish with mint sprigs, if desired. Yield: 8 servings.
SPIRIT NOTE: Bourbon is America's original spirit, made primarily from corn with varying amounts of wheat, barley, and rye. Wild Turkey 80 ($18) may sound like your grandfather's whiskey, but this smooth yet rich bourbon with caramel sweetness, vanilla aromas, and a touch of spice is a superb foundation for a mint julep. For a lighter-bodied, fruitier, and gentler style, choose a bourbon with a lot of wheat, like Maker's Mark ($23).

CALORIES 170 (0% from fat); FAT 0g; PROTEIN 0g; CARB 25g; FIBER 0g; CHOL 0mg; IRON 0mg; SODIUM 0mg; CALC 0mg

Frozen Lemonade with Coconut Rum

1½ cups ice cubes, crushed
3 tablespoons frozen lemonade concentrate
2 tablespoons coconut rum (such as Malibu)
Lime wedge (optional)

1. Place ice, lemonade concentrate, and coconut rum in a blender; blend until slushy. Garnish with lime wedge, if desired. Yield: 1 serving (serving size: about 1 cup).

CALORIES 172 (0% from fat); FAT 0.1g (sat 0g, mono 0g, poly 0.1g); PROTEIN 0.2g; CARB 25.8g; FIBER 0.1g; CHOL 0mg; IRON 0.4mg; SODIUM 2mg; CALC 4mg

Rum Punch

Substitute an additional cup of club soda for the rum if you prefer to turn this summer cocktail into a thirst-quenching tropical fruit punch.

½ cup sugar
½ cup water
4 cups mango juice, chilled (such as Looza brand)
3 cups pineapple juice, chilled
1½ cups dark rum
⅓ cup fresh lime juice (about 3 limes)
¼ cup grenadine
3 cups club soda, chilled

1. Combine sugar and ½ cup water in a small saucepan over high heat; bring to a boil. Cook until sugar dissolves, stirring occasionally. Remove from heat; transfer sugar mixture to a small bowl. Chill.
2. Combine sugar mixture, mango juice, and next 4 ingredients in a large bowl; mix well. Stir in soda. Serve over ice. Yield: 12 servings (serving size: about 1 cup).

CALORIES 191 (0% from fat); FAT 0.1g (sat 0g, mono 0g, poly 0g); PROTEIN 0.3g; CARB 31.1g; FIBER 0.2g; CHOL 0mg; IRON 0.2mg; SODIUM 19mg; CALC 13mg

Kiwi Colada

Here's a fun twist on the classic summertime umbrella drink. Kiwifruit and melon liqueur give the cocktail a green hue and slightly tangy flavor. Although we used green kiwi, you can substitute the golden variety for a sweeter taste and golden color.

5 peeled kiwifruit, divided
3 cups ice cubes
¼ cup light rum
¼ cup Midori (melon-flavored liqueur)
3 tablespoons Cream of Coconut (such as Coco Lopez)
1 (8-ounce) can crushed pineapple in juice, undrained

1. Cut 4 kiwifruit into quarters, and place in a blender. Set remaining kiwifruit aside. Add ice and remaining 4 ingredients to blender; process until smooth. Strain mixture through a sieve into a pitcher; discard seeds. Pour into each of 6 glasses. Cut remaining kiwifruit into 6 slices; garnish each glass with 1 kiwifruit slice. Yield: 6 servings (serving size: about ¾ cup).

CALORIES 143 (10% from fat); FAT 1.6g (sat 1g, mono 0g, poly 0.2g); PROTEIN 0.6g; CARB 23.1g; FIBER 2.5g; CHOL 0mg; IRON 0.4mg; SODIUM 11mg; CALC 17mg

Kiwi Colada

Mango-Avocado Margarita

For extra zip, rub the rim of each empty glass with a lime wedge, then coat the rims with salt and chili powder.

- 2 cups ice cubes
- 1 cup chopped peeled mango (about 1 large)
- 6 tablespoons chopped peeled ripe avocado
- 6 tablespoons fresh lime juice
- ¼ cup tequila
- ¼ cup orange juice
- 2 tablespoons sugar
- 2 tablespoons Triple Sec (orange-flavored liqueur)
- 4 lime wedges (optional)

1. Place first 8 ingredients in a blender; process until smooth.
2. Pour 1 cup mixture into each of 4 glasses. Serve drinks with lime wedges, if desired. Serve immediately. Yield: 4 servings (serving size: 1 cup).

CALORIES 162 (22% from fat); FAT 4g (sat 1.1g, mono 2.1g, poly 0.7g); PROTEIN 1.1g; CARB 23g; FIBER 1.7g; CHOL 0mg; IRON 0.1mg; SODIUM 2mg; CALC 10mg

Mango-Avocado Margarita

Jamaican Margaritas

Hibiscus blossoms can be found at Latin grocery stores. Simmering the blossoms in a sugar-water mixture infuses more flavor than just steeping them in warm water. This drink is especially good when made with premium-quality tequila.

- 1 cup dried hibiscus blossoms (about 2 ounces)
- 3 cups water
- ¾ cup sugar
- 1¼ cups tequila
- ½ cup fresh lime juice
- ⅓ cup Triple Sec or other orange-flavored liqueur
- 8 lime slices

1. Place blossoms in a strainer; rinse with cold water. Combine blossoms, 3 cups water, and sugar in a medium saucepan; bring to a boil. Reduce heat, and simmer 10 minutes. Strain into a bowl; discard blossoms. Cover and chill hibiscus mixture.
2. Combine hibiscus mixture, tequila, juice, and Triple Sec. Serve over ice. Garnish with lime slices. Yield: 8 servings (serving size: ½ cup margarita and 1 lime slice).

CALORIES 205 (0% from fat); FAT 0g; PROTEIN 0.1g; CARB 24.7g; FIBER 0.1g; CHOL 0mg; IRON 0mg; SODIUM 3mg; CALC 4mg

Classic Mojito

This Cuban drink is fast becoming a favorite in Puerto Rico; the mint and sugar go well with traditional dishes. If you have access to Key limes, use those for the most authentic flavor.

- 2 tablespoons sugar
- 15 fresh mint leaves
- ¼ cup white rum
- 1½ tablespoons fresh lime juice
- ¼ cup club soda, chilled
- ½ cup ice cubes

1. Place sugar and mint in a 2-cup glass measure; crush with a wooden spoon. Add rum and juice; stir until sugar dissolves. Just before serving, stir in club soda. Place ice in an 8-ounce glass; pour mint mixture over ice. Yield: 1 serving (serving size: about 1 cup).

CALORIES 234 (0% from fat); FAT 0g; PROTEIN 0.1g; CARB 27.2g; FIBER 0.2g; CHOL 0mg; IRON 0.1mg; SODIUM 14mg; CALC 7mg

Blood Orange Sangría

Any good-quality, fruity red wine works well in this cold sipper; a combination of pinot noir and beaujolais is particularly good. The vermilion flesh of blood oranges (which come into season in December) is lovely. But if they're not available, substitute navel oranges.

  2 cups sliced strawberries
  2 cups apple juice
  ⅔ cup Triple Sec (orange-flavored liqueur)
  ½ cup sugar
  4 whole cloves
  3 seedless blood oranges, each cut into
      16 wedges
  2 (750-milliliter) bottles fruity red wine
  2 (3-inch) cinnamon sticks
  1 lemon, cut into 8 wedges
  1 lime, cut into 8 wedges

1. Combine all ingredients in a large pitcher; stir until sugar dissolves. Cover and chill 8 hours or overnight. Discard cloves and cinnamon sticks. Pour sangría into individual glasses, including fruit. Yield: 16 servings (serving size: about 1 cup).

CALORIES 157 (1% from fat); FAT 0.1g (sat 0g, mono 0g, poly 0.1g); PROTEIN 0.6g; CARB 20.5g; FIBER 1.2g; CHOL 0mg; IRON 0.6mg; SODIUM 7mg; CALC 23mg

Apple Martinis

Make this your signature cocktail for parties year-round. Combine the ingredients for the martini mix in advance so it's ready to go into the shaker as soon as your guests arrive.

  1 cup water
  ¼ cup sugar
  ¾ cup vodka
  1 cup apple juice
  1 cup apple liqueur (such as Sour Apple Pucker)
Crushed ice

1. Combine 1 cup water and sugar in a glass measuring cup. Microwave at HIGH 2 minutes or until sugar dissolves, stirring once; cool. Combine sugar mixture, vodka, apple juice, and liqueur in a pitcher; stir to combine.
2. Place crushed ice in a martini shaker. Add vodka mixture to martini shaker in batches; shake well to chill. Strain about ½ cup vodka mixture in shaker into each of 10 glasses; repeat procedure with remaining vodka mixture, refilling ice as necessary. Serve immediately. Yield: 10 servings (serving size: about ½ cup).

CALORIES 160 (0% from fat); FAT 0g; PROTEIN 0.1g; CARB 16.2g; FIBER 0g; CHOL 0mg; IRON 0mg; SODIUM 0mg; CALC 0mg

Sparkling Pomegranate Cocktail

This simple, delicious cocktail can easily be doubled to serve more guests. For an equally delightful non-alcoholic version, simply mix one part pomegranate juice to two parts sparkling water.

  2 cups pomegranate juice (such as POM
      Wonderful)
1½ cups lemon-flavored sparkling water
  ½ cup berry-flavored vodka or plain vodka
Lemon rind strips (optional)

1. Combine first 3 ingredients in a pitcher. Pour ½ cup into each of 8 ice-filled glasses. Garnish with lemon rind strips, if desired. Yield: 8 servings.

CALORIES 195 (0% from fat); FAT 0g; PROTEIN 0g; CARB 44g; FIBER 0g; CHOL 0mg; IRON 0.7mg; SODIUM 1mg; CALC 1mg

breads

Coconut-Banana
Bread with Lime Glaze,
page 43

Whole-Grain Cornsticks

You can prepare the cornsticks in muffin tins, but a cast-iron cornstick pan yields a crisper crust.

 ¾ cup whole wheat flour
 ¾ cup yellow cornmeal
 3 tablespoons grated fresh Parmesan cheese
 2 teaspoons baking powder
 1½ teaspoons chili powder
 1 teaspoon salt
 ¾ cup plus 2 tablespoons fat-free milk
 2 tablespoons olive oil
 2 tablespoons honey
 1 large egg, lightly beaten
 ¾ cup frozen whole-kernel corn, thawed
 ⅓ cup minced red onion
 2 tablespoons minced jalapeño pepper
 Cooking spray

1. Preheat oven to 425°.
2. Lightly spoon flour into a dry measuring cup; level with a knife. Combine flour and next 5 ingredients in a large bowl. Make a well in center of mixture. Combine milk, oil, honey, and egg. Add to flour mixture, stirring just until moist. Fold in corn, onion, and jalapeño.
3. Place a cast-iron cornstick pan in a 425° oven for 5 minutes. Remove from oven; immediately coat with cooking spray. Spoon batter into pan. Bake at 425° for 18 minutes or until lightly browned. Remove from pan immediately; serve warm. Yield: 1 dozen (serving size: 1 cornstick).

CALORIES 120 (27% from fat); FAT 3.6g (sat 0.8g, mono 2.1g, poly 0.4g); PROTEIN 4g; CARB 19g; FIBER 2g; CHOL 19mg; IRON 0.7mg; SODIUM 325mg; CALC 96mg

Classic Scones

 2 cups all-purpose flour (about 9 ounces)
 3 tablespoons granulated sugar
 1½ teaspoons baking powder
 ½ teaspoon salt
 5 tablespoons chilled butter, cut into small pieces
 ½ cup fat-free milk
 ¼ teaspoon vanilla extract
 1 large egg white, lightly beaten
 ⅓ cup dried currants
 2 teaspoons fat-free milk
 2 teaspoons turbinado or granulated sugar

1. Preheat oven to 425°.
2. Lightly spoon flour into dry measuring cups; level with a knife. Combine flour, sugar, baking powder, and salt in a bowl; stir with a whisk. Cut in butter with a pastry blender or 2 knives until mixture resembles coarse meal.

3. Combine ½ cup milk, vanilla, and egg white in a bowl. Add milk mixture to flour mixture, stirring just until moist (dough will be soft). Turn dough out onto a lightly floured surface. Sprinkle dough with currants. With floured hands, knead 4 times or just until currants are incorporated.

4. Pat dough into an 8-inch circle on a baking sheet lined with parchment paper. Cut dough into 12 wedges, cutting into, but not through, dough. Brush 2 teaspoons milk over dough; sprinkle with turbinado sugar. Bake at 425° for 17 minutes or until golden. Serve warm, or cool on a wire rack. Yield: 12 servings (serving size: 1 scone).

CALORIES 149 (30% from fat); FAT 5g (sat 3g, mono 1.3g, poly 0.3g); PROTEIN 3g; CARB 23.4g; FIBER 0.8g; CHOL 13mg; IRON 1.2mg; SODIUM 203mg; CALC 56mg

Chipotle-Bacon Corn Bread

 1 cup all-purpose flour
 ¾ cup yellow cornmeal
 3 tablespoons sugar
 1 teaspoon baking powder
 1 teaspoon salt
 ½ teaspoon ground cumin
 ¼ teaspoon baking soda
 1⅓ cups fat-free buttermilk
 2 tablespoons butter, melted
 1½ tablespoons chopped canned chipotle chiles
    in adobo sauce
 1 large egg, lightly beaten
 3 bacon slices, cooked and crumbled
 Cooking spray

1. Preheat oven to 425°.
2. Lightly spoon flour into a dry measuring cup; level with a knife. Combine flour and next 6 ingredients in a large bowl, stirring well. Combine buttermilk, butter, chiles, and egg in a medium bowl, stirring with a whisk. Add buttermilk mixture to flour mixture; stir just until moist. Fold in bacon. Pour batter into an 8-inch square baking pan coated with cooking spray.
3. Bake at 425° for 18 minutes or until a wooden pick inserted in center comes out clean. Cool 10 minutes in pan on a wire rack. Cut into squares. Yield: 9 servings (serving size: 1 square).

CALORIES 165 (28% from fat); FAT 5.1g (sat 2.4g, mono 1.6g, poly 0.5g); PROTEIN 4.9g; CARB 25.1g; FIBER 1.2g; CHOL 34mg; IRON 1.3mg; SODIUM 460mg; CALC 82mg

Whole Wheat–Apple Scones

 1 cup plus 2 tablespoons all-purpose flour
    (about 5 ounces)
 1 cup whole wheat flour (about 4¾ ounces)
 ¼ cup sugar
 2 teaspoons baking powder
 1 teaspoon ground cinnamon
 ½ teaspoon baking soda
 ½ teaspoon salt
 Dash of ground nutmeg
 ¼ cup chilled butter, cut into small pieces
 1 cup shredded peeled Granny Smith apple
    (about ½ pound)
 ½ cup 1% low-fat milk
 1 teaspoon vanilla extract
 Cooking spray
 2 tablespoons 1% low-fat milk
 2 teaspoons sugar

1. Preheat oven to 425°.
2. Lightly spoon flours into dry measuring cups and tablespoons; level with a knife. Combine flours, sugar, and next 5 ingredients in a large bowl; stir with a whisk. Cut in butter with a pastry blender or 2 knives until mixture resembles coarse meal. Add apple, ½ cup milk, and vanilla, stirring just until moist (dough will be sticky).
3. Turn dough out onto a lightly floured surface; knead lightly 4 times with floured hands. Divide dough in half; pat each portion into a 6-inch circle on a baking sheet coated with cooking spray. Cut each circle into 5 wedges, cutting into, but not through, dough. Brush tops of wedges with 2 tablespoons milk; sprinkle evenly with 2 teaspoons sugar. Bake at 425° for 15 minutes or until golden. Serve warm. Yield: 10 servings (serving size: 1 wedge).

CALORIES 170 (27% from fat); FAT 5.1g (sat 3g, mono 1.3g, poly 0.3g); PROTEIN 3.7g; CARB 28.1g; FIBER 2.1g; CHOL 13mg; IRON 1.3mg; SODIUM 319mg; CALC 84mg

Apple Muffins with Walnut Streusel

MUFFINS:

1¼ cups all-purpose flour
½ cup whole wheat flour
¾ cup ground flaxseed
¾ cup packed brown sugar
1 teaspoon baking powder
1 teaspoon baking soda
¼ teaspoon salt
½ cup 1% low-fat milk
½ cup orange juice
1 tablespoon butter, melted
1 teaspoon vanilla extract
2 large eggs, lightly beaten
2 cups finely chopped Granny Smith apple (about 1 large)
½ cup golden raisins
Cooking spray

STREUSEL:

¼ cup finely chopped walnuts
2 tablespoons brown sugar
1 tablespoon chilled butter, cut into small pieces

1. Preheat oven to 350°.
2. To prepare muffins, lightly spoon flours into dry measuring cups; level with a knife. Combine flours, flaxseed, and next 4 ingredients in a medium bowl, stirring with a whisk. Make a well in center of mixture.
3. Combine milk and next 4 ingredients, stirring with a whisk; add to flour mixture, stirring just until moist. Fold in apple and raisins. Spoon batter into 18 muffin cups coated with cooking spray.
4. To prepare streusel, combine walnuts, 2 tablespoons brown sugar, and chilled butter in a small bowl, stirring with a fork until crumbly. Sprinkle streusel evenly over batter. Bake at 350° for 20 minutes or until muffins spring back when touched lightly in center. Remove from pans immediately; place on a wire rack. Serve warm or at room temperature. Yield: 1½ dozen (serving size: 1 muffin).

CALORIES 167 (27% from fat); FAT 5g (sat 1.3g, mono 1.1g, poly 2.2g); PROTEIN 3.8g; CARB 27.9g; FIBER 2.6g; CHOL 27mg; IRON 1.4mg; SODIUM 148mg; CALC 54mg

Double-Apple Bran Muffins

Oat bran, the outer casing of an oat, is high in fiber. Apples and applesauce make these healthful muffins sweet and moist. If making them ahead, individually wrap cooled muffins, and freeze up to 1 week.

½ cup packed brown sugar
¼ cup butter, softened
1 large egg
1 large egg white
¾ cup fat-free milk
¼ cup unsweetened applesauce
1 tablespoon molasses
½ teaspoon vanilla extract
1 cup all-purpose flour (about 4½ ounces)
1½ cups oat bran
1½ teaspoons baking powder
¾ teaspoon salt
½ teaspoon ground cinnamon
½ cup coarsely chopped peeled Granny Smith apple
2 teaspoons turbinado sugar (optional)

1. Preheat oven to 400°.
2. Place 12 paper muffin cup liners in muffin cups; set aside. Combine brown sugar and butter in a medium bowl; beat with a mixer at medium-high speed until light and fluffy (about 5 minutes). Add egg; beat 1 minute or until well blended. Add egg white; beat until well blended. Add milk, applesauce, molasses, and vanilla; beat at low speed until well blended.
3. Lightly spoon flour into a dry measuring cup; level with a knife. Combine flour, bran, and next 3 ingredients in a large bowl; make a well in center of mixture. Add milk mixture to flour mixture, stirring just until moist. Gently stir in apple.
4. Spoon batter evenly into prepared muffin cups. Sprinkle evenly with turbinado sugar, if desired. Bake at 400° for 18 minutes or until muffins spring back when touched lightly in center. Yield: 12 servings (serving size: 1 muffin).

CALORIES 174 (29% from fat); FAT 5.6g (sat 2.8g, mono 1.6g, poly 0.8g); PROTEIN 5.2g; CARB 32.5g; FIBER 3g; CHOL 28mg; IRON 1.9mg; SODIUM 258mg; CALC 80mg

Raspberry–Cream Cheese Muffins

⅔ cup (5 ounces) ⅓-less-fat cream cheese, softened

⅓ cup butter, softened

1½ cups sugar

1½ teaspoons vanilla extract

2 large egg whites

1 large egg

2 cups all-purpose flour

1 teaspoon baking powder

¼ teaspoon baking soda

½ teaspoon salt

½ cup low-fat buttermilk

2 cups fresh or frozen raspberries

¼ cup finely chopped walnuts

1. Preheat oven to 350°.

2. Combine cream cheese and butter in a large bowl. Beat with a mixer at high speed until well blended. Add sugar; beat until fluffy. Add vanilla, egg whites, and egg; beat well.

3. Lightly spoon flour into dry measuring cups; level with a knife. Combine flour, baking powder, baking soda, and salt. With mixer on low speed, add flour mixture and buttermilk alternately to cream cheese mixture, beginning and ending with flour mixture. Gently fold in raspberries and walnuts.

4. Place 24 foil cup liners in muffin cups. Spoon batter evenly into liners. Bake at 350° for 25 minutes or until a wooden pick inserted in center comes out clean. Remove from pans; cool on a wire rack. Yield: 2 dozen (serving size: 1 muffin).

CALORIES 142 (32% from fat); FAT 4.7g (sat 2.4g, mono 1.3g, poly 0.7g); PROTEIN 2.7g; CARB 22.6g; FIBER 1.1g; CHOL 19mg; IRON 0.7mg; SODIUM 138mg; CALC 31mg

Cranberry-Orange Muffins

    2 cups all-purpose flour (about 9 ounces)
    1 cup sugar, divided
1 ½ teaspoons baking powder
    1 teaspoon salt
    ½ teaspoon baking soda
    2 teaspoons grated orange rind
    ¾ cup orange juice (about 1 large orange)
    ¼ cup canola oil
    1 large egg, lightly beaten
    2 cups coarsely chopped fresh cranberries
       (about 8 ounces)
    ⅓ cup chopped walnuts, toasted
       Cooking spray

1. Preheat oven to 400°.
2. Lightly spoon flour into dry measuring cups; level with a knife. Set aside 1 tablespoon sugar. Combine flour, remaining sugar, baking powder, salt, and baking soda in a large bowl; make a well in center of mixture.
3. Combine rind, juice, oil, and egg in a bowl, stirring well with a whisk. Add to flour mixture, stirring just until moist. Fold in cranberries and walnuts. Spoon batter into 16 muffin cups coated with cooking spray. Sprinkle evenly with 1 tablespoon sugar. Bake at 400° for 15 minutes or until muffins spring back when touched lightly in center. Run a knife or spatula around outer edge of each muffin cup. Carefully remove each muffin; place on a wire rack. Yield: 16 servings (serving size: 1 muffin).

CALORIES 169 (30% from fat); FAT 5.6g (sat 0.5g, mono 2.5g, poly 2.4g); PROTEIN 2.5g; CARB 27.9g; FIBER 1.3g; CHOL 2mg; IRON 1mg; SODIUM 236mg; CALC 35mg

Oat-Topped Fig Muffins

1 ½ cups all-purpose flour (about 6¾ ounces)
    1 cup whole wheat pastry flour (about 5⅛ ounces)
    ½ cup sugar
    1 teaspoon baking powder
    1 teaspoon baking soda
    ½ teaspoon salt
1 ½ cups low-fat buttermilk
1 ¼ cups chopped dried figs
    2 tablespoons canola oil
    1 teaspoon vanilla extract
    1 large egg
       Cooking spray
    ⅓ cup packed brown sugar
    ¼ cup quick-cooking oats
    1 tablespoon butter

1. Preheat oven to 400°.
2. Lightly spoon flours into measuring cups; level with a knife. Combine flours, sugar, and next 3 ingredients in a large bowl; stir with a whisk. Make a well in center of mixture.
3. Place buttermilk, figs, oil, vanilla, and egg in a food processor; process until well blended. Add fig mixture to flour mixture, stirring just until combined. Spoon batter into 12 muffin cups coated with cooking spray.
4. Combine brown sugar, oats, and butter in a small bowl; toss with a fork until combined. Sprinkle oat mixture evenly over muffins. Bake at 400° for 18 minutes or until a wooden pick inserted in center comes out clean. Cool in pans on a wire rack 5 minutes; remove muffins from pans, and cool completely on rack. Yield: 12 servings (serving size: 1 muffin).

CALORIES 83 (23% from fat); FAT 2.1g (sat 0.7g, mono 0.6g, poly 0.5g); PROTEIN 2.6g; CARB 12.8g; FIBER 0.4g; CHOL 1mg; IRON 0.8mg; SODIUM 247mg; CALC 20mg

Honey and Toasted Pistachio Muffins

Each of these homemade muffins contains almost three grams of fiber.

    1 cup whole wheat flour (about 4¾ ounces)
    1 cup all-purpose flour (about 4½ ounces)
    ¼ cup flaxseed meal
1 ¼ teaspoons baking soda
    ⅛ teaspoon salt
    ⅛ teaspoon ground nutmeg
    ⅛ teaspoon ground allspice
    1 cup buttermilk
    ½ cup packed brown sugar
    2 tablespoons canola oil
    2 large eggs, lightly beaten
    ¼ cup golden raisins
       Cooking spray
    3 tablespoons finely chopped pistachios
    2 tablespoons honey

1. Preheat oven to 350°.
2. Lightly spoon flours into dry measuring cups; level with a knife. Combine flours and next 5 ingredients in a medium bowl, and stir well with a whisk. Make a well in center of mixture. Combine buttermilk, sugar, oil, and eggs; add to flour mixture, stirring just until moist. Stir in raisins. Spoon batter into 12 muffin cups coated with cooking

spray. Sprinkle evenly with pistachios. Bake at 350° for 15 minutes or until muffins spring back when touched lightly in center. Remove muffins from pans immediately; cool on a wire rack. Drizzle honey evenly over tops of muffins. Yield: 12 servings (serving size: 1 muffin).

CALORIES 198 (28% from fat); FAT 6.2g (sat 1.1g, mono 2.4g, poly 2g); PROTEIN 5.2g; CARB 31.9g; FIBER 2.6g; CHOL 38mg; IRON 1.5mg; SODIUM 197mg; CALC 28mg

Millet Muffins with Honey-Pecan Butter

Look for millet, a round, pale yellow grain, in health-food stores or in the organic sections of large supermarkets.

MUFFINS:
  ⅔ cup uncooked millet
  ¾ cup packed brown sugar
  1 large egg
  1 cup fat-free buttermilk
  ¼ cup butter, melted
1½ cups all-purpose flour
  1 teaspoon baking powder
  ¼ teaspoon baking soda
  ¼ teaspoon salt
Cooking spray

BUTTER:
  2 tablespoons butter, softened
  2 tablespoons finely chopped pecans, toasted
  1 tablespoon honey

1. Preheat oven to 375°.
2. To prepare muffins, place millet in a spice or coffee grinder; pulse 6 times or until lightly crushed. Set aside.
3. Place sugar and egg in a large bowl; beat with a mixer at medium speed until well combined. Stir in millet, buttermilk, and ¼ cup butter.
4. Lightly spoon flour into dry measuring cups; level with a knife. Combine flour, baking powder, baking soda, and salt, stirring with a whisk. Make a well in center of mixture. Add buttermilk mixture; stir just until moist. Let batter stand 5 minutes. Spoon batter into 12 muffin cups coated with cooking spray. Bake at 375° for 18 minutes or until muffins spring back when touched lightly in center. Cool in pan 5 minutes on a wire rack. Remove muffins from pan; place on wire rack.
5. To prepare butter, combine 2 tablespoons butter, pecans, and honey, stirring well to combine. Serve with muffins. Yield: 12 servings (serving size: 1 muffin and 1 teaspoon butter).

CALORIES 229 (30% from fat); FAT 7.6g (sat 3.8g, mono 2.4g, poly 0.8g); PROTEIN 4.3g; CARB 36.3g; FIBER 1.5g; CHOL 33mg; IRON 1.5mg; SODIUM 284mg; CALC 67mg

Millet Muffins with Honey-Pecan Butter

Sweet Potato and Pecan Flapjacks

Sweet Potato and Pecan Flapjacks

1¼ cups all-purpose flour (about 5½ ounces)
¼ cup chopped pecans, toasted
3 tablespoons yellow cornmeal
2 teaspoons baking powder
½ teaspoon salt
½ teaspoon ground cinnamon
1 cup fat-free milk
1 cup mashed cooked sweet potato
3 tablespoons brown sugar
1 tablespoon canola oil
½ teaspoon vanilla extract
2 large egg yolks
2 large egg whites
Cooking spray

1. Lightly spoon flour into dry measuring cups; level with a knife. Combine flour and next 5 ingredients in a large bowl, stirring with a whisk.
2. Combine milk and next 5 ingredients, stirring until smooth; add to flour mixture, stirring just until combined. Beat egg whites with a mixer at high speed until soft peaks form; fold egg whites into batter. Let batter stand 10 minutes.
3. Heat a nonstick griddle or nonstick skillet over medium-high heat. Coat griddle or pan with cooking spray. Spoon about ¼ cup batter per pancake onto griddle or pan. Cook 2 minutes or until tops are covered with bubbles and edges look cooked. Carefully turn pancakes over, and cook 2 minutes or until bottoms are lightly browned. Yield: 6 servings (serving size: 2 pancakes).

CALORIES 276 (26% from fat); FAT 7.9g (sat 1.1g, mono 4.1g, poly 2.1g); PROTEIN 7.7g; CARB 43.7g; FIBER 2.8g; CHOL 71mg; IRON 2.7mg; SODIUM 419mg; CALC 166mg

Buttermilk Pancakes

1½ cups all-purpose flour (about 6¾ ounces)
2 tablespoons sugar
1 teaspoon baking powder
½ teaspoon salt
1½ cups fat-free buttermilk
1 tablespoon butter, melted
1 large egg, lightly beaten

1. Lightly spoon flour into dry measuring cups, and level with a knife. Combine flour, sugar, baking powder, and salt in a medium bowl, and stir with a whisk. Combine buttermilk, butter, and egg, and add to flour mixture, stirring until smooth.
2. Pour about ¼ cup batter per pancake onto a hot nonstick griddle or nonstick skillet. Cook 2 minutes or until tops are covered with bubbles and edges look cooked. Carefully turn pancakes over; cook 2 minutes or until bottoms are lightly browned. Yield: 4 servings (serving size: 3 pancakes).

CALORIES 272 (15% from fat); FAT 4.5g (sat 2.2g, mono 1.3g, poly 0.5g); PROTEIN 9.8g; CARB 47.4g; FIBER 1.3g; CHOL 61mg; IRON 2.4mg; SODIUM 583mg; CALC 126mg

White Flour Tortillas

4 cups all-purpose flour
2 teaspoons baking powder
2 teaspoons salt
6 tablespoons vegetable shortening
1½ cups hot water
1 tablespoon nonfat dry milk

1. Lightly spoon flour into dry measuring cups; level with a knife. Combine flour, baking powder, and salt in a large bowl. Cut in shortening with a pastry blender or 2 knives until mixture resembles coarse meal; make a well in center of mixture. Combine hot water and dry milk, and add to flour mixture. Stir until blended. Cover and let rest 20 minutes.
2. Divide dough into 18 equal portions, shaping each portion into a ball (cover remaining dough to prevent drying). Working with one ball at a time, roll ball into a 7-inch round. Heat a cast-iron skillet over medium-high heat. Cook round 1 minute on each side or until lightly browned. Yield: 18 tortillas (serving size: 1 tortilla).

CALORIES 126 (29% from fat); FAT 4g (sat 1g, mono 1.3g, poly 1g); PROTEIN 2.8g; CARB 20.6g; FIBER 0.7g; CHOL 0mg; IRON 1.3mg; SODIUM 306mg; CALC 30mg

Herbed Cracker Bread

We loved the irregular shape of these savory crackers. Store them in an airtight container up to 3 days. Vary the flavor by using other dried herbs in place of herbes de Provence.

2 cups all-purpose flour
⅓ cup (about 1½ ounces) grated fresh Parmesan cheese
2 teaspoons dried herbes de Provence
1½ teaspoons coarsely ground black pepper
1 teaspoon baking powder
1 teaspoon sugar
¾ teaspoon salt
½ cup fat-free sour cream
2 tablespoons butter, melted
1 large egg, lightly beaten
Cooking spray
3 tablespoons yellow cornmeal

1. Preheat oven to 350°.
2. Lightly spoon flour into dry measuring cups, and level with a knife. Combine flour and next 6 ingredients in a large bowl, stirring with a whisk.
3. Combine sour cream, butter, and egg, stirring with a whisk. Add egg mixture to flour mixture; stir to form a soft dough. Turn dough out onto a lightly floured surface; knead lightly 7 or 8 times.
4. Divide dough in half. Place 1 dough portion on each of 2 baking sheets coated with cooking spray and sprinkled with 1½ tablespoons cornmeal; turn to coat top of dough. Roll each portion into a 12 x 8–inch rectangle (about ⅛-inch-thick). Bake at 350° for 15 minutes or until browned and crisp. Remove from pans; cool completely on wire racks. Break into 24 crackers. Yield: 12 servings (serving size: 2 crackers).

CALORIES 132 (25% from fat); FAT 3.7g (sat 2g, mono 1g, poly 0.3g); PROTEIN 4.7g; CARB 19.9g; FIBER 0.9g; CHOL 26mg; IRON 1.4mg; SODIUM 278mg; CALC 89mg

Steamed Brown Bread with Currants and Walnuts

Bread probably isn't what you think of as typical slow-cooker fare, but this method of steaming the bread in the cooker helps the batter cook evenly and makes for a moist texture. Serve this bread as a side to complete a meal or as a light breakfast with coffee. You can substitute sweetened dried cranberries for the currants, if desired.

½ cup all-purpose flour
½ cup whole wheat flour
½ cup yellow cornmeal
¾ teaspoon ground cinnamon
½ teaspoon baking soda
½ teaspoon salt
1 cup low-fat buttermilk
⅓ cup molasses
½ cup dried currants
2 tablespoons chopped walnuts
Cooking spray

1. Lightly spoon flours into dry measuring cups; level with a knife. Combine flours and next 4 ingredients in a large bowl, and make a well in center of mixture. Combine buttermilk and molasses, and stir well. Add to flour mixture, stirring just until moist. Fold in currants and walnuts.
2. Spoon mixture into a 1½-quart round casserole dish coated with cooking spray. Cover with aluminum foil coated with cooking spray; secure foil with a rubber band. Place dish in a 6-quart electric slow cooker; add enough hot water to cooker to come halfway up sides of dish. Cover and cook on HIGH 2½ hours or until a wooden pick inserted in center comes out clean.
3. Remove dish from cooker using oven mitts. Let bread cool, covered, in dish on a wire rack 5 minutes. Remove bread from dish, and let cool completely on wire rack. Yield: 8 servings (serving size: 1 wedge).

CALORIES 170 (13% from fat); FAT 2.4g (sat 0.5g, mono 0.3g, poly 1g); PROTEIN 4.4g; CARB 34.5g; FIBER 2.3g; CHOL 0g; IRON 1.9mg; SODIUM 252mg; CALC 82mg

Steamed Brown Bread with
Currants and Walnuts

Onion and Fontina Beer Batter Bread

    1   tablespoon olive oil
    1   cup diced onion
    3   cups all-purpose flour (about 13½ ounces)
    3   tablespoons sugar
    2   teaspoons baking powder
    1   teaspoon salt
    1   cup (4 ounces) grated fontina cheese
    1   (12-ounce) bottle beer (such as amber ale)
Cooking spray
    ¼   cup butter, melted and divided

1. Preheat oven to 375°.
2. Heat oil in a large nonstick skillet over medium heat. Add onion, and sauté 6 minutes or until tender. Cool to room temperature.
3. Lightly spoon flour into dry measuring cups, and level with a knife. Combine flour, sugar, baking powder, and salt in a bowl; make a well in center of mixture. Add onion, cheese, and beer; stir just until moist.
4. Spoon batter into a 9 x 5–inch loaf pan coated with cooking spray; drizzle evenly with 2 tablespoons butter. Bake at 375° for 35 minutes; brush with remaining 2 tablespoons butter. Bake an additional 23 minutes or until a wooden pick inserted in center comes out clean. Cool 5 minutes in pan on a wire rack, and remove from pan. Cool completely on wire rack. Yield: 16 servings (serving size: 1 slice).

CALORIES 149 (30% from fat); FAT 5g (sat 2.3g, mono 2.1g, poly 0.3g); PROTEIN 3.5g; CARB 22.2g; FIBER 0.8g; CHOL 12mg; IRON 1.2mg; SODIUM 259mg; CALC 61mg

Oatmeal-Molasses Bread

    2   cups fat-free buttermilk
    ½   cup regular oats
    ¼   cup unsulfured molasses
    2   tablespoons vegetable oil
    2¾   cups all-purpose flour
    1   cup whole wheat flour
    2   tablespoons sugar
    1½   teaspoons salt
    1   teaspoon baking powder
    1   teaspoon baking soda
    1   cup raisins
    1   tablespoon yellow cornmeal

1. Preheat oven to 400°.
2. Combine first 4 ingredients in a medium bowl. Lightly spoon flours into dry measuring cups; level with a knife. Combine flours, sugar, salt, baking powder, and baking soda; make a well in center of mixture.
3. Add buttermilk mixture to flour mixture, stirring just until moist; stir in raisins. Stir with a wooden spoon until dough pulls together in a shaggy mass. Let rest 2 minutes.
4. Turn half of dough out onto a lightly floured surface. Knead dough 1 minute with floured hands (dough will feel tacky); shape dough into a 6-inch round loaf. Place on a baking sheet sprinkled with cornmeal. Repeat procedure with remaining dough. Make 3 diagonal cuts ¼-inch-deep across top of each loaf using a sharp knife.
5. Bake at 400° for 20 minutes. Reduce oven temperature to 375° (do not remove loaves from oven); bake an additional 15 minutes or until bottom of each loaf sounds hollow when tapped. Let stand 15 minutes before slicing. Yield: 2 loaves, 12 servings per loaf (serving size: 1 slice).

CALORIES 126 (11% from fat); FAT 1.5g (sat 0.2g, mono 0.3g, poly 0.8g); PROTEIN 3.4g; CARB 25.2g; FIBER 1.6g; CHOL 0mg; IRON 1.3mg; SODIUM 243mg; CALC 50mg

Mini Fruit and Sunflower Loaves

    2   cups all-purpose flour (about 9 ounces)
    1   cup yellow cornmeal
    2   teaspoons baking soda
    ¼   teaspoon salt
    2   cups vanilla fat-free yogurt
    ½   cup canola oil
    ½   cup maple syrup
    ½   cup honey
    1   teaspoon vanilla extract
    1   cup chopped dried mixed fruit
    ½   cup sunflower seed kernels
    1   teaspoon grated orange rind
Cooking spray

1. Preheat oven to 350°.
2. Lightly spoon flour into dry measuring cups; level with a knife. Combine flour and next 3 ingredients in a large bowl. Combine yogurt, oil, syrup, honey, and vanilla. Add to flour mixture, stirring just until moist. Fold in fruit, sunflower seeds, and rind. Spoon into 4 (6-inch) loaf pans coated with cooking spray. Bake at 350° for 35 minutes or until a wooden pick inserted in center comes out clean. Remove from pans; cool completely on a wire rack. Yield: 4 loaves, 8 servings per loaf (serving size: 1 slice).

CALORIES 151 (30% from fat); FAT 5.1g (sat 0.4g, mono 2.4g, poly 2g); PROTEIN 2.6g; CARB 24.5g; FIBER 1.2g; CHOL 0mg; IRON 0.8mg; SODIUM 111mg; CALC 36mg

Coconut-Banana Bread with Lime Glaze

(pictured on page 31)

The tangy lime glaze cuts the sweetness of the bread. Substitute apple juice for the rum, if you prefer.

2 cups all-purpose flour
¾ teaspoon baking soda
½ teaspoon salt
1 cup granulated sugar
¼ cup butter, softened
2 large eggs
1½ cups mashed ripe banana (about 3 bananas)
¼ cup plain low-fat yogurt
3 tablespoons dark rum
½ teaspoon vanilla extract
½ cup flaked sweetened coconut
Cooking spray
1 tablespoon flaked sweetened coconut
½ cup powdered sugar
1½ tablespoons fresh lime or lemon juice

1. Preheat oven to 350°.

2. Lightly spoon flour into dry measuring cups, and level with a knife. Combine flour, baking soda, and salt, stirring with a whisk.

3. Place granulated sugar and butter in a large bowl; beat with a mixer at medium speed until well blended (about 1 minute). Add eggs, 1 at a time, beating well after each addition. Add banana, yogurt, rum, and vanilla; beat until blended. Add flour mixture; beat at low speed just until moist. Stir in ½ cup coconut. Spoon batter into a 9 x 5–inch loaf pan coated with cooking spray; sprinkle with 1 tablespoon coconut. Bake at 350° for 1 hour or until a wooden pick inserted in center comes out clean. Cool 10 minutes in pan on a wire rack; remove from pan. Combine powdered sugar and juice, stirring with a whisk; drizzle over warm bread. Cool bread completely on wire rack. Yield: 1 loaf, 16 servings (serving size: 1 slice).

CALORIES 193 (21% from fat); FAT 4.6g (sat 2.8g, mono 1.1g, poly 0.3g); PROTEIN 2.9g; CARB 35g; FIBER 1.1g; CHOL 35mg; IRON 1mg; SODIUM 179mg; CALC 15mg

Orange-Banana-Nut Bread

Orange rind and juice delicately flavor this bread. For a quick breakfast, spread toasted slices with reduced-fat cream cheese and top with thinly sliced strawberries, peaches, or kiwi.

> 2   cups all-purpose flour
> ¾   teaspoon baking soda
> ½   teaspoon salt
> 1   cup sugar
> ¼   cup butter, softened
> 2   large eggs
> 1½ cups mashed ripe banana (about 3 bananas)
> 1½ tablespoons grated orange rind
> 3   tablespoons fresh orange juice
> ⅓   cup chopped walnuts
>   Cooking spray

1. Preheat oven to 350°.
2. Lightly spoon flour into dry measuring cups, and level with a knife. Combine flour, baking soda, and salt, stirring with a whisk.
3. Place sugar and butter in a large bowl; beat with a mixer at medium speed until well blended (about 1 minute). Add eggs, 1 at a time, beating well after each addition. Add banana, rind, and juice; beat until blended. Add flour mixture; beat at low speed just until moist. Stir in walnuts; spoon batter into an 8½ x 4½–inch loaf pan coated with cooking spray. Bake at 350° for 1 hour and 5 minutes or until a wooden pick inserted in center comes out clean. Cool 10 minutes in pan on a wire rack; remove from pan. Cool completely on wire rack. Yield: 1 loaf, 16 servings (serving size: 1 slice).

CALORIES 178 (27% from fat); FAT 5.4g (sat 2.2g, mono 1.3g, poly 1.5g); PROTEIN 3.1g; CARB 30.5g; FIBER 1.2g; CHOL 34mg; IRON 1mg; SODIUM 170mg; CALC 11mg

Banana–Chocolate Chip–Walnut Bread

Rather than a combination of all-purpose and whole wheat flour, this recipe uses only whole wheat flour. It makes a great healthy after-school snack.

> 2   cups mashed ripe banana (about 4 bananas)
> 1   cup vanilla fat-free yogurt
> ½   cup reduced-fat vanilla soy milk
> ¼   cup canola oil
> ½   teaspoon vanilla extract
> 4   cups whole wheat pastry flour (about 20½ ounces)
> 1   cup sugar
> 2   teaspoons baking powder
> 2   teaspoons baking soda
> 1   teaspoon ground cinnamon
> ½   teaspoon salt
> 1   cup semisweet chocolate chips
> ½   cup chopped walnuts
>   Cooking spray

1. Preheat oven to 350°.
2. Place first 5 ingredients in a food processor; process until smooth.
3. Lightly spoon flour into dry measuring cups; level with a knife. Combine flour and next 5 ingredients in a large bowl. Add banana mixture to flour mixture, stirring just until moist. Stir in chocolate chips and walnuts until well combined. Divide mixture evenly between 2 (9 x 5–inch) loaf pans coated with cooking spray.
4. Bake at 350° for 50 minutes or until a wooden pick inserted in center comes out clean. Cool in pans on a wire rack 10 minutes. Remove from pans; cool completely. Yield: 2 loaves, 16 servings per loaf (serving size: 1 slice).

CALORIES 150 (29% from fat); FAT 4.9g (sat 1.2g, mono 1.8g, poly 1.6g); PROTEIN 3.2g; CARB 25.8g; FIBER 2.7g; CHOL 0mg; IRON 0.9mg; SODIUM 153mg; CALC 41mg

Molasses-Oat-Banana Bread

Molasses gives this bread a rich, deep brown color and distinctly old-fashioned taste. Because of the whole wheat flour and oats, the chewy loaf won't rise very high.

  1 cup all-purpose flour
 ½ cup whole wheat flour
 ⅔ cup regular oats
  1 teaspoon baking soda
  1 teaspoon ground cinnamon
 ½ teaspoon salt
 ⅔ cup sugar
 ¼ cup butter, softened
 ⅓ cup dark molasses
  2 large eggs
  1 cup mashed ripe banana (about 2 bananas)
 ⅓ cup plain low-fat yogurt
  1 teaspoon vanilla extract
Cooking spray

1. Preheat oven to 350°.
2. Lightly spoon flours into dry measuring cups; level with a knife. Combine flours, oats, baking soda, cinnamon, and salt, stirring with a whisk.

About Molasses

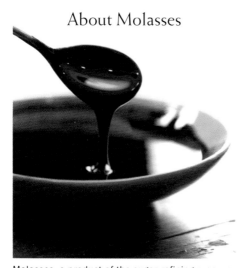

Molasses, a product of the sugar-refining process, is the liquid left behind after sugar crystals have been extracted from boiled sugarcane juice. Several different versions are available. The light variety comes from the first boiling and is usually used to top pancakes. The second boiling creates dark molasses, which has a denser, more assertive flavor; it's most commonly used in gingerbread and barbecue sauces. Avoid blackstrap molasses, which comes from the third boiling; though popular in health-food circles due to its slightly higher mineral content, it's very bitter.

3. Place sugar, butter, and molasses in a large bowl; beat with a mixer at medium speed until well blended (about 1 minute). Add eggs, 1 at a time, beating well after each addition. Add banana, yogurt, and vanilla; beat until blended. Add flour mixture; beat at low speed just until moist. Spoon batter into an 8½ x 4½–inch loaf pan coated with cooking spray. Bake at 350° for 1 hour and 5 minutes or until a wooden pick inserted in center comes out clean. Cool 10 minutes in pan on a wire rack; remove from pan. Cool completely on wire rack. Yield: 1 loaf, 14 servings (serving size: 1 slice).

CALORIES 177 (23% from fat); FAT 4.6g (sat 2.4g, mono 1.3g, poly 0.4g); PROTEIN 3.5g; CARB 31.9g; FIBER 1.6g; CHOL 40mg; IRON 2mg; SODIUM 224mg; CALC 61mg

Date Bread

This bread is easy to make and yields two loaves. Because the dates soak overnight, start the bread the day before serving.

  2 cups chopped pitted dates
  2 cups boiling water
  2 teaspoons baking soda
Cooking spray
  4 teaspoons all-purpose flour
  1 cup sugar
  1 tablespoon butter, melted
  1 teaspoon vanilla extract
  1 large egg, lightly beaten
2¼ cups all-purpose flour
 ½ teaspoon salt

1. Combine first 3 ingredients in a large bowl; cover and let stand 24 hours.
2. Preheat oven to 325°.
3. Coat 2 (8 x 4–inch) loaf pans with cooking spray, and dust each pan with 2 teaspoons flour. Add sugar, butter, vanilla, and egg to date mixture. Lightly spoon 2¼ cups flour into dry measuring cups, and level with a knife. Add flour and salt to date mixture, stirring just until blended. Divide batter evenly between prepared pans.
4. Bake at 325° for 45 minutes or until a wooden pick inserted in center comes out clean. Cool loaves 10 minutes in pans on a wire rack. Remove loaves from pans, and cool completely on wire rack. Yield: 2 loaves, 16 servings per loaf (serving size: 1 slice).

CALORIES 94 (7% from fat); FAT 0.7g (sat 0.3g, mono 0.2g, poly 0.1g); PROTEIN 1.4g; CARB 21.4g; FIBER 1.1g; CHOL 8mg; IRON 0.6mg; SODIUM 122mg; CALC 6mg

Spiced Pumpkin Bread

This recipe makes two generous loaves. Freeze one, or give it as a gift.

 3 cups all-purpose flour (about 13½ ounces)
 2 cups sugar
 2 teaspoons baking soda
 1 teaspoon baking powder
 1 teaspoon ground cinnamon
 ½ teaspoon salt
 ¼ teaspoon ground cloves
 ¼ teaspoon ground nutmeg
 ⅔ cup canola oil
 3 large eggs, lightly beaten
 1 (15-ounce) can pumpkin
 ½ cup dried currants or raisins
 Cooking spray

1. Preheat oven to 350°.
2. Lightly spoon flour into dry measuring cups; level with a knife. Combine flour and next 7 ingredients in a large bowl; make a well in center of mixture. Combine oil, eggs, and pumpkin in a medium bowl; stir with a whisk until smooth. Add to flour mixture, stirring just until moist. Fold in currants.
3. Spoon batter into 2 (9 x 5–inch) loaf pans coated with cooking spray. Bake at 350° for 1 hour or until a wooden pick inserted in center comes out clean. Cool loaves in pans 10 minutes on a wire rack; remove from pans. Cool loaves completely on wire rack. Yield: 2 loaves, 16 servings per loaf (serving size: 1 slice).

CALORIES 150 (31% from fat); FAT 5.2g (sat 0.5g, mono 3g, poly 1.5g); PROTEIN 2g; CARB 24.4g; FIBER 0.9g; CHOL 20mg; IRON 0.9mg; SODIUM 170mg; CALC 18mg

Sour Cream–Raspberry Swirl Loaf

This cake-like loaf freezes well up to 2 months.

 ⅓ cup seedless raspberry jam
 3 tablespoons chopped walnuts, toasted
 1½ cups all-purpose flour
 1 teaspoon baking powder
 ¼ teaspoon baking soda
 ⅛ teaspoon salt
 ¾ cup granulated sugar
 ¼ cup butter, softened
 2 teaspoons grated lemon rind
 1⅛ teaspoons vanilla extract, divided
 1 large egg
 1 large egg white
 ¾ cup fat-free sour cream
 Cooking spray
 ¼ cup sifted powdered sugar
 1½ teaspoons 2% reduced-fat milk

1. Preheat oven to 350°.
2. Combine jam and walnuts in a small bowl.
3. Lightly spoon flour into dry measuring cups; level with a knife. Combine flour, baking powder, baking soda, and salt in a bowl, stirring with a whisk. Combine sugar, butter, lemon rind, 1 teaspoon vanilla, egg, and egg white in a large bowl; beat with a mixer at medium speed until well blended. Add flour mixture and sour cream alternately to sugar mixture, beginning and ending with flour mixture.
4. Spread half of batter into an 8 x 4–inch loaf pan coated with cooking spray. Spoon raspberry mixture over top, leaving a ¼-inch border. Spread remaining batter over raspberry mixture.
5. Bake at 350° for 55 minutes or until a wooden pick inserted in center comes out clean. Cool in pan 10 minutes on a wire rack; remove from pan. Cool completely on wire rack. Combine ⅛ teaspoon vanilla, powdered sugar, and milk in a small bowl, stirring well with a whisk. Drizzle over loaf. Yield: 12 servings (serving size: 1 slice).

CALORIES 184 (26% from fat); FAT 5.4g (sat 2.6g, mono 1.6g, poly 0.9g); PROTEIN 3.2g; CARB 31.2g; FIBER 0.7g; CHOL 28mg; IRON 1.2mg; SODIUM 155mg; CALC 53mg

Sour Cream–Raspberry
Swirl Loaf

Blueberry-Lemon Coffee Cake

Blueberry-Lemon Coffee Cake

Blueberries and lemon are a natural match, and they come together nicely in this fruit-filled snack cake. Almond paste, a sweet mixture of ground almonds and sugar, contributes a mildly nutty flavor and moist texture. Almond paste is found in the baking section of the grocery store. (Don't substitute marzipan, which is sweeter and has a smoother texture.)

CAKE:
1½ cups all-purpose flour
2 teaspoons baking powder
¼ teaspoon baking soda
½ teaspoon salt
½ cup sugar
⅓ cup almond paste
2 tablespoons chilled butter, cut into small pieces
1 large egg
1 tablespoon lemon juice
¾ cup fat-free milk
1½ cups blueberries
2 teaspoons grated lemon rind
Cooking spray

TOPPING:
¼ cup sugar
3 tablespoons sliced almonds, chopped
1½ tablespoons butter, melted
½ teaspoon ground cinnamon

1. Preheat oven to 350°.
2. To prepare cake, lightly spoon flour into dry measuring cups, and level with a knife. Combine flour, baking powder, baking soda, and salt in a small bowl, stirring with a whisk.
3. Place ½ cup sugar, almond paste, and 2 tablespoons butter in a large bowl; beat with a mixer at medium speed until well blended. Add egg and lemon juice, beating well. Add flour mixture and milk alternately to sugar mixture, beginning and ending with flour mixture. Fold in blueberries and rind. Spoon batter into a 9-inch square baking pan coated with cooking spray.
4. To prepare topping, combine ¼ cup sugar and remaining 3 ingredients in a small bowl, tossing with a fork until moist. Sprinkle topping evenly over batter. Bake at 350° for 35 minutes or until a wooden pick inserted in center comes out clean. Cool in pan on a wire rack. Yield: 12 servings (serving size: 1 piece).

CALORIES 196 (30% from fat); FAT 6.5g (sat 2.1g, mono 3.2g, poly 0.8g); PROTEIN 3.8g; CARB 31.6g; FIBER 1.4g; CHOL 27mg; IRON 1.2mg; SODIUM 243mg; CALC 82mg

Banana Coffee Cake with Macadamia Nuts and Coconut

Cooking spray
1⅓ cups all-purpose flour
½ teaspoon salt
½ teaspoon baking powder
¼ teaspoon baking soda
1 cup mashed ripe banana (about 2 large bananas)
¾ cup granulated sugar
3 tablespoons vegetable oil
1 teaspoon vanilla extract
¼ teaspoon ground nutmeg
1 large egg
¼ cup packed dark brown sugar
1 tablespoon water
2 teaspoons butter
2 tablespoons chopped macadamia nuts, toasted
2 tablespoons flaked sweetened coconut

1. Preheat oven to 350°.
2. Coat a 9-inch round cake pan with cooking spray; line bottom of pan with wax paper. Coat wax paper with cooking spray.
3. Lightly spoon flour into dry measuring cups; level with a knife. Combine flour, salt, baking powder, and baking soda in a bowl, stirring with a whisk. Combine banana and next 5 ingredients in a bowl; beat with a mixer at medium speed 1 minute or until well blended. Add flour mixture to banana mixture, and beat until blended. Pour batter into prepared pan.
4. Bake at 350° for 30 minutes or until a wooden pick inserted in center comes out clean. Cool in pan 10 minutes on a wire rack; remove from pan. Carefully peel off wax paper.
5. Combine brown sugar, water, and butter in a small saucepan; bring to a boil. Cook 1 minute, stirring constantly. Remove from heat; stir in nuts and coconut. Spread over cake. Serve cake warm. Yield: 12 servings (serving size: 1 wedge).

CALORIES 189 (28% from fat); FAT 5.8g (sat 1.4g, mono 1.9g, poly 2.1g); PROTEIN 2.3g; CARB 32.6g; FIBER 1g; CHOL 19mg; IRON 0.9mg; SODIUM 159mg; CALC 22mg

Baguettes

Pouring water into the bottom of the oven creates steam and gives the bread a crisp crust.

    1   package dry yeast (about 2¼ teaspoons)
    2   tablespoons sugar
  2½   cups warm water (100° to 110°)
  3¾   cups bread flour, divided
    2   cups whole wheat flour
    ½   cup semolina or pasta flour
  1½   tablespoons salt
        Cooking spray
    1   tablespoon cornmeal
    ¼   cup water

1. Dissolve yeast and sugar in warm water in a large bowl; let stand 5 minutes. Lightly spoon flours into dry measuring cups; level with a knife. Add 3½ cups bread flour, wheat flour, semolina, and salt to yeast mixture; stir with a whisk until well blended.

2. Turn dough out onto a lightly floured surface. Knead until smooth and elastic (about 10 minutes); add enough of remaining bread flour, 1 tablespoon at a time, to prevent dough from sticking to hands (dough will feel tacky).

3. Place dough in a large bowl coated with cooking spray, turning to coat top. Cover and let rise in a warm place (85°), free from drafts, 45 minutes or until doubled in size. (Gently press two fingers into dough. If indentation remains, dough has risen enough.) Punch dough down; cover and let rest 5 minutes. Divide into thirds. Working with one portion at a time (cover remaining dough to prevent drying), roll portion into a 16-inch rope on a floured surface. Place ropes on a large baking sheet sprinkled with cornmeal. Cover and let rise 40 minutes or until ropes are doubled in size. Uncover dough. Cut 3 slits in top of each rope.

4. Preheat oven to 425°.

5. Pour ¼ cup water onto floor of oven (avoiding heating element). Place baking sheet in oven. Quickly close oven door. Bake at 425° for 30 minutes or until loaves are golden brown and sound hollow when tapped. Remove from pan, and cool on wire racks. Cut each loaf into 12 slices. Yield: 3 loaves, 36 servings (serving size: 1 slice).

CALORIES 82 (4% from fat); FAT 0.4g (sat 0.1g, mono 0g, poly 0.2g); PROTEIN 2.9g; CARB 17g; FIBER 1.3g; CHOL 0mg; IRON 1mg; SODIUM 292mg; CALC 5mg

Orange-Cranberry Bubble Bread

    ½   cup dried cranberries
    ⅓   cup granulated sugar
  1½   teaspoons grated orange rind
    6   ounces ⅓-less-fat cream cheese, softened
    2   (10-count) cans refrigerated buttermilk biscuit dough
        Cooking spray
    2   tablespoons butter, melted
    ¼   cup packed brown sugar

1. Preheat oven to 350°.

2. Combine first 4 ingredients.

3. Working with one biscuit at a time (cover remaining biscuits to keep from drying), pat biscuit into a 3-inch circle. Spoon about 1 teaspoon cream cheese mixture into center of circle; gather dough over filling to form a ball, pinching seam to seal.

4. Place filled biscuits, seam sides up, in a 13 x 9–inch baking pan coated with cooking spray. Drizzle melted butter over biscuits; sprinkle with brown sugar.

5. Bake at 350° for 40 minutes or until lightly browned. Yield: 20 servings (serving size: 1 biscuit).

CALORIES 141 (29% from fat); FAT 4.5g (sat 2.3g, mono 1.1g, poly 0.1g); PROTEIN 2.7g; CARB 22.6g; FIBER 0.6g; CHOL 11mg; IRON 0.9mg; SODIUM 280mg; CALC 11mg

How to Make Ciabatta

The slipper-like shape of ciabatta is so easy to achieve. With each oval of dough, simply taper the ends with your fingers to form a slipper shape. Let the dough rise in a warm place (85°), free from drafts, 45 minutes or until doubled in size. Then you're ready to bake.

Ciabatta

Make your own European bread at home for only a fraction of what it would cost at a local bakery. *Ciabatta* (chyah-BAH-tah), a rustic yeast bread which originated in Italy, gets its name from its unique shape—translated, ciabatta means "slipper."

SPONGE:

1 cup bread flour

½ cup warm fat-free milk (100° to 110°)

¼ cup warm water (100° to 110°)

1 tablespoon honey

1 package dry yeast (about 2¼ teaspoons)

DOUGH:

3½ cups bread flour, divided

½ cup semolina or pasta flour

¾ cup warm water (100° to 110°)

½ cup warm fat-free milk (100° to 110°)

1½ teaspoons salt

1 package dry yeast (about 2¼ teaspoons)

3 tablespoons semolina or pasta flour, divided

1. To prepare sponge, lightly spoon 1 cup bread flour into a dry measuring cup; level with a knife. Combine 1 cup flour, milk, and next 3 ingredients in a large bowl, stirring well with a whisk. Cover, and chill 12 hours.

2. To prepare dough, let sponge stand at room temperature 30 minutes. Lightly spoon 3½ cups bread flour and ½ cup semolina flour into dry measuring cups, and level with a knife. Add 3 cups bread flour, ½ cup semolina flour, ¾ cup warm water, ½ cup warm milk, salt, and 1 package yeast to sponge; stir well to form a soft dough. Turn dough out onto a floured surface. Knead until smooth and elastic (about 8 minutes), and add enough of remaining bread flour, 1 tablespoon at a time, to prevent dough from sticking to hands. Divide dough in half.

3. Working with one portion at a time (cover remaining dough to prevent drying), roll into a 13 x 5–inch oval. Place, 3 inches apart, on a large baking sheet sprinkled with 2 tablespoons semolina flour. Taper ends of dough to form a "slipper." Sprinkle 1 tablespoon semolina flour over dough. Cover and let rise in a warm place (85°), free from drafts, 45 minutes or until doubled in size.

4. Preheat oven to 425°.

5. Uncover dough. Bake at 425° for 18 minutes or until loaves are lightly browned and sound hollow when tapped. Remove from pan, and cool on a wire rack. Yield: 2 loaves, 16 servings (serving size: 1 slice).

CALORIES 150 (1% from fat); FAT 0.1g (sat 0g, mono 0.1g, poly 0g); PROTEIN 6.3g; CARB 32.1g; FIBER 1.3g; CHOL 0mg; IRON 2.1mg; SODIUM 227mg; CALC 21mg

Flatbread with Pancetta and Asparagus

DOUGH:

½ cup warm water (100° to 110°)
1 teaspoon dry yeast
1¼ cups all-purpose flour, divided
½ teaspoon sea salt
Cooking spray

TOPPING:

1 teaspoon dried thyme
2 ounces pancetta, finely chopped
1 garlic clove, minced
⅛ teaspoon sea salt
⅛ teaspoon freshly ground black pepper

REMAINING INGREDIENTS:

¼ pound fresh asparagus spears, trimmed
¼ cup (1 ounce) shredded part-skim mozzarella cheese
¼ cup (1 ounce) shaved fresh Parmesan cheese

1. To prepare dough, combine warm water and yeast in a large bowl; let stand 5 minutes. Lightly spoon flour into dry measuring cups; level with a knife. Add 1 cup flour and ½ teaspoon salt to yeast mixture; stir until blended. Turn dough out onto a floured surface. Knead dough until smooth and elastic (about 8 minutes); add enough remaining flour, 1 tablespoon at a time, to prevent dough from sticking to hands (dough will feel sticky).

2. Place dough in a large bowl coated with cooking spray, turning to coat top. Cover and let rise in a warm place (85°), free from drafts, 45 minutes or until doubled in size. (Gently press two fingers into dough. If indentation remains, dough has risen enough.)

3. While dough rises, prepare topping. Heat a small skillet over medium heat. Add thyme, pancetta, and garlic; sauté 5 minutes or until pancetta is crisp. Stir in ⅛ teaspoon salt and pepper.

4. Preheat oven to 475°.

5. Punch dough down; cover and let rest 5 minutes. Roll dough into a 10-inch circle on a floured surface. Place dough on a baking sheet. Spread topping evenly over dough. Arrange asparagus over topping; sprinkle with mozzarella. Bake at 475° for 10 minutes or until crust is golden. Remove from oven. Sprinkle with Parmesan. Yield: 8 servings (serving size: 1 wedge).

CALORIES 132 (31% from fat); FAT 4.6g (sat 2.1g, mono 0.9g, poly 0.2g); PROTEIN 5.8g; CARB 16.2g; FIBER 1.1g; CHOL 9mg; IRON 1.2mg; SODIUM 373mg; CALC 77mg

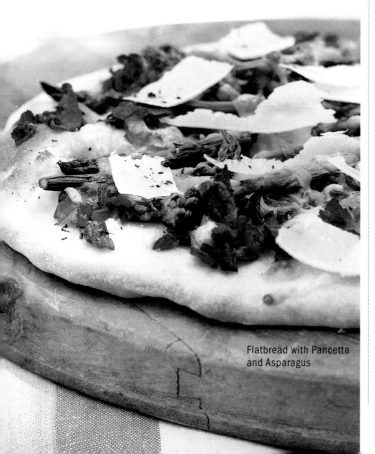

Flatbread with Pancetta and Asparagus

Argentine Black Bean Flatbread with Chimichurri Drizzle

1 red bell pepper
1 tablespoon cornmeal
Cooking spray
1 tablespoon dry yeast
⅛ teaspoon sugar
1 cup warm water (100° to 110°), divided
3 cups all-purpose flour (about 13½ ounces)
1 teaspoon salt
1½ cups Black Bean Spread
½ cup (2 ounces) finely grated fresh Parmesan cheese
¼ cup chopped fresh parsley
¼ cup chopped fresh cilantro
2 tablespoons olive oil
1 tablespoon fresh lemon juice
2 teaspoons minced garlic

1. Preheat broiler.

2. Cut bell pepper in half lengthwise; discard seeds and membranes. Place pepper halves, skin sides up, on a foil-lined baking sheet; flatten with hand. Broil 12 minutes or until blackened. Place in a zip-top plastic bag; seal. Let stand 10 minutes. Peel and cut into 16 strips. Set aside.

3. Reduce oven temperature to 450°.

4. Sprinkle cornmeal over a baking sheet coated with cooking spray. Set aside.

5. Dissolve yeast and sugar in ½ cup warm water in a large bowl; let stand 5 minutes. Lightly spoon flour into dry measuring cups; level with a knife. Add ½ cup warm water, flour, and salt to yeast mixture, stirring until dough forms. Turn dough out onto a floured surface. Knead until smooth and elastic (about 10 minutes).

6. Place dough in a large bowl coated with cooking spray, turning to coat top. Cover and let rise in a warm place (85°), free from drafts, 1 hour or until doubled in size. (Gently press two fingers into dough. If indentation remains, dough has risen enough.) Roll dough into a 14 x 11–inch rectangle; place dough on prepared baking sheet. Spread 1½ cups Black Bean Spread over dough. Sprinkle with cheese. Bake at 450° for 13 minutes or until crust browns and cheese is bubbly. Cool 10 minutes.

7. Combine parsley and remaining 4 ingredients in a small bowl. Drizzle parsley mixture over cheese. Cut bread into 16 squares; garnish each square with 1 bell pepper strip. Yield: 16 servings (serving size: 1 square).

[Totals include Black Bean Spread] CALORIES 126 (19% from fat); FAT 2.7g (sat 0.7g, mono 1.5g, poly 0.3g); PROTEIN 4.3g; CARB 21g; FIBER 1.4g; CHOL 2mg; IRON 1.5mg; SODIUM 248mg; CALC 43mg

BLACK BEAN SPREAD:

Use leftover spread as a dip with baked tortilla chips, a topping for a taco salad, or as a taco or burrito filler.

½ cup coarsely chopped onion
1 (15-ounce) can 50%-less-sodium black beans, rinsed and drained
1 (14.5-ounce) can organic fire-roasted diced tomatoes with green chiles, undrained (such as Muir Glen)

1. Place all ingredients in a blender, and process until smooth. Yield: 3 cups (serving size: ½ cup).

CALORIES 54 (0% from fat); FAT 0g; PROTEIN 2.7g; CARB 10.7g; FIBER 2.4g; CHOL 0mg; IRON 0.8mg; SODIUM 303mg; CALC 25mg

Garlic-Thyme Focaccia

Two kinds of salt add flavor and crunch. For a spicy variation, infuse the oil with ½ teaspoon crushed red pepper along with the garlic; strain through a sieve before brushing the flavored oil onto the dough.

1 teaspoon sugar
1 package dry yeast (about 2¼ teaspoons)
1 cup warm water (100° to 110°)
½ teaspoon fine sea salt
2⅓ cups plus 2 tablespoons all-purpose flour, divided (about 11¼ ounces)
Cooking spray
1 tablespoon olive oil
2 garlic cloves, thinly sliced
1 tablespoon chopped fresh thyme
¾ teaspoon coarse sea salt

1. Dissolve sugar and yeast in 1 cup warm water in a large bowl; let stand 5 minutes. Stir in fine sea salt. Lightly spoon flour into dry measuring cups and spoons; level with a knife. Add 2 cups plus 2 tablespoons flour to yeast mixture, stirring to form a soft dough. Turn dough out onto a floured surface. Knead dough until smooth and elastic (about 8 minutes); add enough remaining flour, 1 tablespoon at a time, to prevent dough from sticking to hands.

2. Place dough in a large bowl coated with cooking spray, turning to coat top. Cover and let rise in a warm place (85°), free from drafts, 45 minutes or until doubled in size. (Gently press two fingers into dough. If indentation remains, dough has risen enough.)

3. Heat oil in a small skillet over medium-low heat. Add garlic; cook 5 minutes or until fragrant. Remove garlic from oil with a slotted spoon; discard garlic, and remove pan from heat.

4. Place dough on a baking sheet coated with cooking spray; pat into a 12 x 8–inch rectangle. Brush garlic oil over dough; sprinkle with thyme. Cover and let rise 25 minutes or until doubled in size.

5. Preheat oven to 425°.

6. Make indentations in top of dough using handle of a wooden spoon or your fingertips; sprinkle dough evenly with coarse sea salt. Bake at 425° for 14 minutes or until lightly browned. Remove from pan; cool on a wire rack. Yield: 10 servings (serving size: 1 piece).

CALORIES 128 (12% from fat); FAT 1.7g (sat 0.2g, mono 1g, poly 0.3g); PROTEIN 3.5g; CARB 24.2g; FIBER 1.1g; CHOL 0mg; IRON 1.6mg; SODIUM 289mg; CALC 7mg

Herbed Focaccia

Ask for focaccia on the Tuscan coast, and you'll get what they call *schiacciata* in Florence: a thin loaf of dimpled bread that's brushed with olive oil and sprinkled with salt. This recipe produces a similar bread. Eat it as a snack, as an accompaniment to a soup or salad meal, or as the base for a sandwich. The coarse texture of kosher salt provides a wonderful crunch and salty flavor that's reminiscent of a big, soft pretzel.

All-Purpose Pizza Dough (recipe on page 55)
1   tablespoon chopped fresh flat-leaf
    parsley
1   teaspoon dried rubbed sage
1   teaspoon dried rosemary
1   teaspoon dried thyme
Cooking spray
1   tablespoon yellow cornmeal
1   tablespoon extravirgin olive oil
½   teaspoon kosher salt

1. Roll prepared All-Purpose Pizza Dough into a 12 x 8–inch rectangle on a floured surface. Sprinkle parsley, sage, rosemary, and thyme over dough. Fold dough into thirds. Knead lightly 1 minute or until herbs are blended into dough. Cover and let stand 10 minutes. Roll dough into a 14 x 12–inch rectangle. Place dough on a baking sheet coated with cooking spray and sprinkled with cornmeal. Cover and let rise in a warm place 35 minutes or until doubled in size.

2. Preheat oven to 450°.

3. Uncover dough. Make indentations in top of dough using the handle of a wooden spoon or your fingertips. Gently brush dough with oil. Sprinkle with kosher salt. Bake dough at 450° for 15 minutes or until browned. Yield: 8 servings (serving size: 1 slice).

CALORIES 209 (11% from fat); FAT 2.5g (sat 0.4g, mono 1.4g, poly 0.5g); PROTEIN 5.7g; CARB 40.2g; FIBER 1.8g; CHOL 0mg; IRON 2.9mg; SODIUM 295mg; CALC 16mg

All-Purpose Pizza Dough

This basic recipe can easily be doubled. You can also make it in a food processor or stand-up mixer with the kneading attachment.

  1 package dry yeast (about 2¼ teaspoons)
1¼ cups warm water (100° to 110°)
3¼ cups all-purpose flour, divided
  ½ teaspoon salt
     Cooking spray

1. Dissolve yeast in warm water in a large bowl, and let stand 5 minutes. Lightly spoon flour into dry measuring cups, and level with a knife. Add 1 cup flour and salt to yeast mixture, and stir well. Add 2 cups flour, 1 cup at a time, stirring well after each addition. Turn dough out onto a floured surface. Knead until smooth and elastic (about 10 minutes), adding enough of remaining flour, 1 tablespoon at a time, to prevent dough from sticking to hands (dough will feel tacky).

2. Place dough in a large bowl coated with cooking spray, turning to coat top. Cover and let rise in a warm place (85°), free from drafts, 1 hour or until doubled in size. (Press two fingers into dough. If indentation remains, dough has risen enough.) Punch dough down; cover and let rest 5 minutes. Shape dough according to recipe directions. Yield: dough for 1 pizza.

CALORIES 1,505 (3% from fat); FAT 5g (sat 0.8g, mono 0.7g, poly 2.1g); PROTEIN 44.6g; CARB 312.7g; FIBER 12.9g; CHOL 0mg; IRON 20mg; SODIUM 1,184mg; CALC 66mg

How to Make Focaccia

Focaccia (foh-KAH-chee-ah), a bread that traditionally contains a fair amount of olive oil, is "dimpled" after rising, giving it a characteristic appearance. This dimpling is done to relieve bubbling on the surface of the bread and to catch olive oil that's drizzled or brushed on before baking. After the dough has fully risen and is ready to be put in the oven, use the handle of a wooden spoon or your fingertips to make indentations evenly across the surface of the dough.

Rosemary Focaccia

The rosemary steeps in boiling water; be sure to let the mixture cool to 100° to 110° before adding the yeast so the dough will rise correctly.

1¼ cups boiling water
  3 tablespoons chopped fresh rosemary, divided
  1 tablespoon honey
  1 package dry yeast (about 2¼ teaspoons)
3¾ cups all-purpose flour, divided
  ¼ cup olive oil, divided
  1 teaspoon salt
     Cooking spray
  1 teaspoon water
  1 large egg yolk
  1 teaspoon sea salt or kosher salt

1. Combine boiling water, 1 teaspoon rosemary, and honey in a large bowl; cool to 100° to 110°. Sprinkle yeast over honey mixture; let stand 5 minutes. Lightly spoon flour into dry measuring cups; level with a knife. Add 3¼ cups flour, 2 tablespoons oil, and 1 teaspoon salt to honey mixture, stirring to form a soft dough. Turn dough out onto a floured surface. Knead until smooth and elastic (about 10 minutes); add enough of remaining flour, 1 tablespoon at a time, to prevent dough from sticking to hands (dough will feel sticky).

2. Place dough in a large bowl coated with cooking spray, turning to coat top. Cover and let rise in a warm place (85°), free from drafts, 45 minutes or until doubled in size. (Gently press two fingers into dough. If indentation remains, dough has risen enough.) Punch dough down. Pat dough into a 14 x 12–inch rectangle on a baking sheet coated with cooking spray. Cover and let rise 20 minutes or until doubled in size.

3. Preheat oven to 350°.

4. Uncover dough. Make indentations in top of dough using handle of a wooden spoon or your fingertips. Combine 1 tablespoon oil, 1 teaspoon water, and egg yolk; brush over dough. Drizzle with 1 tablespoon oil; sprinkle with 8 teaspoons rosemary and sea salt.

5. Bake at 350° for 25 minutes or until lightly browned. Remove from pan; cool on a wire rack. Yield: 14 servings (serving size: 1 slice).

CALORIES 166 (25% from fat); FAT 4.6g (sat 0.7g, mono 3g, poly 0.6g); PROTEIN 3.9g; CARB 27.1g; FIBER 1.1g; CHOL 15mg; IRON 1.7mg; SODIUM 335mg; CALC 9mg

Tomato and Parmesan Focaccia with Caramelized Onions

Serve this tasty appetizer bread warm or at room temperature. While you can make it a day in advance, it's best the day it's baked.

DOUGH:

- 1 cup warm water (100° to 110°)
- 2 tablespoons olive oil
- 1 teaspoon sugar
- 1 package dry yeast (about 2¼ teaspoons)
- 2¾ cups all-purpose flour (about 12⅓ ounces), divided
- ¼ cup yellow cornmeal
- 1 teaspoon salt
- Cooking spray

TOPPING:

- 1 tablespoon olive oil
- 4 cups thinly sliced yellow onion
- 1 teaspoon dried basil
- ½ teaspoon salt
- ¼ teaspoon freshly ground black pepper
- 12 (⅛-inch-thick) slices tomato
- ⅓ cup (about 1½ ounces) grated fresh Parmesan cheese
- ¼ cup thinly sliced fresh basil

1. To prepare dough, combine first 4 ingredients in a large bowl, stirring to dissolve yeast; let stand 5 minutes. Lightly spoon flour into dry measuring cups; level with a knife. Add 2½ cups flour, cornmeal, and 1 teaspoon salt to yeast mixture; stir well. Turn dough out onto a floured surface. Knead until smooth and elastic (about 10 minutes); add enough remaining flour, 1 tablespoon at a time, to prevent dough from sticking to hands.

2. Place dough in a large bowl coated with cooking spray, turning to coat top. Cover and let rise in a warm place (85°), free from drafts, 1½ hours or until doubled in size. (Gently press two fingers into dough. If indentation remains, dough has risen enough.)

3. To prepare topping, heat 1 tablespoon oil in a large nonstick skillet over medium-high heat. Add onion, dried basil, ½ teaspoon salt, and pepper; cook 20 minutes or until onion is golden, stirring occasionally. Cool.

4. Arrange tomato slices between several layers of paper towels. Let stand 10 minutes, pressing down occasionally.

5. Uncover dough. Punch dough down; cover and let rest 5 minutes. Pat dough into an even layer in a 15 x 10–inch jelly-roll pan coated with cooking spray. Cover and let rise 30 minutes.

6. Preheat oven to 425°.

7. Uncover dough. Arrange onion mixture over dough, leaving a ½-inch border. Top with tomato slices; sprinkle with cheese. Bake at 425° for 23 minutes or until browned. Sprinkle with fresh basil. Cool at least 10 minutes before serving. Yield: 16 servings (serving size: 1 piece).

CALORIES 138 (23% from fat); FAT 3.5g (sat 0.8g, mono 2.1g, poly 0.4g); PROTEIN 3.9g; CARB 22.5g; FIBER 1.4g; CHOL 2mg; IRON 1.3mg; SODIUM 266mg; CALC 45mg

Asiago and Balsamic Caramelized Onion Focaccia

For a party, split squares of this moist focaccia and fill them with sliced cooked turkey or pork tenderloin.

- 2 tablespoons plus 2 teaspoons extravirgin olive oil, divided
- 1 cup chopped onion
- 2 tablespoons honey, divided
- ¼ teaspoon dried thyme
- 2 tablespoons balsamic vinegar
- 1½ teaspoons salt, divided
- 1 package dry yeast (about 2¼ teaspoons)
- 1¼ cups warm water (100° to 110°)
- 3¾ cups all-purpose flour (about 17 ounces), divided
- Cooking spray
- ¾ cup (3 ounces) grated fresh Asiago cheese

1. Heat 2 teaspoons oil in a nonstick skillet over medium-high heat. Add onion, 1 tablespoon honey, and thyme; cook 5 minutes or until browned, stirring occasionally. Remove from heat; stir in vinegar and ¼ teaspoon salt. Cool completely.

2. Dissolve yeast and remaining 1 tablespoon honey in 1¼ cups warm water in a large bowl; let stand 5 minutes. Lightly spoon flour into dry measuring cups; level with a knife. Add onion mixture, remaining 2 tablespoons oil, remaining 1¼ teaspoons salt, and 3½ cups flour to yeast mixture; stir until a soft dough forms. Turn dough out onto a floured surface. Knead until smooth and elastic (about 8 minutes). Add enough of remaining flour, 1 tablespoon at a time, to prevent dough from sticking to hands.

3. Place dough in a large bowl coated with cooking spray, turning to coat top. Cover and let rise in a

warm place (85°), free from drafts, 1 hour or until
doubled in size. (Gently press two fingers into
dough. If indentation remains, dough has risen
enough.) Punch dough down; cover and let rest 5
minutes. Gently press dough into a 15 x 10–inch
jelly-roll pan coated with cooking spray. Cover and
let rise 25 minutes or until almost doubled in size.

4. Preheat oven to 400°.

5. Sprinkle dough with cheese. Bake at 400° for 18
minutes or until browned. Cool in pan on a wire
rack 10 minutes. Remove from pan; cool completely
on rack. Yield: 16 servings (serving size: 1 piece).

CALORIES 160 (23% from fat); FAT 4.1g (sat 1.3g, mono 1.7g, poly 0.4g); PROTEIN 4.6g;
CARB 26g; FIBER 1g; CHOL 5mg; IRON 1.5mg; SODIUM 288mg; CALC 46mg

Brown Beer-Rye Bread

Hearty breads like rye and pumpernickel are German culinary standards. This version uses stone-ground rye flour and caraway seeds, a favorite spice in German cooking.

    1   tablespoon olive oil
    ½   cup chopped onion
    1⅛ teaspoons sugar, divided
    2   packages dry yeast (about 4½ teaspoons)
    ¾   cup warm brown beer (100° to 110°)
    ½   cup plain low-fat yogurt
    1   tablespoon white vinegar
    1   tablespoon caraway seeds
    1½ teaspoons salt
    1   large egg, lightly beaten
    2¾ cups all-purpose flour, divided (about
        12⅓ ounces)
    1   cup stone-ground rye flour (about
        4½ ounces) (such as Bob's Red Mill)
        Cooking spray
    1   teaspoon water
    1   large egg white, lightly beaten

1. Heat oil in a large skillet over medium-high heat. Add onion, and sauté 4 minutes or until golden brown. Cool.

2. Dissolve ⅛ teaspoon sugar and yeast in warm beer; let stand 5 minutes. Stir in yogurt and next 3 ingredients. Add 1 teaspoon sugar and egg; stir with a whisk until combined.

3. Lightly spoon flours into dry measuring cups; level with a knife. Add 2½ cups all-purpose flour and rye flour to yeast mixture; stir until a soft dough forms. Stir in onion mixture. Turn dough out onto a floured surface. Knead until smooth and elastic (about 8 minutes); add enough of remaining flour, 1 tablespoon at a time, to prevent dough from sticking to hands (dough will feel tacky).

4. Place dough in a large bowl coated with cooking spray, turning to coat top. Cover and let rise in a warm place (85°), free from drafts, 45 minutes or until doubled in size. (Press two fingers into dough. If indentation remains, dough has risen enough.) Punch dough down; cover and let rest 5 minutes.

5. Shape dough into a 12-inch oval loaf on a lightly floured surface. Place on a baking sheet lined with parchment paper. Lightly coat loaf with cooking spray. Cover with plastic wrap; let rise 30 minutes or until doubled in size.

6. Preheat oven to 400°.

7. Combine 1 teaspoon water and egg white in a small bowl. Gently brush egg white mixture over surface of loaf. Bake at 400° for 28 minutes or until loaf is golden brown and sounds hollow when tapped; let cool on a wire rack. Yield: 1 loaf, 20 servings (serving size: 1 slice).

CALORIES 101 (12% from fat); FAT 1.4g (sat 0.3g, mono 0.7g, poly 0.2g); PROTEIN 3.5g; CARB 18.7g; FIBER 1.5g; CHOL 11mg; IRON 1.1mg; SODIUM 189mg; CALC 20mg

Hearty Sour Rye Bread

Loaves of sour rye were everyday fare for Mennonites living on the Russian steppes. They were made with a natural sourdough starter and baked in ovens that were fueled by prairie grasses. In this recipe, yogurt replaces the sourdough starter.

    2   tablespoons vegetable oil
    ¾   cup chopped onion
    ¼   teaspoon sugar
    1   package dry yeast (about 2¼ teaspoons)
    2   tablespoons warm water (100° to 110°)
    1¼ cups plain low-fat yogurt
    1   tablespoon caraway seeds
    1½ teaspoons salt
    ¾   teaspoon white pepper
    1   large egg, lightly beaten
    2¼ cups bread flour, divided
    1¼ cups stone-ground rye flour (such as
        Bob's Red Mill)
        Cooking spray
    1   tablespoon water
    1   large egg yolk, lightly beaten
    ½   teaspoon kosher salt

1. Heat vegetable oil in a large skillet over medium heat. Add onion; cover and cook 10 minutes or until golden brown, stirring frequently. Remove from heat; cool completely.

2. Dissolve sugar and yeast in warm water in a large bowl; let stand 5 minutes. Stir in yogurt, caraway seeds, salt, and pepper. Add egg; stir well with a whisk.

3. Lightly spoon flours into dry measuring cups, and level with a knife. Add 2 cups bread flour and rye flour to yeast mixture, 1 cup at a time, stirring until a soft dough forms. Stir in onion. Turn dough out onto a lightly floured surface. Knead until smooth and elastic (about 8 minutes); add enough of remaining flour, 1 tablespoon at a time, to prevent dough from sticking to hands (dough will feel tacky).

4. Place dough in a large bowl coated with cooking spray, turning to coat top. Cover and let rise in a warm place (85°), free from drafts, 45 minutes or until doubled in size. (Gently press two fingers into dough. If indentation remains, dough has risen enough.) Punch dough down; cover and let rest 5 minutes.

5. With floured hands, knead dough 5 times. Shape into a round 7-inch loaf. Place loaf on a large baking sheet covered with parchment paper. Cover and let rise 30 minutes or until doubled in size. Make 3 diagonal cuts ¼-inch-deep across top of loaf using a sharp knife.

6. Preheat oven to 350°.

7. Combine 1 tablespoon water and egg yolk; gently brush over dough. Sprinkle with ½ teaspoon kosher salt. Bake at 350° for 35 minutes or until loaf sounds hollow when tapped. Cool on a wire rack. Yield: 1 loaf, 12 servings (serving size: 1 slice).

CALORIES 168 (20% from fat); FAT 3.8g (sat 0.9g, mono 1g, poly 1.6g); PROTEIN 6.5g; CARB 28.1g; FIBER 2.4g; CHOL 37mg; IRON 1.7mg; SODIUM 394mg; CALC 59mg

Prairie Fields Wheat and Soy Bread

In the late 19th century, many farmers milled their own grain for household needs. You can do the same with a food processor or a coffee grinder. To freeze baked loaves, wrap each in foil, then place in a zip-top plastic bag. They will keep about 3 months.

5¼   cups bread flour, divided
  4   cups whole wheat flour
  1   cup soy flour
  1   tablespoon salt
  2   packages dry yeast (about 2¼ teaspoons each)
3½   cups warm water (100° to 110°)
  ½   cup honey
  ⅓   cup olive oil
Cooking spray
  1   tablespoon unsalted butter, melted

1. Lightly spoon flours into dry measuring cups, and level with a knife. Combine 3 cups bread flour, 1 tablespoon salt, and yeast in a large bowl, stirring with a whisk. Stir in water, ½ cup honey, and olive oil. Add 2 cups bread flour, whole wheat flour, and soy flour to yeast mixture, and stir until a soft dough forms. Turn dough out onto a lightly floured surface. Knead until smooth and elastic (about 8

minutes), adding enough of remaining bread flour, 1 tablespoon at a time, to prevent dough from sticking to hands (dough will feel tacky).

2. Place dough in a large bowl coated with cooking spray, turning to coat top. Cover and let rise in a warm place (85°), free from drafts, 1 hour or until doubled in size. (Gently press two fingers into dough. If indentation remains, dough has risen enough.) Punch dough down; cover and let rest 10 minutes.

3. Divide dough into thirds. Working with one dough portion at a time (cover remaining dough to prevent drying), roll portion into a 14 x 7–inch rectangle on a lightly floured surface. Roll up rectangle tightly, starting with a short edge, pressing firmly to eliminate air pockets; pinch seam and ends to seal. Place roll, seam side down, in a 9 x 5–inch loaf pan coated with cooking spray. Cover and let rise 45 minutes or until doubled in size.

4. Preheat oven to 350°.

5. Uncover dough. Bake dough at 350° for 25 minutes or until loaves are browned on bottom and sound hollow when tapped. Remove from pans, and brush tops of loaves with melted butter. Cool on wire racks. Yield: 3 loaves, 12 servings per loaf (serving size: 1 slice).

CALORIES 150 (17% from fat); FAT 2.9g (sat 0.5g, mono 1.5g, poly 0.3g); PROTEIN 5.3g; CARB 27.5g; FIBER 2.7g; CHOL 1mg; IRON 1.7mg; SODIUM 195mg; CALC 9mg

How to Measure Flour

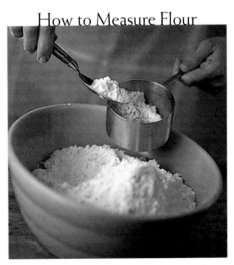

Measuring flour is the single most important factor in light baking. Baked goods made with less fat tend to dry out, so it's crucial to measure flour accurately. First, fluff the flour with a fork to break up any lumps. Then lightly spoon the flour into a dry measuring cup without compacting it, and level with a knife. Don't scoop the flour out of the canister with the measuring cup because you can get up to 3½ tablespoons per cup too much flour that way.

Wheat Berry Bread

This is a hearty sandwich bread. Cooked wheat berries add texture, and the wheat bran gives the surface a nice rustic finish. The recipe makes two loaves, so you can freeze one for later.

3 cups water
¾ cup uncooked wheat berries
1 package dry yeast (about 2¼ teaspoons)
1 cup 2% reduced-fat milk
2 tablespoons dark honey (such as buckwheat)
2½ teaspoons salt
3 cups bread flour, divided
2 cups whole wheat flour
1 cup amaranth flour
Cooking spray
2 tablespoons bread flour
2 tablespoons wheat bran

1. Combine water and wheat berries in a saucepan; bring to a boil. Cover, reduce heat, and simmer 1 hour or until tender. Drain wheat berries in a colander over a bowl, reserving 1 cup cooking liquid; set wheat berries aside.

2. Let reserved cooking liquid stand until warm (100° to 110°). Stir yeast into cooking liquid.

3. Combine milk, honey, and salt in a small, heavy saucepan, stirring with a whisk until honey and salt dissolve. Heat milk mixture over medium heat until warm (100° to 110°). Add milk mixture to yeast mixture, stirring with a whisk; let stand 5 minutes.

4. Lightly spoon 3 cups bread flour, whole wheat flour, and amaranth flour into dry measuring cups; level with a knife. Stir 2½ cups bread flour, whole wheat flour, and amaranth flour into yeast mixture.

5. Turn dough out onto a floured surface. Knead until smooth and elastic (about 10 minutes); add up to ½ cup bread flour, 1 tablespoon at a time, to prevent dough from sticking to hands (dough will feel tacky).

6. Place dough in a large bowl coated with cooking spray, turning to coat top. Cover and let rise in a warm place (85°), free from drafts, 1 hour or until doubled in size. (Press two fingers into dough. If indentation remains, dough has risen enough.)

7. Punch dough down; cover and let rest 5 minutes. Coat 2 (9 x 5–inch) loaf pans with cooking spray; dust each with 1 tablespoon bread flour.

8. Divide dough in half. Working with one portion at a time (cover remaining dough to keep from drying), knead half of wheat berries into dough; place dough in prepared pan. Sprinkle dough with 1 tablespoon wheat bran. Repeat procedure with remaining dough, wheat berries, and wheat bran. Cover and let rise 45 minutes or until doubled in size.

9. Preheat oven to 375°.

10. Bake at 375° for 45 minutes or until golden. Cool loaves in pans 10 minutes on a wire rack; remove from pans. Cool completely on wire rack. Yield: 2 loaves, 9 servings per loaf (serving size: 1 slice).

CALORIES 198 (6% from fat); FAT 1.4g (sat 0.3g, mono 0.2g, poly 0.4g); PROTEIN 7.2g; CARB 39.8g; FIBER 3.9g; CHOL 1mg; IRON 3.6mg; SODIUM 334mg; CALC 37mg

Potato-Dill Bread

1 teaspoon olive oil
2 cups chopped onion
2 packages dry yeast (about 4½ teaspoons)
2 cups warm fat-free milk (100° to 110°)
1 cup mashed cooked peeled Yukon gold potato
2 teaspoons salt
1 (8-ounce) block ⅓-less-fat cream cheese, softened
1 tablespoon chopped fresh dill
7 cups all-purpose flour, divided (about 32 ounces)
Cooking spray
1 teaspoon water
1 large egg, lightly beaten

1. Heat oil in a large nonstick skillet over medium-high heat. Add onion, and sauté 5 minutes. Remove from heat; cool.

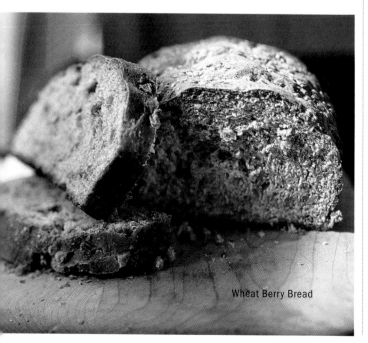
Wheat Berry Bread

2. Dissolve yeast in warm milk in a small bowl; let stand 5 minutes.

3. Combine onion, potato, salt, and cheese in a large bowl. Add milk mixture and dill; stir until well combined.

4. Lightly spoon flour into dry measuring cups; level with a knife. Add 6 cups flour to onion mixture; stir until a soft dough forms. Turn dough out onto a floured surface. Knead until smooth and elastic (about 8 minutes); add enough of remaining flour, 1 tablespoon at a time, to keep dough from sticking to hands.

5. Place dough in a large bowl coated with cooking spray, turning to coat top. Cover and let rise in a warm place (85°), free from drafts, 40 minutes or until doubled in size. (Gently press two fingers into dough. If indentation remains, dough has risen enough.) Punch dough down; cover and let rest 5 minutes.

6. Divide dough into two portions. Roll each portion into a 14 x 7–inch rectangle on a lightly floured surface. Roll up rectangles tightly, starting with short edges, pressing firmly to eliminate air pockets; pinch seams and ends to seal. Place each roll, seam side down, in a 9 x 5–inch loaf pan coated with cooking spray. Coat dough with cooking spray. Cover and let rise in a warm place (85°), free from drafts, 20 minutes or until doubled in size.

7. Preheat oven to 350°.

8. Uncover dough. Combine water and egg, stirring with a whisk. Gently brush loaves with egg mixture. Bake at 350° for 40 minutes or until browned on bottom and sound hollow when tapped. Yield: 2 loaves, 32 servings (serving size: 1 slice).

CALORIES 126 (20% from fat); FAT 2.8g (sat 1.2g, mono 0.9g, poly 0.4g); PROTEIN 4.2g; CARB 21g; FIBER 0.9g; CHOL 12mg; IRON 1.3mg; SODIUM 185mg; CALC 31mg

Cheddar-Asiago-Potato Bread

  3 cups cubed peeled baking potato (about 1 pound)
  1 package dry yeast (about 2¼ teaspoons)
5½ cups all-purpose flour, divided
  2 teaspoons salt
  ¾ teaspoon freshly ground black pepper
  1 cup (4 ounces) shredded extra-sharp Cheddar cheese
  ¾ cup (3 ounces) grated Asiago cheese
Cooking spray

1. Place potato in a saucepan; cover with water. Bring to a boil. Reduce heat; simmer 15 minutes or until tender. Drain in a colander over a bowl, reserving 1¼ cups cooking liquid. Cool liquid to 110°. Mash potato with a potato masher to measure 2 cups; set aside.

2. Combine warm cooking liquid and yeast in a large bowl; let stand 5 minutes. Stir in mashed potato. Lightly spoon flour into dry measuring cups; level with a knife. Gradually stir 5 cups flour, salt, and pepper into potato mixture to form a stiff dough.

3. Turn dough out onto a lightly floured surface. Knead until smooth and elastic (about 10 minutes); add enough of remaining flour, 1 tablespoon at a time, to prevent dough from sticking to hands. Gently knead in cheeses.

4. Place dough in a large bowl coated with cooking spray, turning to coat top. Cover and let rise in a warm place (85°), free from drafts, 30 minutes or until doubled in size. (Gently press two fingers into dough. If indentation remains, dough has risen enough.) Punch dough down; cover and let rest 5 minutes. Divide dough in half. Working with one portion at a time (cover remaining dough to prevent drying), roll each portion into an 11 x 7–inch rectangle on a floured surface. Roll up rectangle tightly, starting with a short edge, pressing firmly to eliminate air pockets; pinch seam and ends to seal. Place roll, seam side down, in an 8 x 4–inch loaf pan coated with cooking spray. Cover and let rise 45 minutes or until doubled in size.

5. Preheat oven to 375°.

6. Uncover dough; bake at 375° for 1 hour or until loaves are browned on bottom and sound hollow when tapped. Remove from pans; cool on a wire rack. Yield: 2 loaves, 12 slices per loaf (serving size: 1 slice).

CALORIES 151 (17% from fat); FAT 2.8g (sat 1.5g, mono 0.8g, poly 0.3g); PROTEIN 5.5g; CARB 25.7g; FIBER 1.1g; CHOL 8mg; IRON 1.6mg; SODIUM 270mg; CALC 67mg

Sweet Challah

Sweet Challah

Allowing the dough to rise three times gives the yeast more time to develop, resulting in a rich, complex flavor.

1 package dry yeast (about 2¼ teaspoons)
1 cup warm water (100° to 110°)
3 tablespoons honey
Dash of saffron threads, crushed
3 tablespoons butter, melted and cooled
1 teaspoon salt
1 large egg
3 cups bread flour (about 14¼ ounces), divided
Cooking spray
1 teaspoon cornmeal
1 teaspoon water
1 large egg yolk, lightly beaten
¼ teaspoon poppy seeds

1. Dissolve yeast in warm water in a large bowl; stir in honey and saffron. Let stand 5 minutes. Add butter, salt, and egg; stir well with a whisk.
2. Lightly spoon flour into dry measuring cups; level with a knife. Add 2¾ cups flour to yeast mixture, and stir until a soft dough forms. Cover and let stand 15 minutes.
3. Turn dough out onto a lightly floured surface. Knead until smooth and elastic (about 8 minutes); add enough remaining flour, 1 tablespoon at a time, to prevent dough from sticking to hands (dough will be very soft).
4. Place dough in a large bowl coated with cooking spray, turning to coat top. Cover and let rise in a warm place (85°), free from drafts, 40 minutes or until doubled in size. (Press two fingers into dough. If indentation remains, dough has risen enough.)
5. Punch dough down. Shape dough into a ball; return to bowl. Cover and let rise 40 minutes or until doubled in size. Punch dough down; cover and let rest 15 minutes.
6. Divide dough into three equal portions. Working with one portion at a time (cover remaining dough to prevent drying), on a lightly floured surface, roll portion into a 25-inch rope with one slightly tapered end. Place ropes lengthwise on a large baking sheet sprinkled with cornmeal; pinch untapered ends together to seal. Braid ropes; pinch loose ends to seal. Cover and let rise 20 minutes or until almost doubled in size.
7. Preheat oven to 375°.
8. Combine 1 teaspoon water and egg yolk, stirring with a fork until blended. Uncover loaf, and gently brush with egg yolk mixture. Sprinkle evenly with poppy seeds. Bake at 375° for 30 minutes or until loaf sounds hollow when tapped. Cool on a wire rack. Yield: 1 loaf, 12 servings (serving size: 1 slice).

CALORIES 157 (24% from fat); FAT 4.1g (sat 2.1g, mono 1.2g, poly 0.4g); PROTEIN 5g; CARB 26.9g; FIBER 0.9g; CHOL 42mg; IRON 1.7mg; SODIUM 202mg; CALC 7mg

Hawaiian Bread

This famous bread is actually a Portuguese sweet bread.

1 (6-ounce) can pineapple juice
1 package dry yeast (about 2¼ teaspoons)
3 cups all-purpose flour, divided
½ cup warm 2% reduced-fat milk (100° to 110°)
½ cup egg substitute
⅓ cup sugar
¼ cup butter, melted
½ teaspoon salt
Cooking spray
2 tablespoons all-purpose flour

1. Place juice in a medium microwave-safe bowl. Microwave at HIGH 45 seconds or until 100° to 110°. Dissolve yeast in warm juice; let stand 5 minutes.
2. Place yeast mixture in the bowl of a stand-up mixer fitted with a paddle attachment. Lightly spoon flour into dry measuring cups; level with a knife. Add 1 cup flour to yeast mixture; beat until combined. Add warm milk, egg substitute, sugar, butter, and salt, beating to combine. Beat in 2 cups flour, ½ cup at a time, until combined (dough will be very soft and sticky). Beat at medium-low speed 2 minutes. Scrape down sides of bowl. Lightly coat sides of bowl with cooking spray.
3. Cover bowl with a damp towel. Let dough rise in a warm place (85°), free from drafts, 1 hour or until doubled in size. (Gently press two fingers into dough. If indentation remains, dough has risen enough.)
4. Coat 2 (8-inch) round pans with cooking spray; dust each pan with 1 tablespoon flour. Divide dough evenly between prepared pans. Cover and let rise in a warm place (85°), free from drafts, 45 minutes or until doubled in size. While dough rises, preheat oven to 350°. Bake at 350° for 30 minutes or until golden brown. Yield: 2 loaves, 12 servings per loaf (serving size: 1 slice).

CALORIES 98 (24% from fat); FAT 2.6g (sat 1.4g, mono 0.7g, poly 0.2g); PROTEIN 2.4g; CARB 16.1g; FIBER 0.5g; CHOL 23mg; IRON 0.9mg; SODIUM 71mg; CALC 12mg

Cinnamon-Raisin Bread

⅔ cup raisins
1 cup plus 2 tablespoons 1% low-fat milk
2½ tablespoons unsalted butter
3 cups bread flour, divided
¼ cup packed brown sugar
1 tablespoon ground cinnamon
¾ teaspoon salt
1 package dry yeast (about 2¼ teaspoons)
2 large eggs, lightly beaten
Cooking spray

1. Place raisins in a small saucepan, and cover with water; bring to a boil. Remove from heat; cover and let stand 15 minutes. Drain well.

2. Heat milk over low heat in a small, heavy saucepan to between 100° and 110°; remove from heat. Add butter to pan; stir until butter melts.

3. Lightly spoon flour into dry measuring cups, and level with a knife. Combine 2¾ cups flour, brown sugar, cinnamon, ¾ teaspoon salt, and yeast in a large bowl, stirring with a whisk. Add warm milk mixture and eggs to flour mixture, and stir until a soft dough forms. Add raisins. Turn dough out onto a lightly floured surface. Knead until smooth and elastic (about 8 minutes); add enough of remaining flour, 1 tablespoon at a time, to prevent dough from sticking to hands (dough will feel tacky).

4. Place dough in a large bowl coated with cooking spray, turning to coat top. Cover and let rise in a warm place (85°), free from drafts, 1 hour or until doubled in size. (Gently press two fingers into dough. If indentation remains, dough has risen enough.) Punch dough down; cover and let rest 5 minutes.

5. Roll dough into a 14 x 7–inch rectangle on a lightly floured surface. Roll up rectangle tightly, starting with a short edge, pressing firmly to eliminate air pockets; pinch seam and ends to seal. Place roll, seam side down, in a 9 x 5–inch loaf pan coated with cooking spray. Cover and let rise 30 minutes or until doubled in size.

6. Preheat oven to 350°.

7. Uncover dough. Bake at 350° for 40 minutes or until loaf is browned on bottom and sounds hollow when tapped. Remove from pan; cool on a wire rack. Yield: 14 servings (serving size: 1 slice).

CALORIES 164 (16% from fat); FAT 3g (sat 1.8g, mono 0.3g, poly 0.1g); PROTEIN 5.5g; CARB 30.6g; FIBER 1.4g; CHOL 37mg; IRON 1.9mg; SODIUM 148mg; CALC 37mg

Sugar-Frosted Cardamom Braid

1⅓ cups 2% reduced-fat milk
½ cup granulated sugar
2 tablespoons butter
2 tablespoons grated lemon rind
½ to 1 teaspoon ground cardamom
½ teaspoon salt
4½ to 4¾ cups all-purpose flour, divided
1 package dry yeast (about 2¼ teaspoons)
1 large egg
Cooking spray
1 large egg white, lightly beaten
1 tablespoon water
1 tablespoon coarse-grain sugar

1. Combine first 6 ingredients in a heavy saucepan over low heat. Cook 5 minutes or until sugar dissolves and a thermometer registers 115°, stirring frequently. Remove saucepan from heat.

2. Lightly spoon flour into dry measuring cups; level with a knife. Combine 2½ cups flour and yeast in a large bowl, stirring well with a whisk. Add milk mixture and egg; beat with a heavy-duty stand mixer at low speed 30 seconds or just until blended. Increase speed to medium; beat 2 to 3 minutes. Gradually add 2 cups flour; beat at low speed until mixture forms a ball.

3. Turn dough out onto a floured surface. Knead until smooth and elastic (about 8 minutes); add enough of remaining flour, 1 tablespoon at a time, to prevent dough from sticking to hands (dough will feel sticky). Place in a large bowl coated with cooking spray, turning to coat top. Cover and let rise in a warm place (85°), free from drafts, 1 hour or until doubled in size. (Press two fingers into dough. If indentation remains, dough has risen enough.) Punch dough down; cover and let rest 5 minutes.

4. Divide dough into three equal portions, shaping each portion into a 20-inch rope. Pinch ends together at one end to seal. Braid ropes on a lightly floured surface; pinch loose ends to seal. Place braid on a baking sheet coated with cooking spray. (The braid should be about 15 inches long.) Cover and let rise 30 minutes or until doubled in size.

5. Preheat oven to 375°.

6. Combine egg white and water; brush over top of loaf. Sprinkle 1 tablespoon sugar over loaf. Bake at 375° for 25 minutes or until golden and loaf sounds hollow when tapped. Remove from oven; cool on a wire rack. Yield: 24 servings (serving size: 1 slice).

CALORIES 130 (13% from fat); FAT 1.9g (sat 0.9g, mono 0.5g, poly 0.3g); PROTEIN 3.6g; CARB 24.5g; FIBER 0.8g; CHOL 13mg; IRON 1.3mg; SODIUM 71mg; CALC 23mg

Sugar-Frosted Cardamom Braid

breads

Potato Rolls

Adding potato to the dough creates a light texture. Bake these rolls up to 1 month ahead. Cool completely, wrap in heavy-duty aluminum foil, and freeze. Thaw completely, and reheat (still wrapped in foil) at 375° for 12 minutes or until warm. Try using the leftover rolls to make miniature sandwiches with turkey and relish.

    2   cups cubed peeled baking potato
    4   teaspoons sugar, divided
    1   package dry yeast (about 2¼ teaspoons)
4¼   cups bread flour, divided
    3   tablespoons butter, melted
1½   teaspoons salt
    1   large egg, lightly beaten
    Cooking spray
    2   tablespoons bread flour

1. Place potato in a medium saucepan; cover with water. Bring to a boil. Reduce heat; simmer 15 minutes or until tender. Drain in a colander over a bowl, reserving 1 cup cooking liquid. Mash potatoes with a fork.
2. Cool reserved cooking liquid to 105° to 115°. Stir in 1 teaspoon sugar and yeast. Let stand 5 minutes.
3. Lightly spoon 4¼ cups flour into dry measuring cups; level with a knife. Combine mashed potato, yeast mixture, 1 tablespoon sugar, 4 cups flour, butter, salt, and egg in a large bowl, stirring until well blended.
4. Turn dough out onto a floured surface. Knead until smooth and elastic (about 10 minutes); add up to ¼ cup flour, 1 tablespoon at a time, to prevent dough from sticking to hands (dough will feel tacky).
5. Place dough in a large bowl coated with cooking spray, turning to coat top. Cover and let rise in a warm place (85°), free from drafts, 45 minutes or until doubled in size. (Press two fingers into dough. If indentation remains, dough has risen enough.) Punch dough down; cover and let rest 10 minutes.
6. Divide dough in half; divide each half into 12 equal portions. Working with one portion at a time (cover remaining dough to keep from drying), shape portion into a 2-inch-long oval on a floured surface. Roll up tightly, starting with a long edge, pressing firmly to eliminate air pockets; pinch seam and ends to seal. Place rolls, seam sides down, on 2 baking sheets coated with cooking spray, placing 12 rolls on each.
7. Sift 2 tablespoons flour over rolls to lightly coat.

Cover rolls, and let rise 45 minutes or until doubled in size.
8. Preheat oven to 350°.
9. Bake at 350° for 10 minutes with 1 baking sheet on bottom rack and 1 baking sheet on second rack from top. Rotate baking sheets; bake an additional 10 minutes or until rolls are browned on bottom, lightly browned on top, and sound hollow when tapped. Remove from pans; cool on wire racks. Yield: 24 servings (serving size: 1 roll).

CALORIES 121 (16% from fat); FAT 2.1g (sat 1g, mono 0.6g, poly 0.3g); PROTEIN 3.6g; CARB 21.6g; FIBER 0.9g; CHOL 13mg; IRON 1.2mg; SODIUM 165mg; CALC 7mg

Mini Cranberry Panettones

This classic Italian holiday sweet bread is a cross between a coffee cake and dessert that's now served year-round the world over. Lining the muffin cups with strips of parchment makes it easy to remove the panettones after baking. You can also prepare this recipe in traditional muffin tins for a yield of 18; trim the parchment paper for the muffin cups to 6 x 2½–inches, and shorten the baking time to 20 minutes.

    2   packages dry yeast (about 4½ teaspoons)
1¼   cups warm water (100° to 110°)
5¾   cups all-purpose flour, divided
    ¾   cup sugar
    7   tablespoons butter
    1   tablespoon finely chopped fresh orange rind
    ½   teaspoon salt
    2   large eggs
2½   cups sweetened dried cranberries
    ¼   cup finely chopped crystallized ginger
    Cooking spray
    2   tablespoons sliced almonds

1. Dissolve yeast in water in a large bowl; let stand 5 minutes. Lightly spoon 1¼ cups flour into dry measuring cups; level with a knife. Add to yeast mixture, stirring with a whisk to combine. Cover; let rise in a warm place (85°), free from drafts, 1 hour.
2. Combine sugar and next 3 ingredients in a large bowl; beat with a heavy-duty stand mixer at medium speed until light and fluffy (about 3 minutes). Add eggs, beating until combined; beat in yeast mixture. Lightly spoon 4½ cups flour into dry measuring cups; level with a knife. Add 4 cups flour to egg mixture, beating at medium speed until smooth. Turn dough out onto a floured surface. Knead until smooth and elastic (about 3 minutes);

Mini Cranberry Panettones

add enough of remaining flour, 1 tablespoon at a time, to prevent dough from sticking to hands (dough will feel sticky). Knead in cranberries and ginger until well incorporated.

3. Place dough in a large bowl coated with cooking spray, turning to coat top. Cover and let rise in a warm place (85°), free from drafts, 1 hour or until doubled in size. (Gently press two fingers into dough. If indentation remains, dough has risen enough.)

4. Coat 6 (1-cup) muffin cups with cooking spray. Cut 6 (5 x 12–inch) strips of parchment paper;

place paper in muffin cups to extend 3 inches from top of muffin cups. Divide dough evenly among muffin cups. Lightly spray each muffin with cooking spray; sprinkle with nuts. Let rise in a warm place (85°), free from drafts, 1 hour or until doubled in size.

5. While muffins rise, preheat oven to 375°.

6. After muffins have doubled in size, bake at 375° for 25 minutes or until muffins are lightly browned. Yield: 24 servings (serving size: $\frac{1}{4}$ muffin).

CALORIES 219 (18% from fat); FAT 4.5g (sat 2.3g, mono 1.2g, poly 0.5g); PROTEIN 4g; CARB 42.6g; FIBER 1.7g; CHOL 26mg; IRON 1.7mg; SODIUM 81mg; CALC 14mg

Olive and Asiago Rolls

A warm, fresh kalamata olive-infused roll sprinkled with rich, nutty-flavored Asiago is an ideal start to just about any meal. You can substitute Parmesan for Asiago and use green olives, if you prefer.

  1   tablespoon sugar
  1   package dry yeast (about 2 ¼ teaspoons)
 ¾   cup warm water (100° to 110°)
3 ⅔ cups bread flour
 ½   cup whole wheat flour
 ¾   cup 1% low-fat milk
  2   tablespoons chopped fresh oregano
  1   teaspoon salt
  1   teaspoon olive oil
Cooking spray
  3   tablespoons chopped pitted kalamata
     olives
  1   tablespoon water
  1   large egg white, lightly beaten
 ½   cup (2 ounces) grated Asiago cheese

1. Dissolve sugar and yeast in warm water in a large bowl; let stand 5 minutes. Lightly spoon flours into dry measuring cups; level with a knife. Add flours, milk, and next 3 ingredients to yeast mixture; beat with a mixer at medium speed until smooth.

2. Turn dough out onto a lightly floured surface. Knead until smooth and elastic (about 10 minutes).

3. Place dough in a large bowl coated with cooking spray, turning to coat top. Cover and let rise in a warm place (85°), free from drafts, 45 minutes or until doubled in size. (Gently press two fingers into dough. If indentation remains, dough has risen enough.)

4. Punch dough down. Cover and let rest 5 minutes. Turn dough out onto a lightly floured surface. Arrange olives over dough; knead gently 4 or 5 times or until olives are incorporated into dough. Cover and let rest 10 minutes.

5. Punch dough down. Divide dough into 16 equal portions. Working with one portion at a time (cover remaining dough to keep from drying), roll portion into a 2-inch ball. Place on baking sheets coated with cooking spray. Cover and let rise 30 minutes or until doubled in size. Uncover rolls, and cut a ¼-inch-deep "X" in top of each roll.

6. Preheat oven to 375°.

7. Combine 1 tablespoon water and egg white; brush over rolls. Bake at 375° for 18 minutes or until golden brown. Remove from oven; immediately sprinkle with cheese. Serve warm. Yield: 16 rolls (serving size: 1 roll).

CALORIES 161 (15% from fat); FAT 2.7g (sat 0.9g, mono 1.1g, poly 0.4g); PROTEIN 6.1g; CARB 27.5g; FIBER 1.3g; CHOL 4mg; IRON 1.6mg; SODIUM 212mg; CALC 58mg

How to Cut Rolls

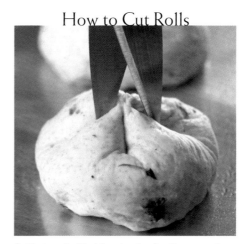

Cutting or slashing the dough after the second rise allows it to expand during baking. Use scissors or a very sharp knife to cut a ¼-inch-deep "X" in the top of each roll.

Freezer Cinnamon-Fruit Rolls

These frozen rolls are good for busy mornings—let them stand at room temperature 30 minutes, then bake 20 minutes. Make them in disposable foil pans for easy gift-giving; present the glaze in a small jar with instructions to microwave at HIGH 15 to 30 seconds, stir until smooth, and drizzle over warm rolls.

DOUGH:

1 package dry yeast (about 2¼ teaspoons)
¼ cup warm water (100° to 110°)
½ cup fat-free milk
⅓ cup granulated sugar
¼ cup butter, melted
1 teaspoon vanilla extract
½ teaspoon salt
1 large egg, lightly beaten
3¾ cups all-purpose flour, divided
Cooking spray

FILLING:

⅔ cup packed brown sugar
½ cup golden raisins
½ cup chopped dried apricots
½ cup chopped pecans
1 tablespoon ground cinnamon
2 tablespoons butter, melted

GLAZE:

1 cup powdered sugar
2 tablespoons fat-free milk

1. Dissolve yeast in warm water in a large bowl; let stand 5 minutes. Stir in ½ cup milk and next 5 ingredients. Lightly spoon flour into dry measuring cups; level with a knife. Add 3½ cups flour to yeast mixture, stirring until blended. Turn dough out onto a floured surface. Knead until smooth and elastic (about 10 minutes); add enough of remaining flour, 1 tablespoon at a time, to prevent dough from sticking to hands (dough will feel sticky).

2. Place dough in a large bowl coated with cooking spray, turning to coat top. Cover and let rise in a warm place (85°), free from drafts, 1 hour or until doubled in size. (Gently press two fingers into dough. If indentation remains, dough has risen enough.) Punch dough down; cover and let rest 5 minutes.

3. To prepare filling, combine brown sugar and next 4 ingredients.

4. Roll dough into an 18 x 10–inch rectangle on a floured surface. Brush 2 tablespoons melted butter over dough. Sprinkle 1½ cups filling over dough, leaving a ½-inch border. Beginning with a long side, roll up dough jelly-roll fashion; pinch seam to seal (do not seal ends of roll).

5. Place a long piece of dental floss or thread under dough ¾ inch from end of roll. Cross ends of floss over top of dough roll; slowly pull ends to cut through dough. Repeat procedure to make 24 rolls. Coat 2 (9-inch) square foil baking pans with cooking spray. Sprinkle remaining filling evenly into bottom of pans. Place 12 rolls, cut sides up, in each prepared pan. Cover and let rise 1½ hours or until doubled in size.

6. Preheat oven to 350°.

7. Uncover rolls. Bake at 350° for 20 minutes or until browned. Invert onto a serving platter.

8. To prepare glaze, combine powdered sugar and 2 tablespoons milk, stirring until smooth. Drizzle over warm rolls. Yield: 24 servings (serving size: 1 roll).

TO FREEZE UNBAKED ROLLS: Prepare through Step 5. Cover with plastic wrap. Wrap tightly with heavy-duty foil. Store in freezer up to 2 months.

TO PREPARE FROZEN UNBAKED ROLLS: Remove rolls from freezer; let stand at room temperature 30 minutes. Uncover and bake at 350° for 20 minutes or until browned.

CALORIES 193 (24% from fat); FAT 5.1g (sat 2g, mono 1.9g, poly 0.8g); PROTEIN 3.1g; CARB 34.4g; FIBER 1.4g; CHOL 17mg; IRON 1.5mg; SODIUM 87mg; CALC 28mg

How to Cut Dough

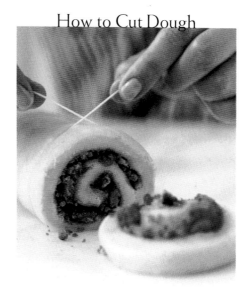

Floss or thread cuts the dough roll much more quickly and easily than a knife.

Parmesan, Garlic, and Basil Twists

Because they begin with refrigerated breadstick dough, these twists are a snap to put together.

1 tablespoon olive oil
2 garlic cloves, minced
1 (11-ounce) can refrigerated breadstick dough
¼ cup chopped fresh basil
¼ cup (1 ounce) grated fresh Parmesan cheese
¼ teaspoon freshly ground black pepper
Cooking spray

1. Preheat oven to 350°.
2. Heat oil in a small saucepan over medium heat. Add garlic; sauté 30 seconds. Remove from heat.
3. Unroll dough, separating into strips. Brush with garlic mixture. Sprinkle with basil, cheese, and pepper, gently pressing into dough. Twist breadsticks, and place on a baking sheet coated with cooking spray. Gently press ends of breadsticks onto baking sheet.
4. Bake at 350° for 15 minutes or until lightly browned. Yield: 1 dozen (serving size: 1 twist).

CALORIES 94 (30% from fat); FAT 3.1g (sat 0.8g, mono 1.4g, poly 0.6g); PROTEIN 2.9g; CARB 13g; FIBER 0.4g; CHOL 2mg; IRON 0.8mg; SODIUM 231mg; CALC 30mg

Bagels

1 (12-ounce) can brown beer (such as Newcastle Brown Ale), divided
1 cup water
1 package dry yeast (about 2¼ teaspoons)
1 large egg white, lightly beaten
4½ cups bread flour, divided (about 21½ ounces)
1½ teaspoons salt
Cooking spray
4 cups water
1 teaspoon brown sugar
1 teaspoon stone-ground yellow cornmeal
1 teaspoon water
1 large egg yolk
1 teaspoon sesame seeds
1 teaspoon poppy seeds

1. Heat ½ cup beer and 1 cup water over low heat in a small, heavy saucepan to between 100° and 110°. Combine beer mixture and yeast in a large bowl, stirring until yeast dissolves. Let stand 5 minutes. Stir in egg white.

2. Lightly spoon flour into dry measuring cups; level with a knife. Add 4¼ cups flour and salt to beer mixture; stir until a soft dough forms. Turn dough out onto a floured surface. Knead until smooth and elastic (about 8 minutes); add enough of remaining flour, 1 tablespoon at a time, to prevent dough from sticking to hands (dough will feel sticky).

3. Place dough in a large bowl coated with cooking spray, turning to coat top. Cover and let rise in a warm place (85°), free from drafts, 1 hour and 15 minutes or until doubled in size. (Gently press two fingers into dough. If indentation remains, dough has risen enough.) Punch dough down; cover and let rest 5 minutes.

4. Turn dough out onto a lightly floured surface. Divide dough into 10 equal portions. Working with one portion at a time (cover remaining dough to prevent drying), shape portion into a ball. Make a hole in center of ball using your index finger. Using fingers of both hands, gently pull dough away from center to make a 1½-inch hole. Place bagels on a baking sheet coated with cooking spray.

5. Lightly coat bagels with cooking spray; cover with plastic wrap. Let rise 10 minutes (bagels will rise only slightly).

6. Preheat oven to 400°.

7. Combine remaining beer, 4 cups water, and sugar in a Dutch oven. Bring to a boil; reduce heat, and simmer. Gently lower one bagel into simmering beer mixture. Cook 30 seconds. Turn bagel with a slotted spoon; cook 30 seconds. Transfer bagel to a wire rack lightly coated with cooking spray. Repeat procedure with remaining bagels.

8. Place bagels on a baking sheet sprinkled with cornmeal. Combine 1 teaspoon water and egg yolk in a small bowl; stir with a fork until blended. Brush bagels with yolk mixture; sprinkle with sesame and poppy seeds.

9. Bake at 400° for 17 minutes or until golden. Transfer bagels to a wire rack to cool. Yield: 10 servings (serving size: 1 bagel).

CALORIES 211 (14% from fat); FAT 3.2g (sat 0.2g, mono 1.1g, poly 1g); PROTEIN 8.3g; CARB 40.8g; FIBER 1.6g; CHOL 20mg; IRON 2.8mg; SODIUM 357mg; CALC 11mg

fish and shellfish

Sautéed Scallops with Parsley
and Garlic, page 93

Grouper with Puttanesca Sauce

Take your taste buds to Italy! The robust, spicy sauce is a chunky mixture of tomatoes, onions, capers, olives, and garlic. The word *puttanesca* (poot-tah-NEHS-kah) comes from puttana, for ladies of the night. Legend has it that the ladies lured men to their houses with this intensely fragrant sauce. It's most often served over pasta, but it tastes terrific spooned over filet mignon, chicken, or fish, or tossed with shrimp. Keep your pantry stocked with the sauce ingredients to make this dish anytime. The prep time is kept to a minimum by capitalizing on high-flavor ingredients. Serve with orzo to soak up the sauce, and enjoy your culinary journey.

Cooking spray
  4 (6-ounce) grouper or flounder fillets
 ⅛ teaspoon salt
 ¼ teaspoon black pepper
1½ teaspoons olive oil
  1 cup thinly sliced onion
  1 tablespoon bottled minced garlic
 ¼ teaspoon dried oregano
  1 (28-ounce) can whole tomatoes, drained
 ⅓ cup chopped pitted kalamata olives
  2 tablespoons capers
 ¼ cup chopped fresh flat-leaf parsley (optional)

1. Heat a nonstick grill pan over medium-high heat. Coat pan with cooking spray. Sprinkle fish with salt and pepper. Add fish to pan; cook 5 minutes on each side or until fish flakes easily when tested with a fork.

2. While fish cooks, heat oil in a large nonstick skillet over medium heat. Add onion; cook 4 minutes or until tender, stirring frequently. Add garlic, oregano, and tomatoes; bring to a boil. Reduce heat, and simmer 6 minutes, stirring frequently. Stir in olives and capers; cook 1 minute. Spoon tomato mixture over fish. Sprinkle with chopped parsley, if desired. Yield: 4 servings (serving size: 1 fillet and ¾ cup tomato mixture).

CALORIES 238 (18% from fat); FAT 4.8g (sat 0.8g, mono 2.5g, poly 0.8g); PROTEIN 35.5g; CARB 12g; FIBER 1.5g; CHOL 63mg; IRON 2.4mg; SODIUM 736mg; CALC 142mg

Peppered Halibut Fillets

Serve these lightly peppered fillets with steamed asparagus and a lemon wedge to add vibrant color to your plate. A side of fluffy, brown rice would be a nice addition as well.

  1 tablespoon coarsely ground black pepper
  1 tablespoon fresh lemon juice
1½ teaspoons canola oil
  4 (6-ounce) halibut fillets
 ¾ teaspoon sea or kosher salt
Cooking spray
  4 lemon wedges

1. Prepare grill.

2. Combine first 3 ingredients; rub over fish. Cover, and let stand at room temperature 10 minutes. Sprinkle fish with salt.

3. Place fish on a grill rack coated with cooking spray; grill 4 minutes on each side or until fish flakes easily when tested with a fork. Serve with lemon wedges. Yield: 4 servings (serving size: 1 fillet and 1 lemon wedge).

CALORIES 210 (24% from fat); FAT 5.7g (sat 0.7g, mono 2.3g, poly 1.8g); PROTEIN 35.6g; CARB 1.9g; FIBER 0.4g; CHOL 54mg; IRON 1.5mg; SODIUM 524mg; CALC 87mg

About Halibut

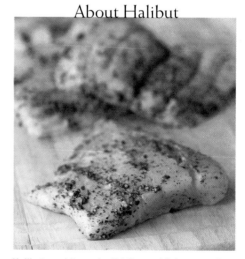

Halibut, a white and mild-flavored fish, comes in steaks and fillets. Although it's a firm fish, halibut is a little more delicate than grouper, sea bass, or mahimahi, so be gentle when turning it on the grill.

Peppered Halibut Fillets

One-Dish Poached Halibut and Vegetables

Prep time, cook time, and cleanup are minimal for this one-skillet meal. Serve with a crisp white wine and your favorite bread to soak up the flavorful sauce.

2 cups thinly sliced fennel bulb (about 6 ounces)

2 cups organic vegetable broth (such as Swanson Certified Organic)

1 (20-ounce) package refrigerated red potato wedges (such as Simply Potatoes)

8 ounces baby carrots

4 (6-ounce) halibut fillets

½ teaspoon paprika

⅛ teaspoon salt

⅛ teaspoon freshly ground black pepper

½ teaspoon chopped fresh thyme

4 lemon wedges

1. Combine first 4 ingredients in a large nonstick skillet; bring to a boil over medium-high heat. Cover, reduce heat, and simmer 4 minutes.

2. Sprinkle 1 side of fish with paprika, salt, and pepper. Add fish, seasoning side up, and thyme to pan; bring to a boil. Cover, reduce heat, and simmer 6 minutes or until fish flakes easily when tested with a fork. Serve with lemon wedges. Yield: 4 servings (serving size: 1 fillet, about 1½ cups vegetable mixture, and 1 lemon wedge).

CALORIES 314 (12% from fat); FAT 4.1g (sat 0.6g, mono 1.3g, poly 1.3g); PROTEIN 39.7g; CARB 26.6g; FIBER 5.6g; CHOL 54mg; IRON 3.3mg; SODIUM 659mg; CALC 115mg

Baked Fish with Chunky Tomato Sauce

Use a heavy ovenproof skillet that can go from stove-top to oven.

3½ cups chopped seeded tomato
     (about 4 medium)
¼ cup chopped green onions
¼ cup dry white wine
1 tablespoon chopped fresh basil
1 teaspoon capers
1 teaspoon bottled minced garlic
1 teaspoon fresh lemon juice
½ teaspoon salt
¼ teaspoon crushed red pepper
¼ teaspoon black pepper
2 teaspoons olive oil
4 (6-ounce) firm white fish fillets
     (such as halibut or grouper)

1. Preheat oven to 425°.
2. Combine first 10 ingredients in a medium bowl.
3. Heat oil in a large, heavy ovenproof skillet over high heat. Place fish in pan; cook 2 minutes. Turn fish over; top with tomato mixture. Bring to a boil. Place pan in oven, and bake at 425° for 8 minutes or until fish flakes easily when tested with a fork. Yield: 4 servings (serving size: 1 fillet and ½ cup tomato mixture).

CALORIES 200 (26% from fat); FAT 5.7g (sat 0.8g, mono 2.7g, poly 1.3g); PROTEIN 28g; CARB 8.6g; FIBER 2.2g; CHOL 41mg; IRON 2mg; SODIUM 400mg; CALCIUM 73mg

How to Seed Tomatoes

Seeding the tomatoes yields a more attractive sauce. To remove the seeds, first cut the tomatoes in half horizontally. Then cup one tomato half in the palm of your hand and gently squeeze out the seeds. You can also scoop out tomato seeds using your fingers or push them out with a spoon.

Broiled Red Snapper with Sicilian Tomato Pesto

In-season tomatoes enliven almost any meal. Plum tomatoes, also called Roma or Italian tomatoes, work best in this recipe because they have a low water content and few seeds; juicier tomatoes would thin the pesto. No need to seed or peel them. You can make the pesto ahead and keep it chilled. Stir in the tomatoes just before serving.

PESTO:
2 cups basil leaves
2 tablespoons pine nuts, toasted
2 tablespoons extravirgin olive oil
2 garlic cloves, minced
¼ cup (1 ounce) grated Parmigiano-Reggiano
     cheese
⅛ teaspoon crushed red pepper
1½ cups chopped plum tomato (about 3 medium)
½ teaspoon salt
½ teaspoon freshly ground black pepper
FISH:
6 (6-ounce) red snapper or other firm whitefish
     fillets
¼ teaspoon salt
Cooking spray
REMAINING INGREDIENT:
3 cups hot cooked orzo

1. To prepare pesto, place first 4 ingredients in a food processor; process until smooth. Add cheese and red pepper; process until blended. Transfer mixture to a bowl. Add tomato, ½ teaspoon salt, and black pepper, stirring gently to combine.
2. Preheat broiler.
3. To prepare fish, sprinkle fish with ¼ teaspoon salt. Arrange fish on a broiler pan coated with cooking spray, and broil 8 minutes or until fish flakes easily when tested with a fork. Place orzo on each of 6 plates, and top each serving with fish and pesto. Yield: 6 servings (serving size: ½ cup orzo, 1 fillet, and ¼ cup pesto).

CALORIES 437 (22% from fat); FAT 10.8g (sat 2.4, mono 4.8, poly 2); PROTEIN 44.9g; CARB 38.9g; FIBER 3.1g; CHOL 67mg; IRON 2.9mg; SODIUM 497mg; CALC 156mg

Salmon Patties

Try adding some chopped fresh dill to fat-free tartar sauce, and spoon it over the patties. Or serve the patties on whole wheat hamburger buns topped with lettuce leaves and slices of tomato for a quick meal.

> 1 (14.75-ounce) can pink salmon
> ½ cup egg substitute
> ½ cup crushed saltine crackers
>   (about 14 crackers)
> ⅓ cup thinly sliced green onions
> 1 tablespoon lemon juice
> ¼ teaspoon salt
> ¼ teaspoon black pepper
> Cooking spray

1. Drain salmon; discard skin and bones. Combine salmon, egg substitute, and next 5 ingredients in a bowl; stir well. Divide mixture into 4 equal portions, shaping each into a ¾-inch-thick patty.

2. Heat a large nonstick skillet over medium-high heat, and coat pan with cooking spray. Add patties, and cook 3 minutes on each side or until lightly browned. Yield: 4 servings (serving size: 1 patty).

CALORIES 163 (22% from fat); FAT 4g (sat 0.2g, mono 0.6g, poly 0.1g); PROTEIN 25.1g; CARB 7.8g; FIBER 0.7g; CHOL 61mg; IRON 1.6mg; SODIUM 638mg; CALC 24mg

Sweet Orange Salmon

Three words describe this dish—quick, easy, and delicious. Add a side of brown basmati rice and throw together a green salad. Finish the meal with a squeeze of orange juice over all, and dinner is ready.

> 2 tablespoons brown sugar
> 1 teaspoon chili powder
> ½ teaspoon grated orange rind
> ½ teaspoon ground cumin
> ½ teaspoon paprika
> ¼ teaspoon salt
> ¼ teaspoon ground coriander
> ⅛ teaspoon black pepper
> 4 (6-ounce) salmon fillets
> Cooking spray
> Orange wedges (optional)

1. Preheat broiler.

2. Combine first 8 ingredients in a small bowl. Rub spice mixture over both sides of fish. Place fish on a broiler pan coated with cooking spray. Broil 8 minutes or until fish flakes easily when tested with a fork. Serve with orange wedges, if desired. Yield: 4 servings (serving size: 1 fillet).

CALORIES 303 (39% from fat); FAT 13.3g (sat 3.1g, mono 5.7g, poly 3.2g); PROTEIN 36.2g; CARB 7.5g; FIBER 0.5g; CHOL 87mg; IRON 1mg; SODIUM 235mg; CALC 33mg

Orange-and-Bourbon Grilled Salmon

To make a complete meal, serve the salmon over a bed of brown rice, with green beans and a salad on the side. Save some orange-and-bourbon marinade and drizzle over the salmon and rice to impart complementing flavors of bourbon and citrus throughout.

> ¼ cup bourbon
> ¼ cup fresh orange juice
> ¼ cup low-sodium soy sauce
> ¼ cup packed brown sugar
> ¼ cup chopped green onions
> 3 tablespoons chopped fresh chives
> 2 tablespoons fresh lemon juice
> 2 garlic cloves, chopped
> 4 (6-ounce) salmon fillets (about 1 inch thick)
> Cooking spray
> Lemon wedges (optional)
> Green onion strips (optional)

1. Combine first 8 ingredients in a large zip-top plastic bag, and add salmon to bag. Seal and marinate in refrigerator 1½ hours, turning bag occasionally.

2. Prepare grill.

3. Remove salmon from bag, reserving marinade. Place salmon on a grill rack coated with cooking spray. Cook 6 minutes on each side or until fish flakes easily when tested with a fork, basting frequently with reserved marinade. Garnish with lemon wedges and green onion strips, if desired. Yield: 4 servings (serving size: 1 fillet).

CALORIES 365 (35% from fat); FAT 14.1g (sat 2.5g, mono 6.8g, poly 3.1g); PROTEIN 36g; CARB 18g; FIBER 0.3g; CHOL 111mg; IRON 1.4mg; SODIUM 575mg; CALC 34mg

Orange-and-Bourbon
Grilled Salmon

Zesty Swordfish Kebabs

- 3 tablespoons low-sodium soy sauce
- 2 tablespoons chopped fresh rosemary
- 2 tablespoons fresh lemon juice
- 1 tablespoon grated lemon rind
- 1½ tablespoons extravirgin olive oil
- 2 teaspoons grated orange rind
- 1 tablespoon fresh orange juice
- 2 teaspoons honey
- 1 teaspoon grated peeled fresh ginger
- ½ teaspoon salt
- ¼ teaspoon freshly ground black pepper
- 5 garlic cloves, chopped
- 1½ pounds swordfish steaks, cut into 1-inch pieces
- ¾ cup (2-inch) sliced green onions
- 12 (1-inch) pieces red bell pepper
- Cooking spray

1. Combine first 12 ingredients in a large zip-top plastic bag; add fish. Seal and marinate in refrigerator 30 minutes, turning once.

2. Prepare grill.

3. Remove fish from bag; discard marinade. Thread fish, green onions, and bell pepper alternately onto each of 4 (10-inch) skewers. Place skewers on a grill rack coated with cooking spray; grill 8 minutes or until desired degree of doneness, turning once. Yield: 4 servings (serving size: 1 kebab).

CALORIES 248 (28% from fat); FAT 7.8g (sat 2g, mono 3.4g, poly 1.7g); PROTEIN 33.8g; CARB 9.7g; FIBER 1.6g; CHOL 64mg; IRON 2mg; SODIUM 711mg; CALC 38mg

About Swordfish

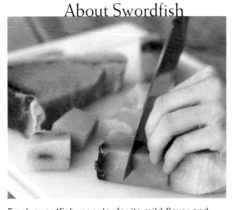

Fresh swordfish, popular for its mild flavor and meaty texture, appears in markets year-round, usually as steak. It's generally best when it's grilled or pan-fried. When you're making kebabs, be sure to cut the swordfish into pieces that are roughly the same size to ensure even cooking on the grill.

Grilled Salmon with East-West Spice Rub and Orange-Soy Glaze

Salmon is an excellent source of omega-3 oil and vitamins A and B, which may help reduce the risk of heart disease—so eat up! This particular recipe is perfect over a bed of white rice and rounded out with sweet steamed snow peas.

SPICE MIXTURE:
- 1 tablespoon sugar
- 1½ teaspoons five-spice powder
- 1½ teaspoons ground coriander
- 1½ teaspoons black pepper
- ½ teaspoon salt

GLAZE:
- 3 (3 x ½–inch) orange rind strips
- ½ cup fresh orange juice
- ½ cup low-sodium soy sauce
- ⅓ cup honey
- 2 tablespoons minced green onions
- 1 tablespoon minced peeled fresh ginger
- 1½ teaspoons dark sesame oil
- 4 garlic cloves, minced
- 1 (3-inch) cinnamon stick

FISH:
- 8 (6-ounce) salmon fillets (about 2 inches thick)
- Cooking spray
- ¼ cup thinly sliced green onions
- 1 tablespoon sesame seeds, toasted

1. To prepare spice mixture, combine first 5 ingredients in a small bowl.

2. To prepare glaze, combine rind strips and next 8 ingredients in a saucepan. Bring to a boil. Reduce heat, and simmer 10 minutes. Strain through a sieve; discard solids.

3. Prepare grill.

4. Rub fillets with spice mixture. Cover; refrigerate 10 minutes. Place fillets, skin sides down, on a grill rack coated with cooking spray. Cover and grill 16 minutes or until fish flakes easily when tested with a fork, basting occasionally with glaze. Remove skin; discard. Arrange fillets on a platter; sprinkle with sliced onions and sesame seeds. Yield: 8 servings (serving size: 1 fillet).

CALORIES 357 (39% from fat); FAT 15.5g (sat 2.7g, mono 7.3g, poly 3.7g); PROTEIN 36.1g; CARB 17g; FIBER 0.3g; CHOL 111mg; IRON 1.5mg; SODIUM 716mg; CALC 32mg

Grilled Striped Bass with Chunky Mango-Ginger Sauce

Tasty, easy, and beautiful—with just the right combination of savory and sweet—this sauce also makes a great salsa for turkey, chicken, or other mild fish. To make the sauce even chunkier, reduce the final cooking time to 10 minutes.

4   (6-ounce) striped bass or other firm white fish
     fillets (such as amberjack or grouper)
1   tablespoon olive oil
½   teaspoon kosher salt
¼   teaspoon black pepper
1   cup Chunky Mango-Ginger Sauce

1. Prepare grill.
2. Brush fillets with oil; sprinkle with salt and pepper. Grill fillets 4 minutes on each side or until fish flakes easily when tested with a fork. Serve with Chunky Mango-Ginger Sauce. Yield: 4 servings (serving size: 1 fillet and ¼ cup sauce).

(Totals include Chunky Mango-Ginger Sauce) CALORIES 296 (34% from fat); FAT 11.3g (sat 2.2g, mono 6.1g, poly 2.1g); PROTEIN 32.9g; CARB 15.3g; FIBER 1.2g; CHOL 116mg; IRON 3mg; SODIUM 363mg; CALC 157mg

CHUNKY MANGO-GINGER SAUCE:

1   tablespoon olive oil
2   cups finely chopped red onion
2   cups cubed peeled ripe mango
1   cup chopped tomato
3   tablespoons minced peeled fresh ginger
2   tablespoons minced garlic (about 6 cloves)
½   cup fresh lime juice (about 2 limes)
¼   cup orange juice
¼   cup dry sherry
3   tablespoons brown sugar
3   tablespoons white vinegar

1. Heat oil in a large nonstick skillet over medium-high heat. Add onion; sauté 7 minutes. Add mango, tomato, ginger, and garlic; cook 5 minutes. Stir in remaining ingredients; bring to a boil. Reduce heat; simmer 20 minutes, stirring occasionally. Yield: 2½ cups (serving size: ¼ cup).

CALORIES 92 (18% from fat); FAT 1.8g (sat 0.2g, mono 1g, poly 0.2g); PROTEIN 0.8g; CARB 18.5g; FIBER 1.4g; CHOL 0mg; IRON 0.3mg; SODIUM 8mg; CALC 19mg

Grilled Tuna over Lemon-Mint Barley Salad

The flavors of the vinaigrette are mirrored in the marinade, so there's a double dose of the refreshing combination of lemon and mint. The salad can be made an hour ahead. You can halve it for two people.

¾ cup finely chopped fresh mint, divided
1 teaspoon grated lemon rind
3 tablespoons plus 1 teaspoon fresh lemon juice, divided
¾ teaspoon salt, divided
½ teaspoon crushed red pepper
3 garlic cloves, minced
4 (6-ounce) Yellowfin tuna steaks
2¼ cups water
1 cup uncooked pearl barley
2 cups chopped tomato
¾ cup chopped green onions
2 tablespoons capers
2 tablespoons chopped pitted kalamata olives
1 tablespoon extravirgin olive oil
Cooking spray

1. Combine ½ cup mint, lemon rind, 4 teaspoons lemon juice, ¼ teaspoon salt, pepper, and garlic in a shallow dish; add tuna, turning to coat. Cover and refrigerate 30 minutes.

2. While tuna marinates, combine ¼ teaspoon salt and water in a medium saucepan; bring to a boil. Stir in barley; cover, reduce heat, and simmer 30 minutes or until liquid is absorbed. Remove from heat; cover and let stand 5 minutes. Spoon barley into a large bowl; cool slightly. Add remaining ¼ cup mint, tomato, green onions, capers, and olives; stir well to combine. Combine remaining ¼ teaspoon salt, remaining 2 tablespoons lemon juice, and oil, stirring well with a whisk. Drizzle over barley mixture; toss gently to coat.

3. Prepare grill.

4. Place tuna steaks on a grill rack coated with cooking spray; cook 2 minutes on each side until tuna steaks are medium-rare or desired degree of doneness. Spoon about 1½ cups barley mixture onto each of 4 plates; top each serving with 1 tuna steak. Yield: 4 servings.

CALORIES 415 (15% from fat); FAT 6.9g (sat 1.2g, mono 3.3g, poly 1.6g); PROTEIN 47.2g; CARB 41.9g; FIBER 10.4g; CHOL 77mg; IRON 4mg; SODIUM 685mg; CALC 88mg

Grilled Lemon-Bay Shrimp

The simplicity of this dish belies its incredible taste. Bay leaves and lemon wedges infuse peppered shrimp with woodsy and citrus flavors. If your grocery store doesn't carry fresh bay leaves, substitute good-quality dried bay leaves (such as Spice Island) soaked overnight in water. Leave the tails on the shrimp for a prettier presentation.

    2   tablespoons fresh lemon juice
    1   tablespoon olive oil
    ½   teaspoon salt
    ½   teaspoon crushed red pepper
    ½   teaspoon freshly ground black pepper
    2   garlic cloves, minced
   32   large shrimp
   32   fresh bay leaves
    4   large lemons, each cut into 8 wedges
  Cooking spray

1. Prepare grill.
2. Peel shrimp, leaving tails intact.
3. Combine first 6 ingredients in a large bowl. Add shrimp; toss to coat. Cover and marinate in refrigerator 10 minutes.
4. Place bay leaves and lemon wedges in a large bowl. Coat with cooking spray; toss to coat.
5. Thread 4 lemon wedges, 4 shrimp, and 4 bay leaves alternately onto each of 8 (10-inch) skewers. Place skewers on a grill rack coated with cooking spray, and grill 2 minutes on each side or until shrimp are done. Yield: 4 servings (serving size: 2 kebabs).

CALORIES 217 (27% from fat); FAT 6.4g (sat 1g, mono 2.9g, poly 1.4g); PROTEIN 34.8g; CARB 3.1g; FIBER 0.3g; CHOL 259mg; IRON 4.3mg; SODIUM 545mg; CALC 94mg

Spicy Grilled Jumbo Shrimp

Make the vinaigrette ahead; then the recipe takes less than 30 minutes to prepare. This dish has a light, citrusy, summertime taste, yet gets an extra jolt of flavor from the hot red pepper sauce.

  2¼   pounds unpeeled jumbo shrimp
   ¾   cup Honeyed Lemon-Dijon Vinaigrette, divided
   ½   teaspoon crushed red pepper
   ¼   teaspoon salt
   ¼   teaspoon coarsely ground black pepper
  Cooking spray
  Lemon wedges

1. Peel shrimp, leaving tails intact. Starting at tail end, butterfly each shrimp, cutting to, but not through, underside of shrimp. Combine shrimp, 6 tablespoons Honeyed Lemon-Dijon Vinaigrette, and red pepper in a large zip-top plastic bag. Seal bag, and marinate in refrigerator 15 minutes, turning bag occasionally.
2. Prepare grill.
3. Remove shrimp from marinade; discard marinade. Sprinkle shrimp with salt and black pepper. Place, cut sides down, on a grill rack coated with cooking spray; grill 2 minutes on each side, basting frequently with 6 tablespoons Honeyed Lemon-Dijon Vinaigrette. Serve with lemon wedges. Yield: 6 servings (serving size: about 4½ ounces).

(Totals include Honeyed Lemon-Dijon Vinaigrette) CALORIES 223 (27% from fat); FAT 6.6g (sat 1.1g, mono 3.2g, poly 1.5g); PROTEIN 34.7g; CARB 4.1g; FIBER 0.3g; CHOL 259mg; IRON 4.2mg; SODIUM 549mg; CALC 93mg

HONEYED LEMON-DIJON VINAIGRETTE:

   ¼   cup chopped fresh dill
   ¼   cup white wine vinegar
    2   tablespoons chopped red onion
    2   tablespoons capers
    1   tablespoon grated lemon rind
    2   tablespoons fresh lemon juice
    4   teaspoons honey
    2   teaspoons Dijon mustard
    1   teaspoon salt
   ¾   teaspoon freshly ground black pepper
   ½   teaspoon hot pepper sauce
    2   garlic cloves, minced
   ⅓   cup boiling water
   ¼   cup extravirgin olive oil

1. Place first 12 ingredients in a blender; process until mixture is smooth. Add water and oil, and process until well combined. Yield: about 1½ cups (serving size: 1 tablespoon).
NOTE: Refrigerate vinaigrette in an airtight container up to five days, and stir well before using.

CALORIES 27 (80% from fat); FAT 2.4g (sat 0.3g, mono 1.8g, poly 0.2g); PROTEIN 0.1g; CARB 1.6g; FIBER 0.1g; CHOL 0mg; IRON 0.1mg; SODIUM 133mg; CALC 2mg

Shrimp with Feta

This simple recipe capitalizes on high-flavor ingredients, such as herbs, wine, and feta cheese. For an elegant presentation, buy peeled shrimp with the tails still on.

    1   (3½-ounce) bag boil-in-bag long-grain rice
    2   teaspoons olive oil
  Cooking spray
  ¼   cup coarsely chopped Vidalia or other sweet
      onion
  ¼   cup chopped fresh parsley
  ½   teaspoon salt
  ½   teaspoon dried basil
  ½   teaspoon dried oregano
  ¼   teaspoon dried dill
  ¼   teaspoon crushed red pepper
    2   (14.5-ounce) cans no-salt-added diced
      tomatoes, undrained
    1   garlic clove, crushed
  ⅓   cup dry white wine
  1½ pounds peeled and deveined large shrimp
    1   (4-ounce) package crumbled feta cheese
  Chopped fresh parsley (optional)

1. Cook rice according to package directions, omitting salt and fat.
2. While rice cooks, heat oil in a nonstick skillet coated with cooking spray over medium-high heat. Add onion, and sauté 4 minutes. Stir in ¼ cup parsley and next 7 ingredients; cook 3 minutes. Stir in wine and shrimp. Cover; cook 3 minutes or until shrimp are done. Remove from heat; sprinkle with cheese. Serve over rice. Garnish with parsley, if desired. Yield: 4 servings (serving size: 1¾ cups shrimp mixture and ½ cup rice).

CALORIES 457 (23% from fat); FAT 11.9g (sat 5.2g, mono 3.6g, poly 1.7g); PROTEIN 43.6g; CARB 42.5g; FIBER 3g; CHOL 284mg; IRON 6.2mg; SODIUM 887mg; CALC 321mg

Cajun Shrimp and Rice

Cajun-seasoned dishes aren't always fiery, but they are always boldly flavored, like this dish. A bagged frozen vegetable stir-fry gives you a head start on your preparations. To thaw the vegetables quickly, place them in a colander and rinse them with cold water. Before sautéing, drain the thawed vegetables on paper towels.

    1   (3½-ounce) bag boil-in-bag long-grain rice
    2   tablespoons olive oil, divided
    2   pounds peeled and deveined large shrimp
    1   tablespoon salt-free Cajun seasoning
    1   tablespoon bottled minced garlic
    1   cup frozen bell pepper and onion stir-fry
      (such as Bird's Eye), thawed
  ¼   cup chopped green onions
  ¼   teaspoon dried thyme
  ½   cup canned Italian-style stewed tomatoes,
      undrained
  ½   teaspoon salt
  ⅛   teaspoon black pepper

1. Cook rice according to package directions, omitting salt and fat.
2. While rice cooks, heat 1 tablespoon oil in a large nonstick skillet over medium-high heat. Sprinkle shrimp with Cajun seasoning, and toss to coat. Add shrimp to pan; sauté 4 minutes or until done. Remove from pan; keep warm.
3. Heat remaining 1 tablespoon oil in pan over medium-high heat. Add garlic; sauté 30 seconds. Add bell pepper stir-fry, green onions, and thyme; sauté 3 minutes or until tender. Stir in cooked rice, shrimp, tomatoes, salt, and black pepper; cook 1 minute or until thoroughly heated. Yield: 4 servings (serving size: 1¼ cups).

CALORIES 354 (25% from fat); FAT 9.8g (sat 1.5g, mono 5.4g, poly 1.8g); PROTEIN 37.4g; CARB 27g; FIBER 1.1g; CHOL 259mg; IRON 5.3mg; SODIUM 658mg; CALC 106mg

Shrimp Pad Thai

Pad Thai is the most popular noodle dish in Thailand. This supereasy recipe is a variation of Thai restaurant fare. Substitute 4 cups hot cooked linguine for the rice stick noodles if you have trouble finding them.

½ pound wide rice stick noodles (*bánh pho*)
¼ cup ketchup
3 tablespoons fish sauce
2 tablespoons sugar
½ teaspoon crushed red pepper
2 tablespoons vegetable oil, divided
1 pound medium shrimp, peeled and deveined
2 large eggs, lightly beaten
1 cup fresh bean sprouts
¾ cup (1-inch) sliced green onions
1 teaspoon bottled minced garlic
2 tablespoons chopped unsalted, dry-roasted peanuts

1. Place noodles in a large bowl. Add hot water to cover; let stand 12 minutes or until tender. Drain.

2. Combine ketchup, fish sauce, sugar, and pepper in a small bowl.

3. Heat 2 teaspoons oil in a large nonstick skillet over medium-high heat. Add shrimp; sauté 2 minutes or until shrimp are done. Remove shrimp from pan; keep warm.

4. Heat 4 teaspoons oil in pan over medium-high heat. Add eggs; cook 30 seconds or until soft-scrambled, stirring constantly. Add sprouts, green onions, and garlic; cook 1 minute. Add noodles, ketchup mixture, and shrimp; cook 3 minutes or until heated. Sprinkle with peanuts. Yield: 6 servings (serving size: 1½ cups).

CALORIES 343 (24% from fat); FAT 9.2g (sat 1.6g, mono 2.6g, poly 3.9g); PROTEIN 21.3g; CARB 42.4g; FIBER 1.4g; CHOL 186mg; IRON 3mg; SODIUM 912mg; CALC 60mg

Singapore Mai Fun

Singapore Mai Fun

A favorite on Chinese take-out menus, this curried noodle dish is a sure hit and ready in a snap—provided you have the ingredients prepped before you start. The leftovers are good cold, as well. You'll find skinny rice noodles in the supermarket's ethnic food section.

　1　(6-ounce) package skinny rice noodles (py mai fun)
　½　cup fat-free, less-sodium chicken broth
　3　tablespoons low-sodium soy sauce
　1　teaspoon sugar
　½　teaspoon salt
Cooking spray
　1　tablespoon peanut oil, divided
　1　large egg, lightly beaten
　½　cup red bell pepper strips
　1　tablespoon grated peeled fresh ginger
　¼　teaspoon crushed red pepper
　3　garlic cloves, minced
　8　ounces skinless, boneless chicken breast, thinly sliced
　1　tablespoon curry powder
　8　ounces medium shrimp, peeled and deveined
　1　cup (1-inch) slices green onions

1. Cook rice noodles according to package directions, omitting salt and fat. Drain.
2. Combine broth, soy sauce, sugar, and salt; stir until sugar dissolves.
3. Heat a large nonstick skillet over medium-high heat; coat pan with cooking spray. Add 1 teaspoon oil. Add egg, and stir-fry 30 seconds or until soft-scrambled, stirring constantly. Remove from pan. Wipe pan clean with a paper towel. Heat 2 teaspoons oil in pan over medium-high heat. Add bell pepper strips, ginger, crushed red pepper, and garlic; stir-fry 15 seconds. Add chicken, and stir-fry 2 minutes. Add curry and shrimp; stir-fry 2 minutes. Stir in noodles, broth mixture, and egg; cook 1 minute or until thoroughly heated. Sprinkle with green onions. Yield: 6 servings (serving size: 1 cup).

CALORIES 237 (17% from fat); FAT 4.6g (sat 1g, mono 1.7g, poly 1.3g); PROTEIN 19.7g; CARB 27.8g; FIBER 1.3g; CHOL 115mg; IRON 2.2mg; SODIUM 646mg; CALC 53mg

Ginger Shrimp with Carrot Couscous

Carrot juice is the secret ingredient in this supereasy recipe. The juice gives the couscous vibrant color and packs this dish with more than 100 percent of the daily recommended amount of vitamin A. Carrots, first cultivated in West Africa and the eastern Mediterranean, are a natural complement to couscous, a staple food in the same area of the world.

　1　tablespoon vegetable oil, divided
　1　(12-ounce) can carrot juice, divided
　¾　cup uncooked couscous
　¼　cup fresh lime juice
　2　to 3 teaspoons minced seeded jalapeño pepper
　2　teaspoons grated peeled fresh ginger
　¼　teaspoon salt
　¼　cup sliced green onions
　4　cups gourmet salad greens
1½　pounds cooked, peeled, and deveined medium shrimp

1. Combine 1 teaspoon oil and 1 cup carrot juice in a medium saucepan; bring to a boil. Gradually stir in couscous. Remove from heat. Cover and let stand 5 minutes.
2. While couscous stands, bring remaining carrot juice to a boil in a small saucepan; cook until reduced to ¼ cup (about 2½ minutes). Remove from heat; stir in 2 teaspoons oil, lime juice, jalapeño, ginger, and salt.
3. Fluff couscous with a fork; stir in ¼ cup reduced carrot juice mixture and onions. Combine remaining carrot juice mixture, greens, and shrimp in a bowl, tossing gently to coat. Place couscous mixture on each of 4 plates; top with shrimp mixture. Yield: 4 servings (serving size: about ½ cup couscous mixture and 1½ cups shrimp mixture).

CALORIES 403 (13% from fat); FAT 5.8g (sat 1.1g, mono 1.2g, poly 3g); PROTEIN 42.7g; CARB 43.4g; FIBER 4.2g; CHOL 332mg; IRON 6.9mg; SODIUM 572mg; CALC 133mg

Shrimp, Tomato, and Basil Linguine with Warm Goat Cheese Rounds

Just a little sugar and red pepper add a sweet-hot note to this dish and complement the acidity of the goat cheese. Prepare the goat cheese rounds a day ahead, and refrigerate to make this recipe extra-easy.

  1   (1-ounce) slice white bread
  1   (4-ounce) package log-shaped goat cheese
  1   tablespoon olive oil
  1   cup coarsely chopped onion
  2   garlic cloves, minced
2½   cups chopped seeded peeled plum tomatoes (about 1½ pounds)
  ¼   cup water
1½   teaspoons sugar
  ¾   teaspoon crushed red pepper
  ½   pound medium shrimp, peeled and deveined
  ½   teaspoon salt
  6   cups hot cooked linguine (about 12 ounces uncooked pasta)
  ½   cup thinly sliced fresh basil
  Basil sprigs (optional)

1. Preheat oven to 400°.
2. Place bread in a food processor; pulse 10 times or until coarse crumbs measure ½ cup. Sprinkle breadcrumbs on a baking sheet; bake at 400° for 2½ minutes or until golden brown. Transfer to a shallow plate; cool completely. Slice goat cheese crosswise into 4 rounds. Press both sides of each round into breadcrumbs. Arrange in a single layer on a baking sheet; chill.
3. While goat cheese rounds chill, heat oil in a large nonstick skillet over medium-high heat. Add onion and garlic; sauté 5 minutes. Stir in chopped tomato, water, sugar, and pepper; cook mixture 15 minutes, stirring occasionally. Add shrimp and salt; cook 4 minutes or until shrimp are done. Remove from heat. Cover; keep warm.
4. Bake cheese rounds at 400° for 10 minutes or until soft but still holding their shape.
5. Add pasta and ½ cup basil to tomato mixture; toss to combine. Place pasta mixture into each of 4 bowls; top with goat cheese rounds. Garnish with basil sprigs, if desired. Yield: 4 servings (serving size: about 2 cups pasta mixture and 1 goat cheese round).

CALORIES 461 (28% from fat); FAT 14.3g (sat 6.7g, mono 4.8g, poly 1.4g); PROTEIN 24.5g; CARB 58.9g; FIBER 4.1g; CHOL 87mg; IRON 4.8mg; SODIUM 562mg; CALC 148mg

Creamy Fettuccine with Shrimp and Bacon

Whisking a couple tablespoons of flour into the milk achieves a texture in the sauce similar to that of cream. A little bit of bacon and drippings contribute smokiness and richness.

  1   pound uncooked fettuccine
  2   bacon slices (uncooked)
  1   pound large shrimp, peeled and deveined
  1   garlic clove, minced
1½   cups frozen green peas, thawed
  1   cup shredded carrot
  2   cups 2% reduced-fat milk
  2   tablespoons all-purpose flour
  ½   teaspoon salt
  ½   teaspoon freshly ground black pepper
  1   cup (4 ounces) grated Parmesan cheese
  ½   cup chopped fresh flat-leaf parsley, divided

1. Cook pasta according to package directions, omitting salt and fat. Drain well; keep warm.
2. Cook bacon in a large nonstick skillet over medium-high heat 6 minutes or until crisp. Remove bacon from pan, reserving 1 tablespoon drippings in pan. Crumble bacon; set aside.
3. Add shrimp and garlic to pan; sauté over medium-high heat 2 minutes. Add peas and carrot; cook 2 minutes or just until shrimp are done. Transfer shrimp mixture to a large bowl; keep warm.
4. Combine milk, flour, salt, and pepper, stirring with a whisk. Add milk mixture to pan; cook over medium heat 3 minutes or until thickened and bubbly, stirring constantly with a whisk. Remove pan from heat; add cheese, stirring until blended. Add milk mixture to shrimp mixture, and stir until combined. Add pasta and ¼ cup parsley, tossing gently to coat. Transfer pasta mixture to a platter, or place on each of 8 plates; sprinkle evenly with ¼ cup parsley and evenly crumbled bacon. Serve immediately. Yield: 8 servings (serving size: about 1¼ cups pasta mixture).

CALORIES 382 (18% from fat); FAT 7.7g (sat 3.7g, mono 1.2g, poly 0.5g); PROTEIN 25g; CARB 52.9g; FIBER 3.6g; CHOL 101mg; IRON 4.1mg; SODIUM 505mg; CALC 218mg

Creamy Fettuccine with
Shrimp and Bacon

Creamy Gruyère and Shrimp Orecchiette

Gruyère has a nutty, slightly sweet flavor; Swiss cheese makes a fine substitute. You can use chopped cooked chicken in place of the shrimp.

    8 ounces uncooked orecchiette pasta
       ("little ears" pasta)
    ¼ cup all-purpose flour
    ½ teaspoon salt
    2 cups 2% reduced-fat milk
 1 ¼ cups (5 ounces) shredded Gruyère cheese,
       divided
    1 tablespoon butter
 1 ½ pounds large shrimp, peeled and deveined
    3 garlic cloves, minced
    2 tablespoons dry white wine
    ¼ teaspoon ground red pepper
    2 cups frozen green peas, thawed
 Cooking spray
 Parsley sprigs (optional)

1. Preheat oven to 375°.
2. Cook pasta according to package directions, omitting salt and fat. Drain well.
3. Combine flour and salt in a Dutch oven over medium heat. Gradually add milk, stirring constantly with a whisk; bring to a boil. Cook 1 minute or until slightly thick, stirring constantly with a whisk. Remove from heat. Stir in ¾ cup cheese, stirring until melted.
4. Heat butter in a large nonstick skillet over medium-high heat. Add shrimp and garlic, and sauté 3 minutes. Stir in wine and pepper, and cook 1 minute or until shrimp are done.
5. Add pasta, shrimp mixture, and peas to cheese mixture, tossing well to combine. Spoon pasta mixture into a 13 x 9–inch baking dish lightly coated with cooking spray; sprinkle evenly with ½ cup cheese. Bake at 375° for 20 minutes or until cheese melts and begins to brown. Garnish with parsley, if desired. Serve immediately. Yield: 6 servings.

CALORIES 459 (27% from fat); FAT 13.8g (sat 7.1g, mono 3.7g, poly 1.6g); PROTEIN 39.6g; CARB 41.2g; FIBER 2.5g; CHOL 210mg; IRON 4.1mg; SODIUM 535mg; CALC 415mg

Linguine with Red Clam Sauce

Clams are harvested all over Italy, and Italians in particular like to cook clams in their shells directly in the sauce. We've adapted that custom, however, to fit the American lifestyle of convenience by using canned clams. Stock your pantry properly, and you'll have items on hand for a last-minute dinner. Ready-to-use ingredients such as dried pasta, olive oil, canned clams, tomato paste, bottled garlic, and pasta sauce have you well on your way to a convenient throw-together meal. While both red and white clam sauces are popular throughout Italy, a red sauce is a healthier choice. There are more calories and fat in a white sauce because of the butter and wine base.

   12 ounces uncooked linguine
    2 teaspoons olive oil
    2 teaspoons bottled minced garlic
    1 (25.5-ounce) bottle fat-free marinara pasta
       sauce (such as Muir Glen)
    2 tablespoons sun-dried or regular tomato paste
    ¼ teaspoon crushed red pepper
    3 (6½-ounce) cans chopped clams, undrained

1. Cook pasta according to package directions, omitting salt and fat. Drain, and keep warm.
2. Heat oil in a medium saucepan over medium heat. Add garlic; sauté 2 minutes. Stir in marinara sauce, tomato paste, and red pepper; bring to a simmer. Drain clams in a sieve over a bowl, reserving liquid; set clams aside. Stir reserved clam liquid into marinara-sauce mixture. Simmer 10 minutes. Stir in clams, and simmer 3 minutes. Serve pasta with sauce. Yield: 6 servings (serving size: 1 cup pasta and about 1 cup sauce).

CALORIES 330 (8% from fat); FAT 3.1g (sat 0.5g, mono 1.4g, poly 0.6); PROTEIN 16.9g; CARB 48.5g; FIBER 3.6g; CHOL 29mg; IRON 6.8mg; SODIUM 833mg; CALC 166mg

Linguine with Red Clam Sauce

Scallops with Roasted
Pepper-Butter Sauce

Scallops with Roasted Pepper–Butter Sauce

Scallops are usually classified into two groups: bay scallops and sea scallops. The larger sea scallops are best for grilling because, like shrimp, they have a meatier texture and can be easily skewered. They cook fast, so keep a close eye on them.

30 sea scallops (about 2¼ pounds)
 4 red bell peppers (about 2 pounds)
 2 cups fat-free, less-sodium chicken broth
 ½ cup dry white wine
1½ teaspoons chopped fresh or ½ teaspoon dried basil, crumbled
 2 tablespoons chilled butter, cut into small pieces
 ¼ teaspoon salt
Cooking spray
Basil sprigs (optional)

1. Thread 5 scallops onto each of 6 (12-inch) skewers. Cover and chill.
2. Preheat broiler.
3. Cut peppers in half lengthwise; discard seeds and membranes. Place pepper halves, skin sides up, on a foil-lined baking sheet; flatten with hand. Broil 15 minutes or until blackened. Place in a zip-top plastic bag. Seal and let stand 10 minutes. Peel peppers; discard skins. Place peppers, broth, and wine in a blender; process until smooth. Combine pepper mixture and chopped basil in a skillet. Bring to a boil; cook until reduced to 1½ cups (about 5 minutes). Reduce heat to medium-low; gradually add butter, stirring until melted. Cover and keep warm.
4. Prepare grill.
5. Sprinkle kabobs with salt; place on a grill rack coated with cooking spray. Grill 2½ minutes on each side or until done. Serve with bell pepper sauce. Garnish with basil, if desired. Yield: 6 servings (serving size: 5 scallops and ¼ cup sauce).

CALORIES 208 (23% from fat); FAT 5.2g (sat 2.5g, mono 1.2g, poly 0.7g); PROTEIN 29.8g; CARB 9.4g; FIBER 1.6g; CHOL 67mg; IRON 0.9mg; SODIUM 970mg; CALC 52mg

Sautéed Scallops with Parsley and Garlic

(pictured on page 73)

Look for scallops that are labeled "dry" or "unsoaked" and that are cream-colored or slightly pink. Avoid purchasing scallops that are pure white, brownish, dull looking, or are labeled "wet."

16 large sea scallops (about 1½ pounds)
 ¼ teaspoon salt
 ¼ teaspoon freshly ground black pepper
1½ tablespoons olive oil, divided
 2 tablespoons butter
 ¼ cup chopped fresh flat-leaf parsley
 2 garlic cloves, minced

1. Sprinkle scallops with salt and pepper. Heat 2¼ teaspoons oil in a large nonstick skillet over medium-high heat. Add 8 scallops; sauté 2½ minutes on each side or until browned. Set aside, and keep warm. Repeat procedure with remaining 2¼ teaspoons oil and 8 scallops. Wipe pan clean with a paper towel.
2. Add butter to pan; reduce heat, and cook until butter melts. Stir in parsley and garlic, and cook 15 seconds. Return scallops to pan; toss to coat. Yield: 4 servings (serving size: 4 scallops).

CALORIES 241 (43% from fat); FAT 11.5g (sat 3.6g, mono 5.7g, poly 1.1g); PROTEIN 28.7g; CARB 4.3g; FIBER 0.2g; CHOL 71mg; IRON 0.8mg; SODIUM 464mg; CALC 48mg

How to Brown Scallops

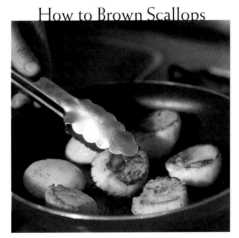

The key to perfectly browned scallops is patience; we recommend cooking them in batches. Begin by patting the scallops with paper towels to remove excess moisture. Heat the oil until it ripples in the pan. Add the scallops, a few at a time, and wait for them to sizzle before adding more. If you add too many at once, the pan will lose heat, the scallops will take longer to brown, and they may overcook, resulting in tough, dry scallops.

Scallops and Pasta with Pistachio-Parsley Pesto

Make the pesto up to two days ahead; cover and chill. Be sure to buy sea scallops, not bay scallops. Sea scallops are bigger than bay scallops (about 1½ inches in diameter compared to about ½ inch in diameter).

1 cup chopped fresh parsley
3 tablespoons coarsely chopped pistachios
1 teaspoon grated lemon rind
¼ teaspoon ground cumin
¼ teaspoon black pepper
⅛ teaspoon salt
⅛ teaspoon paprika
2 tablespoons fresh lemon juice
1¼ teaspoons olive oil
¾ pound sea scallops
¼ cup all-purpose flour
⅛ teaspoon salt
2 teaspoons butter
2 cups hot cooked angel hair (about 4 ounces uncooked pasta)
Freshly ground black pepper

1. Place first 9 ingredients in a food processor; process until smooth, scraping sides of processor bowl occasionally.

2. Combine scallops, flour, and ⅛ teaspoon salt in large zip-top plastic bag; seal and shake to coat.

3. Heat butter in nonstick skillet over medium-high heat. Add scallops; cook 3½ minutes on each side or until scallops are done.

4. Combine pesto mixture and pasta in a large bowl, tossing well. Arrange pasta on each plate, and place scallops on top of pasta. Sprinkle with pepper. Yield: 2 servings (serving size: 1 cup pasta and about 5 ounces scallops).

CALORIES 554 (25% from fat); FAT 15.2g (sat 3.9g, mono 6.4g, poly 3.5g); PROTEIN 41.4g; CARB 64.3g; FIBER 5g; CHOL 66mg; IRON 5.4mg; SODIUM 614mg; CALC 117mg

meatless
main dishes

Grilled Vegetable Lasagna,
page 112

Maple-Hazelnut Oatmeal

Cooked with apples and cinnamon and topped with maple syrup and hazelnuts, this oatmeal is anything but ordinary. This high-fiber breakfast will satisfy your hunger, provide long-lasting energy, and help your mind stay focused.

1½ cups fat-free milk
1½ cups water
  2 Gala apples, peeled, cored, and cut into
       ½-inch cubes (about 3 cups)
  1 cup uncooked steel-cut oats
  2 tablespoons brown sugar
1½ tablespoons butter, softened
  ¼ teaspoon ground cinnamon
  ¼ teaspoon salt
    Cooking spray
  ¼ cup pure maple syrup
  2 tablespoons chopped hazelnuts, toasted

1. Bring milk and water to a boil in a saucepan over medium-high heat, stirring frequently.
2. Place hot milk mixture, apple, and next 5 ingredients in a 3-quart electric slow cooker coated with cooking spray; stir well. Cover and cook on LOW 7 hours or until oats are tender.
3. Ladle oatmeal into individual bowls; top with maple syrup and hazelnuts. Yield: 4 servings (serving size: 1¼ cups oatmeal, 1 tablespoon syrup, and 1½ teaspoons hazelnuts).

CALORIES 341 (24% from fat); FAT 9.2g (sat 3.4g, mono 2.8g, poly 0.5g); PROTEIN 9.9g; CARB 60.6g; FIBER 5.5g; CHOL 13mg; IRON 2.4mg; SODIUM 218mg; CALC 163mg

About Steel-Cut Oats

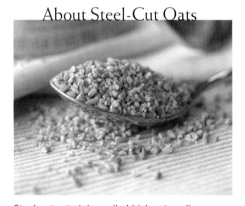

Steel-cut oats (also called Irish oatmeal) are cracked whole-grain oats that have a chewy texture when cooked. Unlike more widely available rolled oats, steel-cut oats are not steamed and flattened. As a result, they take longer to cook, making them an ideal fit for the slow cooker. These oats are wonderfully hearty and are a good source of iron as well as both soluble and insoluble fiber.

Beet Risotto with Greens, Goat Cheese, and Walnuts

Stunning appearance. Satisfying textures. Great flavor. These are just some of this risotto's amazing attributes. The earthiness of the beets and Swiss chard mixed with creamy goat cheese and crunchy walnuts truly make this a one-dish meatless-main wonder. And, unlike a traditional risotto, it's not so labor intensive since it doesn't have to be stirred constantly. Before you sauté the onion, we suggest that you toast the walnuts in the Dutch oven. They will add a nice fragrance.

  2 teaspoons olive oil
  1 cup chopped onion
  1 cup Arborio rice
  1 tablespoon minced peeled fresh ginger
  2 teaspoons finely chopped fresh rosemary
  ½ cup dry white wine
  3 cups finely chopped peeled beets (about
       1 pound)
  ½ cup water
  ¼ teaspoon fine sea salt
  1 (14½-ounce) can vegetable broth
  6 cups finely sliced Swiss chard
  ½ cup (2 ounces) crumbled goat cheese
  ¼ cup chopped walnuts, toasted
    Rosemary sprigs (optional)

1. Heat oil in a Dutch oven over medium-high heat. Add onion; sauté 3 minutes. Add rice, ginger, and rosemary; sauté 1 minute. Add wine; cook 3 minutes or until liquid is nearly absorbed, stirring constantly.
2. Add beets, water, salt, and broth; bring to a boil. Cover, reduce heat, and simmer 20 minutes or until beets are tender, stirring occasionally.
3. Stir in chard; cook 5 minutes. Add cheese, stirring until blended. Sprinkle with walnuts. Garnish with rosemary sprigs, if desired. Yield: 4 servings (serving size: 1½ cups and 1 tablespoon walnuts).

CALORIES 412 (30% from fat); FAT 13.7g (sat 4.9g, mono 4g, poly 3.6g); PROTEIN 14.1g; CARB 57.5g; FIBER 4.1g; CHOL 14mg; IRON 2.1mg; SODIUM 611mg; CALC 92mg

Spring Risotto

6 cups boiling water, divided
1 cup dried morels
2 pounds unshelled fava beans
5 cups vegetable broth or fat-free, less-sodium chicken broth
1 tablespoon olive oil
2 cups thinly sliced leek (about 3 large)
2 garlic cloves, minced
2 cups Arborio rice
2 tablespoons sun-dried tomato paste
1 cup dry white wine
¾ teaspoon salt
½ teaspoon freshly ground black pepper
⅓ cup sliced green onions
¾ cup (3 ounces) finely shredded fresh Romano cheese

1. Combine 3 cups boiling water and morels; cover and let stand 30 minutes. Drain and rinse with cold water. Drain and chop.

2. Remove beans from pods; discard pods. Place beans in a medium saucepan with remaining 3 cups boiling water; cook 1 minute. Drain and rinse with cold water. Drain; remove outer skins from beans. Discard skins.

3. Bring broth to a simmer in a medium saucepan (do not boil). Keep broth warm over low heat.

4. Heat oil in a large saucepan over medium-high heat. Add leek and garlic, and sauté 2 minutes or until leek is tender. Add rice and tomato paste; cook 2 minutes, stirring constantly. Stir in wine, salt, and pepper; cook 1½ minutes or until liquid is absorbed. Stir in 1 cup broth; cook about 2½ minutes or until liquid is nearly absorbed, stirring constantly. Add remaining broth, 1 cup at a time, stirring constantly until each portion is absorbed before adding the next (about 20 minutes total). Stir in morels and beans; cook 30 seconds or until thoroughly heated. Stir in green onions. Sprinkle each serving with cheese. Yield: 8 servings (serving size: 1 cup risotto and 1½ tablespoons cheese).

CALORIES 238 (22% from fat); FAT 5.9g (sat 2.2g, mono 2.9g, poly 0.4g); PROTEIN 9.9g; CARB 29.7g; FIBER 1.6g; CHOL 11mg; IRON 2.6mg; SODIUM 648mg; CALC 135mg

Sweet Pea Risotto
with Corn Broth

Sweet Pea Risotto with Corn Broth

CORN BROTH:

2½ cups water
2 cups fresh corn kernels
¼ teaspoon salt

RISOTTO:

3 cups organic vegetable broth (such as Swanson Certified Organic)
2 tablespoons butter
1 cup uncooked arborio rice
½ cup diced onion
3 tablespoons minced carrot
3 tablespoons minced celery
2 cups fresh green peas
1 cup fresh corn kernels
½ cup diced fresh fennel
2 tablespoons grated Parmesan cheese
2 teaspoons chopped fresh thyme

REMAINING INGREDIENTS:

1 tablespoon sherry vinegar
1 tablespoon olive oil
1 teaspoon sugar
¼ teaspoon salt
1 garlic clove, minced
2 tablespoons grated Parmesan cheese
1 tablespoon chopped fresh parsley
1 tablespoon chopped fresh chives

1. To prepare corn broth, combine 2½ cups water and 2 cups corn kernels in a small saucepan; bring to a boil. Reduce heat, and simmer 5 minutes or until corn is tender. Stir in ¼ teaspoon salt. Place corn mixture in blender; process until smooth. Strain corn mixture through a sieve into a bowl; discard solids. Set aside; keep warm.

2. To prepare risotto, bring broth to a simmer in a medium saucepan (do not boil); keep warm over low heat. Heat butter in a large saucepan over medium-high heat. Add rice; cook 1 minute, stirring constantly. Add onion, carrot, and celery; cook 3 minutes, stirring constantly. Add warm broth, ½ cup at a time, stirring constantly until each portion of broth is absorbed before adding next (about 20 minutes). Add peas and next 4 ingredients, stirring until blended and hot. Keep warm.

3. Combine vinegar and next 4 ingredients in a small bowl, stirring with a whisk until blended. Place about ⅓ cup corn broth in each of 6 bowls. Top each serving with about 1½ cups risotto, and drizzle each with 1 teaspoon vinaigrette. Sprinkle each serving with 1 teaspoon cheese, ½ teaspoon parsley, and ½ teaspoon chives. Serve immediately. Yield: 6 servings.

CALORIES 250 (29% from fat); FAT 8.2g (sat 3g, mono 3.9g, poly 0.9g); PROTEIN 7.8g; CARB 38.9g; FIBER 5.3g; CHOL 13mg; IRON 1.5mg; SODIUM 582mg; CALC 65mg

Arborio Rice, Parmesan, and Green Pea Pancakes

On the side, serve roasted red peppers with olive oil and chopped fresh thyme.

Cooking spray
½ cup finely chopped onion
1 cup uncooked Arborio rice or other short-grain rice
2¾ cups water
¾ teaspoon salt
1 cup fresh or frozen green peas
½ cup (2 ounces) freshly grated Parmigiano-Reggiano cheese
2 large egg whites
1 large egg
2 teaspoons canola oil
Thinly shaved Parmigiano-Reggiano cheese (optional)

1. Heat a large saucepan over medium heat. Coat pan with cooking spray. Add onion; cook 5 minutes or until tender, stirring occasionally. Add rice; cook 1 minute, stirring constantly. Add water and salt; bring to a boil. Cover, reduce heat to low, and cook 15 minutes. Stir in peas and grated cheese; cook 2 minutes, stirring constantly. Cover, remove from heat, and let stand 15 minutes.

2. Combine egg whites and egg in a large bowl. Add rice mixture, stirring until blended.

3. Heat oil in a nonstick griddle or large nonstick skillet over medium heat. Spoon ½ cup rice mixture per pancake onto hot pan, spreading each to a 4-inch diameter. Cook 6 minutes on each side or until bottoms are browned. Garnish with shaved cheese, if desired. Yield: 4 servings (serving size: 2 pancakes).

CALORIES 224 (31% from fat); FAT 7.8g; (sat 2.7g, mono 3.2g, poly. 1.2g); PROTEIN 11.7g; FIBER 2.7g; CHOL 115mg; IRON 1.4mg; SODIUM 677mg; CALC 142mg

Chickpea and Spinach Curry

In less than 10 minutes, this fiber-rich dish is ready for dinner. Serve with warm pitas or over basmati rice. You can top with a dollop of low-fat plain yogurt to contrast the earthy spices.

  1 cup coarsely chopped onion
1½ tablespoons bottled ground fresh ginger (such as Spice World)
  1 teaspoon olive oil
1½ teaspoons sugar
1½ teaspoons red curry powder (such as McCormick)
  1 (19-ounce) can chickpeas (garbanzo beans), rinsed and drained
  1 (14.5-ounce) can diced tomatoes, undrained
  4 cups fresh spinach
½ cup water
¼ teaspoon salt

1. Combine onion and ginger in a food processor; pulse until minced.
2. Heat oil in a large nonstick skillet over medium-high heat. Add onion mixture, sugar, and curry to pan; sauté 3 minutes. Add chickpeas and tomatoes; simmer 2 minutes. Stir in spinach, water, and salt; cook 1 minute or until spinach wilts. Yield: 3 servings (serving size: 1⅓ cups chickpea mixture).

CALORIES 247 (15% from fat); FAT 4g; (sat 0.6g, mono 1.6g, poly. 0.9g); PROTEIN 11.1g; FIBER 8.4g; CHOL 1mg; IRON 5mg; SODIUM 857mg; CALC 194mg

Spicy Black Bean–Corn Casserole

This spicy vegetarian entrée has all the flavors of enchiladas, but instead of using it to fill corn tortillas, you top the saucy black bean and corn mixture with a corn bread batter just before the last hour of cooking. For a complete meal, serve with a salad of mixed greens, orange sections, and sliced avocado dressed in a light vinaigrette.

  3 tablespoons diced green chiles, divided
½ cup salsa
¼ cup chopped green onions
¼ cup chopped fresh cilantro
  1 (15-ounce) can black beans, rinsed and drained
  1 (11-ounce) can corn with red and green bell peppers, drained
  1 (10-ounce) can enchilada sauce
½ cup egg substitute
  1 (8½-ounce) package corn muffin mix
  2 tablespoons chopped bottled roasted red bell peppers
1½ cups (6 ounces) preshredded reduced-fat Mexican blend or Cheddar cheese
  6 tablespoons reduced-fat sour cream
1½ teaspoons thinly sliced fresh cilantro

1. Place 2 tablespoons green chiles and next 6 ingredients in a 3½-quart electric slow cooker; stir well. Cover and cook on LOW 4 hours.
2. Combine remaining 1 tablespoon green chiles, egg substitute, muffin mix, and roasted red bell peppers in a bowl. Spoon batter evenly over bean mixture in cooker. Cover and cook 1 hour or until corn bread is done.
3. Sprinkle cheese over corn bread. Cover and cook 5 minutes or until cheese melts. Top each serving with sour cream; sprinkle with cilantro. Yield: 6 servings (serving size: about 1 cup casserole, 1 tablespoon sour cream, and ¼ teaspoon cilantro).

CALORIES 366 (30% from fat); FAT 12.4g (sat 5.8g, mono 0g, poly 0.1g); PROTEIN 17.2g; CARB 49.6g; FIBER 5.6g; CHOL 28mg; IRON 2.7mg; SODIUM 1,407mg; CALC 307mg

Spicy Black Bean-Corn
Casserole

Barley, Black Bean, and Corn Burritos

There's no need to go out to the local cantina when this wholesome Mexican-style meal is waiting for you at home. Protein-packed black beans and fiber-filled barley come together in this healthy substitute for meat-based burritos. Spicy tomatoes with green chiles, lime juice, cumin, and chili powder add south-of-the-border flavor and intensity.

- 1 (15-ounce) can black beans, rinsed and drained
- 1 (10-ounce) can diced tomatoes and green chiles, undrained
- 1 cup uncooked pearl barley
- 2 cups organic vegetable broth (such as Swanson Certified Organic)
- ¾ cup frozen whole-kernel corn
- ¼ cup chopped green onions
- 1 tablespoon fresh lime juice
- 1 teaspoon ground cumin
- 1 teaspoon chili powder
- ½ teaspoon ground red pepper
- 1 garlic clove, minced
- ¼ cup chopped fresh cilantro
- 18 (6½-inch) flour tortillas
- 1 cup plus 2 tablespoons (4½ ounces) shredded reduced-fat sharp Cheddar cheese
- 9 cups thinly sliced curly leaf lettuce
- 2¼ cups salsa
- 1 cup plus 2 tablespoons fat-free sour cream

1. Place first 11 ingredients in a 3- to 4-quart electric slow cooker; stir well. Cover and cook on LOW 4 to 5 hours or until barley is tender. Stir in cilantro.
2. Heat tortillas according to package directions. Spoon ⅓ cup barley mixture down center of each tortilla; sprinkle each with 1 tablespoon cheese. Roll up. Place 1 cup lettuce on each of 9 plates; top each with 2 burritos. Spoon ¼ cup salsa and 2 tablespoons sour cream over each serving. Yield: 9 servings.

CALORIES 402 (19% from fat); FAT 8.5g (sat 3.3g, mono 0.1g, poly 0.3g); PROTEIN 15.6g; CARB 70.1g; FIBER 10.2g; CHOL 14mg; IRON 2.1mg; SODIUM 1,181mg; CALC 263mg

Black Bean Quesadillas with Corn Salsa

Tex-Mex has never been so easy. A superquick corn salsa completes this tasty vegetarian meal. You might want to make a little extra salsa to have on hand later to serve with chips.

QUESADILLAS:
- 1 tablespoon olive oil
- 1½ teaspoons bottled minced garlic
- 2 cups chopped plum tomatoes
- ½ cup chopped fresh cilantro
- 1 (15-ounce) can black beans, rinsed and drained
- 4 (8-inch) flour tortillas
- Cooking spray
- ¾ cup (3 ounces) preshredded 4-cheese Mexican blend cheese

SALSA:
- 1 cup frozen whole-kernel corn
- ½ cup chopped fresh cilantro
- 2 tablespoons fresh lime juice
- ½ teaspoon bottled minced garlic
- 1 red bell pepper, chopped

1. To prepare quesadillas, preheat broiler.
2. Heat olive oil in a large skillet over medium-high heat. Add 1½ teaspoons garlic; sauté 30 seconds. Add tomatoes, ½ cup cilantro, and beans; cook 5 minutes or until liquid evaporates, stirring occasionally. Place tortillas on a baking sheet coated with cooking spray. Top each tortilla with ½ cup bean mixture and 3 tablespoons cheese; fold in half. Lightly coat tops with cooking spray. Broil 3 minutes or until cheese melts and tortillas begin to brown. Cut each tortilla into 3 wedges.
3. To prepare salsa, combine corn and next 4 ingredients in a small saucepan. Bring to a boil over high heat, and cook 2 minutes, stirring frequently. Serve with quesadillas. Yield: 4 servings (serving size: 3 quesadilla wedges and about ⅓ cup salsa).

CALORIES 420 (31% from fat); FAT 14.4g (sat 5.5g, mono 6.4g, poly 1.3g); PROTEIN 17.8g; CARB 60g; FIBER 10.3g; CHOL 19mg; IRON 4.2mg; SODIUM 590mg; CALC 272mg

Vegetarian Chipotle Nachos

The spicy bean mixture also makes a good filling for tacos and burritos. Look for meatless crumbles near the tofu and other soy products in the produce section.

Cooking spray
1 cup chopped green bell pepper (about 1 medium)
1 cup chopped onion (about 1 medium)
1 (12-ounce) package meatless fat-free crumbles (such as Lightlife Smart Ground)
1 (7-ounce) can chipotle chiles in adobo sauce
1 (15-ounce) can pinto beans, rinsed and drained
1 (14.5-ounce) can diced tomatoes with basil, garlic, and oregano, undrained
¼ cup chopped fresh cilantro
8 cups baked corn tortilla chips (6 ounces)
2 cups shredded romaine lettuce
1 cup diced peeled avocado (about 1 medium)
¾ cup vertically sliced red onion
¾ cup (3 ounces) shredded sharp Cheddar cheese
6 tablespoons fat-free sour cream

1. Heat a large nonstick skillet over medium heat. Coat pan with cooking spray. Add bell pepper, chopped onion, and crumbles; cook 5 minutes, stirring occasionally. Remove 1 chile and 1 tablespoon sauce from can; reserve remaining chiles and sauce for another use. Chop chile; add chile, sauce, beans, and tomatoes to pan. Cover, reduce heat, and simmer 5 minutes. Remove from heat; stir in cilantro. Arrange 1⅓ cups chips on each of 6 plates. Top each serving with 1 cup bean mixture, ⅓ cup lettuce, about 2½ tablespoons avocado, 2 tablespoons onion, 2 tablespoons cheese, and 1 tablespoon sour cream. Yield: 6 servings.

CALORIES 408 (26% from fat); FAT 11.8g (sat 4g, mono 4.2g, poly 2.5g); PROTEIN 23.8g; CARB 53.7g; FIBER 11g; CHOL 16mg; IRON 3.6mg; SODIUM 906mg; CALC 316mg

Eggplant, Tomato, and Smoked Mozzarella Tart

CRUST:

- 1 cup all-purpose flour
- 1 tablespoon toasted wheat germ
- 1 teaspoon baking powder
- ½ teaspoon freshly ground black pepper
- ¼ teaspoon salt
- ¼ cup water
- 1 tablespoon olive oil
- Cooking spray

FILLING:

- 1 (1-pound) eggplant, cut crosswise into ¼-inch-thick slices
- ¾ teaspoon salt, divided
- ½ teaspoon olive oil
- 4 garlic cloves, thinly sliced
- 1 tablespoon chopped fresh basil
- 1½ teaspoons chopped fresh oregano
- 1½ teaspoons chopped fresh mint
- 2 plum tomatoes, thinly sliced (about 6 ounces)
- ½ cup (2 ounces) shredded smoked mozzarella cheese, divided
- 2 tablespoons grated fresh Parmesan cheese

1. Preheat oven to 400°.

2. To prepare crust, lightly spoon flour into a dry measuring cup; level with a knife. Combine flour, wheat germ, and next 3 ingredients in a large bowl, stirring with a whisk; make a well in center of mixture. Add water and 1 tablespoon oil, stirring to form a soft dough. Turn dough out onto a lightly floured surface; knead lightly 4 times. Gently press into a 4-inch circle on plastic wrap; cover and chill 15 minutes.

3. Slightly overlap 2 sheets of plastic wrap on a slightly damp surface. Unwrap dough, and place chilled dough on plastic wrap. Cover with 2 additional sheets of overlapping plastic wrap. Roll dough, still covered, into an 11-inch circle. Remove top sheets of plastic wrap. Fit dough, plastic-wrap side up, into a 10-inch round removable-bottom tart pan coated with cooking spray. Remove remaining plastic wrap. Press dough against bottom and sides of pan. Pierce bottom and sides of dough with a fork; bake at 400° for 10 minutes. Cool completely on a wire rack.

4. To prepare filling, arrange eggplant on several layers of heavy-duty paper towels. Sprinkle with ½ teaspoon salt; let stand 15 minutes. Pat dry with paper towels; brush with oil. Arrange in a single layer on a baking sheet coated with cooking spray. Bake at 400° for 20 minutes. Stack on a plate; cover with plastic wrap. Let stand 7 minutes to steam.

5. Heat a large nonstick skillet coated with cooking spray over medium heat. Add garlic; sauté 1 minute. Remove from heat; stir in ¼ teaspoon salt, basil, oregano, mint, and tomatoes.

6. Sprinkle 2 tablespoons mozzarella evenly in crust. Layer eggplant and tomato mixture in crust; sprinkle with remaining mozzarella and Parmesan. Bake at 400° for 10 minutes or until cheese melts. Cut into 8 wedges. Yield: 4 servings (serving size: 2 wedges).

CALORIES 260 (30% from fat); FAT 8.8g (sat 3.1g, mono 4.2g, poly 0.9g); PROTEIN 9.8g; CARB 37g; FIBER 4.6g; CHOL 13mg; IRON 2.6mg; SODIUM 681mg; CALC 210mg

Hoppin' John

- 2 (16-ounce) packages frozen black-eyed peas
- 2 cups hot water
- ¾ cup sliced green onions
- ¾ cup chopped red bell pepper
- 2 tablespoons minced seeded jalapeño pepper
- 2 teaspoons hot sauce
- ½ teaspoon salt
- ¼ teaspoon black pepper
- 1 vegetable-flavored bouillon cube
- 1 (14.5-ounce) can Cajun-style stewed tomatoes with pepper, garlic, and Cajun spices, undrained
- ⅔ cup uncooked converted rice
- ½ cup sliced green onions

1. Combine first 9 ingredients in a 4-quart electric slow cooker, and stir well. Cover and cook on HIGH 4 hours. Stir in tomatoes and rice; cover and cook 1 hour or until peas and rice are tender and most of liquid is absorbed. Stir in ½ cup green onions. Yield: 6 servings (serving size: 1⅔ cups).

CALORIES 326 (4% from fat); FAT 1.6g (sat 0.5g, mono 0.1g, poly 0.5g); PROTEIN 16.1g; CARB 63g; FIBER 9.9g; CHOL 0mg; IRON 4.5mg; SODIUM 754mg; CALC 76mg

Hoppin' John

Cheese Pie with Peppers

In addition to feta, this Greek specialty traditionally uses kopanisti and graviera cheeses; this version uses more readily available Cheddar and blue. Serve with a mixed greens salad for a light supper. Bell and jalapeño peppers offer sweetness and heat.

Cooking spray
1½ cups chopped green bell pepper
 1 tablespoon finely chopped seeded jalapeño pepper (about 1 medium)
 ½ cup semolina or pasta flour (about 2¼ ounces)
1½ cups fat-free milk, divided
 1 cup plain fat-free yogurt
 1 cup (4 ounces) crumbled feta cheese
 1 cup (4 ounces) shredded reduced-fat extrasharp Cheddar cheese
 ¼ cup (1 ounce) crumbled blue cheese
 ½ teaspoon salt
 ¼ teaspoon freshly ground black pepper
 2 large egg whites
 8 (18 x 14–inch) sheets frozen phyllo dough, thawed

1. Preheat oven to 400°.

2. Heat a large nonstick skillet over medium-high heat. Coat pan with cooking spray. Add bell pepper and jalapeño; sauté 5 minutes. Stir in flour; remove from heat. Set aside 2 tablespoons milk. Gradually add remaining milk to pan, stirring well with a whisk. Stir in yogurt; bring to a boil. Remove from heat; stir 2 minutes or until thick. Cool 5 minutes. Stir in cheeses, salt, black pepper, and egg whites.

3. Working with 1 phyllo sheet at a time (cover remaining dough to keep from drying), place 2 phyllo sheets in a 13 x 9–inch baking pan coated with cooking spray; gently press sheets into bottom and sides of pan, allowing ends to extend over edges of pan. Coat top sheet with cooking spray. Fold 1 phyllo sheet in half crosswise; place on sheets in bottom of pan, and coat with cooking spray. Top with 1 phyllo sheet, gently pressing sheet into bottom and sides of pan; coat with cooking spray. Spread cheese mixture evenly over top of phyllo. Fold 1 phyllo sheet in half crosswise; gently press on cheese mixture in pan, and coat with cooking spray. Top with remaining 3 phyllo sheets, coating each sheet with cooking spray. Cut ends of sheets extending over pan. Fold edges of phyllo to form a rim; flatten rim with fork. Cut 4 slits with a sharp knife in top of phyllo, and brush with reserved 2 tablespoons milk. Bake at 400° for 22 minutes. Reduce oven temperature to 375° (do not remove pie from oven); bake 20 minutes or until browned. Remove from oven; let stand 15 minutes. Yield: 8 servings (serving size: 1 piece).

CALORIES 243 (32% from fat); FAT 8.7g (sat 5.2g, mono 1.7g, poly 0.4g); PROTEIN 13.3g; CARB 27.6g; FIBER 1.4g; CHOL 27mg; IRON 1.5mg; SODIUM 641mg; CALC 292mg

Cheese Pizza

Since this recipe calls for commercial pizza sauce, all you need to prepare is the dough.

Basic Pizza Dough
2 teaspoons olive oil
1 cup fat-free bottled pizza sauce
2 cups (8 ounces) shredded part-skim
    mozzarella cheese
½ cup (2 ounces) grated fresh Parmesan cheese

1. Position one oven rack in the middle setting. Position another rack in the lowest setting, and place a rimless baking sheet on the bottom rack. Preheat oven to 500°.
2. Remove plastic wrap from Basic Pizza Dough, and discard plastic. Brush olive oil over dough. Remove preheated baking sheet from oven, and close oven door. Slide dough onto preheated baking sheet, using a spatula as a guide. Bake on lowest oven rack at 500° for 8 minutes. Remove from oven.
3. Spread sauce in an even layer over crust, leaving a ¼-inch border. Top with mozzarella and Parmesan cheeses. Bake on middle rack an additional 10 minutes or until crust is golden brown and cheese melts. Cut into 12 wedges. Yield: 6 servings (serving size: 2 wedges).

CALORIES 256 (27% from fat); FAT 10.8g (sat 5.8g, mono 3.7g, poly 0.7g); PROTEIN 19.1g; CARB 44.5g; FIBER 2.5g; CHOL 30mg; IRON 3mg; SODIUM 633mg; CALC 357mg

Basic Pizza Dough

Mix up a batch of this dough whenever you're in the mood for homemade pizza. Use it in the recipes here, create your own versions, or add mix-ins to customize the crust. Don't worry about rolling the dough into a perfect circle.

2 teaspoons honey
1 package active dry yeast (about 2¼ teaspoons)
¾ cup warm water (100° to 110°)
2¼ cups all-purpose flour (about 10 ounces),
    divided
½ teaspoon salt
Cooking spray
2 tablespoons stone-ground yellow cornmeal

1. Dissolve the honey and yeast in ¾ cup warm water in a large bowl. Let stand 5 minutes or until bubbly. Lightly spoon flour into dry measuring cups; level with a knife. Add 2 cups flour and salt to yeast mixture; stir until a soft dough forms. Turn dough out onto a lightly floured surface. Knead until smooth and elastic (about 6 minutes); add enough of remaining flour, 1 tablespoon at a time, to prevent dough from sticking to hands (dough will feel slightly sticky).
2. Place dough in a large bowl coated with cooking spray, turning to coat top. Cover and let rise in a warm place (85°), free from drafts, 30 minutes or until doubled in size. (Gently press two fingers into dough. If the indentation remains, the dough has risen enough.)
3. Roll dough into a 12-inch circle (about ¼ inch thick) on a lightly floured surface. Place dough on a rimless baking sheet sprinkled with cornmeal. Crimp edges of dough with fingers to form a rim. Lightly spray surface of dough with cooking spray, and cover with plastic wrap. Place the dough in refrigerator for up to 30 minutes. Bake according to recipe directions. Yield: 1 (12-inch) crust.

(Totals are for 1 [12-inch] pizza crust.) CALORIES 1,155 (3% from fat); FAT 3.4g (sat 0.6g, mono 0.5g, poly 0.7g); PROTEIN 33.8g; CARB 242.5g; FIBER 10.8g; CHOL 0mg; IRON 14.3mg; SODIUM 1,195mg; CALC 49mg

Brie and Egg Strata

Brie and Egg Strata

The night before, assemble and layer the casserole without the egg mixture (steps one and two); cover and refrigerate. Combine the egg mixture (step three), and refrigerate in a separate container. In the morning, pour the egg mixture over the bread mixture; allow the strata to stand for 30 minutes before baking. Substitute a French baguette or sourdough loaf for the flat Italian bread, ciabatta, if desired. Freeze the Brie for about 15 minutes to make chopping easier.

　2　teaspoons olive oil
　2　cups chopped onion
1½　cups diced unpeeled Yukon gold potato
　　　(1 large)
　1　cup chopped red bell pepper
　1　cup halved grape tomatoes
　1　teaspoon salt, divided
　¾　pound ciabatta, cut into 1-inch cubes, toasted
Cooking spray
　4　ounces Brie cheese, rind removed and
　　　chopped
　1　cup egg substitute
　2　large eggs
　1　teaspoon herbes de Provence
　¼　teaspoon freshly ground black pepper
　3　cups 1% low-fat milk
　2　tablespoons chopped fresh parsley

1. Heat oil in a large nonstick skillet over medium-high heat. Add onion, potato, and bell pepper; sauté 4 minutes or until tender. Stir in tomatoes, and sauté 2 minutes. Stir in ½ teaspoon salt. Combine onion mixture and bread.
2. Place half of bread mixture into a 13 x 9–inch baking dish coated with cooking spray. Sprinkle with half of Brie. Top with remaining bread mixture and remaining Brie.
3. Place egg substitute and eggs in a medium bowl. Add remaining ½ teaspoon salt, herbes de Provence, and pepper. Add milk, stirring with a whisk until well blended. Pour egg mixture over bread mixture. Let stand 30 minutes.
4. Preheat oven to 350°.
5. Bake at 350° for 50 minutes or until set. Sprinkle with parsley. Serve immediately. Yield: 12 servings (serving size: 1 piece).

CALORIES 205 (30% from fat); FAT 6.9g (sat 2.7g, mono 3g, poly 0.8g); PROTEIN 10.8g; CARB 26.1g; FIBER 1.7g; CHOL 47mg; IRON 2mg; SODIUM 534mg; CALC 120mg

Angel Hair with Herbed Goat Cheese and Grape Tomatoes

　12　ounces uncooked angel hair pasta
　　1　tablespoon olive oil
1½　teaspoons bottled minced garlic
　　2　cups grape or cherry tomatoes, halved
　　　　(about 1 pint)
　⅔　cup vegetable broth or fat-free, less-sodium
　　　　chicken broth
　　6　tablespoons crumbled garlic and
　　　　herb-flavored goat cheese
　⅓　cup chopped fresh basil
　¼　teaspoon salt
　¼　teaspoon black pepper
Basil sprigs (optional)

1. Cook pasta according to package directions, omitting salt and fat. Drain; place in a large bowl, and keep warm.
2. While pasta cooks, heat oil in a large nonstick skillet over medium-high heat. Add garlic; sauté 30 seconds. Add tomatoes; cook 2 minutes, stirring frequently. Add broth; cook 1 minute. Remove from heat. Add goat cheese, basil, salt, and pepper to pasta; stir until well blended. Add tomato mixture to pasta mixture; toss gently to combine. Garnish with basil, if desired. Yield: 4 servings (serving size: about 1½ cups).

CALORIES 372 (28% from fat); FAT 11.5g (sat 4.9g, mono 4g, poly 0.6g); PROTEIN 16.5g; CARB 51.8g; FIBER 2.5g; CHOL 17mg; IRON 3.1mg; SODIUM 627mg; CALC 75mg

About Grape Tomatoes

Once considered a specialty item, grape tomatoes are now mainstream, competing for shelf space with their large cousins, cherry tomatoes. Grape tomatoes, with their small size and sweet flavor, have become a popular low-calorie snack and salad ingredient. Oven-roasted whole, they make a simple and flavorful side dish. Halved and pan-sautéed, they add rich tomato flavor to pasta dishes.

Fusilli with Roasted Tomato Sauce

Oven-roasting tomatoes with garlic and herbs boosts the flavor in this meatless sauce.

  2   tablespoons extravirgin olive oil, divided
  6   large tomatoes (about 3½ pounds), cored, cut in half crosswise, and seeded
  3   garlic cloves, crushed
  1   teaspoon chopped fresh or ¼ teaspoon dried thyme
  ¾   teaspoon salt, divided
  2   garlic cloves, minced
  2½ tablespoons chopped fresh basil
  ¼   teaspoon black pepper
  3½ cups hot cooked long fusilli (about 8 ounces uncooked twisted spaghetti)
  ¼   cup (1 ounce) shredded fresh Parmesan cheese
      Basil sprigs (optional)

1. Preheat oven to 400°.

2. Brush a jelly-roll pan or shallow roasting pan with 1 tablespoon oil. Arrange tomatoes in a single layer, cut sides down, in pan. Arrange crushed garlic around tomatoes; sprinkle tomatoes with thyme and ¼ teaspoon salt.

3. Bake at 400° for 30 minutes; drain juices from pan. Bake an additional 30 minutes. Remove tomatoes from pan; cool slightly. Discard juice and crushed garlic. Peel and coarsely chop tomatoes.

4. Heat 1 tablespoon oil in a large nonstick skillet over medium-low heat. Add minced garlic, and cook 2 minutes, stirring frequently. Add chopped tomatoes and chopped basil, and cook 3 minutes or until thoroughly heated. Stir in ½ teaspoon salt and pepper. Add pasta, and toss to coat. Sprinkle with cheese; garnish with basil sprigs, if desired. Yield: 4 servings (serving size: about 1 cup pasta mixture and 1 tablespoon cheese).

CALORIES 347 (28% from fat); FAT 10.7g (sat 2.4g, mono 5.8g, poly 1.5g); PROTEIN 11.9g; CARB 54.1g; FIBER 6.6g; CHOL 5mg; IRON 3.7mg; SODIUM 591mg; CALC 121mg

Fettuccine Alfredo

Fettuccine Alfredo was created in the 1920s by Roman restaurateur Alfredo di Lello. In our version of this rich, creamy dish, we used half-and-half instead of whipping cream and decreased the amount of butter and cheese ever so slightly to lower the fat by about 10 grams per serving.

  1   pound uncooked fettuccine
  1   tablespoon butter
  1¼   cups half-and-half
  ¾   cup (3 ounces) grated fresh Parmesan cheese
  ½   teaspoon salt
  ¼   teaspoon black pepper

1. Cook pasta according to package directions, omitting salt and fat.

2. Melt butter in a large skillet over medium heat. Add half-and-half, cheese, salt, and pepper; cook 1 minute, stirring constantly. Reduce heat; add pasta, tossing gently to coat. Yield: 6 servings (serving size: 1½ cups).

CALORIES 427 (31% from fat); FAT 14.6g (sat 7.8g, mono 4.2g, poly 1.3g); PROTEIN 17.2g; CARB 56.5g; FIBER 2.1g; CHOL 105mg; IRON 3.6mg; SODIUM 479mg; CALC 245mg

About Fettuccine

Fettuccine, which translates to "small ribbons," is the perfect match for Alfredo because the smooth sauce can easily coat the long strands. Use a spoon to help swirl the noodles neatly onto your fork.

Fettuccine Alfredo

Grilled Vegetable Lasagna

(pictured on page 95)

Grilled vegetables move from side dish to center stage in this vegetarian entrée. To speed preparation, use no-boil lasagna noodles; the baking time remains the same.

3 eggplants, cut lengthwise into ¼-inch slices (about 3 pounds)
3 zucchini, cut lengthwise into ⅛-inch slices (about 1¼ pounds)
Cooking spray
1 teaspoon salt, divided
¾ teaspoon freshly ground black pepper, divided
2 red bell peppers, quartered and seeded
1 (15-ounce) container fat-free ricotta cheese
1 large egg, lightly beaten
¾ cup (3 ounces) grated Asiago cheese, divided
¼ cup minced fresh basil
¼ cup minced fresh parsley
9 uncooked lasagna noodles, divided
1 (26-ounce) jar tomato-basil pasta sauce (such as Muir Glen)
¾ cup (3 ounces) shredded part-skim mozzarella cheese
¼ cup commercial pesto (such as Alessi)

1. Preheat grill.
2. Coat eggplant and zucchini slices with cooking spray. Sprinkle with ½ teaspoon salt and ¼ teaspoon black pepper. Grill eggplant and zucchini 1½ minutes on each side or just until tender. Cool; combine in a large bowl.
3. Place bell peppers on grill, skin-side down; grill 3 minutes or until tender. Cut into 1-inch-wide strips. Add bell peppers to eggplant mixture.
4. Combine ricotta cheese, egg, ½ cup Asiago cheese, basil, parsley, remaining ½ teaspoon salt, and remaining ½ teaspoon black pepper.
5. Cook lasagna noodles according to package directions, omitting salt and fat.
6. Preheat oven to 375°.
7. Spread ½ cup pasta sauce in a 13 x 9–inch baking dish coated with cooking spray. Arrange 3 noodles over sauce. Top with half of eggplant mixture. Spread half of ricotta cheese mixture over eggplant mixture; sprinkle with ¼ cup mozzarella cheese.
8. Arrange 3 noodles and 1 cup pasta sauce over cheese; cover with remaining eggplant mixture. Top with remaining ricotta mixture. Spread pesto over ricotta, and sprinkle with ¼ cup mozzarella

cheese. Cover with 3 noodles.
9. Spoon 1 cup pasta sauce over noodles. Sprinkle with remaining ¼ cup Asiago cheese and ¼ cup mozzarella cheese.
10. Bake at 375° for 1 hour. Let stand 15 minutes before serving. Yield: 10 servings.

CALORIES 318 (29% from fat); FAT 10.4g (sat 4.2g, mono 1.3g, poly 0.4g); PROTEIN 15.2g; CARB 41.9g; FIBER 3.2g; CHOL 40mg; IRON 2.7mg; SODIUM 728mg; CALC 269mg

Pesto Lasagna with Spinach and Mushrooms

4 cups torn spinach
2 cups sliced cremini mushrooms
½ cup commercial pesto
¾ cup (3 ounces) shredded part-skim mozzarella cheese
¾ cup (3 ounces) shredded provolone cheese
1 (15-ounce) carton fat-free ricotta cheese
1 large egg, lightly beaten
¾ cup (3 ounces) grated fresh Parmesan cheese, divided
1 (26-ounce) jar fat-free tomato-basil pasta sauce
1 (8-ounce) can tomato sauce
Cooking spray
1 (8-ounce) package precooked lasagna noodles

1. Steam spinach, covered, 3 minutes or until spinach wilts. Drain, squeeze dry, and coarsely chop. Combine spinach, mushrooms, and pesto in a medium bowl, and set aside.
2. Combine mozzarella, provolone, ricotta, and egg in a medium bowl, stirring well. Stir in ¼ cup Parmesan cheese, and set aside. Combine pasta sauce and tomato sauce in a medium bowl.
3. Spread 1 cup pasta sauce mixture in bottom of a 6-quart oval electric slow cooker coated with cooking spray. Arrange 3 noodles over pasta sauce mixture, and top with 1 cup cheese mixture and 1 cup spinach mixture. Repeat layers once, ending with remaining 1 cup spinach mixture. Arrange 3 noodles over spinach mixture; top with remaining cheese mixture and 1 cup pasta sauce mixture. Place 3 noodles over sauce mixture; spread remaining sauce mixture over noodles. Sprinkle with remaining ½ cup Parmesan cheese. Cover and cook on LOW 5 hours or until done. Yield: 8 servings.

CALORIES 398 (41% from fat); FAT 18.2g (sat 7.8g, mono 6.6g, poly 2.3g); PROTEIN 22.2g; CARB 38.5g; FIBER 2g; CHOL 56mg; IRON 2.8mg; SODIUM 1,036mg; CALC 407mg

Easy Meatless Manicotti

Because the only preparation this casserole requires is assembly—no chopping or stovetop cooking—it's a great way to get the kids involved in the kitchen. The uncooked shells are easier to handle. If you have trouble stuffing them with a spoon, use a butter knife.

2 cups (8 ounces) shredded part-skim mozzarella cheese, divided
1 (16-ounce) carton fat-free cottage cheese
1 (10-ounce) package frozen chopped spinach, thawed, drained, and squeezed dry
¼ cup (1 ounce) grated fresh Parmesan cheese
1½ teaspoons dried oregano
¼ teaspoon salt
¼ teaspoon black pepper
1 (8-ounce) package manicotti (14 shells)
1 (26-ounce) jar fat-free tomato-basil pasta sauce
Cooking spray
1 cup water

1. Preheat oven to 375°.
2. Combine 1½ cups mozzarella, cottage cheese, and next 5 ingredients in a medium bowl. Spoon about 3 tablespoons cheese mixture into each uncooked manicotti. Pour half of pasta sauce into a 13 x 9–inch baking dish coated with cooking spray. Arrange stuffed shells in a single layer over sauce, and top with remaining sauce. Pour 1 cup water into dish. Sprinkle ½ cup mozzarella evenly over sauce. Cover tightly with foil. Bake at 375° for 1 hour or until shells are tender. Let stand 10 minutes before serving. Yield: 7 servings (serving size: 2 manicotti).

CALORIES 328 (25% from fat); FAT 9g (sat 4.8g, mono 2.2g, poly 0.5g); PROTEIN 23.8g; CARB 38.3g; FIBER 3.9g; CHOL 23mg; IRON 3mg; SODIUM 891mg; CALC 451mg

Pasta with Mushrooms and Pumpkin-Gorgonzola Sauce

Any short pasta will work in this dish. For the sauce, we recommend our favorite brand of cheese—Saladena Gorgonzola; when melted into the other ingredients, it yields a luscious consistency.

  1   pound uncooked pennette (small penne)
  1   tablespoon olive oil
  5   cups thinly sliced shiitake mushroom caps (about ¾ pound whole mushrooms)
  4   cups vertically sliced onion
  4   garlic cloves, minced
  1   teaspoon chopped fresh sage
  1   (12-ounce) can evaporated milk
1½   tablespoons cornstarch
1½   tablespoons cold water
  ½   cup (2 ounces) crumbled Gorgonzola cheese
  ½   cup canned pumpkin
  1   teaspoon salt
  ½   teaspoon freshly ground black pepper
  ⅛   teaspoon grated whole nutmeg
      Sage sprigs (optional)

1. Cook pasta according to package directions, omitting salt and fat. Drain. Keep pasta warm.
2. Heat oil in a Dutch oven over medium-high heat. Add mushrooms, onion, and garlic; cover and cook 3 minutes. Uncover and cook 5 minutes or until tender, stirring occasionally.
3. Combine chopped sage and milk in a medium saucepan over medium heat. Bring to a simmer. Combine cornstarch and water, stirring with a whisk. Add cornstarch mixture and cheese to milk mixture, stirring with a whisk. Cook 2 minutes or until thick and smooth, stirring constantly. Remove from heat; stir in pumpkin, salt, pepper, and nutmeg.
4. Add pasta and pumpkin mixture to mushroom mixture, and toss well to combine. Garnish with sage sprigs, if desired. Yield: 6 servings (serving size: 1½ cups).

CALORIES 462 (13% from fat); FAT 6.5g (sat 2.8g, mono 1.7g, poly 0.4g); PROTEIN 19.9g; CARB 83.1g; FIBER 7.3g; CHOL 11mg; IRON 3.7mg; SODIUM 636mg; CALC 265mg

Pasta and Grilled Vegetables with Goat Cheese

This vibrant vegetable entrée is light and delicious. To ensure even grilling, cut the vegetables into large, similar-sized pieces. After cooking, chop into bite-sized pieces. Substitute yellow squash for zucchini, if desired.

  1   large zucchini, quartered lengthwise (about 8 ounces)
  1   red bell pepper, cut into 4 wedges
  1   leek, trimmed and halved
  1   (14-ounce) can artichoke hearts, drained
  1   head radicchio, quartered
  ½   teaspoon salt, divided
  ¼   teaspoon freshly ground black pepper
  2   garlic cloves, minced
      Cooking spray
  4   cups hot cooked rotini (about 4 cups uncooked corkscrew pasta)
  1   cup grape or cherry tomatoes
  ¾   cup (3 ounces) crumbled goat cheese
  2   tablespoons thinly sliced fresh basil

1. Prepare grill.
2. Arrange first 5 ingredients in a single layer on a jelly-roll pan; sprinkle evenly with ¼ teaspoon salt, black pepper, and garlic. Lightly coat vegetables with cooking spray. Place vegetables on grill rack; grill 3 minutes on each side or until browned and tender. Remove vegetables to a cutting board; chop into bite-sized pieces.
3. Place pasta in a large bowl; sprinkle with ¼ teaspoon salt, tossing well. Stir in grilled vegetables and tomatoes; sprinkle each serving with cheese and basil. Yield: 4 servings (serving size: 2½ cups pasta mixture, 3 tablespoons cheese, and 1½ teaspoons basil).

CALORIES 327 (16% from fat); FAT 5.8g (sat 3.5g, mono 1g, poly 0.3g); PROTEIN 14g; CARB 56.3g; FIBER 3.4g; CHOL 19mg; IRON 3.8mg; SODIUM 682mg; CALC 149mg

Spaghetti Alla Norma

Sicilian legend reveals that this traditional eggplant pasta dish was renamed Spaghetti Alla Norma after the opera *Norma* by composer Vincenzo Bellini. The combination of eggplant and tomato in this pasta sauce is quintessentially Sicilian, and it begs to be served with a classic Sicilian wine.

2 tablespoons olive oil
3 garlic cloves, minced
1½ pounds coarsely chopped peeled tomato (about 2 cups)
1 teaspoon salt
1 pound eggplant, peeled and cut into ½-inch cubes (about 4 cups)
¼ cup thinly sliced fresh basil
¾ pound uncooked spaghetti
6 ounces fresh mozzarella cheese, cut into ¼-inch cubes (about 1 cup)

1. Place oil and garlic in a large skillet; cook over medium-high heat 30 seconds or until garlic begins to sizzle. Add tomato and salt; cook 15 minutes or until liquid evaporates. Add eggplant; cover, reduce heat, and cook 15 minutes or until eggplant is tender. Stir in basil, and set aside.

2. While sauce simmers, cook pasta in boiling water 9 minutes; drain. Toss with sauce and mozzarella cheese. Serve immediately. Yield: 7 servings (serving size: 1 cup).

CALORIES 329 (29% from fat); FAT 10.5g (sat 3.9g, mono 4.6g, poly 1g); PROTEIN 12.2g; CARB 47.3g; FIBER 4.1g; CHOL 19mg; IRON 2.8mg; SODIUM 444mg; CALC 149mg

Four-Cheese Stuffed Shells with Smoky Marinara

1 pound uncooked jumbo shell pasta (40 shells)
Cooking spray
1 (12-ounce) carton 1% low-fat cottage cheese
1 (15-ounce) carton ricotta cheese
1 cup (4 ounces) shredded Asiago cheese
¾ cup (3 ounces) grated fresh Parmesan cheese
2 tablespoons chopped fresh chives
2 tablespoons chopped fresh parsley
¼ teaspoon black pepper
¼ teaspoon salt
1 (10-ounce) package frozen chopped spinach, thawed, drained, and squeezed dry
6 cups Smoky Marinara (recipe on page 117), divided
1 cup (4 ounces) shredded part-skim mozzarella cheese, divided
Parsley sprigs (optional)

1. Cook pasta according to package directions, omitting salt and fat. Drain and set aside.

2. Preheat oven to 375°.

3. Coat 2 (13 x 9–inch) baking dishes with cooking spray; set aside.

4. Place cottage cheese and ricotta cheese in a food processor; process until smooth. Combine cottage cheese mixture, Asiago, and next 6 ingredients.

5. Spoon or pipe 1 tablespoon cheese mixture into each shell. Arrange half of stuffed shells, seam sides up, in one prepared dish. Pour 3 cups Smoky Marinara over stuffed shells. Sprinkle with ½ cup mozzarella. Repeat procedure with remaining stuffed shells, 3 cups Smoky Marinara, and ½ cup mozzarella in remaining prepared dish.

6. Cover with foil. Bake at 375° for 30 minutes or until thoroughly heated. Garnish with parsley, if desired. Yield: 2 casseroles, 5 servings per dish (serving size: 4 stuffed shells and about ½ cup Smoky Marinara).

TO FREEZE UNBAKED CASSEROLE: Prepare through Step 5. Cover with plastic wrap, pressing to remove as much air as possible. Wrap with heavy-duty foil. Store in freezer up to two months.

TO PREPARE FROZEN UNBAKED CASSEROLE: Preheat oven to 375°. Remove foil; reserve foil. Remove plastic wrap; discard wrap. Cover frozen casserole with reserved foil; bake at 375° for 1 hour and 10 minutes or until shells are thoroughly heated.

CALORIES 470 (30% from fat); FAT 15.7g (sat 8.8g, mono 4.7g, poly 0.9g); PROTEIN 28.3g; CARB 52.7g; FIBER 5.3g; CHOL 47mg; IRON 3.8mg; SODIUM 916mg; CALC 508mg

SMOKY MARINARA:

This recipe accompanies Four-Cheese Stuffed Shells on page 116. You can also toss it with penne or other tubular shapes.

1 tablespoon olive oil
3 garlic cloves, minced
¼ cup chopped fresh basil
2 tablespoons chopped fresh parsley
2 tablespoons chopped fresh or 2 teaspoons dried oregano
2 teaspoons balsamic vinegar
⅛ teaspoon salt
⅛ teaspoon pepper
1 (28-ounce) can crushed fire-roasted tomatoes, undrained
1 (28-ounce) can crushed tomatoes, undrained

1. Heat oil in a large saucepan over medium heat. Add garlic, basil, parsley, and oregano; sauté 1 minute, stirring frequently. Stir in vinegar and remaining ingredients. Reduce heat, and simmer 10 minutes. Yield: 6 cups (serving size: ½ cup).

CALORIES 55 (20% from fat); FAT 1.2g (sat 0.2g, mono 0.8g, poly 0.1g); PROTEIN 2.3g; CARB 9g; FIBER 2.3g; CHOL 0mg; IRON 0.9mg; SODIUM 350mg; CALC 49mg

Ziti with Chard

Swiss chard balances the intense combination of grape tomatoes, kalamata olives, and Romano cheese in this refreshing vegetarian dish.

2 tablespoons olive oil
8 cups chopped Swiss chard
4 garlic cloves, minced
4 cups hot cooked ziti (about 8 ounces uncooked short tube-shaped pasta)
2 cups grape or cherry tomatoes, halved
¼ cup chopped pitted kalamata olives
2 tablespoons fresh lemon juice
¾ teaspoon kosher salt
½ teaspoon freshly ground black pepper
¼ cup (1 ounce) shaved fresh Romano cheese

1. Heat oil in a large nonstick skillet over medium-high heat. Add chard and garlic; sauté 2 minutes. Combine chard mixture, pasta, and next 5 ingredients, tossing well. Top with cheese. Yield: 4 servings (serving size: about 2 cups).

CALORIES 336 (28% from fat); FAT 10.5g (sat 2.4g, mono 6.2g, poly 0.8g); PROTEIN 12g; CARB 51g; FIBER 4.2g; CHOL 7mg; IRON 3.9mg; SODIUM 665mg; CALC 132mg

Ziti Baked with Spinach, Tomatoes, and Smoked Gouda

This satisfying meatless casserole oozes with al dente tubes of ziti, bright yellow bell peppers, fire-engine red diced tomatoes, tender baby spinach, and smoky shredded Gouda. You can also bake it in an 11 x 7–inch baking dish. Substitute smoked mozzarella for the smoked Gouda for a more authentic Italian dish.

8 ounces uncooked ziti
1 tablespoon olive oil
1 cup chopped onion
1 cup chopped yellow bell pepper (about 6 ounces)
3 garlic cloves, minced
1 (14.5-ounce) can diced tomatoes with basil, garlic, and oregano, undrained
1 (10-ounce) can Italian-seasoned diced tomatoes (such as Rotel Bold Italian), undrained
4 cups baby spinach
1¼ cups (5 ounces) shredded smoked Gouda cheese, divided
Cooking spray

1. Cook pasta according to package directions, omitting salt and fat. Drain well.
2. Preheat oven to 375°.
3. Heat oil in a Dutch oven over medium-high heat. Add onion and pepper; sauté 5 minutes. Add garlic; sauté 2 minutes or until onion is tender. Stir in tomatoes; bring to a boil. Reduce heat, and simmer 5 minutes, stirring occasionally. Add spinach to pan; cook 30 seconds or until spinach wilts, stirring frequently. Remove from heat. Add pasta and ¾ cup cheese to tomato mixture, tossing well to combine. Spoon pasta mixture into 5 individual casserole dishes lightly coated with cooking spray; sprinkle evenly with ½ cup cheese. Bake at 375° for 15 minutes or until cheese melts and begins to brown. Yield: 5 servings (serving size: 1 casserole).

CALORIES 382 (30% from fat); FAT 12.7g (sat 5.7g, mono 4.6g, poly 0.9g); PROTEIN 17g; CARB 52.3g; FIBER 4.3g; CHOL 33mg; IRON 4.4mg; SODIUM 977mg; CALC 334mg

Green-Chile Ravioli

These nontraditional ravioli with Tex-Mex flair look beautiful on a plate, making this easy entrée an ideal choice for company.

RAVIOLI:

- 1 cup (4 ounces) preshredded reduced-fat Mexican blend cheese
- ¼ cup minced green onions
- ½ teaspoon black pepper
- 1 (4.5-ounce) can chopped green chiles, undrained
- 1 large egg white
- 16 wonton wrappers
- 1 teaspoon cornstarch

Cooking spray

- ⅓ cup vegetable broth or fat-free, less-sodium chicken broth

SAUCE:

- ½ cup minced fresh cilantro
- 2 tablespoons balsamic vinegar
- 2 (14.5-ounce) cans diced tomatoes, drained
- 1 (15-ounce) can black beans, rinsed and drained
- 1 teaspoon olive oil

1. To prepare ravioli, combine first 5 ingredients in a bowl. Working with 1 wonton wrapper at a time (cover remaining wrappers with a damp towel to keep from drying), spoon about 1 tablespoon green chile mixture into center of wrapper. Brush edges of wrapper with water; bring 2 opposite corners together. Press edges together firmly with fingers, forming a triangle. Place ravioli on a large baking sheet sprinkled with cornstarch. Heat a large nonstick skillet over medium-high heat. Coat pan with cooking spray. Add ravioli; cook 2 to 3 minutes on each side or until lightly browned. Add broth; cook, covered, 1 to 2 minutes. Remove ravioli with a slotted spoon, and keep warm.

2. To prepare sauce, combine cilantro, vinegar, tomatoes, beans, and oil in a large saucepan over medium-high heat. Cook 5 minutes or until thoroughly heated. Spoon sauce over ravioli. Yield: 4 servings (serving size: 4 ravioli and ¾ cup sauce).

CALORIES 271 (28% from fat); FAT 8.3g (sat 3.2g, mono 0.9g, poly 0.4g); PROTEIN 16.4g; CARB 41g; FIBER 7.3g; CHOL 23mg; IRON 2.9mg; SODIUM 892mg; CALC 340mg

Ricotta Ravioli with Browned Poppy Seed Butter and Asparagus

Delicate homemade ricotta cheese creates a smooth filling for ravioli. If you can't find round gyoza skins, cut square wonton wrappers into circles with a 3-inch round cutter.

RAVIOLI:

- 1 cup (8 ounces) Homemade Ricotta Cheese (recipe on page 119)
- ¼ cup (1 ounce) grated fresh pecorino Romano cheese
- 2 tablespoons minced fresh flat-leaf parsley
- ⅛ teaspoon salt
- 2 large egg whites
- 48 (3-inch) round gyoza skins
- 6 quarts water

TOPPING:

- 1½ tablespoons butter
- 2 cups (2-inch) slices asparagus
- ¼ teaspoon salt
- 2 teaspoons poppy seeds
- ⅓ cup (about 1½ ounces) crumbled ricotta salata cheese

1. To prepare ravioli, combine Homemade Ricotta Cheese, pecorino Romano, parsley, ⅛ teaspoon salt, and egg whites; mix with a fork until blended. Working with 1 gyoza skin at a time (cover remaining skins to prevent drying), spoon about 2 teaspoons ricotta mixture into center of skin. Moisten edges of skin with water; place 1 skin over filling, stretching slightly to meet edges of bottom skin. Press edges together with a fork to seal; place on a lightly floured baking sheet (cover with a damp towel to prevent drying).

2. Bring 6 quarts water to a boil over medium-high heat. Add 4 ravioli; cook 5 minutes, turning ravioli carefully after 2½ minutes. Remove ravioli from water with a slotted spoon, and place on a platter. Repeat procedure with remaining ravioli; cover and keep warm. Reserve ½ cup cooking water.

3. To prepare topping, melt butter in a large nonstick skillet over medium heat; cook 3 minutes or until lightly browned, shaking pan occasionally. Add ¼ cup reserved cooking water, asparagus, and ¼ teaspoon salt; cook 3 minutes or until asparagus is crisp-tender and water evaporates. Stir in poppy seeds; cook 30 seconds. Add remaining ¼ cup reserved cooking water; cook over medium-high heat 1 minute or until liquid is reduced by about

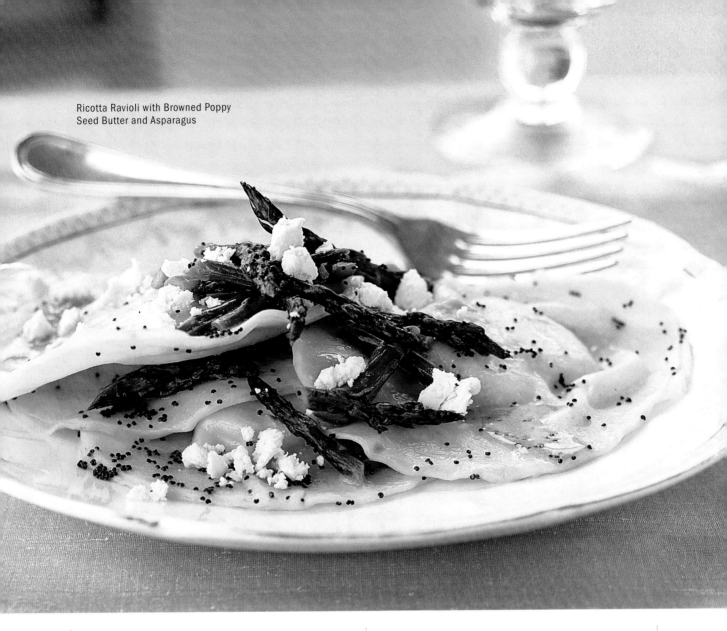

Ricotta Ravioli with Browned Poppy
Seed Butter and Asparagus

half. Add ravioli to pan; toss gently to combine. Sprinkle with ricotta salata; serve immediately. Yield: 6 servings (serving size: 4 ravioli, about ⅓ cup asparagus mixture, and about 1 tablespoon ricotta salata).

CALORIES 356 (30% from fat); FAT 12g (sat 6.6g, mono 2.9g, poly 1.1g); PROTEIN 19.6g; CARB 42.6g; FIBER 2.5g; CHOL 41mg; IRON 3mg; SODIUM 833mg; CALC 288mg

Homemade Ricotta Cheese

    1   gallon 2% reduced-fat milk
    5   cups low-fat buttermilk
    ½   teaspoon fine sea salt

1. Line a large colander or sieve with 5 layers of dampened cheesecloth; place colander in a large bowl. Set aside.
2. Combine milk and buttermilk in a large, heavy stockpot. Attach a candy thermometer to edge of pan so that thermometer extends at least 2 inches into milk mixture. Cook over medium-high heat until thermometer registers 170° (about 20 minutes), gently stirring occasionally. As soon as milk mixture reaches 170°, stop stirring (whey and curds will begin separating). Continue to cook, without stirring, until thermometer registers 190°. Immediately remove pan from heat. (Bottom of pan may be slightly scorched.)
3. Using a slotted spoon, gently spoon curds into prepared cheesecloth-lined colander; discard whey, or reserve it for another use. Drain over bowl 5 minutes. Gather edges of cheesecloth together; tie securely. Hang cheesecloth bundle from kitchen faucet; drain 15 minutes or until whey stops dripping. Scrape ricotta into a bowl. Sprinkle with salt; toss gently with a fork to combine. Cool to room temperature. Yield: about 3 cups (serving size: ¼ cup).

NOTE: Store in refrigerator up to 4 days.

CALORIES 115 (48% from fat); FAT 6.1g (sat 3.8g, mono 1.8g, poly 0.2g); PROTEIN 11.5g; CARB 3.5g; FIBER 0g; CHOL 23mg; IRON 0mg; SODIUM 191mg; CALC 250mg

Ginger-Sesame Grilled
Tofu Steaks

Ginger-Sesame Grilled Tofu Steaks

All you need to complete this meal is a side of steamed snow peas, sugar snap peas, or asparagus. Draining the tofu on paper towels helps it absorb more marinade.

 1 pound reduced-fat extrafirm water-packed tofu, drained and cut crosswise into 8 slices
⅔ cup Ginger-Sesame Vinaigrette
 1 tablespoon finely chopped fresh cilantro
 1 tablespoon low-sodium soy sauce
 8 lime slices
Cooking spray
 2 cups hot cooked short-grain white rice

1. Place tofu slices on several layers of paper towels; cover with additional paper towels. Let stand 20 minutes, pressing down occasionally. Combine Ginger-Sesame Vinaigrette, cilantro, and soy sauce in a 13 x 9–inch baking dish. Remove ¼ cup cilantro mixture; set aside. Add tofu to dish in a single layer, turning to coat. Cover and marinate in refrigerator 30 minutes, turning occasionally.
2. Prepare grill.
3. Add lime slices to marinade, turning to coat. Remove tofu and lime slices from marinade, reserving marinade. Place tofu and lime slices on grill rack coated with cooking spray; grill 2 minutes on each side or until browned and thoroughly heated, basting occasionally with reserved marinade. Spoon ½ cup rice onto each of 4 plates. Top each serving with 2 tofu slices and 2 lime slices; drizzle each serving with 1 tablespoon reserved cilantro mixture. Yield: 4 servings.

CALORIES 307 (27% from fat); FAT 9.3g (sat 0.4g, mono 3.2g, poly 4.4g); PROTEIN 16.3g; CARB 40.6g; FIBER 4.8g; CHOL 0mg; IRON 3.4mg; SODIUM 669mg; CALC 57mg

GINGER-SESAME VINAIGRETTE:

 ½ cup rice wine vinegar
 ¼ cup water
 ¼ cup yellow miso (soybean paste)
 ¼ cup chopped green onions
 2 tablespoons sugar
 2 tablespoons minced peeled fresh ginger
 2 tablespoons low-sodium soy sauce
 4 teaspoons canola oil
 2 teaspoons dark sesame oil

1. Combine first 3 ingredients in a medium bowl, stirring with a whisk until smooth. Stir in green onions and remaining ingredients. Yield: about 1⅓ cups (serving size: 1 tablespoon).

NOTE: Refrigerate vinaigrette in an airtight container up to 5 days; stir well before using.

CALORIES 23 (59% from fat); FAT 1.5g (sat 0.1g, mono 0.7g, poly 0.6g); PROTEIN 0.5g; CARB 2.1g; FIBER 0.1g; CHOL 0mg; IRON 0mg; SODIUM 192mg; CALC 0mg

Versatile Vinaigrette

You'll only need half the vinaigrette for the marinade. Try tossing the remaining vinaigrette with salad greens or rice noodles, or use it as a dipping sauce for pot stickers or spring rolls. Many supermarkets stock miso with the refrigerated foods; if yours doesn't, you'll need to visit an Asian market.

Broccoli-Tofu Stir-Fry

This simple meatless stir-fry has a subtle yet addictive sauce. To cut preparation time, use precut broccoli florets. They're near the salad greens in the supermarket.

    1   (3½-ounce) bag boil-in-bag brown rice
    2   tablespoons low-sodium soy sauce
    2   tablespoons oyster sauce
 2½   teaspoons cornstarch
    2   teaspoons rice vinegar
    2   teaspoons dark sesame oil
    2   teaspoons vegetable oil
    1   pound firm tofu, drained and cut into ½-inch
         cubes
   ¼   teaspoon salt
    2   cups broccoli florets
   ¾   cup water
 1½   tablespoons bottled minced garlic

1. Cook rice according to package directions.
2. While rice cooks, combine soy sauce and next 4 ingredients in a small bowl, stirring with a whisk; set aside.
3. Heat vegetable oil in a large nonstick skillet over medium-high heat. Add tofu, and sprinkle with salt. Cook 8 minutes or until golden brown, tossing frequently. Remove tofu from pan, and keep warm. Add broccoli, water, and garlic to pan. Cover and cook 4 minutes or until crisp-tender, stirring occasionally. Uncover; add soy sauce mixture and tofu, stirring gently to coat. Cook 2 minutes or until sauce thickens, stirring occasionally. Serve broccoli mixture over rice. Yield: 4 servings (serving size: 1 cup stir-fry and ½ cup rice).

CALORIES 451 (17% from fat); FAT 8.3g (sat 1.4g, mono 2.6g, poly 3.8g); PROTEIN 16.2g; CARB 78g; FIBER 4.4g; CHOL 0mg; IRON 2.8mg; SODIUM 581mg; CALC 87mg

Tandoori Tofu and Vegetable Kebabs

Both tofu's subtle flavor and tender texture merge well with a multitude of Western and Asian seasonings.

    1   (16-ounce) package water-packed firm tofu,
         drained and cut into 16 cubes
  Cooking spray
    1   cup finely chopped onion
   ¾   cup plain low-fat yogurt
    2   teaspoons grated peeled fresh ginger
    2   teaspoons canola oil
    2   teaspoons ground coriander
 1½   teaspoons ground cumin
   ½   teaspoon ground turmeric
   ¼   teaspoon freshly ground black pepper
    1   garlic clove, minced
   16   large mushrooms (about 10 ounces)
    2   small red onions, each cut into 8 wedges
 2⅔   cups water
 1⅓   cups uncooked basmati rice
   ⅔   cup golden raisins
    1   teaspoon salt, divided

1. Preheat oven to 375°.
2. Arrange tofu in a single layer on a foil-lined baking sheet coated with cooking spray. Bake at 375° for 25 minutes or until tofu releases 3 or more tablespoons liquid.
3. Combine chopped onion and next 8 ingredients in a large bowl. Add tofu, mushrooms, and onion wedges; toss gently to coat. Let stand at room temperature 30 minutes.
4. While tofu and vegetables marinate, prepare rice. Bring water to a boil in a medium saucepan; stir in rice. Cover, reduce heat, and simmer 15 minutes or until liquid is absorbed. Stir in raisins and ¼ teaspoon salt. Let stand 5 minutes; fluff with a fork.
5. Prepare grill.
6. Remove tofu and vegetables from bowl; discard marinade. Thread tofu cubes, mushrooms, and onion wedges alternately onto 8 (6-inch) skewers. Lightly coat kebabs with cooking spray; sprinkle with ¾ teaspoon salt. Place kebabs on a grill rack coated with cooking spray; grill 4 minutes on each side or until lightly browned. Serve kebabs with rice. Yield: 4 servings (serving size: 2 kebabs and 1 cup rice).

CALORIES 421 (21% from fat); FAT 9.6g (sat 1.7g, mono 1.9g, poly 5g); PROTEIN 20.2g; CARB 72.9g; FIBER 5.4g; CHOL 2mg; IRON 4.9mg; SODIUM 625mg; CALC 190mg

meats

Basic Grilled Steak,
page 133

Southwestern Meat Loaf and Baked Potatoes

    1   pound ground round
    1   cup frozen whole-kernel corn
   ½   cup picante sauce
   ⅓   cup regular oats
   ¼   cup minced fresh cilantro
    1   tablespoon chili powder
  1½   teaspoons ground cumin
    1   large egg white, lightly beaten
Cooking spray
   ¼   cup ketchup
    4   medium baking potatoes (about 1½ pounds)
   ½   cup fat-free sour cream
Fresh chives (optional)

1. Combine first 8 ingredients in a large bowl; stir well. Shape beef mixture into a 9 x 4–inch loaf; wrap in heavy-duty plastic wrap.
2. Preheat oven to 375°.
3. Remove loaf from plastic wrap; place on rack of a broiler pan coated with cooking spray. Brush ketchup over loaf. Arrange potatoes around loaf on pan.
4. Bake at 375° for 50 minutes or until a thermometer registers 160°. Let stand 10 minutes before slicing. Split open potatoes lengthwise. Serve with sour cream and chives, if desired. Yield: 4 servings (serving size: 2 slices meat loaf, 1 potato, and 2 tablespoons sour cream).
NOTE: Place in a zip-top plastic freezer bag; seal. Freeze up to 3 months. Thaw meat loaf in refrigerator overnight.

CALORIES 411 (18% from fat); FAT 8.2g (sat 2.7g, mono 3.2g, poly 0.7g); PROTEIN 34.2g; CARB 50.7g; FIBER 5.6g; CHOL 70mg; IRON 6.1mg; SODIUM 640mg; CALC 59mg

Meat Loaf with Shiitake Mushrooms

    2   (1-ounce) slices whole wheat bread
   ¾   pound ground round
   ¾   pound ground turkey
  1½   cups coarsely chopped shiitake mushrooms
   ½   cup grated fresh onion
    1   teaspoon dried Italian seasoning
   ¾   teaspoon salt
    2   large eggs, lightly beaten
    1   garlic clove, minced
    2   tablespoons ketchup
  1½   teaspoons Dijon mustard
   ⅛   teaspoon ground red pepper

1. Place bread in a food processor, and pulse 10 times or until crumbs measure 1⅓ cups. Combine crumbs, beef, and next 7 ingredients in a large bowl, and shape beef mixture into a 9 x 6–inch loaf. Place loaf in a 3-quart oval electric slow cooker.
2. Combine ketchup, mustard, and pepper in a small bowl, stirring with a fork. Spread ketchup mixture evenly over top of loaf. Cover and cook on HIGH 1 hour. Reduce heat to LOW, and cook 3 hours. Yield: 6 servings (serving size: 4 ounces).

CALORIES 265 (43% from fat); FAT 12.7g (sat 4.2g, mono 5.1g, poly 1.7g); PROTEIN 25.2g; CARB 12.7g; FIBER 1.9g; CHOL 152mg; IRON 3mg; SODIUM 545mg; CALC 41mg

Picadillo

Picadillo is a favorite dish in many Spanish-speaking countries. It always starts with a ground pork, beef, or veal base that is mixed with various ingredients that provide the dish's signature sweet and savory flavors.

    2   pounds ground round
  1½   cups chopped green bell pepper
    1   cup chopped onion
    1   cup sliced green onions
    4   garlic cloves, minced
    1   (14½-ounce) can diced tomatoes, undrained
    1   (8-ounce) can tomato sauce
   ⅓   cup chopped pitted dates
   ⅓   cup chopped dried apricots
   ¼   cup sliced pimiento-stuffed olives
    1   tablespoon ground cumin
    1   teaspoon ground cinnamon
   ½   teaspoon salt
   ½   teaspoon dried oregano
   ¼   teaspoon ground red pepper
   ¼   teaspoon black pepper
   ¼   cup slivered almonds, toasted
  4½   cups hot cooked rice

1. Cook beef, bell pepper, onion, green onions, and garlic in a large nonstick skillet over medium-high heat until beef is browned, stirring to crumble beef. Drain well.
2. Place beef mixture in a 4-quart electric slow cooker. Add diced tomatoes and next 10 ingredients; stir well. Cover and cook on HIGH 3 hours. Stir in almonds. Serve over rice. Yield: 9 servings (serving size: ¾ cup picadillo and ½ cup rice).

CALORIES 391 (29% from fat); FAT 12.5g (sat 4.3g, mono 5.7g, poly 0.8g); PROTEIN 24.7g; CARB 44.2g; FIBER 4.1g; CHOL 66mg; IRON 4.8mg; SODIUM 482mg; CALC 67mg

Meat Loaf with Shiitake
Mushrooms

Chili Mac

Chili Mac

This kid-friendly classic is a staple for school nights, and you can substitute whatever small pasta or cheese you have on hand. For additional convenience, use frozen chopped onion and chopped green bell pepper. Leftovers are even better the next day.

1 pound ground round
½ cup chopped onion
½ cup chopped green bell pepper
3 garlic cloves, minced
2 cups cooked elbow macaroni (about 4 ounces uncooked)
½ cup water
1 tablespoon chili powder
1 teaspoon ground cumin
¼ teaspoon black pepper
1 (15-ounce) can kidney beans, rinsed and drained
1 (14.5-ounce) can whole tomatoes, undrained and chopped
1 (8¾-ounce) can whole-kernel corn, drained
1 (8-ounce) can tomato sauce
1 (6-ounce) can tomato paste
1 cup (4 ounces) shredded sharp Cheddar cheese

1. Cook first 4 ingredients in a large Dutch oven over medium-high heat until browned, stirring to crumble beef.
2. Drain well; wipe drippings from pan with paper towels. Return beef mixture to pan; stir in macaroni and next 9 ingredients. Bring to a boil; cover, reduce heat, and simmer 20 minutes, stirring occasionally. Top individual servings with cheese. Yield: 8 servings (serving size: 1 cup beef mixture and 2 tablespoons cheese).

CALORIES 295 (28% from fat); FAT 9.2g (sat 4.4g, mono 3g, poly 0.8g); PROTEIN 22.6g; CARB 32.5g; FIBER 4.2g; CHOL 50mg; IRON 4.3mg; SODIUM 529mg; CALC 151mg

Cheese and Hamburger Casserole

Pasta and a saucy hamburger mixture are drenched in a two-cheese sauce for a family-pleasing one-dish meal.

1 pound ground round
1 cup chopped onion
3 garlic cloves, crushed
1 (8-ounce) package presliced mushrooms
6 tablespoons tomato paste
1 teaspoon sugar
1 teaspoon dried thyme
1 teaspoon dried oregano
¼ teaspoon black pepper
1 (28-ounce) can whole tomatoes, undrained and chopped
⅓ cup all-purpose flour
2½ cups 2% reduced-fat milk
1 cup (4 ounces) crumbled feta cheese
¾ cup (3 ounces) shredded part-skim mozzarella cheese
4 cups uncooked penne (tube-shaped pasta)

1. Combine first 3 ingredients in a large nonstick skillet; cook over medium-high heat until beef is browned, stirring to crumble. Add mushrooms; cook 5 minutes or until tender. Add tomato paste and next 5 ingredients; stir well. Bring to a boil; reduce heat, and simmer, uncovered, 20 minutes.
2. While beef mixture simmers, place flour in a medium saucepan. Gradually add milk, stirring with a whisk until blended. Place over medium heat; cook 10 minutes or until thick, stirring constantly. Stir in cheeses, and cook 3 minutes or until cheeses melt, stirring constantly. Reserve ½ cup cheese sauce.
3. Pour remaining cheese sauce, beef mixture, and pasta into a 13 x 9–inch baking dish, and stir gently. Drizzle reserved ½ cup cheese sauce over pasta mixture. Cover and refrigerate 24 hours.
4. Let casserole stand at room temperature at least 30 minutes.
5. Preheat oven to 350°.
6. Bake, covered, at 350° for 1 hour and 10 minutes or until thoroughly heated and pasta is tender. Yield: 8 servings (serving size: 1½ cups).

CALORIES 412 (23% from fat); FAT 10.8g (sat 5.5g, mono 3.2g, poly 0.9g); PROTEIN 27.5g; CARB 51.1g; FIBER 3.2g; CHOL 60mg; IRON 4.9mg; SODIUM 448mg; CALC 286mg

Polenta with Bolognese Sauce

These polenta triangles offer a change of pace from the traditional pasta and sauce dish. You can make both the sauce and polenta ahead and reheat before serving.

SAUCE:

Cooking spray
1   cup finely chopped onion
¼   cup finely chopped carrot
¾   pound ground round
3   garlic cloves, minced
⅓   cup dry red wine
¼   teaspoon salt
¼   teaspoon fennel seeds
¼   teaspoon freshly ground black pepper
1   (28-ounce) can diced tomatoes, undrained

POLENTA:

1½   cups 1% reduced-fat milk
½   teaspoon salt
1   (14-ounce) can fat-free, less-sodium chicken broth
1   cup instant polenta
½   cup (2 ounces) finely shredded fresh Romano or Parmesan cheese, divided
¼   cup chopped fresh basil

1. To prepare sauce, heat a large nonstick skillet over medium-high heat. Coat pan with cooking spray. Add onion, carrot, beef, and garlic; cook 6 minutes or until beef is browned, stirring to crumble. Add wine; cook 1 minute. Add ¼ teaspoon salt, fennel, pepper, and tomatoes. Bring to a boil; cover, reduce heat, and simmer 40 minutes.

2. To prepare polenta, combine milk, ½ teaspoon salt, and broth in a medium saucepan. Gradually add polenta, stirring constantly with a whisk; bring to a boil. Reduce heat to medium; cook 3 minutes or until thick, stirring constantly. Stir in 6 tablespoons cheese.

3. Spoon polenta into an 8-inch square baking dish coated with cooking spray, spreading evenly. Let stand 10 minutes or until firm. Loosen edges of polenta with a knife. Invert polenta onto a cutting board, and cut into 4 squares. Cut each square diagonally into 2 triangles. Place 1 triangle on each of 8 plates; top each serving with ½ cup sauce, ¾ teaspoon cheese, and 1½ teaspoons basil. Yield: 8 servings.

CALORIES 263 (30% from fat); FAT 8.8g (sat 3.8g, mono 3g, poly 0.3g); PROTEIN 15.9g; CARB 28.6g; FIBER 3.7g; CHOL 38mg; IRON 2mg; SODIUM 604mg; CALC 183mg

Spaghetti and Meatballs

Italian immigrant restaurateurs developed this dish at the beginning of the 20th century. Meatballs were added to spaghetti to adapt traditional Italian cuisine—mostly vegetables, legumes, and starches—to American tastes. Our quick-and-easy version tastes just like Grandma's.

1   pound ground sirloin
¼   cup minced fresh onion
2   tablespoons dry breadcrumbs
¼   teaspoon garlic salt
¼   teaspoon black pepper
1   large egg white, lightly beaten
1   (25.5-ounce) jar fat-free tomato-and-basil pasta sauce, divided
Cooking spray
5   tablespoons chopped fresh basil
5   cups hot cooked spaghetti or vermicelli (about 8 ounces uncooked pasta)
5   tablespoons grated Parmesan cheese
Basil sprigs (optional)

1. Combine first 6 ingredients and 2 tablespoons pasta sauce in a medium bowl. Shape meat mixture into 25 (1-inch) meatballs. Place a large nonstick skillet over medium heat. Coat pan with cooking spray. Add meatballs, and cook 6 minutes, browning on all sides. Stir in remaining pasta sauce and chopped basil. Cover, reduce heat, and simmer 10 minutes or until meatballs are done, stirring occasionally. Serve meatballs over spaghetti; sprinkle with Parmesan cheese. Garnish with basil sprigs, if desired. Yield: 5 servings (serving size: 5 meatballs, ½ cup sauce, 1 cup pasta, and 1 tablespoon cheese).

CALORIES 476 (19% from fat); FAT 10g (sat 3.8g, mono 3.7g, poly 0.8g); PROTEIN 38.2g; CARB 42.8g; FIBER 4.9g; CHOL 78mg; IRON 5.5mg; SODIUM 651mg; CALC 217mg

Spaghetti and Meatballs

Ragù Alla Bolognese with Fettuccine

Dating back to Renaissance times, ragù (or ragoût in France) had its start as a highly seasoned meat stew served by chefs in noble courts. It was first tossed with pasta in the early 1800s by cooks in what is now Italy's Emilia-Romagna region. While there are countless renditions of ragù, this version is adapted from the renowned sauce from the Italian city of Bologna.

    1   tablespoon olive oil
    1   cup finely chopped onion
    1   cup finely chopped celery
    ½   cup finely chopped carrot
    5   ounces ground pork
    5   ounces ground round
    5   ounces ground veal
    1   cup dry white wine
    ½   teaspoon salt
    ½   teaspoon black pepper
    ¼   teaspoon ground nutmeg
    1   bay leaf
    1   (14-ounce) can fat-free, less-sodium chicken broth
    1   (10¾-ounce) can tomato puree
    1   cup whole milk
    2   tablespoons minced fresh flat-leaf parsley
    2   (9-ounce) packages fresh fettuccine
    2   tablespoons grated fresh Parmesan cheese
Parsley sprigs (optional)

1. Heat oil in a large Dutch oven over medium heat. Add onion, celery, and carrot; cover. Cook 8 minutes, stirring occasionally. Remove onion mixture from pan.
2. Add veal, pork, and beef to pan; cook over medium heat until browned, stirring to crumble. Add wine, salt, pepper, nutmeg, and bay leaf; bring to a boil. Cook 5 minutes. Add onion mixture, broth, and tomato puree; bring to a simmer. Cook 1 hour, stirring occasionally.
3. Stir in milk and minced parsley, and bring to a boil. Reduce heat, and simmer 40 minutes. Discard bay leaf.
4. Cook pasta according to package directions, omitting salt and fat. Add pasta to meat sauce, and toss to coat. Sprinkle evenly with cheese. Garnish with parsley sprigs, if desired. Yield: 8 servings (serving size: 1½ cups).

CALORIES 369 (29% from fat); FAT 11.8g (sat 4.2g, mono 4.8g, poly 1.4g); PROTEIN 21.4g; CARB 44g; FIBER 4.2g; CHOL 87mg; IRON 3.7mg; SODIUM 546mg; CALC 117mg

Basic Grilled Flank Steak

An easy marinade gives this steak robust flavor—yet the seasonings are subtle enough that leftovers work in a variety of applications.

    1   (2-pound) flank steak, trimmed
    2   teaspoons Worcestershire sauce
    ½   teaspoon sea salt
    ½   teaspoon freshly ground black pepper
Cooking spray
Cilantro sprig (optional)

1. Place steak in an 11 x 7–inch baking dish. Sprinkle both sides with Worcestershire sauce, salt, and pepper; rub mixture into steak. Cover and refrigerate at least 20 minutes.
2. Prepare grill.
3. Place steak on a grill rack coated with cooking spray; grill 8 minutes on each side or until desired degree of doneness. Place on a cutting board; cover loosely with foil. Let stand 10 minutes. Cut steak diagonally across grain into thin slices. Garnish with cilantro, if desired. Yield: 8 servings (serving size: 3 ounces).

CALORIES 158 (38% from fat); FAT 6.7g (sat 2.8g, mono 2.7g, poly 0.3g); PROTEIN 22.6g; CARB 0.4g; FIBER 0g; CHOL 45mg; IRON 1.6mg; SODIUM 203mg; CALC 14mg

How to Slice Flank Steak

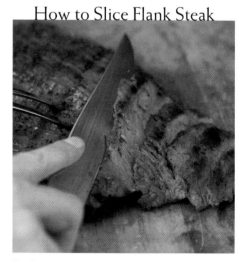

Flank steak has a distinct, visible grain and should be cut across this grain into ⅛- to ¼-inch-thick slices for maximum tenderness. Tilting your knife diagonally and slicing away from you ensures the largest surface area possible for each piece. Allow 10 minutes of stand time before slicing. During this stand time, the flavorful juices are reabsorbed and redistributed, so they won't run out as freely when you carve.

Three-Pepper Beef

This stir-fry gets its color and crunch from a variety of bell peppers. Stir-frying has a frenzied pace, so be sure to prepare all of the ingredients in advance and have them ready to add to the pan. Serve the stir-fry with rice so you can capture all of the sauce's flavor.

2½ teaspoons cornstarch, divided
  1 teaspoon sugar, divided
  ½ teaspoon salt
  1 pound flank steak, trimmed and thinly sliced
     across grain
  ¼ cup less-sodium beef broth
  3 tablespoons low-sodium soy sauce
  1 teaspoon freshly ground black pepper
  1 teaspoon canola oil
  ¼ cup sliced onion
  1 teaspoon minced peeled fresh ginger
  1 garlic clove, minced
1¼ cups cubed red bell pepper
1¼ cups cubed yellow bell pepper
1¼ cups cubed green bell pepper
  1 cup sugar snap peas, trimmed
     Parsley sprigs (optional)

1. Combine ½ teaspoon cornstarch, ½ teaspoon sugar, salt, and steak in a medium bowl; toss to coat. Set aside.

2. Combine remaining 2 teaspoons cornstarch, remaining ½ teaspoon sugar, broth, soy sauce, and black pepper, stirring with a whisk until sugar dissolves; set aside.

3. Heat canola oil in a wok or large nonstick skillet over medium-high heat. Add onion, ginger, and garlic, and stir-fry 10 seconds. Add steak, and stir-fry 3 minutes or until steak is done. Remove steak mixture from pan; cover and keep warm.

4. Add bell peppers and peas to pan; stir-fry 4 minutes or until crisp-tender. Add steak mixture and broth mixture to pan; cook 2 minutes or until thickened, stirring constantly. Garnish with parsley, if desired. Yield: 4 servings (serving size: about 1¾ cups).

CALORIES 238 (31% from fat); FAT 8.3g (sat 3g, mono 3.4g, poly 0.8g); PROTEIN 25.5g; CARB 14.8g; FIBER 3g; CHOL 45mg; IRON 2.5mg; SODIUM 824mg; CALC 49mg

Grilled Porterhouse Steak

Steak and cabernet sauvignon make a classic American combo. The char and meatiness of the steak are beautifully offset by the structure of the wine.

1 (2-pound) porterhouse steak (about 1½ inches thick)
2 tablespoons Worcestershire sauce
1 teaspoon sea or kosher salt
1 teaspoon coarsely ground black pepper
Cooking spray
1 teaspoon unsalted butter, softened

1. Place steak in a dish. Coat steak with Worcestershire sauce. Cover; marinate in refrigerator 30 minutes, turning occasionally.

2. Prepare grill, heating one side to medium and one side to high heat.

3. Remove steak from Worcestershire sauce; discard sauce. Sprinkle steak with 1 teaspoon salt and 1 teaspoon pepper; let stand at room temperature 15 minutes. Place steak on a grill rack coated with cooking spray over high heat; grill 3 minutes on each side. Turn steak, and place over medium heat; grill 3 minutes on each side or until desired degree of doneness. Place steak on a platter. Rub butter over top of steak; let stand 10 minutes. Yield: 6 servings (serving size: 3 ounces).

CALORIES 205 (32% from fat); FAT 7.3g (sat 2.7g, mono 2.8g, poly 0.3g); PROTEIN 33.2g; CARB 0.8g; FIBER 3.1g; CHOL 94mg; IRON 4.2mg; SODIUM 499mg; CALC 15mg

Broiled Flank Steak with Italian Salsa Verde

In Italy, salsa verde is a traditional accompaniment to mildly seasoned broiled or boiled meat. A little goes a long way, so use it sparingly. Serve the steak and salsa with roasted potato wedges.

SALSA:
- 1 cup cilantro leaves
- 1 cup flat-leaf parsley leaves
- 3 tablespoons water
- 2 tablespoons extravirgin olive oil
- 1 tablespoon fresh lime juice
- 2 teaspoons capers, rinsed and drained
- 1 teaspoon Dijon mustard
- 3 cornichons
- 1 garlic clove, peeled

STEAK:
- 1 (1½-pound) flank steak, trimmed
- ½ teaspoon salt
- ½ teaspoon freshly ground black pepper
- Cooking spray

1. Preheat broiler.

2. To prepare salsa, place first 9 ingredients in a food processor; process until smooth, scraping sides of bowl occasionally. Place salsa in a bowl; cover and set aside.

3. To prepare steak, sprinkle each side of steak evenly with salt and pepper. Place on a broiler pan coated with cooking spray; broil 6 minutes on each side or until desired degree of doneness. Cut steak diagonally across grain into thin slices; serve with salsa. Yield: 6 servings (serving size: 3 ounces steak and about 1 tablespoon salsa).

CALORIES 279 (46% from fat); FAT 14.3g (sat 4.6g, mono 7.4g, poly 0.8g); PROTEIN 32g; CARB 3.9g; FIBER 0.3g; CHOL 62mg; IRON 2.9mg; SODIUM 364mg; CALC 37mg

Basic Grilled Steak

(pictured on page 123)

Turn the steaks only once as you cook them. The more time they're in direct contact with the grill, the better. And speaking of better, nothing is better with a grilled steak than sweet, grilled corn-on-the cob. Coat fresh ears of corn with butter-flavored cooking spray; place the corn on the grill rack, and grill over direct heat, covered, 15 to 20 minutes or until the corn is tender, turning occasionally.

- 4 (6-ounce) ribeye steaks, trimmed (about ¾ inch thick)
- 1 teaspoon salt
- ¾ teaspoon freshly ground black pepper
- Cooking spray
- Finely chopped fresh parsley (optional)

1. Sprinkle both sides of steaks with salt and pepper. Let steaks stand at room temperature 20 minutes.

2. Prepare grill.

3. Pat steaks dry with a paper towel. Place steaks on a grill rack coated with cooking spray; grill 2 minutes on each side or until desired degree of doneness. Remove from grill. Cover steaks loosely with foil; let stand 5 minutes. Garnish with parsley, if desired. Yield: 4 servings (serving size: 1 steak).

CALORIES 275 (46% from fat); FAT 14.1g (sat 5.5g, mono 6.1g, poly 0.5g); PROTEIN 34.3g; CARB 0.3g; FIBER 0.1g; CHOL 100mg; IRON 3.7mg; SODIUM 689mg; CALC 19mg

About Tongs

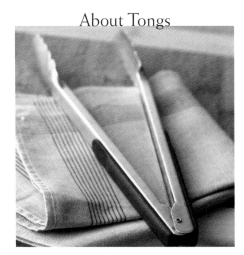

Tongs, especially those with spring-loaded handles, are the ideal tool for grilling. They can be used with any foods—from thick steaks and hamburgers to thin asparagus spears. Tongs help maintain the shape and juiciness of foods. (A fork will pierce food and cause flavorful juices to escape.) Also, their long slender handles are safer to use than a fork because they keep your hands away from the heat.

Slow Cooker Beef Stroganoff

The slow cooker helps make this classic dish a weeknight supper your family will love. You may have most of the ingredients on hand in your pantry, and with minimal prep time, you can have this cooking before you leave for the day.

1   (1-pound) top round steak (1 inch thick), trimmed
1   cup chopped onion
2   tablespoons chopped fresh parsley
2   tablespoons Dijon mustard
¾   teaspoon salt
½   teaspoon dried dill
½   teaspoon black pepper
1   (8-ounce) package presliced mushrooms (about 2 cups)
3   garlic cloves, minced
⅓   cup all-purpose flour
1   cup less-sodium beef broth
1   (8-ounce) container reduced-fat sour cream
2   cups hot cooked medium egg noodles (about 1½ cups uncooked pasta)
Chopped fresh dill (optional)

1. Cut steak diagonally across grain into ¾-inch-thick slices. Place steak and next 8 ingredients in a 3-quart electric slow cooker; stir well.

2. Lightly spoon flour into a dry measuring cup, and level with a knife. Place flour in a small bowl; gradually add broth, stirring with a whisk until blended. Add broth mixture to cooker, and stir well. Cover and cook on HIGH 1 hour. Reduce heat to LOW, and cook 7 to 8 hours or until steak is tender. Turn cooker off; remove lid. Let stroganoff stand 10 minutes. Stir in sour cream. Serve stroganoff over noodles. Sprinkle with chopped dill, if desired. Yield: 4 servings (serving size: about 1 cup stroganoff and ½ cup noodles).

CALORIES 444 (32% from fat); FAT 15.9g (sat 7.4g, mono 3.4g, poly 0.9g); PROTEIN 35.7g; CARB 38.8g; FIBER 2.6g; CHOL 123mg; IRON 4.7mg; SODIUM 737mg; CALC 123mg

Beef Stroganoff

This traditional Russian dish is quick to prepare; use frozen chopped onions and presliced mushrooms to make it even faster. To maintain a creamy consistency, be careful not to bring the sauce to a boil once you stir in the sour cream mixture.

- 1 (8-ounce) carton reduced-fat sour cream
- 3 tablespoons no salt–added tomato paste
- 1 teaspoon Worcestershire sauce
- ½ cup all-purpose flour
- 1 teaspoon salt
- ⅛ teaspoon freshly ground black pepper
- 2 pounds boneless sirloin steak, cut into (2-inch) strips
- 1 tablespoon butter
- ½ cup chopped onion
- 1 (14-ounce) can less-sodium beef broth
- 2 cups sliced mushrooms
- Chopped fresh parsley (optional)
- 8 cups hot cooked medium egg noodles (about 7 cups uncooked pasta)

1. Combine first 3 ingredients in a bowl. Set aside.

2. Combine flour, salt, and pepper in a large zip-top plastic bag. Add beef; seal and shake to coat beef.

3. Melt butter in a large nonstick skillet over medium-high heat. Add onion; sauté 2 minutes or until tender. Add beef and flour mixture; sauté 3 minutes or until beef is browned. Gradually add broth, scraping pan to loosen browned bits. Add mushrooms; cover and cook 5 minutes or until mushrooms are tender. Reduce heat to low; gradually stir in sour cream mixture. Cook, uncovered, 1 minute or until heated (do not boil). Stir in parsley, if desired. Serve over egg noodles. Yield: 8 servings (serving size: ¾ cup beef mixture and 1 cup noodles).

CALORIES 473 (30% from fat); FAT 16g (sat 7g, mono 4.3g, poly 1.1g); PROTEIN 30.2g; CARB 50.6g; FIBER 2.6g; CHOL 129mg; IRON 5.7mg; SODIUM 417mg; CALC 81mg

Hoisin Grilled Sirloin

Hoisin sauce is thick, sweet, and spicy. It's most commonly used as a dipping sauce for a variety of Chinese dishes. Brushing the grilled sirloin with the hoisin mixture gives your meat added flavor. You can find hoisin sauce in Asian markets and large supermarkets. Serve the sirloin with snow peas and rice for a balanced meal.

- 2 tablespoons hoisin sauce
- 1 tablespoon apricot preserves
- 1½ teaspoons fresh lime juice
- ⅛ teaspoon crushed red pepper
- ½ teaspoon salt
- 1 pound top sirloin

1. Heat a grill pan over medium-high heat.

2. Combine first 4 ingredients, stirring with a whisk.

3. Sprinkle salt over beef. Add beef to pan; cook 3 minutes on each side or until desired degree of doneness. Let stand 5 minutes before slicing. Brush both sides of beef with hoisin mixture. Cut beef across grain into thin slices. Yield: 4 servings (serving size: about 3 ounces).

CALORIES 213 (37% from fat); FAT 8.8g (sat 3.4g, mono 3.7g, poly 0.5g); PROTEIN 25.3g; CARB 7g; FIBER 0.3g; CHOL 76mg; IRON 2.9mg; SODIUM 477mg; CALC 13mg

About Grill Pans

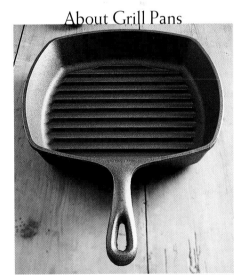

A grill pan is a good alternative to a gas or charcoal grill. With ridges that elevate food so air can circulate underneath and fat can drip away, a grill pan adds more than just pretty grill marks and smoky flavors. Your food doesn't sauté or steam as it does in a plain skillet; instead, flavor is seared into the food. Meat and fish turn out juicy, with no need for added fat. Vegetables stay crisp-tender, and their nutrients don't leach out.

Classic Steak House Rubbed Filet Mignon

Classic Steak House Rubbed Filet Mignon

Filet mignon and beef tenderloin steaks are the same cut of meat. For the leanest, juiciest, and most flavorful steaks, look for those that are richly marbled, but well-trimmed of exterior fat.

> 2 teaspoons black peppercorns
> ¼ teaspoon dried rosemary
> 1 teaspoon dry mustard
> ¾ teaspoon kosher salt
> ½ teaspoon garlic powder
> 4 (4-ounce) beef tenderloin steaks, trimmed (1 inch thick)
> Cooking spray

1. Prepare grill.

2. Place peppercorns and rosemary in a spice or coffee grinder; pulse until pepper is coarsely ground.

3. Combine pepper mixture, dry mustard, salt, and garlic powder; rub evenly over both sides of steaks. Place steaks on a grill rack coated with cooking spray; grill 3 minutes on each side or until desired degree of doneness. Yield: 4 servings (serving size: 1 steak).

CALORIES 188 (43% from fat); FAT 8.9g (sat 3.2g, mono 3.3g, poly 0.3g); PROTEIN 24.5g; CARB 0.8g; FIBER 0.2g; CHOL 72mg; IRON 3.3mg; SODIUM 407mg; CALC 11mg

How to Make Crosshatches

For an attractive presentation, grill crosshatches on the steak. First, place the steak on the grill. After about a minute—or halfway through the cooking time for the first side of the steak—rotate the meat a quarter-turn (45° for diamond-shaped crosshatches, 90° for square-shaped marks). Next, flip the steak over, and complete cooking. Don't flip steak back onto the marked side while grilling. Only one side of the steak will show on the plate, so both sides don't need crosshatches.

Beef Tenderloin with Mushroom Gravy

This superfast family meal is also elegant enough to serve to company. Gradually add the hot mushroom mixture to the cold sour cream to keep the two from separating. Serve the steaks and creamy gravy with low-fat mashed potatoes.

> Cooking spray
> 4 (4-ounce) beef tenderloin steaks, trimmed (½ inch thick)
> ½ teaspoon coarsely ground black pepper
> ¼ teaspoon salt
> 1 cup presliced mushrooms
> ½ cup finely chopped onion
> 1 teaspoon bottled minced garlic
> ½ cup less-sodium beef broth
> ⅓ cup fat-free sour cream
> 2 tablespoons minced fresh parsley

1. Heat a large nonstick skillet over medium-high heat; coat pan with cooking spray. Sprinkle steaks with pepper and salt. Add steaks to pan; cook 3 minutes on each side or until desired degree of doneness. Remove from pan.

2. Add mushrooms, onion, and garlic to pan; sauté 5 minutes. Stir in broth; bring to a boil. Cover, reduce heat, and simmer 3 minutes.

3. Place sour cream in a medium bowl. Gradually add mushroom mixture to sour cream, stirring constantly with a whisk. Stir in parsley. Serve gravy with steak. Yield: 4 servings (serving size: 1 steak and ¼ cup gravy).

CALORIES 182 (38% from fat); FAT 7.6g (sat 2.8g, mono 2.9g, poly 0.4g); PROTEIN 20.3g; CARB 6.5g; FIBER 0.6g; CHOL 57mg; IRON 2.7mg; SODIUM 259mg; CALC 53mg

Argentinean Oak-Planked Beef
Tenderloin with Chimichurri Sauce

Argentinean Oak-Planked Beef Tenderloin with Chimichurri Sauce

Grilled steak topped with emerald-colored chimichurri is one of Argentina's national dishes. Considered the barbecue sauce of Argentina, chimichurri is built on garlic and parsley, and is also a pungent cross between vinaigrette and pesto. Mint gives this version a more delicate taste.

STEAKS:

1   (15 x 6 ½ x ⅜–inch) oak grilling plank
4   (4-ounce) beef tenderloin steaks, trimmed (¾ inch thick)
½   teaspoon salt
¼   teaspoon freshly ground black pepper

SAUCE:

¾   cup fresh flat-leaf parsley leaves
¼   cup fresh cilantro leaves
¼   cup fresh mint leaves
¼   cup chopped onion
¼   cup fat-free, less-sodium chicken broth
3   tablespoons sherry vinegar
2   tablespoons fresh oregano leaves
1   teaspoon olive oil
½   teaspoon salt
½   teaspoon freshly ground black pepper
½   teaspoon crushed red pepper
3   garlic cloves

1. Immerse and soak plank in water 1 hour; drain.
2. Prepare grill, heating one side to medium and one side to high heat.
3. To prepare steaks, sprinkle steaks with ½ teaspoon salt and ¼ teaspoon black pepper. Place plank on a grill rack over high heat; grill 5 minutes or until lightly charred. Carefully turn plank over; move to medium heat. Place steak on charred side of plank. Cover and grill 12 minutes or until desired degree of doneness.
4. To prepare sauce, place parsley and remaining 11 ingredients in a food processor; process until smooth. Serve with steaks. Yield: 4 servings (serving size: 1 steak and 1½ tablespoons sauce).

CALORIES 159 (31% from fat); FAT 5.5g (sat 1.7g, mono 2.4g, poly 0.1g); PROTEIN 23.3g; CARB 5.7g; FIBER 1.4g; CHOL 60mg; IRON 4.4mg; SODIUM 977mg; CALC 52mg

Corned Beef and Vegetables

Rich amber beer, Dijon mustard, and molasses infuse corned beef and its favorite partners—potatoes, cabbage, and carrots—for a palate-pleasing balance of flavors. Corned beef is a brisket cut that's been cured or "corned" in a brine that's usually seasoned with peppercorns and bay leaves. Sometimes corned beef comes with a spice packet. If you can't find one that does, add 1 teaspoon black peppercorns to the cooking liquid.

20   small boiling onions (about 1 pound), peeled
10   medium carrots (about 1¾ pounds), peeled and quartered
10   small red potatoes (about 1¼ pounds)
2   bay leaves
1   (3¾-pound) cured corned beef brisket with spice packet, trimmed and cut in half
1   (12-ounce) bottle amber beer
½   cup Dijon mustard, divided
3   tablespoons molasses
2   large garlic cloves, crushed
1   small cabbage, cut into 10 wedges (about 1½ pounds)

1. Place first 4 ingredients in a 6½-quart electric slow cooker. Reserve spice packet from brisket; place brisket on top of vegetables.
2. Combine reserved spice packet, beer, 3 tablespoons mustard, molasses, and garlic in a bowl; stir well with a whisk. Pour mixture over brisket. Cover and cook on HIGH 1 hour. Reduce heat to LOW; cook 6 hours. Add cabbage; cover and cook 1 hour or until tender. Discard bay leaves.
3. Cut brisket across grain into thin slices. Serve corned beef and vegetables with remaining 5 tablespoons mustard. Yield: 10 servings (serving size: about 3 ounces brisket, 2 onions, 4 carrot pieces, 1 potato, 1 cabbage wedge, and 1½ teaspoons mustard).

CALORIES 340 (44% from fat); FAT 16.5g (sat 5.5g, mono 7.9g, poly 0.7g); PROTEIN 18.5g; CARB 28.8g; FIBER 4.8g; CHOL 83mg; IRON 2.9mg; SODIUM 1,188mg; CALC 84mg

Beef Carbonnade

A staff favorite, this easy recipe relies on the age-old technique of braising, in which less tender cuts of meat, along with aromatic vegetables, slowly cook in liquid. The fork-tender beef will melt in your mouth.

    2   bacon slices, finely diced
 2½   pounds boneless chuck roast, cut into 1-inch
        cubes
    ½   teaspoon salt
    ½   teaspoon black pepper
    1   garlic clove, minced
    5   cups thinly sliced onion (about 4 medium)
    3   tablespoons all-purpose flour
    2   teaspoons white wine vinegar
    ½   teaspoon sugar
    ½   teaspoon dried thyme
    1   (10½-ounce) can beef broth
    1   (12-ounce) bottle light beer
    1   bay leaf
    6   cups hot cooked wide egg noodles
        (about 12 ounces uncooked pasta)

1. Preheat oven to 325°.
2. Cook bacon in a large Dutch oven over medium-high heat until crisp; remove bacon, reserving drippings in pan. Set bacon aside. Add beef, salt, and pepper to drippings in pan; cook 5 minutes, browning beef well on all sides. Add garlic; cook 30 seconds. Remove beef from pan with a slotted spoon; set aside.
3. Add onion to pan; cover and cook over medium heat 10 minutes, stirring occasionally. Stir in flour; cook 2 minutes. Add vinegar and next 5 ingredients; bring to a boil. Return bacon and beef to pan. Cover and bake at 325° for 2 hours or until beef is tender. Discard bay leaf. Serve over noodles. Yield: 6 servings (serving size: 1 cup beef mixture and 1 cup noodles).

CALORIES 540 (26% from fat); FAT 15.3g (sat 5.4g, mono 6.1g, poly 1.8g); PROTEIN 43.3g; CARB 52.1g; FIBER 5.5g; CHOL 147mg; IRON 7.1mg; SODIUM 636mg; CALC 60mg

Herb, Garlic, and Mustard-Crusted Fillet of Beef

For a change of pace, give an Italian-inspired menu a try at your next gathering. With the fillet of beef as the main attraction, complete the meal with a green salad, cheesy polenta, Ciabatta (recipe on page 50), sautéed leeks and broccolini, and a decadent slice of chocolate cake. To make a sauce for the beef, deglaze the pan with red wine, and reduce it. Be sure to use a dry, well-structured, powerful red that can stand up to the beef, such as a cabernet sauvignon.

    1   (2-pound) beef tenderloin, trimmed
Cooking spray
    ¾   teaspoon salt
    ¼   teaspoon freshly ground black pepper
    3   tablespoons Dijon mustard
    ¼   cup chopped fresh basil
    ¼   cup chopped fresh parsley
    1   tablespoon chopped fresh thyme
    1   tablespoon chopped fresh oregano
    3   garlic cloves, minced

1. Preheat oven to 400°.
2. Place beef on a broiler pan coated with cooking spray; sprinkle with salt and pepper. Spread mustard evenly over beef. Combine remaining ingredients; pat evenly over beef.
3. Insert a meat thermometer into thickest portion of beef. Bake at 400° for 40 minutes or until thermometer registers 145° (medium-rare) or desired degree of doneness.
4. Transfer beef to a cutting board. Cover loosely with foil, and let stand 10 minutes before slicing. Yield: 8 servings (serving size: 3 ounces).

CALORIES 154 (43% from fat); FAT 7.4g (sat 2.6g, mono 2.8g, poly 0.4g); PROTEIN 19.8g; CARB 1.4g; FIBER 0.3g; CHOL 57mg; IRON 2.8mg; SODIUM 404mg; CALC 23mg

Company Pot Roast

1 (2-pound) boneless chuck roast, trimmed and cut in half
¼ cup low-sodium soy sauce
2 garlic cloves, minced
1 cup beef broth
1 (.35-ounce) package dried morels or dried shiitake mushrooms
1 tablespoon cracked black pepper
3 tablespoons sun-dried tomato paste or regular tomato paste
2 medium onions (about ¾ pound), quartered
1 (16-ounce) package carrots, cut into 2-inch pieces
16 small red potatoes (about 2 pounds), halved
1 tablespoon canola oil
1½ tablespoons all-purpose flour
3 tablespoons water

1. Combine roast, soy sauce, and garlic in a large zip-top plastic bag; seal bag, and marinate in refrigerator at least 8 hours, turning bag occasionally.
2. Bring broth to a boil in a small saucepan, and add mushrooms. Remove from heat; cover and let stand 20 minutes. Drain mushrooms through a cheesecloth-lined colander over a bowl, reserving broth mixture.

3. Remove roast from bag, reserving marinade. Sprinkle roast with pepper, gently pressing pepper into roast. Combine reserved marinade, mushroom broth mixture, and tomato paste; stir well, and set aside.
4. Place mushrooms, onion, carrot, and potato in a 6-quart electric slow cooker; toss gently.
5. Heat oil in a large skillet over medium-high heat, and add roast, browning well on all sides. Place roast over vegetables in cooker. Pour tomato paste mixture into pan, scraping to loosen browned bits. Pour tomato paste mixture over roast and vegetables. Cover and cook on LOW 10 hours or until roast is tender. Place roast and vegetables on a serving platter; keep warm. Reserve cooking liquid in cooker; increase heat to HIGH.
6. Place flour in a bowl. Gradually add water, stirring with a whisk until well blended. Add flour mixture to cooking liquid in cooker. Cook, uncovered, 15 minutes or until slightly thick, stirring frequently. Serve gravy with roast and vegetables. Yield: 8 servings (serving size: 3 ounces roast, 1 onion wedge, about 3 carrot pieces, 4 potato halves, and about ¼ cup gravy).

CALORIES 358 (33% from fat): FAT 13.2g (sat 3.7g, mono 5.3g, poly 1.1g); PROTEIN 27g; CARB 32.1g; FIBER 4.9g; CHOL 69mg; IRON 4.4mg; SODIUM 746mg; CALC 52mg

Veal Marsala

Vitello al marsala, or veal marsala, is a regional specialty of Sicilian origin. The popular mushroom and wine-based sauce is primarily flavored with Marsala, a dry, dark, and strong fortified wine that gets its name from the town in which the grapes are grown. Serve over vermicelli, linguine, egg noodles, or a blend of white and wild rice.

¼ cup all-purpose flour, divided
⅔ cup beef consommé
1 pound veal cutlets
1 tablespoon butter, divided
½ cup dry Marsala wine
1 cup presliced mushrooms
¼ teaspoon salt
4 cups hot cooked vermicelli (about 8 ounces uncooked pasta)

1. Combine 1 tablespoon flour and consommé, stirring with a whisk, and set aside. Dredge veal in remaining 3 tablespoons flour. Discard any remaining flour.

2. Melt 1½ teaspoons butter in a large nonstick skillet over medium-high heat. Add half of veal; cook 1½ minutes. Turn veal over; cook 1 minute. Remove veal from pan. Repeat procedure with remaining butter and cutlets.

3. Add wine to pan, scraping pan to loosen browned bits. Add consommé mixture, mushrooms, and salt; bring to a boil. Reduce heat; simmer 3 minutes or until thick. Return veal to pan, turning once to coat well with sauce. Serve with pasta. Yield: 4 servings (serving size: 3 ounces veal, about 2 tablespoons sauce, and 1 cup pasta).

CALORIES 406 (13% from fat); FAT 5.9g (sat 2.6g, mono 1.5g, poly 0.8g); PROTEIN 34g; CARB 48.6g; FIBER 2.7g; CHOL 95mg; IRON 3.4mg; SODIUM 512mg; CALC 20mg

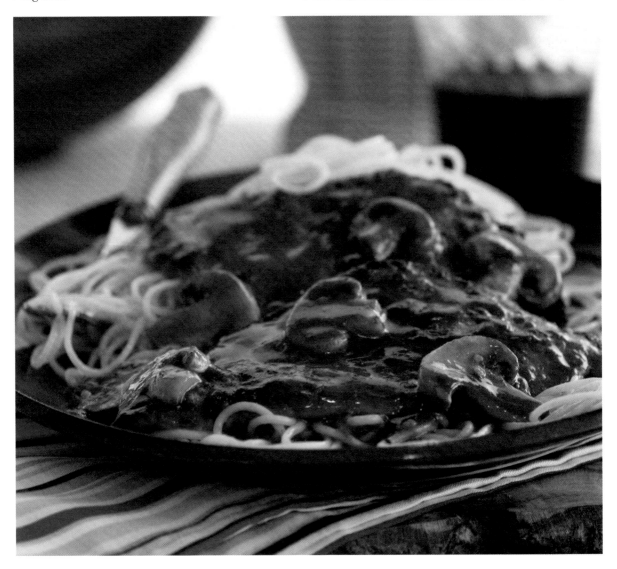

Osso Buco with Gremolata

Veal shanks, called *ossobuco* in Italian, or "bone with a hole," are inexpensive and become a succulent meal in the slow cooker. Even if you aren't an anchovy lover, don't omit the anchovy paste—it adds immeasurably to the flavor. Use the remaining broth mixture in soups and stews.

OSSO BUCO:
- ⅔ cup all-purpose flour
- ¾ teaspoon freshly ground black pepper, divided
- ½ teaspoon kosher salt, divided
- 6 veal shanks, trimmed (about 5 pounds)
- 2 teaspoons butter, divided
- 2 teaspoons olive oil, divided
- 2 cups coarsely chopped red onion
- 1½ cups chopped celery
- 6 garlic cloves, minced
- 4 cups beef broth
- 2 cups dry white wine
- 1 tablespoon chopped fresh rosemary
- 1 tablespoon anchovy paste

GREMOLATA:
- ½ cup chopped fresh flat-leaf parsley
- 1 tablespoon grated lemon rind
- 2 garlic cloves, minced

REMAINING INGREDIENT:
- 8 cups hot cooked pappardelle (wide ribbon pasta; about 1 pound uncooked pasta)

1. To prepare osso buco, combine flour, ¼ teaspoon pepper, and ¼ teaspoon salt in a shallow dish. Dredge veal in flour mixture.

2. Heat 1 teaspoon butter and 1 teaspoon oil in a large skillet over medium heat. Add half of veal; cook 6 minutes, browning on both sides. Place browned veal in a 7-quart electric slow cooker. Repeat procedure with 1 teaspoon butter, 1 teaspoon oil, and remaining veal.

3. Add onion and celery to pan; sauté over medium-high heat 5 minutes or until tender. Add 6 garlic cloves to pan; sauté 1 minute. Stir in broth, wine, rosemary, and anchovy paste, scraping pan to loosen browned bits. Bring to a boil; cook 4 minutes. Pour over veal.

4. Cover and cook on LOW 9 hours or until done. Sprinkle veal with ½ teaspoon pepper and ¼ teaspoon salt. Remove veal from cooker; cool slightly. Remove veal from bones, and cut up.

5. To prepare gremolata, combine parsley, lemon rind, and 2 garlic cloves. Place pasta in each of 8 pasta bowls. Top each serving with veal and broth mixture. Reserve remaining broth mixture for another use. Sprinkle each serving with gremolata. Yield: 8 servings (serving size: 1 cup pasta, ⅔ cup veal, ½ cup broth mixture, and 1 tablespoon gremolata).

CALORIES 443 (25% from fat); FAT 12.2g (sat 4.1g, mono 4.9g, poly 1.1g); PROTEIN 54.9g; CARB 15.9g; FIBER 1.8g; CHOL 200mg; IRON 3.3mg; SODIUM 485mg; CALC 94mg

Grilled Lamb Chops

Lamb pairs well with the bold flavors of many ethnic cuisines, but you'll find it tasty and suitable with simple seasonings, too. Use dry white wine instead of sherry, if you like.

- 3 tablespoons dried oregano
- 1 teaspoon salt
- ½ teaspoon freshly ground black pepper
- 8 (4-ounce) lamb loin chops, trimmed
- 4 garlic cloves, thinly sliced
- 3 tablespoons dry sherry
- Cooking spray
- Lime wedges (optional)

1. Combine first 3 ingredients; sprinkle evenly over lamb. Place lamb in a heavy-duty zip-top plastic bag. Add garlic and sherry; seal bag, turning to coat. Marinate in refrigerator 3 hours, turning occasionally.

2. Prepare grill.

3. Place lamb on a grill rack coated with cooking spray, and cook 5 minutes on each side or until desired degree of doneness. Serve with lime wedges, if desired. Yield: 4 servings (serving size: 2 chops).

CALORIES 273 (31% from fat); FAT 9.4g (sat 3.7g, mono 3.8g, poly 0.5g); PROTEIN 39.1g; CARB 3.4g; FIBER 1.5g; CHOL 120mg; IRON 5.6mg; SODIUM 705mg; CALC 76mg

Rosemary Grilled Lamb Chops

Garlic and fresh rosemary lend a heady fragrant aroma to a humble lamb chop. Marinating the lamb chops in olive oil along with your seasonings of choice allows the meat to soak up a variety of rich flavors, yet doesn't overpower the essence of the lamb.

1 tablespoon chopped fresh rosemary
1 teaspoon olive oil
½ teaspoon kosher salt, divided
1 garlic clove, minced
4 (4-ounce) lamb loin chops, trimmed
⅛ teaspoon freshly ground black pepper
Cooking spray
Rosemary sprigs (optional)

1. Combine rosemary, oil, ¼ teaspoon salt, and garlic; rub mixture evenly over both sides of lamb. Cover and marinate in refrigerator at least 2 hours or overnight.
2. Prepare grill.
3. Remove lamb from bag. Sprinkle both sides of lamb with ¼ teaspoon salt and pepper. Place lamb on a grill rack coated with cooking spray; grill 3 minutes on each side or until desired degree of doneness (145° for medium-rare). Garnish with rosemary sprigs, if desired. Yield: 4 servings (serving size: 1 chop).

CALORIES 278 (54% from fat); FAT 16.8g (sat 7.5g, mono 7.1g, poly 0.8g); PROTEIN 29.3g; CARB 0.4g; FIBER 0.1g; CHOL 96mg; IRON 2.7mg; SODIUM 308mg; CALC 19mg

Apricot and Lamb Tagine

In Morocco, the term *tagine* refers to any slow-cooked meat or vegetable stew that traditionally has a savory-sweet flavor. It also refers to the earthenware cooking dish in which the stew is cooked and served. A tagine has a platelike bottom with a cone-shaped lid that serves as an ideal vessel for stewing tougher cuts of meat. Here, the slow cooker replaces any specialized equipment and renders a thick lamb stew that fills the air with the exotic aromas of North Africa. Serve this over hot couscous, and sprinkle it with crunchy almonds and chopped fresh parsley for an added bit of texture and fresh flavor.

TAGINE:
2 cups diced onion (about 1 large)
½ cup orange juice
½ cup less-sodium beef broth
1 tablespoon grated lemon rind
2 tablespoons honey
1 tablespoon fresh lemon juice
2 teaspoons bottled minced garlic
2 teaspoons grated peeled fresh ginger
1½ teaspoons salt
1 teaspoon ground coriander
½ teaspoon ground cumin
¼ teaspoon freshly ground black pepper
2 pounds boneless leg of lamb, trimmed and cut into bite-sized pieces
2 (3-inch) cinnamon sticks
1 (6-ounce) package dried apricots, halved

REMAINING INGREDIENTS:
4 cups cooked couscous
¼ cup slivered almonds, toasted
¼ cup chopped fresh parsley

1. To prepare tagine, combine first 15 ingredients in a 4-quart electric slow cooker. Cover and cook on HIGH 1 hour. Reduce heat to LOW, and cook 6 hours. Discard cinnamon sticks.
2. Place ½ cup couscous on each of 8 plates. Top each serving with ½ cup lamb mixture, 1½ teaspoons almonds, and 1½ teaspoons parsley. Yield: 8 servings.

CALORIES 451 (37% from fat); FAT 18.7g (sat 7.1g, mono 8.1g, poly 1.7g); PROTEIN 26.2g; CARB 43.2g; FIBER 3.6g; CHOL 81mg; IRON 3.3mg; SODIUM 515mg; CALC 52mg

Yogurt-Marinated Lamb Kebabs

Kebabs create a mouthwatering variation to the routine appearance of your dinner plate, and they're more time-friendly. Because they cook so fast, you'll be able to enjoy your guests instead of standing over a hot grill.

½ pound lean boneless leg of lamb
¼ cup plain fat-free yogurt
1 tablespoon finely chopped onion
2 teaspoons olive oil
1½ teaspoons ground cumin
½ teaspoon dried rosemary
½ teaspoon pepper
¼ teaspoon salt
1 garlic clove, minced
2 cups (1-inch) sliced zucchini
6 large cherry tomatoes
1 small onion, cut into 4 wedges
Cooking spray
2 cups cooked couscous

1. Trim fat from lamb. Cut lamb into 1-inch pieces.
2. Combine yogurt and next 7 ingredients in a large zip-top plastic bag. Add lamb; seal bag, and marinate in refrigerator 8 hours, turning bag occasionally. Remove lamb from bag, reserving marinade.
3. Thread lamb, zucchini, tomatoes, and onion wedges alternately onto 4 (10-inch) skewers.
4. Prepare grill.
5. Place kebabs on a grill rack coated with cooking spray; grill 7 minutes on each side or until done, basting occasionally with reserved marinade. Serve kebabs with couscous. Yield: 2 servings (serving size: 2 kebabs and 1 cup couscous).
NOTE: If using wooden skewers, soak them in water 30 minutes before grilling.

CALORIES 464 (25% from fat); FAT 12.8g (sat 3.1g, mono 6.5g, poly 1g); PROTEIN 35.4g; CARB 53.1g; FIBER 4.3g; CHOL 76mg; IRON 5mg; SODIUM 390mg; CALC 116mg

Pork and Fennel Ragù

With onions, fennel, garlic, and oregano, this traditional ragù, or meat sauce, is reminiscent of Italian sausage.

Cooking spray
  1 cup finely chopped onion
  1 cup finely chopped fennel bulb
  2 garlic cloves, minced
  1 tablespoon fennel seeds
  2 teaspoons sugar
  1 teaspoon dried oregano
  ½ teaspoon salt
  ½ teaspoon crushed red pepper
  ¼ teaspoon ground red pepper
  ¼ teaspoon freshly ground black pepper
  8 ounces lean ground pork
  2 cups chopped tomato
  ½ cup fat-free, less-sodium chicken broth
  4 cups hot cooked rigatoni (about 8 ounces uncooked pasta)
Fennel fronds (optional)

1. Heat a large nonstick skillet over medium-high heat. Coat pan with cooking spray. Add onion, chopped fennel, and garlic; sauté 5 minutes. Add fennel seeds and next 7 ingredients, stirring to combine; sauté 3 minutes.

2. Add tomato and broth; bring to a boil. Reduce heat, and simmer 15 minutes, stirring occasionally. Serve over pasta. Garnish with fennel fronds, if desired. Yield: 4 servings (serving size: 1 cup ragù and 1 cup pasta).

CALORIES 408 (30% from fat); FAT 13.7g (sat 4.7g, mono 5.7g, poly 1.6g); PROTEIN 18.6g; CARB 52.8g; FIBER 5g; CHOL 41mg; IRON 3.5mg; SODIUM 405mg; CALC 64mg

Fennel-Brined Pork Chops

Brining is simply a matter of soaking meat in a saltwater solution, yet the result is the difference between dry and delicious. Unlike marinating, which imparts flavor, brining enhances texture. The process locks in moisture so that the end product is always a succulent, juicy piece of pork or chicken.

  3½ cups water, divided
  ½ cup chopped fennel fronds
  1 tablespoon fennel seeds
  ¼ cup kosher salt
  ¼ cup sugar
  2 tablespoons sambuca or other anise-flavored liqueur
  1 cup ice cubes
  4 (4-ounce) boneless center-cut loin pork chops (about ¾ inch thick)
Cooking spray
  2 teaspoons chopped fresh rosemary
  1 teaspoon freshly ground black pepper
  2 garlic cloves, minced

1. Combine 1 cup water, fennel fronds, and seeds in a small saucepan. Bring to a boil; remove from heat. Pour into a large bowl; cool to room temperature. Add 2½ cups water, salt, sugar, and liqueur, stirring until salt and sugar dissolve. Pour salt mixture into a large zip-top plastic bag. Add ice and pork; seal. Refrigerate 4 hours, turning bag occasionally.

2. Prepare grill.

3. Remove pork from bag; discard brine. Pat pork dry with paper towels. Coat pork with cooking spray. Combine rosemary, pepper, and garlic; rub evenly over both sides of pork. Place pork on a grill rack coated with cooking spray; grill 3 to 5 minutes on each side or until done. Let stand 5 minutes before serving. Yield: 4 servings (serving size: 1 chop).

CALORIES 174 (34% from fat); FAT 6.5g (sat 2.4g, mono 2.9g, poly 0.5g); PROTEIN 24.1g; CARB 3g; FIBER 0.3g; CHOL 65mg; IRON 0.9mg; SODIUM 469mg; CALC 34mg

Fennel-Brined Pork Chops

Grilled Plum and Prosciutto-Stuffed Pork Chops

The flavors of chopped green onion, minced garlic, and white hominy sautéed in butter create a delicious side dish for the pork chops.

4   pitted dried plums, halved
2   very thin slices prosciutto (about ¾ ounce), halved
½   teaspoon crushed fennel seeds
½   teaspoon paprika
½   teaspoon chopped fresh sage
½   teaspoon chopped fresh rosemary
¼   teaspoon kosher salt
¼   teaspoon crushed red pepper
¼   teaspoon freshly ground black pepper
4   (4-ounce) boneless center-cut loin pork chops (about ¾ inch thick)
Cooking spray
2   teaspoons balsamic vinegar
2   teaspoons molasses

1. Prepare grill.
2. Soak plum halves in boiling water 5 minutes. Drain.
3. Wrap 2 plum halves in each prosciutto piece.
4. Combine fennel seeds and next 6 ingredients in a small bowl.
5. Cut a horizontal slit through thickest portion of each pork chop to form a pocket. Stuff 1 prosciutto wrap into each pocket. Sprinkle pork chops with fennel mixture. Place pork chops on a grill rack coated with cooking spray; grill 3 to 5 minutes on each side or until done. Combine vinegar and molasses; brush over pork chops. Yield: 4 servings (serving size: 1 chop).

CALORIES 205 (32% from fat); FAT 7.2g (sat 2.6g, mono 2.9g, poly 0.5g); PROTEIN 25.7g; CARB 8.5g; FIBER 0.9g; CHOL 70mg; IRON 1.3mg; SODIUM 270mg; CALC 42mg

Smoked Paprika Pork Chops with Bell Pepper and Corn Relish

A sweet corn relish with just a bit of heat adorns simply seasoned pork chops. Accompany this dish with refrigerated potato wedges that have been tossed with garlic powder, ground red pepper, and salt and roasted until crisp.

1   tablespoon olive oil
½   cup chopped red onion
2   teaspoons bottled minced fresh ginger
⅓   cup chopped red bell pepper
1   teaspoon ground coriander
¼   teaspoon dried thyme
1   (15.5-ounce) can no-salt-added whole-kernel corn, drained
1   teaspoon cider vinegar
¾   teaspoon salt, divided
¼   teaspoon black pepper, divided
1½ teaspoons smoked sweet paprika
4   (4-ounce) boneless center-cut pork loin chops, trimmed
Cooking spray

1. Heat oil in a large nonstick skillet over medium-high heat. Add onion and ginger, and sauté 2 minutes or until tender. Add bell pepper and next 3 ingredients, and cook 3 minutes or until bell pepper is tender, stirring occasionally. Stir in vinegar, ¼ teaspoon salt, and ⅛ teaspoon black pepper; cook 1 minute, stirring constantly. Spoon relish into a bowl. Wipe pan clean with a paper towel.
2. Combine remaining ½ teaspoon salt, remaining ⅛ teaspoon black pepper, and paprika; sprinkle evenly over pork. Coat pan with cooking spray. Add pork to pan, and cook 4 minutes on each side or until done. Serve with relish. Yield: 4 servings (serving size: 1 chop and about ⅓ cup relish).

CALORIES 263 (30% from fat); FAT 8.9g (sat 2.5g, mono 4.5g, poly 1.2g); PROTEIN 27.2g; CARB 19.8g; FIBER 1.4g; CHOL 62mg; IRON 1.6mg; SODIUM 508mg; CALC 39mg

Psychology

Kenneth Carter, PhD, ABPP
Professor of Psychology
Oxford College, Emory University
Oxford, Georgia

Colleen M. Seifert, PhD
Arthur F. Thurnau Professor of Psychology
University of Michigan
Ann Arbor, Michigan

Contributions by:
Jonna Kwiatkowski, PhD
Assistant Professor of Psychology
Mars Hill College
Mars Hill, North Carolina

JONES & BARTLETT
L E A R N I N G

World Headquarters
Jones & Bartlett Learning
5 Wall Street
Burlington, MA 01803
978-443-5000
info@jblearning.com
www.jblearning.com

Jones & Bartlett Learning books and products are available through most bookstores and online booksellers. To contact Jones & Bartlett Learning directly, call 800-832-0034, fax 978-443-8000, or visit our website, www.jblearning.com.

Substantial discounts on bulk quantities of Jones & Bartlett Learning publications are available to corporations, professional associations, and other qualified organizations. For details and specific discount information, contact the special sales department at Jones & Bartlett Learning via the above contact information or send an email to specialsales@jblearning.com.

Copyright © 2018 by Jones & Bartlett Learning, LLC, an Ascend Learning Company

All rights reserved. No part of the material protected by this copyright may be reproduced or utilized in any form, electronic or mechanical, including photocopying, recording, or by any information storage and retrieval system, without written permission from the copyright owner. Additional photo and illustration credits appear on pages 675-678 which constitute a continuation of the copyright page.

Learn Psychology, Revised First Edition is an independent publication and has not been authorized, sponsored, or otherwise approved by the owners of the trademarks or service marks referenced in this product. Some images in this book feature models. These models do not necessarily endorse, represent, or participate in the activities represented in the images.

Production Credits
Chief Executive Officer: Ty Field
President: James Homer
Senior Vice President: Eve Howard
SVP, Chief Marketing Officer: Alison M. Pendergast
VP, Production and Design: Anne Spencer
Senior Developmental Editor: William Wahlgren
Senior Editorial Assistant: Rainna Erikson
Reprints and Special Projects Manager: Susan Schultz
Associate Production Editor: Tina Chen
Production Assistant: Kristen Rogers
V.P., Manufacturing and Inventory Control: Therese Connell
Manufacturing and Inventory Control Supervisor: Amy Bacus
Rights and Photo Research Supervisor: Anna Genoese
Composition: diacriTech, Inc.
Text Design: Anne Spencer
Cover Design: Timothy Dziewit
Cover Image: © Sofia/ShutterStock, Inc.
Printing and Binding: RR Donnelley
Cover Printing: RR Donnelley

ISBN: 978-1-284-12484-2

The Library of Congress has cataloged the earlier printing as follows
Carter, Kenneth, 1967-
  Learn psychology / Kenneth Carter, Colleen M. Seifert.
    p. cm.
  Includes index.
  ISBN 978-0-7637-9898-7
1. Psychology. I. Seifert, Colleen M. II. Title.
  BF81.C33 2013
  150--dc23
                          2012005228
6048
Printed in the United States of America
20 19 18 17 16   10 9 8 7 6 5 4 3 2 1

Brief Contents

Contents

Contents

Contents

Welcome

Welcome to *Learn Psychology*! Our goal with *Learn Psychology* is to create content for introductory psychology that establishes a new paradigm for student-centered learning.

Learn Psychology is written with the 21st-century student in mind. We have developed a fresh presentation for introductory psychology that is highly interactive, compatible with digital applications, and cognizant of the challenges of an ever-evolving economic landscape. To us, the perfect textbook makes learners want to read it and presents everything they need to know in an easy-to-use format. That's what we've done with *Learn Psychology*. We have drawn on the best practices of educational pedagogy with a "learning by doing" approach that pairs critical analysis of psychological concepts with examples from everyday life and allows readers to actively engage with the curriculum.

About The Learn Series

Learn Psychology is the flagship publication of **The Learn Series**, a completely new course curriculum solution from Jones & Bartlett Learning that aims to provide a fresh, integrated print and digital program solution for general education survey courses. **The Learn Series** is produced with today's "digitally native" students in mind by re-envisioning the learning experience and focusing not just on *what* students learn but also *how* students learn. **The Learn Series** is characterized by authoritative and notable authors; visual, modular design; student-centered pedagogy; and integrated formative and summative assessments that improve learning outcomes—features that allow instructors to easily customize and personalize course curriculum. **The Learn Series** provides the most interactive and advanced curriculum solution for today's student-centered learning environments by emphasizing the skills students need to thrive in the 21st-century knowledge-based economy.

For more information on additional titles in the series, please visit www.TheLearnSeries.com.

Skills for the 21st-Century Workforce

	Sample 21st-Century Addressable Workforce Skills			Supporting Pedagogy in The *Learn Series*
RESEARCH LITERACY	Able to determine the extent of information needed	Able to evaluate information and its sources critically	Can apply evidence to new problem solutions	Group and individual projects Online writing tutorial included in Navigate
INTERPERSONAL COMMUNICATION & PUBLIC SPEAKING	Can convey ideas and meaning through oral communication	Able to speak persuasively in a group	Can effectively work in a team structure to solve problems	Group and individual projects Discussion questions Instructor's Resource Curriculum Guide with additional group projects and activities
PROBLEM SOLVING & CRITICAL ANALYSIS	Able to analyze data Able to synthesize different types of information	Able to evaluate source material for validity, etc.	Able to make decisions based on data	Critical Thinking Applications Short essay questions in Test Bank Interactive exercises in Navigate PAL Psychology
TECHNOLOGY LITERACY	Able to use the Internet critically	Able to retrieve and manage information via technology	Able to use basic word processing and spreadsheet software/tools	Navigate Learn Psychology Chapter Projects Online activities and assignments
WRITTEN COMMUNICATION	Able to organize and outline the main topics or thesis	Uses a variety of simple and complex sentences to create a fluid writing style	Able to write complete, grammatically correct sentences	Online Writing Tutorial included in Navigate Short Essay Questions in Assessment Banks

The Themes and Approach of *Learn Psychology*

The overarching definition of psychology is the science of behavior and mental processes, and the biological, experiential, and sociocultural factors that influence behavior. In *Learn Psychology*, we highlight the multiple influences that affect psychological phenomena. Within each chapter, we explain how biological factors (including genetics, neural processing, hormones, and evolution) combine with environmental factors (such as culture, social context, and experience) to influence psychology. We offer multiple levels of explanation to aid in understanding the "why" of psychology; that is, why do people behave they way they do? In order to understand psychological questions, we must explain the interplay of biological and environmental influences jointly at work in all human behavior.

Each chapter topic is explained in terms of the multiple influences on psychology and concludes with a thought-provoking summary that emphasizes these multiple influences. Learners will see this theme of "multiple influences on psychology" repeated throughout the text, continually underscoring the fact that human psychology has roots in biology, yet is driven by social and cultural context, and that these factors work in concert to explain psychological concepts and questions. Though the field is just beginning to explore how genes and environment interact in development, for example, *Learn Psychology* encourages students to consider multiple influences as explanations for any topic within psychology.

Throughout the book we also emphasize psychological science and explain the methods involved in research. We present state-of-the-art information on psychological topics and the supporting scientific evidence. What we know about psychological phenomena comes from these studies, so it is critical that students learn about the science and the methods. These research discussions require the learner to think critically about conclusions from empirical studies and how results can be applied to behavior in the real world. The scientific foundation includes both classic and recent studies to provide the most accurate, current, and comprehensive coverage possible.

The Structure of *Learn Psychology*

Learn Psychology helps optimize learning through enhanced coverage, study, testing, and review while emphasizing the "doing" that reinforces comprehension. Pedagogical features are designed to provide a preview of the material and ensure key concepts are well understood. Each chapter contains numbered sections, or modules, that address a major concept in the introductory psychology curriculum. These modules are self-contained key content units. Each module has associated learning objectives, preview statement, illustrations, concept learning check, and finally, a summary and test. This modular content unit structure informs the entire *Learn Psychology* program.

All of the content in *Learn Psychology* is highly visual, current, and easy to understand. Visual overviews play to dynamic learning and underscore important points. Our goal with *Learn Psychology* is to present accurate core content rooted in best-in-class pedagogy while avoiding distracting off-topic add-ons. The result is an introductory psychology curriculum that is engaging, consistent, and complete—and which helps students measure their progress at every step.

Learn Psychology is fully comprehensive and designed for cutting-edge coursework. By incorporating opportunities for active learning, Learn Psychology maximizes teaching productivity, enhances student learning, and addresses the challenges of teaching and learning introductory psychology in fresh, new ways.

Pedagogical Aids and Features

Learn Psychology is based on a modular concept format that provides a clear organization of the key topics pertaining to introductory psychology. With this modular format, digital versions of *Learn Psychology* are also fully customizable, allowing faculty full control over the desired curriculum. For more information on customization options, please visit the publisher website at www.jblearning.com.

This essential textbook covers more than 100 introductory psychology topics and divides them into modules linked with learning objectives, providing students with a structured road map for learning, reviewing, and self-assessment.

Every chapter in *Learn Psychology* is organized with the following structure to help learners engage with the concepts in the textbook as they read:

Chapter Sections

The modular format dictates that each chapter opens with a series of learning objectives, which reappear whenever a topic is repeated to help guide students' learning. Each chapter contains several numbered sections that address a major topic or concept; sections are largely self-contained units of content instruction. Any element or feature labeled with a section number reflects and is relevant to that section.

Chapter Overview

Content-specific chapter overviews provide a summary of key chapter concepts and serve as a "master plan" to visually show the scope and sequence of content covered. Students use the Chapter Overviews as a map, to guide them through critical concepts and keep them connected to learning objectives.

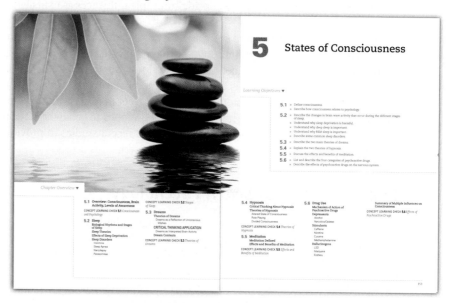

Section Preview Statement

Within each section, a preview statement summarizes the content of the section that follows. These preview statements prepare students for the content ahead, providing advance organization during reading.

14.1 Overview: Understanding Psychological Disorders

Psychologists use a number of different tools to diagnose and understand psychological disorders.

- Define psychological disorders as determined by the American Psychiatric Association (APA) and explain the criteria for abnormal behavior using the *Diagnostic and Statistical Manual of Mental Disorders*.

Figures and Tables

Figures and tables underscore key points or present complex information. They provide an effective alternative mode of instruction, presented schematically to aid the reader visually and reinforce the text. References to figures are in color to make it easier to locate the figure and pop right back into the reading.

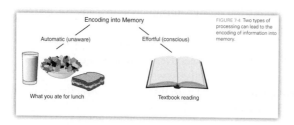

FIGURE 7-4 Two types of processing can lead to the encoding of information into memory.

TABLE 9-1 Psychological Theories of Intelligence

Theorist	Major Concept	Key Points
Charles Spearman (1904)	General intelligence	A single, general intelligence capacity ("g") is the source of all mental abilities
Louis Thurstone (1938)	Primary mental abilities	Discovered a set of seven different factors related to varied task scores
Raymond Cattell (1963)	Fluid and crystalized	Discovered just two underlying abilities: fluid intelligence and crystallized intelligence
Robert Sternberg (1985)	Triarchic theory	Broadened Cattell's concept into three categories of intelligence: analytic, creative, and practical
Howard Gardner (1983)	Multiple intelligences	Proposed a theory of seven separate intelligence abilities operating independently
Mayer, Salovey, Caruso, & Sitarenios (2001)	Emotional intelligence	The ability to perceive, understand, integrate, and regulate emotions to promote personal growth

Concept Learning Check

At the end of every section, a Concept Learning Check is presented to test mastery of the material in that section. These checks focus on "pain points" for students and provide extra coaching on the key concepts in the chapter. This gives learners a chance to apply what they have studied in fresh examples, or to see the material applied from a different perspective.

Critical Thinking Application

The Critical Thinking Applications within each chapter highlight a challenging or topical concept that asks learners to participate and demonstrate their understanding of the concepts.

Summary of Multiple Influences in the Chapter

The final section of each chapter ties together the discussion of biological and environmental factors affecting our psychology and highlights the multiple influences on the topic presented.

Chapter Key Terms

Key Terms appear in blue in the text at point of use and are defined in a way that doesn't interrupt the main idea of the sentence. Key terms are also provided in the margin with sharp definitions that can be used as flashcards. Key terms are also found as an alphabetical list at the very end of the chapter and in the final glossary.

Visual Overview

The Visual Overview provides a dynamic visual diagram of one or more key concepts and helps to tie chapter themes and segments into a cohesive whole.

Visual Summary

The Visual Summary is located at the end of the chapter and recaps the main ideas in each section using brief, bulleted sentences that are highlighted with an image that refers back to the section content.

Chapter Review Test

The Chapter Review Test is a multiple-choice self-quiz covering the entire chapter. Headings correlate to chapter sections as well as objective statements. Answers that provide complete rationales are also included.

Chapter Discussion Questions

Open-ended questions provoke thoughtful discussions in the classroom or in online discussion boards. These questions are carefully chosen to illuminate key concepts of the chapter and to create a constructive experience of discussion, evaluation, and comparison in order to solidify comprehension.

Chapter Projects

Potential projects for individuals, pairs, or small groups are suggested. These can be done either in class or outside of class. They focus on an issue related to students' lives and experience, real-world applications, or media depictions of psychological concepts.

Learn Psychology Digital Curriculum

Learn Psychology is a comprehensive and integrated print and digital solution for courses in introductory psychology. Instructors and students can use the following digital resources in part, or in whole:

Navigate Learn Psychology is a simple-to-use and fully customizable online learning platform combining authoritative content written by the authors of the main text with interactive tools, assessments, and robust reporting and grading functionality. Using content that extends the core text, including objectives organized by lesson, instructors can use Navigate Learn Psychology as part of an on-ground, online, or hybrid course offering requiring little to no start-up time.

PAL Psychology is a powerful new personalized adaptive learning (PAL) program that uniquely combines study planning, homework assignments, and assessment tools all in one easy-to-use application. PAL Psychology helps students study more efficiently so they can make the most of their study time.

For students who prefer electronic textbooks, *Learn Psychology* is also available in digital formats from leading ebook retailers such as Coursesmart, Amazon, and Google.

Learn Psychology Instructor Resource Program

Every element in the Instructor Resource Program maps to chapter and section-level learning objectives. Student learning outcomes are developed by the main authors of the core text ensuring quality and consistency throughout.

The Comprehensive Instructor Resource Program includes:

- **Instructor Resource Curriculum Guide** featuring chapter overviews, chapter outlines, suggested lectures, discussion questions, projects, handouts and media resources—all keyed to chapter section and learning objectives, when and where possible. Additionally, we also include a correlation grid connecting learning objectives to APA outcomes and selected 21st-century workforce skills.

- **Brownstone's *Diploma* Testing Software** with a comprehensive bank of test questions written by the main text authors. The complete bank includes over 160 Critical Thinking, Applied, and Factual questions per chapter, each tagged to chapter learning objectives and Bloom's Taxonomy. Questions can be sorted, selected, and edited based on level of difficulty or question type.

- **PowerPoint™ Presentation Slides** in multiple formats including PowerPoint with chapter images only; PowerPoint with chapter outlines and key narrative; and PowerPoint with outlines, key narrative, and images. All of the PowerPoint slide presentations are written by the main text authors and include references to supported chapter learning objectives.

- **Psychology Instructor Place** for online access to PowerPoints, Instructor Resource Curriculum Guide, APA correlation grid, 21st-century workforce correlation grid, discussion questions file, suggested student projects, video resources links, chapter-by-chapter media bibliography, and sample syllabi.

Contact your Jones & Bartlett Learning Account Representative for more details.

More Free Resources for Students To Support Basic Writing Skills:

A Writing Tutorial for College Students

The ability to organize and outline main topics and write complete, grammatically correct sentences is a critical skill for today's freshman-level student. Combining the best of English composition manuals and various open resources available online, *Learn Psychology* includes a specially developed free resource designed to help students improve basic writing skills, analyze resources on the web, and perform critical analysis of a topic.

The website, www.AWritingTutorialforCollegeStudents.com, distills the essential skills of writing into eight succinct modules:

1. Introduction to College Writing
2. Structure and Thesis Statements
3. Mechanics and Grammar
4. Research, Citation, and Avoiding Plagiarism
5. Making an Argument
6. The Research Paper
7. The Writing Process
8. Elegance and Style

About the Authors

Dr. Antone Minard, PhD

Dr. Minard earned his PhD from the University of California, Los Angeles. He currently resides in Vancouver, British Columbia, where he teaches in the Humanities Department at Simon Fraser University and in the Department of Classical, Near Eastern, and Religious Studies at the University of British Columbia.

Dr. Amy Hale, PhD

Dr. Hale earned her PhD from the University of California, Los Angeles, and teaches introductory students in a variety of courses, disciplines, and delivery systems emphasizing writing projects and assignments.

Acknowledgments

There is an art to aiding in the creation of a textbook like this one. It's an effort that involves encouragement, opportunity, support, and constructive criticism. There are dozens of people who have mastered this art and who made the completion of this project possible. We want to start by thanking Eve Howard, Senior Vice President at Jones & Bartlett Learning. Eve's vision has been the essence of this project, and she provided wonderful motivational speeches, mentorship, understanding, and advice. We would also like to thank our editor, Bill Wahlgren, for his tireless guidance with the manuscript and for his patience and gentility. Without the help extended by each of them, we would not have developed the skills necessary to carry out this project, nor would we have as deep an appreciation of the meaning of collaboration. A special thank-you to the friendly production experts at Jones & Bartlett Learning, including Susan Schultz, Anne Spencer, and Anna Genoese. We would like to especially thank our chief marketing strategist, Alison Pendergast.

Jonna Kwiatkowski of Mars Hill College expertly jumped in and assisted us with the discussion questions and projects at the end of the chapters, taking advantage of her experience with successful online class delivery, and with several of the ancillary elements of the *Learn Psychology* resources. Wendy Ludgewait also contributed to the development of the learning objectives and assessments and the lecture materials.

We also want to thank the reviewers of *Learn Psychology*, who took time out of their hectic schedules to pore over the drafts of the chapters. Your dedication, attention to detail, and expertise helped shape this text. We learned so much from each of you. Thank you!

In-Depth Psychology Faculty Reviewers

Laura Bailey, San Joaquin Valley College
Art Beaman, University of Kentucky
Janice Hartgrove-Freile, Lonestar Community College
John Haworth, Chattanooga State Community College
Linda Jackson, Michigan State University
Jim Johnson, Central New Mexico Community College
Kevin O'Neil, Florida Gulf Coast University
Catherine Snyder, Paradise Valley Community College
John Updegraff, Kent State University

In addition to the reviewers, special thanks to the many instructors who participated in our expanded review and market research, which aided us in rounding out the strategy for **The Learn Series**, as well as refining the pedagogy and chapters of *Learn Psychology*.

Psychology Faculty Analysts

Eric D. Miller, Kent State University
Javier Alonso, Oakton Community College
Jill Norvilitis, Buffalo State College
Richard Shadick, Pace University
Nancy Hartshorne, Delta College
Michelle Russell, University of Tennessee-Knoxville
Jamie Tanner, Valdosta State University
Christine Harrington, Middlesex County College
Dennis A. Gentry, University of Cincinnati Clermont
Cecile Marczinski, Northern Kentucky University
Kim Morris, Athens Technical College

Michael Davis, West Virginia Northern Community College
Steve Ellyson, Youngstown State University
Linda Bajdo, Macomb Community College
Peter Vernig, Suffolk University
Caroline Kozojed, Bismarck State College
Christopher J. Mruk, Bowling Green State University
Bob Reese, Jefferson College of Health Sciences
Amber Amspoker, University of Houston
Teri Fournier, Diablo Valley College

Sean Taylor, Des Moines Area Community College

Scot Hamilton, University of West Georgia

Kevin Kean, Central Connecticut State University

Michael Rader, Northern Arizona University

Jeffrey Green, Virginia Commonwealth University

Diane Reddy, University of Wisconsin-Milwaukee

Jeffrey Baker, Monroe Community College

Karla Lassonde, Minnesota State University, Mankato

Diane Pisacreta, Saint Louis Community College

David Gersh, Houston Community College—Central

Kelie Jones, Odessa College

Cari Cannon, Santiago Canyon College

Andrea Molarius, Shasta College

Ari Grayson, Scottsdale College

Robert Zettle, Wichita State University

Dr. Rebecca Fahrlander, University of Nebraska at Omaha

David Biek, Macon State College

Bonnie Gray, Scottsdale College

Brian Howland, University of Florida

Emily Stark, Minnesota State University, Mankato

Ryan Tapscott, Iowa State University

Mary Fraser, DeAnza College

Susie Sympson, Johnson County Community College

Mary-Ellen O'Sullivan, Housatonic Community College

Dr. Eva Szeli, Arizona State University

Michael Knepp, Mount Union

Karl L. Wuensch, East Carolina University

Barb Corbisier, Blinn College

Autumn Willard, St. Clair County Community College

Sarah Novak, Hofstra University

Lorry Cology, Owens Community College

Laura Jackman, Joliet Junior College

Melissa McCeney, Montgomery College

Jill Berger, Nova Southeastern University

Tamara Hodges, Baylor University

Amy Masnick, Hofstra University

Christine Lofgren, University of California Irvine

William Rick Fry, Youngstown State University

Michael Rader, Northern Arizona University

Aimee Callender, Auburn University

Chris Ruggiero, Tacoma Community College

Rick Howe, College of the Canyons

Finally, a very special thanks to my entire family and many friends, including Jennifer Thompson, Jack Hardy, Teddy Ottaviano, Sharon Lewis, and Susan Ashmore, for providing infinite patience, kindness, and food during adversity.
—Kenneth Carter

To my girls, Lynn Hillger, Julie Boland, and Kim Wheeler, for getting me through it; and my boys, Zeke and Victor Montalvo, for making me do it. I owe you.
—Colleen Seifert

About the Authors

Dr. Kenneth Carter received his PhD in Clinical Psychology from the University of Michigan, Ann Arbor, in 1993 and completed a postdoctoral Masters in clinical psychopharmacology at Fairleigh Dickinson University in 2007. Before joining the faculty at Emory University, Dr. Carter served as a Senior Assistant Research Scientist in the Epidemic Intelligence Service of the Centers for Disease Control and Prevention where he researched smoking as a risk marker for suicidal behaviors in adolescents. Currently he is a Professor of Psychology at Oxford College, Emory University, where he is actively involved in research and teaching. Dr. Carter has been a psychotherapist and researcher for more than 17 years. His work has garnered awards from the National Institutes of Health, the National Heart, Lung, and Blood Institute, and the University of Michigan. Dr. Carter is a past editor of *JCAL: The Journal of Cognitive-Affective Learning*. In addition to his own research, Dr. Carter authors articles in plain language on the latest research in psychology for magazines such as *mental_floss* and *Reader's Digest*, and for news programs such as *Connect With Kids* and NBC's *Today*.

Dr. Colleen Seifert received her BA in Psychology from Gustavus Adolphus College in St. Peter, Minnesota, in 1980, and her PhD in Psychology from Yale University in 1987. After a postdoctoral fellowship at the University of California at San Diego, Dr. Seifert moved to the University of Michigan, Ann Arbor, and was promoted to full Professor of Psychology in 2001. She was named Arthur F. Thurnau Professor of Psychology in 2011. Her research publications address thinking and memory, specifically, how the status and types of past experiences in memory affect current reasoning. Dr. Seifert's investigations are rooted in her interest in how people navigate through complex, real-world tasks, and her research examines planning and problem solving in the domains of legal reasoning, medicine, and creative design. She is a past President and Executive Officer of the Cognitive Science Society, past co-chair of the Institutional Review Board for the Behavioral Sciences at Michigan, and a member of several journal editorial boards.

Chapter Overview ▼

1 Psychology: An Overview

Learning Objectives ▼

1.1 ■ Define the science of psychology.

■ Distinguish between psychological science and popular misconceptions about psychology.

1.2 ■ Discuss the origins and history of psychology.

■ Examine the role of philosophy and physiology in the development of psychology.

■ Contrast structuralism and functionalism.

1.3 ■ Compare and contrast contemporary perspectives in psychology.

■ Describe focused specializations of research and practice.

1.4 ■ Examine the role of critical thinking in the field of psychology.

■ Illustrate the five criteria for critical thinking.

I am one of those people who always knew what I wanted to be when I grew up. Well, not always. It was around fifth grade that I stumbled upon psychology, and I knew that it was the career for me. Little did I know that I would spend the rest of my life as a psychologist and much of my social life preparing myself for a surprise each time someone discovered what I did for a living.

You see, when you are a psychologist, friends, family, and even strangers will bombard you with tons of questions about what kind of people are most compatible in a relationship and which antidepressants are best for poodles and what kind of person would keep a pet monkey and what it means when you dream about the ocean and . . . well, you get the point. Not just questions—theories, too: strange theories about behavior based on the tiniest sliver of psychology, theories based on flawed evidence, and, all too often, theories based on no evidence at all.

Psychology is a field that is vast, but not always in the ways that people think. Why are there so many questions and why so many theories? People have a natural curiosity about behavior and mental processes—a natural curiosity about psychology. But people do not always understand the difference between psychology and other ways to explain behavior. Such was the case back in graduate school one day as I was heading to campus on the shuttle. A fellow passenger noticed I was reading a book on relationships.

"Oh, you are a *psychologist*," she said, with the same kind of lilt in her voice as if I had told her I was going to school to be a pirate.

"Yes, I am just reading about a theory of relationships."

"Is it about Libras? What sign are you?"

"Oh . . . um . . . Well, you know that is astrolo—"

"I bet you are a Capricorn."

"Well, no . . . I am a Taurus."

"That is just what I thought. You are just like a Taurus. They taught you about that in grad school, right?"

"Well, no . . . nothing about Taurus. You see, that's astrolog—"

"They *didn't* teach you about personality? That's stupid. Every psychologist should know about personality."

"Oh . . . no, they did teach me about personality. I had several courses on personality theory, but horoscopes are not really psychology, that's really astrolo—"

"You do not know about personality? I cannot believe you do not know the personality of a Taurus. Exactly what do they teach you about psychology in grad school?"

"Well . . . they teach you science."

1.1 The Science of Psychology

Psychology is the scientific study of behavior and mental processes.

- Define the science of psychology.
- Distinguish between psychological science and popular misconceptions about psychology.

Tell someone you are studying psychology (go ahead—try it) and you are likely to hear some common reactions. Some people suppose you are interested in psychological disorders and may launch into a story about an uncle who collected lost keys or a friend who nibbles her food in careful counter-clockwise bites. Still others may abruptly silence themselves, admitting nervously that they fear that you are going to analyze them. Some might even huff and say that psychology is the science of the obvious. You see, misunderstandings about the field of psychology are deep and wide ranging. Often they are based on popular belief, media portrayals, or assumptions that have little or nothing to do with the science of psychology. **Psychology**, the scientific study of mental processes and behavior, is a fascinating science, and you have come to study it at a very good time. While people have pondered behavior and mental processes for ages, it is only fairly recently that we have examined them scientifically.

The word *psychology* comes from two Greek words: *psych* (meaning *mind*) and *logo* (*study*). The word *psychology* translates to *study of the mind*. Today, psychology has broadened its scope beyond the study of subjective experiences of the **mind** to answer a vast number of questions about mental processes and behavior. To name just a few: What is the best way to treat psychological conditions such as depression? How do children learn to speak? What causes us to fear or to love or to laugh? What motivates people to work hard in school and in their careers? How do we make meaning out of the sounds we hear and the things we see? How do we go about making sense of the world around us? The study of the mind is one of the most important sciences because it addresses something of natural interest to everyone who has a mind. It also offers essential insights into and understanding of what it means to be human.

If you think about it, we are all in the business of examining behavior and mental processes. After all, since we all have minds, we all know something about how they work. It is common to wonder about the attitudes and behavior of those around us, as well as our own. We try to behave appropriately (for the most part) in various situations, and often we try to influence the behavior of others. Some of us are known for understanding, and at times anticipating, the attitudes and behaviors of others. So how are psychologists any different?

Psychologists are different because they are scientists, and their work is based on scientific principles. **Science** is the operation of general laws, especially as obtained and tested through the scientific method. Wilson (1999) says that science "is the organized, systematic enterprise that gathers knowledge about the world and condenses this knowledge into testable laws and principles" (p. 58). Science emphasizes **empiricism**, or knowledge based on observation. We will discuss the principles of scientific study and the scientific method. We have a tremendous arsenal of methods that allow us to systematically

Psychology The scientific study of behavior and mental processes.

Mind Mental processes and our subjective experiences.

Science The operation of general laws, especially as obtained and tested through the scientific method.

Empiricism The theory of knowledge that assumes that knowledge should be based on observation.

THE FIRST CENTURY

of Psychological Science and Practice in America

Dr. Ludy T. Benjamin, Jr.

M	Movement or shift in field
F	Fields
E	Event/major meeting/ milestone
L	Legal or accreditation
P	Publication or new journal
S	Major study

1880s

M Child Study Movement began

M Psychology taught within traditional philosophy departments

E First American psychology laboratories: Johns Hopkins, Pennsylvania, Indiana, Wisconsin, Clark, Nebraska, Kansas

P Publication of George Trumbull Ladd's *Elements of Physiological Psychology* (1887)

P Founding of *American Journal of Psychology* (1887) by G. Stanley Hall

1890s

M Structuralism flourished under Titchener at Cornell University

M Beginnings of American functionalism and its conflict with structuralism

E Psychology laboratories founded at many universities including Columbia, Iowa, Michigan, Wellesley, Harvard, and Texas

E American Psychological Association formed in 1892 by G. Stanley Hall and others

P Coining of the term "mental test" in 1890 by James McKeen Cattell and development of anthropometric mental testing

P Publication of William James's *Principles of Psychology* (1890)

Empirical evidence A type of information that is capable of being confirmed or invalidated by systematic observation.

examine behavior and the psychological factors that drive it. Today's psychology is called psychological science at some universities in recognition of the rigor of its study. The science you will read about in *Learn Psychology* is based on solid, **empirical** observations that are repeatable.

A field of study that uses the scientific method to increase knowledge is a science. Legions of scientists, from astronomers to zoologists, use scientific methodology to investigate and improve our knowledge of the world around us and beyond. For example, physicists, geologists, and astronomers improve our understanding of the universe. Biologists and chemists study the origins of life, its endless variations, and, in medical science, the preservation of life and health in humans. The study of mental processes and human behavior is reserved for psychologists, using scientific methodology to improve our knowledge about *us*, making it one of the most vital, influential, and important sciences. In addition, psychologists are the only scientists who use the *subject* of their investigations—the mind—to *perform* their investigations. It is a unique challenge. As you will learn, designing and conducting experiments that reveal important insights about our mental processes and behavior is a demanding task. For some, it is a life's work. Clearly, this approach to understanding and at times anticipating the attitudes and behaviors of others is far removed from the intuitive "horse sense" that some people seem to have about others. Further, intuition resists explanation and cannot be taught. Often it is just plain wrong. Psychology, being based on scientific principles, welcomes analysis and criticism. Some of the experimental studies you will read about have been performed dozens of times over the years with dozens of different populations. Some of the general laws of psychology you will study may indeed be predictable, but many others are guaranteed to surprise you! We hope that this text engages you in learning about the many ways the science of psychology has advanced far beyond what we as individual "users" know about the mind.

Sometimes, however, the results of scientific inquiry are unsatisfactory. This may be due to our expectations: They may be unrealistic. For example, if you asked a biologist to tell you what a goby fish eats, I am certain that any ichthyologist, a biologist who studies fish, could spout off the favorite meals of the goby quite easily. If, however, I produced a goby from a bowl and asked an ichthyologist to tell you what this specific fish ate yesterday, you would have a different story. The sentences would be full of "probably" and "likely" meals for the fish. Science is pretty good at describing and predicting trends for larger groups, but the more specific you get, the more problems there are. Things get fuzzier the more specific your demands. It is the same for planets, plants, and people. Astronomy, too, is much better at explaining the general than the specific. We can say more confidently, for example, how planets come to be than how our planet, the Earth, came to be. And with psychology, we can say why some people may be shy, but not necessarily why any particular person is or may be shy. We can predict how aggressive people are based on the area of the country they live in (Cohen, Nisbett, Bowdle, & Schwarz, 1996), the temperature on a given day (Anderson & Anderson, 1984), the levels of the hormone testosterone in their saliva (Yu & Shi, 2009), and whether they have just won or lost a soccer game (Rascle et al., 2010). But we cannot predict whether a specific individual

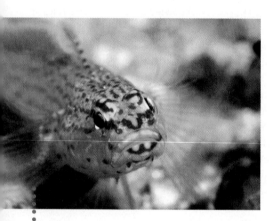

Figuring out what a species of fish eats is much easier than determining what a particular fish had to eat that day.

1890s *(Continued)*

M Edward Thorndike's pioneering work in animal learning

M Dominance of studies of sensation and perception in the study of human consciousness

E Joseph Jastrow organized psychology exhibition at the Chicago World's Fair (1893)

E Founding of the first psychological clinic at the University of Pennsylvania by Lightner Witmer (1896)

P Cattell bought *Science* magazine (1894)

S First study on the psychology of advertising by Harlow Gale (1895)

1900s

M Studies of learning became more prominent, especially animal learning

F Applied areas of study included: child development, educational psychology, abnormal psychology, mental testing

E First psychology laboratory in a mental hospital—McLean Hospital in Belmont, Massachusetts (1904)

P Publication of the four volumes of Titchener's *Experimental Psychology* ("The manuals") (1901–1905)

P First books on social psychology (1909)

M Founding of Titchener's Experimentalists (1904)

M Mental hygiene movement began (1908)

M Formalization of American functional psychology (functionalism) at the University of Chicago and Columbia University

E Sigmund Freud visited America for the Clark University 20th anniversary (1909)

L First eugenic sterilization law in Indiana (1907)

P New journals: *Journal of Philosophy, Psychology, and Scientific Method* (1903), *Psychological Bulletin* (1904), *Journal of Abnormal Psychology* (1906), *The Psychological Clinic* (1907)

will become a domestic abuser, even knowing his or her personal circumstances. It is understandable that this may be disappointing. After all, we are not interested in predictions of behaviors in general as much as we are interested in why people we know do—or do not do—certain things. The limits of prediction are a problem shared by all sciences.

Finally, it is important to recognize that not everything that sounds like science is science. Sometimes we come to believe things because they are dressed up as science. Information that appears scientific but is based on unsound scientific principles is **pseudoscience**. Pseudoscience that can seem somewhat scientific is often appealing. There are some famous examples of pseudoscience. Maybe you have a roommate who listens to classical music when he or she studies. Maybe you listen to it yourself. Take a moment to listen to some classical music. Do you feel yourself getting smarter? Does listening to classical music improve intelligence? Some people in Georgia thought so. They enlisted corporations to donate classical music recordings to expectant mothers. Do a quick search of the Internet for "Mozart effect" and I am sure you will locate dozens and dozens (and dozens) of websites that describe the connection between intelligence and classical music.

A peek into the original study reveals some surprising findings (Rauscher, Shaw, & Ky, 1993). The researchers examined the effect of listening to classical music—namely the first few minutes of "Mozart Sonata for 2 Pianos in D Major"—on a few dozen college students. The researchers found a temporary increase in spatial–temporal reasoning on an IQ test. Since that time, many people have tried, but no one has ever been successful at duplicating the results of the study (Pietschnig, Voracek, & Formann, 2010).

The greatest difficulty in the study of psychology is the vast number of topics that fall under its purview. Everything we do involves our mental processes in some way, so the behaviors of interest include a wide range of topics, from marriage proposals to Google circles. The only limitation to the study of human behavior is figuring out a method for observing it. In this text, we will examine some of the important topics in psychology and introduce you to them. It is a daunting task, nearly like showing a friend your favorite sites on the Internet in only a few moments. We have tried to highlight the most important research findings, the "greatest hits," and the hottest new science, all of which reveal important principles and insights about mental processes and human behavior.

Does listening to Mozart make you smarter? Some researchers thought so. Then their results sparked a pseudoscience theory called the Mozart effect.

Pseudoscience Information that appears scientific but is based on unsound scientific principles.

CONCEPT LEARNING CHECK 1.1　　　*The Scope and Limits of the Science of Psychology*

1. Wilson just read in his psychology text that most people require 8 hours of sleep to be rested, but he feels rested after only sleeping 5. Wilson now believes that the sleep researcher must be wrong. How would you respond to Wilson's claim?

2. Make a list of some topics you are excited to learn about in psychology. Use the table of contents and the index to map out where the topics might appear. Do not be surprised if you find topics in many locations.

1910s

M Rapid growth of industrial psychology

E World War I provided a significant impetus to applied psychology, particularly mental testing and abnormal psychology

E Psychologists were stationed at 40 Army hospitals during the war

E New York Psychoanalytic Society (1911), American Psychoanalytic Association (1911)

P Watson published his behaviorist manifesto (1913)

P New journals: *Journal of Educational Psychology* (1910), *Psychoanalytic Review* (1913), *Journal of Experimental Psychology* (1916), *Journal of Applied Psychology* (1917)

E First internships in psychology were begun at the Boston Psychopathic Hospital under Robert Yerkes (1912)

E Founding of American Association of Clinical Psychologists (1917)

S Research on the nature and origin of sex differences; early work on the psychology of women

P Lewis Terman's version of Binet scale, the Stanford-Binet (1917)

1920s

M Decade of greatest popularity of psychology with the public

M Gestalt psychology ideas crossed the Atlantic

M Structuralism disappeared after the death of Titchener in 1927

L APA established a certification program for consulting psychologists

E Francis Cecil Sumner is first African-American PhD in psychology (1920)

E American Vocational Guidance Association (1921)

P Appearance of several American popular psychology magazines

1.2 The Origins and History of Psychology

Psychology has roots in other disciplines such as philosophy and biology that have influenced both early and contemporary perspectives in psychology.

- Discuss the origins and history of psychology.
- Examine the role of philosophy and physiology in the development of psychology.
- Contrast structuralism and functionalism.

If you wanted to study psychology in, say, the late 1700s, you were pretty much out of luck. Psychology had not grown into its own discipline yet. It was the realm of thinkers in philosophy and biology. Philosophers were interested in what it means to be human, so they began studying the mind, or our subjective experience. Biologists, on the other hand, were busy studying our organs, including the brain. It would not be until much later that *psychological scientists* would emerge to construct a scientific approach to behavior and mental processes.

How did psychology emerge from the fringes of philosophy and biology to become one of the most popular sciences of the 21st century FIGURE 1-1? Changes in psychology were, in part, the result of debates among the early schools of psychology that turned the young discipline to science in order to answer questions about the structure and function of behavior and mental processes. Psychology as an independent discipline did not emerge until the late 19th century (around the time of the invention of the first cash register, blue jeans, and the electric light bulb).

FIGURE 1-1 Psychology has become one of the most popular undergraduate degrees.
Source: Data from Monitor on Psychology, *June 2008, Vol. 39, No. 6.*

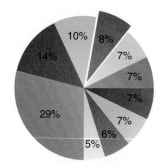

- ■ Business 311,600
- ■ Education 105,500
- ▨ Visual and performing arts 81,000
- ■ Health professions and related clinical sciences 80,700
- ■ Engineering and engineering technologies 78,600
- ▨ Communications, journalism, and related programs 72,700
- ■ Biological and biomedical sciences 64,600
- ▨ Computer and information sciences 54,100
- ■ Social sciences and history 156,900
- ■ Psychology 85,600

1920s *(Continued)*

M Debates over nature-nurture

M Child Guidance Movement began

M Behaviorism became dominant system of psychology

E The Psychological Corporation (1921)

E Ninth International Congress of Psychology—Yale University (1929),

E Psi Chi (1929)

P Rorschach Test (1921), teaching machine (1924), Draw-a-Man Test (1926)

P First textbooks published on the history of psychology (1929)

1930s

M Emphasis on operationism and operational definitions

M Growth of projective testing

M Decade for grand theories of personality (Allport, Murray)

E Association for Consulting Psychologists (1930); Society for Research in Child Development (1933); Society for the Psychological Study of Social Issues (1936); American Association for Applied Psychology (1937)

S Kelloggs' ape and child study (1931; Psychometric Society (1935)

P Thematic Apperception Test (1935)

M Beginning of neobehaviorism (Tolman, Hull, Guthrie, Skinner)

M Beginnings of differential academic training for experimental and clinical psychologists

M Large influx of emigre psychologists from Europe, especially Germany and Austria

E Inez Beverly Prosser—first African-American woman PhD in psychology (1933)

E Boder's Psychological Museum in Chicago (1937)

P Psychological Round Table (1936)

P *Journal of Consulting Psychology* (1937); *Journal of Parapsychology* (1938)

Philosophical Roots

What motivates human behavior? What determines our personality? Psychologists certainly were not the first people to consider questions such as these: Psychology has deep roots in **philosophy**, the study of knowledge and existence, which has long considered what motivates behavior. For example, Aristotle (BCE 384–322) FIGURE 1-2 contemplated the connection of the body and soul (Benjamin, 2008). Ancient philosophers like Plato and Aristotle and even William Shakespeare and Descartes considered many of the same things that psychologists are working on today.

Biological Roots

Psychology also has roots in other sciences. **Physiology**, a branch of biology that studies internal biological processes, has focused attention on the link between the brain and human behavior. In fact, it has only been recently that the biologists and other scientists linked the brain with behavior and personality. Even today, many people point to their chest or heart when they refer to themselves rather to their head or brain. In many cultures, the "me spot" is the heart rather than the head. Ancient Greek physiologists discovered, for example, that damage to one area of the brain created problems in certain parts of the body. The ancient Greek physician Hippocrates (BCE 460–370) FIGURE 1-3 noticed that when people suffered head injuries, their behavior changed, and he surmised that the brain was linked to behavior. Seventeenth-century philosopher and physician John Locke (1632–1704)

Although we currently see the source of our consciousness as the brain. We still point to our heart when talking about ourselves.

Philosophy The study of knowledge and existence.

Physiology A branch of biology that studies internal biological processes.

FIGURE 1-2 Philosophers such as Aristotle pondered many of the same questions that psychologists do today.

FIGURE 1-3 Considered the founder of medicine, Hippocrates considered many questions about behavior and mental processes.

1940s

M Boulder Conference established scientist/practitioner model of training for clinical psychologists (1949)

E Psychologists contributions to World War II: selection of personnel, training, design of equipment, psychological warfare, therapy for victims, etc.

E National Council of Women Psychologists (1941)

L First state psychology licensure law, Connecticut (1945)

P MMPI (1942)

P Strong Vocational Interest Blank (1943)

M Joint APA/VA program to establish accreditation of clinical psychology programs developed (1946)

E New APA formed by merger of several groups (particularly AAAP). Central Office established in Washington, DC (1945)

L National Mental Health Act (1946)

E Educational Testing Service (1947)

E National Institute of Mental Health (1949)

P *American Psychologist* (1946)

S Egas Moniz won the Nobel Prize for work that led to prefrontal lobotomies (1949)

1950s

M Emphases on human factors, physiological psychology, development across the lifespan, scientific method, statistics

M Modern cognitive psychology began

F New fields: space psychology, psychopharmacology, use of computers

L APA began accreditation of counseling psychology doctoral programs (1951)

P First DSM (1952)

P Publication of first APA code of ethics (1953)

S Evelyn Hooker published research that de-pathologized homosexuality (1957)

FIGURE 1-4 suggested that our minds link together ideas that come from the things we see, feel, and experience. Biologists interested in behavior brought with them a set of tools to study biology and behavior: scientific thinking and the scientific method.

Schools of Thought: Structuralism vs. Functionalism

Psychology did not emerge from philosophy and physiology whole and exactly as it is today. Like all sciences, psychology has been shaped by events, reactions, and trends. These influences, including important early thinkers in the field, not only shaped early psychology but also continue to affect contemporary approaches to psychology.

Structuralism

> **Structuralism** The school of psychology that studies human experience by breaking it down into smaller pieces.

The school of **structuralism** studies human experience by breaking it down into smaller pieces. Just as our physical world is made of elements such as iron, copper, and zinc, our mental world, structuralists assumed, was also made of mental elements or structures. The school of structuralism focused on determining just what these mental structures are. Structuralists like Edward B. Titchener and Wilhelm Wundt FIGURE 1-5 suggested that the key to determining mental structures would be to deconstruct human experience by recording the components of an experience, sort of like how you can describe a yummy meal by describing the flavor profiles in a new dish.

FIGURE 1-4 John Locke was an English philosopher who suggested that the mind was a blank slate at birth and knowledge was written on it by our experiences.

FIGURE 1-5 Wilhelm Wundt is often called the founder of modern psychology.

1950s *(Continued)*

M First professional school of psychology: Adelphi University

M Social psychology gained in prominence, perhaps because of psychology's role in 1954 Supreme Court Decision on desegregation, Brown vs. Board of Education

E National Science Foundation (1950), Human Resources Research Organization (1951), Nebraska Symposium on Motivation (1953)

L APA Approved Internships (1956)

L National Defense Education Act (1958)

P *Journal of Counseling Psychology* (1954)

P Wechsler Adult Intelligence Scale (1955)

1960s

M American discovery of Piagetian ideas, especially in education

M Major growth of cognitive psychology (Neisser, Bruner, Simon)

M Humanistic psychology began

E Rogers-Skinner Debate (1962)

L President Kennedy signed the Community Mental Health Centers Act (1963) that called for prevention, community based treatment, and deinstitutionalization

P History of psychology became a specialty field: Archives of the History of American Psychology founded at University of Akron (1965)

M Academic psychology flourished with excellent financial support from business and government

M B. F. Skinner's ideas achieved prominence via applications in education and clinical psychology

L Majority of states passed laws for licensure of psychologists, a process completed in the 1970s

L Texas licensure law (1969)

P *Journal of Humanistic Psychology* (1961)

P DSM-II (1968)

The first laboratory to focus on such studies was founded in 1879 at the University of Leipzig in Germany. The creation of this laboratory by Wilhelm Wundt is sometimes considered the founding of psychology (Benjamin, 2008). Wundt and his colleagues used a technique called introspection to examine the internal components of experience. **Introspection** means "looking inward," and it is a technique used to study subjective experiences such as one's own mental and emotional processes. For example, when you eat a strawberry, what is your experience? A participant would be given a strawberry and asked to speak aloud while eating it: "I am experiencing a feeling of coolness, now tartness . . . Not very sweet . . ." Introspection focuses on what people can report from their experiences. Wundt and his colleagues would, for example, play a trumpet sound and ask the participants to explain their reactions: What did it sound like, how did you feel when you heard it?

The problem—and strength—of introspection is its reliance on subjective experience. Introspection is highly individualized, and the same stimulus can result in varied reactions from different people. If 100 people eat mangoes, each may focus on different components of the experience. What is more, there was no way for the structuralists to sort out how many of these differences are important. No two people would reach the same result following this introspective method. As a result, structuralism proved too messy, and over time, new ways to examine experience were developed.

Today, some researchers use introspective activities such as a "think aloud" protocol in order to peer into the subjective aspects of conscious activities (e.g., Fonteyn, Kuipers, & Grobe, 1993). Introspective activities are useful when researchers want to explore the process of what a person is doing as he or she is doing it. People often report things differently in retrospect because they may not realize what they did. Asking them to report what they do as they are doing it provides a better look at the experience. Critics of introspection say that the technique is unscientific and relies too much on **anecdotal evidence**, or unscientific observation.

Introspection Examination of one's own mental and emotional processes.
Anecdotal evidence A type of information that relies on unscientific observation.
Functionalism A school of psychology concerned with the purposes of behavior and mental processes.

Functionalism

The school of structuralism defined early psychology but gave way in the early 1900s to a new school called functionalism. While structuralism attempted to break down the elements of experience, **functionalism** was concerned with the purposes of behavior and mental processes. William James (1842–1910) FIGURE 1-6, an early functionalist, was inspired by Charles Darwin's (1809–1882) FIGURE 1-7 work on finding meaning behind the behaviors and physical structures of animals. Darwin inspired biologists not only to describe but also to explain why animals have certain biological structures. The goal of structuralism was not simply to identify a structure but also to describe how aspects of the structure increased the likelihood of survival. Functionalists were interested in how behavior functions to adapt to the environment.

FIGURE 1-6 William James.

1970s

M Behavior modification movement

F Formation of first free-standing schools of professional psychology: California School of Professional Psychology

E National Institute of Child Health and Human Development (1963); North American Society for the Psychology of Sport and Physical Activity (1967); Association of Black Psychologists (1968)

S Roger Sperry did initial psychological research on split-brain patients and hemispheric specialization (Nobel Prize 1981)

M Debate over professional training models led to Vail Conference (1974) and development of the Doctorate of Psychology (PsyD); subsequent growth of professional schools

M Heavy government funding of research on alcoholism and drug abuse

L APA began accreditation of school psychology doctoral programs (1970)

P *Cognitive Psychology* (1970)

P *APA Monitor* (1971)

M Government interest in rural mental health care, geropsychology, substance abuse

M Organizational issues achieved prominence in forming industrial/organizational psychology

E Association of Psychologists Por La Raza (1970), became National Hispanic Psychological Association in 1979

P Skinner published *Beyond Freedom and Dignity* (1971)

FIGURE 1-7 Charles Darwin.

William James wanted the field of psychology to examine how people change as a result of their environment. He thought that consciousness, for example, must benefit survival, or it would not exist. To him, that meant that a way to study how consciousness helps us in the world was needed. James believed that consciousness shifts too continually to be studied in the way that the structuralists suggested. Instead, James was inspired to study the "stream of consciousness," because he thought that a constantly shifting consciousness could not be reduced to elements. Because structure and function always go together, James believed that it did not make sense to separate the two. Functionalism brought psychology out of the laboratory and into the real world, attempting to explain how organisms adapt within their environments.

Functionalism was important because it marked the evolution from a focus on subjectivity to an objective study of behavior and mental processes. It led the way for psychologists who later emphasized the importance of empiricism, the theory of knowledge based on observation.

Although structuralism and functionalism are no longer active schools of contemporary psychology, elements of both structuralism and functionalism can be seen in contemporary schools of psychology.

CONCEPT LEARNING CHECK 1.2   *Comparing and Contrasting Structuralism and Functionalism*

Compare and contrast the ways that a structuralist and a functionalist might study the taste of spoiled milk.

1. Structuralist:

2. Functionalist:

1970s *(Continued)*

M Increased Federal Government funding of programs to recruit and train ethnic minorities as psychologists

M Reduction of Federal Government role in training of psychologists, first by the VA, then by NIMH

E Asian American Psychology Association (1972); Society of Indian Psychologists (1973); DSM-III (1973); National Institute on Drug Abuse (1974); National Institute on Alcohol Abuse and Alcoholism (1974); Minority Fellowship Program (1974); Hispanic Journal of Behavioral Sciences (1979)

1980s

F The term psychology dropped from some field names to reflect their interdisciplinary nature, e.g., behavioral neuroscience, cognitive science

E Scientists left APA to form American Psychological Society (1988)

E National conference on psychology and aging held in Boulder, Colorado (1981)

E American Psychological Association of Graduate Students (1988)

E Roger Sperry, David Hubel, and Torsten Wiesel, Nobel Prize 1981

P *Psychology and Aging* (1986); *Journal of Family Psychology* (1987)

1990s

M Managed care altered nature of psychotherapy, significantly reduced insurance coverage of mental health

M Psychologists lobby for prescription privileges

F Executive coaching

E Psychology Exhibition at the Ontario Science Center (1991)

E Teachers of Psychology in the Secondary Schools (1992)

P Advanced Placement Psychology Exam (1992)

1.3 Contemporary Psychology

Contemporary perspectives in psychology offer specialized ways to study behavior and mental processes.

- Compare and contrast contemporary perspectives in psychology.
- Describe focused specializations of research and practice.

People are complex—so complex that there is no single perspective that all psychologists use to describe, examine, explain, and predict behavior and mental processes. Those looking for one simple solution will be disappointed because there *is* no one correct perspective. Instead, interactions of multiple perspectives are required in order to capture the richness of the influences on human behavior. Each perspective will focus on different questions and offer different ways to examine human behavior and mental processes. Perspectives in psychology continue to evolve, and you may even notice overlap in the perspectives.

Each school of psychology focuses on a single approach for behavior and mental processes, which may exclude others that are equally valid. The **eclectic model**, however, pulls together multiple ways of examining a particular problem or question. For example, the **biopsychosocial approach** recognizes three equally important aspects of human mental processes and behavior: biological, psychological, and social. We can use different **levels of analysis** to focus our attention on a part of the story and then step back and appreciate the multiple influences. Let us consider aggression. A biological approach might suggest that aggression is related to the amount of testosterone in the system (Yu & Shi, 2009). However, we also know that culture can influence violence as well (Cohen et al., 1996). What is more, there are studies that suggest that experiential factors such as learning can increase or decrease aggression, too (Rascle et al., 2010). The complex layers of influence are best appreciated when combined to examine how they interact. No one perspective provides the one and only answer, however. Each one focuses on different aspects of behavior and mental processes. A single perspective is very likely incomplete; it may take several overlapping perspectives to get a three-dimensional picture of mental and behavioral processes. **TABLE 1-1** summarizes some of the main research specialties in psychology and the proportion of psychological research that takes place in that area.

Eclectic model An approach that pulls together multiple ways of examining a particular problem or question

Biopsychosocial approach A theory that recognizes three equally important aspects of human mental processes and behavior: biological, psychological, and social.

Levels of analysis Various ways of examining the same psychological phenomenon.

TABLE 1-1 Some of the Research Subfields in Psychology

Percentage	Area	What They Do	Chapter References
36	Clinical	Researches, evaluates, and treats psychological conditions.	14 15
11	Counseling	Helps people achieve greater well-being when they are experiencing difficulty adjusting to life stressors.	14 15
3	Industrial/Organizational	Researches, evaluates, and helps to shape business, employees, and their products.	10
8	Education/School	Researches and evaluates teaching and learning practices and techniques	7
16	Generalist	Crosses the boundaries of many subfields of psychology and integrates research in several areas.	All
3	Psychobiology and comparative	Investigates the physiological processes of behavior and mental processes of humans and other animals	3, 4, 10
6	Developmental	Studies the cognitive, social, and biological changes that emerge with growth over time.	10
3	Cognitive	Examines thinking processes, including knowing, remembering, reasoning, deciding, and communicating.	4

(continues)

Neuroscience The study of the brain and nervous system; also called biological psychology.

Positron emission tomography (PET) A neuroscience imaging technique that uses radioactive glucose to indicate areas of activity.

Functional magnetic resonance imaging (fMRI) Neuroscience imaging technique used to measure changes in blood flow.

Evolutionary psychology A branch of psychology that examines the impact of natural selection on behavioral and mental processes.

Natural selection Varying success in reproduction resulting from the interaction of an organism with the environment.

TABLE 1-1 Some of the Research Subfields in Psychology *(continued)*

Percentage	Area	What They Do	Chapter References
8	Social/Personality	Social psychologist: Studies how the way people think, feel, and behave influences and is influenced by others Personality psychologist: Studies the patterns in the way people think, feel, and behave.	13, 16
2	Experimental	Conducts methods to investigate behavior and mental processes; works closely with professionals in other subfields.	2, 4
1	Health	Researches how psychological factors impact wellness, illness, and medical treatments.	11
1	Forensic	Applies psychological research to the criminal justice system.	16

Source: Data from 2009 Doctorate Employment Survey, APA Center for Workforce Studies. March 2011.

Neurons are the basic building block of the human nervous system.

FIGURE 1-8 MRIs map out brain activity.

The Biological Perspective

The biological perspective examines how physiology connects with the environment to create behavior and mental processes. **Neuroscience**, also called biological psychology, is the branch of psychology that studies the connection between behavior and the body, brain, and nervous system. Neuroscientists help us understand how the brain processes thoughts and emotions, helping to link the physical body with explanations for behavior on many different levels. How are emotions linked to the physical sensations in your body? Neuroscience examines questions like these at the molecular, cellular, organ, and system levels.

While the structuralists had only the tool of introspection, the biological perspective uses a variety of research approaches, including the study of genetics, activity of individual brain cells, and patterns of activation across the brain over time. This is made possible through new tools such as complex imaging techniques, including positron emission tomography and functional magnetic resonance imaging. **Positron emission tomography (PET)** is a neuroscience imaging technique that uses radioactive glucose to indicate areas of activity in the brain, and **functional magnetic resonance imaging (fMRI)** is a noninvasive brain imaging technique that uses powerful magnets and radio equipment to produce detailed images of the soft tissue in your brain. It is particularly useful because it can be used to examine brain activity over time FIGURE 1-8. Along with older techniques such as EEG (electroencephalography) FIGURE 1-9 and FIGURE 1-10, new techniques include MEG (magnetoencephalography), a technique for recording electrical signals from the brain based on changes in magnetic fields.

The Evolutionary Perspective

Evolutionary psychology is a branch of psychology that examines the impact of natural selection on behavioral and mental processes. According to the evolutionary perspective, our behaviors and mental processes are influenced, in part, by information inherited biologically. Influenced by Charles Darwin and the functionalists, evolutionary psychologists assume that behaviors and mental processes must benefit survival. According to **natural selection**, success in reproduction varies depending on the interaction of an organism with the environment. Those with certain behaviors live longer and pass those genes to future generations.

Evolutionary psychologists study **heritability**, or how much of a characteristic can be linked to genetics as opposed to the environment.

How much is intelligence, depression, or personality influenced by your genes as opposed to the environment? The perspective of evolutionary psychology is important because everything in the body—brain structures, hormones, fingers, and toes—are all mapped out by DNA FIGURE 1-11. In addition, comparative psychology studies behavior in other animals as models for our own evolutionary selection. Hoarding behavior in field mice may help us to understand people who save old newspapers, and topics like monogamy and tool use have been studied in animal groups in the wild.

The Psychodynamic Perspective

According to the psychoanalytic perspective, unconscious processes determine your behavior. **Psychoanalytic theory** is a family of theories originated by Sigmund Freud that focus on unconscious motivation and the expression of personality. According to the psychoanalytic perspective, **unconscious**

FIGURE 1-9 The EEG is a noninvasive way to measure electrical activity in the brain.

processes outside of your awareness determine your personality. Before Freud, no one considered that the reasons for one's behavior might not be obvious. But now, this idea is pervasive in everyday thought. You may have heard someone say, "He is in *denial!*" Or, "She is a little *anal* about keeping her room clean." How about, "He tried to hide it, but it *slipped* out." All of these expressions come from Freud's theories. His psychoanalytic approach emphasizes the study of unconscious conflicts that shape behavior. In psychoanalysis, our dreams' hidden meanings and our contradictory actions are studied to reveal our hidden motives.

FIGURE 1-10 EEG patterns map out electrical activity in the brain.

Heritability How much of a characteristic can be linked to genetics as opposed to the environment.

Psychoanalytic theory A family of theories originated by Freud that focuses on unconscious motivation.

Unconscious According to Freud, thoughts, memories, feelings, and wishes that reside outside of awareness.

Imagine someone named Zeke on the day that he opens his new comic book shop to the public. After weeks of stocking his store and months of planning, the big day arrived, and Zeke talked about how excited he was to finally open its door. That morning, he loaded up his car in the driveway and ran back into his house to pick up one more thing. When he came out, he discovered his car running, with all of the doors locked and windows up. He had no spare key, and his roommate was 2 hours away at school; by the time he arrived, Zeke's car had run out of gas. How did Zeke end up 4 hours late for the biggest day of his career? Freud would say Zeke had conflicting feelings that morning. Of course, he was genuinely excited to open his store but perhaps also terrified of failing. While Zeke was not aware of any conflict, his actions gave him away: After all, he had never before or since locked his keys in his running car.

The psychoanalytic school studies topics such as the meaning behind our dreams and the nature of personality. It also posits that the way to change people's behavior is to

FIGURE 1-11 The biological perspective suggests that physiology and our DNA can influence behavior and mental processes.

Sigmund Freud (1856–1939)
is the founder of the
psychodynamic perspective
in psychology and is often
considered the founder of the
first well-organized theory of
personality.

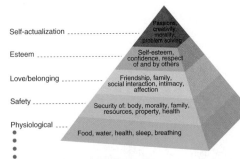

B. F. Skinner (1904–1990), a
major figure in the behavioral
perspective, examined learning
in several species of animals.

Humanists such as Abraham
Maslow suggested that we
are motivated to become good
people. Maslow suggested
these motivations are in
a hierarchy, from basic
physiological needs to
self-fulfillment needs.

understand the conflicting emotions that underlie it. Psychoanalysis relies on the "talking cure," in which a client sees a therapist regularly to talk about his or her concerns and to attempt to understand his or her inner conflicts. Though there are many criticisms of the psychoanalytic perspective, it remains a major force in psychology.

The Behavioral Perspective

Behaviorism, the study of learning based on directly observable actions, was founded by John Watson in 1913. The behavioral perspective suggests that instead of focusing on subjective experiences such as introspection, psychology should emphasize the study of objective behaviors. Behaviorism sought to predict and control behavior and to find a few simple rules for understanding behavior. The behavioral perspective explores the relationship between biological and environmental influences that allow us to learn or change through our experiences. Radical behaviorists were galled at the introspective techniques of the early structuralists and argued that we cannot know what is inside the mind. They proposed that psychologists should study only what is directly observable by others: behaviors in the world. This was, they argued, the best way to make psychology more scientific—by focusing on objective evidence.

The behavioral perspective examines such things as how we learn from the world around us and how we change what we do in response to expected outcomes.

The Humanistic Perspective

According to the **humanistic perspective**, personality, behavior, and mental processes are influenced by an innate capacity for personal growth. The humanists believed that the psychoanalytic and behavioral approaches were too deterministic. The psychoanalytic approach focused on internal, unconscious forces while the behavioral approaches emphasized the external environment. The psychoanalytic and behavioral approaches suggested that humans were at the will of something often too powerful for them to control—either internal drives or external circumstances. The humanistic approach emphasized free will and the pursuit of the best version of ourselves that we can be. Humanists such as Carl Rogers and Abraham Maslow value subjective reality and the importance of human potential.

Humanism's focus can be seen in **positive psychology**, a branch of psychology that emphasizes the constructive features of human strength and healthy living rather than sickness and pathology. Researchers in positive psychology examine human hardiness, optimism, and resilience.

The Cognitive Perspective

The cognitive perspective in psychology emphasizes the internal processes of thought that help us make sense of the world. **Cognition** encompasses all aspects of thinking, including knowing, remembering, reasoning, deciding, and communicating. In addition, the cognitive perspective studies our shortcuts in thinking and the biases and errors that can come from them. Cognitive psychologists study decision-making processes of both slow, deliberative decisions (like choosing the best car you can afford) as well as quick, intuitive choices when we make a snap judgment using our "gut."

Cognitive psychology really took off back in World War II. Knowing how people process and interpret information made psychologists a valuable resource as they helped to design cockpit displays that allowed pilots to recognize and use information from their displays efficiently. Today, cognitive psychologists continue to be interested in questions of internal thought and **cognitive neuroscientists** study brain action linked to thought, perception, and language.

The Sociocultural Perspective

The **sociocultural perspective** (featured throughout *Learn Psychology*) emphasizes the way that social and cultural elements in the world (or environment) influence behavior and mental processes. **Social psychology** is the branch of psychology that focuses on how our thoughts, feelings, and behaviors influence and are influenced by others. The sociocultural perspective helps to make psychology more representative of various cultures and to disrupt the belief that one group is superior to others and the standard by which others are judged, a reflection of **ethnocentrism**.

The sociocultural perspective includes social psychology and cultural psychology, which emphasizes the examination of differences in cultural values and norms. Social and cultural psychology examine the ways that people affect each other (Peplau & Taylor, 1997). **Cross-cultural psychology** examines and compares behaviors and mental processes between different cultures, which helps highlight the various influences of culture. The sociocultural perspective suggests that you cannot really understand behavior in the absence of a person's cultural and social context.

The sociocultural perspective has grown in the United States as the country and psychology have become more diverse. By 2050, ethnic minorities will represent nearly half of the U.S. population (U.S. Census Bureau, 2011). Women now earn three out of four doctorate and undergraduate degrees in psychology (Willard, 2011). It was not always this way. Back in 1895, Mary Calkins (1863–1930) completed all the requirements for a PhD in psychology from Harvard University and had the full support of her committee to earn the degree. But Harvard refused to grant her the degree because, at the time, women were not allowed to earn degrees from Harvard. Calkins was offered a degree from Harvard's sister school, Radcliffe, but she refused it. That did not hold her back. She later became the president of the American Psychological Association. Pioneers like Francis Cecil Sumner (1914–2005), who was the first African American granted a PhD in psychology at Clark University, and contemporary psychological scientists such as Claude Steele have broadened psychology to examine the impact of ethnicity on the individual. The sociocultural perspective is useful because it helps to describe the range of similarities and differences we see in people across the globe.

Professional Specialization and Research Areas in Psychology

The field of psychology is massive. No psychologist can study everything; therefore, many specialize in a particular subfield of psychology. You can take courses that will broaden and deepen your understanding of these topics, and in fact, universities offer doctoral degrees in the subjects of many of the chapters and topics in this book. Some psychological subfields do **basic research**, meaning that the research is driven by the quest for fundamental understanding of the concepts and the theories behind them. Basic research is concerned with expanding knowledge, even if the knowledge has no practical application. Other psychological research is **applied research**, or driven by a need to solve a specific problem. Basic and applied research interact with each other. Often, a psychologist may pursue a research topic in order to get to the bottom of a certain theory (how the eyes adjust to darkness), only to discover a practical application for the research (applications to treat night blindness).

Just knowing that someone is a psychologist might not tell you much. In fact, if someone says that she is a psychologist, the most you can figure is that she may know something about behavior and/or mental processes. Psychologists study people, animals, and even organizations. Psychologists work in clinics, private practices, hospitals, schools, prisons and other government agencies, and large Internet companies. The field of psychology includes several subfields, which are research specialties and work settings for people who research and apply their work. Psychologists in these settings apply their specific research interests to understanding populations and finding solutions to problems.

Psychologists may use data from their research areas to solve or address particular issues and research questions. For example, social psychologists, who focus on how your thoughts, feelings, and behaviors influence and are influenced by others, may apply the results of their research to explain the culture and behavior of juries.

Culture and social settings can impact our behaviors and mental processes.

Behaviorism The study of learning based on directly observable actions.

Humanistic perspective A branch of psychology that emphasizes growth, potential, and self-actualization.

Positive psychology A branch of psychology that emphasizes the constructive features of human strength and healthy living rather than pathology.

Cognition All types of thinking, including knowing, remembering, reasoning, deciding, and communicating.

Cognitive neuroscientist A scientist who studies brain action as it is linked to thought, perception, and language.

Sociocultural perspective A school of psychology that emphasizes the way that social and cultural elements in the world (or environment) influence behavior and mental processes.

Social psychology A branch of psychology that focuses on how our thoughts, feelings, and behaviors influence and are influenced by others.

Ethnocentrism Believing that your own group is superior to others and should be the standard by which other cultures are judged.

Cross-cultural psychology A branch of psychology concerned with the impact that shared attitudes, customs, and behaviors have on individual behavior and mental processes.

Basic research A type of research concerned with expanding knowledge, even if the knowledge has no practical application.

Applied research A type of research concerned with solving everyday problems.

The American Psychological Association (APA) and the Association for Psychological Science (APS) are the field's main professional organizations. The American Psychological Association has 54 divisions or specialized groups. Some of these divisions represent research fields like the ones described above, and others reflect topical interests such as APA Division 18: Psychologists for Public Service. These divisions help members to share research, stay current, and contribute to leading psychological publications. In fact, many divisions publish research journals that highlight the research agendas of the division. **TABLE 1-2** shows the diversity of the divisions of the APA.

TABLE 1-2 List of Divisions of the American Psychological Association

1. Society for General Psychology	32. Society for Humanistic Psychology
2. Society for the Teaching of Psychology	33. Intellectual and Developmental Disabilities
3. Experimental Psychology	34. Society for Environmental, Population and Conservation Psychology
5. Evaluation, Measurement, and Statistics	
6. Behavioral Neuroscience and Comparative Psychology	35. Society for the Psychology of Women
7. Developmental Psychology	36. Society for the Psychology of Religion and Spirituality
8. Society for Personality and Social Psychology	37. Society for Child and Family Policy and Practice
9. Society for the Psychological Study of Social Issues (SPSSI)	38. Health Psychology
10. Society for the Psychology of Aesthetics, Creativity and the Arts	39. Psychoanalysis
12. Society of Clinical Psychology	40. Clinical Neuropsychology
13. Society of Consulting Psychology	41. American Psychology-Law Society
14. Society for Industrial and Organizational Psychology	42. Psychologists in Independent Practice
15. Educational Psychology	43. Society for Family Psychology
16. School Psychology	44. Society for the Psychological Study of Lesbian, Gay, Bisexual and Transgender Issues
17. Society of Counseling Psychology	45. Society for the Psychological Study of Ethnic Minority Issues
18. Psychologists in Public Service	
19. Society for Military Psychology	46. Media Psychology
20. Adult Development and Aging	47. Exercise and Sport Psychology
21. Applied Experimental and Engineering Psychology	48. Society for the Study of Peace, Conflict, and Violence: Peace Psychology Division
22. Rehabilitation Psychology	49. Society of Group Psychology and Group Psychotherapy
23. Society for Consumer Psychology	50. Society of Addiction Psychology
24. Society for Theoretical and Philosophical Psychology	51. Society for the Psychological Study of Men and Masculinity
25. Behavior Analysis	52. International Psychology
26. Society for the History of Psychology	53. Society of Clinical Child and Adolescent Psychology
27. Society for Community Research and Action: Division of Community Psychology	54. Society of Pediatric Psychology
28. Psychopharmacology and Substance Abuse	55. American Society for the Advancement of Pharmacotherapy
29. Psychotherapy	56. Trauma Psychology
30. Society of Psychological Hypnosis	
31. State, Provincial and Territorial Psychological Association Affairs	

Source: Data from the American Psychological Association, http://www.apa.org

When many people think of psychologists, they imagine a therapist who listens to a person who sits on a sofa or who works in a private practice or maybe in a hospital. Psychologists, however, work in various settings, as you can see in FIGURE 1-12.

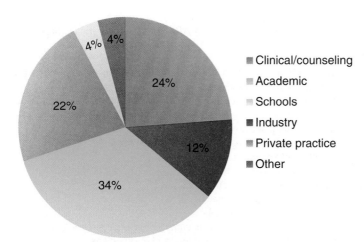

FIGURE 1-12 Settings in which psychologists work. *Source: Data from 2009 Doctorate Employment Survey, APA Center for Workforce Studies, March 2011.*

■ Clinical/counseling
▨ Academic
▨ Schools
■ Industry
▨ Private practice
■ Other

CONCEPT LEARNING CHECK 1.3   *Contemporary Perspectives and Settings in Psychology.*

1. Choose a psychological topic that interests you. Then briefly describe how each of four contemporary perspectives in psychology suggests that one might investigate and analyze the topic.

2. Zoe tells her friend she wants to go to school to become a psychologist. Her friend quips, "You want to be a therapist in a private practice?" Outline a response summarizing at least four areas and three settings in which you are likely to find a psychologist but that do not involve therapy or private practice.

1.4 Critical Thinking and Multiple Influences

An understanding of the science of psychology requires critical thinking.

■ Examine the role of critical thinking in the field of psychology.
■ Illustrate the five criteria for critical thinking.

Good psychology, like all science, demands a certain way of thinking. This way of thinking includes an ability to take in information and decide how credible it is. Not all evidence is equal, and sometimes things can sound convincing or scientific even when they are not.

Critical Thinking

How do you determine what evidence to believe? Critical thinking is important in this process. **Critical thinking** involves identifying and evaluating evidence to guide thoughts and decision making. Critical thinking also helps you to analyze what you have learned and apply this information to unfamiliar situations. Rather than just believing what seems right, critical thinking encourages you to look for problems, assumptions, and biases in the evidence and to make the most reasoned judgments from the evidence. There are many guidelines and tips for critical thinking such as the ones offered by the American Psychological Association in **TABLE 1-3**. Although critical thinking is an important life skill, it is not always easy to apply. As you encounter information, keep the following five criteria (LEARN) of critical thinking in mind.

Critical thinking
Identification and evaluation of evidence to guide thoughts and decision making.

Five Criteria for Critical Thinking in Psychology (LEARN)

1. **L**ook for multiple influences. Often there are many causes for behavior and mental processes. Indeed, there are many levels of analysis, or various ways of examining the same psychological phenomenon.

2. **E**xamine alternatives. It may be possible that other explanations exist. Do not just accept the one that is given or adopt the first one that comes to mind. Keep in mind that many conclusions can be drawn from the same set of circumstances.

TABLE 1-3 Critical Thinking Skills in Psychology from the *APA Guidelines for the Undergraduate Psychology Major*

Respect and use critical and creative thinking, skeptical inquiry, and, when possible, the scientific approach to solve problems related to behavior and mental processes.

Evaluate the quality of information, including differentiating empirical evidence from speculation and the probable from the improbable.
- Identify and evaluate the source, context, and credibility of behavioral claims
- Challenge claims that arise from myth, stereotype, or untested assumptions
- Use scientific principles and evidence to resolve conflicting claims
- Recognize and defend against common fallacies in thinking
- Avoid being swayed by appeals to emotion or authority
- Evaluate popular media reports of psychological research
- Demonstrate an attitude of critical thinking that includes persistence, open-mindedness, tolerance for ambiguity, and intellectual engagement
- Make linkages or connections between diverse facts, theories, and observations

Engage in creative thinking.
- Intentionally pursue unusual approaches to problems
- Recognize and encourage creative thinking and behaviors in others
- Evaluate new ideas with an open but critical mind

Use reasoning to recognize, develop, defend, and criticize arguments and other persuasive appeals.
- Identify components of arguments (e.g., conclusions, premises/assumptions, gaps, counterarguments)
- Distinguish among assumptions, emotional appeals, speculations, and defensible evidence
- Weigh support for conclusions to determine how well reasons support conclusions
- Identify weak, contradictory, and inappropriate assertions
- Develop sound arguments based on reasoning and evidence

Approach problems effectively.
- Recognize ill-defined and well-defined problems
- Articulate problems clearly
- Generate multiple possible goals and solutions
- Evaluate the quality of solutions and revise as needed
- Select and carry out the best solution

Source: From APA Guidelines for the Undergraduate Psychology Major http://www.apa.org/ed/precollege/about/psymajor-guidelines.pdf

3. **A**nalyze the evidence. All evidence should be looked at carefully. Rather than accepting it at face value, inspect evidence for weaknesses, flaws, and shortcomings.

4. **R**easoned skepticism. This is a tough one. As Carl Sagan said, "Keep an open mind, but not so open that your brains fall out" (Sagan, 1986). It is important to be open minded, but if something seems incredible, it might not be credible.

5. **N**otice assumptions. Sometimes we accept evidence because it supports what we already believe. Notice your own assumptions about the supporting evidence as well as the assumptions of the person providing the evidence.

Critical thinking will help you reduce the effects of personal bias when examining evidence. The Critical Thinking Applications in each chapter will ask you to analyze a new question, problem, or situation and use critical thinking techniques to explore and better understand concepts you have studied in the chapter.

The Importance of Multiple Influences

Critical thinking suggests that in psychology it is important to consider multiple influences. Why? Often, a singular perspective is not enough to get the full picture of what is going on. For example, how much of a person's behavior and mental processes are inherited and how much is learned? The relative contributions of nature vs. nurture is a long debate and is older than psychology as an independent discipline. Are people born the way they are, or does what happens to them influence who they are? Those who believe that it is nature, or biology, genes, and evolution, would suggest that those aspects determine behavior and mental processes. On the other hand, those who suggest that nurture is responsible, would explain our behavior and mental processes as being determined by nurture, meaning our environment, learning, and culture.

CRITICAL THINKING APPLICATION

Complete the following quiz on psychological facts and myths, then compute your score by giving yourself one point for each item answered correctly.

Test your Psychology IQ

1. Jet lag is worse going from Hawaii to New York than from New York to Hawaii.

2. Hypnosis is valuable in helping witnesses recall details of a crime.

3. The world's most popular drug is alcohol.

4. People use only about 10% of their brain's capacity.

5. It is not possible to make a gay person heterosexual through psychotherapy.

6. During a full moon, people commit more crimes and behave more abnormally.

7. A few people can use their minds to influence, for example, the way that dice will fall.

8. If two things correlate highly, this does not prove that one causes the other.

9. Hypnosis can reduce the pain of surgery or childbirth.

10. Inside our brains are memories for everything we have experienced.

11. The average IQ in the USA is only about 100.

12. The moon looks much bigger on the horizon than overhead because the atmosphere acts like a magnifying glass.

13. Schizophrenia means split personality.

14. Mentally ill or retarded persons are no more likely to be violent than normal people.

15. Research shows that no significant learning occurs when information is given repeatedly during sleep.

16. As people age, they sleep less.

17. Through hypnosis, some people can remember things from the first 6 months of life.

18. Most German Nazis showed no evidence of serious psychiatric disorders.

19. Among the range of animals, the larger the brain, generally the greater the intelligence.

20. Clear evidence exists to show that a very small percentage of people can receive thoughts of others and predict the future.

Answers: 1. T, 2. F, 3. F, 4. F, 5. T, 6. F, 7. F, 8. T, 9. T, 10. F, 11. T, 12. F, 13. F, 14. T, 15. T, 16. T, 17. F, 18. T, 19. T, 20. F

Source: Standing, L. G. & Huber, H. (2003). Do Psychology Courses Reduce Belief in Psychological Myths? *Social Behavior and Personality,* *31*(6), 585–592. © Society for Personality Research (Inc.).

How did you do? The maximum score is 20, which indicates you do not believe any of the myths. Do not worry if you did not answer all the questions correctly. The score of the average person who has not taken a psychology course is about 13.

Evaluate

1. What was your reaction to some of the answers? Were your answers based on your own experience, scientific research, or a personal theory?

2. Research a few of the topics in several ways. Try an Internet search as well as using scientific journals and psychology books to find the answers. Do you find differences in the evidence presented? Use critical thinking techniques, such as those mentioned above, to reexamine the questions and evaluate the evidence that supports the answers. What conclusions can you draw about your own answers to the quiz? What questions, if any, do you have about your research into some of the topics?

Summary of Multiple Influences on Psychology

Sometimes single perspectives offer flat explanations. More depth occurs when you combine the approaches, as demonstrated by two fluffy cats that share something special with each other. Take a look at the adult cat, Rainbow, and 7-week-old CC in FIGURE 1-13. Cute, are they not? Besides being fluffy, Rainbow and CC have something very special in common: CC (short for copy cat) is a clone of Rainbow. In other words, despite looking very different, Rainbow and CC are genetically identical. If you are wondering how two

FIGURE 1-13 Rainbow (left) is an adult calico cat, CC (right) is genetically identical to Rainbow although she looks different. CC has a spot above her left paw, for example, while Rainbow does not.

genetically identical cats can look so different, the answer lies in the multiple influences between nature and nurture. While genetics or nature influences the fact that CC is a calico, biology only tells part of the story FIGURE 1-14. The influence of CC's growth also influences her calico pattern, but environmental influence cannot explain the pattern either FIGURE 1-15. The exact pattern of her calico is influenced by an analysis of both genetic and environmental factors (Shin et al., 2002) FIGURE 1-16.

FIGURE 1-14 Biology alone can not explain why Rainbow and CC's calico patterns are different.

FIGURE 1-15 Environmental forces alone can not explain why Rainbow and CC's calico patterns are different.

FIGURE 1-16 The multiple influences of biology and environment can provide a more complete explanation than one factor alone.

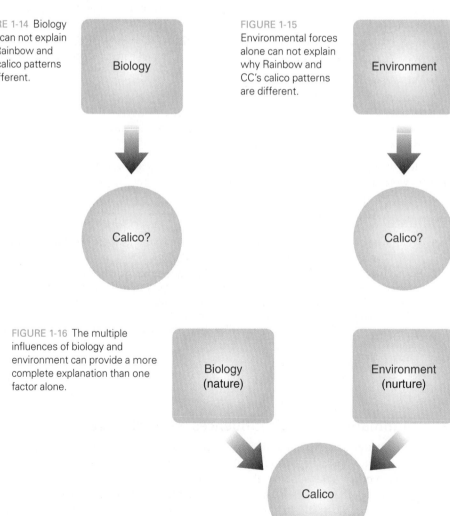

We wrote this book to include information from various sources, including biological, experiential, and cultural. We consider evidence from several types of research, looking at genetics, evolution, biology, environment, social interaction, and culture—integrated throughout the book within each topic. The end of each chapter summarizes this content. You will see a section called "Summary of the Multiple Influences" that highlights a few of the influences on the chapter's topics.

CONCEPT LEARNING CHECK 1.4 | *Applying the Criteria of Critical Thinking*

Harvey has just read an article on the Internet about the influence of the zodiac on personality that suggests that all Tauruses are stubborn and that all Capricorns are hard workers. Use the LEARN approach to critical thinking to analyze and evaluate Harvey's statement.

1. Look for multiple influences:

2. Examine alternatives:

3. Analyze the evidence:

4. Reasoned skepticism:

5. Notice assumptions:

Visual Overview Multiple Perspectives

Multiple perspectives reveal the multiple underlying causes of a psychological function. Each of these perspectives contributes understanding of a vital component of depression, yet none tells a complete story.

Biological
lower amounts of neurotransmitters; genetics

Evolutionary
Depression might be reaction to chronic stress, becoming depressed rather than aggressive might be a better strategy over time.

Positive psychology
Lack of connectedness

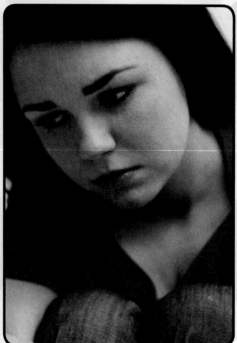

Psychoanalytic
Unresolved conflicts from early life

Behavioral
Learned helplessness

Depression

Sociocultural
Environmental conditions

Cognitive
"Self-talk" and rumination

Humanistic
Lack of unconditional positive regard

1.1 The Science of Psychology

- Psychology is the scientific study of behavior and mental processes.
- The scientific nature of psychology separates it from everyday predictions about behavior and mental processes.
- Pseudoscience is information that seems scientific but is based on unsound scientific principles.

1.2 The Origins and History of Psychology

- Psychology as an independent discipline did not emerge until the late 19th century but has roots in other fields such as philosophy and physiology.
- Structuralism was an early school of thought in psychology that studied human experience by breaking it down into smaller elements.
- Functionalism was an early school of thought in psychology that was concerned with the purposes of behavior and mental processes.

1.3 Contemporary Psychology

- Psychology's multiple contemporary perspectives are used to capture the richness of the influences of human behavior.
- The biological perspective examines how physiology connects with the environment to create behavior and mental processes.
- The evolutionary perspective examines the impact of natural selection on behavior and mental processes.
- The psychodynamic perspective examines how unconscious processes determine your behavior.
- The behavioral perspective explores the relationship between biological and environmental influences that allow us to learn or change through our experiences.
- The humanistic perspective emphasizes the innate capacity for mental growth.
- The positive psychology perspective emphasizes the constructive feature of human strength and healthy living.
- The sociocultural perspective emphasizes the way that social and cultural elements in the world influence behavior and mental processes.
- Psychologists have developed focused specializations of research and practice.
- Psychologists work in several settings, including clinical, industry, academic, private practice, and schools.
- Psychologists have specialty subfields, including clinical, counseling, industrial/organizational, education, developmental cognitive, social, and personality.

1.4 Critical Thinking and Multiple Influences

- Critical thinking involves identifying and evaluating evidence to guide your decision making.
- Principles of critical thinking include looking for multiple influences, examining alternatives, analyzing evidence, reasoned skepticism, and noticing assumptions (LEARN).
- The eclectic model suggests that no single explanation is adequate and it is important to consider multiple levels.

1.1 The Science of Psychology

1. Psychology is the science of:
  A. personality.
  B. humans.
  C. diagnosis and treatment of mental disorders.
  D. behavior and mental processes.

2. Television and radio personalities often give information that sounds as if it is based on psychological science, but it is not. In many cases, this is an example of:
  A. pseudoscience.
  B. introspection.
  C. focusing on the mind rather than the brain.
  D. eclecticism.

1.2 The Origins and History of Psychology

3. Early influences on understanding behavior and mental processes include the fields of philosophy and:
  A. sociology.
  B. anthropology.
  C. physiology.
  D. chemistry.

4. Charles Darwin's theory of evolution influenced the early school of psychology known as:
  A. functionalism.
  B. structuralism.
  C. behaviorism.
  D. psychoanalysis.

5. Contemporary psychological perspectives differ from the classic "armchair" schools because contemporary schools rely heavily on:
  A. modern computers.
  B. the scientific method.
  C. introspection.
  D. determining the cause of a psychological condition.

6. The founding of psychology as an independent discipline is linked to which person?
  A. Aristotle
  B. John Locke
  C. Wilhelm Wundt
  D. Sigmund Freud

7. To test a new website's ease of use, Sam watches as users interact and records the users' spoken reactions to the experience. This technique, called a "think aloud," is rooted in which structuralist technique?
  A. Introspection
  B. Empiricism
  C. Objectivism
  D. Functionalism

8. William James would have believed which of the following statements?
  A. Psychology should study the structures of human experience only.
  B. Structure and function cannot be separated.
  C. Anecdotal evidence should be emphasized over empirical evidence.
  D. Consciousness is an ongoing, rational state for most humans.

1.3 Contemporary Psychology

9. Which contemporary perspective's primary aim is to explain the impact of natural selection on behavior and mental processes?
  A. The biological perspective
  B. The behavioral perspective
  C. The evolutionary perspective
  D. The humanistic perspective

10. Didier's therapist says that Didier is anxious because of unconscious conflicts. His therapist is using the _____ perspective to explain his anxiety.
  A. biological
  B. psychodynamic
  C. evolutionary
  D. humanistic

11. Roberta's therapist says she is anxious because of underactive neurotransmitters in her nervous system. Roberta's therapist is using the _____ perspective to explain her anxiety.
  A. humanistic
  B. behavioral
  C. biological
  D. cognitive

12. Ian is studying the levels of testosterone in the body as they rise and fall during the year. He is investigating this in order to expand knowledge. This research is known as _____ research.
  A. applied
  B. basic
  C. anecdotal
  D. eclectic

13. Which of the following are settings in which you are likely to find a psychologist?
  A. Private practice
  B. Hospitals
  C. Industry
  D. Schools
  E. All of the above

1.4 Critical Thinking and Multiple Influences

14. Katy believes that her brother is stressed because "stress runs in her family." However, her brother points out additional factors that are leading to his stress, such as the extra responsibility she has been given at her job and adjusting to a new neighborhood. Katy refuses to listen. Which principle of critical thinking is Katy ignoring?
A. Reasoned skepticism
B. Looking for multiple influences
C. Noticing assumptions
D. Analyzing the evidence

15. A psychologist who uses an eclectic model emphasizes:
A. biological approaches.
B. environmental approaches.
C. psychodynamic approaches.
D. multiple influences.

CHAPTER DISCUSSION QUESTIONS

1. Notice in Section 1.1 the examples of the types of questions science is better and worse at answering. In general, science is good at predicting trends but gets fuzzier with more specifics. Using this idea of trends versus specifics, examine the questions that will be answered in the chapters of this text (beginning with this section) and identify a trend that a psychologist might answer and a more specific question that would be more difficult to answer.

2. Psychology has strong roots in both philosophy and physiology, as discussed in Section 1.2. After reviewing the main contemporary approaches to psychology in Section 1.3 (biological, evolutionary, psychodynamic, behavioral, humanistic, cognitive, and sociocultural), distinguish a possible philosophical and physiological question that might influence each approach.

3. The LEARN approach is explained in Section 1.4 as a way to think critically, which may lead you to think about it as an approach to science, studying, or other academic endeavors. However, critical thinking can be useful in many realms, including understanding social situations. Assess the value of the LEARN approach in your own social life. Think of a situation in which your social interaction with a person or group was confusing or unclear. Use the LEARN approach to reevaluate the situation. Does this approach bring a new understanding to this situation? Why or why not?

CHAPTER PROJECTS

1. Section 1.3 explains seven of the main approaches to psychology today (biological, evolutionary, psychodynamic, behavioral, humanistic, cognitive, and sociocultural). Review these approaches and then find an example in the news or on the Internet that demonstrates each approach. Your examples should use a technique or make a conclusion that is specific to each approach.

2. Section 1.4 explains the LEARN approach to critical thinking. Dramatize this approach by creating two dialogs: one using the LEARN approach, and one not using the LEARN approach. First, identify a problem that a character would need to think through. Then, explain how s/he might work through the problem without the LEARN approach. Then, write a second dialog in which the character works through the problem using the LEARN approach. For each dialog, include the reflective thoughts of the character at the end of the situation.

CHAPTER KEY TERMS

Anecdotal evidence
Applied research
Basic research
Behaviorism
Biopsychosocial approach
Cognition
Cognitive neuroscientist
Critical thinking
Cross-cultural psychology
Eclectic model
Empirical evidence
Empiricism
Ethnocentrism

Evolutionary psychology
Functionalism
Functional magnetic resonance imaging (fMRI)
Heritability
Humanistic perspective
Introspection
Levels of analysis
Mind
Natural selection
Neuroscience
Philosophy
Physiology

Positive psychology
Positron emission tomography (PET)
Pseudoscience
Psychoanalytic theory
Psychology
Science
Social psychology
Sociocultural perspective
Structuralism
Unconscious

ANSWERS TO CONCEPT LEARNING CHECKS

1.1 The Scope and Limits of the Science of Psychology

1. The researcher has gathered data and made a general claim based upon the nature of sleep. Science is much better at describing general trends than the needs of an individual person.

1.2 Comparing and Contrasting Structuralism and Functionalism

1. Structuralists might break down the components of the taste of spoiled milk.
2. Functionalists would examine why we dislike the taste of spoiled milk. A functionalist might also suggest the disgusting taste might make us not want to drink something that could harm us.

1.3 Contemporary Perspectives and Settings in Psychology

1. Sample answer: Psychologists from different perspectives might investigate humor and laughter in different ways. The biological perspective: What parts of the brain are involved in laughter? How does our brain react when we notice something funny?
   The evolutionary perspective: How does humor offer a reproductive advantage?
   The psychodynamic perspective: Do the things we find funny say something about our unconscious mind?
   The behavioral perspective: In what ways is humor learned? Why is it rewarding when someone laughs at a joke you tell but not when they laugh at a mistake you make?
   The humanistic and positive psychology perspective: Is laughter really the best medicine? Are there benefits to laughing?

The cognitive perspective: What makes something funny? Are there certain thinking processes at play in a joke? The sociocultural perspective: Are there cultural variations in what people find funny?

2. Use the tables in this section to guide your answers. Psychologists research and practice in several areas, including clinical, counseling, industrial/organizational, education, social, and personality. In addition to private practice, psychologists work in clinics, industry, academic settings, and schools.

1.4 Applying the Criteria of Critical Thinking

1. Look for multiple influences. [Many things influence personality, including biological, psychological, cultural, and social characteristics. Personality might be more complex than the explanation suggests.]
2. Examine alternatives. [Maybe people emphasize the kinds of personality characteristics they are hoping to see.]
3. Analyze the evidence. [Do all your friends born in May have the same personality? It might be good to cross-check by examining the "evidence" presented in Harvey's Internet article.]
4. Reasoned skepticism. [This is such a simple theory of personality, it is important to be skeptical about it.]
5. Notice assumptions. [The assumption behind this explanation is that there is something about the personality that is influenced by your birthday.]

ANSWERS TO CHAPTER REVIEW TEST

1.1 The Science of Psychology

1. D. Rationale: Psychology is the scientific study of behavior and mental processes. Although psychology studies humans, it studies nonhumans as well. Psychology does not focus only on psychological conditions like depression.
2. A. Rationale: Pseudoscience is information that appears scientific but is not based on scientific principles.

1.2 The Origins and History of Psychology

3. C. Rationale: Physiology influenced psychology because it acknowledged the role that the health and biology of the brain had on mental processes and behavior.
4. A. Rationale: Functionalism was an early school of psychology that focused on the purpose, or function, of a behavior.
5. B. Rationale: Contemporary perspectives of psychology utilize the scientific method as a way of gathering evidence.
6. C. Rationale: While John Locke and Aristotle discussed topics that might be included in psychology, the founding of psychology is linked to Wilhelm Wundt.
7. A. Rationale: Introspection is a technique used to study subjective experiences such as one's own mental and emotional processes.
8. B. Rationale: James argued against the structuralists, suggesting that structures are there because of the function they serve.

1.3 Contemporary Psychology

9. C. Rationale: The biological perspective's primary aim is to study the body, brain, and nervous system, while the evolutionary perspective seeks to explain the impact of natural selection on behavior and mental processes.
10. B. Rationale: The psychodynamic perspective focuses on unconscious processes.
11. C. Rationale: The biological perspective studies the connection of behavior to the body, brain, and nervous system.
12. B. Rationale: The goal of basic research is to test a theory. The goal of applied research is to find a practical application.
13. E. Rationale: According to the table in Section 1.4, you can find psychologists in all of these settings.

1.4 Critical Thinking and Multiple Influences

14. B. Rationale: Looking for multiple influences is an important factor in critical thinking.
15. D. Rationale: The eclectic model pulls together multiple ways of examining a particular phenonoma.

REFERENCES

Anderson, C. A., & Anderson, D. C. (1984). Ambient temperature and violent crime: Tests of the linear and curvilinear hypotheses. *Journal of Personality and Social Psychology, 46,* 91–97. doi:10.1037/0022-3514.46.1.91

Benjamin, L. T. (2008). *A history of psychology: Original sources and contemporary research.* New York: Blackwell.

Cohen, D., Nisbett, R. E., Bowdle, B. F., & Schwarz, N. (1996). Insult, aggression, and the Southern culture of honor: An "experimental ethnography." *Journal of Personality and Social Psychology, 70*(5), 945–960. doi:10.1037/0022-3514.70.5.945

Fonteyn, M. E., Kuipers, B., & Grobe, S. J. (1993). A description of think aloud method and protocol analysis. *Qualitative Health Research, 3*(4), 430–441. doi:10.1177/104973239300300403

Hughes, W., Lavery, J., & Doran, K. (2009). *Critical thinking: An introduction to the basic skills.* Toronto: Broadview Press.

Peplau, L. A. & Taylor, S. E. (1997). Sociocultural perspectives in social psychology. Englewood Cliffs, NJ: Prentice Hall.

Pietschnig, J., Voracek, M., & Formann, A. K. (2010). Mozart effect Shmozart effect: A meta-analysis. *Intelligence, 38*(3), 314–323. doi:10.1016/j.intell.2010.03.001

Rascle, O., Traclet, A., Souchon, N., Coulomb-Cabagno, G., & Petrucci, C. (2010). Aggressor-victim dissent in perceived legitimacy of aggression in soccer: The moderating role of situational background. *Research Quarterly for Exercise and Sport, 81*(3), 340–348.

Rauscher, F. H., Shaw, G. L., & Ky, C. N. (1993). Music and spatial task performance. *Nature, 365*(6447), 611. doi:10.1038/365611a0

Sagan, C. (1986). *Broca's Brain: Reflections on the Romance of Science* (1st ed.). New York: Ballantine Books.

Shin, T., Kraemer, D., Pryor, J., Liu, L., Rugila, J., Howe, L., Buck, S., et al. (2002). Cell biology: A cat cloned by nuclear transplantation. *Nature, 415*(6874), 859. doi:10.1038/nature723

U.S. Census Bureau. (2008). *United States population projections by race and Hispanic origin: 2000–2050.* Retreived from http://www.census.gov/population/www/projections/methodstatement.html

Willard, C. (2011, January). Men: A growing minority? *gradPSYCH, 9*(1), 40.

Wilson, E. (1999). *Consilience: The unity of knowledge.* New York: Vintage.

Yu, Y. Z., & Shi, J. X. (2009). Relationship between levels of testosterone and cortisol in saliva and aggressive behaviors of adolescents. *Biomedical and Environmental Sciences, 22*(1), 44–49.

Chapter Overview ▼

2 A Scientific Approach to Psychology

My first month of graduate school, I was ready to run my very first experiment. The students in an introduction to psychology course at the school had begun signing up for the open slots I had posted, and I was ready for the first student who agreed to come, a man I will call Jason Porter. When I opened the door to the lab, I saw standing in front of me the most famous person I had ever seen face to face, an Oscar-winning Hollywood star with many important films to his credit. I recalled that he had taken a break from filming to get a degree at this school, and here he was, signed up for *my* experiment! I ushered him in to the observation room and gave him a consent form to sign and a written task to begin the study. Then I left the room, and ran down the hall to tell my fellow graduate students that Jason Porter was in the lab! Several of them followed me back and looked through the one-way mirror at him as he worked on the experimental task. Thinking back to that day, I confess that I am not proud of my star-struck behavior.

What protects people who volunteer for research studies? Do they have the right to confidentiality, so that others will not know what they said or did during the study or even that they participated? How are ethical guidelines enforced in practice? And are there consequences when ethical principles are violated in research? The American Psychological Association provides ethical guidelines, and federal law clarifies the rights of research participants and the responsibilities of researchers. As you will see, scientific research that involves human or animal subjects engaged in tasks that one hopes will offer insights into the mind is among the most demanding types of research in science.

2.1 Psychological Investigation

Psychology uses the scientific method to examine the mind by studying people's behaviors.

- Define psychological science.
- Describe the steps in the scientific method in psychology.
- Discuss the importance of the scientific method.
- Identify design choices in research.

What separates the science of psychology from intuition, opinion, and common sense? Like most of us, you likely have your own ideas about why people behave the way they do, and many are likely correct. For example, women cry more often than men, children are influenced by their parents, and people often want what they cannot have. These observations are of little value precisely because they are so common or obvious. There are many more observations about people's behavior that require more information, or evidence, to confirm. Do people marry others like themselves, or do "opposites attract?" Are we more motivated by money or by meaning in our lives? What is the best way to make a desired change in our behavior?

To answer these questions, psychologists use the **scientific method**. This method tests hypotheses by gathering measurable evidence to determine whether they are true. This often requires designing experiments that capture the behavior of interest and then systematically observing the resulting data. For example, one study had college-age male skateboarders attempt a series of tricks. Half of them did so while an attractive young female experimenter looked on. The skateboarders who saw the woman watching them took more risks with their tricks and had a higher level of testosterone in their saliva

Scientific method A systematic approach to organizing the collection of data and drawing conclusions from a research study.

(Ronay & von Hippel, 2010). Because the experiment kept the situation the same except for the presence of the woman, we can conclude that it was her presence alone that aroused the men and led them to take more risks. **Empirical** studies gain information by carefully collecting observations, or data. Data can include quantitative observations, such as the number of minutes a task takes or a rating on a scale for a survey question. Data can also be qualitative when the "qualities" of data are systematically described rather than counted. For example, interviews collect people's own expressions of their experiences as a source of data. Empirical studies lie at the heart of psychology because they allow us to draw conclusions about human behavior and thinking.

Psychologists want to uncover the "what" of a given phenomenon, such as "intelligence": what is the nature of intelligence? What are its features? What consequences does it have for a person? The research design, or overall structure of a study, depends on the specific questions of interest. And, because the field of psychology is so diverse in its questions, its methods are also highly varied. Psychologists seek universal truths about all people, as well as an understanding of the important differences among them, such as gender, culture, ethnicity, and personality, that result in differing experiences in life. In addition, we want to know the "why" of a phenomenon; that is, an explanation of its causes and the multiple factors that influence it. What does it mean to say that someone is "intelligent," and what causes some people to be judged as more intelligent than others? Using the scientific method, psychologists can add new knowledge about psychology.

Psychological science studies human behavior in order to learn what "makes people tick." Research on psychological topics collects data about human behavior using the same scientific method found in other sciences. This can involve creating a **theory**, with an overarching conceptualization or model about how various factors may influence behavior. Research can also begin with a testable hypothesis, from an observation about human behavior, or with the goal of looking for relationships among possible influences. Then, the scientific method involves relying on empirical evidence provided by impartial procedures and careful measurements of the results. In fact, throughout this book, you will see reference citations—names and dates within parentheses. These are references to studies that support a finding, conclusion, or fact presented in the text. To learn more about the evidence presented, you can look up the reference in the list at the end of the chapter and find a copy to read for yourself. In this chapter, we will cover the major concepts involved in psychological research. The goal is to understand research design well so that you can be an informed, critical reader when considering scientific evidence in this book and wherever it may arise.

The Scientific Method in Psychology

Perhaps you have seen it happen: People gather in a local bar and enjoy an evening of talking, drinking, and meeting new friends. Sometimes, these gatherings result in "hook-ups," or romantic pairings for the evening or longer. A country singer, Mickey Gilley, once observed, "Don't the Girls Get Prettier at Closing Time?" Presumably, the singer meant that a given girl might be viewed as even prettier when the bar is closing and your chance to talk with her tonight is ending. What type of psychological study could test this question? Of course, it is not enough to ask a few people, or make our own guesses; instead, we want to design a research study using scientific principles that allows us to draw a solid conclusion. And we would also want to consider whether "the boys" get more handsome. In fact, such a study was conducted, and we can consider its design and findings in light of the scientific method (Pennebaker et al., 1979).

- Step 1: Formulate a testable hypothesis. First, the question has to be turned into a clear statement that can be shown to be true or false, called a **hypothesis**. For this study, the researchers defined the hypothesis as, "Individuals are seen as more attractive as the time to decide whether to interact with them decreases." Hypotheses are statements about what will happen in a given situation; if the observations do not match the prediction, then the hypothesis is rejected.
- Step 2: Select the research method and design the study. Next, the researchers had to consider how to best test this question. There is no "best" research strategy; rather, each design has its advantages and disadvantages. What people are available to participate in the study? Where should the study take place? How should the behaviors

Empirical Research studies that gain information by carefully collecting observations, or data.

Psychological science Research conducted on topics in the field of psychology.

Theory An overarching conceptualization about how variables may cause behavior.

Hypothesis A clear statement or prediction that can be shown to be true or false in an experiment.

When college students socialize at a bar, what influences attraction?

be measured? Psychological researchers do their best to test their hypotheses in ways that represent the real-world environment in which their question, or hypothesis, has meaning. In this case, the researchers decided to use three bars near a university rather than testing the hypothesis within a laboratory. In the report of the methods used in a study, specific information is given so that someone else can reproduce the same circumstances. For this reason, we know that the researchers were careful in conducting their study.

- Step 3: Collect the data. The researchers approached more than 100 people (half male, half female) of college age in the bars, waiting until they were not engaged in conversation with anyone. They also chose **participants** (people who take part in a research study, also called *subjects*) who were not "intoxicated" or "incapacitated." An experimenter of the same gender approached the potential participant and asked if he or she would mind answering a few questions for a psychology study. Everyone approached agreed to participate. The experimenters asked, "On a scale from 1 to 10, where 1 indicates 'not attractive,' 5 indicates 'average,' and 10 indicates 'extremely attractive,' how would you rate the opposite-sex individuals here tonight?" They then asked, "If you were a member of the opposite sex, how would you rate the other (men or women) here tonight?" The experimenter thanked them and departed. The experimenters looked at the amount of time remaining before "closing time" and collected the data at 9 p.m., 10:30 p.m., and 12 midnight at bars closing at 12:30 a.m. What do you think they found?

- Step 4: Analyze the data and draw conclusions. The ratings provided by the participants were grouped by gender and by the time of the observation. The ratings were analyzed using statistics to compare the ratings based on time of evening. People rated members of the opposite sex as increasingly attractive as closing time approached FIGURE 2-1. While the ratings of their own gender changed a bit from time to time, these differences were not reliable; instead, only the ratings for the opposite gender at 12:00 increased above all of the other ratings. What conclusion is appropriate from this study? The time of night made a difference: The later time produced higher ratings of the opposite sex. So this experiment provides evidence that Mickey Gilley's common-sense observation was right!

Participant A volunteer who agrees to take part in research studies, also called a subject.

Journal A publication containing articles written by scientists that are reviewed before publication by a group of peers.

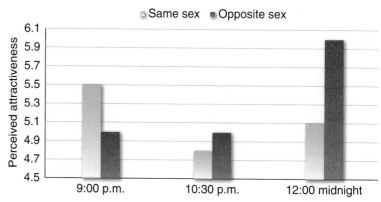

FIGURE 2-1 Bar patrons' ratings of opposite-sex based on time before closing.
Source: Data from Pennebaker, J. W., Dyer, M. A., Caulkins, R. S., Litowitz, D. L., Ackerman, P. L., Anderson, D. B., & McGraw, K. M. (1979). Don't the Girls Get Prettier at Closing Time: A country and western application to psychology. Personality and Social Psychological Bulletin, 5, *122–125.*

- Step 5: Report the findings. When studies are complete, researchers write a full report and submit it to a **journal**, or scientific publication. Peer reviewers—other researchers who had no part in the study—read the report and point out problems with its design or conclusions and with the way they are reported (Wilkinson, 1999). What would you say about this study? Do you think it is good evidence that the hypothesis is true? Can you think of any alternative explanations for why the observations came out this way? For example, as the evening went on, people in the bar likely had more to drink, and were perhaps more tired or more energetic? There was also no attempt to account for the fact that some in the bar may have preferred their own gender rather than the opposite sex. In addition, the study's method had the participants rate the entire group as a whole rather than individuals. As in most studies, questions about the findings remain. For example, would perceiving "the girls get prettier" make any difference in people's actual behavior toward each other? The study cannot answer this question. However, it was reviewed by experts and selected for publication and has been cited by more than 50 other studies published since it appeared.

For any study of human behavior, design choices must be made. These choices often lead to limitations in the conclusions from the study. For example, if they had conducted the study in a laboratory, they would have had more control over the participants but would the subjects have acted as naturally? There are also *confounds* in the design, or factors that may affect the results that are not intended as a part of the study. In this case, the 12 midnight measurement always happens after the participants have spent more time in the bar setting. So the length of time subjects spent in the bar before participating in the study is a confound—that is, a systematic difference between the groups that is not the one the experimenter is measuring (they measured time before closing). So are the girls prettier because the bar is about to close and opportunities to meet someone are vanishing or because you have now drunk a lot more beer?

An important choice in study design is whether to have different people in the comparison groups or whether to have the same people do the experiment more than once. These researchers chose a **between-subjects design**, in which there are different individuals in each of the groups (9 p.m., 10:30 p.m., and 12 midnight) of the study. The people who were in the bar at 9 p.m. may have been a different group than those who stayed on through the closing hour; as a result, their opinions may differ because different types of people make up the three groups. The researchers might have asked the same people to stay at the bar all night and give ratings at each time point, called a **within-subjects design**. If the same person gives a rating at each time, you may have more confidence that the difference you saw is due to the time. In fact, another group of researchers conducted this study again (Johnco et al., 2010), this time asking the same individuals to perform ratings at each time point. They found the same effect—the "girls" still do get prettier—even when blood alcohol levels are taken into account. This shows how studies may suggest further research to refine our understanding of the results and may raise new questions. We can conclude that this closing time effect does occur; however, do we really know *why* it occurs based on these studies?

The results of one study never provide all the information you may need to answer all of the questions you may have. With the scientific method, studies build upon the foundation of other studies to help us reach conclusions. And every research study has limitations in its design. Consider this when you read about studies in this book. Did the researchers make good design choices? Do their conclusions follow from the study? Are there limitations that lead you to question whether it is true in general? While research studies are always fully reported in journals, the results of every study are still open to interpretation. This requires that we be critical thinkers when considering empirical reports.

Why Is the Scientific Method Important?

Researchers in psychology follow the scientific method to perform studies that help explain and may predict human behavior. This is a much more challenging task than studying snails or sound waves. It often requires compromises, such as testing behavior within laboratories rather than natural settings, and asking those readily available (such as introduction to psychology students) to participate rather than collecting data from a true cross-section of the population. It often requires great cleverness to conceive of measures that tap into what people are thinking without altering their thinking, called **reactivity**. Simply knowing they are being observed may cause people to behave differently (such as more politely!). People may give answers they feel are more socially desirable than their true feelings. But for all of these difficulties for psychology, the payoff of the scientific method is that the findings are **replicable**; that is, if you run the same study again following the same procedures, you will be very likely to get the same results. In that sense, the scientific method provides **reliability** for the observations made about human behavior.

However, studies must always be questioned as to their **validity**: Do the research findings offer insight into the psychological question they set out to answer? The scientific

Between-subjects design A research plan in which different individuals take part in differing aspects of the study and the different groups are compared.

Within-subjects design A research plan in which each subject takes part in every aspect of the study.

Reactivity Unintentionally altering people's natural behavior by attempting to measure it.

Replicable Results from a research study that appear the same when the study is repeated.

Reliability The consistency of the results when similar studies are performed.

Validity The degree to which a research experiment captures what it claims to study.

Psychological science follows the same principles of the scientific method found in other fields of science.

Generalizability How well a study's findings can be applied to other people and circumstances.

Meta-analysis A study that examines the results of many earlier studies on a topic and compares their findings to draw conclusions.

method allows other researchers to form their own judgments about a study, and to follow it with their own study if necessary to better identify the underlying causes of behaviors. Incrementally, piece by piece, systematic observations are made and published, and the next research study builds upon them. This provides a solid basis for accumulating evidence across studies, finding consistencies and errors, and coming to a lasting conclusion that is built on fact rather than intuition, personal opinion, or guesswork. The **generalizability** of the results, or how well the findings can be applied to other people and circumstances, is supported by similar findings from other studies. One way to test whether results can be generalized to other situations is to repeat studies while changing the "who," "how," and "where" of the study. Do you think the closing time study would have the same outcome if conducted in a campus coffee shop rather than a bar? Do you think you would find the same results on Sundays, when bars close earlier? The more studies conducted that test the conclusions in new contexts, the more confidence we have that the findings apply to people's behavior in general.

An important contribution to this process is a **meta-analysis** study, in which tens or even hundreds of studies on a single topic are considered together and conclusions drawn about our current knowledge. For example, Petersen and Hyde (2010) conducted a meta-analysis of 834 studies from 87 countries (occurring between 1993 and 2007) to determine gender differences in sexuality. They concluded that men report more permissive attitudes toward casual sex and slightly more sexual experience than did women; however, the difference is disappearing, especially in cultures with greater gender equality. The variety of people participating and the great number of different studies included provide very solid evidence for this meta-analysis conclusion.

CONCEPT LEARNING CHECK 2.1　　　*Within or Between?*

Consider the following descriptions of research designs. For each, identify whether the research design was within-subject, in which each individual participated in every part of the study, or between-subject, in which different people took part in different tasks during the study.

1. A researcher is interested in determining whether using a highlighter helps students during reading. He has his class read a chapter from the textbook using a highlighter while reading and then take a quiz. The next week, he tells them to refrain from using any highlighter or underlining while they read the chapter, and again they take a quiz. The results show highlighters actually produce worse performance on the quizzes.

2. Dr. Brady has a theory that members of all-female groups work more cooperatively together than members of all-male groups. To test this, she assigns participants at random to same-sex groups of five. She asks them to work on a series of tasks. She then has the participants rate their own group members' performances. The results show females are rated as more cooperative, while males are rated as more competitive.

3. Dr. Mertz tries out a new presentation software package on one of his sections of psychology. He gives his traditional blackboard lecture in his morning class and a computerized slide presentation with the same lecture in his afternoon class. He gives the same test to both sections and finds that 15% of the students in the 8 a.m. section fail the test versus 30% in the 2 p.m. section. He concludes that the new presentation method does not improve learning.

4. Dr. Ricardo wants to determine the effects of hunger on aggression in a cat colony. He takes 10 cats from the colony, keeps them in individual cages, and gives them a feeding schedule that results in their losing 20% of their normal weight over a 2-week period. He also isolates 10 other cats in cages but keeps them on a normal feeding schedule. He then tests each hungry cat by putting it back in the colony. The hungry cats show the threat posture that precedes fighting much more frequently than the nonhungry cats. He concludes that hunger increases aggression in cats.

5. Dr. Cleaver believes that children do not show strong preferences for "gender-appropriate" toys. In a testing room, she finds that children often choose gender-appropriate toys, but in interviews, they tell her they like both kinds of toys. She concludes that society pressures children to limit their toy choices.

6. A national study examines factors that determine whether exercise aids weight loss. Subjects are told to begin a rigorous exercise program, and at the end of 3 months, follow-up results are examined. The study finds that people in the study lost an average of 5 pounds.

2.2 Descriptive Research

Descriptive research is intended to accurately observe and systematically define behavior.

- Explain the goals of descriptive research.
- Discuss the components of a naturalistic observation study.
- Compare and contrast case studies, surveys, and correlational studies in terms of descriptive research.

The goal of descriptive research in psychology is to make systematic observations about the "what" of our behavior. As a first step, or for some types of questions, simply observing what happens can be very informative. These studies may take the form of observing behavior as it occurs in the field, or the real world, analyzing a single example case, asking people questions about their behavior, or observing across groups of people or over time. One type of study, called a **comparative study**, looks at behaviors across species. For example, pet dogs were discovered to respond to humans pointing to food locations as a referential gesture (Soproni et al., 2002), even though other primates do not appear to use pointing as a signal. Descriptive studies are concerned with the relationships between and among behaviors, experiences, and individual attributes, also called **variables**.

Naturalistic Observation

When the behavior of interest is complex or has practical importance, it is often first observed as it occurs in "the wild" without any intervention by the researchers, called **naturalistic observation**. Have you ever noticed that the person pulling out from the parking space you are waiting for takes an especially long time once they see you waiting? This is an annoying perception, but is it true?

A naturalistic observational study (Ruback & Juieng, 1997) examined whether the amount of time drivers took to leave a parking space was related to whether another driver was waiting for the space. Two hundred drivers were observed leaving their parking spaces in front of a mall. Two researchers observed the drivers from the time they opened the driver's-side door to the time when the car had completely exited the space. Thirty-eight percent of the drivers were scored as "intruded upon" when they turned their head toward an approaching car before they opened their car door. Drivers departed more quickly (averaging 32 seconds) when *not* intruded upon than when they saw a car waiting (39 seconds on average). So it is true, they are staying longer because you are waiting. However, from a descriptive study, we cannot say *why* this occurs. The authors discuss the territoriality of humans and the need to "mark" or defend their use of the location, but the study does not address these potential explanations.

In fact, observational studies are often employed to discover the behavior of other animals in comparative studies. Naturalist Jane Goodall (1934–) accomplished observations of groups of chimpanzees by spending much of her life following these primates as they moved throughout their natural environment. She noted evidence of territoriality among chimpanzees in which individuals would protect areas and objects they claimed through aggression, postures, gestures, and calls (Goodall, 1982). The "owner" must be prepared at all times to defend his or her claim from others in the group. Somehow, it seems easier to attribute the squabbling of chimpanzees to a display of territoriality, while it is harder to imagine that we ourselves are engaging in the same behavior. Comparative studies of other animals help to identify behaviors in the natural environment that may be removed from our modern awareness.

Naturalistic observation is a method by which the researcher makes no attempt to interact with or change the behavior of those observed. Instead, the research is from the standpoint of a "fly on the wall," making as little impact as possible while noting the behavior of those around them. For example, most people think of themselves as "moral," but do they behave that way? A team of researchers sat outside a university copy room and recorded the number of copies made based on the sound of the copier. Students, faculty, and staff used the copier and self-reported the number of copies they made for

Comparative study A research project that compares similarities and differences between human and animal behavior.

Variable A factor that is manipulated, measured, or controlled during an experiment.

Naturalistic observation Observing human behavior as it occurs in a real-world setting.

Jane Goodall, the world's foremost authority on chimpanzee behavior.

later billing on an honor system. How "honorable" were they? The observers found that people routinely underestimated the number of copies they actually made, with a constant percentage of unreported copies over different copy job sizes. However, when they made a lot of copies, they were more likely to be dishonest. So people seemed to feel competing motivations to maximize financial profits and to behave honestly (Goldstone & Chin, 1993). Observational studies can take place in any public forum, and people can be observed without giving their permission for the study.

Naturalistic studies are important within psychology because many studies are conducted under the controlled conditions of a laboratory or through asking people about their behavior. Then, when a study takes place "in the wild," psychologists sometimes observe that people's behavior in real settings differs. For example, more than 97% of people in Michigan reported that they wear seat belts (National Highway Traffic and Safety Administration, 2008). However, a naturalistic study in which observers watched drivers, found seat belt use ranged from 52 to 90% (Gonzalez et al., 2011). So naturalistic studies provide an important check on the generalizability and validity of research findings. On the other hand, it can be difficult to avoid bias when conducting naturalistic studies. For example, in the study of parking space territory (Ruback & Juieng, 1997), the observers always knew whether a car was waiting or not. They may have been subtly biased by that knowledge when recording the time it took for cars to exit. Objectivity is sometimes difficult to achieve in naturalistic settings.

Case Studies

Case study The extensive examination of the experience of a single individual or group.

Another important type of descriptive study is the extensive examination of the experience of a single individual or group, called a **case study**. These studies are often conducted because the individual's experience is highly unusual, and their behavior allows us to reflect on what must be happening for all individuals. For example, cognitive neuroscientists and clinical neuropsychologists study individuals who have brain injuries that produce specific, characteristic behavior. This allows scientists to infer how the injured areas function within an intact brain. One such case involved a 16-year-old boy called "Adam" (Farah et al., 2000). At 1 day old, Adam contracted meningitis and suffered brain damage to areas of his brain that process visual images FIGURE 2-2. Surprisingly, Adam was able to do well with most visual tasks at age 14, such as recognizing objects; however, he showed extreme difficulty with facial recognition. His favorite television show was *Baywatch*, and he viewed it for an hour daily. In the study, he was given 10 photos of the cast and asked to identify them. He was unable to identify a single face and refused to even guess. This case provides important evidence in support of two separate visual recognition systems in the brain, one for objects (which worked well for Adam) and one for faces (which did not). The case

FIGURE 2-2 Arrows indicate areas of damage (represented by shading) in the occipital lobes. *Source: Adapted from Farah, M. J., Rabinowitz, C., Quinn, G. E., & Liu, G. T. (2000). Early commitment of neural substrates for face recognition.* Cognitive Neuropsychology, 17*(1–3), 117–123.*

also suggests that the brain cannot recover this face recognition function after damage even in a very young infant.

With case studies, there is always a concern that something about the individual other than the brain damage identified may be taking place. Other cases can be compared, but the exact damage is not likely to be the same in other individuals. However, from case studies of adults, damage to this part of the brain is now known to cause prosopagnosia, or the inability to recognize faces (Farah et al., 1995). Damage to other areas of this visual processing region can cause object agnosia, in which individuals are unable to recognize common objects (like hats and toasters) but can recognize faces (Moscovitch et al., 1997). Together, the cases allow us to conclude that the two types of images—faces and objects—rely on separate biological networks of neurons to achieve recognition from memory. Case studies are also undertaken when an individual's life experience is unique, such as individuals who were severely abused as children, who demonstrate exceptional talent, or who display criminal behavior. Case studies address questions about human behavior that cannot be designed as a research study due to the rare qualities of the individuals; however, we can learn much from such studies on a case-by-case basis.

Surveys

We are inundated with surveys, from the "Tell us about your experience" questions when making purchases, to online pop-up surveys, to telephone and e-mailed questionnaires on politics, medical care, and community issues. Within psychology, surveys are a big business, reaching out to sample people across communities in order to register the opinions of a variety of people. **Internet-mediated research**, such as surveys posted online for volunteer respondents, allows researchers to question participants across the world. Why are surveys so popular? A major reason is that a **survey** involves the self-report of behavior, and is much easier to collect than other data. By simply asking people what they do and care about, you can gain interesting information about their psychological lives. Consider a simple survey conducted with 100 students at a mid-size Midwestern university (Ross et al., 1999). In the spring term, they asked 100 students to check items on a list of 40 sources of stress in their lives at college TABLE 2-1. The results can be presented in the form of a bar graph to show the differences among the categories FIGURE 2-3. Simply asking people important questions about their experiences can reveal interesting information for

Internet-mediated research Using the World Wide Web to collect data from remote participants.

Survey A study method in which individuals are asked to respond to a set of questions designed by an experimenter.

TABLE 2-1 Number of College Students Reporting Stress ($n = 100$)

Change in sleeping habits	89
Change in eating habits	74
Financial difficulties	71
Computer problems	69
Lower grade than expected	68
Roommate conflict	61
Public speaking	60
Fighting with boy/girlfriend	41
Personal health problem	26
Change of major	24
Trouble with parents	21
Missing too many classes	21
Death of friend or family	18
Minor law violation	14
Parental divorce	1

Source: Adapted from Ross, S. E., Niebling, B. C., & Heckert, T. M. (1999). Sources of stress among college students. College Student Journal, 33*(2). 312–318.*

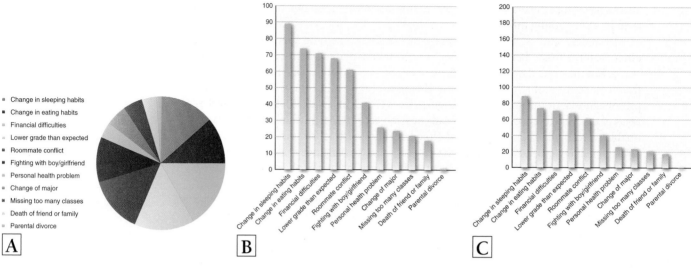

FIGURE 2-3 Results from studies can be displayed in a variety of forms. A. Pie chart showing the frequency of reported stressors. B. Bar graph of the same data. The horizontal axis (x-axis) shows the categories of stressors, and the vertical axis (y-axis) shows the frequency of reports. C. This graph shows the same data again; however this time, the scale has changed to show scores up to 200. As a result, the bars are smaller, so the impact of the stressors may *seem* smaller. Be sure to check scales to interpret carefully the picture you see. *Source: Data from Ross et al., 1999.*

Population The larger group about whom a study would like to draw conclusions.

Sample The subgroup of individuals included in a study to represent a larger population.

Sampling bias The selection of a sample of individuals from within a population that fails to capture an accurate representation of the larger group.

others about what to expect in their own lives. Surveys are used across areas in psychology to assess what concerns people, what inspires them, and what drives their behavior.

However, doing so using well-conceived research designs requires several steps. First, we can ask who we want to draw conclusions about, called the **population** of the study. For example, the survey above addresses college students, while other studies may target the elderly, people in the United States, or people in general. Defining this group is important in selecting a **sample**, or the subgroup of respondents who will take part in the study FIGURE 2-4. In the survey above, one group of 100 students at one university was selected at random for the sample, and the researchers want to conclude that their findings are valid for the population of all college students. How might they improve on the validity of their design? One solution is to increase the number of participants (called *n*) in the study. If many people contribute responses, we can feel more confident we are capturing what most of this population thinks. A second solution is to collect the sample in ways that better represent the population; so they might collect data from campuses at small colleges, big research universities, and community colleges so that all types of college students are included in the sample. Some studies may show a **sampling bias**, or a limitation in the sample selected; for example, studies recruiting participants by calling through the telephone book listings will omit people who do not have listed numbers or home phones.

FIGURE 2-4 A sample, or subset, of individuals are selected from a larger population.

Most commonly, researchers choose a **convenience sample**, or participants who are readily available for the study. Since most researchers are located on college campuses, this means the vast majority of studies conducted use samples composed of undergraduates, often those studying in psychology. They are often selected through their participation in a course or presence in a particular building in which recruiting signs are posted (Schultz, 1969). Are they (and you) "typical" people who are like most other people in the world? Far from it: Study participants are smarter, more involved in volunteer activities, and more financially well off than the rest of the population, even in just the United States (Rosenthal & Rosnow, 1975). Nevertheless, findings from a college student sample are often generalized to all people, assuming a universal truth to the results. Sampling done well represents important factors about the population, including gender, age, ethnicity, and socioeconomic status. In major studies, methods of **random sampling** are used to ensure that every member of the population of interest has an equal chance of selection through the use of randomization. For example, using addresses, one could survey every 10th house listed within a community; however, you would still miss participants who do not live in homes. The cost of good sampling methods often leads to compromises on the selection of the study sample.

Survey data are very easy to collect, and tremendous numbers of psychological studies rely on the self-reports of individuals. However, surveys can have important drawbacks. For example, people can say whatever they want on a survey, so you may not capture their true thoughts or behavior. Sometimes researchers ask the same questions in different forms in order to detect when people might not be giving truthful answers or may be answering without reading the questions carefully. In addition, surveys often depend on our ability to accurately remember our past or recent experiences, and studies have shown that people are not very accurate in recalling when events occurred (Tourangeau et al., 2000). People's answers are also influenced by how the questions are stated and the order of question presentation (Schwarz & Hippler, 1995). Survey methodology is a large specialty area within psychology and provides important descriptive information about people's behavior.

Correlational Studies

Some descriptive studies attempt to determine the relationship between two types of observations. For example, many studies measure "satisfaction with life" (Diener et al., 1985), or your subjective "report card" on how your life is going right now TABLE 2-2. After answering the five test items, you will have a score ranging from 5 to 35. This score is a measure of your subjective well-being (SWB), or your self-perception of how satisfying your life is through evaluating life events (e.g., Diener, 2006). Now we can ask, what variables are related to high SWB? For example, is it true that money brings happiness?

Convenience sample A group of participants who are readily available for a study.

Random sampling Selecting which members of a population will participate in a study through a systematic method that gives every person an equal chance of selection.

TABLE 2-2 Satisfaction with Life Scale

Below are five statements that you may agree or disagree with. Using the 1 to 7 scale below, indicate your agreement with each item by placing the appropriate number on the line preceding that item. Please be open and honest in your response.

7	6	5	4	3	2	1
Strongly agree	Agree	Slightly agree	Neither	Slightly disagree	Disagree	Strongly disagree

1. _____ In most ways my life is close to my ideal.

2. _____ The conditions of my life are excellent.

3. _____ I am satisfied with my life.

4. _____ So far I have gotten the important things I want in life.

5. _____ If I could live my life over, I would change almost nothing.

Scale: Add your scores for the five items.

30–35 Very high score; highly satisfied: Respondents who score in this range love their lives and feel that things are going very well. Their lives are not perfect, but they feel that things are about as good as lives get.

(continues)

TABLE 2-2 Satisfaction with Life Scale *(continued)*

25–29 High score: Individuals who score in this range like their lives and feel that things are going well. Of course their lives are not perfect, but they feel that things are mostly good.

20–24 Average score: The average of life satisfaction in economically developed nations is in this range—the majority of people are generally satisfied, but have some areas where they very much would like some improvement.

15–19 Slightly below average in life satisfaction: People who score in this range usually have small but significant problems in several areas of their lives, or have many areas that are doing fine but one area that represents a substantial problem for them.

10–14 Dissatisfied: People who score in this range are substantially dissatisfied with their lives. People in this range may have a number of domains that are not going well, or one or two domains that are going very badly.

5–9 Extremely dissatisfied: Individuals who score in this range are usually extremely unhappy with their current life. In some cases this is in reaction to some recent bad event such as widowhood or unemployment.

Source: Data from Diener, E., & Biswas-Diener, R. (2008). The science of optimal happiness. *Boston: Blackwell Publishing.*

Scatterplot Graph showing the points observed from scores on two variables.

Correlation coefficient An index, called *r*, of the degree of relationship between two variables, ranging from –1.00 to +1.00.

Correlation A measure of the degree to which different factors are associated with one another.

Positive correlation An association between two variables where higher scores on one go with higher scores on the other.

We can compare people's annual incomes in relation to their SWB scores by graphing them in a **scatterplot**, in which each point represents one person's income and SWB score FIGURE 2-5. To view the pattern of relationship between the variables, the scatterplot includes a line showing the average across the points. Do the points fall close to the average along the line, together, or are they scattered in a very diffuse pattern? This degree of association—how closely the points fall to one another—is measured by the product-moment **correlation coefficient**, invented by Karl Pearson. He named the coefficient *r* to reflect the idea of "reversion," or returning to the average. If the points are clustered along the line, the value of *r* will be high, and if the points are scattered in a more diffuse pattern, the *r*-value will be very low.

In addition, the *r*-value, also called a **correlation**, provides an indicator of the *direction* of relationship between two variables. FIGURE 2-6 shows three possible patterns of scatterplots. How might income relate to SWB scores? One possible pattern reflects a **positive correlation** between the two variables, in which higher scores on one "go with" higher scores on the other, and the value of *r* is between 0.0 and +1.00. It is also possible

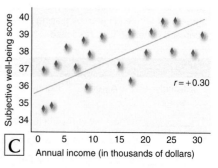

FIGURE 2-5 Three example scatterplots show possible associations between income and SWB, with one point for each observation of a person's income and their SWB score. In A, the correlation (*r* value) is close to +1.00, so each person that is higher in income is also higher on SWB score. B shows a correlation of +0.60, where the points are more scattered. C shows more scatter in the pattern and thus, results with a lower correlation (*r* value of +0.30).

that we may find a **negative correlation** (between 0.0 and –1.00), between income and SWB. What if more money brings *less* happiness; for example, working at better-paying jobs brings more stress? Then *higher* income would be associated with *lower* SWB scores. A final possibility is that there is *no* systematic relationship between income and SWB. If so, then all levels of income would have some people with both high and low SWB scores.

Negative correlation An association between two variables where higher scores on one go with lower scores on the other.

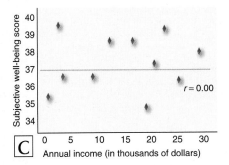

FIGURE 2-6 Correlations can be positive and negative. In A, a positive correlation is found when scores on one variable increase with scores on another. B. A negative correlation is shown, where increasing scores on one variable are matched with decreasing scores on the other. C. When two variables are unrelated, their correlation is close to zero, and there is no pattern to the spread of points in the distribution.

What is your prediction? Over several studies, the average correlation between income and life satisfaction is about +0.20 (Diener & Biswas-Diener, 2002; Lucas & Dyrenforth, 2006; Lucas et al., 2008) FIGURE 2-7. What does this mean? Because it is positive, it means *higher* incomes tend to correlate with *higher* life satisfaction scores. But the numerical size of the correlation also reveals the *strength* of the association. The strength of a correlation is measured by its distance from 0.0 on a scale of 0.0 to +1.0 or –1.0. The further the number is from 0.0, the stronger the correlation. Note that an *r*-value of –0.30 is as strong as one of +0.30; they differ in the *direction* of the correlation. So if you tell me what your income is, I can estimate your life satisfaction score to some degree. But if the *r*-value was higher (say, +0.50), there would be a stronger association between income and SWB scores, giving me a better chance of estimating your life satisfaction more accurately.

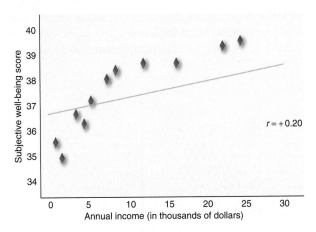

FIGURE 2-7 The actual findings showing the degree of association between income and SWB scores, *r* = 0.20.
Source: Data from Diener, E., & Biswas-Diener, R. (2008). The science of optimal happiness. Boston: Blackwell Publishing.

But knowing the relative strength of a correlation raises other questions we might want to answer. For example, can we interpret the strength of the correlation in terms of how much one variable is tied to the other? To do so, we use the concept of variance, which is an index of the amount of variation among scores. So there is an average SWB score in the United States, and there is a tremendous amount of variance around that average. Each person differs from the average by some large or small amount. What if I knew people's income: Would that help me explain why some of them have high SWB scores and some have low SWB scores? If so, income would provide a good account of the variance in subjective well-being. To determine the amount of the variance in one variable that can be attributed to the other, you can calculate "$r \times r$," or R^2; so the variance in individuals' SWB scores that is due to income is equal to 0.20^2, or 0.04. That means only 4% of the differences in SWB scores are accounted for by income level. That is not very much; however, this small correlation strength reflects a very stable pattern. The richest group (more than $200,000 a year) reports higher happiness scores than the middle group and the poorest group (less than $10,000 a year).

Is this a meaningful finding? Income explains only 4% of the variance in SWB scores. However, when you consider how many other things may also contribute to life satisfaction (e.g., relationships, religion, family, friends, ice cream), the correlation of +0.20 is indeed a helpful finding. It allows us to conclude that money can buy happiness, at least to some small degree. However, the correlation alone does not tell us about the specific patterns within the relationship between two variables. When we examine the subsets of the data, some meaningful patterns emerge. For example, it appears that money *does* make a difference to SWB when income is very low; but, once over $10,000 in annual income, there is less of a difference in SWB attributable to income level. So we might conclude that the relationship between income and SWB depends on the category (very low vs. livable incomes). However, the correlation cannot tell us this: instead, it reveals the association between all levels of both variables at the same time.

Correlations can tell us whether an association exists between two variables, its direction (positive or negative), and its strength, which tells us how well one variable accounts for the variance in the other. But you cannot stop there: You have to look at the scatterplots and examine the *patterns* of association. Consider the scatterplots in FIGURE 2-8. Distributions can have the same correlation value, but the pattern of scores can be very different. For example, age is not correlated with SWB, with no detectable pattern, so that all ages include some people with high and low SWB scores. But the same correlation may be found when there is an underlying pattern; for example, high SWB scores in childhood, young adults, and the elderly, and low scores in teenagers and older adults. The same correlation of 0 could also be found when younger and older people have high SWB and adults have lower scores. So when you see a correlation, think, "These two variables are related;" however, it cannot tell you exactly *how* they are related.

Another question is whether a correlation reveals *why* the two associated variables interact. Does greater subjective well-being cause one to be wealthier, or does greater wealth cause SWB to be higher? One might seem more logical, but a descriptive study with a correlation cannot tell us about the *causality* between the variables. Correlation is not causation; instead,

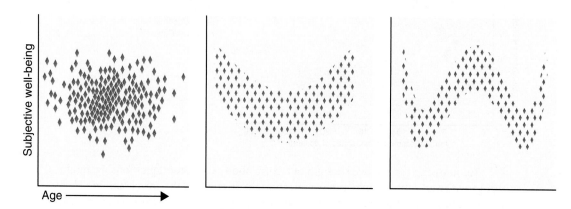

FIGURE 2-8 Three scatterplots of SWB and age with correlations of 0. From the images, it is clear that the correlation does not reveal any information about the shape or pattern of a distribution of scores.

it indicates only that the two variables are associated, or "go together." It may be that a third variable, one we are not measuring, is actually the cause of both observed variables. For example, what if getting married causes both an increase in income (for the family now) and an increase in SWB? We cannot rule out the presence of other, unmeasured factors that may be the cause behind the observed association. So, when you see a correlation, think about what other factors may be causing the relationship between the two correlated variables.

How do we decide whether the correlation strength is large enough to be meaningful to our decisions about behavior? For subjective well-being, the highest correlation found was with self-esteem ($r = +0.55$), along with satisfaction with work ($r = +0.37$) and satisfaction with health ($r = +0.29$; Campbell, 1981). The size of your social network correlates at +0.16 with life satisfaction. A meta-analysis of studies found the correlation between age and SWB to be near zero (Stock, Okun, Haring, & Witter, 1983). How can we interpret the value of these correlations? They may seem small; on the other hand, correlations, even when small, reflect real relationships between variables. For example, the ability of employment interviews to predict job success is just +0.20 (McDaniel, Whetzel, Schmidt, & Maurer, 1994); however, the small size of the correlation does not convince people that they should skip interviews when hiring! Similarly, sugar consumption was reported to be correlated at +0.01 with the behavior and cognitive processes of children (Wolraich, Wilson, & White, 1995). But parents still believe sugar makes their children act more "wired." In large enough samples, even small correlations stand up across studies.

What should our standard be in interpreting the significance of correlation strength? In psychological research, the standard for a correlation is +0.30, meaning one variable accounts for 9% of the variance in the other. As a rule of thumb, this is considered an important finding with implications about and for our behavior (Mischel, 1968). In medical studies, much smaller correlations are considered important (Meyer et al., 2001). For example, women's calcium intake and bone mass are correlated at +0.08, yet it is still recommended that women take calcium supplements to improve bone health (Welten et al., 1995). The correlation of low-level lead exposure and reduced childhood intelligence test scores is +0.11; however, laws are in place to require notification of lead paint use when a home is sold. Even small correlations that predict a small amount of the variance in a variable are important findings if they provide knowledge that is helpful to health and well-being.

A final question to consider about correlation is whether all important variables are included within a study. For example, does subjective well-being differ based on culture, or what part of the world you are living in? Researchers have found very large international differences in life satisfaction, and they appear to be much more related to differences in life circumstances than differences in psychology, or the way these circumstances are evaluated by individuals (Diener et al., 2010). FIGURE 2-9 shows that when the scope of the study is extended across cultures and nations, it is apparent that poverty has an

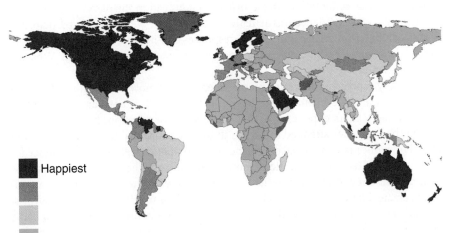

Happiest

Least happy

FIGURE 2-9 A depiction of countries around the world with the average subjective well-being score coded by color, with red as the happiest. *Source: White, A. (2007). A global projection of subjective well-being: A challenge to positive psychology? Psychtalk, 56, 17–20.*

important impact on levels of well-being (White, 2007). SWB correlates most strongly with health (+0.70), followed by wealth (+0.60) and access to basic education (+0.60). The important lesson to learn is that relationships between measured variables, even if small in size, can inform us about psychology. However, the questions we are *not* asking may be even more important in considering the meaning of our findings.

CONCEPT LEARNING CHECK 2.2 | *What Do Correlations Mean?*

For each correlation, write what you conclude from the evidence. Consider the direction, strength, and possible causality of the relationship.

1. Number of minutes studying with others is correlated with course grades, $r = +0.30$.

2. Amount of orange juice consumed is correlated with voting Republican, $r = +0.15$.

3. Number of movies viewed is correlated with number of books read, $r = 0.00$.

4. Hours of video games played each week is correlated with graduation from college, $r = -0.30$.

5. Minutes of aerobic exercise per day is correlated with ratings of mood, $r = +0.50$.

2.3 Experimental Research

In experiments, the researcher intentionally manipulates variables and measures their impact on other variables.

■ Describe the components of a psychological experiment.

Imagine you and a friend are asked to participate in a study of "impression formation" by interacting with people in an online chat room (Gardner et al., 2000). The groups are instructed to "get to know" each other by talking, and you enter comments when your initials come up in turns on the screen. For your friend, the group discusses music, clothing, and movies, and when your friend types in comments, the other group members agree with her ("Cool!") and are approving of her comments. In your case, the topic is marching band, and all four group members enthusiastically discuss the details; but, you were not in band, and your attempts to participate are ignored. You are then asked to rate your impressions of each member.

Now, you and your friend asked to read the same excerpt from a diary and to form an impression of the person who wrote it. The diary includes both social information and individual events. You are both asked to rate your impression of the person and then are given a surprise recall task of the information you read in the diary. Then, you are told your chat room experience was actually "virtual." There were no other participants; instead, a computer program simulated the responses of other individuals. The program produced the same accepting or rejecting messages, no matter what you typed! What are these experimenters up to?

This study represents an **experiment**, where one or more independent factors is manipulated by an experimenter, and the result is measured. The researchers' question was this: Would readers' experience of social acceptance or rejection change what information in the diary they attended to? In the study, the initial chat room experience was intended to manipulate the social experience of participants: feelings of acceptance for some subjects and feelings of rejection for others. In this case, the type of social response is the **independent variable**. This is the factor that *changes* as the experimenter manipulates it to create different experiences for participants. This manipulation works surprisingly well: Even though you think it would not matter, people are sensitive to being ignored in social settings, regardless of the content of the conversation. After participants read the diary excerpt, the researchers measured what participants remembered about the events in the diary. In this case, what participants remembered from the diary is the **dependent variable**. This is a *constant* factor that is measured to determine if there is a

Experiment A method by which one or more independent factors is manipulated by an experimenter, and the result is measured through one or more dependent variables.

Independent variable The factor that an experimenter manipulates to create different experiences for participants.

Dependent variable The measurement collected to determine if there was any effect of the independent variable in an experiment.

relationship between it and the independent variable—the factor that changes. As it turns out, there was a strong relationship between the independent and dependent variables. If rejected, you were *more* likely to remember diary information about social activities than were the "accepted" participants. The "accepted" participants also remembered more information about the individual activities in the diary than did those who had been "rejected." The experimenters concluded that the experience of social acceptance or rejection changed participants' level of interest in the social events of the diary writer.

In a true experiment, the claim from such a study is that the independent variable *causes* the observed differences in the dependent variable. How can we be so sure that it was just the manipulation of social acceptance that caused the social memory differences? The key feature that allows the conclusion of causality is that every participant in the study has an equal chance of being assigned to the groups that make up the independent variable, called **random assignment** FIGURE 2-10. So, when you walked in the door of the study, you had an equal chance of being assigned to the "accepted" experience group or to the "rejected" experience group. Your friend had the same 50% chance of being assigned to each group. This is important, because without the random assignment, other factors may be responsible for causing the outcomes. But if we know that the two groups (those rejected and accepted) only differ in which experience they had, then the outcome must be due to the independent variable. Most experimenters flip a coin or use another method to ensure that the participants are assigned to the independent variable experience at random FIGURE 2-11. So when reading about studies, ask yourself, "Did every participant have the same chance of being in any of the groups?"

Many times, the answer to this question is, "no!" For example, we would often like to compare males and females to find out how gender affects our behavior. But we cannot assign a person to a gender at random! Instead, we accept gender as a quality of an individual and then compare groups of different individuals on measures of behavior. This means that any experiment involving an individual difference, like gender, age, ethnicity, personality, and education, is not a "true experiment." For studies in which

Random assignment
Assigning participants to receive a given treatment or control condition by chance so that each has an equal likelihood of appearing in a given group.

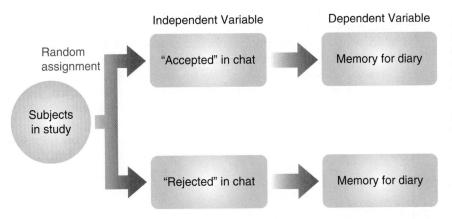

FIGURE 2-10 A true experiment is marked by the random assignment of subjects to conditions. However, for many studies, this is not possible; for example, in the study of gender differences. Such studies may be called "experiments," but they cannot provide the causal conclusions of a true experiment.

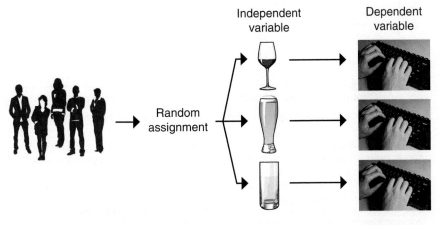

FIGURE 2-11 The design of an experiment involves assigning each participant at random to a group within the independent variable (those who drink wine, beer, or water), while testing all on the dependent variable (typing speed).

Experimental group In an experiment, the group that receives some treatment or experience.

Control group In an experiment, the group that receives no extra treatment or experience.

Interaction between variables When the effect of one independent variable on the dependent variable depends upon the level of another independent variable.

random assignment cannot be done, the question becomes, "To what degree is the variable (e.g., gender) associated with the dependent measure?" For example, a meta-analysis found that girls outperformed boys on math in elementary school and middle school, but large differences with boys outperforming girls show up in high school and college (Hyde et al., 1990). However, because these studies are not true experiments, with the individuals assigned to gender randomly, we cannot conclude that gender per se causes differences in math performance. Many other things (teacher expectations, activities encouraged as interests, societal views of appropriate careers) may be affecting math scores (Eccles & Jacobs, 1986) rather than gender itself. For many important topics in psychology, we have to settle for these indications of relatedness but still think carefully about underlying causes, just as with correlational studies.

In the simplest studies, the independent variable includes an **experimental group** (that receives some treatment or experience) and a **control group** (that receives *no extra* treatment or experience). Control groups are important because of the need to compare those who receive the treatment to those who do not, allowing you to conclude the treatment has an effect. For example, one study compared people who took a campus walk using underground tunnels (the control group walked the normal paths in the cold Canadian setting) to those asked to walk for the same 15-minute period along a canal in a natural setting (the experimental group). After walking, tests showed those who walked along the greenway reported feeling more positive, more relaxed, and more fascinated with life, and reported fewer negative emotions than the tunnel walkers (Nisbett & Zelenski, 2011). The result provides a causal explanation: The level of positive mood *depends upon* the path taken; that is, the score on the dependent variable depends upon the condition of the independent variable.

The experimenters could have chosen to compare a control group of people who did not walk at all. Or perhaps walking through nature would be better compared to walking through an urban environment. Many studies include more than one comparison condition to identify the cause of any observed differences in the dependent variable. But no one study can include enough conditions to answer any question definitively; instead, it takes a series of experiments to arrive at a conclusion. More typically, experiments include more than one independent variable, allowing the exploration of the **interaction between variables**. For example, suppose we repeated the study above but added another independent variable: time stress. Now we can determine whether the positive impact of natural settings on mood is affected by whether you are under time pressure to complete the walk vs. no time pressure FIGURE 2-12. We expect to see the same pattern occur in the control group: With no time restriction, people would rate their mood higher if they walked the natural path than when they walked the

Does walking through an underground tunnel lower your mood?

Walking in the outdoors is hypothesized to improve your mood.

FIGURE 2-12 One study found that walking through natural areas improved people's ratings of their mood. But if we add another independent variable to the study—asking people to walk "as fast as they can"—the pattern of results may change. The control group (without time pressure) may show the same benefit of natural path on mood, but when under time pressure, both path groups may result in negative mood ratings.
Source: Data from Nisbet, E. K., & Zelenski, J. M. (2011). Underestimating nearby nature: Affective forecasting errors obscure the happy path to sustainability. Psychological Science, 22(9), 1101–1106.

control path through the tunnel. However, the time variable makes a difference in the observed pattern: When under time pressure to complete the walk "as fast as they can," *both* groups now rate their moods similarly negative after the walk. Including more variables allows researchers to determine how the impact of one variable might be affected by another.

Confounding variables, or alternative factors that might account for differences in the dependent measure, must be ruled out in order to draw solid conclusions. For example, perhaps the weather on the day of the walk affected the results. Experimenters can try to hold those factors constant in the study or conduct further studies to rule out other potential causes. The use of careful controls within studies is also needed to avoid inaccuracy of measurements due to the researcher's expectations, called **experimenter bias**, or from the participants' expectations. For example, experimenter bias might arise if judgments are made about subjects' performances and the experimenter knows whether they have received the treatment. Participants may alter their behavior in a study to be more **socially desirable** and fail to answer honestly. For example, knowing they received a medication during the study, they may believe the medication has an effect and change their behavior as a result. For this reason, researchers sometimes include placebos, or medications without active ingredients, for one group of subjects so that any **placebo effect** can be separated from the effect of the medication. When subject or experimenter bias is expected to be a problem, a **double-blind procedure** is followed in which neither the subject nor the experimenter knows which condition is assigned for that subject.

The key to a good experiment lies in how the researchers define their independent and dependent variables. In their **operational definitions**, studies attempt to describe and capture the key elements of the variables of interest while still providing a reliable measure of performance. For many areas of psychology, research has broken out in new directions as soon as someone was able to identify new ways of measuring psychological behavior. One example is the use of gaze as a dependent measure. Technology was adapted to allow researchers to pinpoint what someone was looking at and, consequently, to infer what aspect of a situation they were thinking about (called the eye-mind hypothesis; Just & Carpenter, 1980). For example, eye movements have been used to analyze how we interpret information in visual scenes (Henderson, 2003) FIGURE 2-13. This dependent measure has now been employed with infants, web page design, and classroom studies of student–teacher interaction. Examples of the wide variety of behaviors measured by psychologists are shown in **TABLE 2-3**.

Sometimes, it is not possible to do a true experiment given the topic of interest. For example, developmental studies are particularly challenging. Researchers may follow an individual from first grade through high school, measuring the same person each year, and compare behavior over time in a **longitudinal study**. But these studies take a long time to complete (because we have to wait until participants age), and they require staying in contact with people throughout the length of the study. Then, when it's time to compare your performance at age 6 and age 18, many things have changed in addition to their age (the independent variable of interest): The world has changed, too! Alternatively, we can try to understand development by comparing a current group of 6 year olds to others who are now 18, called a **cross-sectional study**. Because we are selecting people for the study based on their age, there is no random assignment to condition. Importantly, there may be **cohort effects**; that is, the life of a 6 year old may be different now than it was for those who are now 18 when they were 6. So the question remains, are differences observed due to age alone, or are they due to differences related to the time period in which people were raised? On questions where the participant comes into the study with their independent variable already determined (by their age,

Confounding variable An alternative factor that might account for observed differences in the dependent measure.

Experimenter bias The introduction of inaccuracy of measurements due to the researcher's expectations.

Social desirability bias Participants may alter their responses if they perceive them as depicting them negatively.

Placebo effect A participant's belief that he or she is receiving a treatment can produce changes in behavior.

Double-blind procedure A method in which both the experimenter and participant are not informed about the subject's assignment to a treatment within a study.

Operational definition The concrete implementation of a psychological concept within a study.

Longitudinal study Following a person through development by studying him or her at different points in time.

Cross-sectional study Comparing people at different ages with different people in the age groups.

FIGURE 2-13 Eye movement durations of one viewer looking at the scene. The circles represent fixations and the lines represent saccades.
Source: Data from Henderson, J. M. (2003). Human gaze control during real-world scene perception. Trends in Cognitive Sciences, 7(11), 498–505.

Cohort effect A difference observed between age groups that may be due to differences in their experiences in addition to age.

TABLE 2-3 Examples of Behavioral Measures in Psychology Studies

Eye movements	Amount of drug self-administered
Galvanic skin reponse	Time spent working
Event-related potentials (electrical activity in the brain)	Hoarding
PET scans (images of oxygen uptake showing high-activity areas in the brain)	Amount of money donated
fMRI scans (images of high neural activity in brain areas)	Number of cookies eaten
EEG (heart rates)	Seat belt use
Cortisol hormone levels in saliva	Time survey was returned
Odor deposited on pads worn under arms	Mailing of postcards
Time to tap a response key	Detection of a stimulus
Recognition of a familiar face	Avoiding shocks
Word identification	Time of awakening
Recall from memory	School grades
Time hand is held in bucket of ice water	Attachment to parents
Decisions to purchase products	Speed of learning
Self-reports of activities, attitudes, thoughts, and feelings	Language use
Ratings of personality	Number of bar presses
Breathing rate	Political themes
Factual quizzes	Perceptions of culture
Driving	Jury decisions
Telephone answers	Hand washing
Facial expressions	Aesthetic judgments
Looking time	Intelligence test scores
Imitation of body movements	Interest in math
Survey questions	Amount of hot sauce added for another
Judgments of liking	Stories told
Distance from another	Mate choices
Group consensus	Photographs of dorm rooms
Number of ideas generated	Picking up another's dropped wallet

gender, personality, experience, etc.), random assignment cannot be accomplished, so the study does not involve a true experiment.

The reason why true experiments with random assignment are so important is that they prove the independent variable alone is the *cause* of observed differences in the dependent variable. This is the most powerful and informative conclusion you can draw from studies of behavior. A true experiment allows conclusive evidence that the independent variable causes differences in the dependent variable.

Another problem with true experiments is that achieving control of the independent variable often involves making compromises about the generalizability of a study. In order to keep elements of the experimental and control conditions constant, you may have to test the participants within a laboratory setting. For example, a study on gender differences in cocaine addiction might employ an animal model, such as a rat, and carefully measure the consequences of the rat's self-administered dosing (Hu et al., 2004). However, will the findings tell us about the differences in men's and women's real life experiences, and how their everyday lives might impact decisions to use cocaine? The ability to conduct controlled studies often requires isolating the target behavior in laboratories in order to ensure proper controls; but, this means some of the important features of real behavior are missing from the simplified (but better controlled) conditions in a study. As shown in **TABLE 2-4**, there are advantages and drawbacks to conducting research using each of these methods.

TABLE 2-4 Comparison of Research Methods

Type of Study	Descriptive	Correlational	Experimental
Goal	Capture existing behaviors	Detect associations between variables	To determine causes
Examples	Case studies Naturalistic observation Surveys	Surveys Group comparisons	Field Laboratory
Key feature	Watch or ask people	Compute correlation of variables	Random assignment
Strengths	Describes in natural setting	Captures existing differences	Determines causality
Weaknesses	Difficult to be objective Hard to compare studies	Can't determine causation, only association	Generalize to behavior in the world

CONCEPT LEARNING CHECK 2.3   *Designing an Experiment*

Design a study to test the hypothesis that men earn higher salaries than women. Fill in the specifics of your study for each of the study elements below.

1. Independent variable

2. Dependent variable

3. Operational definition (of dependent variable)

4. Randomization

5. Sampling

6. Population

7. True Experiment

2.4 Statistical Analysis

The data collected about behavior are summarized by standard numerical measures that describe differences.

- Illustrate the central tendency of, and the variation among, a set of scores in describing data.
- Describe what it means when a study shows an effect that is statistically significant.

To psychologists, the proof is in the data: What do the measurements show about people's actual behavior? My friend Sheri, now a clinical psychologist, demonstrated this approach when she was just a preschooler. The babysitter who cared for Sheri and her little brother sometimes hit him, but when Sheri told her parents, they interpreted this to mean it happened only rarely. So one day, Sheri took the cardboard backing from one of her father's new shirts and made a mark on it with a crayon every time the babysitter struck her brother. That night, confronted with the many markings on the cardboard, her parents quickly grasped the seriousness of the situation. In many important decisions about policies, education, and life improvement, the most convincing evidence is a conclusion drawn from data.

Measures of Central Tendency and Variance

Statistics provide a numerical representation of data, summarizing the nature of all of the observations collected into a shorthand "picture." Rather than describe each data "point" or observation, it is helpful to summarize them into a depiction that describes the most important findings. There are two important ways to describe data: the **central tendency** of, and the variation among a set of scores.

Measures of central tendency describe the "typical" value of a given variable. For example, how many dogs live in the typical American family? The number of dogs in a sample of 45 homes is shown in FIGURE 2-14. How can we summarize the results of the data collected? One measure, called the **mode**, is the most frequently observed score, or one dog per home. A second measure is the **median**, or the middle score of the distribution that divides the sample in two. If we line up the homes from the fewest to the most dogs and take the middle home in this list, the score is 2 dogs. Finally, the most common way to describe the central tendency of a set of scores is the arithmetic average of all the scores (adding up the number of dogs in all, divided by the number of homes), called the **mean**—in this case, 2.8 dogs. Which of these gives the best picture of how many dogs

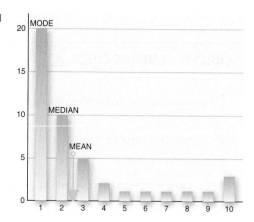

FIGURE 2-14 Measures of central tendency shown on a frequency distribution.

people own? You might say that most families with dogs own just one (the mode), while half own one or two (the median), while the average number is close to three. The best measure of central tendency to report is the one that gives the most useful summary for your purpose. For example, if you are interested in discussing the close bonds formed by people with their dogs, pointing out that most homes have just one (the mode) provides some relevant information.

In addition, we need a way to describe how the scores are distributed around the typical score: Are they spread very far apart, or are they clustered closely together? A bar graph showing the total number of observations in each category is often "smoothed" into a line drawing to show the shape of a distribution of scores. For example, suppose students' scores from a quiz are compiled, and the distribution of their scores shows that most people score close to the average score FIGURE 2-15. We might conclude that most of the students are learning the material well. On the other hand, the same average score might occur with a distribution of scores that is much more "spread out": While the central tendency is the same, there may be many more higher and many more lower scores. This suggests that the group shows more differences between scores, called **variance**. So in addition to the central tendency, it is important to give a summary of the variance observed in the data sample. A simple measure of variance is the **range**, or the

---

Statistic A numerical summary of the results of data collection.

Central tendency The "typical value" of a group of scores, described by the mean, mode, or median.

Mode The most frequently observed score in a data sample.

Median The score at the middle of a distribution of scores from a sample.

Mean The arithmetic average, or the sum of all scores in a sample divided by the number of scores.

Variance The variability between scores observed on a given dependent variable.

Range A measure of variation in a data sample determined by subtracting the lowest score from the highest score.

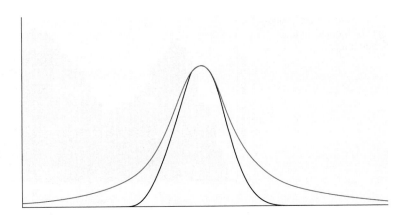

FIGURE 2-15 Scores from two quizzes demonstrate that data with the same mean can have a different variation within the group—the red group's data is much more spread out.

highest score minus the lowest score. The most frequently used measure of variation is the **standard deviation**, a measure tracking how each score in a sample differs from the mean TABLE 2-5. This calculation reveals in a single number whether the distribution of scores is close together or more spread out.

The pattern of scores can take on many shapes, such as a **bimodal distribution**, in which there are two clusters of frequently occurring scores FIGURE 2-16. Often, the distribution of scores in a large sample takes the shape of an upside-down bell, called the **normal distribution**. It takes this name because many common measurements fall into this distribution shape, such as people's heights FIGURE 2-17. For this special pattern of

The frequency of each category observed is shown as a bar; then, the shape of the tops of the bars is smoothed into a line drawing.

TABLE 2-5 Example of Standard Deviation in Two Samples

	BOYS			GIRLS		
	Test Score	Difference from Mean	Squared Difference	Test Score	Difference from Mean	Squared Difference
	110	10	100	110	10	100
	109	9	81	110	10	100
	108	8	64	110	10	100
	107	7	49	110	10	100
	106	6	36	110	10	100
	94	−6	36	90	−10	100
	93	−7	49	90	−10	100
	92	−8	64	90	−10	100
	91	−9	81	90	−10	100
	90	−10	100	90	−10	100
Mean =	100			100		
Range =	90–100			90–110		
Sum of Deviations^2 =		660			1,000	
Sum of Deviations^2/ (n−1)		73.33			111.11	
Standard Deviation =		8.56			10.54	

Standard Deviation = $\sqrt{(\text{Sum of Deviations}^2/n-1)}$.

Standard deviation A statistical measure tracking how each score in a sample differs from the mean.

Bimodal distribution A pattern of scores with two distinct clusters with different modes (frequently occurring scores).

Normal distribution The inverted bell-shaped frequency distribution that often occurs for psychological tests and variables such as height.

FIGURE 2-16 Example distribution showing two "modes," or a bimodal distribution.

FIGURE 2-17 The normal curve has a specific distribution where certain percentages of scores fall within one, two, or three standard deviations.

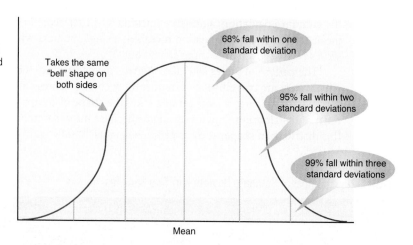

distribution, the mean and the median are the same; that is, half of the scores fall lower than the mean and half higher. The "spread" of the normal distribution is related to the standard deviation. Approximately 68% of the scores lie within one standard deviation of the mean, 95% within two, and 99% within three standard deviations of the mean. Research reports often include the means and standard deviations in order to provide a complete picture of the data observed. For example, the study on nature walks found that an indoor walk produced an average positive mood rating of 2.01, with a standard deviation of 0.82, while an outdoor walk produced an average mood rating of 3.21, with a standard deviation of 0.84 (Nisbett & Zelenski, 2011). From this, we can depict the distributions of the two sets of data for indoor and outdoor walkers and about how much the two overlap FIGURE 2-18.

FIGURE 2-18 Walkers who were mostly indoors had a lower mean mood rating (in blue) than walkers out in nature (shown in red), though the variance in the two groups (shown by the spread of the frequency distributions) was very similar.
Source: Data from Nisbett, E. K., & Zelenski, J. M. (2011). Underestimating nearby nature: Affective forecasting errors obscure the happy path to sustainability. Psychological Science, 22(9), 1101–1106.

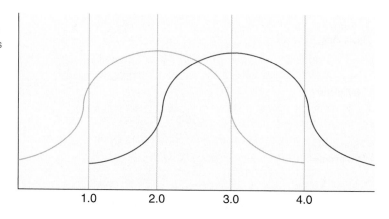

Making Inferences with Statistics

The point of using **inferential statistics** is to guide us in making conclusions from data, and to help us decide whether any differences observed are meaningful or due to random variation. In other words, can we believe the differences in the groups within an experiment, or could we be mistaken? When drawing conclusions, we want to ensure that the differences we observe are reliable and not simply a result of chance. Suppose you wanted to test whether college athletes have lower grade point averages than nonathletes. You could stop by the gym, ask five athletes and five nonathletes their GPAs, and see if the averages differ. Suppose you found that the GPAs of the five athletes were actually higher. Would you believe the result? What would it take to convince you that an observed difference between the two groups is "real" and not a result of chance?

What leads us to believe that the difference between two groups is real? One factor is the size of the difference between the two groups. A recent study found the average GPA of male recruited athletes was 2.84, while nonathletes averaged 3.04 (College Sports Project, 2010). This is a fairly small difference on a small (4.0) scale. If the averages of the two groups are even close together ("walk-on" male athletes averaged 2.97), we might be less inclined to believe there is a real difference between the groups. A second factor is the variability within each of the groups. The standard deviation for nonathletes was very small, while the GPAs among athletes had more spread from high to low. That means the nonathletes are more similar in their GPAs as a group, while the athletes show a lot more variation among them. But the variance in both groups was small in comparison to the size of the averages. That suggests reliable measurement. A third factor to consider is how many observations were collected. In the study, there were 8,951 recruited athletes and 22,734 nonathletes. With so many observations, you might feel much more confident that the differences observed are reliable differences compared to the locker room study.

These factors are combined in statistical formulas that capture the size of the difference between groups, the amount of variation observed within each, and the number of observations collected, all at the same time. From the resulting statistical value, we can determine the probability that the finding may have occurred just by chance or whether occurring by chance alone is unlikely. There may be a 1 in 10 chance of observing this data pattern or a 1 in 100 chance; so we need to set a criterion or standard to use as a cutoff for accepting that an outcome is "unlikely." For example, say you have a bag with 100 marbles inside, with 99 blue and 1 red marble. You pull 1 marble out, and it is the red one. We might agree that is highly unlikely to happen! What if there were 10 marbles that were red and 90 blue, and you pull out one that is red? Still surprised? The standard used by psychologists—purely an arbitrary convention—is a probability of less than 5%. When an observed difference occurs and the probability of its occurrence is determined to be less than 5%, psychologists call it **statistically significant**, noted as the "alpha level," or *p*-value. Psychologists agree that when the likelihood of finding the observed difference is less than 5%, they will consider the differences as "real" and not a fluke occurrence. So the study on GPA found a statistically significant difference (a *p*-value less than 0.05) and was judged not likely to be caused by chance. Though recruited male athletes do have lower GPAs than male nonathletes, the size of the difference is fairly small; in fact, the study authors concluded athletes had ". . . GPAs only slightly below those of nonathletes."

Statistics are tools used to describe the results of research and to make inferences about how likely the observations are to reflect real differences (or the result of chance alone). For each study, researchers ask whether the results could be due to chance alone, whether the findings are robust (of a large size), and whether the study was sensitive enough to detect a real difference if it was there. Statistical significance is a standard the field accepts to say that the findings are likely to be real; however, errors do occur. A replication is the running of a study again under similar circumstances to see whether the same results are found. Sometimes, results cannot be replicated, pointing out errors or important features in studies. One study found a "Mozart effect," in which 10 minutes of listening to classical music by Mozart led to a three-point improvement on a spatial reasoning test FIGURE 2-19 (Rauscher et al., 1993). Many researchers attempted

Inferential statistic
A numerical test to determine what conclusions can be drawn from observed data.

Statistically significant
When the probability (*p*) of an observed difference occurring is determined to be less than 5% ($p < 0.05$).

FIGURE 2-19 A. Performance on a spatial reasoning task improved more after listening to Mozart's music for a brief period. Note that the scale begins at "5;" if the scale began at "0," as in B, the small size of the "Mozart effect" is more apparent.

Source: Data from Rauscher, F., Shaw, G., & Ky, K. (1993). Music and spatial task performance. Nature, 365, 611.

to benefit from this finding by playing classical music for babies to boost their reasoning abilities. However, further studies showed the effect was difficult to replicate and did not generalize to other reasoning tasks (Steele et al., 1999). Other times, studies may show a statistically reliable result that has little importance in the world. For example, a study of swimming showed people move as quickly through syrup as they do through water (Gettelfinger & Cussler, 2004). Though statistically significant, the question of the study's significance to our understanding of psychology is an entirely separate question. This demonstrates that even statistically significant findings have to be considered for their real-world validity.

CONCEPT LEARNING CHECK 2.4   *Summarizing with Statistics*

1. For the set of data below, compute the mean, median, mode, and range.

1, 1, 1, 1, 2, 2, 2, 3, 3, 5

  A. Mean

  B. Median

  C. Mode

  D. Range

Explain

2. In your own words, describe what it means when a study shows an effect that is "statistically significant."

2.5 Ethics in Psychological Research

Psychological research requires careful judgments and regulation regarding appropriate participation by humans and animals in studies.

  ▪ Examine the rights of participants in research identified in the Belmont Report.

  ▪ Contrast the ethical guidelines for human research studies and animal research studies.

Psychologists are interested in studying all kinds of human behavior, from our finest to our worst moments. Is it ethical to experiment on people? In order to study behavior using the scientific method, researchers sometimes create conditions in their studies that may be uncomfortable for participants. At the same time, the benefits of the research may be new psychological knowledge that not only increases our understanding but has the potential to help solve problems in the world. Do these positive ends justify the means? How do researchers protect their research participants and, at the same time, conduct studies that probe difficult issues in human behavior?

Human Participants

Historically, scientists had no guidance or regulation regarding how to treat human participants. For example, in the 1920s and 1930s, when laboratory studies were beginning in the United States, studies were conducted by well-meaning psychologists that would never be allowed now. In one, studying the experience and expression of emotion, participants were subjected to a variety of treatments designed to elicit strong emotion: plunging their hand into a pail of shallow water that, unbeknownst to them, contained three live frogs; viewing a pornographic picture; dropping a lit firecracker underneath an unsuspecting subject's chair; and a request to cut off a live rat's head with a butcher knife (Landis & Hunt, 1939). Other famous studies raised concerns about how participants were treated in research studies and motivated a national movement to regulate behavioral research.

In 1974, the National Research Act was signed into law, creating the National Commission for the Protection of Human Subjects of Biomedical and Behavioral Research. This *Common Rule* requires federally funded investigators to obtain and document the informed consent of research subjects, and describes requirements for institutional review boards at unversities and hospitals to review research before it is conducted. Other subparts address additional requirements when conducting research with vulnerable populations such as pregnant women, children, and prisoners. In 1979, the National Commission published the Belmont Report (Department of Health and Human Services, 1979), identifying the rights of participants in research, including:

1. Respect for persons. Treat individuals as autonomous agents, and protect those who may not be able to make independent decisions. Respect means that subjects enter into the research voluntarily and are given adequate information. If someone has a diminished ability to give consent (children, prisoners, mentally ill), take extra steps to protect that individual's rights.

2. Beneficence. Treat people ethically by not only respecting their decisions and protecting them from harm but also making efforts to secure their well-being. First, do no harm, and second, maximize possible benefits and minimize possible harms.

3. Justice. Out of a sense of fairness, it is important to distribute both the burdens and the benefits of research. Since all of society benefits from research, all should be asked to bear the costs of participating in research.

From the principles of the Belmont Report, procedures to guide researchers in conducting their studies were created. Institutional review boards (IRBs) were created to examine planned experiments to ensure the rights of the participant are preserved. For behavioral studies, each researcher must provide information to the IRB for review, and the board determines the risk–benefit analysis for the research. In addition, each researcher commits to offering every participant privacy and confidentiality so that their participation and the data they contribute to the research are not revealed to others outside of the research team. This was the rule I breached when I revealed to other graduate students that a Hollywood star was participating in my research study. Along with the nature of participation and the contributions made, the fact that someone participated at all is also treated confidentially.

Research studies now begin with a key step called the **informed consent** process. In this process, the participants are given information about the nature of the tasks they will be asked to complete, disclosure of any risks and benefits to them, their rights to privacy and confidentiality, the length of participation requested, and any compensation provided for their participation. They are also told they have the right to withdraw from participating at any time. The participants can ask questions of the researcher, and the process concludes with signatures from the participants who decide to volunteer for that study. These consent forms document that the subjects indicated they understand their rights; however, even after signing, they may choose to end their participation at any time without consequences.

These steps help to ensure that there are no surprises in research studies; rather, the participants know what they are getting into when they decide to join a study, and they know they can choose to stop. Of course, for most studies, the participants cannot be informed about the hypothesis beforehand; otherwise, they may behave differently based on their knowledge of the study. But they can know what they will be asked to do (answer questions about their personality, solve math puzzles, talk in a chat room).

Informed consent The process through which an experimenter describes the nature of study participation to the potential volunteer, including his or her right to stop at any time.

For most behavioral research in psychology, these tasks are uncontroversial. In fact, for studies involving surveys alone, informed consent is not always needed; instead, your willingness to answer a question indicates your consent to participate. But the researcher is obligated to remind you that you may choose not to answer any question at any time. Other studies fall into the realm of "public behavior": When you are in a public place, you do not have a right to privacy! Your behavior can be observed by anyone and used (anonymously) in a study report.

A more difficult situation arises when the researcher plans to use **deception** in the experiment; that is, to actively provide information to the participants that is untrue. You have already read about such an experiment in this chapter. Can you identify which study it was? The "online chat room" study used active deception because the researchers told the participants they were having a conversation with others online, while it was actually a computer program that was generating the conversation. This deception seems innocuous; that is, no one is likely to be upset when they learn the truth. However, other studies may use deception that is troubling to participants. In one study, subjects were told, "You are the type who will end up alone later in life. You may have friends and relationships now, but by your mid-20s, most of these will have drifted away. You may even marry or have several marriages, but these are likely to be short-lived and not continue into your 30s" (Baumeister et al., 2002). The experimenters argue these manipulations are necessary to create emotional responses within laboratory studies.

To deal with this problem, a standard has emerged: Is the experience one you may encounter within everyday life? It is possible you may hear swear words directed at you or have a palm reader tell you negative things about your future in the course of day-to-day living. These types of events may occur, and most people are able to withstand the short-term stress caused by such studies. In addition, the Belmont regulations require that studies using deception provide a full **debriefing** following the study, through which the untrue information is revealed and the participants can ask any questions. So, in the chat room study, researchers fully informed the participants that the conversation was a computer program and explained why it was necessary to keep that information from them (because it was intended to make them feel socially excluded). A process debriefing is used to walk the participants through the study, ensuring they understand that they were assigned to the treatment they received at random, that they know the manipulation (such as the false test results) had nothing to do with them personally, and they can have any questions answered before they leave the study.

It has been more than 30 years since the Common Rule was established, and the safety and well-being of human and animal participants has been greatly improved. However, to some, this increased regulation of behavioral research may have gone too far. Most universities review all research under the same guidelines, and the process is costly and time consuming. In most psychology studies, little or no risk is involved, so perhaps less regulation is needed. In addition, the regulations may mean that some studies of great benefit to society may never be conducted because they invoke ethically questionable procedures. For example, teenage pregnancy interventions could be tested to determine which are most successful. However, because they are under the age of consent (18), studies of teenagers require parental consent for their participation. And, for example, if parents will not approve a study plan that makes condoms accessible to their children, the possible benefits to the children cannot be determined. In some situations of urgent need, such as behaviors related to HIV transmission, lack of scientific knowledge may result in more human suffering, while studies may be conducted in areas of the world with fewer ethical protections for participants (Angell, 2000; Lurie & Wolfe, 1997).

The ethical conduct of psychological studies has come a long way since the 1920s; however, it is important to recognize that dilemmas still exist. For example, the principle of justice says that everyone in a society should bear the burden of contributing to research. In practice, however, individuals who are willing to participate for small financial payments or for credit in college courses are the ones most often recruited. In addition, studies of special populations may approach some individuals multiple times in order to recruit participants. Further, there is a difficulty in recruiting those with psychological disorders (such as bipolar disorder or schizophrenia) to participate in a study when, by definition, their thinking may be disordered. Finally, other ethical dilemmas in psychology

Deception To actively provide information to the participant that is untrue.

Debriefing The process by which any deception used by researchers is fully disclosed to participants at the end of a study.

include the fact that many potential questions are not asked, and many important members of society are not included in studies. Across all fields, university professors at doctoral institutions are still predominantly male (68%) and White (78%) (Forrest Cataldi et al., 2005). Since the lived experiences of researchers contribute to their research questions, it is important to broaden the diversity of those engaged in psychological research.

Animal Studies

Animal subjects (mostly laboratory-bred rats and mice, but also cats, dogs, and monkeys) are employed in a wide array of psychological studies. Research topics include exposure to addictive drugs, sleep, diet, stress, hormones, and disease. Increasingly, the link between behavior and genetics is examined, and animal models are much more practical for these studies due to their shorter natural lifespan. The interest in measures of neural function often involves invasive procedures such as surgery to determine how behavior relates to physiological function and performing brain anatomy studies after death. The use of animal models allows us to gain knowledge that would not be possible with human subjects based on ethical or practical concerns. The results from animal studies have been shown to greatly benefit human health and medical treatments (Miller, 1985).

The white lab rat shown here in containers, is a staple of many psychology studies.

However, animals are not given the same rights that human participants enjoy: They cannot consent to participation. Efforts are made to ensure humane treatment of research animals, and safeguards are put in place to make certain they receive adequate care. Ethical boards review all animal research treatments, and federal laws specify how animals are housed and fed in protected facilities. Animal testing is much more prevalent in consumer product testing, through which substances are proven safe for human consumption or use. However, the practice of testing animals for purely research purposes is controversial, and some argue that it is not appropriate, even if human lives are saved by the outcome of research (Shapiro, 1990). Even within the field, people differ in their opinions: A survey of researchers in the field of psychology found that a majority support animal studies involving observation but disapprove of studies involving pain or death (Plous, 1996).

In behavioral research, laboratory animals have played critical roles in developing new theories that are now improving research into human behavioral disorders. One example is research on brain activity in monkeys. In the studies, monkeys undergo testing with wires implanted in specific brain areas that record neural activity. One researcher noted that a monkey's brain responded as if it had eaten a peanut even though it was only *watching* someone else eat one (Rizzolatti, Fogassi, & Gallese, 2006). This uncovered a network in the brain that reflects others' behavior and may be responsible for creating empathy with others. Researchers are now exploring how disruptions of this "mirror neuron" system may be related to the development of autism in humans, a growing health concern (Iacoboni, 2008).

Another example comes from a study of dogs that first underwent training in which escaping from shock was impossible (Seligman & Maier, 1967). After this training, the dogs were placed in an escape learning setting where they could easily escape the coming shock by jumping over a low barrier. But the dogs had given up, a phenomenon that is termed *learned helplessness*. This behavior was tied to theories of human behavior in depression, in which people lose the sense that they can have a positive impact on their own success or environment. Many years later, Seligman is now leading a research-based movement, called positive psychology, that is using some of these insights to help change lives for the better around the world (Peterson, 2006; Seligman, 2006).

Increasingly, scientists are looking for alternatives to animal studies in psychology (Gallup & Suarez, 1985). For example, experimental methods are being devised that can tie behavior to human brain function through neuroimaging. While studies of human behavior have produced many important findings about mental processes, the ability to tie those processes to specific structures and systems within the brain has been limited. However, brain imaging devices from medicine have now been used in behavioral research to measure thinking through correlates in the brain's activity. These include measuring the uptake of oxygen (positron emission technology, or PET scans), changes in blood flow (functional magnetic resonance imagery, or fMRI scans), and electrical patterns of activity across the scalp (event-related potentials, or ERPs) that are produced by neural activity. These new methods have allowed psychologists to ask questions with human subjects that were not possible in the past.

Dogs unable to escape from shocks appeared to "give up," and did not attempt to escape when tested in a new situation.

For example, when people diagnosed with schizophrenia hear voices in hallucinations, are they actually "hearing" them? A study had volunteers lie in MRI machines and depress a button for the duration of time they were hearing voices. The results showed that the brain activity taking place during hallucinations is in the same areas that are active when we actually hear voices (Kircher et al., 2005) FIGURE 2-20. The development of new technologies for measuring human brain function may reduce the need for the use of animal models in psychology.

FIGURE 2-20 Positron emission tomography (PET) brain scan of a schizophrenic male patient aged 23 during an active hallucination. Highlighted in orange are areas of brain activity in the visual (right) and auditory processing (upper central) areas of brain, showing the patient has "seen" and "heard" during an hallucination.

Research in psychology strives to identify the factors that influence human behavior. The underlying model is that all humans are alike and that there are *universal* truths about psychology that apply to all humans. Clearly, this is true for many research conclusions. For example, psychologists have concluded that

- There is a special area of the human brain devoted to learning and recognizing human faces (Farah, 1996).
- People have a deep need to belong to a social group or relationship (Baumeister, 1991).
- The basic human emotions are displayed in characteristic facial expressions (Ekman et al., 1987).

At the same time, many conclusions about behavior depend upon the ways individuals *differ* from one another, including by gender, age, ethnicity, nationality, education, socioeconomic status, environment, personality, and culture. Many findings must be qualified by noting that the research studies included only Americans or college students, meaning that the validity for other groups has not yet been verified. In fact, the attempts to verify "universal" findings across cultures have quickly uncovered major differences in how individuals respond based on the culture surrounding them.

For example, social psychologists identified a reasoning pattern so pervasive it was named the "fundamental attribution error" (Nisbett & Borgida, 1975; Ross, 1977). This error is to assume that people act the way they do because the behavior is an inherent part of their nature and not because of the particular situation in which they find themselves. For example, you observe your professor lecturing in class and infer that he or she is very comfortable giving public speeches. You see the behavior and attribute it to who she or he is as a person. Then you attend a friend's wedding and see the same professor nervously reciting poetry as part of the ceremony. This tells you that the situation also plays a role: Though your professor is comfortable in the lecture hall, he or she is not likely to win a poetry slam. The "fundamental attribution error" we all make is to assume that what we see is a reflection of the person's qualities and not the situation he or she is in.

Or do we? In a study comparing American and Chinese students, a video of an individual fish swimming in front of a group of fish was shown. More American than Chinese participants described the activity of the fish as internal to the fish ("the fish is leading the group") rather than externally caused ("the school of fish is avoiding a predator;" Morris & Peng, 1994). Cultural values like individualism (in Western cultures) and collectivism (in Eastern cultures) appear to alter the inferences people draw to explain the behavior of others (Miller, 1984). In several studies, East Asians tended to attribute behavior to the situation, while Westerners attributed the same behavior to the person (Masuda & Nisbett, 2001). One explanation for this difference in attribution is that people in different cultures are more or less oriented toward perceiving themselves within a holistic environment. The fundamental attribution error was not so fundamental after all!

Summary of Multiple Influences on a Scientific Approach to Psychology

Currently, explorations of culture and psychology are burgeoning as researchers seek to compare how individuals are affected by the social environment around them. Throughout this book, we will bring to bear evidence of multiple influences on human behavior. Many influences from biology, such as genetics, heredity, hormones, and brain structure and function, unite our behavior under explanations that apply to all humans. These same biological influences may account for many differences across individuals, such as gender, age, and personality differences. Other influences from our lived experiences may similarly evoke universal behavior across individuals, such as learning to speak and forming bonds with others. At the same time, psychologists are uncovering many more ways that our lived experiences, including our culture, education, and socioeconomic environment, may give rise to differences in our behavior.

The methods available to psychologists for exploring the causes of human behavior are varied, each with strengths and limitations. Consequently, it is critical to examine evidence about multiple influences on behavior through as many different methods as possible. Throughout this book, we will bring to bear evidence from biological, environmental, cultural, and experiential influences to provide a more complete picture of psychology.

CONCEPT LEARNING CHECK 2.5   *Ethics in Psychological Studies*

Define and describe these concepts of ethical conduct in research studies.

1. Respect for persons

2. Beneficence

3. Justice

4. Informed consent

5. Deception

6. Debriefing

CRITICAL THINKING APPLICATION

Students sometimes serve on the IRB committees that review research. Their job is to consider the risks and the potential benefits of studies, along with ensuring the researchers follow the informed consent guidelines. For each of the studies, consider whether you would approve it or whether you would stop an ongoing study. What issues might raise questions in your mind? Finally, guess whether the description came from an actual study or is an example created for illustration.

1. A subject comes to an approved experiment on hypothesis testing. The experimenter has a hidden rule that produces a number sequence, and the subject must try to figure out the rule by generating examples and asking if they fit the experimenter's rule. One subject starts using the same examples over and over again and gets very agitated when he cannot guess the experimenter's rule. He becomes unresponsive and has to be taken to the ER. Should the study be stopped?

This event happened in a famous study taking place around 1960. The pressure of the very difficult task was too much for one participant. However, it was reasonable to expect that people would be able to respond without such a reaction, and this was the only participant to have difficulty. Therefore, the study was continued (Wason & Johnson-Laird, 1968).

2. Some psychologists are interested in the effect of frustration on preschool children. They propose a study in which a 3-year-old child is able to see a desired toy through a transparent plastic box and is left alone to work on opening the box with a ring of wrong keys. After 3 minutes, the experimenter returns with the correct key and explains, "I guess I gave you the wrong keys. Let's try this one." The box is then opened; the child is encouraged to play for 1 minute with the toy. Do you think this causes harm to the child subjects?

The frustration tolerance required by this task has been used as a dependent measure in many studies (Dennis, 2006). Parents must always give permission for minors to participate in studies; however, very young children are not able to give their own assent to participate.

3. A researcher is interested in examining gender differences in attitudes toward sex. An attractive research assistant approaches students (of the opposite sex) on campus. She or he strikes up a conversation and then asks one of the following three questions: "Will you go on a date with me tonight?" "Will you come to my apartment tonight?" Or "Will you have sex with me tonight?" After the subject's response is noted, the research assistant debriefs the subject. Is it fair to ask such a question on a street corner?

This study was conducted at a major Midwestern university. Because the participants were approached in a public place and the content of the discussion was not outside of everyday experience, no consent was required for the study. The study found that almost all of the male participants said, "Yes!" (Clark & Hatfield, 1989).

4. Observations will be collected of public behavior in restrooms—specifically, of males standing at urinals. A confederate will be in the restroom and will approach the subject by standing at either a nearby urinal or two urinals away. A nearby experimenter will record latency and duration of urination by the subject. Do the investigators need consent from the participants?

This study was conducted using public restrooms, so no consent was needed from participants. The results showed the effects of social stress from violating "personal space" (Middlemist et al., 1976).

5. A researcher interested in what provokes violence invited students into the lab. Once there, they were "accidentally" bumped into by a confederate, who muttered a curse word at the student. The subjects' response to the incident ranged from ignoring it completely to chasing the confederate down the hall and pounding on the door. Is this experience along the lines of what you encounter in daily life?

This study was conducted at a major university and approved by the IRB after some consideration of what words were appropriate to use as the insult in the study. The results showed subjects from northern U.S. states were less reactive to the insult than were subjects from southern U.S. states (Cohen et al., 1996).

6. Participants in a study were asked to try on "clothing samples" in a locked laboratory room, where they were alone. They were given either a basket of sweaters or a basket of revealing swimsuits and told to put one on. Then they completed some surveys and a math test.

Because subjects were alone in the lab room, this was considered an acceptable request of participants. This study was approved by the IRB, and its findings were that women did more poorly on the math test when wearing swimsuits rather than sweaters, but for men, there was no difference (Fredrickson et al., 1998).

From the variety of studies you have seen here, it is clear that people differ in their judgments of what they consider appropriate for psychological experiments. While the guidelines help to ensure that subjects are informed about the study and that they may not be told everything until the study ends, the many studies being conducted will mean that some people become offended by the procedures. As a last resort, there is comfort in knowing that participants may always stop their participation at any time or may decide not to answer any given question. But, just like everyday experiences in the world, experiments may evoke unexpected emotions. Concerns about studies can be reported directly to the experimenter and to the IRB at any institution.

Visual Overview Sampling from a Population for a Scientific Study

The population includes all individuals for whom you would like to draw conclusions from the study. In a sample, you select a smaller group from the population for the purpose of the research study. Random sampling ensures that all members have a equal chance of being chosen for the study, so that no subgroups within the population are left out. Convenience samples (e.g., volunteers on college campuses) are often used as a shortcut due to the cost of true random sampling.

Convenience Sample

Small subset that is easy to access (e.g., college students)

Random Sample

Every person has an equal chance of being selected

Nonrandom Sample

A small subgroup that may not represent all in the population; may be biased in selection.

2.1 Psychological Investigation

- Psychological science is the study of human behavior and its underlying causes.
- The scientific approach to investigation consists of five steps.

  Step 1: Formulate a testable hypothesis.

  Step 2: Select the research method and design the study.

  Step 3: Collect the data.

  Step 4: Analyze the data and draw conclusions.

  Step 5: Report the findings.

- Every research study has limitations in its design.
- *Reliability* is the degree to which an experiment can be repeated under similar circumstances and produce the same results.
- *Validity* refers to how well the research reflects and captures what it set out to measure.
- *Generalizability* tells how well research findings can be applied to other people and circumstances.

2.2 Descriptive Research

- Descriptive studies are concerned with the qualities of human behaviors, experiences, and individuals, called variables.
- Naturalistic observation studies behavior as it occurs in "the wild", without any intervention by the researchers.
- The extensive examination of the experience of a single individual or group is called a case study.
- A well-conceived survey draws conclusions about the population from a selected sample.
- Methods of random sampling are used to ensure that every member of the population of interest has an equal chance of selection through the use of randomization.
- A scatterplot provides a graph showing each person's score on two variables.
- The correlation coefficient r provides an indicator of the type of relationship between two variables.

- A positive correlation between two variables means that the scores of both variables rise together, and the value of r is between 0.0 and +1.00.
- A negative correlation means that as the score of one variable rises, the score of the other drops, and the value of r is between 0.0 and −1.00.
- When there is *no* systematic relationship between the two variables, r is close to 0.
- A correlation can tell us whether an association exists between two variables, the direction (positive or negative), the strength of the association, and even how well one variable accounts for variance in the other.
- A correlation cannot tell us about *causality* between the variables.

2.3 Experimental Research

- In experiments, the researcher intentionally manipulates variables and measures their impact on other variables.
- The independent variable is a factor that the experimenter manipulates to create different experiences for participants.
- The dependent variable measures any effect of the independent variable. Change in the dependent variable *depends* on the independent variable.
- The key feature that allows the conclusion of causality is that every participant in the study has an equal chance of being

assigned to the groups of the independent variable, called random assignment.
- In the simplest studies, the independent variable includes an experimental group (that receives some treatment or experience) and a control group (that receives no extra treatment or experience).
- The advantage of a true experiment is that the scientific method proves that the independent variable alone is the cause of observed differences in the dependent variable.

2.4 Statistical Analysis

- The data collected about behavior are summarized by standard statistics that describe differences in measurements.

- Measures of central tendency describe the "typical" value of a given variable. These include the mode, the median, and the mean.

- The variance describes how the scores are distributed around the typical score, including statistics called the range and standard deviation.

- The point of using statistics is to guide us in making generalizations from samples, and to help us decide whether any differences observed are significant.

- When the probability of a finding is determined to be less than 5%, psychologists say it reaches statistical significance, noted as the "alpha level" or $p < 0.05$.

2.5 Ethics in Psychological Research

- The Belmont Report (Department of Health and Human Services, 1979) identified the rights of participants in research, including *Respect for persons, Beneficence,* and *Justice.*

- Institutional review boards (IRBs) were created to examine planned experiments to ensure the rights of the participants are preserved.

- Research studies now begin with a key step called the informed consent process.

- In deception experiments, the researcher actively provides information to the participant that is untrue, and provides a full debriefing following the study.

- Animal subjects (mostly laboratory-bred rats and mice, but also cats, dogs, and monkeys) are employed in a wide array of psychological studies.

- Ethical boards review all animal research treatments, and federal laws specify how animals are housed and fed in protected facilities.

- The underlying model is that there are *universal* truths about psychology that apply to all humans. At the same time, many conclusions about behavior depend upon the ways individuals *differ* from one another.

- Many influences from biology, such as genetics, heredity, hormones, brain structure and function, underly our behavior.

2.1 Psychological Investigation

1. The ability to draw a conclusion from a study that will also be true in other settings is called:
A. reliability.
B. validity.
C. generalizability.
D. probability.

2. The first step in designing a research study is to:
A. formulate a hypothesis.
B. collect data.
C. report findings.
D. select a research method.

2.2 Descriptive Research

3. A descriptive study that includes only a single subject is called:
A. a case study.
B. a survey.
C. naturalistic observation.
D. an experiment.

4. Which of the following is an example of a negative correlation?
A. People who exercise regularly live longer than those who do not.
B. There is no relationship between violent crime and whether a state has a death penalty.
C. The more children watch television, the less they read.
D. Men with high testosterone levels are more prone to violence.

5. Which of the following is an example of a positive correlation?
A. If you take vitamin C, you are less likely to catch a cold.
B. The more classes you attend, the higher your grades will be.
C. People who smoke have poorer health.
D. The more you exercise, the less you eat.

6. Sample is to population as:
A. large is to small.
B. not representative is to representative.
C. valid is to invalid.
D. part is to whole.

2.3 Experimental Research

7. The variable that an experimenter manipulates in order to measure its effects is called the _____ variable.
A. independent
B. controlled
C. random
D. dependent

8. A group of researchers wanted to determine if people tend to eat more food when they are with others, so half the participants ate in a room together and half ate in a room alone. They then measured how much food was consumed. In this study, the independent variable was:
A. the amount of food that was consumed.
B. how hungry the participants felt at the end.
C. whether they ate with others or alone.
D. the type of room that they ate in.

9. A group of researchers tested whether children's performance is affected by the presence of the experimenter. Half of the children were tested in a room alone and timed while they completed a puzzle. In this study, the length of time it takes to complete the puzzle would be:
A. the independent variable.
B. a confounding variable.
C. a control variable.
D. the dependent variable.

10. A true experiment requires:
A. the use of humans.
B. the research participants to manipulate the independent variable.
C. at least three comparison groups.
D. random assignment of research participants to conditions.

11. A researcher is carrying out a study on procrastination. In the research process, she must specify, in concrete "how-to" terms, how the dependent variable will be measured. In other words, she must provide:
A. hypotheses.
B. theories.
C. operational definitions.
D. archival records.

2.4 Statistical Analysis

12. The measure of central tendency that indicates which response occurred most frequently is the:
- **A.** mean.
- **B.** median.
- **C.** mode.
- **D.** average.

13. The measures of variation within a group of scores include the:
- **A.** range.
- **B.** significance.
- **C.** *r*-value.
- **D.** average.

14. The level of statistical significance used as a standard in psychological research is:
- **A.** 0.05.
- **B.** 0.50.
- **C.** 1.00.
- **D.** 100.

2.5 Ethics in Psychological Research

15. Stan is in a study in the subject pool in which the experimenter seems to rush him through the tasks. As a result, Stan started feeling uncomfortable. Stan should know he has a right to:
- **A.** demand more time.
- **B.** stop the experiment.
- **C.** take a break for as long as he needs.
- **D.** complain to the experimenter.

16. Mackenzie agreed to take part in an experiment in which she was asked to drink two glasses of beer over 30 minutes, was given a blood test, and then was given a questionnaire. When finished, she was not told the purpose of the study, nor that the drinks had no alcohol. In this case, the researchers:
- **A.** failed to obtain informed consent.
- **B.** violated Mackenzie's right to privacy.
- **C.** did not use an adequate debriefing procedure.
- **D.** did not provide adequate protection from harm.

17. The process at the start of a study in which the experimenter and participant discuss what will occur in the session is called the:
- **A.** introduction to the study.
- **B.** formulation of hypothesis.
- **C.** informed consent process.
- **D.** warm-up session.

CHAPTER DISCUSSION QUESTIONS

1. The scientific method is a formal approach to designing a research study with the goal of better understanding a topic, question, or problem. You may find that when you work on problems in your everyday life, you use some of the same steps. Think of a problem that you solved and compare the steps of the scientific method to the steps that you used. Are the steps the same? Did you follow the same order as the scientific method? What was different about your problem-solving approach?

2. Think of a career or job that you might like and then consider the various descriptive research techniques covered in Section 2.2 (naturalistic observations, case studies, surveys, and correlational studies). For the career you have picked, identify how someone might use each of the descriptive research techniques. In other words, for this career, describe some topics, questions, or problems for which you could investigate solutions using these descriptive research techniques.

3. One of the most interesting challenges for psychological research is figuring out how to create operational definitions for the topics we want to study. An operational definition explains how a researcher intends to measure the independent or dependent variable, an important step in developing an experiment. Identify a possible way to measure, or operationally define, each of the following topics of interest to psychology: memory, happiness, learning, depression, and motivation.

4. *Statistical significance* is used to describe research results that exceed the probability of chance. When researchers claim to have statistically significant results, it means they believe their results would happen again if they did their experiment again. In comparison, the term significant is used often in situations that have nothing to do with research (e.g., "she thought that was a significant change in his attitude"). Describe at least three situations in which it would be appropriate to call something statistically significant versus significant.

5. Review the informed consent process discussed in Section 2.5 and consider how the same type of process might be useful in nonresearch situations. Think of a situation in which you would have liked to have informed consent before participating. Relate the parts of informed consent to your own situation and describe what the informed consent process would have discussed.

CHAPTER PROJECTS

1. Think about something in psychology that you would be interested in studying. Then, starting with the steps of the scientific method discussed in Section 2.1, plan a research project. In your response, fill in details for each step of the scientific method, making sure to include information from the other sections of this chapter. For example, in step 2 of the scientific method, make sure to add information about which type of research method you would use.

2. Popular media sources often report on research results, but they try to present the results in very general terms so that many people can understand. Sometimes, these popular media sources end up misrepresenting research results through their simplification or because they want to create a more sensational story. Think about the long-term problems of popular media sources misrepresenting research results. Demonstrate how sensationalizing research results could be harmful. Imagine and describe a scenario in which a false representation of a research result could be damaging to a person or a community.

Between-subjects design
Bimodal distribution
Case study
Central tendency
Cohort effect
Comparative study
Confounding variable
Control group
Convenience sample
Correlation
Correlation coefficient
Cross-sectional study
Debriefing
Deception
Dependent variable
Double-blind procedure
Empirical
Experiment
Experimental group
Experimenter bias
Generalizability

Hypothesis
Independent variable
Inferential statistic
Informed consent
Interaction between variables
Internet-mediated research
Journal
Longitudinal study
Mean
Median
Meta-analysis
Mode
Naturalistic observation
Negative correlation
Normal distribution
Operational definition
Participant
Placebo effect
Population
Positive correlation
Psychological science

Random assignment
Random sampling
Range
Reactivity
Reliability
Replicable
Sample
Sampling bias
Scatterplot
Scientific method
Social desirability bias
Standard deviation
Statistically significant
Statistic
Survey
Theory
Validity
Variable
Variance
Within-subjects design

2.1 Within or Between?

1. Within

2. Between (males and females were compared)

3. Between

4. Within

5. Within (boys and girls did the same activities and were not compared)

6. Within (all exercised)

2.2 What Do Correlations Mean?

1. Studying with others may be an effective way to improve grades.

2. More conservative people are somewhat more likely to have a daily breakfast.

3. There is no relationship between viewing movies and reading.

4. More video game playing is related to lower likelihood of graduation.

5. Daily aerobic exercise may effectively improve mood.

2.3 Designing an Experiment

1. Independent variable. [Gender]

2. Dependent variable. [Salary]

3. Operational definition (of dependent variable). [Hourly wage paid over past 3 months]

4. Randomization. [None]

5. Sampling. [Select 100 males and 100 females from an executive education conference]

6. Population. [Employed adults]

7. True experiment. [No, because we cannot assign people at random to the independent variable groups]

2.4 Summarizing with Statistics

1. **A.** Mean. 21/10, or 2.1

   B. Median. Middle score, or 2

   C. Mode. Most frequent score, or 1

   D. Range. 1 to 5

2. The findings from the study are unlikely to occur by chance.

2.5 Ethics in Psychological Studies

1. Respect for persons. [Make sure everyone has a free, independent choice about participating.]

2. Beneficence. [Make sure you minimize any harm, and try to treat participants well.]

3. Justice. [Provide the opportunity to participate as fairly as possible.]

4. Informed consent. [Tell the participants what they will be asked to do and what the risks are. Give them a chance to ask questions, and remind them they can stop at any time.]

5. Deception. [If you give false information to participants, you must fully inform them about it after the study in the debriefing.]

6. Debriefing. [Informing the participant about the study's purpose and procedures at the conclusion of their session.]

ANSWERS TO CHAPTER REVIEW TEST

2.1 Psychological Investigation

1. C. Rationale: Generalizability; though validity is a closely related concept, it refers to the meaning of the finding.

2. A. Rationale: Formulate a hypothesis; before a study method can be selected, the hypothesis must be known.

2.2 Descriptive Research

3. A. Rationale: A case study.

4. C. Rationale: The more children watch television, the less they read; a high score on one variable goes with a low score on the other.

5. B. Rationale: The more classes you attend, the higher your grades will be; a high score goes with a high score.

6. D. Rationale: Part is to whole; a sample is a subset of the population.

2.3 Experimental Research

7. A. Rationale: Independent; it is assigned to participants and acts independently.

8. C. Rationale: Whether they ate with others or alone; it was assigned to subjects.

9. D. Rationale: The dependent variable; it is measured to determine if there were any effects.

10. D. Rationale: Random assignment of research participants to conditions; a key to true experiments.

11. C. Rationale: Operational definitions; exactly how to measure the effects.

2.4 Statistical Analysis

12. C. Rationale: Mode; it comes from the French word for "fashion" and is related to the idea of "most popular."

13. A. Rationale: Range; another is the standard deviation.

14. A. Rationale: 0.05, meaning that 5 times out of 100 studies, this finding might occur by chance.

2.5 Ethics in Psychological Research

15. B. Rationale: Stop the experiment; the participant can decide to stop at any time.

16. C. Rationale: Did not use an adequate debriefing procedure; because deception was used, debriefing is required.

17. C. Rationale: Informed consent process; this initial information is required for many studies.

REFERENCES

Angell, M. (2000). Investigators' responsibilities for human subjects in developing countries. *New England Journal of Medicine, 342,* 967–969.

Baumeister, R. F. (1991). The need to belong: Desire for interpersonal attachments as a fundamental human motivation. *Psychological Bulletin, 117*(3), 497–529.

Baumeister, R. F., Twenge, J. M., & Nuss, C. K. (2002). Effects of social exclusion on cognitive processes: Anticipated aloneness reduces intelligent thought. *Journal of Personality and Social Psychology, 83,* 817–827.

Campbell, A. (1981). *The sense of well-being in America: Recent patterns and trends.* New York: McGraw-Hill.

Clark, R. D., III, & Hatfield, E. (1989). Gender differences in receptivity to sexual offers. *Journal of Psychology and Human Sexuality, 2,* 39–55.

Cohen, D., Nisbett, R. E., Bowdle, B., & Schwarz, N. (1996). Insult, aggression, and the Southern culture of honor: An "experimental ethnography." *Journal of Personality and Social Psychology, 70,* 945–960.

College Sports Project. (2010). College Sports Project updates findings about athletics and academics in NCAA Division III. Retrieved from http://www.collegesportsproject.org/

Dennis, T. (2006). Emotional self-regulation in preschoolers: The interplay of child approach reactivity, parenting, and control capacities. *Developmental Psychology, 42*(1), 84–97.

Department of Health and Human Services. (1979). *Belmont report: Ethical principles and guidelines for the protection of human subjects of research, report of the National Commission for the Protection of Human Subjects of Biomedical and Behavioral Research.* http://www.hhs.gov/ohrp/archive/documents/19790418.pdf

Diener, E. (2006). Guidelines for national indicators of subjective well-being and ill-being. *Applied Research in Quality of Life, 1,* 151–157.

Diener, E., & Biswas-Diener, R. (2002). Will money increase subjective well-being?: A literature review and guide to needed research. *Social Indicators Research, 57,* 119–169.

Diener, E., & Biswas-Diener, R. (2008). *The science of optimal happiness.* Boston: Blackwell.

Diener, E., Emmons, R. A., Larsen, R. J., & Griffin, S. (1985). The Satisfaction With Life scale. *Journal of Personality Assessment, 49*(1), 71–75.

Diener, E., Kahneman, D., & Helliwell, J. (2010). *International differences in well-being.* New York: Oxford University Press.

Eccles, J. S., & Jacobs, J. E. (1986). Social forces shape math attitudes and performance. *Signs, 11*(2), 367–380.

Ekman, P., Friesen, W. V., O'Sullivan, M., Chan, A., Diacoyanni-Tarlatzis, I., Heider, K., Krause, R., LeCompte, W. A., Pitcairn, T., Ricci-Bitti, P. E., Scherer, K. R., Tomita, M., & Tzavaras, A. (1987). Universals and cultural differences in the judgments of facial expressions of emotion. *Journal of Personality and Social Psychology, 53*(4), 712–717.

Farah, M. J. (1996). Is face recognition special? Evidence from neuropsychology. *Behavioral Brain Research, 76*(1–2), 181–189.

Farah, M. J., Levinson, K. L., & Klein, K. L. (1995). Face perception and within-category discrimination in prosopagnosia. *Neuropsychologia, 33,* 661–674.

Farah, M. J., Rabinowitz, C., Quinn, G. E., & Liu, G. T. (2000). Early commitment of neural substrates for face recognition. *Cognitive Neuropsychology, 17*(1–3), 117–123.

Forrest Cataldi, E., Fahimi, M., & Bradburn, E. M. (2005). *2004 National Study of Postsecondary Faculty (NSOPF:04) Report on Faculty and Instructional Staff in Fall 2003* (NCES 2005–172). U.S. Department of Education. Washington, DC: National Center for Education Statistics. Retrieved from http://nces.ed.gov/pubsearch

Fredrickson, B. L., Roberts, T. A., Noll, S. M., Quinn, D. M., & Twenge, J. M. (1998). That swimsuit becomes you: Sex differences in self-objectification, restrained eating, and math performance. *Journal of Personality and Social Psychology, 75*(1), 269–284.

Gallup, G. G., & Suarez, S. D. (1985). Alternatives to the use of animals in psychological research. *American Psychologist, 40*(10), 1104–1111.

Gardner, W. L., Pickett, C. L., & Brewer, M. B. (2000). Social exclusion and selective memory: How the need to belong influences memory for social events. *Personality and Social Psychology Bulletin, 26*(4), 486–496.

Gettelfinger, B., & Cussler, E. L. (2004). Will humans swim faster or slower in syrup? *American Institute of Chemical Engineering Journal, 50,* 2646–2647.

Goldstone, R. L., & Chin, C. (1993). Dishonesty in self-report of copies made: Moral relativity and the copy machine. *Basic and Applied Social Psychology, 14*(1), 19–32.

Gonzalez, R., Seifert, C. M., Manzon, E., Yoon, C., & Cho, S. (2011). *From "part-time" to "rolling" belters: Social promotions of seat belt use.* Unpublished manuscript.

Goodall, J. (1982). Order without law. *Journal of Social and Biological Structures, 5*(4), 353–360.

Henderson, J. M. (2003). Human gaze control during real-world scene perception. *Trends in Cognitive Sciences, 7*(11), 498–505.

Hu, M., Crombag, H. S., Robinson, T. E., & Becker, J. B. (2004). Biological basis of sex differences in the propensity to self-administer cocaine. *Neuropsychopharmacology, 29,* 81–85.

Hyde, J. S., Fennema, E., & Lamon, S. J. (1990). Gender differences in mathematics performance: A meta-analysis. *Psychological Bulletin, 107*(2), 139–155.

Iacoboni, M. (2008). *Mirroring people: The new science of how we connect to others.* New York: Farrar, Straus, & Giroux.

Johnco, C., Wheeler, L., & Taylor, A. (2010). They do get prettier at closing time: A repeated measures study of the closing-time effect and alcohol. *Social Influence, 5*(4), 261–271.

Just, M., & Carpenter, P. (1980). A theory of reading: From eye fixations to comprehension. *Psychological Review, 87,* 329–354.

Kircher, T. T. J., & Thienel, R. (2005). Functional brain imaging of symptoms and cognition in schizophrenia. *Progress in Brain Research, 150,* 299–308, 604.

Landis, C., & Hunt, W. (1939). *The startle pattern.* Oxford, UK: Farrar & Rinehart.

Lucas, R. E., & Dyrenforth, P. S. (2006). Does the existence of social relationships matter for subjective well-being? In K. D. Vohs & E. J. Finkel (Eds.), *Self and relationships: Connecting intrapersonal and interpersonal processes* (pp. 254–273). New York: Guilford Press.

Lucas, R. E., Dyrenforth, P. S., & Diener, E. (2008). Four myths about subjective well-being. *Social and Personality Psychology Compass, 2*(5), 2001–2015.

Lurie, P., & Wolfe, S. M. (1997). Unethical trials of interventions to reduce perinatal transmission of the human immunodeficiency virus in developing countries. *New England Journal of Medicine, 337*(12), 853–856.

Masuda, T., & Nisbett, R. E. (2001). Attending holistically vs. analytically: Comparing the context sensitivity of Japanese and Americans. *Journal of Personality and Social Psychology, 81,* 922–934.

McDaniel, M. A., Whetzel, D. L., Schmidt, F. L., & Maurer, S. D. (1994). The validity of employment interviews: A comprehensive review and meta-analysis. *Journal of Applied Psychology, 79,* 599–616.

Meyer, G. J., Finn, S. E., Eyde, L. D., Kay, G. G., Moreland, K. L., Dies, R. R., Eisman, E. J., Kubiszyn, T. W., & Reed, G. M. (2001). Psychological testing and psychological assessment: A review of evidence and issues. *American Psychologist, 56,* 128–165.

Middlemist, R. D., Knowles, E. S., & Matter, C. F. (1976). Personal space invasions in the lavatory: Suggestive evidence for arousal. *Journal of Personality and Social Psychology, 33*(5), 541–546.

Miller, J. G. (1984). Culture and the development of everyday social explanation. *Journal of Personality and Social Psychology, 46,* 961–978.

Miller, N. E (1985). The value of behavioral research on animals. *American Psychologist, 40,* 423–440.

Mischel, W. (1968). *Personality and assessment.* New York: Wiley.

Morris, M. W., & Peng, K. (1994). Culture and cause: American and Chinese attributions for social and physical events. *Journal of Personality and Social Psychology, 67,* 949–971.

Moscovitch, M., Winocur, G., & Behrmann, M. (1997). What is special about face recognition? Nineteen experiments on a person with visual object agnosia and dyslexia but normal face recognition. *Journal of Cognitive Neuroscience, 9,* 555–604.

National Highway Traffic Safety Administration (2008). *Seat belt use in 2008: Use rates in the states and territories.* (DOT-HS-811-106). Washington, DC: U.S. Department of Transportation.

Nisbett, E. K., & Zelenski, J. M. (2011). Underestimating nearby nature: Affective forecasting errors obscure the happy path to sustainability. *Psychological Science, 22*(9), 1101–1106.

Nisbett, R. E., & Borgida, E. (1975). Attribution and the psychology of prediction. *Journal of Personality and Social Psychology, 32,* 932–943.

Pennebaker, J. W., Dyer, M. A., Caulkins, R. S., Litowitz, D. L., Ackerman, P. L., Anderson, D. B., & McGraw, K. M. (1979). "Don't the girls get prettier at closing time": A country and western application to psychology. *Personality and Social Psychological Bulletin, 5,* 122–125.

Petersen, J. L., & Hyde, J. S. (2010). A meta-analytic review of research on gender differences in sexuality, 1993–2007. *Psychological Bulletin, 136,* 21–38.

Peterson, C. (2006). *A primer in positive psychology.* New York: Oxford University Press.

Plous, S., (1996). Attitudes toward the use of animals in psychological research and education: Results from a national survey of psychologists. *American Psychologist, 51*(11), 1167–1180.

Rauscher, F., Shaw, G., & Ky, K. (1993). Music and spatial task performance. *Nature, 365,* 611.

Rizzolatti, G., Fogassi, L., & Gallese, V. (2006, November). Mirrors in the mind. *Scientific American,* 54–61.

Ronay, R., & van Hippel, W. (2010). The presence of an attractive woman elevates testosterone and physical risk-taking in young men. *Social Psychological and Personality Science, 1,* 57–64.

Rosenthal, R., & Rosnow, R. L. (1975). *The volunteer subject.* Oxford, UK: John Wiley & Sons.

Ross, L. (1977). The intuitive psychologist and his shortcomings: Distortions in the attribution process. In L. Berkowitz (Ed.), *Advances in experimental social psychology* (vol. *10,* pp. 173–220). New York: Academic Press.

Ross, S. E., Niebling, B. C., & Heckert, T. M. (1999). Sources of stress among college students. *College Student Journal, 33*(2), 312–318.

Ruback, R. B., & Juieng, D. J. (1997). Territorial defense in parking lots: Retaliation against waiting drivers. *Journal of Applied Social Psychology, 27*(9), 821–834.

Schultz, D. P. (1969). The human subject in psychological research. *Psychological Bulletin, 72*(3), 214–228.

Schwarz, N., & Hippler, H.-J. (1995). Subsequent questions may influence answers to preceding questions in mail surveys. *The Public Opinion Quarterly, 59*(1), 93–97.

Seligman, M. E. P. (2006). *Learned optimism: How to change your mind and your life.* New York: Vintage.

Seligman, M. E. P., & Maier, S. F. (1967). Failure to escape traumatic shock. *Journal of Experimental Psychology, 74,* 1–9.

Shapiro, K. J. (1990). Animal rights vs. humanism: The charge of speciesism. *Journal of Humanistic Psychology, 30,* 9–37.

Soproni, K., Miklósi, Á., Topál, J., & Csányi, V. (2002). Dogs' (*Canis familaris*) responsiveness to human pointing gestures. *Journal of Comparative Psychology, 116*(1), 7035–7036.

Steele, K. M., Bella, S. D., Peretz, I., Dunlop, T., Dawe, L. A., Humphrey, G. K., Shannon, R. A., Kirby, J. A. Jr., & Olmstead, C. G. (1999). Prelude or requiem for the 'Mozart effect'? *Nature, 400,* 827.

Stock, W. A., Okun, M. A., Haring, M. J., & Witter, R. A. (1983). Age and subjective well-being: A meta analysis. In R. J. Light (Ed.), *Evaluation studies: Review annual* (vol. *8,* pp. 279–302). Beverly Hills, CA: Sage.

Schwarz, N., & Hippler, H. -J. (1995). Subsequent questions may influence answers to preceding questions in mail surveys. *The Public Opinion Quarterly, 59*(1), 93–97.

Tourangeau, R., Rips, L. J., & Rasinski, K. (2000). *The psychology of survey response.* Cambridge, UK: Cambridge University Press.

Wason, P. C., & Johnson-Laird, P. N. (1968). *Thinking and reasoning.* Harmondsworth, UK: Penguin.

Welten, D. C., Kemper, H. C. G., Post, G. B., & Van Staveren, W. A. (1995). A meta-analysis of the effect of calcium intake on bone mass in young and middle-aged females and males. *Journal of Nutrition, 125,* 2802–2813.

White, A. (2007). A global projection of subjective well-being: A challenge to positive psychology? *Psychtalk, 56,* 17–20.

Wilkinson, L., & Task Force on Statistical Inference. (1999). Statistical methods in psychology journals: Guidelines and explanations. *American Psychologist, 54*(8), 594–604.

Wolraich, M. L., Wilson, D. B., & White, J. W. (1995). The effect of sugar on behavior or cognition in children. *Journal of the American Medical Association, 274,* 1617–1621.

Chapter Overview ▼

3 Neuroscience: The Biology of Behavior

Learning Objectives ▼

3.1
■ Describe how neuropsychology and neuroscience relate to the study of psychology.
■ Explain how the nervous system conducts signals to and from various parts of the body and brain.

3.2
■ Identify the structural elements of the nervous system.
■ Recognize the types and structure of neurons.

3.3
■ Compare and contrast the peripheral nervous system and the central nervous system.

3.4
■ Identify the different areas of the brain and the functions they control.

3.5
■ Discuss the role of endorphins and the endocrine system as communication mechanisms in the nervous system.

3.6
■ Discuss the role of genetics in psychology.

It was history-making surgery—the surgery that would restore his sight. Forty-six-year-old Mike May had been blind since he was 3, when a freak chemical explosion had damaged both of his eyes. This surgery would correct that. Stem cells, multiple operations, and even a transplanted cornea would be used—the stuff of science fiction. All of these technologies would come together for this miracle operation. News magazine shows were on hand as the doctors removed the bandages from Mike's eyes. You could hear the rapid-fire clicks of a crush of cameras. He had functioning eyes and would see his wife's face for the very first time.

Faces, Mike would later realize, would be a problem for him. A few weeks after his operation, he noticed that he had trouble distinguishing one person from another—he could not really tell his two children apart. Two months after the operation, although his eyesight was good enough for driving, he still could not tell men's faces from women's faces or that his sister was wearing Groucho glasses. Faces were enigmas. Something was wrong. His eyes were fine, but his brain had trouble interpreting what he was seeing.

We see with more than just our eyes. We see with our brains, too. Our brains have to process the information that comes in through not only our eyes but our other senses as well. Mike's brain had adapted to help him get along quite well without being able to see. After all, he set a world's record for downhill skiing by a totally blind person and received numerous medals in the Paralympic Games. It is as if the parts of his brain that might have processed sight had been reassigned new duties. We'll hear more about Mike May's story later and how the tools of neuroscience help to explain his perceptions.

3.1 Overview: The Components of Biological Bases of Behavior

The nervous system conducts signals to and from various parts of your body.

- Describe how neuropsychology and neuroscience relate to the study of psychology.
- Explain how the nervous system conducts signals to and from various parts of the body and brain.

Biological psychology
The branch of psychology that studies the connection of bodily systems and behavior.

Neuroscience The study of the brain and nervous system.

You cannot study much psychology without some understanding of biology. It is like trying to explain the plot of a favorite book or movie without being able to name any of the characters. Know just a little about the biology of psychology, and you've added critical depth and dimension to your understanding of psychology.

Biological psychology, also called neuropsychology, is the branch of psychology that studies the connection of bodily systems and behavior with **neuroscience**, the study of the brain and the nervous system. Neuropsychology helps to link your physical body with explanations for behavior on many different levels. Neuropsychologists help us understand how the brain processes our thoughts and emotions. It also can aid in explaining how our emotions are linked to the physical sensations in our body. Why does your stomach hurt when you are nervous? Neuropsychology examines questions like these at the molecular, cellular, organ, and system levels.

Biologists organize the human body into different organ systems. As you know, you have a digestive system that breaks down and processes foods, a circulatory system that distributes blood to and from the various organs in your body, and a respiratory system that brings oxygen in and carbon dioxide out of your body. Neuroscientists are most interested in the **nervous system**, which is a network of organs, nerves, and supportive systems that send and receive neural signals to and from various parts of the body.

The nervous system links our experience of a changing world with our actions and attitudes. Its main job is communication. The several million signals, or messages, that the nervous system sends and receives every minute are really just electrochemical activity. The nervous system's power and complexity lie in the many ways these signals, or messages, are processed.

Communication within the nervous system generally occurs through messages between **neurons**, or nerve cells, which act like instant messengers, delivering messages that activate or deactivate parts of your nervous system. Communication also occurs through long-distance messengers, such as **hormones**, that communicate with areas of the body that lie beyond the nervous system. The central hub of activity, however, is in your brain. We'll discuss each of these aspects of the nervous system in detail and end with a discussion of genetics that highlights the interconnection of biological and environmental influences.

This chapter has a lot of terms, many of which may be unfamiliar. But like the characters in a book or a movie, once you know how they're related, they'll be less intimidating. We'll start with the basics and work our way to larger, more complex systems. By the end of this chapter, you will understand the molecules, cells, organs, and systems that underlie the biology of behavior.

Nervous system
A collection of organs including neurons and supportive systems.

Neuron A nerve cell.

Hormone A chemical messenger that is produced by endocrine glands.

CONCEPT LEARNING CHECK 3.1 | *Reviewing the Terminology of Neuroscience*

Match the term with the correct definition.

A. Nervous system

B. Neuroscience

C. Neurons

D. Hormones

E. Biological psychology

1. _____ The collection of organs including neurons and supportive systems that creates and conducts signals to various parts of our body

2. _____ The long-distance messengers of our nervous system

3. _____ The branch of psychology that studies the connection of bodily systems and behavior

4. _____ The study of the brain and the nervous system

5. _____ Nerve cells that provide fast communication

3.2 Neural Communication

The nervous system is composed of glia and neurons. Glia support and protect neurons. Neurons communicate messages throughout the nervous system and the rest of the body.

- Identify the structural elements of the nervous system.
- Recognize the types and structure of neurons.

Like the rest of your body, your nervous system is composed of millions upon millions of highly specialized cells. In general, nervous system cells fall into two major categories: glia and neurons.

Glia

Glia cells are cells of the nervous system that support and protect our neurons. *Glia*, from the Greek word for *glue*, were once thought to be the paste that held neurons together. New research has expanded our understanding of glia (sometimes referred to as glial cells). Although smaller than neurons, glial cells are more numerous. Estimates suggest that glial cells make up about 50% of the total volume of the brain (Jessen, 2004). Glial cells provide nutrients, insulation, and protection to neurons. They do not stop there—glial cells also manage and organize your nervous system by directing where neurons grow. They send survival signals to some neurons and perish signals to others to direct **neural pruning**, or the destruction of certain neurons to increase the processing speed of the nervous system. Glial cells also play a strong role in controlling how neurons communicate and in the formation of connections between neurons. In addition to this supportive role, some recent research suggests that glial cells might send communication signals of their own. Damage to glial cells can leave neurons exposed to destruction, inflammation, or slowed processing. Glial malfunction may be partially responsible for such diseases as multiple sclerosis, brain tumors, and Alzheimer's disease (Jessen, 2004).

Although we are beginning to appreciate the complex role that glial cells play, the neuron is the star of the nervous system.

Neurons

Your brain consists of tens of billions (by some estimates, up to 100 billion) of neurons, each with thousands of connections, as can be seen in FIGURE 3-1. Neurons, or nerve cells, are the basic cells of the nervous system. Groups of neurons form nerve fibers that communicate information, or special messages, throughout the nervous system. Many of these neurons communicate with other types of cells throughout the body, such as muscle cells or gland cells. Most neurons in your body, however, are **interneurons**, which are neurons that communicate only with other neurons to help you do all that you do each moment of the day.

FIGURE 3-1 Neurons are the basic cell of the nervous system.

Your nervous system also requires that certain neurons be specialized in order to get the job done. In the same way you have arteries that move blood away from the heart and veins that move it back, you have **afferent nerve fibers** that move information toward the brain and spinal cord as well as **efferent nerve fibers** that carry impulses away from the brain and spinal cord.

To perform a simple physical task, such as turning a page in a book, you use different kinds of neurons. First, you use **sensory neurons**, one type of *afferent* nerve fiber. These are neurons that translate external stimuli into messages to be sent to the central nervous system for processing. When you touch the page of a book, sensory neurons send messages to your brain, allowing it to recognize the single page you intend to turn. Then you employ **motor neurons**, an example of *efferent* nerve fibers. These are the neurons that send messages to muscles and glands to activate the muscles in your hand as you pull the page toward you.

Glia cells Cells in the nervous system that provide support and protection for neurons.

Neural pruning The destruction of certain neurons to increase the processing speed of the nervous system.

Interneuron A neuron that communicates only with other neurons.

Afferent nerve fibers Neurons that move information toward the brain and spinal cord.

Efferent nerve fiber A type of neuron that carries impulses away from the central nervous system.

Sensory neuron A neuron that is responsible for carrying external stimuli to the central nervous system for processing.

Motor neuron A type of neuron that interfaces with muscles and glands.

You even have specialized neurons that are activated when you watch another person perform a task. Called **mirror neurons**, they are active both when you perform a task yourself and also when you watch another person perform an action. Mirror neurons make it easier for you to perform an action while watching another person do the same action, which is very handy when in a group exercise class. In fact, new research on mirror neurons suggests that their role may include monitoring our own movements so that we are aware of the movements we make (Bonaiuto & Arbib, 2010).

The Structure of a Neuron

With more than 10,000 specialized types of neurons come various neuron structures as well. Most neurons, however, have a few things in common: dendrites, a soma, and an axon.

Dendrites are the nerve cell structures that receive messages from other neurons. They look a little like tree roots and funnel messages from other neurons to the **soma**, or **cell body**. The soma is the central part of the neuron. It keeps the cell alive and contains the genetic material for the cell. The **axon** is a long tubelike structure that carries the message away from the soma on its way to another neuron. Although axons are infinitesimally narrow, some are also infinitesimally short, while others, such as those between your spine and your toes, extend several feet. As a collection, the axons of neurons form cablelike bunches in the peripheral nervous system called **nerves**. To keep the message moving smoothly, glial cells envelop a neuron's axon in a white fatty substance called myelin. This **myelin sheath** insulates the axon and enables efficient communication along the axon. The myelin sheath also divides axons into little capsulelike sections, like sausages on a string. At the very end of the axon is the **axon terminal**, sometimes called the terminal button or terminal end bulb.

This is just a basic blueprint. As you can see in FIGURE 3-2, some neurons do not have axons and some have two, but in general, most neurons follow the same basic structure.

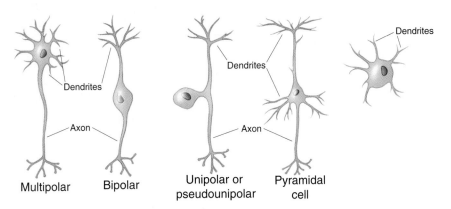

FIGURE 3-2 Neurons come in many shapes, sizes, and configurations.

Neurotransmitters

Although the billions of neurons in your body are in constant communication with each other, they do not touch to communicate; they use (and recycle) chemicals to bridge the incredibly tiny space between one neuron and the next. Neurons communicate messages by discharging neurotransmitters. **Neurotransmitters** are molecules and act as chemical messengers that communicate, or transmit, messages from one neuron to the next. Neurotransmitters can directly or indirectly influence neurons in particular areas of the brain and therefore affect behavior.

Synapses

The space between neurons is part of an area called the **synapse** FIGURE 3-3. The synapse consists of three parts: the terminal button of the sending or **presynaptic neuron**; the space between one neuron and the next (called the synaptic gap or **synaptic cleft**); and the receptor sites on the dendrites of the receiving or **postsynaptic neuron**.

Mirror neuron A type of neuron that fires when an individual watches an action and when performing the action.

Dendrite Nerve cell structure that receives information from other cells.

Soma The part of the neuron that keeps the cell alive and contains the genetic material for the cell.

Cell body The part of a nerve cell that keeps the entire cell alive; also called the soma.

Axon The part of the neuron that carries the nerve impulse away from the soma.

Nerves Bundles of neurons.

Myelin sheath A fatty substance that insulates the axon and enables efficient transmission.

Axon terminal The part of the neuron that discharges and recycles neurotransmitters; also called the terminal button.

Neurotransmitter Chemical messenger that transmits information from one neuron to another.

Synapse An area that includes three structures; the terminal button of the sending neuron, the synaptic gap, and the dendrite of the receiving neuron.

Presynaptic neuron A neuron that sends a signal to another neuron.

Synaptic cleft The small space between the axon terminal of a sending neuron and the dendrite of the receiving neuron.

Postsynaptic neuron A neuron that receives a signal from another neuron.

How Neurons Communicate

Neural communication is fast—really fast. Our fastest neurons communicate across incredibly tiny spaces, transmitting messages at rates of up to 268 miles an hour—the top speed of the world's fastest trains. Let us take a close look at how this communication works. Neurons communicate by way of **synaptic transmission** FIGURE 3-4, meaning they use neurotransmitters to send messages across the synapse to the next neuron. The message the neuron sends can generate or prevent an **action potential**. Neurons send just two types of messages: The message is either *excitatory*, which tells the next neuron, "Fire!" or *inhibitory*, which tells the next neuron, "Don't fire!" If the sum of excitation from excitatory neurons minus the sum of inhibition from inhibitory neurons is greater than the next neuron's **threshold**, then the postsynaptic neuron fires (creates an action potential). If a neuron is communicating with, say, a muscle cell, an excitatory message might cause the muscle cell to contract so you can flex your biceps in the mirror. An inhibitory message might cause a muscle to release so you can place your grocery bags on the kitchen table.

Action Potentials

So neurons send excitatory or inhibitory messages—called action potentials—that say to the next neuron, "Fire!" or "Don't fire!" But what sets these messages in motion? It is both an electrical and chemical reaction. All around the neuron, both inside and outside of a neuron's axon, are fluids that contain electrically charged atoms (or ions) of sodium and potassium. The movement of these ions determines whether a neuron generates an action potential FIGURE 3-5. When a neuron is not firing or is at rest, sodium and potassium ions flow back and forth through tiny holes in the axon's wall, or membrane.

Synaptic transmission
The process by which one neuron communicates with another by using neurotransmitters.

Action potential The electrical message or neural impulse that flows along a neuron's axon.

Threshold The point at which a neuron will respond to an action potential.

FIGURE 3-3 The synapse is the junction between two neurons.

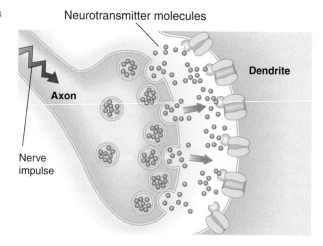

FIGURE 3-4 Neurons don't touch, instead they communicate through synaptic transmission.

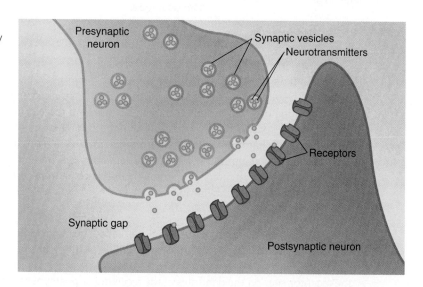

These holes are called channels. They allow sodium and potassium to move from areas of higher concentration to areas of lower concentration on their own. Think of a drop of red dye in a glass of water. The dye will disperse through the water, moving from an area of higher concentration (where there is a lot of dye) to areas of lower concentration (where there is little or no dye). The ions of our neurons move around in the same way. The axon's membrane also contains a channel that acts like a pump, sending some of the potassium and sodium ions against the flow, back to their respective sides of the axon. This pump ensures that the inside of an axon is more negatively charged than the outside of the axon. In a resting neuron, this charge is about –70 millivolts (by contrast, a small watch battery is more than 10 times stronger at about 880 millivolts). Maintaining the negative charge, by the way, takes a huge amount of energy. It is estimated that up to one-third of our energy, even when we are sedentary, is used to power this sodium/potassium pump (Laughlin, van Steveninck, & Anderson, 1998). The inactive neuron's negative charge is called the **resting potential** FIGURE 3-6.

When a neuron is stimulated to fire, potassium channels in the first section of the axon close. Then sodium rushes into the axon and causes this section of the axon to **depolarize**, or become more positive. This generates an action potential. Once the action potential is generated and starts hurtling down the axon, it does not grow stronger or weaker, and it cannot be stopped. This is called the **all-or-nothing law**, because an action potential either happens or it does not.

The action potential continues hurtling down the axon, changing the polarity of each axon section as it passes through. Once the action potential has passed, the opened channels in the axon's membrane now close, and that section of the axon resets or **repolarizes**

Resting potential An inactive neuron's negative charge.

Depolarizes The process by which an axon becomes more positive.

All-or-nothing law The concept that either a neuron fires or it doesn't. There is no partial firing.

Repolarizes The process by which a neuron's axon will return to the resting potential.

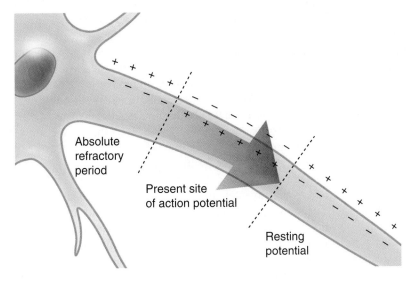

FIGURE 3-5 The action potential will determine if a neuron will fire.

FIGURE 3-6 Resting potential.

Absolute refractory period The point after an action potential when the neuron cannot produce another action potential no matter the intensity of the stimulation.

Synaptic vesicle A sac that contains neurotransmitters in the axon terminal.

Receptor site An area on the dendrite that receives neurotransmitters.

Stimulus threshold The point at which the neuron responds by changing its voltage.

Postsynaptic potential (PSP) Changes in the dendrite of the receiving neuron as the result of its binding with neurotransmitters.

Excitatory postsynaptic potential (EPSP) A voltage change caused by the binding of neurotransmitters that causes a positive voltage shift in the resting potential of the postsynaptic neuron triggering the neuron to fire.

Inhibitory postsynaptic potential (IPSP) A voltage change caused by the binding of neurotransmitters that causes a negative voltage shift in the resting potential of the postsynaptic neuron preventing the neuron from firing.

Reuptake The reabsorption of neurotransmitters back into a presynaptic neuron.

Synaptic pruning The destruction of less active synapses to organize and improve efficiency of the neural connections.

and returns to the resting potential. This reset period is called the **absolute refractory period**. It is the point after an action potential when the neuron cannot produce another action potential, regardless of the intensity of the stimulation. During this time, the action potential cannot regenerate. It is really a short time, maybe 1 to 2 milliseconds. The absolute refractory period prevents the action potential from moving backward and ensures that the action potential flows only in one direction.

This change in polarity is constantly regenerated as the action potential travels from section to section along the axon. It is somewhat like a kid careening down a water slide: The polarity of the axon returns to its resting potential after the action potential has passed—just as the water flow in a section of the slide returns to normal after the kid passes by. The action potential continues in this way until it reaches the axon terminal, where it performs a final trick.

When the action potential reaches the axon terminal, it ends at **synaptic vesicles**, which are small sacs that contain the neurotransmitters, floating down to the very end of the axon terminal or the terminal end bulb. There, the synaptic vesicles fuse with the terminal button. At this point, the neurotransmitters spill out into the synaptic gap, where they float and bounce around like Ping-Pong balls. Some will find their way to another neuron's receptor sites. **Receptor sites**, located on the neuron's dendrites, are areas that receive neurotransmitters. There, the neurotransmitters from the sending neuron bind with the receiving neuron's receptor site and deliver the message to fire or not to fire.

Once the neurotransmitter binds to the receiving, or postsynaptic, neuron's receptor site, it can help change the voltage of the postsynaptic neuron. If enough bind, the postsynaptic neuron will reach its **stimulus threshold**, the point at which it responds by changing its voltage. This change in voltage is called a **postsynaptic potential (PSP)**. A PSP is a change in the postsynaptic neuron that was the result of neurotransmitters from another neuron binding with it. The postsynaptic neuron may generate an action potential of its own, in which case the entire process repeats itself, and the postsynaptic neuron becomes a presynaptic neuron, and so on and so on.

There are two kinds of postsynaptic potentials, or PSPs: excitatory and inhibitory. **Excitatory postsynaptic potentials (EPSPs)**, cause a positive voltage shift in the resting potential of the next (postsynaptic) neuron. This triggers the channels in the axons to open and depolarize them, causing the neuron to fire. **Inhibitory PSPs (IPSPs)**, cause a negative voltage change and make the resting potential even more negative. In this case, the neuron does not fire. In fact, it may take even more stimulation for the neuron to fire because the current resting potential may be below its usual −70 millivolts.

Postsynaptic neurons do not absorb or pass on the neurotransmitters that they receive and that bind with them. Therefore, they need to be discarded or put to good use. There are two primary cleanup mechanisms in the synapse. Some neurotransmitters get gobbled up (metabolized) by an enzyme called monoamine oxidase (MAO), while some others get recycled and repackaged into new synaptic vesicles by transport proteins located on the presynaptic terminal buttons. This process of reabsorbing the neurotransmitters into a presynaptic neuron is called **reuptake**.

Neural Networks

You'll recall that neurons receive signals from a lot of other neurons all at the same time. Rather than simply passing along the signal, neurons integrate signals. An IPSP, under the right circumstances, could cancel out an EPSP. In this way, neurons incorporate information from many sources.

In addition, there are specific neurotransmitter pathways that connect various areas of the brain. These pathways are sort of like highways that connect certain brain areas and allow neurotransmitters to influence behavior in many parts of the brain.

Pruning of Networks

You might think that the more synaptic connections we have, the better. However, the nervous system forms more synapses than it needs, so, over time, it gradually gets rid of the less active synapses. This is referred to as **synaptic pruning**. Newborns, for example, have about 11 million neurons in their thalamus, a part of the brain that acts as a relay station. By adulthood, they have lost about 41% of those neurons (Abitz et al., 2007) FIGURE 3-7. Getting rid of less active connections helps to organize and improve the efficiency of the whole system. In fact, neural networks peak when a person is 1 year old and then begin their decline.

Multitasking Neurotransmitters

Neurotransmitters act like keys to the locks of receptor sites, with only certain neurotransmitters activating certain receptor sites to create inhibitory or excitatory PSPs.

Since neurotransmitters can only create either an excitatory postsynaptic potential or an inhibitory postsynaptic potential, it would seem logical that you would only need two types of neurotransmitters—one for the gas and one for the brakes. In actuality, more than 100 different types of substances play the role of neurotransmitters at least some of the time (Greengard, 2001). There are a few "classic" neurotransmitters whose functions can be found in **TABLE 3-1**. A single neurotransmitter can be involved in many functions and thus may have overlapping responsibilities in the nervous system. **Acetylcholine** and **norepinephrine**, for example, are both involved in memory.

In addition to influencing postsynaptic neurons, some drugs can influence the effect of neurotransmitters. An **agonist**, for example, is a substance that mimics or increases the effect of a neurotransmitter. **Gamma-aminobutric acid (GABA)** is the nervous system's primary inhibitory neurotransmitter. GABA agonists like Valium can slow down the nervous system and relax us. **Antagonists**, on the other hand, are substances that block the action of a neurotransmitter. Botulinum toxin, for instance, acts as an antagonist and blocks the release of acetylcholine. This interference with acetylcholine can cause paralysis of muscles and result in the illness known as botulism. Agonists and antagonists each can act directly (by binding or blocking) at receptor sites or indirectly (by increasing or decreasing the release of the neurotransmitter, blocking reuptake, or destroying transmitters in the synapse).

Acetylcholine Neurotransmitter that is involved in memory and muscle functions.

Norepinephrine A neurotransmitter responsible for learning and memory.

Agonist A substance that mimics or increases the effect of a neurotransmitter.

Gamma-aminobutric acid (GABA) The nervous system's primary inhibitory neurotransmitter.

Antagonist A substance that blocks the action of a neurotransmitter.

Dopamine Neurotransmitter that is involved in movement and reward systems.

Serotonin A neurotransmitter involved in sleep, mood, and appetite.

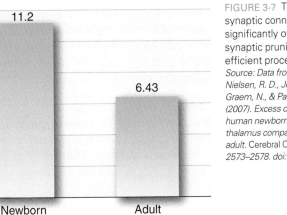

FIGURE 3-7 The number of synaptic connections declines significantly over time, but this synaptic pruning leads to more efficient processing. *Source: Data from Abitz, M., Nielsen, R. D., Jones, E. G., Laursen, H., Graem, N., & Pakkenberg, B. (2007). Excess of neurons in the human newborn mediodorsal thalamus compared with that of the adult. Cerebral Cortex, 17(11), 2573–2578. doi:10.1093/cercor/bhl163*

TABLE 3-1 Neurotransmitters and Their Functions

Neurotransmitter	Function
Acetylcholine	Involved in memory and muscle functions.
Dopamine	Involved in movement and reward systems.
GABA	The nervous system's primary inhibitory neurotransmitter.
Norepinephrine	Responsible for learning and memory.
Serotonin	Involved in sleep, mood, and appetite.

CONCEPT LEARNING CHECK 3.2 | *Recognizing the Parts of the Neuron*

Match the parts of the neuron and synapse with the correct area.

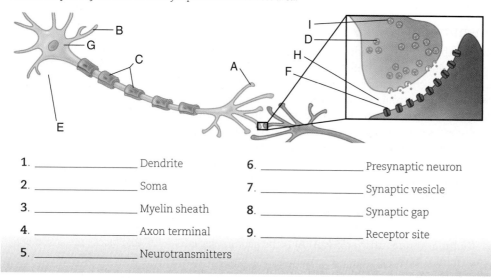

1. _____ Dendrite

2. _____ Soma

3. _____ Myelin sheath

4. _____ Axon terminal

5. _____ Neurotransmitters

6. _____ Presynaptic neuron

7. _____ Synaptic vesicle

8. _____ Synaptic gap

9. _____ Receptor site

3.3 Nervous System Organization

Our nervous system is composed of two main branches: The central nervous system integrates and controls the body and the peripheral nervous system links the rest of your body to the central nervous system.

■ Compare and contrast the peripheral nervous system and the central nervous system.

Peripheral nervous system A division of the nervous system excluding the brain and spinal cord.

Somatic nervous system The division of the peripheral nervous system that connects to voluntary muscle movement and communicates sensory information.

Autonomic nervous system Part of the peripheral nervous system that interfaces with the heart, intestines, and other organs.

Sympathetic nervous system A branch of the autonomic nervous system that prepares the organs for vigorous activity.

Parasympathetic nervous system A component of the autonomic nervous system that conserves bodily functions and energy.

Your nervous system is composed of two main branches: the central nervous system FIGURE 3-8, which integrates and controls the body, and the peripheral nervous system, which links the rest of the body to the central nervous system. The two parts of your nervous system work together to connect and operate the body.

Peripheral Nervous System

It might be easier to think about the peripheral nervous system in terms of what it is not. The **peripheral nervous system** consists of all the parts of the nervous system *excluding* the brain and the spinal cord. What is left? A lot. The peripheral nervous system includes miles and miles of nerves, or bundles of neurons that connect to the muscles, glands, and organs of your body.

The peripheral nervous system itself is organized into two parts: a **somatic nervous system**, which controls the voluntary movement of your muscles, and the **autonomic nervous system**, which controls internal organs and glands.

The autonomic nervous system, in turn, has two components: The **sympathetic nervous system** speeds you up to fight, freeze, or flee; the **parasympathetic nervous system** calms you down and conserves your bodily functions.

Imagine that you are in class and suddenly your professor says the words that all students fear: "Pop quiz!" All of a sudden, your sympathetic nervous system fires up. Your hands become cold and clammy; your heart rate and blood pressure shoot up. Your sympathetic nervous system is getting you ready to rumble. The problem is, there is no one to fight and nowhere to flee. In these situations, some people do freeze with test anxiety. There is some evidence that this is the kind of stress that might be linked to cardiovascular disease (Macleod et al., 2002).

Events like a pop quiz, a fender bender, or even a day of riding roller coasters may lead to exhaustion. Some people attribute this tiredness to all the work their body did. However, some of your exhaustion may be due to the effects of your parasympathetic nervous system calming you down. FIGURE 3-9 highlights the features and organs that are affected by the sympathetic and parasympathetic nervous systems.

Central Nervous System

The **central nervous system** consists of your brain and your spinal cord, and it has a support system of its own. In addition to the bony skull and spinal column, the central nervous system is protected by **cerebrospinal fluid (CSF)**, a clear liquid created in the brain's ventricular system that supports and protects the central nervous system. Cradling the brain in cerebrospinal fluid creates buoyancy and reduces the net weight of the brain from around 3 pounds (about the weight of a large pineapple) to less than 2-tenths of a pound (about the weight of one medium-sized banana) because of buoyancy. CSF also acts as a transportation medium to carry hormones in and out of the brain and wash away toxins. We will explore the brain in more detail later on.

Spinal Cord

Although our brain often gets top billing, the spinal cord is no bit player. The **spinal cord** is a collection of neurons that run from the base of the brain and down your back and is protected by a spinal column. Your spinal cord can initiate actions all by itself. These **reflexes**, or involuntary motor responses, coordinated by the spinal cord are known as **spinal reflexes**. When you touch a hot stove, for example, it is easy to think that your brain coordinates your response—jerking your arm back—but it does not. The information goes directly to the spinal cord, and your spinal cord sends the signal to pull your hand back before you do any more damage to your poor finger. In the next section, we'll examine how the spinal cord does what it does.

FIGURE 3-8 The nervous system consists of a central (red) and peripheral (blue) nervous system.

Central nervous system
A division of the nervous system that is comprised of the brain and spinal cord.

Cerebrospinal fluid (CSF)
Clear liquid created in the ventricular system that supports and protects the central nervous system.

Spinal cord A collection of neurons that run from the base of the brain down the back.

Reflex An involuntary motor response.

Spinal reflex An involuntary motor response coordinated by the spinal cord.

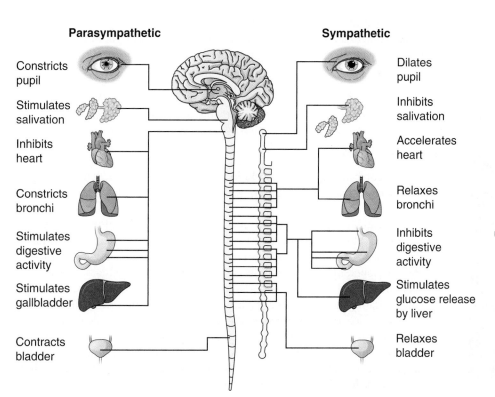

FIGURE 3-9 The sympathetic nervous system gets us ready to fight, freeze, or flee, while the parasympathetic nervous system calms us down.

CONCEPT LEARNING CHECK **3.3** | *The Organization of the Nervous System*

Fill in the blanks of the nervous system organization chart.

Phrenology A procedure that uses bumps on an individual's head to determine and predict personality characteristics.

Lesion A natural or intentional destruction of brain tissue.

Electrical stimulation of the brain A technique used to stimulate neural networks in the nervous system. Also known as deep brain stimulation.

3.4 The Brain

The brain is divided into three major structures, each involved in important daily functioning.

■ Identify the different areas of the brain and the functions they control.

The champion of the nervous system (and maybe of the entire body) is the brain—and it is an amazing organ. Weighing in at only 3 pounds, it packs in trillions of glial cells and easily 100 billion neurons. Your brain uses about 20% of all the oxygen you breathe in every day. It is staggeringly complex. Your brain controls your organs and muscles and integrates all the information you know, to name just a few things. This section is really just an initiation to the general structures, functions, and organization of this organ. Honestly, scientists are only just beginning to understand how the brain works.

Organization

The best way to introduce how the brain works is to orient you to the location of the structures and their functions. As remarkable and as functionally distinct as the structures are, at first glance everything looks . . . well, the same.

Research on the Brain

Many people wonder how psychologists know that a particular part of the brain is associated with a certain function. Researchers have used different techniques to study the brain.

Researching the brain is not new. Back in the 1800s, phrenology was a popular technique. **Phrenology** was a procedure that used bumps on an individual's head to determine and predict personality characteristics. Unfortunately, it is not very accurate. We have found more reliable information from lesions in the brain. A **lesion** is the natural or intentional destruction of brain tissue. Knowing what happens when a part of the brain is damaged or destroyed is a key to knowing its function when it works correctly. In 1848, a railroad worker named Phineas Gage FIGURE 3-10 suffered an accident when an explosion drove a 1-pound steel rod straight through his head, destroying much of the front part of his brain. Some of the reports after the accident suggested that his personality was altered. Gage's case underscores the fact that examining lesions is an important way to study the functions of various parts of the nervous system.

Today, more sophisticated technologies are employed to study and treat the brain. For example, **electrical stimulation of the brain** is a technique used to stimulate neural

FIGURE 3-10 Phineas Gage suffered an accident that damaged his frontal lobe.

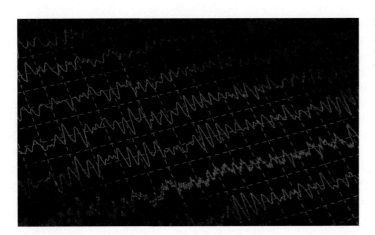

FIGURE 3-11 EEGs produce distinctive patterns that can be analyzed.

Transcranial magnetic stimulation (TMS) A procedure that uses electromagnetic coils to activate nerve cells in the brain.

Electroencephalogram (EEG) A device that measures the electrical activity in the brain.

Computed tomography scans (CT scans) A neuroscience imaging technique that uses computer-enhanced X-rays that are helpful at examining brain structures.

Positron emission tomography (PET scan) A neuroscience imaging technique that uses radioactive glucose to indicate areas of activity.

Magnetic resonance imaging (MRI) A non-invasive neuroscience imaging technique that uses magnets and radio equipment to produce detailed images.

Functional magnetic resonance imagining (fMRI) Neuroscience imaging technique used to measures changes in blood flow.

networks in the nervous system. Also known as deep brain stimulation, it uses electrical signals to trigger areas of the brain. Instead of using electricity, **transcranial magnetic stimulation (TMS)** is a procedure that uses magnetic fields generated by electromagnetic coils to activate nerve cells in the brain. TMS can be used to activate or momentarily depress or deactivate activity in a specific area of the brain.

The **electroencephalogram (EEG)** is a device that measures the electrical activity in the brain. Using electrodes on the scalp, the machine records the electrical activity or brain waves produced by the action potential of the neurons. These brain waves produce distinct images that can be analyzed FIGURE 3-11. **Computed tomography scans (CT scans)** are another neuroimaging technique. CT scans are computer-enhanced X-rays and are good at examining structures. **Positron emission tomography (PET scan)**, is a neuroscience imaging technique that uses radioactive glucose to indicate areas of activity. Patients are injected with glucose that is tagged with small amounts of radiation. The parts of the brain that are more active use more glucose, and the PET scanner can indicate those areas with different colors. The PET scan examines areas of the brain that are using more energy FIGURE 3-12. **Magnetic resonance imaging (MRI)** FIGURE 3-13 is a noninvasive imaging technique that uses magnets and radio equipment to produce detailed images. MRIs are good at producing details of soft tissue. **Functional magnetic resonance imaging (fMRI)** is like MRI but can examine brain activity over time. Remember the story of Mike May at the beginning of the chapter? Psychologists utilized fMRI techniques to discover that May used the part of his brain that processes visual images differently than other people do. This might explain why he had difficulty interpreting faces. In fact, the parts of the brain that are active in individuals who can recognize faces were inactive in Mike (Fine et al., 2003).

The Brainstem

Many neuroscientists divide the brain into three structures: a hindbrain and a midbrain (sometimes together called the **brainstem**) and the larger forebrain. Each of those other structures is further divided as well. It all looks very complex and unfamiliar, but, as with any new map, once you have a general lay of the land, it is much easier to find your way around. Let us get started with the hindbrain.

A few years ago in western Colorado, a farmer named Lloyd was getting ready to make dinner for his wife. The meal featured chicken, and Lloyd's wife's favorite part of the chicken was the neck. He decided to cut the head off of the chicken so that there would be as much neck as possible for his wife (gruesome, if not kind). With one blow he chopped off the head. He did a wonderful job at saving the neck—too wonderful. In aiming for maximum neck, the farmer managed to preserve the brainstem structures of the chicken. It lived—not just overnight but

FIGURE 3-12 Images from a PET scan show areas of greater brain activity in red, moderate in yellow, and low in blue.

Brainstem The part of the brain between the cerebral cortex and the spinal cord responsible for survival functions.

Hindbrain A region of the brain that includes the cerebellum, the pons, and the medulla. It supports vital bodily processes.

Medulla Part of the hindbrain that is involved in breathing, heartbeat, and other essential functions.

Pons Part of the hindbrain that is involved in relaying information from the cortex, as well as in sleep and arousal.

Reticular formation A network of nerve fibers involved in sleep and wakefulness. Also called the reticular activating system (RAS).

Cerebellum A part of the hindbrain involved in the development and coordination of movement.

for over a year. Nutritionists were consulted, vets were retained, and Mike the Headless Chicken hit the road. Mike died about 18 months later after choking on a piece of corn.

This seemingly improbable story (there is a documentary about it) reveals the brainstem's function. The brainstem connects our spinal cord to the rest of the central nervous system and houses many structures needed for survival. The brainstem consists of hindbrain and midbrain structures. Mike the Headless Chicken was able to survive as long as he did because his brainstem handled all the essential functions that his body needed to live.

The **hindbrain** FIGURE 3-14 is a central intersection for nerves that come up through the spinal cord. Its structures support vital bodily processes. Nerves cross over from left to right in the hindbrain. This results in the left side of your brain controlling the right side of your body. The hindbrain contains four important structures: the medulla, the pons, the reticular activating system, and the cerebellum. The **medulla** is the part of the hindbrain that is involved in breathing, heartbeat, and other essential functions. It also coordinates certain reflexive behaviors such as swallowing, coughing, vomiting, and sneezing. Above the medulla is the pons. The **pons** is the part of the hindbrain that is involved in relaying messages from the cerebral cortex and is involved in sleep and arousal. The reticular activating system (RAS) or the **reticular formation** is a network of nerve fibers critical in sleep and wakefulness. It also helps you filter out or ignore what is not important to focus on.

The **cerebellum** is a part of the hindbrain involved in the development and coordination of movement. About the size of two golf balls, it has a role in balance, muscle movements, and routines like typing and writing. In addition, it is also responsible for

FIGURE 3-13 Neuroscientists can analyze MRIs to determine information about brain structures.

FIGURE 3-14 Hindbrain structures support vital bodily processes.

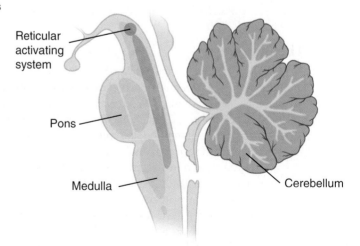

coordinating rhythm timing (Courchesne et al., 1994). Chronic alcoholism can cause damage to the cerebellum and cause **ataxia**, or loss of coordination of muscle movements (Melgaard & Ahlgren, 1986).

Midbrain

The **midbrain** is a major relay station for processing auditory and visual information. It is also helpful in tracking movements. An important midbrain structure is the **substantia nigra**. Meaning dark substance because of its dark color, the substantia nigra is responsible for the initiation of movement.

Knowing what the brainstem does for the body, you can see how Mike the Headless Chicken managed to survive for so long. His brainstem made sure that his heart could still beat, his lungs could still breathe, his reflexes could still respond to stimuli, and he could still sleep and move around.

Forebrain

The **forebrain** FIGURE 3-15 is the largest part of the brain. The forebrain consists of the thalamus, the hypothalamus, the limbic system, and the cerebrum.

Thalamus

The **thalamus** is a forebrain structure that is a major relay station for all sensory information (except smell). It acts like a router, sorting and distributing information to other areas of the brain. In addition to this sorting function, the thalamus plays a role in how we notice and react to the sensations around us.

Hypothalamus

The **hypothalamus** is the forebrain structure that detects need states and drives such as the fight-or-flight response and hunger. The hypothalamus controls the autonomic nervous system and pituitary hormone production. The hypothalamus controls blood flow and regulates metabolic activity such as hunger and reproductive activity such as sexual appetite and menstrual cycles. It helps us coordinate our responses to threats by releasing stress hormones and helps us balance the influence of our sympathetic and parasympathetic nervous systems.

Limbic System

The **limbic system** FIGURE 3-16 is a group of structures surrounding the brainstem that governs emotions such as anger, happiness, and fear. It also stores and retrieves new memories. Although the limbic system has many structures, we'll look at just two—the amygdala and the hippocampus.

Amygdala

The **amygdala** is a cluster of neurons in an area of the brain called the temporal lobe. Neurons in the amygdala are linked to emotions such as anger and fear. The amygdala integrates the emotional significance of sensory stimuli and guides our behavior.

Ataxia Loss of coordination of muscle movements.

Midbrain Part of the brainstem involved in control of sensory processes.

Substantia nigra A midbrain structure that is responsible for initiation of movement.

Forebrain The largest part of the brain, consisting of a number of structures including the cerebrum, the thalamus, and the limbic system.

Thalamus A forebrain structure that is a major relay station for sensory information.

Hypothalamus A forebrain structure that detects need states and controls the autonomic nervous system and pituitary hormone production.

Limbic system A group of structures surrounding the brainstem that governs emotions such as anger, happiness, and fear, and stores and retrieves new memories.

Amygdala A cluster of neurons in the temporal lobe linked to emotions such as anger and fear.

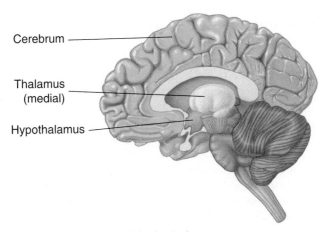

FIGURE 3-15 Structures of the forebrain.

FIGURE 3-16 The limbic system is a group of structures that surround the brainstem.

Hippocampus Part of the limbic system that is involved in processing new memories.

Cerebrum The cerebrum is the largest part of the forebrain and consists of left and right hemispheres, each made up of four lobes.

Corpus callosum A dense network of fibers that connects the left and right cerebral hemispheres.

Cerebral cortex The part of the brain involved in complex cognitive functioning.

Occipital lobe An area in the back of the cerebral cortex. Its visual cortex processes image information.

Temporal lobe An area of the cerebral cortex near the temples. Includes primary auditory cortex, and language centers.

Frontal lobe The front part of the cerebral cortex involved in planning, organization, and personality.

Motor cortex A region of the cerebral cortex involved in planning, controlling, and executing motor functions.

Parietal lobe An area of the cerebral cortex located behind the frontal lobe. Its somatosensory cortex processes body sensation information.

Somatosensory cortex An area of the parietal lobe that processes body sensation information.

Association areas Areas of the cerebral cortex involved in integration of information.

Hippocampus

Being on a national news television program would be an exciting day for anyone, but Michelle would not remember it. A car crash left her hippocampus damaged. The **hippocampus** is part of the limbic system that is involved in processing new memories. Because of this damage, she cannot record any new memories. She remembers everything up until the time of the car accident that damaged her hippocampus—everything until 1994. After that, things get fuzzy—even her wedding to her husband in 1997. In fact, her memory seems to reset every day. She uses sticky notes, her cell phone, and a GPS system to get around most days. It is incredibly frustrating for her. When reading a book, by the time she gets to the middle, she may have totally forgotten how the story started. When shopping, by the time she gets to the store, she may have forgotten why she went there in the first place. Michelle's story demonstrates how important the hippocampus is to each of us in our everyday life.

Cerebrum and Cerebral Cortex

The **cerebrum** is the area most responsible for thinking and language. It is the largest part of the forebrain and is involved in complex cognitive functioning. Containing about 90% of the brain's volume, the cerebrum is only about a fourth of an inch thick (about the thickness of a cushy yoga mat). Its hills (gyri) and valleys (sulci) make it more compact and easier to carry around with you. Without this folding, the cerebrum would be about 3 feet wide by 3 feet long. The cerebrum consists of two hemispheres (left and right), each of which contains four lobes. The two hemispheres are connected by a dense network of nerve fibers called the **corpus callosum**.

Lobes of the Cerebrum

When we picture a brain, the image most of us have is of the **cerebral cortex**, the outside layer of the cerebrum. The cerebral cortex, or cortex, is the rounded mass of "gray matter" just beneath the skull. There are four lobes, or regions, in each hemisphere of the cerebral cortex FIGURE 3-17. Each lobe has been linked to different tasks. The **occipital lobes** are an area in the rear of the cerebral cortex. At the very back of the occipital lobes is the visual cortex, which processes image information. The **temporal lobes** are an area near the temples. The temporal lobes contain the primary auditory cortex, which processes sounds. The **frontal lobes** are at the front of the cerebral cortex and play a role in personality, organization, and planning. The frontal lobes also contain the **motor cortex**, which is an area that has a role in planning, controlling, and executing movements. The **parietal lobe** is located behind the frontal lobe, at the top of your head. The parietal lobes contain the **somatosensory cortex**, which processes body sensation information such as texture, warmth, weight, and how things feel. The parietal lobes also contain **association areas** that are critical in the integration of information.

Hemispheres

The cerebrum's two hemispheres, left and right, are sometimes referred to as the left brain and right brain. Each hemisphere is divided into the four lobes. These **cerebral hemispheres** operate relatively independently even though they are connected by the corpus callosum FIGURE 3-18. This highway of nerve fibers allows the hemispheres to be in constant contact with each other. The discovery of **lateralization of function**, the idea that there are hemispheric specialties, was made quite by mistake. Severing the corpus callosum, also called a callostomy, is an operation that is sometimes performed to control epileptic seizures. Seizures in epilepsy can sometimes be like electrical storms that spread across the brain. Cutting the corpus callosum, it was believed, could contain the seizure on one side of the brain. The first surgeries were done in the 1940s but did not really help those with epilepsy. Because of this, the idea was abandoned and the resulting hypothesis was that it caused no perceptible difference in thoughts or actions of the patients. It was not until 30 years later that other physicians realized that in the previous operations, the corpus callosum was not completely severed. Once that new operation was done, the seizures were controlled and researchers started noticing some differences between these new "**split-brained**" patients and those who had not had this operation.

Cerebral hemisphere One of the two regions of the cerebral cortex.

Lateralization of function The concept that each hemisphere of the cerebral cortex is primarily responsible for certain activities.

Split brain The result of severing the corpus callosum, so that the hemispheres of the cerebral cortex cannot communicate through the nerves that would usually connect them.

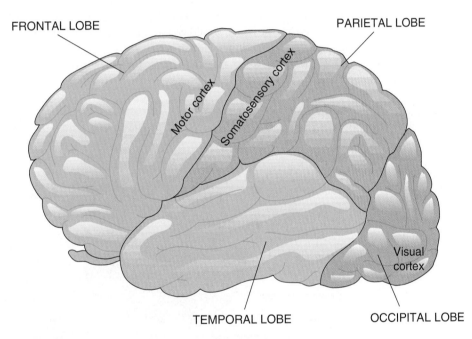

FRONTAL LOBE   PARIETAL LOBE
Motor cortex   Somatosensory cortex
Visual cortex
TEMPORAL LOBE   OCCIPITAL LOBE

FIGURE 3-17 Lobes of the cerebral cortex.

FIGURE 3-18 A photograph of the brain showing the cerebral hemisphere (purple) and the corpus callosum (green).

Severing the connection between the left and right hemispheres gave researchers a peek at how each hemisphere operates because information could no longer flow between the two hemispheres. As a result of this operation, the left hemisphere could not communicate with the right hemisphere. Lateralization of function is the concept that each hemisphere is primarily responsible for a certain function FIGURE 3-19. For example, scientists discovered a left-hemispheric dominance for language, both written and verbal. While the right hemisphere can understand some written words, it has a much harder time changing words into spoken language, something that is no problem for the language-loving left hemisphere. Despite that, the right hemisphere has some of its own strengths, including visual and spatial tasks.

Destruction of parts of the corpus callosum can stop the transfer of certain signals from the left hemisphere to the right. The back part of the corpus callosum, for example, relates to the transfer of sight, hearing, and body sensation. The frontmost part of the corpus callosum is responsible for things like attention.

Once the **split-brain surgery** is completed, the hemispheres operate independently FIGURE 3-20. Since the left hemisphere is in control of the right side of the body, and the right hemisphere is in charge of the left, combined with lateralization of function, researchers came up with some interesting findings. If researchers showed an image, let us say of a key, to only the right visual field of the patient, the patient could easily describe what he saw. The reason was that the image would go into the right visual field, get processed by the brain's left hemisphere, and the left hemisphere's strength in language could easily describe the key. However, when shown an image to the left visual field, the patient

Split-brain surgery An operation that involves severing the corpus callosum. Also called a corpus callostomy.

FIGURE 3-19 Lateralization of function suggests hemispheric specialties.

LEFT BRAIN FUNCTIONS

Right-handed control

Analytic thought

Logic

Reasoning

Language

Writing

Science and math

Number skills

RIGHT BRAIN FUNCTIONS

Left-handed control

Music awareness

Art awareness

Creativity

Imagination

3-D forms

Holistic thought

Intuition

Insight

FIGURE 3-20 An example of a split-brain experiment.

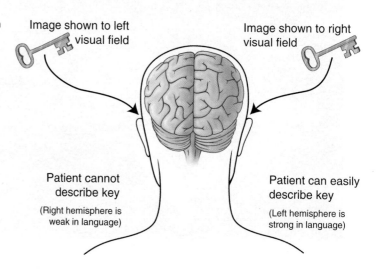

Image shown to left visual field

Image shown to right visual field

Patient cannot describe key

(Right hemisphere is weak in language)

Patient can easily describe key

(Left hemisphere is strong in language)

did not recognize the image because the right hemisphere is not too great at producing language. However, if given a list of images to point to, he could find the image easily.

Even though most of us have an intact corpus callosum, there are some artifacts of the left and right hemispheric dominance for certain tasks. This means that the left and right brains' particular talents can show up in everyday tasks. Since our right hemisphere is better at visual spatial tasks, for example, we tend to pay more attention to the facial information processed in our left visual field. These artifacts lead to **perceptual asymmetries** or differences in the speed of processing depending on the laterality of function. (For example, we tend to pay more attention to the left side of the face when we recognize people we know).

Plasticity

Our nervous system has an astounding ability to grow and adjust. **Plasticity** refers to the ability of the nervous system to adapt by creating new neural pathways. I'm sure you've noticed from our discussion of the biology of the brain that the structure and functions of brain areas are linked. The idea that certain areas of the brain are responsible for specific processes is known as **cortical localization**. Because of this, scientists can predict what kind of problems a person might have due to damage to certain brain areas. For example, damage to an area of the brain that processes language can lead to **aphasia**, which is an inability to understand or produce language.

But the nervous system can also change and grow. Reading this textbook can cause changes to your brain. As you learn new ideas, new synaptic connections are made. Learning a second language, for example, can create denser areas of brain matter in your left parietal lobe (Mechelli et al., 2004). In fact, the earlier you learn a second language, the denser this area becomes from that experience.

Your life experiences can alter the actual structure as well as the tasks that these structures can accomplish. **Structural plasticity** is the brain's ability to change in response to the environment. fMRIs indicate, for example, that learning to play a musical instrument can make areas in your hippocampus more dense. The environment can change the function of certain areas of the brain, too. **Functional plasticity** is the capacity to change areas of the brain that are responsible for activities. When you learn how to read, for example, there are changes to the way your brain processes information that may improve brain functioning.

It used to be thought that we were born with all of the neurons we'll ever have. More recent research, however, has suggested that **neurogenesis**, the process of the development of new neurons, is not only possible but also can be influenced by our environment. Exercise, for example, can create new neurons in the hippocampus of mice (van Praag, Shubert, Zhao, & Gage, 2005).

But what about Mike May at the beginning of this chapter? Why did Mike have so much difficulty in recognizing faces? Unfortunately, when certain experiences do not occur, this could result in some areas of the brain not developing fully. For many structures and functions, there may be a **critical period** or a window of opportunity in which certain experiences will result in the development of functions and structures in our brain. Mike May could have missed the many early experiences that would have allowed his developing brain to interpret and distinguish faces (Fine et al., 2003).

Perceptual asymmetry Because of imbalances between the left and right cerebral hemispheres, visual or auditory processing happens at different speeds depending on whether sensory input is coming from the left or right side of the body.

Plasticity The ability of the nervous system to adapt by creating new neural pathways.

Cortical localization The observation that certain areas of the brain are responsible for specific processes.

Aphasia An inability to understand or produce language based on damage to the language areas of the brain.

Structural plasticity The brain's ability to change in response to the environment.

Functional plasticity The capacity to change areas of the brain that are responsible for activities.

Neurogenesis The process of the development of new neurons.

Critical period A time when a property is most vulnerable to being established or altered.

CONCEPT LEARNING CHECK 3.4 | *Identifying the Structures and Functions in the Brain*

Match the area of the brain with the function.

A. Medulla

B. Pons

C. Reticular activating system

D. Cerebellum

E. Substantia nigra

F. Thalamus

G. Hypothalamus

H. Hippocampus

1. _____ Involved in the creation of new memories

2. _____ Relays information from the cortex and is involved in sleep and arousal

3. _____ Detects need states

4. _____ Sleep and wakefulness

5. _____ Relay station for sensory information

6. _____ Breathing, heartbeat, and other essential functions

7. _____ Initiation of movement

8. _____ Coordination of movement

Endocrine system A collection of glands involved in releasing hormones into the bloodstream.

3.5 The Endocrine System

The endocrine system uses endorphins and hormones to communicate over long distances and time.

- Discuss the role of endorphins and the endocrine system as communication mechanisms in the nervous system.

While neurotransmitters work their magic at the synapse level, other communication mechanisms transfer messages over much greater distances and over longer periods of time. The **endocrine system** FIGURE 3-21 is a separate and slower communication sys-

FIGURE 3-21 Structures of the endocrine system.

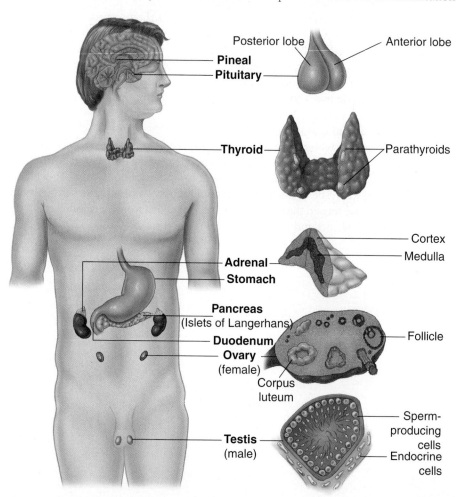

tem that uses hormones, which are chemical messengers released into the bloodstream. By releasing hormones into the bloodstream, the endocrine system can exert influence not only from long distances but for a long period of time as well. Once the body begins to produce **testosterone**, for example, there are changes in the male that last for years (such as the growth of facial hair). These chemicals can also function as or influence neurotransmitters. For example, norepinephrine, secreted by the adrenal gland, can be a neurotransmitter or a hormone depending on what function it is performing. When you are getting ready to fight, freeze, or flee because of a stressor, many parts of your body need to react. Your heart beats faster, you breathe more heavily, and your pupils dilate. Many of these changes are controlled by hormones rather than by neurotransmitters.

The endocrine system and nervous system are linked via the hypothalamus and pituitary gland for communication. The endocrine system relies on the brain's hypothalamus to regulate the production and release of hormones. It is the hormone control center for the rest of the body. The hypothalamus, in turn, relies on the pituitary gland to activate the other endocrine glands. The pituitary gland is often called the "master gland" since it influences so many other glands.

Endorphins

Endogenous opioid peptides, or **endorphins**, can reduce pain and promote pleasure. During extreme exercise, pain, or even excitement, the **pituitary gland** and hypothalamus both pour endorphins into the blood stream. Endorphins are naturally produced painkillers and get their name because they mimic the action of synthetic painkillers. The word *endorphin* is a cross between *endo*genous, meaning coming from within the body, and *morphine*, a medicine used to decrease pain. Endorphins are neither neurotransmitters nor hormones. Rather, they are neuromodulators that influence the effects of neurotransmitters. Some endorphins function like neurotransmitters when they operate in the synapse, and most will alter the effects of neurotransmitters. At other times, endorphins will be released directly into the bloodstream.

Perhaps the most common notion of endorphins comes from the idea of the "runner's high," a feeling of pleasure some report from extensive exercise. Recently, some researchers have questioned whether endorphins are linked to a runner's high at all. The discovery of endorphins in the early 1970s coincided with the start of a running and jogging craze in the United States. Some researchers believed that this may have been the origin of the idea of the runner's high. Researchers do admit that exercise can be addicting. Rats, for example, in the proper context will run themselves to death (up to 12 miles a day) if allowed to do so.

Other research (Sparling, Giuffrida, Piomelli, Rosskopf, & Dietrich, 2003) indicates that the pain-killing and out-of-body sensations experienced by some runners may be linked to another part of the brain, and the runner's high might be linked to tetrahydrocannabinol, or THC, the psychoactive substance in marijuana. THC does have mild pain-reducing effects, but it is not morphine.

Adrenal Glands

The **adrenal glands** are important glands of the endocrine system. The two adrenal glands are at the top of the kidneys (*ad* meaning adjacent and *renal* referring to the kidneys). There are two parts to the adrenal glands: an outer **adrenal cortex** (*cortex* means the outside like bark) and an inner **adrenal medulla** (*medulla* referring to the middle of the structure like marrow, the inside of a bone). The sympathetic nervous system stimulates the adrenal medulla, and it releases epinephrine and norepinephrine (more commonly known as adrenaline). Hormones secreted by the adrenal glands have a broad influence over many organs in the body. For example, the adrenal glands, in times of stress, will secrete stress hormones like epinephrine that increase blood pressure, heart rate, and the other parts of the fight, freeze, or flee response of the sympathetic nervous system.

Gonads

Gonads are organs that release male and female sex hormones. In women, the ovaries secrete **estrogen**, progesterone, and a small amount of testosterone. In men, the testes secrete testosterone. Testosterone is also produced in the adrenal glands of men and women.

Testosterone A sex hormone produced by the testes, adrenal cortex, and ovaries that is important in the male sex characteristics of the male body.

Endorphins Chemicals linked to pain perception and reward.

Pituitary gland The endocrine system's master gland.

Adrenal glands Important glands of the endocrine system consisting of the adrenal cortex and the adrenal medulla.

Adrenal cortex The outer layer of the adrenal gland that secretes hormones during stress.

Adrenal medulla The interior layer of the adrenal gland that secretes epinephrine and norepinephrine.

Gonads An organ that secretes sex hormones.

Estrogen A sex hormone produced primarily by the ovaries that is an important female sex hormone.

CONCEPT LEARNING CHECK 3.5 | *Identifying the Role of Endorphins and the Endocrine System Functions*

Match the chemical or structure with the correct function.

A. Hypothalamus

B. Pituitary gland

C. Epinephrine

D. Testosterone

E. Estrogen

1. _____ Associated with stimulation of the sympathetic nervous system

2. _____ A structure that detects need states

3. _____ Sometimes called the "master gland" because it influences hormone production in other parts of the body

4. _____ A sex hormone produced primarily by the ovaries that is an important female sex hormone

5. _____ A sex hormone produced by the testes, adrenal cortex, and ovaries that is important in the male sex characteristics in the male body

---

3.6 Genetics

Our DNA, in combination with the environment, allows us to pass along traits from parents to offspring.

■ Discuss the role of genetics in psychology.

The Basic Concepts of Genetics

Packed inside nearly all of your cells is a special message—in code. This message is locked away in deoxyribonucleic acid or DNA and contains the directions to make every substance and structure in your body. There are nearly 6.5 feet of tightly bundled DNA in each cell of the body. In essence, your DNA contains the unique list of ingredients and the specific recipe to make you *you*. Anyone who has watched a crime drama lately knows that DNA is unique to each person in the world who has ever lived.

All parts of your body are produced from this instruction manual—from your earwax to the endoplasmic reticulum and from your toes to your tears. A **genome** is the sum of an organism's hereditary information, like an instruction manual for assembling the body. Our genes are the letters, each offering up a part of the story of you. Put the letters together in a genome and you have the story—provided you've put the letters together in the right order. In this section, we'll look at genetics and behavioral genetics and examine the ways in which the biology of behavior is influenced by both genetic and environmental factors.

Chromosomes are the parts of the cell that contain segments of DNA called **genes** FIGURE 3-22. You got half of your chromosomes from your mom and the other half from your dad back when you were a **zygote**, or a fertilized egg. This means, of course, that half your genes came from each of your biological parents. Our genes' ability to make copies of themselves lets our parents give us certain characteristics like freckles or big feet. But with half from mom and half from dad, what decides what gets expressed? This answer depends on many factors.

First, it is important to know that most traits are **polygenic**, meaning that multiple genes influence their expression. It is unlikely that there is only one gene for shyness, for example.

Genome The sum of an organism's hereditary information.

Chromosome Cellular organelle that contains genes.

Gene A segment of DNA.

Zygote A fertilized egg.

Polygenic Characteristics that multiple genes shape.

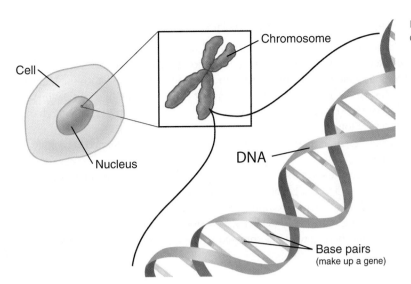

FIGURE 3-22 Basic genetic structures include DNA, chromosomes, and genes.

How traits are expressed also depends on the characteristics of the genes that are linked to the traits. Certain genes are more assertive than others. A **dominant gene** exercises its influence over other genes and overpowers recessive genes. This is called a **heterozygous condition**. A **recessive gene's** influence will only be seen when it teams up with an identical recessive gene. When two recessive genes pair up, the trait is likely to be expressed. When genes are alike, it is called a **homozygous condition**. Sometimes when a trait is heterozygous, the recessive trait lurks in the background. It is genetically present but not expressed. You'd never know you had it. Your **phenotype**, the expression of genetic influence, may not match your **genotype** or your personal genetic makeup. Then, if you pass on your genes to your kids by mating with someone who also has a recessive gene for the same trait, the trait may pop up. That explains how two people with straight, dark brown hair can have a child with curly red hair.

But after that, what determines which traits are expressed? According to scientists since Darwin, it is the environment. Each time an organism produces an offspring, a unique combination of DNA from the male and female parent is passed down. Some combinations of DNA can lead to infertility, diseases, or a shorter life. But, by chance, some combinations of DNA cause the offspring to remain healthier in a particular environment. Therefore, they live longer and are more likely to appear in future generations. In such cases, the combined DNA is an **adaptation**, a characteristic that increases in a population because it makes reproduction or survival more likely. These adaptations can accumulate over generations in both individuals and populations of individuals, giving them a distinct advantage.

For example, combinations of DNA caused some people in certain parts of Africa to have genes that protected them from malaria. This gene was more likely to appear in some of their children. Children who received the malarial protection gene survived and were able to pass it along to their children. The kids who did not get the trait may have died sooner and therefore were less likely to have kids of their own. Those who passed along the adaptive, malaria-resistant genes increased their family's **fitness**, or their contribution to the genetic pool of the next generation. As a group, this is called **inclusive fitness**, or kin selection, which is your family's contribution to the entire gene pool of the population.

So what do these notions of heredity and **natural selection** have to do with psychology? Everything. Earlier in this chapter, we discussed the importance of neurotransmitters, neurons, neural pathways, brain structures, other chemicals, and their links to behaviors and actions. All of these structures and molecules are mapped out by DNA. How it all comes together is influenced by the interplay of biology and the environment.

Dominant gene A unit of heredity whose influence is exerted over other genes.

Heterozygous condition A circumstance where genes are different for a given trait.

Recessive gene A unit of heredity whose influence is exerted only when paired with an identical gene.

Homozygous condition A circumstance where both genes are the same for a given trait.

Phenotype Expression of genetic influences.

Genotype An individual's genetic makeup.

Adaptation A process by which a characteristic increases in a population because it makes reproduction or survival more likely.

Fitness The contribution an individual makes to the gene pool of the next generation.

Inclusive fitness Also known as kin selection, the contributions to the next generation's gene pool of both an individual and his or her relatives.

Natural selection Varying success in reproduction resulting from the interaction of an organism with the environment.

The Research Methods of Genetics

Heritability The amount of a trait or characteristic that you can link to genetics as opposed to the environment.

Family study A method that allows researchers to test hypotheses concerning the contribution of genetic and environmental factors by examining biological relatives.

An inheritance is something that is passed down from parents to children. Heritability is much the same. **Heritability** refers to the amount of a trait or characteristic that you can link to your genetics as opposed to your environment. FIGURE 3-23, for example, shows what scientists believe is the link between our genes and intelligence (Devlin, Daniels, & Roeder, 1994; Norrgard, 2008) as well as genes and certain personality characteristics FIGURE 3-24 (Plomin, 1999).

Several research methods are used to tease apart the influence of biology versus the environment.

Family studies, for example, allow researchers to test hypotheses concerning the amount of influence that genetic factors have versus environmental factors by examining biological relatives. But just examining families cannot tell us everything. Perhaps members of one family are more likely to have depression, for example, because the family lives in an atmosphere charged with unexpressed rage. This is an environmental factor that makes

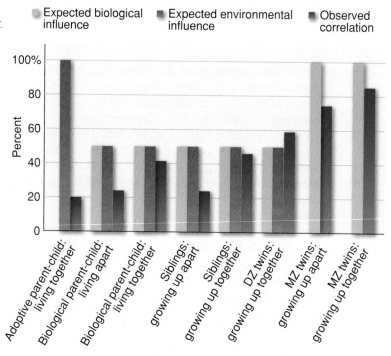

FIGURE 3-23 Heritability of human intelligence.
Source: Data from Devlin, B., Daniels, M., & Roeder, K. (1994). The heritability of IQ. Genetics, 137, 597–606.

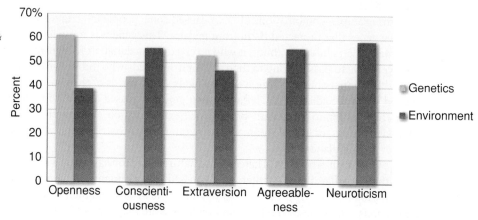

FIGURE 3-24 Heritability estimates for personality traits.
Source: Data from Jang, K.L., Livesly, W.J., & Vernon, P.A. (1996). Heritability of the big five personality dimensions and their facets: a twin study. Journal of Personality, 64(3), 577–591.

it more likely that the family's members will be depressed. Here is where **adoption studies** come in. In an adoption study, researchers examine characteristics between children and their biological and adopted parents. These studies compare characteristics of parents to the characteristics of their biological or adopted kids.

Family and adoption studies are often compelling; however, they still only reveal part of the story. While family members do share genetic makeup, they are not identical. Each child has a unique combination of genes from mom and dad. To reveal the various contribution factors of the environment and biology, it would help if all mom and dad's children were exactly the same. This is the case in **twin studies**. There are two kinds of twins. One kind is **monozygotic (MZ)** (from one-egg, or identical twins). Identical twins come from a single fertilized egg that splits apart. MZ twins share 100% of their genetic material. Only 1 in 250 births are identical twins (Segal, 2010). The other types of twins are **dizygotic (DZ)** (from two-egg, or fraternal twins; FIGURE 3-25). DZ twins come from two eggs and two sperm and really are not any more genetically similar than two nontwin siblings from the same parents. Fraternal twins do have the research advantage of having the same prenatal environment. Twin studies are the gold standard, used to tease apart environmental and biological influences. Since identical twins share 100% of their genes, and twins raised together share 100% of their environment, examining twins in different families might be the ideal way to tease out the relative strength of genes versus environmental contribution. The idea of using twins to examine the relative strength of environmental and genetic influences has been around for a long time. Some classic adoption studies looked at identical twins whose natural parents had schizophrenia. Although the twins were adopted by different families with no history of schizophrenia, the studies revealed the presence of heritable genes for schizophrenia. These studies demonstrated that children whose parents had schizophrenia were still at risk for having the disorder (Heston, 1966).

As impressive as these estimates of heritability are, there may be problems with assumptions behind the twin study model. Although identical twins may share a family environment, should we assume that each twin's experience of this environment is the same? Some critics of the family study method suggest we should not (Hoffman, 1991). Birth order, gender differences, and varied experiences with teachers, friends, sports, interests, and siblings

Adoption study A method that allows researchers to test hypotheses concerning the contributions of genetic and environmental factors by examining characteristics between children and their biological and non-biological parents.

Twin study A research design in which the influences of heredity and environment are examined by comparing monozygotic or dizygotic twins.

Monozygotic (MZ) twins Twins from a single fertilized egg; also known as identical twins.

Dizygotic (DZ) twins Twins who are formed from two fertilized eggs; also known as fraternal twins.

1 egg
1 sperm

2 eggs
2 sperm

Shared placenta

Separate placentas

IDENTICAL TWINS
Separate amniotic sacs

FRATERNAL TWINS
Separate amniotic sacs

FIGURE 3-25 Monozygotic (identical) twins come from one egg, while dizygotic (fraternal) twins come from two.

all conspire to make your family environmental experience unique to you—maybe as unique as your mix of genes. Siblings' individual experiences within the same family can be as different as if they came from totally different families. On the other hand, some researchers have suggested that there is a "twin effect." The idea here is that twins, *because* they are twins, are raised a little differently than nontwin children. This, researchers note, makes it difficult to compare twins to nontwins (Plomin, Asbury, & Dunn, 2001). After all, how many people in the same family are routinely mistaken for one another or dress in identical clothes?

Summary of Multiple Influences on the Biology of Behavior

As this chapter has shown, neuroscientists and behavioral biologists examine behavior at many levels, as summarized in **TABLE 3-2**.

It has been a few years since Mike May's operation. The critical period has passed for his occipital lobe to be able use vision in the same way he would have before the accident. Even a year after the operation, he can correctly identify only about 25% of common objects. He has trouble discerning facial expressions most of the time, and he still has difficulty telling men's faces from women's faces. People, however, are amazingly flexible. Mike relies on secondary features such as the length of a person's hair or the shapes of eyebrows to make these judgments.

Psychology cuts across several fields. In this chapter, we have touched on many of the disciplines that help us to understand human behavior—chemistry, biology, and genetics, to name just a few. People are complex as well. You cannot separate a person from his or her body any more than you can separate psychology from neuroscience.

TABLE 3-2 What Neuroscientists Study

Level	What Does It Examine?
Behavioral	What people do
System	Systems such as the sympathetic or sympathetic nervous system reactions
Local circuit	Groups of neurons
Single neuron	An individual neurons reaction to an event such as exposure to a medicine or a neurotransmitter
Synapse	What occurs at the synapse
Membrane	Ion channels on neurons
Genetic	How genes influence the how neurons work

Source: Adapted from E. H. Chudler. Neuroscience for Kids. http://faculty.washington.edu/chudler/what.html

---

CONCEPT LEARNING CHECK 3.6 | *Reviewing the Role of Genetics in Psychology*

Fill in the blank with the key term that fits the statement best.

1. _____ are the parts of the cell that contain segments of DNA called _____.

2. _____ refers to the amount of a trait that is linked to your genetics rather than to your environment.

3. _____ twins come from one egg and _____ come from two eggs.

4. _____ refers to the expression of your genes while _____ refers to your actual genetic makeup.

5. Most traits come from multiple genes, meaning they have a _____ influence.

CRITICAL THINKING APPLICATION

Aquick review of news magazine articles about genetics yields some interesting claims—there seems to be a gene for everything from laziness to racism to liberalism. These stories do their best to extrapolate from recent findings in neuroscience and genetics, with a hope of linking biology with our behaviors in a clean, unmuddled, precise way. But is it really that simple?

A 1980 *Science* magazine article, for example, related superior mathematical performance in men to biological factors, suggesting the male brain was better for math (Benbow & Stanley, 1980).

Biodeterminism is the belief that only your biology influences your future. It is the notion that some things are purely biologically derived and that other things come only from environmental factors. As you have learned in this chapter, there's no single part of the brain that is associated with math. There is also no single gene associated with math ability. In fact, a recent study examined nearly 500,000 individuals and found no link between math ability and gender (Else-Quest, Hyde, & Linn, 2010). There were some countries in which women were better in math and some countries in which men were better.

Evaluate

1. What examples of biodeterminism do you see stated in the nightly news about new studies?

2. What other explanations can you think of for laziness, racism, and liberalism? Are genetics the most compelling explanation?

Visual Overview Nervous System

Our nervous system is composed of two main branches: the **central nervous system** integrates and controls the body, and the **peripheral nervous system** links the rest of the body to the central nervous system.

3.1 Overview: The Components of Biological Bases of Behavior

- The nervous system conducts signals to and from various parts of your body.
- Neuropsychology and neuroscience add depth and dimension to the science of psychology.
- Neuropsychology helps us to link our physical body with explanations for behavior on many different levels.

Neurotransmitter molecules

Dendrite

Axon

Nerve impulse

3.2 Neural Communication

- The nervous system is composed of glia and neurons.
- Glial cells are the cells of the nervous system that support and protect our neurons.
- Neurons are the basic cells of the nervous system.
- The basic structure of neurons includes the soma, dendrites, and axons.
- Neurons communicate via synaptic transmission.
- The action potential determines the message a neuron will send.
- Neurons integrate the messages they receive.
- Synaptic pruning results in more efficient neural networks.
- Neurotransmitters are involved in synaptic transmission.

3.3 Nervous System Organization

- Our nervous system is composed of a peripheral nervous system and a central nervous system.
- The peripheral nervous system includes nerves that connect to all the glands and organs of our body.
- The peripheral nervous system is divided into the somatic and the autonomic nervous systems.
- The autonomic nervous system is divided into the sympathetic and parasympathetic nervous systems.
- The central nervous system consists of the brain and the spinal cord.

Cerebrum

Thalamus (medial)

Hypothalamus

3.4 The Brain

- Researchers use many tools to examine the inner workings of the brain, including examining lesions and the effect of electrical and magnetic stimulation, EEGs, CTs, PET scans, and MRIs.
- The brainstem consists of the hindbrain and midbrain and is involved with structures that support vital body processes.
- The midbrain is a major relay station for processing auditory and visual information and includes the substantia nigra, which is responsible for the initiation of movement.
- The forebrain is the largest part of the brain and includes the thalamus, the hypothalamus, the limbic system, and the cerebrum.
- The limbic system is a group of structures that surround the brainstem and governs emotions such as anger, happiness, and fear and stores and retrieves new memories.
- The cerebrum contains about 90% of the brain's volume. It consists of four lobes and two hemispheres that are connected by a dense network of nerve fibers called the corpus callosum.
- The occipital lobes of the cerebrum contain the visual cortex, which processes visual images.
- The temporal lobes of the cerebrum house the primary auditory cortex, which processes sound.
- The frontal lobes of the cerebrum contain the primary motor cortex, which

is an area that has a role in planning, controlling, and executing movements.

- The frontal lobes of the cerebrum play a role in personality, organization, and planning.
- The parietal lobes of the cerebrum contain the somatosensory cortex, which processes body sensation information.
- The cerebrum has a left and right hemisphere that are expert at certain tasks; this is known as lateralization of function.

- Lateralization of function was discovered by research into split-brained patients whose corpus callosum was severed. The result was that the left and right hemispheres operated without communicating to the other hemisphere.
- The brain has an amazing ability to grow and adjust. This results in both structures and functions adapting to environmental influences.

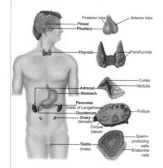

3.5 The Endocrine System

- The nervous system uses endorphins and hormones to communicate over longer distances and time.
- Endorphins can reduce pain and promote pleasure.

- The endocrine system consists of glands that create hormones.
- Hormones are chemical messengers that have a broad influence over many organs in the body.

3.6 Genetics

- Chromosomes are parts of the cell that contain segments of DNA called genes.
- Most traits are polygenic, meaning they arise from multiple genes.
- Dominant genes will exercise their influence over other genes and overpower recessive genes, whose influence will only be seen when teamed up with an identical gene.
- The environment has an influence on which genes are expressed.
- A gene is considered adaptive because it leads to a characteristic that makes reproduction or survival more likely.

- Heritability refers to the amount of a trait that you can link to your genes as opposed to your environment.
- Research methods for examining heritability include family studies, adoption studies, and twin studies.
- The human brain is amazingly complex and flexible.
- Psychology draws from several fields, such as chemistry, biology, and genetics.
- A person's psychological makeup cannot be understood separately from his or her physiological makeup.

3.1 Overview: The Components of Biological Bases of Behavior

1. The branch of science that studies the connections between the brain and behavior is called:
- **A.** biological psychology.
- **B.** neuroscience.
- **C.** biopsychology.
- **D.** All of the above.

3.2 Neural Communication

2. Which of the following structures is involved in providing nutrients, insulation, and protection to neurons?
- **A.** Axon terminal
- **B.** Neurotransmitters
- **C.** Dendrites
- **D.** Glia

3. The sodium-potassium pump moves sodium ions _____ and potassium ions _____.
- **A.** out of the cell; out of the cell
- **B.** out of the cell; into the cell
- **C.** into the cell; into the cell
- **D.** into the cell; out of the cell

4. What is the approximate resting potential of the inside of a neuron?
- **A.** –70 millivolts
- **B.** +70 millivolts
- **C.** –10 millivolts
- **D.** +10 millivolts

5. What determines if a neuron has an action potential?
- **A.** Glial cells
- **B.** Both EPSPs and IPSP
- **C.** Only EPSPs
- **D.** Only IPSPs

3.3 Nervous System Organization

6. After her students surprised her, Dr. Morgan's blood pressure increased and her heart rate sped up. These physical reactions were most likely regulated by her:
- **A.** hippocampus.
- **B.** parasympathetic nervous system.
- **C.** sympathetic nervous system.
- **D.** spinal cord.

3.4 The Brain

7. The limbic system is important for:
- **A.** motor coordination.
- **B.** creating cerebrospinal fluid.
- **C.** connecting the cerebral hemispheres.
- **D.** emotional behaviors.

8. One function of the thalamus is to:
- **A.** regulate sleep.
- **B.** relay sensory information.
- **C.** encode new memories.
- **D.** motor coordination.

9. Dr. Anton is experimenting on brain function by injecting subjects with a radioactive glucose substance and then asking them to listen to recordings of sounds. The subject's heads are then scanned to determine the areas of the most radiation. What is the method being used by Dr. Anton?
- **A.** Electroencephalogram
- **B.** Computed axial tomography
- **C.** Positron emission tomography
- **D.** Magnetic resonance imaging

10. After a car accident, Roman had damage to his cerebellum. Roman is likely to have difficulty with which of the following activities?
- **A.** Yoga
- **B.** Reading
- **C.** Following conversations
- **D.** Understanding emotions

11. Memories of emotional events are especially likely to be facilitated by activation of the:
- **A.** amygdala.
- **B.** hypothalamus.
- **C.** sensory cortex.
- **D.** motor cortex.

3.5 The Endocrine System

12. People who feel a runner's high after participating in long, strenuous exercise sessions can thank which of the following chemicals?
- **A.** Estrogen
- **B.** Endorphins
- **C.** Pons
- **D.** Reticular activating system (RAS)

13. The endocrine system consists of glands that create _____.
- **A.** hormones
- **B.** neurotransmitters
- **C.** endorphins
- **D.** myelin

3.6 Genetics

14. When a trait is _____, it may increase in the population because it makes reproduction or survival more likely.
- **A.** heritable
- **B.** homozygous
- **C.** recessive
- **D.** adaptive

15. In order to determine how much the environment, as opposed to genes, influences behavior, the best type of study would compare which types of children?
- **A.** MZ twins growing up together
- **B.** DZ twins growing up apart
- **C.** DZ twins growing up together
- **D.** MZ twins growing up apart

CHAPTER DISCUSSION QUESTIONS

1. What examples from your own family suggest recessive and dominant gene expression?

2. In what ways does integrating neuroscience with psychology help psychology as a science?

3. In what ways does psychology influence the study of biology?

4. Structure and function are major themes in neuroscience. Discuss some examples.

CHAPTER PROJECTS

1. Design and construct an experiment to examine the link between psychological states and physiological response when viewing natural versus constructed environments. Collect pictures from online sources of natural environments like woods and animals versus constructed environments like cities. Consider measuring heart rate and blood pressure. Be sure in your report to indicate any confounds that may have influenced your results.

Adapted from Rowland, D. L., Kaariainen, A., & Houtsmuller, E. J., 2000. Interactions between physiological and affective arousal: A laboratory exercise for psychology. Teaching of Psychology, 27, 34–37.

2. Make a model of the brain or a neuron out of common everyday objects. See if you can link the function to the structure of what you have created.

3. Research the history of certain discoveries or technologies in neuroscience. What led to the discovery of the electroencephalogram, for example?

CHAPTER KEY TERMS

Absolute refractory period	Cerebral hemispheres	Frontal lobe
Acetylcholine	Cerebrospinal fluid (CSF)	Functional magnetic resonance imagining (fMRI)
Action potential	Cerebrum	
Adaptation	Chromosome	Functional plasticity
Adoption study	Computed tomography scans (CT scans)	Gamma-aminobutric acid (GABA)
Adrenal cortex		
Adrenal glands	Corpus callosum	Gene
Adrenal medulla	Cortical localization	Genome
Afferent nerve fibers	Critical period	Genotype
Agonist	Dendrite	Glia cells
All-or-nothing law	Depolarizes	Gonads
Amygdala	Dizygotic (DZ) twins	Heterozygous condition
Antagonist	Dominant gene	Heritability
Aphasia	Dopamine	Hindbrain
Association areas	Efferent nerve fibers	Hippocampus
Ataxia	Electrical stimulation of the brain	Homozygous condition
Autonomic nervous system	Electroencephalogram (EEG)	Hormone
Axon	Endocrine system	Hypothalamus
Axon terminal	Estrogen	Inclusive fitness (kin selection)
Biological psychology	Endorphins	
Brainstem	Excitatory postsynaptic potential (EPSP)	Inhibitory postsynaptic potential (IPSP)
Cell body		
Central nervous system	Family study	Interneuron
Cerebellum	Fitness	Lateralization of function
Cerebral cortex	Forebrain	Lesion

Limbic system
Magnetic resonance
 imaging (MRI)
Medulla
Midbrain
Mirror neuron
Monozygotic (MZ) twins
Motor cortex
Motor neuron
Myelin sheath
Natural selection
Nerves
Nervous system
Neural pruning
Neurogenesis
Neuron
Neuroscience
Neurotransmitter
Norepinephrine
Occipital lobe
Parasympathetic nervous
 system
Parietal lobe

Perceptual asymmetry
Peripheral nervous system
Phenotype
Phrenology
Pituitary gland
Plasticity
Polygenic
Pons
Positron emission tomography
 (PET scan)
Postsynaptic neuron
Postsynaptic potential (PSP)
Presynaptic neuron
Receptor site
Recessive gene
Reflex
Repolarize
Resting potential
Reticular formation
Reuptake
Sensory neuron
Serotonin
Soma

Somatic nervous system
Somatosensory cortex
Spinal cord
Spinal reflex
Split brain
Split-brain surgery
Stimulus threshold
Structural plasticity
Substantia nigra
Sympathetic nervous system
Synapse
Synaptic cleft
Synaptic pruning
Synaptic transmission
Synaptic vesicle
Temporal lobe
Testosterone
Thalamus
Threshold
Transcranial magnetic
 stimulation (TMS)
Twin study
Zygote

ANSWERS TO CONCEPT LEARNING CHECKS

3.1 Reviewing the Terminology of Neuroscience

1. A. Nervous system
2. D. Hormones
3. E. Biological psychology
4. B. Neuroscience
5. C. Neurons

3.2 Recognizing the Parts of the Neuron

1. B. Dendrite
2. G. Soma
3. C. Myelin sheath
4. A. Axon terminal
5. D. Neurotransmitters
6. E. Presynaptic neuron
7. F. Receptor site
8. I. Synaptic vesicle
9. H. Synaptic gap

3.3 The Organization of the Nervous System

1. Central nervous system
2. Spinal cord
3. Somatic nervous system
4. Sympathetic nervous system
5. Parasympathetic nervous system

**3.4 Identifying the Structures and Functions
 in the Brain**

1. Hippocampus
2. Reticular activating system

3. Hypothalamus
4. Pons
5. Thalamus
6. Medulla
7. Substantia nigra
8. Cerebellum

**3.5 Identifying the Role of Endorphins and the
 Endocrine System Functions**

1. Epinephrine
2. Hypothalamus
3. Pituitary gland
4. Estrogen
5. Testosterone

3.6 Reviewing the Role of Genetics in Psychology

1. **Chromosomes** are the parts of the cell that contain
 segments of DNA called **genes**.
2. **Heritability** refers to the amount of a trait that is linked to
 your genetics rather than to your environment.
3. **Monozygotic** twins come from one egg and **dizygotic**
 come from two eggs.
4. **Phenotype** refers to the expression of your genes while
 genotype refers to your actual genetic makeup.
5. Most traits come from multiple genes, meaning they have a
 polygenic influence.

3.1 Overview: The Components of Biological Bases of Behavior

1. D. Rationale: Biological psychology, biopsychology, and neuroscience are all areas that study the connections of the brain and behavior.

3.2 Neural Communication

2. D. Rationale: Glial cells are the cells in the nervous system that provide support and protection for neurons.

3. B. Rationale: The sodium-potassium pump moves sodium ions out of the cell and potassium ions into the cell.

4. A. Rationale: The resting potential inside of the neuron is −70 millivolts

5. B. Rationale: Since neurons receive and integrate signals from many different other neurons, both excitatory post-synaptic potentials and inhibitory postsynaptic potentials will determine if a neuron has an action potential.

3.3 Nervous System Organization

6. C. Rationale: The sympathetic nervous system is a branch of the autonomic nervous system that prepares the organs for vigorous activity.

3.4 Brain

7. D. Rationale: The limbic system is a group of structures that surround the brainstem and governs emotions.

8. B. Rationale: The thalamus is a forebrain structure that is a major relation station for sensory information.

9. C. Rationale: Dr. Anton is using positron emission tomography or a PET scan. A PET scan is a neuroscience imaging technique that uses radioactive glucose to indicate areas of activity.

10. A. Rationale: The cerebellum is part of the hindbrain involved in the development and coordination of movement.

11. A. Rationale: The amygdala is linked to emotions like anger and fear.

3.5 Endocrine System

12. B. Rationale: Endorphins are chemicals linked to pain perception and reward.

13. A. Rationale: The endocrine system is a collection of glands involved in releasing hormones into the bloodstream.

3.6 Genetics

14. D. Rationale: Adaptation is the process by which a characteristic increases in a population because it makes reproduction or survival more likely.

15. D. Rationale: Looking at monozygotic twins growing up apart would be the best way to examine heritability.

REFERENCES

Abitz, M., Nielsen, R. D., Jones, E. G., Laursen, H., Graem, N., & Pakkenberg, B. (2007). Excess of neurons in the human newborn mediodorsal thalamus compared with that of the adult. *Cerebral Cortex, 17*(11), 2573–2578. doi:10.1093/cercor/bhl163

Benbow, C., & Stanley, J. (1980). Sex differences in mathematical ability: Fact or artifact? *Science, 210*(4475), 1262–1264. doi:10.1126/science.7434028

Bonaiuto, J., & Arbib, M. A. (2010). Extending the mirror neuron system model, II: What did I just do? A new role for mirror neurons. *Biological Cybernetics, 102*(4), 341–359. doi:10.1007/s00422-010-0371-0

Courchesne, E., Townsend, J., Akshoomoff, N. A., Saitoh, O., Yeung-Courchesne, R., Lincoln, A. J., James, H. E., et al. (1994). Impairment in shifting attention in autistic and cerebellar patients. *Behavioral Neuroscience, 108*(5), 848–865.

Devlin, B., Daniels, M., & Roeder, K. (1994). The heritability of IQ. *Genetics, 137,* 597–606.

Else-Quest, N. M., Hyde, J. S., & Linn, M. C. (2010). Cross-national patterns of gender differences in mathematics: A meta-analysis. *Psychological Bulletin, 136*(1), 103–127. doi:10.1037/a0018053

Fine, I., Wade, A. R., Brewer, A. A., May, M. G., Goodman, D. F., Boynton, G. M., Wandell, B. A., et al. (2003). Long-term deprivation affects visual perception and cortex. *Nature Neuroscience, 6*(9), 915–916. doi:10.1038/nn1102

Greengard, P. (2001). The neurobiology of slow synaptic transmission. *Science, 294*(5544), 1024–1030. doi:10.1126/science.294.5544.1024

Herdener, M., Esposito, F., di Salle, F., Boller, C., Hilti, C. C., Habermeyer, B., Scheffler, K., et al. (2010). Musical training induces functional plasticity in human hippocampus. *Journal of Neuroscience, 30*(4), 1377–1384. doi:10.1523/JNEUROSCI.4513-09.2010

Heston, L. L. (1966). Psychiatric disorders in foster home reared children of schizophrenic mothers. *British Journal of Psychiatry, 112*(489), 819–825. doi:10.1192/bjp.112.489.819

Hoffman, L. (1991). The influence of the family environment on personality: Accounting for sibling differences. *Psychological Bulletin, 110*(2), 187–203.

Jessen, K. R. (2004). Glial cells. *The International Journal of Biochemistry & Cell Biology, 36*(10), 1861–1867.

Laughlin, S. B., van Steveninck, R. R., & Anderson, J. C. (1998). The metabolic cost of neural information. *Nature Neuroscience, 1*(1), 36–41.

Macleod, J., Davey Smith, G., Heslop, P., Metcalfe, C., Carroll, D., & Hart, C. (2002). Psychological stress and cardiovascular disease: Empirical demonstration of bias in a prospective observational study of Scottish men. *BMJ (Clinical Research Ed.), 324*(7348), 1247–1251. Retrieved from http://www.ncbi.nlm.nih.gov/pubmed/12028978.

Mechelli, A., Crinion, J. T., Noppeney, U., O'Doherty, J., Ashburner, J., Frackowiak, R. S., & Price, C. J. (2004). Neurolinguistics: Structural plasticity in the bilingual brain. *Nature, 431*(7010), 757. doi:10.1038/431757a

Melgaard, B., & Ahlgren, P. (1986). Ataxia and cerebellar atrophy in chronic alcoholics. *Journal of Neurology, 233*(1), 13–15.

Norrgard, K. (2008). Heritability of human intelligence: IQ and eugenics. *Nature Education, 1*(1). Retrieved from http://www.nature.com/scitable/topicpage/heritability-of-human-intelligence-iq-and-eugenics-796

Plomin, R. (1999). IQ and human intelligence. *American Journal of Human Genetics, 65*(5), 1476–1477.

Plomin, R., Asbury, K., & Dunn, J. (2001). Why are children in the same family so different? Nonshared environment a decade later. *Canadian Journal of Psychiatry, 46*(3), 225–233. Retrieved from http://www.ncbi.nlm.nih.gov.proxy.library.emory.edu/pubmed/11320676

Rowland, D. L., Kaariainen, A., & Houtsmuller, E. J. (2000). Interactions between physiological and affective arousal: A laboratory exercise for psychology. *Teaching of Psychology, 27,* 34–37.

Segal, N. L. (2010). Twins: The finest natural experiment. *Personality and Individual Differences, 49*(4), 317–323. doi:10.1016/j.paid.2009.11.014

Sparling, P. B., Giuffrida, A., Piomelli, D., Rosskopf, L., & Dietrich, A. (2003). Exercise activates the endocannabinoid system. *Neuroreport, 14*(17), 2209.

van Praag, H., Shubert, T., Zhao, C., & Gage, F. H. (2005). Exercise enhances learning and hippocampal neurogenesis in aged mice. *Journal of Neuroscience, 25*(38), 8680.

4 Sensation and Perception

Learning Objectives ▼

4.1 ■ Examine how sensations and perceptions work together to process a stimulus.

4.2 ■ Apply the principles of transduction, sensitivity, and adaptation across the senses.

4.3 ■ Identify the five main external senses.

■ Describe how each sensory organ achieves transduction.

■ Follow the path of signals within the brain.

4.4 ■ Describe the principles that organize perception of images.

4.5 ■ Give examples of how perception may be altered by experience.

4.6 ■ Describe how attention enhances and limits perception.

Just at dusk, I arrived for my first college night class. I walked slowly down the shadowy, unfamiliar sidewalk. Passing under a light, an older man crossed my path. He wore thick glasses and sported a cardigan sweater with the buttons misaligned. Strangely, his tongue protruded out of his mouth as he hurried down the walk. Alarmed, I stopped in my tracks, and waited for him to proceed into the building ahead of me. "You have to be careful on campus," I remembered being told, "Sometimes people are attracted to campus and they are up to no good!"

I entered and found my classroom, sitting in the front row. I looked up to see the instructor writing on the chalkboard, and when he turned around, I was stunned to see it was the man from the sidewalk. I had perceived him as distinctly odd, somewhat threatening, and not very sharp. I learned over the term that my perceptions were quite inaccurate (well, maybe not the "odd" part): My new professor was a brilliant and gentle man.

Why do we sometimes see things that aren't really there and sometimes miss seeing what is actually out there in the world?

Sensation and perception are processes that translate what's "out there" in the world into patterns we can recognize in our minds. You might expect that our sensory processes provide a literal copy of the physical world for us to internalize in mental images. However, that is not how the human perceptual system works: Instead, what is "out there" in the external world is not at all the same as the image we form "inside" our minds. Sensation—receiving information from the environment—and perception—selecting and interpreting this information—work together to form an understanding of the world around us.

4.1 The Interaction of Sensation and Perception

We create an understanding of the world around us by combining incoming sensations from the physical world with our expectations based on past experience.

- Examine how sensations and perceptions work together to process a stimulus.

Consider the photograph in FIGURE 4-1. You probably notice a father and his children and guess they are in the country, perhaps on vacation, relaxed and casual. It appears to be a typical family snapshot. That is what you expect to see, and what you perceive in the photograph. But take another look: It requires some closer inspection. Look at the area between the daughter leaning in and her father. Something is in her way, but what? You see a circular shape, with a small dark area, but it's hard to recognize: It's her brother's fist! The subjects, brother and sister, fought constantly, so she was not surprised to see he had done this in the photo. But like the now grown-up girl, we can look at the photograph many times and never "see" it, even though it's right there in black and white. We can only perceive the information we attend to. As a result, we will often miss important information that was "out there" in the physical environment but somehow failed to make it inside, to the world within our minds.

Sensation and perception work together to help us sort out the complex information available to us. **Sensation** refers to the stimulation of a sense organ by an external physical stimulus: for example, a light, smell, or sound. **Perception** refers to organizing sensory information to form an understanding. These two processes direct how we take in information from our senses and form our perceptions of the world around us.

Sensation The process of registering the stimulation of sensory receptors by an external physical stimulus.

Perception The process of organizing sensory information to form a meaningful interpretation.

Imagine bending down to get in a car and seeing a shiny quarter on the pavement. How did you recognize it? It seems you instantly recognize the coin, even though you don't expect to see it there. This is processing based on information presented to you in the world, called **bottom-up processing**. The physical energy of the light waves to your eyes provides a sensory **stimulus**. And receptors within the eye translate the physical energy (e.g., light waves) into the firing of neurons. These signals then travel to the specific areas in the brain devoted to visual information.

At the same time, your perception is guided by **top-down processing**. This means that past experiences in memory provide expectations about what you are seeing, and these help to organize the incoming sensations. You know that round, shiny objects on the ground are likely to be coins. So your perceptual processes direct your sense organs to look more to determine what kind of coin it is. These "top-down" expectations of what the coin will look like help you quickly recognize it, and also make you more likely to mistake a subway token as a quarter. Top-down perceptual processes meet and interact with our bottom-up, sensation-driven processes somewhere in the middle of this continuum (see FIGURE 4-2). The two processes work together to create an interpretation of the information around us.

Let's take an example of an unfamiliar image, shown in FIGURE 4-3 (left). Since you don't have a way to organize the objects in the image, you begin to notice individual

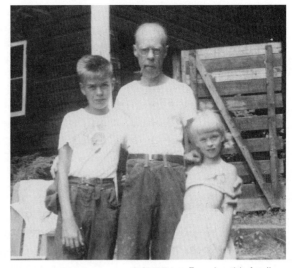

FIGURE 4-1 Examine this family photo (from R. U. Akeret's *Photoanalysis*, 1973). What is your impression from this visual image?

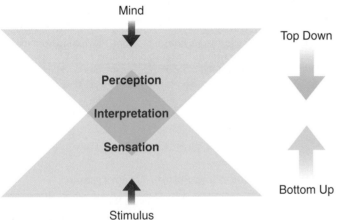

FIGURE 4-2 Incoming energy from the physical stimulus provides sensation, which is met by perceptual processes based on our expectations of the world.

Bottom-up processing The stimulus-driven process of sensation that registers external physical energy and translates it into neural encoding.

Stimulus Physical energy in the world registered by a sensory organ, including light, sound, and smell.

Top-down processing Perception through the use of information in memory to organize incoming sensations.

FIGURE 4-3 This image (left), illustrating the perceptual process, is an inverted painting in the style of 16th-century artist Giuseppe Arcimboldo. Depicting fruits and vegetables, it takes on more meaning when inverted (right), where a face is detectable. The different perceptions of the two images show that our top-down perceptual processes are bringing meaning to the incoming sensory information.

pieces—a pear, a cabbage leaf, and is that a gourd? You finally decide you're looking at a pile of fruits and vegetables. Examine the same image now that it has been inverted (right): This time, look for a face in the image! Do you see its eyes, nose, and hair? This time, your expectation provided a "face" organization to help you process the image. This example illustrates that what we see is not *solely* determined by what is "out there" on the page; instead, we *create* an interpretation through the interaction of top-down perceptions and bottom-up sensations.

A learned skill such as reading demonstrates how top-down perceptual processes actively guide understanding, overriding the actual information provided by sensation. For example, you can still read this sentence even though the letters are scrambled as long as the first and last letter appear in the right place: "Tihs is bcuseae the huamn mnid deos not raed ervey lteter by istlef, but the wrod as a wlohe" (Rawlinson, 1976). Another source of expectations arises from our most recent processing, called **perceptual set**. This refers to a "mindset" of top-down expectations based on your experience. For example, while reading handwriting, we interpret small black marks on the page as forming letters. The influence of perceptual set is so strong that even ambiguous figures can still be interpreted. For example, in one experiment, people viewed ambiguous figures as a different image depending upon the image they started with FIGURE 4-4 (Fisher, 1968). This suggests our recent perceptions provide top-down expectations about what is about to occur.

Perceptual set The influence of recent processing as a framework for continuing perception.

FIGURE 4-4 The phenomenon of perceptual set is demonstrated by viewing these images from left to right. Processing from the left to right allows us to continue to recognize the bird in the more ambiguous middle drawings. However, processing from the right generates a different form (a cat), and that form is maintained as you continue to look leftward at the more ambiguous images in the middle.

CONCEPT LEARNING CHECK 4.1   *Comparing Top-Down and Bottom-Up Processing*

Identify aspects of these experiences that correspond to top-down and bottom-up processing:

A. Reading a book

B. Walking down the street and recognizing a friend

C. Listening to a new song

D. Being tapped on the shoulder when you didn't notice anyone behind you

E. Taking the first spoonful of your favorite food into your mouth

4.2 Sensory Principles

Sensory organs register physical energy using very different mechanisms that share common principles of operation.

■ Apply the principles of transduction, sensitivity, and adaptation across the senses.

Though very different in physical structure, our senses share some key defining features in their task of relating our psychological experience to the reality of the external world.

Transduction of Physical Energy into Neural Stimulation

Each of our sensory organs—eyes, ears, nose, mouth, and skin—has its own method for translating external physical stimulation into neural stimulation. **Transduction** is the process in which physical energy in the world is translated into an electrochemical signal—neurons firing—that represents the incoming sensation in the brain. For example, a touch on your fingertip causes receptors within the skin to register "pressure," which in turn causes neurons located there to begin firing. These neural signals are passed through the body to the brain, where the construction of meaning takes place.

Each sense organ responds to a different type of physical energy in the world, such as sound waves, chemical molecules in the air, or light waves. So the sense organs have specialized **sensory receptor** cells that react only to particular kinds of physical stimulation. For example, in the ear, tiny hair cells move, registering a pattern of sound waves and converting this to neural firing. All five of these major sense organs register two specific features of the incoming sensation: Sensations are coded for their *intensity* (strong versus weak) and *quality* (e.g., a foul versus a pleasant smell). Typically, much of this coding about the nature of the sensation happens *after* transduction. Once in neural form, sensations follow neural pathways from the receptors to specific areas in the brain, particularly in the outer cortex. So the experience of sensation begins with the sensory receptors in the sense organs and continues in the brain.

Detection Thresholds Reflect Sensitivity

How good are our sensory systems? Humans compare unfavorably to the impressive sense of smell in dogs or the superior distance vision in birds of prey. The field of research called psychophysics examines the properties of our external sensory systems. What is the smallest sensation we can detect? **Absolute thresholds** are the lowest amount of physical energy we can detect reliably (50 percent of the time) using a given sense organ. For example, standing on the top of a building on a clear, dark night, a person can detect a lighted candle 30 miles away (Galanter, 1962). We can taste a teaspoon of sugar in 2 gallons of water, and smell a drop of perfume inside a three-room apartment. We can hear a ticking watch 20 feet away, and feel a bee's wing fall onto a cheek from a centimeter away. However, there are some problems with measuring absolute thresholds.

For example, you may recall taking a hearing test, during which you wear headphones and raise your hand whenever you hear a tone. Suppose that some time passes and you don't hear any tones. Now you may be expecting that a tone must be coming soon and be straining to hear it. This may make you *too* ready to respond and say, "Yes, I heard something." So your criterion for deciding that you did hear a very faint tone changes based on your top-down expectations. Your sensitivity—how many tones you miss and how many tones you incorrectly say you heard—will vary. **Signal detection theory** (Green & Swets, 1966) is a testing method that takes your readiness to respond into account. On some trials, a tone is played and you say, "Yes, I heard it," called a "hit." Other times, no tone is played, but you think you did hear one, called a "false alarm" **TABLE 4-1**. By comparing these trials, your ability to detect a tone can be measured along with your tendency to be more or less conservative. By correcting for changes in your top-down expectations and criteria for responding, signal detection theory can provide a more accurate measure of thresholds.

We can also define the sensitivity of our senses by examining how accurately we can detect *changes* in stimulation. If you turn up the volume on your iPod, how much louder

Transduction The process in which physical energy in the world is translated into an electrochemical signal—neurons firing—that represents sensation in the brain.

Sensory receptor Specialized cells in each sense organ that react to only particular kinds of external physical stimulation.

Absolute threshold The lowest amount of physical energy that can be detected reliably 50 percent of the time using a given sense organ.

Signal detection theory A sensory testing method that takes into account both the actual stimulus intensity and your readiness to respond.

TABLE 4-1 Signal Detection Theory

Signal Is Played		
You say:	"Yes"	"No"
	Hit	Miss
Signal Is Not Played		
You say:	"Yes"	"No"
	False alarm	Correct rejection

Source: Adapted from Green, D. M., & Swets, J. A. (1966). Signal detection theory and psychophysics. New York: Wiley.

is perceived as "louder?" If you have ever been fitted for eyeglasses or contact lenses, you have experienced a test of your ability to detect subtle differences in sensation. As you sat in a chair, you looked through a lens to find the best correction for your vision. You were asked repeatedly, "Which is better, the first lens or the second?" The doctor was, in effect, checking whether adding more correction to your lenses results in any noticeable improvement in your vision. When you can no longer detect a difference with additional lenses, the best correction to your vision has been found. A **difference threshold** is defined as the difference in stimulus strengths that you can correctly identify at least 50 percent of the time. The smallest amount of change between two stimuli that a person can detect at least half of the time is defined as the **just noticeable difference (jnd)**.

Your ability to notice a difference between sensations depends directly upon the *strength* of the stimulus. For example, turning your headphones down may be quite noticeable when the sound is already low, whereas turning it down by the same amount when it's blasting loudly might not be noticeable. As the stimulus becomes stronger or larger, so, too, does the *jnd*, and vice versa, a relationship known as **Weber's Law** (Hess & Hayes, 1993). Imagine carrying a heavy (20-pound) bag of groceries and adding a 1-pound bag of coffee to it. The difference in the weight of the bag is not as noticeable compared to adding the same coffee bag to a very light (2-pound) grocery bag. It is the *proportion* of the difference between the two stimuli (20 vs. 21 pounds or 2 vs. 3 pounds) that matters in detecting differences, not the *size* of the difference (adding 1 pound to both bags). Weber's Law says that the size of the *just noticeable difference* (i.e., the change in stimulus intensity) is a constant proportion of the original stimulus value. And this proportion is different for each sense modality (e.g., hearing, seeing, touch). For example, a 10-decibel difference in volume is easy to notice at low volumes, so you may hear a mosquito buzzing in a quiet room. But at high volumes, the 10-decibel difference between a jet engine and a machine gun may be harder to detect **TABLE 4-2**.

If sensation falls "below threshold," we may be unaware that it occurred, called **subliminal perception** (without conscious awareness). We may be unsure that we even *saw* a particular stimulus; however, its effect can be measured. In one study, pairs of kaleidoscope images were flashed on a screen for 2 seconds. Later, the volunteers couldn't say which of the pair they had seen, but when told to "just guess," they were up to 80 percent accurate (Voss & Paller, 2009). Advertisers sometimes use subliminal perception to attempt to influence consumers **FIGURE 4-5**. Does it work?

In 1957, an advertising expert named James Vicary reported he had secretly flashed, at a third of a millisecond, the words "Eat Popcorn" and "Drink Coke" onto the screen during a movie at a public theater (Pratkanis, 1992). His studies involved thousands of moviegoers who received a subliminal message every 5 seconds during the film. Vicary claimed an increase in Coke sales of 18 percent and a rise in popcorn sales of almost 58 percent. However, this was too good to be true for advertisers: 5 years later, after investigation by the Federal Communications Commission, Vicary admitted his studies were a "gimmick" intended to save his failing business and that they had no scientific or practical validity.

Difference threshold The smallest difference in sensation that is reliably detectable.

Just noticeable difference (jnd) The smallest amount of change between two stimuli that a person can detect at least half of the time.

Weber's Law As the stimulus becomes stronger or larger, so does the just noticeable difference between it and other similar stimuli.

Subliminal perception Sensation registered "below threshold," without conscious awareness of its occurrence.

FIGURE 4-5 In the 2000 presidential campaign, a 30-second televised advertisement discussed a prescription drug plan for the elderly. Alongside images of Vice-President Al Gore, the ad shows fragments of the slogan, "Bureau**rats** decide." The letter string "RATS" was flashed for a split second. The advertisement was withdrawn after complaints.

TABLE 4-2 Weber's Law

Sound	Decibel Level	Times Louder than Threshold
Jet engine	140	100,000,000,000,000
Threshold of pain	120	1,000,000,000,000
Rock band	110	100,000,000,000
Vacuum cleaner	80	100,000,000
Traffic	70	10,000,000
Conversation	60	1,000,000
Mosquito	40	10,000
Breathing	10	10
Threshold of hearing	0	1

Source: Data from Center for Hearing and Communication, 2012, http://www.chchearing.org/noise-center, Retrieved 2/22/12.

There is little evidence that subliminal perception leads to actual changes in behavior (Vokey & Read, 1985). For example, one claim for subliminal perception is that you can learn while you sleep! Commercials for self-help and language recordings claim you can play them while you sleep, and your subliminal perception will take in the information. In double-blind procedures (in which both subject and tester don't know what was on the recordings), no benefit from listening while sleeping has been found (Greenwald et al., 1991). So save your money!

Sensory Adaptation

Another important principle is that our sense organs *adapt* to the stimulation they receive over time. For all senses, repeated exposure to a stimulus will lead, over time, to reduced responding. For example, if you are exposed to the smell of a skunk, you will initially find it noxious; but, over time, your sense of smell will adapt so that the odor is much less noticeable. **Sensory adaptation** is change in responsiveness to the same sensation over time. For example, are you wearing a watch right now? If so, you were likely unaware of the sensation of the pressure it causes on your skin because your sense of touch adapted to its presence over time. Adaptation allows you to ignore the ever-present watch and to notice immediately when your watch falls off. Sensory adaptation results in sense organs that are great at detecting *changes* in sensation rather than at maintaining the same sensation over time.

For example, if you could stabilize your eye so that it remained completely still while you stared at this page, you would only be able to see it for about 10 seconds; then everything would go dark. Sensory receptors that are repeatedly stimulated in exactly the same way will begin to adapt and will stop passing forward the neural message to the brain (Martinez-Conde et al., 2004). We don't experience this because our eyes make automatic movements called *saccades*, creating a fresh sensation to process FIGURE 4-6.

> **Sensory adaptation** A change in responsiveness to the same stimulation in a sensory organ over time.

FIGURE 4-6 When viewing a still image, our eyes move across it quickly, stopping briefly at points, and then moving on to refresh the sensations. The movement of the eye fixations is depicted by the dots and lines shown in the figure on the right.

Our perceptual processes experience fatigue when a sensation remains the same and excite when sensation changes. Consider the image in FIGURE 4-7. Once information is perceived, we don't need to attend closely to it. However, if some portion of the image moves, this may provide vital information about a threat (or food source) that requires immediate attention. Our sensory processes are adapted through evolution to process changes in sensation, increasing our chances of survival.

In summary, our experience of the external world is created by the transduction of physical energy into neural stimulation, by the sensitivities of our sense organs, and by our adaptation to stimulation over time. These principles are consistent across each of our sensory systems; however, each sense has its own "hardware" for implementing these principles. Said another way, the transduction of physical to neural energy is accomplished in different ways within each sensory organ.

FIGURE 4-7 In a visual scene, movement may be the only visual cue that reveals the presense of danger; in this case, an alligator in a plant-covered swamp.

Answer the following question.

1. How would you determine the absolute and difference thresholds for the sense of taste? Describe the testing method you would use to measure the sensitivity of your sense of taste.

4.3 The Five Major Senses

Five major sources of external information provide sensory data.

- Identify the five main external senses.
- Describe how each sensory organ achieves transduction.
- Follow the path of signals within the brain.

Virtual reality devices present visual images adjusted to show what you would see if you moved your head and body within a simulated world.

How many senses are there, and what defines a "sense?" By convention, we often describe "the five senses"—seeing, hearing, smelling, tasting, and touching—as the main sources of sensations from the world. These relate to five external sense organs on the body, namely, the eyes, ears, nose, mouth, and skin (see **TABLE 4-3**). However, there are additional sources of information about the world that are internal to the body.

For example, the vestibular sense (based on movement of fluid within the ear canals) provides sensations of balance and indicates the position of your body relative to the ground. Imagine a gymnast tumbling through the air; with eyes closed, the vestibular sense provides information about where the body is in space. Another internal body sense, kinesthetic sense, provides you with information about the movement and position of your muscles and joints. Motion simulators used in entertainment rides make use of these bodily senses to give you the impression of driving fast around a curve; the seat tilt provides the same internal sensations you would have in a real car. We also have internal detectors of muscle stretch. So our bodies provide some internal senses to help us relate to the external world.

In this chapter, we will focus on our five main external senses to illustrate the most relevant principles of sensation for psychology. Keep in mind, however, that we rarely function in the world using only one sense. Texting on your cell phone combines sight and touch; eating combines smell and taste. And understanding speech involves both visual and auditory cues, which explains why it's easier to understand each other when talking face to face (McGurk & MacDonald, 1976). And for a small number of people, perceptions can appear to blend across modes, such as smelling a color or hearing a visual movement (Simner et al., 2006). Synesthesia refers to a rare, genetic neurological condition in which stimulation of one sensory or cognitive pathway leads to automatic experiences in a second (Sagiv & Robertson, 2005). Often, this involves combining types of stimuli, like seeing colors around days of the week or saying words that evoke tastes

TABLE 4-3 Overview of the Five Major Senses

Sense	Stimulus	Receptors	Location	Psychological Phenomenon
Seeing	Visible light waves	Rod and cone cell	Retina	Color vision
Hearing	Sounds waves	Hair cells	Cochlea	Locating sound sources
Smelling	Chemicals floating in air	Receptor cells	Olfactory bulb	Pheromones
Tasting	Chemicals dissolved in water	Taste buds	Papillae	Supertasters
Touching	Pressure	Pacinian corpuscles	Skin	Differing sensitivity of body surfaces

in the mouth (Ward & Simner, 2003). But only 1 percent of us have such experiences, so we will focus on five major senses separately in this chapter.

The Sense of Vision

Humans are visual creatures; for us, "seeing is believing." In the span of evolutionary time, vision went from a primitive recognition of light versus dark to the detection of features like shape, texture, motion, and color in higher-order animals (Land & Fernald, 1992). What makes the sense of vision in humans possible? Light waves have three physical properties that create sensations: The **wavelength** of light—the horizontal distance between wave peaks—determines its color or hue. The amplitude—how high the peaks are—determines its brightness. And the number of different wavelengths present determines its saturation, or the purity and richness of color. For example, red, green, and blue light each have a characteristic wavelength, and white light combines all three. The physical properties of the external stimulus—the light—result in our internal sensation of color, brightness, and richness. But how does light in the external world form our psychological experience?

We commonly describe vision as taking place in the eye, but it only begins there. Light from an object comes in through the eye's pupil and passes through the lens (a transparent organ that helps to focus light). It is then flipped upside down and falls onto the back wall of the eyeball, a layer of nerve cells called the **retina** FIGURE 4-8.

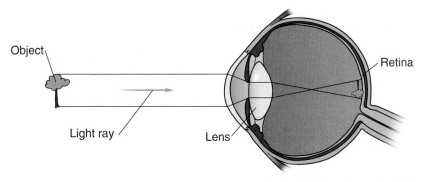

Object

Light ray

Lens

Retina

FIGURE 4-8 Rays of light entering the eye pass through the lens to fall on the back wall of the eyeball, called the retina.

So an image of a person actually falls on the retina with the feet at the top of the retina and the head at the bottom. Two types of cells line the interior wall of the retina: **rod cells**, which recognize degrees of darkness and light, and **cone cells** that recognize colors (see FIGURE 4-9). The rod cells operate under low illumination, and night vision occurs using this type of receptor. Located around the periphery of the eye, the rod cells detect light but are not good at sharp images. As you enter a dark room, your rod cells become more than 10,000 times more sensitive to light after time passes, and you experience **dark adaptation**. Similarly, when you go from a dark to light room, you experience light adaptation, in which your eyes adjust to the higher illumination of a room.

The cone cells operate under high illumination. These cells are packed around the **fovea**, or focal point of the eye. This means the perception of sharp images is best in the area at the center of our gaze. Rod and cone cells are known as **photoreceptors**: cells that respond to the electromagnetic energy of light. Photoreceptor cells *transduce*, or translate, the light's energy into neural signals. These neural signals pass to another layer of cells, called **bipolar cells**, which process and pass them to another layer called **ganglion cells**. More than 130 million photoreceptor cells feed neural signals into about one million ganglion cells. So within the retina itself, layers of connected cells begin to process sensory information first absorbed by the photoreceptors (Palmer, 1999).

Wavelength The distance between peaks of incoming light waves that determines their color.

Retina The layer of sensory receptor cells lining the back wall of the eye.

Rod cells Rod-shaped cells in the retina that register degrees of lightness and darkness.

Cone cells Cone-shaped cells on the retina that recognize colors.

Dark adaptation The increased sensitivity experienced when your eyes adjust to lower levels of available light.

Fovea The focal point of the retina where image processing is sharpest due to more cone cells.

Photoreceptors The rod and cone cells in the retina that register the presence of light waves.

Bipolar cells Cells that process incoming information from the rods and cones in the retina.

Ganglion cells More complex cells that process patterns of receptor activation within the retina.

FIGURE 4-9 This image shows the distinctive shapes of rod and cone cells. There are 20 rod cells for every one cone cell, and the cones are clustered in the center of the retina. Rods respond to dim light, and cones detect color and detail.

Because the photoreceptor cells lie at the back, or interior wall, of the retina FIGURE 4-10, incoming light must pass through the ganglion and bipolar cell layers to reach the photoreceptor cells. It's as if the wiring of a car headlight was placed in front of rather than behind the light. Ganglion cells' axons then carry neural signals within a complex strand of neural pathways, called the **optic nerve**, that leaves the back of the eye and extends into the brain. The point at which the optic nerve leaves the back of the eye causes a **blind spot**, where light falling on that part of the retina cannot be processed (see FIGURE 4-11). As neural activity exits the eyes through the optic nerves, the signals travel to visual centers in the brain FIGURE 4-12.

Close one eye and imagine a vertical line in the middle of what you can see. Everything to the left of that line is in your left visual field and on the right, your right visual field. Each eye has its own left and right visual fields. So the neural pathway from each eye crosses

Optic nerve The bundle of neural fibers collecting sensation in the retina that passes out of the eyeball in a pathway to the brain.

Blind spot The small area of the retina where the optic nerve leaves the eyeball.

FIGURE 4-10 A depiction of the eye, where the layers of cells in the retina are enlarged.

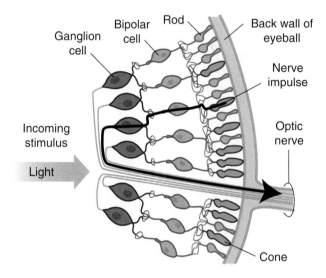

FIGURE 4-11 To experience your blind spot, close your right eye and look at the red dot on the right with your left eye. From about 18 inches away, move your face slowly towards the page. At a critical distance, the circle on the left will fall entirely on your blind spot, the area of the retina where there are no receptor cells (where the optic nerve leaves the eye). When the circle disappears it is seen as the same as the background because that area is "filled in" by nearby receptors.

FIGURE 4-12 Neural stimulation takes place in the retina, where the processing of signals begins. From there, signals travel to a cross-over point called the optic chiasm, the thalamus "relay center," and finally to the occipital lobes of the cortex.

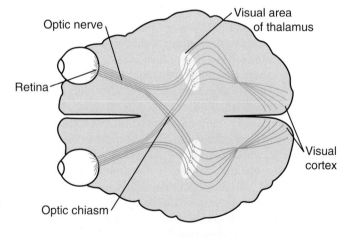

over at a point called the **optic chiasm**. Here, all the neural signals from the left visual fields of both eyes are gathered and sent to the right hemisphere of the brain. Similarly, all the neural signals from the right visual fields of both eyes are gathered and sent to the brain's left hemisphere. Then neural pathways within each hemisphere send the neural signals to the thalamus, the "sensory relay center" of the brain. The thalamus reroutes incoming neural messages to processing areas in the visual cortex and then to more than 30 different areas of the occipital cortex.

Within the occipital cortex, groups or "columns" of cells further analyze the neural signals to make sense of the incoming information. These cells are called **feature detectors**. Each feature detector cell responds to a unique, specific aspect, or feature, of the visual stimulus (e.g., a horizontal line, a vertical line, or line at a specific angle). Each feature detector cell performs its task independently from all other feature detector cells, known as **parallel processing**. However, a feature detector also sends messages to nearby cells, acting to amplify and inhibit the action of its neighbors.

Nobel Prize–winning research (Hubel & Weisel, 1962) studied the function of these feature detector cells in the visual cortex. The experiment involved tapping into individual cells with microelectrodes. Anesthetized (unconscious) cats (with their eyes open) saw a stimulus projected on a screen in front of them. The microelectrode captured the activity of an individual feature detector cell while a stimulus was displayed in different places on the screen. By carefully testing which stimuli activated each cell, the experimenters determined that individual cells in the visual cortex responded only to certain types of visual information. For example, a cell may respond only to a line moving up and down at a 45-degree angle. This particular cell's receptive field is limited only to a small area that, when stimulated in a specific way by specific visual information, causes a change in its firing rate.

Each feature detector cell looks for a specific pattern, such as color, form, movement, and depth (Hubel, 1996). The visual cortex is made up of millions of these cells, each tuned to recognize simple or complex features. Other cells look at the results of this process and attempt to recognize patterns formed by overlapping fields of feature detectors (Tanaka, 1996). It's a bit like putting together the pieces of a jigsaw puzzle: By detecting the edges of forms—abrupt transitions between light and dark—the visual system begins to put together the outlines of an image, and the stimulus takes on a recognizable form.

For example, a simple stimulus like the letter "A" consists of three separate lines. Using bottom-up processing, feature analysis by the differing types of detector cells identifies each separate line (/ - \), and the pattern they form is pieced together by further processing in the visual cortex (A). At the end of this (split-second) journey from retina to cortex, the pattern, spread across columns of cells, is recognized as the letter "A." Now, imagine how much easier this process would be had you just read the letters "B – A – N – A – N –"! Your top-down expectations for the letter to come would help you tie the pieces into a pattern much more quickly!

To perceive color, our eyes use the same method as television and computer screens. In order to produce the entire spectrum of colors, only three primary colors of light are needed: red, blue, and green. This **trichromatic theory** of color vision—that the eye contains only red, blue, and green color detectors—was advanced by Thomas Young (1773–1826) and Hermann von Helmholtz (1821–1894). In fact, evidence shows that each cone in the retina is tuned to detect only red, or blue, or green light (Bowmaker & Dartnall, 1980). The patterns of light detected by cones are then analyzed to capture individual hues made up of varying combinations of these three colors. Color mixing with light is *additive*, in that two colors with different wavelengths combine to produce a new color; so, red and blue light together make pink light

However, there is more to color vision than cones. For example, consider the images comprised of dots in FIGURE 4-13. Some individuals (about 8 percent of men and 0.5 percent of women, with men more at risk because of mutations linked to X chromosomes) cannot see numbers formed by certain colors of dots. This indicates a form of **colorblindness**, a condition marked by difficulty in distinguishing one color, such as red, from others, such as green. If trichromatic theory were the correct account of color vision, these patterns should not be problematic.

Optic chiasm The place in the front of the brain where the neural tracts following from the optic nerve of each eye cross over so that some tracts lead to both the right and left hemispheres.

Feature detectors Individual cells in the visual cortex that respond only to certain types of visual patterns, such as lines, circles, or angles.

Parallel processing Analyzing information in groups or "columns" of cells in the cortex at the same time in order to understand an overall pattern.

Trichromatic theory The notion that color vision relies on sensory receptors in the retina that process only red, blue, and green.

Colorblindness A condition marked by difficulty in distinguishing among some shades of red, green, or, more rarely, blue.

Opponent process theory The theory that opposing, or complementary, colors (yellow/blue, white/black, and red/green) are produced by differences in firing rates by complex cells within the retina.

Afterimage The appearance of an illusion of color (e.g., red) on a white surface after viewing its complementary color (e.g., green) for a prolonged period.

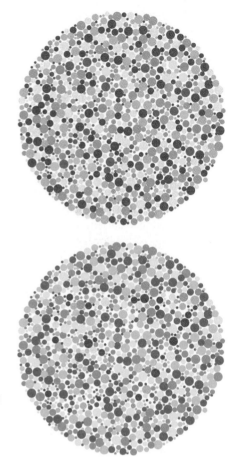

FIGURE 4-13 Some individuals have trouble picking out the numbers "23" in the image (top) and the number "57" (bottom) among the dot patterns, indicating an impairment of color processing that can't be explained by trichromatic theory.

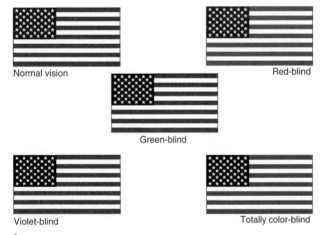

Normal vision

Red-blind

Green-blind

Violet-blind

Totally color-blind

Most people see the American flag in the colors shown on the flag labeled "normal vision". With variants of color blindness, people have difficulty in distinguishing among colors due to a problem in one type of receptor, causing the flag to appear in different colorations.

A different theory of color vision was proposed by Ewald Hering (1834–1918), called **opponent process theory**. This arose from observation of phenomena called negative **afterimages**. In some conditions, viewing red for a time leads to seeing its complementary color, green, on a white background. Similarly, viewing blue can lead to an afterimage of its complementary color, yellow, and black to white. When processing the same stimulus over a period of time fatigues the receptor cells on the retina, they respond by presenting the *opposing* color to what was processed. This "opponent process" suggests that yellow and blue are linked, as are red and green, and black and white. The occurrence of afterimages demonstrates a link in our sensation of color that cannot be explained by trichromatic theory FIGURE 4-14.

What accounts for afterimages? The answer lies in the characteristics of the ganglion cells that process information coming from the cone cells. There are three types of ganglion cells: red/green cells, blue/yellow cells, and black/white cells. When cones sensitive to one color fire, the ganglion cell inhibits the processing of the opposing color. So a single ganglion cell that fires faster when a red cone is active may fire slowly when the complementary green cones become active FIGURE 4-15. As a result, the color we see as an afterimage is a reflection of the processing in ganglion cells adapting to the repeated neural messages from the cones. For example, a ganglion cell firing rapidly to signal "red" will eventually fatigue and slow down, resulting in the passing on of a signal from that cell as "green" (Vimal et al., 1987).

The occurrence of afterimages shows that as soon as cones register information, the next layer of cells has already begun to piece together information and transmit an interpretation of the stimulus. So both the trichromatic theory and the opponent process

FIGURE 4-14 To see an afterimage, focus on the cross in the middle of the left figure. Be sure to keep your eyes as still as possible. Stare at the cross for at least 30 seconds. Then, switch your eyes quickly to the white box on its right. You should see an afterimage of the American flag!

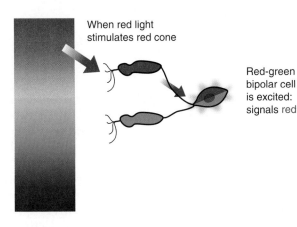

When red light stimulates red cone

Red-green bipolar cell is excited: signals red

FIGURE 4-15 Opponent process theory posits the presence of processing cells that respond to pairs of complementary colors: red or green, blue or yellow, or black or white. These cells help to refine the color detected in the red, blue, and green cone cells.

theory together help to explain color vision (Abramov & Gordon, 1994). Perceptual **illusions** like afterimages remind us that our sensory systems can go astray. By examining some of these exceptions, we can glimpse how our sensory and perceptual systems build our internal sense of the external world.

The Sense of Hearing

Audition, or the sense of hearing, depends on the movement of air in the external world. As the proverbial question goes, "If a tree falls in the forest and no one is around to hear it, does it make a sound?" The falling tree does make sound waves, but audition occurs when someone hears it.

Our sense of hearing registers a sound when an object in the world vibrates, setting air molecules into motion against the ear. Imagine striking a metal bar; as it vibrates, it creates small pressure waves of air that travel out in all directions. These are called *sound waves* and are invisible to the eye. These waves have amplitude or height, which creates the experience of loudness (Knight, 1960). The number of sound waves arriving within a given time period reflects their **frequency**, which we experience as pitch (whether a sound is high or low). Combinations of sound waves contribute to our psychological sense of the complexity or purity of sound, called *timbre* (pronounced "TAM-ber"). To accomplish this, our ears rely on a lot of "hardware" to amplify the incoming sound waves and detect the three major properties of sound.

FIGURE 4-16 shows the ear, its internal canal, and a delicate translation system that captures the sound waves on the eardrum in the outer ear and replicates them in the middle ear through a mechanism involving the hammer, anvil, and stirrup bones to produce pressure on a membrane called the **oval window**. The **cochlea** is a semicircular canal formed by three spiral-shaped fluid-filled tubes. Movement of the oval window causes the fluid in the cochlea to move, reproducing the sound wave that struck the eardrum. The cochlea is lined with the **basilar membrane**, which includes tiny hair cells on its surface. Each of these **hair cell receptors** is connected to the auditory nerve. When sound waves

Illusion A visual image that creates a misperception of the world.

Frequency The wavelength of sound or light waves (the time distance between peaks).

Oval window Membrane in the ear that collects sound waves and translates them into fluid movement in the cochlea.

Cochlea The semicircular canal of fluid-filled tubes that captures movements of the oval window to transduce vibrations into neural firing.

Basilar membrane A neural pathway within the cochlea that registers the movement of fluid through tiny hair cells on its surface.

Hair cell receptors Sound receptors in the cochlea that transduce fluid movement into neural impulses.

FIGURE 4-16 The external portion of the ear acts to collect sound waves, while the middle ear replicates them on an internal mechanism called the basilar membrane. The movement of this membrane stimulates receptor cells that create neural impulses.

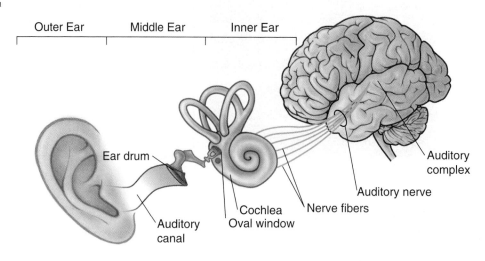

Place theory The notion that the pitch of a sound is determined by the location of the stimulation on the basilar membrane inside the ear.

Frequency theory The notion that the firing rate of neurons is determined directly by the frequency (length of time between sound waves) of the sound.

Chemical senses The two external senses that involve the detection of chemical molecules either dissolved in water (taste) or floating in the air (smell).

cause them to move, the hair cells transduce these signals into patterns of neural activity. This activity then follows a pathway from the inner ear to the thalamus. From there it travels on to either the left or the right *auditory cortex* in the temporal lobes of the brain. All of the neural connections from the right ear go to the left auditory cortex, and all of the connections from the left ear go to the right auditory cortex.

How does the stimulation of hair cell receptors create the experience of hearing? Loudness is recorded by the firing rate of the individual nerve cells and in the total amount of neural activity occurring. However, two theories attempt to explain how we hear pitch. **Place theory** proposes that sound waves of differing frequencies affect different locations along the basilar membrane (Bekesy, 1947). High-frequency sounds move the part of the membrane nearest the oval window, while low-frequency sounds move the entire membrane. **Frequency theory** (Wever, 1949) suggests the firing rate of neurons is determined directly by the frequency (length of time between sound waves) of the sound. In fact, both factors are at work, depending on the particular pitch of the incoming sound: Lower-pitched sounds are detected through increased firing rates, and higher-pitched sounds are detected according to where the neurons are located. Intermediate pitches use both methods. Unlike light, sound is not additive; instead, we hear each low and high pitch in sound separately rather than mixed into a single pitch.

Given this delicate system, our sense of hearing can be very vulnerable to overstimulation. How loud is "too loud"? The measurement unit of sound is the decibel (dB). Daily exposure to sounds over 85 decibels (vacuum cleaners, subways, and lawnmowers) can flatten hair cells over time and cause a gradual hearing loss. Even brief exposure to stimuli over 140 dB (gunshots, amplified rock band, rocket launch) can cause permanent hearing loss (Kryter, 1994). Listening to music at high volumes through the earphones of MP3 players and similar devices can also cause hearing loss (Vogel et al., 2009), and this loss is permanent.

Why are our ears on the sides of our heads? Imagine walking through the woods and hearing a sound nearby. Immediately, you swing your head in the direction of the sound. How does our sense of hearing tell us which way to look? The positions of the ears on opposite sides of the head results in differences in the timing of the sensations they register. The brain calculates a sound's location—below or above; right or left; near or far—by using these differences in the volume and timing of the arrival of sound waves at each ear (Phillips & Brugge, 1985). In trying to find sound sources, we often tilt our heads one way or another, providing further cues about where sounds are occurring in the world around us.

The Sense of Smell

Taste and smell are **chemical senses** because they involve the detection of chemical molecules either dissolved in water (taste) or floating in the air (smell). The proximity of the mouth and nose also means that the two senses work together to produce the sensations we experience in a process called **sensory interaction**. If you can recall eating a meal when you have a cold, the food may have seemed less tasty. These two senses provide important clues about the foods we eat, such as whether they are potentially nutritious or poisonous. These sensory systems also help motivate us to eat.

Olfaction is far less important to us than to other mammals; for example, dogs have about 100 million smell receptors, compared to just 10 million in people. We take in odors through olfactory receptors located at the top of our nasal cavity (and some in the throat). The neurons leading from these receptors are bundled together in the olfactory nerve, which travels to the **olfactory bulb** located at the base of the brain FIGURE 4-17. The receptors for odors appear to be highly specialized, with thousands of different types, each responding to a different odor molecule in the air (Buck & Axel, 1991). The *lock-and-key theory* (Amoore et al., 1964) suggests that odor molecules may fit into differently shaped sites on the receptors, triggering the transduction to neural stimulation. Unlike the visual and auditory senses, much of the processing of the neural activity from odor receptors occurs in the sensory organ rather than the brain. Olfaction is the only sense that does not pass through the thalamus for further processing in the cortex but is sent directly to the amygdala within the limbic system, which processes emotion and memory. As a result, smell is a link to memories and feelings, even after many years (Chu & Downes, 2000).

Olfaction The sense of smell.

Olfactory bulb The processing center for smell located at the base of the brain.

Olfactory bulb

Olfactory nerve

Receptor cells

FIGURE 4-17 Unlike other senses, much of the neural processing of smell takes place in the sense organ itself, rather than the cortex.

You may find there are some smells you react to strongly and others you can't detect. Studies have found that individuals can't be characterized as more or less sensitive to odors than others (Koelega, 1994); instead, you may be more sensitive than someone else to some specific odor. **Pheromones** are biochemical odors emitted by people that others can recognize. Parents can recognize their children by smell, and infants respond to the smell of their mother's breast (Russell, 1976). Women are sensitive to the pheromones produced during the menstrual cycle. In one study, women were exposed to armpit sweat (applied to their upper lips) from other women, and they developed coordinated menstrual cycles even though they had no other contact (Stern & McClintock, 1998). Pheromones may also play important roles in sexual attraction, so our sense of smell may affect our social relationships.

The Sense of Taste

Clearly, our sense of taste, or **gustatory** sense, greatly affects our behavior, motivating us to eat when we're not hungry, to choose some foods over others, and to avoid some foods completely. Taste buds are neural receptors located mostly on the tongue FIGURE 4-18, and they are shaped like the segments of an orange. The buds have tiny hair-like projections through a central pore. Water-soluble chemicals in food stimulate the taste buds to transduce this chemical energy into neural signals. There can be several hundred buds located in and around each **papillae** (the visible bumps we see on the tongue). If you've ever burned your tongue on hot food or liquids, you've experienced the death of some of your taste buds! Fortunately, our bodies regenerate taste buds constantly in order to repair the damage.

Pheromone A characteristic biochemical odor emitted by an individual.

Gustatory The sense of taste.

Papillae Visible bumps on the tongue.

FIGURE 4-18 Taste buds are the chemical receptors located in and around papillae in the tongue and mouth. The taste buds are embedded within the papillae, and are made up of taste receptor cells.

Our sense of taste registers at least five primary qualities: sweet, salty, sour, bitter, and "umami," thought to relate to tastes with high concentrations of proteins (Yamaguchi & Ninomiya, 2000). These tastes may help us to select food, because sweet-tasting foods like fruit are generally safe to eat, while the "salty" detectors help us maintain levels of sodium needed in the blood. "Sour" detectors may aid in avoiding spoiled foods, and "bitter" usually signals something poisonous, or at least something to be avoided. However, a wide range of chemical stimuli can activate each type of receptor. For example, more than 50 different binding sites are activated by an equal number of different bitter-tasting chemicals. Our experience of different tastes arises from the combinations of stimulated receptors.

While people don't differ in the qualities of receptors, they do show a large variation in the number of taste buds present. Some individuals have as few as 500 taste buds, while others have as many as 10,000 (Bartoshuk, 1993). No other sense involves such large differences in numbers of receptors among individuals. Researchers have found that 25 percent of us are "supertasters" and have a greater number of structures that house taste buds FIGURE 4-19. If you're a supertaster, you may experience an overall higher level of tasting ability than others (Bartoshuk, 2000). And the burning heat set off by the chili pepper ingredient, capsaicin, is more intense in supertasters than in others. But be careful how you test yourself: An aspiring chef challenged his friend to a chili-eating contest and ate a plateful of his hottest sauce to his friend's spoonful. Later that night, the chef was found unconscious and died just hours later (Sims, 2008). Mild adverse reactions to chili peppers can include burning eyes, a streaming nose, and uncontrollable hiccups.

FIGURE 4-19 Some people, called supertasters, are born with many more taste buds. This figure shows two tongues stained with blue food coloring. The top image shows a supertaster, with about 60 fungiform papillae within a 6 mm circle (shown in red). The bottom image shows a tongue with just 16 in the same size area.

Is it good to be a supertaster? It may not help you, but to a social group, having some individuals who can detect poisonous food would be an advantage. Supertasters appear to be more responsive to many bitter compounds, including those in coffee, grapefruit juice, and green tea. So supertasters may have an advantage in detecting the poisonous compounds in plants, which often taste bitter. They also perceive saccharin and sucrose as sweeter than other people do and are more sensitive to oral pain. It is possible to self-diagnose supertasters at home by careful examination of the tongue. Use blue food dye and look for the number of papillae. Being a supertaster or nontaster represents normal variation in the human population, just like eye or hair color.

The Sense of Touch

Touch is a very important sense for psychology because it connects us to other people. Consider this example: Can you tickle yourself? Tickling is defined as the act of touching a part of the body so as to cause involuntary twitching movements or laughter. Harris and Christenfeld (1999) presented subjects with a "mechanical tickle machine," and found that people laughed just as much when they believed a machine was tickling them. But the tickle response is something you can't do for yourself: It may be a reflex, similar to the startle reflex, that is contingent upon the element of surprise. You can't tickle yourself because you can't surprise yourself in this way. This shows that the physical stimulus—the touch—is interpreted differently based on your knowledge of its source. Clearly, top-down expectations play a role in determining how incoming sensations are perceived and whether sensation is pleasurable.

Our perception of touch relies on separate sensory systems for pressure, temperature, and pain. The entire surface of our bodies responds to pressure against it. Tiny receptors, called **Pacinian corpuscles**, are located in the fatty layer beneath the surface of the skin FIGURE 4-20. These receptors transduce changes in pressure on the skin into neural signals that travel to the brain and "tell" it how much force has been applied and where it is located. Pacinian corpuscles send the brain a pattern that looks exactly like the object itself. So pressing a coin onto the skin registers in the brain as the shape of a circle, called **isomorphic** perception (Burton & Sinclair, 1996).

Pacinian corpuscles are not evenly distributed across the skin; instead, they are gathered more densely in some areas where more sensitivity to touch is required. Think for a minute about what parts of your skin are most sensitive. Your fingers and face are more sensitive than the calf, trunk, and arm, so less pressure is required to register sensation. It makes sense that the face and hands are most sensitive when you consider how important they are for eating, social behavior, and fine movements. FIGURE 4-21 shows how pressure sensation differs across the body, where the lips, hands, feet, and sex organs have more sensory neurons than other parts of the body. To demonstrate this difference in sensitivity, try this experiment: Hold two toothpicks together and press them gently onto to your skin, beginning at your shoulder. Reposition the toothpicks, advancing a little farther down your arm and toward your hand and fingers. At your shoulder, the two toothpick points should feel like one. By the time you reach your hand and fingers, you should clearly feel two separate points of pressure.

FIGURE 4-20 A sensory receptor called the Pacinian corpuscle is located within the skin.

Pacinian corpuscles Tiny pressure receptors located in the fatty layer beneath the skin.

Isomorphic A representation taking on the same shape or form as the object itself.

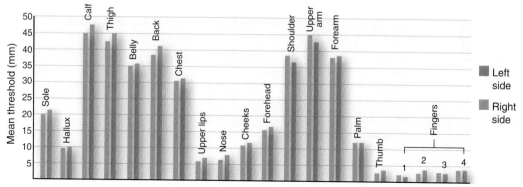

FIGURE 4-21 This map of the body shows that some areas have greater sensitivity (require less pressure to recognize touch, shown by shorter bars) than others. For example, touch on the face is easier to detect than on the trunk of the body.
Source: Data from Weber, E. H. (1978.) E. H. Weber: The sense of touch. [translated from De pulsu, resorptione, auditu et tactu: Anatationes anatomicae et physiologicae by E. H. Weber, 1834]. New York: Academic Press.

Imagine grasping a toasted marshmallow and an ice cube in your hand at the same time. What sensation would you expect to feel? When a person grasps two braided water pipes—one with cold water running through it and one with warm water—the sensation they experience is, "very hot!" This surprising result is based on how the sensory receptors recognize temperature (Casey et al., 1993). Parts of the skin have receptors responding to cold, while nearby areas have receptors responding to warmth. When both types of responses occur at the same time, the brain interprets simultaneous firing as "burning hot." Neuroimaging studies show that gripping warm and cold bars at the same time activates brain regions responsive to pain (Craig et al., 1996). While you may think of pain as occurring on the skin, pain can and does register through any sensory receptor. Deafening sounds, blinding lights, and spicy-hot foods produce pain as readily as sunburn. But most importantly, pain goes beyond sensation in that many psychological factors affect our perception of pain. When asked by his dentist "Where does it hurt?" the philosopher Bertrand Russell replied, "In my mind, of course." Our top-down expectations about pain can greatly change our experience of it.

How does sensation translate to the perception of pain in the mind? Pain is critically important for survival, as it indicates damage to the body. Unlike other senses, there are multiple sensory receptors that detect pain and multiple routes for the processing of pain sensations. First, there is a simple reflex in the interneurons located in the spine that connect incoming sensory fibers and outgoing movement fibers. This circuit allows us to rapidly respond to a painful stimulus even before the perception of pain occurs in the brain FIGURE 4-22. Second, there are pain receptors of two types: fast-acting ones

Gate-control theory The notion that interneurons in the spinal cord act as a gate to block some sensory signals from going to the brain.

FIGURE 4-22 Pain messages can be quickly responded to based on "interneurons" in the spinal cord that link incoming sensory and motor neurons. As a result, the movement away from the painful stimulus happens well before the pain message reaches the brain.

Sensory neuron

Motor neuron

Interneuron

FIGURE 4-23 This drawing shows an area of the cortex called the anterior cingulate cortex. In a study where people played a virtual ball-tossing game, social exclusion showed activation in this area, just as when experiencing physical pain.

that transmit sharp initial pains and slower-acting receptors that provide the sensation of longer-lasting, duller pain. These neural signals for pain travel through two separate pathways and cause two different psychological experiences (Treede et al., 1999). The sensation of pain involves not just a registration of where and what is happening but also an emotionally aversive response that motivates us to avoid the stimulus. In fact, there is some evidence that social pain, such as being rejected by a partner in a game, can cause the same brain response as the perception of physical pain (Eisenberger et al., 2003). The reaction to both social and physical pain activates the same area of the cortex, known as the anterior cingulate (see FIGURE 4-23).

Gate-control theory (Melzack & Wall, 1965) proposes that too much sensory information coming in can overwhelm the nervous system. When that happens, the interneurons in the spinal cord act as a gate, blocking some signals from going to the brain while letting others pass through. The brain may also send messages to the spinal cord to open or close these gates, controlling the amount of sensation transmitted. Pain can be also be "gated" by skin receptors, so that massaging your bumped elbow acts to "close the gate" and prevent pain signals from reaching the brain. Top-down processing can be very influential in the processing of pain signals. For example, while playing a sport, you may not feel a cut until after you stop playing. Pain can be controlled by changing the context, such as the generation of endorphins, drugs, massage, acupuncture, and competing stimulation. One particularly helpful method is distraction. In studies of pain tolerance, managing intense discomfort is aided by focusing attention on a pleasant picture, music, film, or even just a familiar mental image (Villemure & Bushnell, 2002). Expectant mothers are taught this "focal point" technique, along with breathing exercises, to help cope with labor pain.

The mind exerts plenty of control over what we experience as pain. In the **placebo effect**, people are given a treatment that is known to have no effect on pain, such as a sugar pill; nonetheless, some report their experience of pain is reduced significantly. This is a great example of how top-down processing provides expectations for our experience. In the placebo effect, expectations are so strong that we actually experience what we believe we should! One study of postoperative pain following the extraction of a molar tooth found that a saline injection was as potent as a 6- to 8-mg dose of morphine (Levine et al., 1981). In addition, our memory for pain may be quite inaccurate, focusing on the peak amount of pain and the amount of pain perceived at the end of an experience, called the "peak-end rule" (Kahneman et al., 1993). What if you had to choose whether to have your colonoscopy extended for a short interval? It would seem obvious that a shorter duration would be less painful; however, people with the added time reported less pain because the extra period involved less pain at the end of the experience. Tapering the experience so that the end period was less painful actually changed people's perception of the total pain they endured (Redelmeier et al., 2003). Pain perception clearly demonstrates the interaction of bottom-up sensory processes and top-down perceptional processes. It is to these perceptional processes that we now turn.

> **Placebo effect** Feeling benefit or improvement from a treatment known to have no effect.
>
> **Extrasensory perception (ESP or psi)** Detecting information without knowing its sensory source.

CONCEPT LEARNING CHECK 4.3 | *Methods of Sensory Transduction*

Each of the five sensory organs has a different means of transducing physical energy to neural stimulation. Identify which sense fits with each description of neural stimulation:

1. _____ Movement of a tiny hair cell on a membrane

2. _____ Fitting of a chemical molecule into a specific site

3. _____ Breakdown of pigment after exposure to light

4. _____ Compression of a receptor's shape

5. _____ Dissolved chemicals matching one of five qualities

CRITICAL THINKING APPLICATION

As we've seen, sensation and perception involve the interaction of the external stimulus with internal expectations. If we don't know or recognize the sensory source of our perception, it is termed **extrasensory perception (ESP or psi)**. People have reported having the experience of clairvoyance (knowing something beyond the usual senses), telepathy (transferring information between people), psychokinesis (influence of thought on physical events), and premonition (awareness of a future event; Bem, 2011).

For example, one student reported having a premonition: "A week before my grandma died I was on my way to school and for some reason felt compelled to think about her. And then, a week later, she died. I always knew she had health problems, but for some reason, I knew her time was up."

It's tempting to apply a mystical interpretation to these experiences and decide that ESP must be involved. About 57 percent of U.S. adults believe in some form of ESP (CBS News, 2002). Moreover, over one-quarter of Americans say they believe in psychic phenomena, such as communicating with someone who has died,

(Continues)

CRITICAL THINKING APPLICATION *(Continued)*

FIGURE 4-24 The set of five distinct "Zener" cards created by Rhine and Zener to test for extrasensory perception in laboratory studies.

that extraterrestrials have visited earth, or that houses can be haunted (Lyons, 2005). Others enjoy psychics, astrology, and palm-reading sessions. What is the basis for these beliefs?

Parapsychology, the study of extrasensory phenomena, has produced hundreds of controlled studies attempting to document extrasensory perception. In the 1930s, J. B. Rhine and K. Zener created a set of cards with symbols on one side FIGURE 4-24. One procedure tested for *telepathy*, where a "sender" would look at each card in sequence and the "receiver" would try to read the sender's mind. In another procedure, the subject would try to read the card face down (*clairvoyance*, detecting something hidden from view) or try to predict the sequence of cards before they were shuffled (*precognition*). Rhine accumulated more than 100,000 responses from a variety of subjects. In 1934, he reported the results: Using a 25-card deck, his subjects averaged 7.1 correct card identifications, a better-than-chance performance. Another procedure had a sender concentrate on a single visual

stimulus, and the receiver chose the stimulus that "matches their thoughts the best" from among four stimuli. Receivers were found to be 32 percent correct, higher than the 25 percent expected by chance (Bem & Honorton, 1994).

Most recently, Bem (2011) presented a set of studies in which people guessed which of two positions on the screen would show a stimulus; after their guess, the position was determined at random by a computer program. Some of the pictures were erotic and others nonerotic. The results were that for erotic pictures only, a very small (53 percent vs. 50 percent expected by chance) but reliable effect occurred in which subjects guessed better than chance. Despite these findings, the vast majority of existing documented studies fail to find evidence of ESP.

It is difficult to conduct rigorous research on ESP and avoid alternative interpretations. Great care must be taken to ensure that no other sensory information is reaching the recipient and that no other non–ESP information will allow them to select their responses (Swets & Bjork, 1990).

Evaluate

1. How would you account for experiences such as those cited previously without appealing to ESP?

2. What type of study would provide convincing evidence about extrasensory perception? Think through the details of your study and how you would rule out any alternative explanations.

3. What type of study would convince you that ESP does not exist?

4.4 Perception Organizes Sensations

Perceptual processes organize incoming sensations by providing patterns and organizing principles to help us navigate and understand the outside world.

■ Describe the principles that organize perception of images.

In order to make sense of the incoming flow of sensations, we need the help of top-down perceptual processes. Sensation and perception processes work together to interpret information using bottom-up sensory stimulation and top-down expectations about what we are going to see or experience. Much of the research on perception has examined the visual system and the cues we use to make sense of incoming images, and we will focus on examples of visual perception.

Form and Pattern Perception

As we saw, the visual system picks out specific features from the stimulus for further processing; then, these features have to be reassembled to recognize objects. To do this, our perception relies on organizational principles—that is, ways of putting together information. As we've seen, visual sensations begin at the retina and are pieced together by feature detectors to create a neural pattern. But how do we then recognize the neural pattern as a familiar form or object, such as an apple? Our perceptual processes have to give meaning to the pattern.

One theory argues that objects are represented in memory by **distinctive features**— that is, those essential physical features that uniquely specify an object (Treisman, 1999). For example, there is a distinctive set of features that allows you to identify a letter even

Parapsychology The study of paranormal or extrasensory phenomena.

Distinctive features The essential physical properties that uniquely identify an object.

M N **M** *M* *N* N M *N* **N M** **M** **N**

FIGURE 4-25 Feature analysis tolerates variation in specific features, while detecting the distinctive features that distinguish among similar objects like letters.

though many specific aspects of the image may vary FIGURE 4-25. The more distinctive the differences from objects around it, the easier it is to pick out a given object. On the other hand, the presence of more perceptual cues may make some features "pop out" during a visual search, indicating that some features are just easier to detect than others FIGURE 4-26. The feature detection cells in the occipital lobe detect more complex patterns of features, and may look for complex forms called **geons** that capture geometrical shapes like cylinders and pyramids (Biederman, 1987; see FIGURE 4-27). Organizing principles help by providing top-down expectations for the objects we're looking for within the incoming stimulus information.

Gestalt Organizing Principles

Gestalt psychologists (Wertheimer, 1912) identified organizing principles we use to identify objects. **Gestalt** means "whole," reflecting the belief that the whole emerges in perception and is more than simply "the sum of its parts." In other words, perception involves both what is "out there" and what comes from "inside the mind." Both bottom-up information from a sensory system and top-down perceptual processes are needed to create understanding.

Figure and Ground

A major problem that must be solved by our visual system is figure and ground—that is, determining what aspects in a scene are the figure (the object of interest) and what parts comprise the background. Sometimes the difference between a target figure and its surrounding ground is unclear. To the retina, the patterns of brown and white in this illustration have no meaning. The retina can only faithfully reproduce where the shapes occur on the image. To perceive the figure, our sense of sight draws on organizational principles.

Geon A simple three-dimensional form that, in combination, can create any shape.

Gestalt The "whole," reflecting the belief that the whole emerges in perception and is more than simply "the sum of its parts."

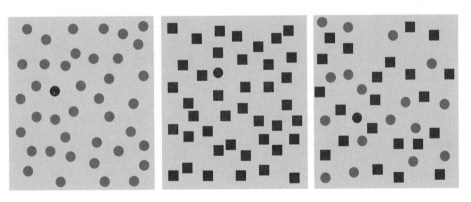

FIGURE 4-26 Scan through the figures looking for a red circle. Is it equally easy to find in all three panels? Chances are good you found the red circle easiest to find in the first panel, where it "pops out," and hardest in the last where it blends in with other red objects.

Geons

Objects

FIGURE 4-27 Recognition of the form of an object like a cup may require piecing together constituent parts, represented as "geons."

Our top-down expectations lead us to "fill in" missing edges of shapes, and finally to pick out the figure of interest from the background.

Perceptual Grouping

Our perception of visual images depends on organizing principles called the **laws of perceptual grouping**. One principle is *similarity*, in which pieces of images that appear similar in some way (in color, size, or orientation) are assumed to part of the same object. A second principle is *proximity*: If images are close together, they are likely to be part of the same object. The principle of *continuity* tells us that objects that touch each other are also likely to be parts of the same object. Finally, closure helps us fill in missing parts of images in order to perceive a whole object. These perceptual organization principles, summarized in FIGURE 4-28, help us to group related information within an image and figure out what parts belong to which objects.

These laws of perceptual grouping take us beyond what we physically see in the world to a pattern of perception based on expectations about visual objects. When patterns are incomplete, we tend to fill in the missing information in order to perceive the whole we expect to see (Rumelhart et al., 1986; FIGURE 4-29). The laws of perceptual grouping allow us to perceive a whole based on fragments and create an image where nothing is actually visible. The importance of organizational principles is illustrated by **reversible figures** in which two separate interpretations are suggested by the same image FIGURE 4-30. Another example of how organizational principles operate comes from **impossible figures**, which employ cues suggesting multiple, conflicting organizing principles FIGURE 4-31.

Visual **illusions** are images that create a misperception of the world. They make the point that what is "out there" in the stimulus goes through a great deal of perceptual processing to arrive at a meaningful interpretation of an image. By examining how illusions mislead our perceptions, we gain insight into how perceptual processing works. For the

Laws of perceptual grouping Simple organizational principles that help to interpret image elements, including similarity, proximity, continuity, and closure.

Reversible figure An image that can be understood with two different interpretations.

Impossible figure An image that can't be resolved into a single consistent interpretation.

Similarity | Proximity | Continuity | Closure

FIGURE 4-28 Organizing principles help us create a coherent image. **A** is seen as rows of dots, while **B** is seen as columns of dots. The *similarity* of their color helps to organize the image. The second image shows "four sets of double lines" rather than "eight lines" because *proximity* organizes the information. The *continuity* of line segments helps us see two lines overlapping in the top image; however, the two images below it suggest they could be two non-overlapping lines. Finally, the principle of *closure* fills in missing parts to help us perceive a whole object.

FIGURE 4-29 Missing information is readily filled in by our perceptual processes based on what we expect to see.
Source: Adapted from Kanizsa, G, (1955). Margini quasi-percettivi in campi con stimolazione omogenea. Rivista di Psicologia 49(1): 7–30.

FIGURE 4-30 Two opposing images. One shows a series of white urns, while the other shows two figures facing one another in silhouette.

Depth perception The detection of the distance of a stimulus from the body.

Binocular cues Ways to determine depth of field that require having two eyes.

Retinal disparity Two slightly different images falling on each retina because of their distance from one another on the face.

most part, the laws of perceptual grouping work so well at processing outside stimuli that we don't even notice occasional inconsistencies in our perception.

Depth Perception

Accurately estimating how far away an object is may be useful and sometimes essential. **Depth perception** tells us how far to reach for an object, how to navigate through space, or whether to duck when a ball is flying at us (Gibson, 1988). We perceive depth through principles that make the best use of the limited information that reaches our sensory organs. Remember that the retina provides only two dimensions (height and width in a two-dimensional plane), while the world has three! The missing dimension, depth, is the distance to a given object. We need ways to translate a proximal (nearby) stimulus (the

FIGURE 4-31 In some visual illusions, the laws of perceptual organization help to construct an image that is impossible in the physical world. In this image space between a series of orange foxes becomes a series of white foxes.

sensations registering on our receptors) into a perceived distal (distant) stimulus—the actual object out there in the world. Our visual system uses two sources of information for depth: binocular cues and monocular cues.

You might expect that having two eyes is a big advantage in perceiving depth, but **binocular cues** are of limited use. One such cue, **retinal disparity**, arises from our eyes being a couple of inches apart. Close both of your eyes, then open one at a time. You can see that each eye has a slightly different image. Your brain merges the images, and as it does so, it uses their differences to create an effect of depth. You can prove this to yourself by rapidly blinking first one eye, then the other. This provides some information about how far away the object is because the closer the object is, the more the locations of the images on the two retinas will differ. However, very distant objects will produce very similar images on the two retinas. Special neurons located in the visual cortex use this retinal information to determine depth (Cumming & DeAngelis, 2001). Technology for three-dimensional viewing of movies makes use of retinal disparity cues by projecting a slightly different image to each eye using special viewing glasses.

The second binocular cue is literally right in front of your face: **convergence**. Your eyes provide muscle movement cues as they work to coordinate focus on objects just in front of you. If you hold your arm out to focus on your finger and then draw your finger close to your nose, you reach a point where your eyes appear to "cross" the images. This muscular cue tells you when an object is very close to you.

Most commonly, we judge distance from cues that are available to a single eye, called **monocular cues**. If you close one eye, you can still use all of these cues to detect the distance of an object on the single retinal image you see. These cues have long been used in art to portray three dimensions on the two-dimensional surface of a canvas FIGURE 4-32. Our visual system uses these same cues to give us the impression of depth in the physical world FIGURE 4-33. By exaggerating these same cues, artists can create two-dimensional

Convergence A cue to depth based on the muscle movement of your eyes as they work to coordinate focus on objects in front of you.

Monocular cues Ways of determining the distance of an object that require a single eye.

FIGURE 4-32 Pictorial cues are used to suggest the depth of field in artistic images. Spot the depth cues in this image. We automatically perceive the foreground as closer to us because of its coarser texture, its greater detail, the relative size of the posts, relative heights of objects in the image, the interposition of objects, and the linear perspective of walls appearing to converge in the distance.

images that convey the illusion of three-dimensionality in an extremely realistic way FIGURE 4-34. In addition to pictoral cues, **accommodation** of the eye muscles as we focus our vision on near or far objects also provides a monocular cue about depth of field. These binocular and monocular cues to depth, and those for detection of motion, are shown in **TABLE 4-4**.

Perception of Motion

Motion perception involves only monocular cues, even though the objects are moving in three-dimensional space. In perceiving real movement, we rely on two types of cues to tell us how far away objects are. **Motion parallax** involves noting that objects close to you are moving past you faster than objects farther away. This effect is seen along the road where the edges of the roadway move past you faster than faraway objects on the horizon FIGURE 4-35. The second movement cue to depth is called **kinetic depth effect**. Imagine watching the shadow from an object (like a cat) lit by a car headlight. If the object rotates, a viewer can readily perceive the shape of the object just from seeing the changing shadow pattern (Wallach & O'Connell, 1953). We also readily extract structure from motion of points of light we see in a moving image, even with little information available. When viewed as a video, people can readily see a dozen moving light points, attached to the joints of the body, as a moving human figure (Johansson, 1973). Biological motion is a highly complex motion pattern and demonstrates the sophistication of pattern analysis in the brain.

FIGURE 4-33 We use a variety of cues to interpret visual depth in the physical world. A. Relative height: Objects higher in the image are more distant. B. Texture gradient: Closer images have more coarse texture. C. Linear perspective: Parallel lines appear to converge in the distance. D. Shading: Patterns of light and shadow suggest angles and shapes.

FIGURE 4-34 Artist Julian Beever demonstrates how three-dimensional perception can be created from two-dimensional cues in his art using chalk drawings on pavement. From the perspective shown, the image appears to be three dimensional; however, the actual drawing exaggerates the swimmer's extended leg disproportionately in order to create the impression of depth.

TABLE 4-4 Summary of Distance Cues

	Cues
Binocular (requires both eyes)	Convergence
	Retinal disparity
Monocular (requires one eye)	
Eye muscle	Accommodation
Movement	Motion parallax
	Kinetic depth effect
Pictorial	Size of object
	Height in plane
	Linear perspective
	Interposition
	Texture gradient
	Shading
	Atmospheric perspective

Accommodation Movement in an eye's muscles as we focus our vision on near or far objects provides a monocular depth cue.

Motion parallax The interpretation that objects close to you are moving past you faster than objects farther away.

Kinetic depth effect The movement of a three-dimensional object reveals its shape.

Phi phenomenon A series of static images viewed in sequence are interpreted as a moving image.

Constancy The assumption that objects in the physical world do not change spontaneously, but maintain their size, shape, color, and brightness over time.

Interestingly, our perception of motion is independent of retinal motion. An early demonstration of this was the **Phi phenomenon**, in which light bulbs turned on and off in a series appear to us as a moving light. For example, a lighted sign with bulbs flashed on and off in sequence appears as a moving light to the viewer. Following the Gestalt principle of continuity, we "see" a moving light rather than the actual independent sources in sequence. Film presents a series of still images to the eye, and the mind connects them to give the perception of continuous movement. Another type of motion illusion arises when a static image appears to be moving due to the effects of interacting color contrasts. If you look at the image in FIGURE 4-36, it appears that the forms are moving; however, if you keep your eyes still on a corner of the image, you will see that it is not. The illusion of motion results primarily from differences in the speed of processing the contrast in colors where the neurons respond faster to the higher-contrast white and black elements than to the lower-contrast light gray and dark gray elements (Backus & Oruc, 2005). But even these movement illusions depend only on monocular cues. We rely on organization provided by the laws of perceptual grouping to perceive three-dimensional objects from two-dimensional retinal images.

Perceptual Constancy

We assume that objects in the physical world don't change spontaneously. Instead, real objects maintain **constancy** in their size, shape, color, and brightness over time. Our perceptual system uses this knowledge to account for the many changes in form or shape that appear on the retina, and we automatically link them together to produce a mental image in which the object remains constant. For example, if you hold a coin in your fingers, you can turn it from a front view, where you see a circle shape, to a side view, where you see only the thin edge. That means the shape of the coin on the retina has drastically changed, but it still looks like the same quarter to you. Shape constancy allows us to recognize an object even though its shape might appear quite different. The sensations registered on the retina are overridden by the higher-order, top-down processing in the brain, which is saying, "Yes, this looks a little different now than before, but it's really the same object. It must have spun in the air." Constancy is important because it allows us to see very different sensory input as part of the same external object.

We perceive an object as having a set size even though its size on the retina changes with its distance, a principle known as size constancy. As a person walks towards you,

FIGURE 4-35 The faster moving objects near to you, such as the car, are compared to objects in the distance (such as the trees behind) in the depth cue of motion parallax.

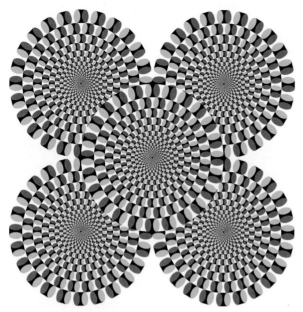

FIGURE 4-36 This image uses color contrast to give the impression of concentric movement. As your eyes naturally move while examining the image, the change in color contrast falling on receptors gives you the illusion that the circles are moving.

their image on the retina gets larger; however, we know people don't grow or shrink instantly in the world. We rely on this knowledge to conclude that a person that appears larger on the retina must be closer to us. The relative size of each person in the figure provides a cue about how far away each person is from the viewer. Since physical size stays constant, the perceived size on the retina as we move closer or farther away from an object tells us how far away it is. However, we have no problem recognizing that it's the same object even though its shape on the retina is quite different. These constancies in shape and size are important because, as observers, we move around in the world and our sensory information changes however, we don't perceive the objects themselves as changing.

Light and shadow also produce different patterns on the retina, where the brightness of parts of an object may make it appear dramatically different in the image formed on the retina. However, we have no trouble recognizing the whole object based on our assumption of brightness constancy. We are adept at "filling in" our perception so that the object appears as a whole even if we actually see only its parts. Similarly, inconsistencies in color are "filled in" by the perceptual processes so that missing spots of color are not detected, called color constancy. For example, a shadow falling across the hood of a car doesn't change your perception of the car as a single solid color.

The **Ames room** illusion (named after American ophthalmologist Adelbert Ames, Jr., in 1934) plays with our sense of size constancy by making two people look very different in size FIGURE 4-37. The room's normal cues about depth (the straight line of the floor and window sills) are hidden by distortions. This illusion shows that our usual perceptual processes can be fooled. Most of the time, however, our perceptual system effectively provides us with the information we need to recognize objects, to determine where they are in space, and to coordinate our actions in relation to them. The key to its success is our ability to provide top-down perceptual processing of incoming, bottom-up information to make sense of the world around us.

CONCEPT LEARNING CHECK 4.4   *Perceptual Organization Principles*

Match the example to the perceptual organization principle.

A. Laws of perceptual grouping: similarity, proximity, continuity, and closure

B. Binocular depth cue: retinal disparity and convergence

C. Monocular depth cue: linear perspective, relative height, interposition, texture gradient, shading, atmospheric perspective, and relative size

D. Motion cues: kinetic depth and motion parallax

E. Constancy: size, shape, brightness, and color

1. _____ Noticing the faces of the first few rows of people sitting in a stadium

2. _____ Seeing a "double" image of a pencil held close to your face

3. _____ Recognizing a globe from the half of a sphere lit by a flashlight

4. _____ Finding two groups of three people sitting near each other in a waiting room

5. _____ Stopping to pick up a quarter stuck on its edge in a sidewalk grate

6. _____ Noticing which wolf standing in a pack is the closest to you

7. _____ Detecting the shape of a tumbling box by watching its shadow

8. _____ Seeing a large train approaching at a distance

9. _____ Recognizing a black snake as it moves through the shadows of a bush

10. _____ Following a straight line when two paths in the wood intersect

4.5 Experience and Perception

Perception can be influenced by biological and experiential factors.

■ Give examples of how perception may be altered by experience.

We've seen that perceptual processes rely on experience. Researchers have confirmed that perception is also determined by the habits, tendencies, and styles we bring to bear on our sensations (Wehner & Stadler, 1994).

Development

Are we born with the ability to construct perceptions, or do they depend on experience with the world? In other words, is perception based on "nature," our built-in biology, or on "nurture," the experiences we have? An early experiment tested the relative contributions of nature and nurture in the perceptual ability of babies who can crawl (Gibson & Walk, 1960). A "visual cliff" was designed on a tabletop with a patterned surface on one half and a glass surface on the other half, with the patterned area on the floor below. Would a 6- to 14-month-old baby placed on the table perceive the apparent dropoff and refuse to crawl across it? (See FIGURE 4-38.) Even with their mothers calling them from the "cliff" side, most babies refused to crawl onto the glass surface. This suggests that the ability to perceive depth—so important to survival—may be inborn and not require any experience with the world.

However, 6-month-old babies do have some experience with perception, which may amplify an innate fear of heights. What about younger babies? The difficulty is determining how to ask an infant what she perceives when she is as yet unable to perform many actions upon the world. In a follow-up study with the visual cliff, 2-month-olds showed changes in heart rate when placed over the glass top but not over the patterned top (Campos et al., 1970). These infants showed signs of noticing the difference in depth. So some perceptual abilities are built in to our perceptual system.

Learning

A key aspect of perception that demonstrates the importance of experience is identifying faces (LeGrand et al., 2010). Based on our experience, we "fill in" the expected details of the face and may miss details that differ from our expectations. In FIGURE 4-39, the top two images of an upside-down face may look the same; however, when viewed right side up, as we normally see them, we readily detect the differences in the two images. Unlike most objects, faces are processed holistically rather than as a collection of independent features. Our tendency to see patterns of features as faces, even when occurring in objects like rocks and trees, is illustrated by FIGURE 4-40. This suggests

Ames room An illusion created by adding physical distortions to make a room appear to have a normal rectangular shape so that its contents appear to violate size constancy.

FIGURE 4-37 This room is designed to give the appearance of a level floor, with parallel lines formed by the juncture of the wall and ceiling. The person on the left is thus perceived as bigger because the distance cues are hidden from us. The left corner is actually closer and has a lower ceiling than the right.

FIGURE 4-38 The "visual cliff" apparatus is a table with one half covered by a patterned surface. The other half is made of glass, and the patterned surface is dropped down to the floor. A baby is placed on the patterned side, and its mother attempts to coax the baby to crawl over the glass top to reach her.

FIGURE 4-39 When faces are viewed in an unusual orientation (two top images), they look similar. When viewed right side up, our experience allows us to readily detect the alterations in the left hand image.

Müller-Lyer illusion Two lines of the same length appear to be different if one has inward "arrowhead" extensions compared to outward extensions.

face recognition may be built into the development of perception. In addition, our experience seeing specific faces and similarities among those faces can lead to difficulties in detecting specific kinds of differences among faces. Many studies have shown an "own race" bias in which people are much more accurate in remembering faces of individuals from their own racial group (Meissner & Brigham, 2001). Presumably, greater familiarity with individual faces within your family and ethnic group (called kinship) makes it easier to recognize the subtle variations in new faces.

Culture

Because perception is informed by our experience, culture also plays a role in altering our perception. One example from anthropologist Colin Turnbull (1961) describes a man from the BaMbuti pygmy people, Kenge, whose life experience was limited to densely forested settings. For someone growing up in a rainforest, a view with a very distant horizon perspective would be rare. Turnbull describes taking Kenge from the rainforest to a savanna, where for the first time he viewed a wide plain with very distant objects, such as trees FIGURE 4-41. One of the objects was a large buffalo that was completely unfamiliar to him. Kenge referred to the buffaloes as "insects." To him, their small size on the retina was a cue about their physical size. Because he had no experience with the animal or this depth of perspective, he was unable to interpret the large animal in the distance as different from closer, small insects. This example suggests that the way we interpret objects and scenes depends heavily on our experience within those environments.

Research in anthropology suggests that some perceptual illusions may arise from our experiences with the world and are therefore potentially different among different cultures. The **Müller-Lyer illusion** is experienced by people in Western cultures as the appearance of the "arrowhead" line as shorter than the same line with outward ends FIGURE 4-42. But where does this illusion come from? One theory is

FIGURE 4-40 We readily notice facial images even where unexpected.

FIGURE 4-41 The long distance perspective of a savanna (left) provides many different depth cues than the shorter views in the rain forest (right).

FIGURE 4-42 The Müeller-Lyer figure embedded in the "carpentered world," where the angles adjacent to the vertical line provide information about its distance from the viewer. In contrast, experience with alternative architecture, such as this Zulu kraal, would not provide the same visual experiences.

that these figures suggest depth by perspective, representing familiar lines seen in the world that correspond to depth (Nijhawan, 1991). So the "arrowhead" lines suggest the vertical line is nearer to the viewer, while the open-ended line suggests the vertical line is at a greater distance. Early research suggested that those in environments without these "carpentered world" characteristics would not necessarily see the same meaning in the lines. People from non-Western cultures were found to be less susceptible to the Müller-Lyer illusion (Segall et al., 1966). Perhaps experience with straight lines, rectangular rooms, and right angles is required to develop this organizing principle in perception. The **Ponzo illusion** also relies on the linear perspective cue to judge the distance of objects FIGURE 4-43. Even though all three figures are the same size, the one furthest to the right appears larger because the linear perspective cue makes it appear farther away. Because it relies on constructed lines in the world, this illusion is strongest in Western cultures (Leibowitz et al., 1969).

Comparing people with East Asian and Western cultural backgrounds has revealed other differences in interpretations of images. When asked to describe a simple scene of fish swimming in a tank, Japanese students were much more likely to include descriptions of the context information, while American students described the more salient, focal objects first FIGURE 4-44. Overall, Japanese made 65 percent more observations about the background than did Americans (Masuda & Nisbett, 2001). Cultural experiences may include how information is attended to and processed, resulting in differences in how we see the world based on the social and physical world in which we live.

Ponzo illusion The misjudgment based on linear perspective that identical objects placed within converging lines appears to be of different sizes.

FIGURE 4-43 How do the three men compare? If you perceive the top as bigger than the bottom, you are subject to the Ponzo Illusion, because all three cast the same size image on the retina. The linear perspective cue makes it seem as though the top figure is farther away, and thus it is perceived as larger.

FIGURE 4-44 After viewing a short video of fish moving in a tank, people were asked to describe what they saw. American and Japanese participants differed in what they emphasized in their reports, and how much attention they paid to the background context.

All instances of perception involve the interpretation of the incoming sensory information based on our experiences, cultural definitions, and recent perceptual processing. Perceptual habits develop over time so that the ways we structure our sensations reflect our life history (Gibson, 1992). Further, our beliefs about what we *expect* to perceive play a critical role in matching the incoming sensations to our perceptions. Think back to the story at the beginning of the chapter: My expectations about professors did not yet include an individual like the one I encountered on the sidewalk. Examples like this illustrate that our perception depends heavily on the interaction of the external sensation and the top-down perceptual expectations we bring to bear on our experiences.

CONCEPT LEARNING CHECK 4.5 | *The Role of Experience in Perception*

1. Imagine that you were raised in a rainforest environment. The vegetation is very dense, little light reaches the ground, and the coloration of plants and animals is vivid. Now, imagine you are transplanted at your current age to Greenland, an open plain with little vegetation ringed with jagged cliffs. Based on your experience, what specific perceptual cues would be more difficult to make use of in your new home?

4.6 The Role of Attention

Sensation and perception depend on our choices about what available information to attend to given the limits of our capacity for attention.

■ Describe how attention enhances and limits perception.

To further understand our perceptions, we return to the idea that all of the information available in the physical world—what's "out there"—is not necessarily included in the internal representation created in the mind—what's "in here." **Attention** involves awareness of the sensations and perceptions that are a focus of thinking at any given time. When we miss information in the world that could be detected, it reveals more about how normal perceptual processing takes place.

Attention Awareness of the sensations and perceptions that are a focus of thinking at any given time.

Inattentional blindness Failing to process an object clearly present in a scene.

Selective Attention

A compelling demonstration of this phenomenon is provided by research on **inattentional blindness**. Imagine watching a video in which six people throw two basketballs to each other. Your job is to pay attention to the team of three people wearing black t-shirts and to count the number of passes that take place among them throughout the video. Most people focus on the team they are assigned to, and they closely monitor the number of passes that take place within the two-minute video. Now suppose that, midway through the video, someone in a gorilla suit enters the scene, stands in the middle of the picture, and pounds his chest. Surely anyone would notice something so unusual! However, most of the subjects in the study did not notice the gorilla shown in FIGURE 4-45. For those counting the passes, more than 70 percent completely missed the presence of the gorilla in the midst of this

FIGURE 4-45 Three frames from the opaque "gorilla" event in the selective-looking paradigm. The unexpected object (a person in a gorilla suit) was visible for 5 seconds as it traversed the visual scene.

scene (Simons & Chabris, 1999). When not told to count passes, everyone watching the video readily detects the presence of the gorilla. This study demonstrates that what appears in front of us is not necessarily what appears in our perception of the world. Rather, our impressions of the world around us are caused by our attention to sensory information as well as the perceptual principles we use to process sensations in the physical world.

We have the ability to focus on some information while ignoring other stimuli. Our attention to external stimulation is selective, meaning we do not simultaneously attend to all of the stimuli occurring around us (Lavie & Tsal, 1994). In **selective attention**, you choose to perceive only what's currently relevant to you (Johnston & Dark, 1986). For example, you listen to your friend's voice in a crowded restaurant, ignoring the many other sounds present. Selective attention narrows your awareness to particular sensations, at the same time leaving you unaware of others. Your perception depends both on what sensory information is present around you and which stimuli you decide to attend to and which you decide to ignore (Simons & Levin, 1998).

The fact that we often miss very obvious external stimuli may lead to some concerns about our abilities to process needed information. Why don't we simply process all of the information our sensory receptors capture? The reason is that our capacity for processing sensory information is limited. Only so much information can be processed at one time. It is as if we have a "gatekeeper" to control the flow of information over time (Broadbent, 1958). Therefore, we sometimes experience **change blindness**, in which some features of a scene change (such as a car pulling in front of you), but you fail to notice because you are not attending to that information. Even though real objects are there in the environment, we may sometimes completely miss them because we choose not to pay attention (Galpin, Underwood, & Chapman, 2008).

At the same time, we may be unable to resist processing some information despite our intention to ignore it. When experienced readers look at a familiar word, they process its name and meaning automatically. It is very difficult to look at a word and not think about its name, even when doing so interferes with a task. In a classic study, Stroop (1935) demonstrated this by asking people to look at a series of words and report only the color of the ink for each FIGURE 4-46. Most people cannot completely ignore the words and simply name the colors, even when we try to suppress this well-practiced skill of reading. Somtimes, automatic processes break through our attempts to control attention.

However, most often, we can decide to select and focus our attention on specific aspects of the world around us. Doing so allows us to process some information deeply and to use our cognitive resources to our best advantage. It also means that we may miss important information even when it's right in front of us. As we've seen, some aspects of our environment seem to demand our attention, especially when their use is well practiced. The result is that we are not always in control of whether important information in our environment becomes part of our perception of the world.

Divided Attention

What happens to those sensations that are not given attention? It appears they are not "turned off" but continue to receive some level of processing. For example, if you are

Selective attention Intentionally attending to one specific task.

Change blindness A change occurs between two viewings of a scene, but it is not noticed.

Blue Red Yellow **Green** **Orange** Purple

Yellow **Blue** Orange **Blue** **Purple** Red

Red Green Purple Yellow Blue **Orange**

Purple Red **Green** **Blue** Yellow Purple

FIGURE 4-46 Try to say the name of the color of ink only, as quickly as you can, for each of the words in the figure. You will find it difficult to ignore what the words say.

Cocktail party phenomenon
Hearing your name mentioned despite not attending to its source.

Divided attention The process of attending to two or more tasks to perform them at the same time.

listening to a conversation at a party, you may be aware of a nearby conversation but not of its content. Then, when someone in the other group mentions your name, your attention is immediately and automatically drawn to that conversation, referred to as the **cocktail party phenomenon** (Cherry, 1953; Moray, 1970). So if the unattended information is being filtered out at some level, it must occur after the sounds have been identified as words.

But how do we sort out one message from several others? And when do we become overloaded by incoming information? People often report that they are quite good at doing two things at once, such as listening to music while studying or having a conversation while watching a movie. When you try to do two things at once—say, driving while talking on a cell phone—you are juggling two different sources of sensory input at the same time. **Divided attention** is the process of attending to two or more tasks to perform them at the same time (Pashler, 1998). Coordinating senses often works well; however, when you must react suddenly to changes in sensation, your response time is slowed if you are trying to follow two sources of sensory input. For example, people in driving simulators showed slower reactions to brake lights and stop signs when talking on cell phones (Strayer et al., 2003).

An active task like a cell phone conversation detracted from driving performance, while a passive task like listening to the radio did not. Using a phone—hands free or not—resulted in dangerous delays in driving responses. One study estimated that using a cell phone while driving makes an accident four times more likely (McEvoy et al., 2005). A University of Utah study found motorists who talk on cell phones while driving are as impaired as drunken drivers with blood-alcohol levels at the legal limit of 0.08 percent (Strayer et al., 2006). Dividing attention between tasks is sometimes possible, but not when one of the tasks requires full attention in order to respond to important changes (Levy & Pashler, 2008). Studies show that, while practice improves performance, it is simply not as good as undivided attention (Wickens et al., 1983).

Summary of Multiple Influences on Sensation and Perception

Our minds direct our perception, piecing together information, filling in missing pieces, and looking for confirming evidence that gives us our psychological sense of constancy in the world. These top-down processes work to provide organization for the incoming bottom-up information arriving from the sensory organs.

Multiple influences contribute to our sensations and perceptual processes. We share many biological features of our sensory organs with other animals. However, we differ from them, and even from other mammals, in our use of these organs; for example, we are much less likely to use our sense of smell to recognize others. Human evolution presumably led to our greater emphasis on visual and auditory processing. Biological influences have created specific sensory receptors capable of transducing different forms of physical energy (e.g., light waves, odor molecules) into neural impulses. Similarly, areas of the brain in the cortex have specialized to process sensory information, such as visual information in the occipital lobe and auditory information in the temporal lobe. However, the environment we experience also plays an important role in sensation and perception. We recognize objects and sensations through our familiarity with them, and choose to attend to them or ignore them. Our experiences provide key principles to help us organize the chaotic information coming from our senses into patterns we recognize. And interpreting these patterns often depends on the special, formative social and cultural experiences that shape our understanding of the external world.

Our minds make sense of what is "out there" in the world to produce our internal psychological experience. Said another way, we tend to "see what we believe" rather than "believe what we see." As Albert Einstein said, "Reality is merely an illusion, albeit a very persistent one."

CONCEPT LEARNING CHECK 4.6   *The Role of Attention in Perception*

1. Design a cell phone system that would be safe to use while driving. How would you use the principles of attention to help organize the incoming and outgoing information?

Visual Overview Transduction from Physical Energy to Neural Signals

Each of the sensory organs—eye, ear, nose, mouth, and skin—has a unique receptor for transforming a form of physical energy (e.g., light and sound waves, chemical molecules, pressure and temperature) into a neural code that is interpreted in specific areas within the cortex.

Touch

Vision Hearing Taste

Smell

Pacinian Corpuscle

Light

Retina

Olfactory Bulb

Taste Bud

Basilar Membrane

4.1 The Interaction of Sensation and Perception

- We actively create our understanding of the external world around us.
- Sensations result from the stimulation of a sense organ by a stimulus.
- Perception makes use of expectations based on experiences in memory.
- Sensation occurs through bottom-up processing of incoming information,

while perception organizes sensations into patterns through top-down processing.
- Sensations and perceptual processes interact to create a meaningful interpretation.
- Perceptual set occurs when recent processing guides continuing perception.

4.2 Sensory Principles

- Our sensory organs share common principles of operation, but each has its own specialized receptor cells to encode stimulus intensity and quality.
- Transduction is the process through which physical energy in the world is translated into neural firing.

- Signal detection theory helps to measure the sensitivity of the senses, called absolute and difference thresholds.
- Some sensation is registered subliminally, without conscious awareness.
- Sensory adaptation occurs quickly when the same stimulation is present over time.

4.3 The Five Major Senses

- The five major sources of external sensations are the eye, ear, nose, mouth, and skin; internal sources include vestibular and kinesthetic senses.
- The sense of vision occurs through the retina, a layer of rod and cone nerve cells lining the back wall of the eye that registers the wavelengths of light.
- Feature detector cells in the visual cortex of the brain pick out patterns and piece them together to recognize objects.
- Color vision is based on a trichromatic theory of red, blue, and green color detectors, and on opponent process theory in which opposing colors are tied together in processing by complex cells.
- The sense of hearing registers sound waves originating from the vibrations of an object.
- Hair cell receptors detect vibrations in the ear's basilar membrane, and recognition of sounds depends on the location and frequency of vibrations.

- Taste and smell involve the detection of chemical molecules in water or air, and they work together in a process called sensory interaction.
- Smell receptors located at the top of the nasal cavity lead into the olfactory bulb and are adept at recognizing individual biochemical odors called pheromones.
- Taste buds are neural receptors located mostly on the tongue's visible bumps called papillae.
- The sense of touch occurs through Pacinian corpuscle receptors located in the fatty layer beneath the skin surface.
- The perception of pain depends on sensory receptors as well as on other psychological influences.
- Information detected without a known sensory source is called extrasensory perception (ESP).

4.4 Perception Organizes Sensations

- Perceptual processes organize incoming sensations into recognizable patterns through a variety of principles.
- We recognize objects by piecing together forms and patterns of distinctive features.
- The whole ("Gestalt") that emerges is more than simply "the sum of its parts."
- In every image, we determine what aspects represent the figure of interest vs. the background.
- Organizing pieces into images is aided by the laws of perceptual grouping, including similarity, proximity, continuity, and closure.
- Depth perception is important to perception because it helps us decide how far away objects are in the world.

- Binocular cues depend on two eyes and include retinal disparity and convergence.
- Most often, we judge distance from monocular cues that are available to a single eye, including linear perspective, relative height, interposition, texture gradient, shading, atmospheric perspective, relative size, and accommodation.
- Perception of motion involves cues including motion parallax and the kinetic depth effect.
- Perceptual constancy is the assumption that real objects don't change their shape, size, brightness, or color despite changes in how they appear to our senses.

4.5 Experience and Perception

- Biology determines the sensations we can detect, and inborn tendencies to detect depth and faces may exist.
- Perception can be altered by culture, context of processing, and experience.

- Cultural differences in perceptions have been demonstrated with illusions related to a "constructed world."

Blue Red Yellow **Green** Orange Purple

Yellow **Blue** Orange **Blue Purple** Red

Red Green Purple Yellow Blue **Orange**

Purple Red **Green Blue** Yellow Purple

4.6 The Role of Attention

- Our perception is affected by what we choose to attend to and the limits to our attentional capacity.
- Inattentional blindness results from ignoring stimuli, and change blindness occurs when we fail to notice changing features in a scene.
- Selective attention allows us to choose to perceive only what's currently relevant.

- The cocktail party phenomenon shows some sensations may be processed even without attention.
- We are limited in our ability to divide attention across different sources of sensory input or tasks at the same time.

4.1 The Interaction of Sensation and Perception

1. Your ability to sing along in time with your favorite song on the radio relies on:
 A. perceptual constancy.
 B. top-down processing.
 C. auditory pitch.
 D. absolute thresholds.

2. When getting up at night to use the bathroom, you can navigate in the dark hallway and return without running into any obstacles by using your memory of the rooms. This is an example of:
 A. top-down processing.
 B. bottom-up processing.
 C. perceptual constancy.
 D. absolute threshold.

3. When perceiving our surroundings, we use both top-down and bottom-up processes to make sense of the stimuli. But we rely even more on top-down processing when we find ourselves in _____ contexts.
 A. familiar
 B. unfamiliar
 C. perceptual
 D. artistic

4.2 Sensory Principles

4. Sonja put on a new watch this morning and found it uncomfortable because it was so heavy. However, later, when a friend asked her what time it was, she forgot she was even wearing a watch. This change in sensitivity is known as:
 A. perceptual constancy.
 B. sensory adaptation.
 C. absolute threshold.
 D. just noticeable difference.

5. The smallest difference between two sounds that you can reliably detect (at least half the time) is called the:
 A. absolute threshold.
 B. just noticeable difference.
 C. signal detection.
 D. transduction.

4.3 The Five Major Senses

6. The retina can detect color images with red, blue, and green detector cells called:
 A. cones.
 B. rods.
 C. feature detectors.
 D. ganglions.

7. Each of the five main external senses travels from the sensory organ through the sensory relay station in the brain, the thalamus, and then on to cortical areas, except for:
 A. vision.
 B. hearing.
 C. smell.
 D. touch.

8. Eric has been wearing yellow welding goggles for the past 30 minutes. Based on the opponent-process theory of color vision, when Eric takes off the goggles, he should expect that white objects may temporarily appear to be:
 A. more distant.
 B. less distant.
 C. blue.
 D. green.

4.4 Perception Organizes Sensations

9. The sand at Jason's feet appeared coarse, and he could see the individual grains of sand. However, the sand farther down the beach appeared to be a smooth, tan surface. This apparent difference provides the depth cue of:
 A. light and shadow.
 B. interposition.
 C. texture gradient.
 D. relative size.

10. One binocular visual cue that provides information about how far away something is called:
 A. linear perspective.
 B. interposition.
 C. convergence.
 D. relative size.

11. An oil painting itself can include all of the following cues to depth perception except:
 A. linear perspective.
 B. retinal disparity.
 C. texture gradient.
 D. relative image size.

4.5 Experience and Perception

12. When viewing a complex scene, students from East Asian cultures tended to describe _____ more than those from Western cultures.
  A. the focal figure
  B. carpentered figures
  C. binocular cues
  D. the background context

13. The Müller-Lyer illusion may be interpreted differently by some people based on their:
  A. experience with constructed corners.
  B. artwork.
  C. reading.
  D. perceptual set.

4.6 The Role of Attention

14. People feel able to divide attention between highly practiced, automatic tasks, like reading or driving, and more demanding tasks, like conversation. A recent study of motorists in accidents found:
  A. the accident rate was higher when on the phone.
  B. the accident rate was the same for callers and noncallers.
  C. the accident rate was higher for callers but not those with speakerphones.
  D. the accident rate was lower for those on the phone.

15. Failing to notice the sudden disappearance of an object within a scene is a phenomenon known as:
  A. change blindness.
  B. perceptual set.
  C. selective attention.
  D. divided attention.

CHAPTER DISCUSSION QUESTIONS

1. A surprising fact about human perception is that top-down processes can change how we understand external sources of sensation. Why do you think top-down processes are so important? What advantages and disadvantages does it provide?

2. If you had to live without one of your senses, which one might you choose, and why? How would the lack of that sense affect your everyday life? How might your other senses begin to compensate for the loss?

3. Think of a perceptual illusion you have experienced. What caused the illusion? What does it suggest about how our perceptual processes normally operate?

4. What differences in perception may arise from differences in cultural perspectives? How do culture and experience play roles in sensation and perception? Think of specific examples of how top-down processing may result in two people having different perceptions.

5. Eyewitnesses are often called upon to testify about specific elements of their experiences, such as whether a door was open when they arrived at home or what color shirt a person was wearing. Based on what you read about attention, what kinds of information do you think eyewitnesses will be *inaccurate* about?

CHAPTER PROJECTS

1. Try to experience limited or altered sensation in one of your sensory organs. For example, wear a thick pair of work gloves, smear Vaseline on a pair of sunglasses, or wear earplugs. See if you can describe the specific problems that arise from your changed sensory processes. What evidence do you find about how other senses make up for the lost sensation?

2. Watch the movie *Rashomon* (1950) by Akira Kurosawa. The film depicts the assault of a woman and her samurai husband through the mutually contradictory accounts of four people. It was remade as a Western, *The Outrage* (1964), and has influenced a variety of subsequent films, such as *Hero*, *Vantage Point*, *Courage Under Fire*, *Basic Instinct*, and *One Night at McCool's*. How is the difference between sensation and perception illustrated by differences in how people perceive the same external event?

CHAPTER KEY TERMS

Absolute threshold	**Bipolar cells**	**Colorblindness**
Accommodation	**Blind spot**	**Cone cells**
Afterimage	**Bottom-up processing**	**Constancy**
Ames room	**Change blindness**	**Convergence**
Attention	**Chemical senses**	**Dark adaptation**
Basilar membrane	**Cochlea**	**Depth perception**
Binocular cues	**Cocktail party phenomenon**	**Difference threshold**

Distinctive features
Divided attention
Extrasensory perception
  (ESP or psi)
Feature detectors
Fovea
Frequency
Frequency theory
Ganglion cells
Gate-control theory
Geon
Gestalt
Gustatory
Hair cell receptors
Illusion
Impossible figure
Inattentional blindness
Isomorphic
Just noticeable difference (jnd)
Kinetic depth effect

Laws of perceptual grouping
Monocular cues
Motion parallax
Müller-Lyer illusion
Olfaction
Olfactory bulb
Opponent process theory
Optic chiasm
Optic nerve
Oval window
Pacinian corpuscles
Papillae
Parallel processing
Parapsychology
Perception
Perceptual set
Pheromone
Phi phenomenon
Photoreceptors
Placebo effect

Place theory
Ponzo illusion
Retina
Retinal disparity
Reversible figure
Rod cells
Selective attention
Sensation
Sensory adaptation
Sensory receptor
Signal detection theory
Stimulus
Subliminal perception
Top-down processing
Transduction
Trichromatic theory
Wavelength
Weber's Law

ANSWERS TO CONCEPT LEARNING CHECKS

4.1 Comparing Top-Down and Bottom-Up Processing

A. Reading a book. [Bottom-up: Piecing together lines to recognize letters; top-down: Anticipating the next word.]

B. Walking down the street and recognizing a friend. [Bottom-up: Identifying the features of a face; top-down: Looking for that friend in the crowd.]

C. Listening to a new song. [Bottom-up: Piecing together tones to recognize melody; top-down: Anticipating the next lyric.]

D. Being tapped on the shoulder when you didn't notice anyone behind you. [Bottom-up: Feeling pressure on your skin at the shoulder; top-down: Recognizing someone wants your attention.]

E. Taking the first spoonful of your favorite food into your mouth. [Bottom-up: Processing the taste spreading on your tongue; top-down: Anticipating what the taste will be.]

4.2 Testing Sensory Thresholds

1. For absolute threshold, you might begin by tasting a sample of 1 ounce of water with no sugar added; then, a sample with one grain of sugar added, then two, and so on until you notice a sweet taste in the water. For difference thresholds, compare the difference between two samples in the series. Does a sample with one more grain taste sweeter to you? Once the water solution is already sweet (contains many grains), adding one more grain to the sample might not make it noticeably sweeter.

4.3 Methods of Sensory Transduction

1. Movement of a tiny hair cell on a membrane. [Hearing]

2. Fitting of a chemical molecule into a specific site. [Smell]

3. Breakdown of pigment after exposure to light. [Vision]

4. Compression of a receptor's shape. [Touch]

5. Dissolved chemicals matching one of five qualities. [Taste]

4.4 Perceptual Organization Principles

1. C [texture gradient]

2. B [retinal disparity]

3. D [kinetic depth]

4. A [proximity]

5. E [shape constancy]

6. C [interposition]

7. D [kinetic depth]

8. E [size constancy]

9. E [brightness constancy]

10. A [continuity]

4.5 The Role of Experience in Perception

1. Living in a dense rainforest would provide little experience with some visual depth cues due to the limited distance you can view. These cues include atmospheric perspective, linear perspective, relative height, relative size, and texture gradient. Once in Greenland, the newness of the open sky perspective would make it harder to make use of the available distance cues.

4.6 The Role of Attention in Perception

1. From studies, we know that talking on a cell phone can compete with responding to visual cues while driving. One solution might be to add tactile or touch alarms to grab attention from drivers when needed. The rumble strips on highways before tollbooths act as an attentional cue using a different physical modality (the sensations of movement produced when the car tires roll over studded cement strips).

4.1 **The Interaction of Sensation and Perception**

1. B. Rationale: Singing along requires anticipating what stimulus is going to occur next. This requires top-down processing using expectations about what you will perceive.

2. A. Rationale: Navigating from memory involves using your expectations about where objects are, a top-down process, rather than your sensations arising from the actual objects.

3. A. Rationale: Because top-down processing involves expectations from memory, they are made possible by what we already know: the familiar.

4.2 **Sensory Principles**

4. B. Rationale: The sensations arising from the pressure of the watch on the skin are quickly adapted to by our sensory processing so that the same stimulus over time stops receiving attention, known as sensory adaptation.

5. B. Rationale: The just noticeable difference is defined as the ability to notice a difference between two similar stimuli at least half of the time.

4.3 **The Five Major Senses**

6. A. Rationale: The cones are the receptor cells in the retina that respond to these three color wavelengths.

7. C. Rationale: Smell is a unique sense in that more of its perceptual processing takes place in the sense organ and in the limbic system rather than in the cortex.

8. C. Rationale: The opponent process theory states that some cells process the presence of opposing colors, blue or yellow and red or green, resulting in afterimages of the opposing color.

4.4 **Perception Organizes Sensations**

9. C. Rationale: The fine detail of texture that can be detected nearby fades to a more smooth appearance on surfaces farther away.

10. C. Rationale: The only binocular cue (requiring two eyes) is convergence, the muscle movements that coordinate focus on nearby objects.

11. B. Rationale: Retinal disparity is a binocular cue in which the images on the two retinas are slightly different, and unlike the other cues, this cannot be depicted in a two-dimensional image like a painting.

4.5 **Experience and Perception**

12. D. Rationale: Cultural experiences may include how information is attended to and processed, resulting in differences in how we see the world based on the social and physical world in which we live.

13. A. Rationale: Studies show people are more likely to experience this illusion if they have experience viewing the right angles of constructed rooms.

4.6 **The Role of Attention**

14. A. Rationale: Dividing attention by talking on the phone while driving showed problems regardless of whether the mode was hands free.

15. A. Rationale: The study involved showing two scenes that were identical except for a missing object. This type of change blindness may be caused by divided or selective attention.

REFERENCES

Abramov, I., & Gordon, J. (1994). Color appearance: On seeing red, or yellow, or green, or blue. *Annual Review of Psychology, 45,* 451–485.

Amoore, J. E., Johnston, J. W., & Rubin, M. (1964). The stereochemical theory of odor. *Scientific American, 210,* 42–49.

Backus, B. T., & Oruc, I. (2005). Illusory motion from change over time in the response to contrast and luminance. *Journal of Vision, 5*(11), 1055–1069.

Bartoshuk, L. M. (1993). The biological basis of food perception and acceptance. *Food Quality and Preference, 4,* 21–32.

Bartoshuk, L. M. (2000). Comparing sensory experiences across individuals: Recent psychophysical advances illuminate genetic variation in taste perception. *Chemical Senses, 25,* 447–460.

Bekesy, G. V. (1947). The variation of phase along the basilar membrane with sinusoidal vibration. *Journal of the Acoustical Society of America, 19,* 452–460.

Bem, D. J. (2011). Feeling the future: Experimental evidence for anomalous retroactive influences on cognition and affect. *Journal of Personality and Social Psychology, 100,* 407–425.

Bem, D. J., & Honorton, C. (1994). Does psi exist? Replicable evidence for an anomalous process of information transfer. *Psychological Bulletin, 115,* 4–18.

Biederman, I. (1987). Recognition-by-components: A theory of human image understanding. *Psychological Review, 94,* 115–147.

Bowmaker, J. K., & Dartnall, H. J. (1980). Visual pigments of rods and cones in a human retina. *Journal of Physiology, 298,* 501–511.

Broadbent, D. E. (1958). *Perception and communication.* London: Pergamon Press.

Buck, L., & Axel, R. (1991). A novel multigene family may encode odorant receptors: A molecular basis for odor recognition. *Cell, 65,* 175–181.

Burton, H., & Sinclair, R. (1996). Somatosensory cortex and tactile perceptions. In L. Kruger (Ed.), *Pain and touch* (pp. 105–177). San Diego: Academic Press.

Campos, J. J., Langer, A., & Krowitz, A. (1970). Cardiac responses on the visual cliff in prelocomotor infants. *Science, 170,* 196–197.

Casey, K. L., Zumberg, M., Heslep, H., & Morrow, T. J. (1993). Afferent modulation of warmth sensation and heat pain in the human hand. *Somatosensory and Motor Research, 10,* 327–337.

CBS News. (2002, April 28). Poll: Most believe in psychic phenomena. CBSNEWS.com.

Cherry, E. C. (1953). Some experiments on the recognition of speech, with one and two ears. *Journal of the Acoustical Association, 25,* 975–979.

Chu, S., & Downes, J. J. (2000). Odour-evoked autobiographical memories: Psychological investigations of Proustian phenomena. *Chemical Senses, 25,* 111–116.

Craig, J. C., Reiman, E. M., Evans, A., & Bushnell, M. C. (1996). Functional imaging of an illusion of pain. *Nature, 384,* 258–260.

Cumming, B. G., & DeAngelis, G. C. (2001). The physiology of stereopsis. *Annual Review of Neuroscience, 24,* 203–238.

Eisenberger, N. I., Lieberman, M. D., & Williams, K. D. (2003). Does rejection hurt? An fMRI study of social exclusion. *Science, 302*(5643), 290–292.

Fisher, G. H. (1968). Ambiguity of form: Old and new. *Perception and Psychophysics, 4,* 189–192.

Galanter, E. (1962). Contemporary psychophysics. In R. Brown, E. Galanter, H. Hess, & G. Mandler (Eds.), *New directions in psychology.* New York: Holt, Rinehart, & Winston.

Galpin, A., Underwood, G., & Chapman, P. (2008). Sensing without seeing in comparative visual search. *Consciousness and Cognition, 17,* 672–687,

Gibson, E. J. (1988). Exploratory behavior in the development of perceiving, acting and the acquiring of knowledge. *Annual Review of Psychology, 39,* 1–41.

Gibson, E. J. (1992). How to think about perceptual learning: Twenty-five years later. In H. L. Pick, P. van den Broek, & D. C. Knill (Eds.), *Cognition: Conceptual and methodological issues* (pp. 215-237). Washington, DC: American Psychological Association.

Gibson, E. J., & Walk, R. D. (1960, April). The "visual cliff." *Scientific American,* 153–154.

Green, D. M., & Swets, J. A. (1966). *Signal detection theory and psychophysics.* New York: Wiley.

Greenwald, A. G., Spangenberg, E. R., Pratkanis, A. R., & Eskenaz, J. (1991). Double-blind tests of subliminal self-help audiotapes. *Psychological Science, 2*(2), 119–122.

Harris, C. R., & Christenfeld, N. (1999). Can a machine tickle? *Psychonomic Bulletin & Review, 6,* 504–510.

Hess, R. F., & Hayes, A. (1993). Neural recruitment explains "Weber's law" of spatial position. *Vision Research, 33,* 1673–1684.

Hubel, D. H. (1996). A big step along the visual pathway. *Nature, 380,* 197–198.

Hubel, D. H., & Weisel, T. (1962). Receptive fields, binocular interaction and functional architecture in the cat's visual cortex. *Journal of Physiology, 160,* 106–154.

Johansson, G. (1973). Visual perception of biological motion and a model of its analysis. *Perception and Psychophysics, 14,* 201–211.

Johnston, W. A., & Dark, V. J. (1986). Selective attention. *Annual Review of Psychology, 37,* 43–75.

Kahneman, D., Fredrickson, B. L., Schreiber, C. A., & Redelmeier, D. A. (1993). When more pain is preferred to less: Adding a better end. *Psychological Science, 4,* 401–405.

Knight, D. C. (1960). *The first book of sound: A basic guide to the science of acoustics.* New York: Franklin Watts.

Koelega, H. S. (1994). Sex differences in olfactory sensitivity and the problem of the generality of smell acuity. *Perceptual and Motor Skills, 78,* 203–213.

Kryter, K. D. (1994). *The handbook of hearing and the effects of noise.* San Diego: Academic Press.

Land, M. F., & Fernald, R. D. (1992). The evolution of eyes. *Annual Review of Neuroscience, 15,* 1–29.

Lavie, N., & Tsal, Y. (1994). Perceptual load as a major determinant of the locus of selection in visual attention. *Perception and Psychophysics, 56,* 183–197.

Le Grand, R., Mondloch, C. J., Maurer, D., & Brent, H. P. (2010). Impairment in holistic face processing following early visual deprivation. *Psychological Science, 15*(11), 762–768.

Leibowitz, H. W., Birslin, R., Perlmutter, L., & Hennessy, R. (1969). Ponzo perspective illusion as a manifestation of space perception. *Science, 166,* 1174–1176.

Levine, J. D., Gordon, N. C., Smith, R., & Fields, H. L. (1981). Analgesic responses to morphine and placebo in individuals with postoperative pain. *Pain, 10*(3), 379–389.

Levy, J., & Pashler, H. (2008). Task prioritization in multitasking during driving: Opportunity to abort a concurrent task does not insulate braking responses from dual-task slowing. *Applied Cognitive Psychology, 22,* 507–525.

Lyons, L. (2005). Paranormal beliefs come (super) naturally to some. *Gallup News,* November 1.

Martinez-Conde, S., Macknik, S. L., & Hubel, D. H. (2004). The role of fixational eye movements in visual perception. *Nature Reviews Neuroscience, 5*(3), 229–240.

McGurk, H., & MacDonald, J. (1976). Hearing lips and seeing voices. *Nature, 264*(5588), 746–748.

McEvoy, S. P., Stevenson, M. R., McCartt, A. T., Woodward, M., Haworth, C., Palamara, P., & Cercarelli, R. (2005). Role of mobile phones in motor vehicle crashes resulting in hospital attendance: A case-crossover study. *British Medical Journal, 331,* 428–433.

Masuda, T., & Nisbett, R. E. (2001). Attending holistically vs. analytically: Comparing the context sensitivity of Japanese and Americans. *Journal of Personality and Social Psychology, 81,* 922–934.

Meissner, C. A., Brigham J. C. (2001). Thirty years of investigating the own-race bias in memory for faces: A meta-analytic review. *Psychology, Public Policy, and Law, 7*(1), 3–35.

Melzack, R., & Wall, P. (1965). Pain mechanisms: A new theory. *Science, 150,* 971–979.

Moray, N. (1970). *Attention: Selective processes in vision and hearing.* New York: Academic Press.

Nijhawan, R. (1991). Three-dimensional Müeller-Lyer illusion. *Perception and Psychophysics, 49,* 333–341.

Palmer, S. E. (1999). *Vision science: Photons to phenomenology.* Cambridge, MA: MIT Press.

Pashler, H. (1998). The psychology of attention. Cambridge, MA: MIT Press.

Phillips, D. P., & Brugge, J. F. (1985). Progress in neurophysiology of sound localization. *Annual Review of Psychology, 36,* 245–274.

Pratkanis, A. R. (Spring 1992). The cargo-cult science of subliminal persuasion. *Skeptical Inquirer* (Committee for the Scientific Investigation of Claims of the Paranormal), 260–272.

Rawlinson, G. E. (1976). The significance of letter position in word recognition. Unpublished PhD Thesis, Psychology Department, University of Nottingham, Nottingham UK.

Redelmeier D. A., Katz, J., & Kahneman, D. (2003). Memories of colonoscopy: A randomized trial. *Pain, 104*(1–2), 187–194.

Rumelhart, D. E., McClelland, J. L., Hinton, G., & the PDP Research Group. (1986). *Parallel distributed processing: Vol. 1. Foundations.* Cambridge, MA: MIT Press.

Russell, M. J. (1976). Human olfactory communication. *Nature (London), 260,* 520–522.

Sagiv, N., & Robertson, L. C. (2005). *Synesthesia: Perspectives from cognitive neuroscience.* Oxford: Oxford University Press.

Segall, M. H., Campbell, D. T., & Herskovits, M. J. (1966). *The influence of culture on visual perception.* Indianapolis, IN: Bobbs-Merrill.

Simner, J., Mulvenna, C., Sagiv, N., Tsakanikos, E., Witherby, S. A., Fraser, C., Scott, K., & Ward, J. (2006). Synaesthesia: The prevalence of atypical cross-modal experiences. *Perception, 35*(8), 1024–1033.

Simons, D. J., & Chabris, C. E. (1999). Gorillas in our midst: Sustained inattentional blindness for dynamic events. *Perception, 28,* 1059–1074.

Simons, D. L., & Levin, D. T. (1998). Failure to detect changes to people in real world interaction. *Psychonomic Bulletin and Review, 5,* 644–649.

Sims, P. (2008). Aspiring chef dies hours after making ultra-hot sauce for chili-eating contest. Daily Mail Online, 29th September 2008. http://www.dailymail.co.uk/news/article-1063598/Aspiring-chef-dies-hours-making-ultra-hot-sauce-chilli-eating-contest.html.

Stern, K., & McClintock, M. K. (1998). Regulation of ovulation by human pheromones. *Nature, 392,* 177–179.

Strayer, D. L., Drews, F. A., & Crouch, D. J. (2006). Comparing the cell-phone driver and the drunk driver. *Human Factors, 48,* 381–391.

Strayer, D. L., Drews, F. A., & Johnston, W. A. (2003). Cell phone induced failures of visual attention during simulated driving. *Journal of Experimental Psychology: Applied, 9,* 23–52.

Stroop, J. R. (1935). Studies of interference in serial verbal reactions. *Journal of Experimental Psychology, 18,* 643–662.

Swets, J. A., & Bjork, R. A. (1990). Enhancing human performance: An evaluation of "new age" techniques considered by the U.S. Army. *Psychological Science, 1,* 85–96.

Tanaka, K. (1996). Inferotemporal cortex and object vision. *Annual Review of Neuroscience, 19,* 109–139.

Treede, R. D., Kenshalo, D. R., Gracely, R. H., & Jones, A. K. (1999). The cortical representation of pain. *Pain, 79*(2–3), 105–111.

Treisman, A. (1999). Feature binding, attention, and object perception. In G. W. Humphrys, J. Duncan, & A. Triesman (Eds.), *Attention, space, and action* (pp. 91–111). New York: Oxford University Press.

Turnbull, C. M. (1961). *The forest people: A study of the Pygmies of the Congo.* New York: Clarion.

Villemure, C., & Bushnell, M. C. (2002). Cognitive modulators of pain: How do attention and emotion influence pain processing? *Pain, 95,* 195–199.

Vimal, R. L. P., Pokorny, J., & Smith, V. C. (1987). Appearance of steadily viewed lights. *Vision Research, 27,* 1309–1318.

Vogel, I., Verschuure, H., van der Ploeg, C. P. B., Brug, J., & Raat, H. (2009). Adolescents and MP3 players: Too many risks, too few precautions. *Pediatrics, 123,* e953–e958.

Vokey, J. R., & Read, J. D. (1985). Subliminal messages: Between the devil and the media. *American Psychologist, 40*(11), 1231–1239.

Voss, J. L., & Paller, K. A. (2009). An electrophysiological signature of unconscious recognition memory. *Nature Neuroscience, 12,* 349–355.

Wallach, H., & O'Connell, D. N. (1953). The kinetic depth effect. *Journal of Experimental Psychology, 45*(4), 205–217.

Ward, J., & Simner, J. (2003). Lexical-gustatory synaesthesia: Linguistic and conceptual factors. *Cognition, 89*(3), 237–261.

Wehner, T., & Stadler, M. (1994). The cognitive organization of human errors: A Gestalt theory perspective. *Applied Psychology: An International Review, 43,* 565–584.

Wertheimer, M. (1912). Experimentelle Studien über das Sehen van Bewegung. *Zeitschrift für Psychologie, 60,* 321–378.

Wever, E. G. (1949). *Theory of hearing.* New York: Wiley.

Wickens, C. D., Kramer, A. F., Vanasse, L., & Donchin, E. (1983). Performance of concurrent tasks: A psycho-physiological assessment of the reciprocity of information-processing resources. *Science, 221,* 1080–1082.

Yamaguchi, S., & Ninomiya, K. (2000). Umami and food palatability. *Journal of Nutrition, 130*(4S Suppl.), 912S–962S.

Chapter Overview ▼

5 States of Consciousness

Learning Objectives ▼

5.1
- ■ Define consciousness.
- ■ Describe how consciousness relates to psychology.

5.2
- ■ Describe the changes in brain wave activity that occur during the different stages of sleep.
- ■ Understand why sleep deprivation is harmful.
- ■ Understand why deep sleep is important.
- ■ Understand why REM sleep is important.
- ■ Describe some common sleep disorders.

5.3
- ■ Describe the two main theories of dreams.

5.4
- ■ Explain the two theories of hypnosis.

5.5
- ■ Discuss the effects and benefits of meditation.

5.6
- ■ List and describe the four categories of psychoactive drugs.
- ■ Describe the effects of psychoactive drugs on the nervous system.

$\mathcal{E}$verything in the room was perfect: the temperature, a cool 68 degrees; silence—not a peep from anything except the purring of my two cats; darkness, no light anywhere, and comfy sheets and pillows. But there was still a problem, a big one. I couldn't sleep. More specifically, I couldn't quiet my mind. I kept thinking of all the things I had to do the next day. *Get those exams back to the students…lecture on Freud …where did I stop last time? Let me think, I was teaching, and then Freud came into class …wait, Freud was there? Oh, I must be asleep…wait …not anymore. Okay… what else?…I need to finish the chapter on sleep…sleep. That's what I should be doing. If I go to bed now…what time is it …1 a.m.? That will give me 5 hours of sleep. I'll have a terrible day tomorrow if I don't fall asleep now. Why am I not sleepy? I was so tired earlier in the day.*

If those ramblings sound familiar, you are in good company. More than half of us have a problem sleeping at least a few nights a week (Doghramji, 2006). And people do a lot to counter insomnia. We reach for sleeping remedies like melatonin, pillow-top mattresses, meditation, and self-hypnosis. But what *is* sleep? In this chapter, we will investigate sleep as well as other states of consciousness. We will look at how psychologists study states of consciousness and, finally, some techniques to help make sleep easier. In addition, you will learn why that PM capsule might not be the best remedy to coax the sandman your way.

5.1 Overview: Consciousness, Brain Activity, Levels of Awareness

Consciousness is a person's awareness of the internal and external environment at any given moment.

- Define consciousness.
- Describe how consciousness relates to psychology.

Consciousness A state of awareness of the internal and the external world.

Consciousness is our subjective state of awareness of our internal and external environment, experience, and reality. It's been a topic of interest for psychologists and philosophers for hundreds of years. In fact, a professor teaching psychology back in the late 1800s might have defined psychology as the study of consciousness. Since the focus of psychology was on internal and external awareness, psychology developed techniques and methods suited to gather data on things we notice. Since then, psychology has shifted from a primary focus on consciousness to a primary focus on behavior. But consciousness is still a major topic in psychology. This chapter addresses many of the current issues in states of consciousness as well as altered states of consciousness.

There are many facets of consciousness. Consciousness includes the state of awareness of your internal sensations. When you feel hungry, tired, or restless, you know how you feel because you are aware of your own sensations. In addition, consciousness includes your knowledge of your own thoughts and internal dialogue. You may think to yourself, "Oh I need to get shampoo" when at the grocery store or "Where did I put my cell phone?" in the morning as you get ready for your day. Consciousness also refers to your cognizance of yourself as a person separate from others. This state of self-awareness isn't something that many animals have, and it's an ability we are not born with. However once we are aware of ourselves as separate from others, it becomes part of our conscious experience. For example, you know that when you are hungry, this doesn't mean that other people are hungry too. Finally, consciousness includes your understanding of your external environment, including all your sensations and perceptions. Consciousness is subjective and internal; perhaps nothing is more so.

Your entire brain is involved in your consciousness. Neuroscientific imaging techniques including the **electroencephalogram (EEG)**, a device that measures and graphs the electrical activity in the brain, have been helpful in taking a peek into what's going on in your nervous system during different consciousness states.

Each moment of the day, you are under a constant sensory assault. Consciousness isn't all or nothing. Events and sensations can poke through awareness. One moment, you are diligently focused on reading; the next, you are in an internal deep debate on where you will go for a snack because you caught a whiff of a french fry-like aroma. Luckily, you have an ability to focus your thoughts and perceptions to filter out stimuli, known as **selective attention**. We are even good at ignoring things entirely, as in **inattentional blindness**, in which you narrow your awareness to particular sensations and become unaware of others, and **change blindness**, in which some features of a scene change between two views, but you fail to notice because you are not attending to that information.

You can integrate several sources of sensory input at the same time. Although your attention is divided, you can process all these sensations at the same time. The idea of **dual processing** suggests that you not only attend to but also manage the stimuli all at once— some automatically (out of consciousness) and some more intentionally in your awareness.

There are times when you are not fully aware of your consciousness. When you sleep, for example, you experience minimal consciousness. You are aware enough to pull up the blankets when you feel chilly or push them off when too warm. But when asleep, you are probably not the best conversationalist.

The methodological study of brain action linked to thought, perception, and language is called **cognitive neuroscience**. Those who study cognitive neuroscience are interested in the biological underpinnings of cognition. It brings together many fields such as psychology, psychiatry, and linguistics, to name a few.

Electroencephalogram (EEG) A device that measures and illustrates the electrical activity in the brain.

Selective attention The ability to focus thought or perception while filtering extraneous stimulation.

Inattentional blindness Failing to report an object clearly present in a scene.

Change blindness A change occurs between two viewings of a scene, but it is not noticed.

Dual processing The ability to attend to and manage several stimuli at once, some automatically (out of consciousness) and some intentionally in your awareness.

Cognitive neuroscience The methodological study of brain action linked to thought, perception, and language.

CONCEPT LEARNING CHECK 5.1 | *Consciousness and Psychology*

Indicate whether the statement is true or false.

1. The study of consciousness is relatively new in psychology.

2. Cognitive neuroscience studies brain action linked to thought, perception, and language.

3. Humans can usually only attend to one thing at a time.

4. An electroencephalogram can be used to study consciousness.

5. Consciousness is the state of awareness of only our external environment.

5.2 Sleep

During sleep, your brain and body progress through distinct stages.

- Describe the changes in brain wave activity that occur during the different stages of sleep.
- Understand why sleep deprivation is harmful.
- Understand why deep sleep is important.
- Understand why REM sleep is important.
- Describe some common sleep disorders.

We spend a third of our lives in a state of altered and minimal consciousness called sleep. However, despite sleep's universality, scientists understand surprisingly little about sleep and even less about dreams. We know that **sleep** is a state of minimal consciousness that is associated with reduced motor and sensory activity. But why do we sleep? What do our dreams mean, and what's the effect of sleeping too little or too much? Recent advances in technology have increased what we do understand about this mysterious state.

Although you seem restful, your brain is active and dynamic during sleep.

Sleep A natural loss of consciousness that is associated with reduced motor and sensory activity.

Circadian rhythm A biological process that occurs on a daily cycle.

Alpha waves A type of brain wave linked to relaxed wakefulness.

Stage 1 A phase of sleep between relaxed wakefulness and being asleep.

Theta An EEG pattern that is associated with relaxed wakefulness.

Sleep spindle A type of brain wave pattern associated with Stage 2 sleep and the consolidation of new memories.

K-complex An EEG waveform that is characteristic of Stage 2 sleep.

FIGURE 5-1 The EEG records distinctive patterns during sleep.

Delta waves A type of brain wave pattern linked to Stage 4 sleep.

Rapid eye movement (REM) sleep A period of sleep that is characterized by rapid eye movements and dreams.

Biological Rhythms and Stages of Sleep

Your body loves routines. For example, every day, your core body temperature will rise during the day and then start to fall, hitting the lowest point early in the morning. In fact, there are well over 100 human **circadian rhythms** (daily) that ebb and flow in a 24-hour period, many of which are controlled by the hypothalamus. One of the rhythms that we are most aware of is our daily sleep and wake cycle.

When most people think about sleep, they imagine that you slowly drift off to sleep, sleep deeply through the night, and then wake up in the morning. They imagine that the body and mind are resting all through the night. You wake refreshed and restored because your body was being renewed like a set of rechargeable batteries. Measuring the activity of the brain tells a different story entirely. When psychologists use an electroencephalogram (EEG), they discover an active and dynamic brain. In fact, your brain is very active during the night, and you career through four distinct realms of sleep with various levels of activity.

Truth is, you do *fall* asleep. You can go from being awake and relaxed and emitting **alpha waves** on the EEG to the first sleep stage, Stage 1, quite suddenly (I've seen it in my class). **Stage 1** is a phase between relaxed wakefulness and being asleep. You are calm, your muscles are loose, and your breathing and heart rate have slowed down. You may have strange and wandering thoughts, and your brain generates an EEG pattern called **theta**. Some people with insomnia may confuse this light sleep with wakefulness.

After a few minutes in Stage 1, you enter Stage 2. In Stage 2, the body is more relaxed, and it's harder for outside noises to wake you up. The brain emits **sleep spindles**, which are small bursts of brain activity, and **K-complexes** FIGURE 5-1 on the EEG. K-complex patterns have been associated with memory consolidation and inhibition of activity (Cash et al., 2009).

You spend about 45 minutes in Stage 2 before you enter an even deeper sleep—Stage 3 and Stage 4. During Stages 3 and 4, the EEG will show a new kind of pattern called **delta waves**. Delta waves are introduced in Stage 3 and become more prominent in Stage 4. Your breathing, blood pressure, heartbeat, and use of oxygen are at their lowest levels of the night, reflecting the rested state of your body. During deep sleep, loud noises such as city traffic or even a train won't rouse most people, and it can take some people up to 15 minutes to regain full consciousness from Stage 4 due to the lowered levels of oxygen in the brain.

Stage 4 is your deepest sleep, but you won't be there for long. After around 45 minutes in Stages 3 and 4, you go back to Stage 2. But this time instead of entering Stage 1, something is different. Your eyes dart back and forth under your closed eyelids. Anyone who is awakened at this point will report having a vivid dream. In addition, blood pressure, heartbeat, and respiration increase, and penile and clitoral arousal may occur. Although your motor cortex is hard at work, during these periods, the brain stem inhibits the signals that come out of it. Your brain waves, as measured by EEG, look a lot like they do when you are awake, but you're not. You've entered a mentally active but physically restful state of known as **rapid eye movement (REM) sleep**. REM sleep is a period of sleep that is characterized by darting eye movements and dreams. After a few minutes in this new type of sleep, you make your way back through the stages a second time. You work through the stages in about 90 minutes. Over a typical night of sleep, you'll have up to six of these cycles during the night.

But the cycles are all not the same. During the start of the night, your Stage 3 and 4 periods are very long, lasting up to an hour, and REM periods are short—only a few minutes. As the night goes on, your Stage 4 periods become shorter and shorter, diminishing altogether by the middle of the night. Your REM periods get longer and longer—up to an hour. This means you get most of your deep sleep at the beginning of your sleep cycle and most of your REM sleep near the end. Unfortunately, because your REM periods occur during lighter sleep, it's pretty normal to wake up after a particularly startling dream. In fact, most people wake up about a half dozen times or so during the night. You end up spending about 5% of the night in non-REM or **nREM sleep** Stage 1, 50% in Stage 2, 20% in deep Stages 3 and 4, and about 25% in REM sleep.

Outside factors can influence your sleep patterns, too. When light enters your eyes, it sends signals to the **suprachiasmatic nucleus**, a part of your hypothalamus that is involved in sleep and wakefulness. This causes the pineal gland to stop making **melatonin**, a hormone that promotes sleepiness, in the morning and to increase it in the afternoon. So too much nighttime light can disrupt this sleep regulatory system (Dement & Vaughan, 2000).

Knowing a bit about sleep stages will help you to understand how best to manage your sleep. Wake up from Stage 1 sleep and you might not even know you were asleep. The later stages, like Stage 3 or 4, are associated with a much deeper level of sleep. It's pretty hard for many people to wake up in the midst of Stage 4 sleep, and many who do wake up confused and disoriented. Think back to the last time you decided to take a nap. Did you set your alarm for about an hour? Did you wake up feeling worse than you did when you fell asleep? If you set your alarm for about an hour, you may have unintentionally set your alarm to wake you up in the middle of Stage 4 sleep, perhaps guaranteeing a grumpy welcome back into consciousness. What's the solution—a 3-hour nap? Probably not. When it comes to naps, more is not necessarily better. In fact, a quick 20-minute nap can increase your energy and restore a mood battered by a poor night's sleep the night before.

Sleep Theories

As you have read, we know quite a bit about the physiology of sleep, including the parts of the brain, the kind of brain waves that are associated with different phases, and the various systems associated with sleep. That being said, we know much less about why we sleep. The biopsychosocial and evolutionary models, however, may give insight into the mystery of why we sleep.

The **restorative theory of sleep**, for example, maintains that sleep is intended to regenerate your body. Research shows that Stage 3 and 4 sleep does appear to help restore various body processes (Jacobs, 2009). During deep sleep, blood is directed away from the brain to your muscles. This is great for your muscles, as it helps to repair and nourish them. The immune system is also more active during this stage, which might explain why you sleep more when you aren't feeling well. Since the brain is less active, it requires less blood. This might explain why you feel so dopey if you wake up during Stage 3 or 4 sleep.

The **adaptive theory of sleep** suggests that our sleep-wake patterns are shaped by an evolved biological process (Siegel, 2009). Evolutionary perspectives suggest that certain behaviors are more likely to be passed down if they increase the likelihood of survival. It's easy to see why sleeping at night, for example, might be adaptive in some way: In the wild, it's easier to hunt during the day when you can see what you're hunting. Sleeping at night might also contribute to reproductive success by keeping early humans out of sight of predators. It's better to be asleep and safe in your cave than to be roaming the jungle at night, where nocturnal predators may put an end to your contribution to the gene pool.

Both of these theories might explain why sleep is structured the way it is. Deep sleep is considered to be essential because it happens early in the night. This means you are less likely to miss deep sleep. You also tend to "make up" the most important aspects of sleep. Miss a few hours of sleep one night, and the next night you will have longer periods of REM sleep (known as **REM rebound**) and more deep sleep, suggesting these are the most important parts of the sleep cycle. Other observations support the idea that REM and deep sleep are most important as well. Interruptions early in the night have a greater impact on our daily functioning than missing sleep later in the night (Jacobs, 2009).

---

nREM sleep Stages of sleep in which dreams are unlikely to occur and that are not associated with rapid eye movement.

Suprachiasmatic nucleus A part of the hypothalamus that controls daily rhythms for sleep and wakefulness.

Melatonin A hormone manufactured by the pineal gland that promotes sleepiness.

Restorative theory of sleep The view that sleep is needed in order to maintain mental and physical operations.

Adaptive theory of sleep A theory of sleep that suggests that our sleep-wake patterns are shaped by an evolved biological process.

REM rebound After periods of loss of sleep, the tendency to increase the length of REM.

Chronic lack of sleep can cause problems in thinking and concentration, and impaired driving.

Effects of Sleep Deprivation

Given the importance of sleep, it's good to know how much you need to get. I'm sure you've heard before that everyone needs 8 hours of sleep every night. But it's a bit more complicated than that. Different people need different amounts of sleep to feel rested. Indeed, some sleep researchers have argued that some people need up to 9 hours of sleep. There is considerable variation among individuals on the required amount of sleep. In fact, as you get older, the amounts of total sleep and REM sleep you get will change, as you can see in FIGURE 5-2.

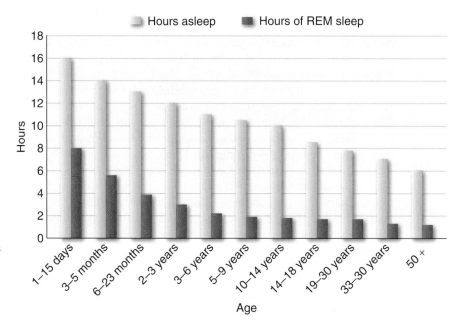

FIGURE 5-2 The percentage of time in REM sleep decreases dramatically in the first few years of life, but remains relatively constant after age 9.
Data from Parkes, J. D. (1985). Sleep and its disorders. W. B. Saunders Company: England, p. 20.

Sleep debt The difference between how much you should sleep and your actual amount of sleep.

Sleep disorder A condition in which the amount or quality of sleep is disturbed, resulting in distress or impairment.

There are effects of extreme sleep deprivation. Studies suggest that those who are prevented from sleeping are irritable and have decreased reaction time and memory loss. This is consistent with research that suggests that REM sleep helps us to process and store new memories (Saxvig et al., 2008).

More extreme effects of sleep deprivation include an increased risk of disease, including heart disease, type II diabetes, and obesity (Gangwisch, Malaspina, Boden-Albala, & Heymsfield, 2005).

Much less, however, has been made of **sleep debt**, a chronic lack of sleep. The size of your sleep debt is related to how much sleep you have lost. For example, if you normally need 8 hours to feel rested and you get only 6 hours one night because you stayed up studying for a biology exam, then you've racked up a 2-hour sleep debt. That means you'll need your normal 8 plus an extra 2 in order to feel rested. Researchers suggest that the average person in the United States has a sleep debt of about 2 weeks. This debt results in cognitive, physical, and emotional deficits that include problems with thinking and concentrating as well as impaired driving. This might explain why 75% of adults in the United States experience daytime sleepiness and 34% report that the daytime sleepiness is so bad that it interferes with their daily lives. How do you pay off this sleep debt? Easy—sleep more. Increasing sleep time as little as 2 hours a night over a few weeks can help reduce your sleep debt (Dement & Vaughan, 2000). Although there has been mixed evidence on how much you can pay down your sleep debt, according to some sleep researchers, paying off this sleep debt and getting enough sleep can have tremendous benefits such as improved self-esteem, increased immune system functioning, increased energy (Dement & Vaughan, 2000), improved memory, and improved ability to think creatively (Cai et al., 2009).

Sleep Disorders

Sleeping isn't always a pleasant experience. People with chronic problematic sleep may develop a **sleep disorder**, a condition in which the amount or quality of sleep is disturbed. Sleep disorders can lead to distress and interference with daily functioning.

Sleep specialists have constructed criteria for more than 80 sleep disorders. These include **dyssomnias**, which are conditions that can affect the quantity, quality, or timing of sleep (like insomnia, sleep apnea, and narcolepsy), and **parasomnias**, which are abnormal behaviors associated with sleep (such as tremors, nightmares, and sleepwalking). In this next section, we'll examine some common sleep disorders including insomnia, sleep apnea, narcolepsy, and a few parasomnias.

Insomnia

Insomnia is characterized by difficulty falling asleep, difficulty staying asleep, waking up too early, or having nonrefreshing sleep. There are various types of insomnia. Insomnia can be transient, lasting just a few nights; short term, which might last less than 3 weeks; or chronic, lasting greater than 3 weeks.

While insomnia can be frustrating during the night, there are, as you can imagine, also daytime consequences of insomnia. Tiredness, lack of daytime energy, difficulty concentrating, and even irritability are common.

Much of the time, short-term or **acute insomnia** is due to emotional or physical dysfunction (such as an illness or jet lag). Drugs such as caffeine, alcohol, antidepressants, decongestants, and nicotine can also cause problems. Alcohol can enhance the onset of sleep but can lead to sleep disturbances and restless, fitful sleep. Food habits may also affect sleep. Eating high-fat meals, acid reflux, or eating late at night can all cause problems (Jacobs, 2009).

Primary insomnia is diagnosed after all other associated causes of insomnia are ruled out, such as chronic stress, depression, or other conditions. **Secondary insomnia** occurs when the sleeplessness is an associated symptom of another condition.

There are many consequences of insomnia, some short and some long term. Of course, sleepiness and impaired mood and performance are common complaints. After that, long-term fatigue can set in, along with longer-term mood changes, difficulty concentrating, and greater impairment in daytime functioning.

Many people turn to medications to help them sleep. The problem with most sleeping pills, like over-the-counter sleep medicines or even prescription sleep medicines, is that they decrease Stage 1 and Stage 4 sleep and may lead to the need to take more and more sleep medication in order to get to sleep. Sleep medications may also produce daytime grogginess, headaches, or even an unpleasant taste in your mouth (Stahl, 2009).

Sleep Apnea

Associated with snoring, daytime sleepiness, and obesity, **sleep apnea**, or obstructive sleep apnea, is a sleep disorder in which your breathing stops (*apnea*—from Greek "without breath"). Apneas can last from just a few seconds to more than a minute (Friedman, 2008). About 9% of women and 24% of men have sleep apnea (Ulualp, 2010). People tend to have more apneas as they get older and also in certain sleep positions (like sleeping on your back). Some people with severe sleep apnea may have dozens of apneas during the night. During an apnea, the body is starved of oxygen. Because there is less oxygen in the blood, the heart has to work harder to keep the little oxygen that's in the blood moving around the body. The extra burden put on the heart by the reduced oxygen puts those with sleep apnea at higher risk for cardiovascular diseases such as high blood pressure. In addition, those with sleep apnea may have significant daytime sleepiness.

Sleep apnea may be caused by a number of factors. Some theories suggest a central nervous system issue associated with the control of breathing (Chokroverty, 2008). Others think a physical problem with the throat is the source of the condition. Luckily, there are many effective treatments for sleep apnea. Avoid sleeping on your back, keep your head elevated, and cut back on alcohol or sleeping pills, which could make the problems worse or be dangerous (Chokroverty, 2008). For moderate to severe sleep apnea there are other treatments, including **continuous positive airway pressure (CPAP)** FIGURE 5-3, in which a small machine and mask keep the airway open by sending a constant stream of compressed air. More serious cases of sleep apnea may require surgery to increase the size of the airway (Olsen, Smith, Oei, & Douglas, 2010).

Certain foods and beverages can make insomnia worse.

Dyssomnia A condition that affects the quantity, quality, or timing of sleep.

Parasomnia Abnormal behaviors associated with sleep.

Insomnia A condition in which a person is unable to fall or stay asleep.

Acute insomnia Short-term inability to fall or stay asleep.

Primary insomnia Difficulty falling asleep, staying asleep, or waking up too early that is not associated with another medical or psychological condition.

Secondary insomnia Lack of sleep associated with another medical or psychological condition.

Sleep apnea A sleep disorder characterized by abrupt gaps in breathing during sleep, causing momentary wakefulness; also called obstructive sleep apnea.

Continuous positive airway pressure (CPAP) A treatment for insomnia utilizing a small machine and mask to keep the airway open.

FIGURE 5-3 CPAP is a device to treat sleep apnea.

Narcolepsy

Narcolepsy is a condition characterized by daytime sleepiness and sudden lapses into sleep during the day. Narcolepsy is fairly rare, affecting only one out of 2,000 people in the United States (Ahmed & Thorpy, 2010). Often those with narcolepsy have **cataplexy**, an abrupt and temporary muscle weakness often following a strong emotional experience (such as being surprised or very upset). The weakness can cause the person to fall and can be dangerous. Luckily, cataplexy tends to decline over time as people tend to learn to avoid situations that would bring on cataplexy (Ahmed & Thorpy, 2010). When people with narcolepsy do suddenly fall asleep (sometimes called sleep attacks), they may enter REM sleep straightway. One moment, they may be in class listening to a lecture, and the next moment, in the middle of a terrifying dream. They may even experience **hypnagogic hallucinations**, which are sensory experiences that occur between being asleep and being awake. Although not all forms of narcolepsy cause one to suddenly lapse into sleep, studies suggest that around 60% of those diagnosed with narcolepsy have experienced sudden sleep.

The symptoms of narcolepsy that people notice first include sleeping a lot and not feeling rested, fatigue, impaired daytime performance, and disturbed nighttime sleep. Recent research has pointed to deregulations in **hypocretin**, a hormone linked to regulating wakefulness, as a possible cause of narcolepsy. The absence of hypocretin-producing neurons in those with narcolepsy helps to make the case that it is a possible cause for narcolepsy (Siegel & Boehmer, 2006). Stimulants to combat daytime sleepiness, such as modafanil and methylphenidate, may prevent daytime sleep attacks (Stahl, 2009).

Parasomnias

Parasomnias are sleep disorders that often involve problematic movements and dreams or problems with sleeping and wake patterns. They are generally divided into two areas: Parasomnias that occur during REM periods are also known as REM parasomnias, and those that occur during non-REM periods like Stage 3 and 4 deep sleep are sometimes called nREM parasomnias.

Sleep Paralysis

While you are asleep, your brain sends a signal to your body to inhibit your movement while you're dreaming. This keeps you from thrashing around and possibly hurting yourself while you are sleeping. But when sleep paralysis occurs, the brain either switches on your muscle inhibition feature too soon or doesn't switch it off when you wake up.

Sleep paralysis is a condition characterized by a temporary inability to move upon wakening. In addition to being unable to move, many people will experience hypnagogic hallucinations. The most common hallucinations that occur with sleep paralysis include sensing or seeing another person in the room, being touched, hearing footsteps, floating, or even hearing someone call your name. And for some people, the sensation is so strong and frightening they think they've had a stroke and are really paralyzed. Episodes of sleep paralysis can last anywhere from 10 seconds to a terrifying 70 minutes.

Studies suggest that about half of us have experienced at least one episode of hypnagogic sleep paralysis of the kind that occurs soon after we fall asleep (Avidan & Kaplish, 2010). Generally, the disorder is related to jet lag, sleep deprivation, stress, or even your sleeping position. It's believed that sleeping on your back can make a person much more likely to have an episode of sleep paralysis than any other position (Cheyne, 2002). If you are prone to sleep paralysis, try sleeping with a pillow between your legs and sleep on your side.

If you do happen to wake and find yourself with a bout of sleep paralysis, try wiggling your toes. The paralysis seems to affect larger muscles more than smaller ones, so a good way to get out of it is to try to make small movements to wake yourself up.

Narcolepsy A condition characterized by daytime sleepiness and sudden lapses into sleep during the day.

Cataplexy An abrupt and temporary weakness often following a strong emotional experience.

Hypnagogic hallucinations Sensory experiences that occur between being awake and asleep.

Hypocretin A hormone that is linked to wakefulness.

Sleep paralysis A sleep condition characterized by a temporary inability to move upon wakening.

REM Sleep Behavior Disorder

REM sleep behavior disorder is a type of REM parasomnia in which a person will act out her or his dreams. In some ways, it is the opposite of sleep paralysis. While you are asleep, your brain fails to send a signal to your body to inhibit your movement while you're dreaming. Instead of just rapid eye movement, those with REM sleep behavior disorder may kick, punch, or do other things that could cause harm to themselves or others while they dream. REM sleep behavior disorder affects around 0.5% of people in the United States (Avidan & Kaplish, 2010).

Sexsomnia

Sexsomnia, or **sleepsex**, is a type of nREM parasomnia associated with engaging in sexual activity while asleep. Researchers have classified the sexual behaviors that occur during sleep into three categories. The first involves actions that the researchers describe as "annoying," though not harmful. Cases in this category include sexual moaning loud enough to be heard in adjoining rooms, attempts to remove clothing, and mumbling sexually inappropriate phrases. The second category includes behaviors that are also considered annoying but are, at times, harmful to the person suffering from sexsomnia. Often, this involves violent masturbation that can cause bruising and soreness the next morning. The last, and most severe, category is for actions that are harmful to others. These cases involve inappropriate and violent sexual behavior.

Some people think that the diagnosis of sexsomnia is used to justify inappropriate sexual advances. However, in nearly every case, doctors were able to document abnormal patterns of REM or nREM sleep, something impossible to fake. The majority of cases also had other psychiatric diagnoses. Fortunately, most patients with sexsomnia can be successfully treated with psychotropic medications (Ebrahim, 2006).

Sleep Terrors

Everyone knows that nightmares can be horrifying. You wake terrified, sometimes in the midst of your own screaming, remembering vividly disturbing images. But nightmares, which occur late in our sleep cycles, are very different from sleep terrors, which happen earlier during nREM sleep. **Sleep terrors**, also known as night terrors, are a sleep condition in which people experience sudden episodes of panic during Stage 4 sleep. This is different than a **nightmare**, a type of dream that is frightening and often will wake up the dreamer. Nightmares will often occur during REM sleep, whereas night terrors occur during Stage 4.

To someone else, the person experiencing a sleep terror will seem wide awake, but he is not. With eyes wide open, his breathing is intense and his heart rate has shot through the roof. He might even scream at the top of his lungs in fear, look panicked, and act as if he is in excruciating pain. It's okay to wake the person . . . if you can. But it's very difficult to rouse some sleepers out of these episodes. When they do wake up, most of the time they have no memory of the experience or the emotional upheaval it caused them (and, most likely, the people around them). Sleep terrors usually occur in children and can last between a few seconds to 5 minutes. The highest rates of sleep terrors occur in children aged 4 to 12 with up to 6.5% of children in the United States experiencing symptoms. Although most people tend to grow out of sleep terrors as they get older, about 4% of adults continue to suffer from them (Avidan & Kaplish, 2010).

Sleepwalking and Sleep Eating

Sleepwalking is a type of nREM parasomnia in which a person will leave her bed and perform activities while still asleep. Sleepwalking is common in kids, with up to 17% of children having experienced symptoms at some point. The rate decreases in adults to around 3% (Avidan & Kaplish, 2010). Nocturnal sleep-related eating disorder, or **sleep eating**, is a condition similar to sleepwalking in which affected people will engage in nightly meals while partially or totally asleep. The most common sleep eating episodes entail a person sleepwalking to the refrigerator and having a meal she or he will probably never remember. Other times, the episodes are more elaborate, and the fully asleep sufferers head to the kitchen and prepare a meal.

The disorder is fairly rare, occurring in only about 1.5% of the population. Two out of three people with sleep eating are women, and three out of four eat nightly (some up

REM sleep behavior disorder A type of REM parasomnia in which a person will act out a dream.

Sleepsex A type of nREM parasomnia associated with engaging in sexual activity while asleep. Also called sexsomnia.

Sleep terror A type of nREM parasomnia characterized by observed panic and terror while asleep, often associated with amnesia about the situation. Also called night terror.

Nightmare A type of dream that is frightening and often will wake up the dreamer.

Sleepwalking A type of nREM parasomnia in which a person will leave his or her bed and perform activities while still asleep.

Sleep eating A type of nREM parasomnia associated with preparing and consuming food while still asleep.

to eight times a night). Most of them (84%) are completely unaware of their nighttime snacks. In almost all cases, the behavior doesn't appear to be hunger related (Howell, Schenck, & Crow, 2009).

The food choices of sleep eaters can be, at times, peculiar. Case studies have revealed nighttime meals that include cat food, raw chicken, coffee grounds and milk, sandwiches made from fistfuls of salt, and even inedibles such as ammonia or buttered soda cans.

Lots of things can be done to limit the impact of sleepwalking and sleep eating. Bedrooms should be made safe by blocking windows or locating them on the first floor if possible. It's best to try to get enough sleep, cut back on alcohol and caffeine, and avoid stressful situations. For more severe conditions, medications that inhibit GABA such as low-dose benzodiazepines (such as diazepam), have been effective (Avidan & Kaplish, 2010).

CONCEPT LEARNING CHECK 5.2 | *Stages of Sleep*

Match the concept with the proper stage.

A. Stage 1

B. Stage 2

C. Stage 3

D. Stage 4

E. REM sleep

1. Sleep spindles begin during _____.

2. During _____, the body has increased heart rate and rapid breathing.

3. _____ is when delta waves begin.

4. _____ is the most difficult stage to wake up from.

5.3 Dreams

The psychoanalytic theory of dreams suggests that dreams are unconscious wishes and/or conflicts. The activation synthesis hypothesis of dreams implicates neurological activity and cortical interpretation.

- Describe the two main theories of dreams.

What's more immersive than any computer videogame, perhaps more exciting than an action movie, filled with romance, violence, intrigue, and with more twists and turns than any reality TV show? Oh, and it's on every night and it's free? It's your dreams. **Dreams** are an array of sensory events experienced during sleep. Although some people say they don't dream, if roused during REM sleep, nearly all will report having had a vivid dream. Dreams are universal and enigmatic, and psychologists have a few theories to explain the purpose of dreams. Dream researchers caution that the meaning and purpose of dreams are different things. Your dreams may have a special meaning or significance to you apart from the reason why you dream.

Theories of Dreams

There are two main theories of the purpose of dreams: dreams as a reflection of unconscious wishes and dreams as a byproduct of mental housekeeping in the form of interpreted brain activity.

Dreams as a Reflection of Unconscious Wishes

The **psychoanalytic theory of dreams** suggests that dreams are unconscious wishes. To understand this theory, you need to know just a little about Freud, since it's

Dream An array of sensory events experienced during sleep.

Psychoanalytic theory of dreams A theory of dreams that suggest that dreams are unconscious wishes and/or conflicts.

CRITICAL THINKING APPLICATION

Researchers in Canada discovered that people with insomnia spend more money on alcohol as a sleep aid ($340 million Canadian) than they spent on over-the-counter and prescription sleep medicines ($14.7 million) and on visits to the doctor for insomnia ($69.4 million) combined (Daley, Morin, LeBlanc, Grégoire, & Savard, 2009), despite the fact that alcohol isn't an effective treatment for insomnia.

What can you do to fight insomnia? **Stimulus control therapy** is a treatment for insomnia that includes associating bedtime with sleep to reestablish a consistent sleep-wake schedule. There are a few things we all know that can be helpful. These are in the category of good **sleep hygiene**, or behaviors that lead to quality sleep.

- Wake up and go to bed at the same time every day (including weekends).
- Limit caffeine intake, especially between 4 and 6 hours before bedtime.
- Avoid nicotine and alcohol, especially late in the evening.
- Avoid heavy meals close to bedtime.
- Exercise (but not too close to your bedtime).
- Adjust surroundings; make sure to limit nighttime distractions such as light, excess heat, and loud noise. Some noise can get you to sleep, so try a low-emotional TV program (like those that feature home improvement; avoid nighttime crime dramas) and put your television on the "sleep" setting so it turns itself off after about an hour.

Evaluate

After reviewing resources on improving sleep, consider the following questions:

1. If stimulus control techniques are so effective, why do you think more people don't utilize them to improve sleep?
2. Why do you suppose alcohol is used more often than medical services and medications for insomnia?
3. What could you do to help someone who is using alcohol as a sleep medication to switch to a more helpful intervention?

based on his theory of personality. We'll learn more about Freud later on. To begin with, I'd like you to imagine that for about 7 hours, you could do whatever you wanted that was humanly possible (sorry, flying is out). I mean anything. You could do anything you wanted and no one would ever find out and you wouldn't get into trouble. What would you do? When most people are asked to think about this, many will say "rob a bank" or "run naked through the college quad." The part of your personality that is responsible for these choices, according to Freud, is your id. It's the part of the personality that wants to reduce tension and to seek pleasure. While you are sleeping, the part of your personality that is involved in your wishes is more active. Freud believed if you had full access to all the terrible, horrible things that your id wanted to do, you would never get any sleep. Freud thought that the purpose of dreaming was to protect sleep.

There is another part of your personality, according to Freud—your superego. While the id is interested in the pleasure principle, or reducing tension, the superego operates on the perfection principle. It wants us to be perfect all of the time. It makes us feel guilty when we aren't and proud when we are. As you might imagine, the superego would be none too pleased with the id's party time during sleep. It's the responsibility of the ego to protect the sensitive superego.

The ego is the part of your personality that is responsible for getting things done; it operates on the reality principle. It also is responsible for compromise. It somehow has to handle the demands of the id and the prohibitions of the superego. Since the superego would be shocked and awakened by the id's fantasies, the ego agrees to disguise the id's wishes. And that disguise, more often than not, ends up being your dream.

Stimulus control therapy A treatment for insomnia that includes associating bedtime with sleep to reestablish a consistent sleep-wake schedule.

Sleep hygiene Sleep habits.

Latent content In psychoanalytic theory, the true, underlying, undisguised meaning of a dream.

Manifest content In psychoanalytic theory, the dream as the dreamer reports it.

Activation-synthesis model of dreaming A theory of dreams that suggests that dreams are interpreted brain activity.

Consolidation The stabilization of information in long-term memory through structural changes in the brain.

Sleepthink Generic thought about the day during sleep.

According to Freud, dreams have two kinds of content: undisguised material and disguised material. Freud called the undisguised dream **latent content**. It represents the pure id wish. The disguised dream is the **manifest content**, or the dream as it is often reported. The disguised dream reveals not only the id's wishes but also the superego's problems with the id's wishes. When the latent content and the manifest content are too similar, we have a nightmare and wake up. A nightmare, according to Freud, is a totally undisguised dream.

Dreams as Interpreted Brain Activity

Look at the three images in FIGURE 5-4. Can you make up a story that links the images together? I bet you can. What you've done is to synthesize or link the images together into a coherent story. Your brain likes to make sense of things.

The activation-synthesis hypothesis of dreaming is based on the brain's desire to make sense out of randomness. The **activation-synthesis model of dreaming** (Hobson & McCarley, 1977) suggests that dreams are interpreted brain activity and have no particular significance. The activation part has to do with the mental housekeeping that is done during REM sleep. You'll recall that during REM sleep, the part of the brain that is involved in sorting out your memories and making them easier to retrieve is very active. It's like organizing files on a computer or a flash drive. Your brain is looking at each memory and tagging it with information to make it easier to pull out for retrieval later. This process, called **consolidation** helps to stabilize the information in long-term memory. While you access (or activate) those memories, you synthesize images, thoughts, and sensations into stories you recall in the morning.

FIGURE 5-4 Because your brain likes to make sense of things, it is likely that you can easily make up a story that links these random images.

So what do dreams mean according to this theory? Pretty much nothing. You are just doing mental housekeeping and making up a story along the way. MRI scans of people while they sleep indicate lots of brain activity in the memory consolidation areas during REM sleep, which lends plenty of support to this theory (Saxvig et al., 2008).

Dream Contents

So what do people dream about? An average person spends about 6 years dreaming, mostly consisting of **sleepthink** or generic thoughts about their day. Several studies have collected themes of dreams FIGURE 5-5. Studies have found that about 84% of students dream about being attacked or followed, 78% of falling, and 79% of trying over and over to do something (Griffith, Miyagi, & Tago, 1958). Recent research suggests that rates of typical dreams seem to be similar across different ethnic groups (Maggiolini, Cagnin, Crippa, Persico, & Rizzi, 2010).

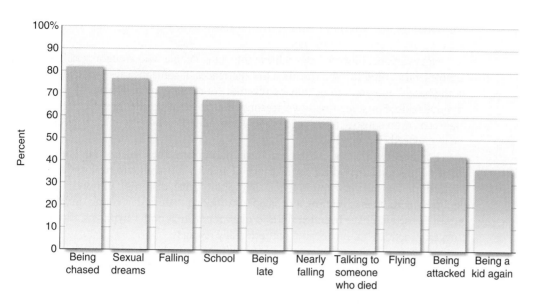

FIGURE 5-5 Top 10 reported
dream contents.
*Data from Nielsen, T. A., Zadra, A. L.,
Simard, V., Saucier, S., Stenstrom,
P., Smith, C., & Kuiken, D. (2003).
The typical dreams of Canadian
university students. Dreaming,
13(4), 211–235.*

CONCEPT LEARNING CHECK 5.3   *Theories of Dreams*

Fill in the blank with the correct key term.

1. _____ is the theory of dreams that suggests that dreams are interpreted brain activity.

2. _____ is the theory of dreams that suggests that dreams are a reflection of unconscious wishes.

3. According to the Freudian theory of dreams, a dream's _____ content is the dream as it is often reported.

4. According to the Freudian theory of dreams, a dream's _____ content is the underlying meaning of the dream.

5.4   Hypnosis

Hypnosis is a trancelike state in which a person is susceptible to suggestion.

■ Explain the two theories of hypnosis.

A dark figure with intense eyes dangles a pocketwatch in front of a nervous-looking subject. "You are getting veeery sleepy," he commands. The subject's eyes are blank as he stares forward. The man with the pocket watch says, "When you wake up, you will take your roommate's ATM card. You will remember the code from the last time you looked over your roommate's shoulder. You will then withdraw $20 dollars and mail it to me and have no memory of doing so. Three, two, one, now open your eyes!" The man with the pocketwatch snaps his fingers.

This portrayal of hypnosis is common in popular literature, mocked on TV shows, and even likely to be found in college orientation schedules, but how accurate is it? Is hypnosis the magical state of consciousness that these depictions suggest? Are there practical psychological explanations and applications to this technique, or is it just a nifty parlor trick?

Although the word *hypnosis* has its roots in the name of the Greek god for sleep, Hypnos, the hypnotic state is quite different from sleep. In **hypnosis**, a trancelike state, the subject readily accepts the hypnotist's suggestions of changes in consciousness or sensations.

Critical Thinking About Hypnosis

Hypnotic induction often begins with relaxing the subject and encouraging him or her to focus on an object or a sensation. Although subjects remain fully aware of their

Hypnotic induction often begins with encouraging the subject to relax and focus on an object.

Hypnosis A trancelike state in which the subject readily accepts the hypnotist's suggestion of changes in consciousness or sensations.

surroundings, many report feeling fully immersed in the experience, like when reading a great story or watching a movie.

Not everyone, however, can achieve this state. People who are more easily hypnotizable tend to be able to be absorbed in experiences. If someone says, "imagine you are at the beach" and you can be fully involved in your own imagination, it's likely you are hypnotizable. For some unknown reason, about 20% of people, however, report that they can't even construct an image of the waves and sea. Those people are not likely to be hypnotized (Barrett, 2010).

For those who can be coaxed into the hypnotic state, there are several types of hypnotic suggestions, including performance of an action, inability to perform an action, distortion of normal perception (such as stopping pain), distortion of normal memory, and **posthypnotic suggestion**, a behavior or thinking pattern that comes out after hypnosis. Those who have been hypnotized often report that under hypnosis, they did the suggested actions "automatically" without really trying to.

The hypnotic suggestions create opportunities for psychological and medical applications. Perhaps the greatest uses of hypnosis are for chronic pain and conditions that are linked to or exacerbated by stress such as anxiety, asthma, and nausea (Hammond, 2010).

There are a few things, however, that hypnosis cannot do. There is no evidence that people under hypnosis will do things that are against their principles, like murder or steal. **Hypermnesia** or elevated memory recall isn't universal for hypnosis. Memory tests for high-sense stimuli such as pictures almost always produce increased recall under hypnosis. The story changes for things like words. Hypnosis does not appear to be able to produce increased memory for low-sensory things like nonsense syllables and word lists (Erdelyi, 1994).

Theories of Hypnosis

There are several major theories of hypnosis, including hypnosis as a special state of consciousness, role playing, and a dissociated state.

Altered State of Consciousness

The altered state of consciousness (ASC) theory of hypnosis suggests that hypnosis is a distinctive kind of consciousness (Lynn, Fassler, & Knox, 2005) and that those who are hypnotized are in a unique kind of psychological trance. This theory was popular during the early days of hypnosis, back when those under the hypnotic state were thought to have amazing abilities such as communicating with the dead, spotting illnesses, and teleportation. More contemporary theories suggest that behavior under hypnosis may not require a distinctive state of consciousness to be effective. They still, however, speculate that a unique hypnotic trancelike state may exist for some people. Some research does support the ASC theory. Under an MRI, for example, pain induced under hypnosis looks more like real pain than imagined pain.

Although people refer to those who are hypnotized as being in a trance, most research suggests that hypnotized people are not necessarily in a special state of consciousness. Researchers have not consistently found changes in the brain that are unique to the hypnotic state (Kirsch & Lynn, 1995).

Role Playing

The sociocognitive theory of hypnosis suggests that you respond to the suggestion of the hypnotist because you are expected to do so (Orne, 1959). Hypnosis is, according to this theory, more role playing than anything else. This isn't to suggest that hypnosis is fake or a trick; the power of the role and the situation can be very compelling. In class, I've told students, "Put down your pens and cover your right ear with your right hand." About 90% of students will do it. When I asked them why they did what they did, they responded, "Because you told us to." If I barged into a calculus class and did the same thing, it is unlikely that the students would be as compliant. It doesn't appear to work very well in the grocery store, either. Why? The social context of my own classroom creates an atmosphere in which my suggestions are more readily followed. The social environment of the hypnotic experience, according this theory, works in much the same way.

Posthypnotic suggestion A behavior or thinking pattern that comes out after hypnosis.

Hypermnesia Elevated memory recall by means of hypnosis.

Researchers show that hypnosis can create MRI patterns similar to pain (shown here) but different to imagined pain. Proponents that suggest hypnosis as an altered state of consciousness use such research as support for their theory.

Divided Consciousness

Your brain has an **executive control system**, an assortment of brain processes that plan and initiate actions, especially well-learned ones. When you drive, for example, your executive control system might tell you when to use your turn signal and when to step on the brakes. Much of this happens outside of your awareness. This is the sense in which consciousness is "divided"; some things you consciously attend to, while others you don't. The **dissociation theory of hypnosis** (Hilgard, 1992) suggests that the hypnotic state reduces the influence of the executive control system, allowing you to be more easily influenced by external stimulation. Your normal executive control system becomes a **hidden observer** and passively watches what you are doing, without being involved in carrying out the behavior.

Related to the dissociative theory is a **neodissociation theory of hypnosis**. This suggests that hypnosis causes the subjects to divide their consciousness voluntarily. One part responds to the hypnotist while the other retains awareness of reality.

> **Executive control system** An assortment of brain processes that plan and initiate actions.
>
> **Dissociation theory of hypnosis** A theory of hypnosis that suggests that the hypnotic state produces a split in consciousness and separates the executive control system from the rest of the brain.
>
> **Hidden observer** In the dissociation theory of hypnosis, the executive control system that witnesses without being involved.

CONCEPT LEARNING CHECK 5.4 | *Theories of Hypnosis*

Fill in the blank with the correct key term.

1. The _____ suggests that the hypnotic state produces a split in consciousness and separates the executive control system from the rest of the brain.

2. The _____ suggests that you respond to the suggestion of the hypnotist because you are expected to do so.

3. He calls the orphaned executive control system a(n) _____.

4. _____ or elevated memory recall isn't universal for hypnosis.

5.5 Meditation

Meditation is a mental practice that regulates attention, awareness, and relaxation.

- Discuss the effects and benefits of meditation.

Meditation refers to any number of mental practices or techniques that focus on regulating attention and awareness. Although many people link meditation with religious practices, the techniques of meditation aren't tied to any particular religion and can be nonreligious in nature. Like hypnosis, meditation involves an alteration of consciousness.

Meditation Defined

Meditation can take many forms but often involves controlling, retraining, monitoring, or redirecting attention. While many people meditate for spiritual reasons, there are quite a few health benefits to meditation practice, as you will learn later. There are several types of meditation, including those involving concentration techniques in which you focus your awareness and those involving observation and acknowledgement of thoughts and sensations without judging them.

Effects and Benefits of Meditation

Quite a bit of evidence suggests that mediation is an effective treatment for many conditions, including hypertension (Anderson, Liu, & Kryscio, 2008) and chronic pain (Zeidan, Gordon, Merchant, & Goolkasian, 2010). Meditation is associated with reduced subjective and physiological reactions to stress in healthy adults. Benefits include increased perception of control, enhanced empathy, improvement in eating disorders, and the alleviation of chronic anxiety, severe psoriasis, tension headache, and depression (Majumdar, Grossman, Dietz-Waschkowski, Kersig, & Walach, 2002). One advantage to meditative practices is

Meditation can be religious or nonreligious and can be helpful for many conditions.

> **Neodissociation theory of hypnosis** A theory of hypnosis that suggests that hypnosis causes subjects to divide their consciousness voluntarily.
>
> **Meditation** A mental practice that regulates attention and awareness.

Progressive relaxation
A method for reducing stress by contracting and then releasing groups of muscles.

Attentional blink
Difficulty in detecting new information after a information is presented.

Psychoactive drug A chemical that alters consciousness.

Drug abuse A condition in which a person uses psychoactive substances that results in distress or impairment in their social, work, or school functioning.

Drug addiction
A situation in which taking a psychoactive substance leads to habitual use and craving even though the use causes distress or impairment.

that benefits may occur even with limited practice. In one study, the benefits of increased pain tolerance were seen after only three 20-minute training sessions (Zeidan et al., 2010).

Some suggest that the benefits of meditation aren't much different from **progressive relaxation** (Benson & Klipper, 2000), a technique for reducing anxiety by alternately tensing and relaxing the muscles. Progressive relaxation and meditation can lead to decreases in distress as well as increases in positive mood states over time. However, one advantage to meditation over progressive relaxation may be in its ability to reduce sidetracking thoughts and behaviors (Jain et al., 2007).

There are several long-term benefits to regular meditation. Regular meditation is associated with lower stress hormones such as cortisol, increased immune response, increased self-esteem, and lower blood pressure (Ospina et al., 2007).

Researchers have discovered that meditation can help us to focus our attention (Slagter et al., 2007). They presented subjects with a series of letters one at a time. Interspersed in the letters were two numbers. When the numbers were presented close in sequence, many of the subjects missed the second number. This is due to a phenomenon called **attentional blink**. Attentional blink occurs when we focus so closely on one thing that we miss something that comes immediately after it.

In addition to doing better on the letter-number task, the researchers found differences in the way the subjects' brains reacted to the activity. The researchers used an EEG to measure the brain waves of individuals during the attentional blink task. The researchers noticed a spike in brain activity when the subjects saw the first object they were to recognize. After the meditation practice, subjects had less EEG activity when they recognized the first number, allowing the subjects to do better on the task. This research suggests that mediation can allow you to have more control over the things that you want to focus your attention on and perhaps to notice more things around you.

CONCEPT LEARNING CHECK 5.5   *The Effects and Benefits of Meditation*

Indicate whether each of the statements is true or false.

1. _____ Meditation only refers to religious practices that focus on regulating attention and awareness and spirituality.

2. _____ Progressive relaxation is a technique for reducing anxiety by alternately tensing and relaxing the muscles.

3. _____ Regular meditation is associated with lower stress hormones such as cortisol, increased immune response, increased self-esteem, and lower blood pressure.

4. _____ There is evidence that mediation offers additional benefits beyond those of progressive relaxation.

5.6 Drug Use

Psychoactive drugs are chemicals used to alter consciousness.

- List and describe the four categories of psychoactive drugs.
- Describe the effects of psychoactive drugs on the nervous system.

According to the Substance Abuse and Mental Health Services Administration (SAMHSA), more than 22 million Americans aged 12 and over abuse or are dependent on a nonprescribed psychoactive drug (http://www.samhsa.gov/). A **psychoactive drug** is a chemical used to alter consciousness. Many psychoactive drugs can have a beneficial aspect to them. Often, misuse of a psychoactive drug can lead to **drug abuse** and cause distress or impairment in social, work, or school functioning. Drug abuse can also lead to **drug addiction**, which is a habitual use or craving of a drug even though it causes distress or impairment. The development of drug addiction has many factors. While the direct effects of the psychoactive drugs are biological, there are multiple influences on a person's motivation to take psychoactive substance for the first time. Chaotic living conditions, poor coping skills, and involvement with peers who use drugs can all be risk factors for drug abuse and addiction (www.drugabuse.gov). Drug abuse and addiction can tear apart families and cause significant health, financial, and social problems.

The abuse of psychoactive substances can lead to physical changes such as **tolerance**, which is a reduction in a person's sensitivity to a drug over time. Tolerance may lead to a person's needing more of the drug to generate the original effect.

Though there are many ill effects of psychoactive drugs, stopping them is difficult. Many substances have strong **withdrawal symptoms**, which are distressing side effects and cravings associated with the rapid discontinuation of certain psychoactive substances. **Drug rebound effects** can also occur, so that stopping the use of a drug has the reverse effect, making you feel worse. All of these symptoms combine to explain drug dependency. **Drug dependence** occurs when a person's drug use has led to distress or impairment, including drug tolerance, significant withdrawal symptoms, and unsuccessful efforts to reduce drug use. Dependence can come in many forms, including **physical dependence**, a condition in which a drug must be taken continually to avoid symptoms of withdrawal, and **psychological dependence**, in which a person's use of a substance leads to cravings, distress, and impairment in the absence of physiological dependence.

TABLE 5-1 lists the common psychoactive drugs and their effects. **TABLE 5-2** details the common psychoactive drugs and numbers of users.

Tolerance A reduction in a person's sensitivity to a drug over time.

Withdrawal symptoms Distress and cravings associated with the rapid discontinuation of certain psychoactive substances.

Drug rebound effect A situation in which stopping the use of a drug can have the reverse effect of the action of the drug.

Drug dependence A situation in which a person's drug use has led to distress or impairment including drug tolerance, significant withdrawal symptoms, and unsuccessful efforts to reduce drug use.

Physical dependence A condition in which a drug must be taken continually to avoid symptoms of withdrawal.

Psychological dependence A situation in which a person's use of a substance leads to cravings, with distress and impairment in the absence of physiological dependence.

TABLE 5-1 Psychoactive Drugs and Their Effects by Class

Type of Drug	Description	Methods of Ingestion	Principal Medical Uses	Desired Effects	Known and Potential Short-Term Side Effects
Stimulants					
Amphetamines	A class of stimulant drugs that activates the central nervous system	Oral	Narcolepsy	Alertness, elevated mood	Anxiety, headaches, blunted appetite, high blood pressure, psychosis
Cocaine	A stimulant drug made from the coca plant	Oral, sniffed, injected, smoked	Local anesthetic	Euphoria, confidence, energy, depressed appetite	Insomnia, sweating, anxiety, panic, depression, cardiovascular stress
Nicotine	A type of drug that targets the nicotinic receptors. Found in tobacco	Smoked, gum, buccally (through the inside of the cheek).	Cessation of smoking habit	Euphoria, increased confidence, energy, decreased appetite	Heart disease, cancer, high blood pressure
Caffeine	A type of stimulant drug that is associated with increased central nervous system activity	Oral, drinking	Painkiller	Alertness, increased reaction time	Insomnia, high blood pressure
Methamphetamine	A stimulant drug that is associated with increased nervous system activity, elevated libido, and increased self-esteem	Oral, smoked	None	Euphoria, alertness, energy	Irritability, insomnia, hypertension, seizures, nervousness, headaches, decreased appetite, psychosis

(continues)

TABLE 5-1 Psychoactive Drugs and Their Effects by Class *(continued)*

Type of Drug	Description	Methods of Ingestion	Principal Medical Uses	Desired Effects	Known and Potential Short-Term Side Effects
MDMA (ecstasy)	A stimulant-hallucinogenic drug that can induce euphoria and diminish anxiety	Oral	None	Increased mood, alertness and wakefulness, disinhibition	Anxiety, agitation, and insomnia in high doses; Dehydration, sweatiness, depressed mood, impaired cognitive and immune functioning
Depressants					
Alcohol	A type of depressant drug that is associated with reduced inhibition, slurred speech, and impairments in balance	Oral	Antiseptic	Relaxation and disinhibition	Depression, memory loss, liver damage, impaired reaction time
Barbiturates	A type of depressant drug that reduces stress induces sleep	Oral, injected	Sedative, sleeping pill,	Reduced anxiety, reduced tension, sedation	Memory difficulties, withdrawal symptoms, convulsions
Hallucinogens					
Heroin	A psychoactive substance made from opium that relieves pain and reduces the activity of the nervous system	Injected, smoked, oral	None	Euphoria, pain relief	Reduced appetite, nausea, convulsions, coma
LSD	A synthetic psychedelic hallucinogenic drug that produces altered states of consciousness	Oral	None	Hallucinations	Psychosis, paranoia, panic
Marijuana	A drug that has both painkilling as well as stimulating effects on the nervous system	Smoked, oral	Nausea associated with chemotherapy; treatment of nausea, insomnia, and lack of appetite.	Enhanced sensation, relief of pain, distortion of time, relaxation,	Memory difficulties

If you are concerned that you or someone you know has become addicted to a psychoactive substance, talk to a trained professional like someone at your college's counseling center and request a confidential assessment. They can discuss treatment options with you.

TABLE 5-2 Number of People Using Psychoactive Drugs in the United States (2009)

Type of Drug	Millions of People Who Use This Drug
Illicit drugs	21.8
Marijuana	16.7
Psychotherapeutics	7
Cocaine	1.6
Hallucinogens	1.3
Inhalants	0.6
Heroin	0.2

Source: Data from 2009 Substance Abuse and Mental Health Services Administration.

Mechanism of Action of Psychoactive Drugs

A **mechanism of action (MOA)** of a drug describes the way a drug functions. The mechanism of action of most psychoactive drugs is on the neurotransmitters in the nervous system. Neurotransmitters are the chemical messengers of your nervous system. Psychoactive drugs can influence the functioning of the nervous system in various ways. They can:

1. Block the action of neurotransmitters

2. Prevent reuptake, causing excess neurotransmitters to flood the synaptic gap

3. Increase the effect of a neurotransmitter

4. Decrease the effect of a neurotransmitter

5. Bind to receptor sites normally used by neurotransmitters

Many psychoactive drugs influence the neurotransmitter dopamine, a neurotransmitter associated with the nervous system's reward structure, which can make the drugs highly addictive. In general, there are three main classes of psychoactive drugs: **depressants**, which reduce activity in the nervous system; **stimulants**, which increase activity in the nervous system; and **hallucinogens**, which distort conscious experiences.

Depressants

Depressants work by reducing the level of activity in the nervous system. Drugs in this class include alcohol, narcotics, and opiates. Those who use these drugs report feelings of reduced inhibition, reduced anxiety, and lethargy. Also in this class are **tranquilizers**, a type of drug used for sedation and reducing anxiety.

Moderate use of depressants is associated with listlessness, confusion, slowed pulse and breathing, and impairments in coordination, memory, and judgment. Abuse of depressants can lead to addiction, insomnia, brain damage, and stress or damage to the liver as it attempts to clear the substance from the body. Heavy abuse of depressants can interfere with nervous system function, shut down the cardiovascular system, and cause death.

Alcohol

The nervous system has a few all-purpose neurotransmitters: GABA for inhibition and glutamate for excitation. **Alcohol**, an ethanol-containing beverage, increases the power of GABA, making it work better. In addition, it can reduce the effectiveness of **glutamate**, an all-purpose excitatory neurotransmitter. The result is that there is more general inhibition in the nervous system, slowing everything down. This results in the telltale symptoms of alcohol intoxication, including slurred speech, reduced inhibition, and impairments in balance. Heavy use of alcohol can cause a slowing down of the central nervous system, including the nerves that control breathing and the gag reflex. Large amounts of alcohol can stop these functions, which is why passing out from excessive alcohol use can be so dangerous.

Mechanism of action (MOA) A description of the way a drug functions.

Depressants A class of drugs that reduces the activity in the nervous system.

Stimulants A class of psychoactive substances that increases activity in the nervous system.

Hallucinogens A type of drug that distort conscious experiences.

Tranquilizers A type of drug used for sedation and reducing anxiety.

Alcohol A type of depressant drug that is associated with reduced inhibition, slurred speech, and impairments in balance.

Glutamate An excitatory neurotransmitter.

Caffeine is a common stimulant.

Narcotics/Opiates

Barbiturates are a type of depressant drug that reduces stress and induces sleep. **Opiates** are psychoactive substances made from opium that relieve pain and reduce the activity of the nervous system. Both are similar to your body's natural opiate painkillers and both activate opiate receptor sites. When this occurs, the natural inhibition of dopamine is turned off, which allows dopamine to be released. Since dopamine is involved with the body's reward system, it is often associated with feelings of well-being and reduction of pain. With their pain-relieving ability, opiates act like endorphins, but they can also act on your moods. People report feelings of euphoria, reduction of anxiety, and increasing motivation. Large doses can have disastrous effects including respiratory depression, hypothermia, and coma. Withdrawal from barbiturates can cause elevation of body temperature, blood pressure, heart rate, and breathing. In addition, some people experience disorientation, psychotic behavior, and hallucinations from barbiturate withdrawal.

Stimulants

Stimulants are a group of psychoactive substances that increase activity in the nervous system. Drugs in this class include common things such as caffeine and nicotine, along with **amphetamines**, methamphetamine, cocaine, and ecstasy.

Small doses of stimulants can produce feelings of increased energy and euphoria. Moderate doses can lead to **stimulant-induced psychosis**, which involves hallucinations and delusions caused by this class of substances. Larger doses can lead to convulsions, cardiovascular failure, and death.

Caffeine

Caffeine is one of the most widely used stimulants in the world. It's present in a variety of products including chocolate, coffee, tea, nonprescription medications, and energy drinks. Caffeine stimulates the cerebral cortex and boosts energy and alertness. Even small doses of caffeine can stay in your system for up to 4 hours. Mild doses of caffeine taken too late in the day can impair sleep, and higher doses can lead to anxiety, headaches, and digestive problems. If you feel like you need to reduce your caffeine intake, do it slowly; rapid decreases in caffeine can lead to lethargy, headaches, and difficulty concentrating.

Nicotine

About one in four American adults smoke tobacco. The psychoactive substance in tobacco is a naturally occurring amount of nicotine. **Nicotine** reduces activity in many areas of the brain including the amygdala, the hippocampus, and the frontal lobes (Sharma & Brody, 2009). A dose of nicotine can stimulate the central nervous system in less than 7 seconds and increases the release of the neurotransmitter dopamine that can increase energy, pain tolerance, and alertness and reduce anxiety, appetite, and anger (Heishman, Kleykamp, & Singleton, 2010). Unfortunately, the use of tobacco is related to many illnesses, and each year, 4.5 million tobacco users die from a variety of tobacco-related illness. Also unfortunately, it is very difficult to stop using tobacco products. Quitting can cause anxiety, irritability, and cravings, and the mood-boosting effects of nicotine only last about 30 minutes.

Cocaine

Cocaine can increase the availability of dopamine and norepinephrine by blocking the transport proteins that normally clear these neurotransmitters from the synaptic cleft. This results in fewer ways of dopamine being cleared from the synaptic cleft. This allows dopamine and to bind with the dopamine receptor sites over and over. Cocaine use leads to increased energy, decreased appetite, alertness, anxiety, and feelings of euphoria. Abuse and long-term use of cocaine can result dependence, depression, tremors, hallucinations, and convulsions.

Methamphetamine

Methamphetamine is a stimulant drug associated with increased nervous system activity and elevated libido and self-esteem. Methamphetamine resembles dopamine, a neurotransmitter linked to pleasure. Because of its similarity to dopamine, methamphetamine is easily reabsorbed into the presynaptic neuron by the reuptake transport proteins that normally recycle dopamine neurotransmitters. Once inside the presynaptic neuron,

Barbiturates A type of depressant drug that reduces stress and induces sleep.

Opiates A psychoactive substance made from opium that relieves pain and reduces the activity of the nervous system.

Amphetamines A class of stimulant drugs that activates the central nervous system.

Stimulant-induced psychosis Symptoms of hallucinations and delusions that are caused by medication that activates the nervous system.

Caffeine A type of stimulant drug that is associated with increased central nervous system activity.

Nicotine A type of drug that targets the nicotinic receptors. Found in tobacco.

Cocaine A stimulant drug made from the coca plant.

Methamphetamine A stimulant drug that is associated with increased nervous system activity and elevated libido and self-esteem.

methamphetamine gets packaged into synaptic vesicles and displaces the dopamine. Because of this displacement, dopamine builds up at the end of the presynaptic neuron and causes the transport proteins to reverse and pump dopamine back into the synaptic gap. Once the dopamine gets trapped in the synaptic gap, it binds to receptor sites on the postsynaptic neuron over and over again and overstimulates the system.

Hallucinogens

Consciousness is the lens through which you experience yourself and your world. Change your consciousness and you've changed yourself. Hallucinogens are a class of psychoactive drugs that distort conscious experiences and can produce changes in how we perceive reality. People have used hallucinogenic agents for thousands of years for cultural and spiritual ceremonies to modify experience, often in surreal and inexpressible ways. Used recreationally, these drugs can produce unwanted effects.

Methamphetamine addiction can cause dramatic differences in a person's appearance.

Drugs in this class include lysergic acid diethylamide (LSD), mescaline, and marijuana. Although they are called hallucinogens, not every drug in this class will actually produce a hallucination, or a sensory experience without sensory input, at every dose. Rather, hallucinogens alter regular sensory experiences. Effects of hallucinogens can vary widely depending on the drug, the dose, the person, and even the environmental setting. Hallucinogens use can produce a myriad of emotions all converging at the same time.

Hallucinogens can also create distortions in the perception of time and sense of self. The effects of hallucinogens can last from a few moments to several days. Physical effects of hallucinogens include dilated pupils, dry mouth, tremors, and increases in blood pressure, breathing, and heart rate. Researchers have found changes in central nervous system functioning in heavy users, including impairments in attention, memory, and abstract thinking. Hallucinogens can cause changes in perception and thought. Some people report good hallucinations and distortions of time and perception, while others report upsetting hallucinations.

Some hallucinogens, like LSD, are synthetic, while others like mescaline, salvia, and psilocybin (sometimes called mushrooms) can be found in nature. Remember, though, that not everything natural is good for you or safe (like hemlock or cyanide). Responses to hallucinogens, either synthetic or natural, can vary widely from dose to dose and person to person. Experiences from psychedelics can range from pleasant to nightmarish.

LSD

Lysergic acid diethylamide (LSD) is a synthetic hallucinogenic drug that produces altered states of consciousness. The effects of LSD are usually felt within 30 to 60 minutes after the drug is taken. The effects of LSD include physiological changes such as an increase in heart rate, blood pressure, and body temperature, and dizziness. The psychoactive effects include a bending of sensory experiences and hallucinations from all five senses. LSD can produce flashbacks to experiences with the drug months after the drug was taken (Jaffe, 1990).

The mechanism of action of LSD is on serotonin pathways, mostly by binding to serotonin receptor sites. Sometimes LSD will activate the receptor and sometimes it won't, which makes LSD unpredictable. Most hallucinogens, including LSD, will activate many parts of the brain and various sensory areas in the brain.

Marijuana

While commonly listed as a hallucinogen, the active ingredient in **marijuana, tetrahydrocannabinol (THC),** has both mild painkilling as well as stimulating effects on the nervous system. It can lead to increased heart rate and altered perceptions, making those who have taken it feel relaxed, sleepy, and content. Under the effects of marijuana, people may spontaneously laugh, have disconnected rambling thoughts, and experience a distortion of time. Like other drugs, it can have multiple routes of administration, or ways to take it. It can be taken orally, as in a pill, in foods, or as an **inhalant** when its vapors are breathed in to produce its effect.

Lysergic acid diethylamide (LSD) A synthetic psychedelic hallucinogenic drug that produces altered states of consciousness.

Marijuana A drug that has both painkilling as well as stimulating effects on the nervous system.

Tetrahydrocannabinol (THC) A psychoactive substance that is the active ingredient in marijuana.

Inhalants Drugs whose vapors are breathed in to produce their intoxicating effect.

Larger doses of marijuana are associated with hallucinations and dissociative experiences. While some research suggests that marijuana can cause problems with long-term memory and motor coordination, others find only minor impairment in memory and learning in a group of long-term users versus nonusers (Grant, Gonzalez, Carey, Natarajan, & Wolfson, 2003).

The medicinal benefits of marijuana have led to its use in some medical areas. Medicinal benefits include increased appetite and reduction of nausea and vomiting, tremors, and the number and severity of seizures (Voth & Schwartz, 1997).

Ecstasy

Ecstasy (MDMA) A stimulant-hallucinogenic drug that can induce euphoria and diminish anxiety.

Methylenedioxymethamphetamine (**MDMA**) or **ecstasy** is a stimulant-hallucinogenic drug that can induce euphoria and diminish anxiety. Under the influence of ecstasy, users report feelings of enhanced intimacy, increased sensitivity to sensory stimuli, and more emotional openness. Ecstasy produces its full effect about an hour after it is ingested and lasts about 4 to 6 hours. Long-term use of MDMA is associated with dehydration, depression, and insomnia and can create long-term damage to serotonin neurons. Some people experience heart, liver, or kidney failure from taking large doses.

Transport proteins are one of the cleanup mechanisms in the synapses. Molecules of ecstasy are attracted to these sites and are taken into the axon terminal. This can cause changes in the reuptake site, causing the transport proteins to work backward. Instead of recycling serotonin, the axon terminal pumps it out of the cell. With fewer ways to clean up the synaptic gap, serotonin floods the synapse, overstimulating the receptor sites. This overstimulation can produce permanent damage and reduce the amount of healthy serotonin in the brain.

Serotonin pathways in the cerebral cortex influence multiple areas. Because there's so much serotonin in the synapse, ecstasy affects the user's emotions, appetite, sleep, wakefulness, and consciousness. In addition to serotonin, ecstasy can also impact dopamine, which is involved in our nervous system's reward system.

Summary of Multiple Influences on Consciousness

Eventually I did get to sleep. Turns out I was worried about a television interview that I was scheduled for later on that week. It's probably not a big surprise that something as simple as that, even though I wasn't thinking about it, could have such an impact on my ability to get to sleep. In this chapter, we have seen how our awareness of our internal and external environments is influenced by biological factors like the effects of psychoactive substances and natural sleep cycles but also by environmental factors like meditation and hypnosis. Social and cultural influences have an impact not only on your wanting to alter your consciousness through psychoactive drugs, but as in the case of LSD, your actual experience of the drug. Our awareness and experiences of our internal and external worlds depend on how we interact with these experiences. There are multiple influences on our awareness of both.

CONCEPT LEARNING CHECK **5.6** | *The Effects of Psychoactive Drugs*

Match the class of psychoactive drug to the specific substance.

A. Depressant

B. Stimulant

C. Hallucinogen

1. _____ Alcohol

2. _____ Amphetamines

3. _____ Caffeine

4. _____ Cocaine

5. _____ Ecstasy

6. _____ LSD

7. _____ Marijuana

8. _____ Methamphetamines

9. _____ Narcotics

10. _____ Nicotine

11. _____ Opiates

Visual Overview Sleep Cycles

	Easy to wake up
	More difficult to wake up
	Hard to wake up, may feel disoriented
REM	Low voltage, mixed frequency + rapid eye movement and muscle atonia

5.1 Overview: Consciousness, Brain Activity, Levels of Awareness

- Neuroscience imaging gives us a peek into what occurs in consciousness.
- Consciousness is dynamic and fluid.
- Our ability to selectively attend helps us to focus and attend.
- Dual processing ability of your nervous system helps you to attend to and manage stimuli from a variety of sources.
- Cognitive neuroscience is the science that studies thought, perception, and language from a biological perspective.

5.2 Sleep

- Your brain is active during sleep.
- You progress through four distinct phases during sleep.
- Stage 1 is the phase between relaxed wakefulness and sleep.
- Stage 2 is distinguished by sleep spindles and K-complexes on the EEG.
- In Stage 3, delta waves emerge on the EEG.
- In Stage 4, delta waves are more prominent on the EEG.
- REM sleep emerges the second time you enter Stage 1 sleep and is associated with memory sorting and dreams.
- The restorative theory of sleep suggests that sleep regenerates the body.
- The adaptive theory of sleep maintains that sleep is an evolved biological process.
- Sleep deprivation can cause many psychological and physical problems.
- Chronic sleep deprivation and sleep debt can also cause problems in daily functioning.
- Sleep disorders are conditions in which the quality or quantity of sleep is disturbed.
- Parasomnias are abnormal behaviors associated with sleep.
- Dyssomnias are conditions that affect the quantity or timing of sleep.
- Insomnia is characterized by difficulty falling or staying asleep.

5.3 Dreams

- Dreams are an array of sensory events experienced during sleep.
- The Freudian theory of dreams suggests that dreams are a reflection of unconscious id wishes.
- The activation-synthesis theory of dreams maintains that dreams are the result of interpreted brain activity during the consolidation of our memories.

5.4 Hypnosis

- Hypnosis is a trancelike state induced by a person whose suggestions of changes in consciousness or sensations are readily accepted by the subject.
- Not everyone is hypnotizable; about 20% of people can't be hypnotized, even by highly skilled practitioners.
- Hypnosis can help many medical conditions like pain.
- Researchers can't consistently find changes in the brain that would indicate that hypnosis is a special state of consciousness.
- The sociocognitive theory of hypnosis suggests that you respond to the suggestions of the hypnotist because you are expected to do so.
- Dissociation theories of hypnosis suggest that the hypnotic state produces a split in consciousness and separates the executive control system from the rest of the brain.

5.5 Meditation

- Meditation refers to any mental practice that focuses on regulating attention and awareness.

- The techniques of meditation hold promise for the treatment of several conditions.

5.6 Drug Use

- A psychoactive drug is a chemical used to alter consciousness.
- The abuse of psychoactive substances can lead to addiction, tolerance, and symptoms of withdrawal.
- A mechanism of action refers to the way a drug functions, and psychoactive drugs influence the functioning of the nervous system through their influence on neurotransmitter functioning.

- Depressants are drugs that reduce the level of activity in the nervous system and include tranquilizers, alcohol, narcotics, barbiturates, and opiates.
- Stimulants are drugs that increase activity in the nervous system and include caffeine, nicotine, amphetamines, methamphetamine, cocaine, and ecstasy.
- Hallucinogens are a class of drugs that distort conscious experience and include LSD, mescaline, and marijuana.

5.1 Overview: Consciousness, Brain Activity, Levels of Awareness

1. The interdisciplinary study of how brain action is linked to thoughts, perception, and language is called
 A. change blindness.
 B. cognitive neuroscience.
 C. dual processing.
 D. selective attention.

2. Your ability to pay attention to only one voice among many is called
 A. change blindness.
 B. dual processing.
 C. selective attention.
 D. consciousness.

3. Consciousness includes which of the following?
 A. Awareness of your internal sensations
 B. Awareness of your own thoughts
 C. Your awareness of yourself as a person separate from others
 D. All of the above

5.2 Sleep

4. As the night goes on:
 A. it becomes increasingly difficult to wake up.
 B. REM periods get longer.
 C. Stage 4 periods get longer.
 D. Stage 3 periods get longer.

5. About an hour after falling asleep, Dane sits up in bed screaming. After his roommate wakes him, he doesn't remember anything. It seems that Dane is suffering from
 A. narcolepsy.
 B. nightmares.
 C. night terrors.
 D. sleep apnea.

6. The bursts of EEG activity that occur during Stage 2 sleep are called
 A. night terrors.
 B. REM sleep.
 C. sleep spindles.
 D. sleep apnea.

7. The part of your hypothalamus that is involved in sleep and wakefulness is called
 A. suprachiasmatic nucleus.
 B. circadian.
 C. melatonin.
 D. CPAP.

8. A person who experiences sleep attacks where he or she suddenly lapses into sleep during the day is likely suffering from which sleep disorder?
 A. Sleep apnea
 B. Narcolepsy
 C. Primary insomnia
 D. Night terrors

9. Sarah snores a lot when she sleeps. In addition, she has periods during which her breathing will stop. It's likely that Sarah suffers from which sleep disorder?
 A. CPAP
 B. Cataplexy
 C. Obstructive sleep apnea
 D. Hypocretin

10. Stopping someone from getting REM sleep would result in what changes in sleep when the person is then allowed to sleep normally?
 A. More restful sleep
 B. No change in REM when allowed to sleep normally
 C. Increased REM in Stage 4 sleep when allowed to sleep normally
 D. Increased REM in Stage 1 sleep when allowed to sleep normally

5.3 Dreams

11. As Anton remembered his dream, he was running a race. A person utilizing the psychoanalytic or Freudian theory of dream would say that Anton's account of the dream represents the _____ content of the dream.
 A. manifest
 B. latent
 C. activated
 D. synthesis

12. Roberta had a dream in which she was ice skating while reading a psychology book. Earlier that day, she was watching ice skating on TV while reading her book. Which model or theory of dreams would suggest that this dream is just a way to combine the memories she had that day?
 A. Manifest content
 B. Latent content
 C. Psychoanalytic
 D. Activation-synthesis

5.4 Hypnosis

13. The theory of hypnosis that suggests that the hypnotic state that separates the executive control system from the rest of the mind is called
 A. the dissociative theory of hypnosis.
 B. the role-playing theory of hypnosis.
 C. hypermnesia.
 D. the sociocognitive theory of hypnosis.

5.5 Meditation

14. The benefits of meditation include
   A. reduction of inflammation.
   B. reduction of hypertension.
   C. enhanced empathy.
   D. all of the above.

5.6 Drug Use

15. Psychoactive drugs produce their actions in the nervous system by
   A. blocking the action of neurotransmitters.
   B. preventing the reabsorption of neurotransmitters.
   C. binding to a receptor site normally used by neurotransmitters.
   D. All of these are examples of how psychoactive drugs produce their actions on the nervous system.

16. Don has a morning coffee to keep himself going at work. Lately he has noticed that he needs more and more caffeine to get the same effect. Don is beginning to develop _____.
   A. a tolerance to caffeine
   B. rebound symptoms
   C. withdrawal symptoms
   D. abuse of caffeine

CHAPTER DISCUSSION QUESTIONS

1. A lot has been made of dream interpretation. Why do you think that people are so interested in dreams? What do the theories presented in the text add to your understanding of your own dreams?

2. Practice meditation or progressive relaxation for 2 weeks and keep a diary of your sleep and level of anxiety. Record what you've learned in a blog.

3. Despite the evidence that sleep is greatly improved by stimulus control techniques and sleep hygiene, why do you think most people focus on biological interventions (like PM capsules) to induce sleep?

4. Many sections in this chapter focus on altering consciousness by either biological (drugs) or behavioral (hypnosis and meditation) means. Why do you think that we try so hard to alter our consciousness?

CHAPTER PROJECTS

1. After reviewing the information on insomnia and on ways to improve sleep, interview a friend and develop a sleep improvement plan that lists the things that she or he could do to improve sleep. Be sure to examine psychological, social, and biological issues that could impair sleep.

CHAPTER KEY TERMS

Activation-synthesis model of dreaming
Acute insomnia
Adaptive theory of sleep
Alcohol
Alpha waves
Amphetamines
Attentional blink
Barbiturates
Caffeine
Cataplexy
Change blindness
Circadian rhythm
Cocaine
Cognitive neuroscience
Consciousness
Consolidation
Continuous positive airway pressure (CPAP)
Delta waves
Depressants
Dissociation theory of hypnosis
Dream

Drug abuse
Drug addiction
Drug dependence
Drug rebound effect
Dual processing
Dyssomnia
Ecstasy (MDMA)
Electroencephalogram (EEG)
Executive control system
Glutamate
Hallucinogens
Hidden observer
Hypermnesia
Hypnagogic hallucinations
Hypnosis
Hypocretin
Inattentional blindness
Inhalants
Insomnia
K-complex
Latent content
Lysergic acid diethylamide (LSD)
Manifest content

Marijuana
Mechanism of action (MOA)
Meditation
Melatonin
Methamphetamine
Narcolepsy
Neodissociation theory of hypnosis
Nicotine
Nightmare
nREM sleep
Opiates
Parasomnia
Physical dependence
Posthypnotic suggestion
Primary insomnia
Progressive relaxation
Psychoactive drug
Psychoanalytic theory of dreams
Psychological dependence
Rapid eye movement (REM) sleep
REM rebound

REM sleep behavior disorder
Restorative theory of sleep
Secondary insomnia
Selective attention
Sleep
Sleep apnea
Sleep debt
Sleep disorder
Sleep eating

Sleep hygiene
Sleep paralysis
Sleepsex
Sleep spindle
Sleep terror
Sleepthink
Sleepwalking
Stage 1
Stimulant-induced psychosis

Stimulants
Stimulus control therapy
Suprachiasmatic nucleus
Tetrahydrocannabinol (THC)
Theta
Tolerance
Tranquilizers
Withdrawal symptoms

ANSWERS TO CONCEPT LEARNING CHECKS

5.1 Consciousness and Psychology

1. The study of consciousness is relatively new in psychology. [F]
2. Cognitive neuroscience studies brain action linked to thought, perception, and language. [T]
3. Humans can usually only attend to one thing at a time. [F]
4. An electroencephalogram can be used to study consciousness. [T]
5. Consciousness is the state of awareness of only our external environment. [F]

5.2 Stages of Sleep

1. Sleep spindles begin during **Stage 1**.
2. During the **REM sleep** stage, the body has increased heart rate and rapid breathing.
3. **Stage 3** is the stage when delta waves begin.
4. **Stage 4** is the most difficult stage to wake up from.

5.3 Theories of Dreams

1. **Activation synthesis** is the theory of dreams that suggests that dreams are interpreted brain activity.
2. **Freudian or psychodynamic** is the theory of dreams that suggests that dreams are a reflection of unconscious wishes.
3. According to the Freudian theory of dreams, a dream's **manifest** content is the dream is it is often reported.
4. According to the Freudian theory of dreams, a dream's **latent** content is the underlying meaning of the dream.

5.4 Theories of Hypnosis

1. The **dissociation theory of hypnosis** suggests that the hypnotic state produces a split in consciousness and separates the executive control system from the rest of the brain.

2. The **sociocognitive theory of hypnosis** suggests that you respond to the suggestion of the hypnotist because you are expected to do so.
3. He calls the orphaned executive control system a **hidden observer**.
4. **Hypermnesia** or elevated memory recall isn't universal for hypnosis.

5.5 The Effects and Benefits of Meditation

1. Meditation only refers to religious practices that focus on regulating attention and awareness and spirituality. [F]
2. Progressive relaxation is a technique for reducing anxiety by alternately tensing and relaxing the muscles. [T]
3. Regular meditation is associated with lower stress hormones such as cortisol, increased immune response, increased self-esteem, and lower blood pressure. [T]
4. There is evidence that meditation offers additional benefits beyond those of progressive relaxation. [T]

5.6 The Effects of Psychoactive Drugs

1. Alcohol [depressant]
2. Amphetamines [stimulant]
3. Caffeine [stimulant]
4. Cocaine [stimulant]
5. Ecstasy [stimulant-hallucinogen]
6. LSD [hallucinogen]
7. Marijuana [hallucinogen]
8. Methamphetamines [stimulant]
9. Narcotics [depressant]
10. Nicotine [stimulant]
11. Opiates [hallucinogen]

ANSWERS TO CHAPTER REVIEW TEST

5.1 Overview: Consciousness, Brain Activity, Levels of Awareness

1. B. Rationale: Cognitive neuroscience is the methodological study of brain action linked to thought, perception, and language. Those who study cognitive neuroscience are interested in the biological underpinnings of cognition.
2. C. Rationale: Selective attention is your ability to focus your thoughts and perceptions to filter out stimuli.
3. D. Rationale: Consciousness is the state of awareness of the internal and external environment and includes all of the examples listed.

5.2 Sleep

4. B. Rationale: As the night progresses, deeper sleep decreases while Stage 1 and REM periods increase in length.
5. C. Rationale: Sleep terrors, also known as night terrors, are a sleep condition in which a person has the appearance of panic; occurs during the early part of the night. Nightmares will more often occur later in the night during REM sleep.
6. C. Rationale: Sleep spindles are small bursts of brain activity that are recorded on the EEG.

7. A. Rationale: The suprachiasmatic nucleus helps regulate the pineal gland's melatonin production.

8. B. Rationale: Narcolepsy is a condition characterized by daytime sleepiness and, in some cases, sudden lapses into sleep during the day.

9. C. Rationale: Obstructive sleep apnea is a sleep disorder in which your breathing will stop.

10. D. Rationale: REM rebound is the increased amount of REM sleep in Stage 1 when deprived of REM sleep.

5.3 Dreams

11. A. Rationale: The manifest content of a dream is the dream as it is remembered by the dreamer.

12. D. Rationale: The activation-synthesis model of dreaming suggests that dreams are interpreted brain activity.

5.4 Hypnosis

13. A. Rationale: Dissociative theories of hypnosis suggest that hypnosis produces a dissociated "hidden observer" or split-off executive control system.

5.5 Meditation

14. D. Rationale: Research suggests that all of these are benefits of meditation.

5.6 Drug Use

15. D. Rationale: All of these are examples of how psychoactive drugs produce their actions on the nervous system.

16. A. Rationale: Drug tolerance is indicated by a reduction in sensitivity to a drug over time, which may lead to needing more and more to produce the original effect.

REFERENCES

Ahmed, I., & Thorpy, M. (2010). Clinical features, diagnosis and treatment of narcolepsy. *Clinics in Chest Medicine, 31*(2), 371–381. doi:10.1016/j.ccm.2010.02.014

Anderson, J. W., Liu, C., & Kryscio, R. J. (2008). Blood pressure response to transcendental meditation: A meta-analysis. *American Journal of Hypertension, 21*(3), 310–316. doi:10.1038/ajh.2007.65

Avidan, A. Y., & Kaplish, N. (2010). The parasomnias: Epidemiology, clinical features, and diagnostic approach. *Clinics in Chest Medicine, 31*(2), 353–370. doi:10.1016/j.ccm.2010.02.015

Barrett, D. (Ed.) (2010). *Hypnosis and hypnotherapy.* Santa Barbara, CA: Praeger.

Benson, M. H., & Klipper, M. Z. (2000). *The relaxation response* (Rev. ed.). New York: Harper Paperbacks.

Cai, D. J., Mednick, S. A., Harrison, E. M., Kanady, J. C., & Mednick, S. C. (2009). REM, not incubation, improves creativity by priming associative networks. *Proceedings of the National Academy of Sciences of the United States of America, 106*(25), 10130–10134. doi:10.1073/pnas.0900271106

Cash, S. S., Halgren, E., Dehghani, N., Rossetti, A. O., Thesen, T., Wang, C., Devinsky, O., et al. (2009). The human K-complex represents an isolated cortical down-state. *Science, 324*(5930), 1084–1087. doi:10.1126/science.1169626

Cheyne, J. A. (2002). Situational factors affecting sleep paralysis and associated hallucinations: Position and timing effects. *Journal of sleep research, 11*(2), 169–177.

Chokroverty, S. (2008). *Questions & answers about sleep apnea* (1st ed.). Sudbury, MA: Jones and Bartlett Publishers, Inc.

Daley, M., Morin, C. M., LeBlanc, M., Grégoire, J., & Savard, J. (2009). The economic burden of insomnia: Direct and indirect costs for individuals with insomnia syndrome, insomnia symptoms, and good sleepers. *Sleep, 32*(1), 55–64.

Dement, W. C., & Vaughan, C. (2000). *The promise of sleep: A pioneer in sleep medicine explores the vital connection between health, happiness, and a good night's sleep* (1st ed.). New York: Dell.

Doghramji, K. (2006). The epidemiology and diagnosis of insomnia. *American Journal of Managed Care, 12*(8 Suppl), S214–S220.

Ebrahim, I. O. (2006). Somnambulistic sexual behaviour (sexsomnia). *Journal of Clinical Forensic Medicine, 13*(4), 219–224. doi:10.1016/j.jcfm.2006.02.001

Erdelyi, M. H. (1994). Hypnotic hypermnesia: The empty set of hypermnesia. *International Journal of Clinical and Experimental Hypnosis, 42*(4), 379–390.

Friedman, M. F. (2008). *Sleep apnea and snoring: Surgical and non-surgical therapy* (1st ed.). Philadelphia, PA: Saunders.

Gangwisch, J. E., Malaspina, D., Boden-Albala, B., Heymsfield, S. B. (2005). Inadequate sleep as a risk factor for obesity: Analyses of the NHANES I. *Sleep, 28*(10), 1289–1296.

Grant, I., Gonzalez, R., Carey, C. L., Natarajan, L., & Wolfson, T. (2003). Non-acute (residual) neurocognitive effects of cannabis use: A meta-analytic study.

Journal of the International Neuropsychological Society: JINS, 9(5), 679–689. doi:10.1017/S1355617703950016

Griffith, R. M., Miyagi, O., & Tago, A. (1958). The universality of typical dreams: Japanese vs. Americans. *American Anthropologist, 60*(6), 1173–1179. doi:10.1525/aa.1958.60.6.02a00110

Hammond, D. C. (2010). Hypnosis in the treatment of anxiety- and stress-related disorders. *Expert Review of Neurotherapeutics, 10*(2), 263–273. doi:10.1586/ern.09.140

Heishman, S. J., Kleykamp, B. A., & Singleton, E. G. (2010). Meta-analysis of the acute effects of nicotine and smoking on human performance. *Psychopharmacology, 210*(4), 453–469. doi:10.1007/s00213-010-1848-1

Hilgard, E. R. (1992). Divided consciousness and dissociation. *Consciousness and Cognition, 1*(1), 16–31. doi:16/1053-8100(92)90041-8

Hobson, J. A., & McCarley, R. W. (1977). The brain as a dream state generator: An activation-synthesis hypothesis of the dream process. *American Journal of Psychiatry, 134*(12), 1335.

Howell, M. J., Schenck, C. H., & Crow, S. J. (2009). A review of nighttime eating disorders. *Sleep Medicine Reviews, 13*(1), 23–34. doi:10.1016/j.smrv.2008.07.005

Jacobs, G. D. (2009). *Say good night to insomnia* (1st ed.). New York: Holt Paperbacks.

Jain, S., Shapiro, S. L., Swanick, S., Roesch, S. C., Mills, P. J., Bell, I., & Schwartz, G. E. R. (2007). A randomized controlled trial of mindfulness meditation versus relaxation training: Effects on distress, positive states of mind, rumination, and distraction. *Annals of Behavioral Medicine: A Publication of the Society of Behavioral Medicine, 33*(1), 11–21. doi:10.1207/s15324796abm3301_2

Jaffe, J. H. (1990). Drug addiction and drug abuse. In A. G. Gilman et al. (Eds.), *Goodman Gilman's the pharmacological basis of therapeutics* (8th ed.). New York: Pergamon.

Kirsch, I., & Lynn, S. J. (1995). Altered state of hypnosis: Changes in the theoretical landscape. *American Psychologist, 50*(10), 846–858. doi:10.1037/0003-066X.50.10.846

Lynn, S. J., Fassler, O., & Knox, J. (2005). Hypnosis and the altered state debate: Something more or nothing more? *Contemporary Hypnosis, 22*(1), 39–45. doi:10.1002/ch.21

Maggiolini, A., Cagnin, C., Crippa, F., Persico, A., & Rizzi, P. (2010). Content analysis of dreams and waking narratives. *Dreaming, 20*(1), 60–76. doi:10.1037/a0018824

Majumdar, M., Grossman, P., Dietz-Waschkowski, B., Kersig, S., & Walach, H. (2002). Does mindfulness meditation contribute to health? Outcome evaluation of a German sample. *Journal of Alternative and Complementary Medicine, 8*(6), 719.

Olsen, S., Smith, S., Oei, T. P., & Douglas, J. (2010). Cues to starting CPAP in obstructive sleep apnea: Development and validation of the cues to CPAP use questionnaire, *Journal of Clinical Sleep Medicine 6*(3), 229–237.

Orne, M. T. (1959). The nature of hypnosis: Artifact and essence. *Journal of Abnormal and Social Psychology, 58*(3), 277.

Ospina, M. B., Bond, K., Karkhaneh, M., Tjosvold, L., Vandermeer, B., Liang, Y., Bialy, L., et al. (2007). Meditation practices for health: State of the research. *Evidence Report/Technology Assessment,* (155), 1–263.

Saxvig, I. W., Lundervold, A. J., Grønli, J., Ursin, R., Bjorvatn, B., & Portas, C. M. (2008). The effect of a REM sleep deprivation procedure on different aspects of memory function in humans. *Psychophysiology, 45*(2), 309–317. doi:10.1111/j.1469-8986.2007.00623.x

Siegel, J. M. (2009). Sleep viewed as a state of adaptive inactivity. *Nature Reviews Neuroscience, 10*(10), 747–753. doi:10.1038/nrn2697

Siegel, J. M., & Boehmer, L. N. (2006). Narcolepsy and the hypocretin system—where motion meets emotion. *Nature Clinical Practice Neurology, 2*(10), 548–556. doi:10.1038/ncpneuro0300

Sharma, A., & Brody, A. L. (2009). In vivo brain imaging of human exposure to nicotine and tobacco. *Nicotine Psychopharmacology, 192*(2) 145–171. doi:/10.1007/978-3-540-69248-5_6

Slagter, H. A., Lutz, A., Greischar, L. L., Francis, A. D., Nieuwenhuis, S., Davis, J. M., & Davidson, R. J. (2007). Mental training affects distribution of limited brain resources. *PLoS Biol, 5*(6), e138. doi:10.1371/journal.pbio.0050138

Stahl, S. (2009). *The prescriber's guide* (3rd ed.). Cambridge, MA: Cambridge University Press.

Ulualp, S. O. (2010). Snoring and obstructive sleep apnea. *Medical Clinics of North America, 94*(5), 1047–1055.

Voth, E. A., & Schwartz, R. H. (1997). Medicinal applications of delta-9-tetrahydrocannabinol and marijuana. *Annals of Internal Medicine, 126*(10), 791–798.

Zeidan, F., Gordon, N. S., Merchant, J., & Goolkasian, P. (2010). The effects of brief mindfulness meditation training on experimentally induced pain. *Journal of Pain: Official Journal of the American Pain Society, 11*(3), 199–209. doi:10.1016/j.jpain.2009.07.015

Chapter Review

Chapter Overview ▼

6 Learning

At 6, my son Victor just barely reached the "You must be this tall to ride!" sign at the community pool. He eagerly climbed the stairs after his older cousins, excited for his first trip on a waterslide. He jumped on at the top, rode the waterslide down twisting turns, and landed on his back in the foot-deep pool of water at the bottom. Completely, and unexpectedly, submerged, Victor coughed and cried from the rush of water into his nose. He was done riding the slide, but not just for the day: Two years later, Victor doesn't recall that August day, but he still avoids waterslides, saying, "I just don't like them."

Something happened during Victor's first waterslide experience: He learned an enduring connection between waterslides and feelings of discomfort. In what ways does our biological heritage explain how we learn basic responses like "fear?" And how does our experience in the world shape what we learn about it? As we'll see in this chapter, our biological tendencies interact with environmental factors to produce learning like Victor's. Psychologists investigate events like these to understand the processes underlying learning. Their research explores topics such as:

- how emotional experiences affect our actions and attitudes
- how we learn to change our behavior in response to expected outcomes
- how we learn from the behavior of others around us.

In this chapter, we'll explore the relationships between the biological and environmental influences that allow us to change through our experiences; that is, to learn from them.

6.1 How We Learn

Learning can occur through associating events that occur together, responding to the consequences of our behavior, and observing the behavior of others.

■ Distinguish among three major types of learning theories focusing on behavior.

Learning A lasting change in knowledge or behavior based on experience.

Acquisition Gaining new knowledge or behavior to use in the future.

Psychologists think about **learning** as a lasting change in knowledge and/or behavior as a consequence of experience. It is a central problem for psychology because people, and in fact all living things, must learn in order to survive. The world is constantly changing, and our capacity to learn means we can adjust to a changing world by changing our behaviors accordingly. The field of psychology has devoted an immense amount of research to the ways in which we learn from experience. Learning is certainly a central, defining topic within psychological science.

At the heart is a basic question: How can I, as a scientist, determine that you, as a research subject, have learned? Right now, as you're reading this text, you are learning (I sincerely hope!), forming connections to what you already know, and creating new memories containing this new information, called **acquisition** of information or behaviors. But to an outside observer, how can your change in knowledge be verified? Typically, we use language to demonstrate whether we have learned something. But people are often unable to report how or why they know something; for example, Victor can't say how he learned to avoid waterslides. So historically, psychologists focused on defining learning in a way that does not depend on language. If you meet someone who doesn't speak your language, how could you determine what he or she can learn? You would have to depend on the person's behaviors, or actions that can be directly observed in the world.

For this reason, a well-established psychological theory, called **behaviorism**, argues that we can't know what is inside the mind, but we can know what actions are observable in the world (Watson, 1913).

"Radical behaviorists" thought we should investigate the basic processes of learning by completely ignoring what people are thinking and study only their discrete, observable behaviors. They chose to refer to learning as **conditioning**, emphasizing the role of training to produce changes in behavior. In addition, behaviorists study the properties of human learning by testing animal behaviors, arguing that the important processes of learning are just as evident in animals as they are in humans. To understand why people do what they do, behaviorists argue, we don't need language; instead, we need only observe behavior as it changes with experience.

From this behaviorist perspective, there are two types of learning exhibited by humans and other animals: classical conditioning and operant conditioning FIGURE 6-1. In **classical conditioning**, we learn through our experience with the world that two things are associated with one another, just as a flash of lightning goes with the roar of thunder. By watching for signs that predict what will happen next, we can learn to seek out or avoid situations that may benefit or harm us. This type of learning is basic to survival, helping us seek out the good and avoid the bad. For example, if you eat a new food and then become sick, you will quickly associate sickness with that food and avoid it in the future. Classical conditioning involves *instinctive and reflexive* behaviors that are elicited (or brought out) by specific events. The key to classical conditioning is to remember that it involves only reflexive behaviors: specifically, our basic physiological responses, such as feeling sexually aroused, nauseated, anxious, or startled.

The second type of learning from the behaviorist perspective ties a behavior to its consequence in the world. In **operant conditioning**, we "operate" on our environment, and our behavior is rewarded with consequences; if we are positively rewarded, we will perform this behavior again, and more often. Operant conditioning involves behaviors that we emit (*freely choose*) to perform. Why do you put change in the soda machine or talk to that cute student or read this assignment? Because these behaviors have been rewarded, or **reinforced**, in the past. For example, drinking a soda tastes good, so that behavior is likely to be repeated. The key to operant conditioning is to remember that it predicts how we will behave based on how we've been rewarded for these behaviors in the past.

Following the behaviorist approach, a second approach to learning, the **cognitive** approach, focused on learning as changes in knowledge within the mind. Cognitive theories of learning address mental processes that cannot be accounted for in strictly behavioral terms. Even in rats, learning can occur without behavior, so we need explanations for how

Behaviorism The study of learning based on directly observable actions.

Conditioning Training, or learning as displayed by an animal's or human's behavior.

Classical conditioning A neutral stimulus is associated with an unlearned stimulus and its automatic response.

Operant conditioning Training emitted behaviors to make them more likely to occur again.

Reinforce To strengthen behavior, making it more likely to occur again.

Cognitive The explanations of behavior based on changes in knowledge within the mind.

Classical Conditioning

The monkey avoids snakes after being bitten by one.

Operant Conditioning

The monkey works to peel the banana, and is rewarded with food.

Observational Learning

The monkey copies a new method for cracking open coconuts

FIGURE 6-1 Learning theories in psychology address only observable behaviors and apply to all types of organisms.

Observational learning Acquiring new behaviors from watching a model.

changes occur in knowledge within the mind. For example, **observational learning** allows us to watch and learn from the behaviors of others without moving a muscle. In fact, it appears that our brains are wired with special neural systems that "mirror" the experiences of others within our own minds. By observing others, we can quickly gain knowledge about which behaviors are likely to lead to good outcomes. For example, wild monkeys have been shown to rapidly learn to fear snakes from watching other monkeys (Mineka, Keir, & Price, 1980). In fact, studies of animal groups show the benefits of "culture" similar to ours, in which a chimp that learns to swim leads to a whole pack of swimming chimps, while other groups never venture into the water. The phrase "Monkey see, monkey do" is not about humans, but it aptly describes how readily we learn from others around us.

Behavioral theories of learning describe how behavior changes with experience (see **TABLE 6-1**). Because they focus on our external, observable actions in the world, they do not take into account the thinking we do or the language we use. In later chapters, we will more fully explore cognitive theories of learning in terms of memory processes and language. In this chapter, we will see how far theories of learning can go in accounting for our behavior without appealing to the special cognitive abilities of the human animal.

TABLE 6-1 Summary of Behavioral Learning Theories

Type of Learning	Training Method	After Training	Example
Classical conditioning	A neutral stimulus is paired with an unconditioned stimulus that elicits an unconditioned response.	The neutral stimulus becomes the conditioned stimulus and elicits the conditioned response.	A bell now elicits salivation just like meat does.
Operant conditioning	A behavior is followed by reinforcement.	The behavior is now more likely to occur.	A rat presses a bar for food.
Observational learning	A behavior is modeled for the learner.	The observer performs the same behavior at will.	A child hits a doll just like what was seen on a video.

CONCEPT LEARNING CHECK 6.1   *Comparing Types of Learning*

For each example, determine whether it best fits classical conditioning, operant conditioning, or observational learning theory.

1. Sydney liked the comments and attention she received when she wore provocative clothing, so she started wearing even shorter skirts to school.

2. Raoul was home alone when a bad storm brought down the power lines, leaving him in the dark for several hours. Now, he insists that his roommate stay in whenever it's raining.

3. Mandy was very disappointed when her daughter was caught playing hooky from middle school. The school had to send a letter to their home because Mandy herself was not at work on the days that the school attempted to call her.

4. Dedre had several humiliating moments when her history teacher called on her to explain concepts in class. Now, whenever he calls on her during class, she starts trembling uncontrollably.

5. When Pete went to his girlfriend's home for dinner, he watched to see which fork she used for the salad.

6. Malay was trying to study, but every time she answered one of her sister's comments, her sister talked even more.

6.2 Classical Conditioning

We learn to connect events that predict our important physiological responses, including reflexes and fear.

- Identify the principles of classical conditioning involving reflexive behaviors.

In associative learning, we learn that when Event A happens, Event B is likely to follow soon after. For example, you may learn to stay out of dusty attics after finding a spider lurking in one. How we learn these sorts of associations between events is called classical conditioning, because it was the first modern learning theory developed. It was originally discovered—by accident—by a Russian physiologist, Ivan Pavlov. You may have heard of the famous "Pavlov's dogs," as they provided the insight behind this learning theory (Pavlov, 1927).

Pavlov's Experiments

Pavlov was interested in digestion in dogs, not in psychology. In fact, he later won a Nobel Prize for his studies of the reflexes involved in digestive functioning. Part of his scientific procedure involved putting food (in this case, meat powder) on dogs' tongues and measuring their salivary secretions in long tubes hanging from the corners of their mouths. Dogs naturally produce saliva, or drool, whenever they are exposed to food. But Pavlov soon noticed a surprising thing: The dogs salivated as soon as they saw the assistant entering the lab! The dogs learned to associate the sight of the attendant with food because the two occurred together in time. This phenomenon, called psychic secretions by Pavlov and Pavlovian conditioning by others, came to be called classical conditioning.

Acquisition

Let's walk through the steps involved in the process of classical conditioning for Pavlov's dogs. Before any learning takes place, there is an existing link between the food, called the **unconditioned stimulus** (the event that elicits a response) and the resulting salivating, called the **unconditioned response** (the reflexive behavior elicited by the stimulus). When dogs are exposed to food, they automatically begin to salivate as a basic physiological reflex. Conditioning refers to the learning and training that results in this response. Whenever you see the term *conditioned*, think *learned*, and for *unconditioned*, think *unlearned* (occurring without learning).

The first step in conditioning involves a new stimulus, called the **neutral stimulus** because it does not yet cause any response. For example, Pavlov rang a bell, which at first caused no salivary reaction in the dogs at all. During the conditioning trials, the neutral stimulus (the bell) was presented with the unconditioned stimulus (the food). So on each trial, a bell was rung just before food was given to the dogs, which produced the unconditioned response (salivating). By repeatedly pairing the neutral stimulus with the unconditioned stimulus, the dogs learned that the bell reliably predicts the arrival of food. Soon, the dogs didn't wait for the food but began salivating as soon as they heard the bell. After conditioning, the bell is called a **conditioned stimulus**. That is, the bell changes from a neutral or meaningless stimulus into a stimulus that, on its own, now leads to a **conditioned response** (salivation). In addition, salivation changes from a reflexive, unconditioned response into a trained or "conditioned" response. This sequence of learning trials in classical conditioning is shown in FIGURE 6-2. The key is to remember that *unconditioned* refers to the *unlearned*, already-present connection between a stimulus and a reflexive response. *Conditioned*, then, refers to the *learned* association acquired between a new stimulus and the reflexive response.

Unconditioned stimulus An unlearned signal that leads to an automatic, reflexive response.

Unconditioned response A physiological behavior that is involuntarily elicited by a stimulus.

Neutral stimulus An event or signal that causes no reflexive, automatic response.

Conditioned stimulus A learned signal that predicts another stimulus is about to occur.

Conditioned response A physiological behavior that is associated with a learned stimulus.

Before learning

Food
Unconditioned stimulus

→ Response →

Salivation
Unconditioned response

Bell

→ Response →

No response

During learning

Food

+

Bell

→ Response →

Salivation
Unconditioned response

After learning

Bell
Conditioned stimulus

→ Response →

Salivation
Conditioned response

FIGURE 6-2 The sequence of events in Pavlov's classical conditioning experiment.

The famous example of Pavlov's dogs is all well and good, but what does it tell us about learning by people? Classical conditioning is very specific in terms of what you can learn with it: It refers *only* to learning that involves an existing reflex, instinct, or automatic response. An example of a reflex that can be classically conditioned is the "startle" response, induced by any loud, sudden noise. Imagine you're driving along in your car, and you suddenly hear a police siren behind you: You will feel an unsettling startle reflex in response. The loud sound (the unconditioned stimulus) will cause your body to become active, alert, alarmed, and likely upset (the unconditioned response). Now imagine you drive past a police car sitting on the side of the road (a previously neutral stimulus). You may cringe and feel the same unpleasant startle reaction. Through classical conditioning, you have learned that police cars (now the conditioned stimulus) signal the unconditioned stimulus (the siren), which evokes your startle response. Now, just seeing a police car is enough to cause the (conditioned) startle response, even without hearing the siren.

Through **higher-order conditioning**, a neutral stimulus can become a new conditioned stimulus just by being paired with an existing conditioned stimulus FIGURE 6-3. In Pavlov's study, after the connection between the bell and salivation is well established, he added a new neutral signal, a flashing light, *before* the bell rang. Any signal that predicts the conditioned stimulus (the bell) will *itself* be learned as a conditioned stimulus. These second-order associations can have important consequences in our everyday lives. For instance, you may later feel an unpleasant startle reaction just from seeing a police officer. Anything related to the conditioned stimulus can be a signal that it may now occur.

Classical conditioning theory states that we are ready to associate *any* sign with our reflexive, unconditioned responses. And we may learn the association, as Victor did with the waterslide, through a single trial. Victor's unpleasant experience of being unexpectedly submerged at the bottom of the slide (the unconditioned stimulus) naturally resulted in fear and pain (the unconditioned response). This experience turned a previously neutral stimulus (going on the waterslide) into a conditioned stimulus that now, by itself, elicits fear (the conditioned response). He may also associate other signals with that event, such as the specific pool where it took place. We are often unaware of the higher-order associations we develop, but our physiological responses can be so pleasant or unpleasant that we quickly learn to associate new cues that predict their occurrence. A familiar signal like the smell of a favorite food can be enough to evoke our conditioned responses from past experiences.

Extinction and Spontaneous Recovery

It's important to realize that, just as we learn an association between a signal and our physiological reaction, we can *unlearn* it. In the process of **extinction**, the conditioned stimulus is repeatedly presented without the unconditioned stimulus. For example, if

The positive emotions from cooking with family may become associated with specific foods, which later give rise to the same feelings on their own.

Higher-order conditioning Learning to associate a neutral stimulus with an already-learned conditioned stimulus and conditioned response.

Extinction The tendency to stop responding to the conditioned stimulus when repeatedly presented without the unconditioned stimulus.

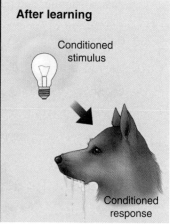

FIGURE 6-3 In higher-order conditioning, a new neutral stimulus (a light) is paired with an already learned conditioned stimulus (the bell) instead of with the unconditioned stimulus (the food).

Victor were to go down that waterslide every day and never again experience that painful submersion, he would eventually unlearn that association. However, it also appears that past associations "wait in the wings," ready to reappear if needed. New learning appears to suppress but not erase previous learning. If some time goes by without any experience of the conditioned stimulus, and then it suddenly occurs again, it may again evoke the conditioned response. This partial recovery of an association, called **spontaneous recovery**, occurs even after the conditioned stimulus has undergone extinction FIGURE 6-4. When in doubt, we fall back on the strength of prior associations. In fact, conditioned responses can show resistance to extinction, where the conditioned response is particularly difficult to unlearn.

Generalization

Classically conditioned responses may occur with a new stimulus even though it is not exactly the same as the one first learned. For example, you may have heard the whining tone of the dentist's drill as its painful work on your teeth was about to occur. After acquisition, the sound of the drilling tone has become a conditioned stimulus, eliciting a feeling of fear whenever you hear it. But what about other drilling sounds? In classical conditioning, you may **generalize** learning so that you have the same conditioned response (fear) to other, similar sounds, a process called stimulus generalization. The process of generalization in classical conditioning forms a reliable relationship, called the generalization gradient: The closer the new stimulus is to the one you learned, the more likely you are to experience the same conditioned response. FIGURE 6-5 shows this pattern, in which the strength of a conditioned response is highest when the stimulus is most similar to the conditioned stimulus. When new stimuli are less like the original, the conditioned response is weaker.

Discrimination

The opposite side of generalization is the process of **discrimination**, in which the learner comes to recognize differences among similar stimuli. Perhaps the dentist's drill has led you to fear all such sounds; but over time, you may demonstrate a reduced fear response when

Spontaneous recovery The reappearance of an extinguished conditioned response.

Generalization Learning to respond to stimuli similar to the one experienced.

Discrimination Learning to see the difference between two similar stimuli.

The sounds of the dentist's drill become associated with pain, so that the sound alone may give rise to fear in the future.

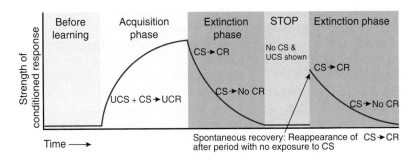

FIGURE 6-4 The rising line shows an increase in the conditioned response during acquisition, and a decrease during extinction. Then, after some time passes, the response may return, called "spontaneous recovery."

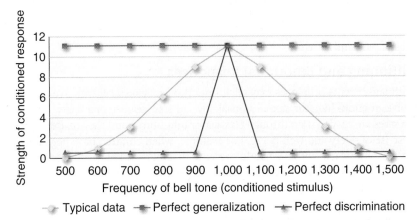

FIGURE 6-5 If Pavlov's dogs only responded to a bell tone like the one they learned, they would show a steep generalization gradient (the green line). If they generalized their learning so that similar sounding bells also produced the conditioned response, a pattern like the blue line would be observed. And, if they responded to any bell at all, they would show the complete generalization indicated by the orange line.

you hear a woodworking drill. As you learn stimulus discrimination, the generalization gradient narrows so that a smaller range of stimuli elicits the same conditioned response. This allows us to learn which aspects of the earlier experience predict real danger.

Review of Terminology, Processes, and Factors That Affect Classical Conditioning

An example will help to illustrate the terms and processes just described FIGURE 6-6. Classical conditioning is learning that two events go together; when one happens, the other happens. But most importantly, classical conditioning happens with behaviors that are elicited from the learner and are *not* voluntary. For example, if a strange dog bites you, you will have the automatic response of pain and fear, and that is not a choice or decision on your part. It occurs because an unconditioned stimulus—the dog bite—produces an unconditioned response—pain and fear. This existing link is the cornerstone of classical conditioning, and new learning builds upon this unconditioned association.

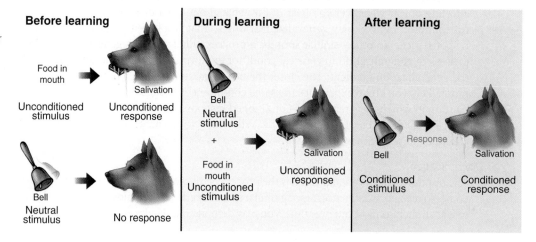

FIGURE 6-6 The three stages in classical conditioning are depicted: before, during, and after conditioning (learning).

Now, in this example, we pair the dog's bark—a neutral stimulus—with the bite. Before learning, the bark is neutral because it elicits no response from you. But after your experience of hearing barking, then of being bitten and feeling the resulting pain and fear, you have now learned that the bark is associated with the bite. Now, even when no bite occurs, a barking dog—the conditioned (or learned) stimulus—elicits the conditioned (learned) response: You feel fear! Remember that the unconditioned (unlearned) response becomes the conditioned (learned) response, so they are always the same behavior. And, in classical conditioning, this is always a basic physiological response such as a reflex or an emotion.

Once learned, these associations can undergo extinction. If a barking dog never bites, you may get used to the bark eventually. On the other hand, you may generalize your fear response to any animal that makes noise or you may learn to discriminate among noises that signal danger. What is most impressive about classical conditioning is that an experience can occur only once, but the learning from it can stay with you forever. Classical conditioning helps us readily learn the signs associated with our intense experiences of pain and pleasure.

Conditioning and Emotional Responses

In humans, events or images may elicit important reflexes or instinctive responses that involve emotions like fear, sexual arousal, joy, sadness, disgust, or anxiety. Our emotional responses are easy to train through classical conditioning, and they matter very much to our sense of safety and well-being. For example, when children have been abused, they associate angry faces with the painful violence that follows. Pollak and colleagues (1998) found that abused children's brain wave responses to angry faces were much stronger and longer lasting compared to those of nonabused children. A similar phenomenon may occur in couples experiencing marital discord. Repeated experiences of conflict and pain may lead to deep, emotional responses becoming associated with the other

Reflexive or automatic emotional arousal may occur from some events; in this case, a fly in your soup elicits the emotion of disgust.

partner (Gottman, 1998; Driver & Gottman, 2005). As a result, even when not engaged in fighting, the mere presence of the partner may evoke the emotional discomfort they have experienced so often. Through classical conditioning, we quickly learn the signs that predict upcoming emotional pain or pleasure, and we remain sensitive to those cues long after the original learning takes place.

Associations may also be positive. Using the principles of classical conditioning, it is easy to explain why specific associations occur with feelings of sexual arousal. For example, an unconditioned stimulus, such as a kiss, will lead to the unconditioned response of sexual arousal FIGURE 6-7. Through experience, however, another stimulus associated with the kiss may on its own lead to feelings of sexual arousal. For example, the smell of perfume, when paired with the kiss, can become associated with the resulting sexual arousal. Eventually the scent of the perfume alone leads to the conditioned response of sexual arousal.

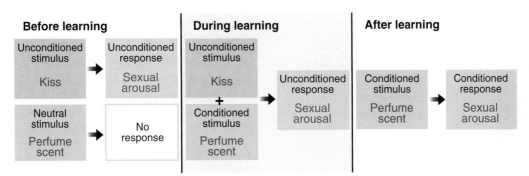

Before learning

| Unconditioned stimulus | Unconditioned response |
| Kiss | Sexual arousal |

| Neutral stimulus | No response |
| Perfume scent | |

During learning

Unconditioned stimulus	
Kiss	Unconditioned response
+	Sexual arousal
Conditioned stimulus	
Perfume scent	

After learning

| Conditioned stimulus | Conditioned response |
| Perfume scent | Sexual arousal |

FIGURE 6-7 Through classical conditioning, a perfume scent (conditioned stimulus) can become associated with sexual arousal (conditioned response).

In addition, we may be drawn to particular people without realizing they have tapped into classically conditioned responses from our past. For example, you may really enjoy listening to a new friend's deep voice as he tells you about his life and find his manner reassuring and supportive. The similarity to your long talks with your own father may not be apparent until you see them together. Or a friend stopping by with fresh-baked chocolate chip cookies may bring out warm feelings not just for the taste but also for the feelings of comfort you experienced when your Mom baked the same cookies for you. A "lucky" sweater or beat-up old car may become tied to intense feelings from experiences in which they happened to be with you, leading to a residue of past emotions on familiar objects. It is easy to underestimate the influence of our associations to past emotional experiences. We even prefer specific numbers and letters of the alphabet; specifically, those of our own birthdates and letters from our own names (Koole et al., 2001)!

In fact, we learn so well from classical conditioning that changes may occur in our physiological responses below our conscious awareness. In particular, it may be possible to train the body's immune system, affecting our general health (Ader & Cohen, 1985). Using classical conditioning procedures, sugar water was paired with a drug that caused nausea. As expected, rats quickly developed an aversion to the taste of the sugar water. Many of these rats died because this drug weakens the immune system by destroying white blood cells. Later, surviving rats were then fed sweetened water on its own (the conditioned stimulus) without the drug (the unconditioned stimulus). Consuming the sweetened water associated with the drug was enough to suppress the immune system (the conditioned response), leading to sickness and death in these rats FIGURE 6-8. Other studies show promise in *increasing* activity levels in the immune system through classical conditioning (Miller & Cohen, 2001). **Biofeedback** methods, which provide external signals of physiological responses, have been successfully used to train people to lower their blood pressure, slow their heartbeat, relax muscle tension, and control pain (deCharms et al., 2005).

Another place where emotional conditioning takes place is in advertising. One technique is to pair images that evoke pleasant responses (such as sexual images, the unconditioned stimulus) with a neutral product image (which becomes the conditioned stimulus). By repeatedly associating the product with an image that elicits a positive unconditioned response (arousal), advertisers hope their products will also come to evoke

Biofeedback Using instruments that display physiological functions to help learn to control responses.

FIGURE 6-8 Suppression of the immune system occurred through classical conditioning when a sweet taste was paired with exposure to an immune-suppressing drug. Later, the animals experienced immune suppression from drinking the sweetened water alone. *Source: Data from Miller, G., & Cohen, N. (2001). Psychological interventions and the immune system: A meta-analytic review and critique. Health Psychology, 20, 47–63.*

Car advertisements with sexy models are intended to build your positive associations with the automobile.

Taste aversion Learning to dislike foods that were followed by nausea.

Avoidance learning Learning to stay away from stimuli that predict negative events.

the same reaction. Car ads, for example, often feature an attractive female model draped across the hood; since the model is not for sale, her purpose in the ad must be to evoke positive sexual feelings and, by association, boost your feelings about the car. Advertisers know (and research confirms) that car ads including an attractive female are rated (by men) as more appealing, better designed, and more desirable.

Contemporary Views of Classical Conditioning

The dominance of behaviorism in the early years of psychology gave way to the cognitive revolution in the 1960s and 1970s. Behaviorists focused only on external behavior and worked mainly with animal models; as a result, they sometimes underestimated the importance of both cognition (thoughts, beliefs, language) and biology (built-in and evolutionary constraints).

Learning to Predict

Pavlov's account of dogs responding to bells led to a view of learning as a mindless, mechanical process. Yet even dogs may be thinking more than Pavlov would suggest: Perhaps what the dogs learned about the bell was not a simple association but, rather, the *prediction* that food was about to arrive. Based on years of research in animal learning, Rescorla (1988) concluded that the simple pairing of events is not sufficient for conditioning to occur. Instead, classical conditioning results in *predicting* that Event A (the conditioned stimulus) will be followed by Event B (the unconditioned stimulus). A study demonstrated the difference by pairing a tone and an electrical shock. For one group of rats, the tone always perfectly predicted the shock, while for another group, the shock occasionally occurred without the tone. Only the first group learned to fear the tone; for the second group, the conditioned stimulus simply didn't reliably predict the unconditioned stimulus. Classical conditioning requires more than a simple association or pairing of stimuli; rather, it requires a *reliable, predictive* relationship.

Biological and Evolutionary Predispositions

Pavlov and other early behaviorists assumed that any organism (pigeon, rat, or human) can be conditioned with any stimulus (bell, light, or odor). But can we learn to associate any signal with any physiological response? Imagine dining out in a restaurant where you happen to try a dish with hollandaise sauce. At home later that night, you become violently ill. How do you think you will feel about eating hollandaise sauce again? Most likely, you will not be eager. However, you could have associated many other things in the situation with your illness, such as the people you dine with or the music playing in the restaurant. John Garcia proposed an explanation for this experience: People—and all animals—develop **taste aversions** that associate feelings of nausea with whatever food was last consumed, and this causes them to avoid that taste in the future. He suggested that we are biologically prepared to easily learn some signals and not others as predictors for some responses.

To test his theory, Garcia and Koelling (1966) exposed rats to an unconditioned stimulus (radiation), and they experienced an unconditioned response (illness). For different groups of rats, he provided different neutral stimuli as potential cues: clicking noises, flashing lights, and sweet-tasting water. Would the rats learn to associate these neutral stimuli with illness equally well? The measure of their associations would be their **avoidance learning**; that is, whether the animals tried to escape from these cues. As Garcia suspected, some pairings were easier to learn than others: The rats were much quicker to learn that the taste of sugar water predicts nausea compared to lights or sounds FIGURE 6-9. Garcia also performed versions of the study in which the unconditioned stimulus was electrical shock and the unconditioned response was pain and fear. For these rats, it was much easier to learn that lights predicted the shock and difficult to learn that sweetened water did. His conclusion was that not all conditioned stimuli are equal; rather, some associations between stimuli and responses are easier to learn than others.

Our readiness to learn the signals for important physiological responses can result in problems in real-world situations. One example comes from the administration of chemotherapy to patients with cancer FIGURE 6-10. When patients begin treatment, the drugs given to fight the cancer frequently cause terrible nausea as a side effect. The patient experiences this unconditioned stimulus—the drug—that produces the unconditioned response of nausea. However, this occurs repeatedly in the presence of the same neutral stimulus: a waiting room. Over time and experience, the patient begins to associate the waiting room itself with the impending nausea that will result from the drug. Eventually, even when no drug is administered, the patient will enter the waiting room (the conditioned stimulus) and begin to feel the nausea that usually results (the conditioned response). Humans are so good at pairing signals to physiological reactions that events far removed from the unconditioned stimulus, such as the freeway exit sign on the way to the treatment center, may become conditioned to begin the unpleasant response. Many cancer patients report that they continue to feel nauseous in response to any reminders of their treatment, even 20 years later (Cameron et al., 2001).

Biological preparedness describes inborn tendencies that point us toward the signals that are most likely to be related to the cause of our reactions. These tendencies vary across species and play a very valuable role in preserving us from harm. It makes sense that the scavenging rat would be quick to learn to avoid foods that make it sick, while birds, on the other hand, are more likely to learn visual cues. We humans also show preparedness to learn to fear specific dangerous objects and situations, such as spiders, thunder, snakes, darkness, and heights. Öhman and Mineka (2001) proposed that we have "fear modules" to protect us from the dangers experienced by our ancestors. As a result, we are biologically prepared to learn associations that help us adapt to our world.

Biological preparedness
Built-in tendencies to learn some associations more easily.

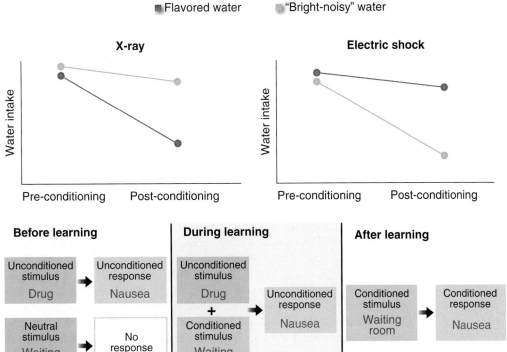

FIGURE 6-9 Water intake is shown before (pre-) and after (post-) conditioning. The left panel shows learning when X-rays were the unconditioned stimulus, and the right panel shows learning when electric shock was the unconditioned stimulus. The results show that the rats learned some pairings more readily: the taste of flavored water to nausea, and "bright lights and noise" to shock. *Source: Data from Garcia, J., & Koelling, R. A. (1966). Relation of cue to consequence in avoidance learning. Psychonomic Science, 4, 123–124.*

FIGURE 6-10 Through classical conditioning, a waiting room (conditioned stimulus) can become associated with nausea (conditioned response).

Humans appear to be biologically prepared to respond to some stimuli; in particular, we often feel emotional arousal for spiders, lightning and thunder, snakes, heights, and darkness.

Phobia A generalized fear from classical conditioning.

For example, poisonous substances often taste bitter, and spoiled foods become sour, so our taste aversions lead us away from harmful foods. And the world is a somewhat predictable place in which events that occur together are often related by an underlying cause rather than an arbitrary association. This research shows that learning is not solely due to nurture or to our experiences in the world; instead, learning is also influenced by our nature, or our biological predispositions.

Applying Principles of Classical Conditioning

The early learning theorist John Broadus Watson felt that Pavlov's work with dogs could go a long way toward explaining **phobias**, the irrational fears that people seem to develop based on their experiences.

Watson and Behaviorism

Watson became associated with the behaviorism movement in psychology as one of its leading proponents. He believed so strongly in it that he claimed, "Give me a dozen healthy infants, well-formed, and my own specified world to bring them up in and I'll guarantee to take any one at random and train him to become any type of specialist I might select—doctor, lawyer, artist, merchant-chief, and yes, even beggar-man and thief, regardless of his talents, penchants, tendencies, abilities, vocations, and race of his ancestors" (Watson, 1925, p. 248). He clearly believed that people became who they were based on what they learned from life experiences.

With his assistant, Rosalie Rayner, Watson set out to see if he could create a phobia in a child using a classical conditioning process (Watson & Rayner, 1920). So he took a 9-month-old child, called Little Albert, into his lab. Albert had been raised in a hospital as an orphan from birth. Watson described Little Albert as a hearty child, "stolid and unemotional," who seldom cried and was not afraid of novel things. Watson showed him a white rat, a rabbit, a dog, monkey, masks, a ball of white cotton wool, and a newspaper set on fire. Little Albert had never seen any of these objects before, and his general reaction was to reach out and try to touch them. Clearly, Albert had no fear of any of these items (neutral stimuli).

Little Albert Experiment

Next, Watson began his conditioning experiment: Could he classically condition an emotional reaction to one of these neutral stimuli? In a series of trials, he showed Little Albert a white rat and waited until Albert reached out to touch it. Then, directly behind Little Albert's head, Watson hit a hammer against a 4-foot metal bar (the unconditioned stimulus)! Of course, Albert was incredibly startled: In Watson's words, he "jumped violently and fell forward, burying his face in the mattress. He did not cry, however."

Watson then repeated the procedure three times, each time producing a more pronounced response from Albert. After a week to rest, he began a new set of four trials in which he showed the rat—now a conditioned stimulus—again to Little Albert along with the unconditioned stimulus. Then, he presented the rat (the conditioned stimulus) to Albert alone, without the noise. When Little Albert saw the rat, he started to cry, and crawled away from the rat so fast that Watson reports he was caught before he fell off the table only with great difficulty! Essentially, Watson had shown that he could create a rat phobia in a child through the process of classical conditioning. By repeatedly pairing the neutral stimulus—the rat—with an unconditioned stimulus—the loud clanging sound—he turned the neutral rat into a conditioned stimulus that evoked the conditioned response of fear.

Watson also found that this phobia was not limited to just rats; instead, it showed generalization to other kinds of white or furry things. A week later, Little Albert was shown a white rabbit, and as Watson noted, "He leaned as far away from the animal as possible, whimpered, and then burst into tears." Little Albert was also afraid of the white cotton wool, a Santa Claus beard, and a white fur coat. To determine whether Little Albert's phobia would persist over time, he was tested 1 month later. Albert remained very afraid of all of these objects. Little Albert was then scheduled to leave the hospital and be adopted by a family. Watson does not report any assistance with Little Albert's newly acquired phobia or attempts to recondition him to handle these acquired fears. Today, this type of experiment would raise serious ethical concerns and would not be permitted.

Watson's demonstration showed that phobias are indeed created through experience (Watson, 1924). This work also led to the idea of using classical conditioning to unlearn, or treat, phobias. For example, people often come to fear their dentist's office because they repeatedly experience an unconditioned stimulus (cavity repair) that causes an unpleasant response (pain or discomfort). However, classical conditioning can also be used to associate *good* feelings with the dentist's office. For example, dentists often offer a small toy to children when they visit, and the pleasant experience of the toy helps associate positive feelings to counteract the negative. Another technique, called **flooding**, involves immersing yourself in a feared situation. For example, if Little Albert were to sit in front of a dozen rats and no unconditioned stimulus ever occurred, eventually he would learn that the rat is not a predictor of the feared event. By being in the presence of the conditioned stimulus with no harmful consequences, fear eventually subsides, calm sets in, and then calm can be associated with the recently feared object.

Another application for treatment of phobia is called **systematic desensitization** (Wolpe, 1961). The idea is to learn to maintain a calm, relaxed attitude in the presence of the feared stimulus. For example, suppose you have a fear of flying. First, the clinician would ask you to construct an "anxiety hierarchy," listing each of the steps leading up to the conditioned response (packing your bags, driving to the airport, going to the gate, etc.) in the order of how fearful you feel with each step. Then, you begin "unlearning" the fear. You imagine each step, such as driving to the airport, and learn to relax in the presence of each stage of the activity. For example, you may visualize sitting in the gate area without going on the plane and practice feeling relaxed with that image in mind. The goal is to achieve relaxation in the presence of each part of the feared sequence, progressing through the hierarchy of stages from least to most feared. By systematically relaxing in the presence of the feared stimulus, you can accomplish the extinction of these fearful associations.

Watson showed that what was considered a complex psychological disorder can instead result from a simple learning experience and that learning theory—classical conditioning—can explain and treat the emotional consequences of our experiences.

Flooding A therapy to treat phobias based on intense exposure to the feared stimulus.

Systematic desensitization Treatment for phobia that practices relaxation to progressively more feared stimuli.

CONCEPT LEARNING CHECK 6.2 | *Applying Principles of Classical Conditioning*

For each scenario presented below, identify the four major elements of classical conditioning. Specify for each example (a) the unconditioned stimulus, (b) the unconditioned response, (c) the conditioned stimulus, and (d) the conditioned response.

1. As part of an experiment, researchers give mice an electrical shock preceded by a flash of light. The mice feel pain and fear in response. After several trials, the mice try to hide whenever the flashing light is presented, even without the shock.

2. Scientists feed coyotes small pieces of sheep meat tainted with poison that, when ingested, cause nausea. Later, when coyotes approach sheep, the mere smell of the sheep causes the coyotes to run frantically away from their former prey.

6.3 Operant Conditioning

We learn based upon the consequences that follow our behavior in the world.

- Apply the principles of operant conditioning based on the consequences of behavior.

As we know, classical conditioning always involves an unconditioned, involuntary response *elicited from* the individual whenever an unconditioned stimulus occurs. These reflexes involve important physiological reactions that greatly affect our everyday lives, particularly in our experience of emotion. However, a second theory of learning involves voluntary responses *emitted by* the subject: That is, the individual freely chooses to make a particular response at a given time. This kind of conditioning is called operant conditioning, where **operant** refers to a behavior "operating" in the world. The choice of whether and when to perform a given behavior is purely at the discretion of the individual. So what controls operant behavior, or the decision to perform a given action?

Thorndike's Law of Effect

In 1898, Edward Thorndike decided to look at this problem using cats as his subjects. Thorndike put cats into large wooden crates containing an escape lever inside. These puzzle boxes required the cat to pull on a lever to release the latch and open the door to escape. Thorndike was interested in animal intelligence and wanted to see how long it would take the cats to learn to open the box. What he found was that the behaviors followed by pleasant consequences were more likely to be repeated in that situation FIGURE 6-11. So when the cat was first trapped inside the puzzle box, it scratched at the bars, pushed at the ceiling, nosed the floor, howled, and performed many other behaviors, until finally it happened to press the lever that opened the door. After many trials, the cat learned to press the lever right away to release itself from the box. The animal had learned

Operant A behavior freely initiated or displayed, which can be conditioned.

Law of Effect Behaviors that lead to positive outcomes are likely to be repeated.

Reinforcer A consequence (either positive or negative) following a behavior that makes it *more* likely to occur again.

FIGURE 6-11 The cat in a puzzle box would perform many different behaviors, until finally it learned to press the lever and escape.
Source: Data from Thorndike, E. L. (1898). Animal intelligence: An experimental study of the associative processes in animals. Psychological Monographs, 2 *(Whole No, 8).*

First trial

Scratch at sides
Push at ceiling
Dig at floor
Cry
Other
Press lever

Cat trapped in box

After many trials

Scratch at sides
Push at ceiling
Dig at floor
Cry
Other
Press lever

Cat trapped in box

FIGURE 6-12 B. F. Skinner was very influential learning theorist, and a major figure in 20th-century American culture.

to perform the specific actions that led to positive outcomes. Thorndike summarized his findings as the **Law of Effect**: Behaviors that lead to positive outcomes in a situation are likely to be repeated again in the future (Thorndike, 1898).

Skinner's Experiments

B. F. Skinner FIGURE 6-12, another major figure in behaviorism, pursued this finding to determine how individuals learn from the consequences of their actions. In Skinner's theory, the individual freely chooses to emit some behavior, which is followed by some kind of consequence (Skinner, 1938). When the consequences are pleasant, the individual is much more likely to do that behavior again. Skinner called this "reinforcement learning," because positive outcomes reinforce, or strengthen, the chance of performing that specific behavior again. This comes from its everyday meaning: If something is reinforced, it is made stronger. So if your dog sits and you hand him a treat, the treat is the **reinforcer**: It acts to make the behavior (sitting) more likely to occur again.

Skinner conducted the bulk of his research using laboratory rats and pigeons. The tasks they learned to perform and the reinforcers he used in the studies were very simple. However, by varying which behaviors received reinforcement and how the rewards were provided, Skinner was able to characterize many important principles that predict the behaviors people do even in complex situations. He started with the simplest design possible, known as the **Skinner box (operant chamber)** FIGURE 6-13. The box was large enough for the animal to move about but was starkly empty except for a single response mechanism and a feeding tray. For the rat, the response bar could be pressed with its paws, and for a pigeon, a disk could be pecked to register a response. When the animal performed the desired response (pushed down the bar or pecked the disk), the box would automatically drop a pellet of food into the tray. This food served as the reinforcer: The animal learned to perform whatever action led to the appearance of the food. A recorder was connected to the box to measure the animal's responses over time. This simple setup allowed Skinner to investigate how reinforcement affected behavior.

FIGURE 6-13 The Skinner box is a controlled environment where animals could be trained while recording their responses automatically.

Reinforcement

Skinner studied how animals learned to perform specific behaviors and how their learning was affected by reinforcement FIGURE 6-14. The key idea about reinforcement is that it always brings on a more pleasant state for the learner. **Positive reinforcement** is like getting a reward, where a behavior is followed by a pleasant stimulus (for example, a food pellet). Behavior can also be reinforced—made stronger—by a "negative reinforcer." **Negative reinforcement** occurs when a behavior is followed by the termination of a negative stimulus. For example, a loud noise may be sounding in the box, and when the rat pushes down the lever, the noise stops. This is "negative" because it means taking something away from the learner, but it results in a more pleasant outcome (no loud noise). It is important to remember that reinforcement always makes the behavior stronger and more likely to happen again because it produces a desirable outcome for the learner. *Positive* refers to applying a reinforcer (like giving a medal), and *negative* refers to taking away something as a reinforcer (like a loud noise). But both always lead to increases in the target behavior.

Skinner box (operant chamber) A testing apparatus with a response mechanism that also delivers reinforcement.

Positive reinforcement A consequence that creates a pleasant state, making behavior more likely to occur.

Negative reinforcement A consequence that takes away an unpleasant state, making behavior more likely to occur.

Primary reinforcer A reward that provides basic needs.

FIGURE 6-14 Skinner's view was that "reinforcement" always makes the behavior grow stronger.

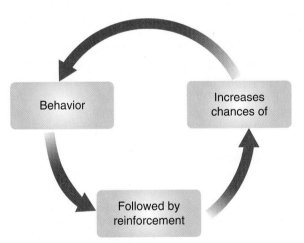

These examples work well within the Skinner box, but do human behaviors also receive positive and negative reinforcers? Yes! An example of a positive reinforcer is a smile; when you receive one, you are more likely to keep doing whatever behavior you are doing. An example of a negative reinforcer is the mechanism in your car that encourages you to put on your seatbelt. If you sit in the car without your belt, a pinging sound will occur that is unpleasant, and it will continue until you click on your seatbelt. Immediately, the obnoxious pinging noise is terminated. Therefore, your behavior of buckling up is negatively reinforced; that is, the annoying noise ends once you perform the desired behavior. In both cases, the reinforcement strengthens the behavior (makes it more likely to occur again); however, reinforcement occurs both by applying a positive reward and by removing a negative stimulus (see **TABLE 6-2**).

Skinner defined two types of reinforcers. **Primary reinforcers** bring about a pleasant state by fulfilling some biological need. These reinforcers are the basics—food, water,

TABLE 6-2 Reinforcement Learning

	Positive	Negative
Pleasant outcome increases behavior	Add something "Give a medal"	Take something away "Turn off alarm"

FIGURE 6-15 Food is a primary reinforcer because its positive value to the learner is already established.

FIGURE 6-16 A kiss is a secondary reinforcer for this dolphin because it had to learn that affection from its trainer means positive consequences for it.

Secondary reinforcer (conditioned reinforcer) A reward that can be exchanged for ones meeting basic needs.

Shaping Reinforcing an approximation of a behavior initially, and then increasing successively to reach the target behavior.

air—so any behavior that brings these primary reinforcers is quickly repeated FIGURE 6-15. **Secondary reinforcers** (also called **conditioned reinforcers**, because they are learned) are pleasing because they are associated with a primary reinforcer. They don't, in and of themselves, fulfill any biological need, but they are positively viewed because they can be turned into a primary reinforcer FIGURE 6-16. The secondary reinforcer that is very effective for people is money. Money is not a primary reinforcer because you can't eat it; however, people will work hard for it because it can buy the primary reinforcers you need. Examples of secondary reinforcers used by Skinner in his studies include tokens that are given meaning because they can be exchanged for primary reinforcers like food. So a monkey will happily work for a pile of tokens it can exchange for a banana.

Acquisition and Shaping

The acquisition of behaviors in Skinner boxes was straightforward: The researcher would wait until the animal (say, a rat) did the desired behavior (let's say, pushed down on the response bar), and then she would press a button to release the food pellet into the tray. The rat would quickly learn to perform that behavior (push the bar) in order to receive the food reinforcer. But what if the animal in training never does push the bar? How can behaviors be acquired if you have to wait until the animal does them before you can reinforce them? Skinner's answer is a procedure called **shaping**, or rewarding successive approximations of the target behavior. The trainer chooses a target behavior that is short of the eventual goal; so, rather than pushing the bar, the initial goal would be to move in the direction of the bar. As soon as this behavior occurred, the rat would be reinforced. Then the trainer would change the goal to be closer to pushing, such as touching the bar. The rat would then be reinforced only if it touched the bar with its paw. By successively meeting and then changing the goal, shaping allows a complex behavior to be gradually trained.

Using shaping, Skinner demonstrated that pigeons can learn to play Ping-Pong! Initially, the pigeons received rewards whenever their beaks touched the ball. Eventually, they received food only when they actually scored a point on the pigeon across the table. Shaping allows the development of behaviors that may not occur on their own. And because operant conditioning can only reinforce the behaviors the animal emits, it is critical to come up with a way to establish partial forms of the behavior, eventually requiring the complete behavior. Shaping in human behavior occurs all of the time; for example, a child learning to talk will often receive reinforcement from its mother whenever it makes any sound. Over time, the mother reinforces it only when the child makes a "Ma" sound. Eventually, the mother waits until a full "Mama" is heard before rewarding her with attention. Skinner believed that the principles of learning he studied in his boxes were all that were needed to explain even the most complex human behaviors.

Generalization and Discrimination

Just as with classical conditioning, operant conditioning follows the principles of generalization and discrimination. When the rat learns to press the lever for a food reward, it may press it with its left paw, then its right, and then its nose; as long as the pellets keep falling with each bar press, the actual behavior can be of a general type that works to depress the bar. Alternatively, behaviors can be discriminated so that only a particular type of press—say, using both paws—releases the food. The rats will quickly learn which aspects of their behaviors are required and which can be varied. With any learning task, the learner will adapt to perform what is necessary to achieve the reinforcer and will stop performing behaviors that don't lead to reinforcement.

But what happens when reinforcement occurs by accident? Skinner (1948) discussed the problem of superstition through reinforcement. He set up a Skinner box that dropped a food pellet at varied time intervals. The reinforcement in this case had nothing to do with the animal but simply occurred on a random, predetermined basis. Now, imagine you are the pigeon in the box. You are waiting around for food and decide to try bobbing your head. Coincidentally, the food drops, reinforcing your head bobbing. Now you think you've got it: Keep bobbing, and the reinforcer will come. It may take some repetitions, but again, food drops, and you become convinced that your bobbing is the cause. In this way, Skinner argues, learners can become convinced that certain behaviors lead to reinforcements because it has happened in the past. Baseball players, for example, are known to repeat the meals they ate and actions they performed just before hitting that home run. Then, because they believe in the connection, they perform these rituals every time, and consequently, they again occur before the reinforcement of a home run happens. Learners are on the watch for reinforcements, and consequently they may "learn" from them even when no real connection to the outcome exists!

Extinction

As in classical conditioning, operant conditioning uses the term *extinction* to refer to "unlearning" the behavior. Imagine that you've trained a rat to press a bar for food. Now you unplug the box, and no more food will fall. How long do you think the rat will continue pressing, hoping for its food reward? It may do so for quite a while, but eventually, the rat will give up and stop emitting the bar-pressing behavior. When it does, we say that the behavior has been **extinguished**. Animals are fairly quick to learn that the gravy train has stopped and are efficient with their efforts. People, on the other hand, are notorious for not giving up in the face of extinction. For example, Orne (1962) did a study to determine how long people would continue working on a task with no clear reward. He sat his subjects in a room full of papers with multiplication problems on them and asked them to begin working. Then he asked them to begin tearing up each piece of paper once they had solved the problems to show them that their work had no purpose. Still, they continued working. After 3 hours, Orne called a halt to the study, failing to see the extinction point any other animal would have reached. When asked, the people in the study said they had developed their own rationales for why they were asked to do the problems, and they kept going even though no reinforcement appeared to be coming. Later in this chapter, we will return to the role that cognition plays in learning.

Schedules of Reinforcement

Ideally, you would follow every behavior with a reinforcer every time it occurs, called **continuous reinforcement**. This makes the behavior very reliable, and very rapid, in response. Immediately reinforcing the behavior is much more effective than delaying it until later. In fact, for some animals like rats, a 30-second delay in delivering the reinforcement may mean they fail to learn the behavior. People, however, are much better at working for delayed reinforcement. (For example, some students work for 4 years to receive their college degrees!)

However, it may not be practical to provide reinforcement with every behavior. Instead, an **intermittent reinforcement** may be used, in which the reinforcer is delivered after only some of the responses. The benefit of using intermittent reinforcement, also called partial reinforcement, is that you don't have to supply the reinforcer each time the desired behavior occurs. For example, if a rat is working for food pellets, it may eventually become full and stop the behavior. However, if it must perform the behavior multiple times in order to receive the reward once, it will be able to work longer. Another benefit is that intermittent reinforcement is more resistant to extinction. If you are paid $10 every time you mow the lawn, it only takes one time of not getting paid for you to notice. But if you are paid only every 10th time, it may be a while before you notice that the reinforcement has stopped.

A **schedule of reinforcement** refers to planning the timing of the application of reinforcers **TABLE 6-3**. If the reinforcement occurs, for example, after every other response, or every fifth response, the schedule is called a **fixed-ratio schedule** FIGURE 6-17. If you frequent a particular coffee shop, you may be given a card with which, after 10 purchases, you

Extinguish To stop the display of a given behavior.

Continuous reinforcement Following every behavior with a consequence.

Intermittent reinforcement Following behavior with a consequence sometimes, but not every time.

Schedule of reinforcement A plan for applying consequences following a behavior.

Fixed-ratio schedule Providing reinforcement after a set number of repeated behaviors.

TABLE 6-3 Schedules of Reinforcement

Name	Time of Reinforcement
Continuous	After each behavior occurs
Intermittent (partial)	Only after some repetitions of the behavior
Fixed ratio	Only after a set number of repeated behaviors
Variable ratio	After an average (with some variation) number of repetitions
Fixed interval	Only after a set time has passed and the behavior occurs
Variable interval	Only after an average (with some variation) amount of time has passed and the behavior occurs

JAVA JAVA JAVA!!
Buy ten cups, get one FREE!

FIGURE 6-17 A fixed-ratio schedule of reinforcement.

receive a free coffee. This fixed-ratio schedule provides a reward—the free coffee—only after you perform the behavior 10 times. Another type of reinforcement schedule is the **variable-ratio schedule** FIGURE 6-18. This involves setting an average number of times the behavior must occur before the reward is given, but the actual number varies around that average. An effective example of a variable-ratio schedule is a slot machine found in casinos. The machines are set to pay off on a variable ratio: For example, after an average of 10,000 quarters are played, a payout of winnings will occur. But it is not predictable exactly when that will occur, because the payoff may occur much earlier or much later than that average. This variable-ratio schedule works well to keep the response coming because of the uncertainty about exactly when the reward will occur.

Both of these **ratio schedules** are based on the number of times the behavior occurs. As a result, the learner tends to perform frequent, rapid responses because the reward is contingent—depends upon—the number of responses made. The ratio schedules are very effective in motivating fast responses, with the fixed-ratio schedule producing the most responses over the shortest amount of time FIGURE 6-19. For example, with your coffee card, you know exactly how many more coffees you have to buy before you will get your free one! But with the variable-ratio schedule, you are never certain about how many times you'll have to repeat the behavior before the reinforcement will come your way. As a result, variable-ratio schedules show greater resistance to extinction. It's harder to know when reinforcements have actually ended!

Two other reinforcement schedules are based on the amount of time that elapses between rewards. On time **interval schedules**, no amount of responding is going to hurry the reward; instead, some time must pass before the reinforcer is given. Most of

FIGURE 6-18 A variable-ratio schedule of reinforcement.

Variable-ratio schedule Providing reinforcement after an average number of repeated behaviors.

Ratio schedules Reinforcement is provided after behaviors are repeated a number of times.

Interval schedule Reinforcement is provided after time passes, and then a behavior is repeated.

FIGURE 6-19 The delivery schedule for reinforcement makes a difference in how quickly the learner will perform the behavior.

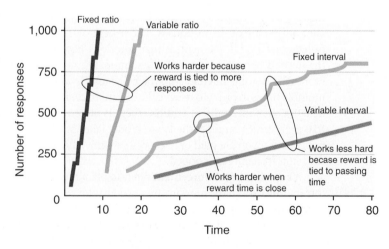

us are employed on a **fixed-interval schedule**—that is, we receive a paycheck after some period of work FIGURE 6-20. So, for example, our reward—the check—comes every 2 weeks, even though our behavior of working is spread over that 2-week interval. This type of schedule is more convenient for administering the reinforcement. But it is not as effective in getting frequent, fast behavior to occur because the learner knows he or she has to wait, and that the speed or frequency of responding does not determine when the reinforcement will occur. The slowest responding is seen in the **variable-interval schedule**, in which a reward will occur after a variable period of time FIGURE 6-21. An example is checking your mailbox for new mail: After time passes, you will likely receive more mail, but you can't predict when, and the number of times you check for the mail does not affect whether you will receive it. What is the best schedule of reinforcement for motivating fast, frequent responding? Continuous reinforcement! That way, you know you will be reinforced as soon as you perform the response.

Punishment

In reinforcement learning, you are attempting to strengthen or increase the likelihood of the behavior occurring again. Unlike the reinforcement learning we've been discussing, the goal of punishment is to *extinguish* a behavior rather than reinforce it. That is, you want the behavior that is punished to stop and never occur again. This key difference separates reinforcement learning from punishment FIGURE 6-22. Punishment places the learner in a more negative situation by either applying a bad consequence or removing a positive state. In contrast, the outcome for learners is always more *positive* following reinforcement. That is, they are enjoying their reinforcer (such as food), or they are enjoying the removal of a negative reinforcer (the absence of the pinging noise now that their seatbelts are latched). Punishment creates a negative state in the learner through **punishment by application** of a negative event, such as a spanking, or **punishment by removal** of a positive event or state, such as being grounded (not allowed to leave the house).

Studies of learning show that punishment is not an effective tactic for learning. One reason is that punishment informs the learner about what *not* to do, but it does not inform him or her about what to do instead. So if someone steals food for her family and is then arrested, the punishment may stop the behavior of stealing, but it does not solve the problem of needing food. Another problem with punishment is that it may lead to imitation of the

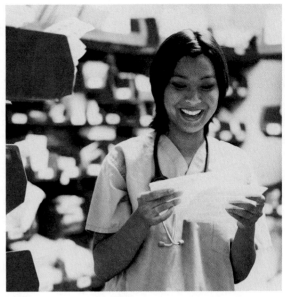

FIGURE 6-20 A fixed-interval schedule of reinforcement.

FIGURE 6-21 A variable-interval schedule of reinforcement.

	Add to situation	Remove from situation
Reinforcement (always increases behavior)	Positive reinforcement	Negative reinforcement
Punishment (may decrease behavior)	Punishment by application	Punishment by removal

FIGURE 6-22 The key difference is that reinforcement always strengthens behavior, while punishment is intended to decrease it.

Fixed-interval schedule Providing reinforcement for the first behavior after a set amount of time passes.

Variable-interval schedule Providing reinforcement for the first behavior after a set average amount of time has passed.

Punishment by application Attempting to extinguish a behavior by applying a negative consequence.

Punishment by removal Attempting to extinguish a behavior by removing a positive state.

Yelling at children may teach them to act similarly toward others.

punisher rather than stopping the targeted behavior. For example, if a child hits another child and then receives a spanking, the child may have difficulty learning to stop hitting others due to modeling (discussed in the next section).

A review of studies on physical punishment concluded that children subjected to physical punishment tend to become more aggressive themselves (Gershoff, 2002). Many countries have made physical punishment illegal (such as Germany, Norway, Finland, and Israel), while others employ physical punishment for mild transgressions such as vandalism. In the United States, a parent can be prosecuted for injuring a child through physical punishment. According to Alan Kazdin (2008), "More than one-third of all parents who start out with relatively mild punishments end up crossing the line drawn by the state to define child abuse, such as hitting with an object, harsh and cruel hitting, and so on."

Finally, punishment may also lead to negative emotional consequences through classical conditioning. The application of punishment, such as a spanking by a parent, may lead to emotional responses and fear in the child. These feelings then become associated with the parent who performs the punishment. So, through punishment, the child may feel fearful in the presence of the parent as a classically conditioned response to the experience of being punished. However, there are some situations in which some form of punishment may be necessary. If so, punishment that removes the learner from a desirable situation, such as having to sit on a "time out" chair rather than play, are much less problematic than physical punishment. In addition, some behaviors may post a danger to the learner. For example, some disturbed clinical patients may pull their own hair or hit themselves repeatedly; in these situations, punishments such as a short burst of sprayed water or even a mild electrical shock have been employed (Lovaas, 1987).

If punishing undesirable behavior is not effective, then what does work? It is much more effective to stop "attending to" undesirable behaviors and start rewarding desired ones. This can be tricky, because to the learner, punishment may be interpreted as a positive reinforcer. A classic example is a child having a tantrum in the grocery store aisle. This is undesirable behavior, and the parent wants it to stop. However, the actual response may be to stop shopping, pay attention to the child, soothe him, and perhaps bargain with him to gain his cooperation. The parent may feel she is obviously displeased by the behavior, but to the child, the response is reinforcing the tantrum: The child received attention, appeasement, and an early exit from shopping following the tantrum. In any learning situation, it is important to look at what outcome follows the behavior: If the behavior increases in frequency, it is likely that something about the situation is providing reinforcement to the learner. Solving behavior problems often requires careful attention to what response is occurring after a behavior. From years of study of reinforcement learning, we know that behaviors that are reinforced—in any way—are more likely to happen again. Consequently, the advice from learning theorists is that undesired behaviors should be absolutely ignored. Then quickly jump in to reinforce any positive behaviors once they occur.

Review of Terminology, Processes, and Factors That Affect Operant Conditioning

Operant conditioning refers to the ways we "operate" on our environment: We do behaviors and then experience their reinforcement or lack thereof. Here's an example of reinforcement in its purest form: karaoke. You stand in front of a room full of friends and strangers and belt out "I Wanna Know What Love Is" by Foreigner. How do you know whether to do that ever again? By the tremendous applause that follows your performance! Your behavior is reinforced by the clapping, and you're much more likely to sing again. If, instead, your performance is followed by painful silence, you may be less likely to volunteer again. Our behavior in the world is constantly shaped by the reinforcement we receive: Do something, see what the result is, and act based on that feedback. Reinforcement can be positive, where a good thing is given, or negative, where a bad thing is taken away. The key is that reinforcement always makes the behavior more likely to happen again.

Shaping is important in operant conditioning because you have to wait until the learner emits the desired behavior—voluntarily—before you can reinforce it. So you might start by rewarding her for doing part of the behavior at first, then hold off until she does more of it, and so on, shaping the behavior into what you want to see. Just as with classical conditioning, you may see generalization (now you are happy to dance as well as sing) or discrimination (you learn to sing only when your mom is in the crowd to start the applause). But if the applause stops, you will also eventually stop singing. Operant conditioning depends on the reinforcement to maintain the behavior, and a variety of schedules for reinforcement have been identified. Reinforcing behaviors you want to see again works much better for learning than punishing behaviors you want to extinguish.

Contemporary Views of Operant Conditioning

B. F. Skinner was one of the most important intellectual figures in psychology, but his theory was quite controversial. He raised the question of whether we ever truly act without expectations of consequences or whether "free will" is limited by the realities of reinforcement:

> "In the traditional view, a person is free. He is autonomous in the sense that his behavior is uncaused. He can therefore be held responsible for what he does and justly punished if he offends. That view, together with its associated practices, must be re-examined when a scientific analysis reveals unsuspected controlling relations between behavior and environment" (Skinner, 1972, p. 17).

If our behavior is determined by the reinforcements it will receive, then are we really free to do as we choose?

Skinner's strong beliefs in the power of the environment in controlling behavior led him to minimize any contributions of internal, cognitive processes. At one point, he claimed that the mental thoughts we experience are also behaviors, in the form of "sub-vocal" speech (Skinner, 1957; 1990). He remained unwilling to consider any role for cognition in determining behavior or that the principles of operant conditioning might be altered by biological influences. However, other researchers quickly found evidence that operant conditioning is not the only influence on our behavior.

Learned Helplessness

Some studies of operant conditioning use an **escape learning** procedure (Durgam, 2001). Animals are placed in a shuttle box with two compartments. An electrical current, mildly painful but not harmful, is passed through the floor on one side of the box, and the animal quickly learns to jump over a partition or through an opening to the other side to escape the shock. Rats quickly learn signals, such as flashing lights or buzzers, that predict when the shocks will occur and jump into the safe area in advance ("avoidance learning"). However, Seligman and Maier (1967) altered this procedure by giving dogs advance training. First, they were exposed to electrical shocks that they could neither control nor escape from. After this initial training, they were placed in the shuttle box for the escape learning procedure. However, these dogs acted in a way that no previous animal had: They simply failed to learn to escape from the shocks, even when escape was easy and readily learned by dogs without the initial training.

Seligman called this phenomenon "**learned helplessness**." The dogs initially unable to escape the shock seemed unable to learn that they were *now* able to escape. They seemed to have generalized their learning to feel they no longer had any control of consequences. As a result, they were unable to learn to respond when the consequences changed. Seligman extended this concept to human behavior in people suffering from depression. When you feel your efforts at controlling events in your life repeatedly fail, you may become depressed and give up at even trying to succeed. Later, you may be in situations in which you can control the consequences, but you may still fail to act, believing you are not able to control the outcome. For example, if you were to enroll in an advanced language course without any background and receive failing grades on every assignment, you may quickly give up on your efforts. Later, even if the instructor makes the assignments much easier, you may still put out little effort, believing you have no control over whether you will do well in the course.

The feeling of personal control over outcomes—that your behaviors will lead to appropriate reinforcements—is key to feeling effective and in control in life. When people feel their setbacks are temporary and are limited to a specific area, they are more motivated to keep working and may then end up successful. People are more likely to become depressed if they believe that their lack of control over outcomes is permanent or a part

Escape learning An acquired behavior performed to avoid a noxious stimulus.

Learned helplessness When an animal fails to take action to escape a noxious stimulus.

of their own basic personality rather than based in the situation (Abramson, Seligman, & Teasdale, 1978). These findings were important because operant conditioning theory would never have predicted them. In reinforcement learning, no animal would stop trying to repeat behaviors that lead to good outcomes. The results showing that dogs—and people—can give up trying to learn posed a problem for operant conditioning theory. It also led Seligman to develop the field of positive psychology to counteract these effects.

Intrinsic Motivation

It would seem that rewards are always good, leading to more of the desired behavior. But rewards can also result in discouraging rather than reinforcing behavior. A classic study (Lepper, Greene, & Nisbett, 1973) gave preschool children felt markers to play with, and most children enjoyed this new toy. One week later, the children were divided into three groups. Children in the first group were told they would receive a reward (a gold star and a ribbon) for playing with the markers. Children in the second group were not told about the reward but received one when they finished playing, just like the first group. Children in the third group were not told about the reward, nor did they receive one when they finished playing. After a week, their teachers put out the markers in the classroom with no instructions. How much time would the children spend playing with the markers? The children who had played with them for the reward—Group 1—now played with them less! Those who had no reward or had the surprise reward (so they didn't feel they had participated just for the reward) chose to play more. What explains why reinforcing the first group backfired?

One possible explanation is that pleasurable activity (like playing with the markers) feels less so when it is rewarded. Lepper and colleagues argued that "playing" follows from **intrinsic motivation**, in which an internal drive or interest gives rise to the behavior. By providing **extrinsic motivation**—giving the reward—for this behavior, the reinforcement had provided an external source to account for their behavior. This explanation is quite cognitive: When considering whether to play with the markers again, the children who received rewards could justify their earlier playing as driven by the reward, not by their own interest. As a result, they may conclude they don't really have an inherent, or intrinsic, interest in playing with them. Providing reinforcements for behaviors that people would choose to do anyway may backfire, convincing them that the only reason to behave in this way is to receive the reward. Then, when the reward is withdrawn, the behavior stops. When people are intrinsically motivated to read, to create, and to learn, adding artificial reinforcements may take away the joy that arises from the behavior itself. Consequently, adding external rewards can decrease the performance of some behaviors.

These studies raise issues about the role of cognition in learning, and their results are clear: People do not simply and mindlessly repeat behaviors that are followed by reinforcements. Accounting for learning will require that we include more cognitive variables in the mix.

Biological Influences on Operant Conditioning

Biological influences are also apparent in the use of operant principles for training animals. In movies and television, live animal shows at outdoor aquariums, theme parks, and zoos, and in our homes, the principles of operant conditioning have been successfully applied to train animals to do very unusual things. Two of Skinner's students, Keller and Marian Breland (1961), successfully trained a wide variety of animals, including dogs, cats, chickens, parakeets, turkeys, pigs, ducks, hamsters, porpoises, and killer whales—eventually training more than 10,000 animals from more than 100 different species. However, in their work, the Brelands noticed that not all behaviors were readily learned by all species. For example, it was quite simple to train a dog or cat to jump, since that is a behavior it naturally performs. However, teaching them to crawl on their bellies proved much more difficult.

The reason is that animals are biologically predisposed to perform certain actions related to their survival, and those behaviors are specific to the ways each animal hunts for food and defends itself. In addition, the animals showed a tendency to revert to their typical behaviors, called **instinctual drift** (see FIGURE 6-23). For a bank commercial, trainers attempted to teach a raccoon to pick up coins and deposit them in a piggy bank. However,

---

Intrinsic motivation
Behavior is repeated without any external reinforcement.

Extrinsic motivation
Behavior is repeated only when external reinforcement is provided.

Instinctual drift The tendency for new behaviors to revert to ones familiar to that species.

FIGURE 6-23 It is easier to train a pig to play soccer than other sports because they naturally "root" into the ground, behavior that helps them learn to move the ball.

while readily able to manipulate the coins, the raccoon proved reluctant to release the shiny objects into the bank, pulling them back out again and again. Contrary to operant principles, you can't train every response in every animal equally easily. As with classical conditioning, biological constraints intervene to guide learning.

Applying Principles of Operant Conditioning

Because reinforcement learning is so effective, it has been applied in many circumstances in which other types of learning are not possible. For example, in training animals, the principles of operant conditioning work well to produce the desired behavior. The same principles are applied to humans in a therapy called behavior analysis, or **behavior modification**. In this therapy, concrete rewards are offered for specific, easy-to-perform behaviors, allowing the establishment of successful change. For example, Ivar Lovaas (1987) worked with children with severe forms of autism. He was able to use immediate rewards, such as food, drink, and hugs, to reinforce simple requests such as sitting in a chair. By working on these simple, successful behaviors, other types of learning experiences were then possible. Behavior modification is especially effective for individuals for whom language-based instruction is not possible. Because all organisms can understand positive outcomes, reinforcement learning can train all types of learners. Behavior modification is in widespread use in clinical therapy and now has gained favor for encouraging socially beneficial activities. In Ann Arbor, Michigan, recycling behaviors are tracked by weighing containers from each household, and points are awarded that can be used to purchase prizes. In schools, sports, and clinics, operant conditioning is working to help people learn to perform beneficial behaviors.

One prominent example of operant conditioning occurs in the workplace. You may have noticed that salespeople are sometimes paid on commission rather than by the hour; that is, their pay is based on the number of sales they make while on the job. Realtors, too, earn money only once they successfully sell a house. Does making your paycheck contingent upon making a sale motivate people to sell more? A study in a major department store set out to test this idea (Luthans, Paul, & Baker, 1981). More than 80 retail clerks were observed on the job over a period of 60 days, and their performance was scored for sales, stock work, idle periods, and absence from their stations. After 20 days, half of the staff were told about a new incentive program that would take place for the next 20 days: Those with the best performance would earn paid time off, equivalent cash, and a chance for a paid vacation. After the incentive period ended, both groups were still monitored for another 20 days. FIGURE 6-24 shows the results of the study. In the "baseline" period, before the incentives were introduced, performance measures in the control and experimental groups looked very similar. But beginning on day 20, and for the next 20 days while the incentives were given, the experimental group outperformed the control group by a large margin. Reinforcements worked to motivate better performance in the salespeople. Interestingly, this improved performance continued in the final phase even

Positive reinforcement has been shown to be effective in changing behaviors of children with severe autism.

Behavior modification An operant conditioning program designed to achieve a goal.

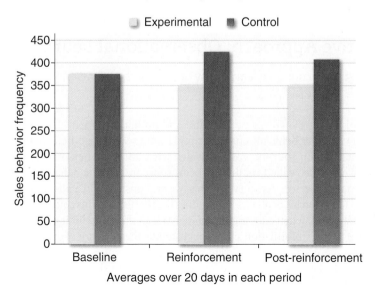

FIGURE 6-24 In the baseline period, both groups performed the same. However, once the experimental group began receiving reinforcements, their performance was much better than that of the control group, even when the reinforcement period ended.
Source: Data from Luthans, F., Paul, R., & Baker, D. (1981). An experimental analysis of the impact of contingent reinforcement on salesperson's performance behavior. Journal of Applied Psychology, 66 *(3). 314–323.*

when no incentives were offered. The experimental group maintained better performance even when the reinforcement ended.

Token economies are another method for developing long-term behavior changes. Tokens redeemable for privileges or rewards can be given out to reinforce behaviors on the spot. One example of a token economy occurs at a language-learning camp in Minnesota, where teachers reward campers when they attempt to speak in the new language. Then, when camp ends, tokens are traded in for large prizes. Token economies help by reinforcing the behavior whenever it occurs with an immediate symbol of reward, even though the reward itself is not given until later. For children, tokens such a ribbons, trophies, and gold stars are used to reinforce new behaviors, such as completing assignments, competing in sport, or participating in science fairs. Even for adults, the use of token economies can help people to reinforce new behaviors immediately and learn to maintain them over time. For individuals who have difficulty understanding the consequences of their behavior, a **behavioral contract** may be created to make an explicit link from behavior to reward. For example, a homeless shelter may require specific behaviors every day in order to stay overnight, such as making beds or returning by a certain time. Contracts may be especially helpful for adolescents or individuals with communicative or emotional disorders. Clear expectations that can be successfully met can help individuals establish desired behaviors.

> **Token economies** Situations in which easy-to-use secondary reinforcers are traded in for a meaningful reward.
>
> **Behavioral contract** The learner signs a written specification of an operant conditioning program.

CONCEPT LEARNING CHECK 6.3 | *Comparing Consequences of Behavior*

For each example below, determine what type of operant conditioning has occurred. First, identify the subject and his or her behavioral response. Decide whether the response was (a) strengthened through reinforcement or stopped through punishment. If the response was strengthened through reinforcement, decide whether it was (b) the result of positive (something added) or negative (something taken away) reinforcement.

1. Every time Billy says "please" when he makes a request, his parents do as he asks. After 1 week, Billy almost always remembers to say "please."

2. When Sarah interrupts her mom when she's talking on the phone, her mom stops the conversation to tell Sarah not to do that, and asks, "What is so important it can't wait?" After a month, Sarah interrupts her mom every time she makes a call.

3. Whenever Pete brings home a paper with an "A," he is excused from doing his usual household chores for the rest of the week. He begins to get more "A" grades.

4. Maxell did a terrific job on a sales report in just 1 day, so her boss asked her to do all of the reports for the office. A week later, Maxell had not yet finished any more reports.

6.4 A Cognitive Approach: Observational Learning

We readily benefit in our own learning by observing the behavior of others.

- Explain the evidence that learning can occur without acting out behavior.

A third type of learning involves no response and no reinforcement: In observational learning, knowledge or behavior changes simply from watching others. Without ever experiencing a situation yourself, you can watch what unfolds when others take action around you. This is also called **modeling**, because we imitate the behavior of a model provided by another person. As social animals, we are constantly in a position to observe and learn from the behavior of others. Where does the line form in this coffee shop? Should you take your shoes off when entering this home? What's the speed limit on this road? We constantly gain needed information simply by matching the behavior of others around us.

Behavioral theorists would never agree to such a cognitive description of learning. But a great deal of evidence has accumulated to suggest that what the animal—or human—*knows* about events matters. Modern behaviorists see that it is necessary to make

> **Modeling** Performing specific behaviors that others observe.

inferences about what is occurring in the mind, or cognition, even to explain learning in rats. As Rescorla (1988) stated, "Conditioning is not a stupid process by which an organism willy-nilly forms associations between any two stimuli that happen to co-occur. Rather the organism is better seen as an information seeker using logical and perceptual relations among events and its own preconceptions to form a sophisticated representation of its world" (p. 154).

How did learning theories change from the radical view that only external behavior matters?

CRITICAL THINKING APPLICATION

Can the principles of operant conditioning be used to change your own behavior? Here's an experiment on behavior modification you can attempt. First, review the major terms from our discussion of operant conditioning. Can you design a behavior modification program to help you achieve a goal?

Step 1: Goal. First, think about your goal. Select a behavior that you want to perform more often (e.g., floss your teeth), not one that you want to stop (e.g., smoking). Ideally, the behavior would be something you do at least several times a day; for example, "Increase the amount of time I study every day." Then, propose an operational definition (quantitative rather than qualitative) of your target behavior so you can measure the change. For example, if your target behavior is to study more, how many hours each day would constitute studying "more"?

Step 2: Baseline. Next, keep a written record of your behavior for 3 days without beginning any conditioning. Just note whenever you do the behavior (e.g., study, and for how long), for several days.

Step 3: Conditioning. Now you are ready to begin the conditioning. But first, you have to identify a reinforcer that works for you. It must be something that you can control, that you will make use of only when you do the target behavior, and that you find pleasurable. Some examples might be watching a video, calling a friend to talk, or eating a cookie. Decide on the contingencies, or how you will administer the reinforcer; for example, "For every hour I study, I can eat one cookie." Or, "For every day I study for 4 hours, I can watch 1 hour of television." Try to think of a variety of possible reinforcers, and choose one that will motivate you but will not be too expensive or have harmful, unpleasant, or unintended consequences. Be very specific about what you must do to receive the reinforcement. If you can't trust yourself as your own trainer,

ask a roommate or friend to apply the reinforcer for you. Next, think about the schedule of reinforcement: Will it be continuous, such as eating a cookie after every assignment you complete? Or will it be a partial reinforcement schedule in which you receive the reinforcement only after some responses? Will it be a ratio (depending on the number of responses that occur) or interval (depending on how much time has passed) schedule? Then, for at least 5 days, follow the reinforcement plan you designed.

Step 4: Extinction. During this period, no reinforcement is given. Continue writing down the number (or length) of times your behavior occurs. Keep a record for at least 3 days.

Step 5: Principles of operant conditioning. Now examine your records. How much did you do your target behavior before conditioning started? How many times did you receive reinforcement during the training period? And how often did you perform the behavior when it was no longer being reinforced? What do you conclude about your behavior modification program? Did your desired behavior decrease during extinction, when the reinforcement period stopped? If so, perhaps reinforcement will be required to maintain your new behavior. If your desired behavior continued even though it was no longer being reinforced, what do you conclude about operant conditioning? Are there other aspects of the situation that may be providing rewards for your new behavior? For example, perhaps you are enjoying your studying more, and that is causing you to continue studying more even without the cookies!

Tolman's Latent Learning

One learning theorist who raised issues with behaviorist theories was Edward C. Tolman (1886–1959). He identified **latent learning**, in which learning takes place without any

Latent learning
Knowledge that is not displayed in behavior until reinforcement is provided.

change in displayed behavior (Tolman, 1948). One study (Tolman & Honzik, 1930) had rats learn to run through mazes for a food reward at the goal box. With the reward, this group showed steady improvement by making fewer errors over the 17 days in the study FIGURE 6-25. Another group was allowed to run the maze each day, but there was no food in the goal box. This group showed continued wrong turns and errors, and just a small improvement in their performance over the days. This result appears to support operant conditioning theory because they didn't improve without reinforcement. But a third group started out with no reinforcement for their first 10 days in the maze. On the 11th day, and every day after that, a food reward awaited them in the goal box. If these rats had learned nothing in the first 10 days without reward, as predicted by operant theory, they should now begin to learn just like the first group of rats did on Day 1 and show the same steady improvement over days.

FIGURE 6-25 Tolman and Honzik's results showed that rats that were reinforced only after 11 days of wandering the maze (the no reinforcement then reinforcement group) quickly responded to reinforcement, performing better than rats always reinforced (the always reinforced group). The never reinforced group never received any reinforcement. *Source: Data from Tolman, E. C. (1948). Cognitive maps in rats and men. Psychological Review, 55, 189–208; Tolman, E. C., & Honzik, C. H. (1930). Introduction and removal of reward and maze performance in rats. University of California Publications in Psychology, 4, 257–275.*

But they didn't! On the remaining days of the study, these rats showed an immediate reduction in errors and even performed better than the rats that had received reinforcement all along. Clearly, this third group had learned from its "purposeless" wanderings in the maze, because as soon as there was a reward, the rats quickly found it. The evidence Tolman collected showed that learning does take place without reinforcement. In addition, the studies showed that learning can occur in the absence of any displayed behavior. Tolman suggested the rats had developed **cognitive maps** of the maze, so that when they wanted to reach the goal quickly for the reward, they had an internal representation leading them there. As evidence from these and other studies accumulated, learning psychologists were forced to begin incorporating cognitive processes into their theories.

Tolman demonstrated that cognition must be incorporated into learning theories. His rats learned about the maze without any reinforcement taking place and were ready to use their knowledge when needed. This opened the door for theories that explicitly discussed the cognitive changes taking place during learning.

Cognitive map A mental representation of a physical path to a goal location.

Bandura's Social-Cognitive Learning Theory

In an experiment to demonstrate this point, a researcher named Albert Bandura set out to test observational learning in a study with 5- and 6-year-old children (Bandura, Ross, & Ross, 1961). In this study, children watched a videotape in which an adult model played with a large inflatable doll called a Bobo doll. In the video, the adult model performed violent actions upon the doll: kicking it, punching it, lifting it up and throwing it, and so forth. Next, the child was brought into a second room full of toys, and to introduce a feeling of frustration, they were told the toys in that room were for "the other children." Left alone in a third playroom, they soon found one of the toys there was the same Bobo doll shown in the video. Would there be any effects of seeing the violence in the video when the children were allowed to play on their own?

Bandura found plenty of evidence that the children were affected by the modeling they saw in the video. Not only were the children more violent with the Bobo doll, but they

Mice who wander in a maze without any reward will then run through it quickly once cheese is added to the goal box as a reward.

also performed actions very similar to the model's actions FIGURE 6-26. For example, they also lifted the large doll up and threw it and repeated phrases the model used ("Sock him in the nose!"). The children appeared to learn how to behave with this novel toy by copying the actions they had seen in the video. Learning, in the form of acquiring specific behaviors, had taken place simply through observing the model's behavior.

FIGURE 6-26 The results of Bandura's study of modeling aggression. Control (green) and nonaggressive model subjects (orange) showed less aggressive behaviors than the aggressive model subjects (blue). *Source: Data from Bandura, A., Ross, D., & Ross, S. A. (1961). Transmission of aggression through imitation of aggressive models.* Journal of Abnormal and Social Psychology, 63, *575–582.*

Acquisition vs. Performance

Bandura proposed that two stages are required in observational learning: an acquisition stage and a performance stage. Recall the rats in Tolman's demonstration of latent learning: First, they wandered through the maze without any rewards. However, when the reward trials began, the rats were quick to find them, showing they had learned (during an acquisition stage) but had not demonstrated their knowledge until the rewards appeared (in the performance stage). Similarly, Bandura noted that observational learning can take place in an acquisition phase without any display of behavior from the learner. Then, in a performance stage, their behavior reveals the change they gained from having observed the model. Any parent can verify that children readily learn from observation but can show no sign until they perform the behavior—usually at a most embarrassing time!

Basic Processes

In later work, Bandura proposed four processes required for successful learning by observation (Bandura, 1977).

1. Attention. To learn by observation, you have to pay attention to the behavior being modeled and to the consequences of the behavior. While you may have witnessed someone preparing a meal many times, you may not have attended closely enough to perform the actions on your own. We also choose our models; so peers, movies, and celebrities may become effective models because they capture our attention.

2. Retention. Once observed, time may pass before you have the opportunity to take action. Will you recall the behavior you observed and remember its specific nature? Taking steps to mentally rehearse or think about the observations will aid in recall.

3. Reproduction. Even though you saw the necessary behaviors, you must be able to perform them yourself. You may have watched a chef throw pizza dough into the air, but you may not be able to reproduce that behavior and execute it correctly.

4. Motivation. Whether an observer ever takes action will be determined by whether he or she feels the behavior will be reinforced, or lead to a desirable consequence. People are more likely to imitate when models are rewarded for their behavior and observers see the behavior as accomplishing something they desire.

Observational learning proves that learning can occur without firsthand experience. The real question is what behaviors people will choose to imitate and where those behaviors will lead.

FIGURE 6-27 Some of the same neurons fire when a monkey watches an action as when it performs the same action.

Mirror neurons Neurons in the frontal lobe that respond to motor behavior in oneself and in others.

Biological Basis: Mirrors in the Brain

Recent evidence suggests that not only are we prepared to imitate others, but we also may have a built-in biological advantage in doing so. Researchers in Parma, Italy, were studying motor behavior in monkeys. A laboratory monkey undergoing testing had wires implanted in its motor cortex that recorded neural activity. This motor region is in the frontal lobe, the brain region that enables planning and action. When the monkey put a peanut into its mouth, a monitoring device would record the activity in this motor area. At one point, the monkey simply watched while a human experimenter grabbed a peanut and ate it. Much to their surprise, the researchers found that the same brain region active when the monkey grabbed and ate a peanut was made active by simply watching the human (or another monkey) do it FIGURE 6-27.

Eventually, the scientists realized they had discovered a previously unknown type of neuron, called **mirror neurons** (Rizzolatti, Fogassi, & Gallese, 2006). These neurons form the basis for imitation and observational learning. For example, when a monkey grasps, touches, or pushes something, neural activity occurs. The neurons fire in the same way when the monkey observes another monkey (or a person) performing the same behaviors. Brain scans reveal that humans, like monkeys, have a mirror neuron system (Iacoboni, 2008). As we observe others' actions, our brains generate an internal simulation of their activity. For example, watching a child eat an ice cream cone, we can imagine the sense of pleasure it generates, along with the sense of loss when she drops it to the ground. We may learn to understand another person's feelings by imitating them within our own neural system and playing out their consequences. Our mirror neurons may help us understand how others are feeling when we see a smile, a passionate kiss, or a painful blow. Some scientists speculate this system may be involved in our ability to develop empathy for others. In fact, the lack of connection to others displayed by individuals with autism may be linked to "broken mirrors" in this system (Iacoboni & Dapretto, 2006; Oberman & Ramachandran, 2007).

Certainly, the discovery of mirror neurons identified a potential biological mechanism to support our ability to learn by observing others.

Applying Principles of Observational Learning

By the time most children in this country reach adolescence, they have seen countless acts or portrayals of violence in the media. Think about your own exposure to violence. How many fights, gunshots, and killings have you seen depicted? Do you think this exposure has ever led to violence on your part? In the 1970s, it was believed that watching violence might lead to less aggression. The idea was that seeing violence was cathartic: It released your aggressive feelings to see aggression by others. However, experiments like Bandura's suggest that simply observing violence may make violence less offensive. Are we perhaps more accepting of violent behavior and therefore more likely to respond aggressively in some situations? Recent studies using video have shown that people do act more aggressively following viewing of aggression (Bushman & Huesmann, 2001). For example, in one study, college students' aggressive cognitions increased with the level of violence in a video, and their measured hostility and systolic blood pressure were higher in response to the most violent video (Bushman & Geen, 1990).

What about the effects of exposure to violent models on your sensitivity toward violence? One study (Carnagey, Anderson, & Bushman, 2007) tested college students who played 20 minutes of either violent (*Duke Nukem*, *Mortal Kombat*, and *Future Cop*) or nonviolent (*3D Pinball*, *3D Munch Man*, and *Tetra Madness*) games FIGURE 6-28. The researchers found that both groups showed similar results when having their heart rate and galvanic skin response tested. Next, they watched a 10-minute videotape of real-life violence, including police confrontations, fights among prisoners, people shooting at each other, and the like. Results showed that those who had played violent video games had weaker physiological responses to images of violent, real-life events than those who

FIGURE 6-28 Frequent exposure to violent images results in lowered physiological, and therefore psychological, responses.

played nonviolent games. Their findings suggest that violent video game exposure can cause a psychological desensitization to violence. The researchers warn: "It appears that individuals who play violent video games habituate, or 'get used to,' all the violence and eventually become physiologically numb to it. The modern entertainment media landscape could accurately be described as an effective systematic violence-desensitization tool." After repeated exposure in video games, violent images may no longer evoke the same psychological response (Carnagey et al., 2007).

A meta-analysis of studies of video game play across cultures found that exposure to violent video games is a causal risk factor for increased aggressive behavior and decreased empathy (Anderson et al., 2010). These studies show a direct relationship between violent media and feelings of aggression. Considering how much exposure to violence occurs in our everyday lives, these studies pose real concern. Based on a review of more than 50 years of research, violence depicted on television, in films, and in video games raises the risk of aggressive behavior in adults and young viewers (Huesmann, 2007). It also poses a public health risk second only to smoking as a risk factor. The health of young people is placed at greater risk by media violence than by unprotected sex among populations at risk of contracting AIDS, or by passive smoking. However, in 2011, the U.S. Supreme Court struck down a California law that banned the sale of violent video games to children on the grounds that it violated the right to free speech (Liptak, 2001).

Violent images in emotionally arousing video games may lead to desensitization toward aggression.

Observational learning can also be used to motivate positive social encounters, called **prosocial behavior** (Rosenhan, 1972). Seeing others donate to charity, volunteer in the community, or help others can motivate the imitation of that behavior. Unfortunately, there has been relatively little research on purely prosocial video game effects, largely because there are few games that have the main characters modeling helpful behavior. However, one recent study found that playing a prosocial (relative to a neutral) video game reduced hostile expectations and decreased the accessibility of antisocial thoughts (Greitemeyer & Osswald, 2009). Prosocial behavior is another instance in which the main tenants of operant conditioning may not appear to hold. In charitable giving, for example, you are performing an action that is not rewarded by an external reinforcer but actually results in a financial loss. However, giving can be its own reward, pointing out how any account of learning must also provide for internal motivations, cognition, and emotions as influences on our behavior.

Prosocial behavior Actions that help others at a cost to oneself.

Observational learning greatly speeds the amount of information and behavior we can acquire by benefitting from the behavior of others. In some social animals, a "culture" develops in which new behaviors are shared among the group but may never be picked up by other groups. For example, chimpanzees were thought to be unable to swim; however, one individual tried it and liked the water play. Soon, the entire group was in the water, and this behavior was maintained over time. However, no other chimpanzee group has been observed playing in water. A recent study introduced new foraging techniques to individual chimps in different groups (Whiten et al., 2007). They found that foraging behaviors carried across two separate groups of chimpanzees, and within a group, most of the troop were observed using the special techniques. This suggests other social animals can gain the advantage of cultural learning, which provides faster adaptation than genetic changes through generations.

Summary of Multiple Influences on Learning

Like the other forms of learning, observational learning again demonstrates how biological (in the form of mirror neurons) and environmental factors (in the form of other people whose behavior we model) work together to produce learning. Throughout this chapter, both in the behavioral theories of classical and operant conditioning and in the cognitive theory of observational learning, we've seen the multiple causal influences determining whether learning occurs. We have seen how learning depends on biological factors (e.g., physiological reflexes, biological preparedness, mirror neurons) and environmental factors (e.g., associations, experiences, reinforcements) including social factors (observation of others). What and how we learn depends on our biological and evolutionary heritage, and to a very large extent, on the experiences we have in the world. The theories of learning in this chapter point out the complex interweaving of biological and environmental influences in psychology.

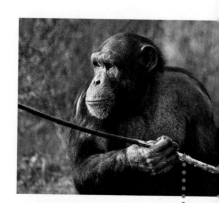

Chimpanzees have been found to develop novel methods of foraging for foods that are shared within social groups.

CONCEPT LEARNING CHECK **6.4** | *Learning by Observing*

Consider the principles of observational learning. Which of these outcomes may follow from observation? Explain how each of these relates to the principles of observational learning.

1. New behaviors

2. Stopping of previously learned behaviors

3. Start of previously forbidden behaviors

4. Similar behaviors

Visual Overview Three Types of Learning

There are three basic types of learning exhibited by humans and other animals: classical conditioning ("learning"), operant conditioning, and observational learning. In classical conditioning, we learn to anticipate events that cause basic physiological responses (UCS: Unconditioned Stimulus, UCR: Unconditioned Response, CS: Conditioned Stimulus, CR: Conditioned Response). In operant conditioning, whether we perform a given behavior again depends on its "reinforcement," or reward. Finally, observational learning occurs by "mirroring" the experiences of others within our own minds. These three methods of learning explain how our behavior changes with experience.

Classical Conditioning

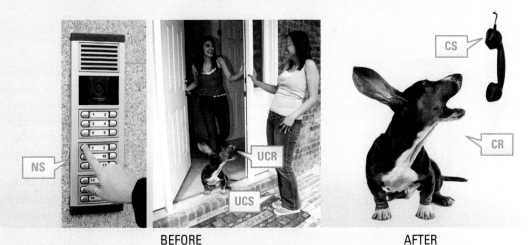

BEFORE   AFTER

Operant Conditioning

BEFORE   AFTER

Observational Learning

BEFORE   AFTER

6.1 How We Learn

- Learning describes a lasting change in knowledge or behavior based on experience.
- Behaviorism defines learning based on changes in observable behaviors.
- Classical conditioning describes linking events that occur together.

- Operant conditioning describes responding to the consequences of our behavior.
- In observational learning, a cognitive theory, new behaviors are modeled by others.

6.2 Classical Conditioning

- We learn to connect events that signal important physiological responses.
- Pavlov's dogs learned to associate a bell with receiving meat and began salivating.
- Acquisition takes place by pairing a neutral stimulus with the unconditioned stimulus.
- After learning, the neutral stimulus becomes the conditioned stimulus.
- After learning, the unconditioned response becomes the conditioned response.
- Higher-order conditioning builds more associations upon conditioned stimuli.
- Extinction happens if a conditioned stimulus repeatedly appears alone.
- After a rest, a conditioned response can occur again, called spontaneous recovery.

- In generalization, similar stimuli evoke the same conditioned response.
- In discrimination, distinctions between meaningful stimuli (signs) are made.
- Emotional responses like fear, arousal, and anxiety can be classically conditioned.
- More recent work suggests classical conditioning is more like learning a prediction.
- Taste aversion shows we are biologically prepared to more easily learn some associations.
- Phobias can be classically conditioned and treated using these techniques.

6.3 Operant Conditioning

- Operant conditioning is learning from consequences.
- Thorndike's Law of Effect predicts behaviors leading to good outcomes are repeated.
- B. F. Skinner's experiments show the principles of operant conditioning.
- Reinforcement (or reward) of behavior leads to learning.
- Shaping involves rewarding partial behavior in successive approximations.
- Operant or voluntary behaviors also show generalization and discrimination.

- When behaviors no longer occur, they enter extinction.
- Schedules of reinforcement are training programs for delivering rewards.
- Punishment is not an effective method of operant learning.
- Intrinsic motivation can make external reinforcers more complicated to apply.
- Not all behaviors are equally easy to learn for every species of animal.
- Behavior modification programs can change problematic behaviors.

6.4 A Cognitive Approach: Observational Learning

- We readily learn by observing the behavior of others.
- Cognition is evident in even animal learning as shown in latent learning.
- Both negative and prosocial behavior can be acquired from models.
- Bandura's experiments showed children learn aggressive behavior from models.
- Learning can take place well before performance shows it has occurred.

- Basic processes include attention, retention, reproduction, and motivation.
- Mirror neurons in the brain respond the same whether you are performing or observing.
- Observational learning provides the benefit of others' experiences.

6.1 How We Learn

1. When 2-year-old Clarice was playing in the basement, a large burst of thunder scared her at the same time she saw a cat. Now Clarice has a cat phobia. Clarice's experience is an example of which type of learning?

A. operant conditioning

B. observational learning

C. superstition

D. classical conditioning

2. When Harold watched the cheerleaders at the first Michigan football game he attended, he learned to do their new cheer flawlessly. This type of learning is most likely due to:

A. operant conditioning.

B. mirror neurons.

C. classical conditioning.

D. observational learning.

3. Your coworker gives you a compliment, and you smile back. The probability that she will give you another compliment now increases. This is an example of the type of learning called:

A. mirror neurons.

B. operant conditioning.

C. observational learning.

D. classical conditioning.

6.2 Classical Conditioning

4. After several visits to the doctor for chemotherapy treatments, Courtney finds she begins to feel nauseous just sitting in the waiting room before her appointment begins. According to the principles of classical conditioning, Courtney's feeling of nausea in the absence of any chemotherapy drugs is:

A. an unconditioned stimulus.

B. an unconditioned response.

C. a conditioned stimulus.

D. a conditioned response.

5. In Little Albert's experience with classical conditioning, a neutral stimulus (the white rat) was paired with a very loud crash of metal, which startled him and made him cry. After Little Albert learns this, the rat will become a(n):

A. unconditioned stimulus.

B. conditioned stimulus.

C. controlled stimulus.

D. generalized stimulus.

6. In a classic study on taste aversion, rats tasted sweetened water, saw a flash of light, and heard a loud clicking noise simultaneously. When they were then exposed to X-rays, which caused nausea, the rats learned to avoid the:

A. loud clicking noise.

B. sweetened water, light flashes, and clicks.

C. sweetened water.

D. flashes of light.

7. Wolpe's research on treating phobias with systematic desensitization showed that the best way to "unlearn" an association developed through classical conditioning is to:

A. focus on consistent training.

B. add learning by rewards.

C. retrain with relaxation training.

D. understand the basis for irrational fears.

6.3 Operant Conditioning

8. Denisa works hard on studying for her psychology exam. As a result, she gets an "A" on the first exam. Now, she is much more likely to study hard for the second exam. In this example, the grade is:

A. positive punishment.

B. positive reinforcement.

C. negative reinforcement.

D. superstitious behavior.

9. Stanley gets annoyed when his mom nags him to do his homework. When he finally does it, his mom stops nagging. Now he does his homework without any nagging. "Nagging" has served as a:

A. punishment by application.

B. positive reinforcement.

C. negative reinforcement.

D. punishment by removal.

10. You are a manager at a telemarketing firm and want to get your employees to make the most calls possible while at work. To do so, you should provide bonus money after they make calls using a schedule of reinforcement called:

A. variable ratio.

B. fixed ratio.

C. fixed interval.

D. variable interval.

11. Oskar listens regularly to a radio station that gives prizes to listeners who are asked to call in once every few hours, after either 1, 2, or 3 hours have gone by. This is an example of a schedule of reinforcement called:

A. fixed interval.

B. variable interval.

C. variable ratio.

D. fixed ratio.

6.4 A Cognitive Approach: Observational Learning

12. In a classic experiment by Bandura, nursery-school children observed an adult model interact with a Bobo doll, an inflatable clown-like toy, and then were given a chance to play with Bobo. The results of this research showed that:

    A. classical conditioning explains kids' behavior.

    B. rewards can provide reinforcements for learning.

    C. antisocial actions are instinctual action patterns.

    D. exposure to aggression leads to aggression.

13. Scientists were surprised to find activation in prefrontal cortex neurons involved in planning motor actions whenever a monkey in their experiment:

    A. saw a picture of a peanut.

    B. saw a peanut.

    C. saw a man reach for and eat a peanut.

    D. went for a swim in a pond.

14. Observational learning is distinguished from both classical conditioning and operant conditioning by the fact that:

    A. no behavior occurs during learning.

    B. another person is usually present.

    C. no "conditioning" (training or learning) takes place.

    D. more repetitions or trials are needed to learn.

CHAPTER DISCUSSION QUESTIONS

1. A surprising fact about theories of human learning in this chapter is that they focus on behavior rather than on knowledge. How far can a behavioral theory go in explaining learning? What aspects of learning are not well addressed by the theories here, and what must knowledge-based theories account for?

2. Think of an example of your own emotional experience. Were any associations made to the experience? Do any of those associations elicit an emotional reaction now? How can you "unlearn" undesirable associations?

3. Is punishment ever a useful training technique? What are the arguments against using punishment? Do you feel physical punishment should be illegal in your country?

4. What differences in cultural perspectives may arise from experience? How do culture and experience play roles in how people learn in a given situation? Think of specific examples of how two people may learn differently in the same situation based on cultural experiences.

5. Based on what you read about aggression arising from violence in videos, do you think some behaviors should be banned from entertainment media for children?

CHAPTER PROJECTS

1. Read an article or book about the experiences of people who have social phobia. How would a treatment technique like systematic desensitization work for social phobia? Would a behavior modification program also address issues with social interaction? What would a behavioral contract to increase social behaviors look like?

2. Read the short story "Flowers for Algernon" (1959) by Daniel Keyes or see the Hollywood film called *Charley* (1968) directed by Ralph Nelson. The story captures issues of animal ethics, cognitive maps and operant training, and the treatment of the disabled. How is the intelligence of people perceived as different from that of animals, and what does that imply about people who are less able to learn?

Acquisition
Avoidance learning
Behavior modification
Behavioral contract
Behaviorism
Biofeedback
Biological preparedness
Classical conditioning
Cognitive
Cognitive map
Conditioned response
Conditioned stimulus
Conditioning
Continuous reinforcement
Discrimination
Escape learning
Extinction
Extinguish
Extrinsic motivation
Fixed-interval schedule
Fixed-ratio schedule

Flooding
Generalization
Higher-order conditioning
Instinctual drift
Intermittent reinforcement
Interval schedule
Intrinsic motivation
Latent learning
Law of Effect
Learned helplessness
Learning
Mirror neurons
Modeling
Negative reinforcement
Neutral stimulus
Observational learning
Operant
Operant conditioning
Phobia
Positive reinforcement
Primary reinforcer

Prosocial behavior
Punishment by application
Punishment by removal
Ratio schedules
Reinforce
Reinforcer
Schedule of reinforcement
Secondary reinforcer (conditioned reinforcer)
Shaping
Skinner box (operant chamber)
Spontaneous recovery
Systematic desensitization
Taste aversion
Token economies
Unconditioned response
Unconditioned stimulus
Variable-interval schedule
Variable-ratio schedule

6.1 Comparing Types of Learning

1. This fits operant conditioning because the behavior is followed by consequences that make performing the behavior again more likely.

2. This fits classical conditioning because the storm has become associated with the fear from the electrical outage.

3. This fits observational learning because the mother's behavior is the model for the daughter's (not going to work or school).

4. This fits classical conditioning because an emotional response is elicited by a conditioned stimulus (the teacher calling her name).

5. This fits observational learning because he learns what to do by watching his girlfriend.

6. This is operant conditioning because Malay's responses reinforce her sister's talking.

6.2 Applying Principles of Classical Conditioning

1. Unconditioned stimulus: shock

   Unconditioned response: fear

   Conditioned stimulus: flash of light

   Conditioned response: fear

2. Unconditioned stimulus: poison

   Unconditioned response: nausea

   Conditioned stimulus: smell of sheep

   Conditioned response: nausea

6.3 Comparing Consequences of Behavior

1. **a.** Reinforcement: It led to more of the behavior.

   b. Positive reinforcement: His requests with "please" always led to a pleasant outcome by his parents doing what he wanted.

2. **a.** Reinforcement: It led to more of the behavior.

   b. Positive reinforcement: Her mother's attention when interrupted was positive for Sarah.

3. **a.** Reinforcement: It led to more of the behavior.

   b. Negative reinforcement: A negative (chores) is removed after the behavior, leading to a positive outcome for the learner.

4. **a.** Punishment: The behavior decreased or stopped.

   b. Not applicable

6.4 Concept Learning Check 6.4 Learning by Observing

1. Observation is good at helping learners gain new behaviors they see modeled by others.

2. Observation does not involve any behavior during learning, so it is difficult to observe that a behavior is not happening.

3. Studies on aggression show that people can learn negative behaviors they see modeled.

4. Observing behaviors may result in the learner acquiring similar behaviors to what is modeled; for example, they may try their own aggressive actions on the Bobo doll in Bandura's study.

6.1 How We Learn

1. D. Rationale: The thunder elicited fear and now the cat is associated with fear. The automatic response signals that this is classical conditioning.

2. D. Rationale: The learner didn't perform any actions but watched another perform the behavior. So this is an example of observational learning.

3. B. Rationale: The smile worked to reinforce the behavior of smiling in the learner, making her more likely to smile again. So this is reinforcement learning, also called operant conditioning.

6.2 Classical Conditioning

4. D. Rationale: The drugs (unconditioned stimulus) elicited nausea (unconditioned response). After learning, the waiting room (conditioned stimulus) elicits the same nausea, now a conditioned (learned) response.

5. B. Rationale: The loud crash (unconditioned stimulus) elicited fear (unconditioned response), and now, after learning, the rat (conditioned stimulus) is associated with fear (conditioned response).

6. C. Rationale: Not all associations are equally easy to learn. For taste aversion, animals are biologically prepared to associate taste with nausea and have a harder time learning to associate other neutral stimuli (like light or sound) with nausea.

7. C. Rationale: The presence of the conditioned stimulus now elicits a conditioned response. Systematic desensitization provides gradual practice being in the presence of the conditioned stimulus while learning to relax.

6.3 Operant Conditioning

8. B. Rationale: The grade is a reinforcement because it makes the behavior more likely to occur again. It is a positive reinforcement because it is the introduction of a positive reward for the learner.

9. C. Rationale: The nagging makes the behavior (doing homework) more likely to happen again, so it is a reinforcement. When the nagging stops, it is the removal of a negative feature, so it is negative reinforcement.

10. B. Rationale: The schedules of reinforcement vary in how quickly the learner responds and works for further reinforcement. The schedule that motivates the fastest responses is a fixed-ratio schedule.

11. B. Rationale: The reinforcement occurs to a behavior that happens after a given time interval, which varies (1, 2, or 3 hours), so it is a variable-interval schedule.

6.4 A Cognitive Approach: Observational Learning

12. D. Rationale: The children in the study showed the same aggressive play behaviors they had observed in the models, so that watching aggressive behavior led to more aggressive actions by the children.

13. C. Rationale: The mirror neurons respond to actions that the animal plans and performs itself and to the same actions when performed by another. They likely play a role in learning by observation.

14. A. Rationale: Unlike the two other types of learning, observational learning occurs without the learner performing any behaviors, but simply by watching a model. Other people can be involved in all three types of learning, and all three types may produce learning within a single trial.

REFERENCES

Abramson, L., Seligman, M., & Teasdale, J. (1978). Learned helplessness in humans: Critique and reformulation. *Journal of Abnormal Psychology, 87,* 49–74.

Ader, R., & Cohen, N. (1985). CNS-immune system interactions: Conditioning phenomena. *Behavioral and Brain Sciences, 8,* 379–426.

Anderson, C. A., Ihori, N., Bushman, B. J., Rothstein, H. R., Shibuya, A., Swing, E. L., Sakamoto, A., & Saleem, M. (2010). Violent video game effects on aggression, empathy, and prosocial behavior in eastern and western countries: A meta-analytic review. *Psychological Bulletin, 136*(2), 151–173.

Bandura, A. (1977). *Social learning theory.* Englewood Cliffs, NJ: Prentice-Hall.

Bandura, A., Ross, D., & Ross, S. A. (1961). Transmission of aggression through imitation of aggressive models. *Journal of Abnormal and Social Psychology, 63,* 575–582.

Breland, K., & Breland, M. (1961). The misbehavior of organisms. *American Psychologist, 16,* 661–664.

Bushman, B. J., & Geen, R. G. (1990). Role of cognitive-emotional mediators and individual differences in the effects of media violence on aggression. *Journal of Personality and Social Psychology, 58*(1), 156–163.

Bushman, B. J., & Huesmann, L. R. (2001). Effects of televised violence on aggression. In D. G. Singer and J. Singer (eds.), *Handbook of children and the media* (pp. 223–254). Thousand Oaks, California: Sage.

Cameron, C. L., Cella, D., Herndon, J. E. II, Kornblith, A. B., Zuckerman, E., Henderson, E., Weiss, R. B., Cooper, M. R., Silver, R. T., Leone, L., Canellos, G. P., Peterson, B. A., Holland, J. C. (2001). Persistent symptoms among survivors of Hodgkin's disease: An explanatory model based on classical conditioning. *Health Psychology, 20,* 71–75.

Carnagey, N. L., Anderson, C. A., & Bushman, B. J. (2007). The effect of video game violence on physiological desensitization to real-life violence. *Journal of Experimental Social Psychology, 43,* 489–496.

deCharms, R. C., Maeda, F., Glover, G. H., Ludlow, D., Pauly, J. M., Soneji, D., Gabrieli, J. D. E., Mackey, S. C., & Raichle, M. E. (2005). Control over brain activation and pain learned by using real-time functional MRI. *Proceedings of the National Academy of Sciences of the United States of America, 102*(51), 18626–18631.

Driver, J. L., & Gottman, J. M. (2005). Dysfunctional marital conflict and everyday marital interaction. *Journal of Divorce & Remarriage, 43*(3–4), 63–77.

Durgam, R. C. (2001). Rodent models of depression: Learned helplessness using a triadic design in rats. *Current Protocols in Neuroscience,* 8.10B.1–8.10B.12.

Garcia, J., & Koelling, R. A. (1966). Relation of cue to consequence in avoidance learning. *Psychonomic Science, 4,* 123–124.

Gershoff, E. T. (2002). Corporal punishment by parents and associated child behaviors and experiences: A meta-analytic and theoretical review. *Psychological Bulletin, 128*(4), 539–579.

Gottman, J. M. (1998). Psychology and the study of marital processes. *Annual Review of Psychology, 49,* 169–197.

Greitemeyer, T., & Osswald, S. (2009). Prosocial video games reduce aggressive cognitions. *Journal of Experimental Social Psychology, 45,* 896–900.

Huesmann, L. R. (2007). The impact of electronic media violence: Scientific theory and research. *Journal of Adolescent Health, 41*(6), S6–S13.

Iacoboni, M. (2008). *Mirroring people: The new science of how we connect to others.* New York: Farrar, Straus, & Giroux.

Iacoboni, M., & Dapretto, M. (2006). The mirror neuron system and the consequences of its dysfunction. *Nature Review Neuroscience, 7,* 942–951.

Kazdin, A. E. (2008). *The Kazdin method for parenting the defiant child: With no pills, no therapy, no contest of wills.* Boston: Houghton Mifflin Harcourt.

Koole, S. L., Dijksterhuis, A., & van Knippenberg, A. (2001). What's in a name: Implicit self-esteem and the automatic self. *Journal of Personality and Social Psychology, 80*(4), 669–685.

Lepper, M. R., Greene, D., & Nisbett, R. E. (1973). Undermining children's intrinsic interest with extrinsic reward: A test of the "overjustification" hypothesis. *Journal of Personality and Social Psychology, 28,* 129–137.

Liptak, A. (2011). Minors can buy violent games, justices decide. *New York Times,* June 27, p. A1.

Lovaas, O. I. (1987). Behavioral treatment and normal educational and intellectual functioning in young autistic children. *Journal of Consulting and Clinical Psychology, 55*(1), 3–9.

Luthans, F., Paul, R., & Baker, D. (1981). An experimental analysis of the impact of contingent reinforcement on salesperson performance behavior. *Journal of Applied Psychology, 66*(3), 314–323.

Miller, G., & Cohen, N. (2001). Psychological interventions and the immune system: A meta-analytic review and critique. *Health Psychology, 20,* 47–63.

Mineka, S., Keir, R., & Price, V. (1980). Fear of snakes in wild- and laboratory-reared rhesus monkeys (*Macaca mulatta*). *Animal Learning and Behavior, 8,* 653–663.

Öhman, A., & Mineka, S. (2001). Fears, phobias, and preparedness: Toward an evolved module of fear and fear learning. *Psychological Review, 108,* 483–522.

Orne, M. T. (1962). On the social psychology of the psychological experiment: With particular reference to demand characteristics and their implications. *American Psychologist, 17,* 776–783.

Pavlov, I. P. (1927). *Conditioned reflexes.* London: Oxford University Press.

Pollak, S., Cicchetti, D., & Klorman, R. (1998). Stress, memory, and emotion: Developmental considerations from the study of child maltreatment. *Developmental Psychopathology 10,* 811–828.

Oberman, L. M., & Ramachandran, V. S. (2007) The simulating social mind: The role of the mirror neuron system and simulation in the social and communicative deficits of autism spectrum disorders. *Psychological Bulletin, 133,* 310–327.

Rescorla, R. A. (1988). Pavlovian conditioning: It's not what you think it is. *American Psychologist, 43,* 151–160.

Rizzolatti, G., Fogassi, L., & Gallese, V. (2006). Mirrors in the mind, *Scientific American,* 54–61.

Rosenhan, D. L. (1972). Learning theory and prosocial behavior. *Journal of Social Issues, 28*(3), 151–163.

Seligman, M. E. P., & Maier, S. F. (1967). Failure to escape from traumatic shock. *Journal of Experimental Psychology, 74,* 1–9.

Skinner, B. F. (1938). *The behavior of organisms.* New York: Appleton-Century-Crofts.

Skinner, B. F. (1948). "Superstition" in the pigeon. *Journal of Experimental Psychology, 38,* 168–172.

Skinner, B. F. (1957). *Verbal behavior.* New York: Appleton-Century-Crofts.

Skinner, B. F. (1972). *Beyond freedom and dignity.* New York: Bantam Vintage.

Skinner, B. F. (1990). Can psychology be a science of mind? *American Psychologist, 45,* 1206–1210.

Thorndike, E. L. (1898). Animal intelligence: An experimental study of the associative processes in animals. *Psychological Monographs, 2*(Whole No, 8).

Tolman, E. C. (1948). Cognitive maps in rats and men. *Psychological Review, 55,* 189–208.

Tolman, E. C., & Honzik, C. H. (1930). Introduction and removal of reward and maze performance in rats. *University of California Publications in Psychology, 4,* 257–275.

Watson, J. B. (1913). Psychology as the behaviorist views it. *Psychological Review, 20,* 158–177.

Watson, J. B. (1924). The unverbalized in human behavior. *Psychological Review, 31,* 339–347.

Watson, J. B. (1925). *Behaviorism.* New York: W. W. Norton.

Watson, J. B., & Rayner, R. (1920). Conditioned emotional responses. *Journal of Experimental Psychology, 3,* 1–14.

Whiten, A., Spiteri, A., Horner, V., Bonnie, K. E., Lambeth, S. P., Schapiro, S. J., & de Waal, F. B. (2007). Transmission of multiple traditions within and between chimpanzee groups. *Current Biology, 17*(12), 1038–1043.

Wolpe, J. (1961). The systematic desensitization treatment of neuroses. *Journal of Nervous and Mental Diseases, 132,* 180–203.

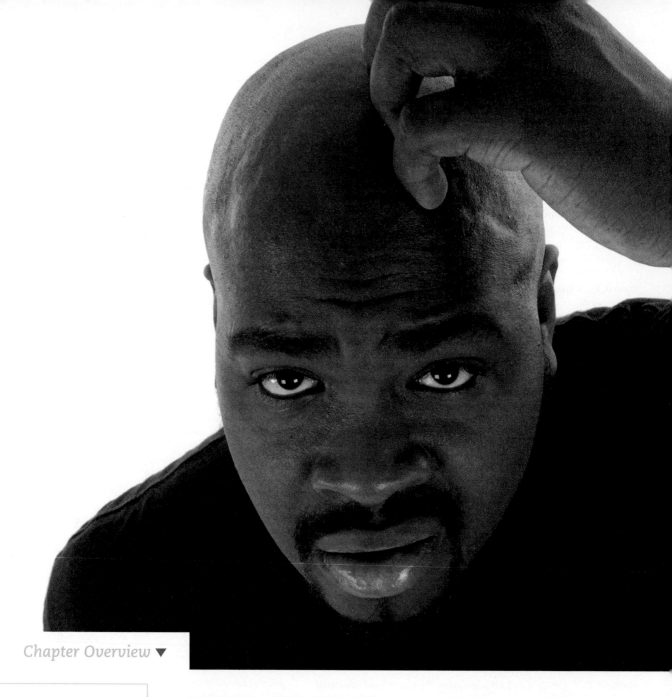

7 Memory

Learning Objectives ▼

7.1 ■ Explain how human memory differs from an objective video recording of events.

7.2 ■ Identify the ways that effortful processing can help to encode information into memory.

7.3 ■ Discuss how the three memory stages are involved in encoding new information into memory.

7.4 ■ Describe the main ways that information is organized in long-term memory.

7.5 ■ Examine the successful retrieval of information from long-term memory.

7.6 ■ Explain how information from long-term memory may include misinformation.

7.7 ■ Analyze how forgetting improves memory.

7.8 ■ Identify principles that can improve memory.

One December day, I spent a lunch hour buying Michigan sweatshirts as holiday gifts for my nephews. At the end of the workday, I returned to my car and was startled to find the bag of gifts missing. Living in a small college town, security was not on my mind, and I had left my car unlocked. I filed a police report by phone, and sent an e-mail to the entire department: "The Grinch Has Stolen Christmas," I warned, cautioning them not to leave their vehicles open.

The next day at lunch, I returned to the local college sportswear store, and approached the counter to tell them what had happened. "There you are!" the clerk immediately said, handing over a large package, "You forgot your purchase yesterday!"

I returned to the office and e-mailed the police and department, revealing that the missing bag had been my error alone. But that night, after I got out of my car, I locked the door behind me—for the first time ever.

7.1 Overview: What Is Memory?

Memory is an active process that constructs, encodes, stores, alters, and retrieves information.

- Explain how human memory differs from an objective video recording of events.

Is memory accurate? I know perfectly well that there was no theft from my car, and yet my sense of possible danger was inflated by an event I know never actually occurred. We may want to believe our memory is like a videotape of the past that we can call to mind at will. However, as we will see in this chapter, memory is not at all a static "picture;" instead, **memory** is an active, constructive, and dynamic process. When we examine the psychology of memory, we discover that vivid memories can be true and untrue, accurate and distorted, all at the same time. How can an experience become a life-long memory when it never really happened? In this chapter, we'll discover how memory processes shape what we know and remember about the world.

As a student, you already know a lot about memory; in fact, you are an expert at getting information into memory and ways of testing whether it is there. But in psychology, memory refers to the much broader topic—the enduring consequences in the mind of our experiences with the world. Every event you witnessed, fact you read, view you have seen, voice and song you have heard, and step you've taken has passed through your memory system, even if only for an instant. What is left behind in memory for you to now recall? The processing of our experiences can lead to little effect on memory; for example, what did you eat for lunch last Wednesday? Alternatively, it can lead to memories that last a lifetime, such as the day you met your boy or girlfriend for the first time. Memories are created through actions we take in the world, such as how to execute your improved tennis stroke. And memories are formed from wholly internalized processes, such as thinking about what has happened in the past and what you would like to have happen in the future.

With every new experience, memory effortlessly brings our past to mind. In many ways, the person you are is entirely determined by what you remember about your past. Do you like lemonade? Have you ever been to Ohio? Do you speak Spanish? Our memories define us as individuals and give us our sense of belonging in our relationships to others, and in our own personal histories. Should you become completely unrecognizable through physical characteristics, your memory identifies you as the unique person you are.

Memory plays a role in every other psychological function. Consciousness involves thinking about experiences in memory, and perception requires recognizing when an

Memory The enduring consequence in the mind of our experiences with the world.

object is familiar. Learning requires remembering that a behavior was previously rewarded. It is difficult to imagine how thinking occurs without relying on memory, even if just in the language we might use to express a current thought. Later, we'll address how cognitive processes such as thinking and deciding go hand in hand with memory processes. In this chapter, we will focus specifically on how memory internalizes the world within the mind.

CONCEPT LEARNING CHECK 7.1 | *Defining Memory*

As an experienced student, you've likely taken many tests designed to capture your memory for knowledge. The formats of some test items commonly used include:

A. Essay

B. Multiple choice

C. Fill in the blank

1. _____ Which of these is the most difficult type of question to answer, and why?

2. _____ Which is the easiest type of question to answer, and why?

3. _____ Which question type aids memory retrieval by providing cues?

7.2 Constructing Memory

Adding information into memory can be automatic, but constructing new memories requires effortful processing.

■ Identify the ways that effortful processing can help to encode information into memory.

Learning brings new knowledge into memory. A first question to consider is how information enters memory, a process called **encoding**. Many things seem to enter memory with no effort on our part; for example, you can probably draw a floor plan of your current bathroom even though you've not likely thought about it before now. However, other things seem to require a great deal of effort to encode into memory. For example, what is the name of the person you last met? While it seems like memory should be a record of whatever occurs around us, memories are not passive observances. Instead, we actively construct our memories based on information around us. Encoding information into memory often requires much more effort in its construction.

Encoding The process of taking new information and storing it in short- and long-term memory.

Automatic processing Information made available without conscious effort.

Incidental memory Explicit knowledge you did not intentionally encode.

Automatic Processing

We can encode large amounts of information without conscious effort, called **automatic processing**. Many things are encoded into memory even though little interest is paid to them. **Incidental memory** includes information you process and remember without any specific effort to do so. For example, advertisements are designed to be memorable even though you are explicitly not trying to remember them FIGURE 7-1. They are frequently repeated, designed to be "catchy," and sometimes add music or emotional cues to aid recall. Given examples like these, it's easy to think information lands in memory with little effort on our part. But you know, for example, from attempting to learn the names for

1. Reach out and touch someone.
2. The real thing
3. Finger lickin' good
4. He keeps going and going and going . . .
5. It's everywhere you want to be.
6. Live in your world, play in ours.
7. When it absolutely, positively has to be there overnight
8. Snap, Crackle, Pop!
9. Just do it.

A. AT&T®
B. Coca-Cola®
C. KFC®
D. Energizer® batteries
E. VISA®
F. Sony PlayStation®
G. FedEx®

H. Kellogg's® Rice Krispies®
I. NIKE

FIGURE 7-1 Identify the brand name associated with each of these advertising slogans. What factors help you recall them even though you are not trying to remember them?

all of the parts of the brain, that even repetition is not enough to ensure that information will "stick" in memory.

Often, information is encoded automatically, without your conscious attempt to attend to it. You may find yourself humming the song you keep hearing on the radio. Or you may think about fortune cookies when you pass the pungent smells of a Chinese restaurant. **Priming** refers to the activation of information in memory from a related cue (Meyer & Schvaneveldt, 1971). We are often unaware of these memory associations acquired from our environment, but they constantly bring past memories to mind. Automatic associations predict what will happen next, and that can influence our behavior. In one study (Bargh et al., 1996), students performed a laboratory task, and for some, it included the words, "worried, Florida, old, lonely, grey, sentimental, wise, bingo, retired, wrinkle." After the study, the time it took the students to walk down the hallway to the exit was measured (see FIGURE 7-2). Those who had read the elderly-related words took longer to exit, even though they were unaware of the stereotype contained in the task. We constantly encode and recall associations from information in the world without our conscious awareness.

> **Priming** The activation of information in memory from a related cue.

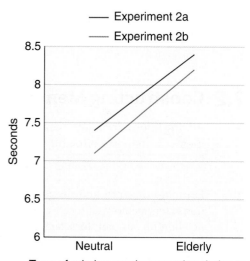

FIGURE 7-2 Mean time (in seconds) to walk down the hallway after the conclusion of the experiment for subjects primed by "elderly" stereotyped words compared to neutral words. The graph shows a replication in experiment 2a and 2b.
Source: Data from Bargh, J. A., Chen, M., & Burrows, L. (1996). Automaticity of social behavior: Direct effects of trait construct and stereotype activation on action. Journal of Personality and Social Psychology, 71(2), 230–244.

However, most often, we must put effort into constructing a memory for an event. This is not a videotape of our experience that we can replay later. Instead, constructing memories requires paying attention, or focusing our mental "spotlight" on specific information. In fact, the fundamental requirement for encoding information into memory is paying attention to it. This fact is illustrated by information we believe to be in memory but that may not be there. What does a penny look like? You have handled them countless times, but can you recall the correct face of a penny? (See FIGURE 7-3.) Why is this information hard to recall? Most likely, it was never encoded into your memory in the first place. After all, to use a penny, all you need to know is its color and size to distinguish it from other coins. So your memory for a penny is constructed from the available information but does not include everything that could have been encoded. Constructing memories involves attending to, selecting from, and encoding specific information

FIGURE 7-3 What does a penny look like? You have used it many times, and can surely recognize one when it is shown to you. But can you identify which of the drawings accurately depicts the face of the coin?
Source: Reproduced from Nickerson, R. S., & Adams, M. J. (1979). Long term memory for a common object. Cognitive Psychology, 11, 287–307.

about your experiences. In this sense, memory is highly selective: It depends on you to construct the information, and it requires your effort.

Effortful Processing

In contrast to automatic processing, memory construction requires a great deal of effortful processing in order to ensure that information is encoded into memory. As experienced learners, you know this very well: Simple repetition, or experience with information, is not sufficient to guarantee that the target information will be encoded (see FIGURE 7-4). One fundamental finding is that we tend to remember the *meaning* of an experience rather than the incidental details surrounding its encoding. In other words, people perform effort after meaning, attempting to understand the point of a communication or experience, and we tend to encode the meaning that we assign to it.

Encoding into Memory

Automatic (unaware)

Effortful (conscious)

What you ate for lunch

Textbook reading

FIGURE 7-4 Two types of processing can lead to the encoding of information into memory.

This is illustrated by an early study of reading (Sachs, 1967), where this story was presented: "There is an interesting story about the telescope. In Holland, a man named Lippershey was an eyeglass maker. One day his children were playing with some lenses. They discovered that things seemed very close if two lenses were held about a foot apart. Lippershey began experimenting and his "spyglass" attracted much attention. He sent a letter to Galileo, the great Italian scientist. Galileo at once realized the importance of the discovery and set about to build an instrument of his own. He used an old organ pipe with one lens curved out and the other in. On the first clear night he pointed the glass toward the sky. He was amazed to find the empty dark spaces filled with gleaming stars! Night after night Galileo climbed to a high tower, sweeping the sky with his telescope. One night he saw Jupiter, and to his great surprise discovered near it three bright stars" (Sachs, 1967).

What will you remember about this story in a few minutes? In the study, students read the passage sentence by sentence and were interrupted for a test at various points. The results (see FIGURE 7-5) show that, after some further sentences were read, memory for the words, ordering, and syntax of the sentences was poor: Only the meaning of the

FIGURE 7-5 The results show that as more syllables were presented, memory for the literal words seen, word order, and syntax of the sentences grew worse. Only the meaning remained in memory after reading further sentences.
Source: Data from Sachs, J. (1967). Recognition memory for syntactic and semantic aspects of connected discourse. Perception and Psychophysics, 2, *437–442.*

sentences was remembered after further reading. This shows that, though we process many types of information, we are most likely to recall the gist, or meaning, of the information we comprehend. In many other studies, information presented in a variety of formats such as visual, auditory, text, or multimedia tends to be "boiled down" to its gist when encoded into memory. So you may not remember much of what was actually said during an important conversation, but you will encode the main "point" of the experience into memory.

In this sense, a memory is a construction of available information. Two people watch the same YouTube clip, but what they recall about the video may differ. Each will construct his or her own "take" on the information, organize the pieces in a way that make sense to him or her, and then encode his or her own version into memory. In a sense, a memory is a "story" that we tell ourselves about what we experienced (Schank & Abelson, 1995). As an example, consider the congressional testimony of Supreme Court Justice Clarence Thomas and Anita Hill, a lawyer who had worked for years with Thomas. Hill testified that Thomas had subjected her to sexually explicit comments that she felt constituted harassment. Thomas denied making each of the specific comments Hill attributed to him and blamed politicians for trying to derail his nomination to the court. Though these two people have many shared memories, the memories they constructed for themselves about their experiences were very different. In this way, memory is always "subjective," relying on the meaning we take from the events we experience. The memory we construct is not necessarily the same as the events that actually happened (Bartlett, 1932).

Suppose your goal is to construct a memory that will be available to you in the future. How can you best construct and encode information? Let's say you want to use a new password for your online bank account, "bandit." What is the best way to encode this new password into memory so you will remember it next time you try to log in? Most people will say that repeating it over and over is the best way to "burn" something into memory. But repetition is a fairly "shallow" way to process the information. A "deeper" level of processing would be to think about the *meaning* of the new password: A "bandit" steals money, and money is what you're storing in the online bank account you are setting up; so, you hope the password will keep out any "bandit" that tries to steal your money. Now, which of these encoding methods will be better for helping you remember your new password? A study of **levels of processing** demonstrated that the deepest, most meaningful level for encoding information results in the best recall (Craik & Tulving, 1975). One group read words and thought about whether they were shown in all capital letters versus all lowercase letters. This visual encoding task is a "shallow" process, since they didn't even need to read the words to perform this task. A second group made up rhymes for each word, focusing on the acoustic sounds. The final group was told to think about the semantics, or meaning, of each word they read. The results (see FIGURE 7-6) show the deepest level of encoding, thinking about meaning, produced the best recall. Thinking about deep, meaningful associations with information is the best way to fully process it, and deeper thinking results in better memory.

Levels of processing The depth of thinking with new information affects the likelihood of remembering it.

FIGURE 7-6 Processing a word by encoding its meaning (semantic encoding) results in better recognition at test time than more shallow processing of its visual appearance or sound. *Source: Data from Craik, F. I. M, & Tulving, E. (1975). Depth of processing and the retention of words in episodic memory.* Journal of Experimental Psychology: General, 104, *268–294.*

Suppose you want to remember the date of the first moonwalk. Another principle of memory, called **elaboration**, involves drawing connections to information already in memory. This helps encoding because establishing multiple, meaningful links to information provides more ways to access it again in the future. For example, you might think about the circumstances of the first moonwalk—that it was televised at 8:17 p.m., so many people were able to watch it as it happened in real time. That same year, Richard Nixon became U.S. president, and the Beatles gave their last live performance on the rooftop of Apple Records. Adding connections to "play out" the meaning of the timing of the first moonwalk elaborates its connections to other information in memory, and so makes it more memorable.

There are many ways to elaborate on meaning, such as thinking of examples ("An example of an *aphorism* is, 'No good deed goes unpunished'"), implications ("What happened after the Civil War ended in 1863?"), or comparisons ("Prime numbers have only two divisors, while even numbers always have 2 as a divisor"). Focusing on meaning helps encode information by tying it to information that is already present in memory, providing multiple ways to link the new information into memory. More links means it's well encoded, and more ways to access it are available. Surprisingly, you can spend *less* time studying if you are careful to elaborate on new information rather than attempting to memorize it in isolation.

What is the easiest way to elaborate on new information? To think about how it relates to you! Like all humans, we are attuned to information that reflects upon us personally. So a very helpful method of encoding is to tie new information to personally relevant information, called the **self-reference effect**. You will likely remember who the candidates were in a presidential election if you were able to place your first vote that year. If you are female, you may be more likely to recall that one vice-presidential nominee was also a woman. And you'll be more likely to remember your college football team's season if you attended games. Since we are (necessarily) thinking a lot about ourselves, tying information into our personal memories really helps in constructing memories. In one study, the self-reference effect was examined by having subjects rate 40 personality traits (for example, "friendly, hostile, ambitious"). Some subjects judged whether the words were self-descriptive. Others judged the same words' length, sound, or meaning. Later, subjects remembered more of the words if they were asked to think about them with regard to themselves (Rogers, Kuiper, & Kirker, 1977). This is not surprising when you consider we are most interested in information about ourselves.

In fact, our memory is better for information that we have to *construct* ourselves instead of having it simply given to us. This is called the **generation effect**. For example, imagine being introduced to someone new and having a conversation with him or her. If you say his or her name yourself during the conversation, you'll be more likely to recall it later than if you hear someone else say it. The reason is that the act of generating the name is more cognitively active than simply passively hearing it. A study by Slamecka and Graf (1978) demonstrated this effect by asking some subjects to generate rhymes, such as, "nose - r ___." Other subjects had the same word pairs read aloud to them. Who showed better memory? Even though the generation of rhymes required little effort, the simple act of generating the associated word improved memory by 28%. This suggests that testing your memory by simply reading over the material is not as effective as trying to generate the answers for yourself.

Active construction works to get information encoded into memory. "Watching" the information pass by is ineffective at making an impression on your memory. College texts are often resold covered in highlighter markings; however, while highlighting key information is better than just reading (Fowler & Barker, 1974), effective studying involves far more than simply underlining (Wade & Trathen, 1989). The reason is that the amount of cognitive processing you do with new information and how you construct the information for yourself makes a huge difference in your memory for the material. In fact, research on college learning in physics has shown the value of memory construction in the form of self-explanation. In one study, college students read physics texts including worked-out examples (Chiet et al., 1989; 1994). Some students were asked to explain, or talk through, the worked-out problem to themselves rather than simply reading through it. These students learned new problem-solving skills and showed superior performance on

Elaboration Tying new information to that already stored in memory.

Self-reference effect Associating information with oneself to aid in retrieval.

Generation effect Memory is better for information that we create ourselves.

posttests compared to students who simply studied the material for the same amount of time. By talking through the example in their own words, the self-explanation students were able to tie the new problem skills to their previous knowledge in memory.

Mnemonics

Mnemonic Encoding "trick" that ties to-be-remembered information to something familiar.

Method of loci Mnemonic for remembering items by placing them on a familiar path.

Link method Forming links between concepts to make them more memorable.

Sometimes, the information we would like to encode is difficult to tie to our past knowledge. Constructing memories sometimes calls for the use of strategies to make information more memorable, called **mnemonics** (nih-MON-iks). These "tricks" make use of our ability to construct and organize information to help us encode it into memory. One mnemonic, called the **method of loci**, uses imagery to construct a memory including specific items. The trick is to think of a very familiar path, such as the route you take often between your home and your classroom. Picture the route, the turns you take, the street names and buildings. Then you can add in visual images of the set of items you want to remember (such as a grocery list). So you imagine leaving your home and picture a newspaper propped across the doorframe. Next, you turn at the sidewalk and have to step over a giant loaf of bread. On the corner where you turn left, you imagine a tall salami serving as the light pole. After encoding all of the items, you needn't think about the list again. Later, at the store, you simply "walk" the imagined path again in your mind and notice the objects you have placed in your path. Newspaper, bread, salami—your constructed list is easy to recall.

Mnemonics are a great method for constructing memories that include pieces that are difficult to connect together. Another mnemonic, called the "first letter" mnemonic, associates a set of things together with an acronym created by the first letter of each item. For example, the order of colors in the visual spectrum (red, orange, yellow, green, blue, indigo, and violet) may be hard to recall. So the phrase "ROY G BIV" can be constructed, and that serves as a cue to help you remember all of the colors in order. Or, if you need to recall all of the Great Lakes, you can construct the acronym "HOMES" to help recall lakes Huron, Ontario, Michigan, Erie, and Superior. One reason mnemonics work is that you can create associations between items in a way that is unusual and therefore memorable. For example, the whimsical phrase, "Never Eat Soggy Waffles," helps to recall the directions on the compass starting at the top and going clockwise. We tend to have better memory for items that "stick out" as different or unusual compared to other items in memory (von Restorf, 1933).

Another mnemonic, called the **link method**, can help you construct organization in memory, such as, "Hippos are like elephants, which never forget; and, the "hippocampus" is the brain area where memories are formed." Constructions of memory are often culturally based, where tricks for creating memories are passed on to other people. Remembering the spelling trick, "I before E, except after C"? Or the tip for recalling how to change the clocks for Daylight Savings Time ("spring forward, fall back")? Mnemonic tricks are very helpful in constructing memories of information you need in courses, such as the bones of the hand or the orders of the animal kingdom.

A mnemonist is an expert at using these methods to learn new information. One college student practiced for more than 200 hours over several months and then was tested. He was able to correctly repeat a string of 80 individual digits in order (Ericsson & Chase, 1982). His mnemonic trick was based on his extensive knowledge of long-distance running. He encoded the digits in clumps that matched times he recognized; for example, "3492" was recalled as "3 minutes and 49.2 seconds, a near world-record time for the mile." With practice, he established an elaborate set of mnemonic associations he could use to recall groups of digits. With practice and the right mnemonics, anyone can become an exceptional mnemonist.

Any mnemonic that adds meaning to the material can be helpful; for example, you might make up a story of "The Three Little Memory Stages" along the lines of "The Three Little Pigs." Special tricks include using vivid visual imagery (your mom jumping out of a giant cake with 16 candles on it to remember her birthdate) and exaggerated, even silly associations ("Obama rhymes with llama") as ways of making memories stand out.

Memories are not like videos; instead, they are "stories" we create for ourselves to tie information together for later recall. This requires not only attention but also active, effortful processing.

CONCEPT LEARNING CHECK 7.2 | *Applying Methods of Encoding*

For each example, determine which type of effortful encoding strategy is illustrated.

Strategies

A. Elaboration

B. Generation

C. Depth of processing

D. Self-reference effect

E. Self-explanation

F. Mnemonic devices

1. _____ "Let me try to think of an example of when classical conditioning happens in my everyday life."

2. _____ "Observational learning reminds me of when I learned how to make pancakes, and I watched my Dad cook them for me until I remembered all of the steps."

3. _____ "I remember it's called 'operant conditioning' because the learner 'operates' in the environment and gets reinforced for it."

4. _____ "Once I read a book section, I draw my own visual outline to understand the meaning of the material."

5. _____ "The answer is classical conditioning. Let me trace through the problem so I can see for myself which stimulus is the UCS, and which is the CS."

7.3 The Three Stages of Memory

There are three different memory stages for the conscious processing of memories.

■ Discuss how the three memory stages are involved in encoding new information into memory.

How is new information processed and stored in memory? One proposed model is the **stage model of memory** (Atkinson & Shiffrin, 1968), in which three separate stages are involved in consciously forming a lasting memory (see FIGURE 7-7). The three stages include:

1. We experience a flash of input information through our senses, called **sensory memory**.
2. Some information from this stage is encoded into a short-term memory buffer, where we hold it in our current thoughts.
3. Some information from this stage is encoded into a long-term memory store, where it remains indefinitely for future access.

Stage model of memory Atkinson and Shiffrins's three stages of memory—sensory, short-term, and long-term memory.

Sensory memory The brief flash of input information through the senses.

Working memory Synonym for short-term memory that reflects its role in thinking.

FIGURE 7-7 The Atkinson-Shiffrin (1968) stage model proposes three separate memory storage areas. Information moves between them as shown by the green arrows, within short-term memory as shown by the red arrows, and out of long-term memory as shown by the blue arrow. *Source: Data from Atkinson, R. C., & Shiffrin, R. M. (1968). Human memory: A proposed system and its control processes. In K. W. Spence & J. T. Spence (Eds.), The psychology of learning and motivation, 2, 89–195. New York, NY: Academic Press.*

A wealth of research has taken place since the model was proposed, and many aspects have been updated. For example, short-term memory is now called **working memory** to reflect the "work" it performs in our thinking processes (Baddeley, 2001). This middle stage is the "hot seat" of action, where new information is constantly flowing in through sensory memory, and past information is also constantly brought in from long-term memory.

For example, imagine you are searching online for a present for your young niece or nephew. You come across a picture of a book, *Green Eggs and Ham*. The entire image of the book enters into your sensory memory as you view the page. However, most of this information falls away while you pay attention to just the author's name, Dr. Seuss. Only that information enters into short-term memory, where you retain the name while thinking about it. That leads to retrieval from long-term memory—specifically, the memory that you once read and liked the book as a child. You stop thinking about the author as a writer, so that information falls out of short-term memory; but meanwhile, you decide you want the book for your relative. In the end, you encode your intention to buy the book, and that is stored in your long-term memory. This example shows how selective the memory processes can be: A great deal of information is presented in sensory memory, but a limited piece is attended to in short-term memory, and then finally, a different piece stored in long-term memory. In the next sections, we will further discuss each of these three stages and their operations.

Sensory Memory

The first stage of memory is essentially a sensory register. The sensory memory stage is capable of taking in a large amount of information, but it retains it only very briefly. For example, lift your eyes from the page to take in the scene in front of you right now, and then shut your eyes. Your memory for the visual scene rapidly fades from sensory memory in less than a second. However, there can be quite a bit of information contained in that visual scene, including all of the objects in a room, the lights, furniture patterns, people, and many other details. If it fades so fast, how do we make use of the impressions provided by our senses?

Consider the display in FIGURE 7-8. At a glance, then looking away, can you report all 12 letters correctly? Most can't because even though complete, the sensory image fades quickly, before you can report all of the letters. However, Sperling (1960) devised a way to show that we can selectively access parts of the complex stimulus and read some information from it in time. Just *after* the stimulus in the figure was flashed on a screen, subjects were signaled with a high tone to report the top row, a medium to report the middle row, or a low tone to report the bottom row. With the tone signal, subjects were able to report all four digits on the specified line before the image faded. This study demonstrates that our sensory store has a very large capacity for holding information; but it decays, or fades from memory, very quickly (in a fraction of a second). In order to "read" in any information from it (or, in other words, to perceive it), we have to *select* which information we want by attending to it.

FIGURE 7-8 When an image of letters is flashed for just 1/20th of a second, subjects remember less than half of the letters. But, when a tone follows the flash to signal which row to report, their performance is nearly perfect. *Source: Adapted from Sperling, G. A. (1960). The information available in brief visual presentation.* Psychological Monographs: General and Applied, *74(11), 1–29.*

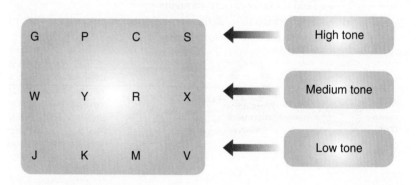

So we can select out a small amount of information from the sensory register before the information disappears. This **iconic memory** registers what the eye sees in vivid detail, but very briefly. These properties hold true for other senses like audition. **Echoic memory** holds the last few sounds that arrived at your ears for a fleeting moment before it, too, is wiped clean. While sensory memory is quite short, it allows us to select out the information we want—to perceive its meaning—if we attend to it while it is there. Thus, attention is the key to what gets encoded from sensory memory into short-term memory. Unfortunately, though many have claimed it, no one has been shown to have a long-lasting "photographic memory" (FIGURE 7-9).

Iconic memory Sensory memory for visual information taken in.

Echoic memory Sensory memory for the sound reaching your ears.

Short-term memory (STM) The memory stage consisting of whatever information is in consciousness.

Short-Term Memory or Working Memory

The second stage of memory is called short-term memory, more recently also referred to as "working memory." **Short-term memory (STM)** consists of the conscious thoughts

FIGURE 7-9 A true photographic memory would not fade, but would persist in the "mind's eye" so that you could pass this test: View the image in A, then look at the image in B. With a photographic memory, you could combine the features and produce the image in C.
Source: Adapted from Miller, S., & Peacock, R. (1982). Evidence for the uniqueness of eidetic imagery. Perceptual and Motor Skills, 55, 1219–1233.

you can keep in mind at any given moment. STM has multiple components, including a phonological buffer that holds the sounds of speech and a visuo-spatial sketch pad that stores information like a mental map of a route (Baddeley & Hitch, 1974). How much information can be held in short-term memory at one time? Let's "seed" your short-term memory with a series of numbers. Look at the numbers presented in FIGURE 7-10. First, read only the row labeled "A." Read the set of numbers aloud, one at a time, slowly, until

A: 7   3   5   6   2   1   8   4   9

B: 9   5   6   2   7   4   1   8   3

C: 1   8   3   2   9   5   4   6   7

FIGURE 7-10 Read the line of numbers next to the letter, and then look away, trying to keep the numbers you read in mind.

you reach the end of the series. Then, look away from the book, and try to keep the numbers in mind for 30 seconds. Then, try to say all of the numbers out loud, in order. Most people find they can't keep all nine digits in memory, and they work hard to maintain them in their conscious mind. **Maintenance rehearsal** is the practice of saying the numbers over and over to yourself to refresh their activation and keep them available to your conscious mind. You can keep them in mind as long as you keep rehearsing them. If you stop and wait about a minute, you will find you now have little memory for the series. Short-term memory decays within 15 to 30 seconds unless you actively rehearse the information.

Now, look back at Row B, read through it completely, and then go on to Row C. Certainly, there are too many numbers now to keep them all in mind in the correct sequence. This demonstrates that short-term memory has a limited capacity. As new numbers in the sequence come in, they displace the earlier items from memory and are now remembered while the old information is lost. FIGURE 7-11 illustrates displacement with a grocery list. As new items fill up the list, the earlier items are bumped off. Our short-term

Maintenance rehearsal
Reactivating information in short-term memory to keep it in mind.

FIGURE 7-11 Imagine hearing a list of groceries you need to pick up on your way home. The list includes: bread, cheese, eggs, peas, syrup, apples, flour, milk. Because short-term memory is limited to around seven items, early items (bread) can be displaced, losing them from memory.

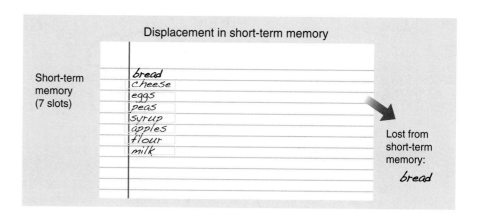

memory appears to be limited to approximately seven items at any one time, with a range from five to nine. This very limited capacity was called "The Magical Number Seven, plus or minus two" by George Miller (1956). To illustrate, listen to someone speaking. How many of their actual words can you recall at the end of a sentence? Usually, the later words can be retrieved, but the earlier items are quickly lost from your short-term memory. In fact, the original telephone numbers created by Bell Telephone used this limited-capacity principle to design seven-number sequences for local phone numbers. These seven digit strings were short enough to look up in a phone book and keep in mind while people dialed the number.

But you may be wondering, "7 ± 2 *what*?" We can remember seven digits, or letters, or even seven grocery items: What matters is the number of items. However, the same information can be presented as a list of seven separate items ("R – E – C – E – I – V – E") or as a single item ("receive"). By grouping items into larger sets of information, through a process known as "**chunking**," more information can be maintained in short-term memory. A chunk is a meaningful memory unit consisting of related elements (Cowan, 2001). By changing digit strings into meaningful units (like the "Zip code plus 4"), you can keep more items in short-term memory (see FIGURE 7-12).

The synonymous concept of "working memory" emphasizes that this second memory stage is where the real "work" of thinking takes place. Imagine trying to perform mental arithmetic by adding a series of numbers in your head: 897 + 364 = ? To accomplish this, you must recall the operations you need (7 + 4 = 11) and then maintain memory of this result while you move to the tens column, and so on. If you are unable to keep results in mind while recalling and applying operations, you will be unable to complete the task. So your **working memory span**, or the number of items you can keep in mind at once, will have a direct impact on the thinking you can do. FIGURE 7-13 provides an example of an intelligence test item that depends on short-term memory span for success (Raven, 1936).

Chunking Grouping separate elements into a related unit in memory.

Working memory span The amount of different pieces of information (such as digits) that can be held in conscious memory for a short time and reported back correctly.

FIGURE 7-12 While each digit can be considered as one item to remember, four together as a year can be recalled as a single "chunk" in memory.
Source: Data from Miller, G. A. (1956). The magical number seven, plus or minus two: some limits on our capacity for processing information. Psychological Review, 63*(2), 81–97.*

Raven's Matrices

FIGURE 7-13 Raven's matrices.
Source: Adapted from Raven, J. C. (1936). Mental tests used in genetic studies: The performance of related individuals on tests mainly educative and mainly reproductive. MSc Thesis, University of London.

Raven's matrices show a set of figures that are related, with the final figure missing. Select the final shape that completes the set from the group shown above. Look across rows and then look down the columns to determine the rules. Then, use the rules to determine the missing figure.

1. The background figures in each row are a rectangle, a triangle, and a diamond. So the third row needs a square.
2. The bar has three possible orientations. The third figure in the third row needs a bar oriented obliquely.
3. The bar has three possible patterns: clear, striped, and solid. The bar in the third figure in the third row must be solid.
4. So, the answer is alternative 5.

Working memory allows you to store partial information, information you have to keep in mind as you are analyzing each row.

You also need to process the information, and "work" on it (hence "working" memory). For example, you not only need to hold the geometric figures in mind, but you also need to compare them.

Holding all of this information in mind to successfully complete the task is the function of working memory. Much of the variation in problem difficulty and in differences among people in problem solving ability is due to working memory, according to this model.

People differ on the size of their memory span when tested. The memory span test FIGURE 7-14 was created to test individuals on their ability to remember sequences. For most of us, on richer tasks, four is a more likely span than the seven that Miller claimed (Cowan, 2001). But interestingly, individual differences in the size of memory span have been shown to relate to measures of thinking ability. Reading is correlated with memory span because it's easier to process complex sentences when you can keep more information in mind. For example, reading the sentence "There is a sewer near our house who makes terrific suits" requires the reader to back up and find an alternate meaning for *sewer*. Having a larger short-term memory span makes initially ambiguous sentences easier to process. One longitudinal study found that a child's working memory span at age 5 is a better predictor of later academic success than her or his IQ score (Alloway & Alloway, 2010).

Sequence Test

FIGURE 7-14 Memory span test.

1	9 2 4 1
2	6 3 8 5
3	2 7 9 4 1
4	5 3 2 6 9
5	4 9 5 2 8 3
6	1 8 4 6 3 5
7	7 4 2 9 6 8 1
8	3 5 8 4 6 9 2
9	2 6 9 7 4 1 3 5
10	5 8 3 7 6 9 2 4
11	3 8 2 5 4 6 7 9 1
12	9 7 1 6 2 4 8 5 3
13	3 4 9 1 6 2 8 7 5 3
14	9 4 3 4 5 2 8 1 7 6
15	7 3 4 6 9 2 7 1 4 5 8
16	4 1 9 3 8 2 7 1 9 6 5

For this test, take a blank piece of paper and number the lines 1 through 16. To begin the test, read the top row of digits, at a pace of one per second; then, look away, and write them down in order on the paper. Next, try the second row, and the third, until you have tested yourself on all of the lines. Compare your paper to the figure: the highest number of digits where you got both lines correct is your short-term memory span.

Long-Term Memory

Most importantly, the processing that takes place in short-term memory also determines whether the information gets encoded into the next stage, called long-term memory. As long as you keep rehearsing information in short-term memory, it will stay there. However, eventually, you will want to encode the information into long-term memory, where it can remain available for an unlimited amount of time. **Long-term memory (LTM)** refers to what most people mean when they talk about "memory": an essentially limitless store of information that appears to persist indefinitely. In this way, long-term memory appears to be like the hard drive of a computer: Once information is written on a computer disk, it stays forever. However, while short-term memory feeds information into long-term memory, encoding it into long-term memory takes effort. As a student, you are well aware of this! A summary of each of the three memory stages and their characteristic features is shown in **TABLE 7-1**.

Long-term memory (LTM) The enduring stage of memory that is unlimited in capacity and duration.

TABLE 7-1 The Atkinson-Shiffrin Stage Model of Memory

	Sensory Information Storage	Short-Term Memory	Long-Term Memory
Nickname	Register	"Working memory" buffer	Storehouse
Function	Get information in	Hold in current thought	Hold for later use
Format	Literal image	Labels	Semantic meaning
Capacity	Unlimited	7 ± 2 items	Unlimited
Duration	Less than a second	15–30 seconds	Unlimited
Retains	Attention selects information	Attention maintains information	Attention required to encode
Input source	External senses	Sensory and long-term memory	Short-term memory
Forgetting	Decay	Displace	Interference

Source: Atkinson, R.C., & Shiffrin, R.M. (1968). Human memory: A proposed system and its control processes. In K.W. Spence (Eds.), The psychology of learning and motivation, 2, 89–195. New York, NY: Academic Press.

Storing Memories in the Brain

To understand how information is written into your long-term memory, we will have to investigate the biology of human memory. You may think of the information in the brain as a library full of books, each in its own place. However, from the earliest days of brain research, it seemed that memory for information is not organized into specific places. In a series of experiments, rats were trained to find their way out of mazes, and then a portion of the cortex was removed. No matter which area was taken out, the rats were still able to solve the mazes (Lashley, 1950). The *amount* of cortical tissue removed affected their performance, but the *location* of the removed cortex had no effect on later performance in the maze. This led Lashley to conclude that memories are not localized but widely distributed across the cortex.

Synaptic Changes

Neuroscientists searched for the "engram," the neuronal processes that form and store new memories. We know from studies of other species that synapses between neurons show changes as a result of experience. Working with sea slugs, which have only 20,000 nerve cells, or neurons, Kandel and Schwartz (1982) trained the animals through classical conditioning. They then observed changes in the amount of the neurotransmitter serotonin at certain synapses. These synapses then became more efficient at passing signals to the dendrites of other neurons. Specifically, the sending neurons became more sensitive, so it took less stimulation to cause them to fire; at the same time, the receiving neurons developed more receptor sites. As a consequence, the neural circuit is more sensitive and more responsive to the specific patterns of neural activities that have been experienced.

This change in neurons is called **long-term potentiation**, reflecting greater potential for transmitting neural signals in the future (Lynch & Stabli, 1991). So synapses are responsible for **consolidation**, the process that converts information into structural changes in the brain to form long-term memories (Dudai, 2004).

The Anatomy of Memory

While synapses change all over the cortex to reflect the specifics of learning, there is an anatomical structure that is critical in the formation of all new memories: the **hippocampus** (see FIGURE 7-15). This structure, part of the limbic system deep in the brain, is highly interconnected with every area of the cortex (Gluck & Myers, 1997). Through these connections, the hippocampus plays an essential role in consolidating or forming long-term memories. This consolidation process takes more time, but once it is accomplished, the hippocampus is no longer needed to access the learned information. So the hippocampus appears to play its role in developing the long-term structural changes in the cortex that maintain information over time.

How do we know that the hippocampus plays this unique role in memory consolidation? The main evidence comes from an inadvertent experiment with a human subject known as "H.M." Treated surgically for extreme epileptic seizures in 1953 when he was 27, H.M. awoke to life with his hippocampus removed from both hemispheres. The surgery was successful in its primary goal of controlling his epilepsy. However, its side effects were catastrophic: Since the operation, H.M. was unable to learn anything new. He could not

Long-term potentiation The process of changes in neuronal receptivity that encodes information into memory.

Consolidation The stabilization of information in long-term memory through structural changes in the brain.

Hippocampus Limbic system structure that acts to consolidate information into long-term memory.

FIGURE 7-15 The hippocampus, part of the limbic system, plays a vital role in the formation of new memories.

Hippocampus

identify by name the researchers he worked with daily until his death in 2008. His family moved to a new home, but he was unable to learn his way around the new neighborhood. He read the same newspaper over and over again and always found it of interest. He remained quite amiable and was able to hear the same joke repeatedly, laughing every time.

H.M.'s short-term memory appeared to be intact, so that he could remember a small amount of verbal information as long as he was not distracted. So he could carry on a conversation as long as the content remained in his short-term memory. However, a few minutes later, he had no memory for the conversation he just had.

Researcher: Do you know what you did yesterday?

H.M.: No, I don't.

R: How about this morning?

H.M.: I don't even remember that.

R: Could you tell me what you had for lunch today?

H.M.: I don't know, to tell you the truth.

Interestingly, all of his memories for events before the surgery were intact, and he remembered earlier life experiences, such as schoolyard events, quite easily. However, he remained completely unable to form any new memories following his surgery.

In his own words, H.M. described his conscious experience:

"Every day is alone in itself, whatever enjoyment I've had, and whatever sorrow I've had . . . Right now, I'm wondering. Have I done or said anything amiss? You see, at this moment everything looks clear to me, but what happened just before? That's what worries me. It's like waking up from a dream; I just don't remember." (Milner, 1970, p. 37)

For H.M., his conscious experience was limited to what he could keep in short-term memory or recall from long-term memory prior to the surgery. Each moment was sensible, but he had no memory at all for what happened a few minutes, hours, days, or years ago. The loss of memory in clinical patients is called **amnesia**. H.M.'s complete inability to form new memories proved conclusively that the hippocampus is the seat of new memory formation. Many other clinical cases since have replicated this finding, and we'll return to this topic in the section on forgetting.

Amnesia The loss of memory in clinical patients.

CONCEPT LEARNING CHECK 7.3   *Movement of Information Through the Stages of Memory*

For each scenario presented below, identify how information flows through the three memory stages by indicating which stage the information resides in during the example.

Sensory Memory   Short-Term or Working Memory   Long-Term Memory

A. Sensory memory

B. Long-term memory

C. Non-working memory

D. Short-term or working memory

1. You see a flash of lightning out of the corner of your eye and go back to your conversation. The flash likely made it into your memory system only to _____.

2. You are introduced to Peter and talk to him for a while, but you forget his name after a minute. Peter's name likely made it as far as _____.

3. You study neurotransmitter properties and tie them in with their functions within psychology, along with thinking of examples. You score an "A" on the quiz the next day. The neurotransmitter information likely made it into _____.

7.4 Organizing Information in Memory

Different kinds of knowledge are organized in different ways in long-term memory.

■ Describe the main ways that information is organized in long-term memory.

This stage model of memory provides a good account of how sensory information is taken into conscious short-term memory and eventually encoded into long-term memory. However, studies on human memory quickly uncovered the fact that the content of memory, that is, the type of information our memory contains, resulted in differences in how that information was organized and stored in long-term memory. Remembering how to ride a bike involves qualitatively different knowledge than remembering that a fox has pointed ears or that waiters will come to take your order in a restaurant. In this section, we discuss different ways of organizing information in long-term memory.

Within long-term memory, are there different kinds of memories? Yes, there are different kinds of information stores, and their organization is accomplished in different ways. This has consequences for how the information is encoded and recalled. The organizational structure that is imposed on information influences what is "remembered." Organization seems to be the key to finding things in memory again. For finding your favorite pair of socks, or information about your bank PIN in long-term memory, organizing the information makes it much easier to locate than having it thrown together in a heap. And a lot of evidence suggests that information in long-term memory is not stored in a haphazard fashion, but is instead highly organized.

Different types of memory organizations hold different forms of memory. The major divisions in long-term memory are shown in FIGURE 7-16. The major division in long-term memory is between memories that are declarative and those that are procedural. **Declarative memory** is information that can be explicitly stated; for example, your name, the date for Halloween each year, and a recipe for carrot cake. This is also called explicit memory in that you can identify clearly exactly what information is contained in each idea (see FIGURE 7-17). Nondeclarative memory includes information that can't be stated. This includes **procedural memory**, which contains information about how to do specific tasks, such as riding a bike, styling your hair, or flipping pizza dough. You can describe what the task is, but you can't describe the specific muscle movements that produce the activity. In this sense, procedural knowledge is implicit memory; you can ride a bike or tie a bow in your shoelace, but you can't just tell someone how to do it. Procedural memories arise from repeated practice with actions.

Declarative memory Memory for knowledge of which we are consciously aware; also called explicit memory.

Procedural memory Implicit, nonstated memory for how to do things; also called implicit memory.

Stages of Memory

```
Sensory memory        Short-term memory      Long-term memory
(Incoming)            (Working memory)       (Stored)
                                                   │
                                                   ▼
                            Content of
                            memory
                         ╱           ╲
                        ▼             ▼
              Declarative memory   Procedural memory
                 (Explicit)          (Implicit)
               ╱          ╲
              ▼            ▼
       Semantic memory   Episodic memory
         (Meaning)       (Autobiographical)
```

FIGURE 7-16 A taxonomy of types of knowledge in long-term memory.

Procedural Memory

Knowledge of "how to do"

Skills, implicit, hard to verbalize

Declarative Memory

Knowledge "that . . ."
Factual, explicit, accessible

Republic of Chile

FIGURE 7-17 An important distinction between types of knowledge in long-term memory is that of declarative vs. procedural memories.

Declarative Memory

Several different types of knowledge are encoded in the declarative memory system, which captures explicit knowledge of which we are consciously aware. One is called **semantic memory** because it refers to the meaning, or semantics, we associate with concepts. Semantic memory is also broken down into distinct types.

Semantic Memory

One of the basic "building blocks" of declarative memory is the **concept**, or a grouping of similar objects and events. Consider the idea of the "chair": What does this concept involve? You can describe the act of sitting and conclude that chairs must have a flat area. But must they have seat backs, legs, or arms? When you see an object, even if it is entirely new to you, you have no difficulty recognizing that it can be used as a chair (see FIGURE 7-18). So, for example, even though each of these instances looks different, we recognize them all as chairs. One of the most powerful aspects of concepts is that they allow us to know things about new instances. And therefore we can make inferences about them. For example, we know about how big each one is in life, that it is for sitting on, that it is likely to be movable, and that it is a designed piece of furniture. Concepts are central to how we understand the world. So it's natural and effective for us to divide the world into concepts.

Concepts can also be organized into categories based on their common properties. A **category** is a hierarchical cluster of similar concepts; for example, the category "birds" includes its members, (e.g., robins, sparrows, and cardinals). Knowing from memory that a concept fits into a category can provide useful knowledge (see FIGURE 7-19). For example, if I am told that an object is a pomegranate, a type of fruit, I know I can eat it. Categories provide information at a general level for the entire group of concepts within them and efficiently store information at the group level. So I know my new pomegranate can be made into juice, that it will ripen and then decay, and that it should be stored in a cool place. By grouping concepts into categories or **conceptual hierarchies**, information can be shared across concepts. This memory organization is more efficient, because the shared information (e.g., that fruit can be made into juice) only has to be stored in one place (e.g., with "fruit") rather than with each concept.

Semantic memory
Memory for the meaning of material.

Concept A "building block" or basic unit of knowledge.

Category A cluster of similar concepts.

Conceptual hierarchy Organization of related concepts into levels of categories.

FIGURE 7-18 The concept of "chair" includes a diverse set of objects that may appear hard to define; but, we recognize a chair instantly.

Concept

A mental grouping of persons, ideas, events, or objects that share common properties.

FIGURE 7-19 This concept hierarchy shows the sets of concepts grouped under "foods," and the set of concepts grouped under "fruits." The importance of this memory organization is that shared information has to be stored in only one place—with the higher level concept.

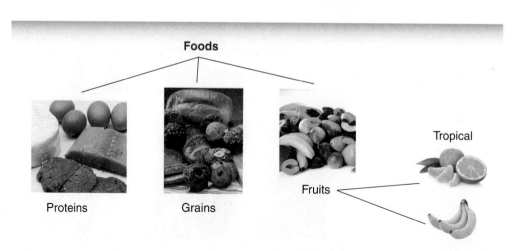

How do we know that long-term memory makes use of these efficient concept hierarchies? A series of studies used the speed of finding needed information to uncover its organization (Collins & Loftus, 1975). For example, which would you answer faster: (a) Does a chicken have wings? or (b) Does a bird have wings? The results show that knowledge about the properties of birds (flies, have wings) is stored in memory with "bird," and the concept of "chicken" is stored as an associated concept. So to answer the question about chickens having wings, this link between the concepts has to be searched, taking more time. (This is true even though "chickens" and "wings" are associated through experiences with eating them!) In FIGURE 7-20, we see what a small part of a concept hierarchy, also called a **semantic network**, of related ideas might look like. As you can see, the concept "bird" is closely associated with "flies, wings, and feathers." It is more distantly connected to "blood" (stored with "animals") or "farm" (stored with "chicken"). The result is that related concepts are clustered together in ways that reflect their meaningful associations.

> **Semantic network model** Organization of information that captures meaningful relationships between concepts.

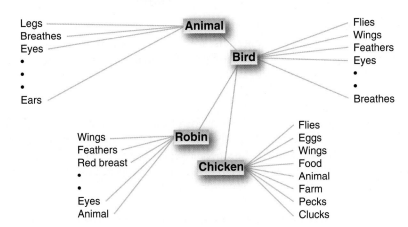

FIGURE 7-20 A semantic network showing the organization of the concept hierarchy for "birds."
Source: Reproduced from Collins, A. M., & Loftus, E. F. (1975). A spreading activation theory of semantic processing. Psychological Review, 82, 407–428.

Another consequence of organization in long-term memory is that concepts that are frequently accessed together are more tightly linked, so that accessing one makes it easier to access the other. For example, think of a "bird": You are much more likely to answer "robin" than "ostrich," because the first is much more frequently accessed. Try again: Think of a fruit. Did "apple" come to mind, or the more unusual "kiwi"? Our long-term memory keeps track of the associations between concepts simply by tracking the frequency of their occurrence together. Then, the strength of the links between concepts aids in accessing one given the other, in the form of priming (Meyer & Schvaneveldt, 1971). This process, also called **spreading activation**, is very important in bringing the right concepts to mind to help us process what is happening in the world around us. For example, when you are seeing a zebra, you are much more likely to access a related concept like "tiger" than "dentist" (Bousfeld, 1953). Theories of memory that embody these interconnections are called **connectionist models**, or parallel distributed processing (PDP) models. These approaches focus on representing every level of information in memory as interconnected elements, so that the activation of a concept creates an active network of smaller pieces of knowledge.

Another idea about how we store information in memory is the **schema** (Bartlett, 1932), a pattern of knowledge that occurs across experiences. Consider an example story using a schema called the "restaurant script" (Schank & Abelson, 1977): "John went into a restaurant and sat down. He ate spaghetti. He left." Not exactly a scintillating story, but if I ask you about it later, you are likely to add lots of substance to its bare bones. Did he order from a waitress? Did he leave a tip? Was he satisfied with his meal? Schemas provide a scaffold for events so that you can track the action as it occurs and make assumptions to fill in any gaps. And it helps to organize our behavior by shaping perceptions and encoding our experiences (e.g., "Why is this waiter giving me a list of sushi?").

So, if you have a schema, you have a basic framework to fit new experiences into as they occur. We have thousands of schemas in memory, organizing our memories for

> **Spreading activation** The links between concepts in memory help to access one given another.
>
> **Connectionist models** Memory theories that capture the distributed interconnections between concepts.
>
> **Schema** Organizer for information about events, people, and groups.

Think of a . . .

bird?

fruit?

Concepts that are frequently accessed together are more tightly linked, thus, when you think of "bird" you are much more likely to think of the common robin, rather than the more unusual ostrich. What if you were asked to think of a fruit?

experiences with individuals (Michael Jackson), groups (college football fans), and events (weddings, baseball games, bat mitzvahs; see FIGURE 7-21). Rather than remembering every experience separately, schemas group them together in memory and so provide a general description of what usually happens. Studies show that people agree on the knowledge included in schemas, such as the ordering of steps (e.g., you eat before you pay in a restaurant; Bower et al., 1979).

Schemas play an important role in reconstructing memories, filling in the usual events when we can't recall the specifics (e.g., did you wait in the waiting room at the dentist's office on your last visit?). Studies show people report parts of schemas even when not actually mentioned in a story (Bower et al., 1979). Imagine you are brought into a graduate student's office shown in FIGURE 7-22. You are left there for 10 minutes and then brought into

FIGURE 7-21 Schemas in memory organize information and guide our behavior.

Person Schema
About particular people

Group Schema
About groups of people

Event Schema
About particular events

FIGURE 7-22 Look around in this office, then look away. Write down everything you can remember in the office.

another room and asked to now write down everything you can remember in the office. What will you recall? People tend to remember items consistent with their schema for an office, like the desk and chair, but not the basket (Brewer & Treyens, 1981). More interestingly, people often report items not in the actual office, but typically found there (for example, books!). So, while schemas aid memory by facilitating the recall of related items, they can also result in the intrusion of items that were not present in the scene.

In this way, schemas introduce distortions or inaccuracies in memory. Many times, we may "remember" something because it is consistent with a schema, not because it really happened. For example, you may recall that you have eaten at a particular restaurant and so must have ordered there. Or you may remember that you once didn't have enough money to leave a tip but not recall which restaurant you were in. The power of the schema is that it organizes information very efficiently. Rather than storing a complete record of each restaurant visit, your schema for restaurants preserves the common elements (e.g., ordering, eating, paying) while leaving out details that appear unimportant.

Episodic Memory

So far, we have been discussing types of semantic memory, such as concepts, categories, semantic networks, and schemas. All of these memory structures work to organize information and bring it to mind just when it is needed. A second type of declarative memory is episodic memory (see FIGURE 7-23). **Episodic memory** refers to the recall of

Episodic memory Recall of your own personal, autobiographical experiences.

Semantic Memory

Definitions, knowledge, and facts

A 15-year-old invented ear muffs because his ears were cold

 = Dog

Episodic Memory

Personal experiences

FIGURE 7-23 Declarative memory includes both semantic (meaning-based) and episodic (autobiographical) memories.

your own personal experiences, also called autobiographical memory. The events from your last birthday, your walk home last night, and your earliest childhood memories are all examples of this special type of memory. We saw that declarative memory structures were focused on grouping similar information together for greater efficiency. In episodic memory, the focus is on the distinctive differences between experiences. The more your experience is novel, unusual, and unlike any other, the more likely you will recall it well. For example, can you recall what you ate for lunch last Thursday? How about what you ate for lunch last Thanksgiving? Or the first time you ate octopus, or a special meal someone made for you? We're more likely to remember the personal experiences that mean the most to us and so stand out from the everyday experiences we enjoy.

"Flashbulb" Memories

One type of episodic memory stands out from all others due to its vividness. Consider for a moment where you were when you first heard the news about 9/11, when two airliners crashed into the Twin Towers in New York City in 2001 FIGURE 7-24. I can still clearly recall my spouse coming into the room and asking me to turn on the television because a plane had crashed into the towers. I was very skeptical, and we watched together as the second plane later crashed into the buildings. This is called a **flashbulb memory** because the notion is that this moment is indelibly recorded in your memory, just like a flashbulb went off to capture a photograph of that specific moment. You likely had the feeling that you will never forget where you were when you heard about the events of 9/11. The heightened emotion we feel during some episodes in life signals to us that the

Flashbulb memory An emotional or vivid event that appears to be well remembered.

FIGURE 7-24 The attack on the World Trade Center on 9/11 was a surprising event that many people experienced as a "flashbulb memory" that they will never forget.

event is salient and should be paid attention to and remembered. In fact, the place where memory consolidation takes place, the hippocampus, is adjacent to the amygdala, the area of the brain that processes primitive emotions like fear. Our emotions appear to highlight special memories.

You likely also believe that your memory for that episode is highly accurate. One research group set out to examine this assumption through a controlled study. In 1986, millions watched the launch of the space shuttle *Challenger*. One crew member aboard was a schoolteacher, Christa McAuliffe, who was chosen as the first member of the Teacher in Space Project. Disaster occurred when the spacecraft broke apart 73 seconds into its flight, leading to the deaths of its seven crew members. Media coverage of the accident was extensive, and 85% of Americans heard the news within an hour of the accident. Researchers at Emory University then surveyed students in psychology the next day, and again several years after that day (Neisser & Harsch, 1992). Here are two examples of reports from students who were asked, "Where were you when you heard the news about the *Challenger* disaster?"

A: "I was in my religion class and some people walked in and started talking about [it]. I didn't know any details except that it had exploded and the schoolteacher's students had all been watching which I thought was so sad."

B: "When I first heard about the explosion I was sitting in my freshman dorm room with my roommate and we were watching TV. It came on a news flash and we were both totally shocked."

Which report do you think is the most accurate? In fact, both reports are from the same student! She wrote the first report a day after the explosion, and the second two and a half years later. She was so confident in her later report that she asked to see her earlier one from the day after the disaster. Even seeing her own handwriting, she could not explain why she had such a different flashbulb memory after time had passed. Memories, especially emotional ones, may seem quite salient, and we may indeed never forget. But studies like this one show that people do forget even very vivid memories and can be very mistaken about what they believe to have experienced at the time.

Procedural Memory

Episodic and semantic memories involve explicit knowledge. We can state the content of the memories and describe exactly what they involve. Another type of memory, procedural memory, captures actions: how we move, perform, and manipulate objects. For procedural knowledge, we learn through practicing sequences of actions over time. As a result, we are left unable to describe the content of procedural memories even though we can demonstrate the knowledge. For this reason, it is called implicit memory, evident in our actions even if we can't describe its content.

Procedural memory is the type of memory that allows you to remember how to tie your shoelaces or play a guitar without consciously thinking about these activities. After many sessions of practice, your fingers fly through the procedures on autopilot, expertly performing well-tuned actions in a very specific manner. Becoming truly expert at an activity such as playing the piano appears to take on the order of 10,000 hours of practice (Ericsson, Krampe, & Tesch-Romer, 1993). That would mean 10 years of practicing more than 2 hours a day! After all of that practice, your fingers move automatically as you think, just as when you're typing or texting on a cell phone. Procedural memories are also very durable, so that skills you learned as a child are still "in there" waiting to be used again. As they say, "Once learned, you never forget how to ride a bicycle." In a sense, it's "muscle memory," stored in the cerebellar area at the base of the brain.

The strongest evidence that suggests a separation of implicit and explicit memory focuses on studies of amnesic patients. Amnesia, as illustrated by the case of H.M., demonstrated the critical role of the hippocampus in forming new memories. Yet H.M. would provide another startling finding about memory. Psychologist Brenda Milner tested H.M. on a task called "mirror tracing." A device holds an image of a large star, but you can only see its reflection through a mirror while you trace it on a blank page. It's a hard task for anyone, but with practice, people learn to do it. The first time H.M. tried it, he performed poorly. But the next time he tried, he did it a little better. Soon, after practicing the task over a 3-day period, he completed the task as well as anyone (see FIGURE 7-25).

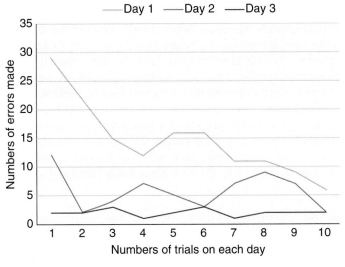

FIGURE 7-25 H.M. showed improvement in learning skilled movements in this mirror-tracing task. He was taught to trace a line between the two outlines of a star while viewing his hand and the star in a mirror. He showed steady improvement over the 3 days of testing, though he continued to have no memory of having attempted the task before. *Source: Data from Milner, B., Squire, L. R., & Kandel, E. R. (1998). Cognitive neuroscience and the study of memory. Neuron, 20, 445–468.*

However, H.M. showed no memory for his experiences tracing the star. He was asked to do so again, and after tracing it almost perfectly, said, "I thought this would be difficult, but I seem to have done this well" (Milner, Squire, & Kandel, 1998). Because H.M. was incapable of consciously remembering the task but seemed to be able to unconsciously remember how to perform it, the human mind must contain at least two separate and independent memory systems. One system, explicit memory, appears to be processed through the hippocampus. In H.M.'s case, the surgery removing his hippocampus in both hemispheres completely obliterated his ability to form new memories. However, another memory path exists in the brain, involving the cerebellum (the area at the base of the brain controlling complex, voluntary movements) and the nearby basal ganglia. Studies on other amnesic patients also support the possibility of an intact implicit memory despite a severely impaired explicit memory (Cohen et al., 1985).

CONCEPT LEARNING CHECK 7.4   *Organizing Information in Memory*

Determine what type of memory organization is illustrated in each example and match it to this list:

A. Concepts

1. _____ A pig has a curly tail.

B. Concept hierarchies

2. _____ The moment you found out you got into college.

C. Semantic networks

3. _____ Taking a seat in the waiting room at the dentist.

D. The schema

4. _____ A whale is a mammal, not a fish.

E. Episodic memory

5. _____ Name a vehicle that is red and has a siren: a fire truck.

7.5 Retrieval from Memory

The key to retrieving information from memory is to think about the context surrounding learning.

- Examine the successful retrieval of information from long-term memory.

In the last sections, we saw the many ways information is organized in long-term memory and the processes involved in adding information to this enduring store. So why can't we remember everything that was once placed in long-term memory? Think back on courses you have completed in the past. Even though you may have correctly recalled the information on the final exam, can you recall it now? Your high school French may be "in there," but what does it take to successfully gain access to it again? *Retrieval* refers to the process of bringing information from long-term memory back into consciousness in short-term or working memory (see FIGURE 7-26). Sometimes, retrieval of memories occurs spontaneously and without effort. When your favorite song is playing, you can sing along without having to concentrate on the lyrics. Many other times, retrieving information from long-term memory, just like encoding into it, requires a lot of work!

The **tip-of-the-tongue phenomenon** (James, 1890) illustrates this difficulty. James described it as "a gap that is intensely active," where a word appears to be known but cannot be recalled from memory. You would be able to recognize the right answer, but you couldn't retrieve it from memory on your own. The examples listed in FIGURE 7-27 are selected based on the difficulty of retrieving the appropriate word from memory (Yaniv & Meyer, 1987). When you have entered a state in which you feel you know an answer but cannot recall it from long-term memory, you are having a tip-of-the-tongue experience. Studies suggest these (1) are a nearly universal experience, across languages, (2) happen to most people about once a week, (3) increase with age, (4) frequently occur when one is trying to think of a person's name, and (5) are resolved during the experience about half of the time (Brown, 1991).

Tip-of-the-tongue phenomenon The feeling of knowing a word but being unable to recall it from long-term memory.

Retrieval Cues

What "work" can you do at the time of retrieval to help bring information to mind? You need a way to "prime" the information, just like you prime a pump by pouring water into it, so that the target word will become active in memory. This can be accomplished

FIGURE 7-26 Retrieval involves reactivating information in long-term memory and placing it within conscious access in short-term or working memory. *Source: Data from Atkinson, R. C., & Shiffrin, R. M. (1968). Human memory: A proposed system and its control processes. In K. W. Spence & J. T. Spence (Eds.), The psychology of learning and motivation, 2, 89–195. New York: Academic Press.*

Recall the word.

1. A navigational instrument used in measuring angular distances, especially the altitude of the sun, moon, and stars at sea.
2. A small boat used in the river and harbor traffic of China and Japan, propelled with an oar.
3. An infectious and usually fatal bacterial disease of animals, especially cattle and sheep.
4. A person who believes that nothing can be known about God; expressing ignorance of God; not an atheist.
5. In old Greek stories, the food of the Gods; supposed to give immortality to any human who eats it; anything that has a delightful taste.

Answers: 1. Sextant, 2. Sampan, 3. Anthrax, 4. Agnostic, 5. Ambrosia.

FIGURE 7-27 Read these definitions one at a time and try to think of the word. When you can't, but feel you do know the answer, you will have reached a "tip-of-the-tongue" phenomenon, where you can recognize the answer but can't retrieve it from long-term memory.
Source: Adapted from Yaniv, I., & Meyer, D. E. (1987). Activation and metacognition of inaccessible stored information: Potential bases for incubation effects in problem solving. Journal of Experimental Psychology: Learning, Memory, and Cognition, 13(2), 187–205.

by trying to access information related to the word you are trying to recall. Suppose you are stuck while trying to retrieve author Mark Twain's real name. You might think about other facts you know about him, such as the names of his books, famous quotes, the time in history when he lived, and so forth. Each of these facts can serve as a retrieval cue or an aid in recall. One cue would be his first name, "Samuel." Does this cue help you retrieve the name? By continuing to add as many related cues as possible, you may use **cued recall** to finally retrieve his name.

Retrieval cues can help in recall by providing activation of related concepts, boosting the activation of the target concept through spreading activation (see FIGURE 7-28) (Collins & Loftus, 1975). These principles work the same no matter how complex the target information in memory. If you need to recall the name of the brain structure responsible for encoding new long-term memories, you can aid its retrieval by thinking about related concepts, which then serve as retrieval cues. Remember H.M. and his tragic amnesia, living each day without remembering what occurred. Did you recall "hippocampus?" Retrieval cues work by filling out the network of concepts related to the target you are trying to recall. Imagine playing a heated game of charades with your friends. A wide variety of unusual cues can work to help you access a particular piece of knowledge in memory.

These memory principles also explain why encoding strategies work the way they do. Elaboration, for example, is tying a new concept to other concepts already in memory. So, rather than learn about canaries in isolation, comparing them to other types of birds and thinking about how they differ in size, eating behavior, and singing helps to tie the new concept into the network of past concepts. Then, the ties from encoding can serve as cues at the time of retrieval, "retracing" your steps during encoding to bring the target concept to mind. In fact, the more you can tie the cues at retrieval to the ones you used during encoding, the more likely you are to retrieve the information. This principle, called **encoding specificity**, says that the cues present at encoding will be the best cues at retrieval (Thompson & Tulving, 1973). In that experiment, people learned two separate lists of words, one while sitting on the side of a pool and one while underwater, in scuba gear! Next, they were tested for both lists, either in the water or on the deck. The results showed

Cued recall Retrieving information from related pieces of information.

Encoding specificity The principle that cues present at encoding will be the best cues for retrieval.

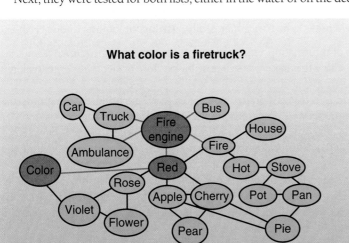

What color is a firetruck?

FIGURE 7-28 In a semantic network, accessing concepts tied to your target concept in memory spreads activation to it, making successful retrieval more likely. To remember "fire engine," for instance, you can add retrieval cues like "color" and "red" to make the concept more active.
Source: Adapted from Collins, A. M., & Loftus, E. F. (1975). A spreading activation theory of semantic processing. Psychological Review, 82, 407–428.

that more words were retrieved when the encoding conditions (e.g., being underwater) *matched* the retrieval conditions (e.g., being in the water).

Physiological states, such as being under the influence of alcohol, can similarly serve as a cue in memory (Goodwin et al., 1969). Finally, there is a role for mood in memory. Perhaps you had an unpleasant experience during which you felt very afraid; luckily, this experience may not come to mind very often. However, at future times when you experience that emotion again, the unpleasant memories may come quickly to mind. Bower (1981) documented this effect by inducing pleasant or depressed states in subjects and found that the emotional state during learning could aid in the retrieval of word lists. Depending on their mood, their free associations, imaginative fantasies, social perceptions, and snap judgments about others' personalities changed. And, when the feeling-tone of a narrative agreed with the reader's emotion, the salience and memorability of events in that narrative were increased. So the **mood congruence** of information at encoding and retrieval can serve as a memory cue.

Mood congruence
Matching emotional mood as a cue at encoding and retrieval to improve memory.

Adding Context

Just like specific cues, encoding specificity suggests the *context* of an event, or the circumstances surrounding it, is very important for retrieval. For example, returning to your childhood home may lead to the retrieval of memories you may not have thought about in a long time. The specific place cues help to retrieve memories that took place in that location. Reinstating the context of an event, even if only in your mind, can help with retrieval. For example, if you try to recall events from the year you were 5, you may have a difficult time recalling many. But if I help you to reinstate the context by talking about kindergarten, your first teacher, how you got to school every day, whether you went on any field trips, and so on, memories may start to come back to you. The idea is that long-term memories are still "in there," but they may require cues from their original encoding to bring them to mind again.

In everyday life, this suggests you're likely to remember more of that high school algebra if you return to the classroom where you learned it! In fact, some studies have shown a (very) small benefit to studying in the same classroom in which the test takes place. However, the power of encoding specificity lies more in the specific set of features related to a specific memory than in a general cue like where you learned it. The key to retrieval is to have ways to label memories so that you can bring them back up again by thinking about those labels. For example, one study asked people to recall other students from their yearbooks between 5 and 20 years after graduating from high school (Williams & Hollan, 1981). People recalled some names immediately, and then used contextual cues to help recall other names; for example:

> "trying . . . I'm—Okay I was imagining the whole room and we were imagining the instruments set up and I'm trying to remember the name of this guy—who used to . . . Art! And he was also in our 10th-grade art class . . . he would also bring a whole lot of people to—first on that—what's his name now? Let's see—[whistle] I'm trying to—remember his name. At his house was the first time I heard a Jefferson Airplane album. Umm . . . the bass guitar, really a strungout looking dude . . . uhh . . . wow."

Clearly, lots of information remained in memory, though the name was not accessible; however, recalling the name was still possible because of all of the contextual information that served as retrieval cues.

The need to reinstate context in order to recall experiences in memory may be the cause of an amnesia we all suffer from: childhood amnesia (Usher & Neisser, 1993). Think back now to your earliest memory in life. For most people, this dates between ages 2 and 5 (Barrett, 1980). Why? A possible cause may be the difficulty in reinstating the context of early memories to help to retrieve them. What else was on your mind when you were 4? What were the salient moods, places, and thoughts at that time? What labels, if any, were you likely to have created for your memories? If we were able to reinstate the context for those memories, we may find they are indeed still there in our long-term memories, awaiting the right cues to unlock them.

Another explanation is that memory may improve as we develop our sense of "self" (around age 2), since we organize memories autobiographically (Howe & Courage, 1997). Similarly, language learning at about the same age may allow children to describe experiences in ways that add to memorability (Hayne & Simcock, 2002). A final possibility is biological: Perhaps the networks of neurons that encode memories may require some time to fully mature (Bachevalier & Vargha-Khadem, 2005).

Very often, we have the sense of knowing information is in memory but being unable to explicitly state it. An example is the "50 states problem": You are likely able to recognize that Alabama and Arkansas are states in the United States, but can you name the other 48? What can we do when "it's in there," but we can't quite recall it from memory? As noted about retrieval, putting in effort to try to retrieve the information can lead to success. Accessing related information in memory (thinking about road trips you've made), invoking the context in which the information was originally encoded (remembering your fifth grade classroom), and generating retrieval cues (there must be other states that start with "A") are all ways to work at retrieval. When you are being tested and experience a retrieval cue failure, try to keep this playful perspective in mind and vary the cues you use to help with retrieval.

Retrieval Practice

Recent studies have shown that testing can be a means of improving learning, not just of assessing its results. Suppose you are given the task of learning 40 new words in a new language, say, Swahili. Most people would spend the entire time allotted to studying the words and their meanings. However, if you spent the same amount of time but used it to repeatedly test your recall of the words, you would actually learn more (Karpicke & Roediger, 2008). Taking a memory test enhances later retention, a phenomenon known as the *testing effect*. The simple act of practicing recall can boost your ability to retrieve the information later (Carrier & Pashler, 1992). The steps involved in retrieval benefit from practice.

But testing facilitates learning beyond offering an opportunity to restudy the material. In one experiment, students studied prose passages and took either one or three immediate free-recall tests, without any feedback, or restudied the material the same number of times. Students then took a final retention test 5 minutes, 2 days, or 1 week later. When the final test was given after only 5 minutes, repeated studying produced the best performance. However, on the delayed tests, repeated testing produced substantially greater retention than studying, even though repeated studying increased students' confidence in their ability to remember the material. Testing is a powerful means of improving learning (Roediger & Karpicke, 2006).

In fact, testing helps even if you don't know the answers! Studies of pretesting, where you attempt to answer questions about material you haven't read yet, find substantial benefits simply from considering the questions. Unsuccessfully attempting to answer questions about new topics proved more beneficial than having extended time to study the text (Richland et al., 2009). For example, a question such as, "What is total color blindness caused by brain damage called?" was posed before reading. The subjects who saw the question were more likely to learn the answer (cerebral achromatopsia) from the text than those who simply studied it on their own. The pretest questions served to prepare learners to look for important information in the text.

Once information appears to be solidly in memory, it is tempting to stop studying. However, the **overlearning** principle shows that performance can still be improved even when accuracy is at 100%. When you keep practicing retrieval past the point of perfect recall, you are still strengthening connections between concepts. So we can continue to learn even after we think we know the information perfectly.

Overlearning Continuing learning even when recall appears successful.

CONCEPT LEARNING CHECK 7.5 | *Practicing Retrieval*

Consider the principles of memory retrieval. Explain how these strategies would help you recall a word on the tip of your tongue.

1. Generating retrieval cues

2. Adding context

3. Retrieval practice

7.6 Reconstructing Memories

Memory is a dynamic process that constructs both old and new information.

- Explain how information from long-term memory may include misinformation.

Reconstruction Creating a memory of what likely occurred based on information you can recall.

Source monitoring Memory for the circumstances of acquiring information.

As we learned about perception, what is "out there" is not necessarily what makes it into the mind, and so with memory. Our experience of an event is not wholly encoded into memory, but may be "filled in" using our schemas. So when you attempt to recall a particular time you were in a restaurant, you may recall elements of the event, but you may also reconstruct, or regenerate, memories of the event using your knowledge of what usually happens. This process of "filling in" the details of a memory is called **reconstruction**.

For example, think of a family holiday that took place several years ago. Can you actually recall the details of the event, such as who was there, what time you gathered, what food was served and what you ate and drank, and what was discussed? While some notable details may be recalled ("the ham Mom cooked all day that turned out looking like a football"), most of our "memory" for the event is constructed by what we know must have occurred: "Surely Uncle Bob was there because he always comes, and we always have turkey, and we gather at noon. . . ." We can construct, or reconstruct, a memory for that holiday, and bits of actual memories may be included; however, a large part of our memory for that day is filled in by knowledge rather than specific recollection. In a study of college students, Brewer (1988) had students and their roommates keep detailed diaries of their daily lives. While they could recall specific memories that same day, the common events were likely to be reconstructed memories. We seem to keep vivid memories of unusual, surprising, and important events (such as flashbulb memories), while our everyday experiences are grouped together under schemas, recording only minimal information from each event. Reconstruction is a guess at what happened based on the frequency of occurrence; as a result, it can be incorrect. We lose many details of our experiences and combine reconstruction with recall when remembering, potentially introducing inaccuracies in memory.

Source Monitoring

When we reconstruct memories, we may get some of the specifics wrong. A common error is remembering some information but being unable to recall its source. **Source monitoring** errors refers to recalling information without identifying its original source (Lindsay & Johnson, 1991). If I ask you to do a series of mundane tasks, such as lick an envelope and staple some papers, or ask you to watch while someone else does those actions, will you remember which you did? Laboratory studies show that it's easy to forget such inconsequential actions and to recall that you did them when you actually watched (Johnson, Hashtroudi, & Lindsay, 1993). Source-monitoring error is observed for important events as well, such as when people incorrectly recalled how they heard about the *Challenger* disaster.

An example of a source monitoring error with important consequences occurred when psychologist Donald Thompson was identified by a rape victim as a physical match for the face of her attacker. Just before the attack, Thompson had appeared on a live television show to discuss his work (ironically) on face recognition. The police determined that the victim must have accurately remembered his face but mistaken the source as the attacker rather than the show (Powell & Freckelton, 2008). Other studies suggest simply imagining possible events make you more likely to misremember them as occurring. For example, after the crash of an El Al Boeing 747 into an apartment building in the Netherlands, 60% of study participants reported seeing video of the crash on television (Crombag et al., 1996). However, no such video exists! This suggests we should be suspicious of our memories and seek to validate them externally rather than believing whatever we recall. Though it goes against our belief that our memories are the truth, we have seen that memory is far from a videotape of our experiences.

The Misinformation Effect

Can memory for a specific episode be altered by new information? In one study (Loftus, Miller, & Burns, 1978), subjects were shown a series of color slides depicting an accident in which an automobile hit a pedestrian. At the beginning, a sports car is seen passing a yield sign, then moving on to where the accident occurred. FIGURE 7-29 Later, the subjects were asked questions about what they remembered. One of the questions included a "presupposition," or a phrase that is assumed to be true when it was not: "Did another car pass the red car while it was stopped at the stop sign?" This information was misleading because it was actually a yield sign, but most people don't notice the contradiction. For other subjects, consistent information was presented ("the yield sign") or no sign was mentioned. Then, after a delay, subjects were tested again about their memory for the accident. The partcipants had to say whether they had seen the image with a stop sign or the yield sign before. If the subjects never saw the misinformation, they said the correct sign 75% of the time; however, if they saw the question asking about the stop sign, fewer people (41%) correctly reported the yield sign. FIGURE 7-30 shows that misinformation led to even poorer performance on giving correct answers if introduced after a delay rather than right after seeing the slides. Overall, the results suggest that information seen after an event, whether consistent or misleading, is integrated into the witness's memory of the event.

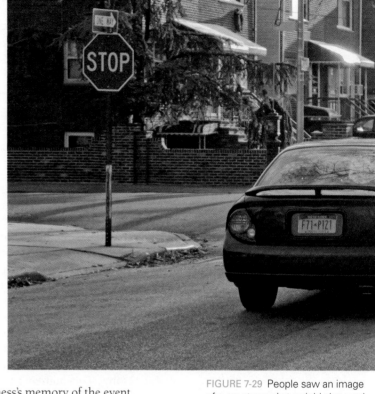

FIGURE 7-29 People saw an image of a car stopped at a yield sign, and were later asked if anyone passed the car when it was at the stop sign.

FIGURE 7-31 shows what may be happening in memory when new information is added after an event. If a contradiction is not detected, the misinformation may remain in memory and may change later descriptions of the event. This **misinformation effect** (Loftus, 1979) leads to the inclusion of incorrect information along with the original memory in a way that the person can't distinguish. Then, when they reconstruct the original event, they may include other information that came later within their own account. This means that memories can include information encoded at the original time of the event and information that is added to that memory when it is discussed or thought about at a later time. This is strong evidence that memory is dynamic (Schank, 1982); that is, it is changeable based on reaccessing it and adding to it at later times. Studies show that questions about events, even if they occur long after the events took place, can influence memory by adding misinformation (Loftus, 1975; 1979; 1980).

Misinformation effect
Adding new, incorrect information to a memory after the event.

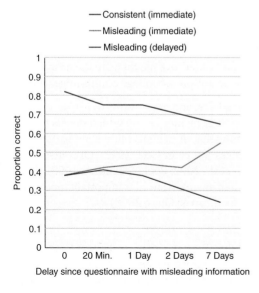

— Consistent (immediate)
— Misleading (immediate)
— Misleading (delayed)

Proportion correct

Delay since questionnaire with misleading information

FIGURE 7-30 Introducing misleading information during later questions impacts the accuracy of memory for the original event. In a control group, no misinformation was introduced. In another group of participants, misleading information was given immediately following viewing the slides of an accident. In a third group, the misleading information came after a 20-minute filler test. Some participants in all three groups were tested for their memory of the original slides either immediately, after 20 minutes, 1 day, 2 days, or 1 week later. The results show the misled groups were significantly less accurate than the control groups.
Source: Data from Loftus, E. F., Miller, D. G., & Burns, H. J. (1978). Semantic integration of verbal information into a visual memory. Journal of Experimental Psychology: Human Learning and Memory, *4(1), 19–31.*

FIGURE 7-31 When new information is added about a past episode, it may become incorporated into memory without noting an inconsistency.

Loftus (1996) points out that questions asked of eyewitnesses may commonly introduce error by including information that the witness unwittingly incorporates into his or her memories of events. In a typical investigation, witnesses may be questioned multiple times, and hypotheses about what occurred are often expressed. Even when trying to accurately report what you witness, you may be influenced by the questions posed by the police, lawyers, and other authorities. In a dramatic 1984 case in Scott County, Minnesota, prosecutors investigated a child-abuse ring (Press et al., 1985). It started when two mothers accused a local trash collector of sexually abusing their girls; he, in turn, confessed and accused 15 others (he later recanted). As the investigation continued, 45 adults were targets, and 24 were eventually charged. Many of the children involved were taken from their parents and placed in foster homes. There, they were repeatedly interviewed by prosecutors or social workers, who encouraged them to recall detailed stories. For children, and even for adults, the questions asked by authorities, even when well intentioned, can lead to answers that the questioner seeks.

In the end, only one trial of two adults was held in Scott County, and they were acquitted; all remaining charges were dropped. Cases like this raise the question of whether a child's testimony about events can be trusted. To investigate, Loftus and others conducted a study in which preschoolers were asked repeatedly (7–10 times over a 10 week period) about a fictitious event (Ceci et al., 1994). They were told, "I'm going to read some things that may have happened to you, and I want you to think real hard about each one of them that I am going to read. Try to remember if it really happened. Think real hard, and tell me if this ever happened to you." Then, they were asked about several events, some provided by parents such as a sibling's birth or vacation, and some fictitious. In particular, one event was getting their hand caught in a mousetrap and going to the hospital to have it removed.

The results showed the children's memory for true events was very nearly always accurate. But, by the seventh questioning, around one-third of the children reported recalling the fictitious event actually happening to them. One 4-year-old's statement describes his report (Ceci et al., 1994, p. 399):

> "My brother Colin was trying to get Blowtorch (an action figure) from me, and I wouldn't let him take it from me, so he pushed me into the wood pile where the mousetrap was. And then my finger got caught in it. And then we went to the hospital, and my mommy, daddy, and Colin drove me there, to the hospital in our van, because it was far away. And the doctor put a bandage on this finger [indicating]."

Perhaps because they trusted the source, and other events were true, some preschool children incorporated the story into their memories and added details to establish its reality. Later studies support the finding that preschool children are particularly vulnerable to a variety of suggestive influences (Bruck & Ceci, 1999). Of course, children can be accurate witnesses to events (Ceci et al., 2002; Poole & Lindsay, 1998). Studies show that when, how, and how often children are interviewed is important for the accuracy of their reports. (Garven et al., 1998; Goodman & Quas, 2008).

False Memories

False memory Inaccurate information incorporated into memory.

What about memory accuracy in adults? They, too, may create new, **false memories** for events that never actually occurred. An innocuous example is provided by studies in which words are presented (e.g., *bed, rest, awake*) and other words are recalled as presented (e.g., *sleep*; Deese, 1959; Roediger & McDermott, 1995), a phenomenon called *implicit memory*. However, adults are also capable of generating false memories for episodic events (Loftus, 1997). Suppose you are told, "I talked to your parents, who shared a story about how you had been lost in the mall when you were about 5 years old. You may not feel like you remember this event. But you were lost for an extended period, were crying, and found aid and comfort in an elderly woman who finally reunited you with your family. Now, try to recall as much detail as possible about that event. Are you starting to remember now?" Twenty-nine percent of college students stated they remembered, either partially or fully, the false event constructed for them. Another study provided false photographs of subjects on a hot air balloon ride as a child, and more than 50% recalled specifics of the event (Wade et al., 2002).

Suggesting memories that never happened and coming to feel you can recall them is a very rare experience. But you may have experienced something like this; for example, perhaps you have heard a family story about your childhood so often you become convinced you remember the scene. Or, while you remember an event, discussing it with others adds information to that memory so that it contains new elements not there when you initially experienced it. It is even possible to imagine events so vividly that you may misremember them as something that happened, called *imagination inflation* (Loftus & Davis, 2006). This points out a danger in our memory system: We may have vivid memories of events that never actually occurred. For example, spurious memories of unidentified flying object (UFO) abductions are created and maintained, and in these cases, there is at least some reason to doubt their literal accuracy (Newman & Baumeister, 1996).

In fact, even when we know information in memory is incorrect, it can still affect our thinking. In the *continued influence effect*, people rely on information they *know* is not true when making later decisions (Johnson & Seifert, 1994). For example, imagine you heard about a family of four found dead in their home, having dined the night before at a local Chinese restaurant. The police report that food poisoning was not the cause of their deaths, and you believe that. But do you want to go eat at that restaurant? No! The best way to counteract misinformation is to provide an alternative account for the cause; in this case, it was carbon monoxide poisoning. Even information known to be incorrect stays in memory, and we may fall back on it. Think about the example of the "stolen" Christmas gifts at the beginning of the chapter; even though I knew perfectly well there was no theft, I still believed the parking lot was more dangerous after this event! This use of asserted information, even when corrected, can have serious consequences for our reasoning about events in the world (Lewandowsky et al., 2005).

After learning about the processes involved in memory, it may be surprising that memory is ever really accurate; rather, we each carry in our minds a changing version of the reality we experienced. But memory is most often surprisingly accurate. In one study, people saw a series of travel scenes for just a second or two but were very accurate in identifying whether they had seen them before—more than 90% correct—even when thousands of pictures were shown (Shepard, 1967; Standing, 1973). Memory for familiar faces surpasses 95% accuracy (Bruce & Le Voi, 1983). Procedural memory is maintained for very long periods of time; in fact, it is often said that you never forget how to ride a bicycle once you have learned. And your own test scores should convince you that, if you put in effort, it is possible to encode and maintain any information in memory. In this section, we have focused on the question of how distortions enter into memory because they have important consequences. But even so, your memory most often serves as an accurate record of your experiences, preferences, and emotions over time.

CONCEPT LEARNING CHECK 7.6 | *Introducing Error in Memory*

For each example, identify the principle involved in introducing error into memory.

A. Reconstruction

B. Source-monitoring error

C. Misinformation effect

D. False memory

1. _____ Carrie mistakenly thinks her roommate was along when she saw Third Eye Blind perform because she does everything with her roommate.

2. _____ The professor told the class when the quiz would take place but gave a different date on the syllabus.

Peter recalls the syllabus date and is upset that the quiz is a surprise.

3. _____ Raoul sees a woman who looks very familiar but can't think of how he knows her. Later, he sees her picture on a poster for school election candidates.

4. _____ Little Colleen always shudders when her family drives by the municipal trash facility. She recalls the smell inside the trucks because her brothers always tell her that when she was born, they picked her up at the garbage dump.

CRITICAL THINKING APPLICATION

A witness to a crime says, "I'll never forget that face!" As jurors, we believe them. Eyewitness testimony is the gold standard in the courtroom and the most convincing short of DNA evidence (Loftus, 1996). But after what you have learned about memory in this chapter, what do you predict about the veracity of eyewitness memory?

Very influential in trials, juries find eyewitnesses quite convincing (Kassin et al., 1989). How could someone be wrong about identifying an attacker at the center of an extremely traumatic event? One case involved a woman (see FIGURE 7-32) who identified her male attacker in court. Based largely on her testimony, he served more than 10 years in jail for the crime; however, he was then freed based on DNA evidence. FIGURE 7-33 shows the actual assailant and the man she mistakenly identified. Remarkably, the accused man and the victim have written a book together describing their painful journey through this case (Thompson-Cannino & Cotton, 2009). In recent years, hundreds of cases have been overturned based on DNA testing, and more than 80% of these contained mistaken identifications (http://www.innocenceproject.org/).

A great deal of psychological research has identified factors that influence the accuracy of eyewitnesses (see **TABLE 7-2**), and there is a strong consensus among legal professionals that these principles are sufficiently reliable to present in court. However, jurors are still most influenced by the apparent confidence of the eyewitness in their identification (Penrod & Cutler, 1995). Unfortunately, an eyewitness's confidence is not a good predictor of accuracy; in studies of actual crime witnesses, very confident identifications occurred even when the witness was wrong. This suggests our judgments about eyewitness memory may not be very different from other types of memory. If it feels real, we believe it must be, despite plenty of psychological evidence to the contrary.

FIGURE 7-32 Jennifer Thompson identified the man she believed attacked and raped her during an assault in 1984.

FIGURE 7-33 Ronald Cotton (right), is shown in this 1984 police photo. Cotton was convicted of the rape of Jennifer Thompson, but DNA testing eventually showed the real rapist was Bobby Poole (left).

TABLE 7-2 Factors that Impair the Accuracy of Eyewitness Testimony

- Very high levels of stress during the event
- The occurrence of violence during the event
- The presence of a weapon that captures attention
- The duration of the event
- Longer amount of time since the event until questioning occurs
- Identification of a person from a race other than your own
- Information about the event is provided by others after it occurred
- Exposure to a person is experienced in other settings
- The witness's own attitudes and beliefs about the event

Source: Kassin, S. M., Ellsworth, P. C., & Smith, V. L. (1989). The "general acceptance" of psychological research on eyewitness testimony: A survey of the experts. American Psychologist, 44*(8), 1089–1098.*

7.7 Forgetting

The ability to forget informs us about the processes of remembering.

- Analyze how forgetting improves memory.

We often think of "forgetting" as a mistake, as in forgetting our keys or a phone number. But the ability to forget may be a key feature of human memory that aids, rather than inhibits, our intelligence (Schank & Abelson, 1977). A case study illustrates how important it is to select out information for later recall versus recalling everything that occurs. A woman was identified who spends an excessive amount of time recalling autobiographical memories. If given a date, she can tell you what she was doing and what day of the week it fell on. Based on hers and other cases, a syndrome called **hyperthymesia** was identified (Parker et al., 2006). However, this special memory ability is not very helpful; indeed, it gets in the way of thinking about life. While it can take work to encode information into memory, the fact that we can also forget a great deal of information may be the feature of human memory that makes us "smart."

Measures of Forgetting

As students, you are experts in memory tests: Free recall of information is tested by writing essays, recognition by a multiple-choice test, and cued recall by fill-in-the-blank and matching questions. All of these methods are used in education to see how much a student remembers from information in lessons. But what if you wanted to study how much information students *forget*?

In the early days of psychology, Herman Ebbinghaus (1885) attempted to look at memory performance using novel stimuli, ones that he had never been exposed to before. So he created the nonsense syllable, three-letter strings that did not form recognizable words (e.g., *puh*, *ret*, and *miw*). He then tested his own memory for them after varied amounts of time and measured what information was lost or forgotten. The result was a **forgetting curve** (see FIGURE 7-34), the shape of which holds true for just about any learned material. Initially, there is a steep loss in the amount of information retained, and then this levels out to a baseline maintained over time. Other, more meaningful material shows the same type of forgetting curve. For example, Bahrick's (1984) study of high school Spanish students showed that they forgot a lot in the initial years after studying (see FIGURE 7-35), but surprisingly still retained around 40% of the material up to 50 years later! Most relevant for you, a similar pattern was found for material from an introduction to psychology class up to 12 years later (Conway, Cohen, & Stanhope, 1991).

The speed of forgetting depends on the difficulty of the learned material (e.g., how easy it is to encode deeply), its organization, and physiological factors such as stress and sleep. This basal forgetting rate differs little between individuals. However, improvement in forgetting rates occurs through the repetition of learning (see FIGURE 7-36). With each study session, the starting point of full recall (at the end of the study session) falls off, but not as far with the second repetition and even less with the third. The notion is that each session is raising the "floor" of the forgetting function, even though each session shows a

Hyperthymesia Recalling past autobiographical events to an excessive degree and accuracy.

Forgetting curve Graph showing that much information is immediately lost from memory after study.

FIGURE 7-34 Ebbinghaus's forgetting curve is characterized by an initial sharp dropoff in remembered material, which then levels off to a baseline maintained over time.
Source: Data from Ebbinghaus, H. (1885; reprinted in 1913). Memory: A contribution to experimental psychology. (Translation by H. Roger & C. Bussenius). New York: Teacher's College Press.

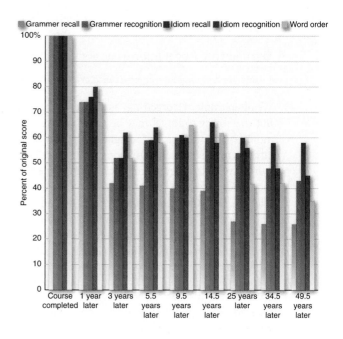

FIGURE 7-35 Bahrick's (1984) study of high school Spanish students showed that they forgot a lot in the initial years, but still retained around 40% of the material 50 years later.
Source: Data from Bahrick, H. P. (1984). Semantic memory content in permastore: Fifty years of memory for Spanish learned in school. Journal of Experimental Psychology: General, 113, 1–35.

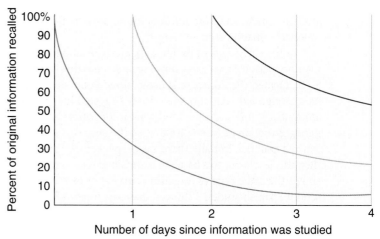

FIGURE 7-36 Forgetting curves showing repeated study sessions, where each acquires the maximum, and then the fall off to the base rate is less with each session.

Relearning A measure of forgetting and learning that is based on how easy it is to learn information again at a later time.

marked dropoff immediately following learning. Each repetition in studying increases the optimum interval before the next repetition is needed (for near-perfect retention, initially repetitions may need to be made within days, but later they can be made after years).

Since a great deal of forgetting happens right away, this may suggest a strategy of studying just before exams, before the dropoff happens. However, that would result in a very big dropoff! With each repetition of study, the recall floor is boosted so that the retention of information in long-term memory stays at a fairly constant level for days, weeks, and years after study. So the best strategy is to study repeatedly, picking up after the initial forgetting has occurred, and adding to the baseline. This pattern will help you to recall the information on tomorrow's quiz, on the final exam, and in later life!

Another measure of forgetting is **relearning**, in which information seems to be forgotten but is evident in memory because learning it a second time is faster. Think back on any lessons you learned in a second language. While it may seem like you don't recall much of your high school French, you will see some benefits of that past learning if you study it again. The speed of relearning information is another way to demonstrate that we have information in memory that we appear to have forgotten.

Forgetting appears to be inevitable, but why should it be? Judging from computer memory systems, the drawback of not forgetting is that you quickly run out of storage space. In addition, the usability of knowledge grows increasingly difficult, with longer access times as more information is added. However, human memory doesn't appear to have these drawbacks. Instead, only some current information makes it into our long-term memory store, and, once there, remains highly organized. The advantage of human memory is that the material we think about the most is the most likely to be encoded into long-term memory and is therefore less likely to be forgotten.

Theories of Forgetting

There are many reasons we remember some information, such as its personal importance, its emotional tone, and the frequency of thinking about it. Similarly, there are many reasons we may forget. The endless details we experience, such as where the ketchup is found in the cafeteria, are arguably not needed. Indeed, retaining that information in memory would work against our ability to focus on meaningful information we may need again. Through the efficient organization of information in memory, we don't need to remember all the times we've seen a robin or every trip to the dry cleaner's; instead, we remember only general information about some episodes in life. A memory without the ability to forget would face an overwhelming problem of organization (a glance at your computer storage drive should convince you that keeping everything quickly becomes a problem for retrieval)! But if information is desirable, why is it sometimes forgotten?

The primary reason we can't recall information we want—the formula for the circumference of a circle, the name of your new neighbor, or where you left your car keys—is that the information was never encoded into long-term memory in the first place. Think about meeting someone new: Are you attending to his or her name and attempting to tie it into your existing knowledge? Most often, we're too busy shaking hands and preparing what we'll say to fully encode their name. We have identified a number of ways you can increase the odds of getting information into long-term memory, and the key factor is effort. Some things go right without any help, and some things stay in memory that we wish we could forget. But for the most part, forgetting happens because the current contents of short-term memory never make it any further into long-term memory, causing encoding failure.

If information is encoded into long-term memory, it appears to endure there. There is no evidence that memories decay, or fade in their strength over time. Based on **decay theory**, we would expect all memories to fade over time; however, there are some old memories that you still vividly recall. No physiological evidence has been discovered that suggests well-encoded memories fade over time. Instead, memories appear to be retained: The problem with forgetting seems to involve getting information encoded in the first place or regaining access to it.

Another important factor in forgetting is **interference** from other information. Neuropsychological evidence suggests that sleep is necessary in order to allow the consolidation process in the hippocampus to occur (Stickgold, Hobson, Fosse, & Fosse, 2001). In a very early study of learning, Jenkins and Dallenbach (1924) compared learning a set of new concepts (A) to learning those concepts followed by a new set (B). They found subjects remembered more information from set A if they went to sleep rather than learning another set. They concluded that "forgetting is not so much a matter of the decay of old impressions and associations as it is a matter of interference, inhibition, or obliteration of the old by the new." If the two sets of information are very similar, such as sets of nonsense words as in Ebbinghaus's study, learning one may cause interference with memory for the other. As long as the materials are distinctive, interference between study sessions is not a major problem.

This raises the question of how to schedule study sessions so as to maximize what is recalled. A great wealth of evidence indicates that spacing out your study sessions produces much better performance than studying once for the same amount of time (Cepada et al., 2006). This **spacing effect** is that we retain information better if the learning effort is distributed over time (see FIGURE 7-37). Many students plan to cram their learning into a long session just before a test, called "massed practice." This can feel like it's leading to a lot of progress, but it is actually an inefficient process. In general, shorter practice sessions spaced widely apart produce the best memory. There are few findings in psychology as robust as the spacing effect; even so, many modern educational systems fail to build in repeated practice sessions as part of learning (Dempster, 1988). In many cases, two spaced presentations are about *twice* as effective as one massed session (Hintzman, 1974). Now that you know how important it is to space out your learning sessions, you can build this principle into your study habits.

Decay theory The notion that information fades from memory on its own.

Interference theory New knowledge can disrupt recently learned memories.

Spacing effect Learning is improved if study effort is distributed over time.

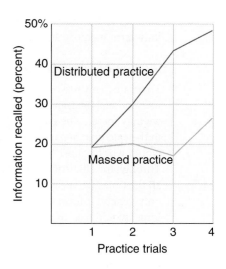

FIGURE 7-37 Graph showing the advantage of spaced vs. massed practice for long-term memory retention.
Source: Data from Cepada, N. J., Pashler, H., Vul, E., Wixted, J. T., & Rohrer, D. (2006). Distributed practice in verbal recall tasks: A review and quantitative synthesis. Psychological Bulletin, 132(3), 354–380.

Motivated Forgetting

Can our conscious intention to forget an event be helpful in making it disappear from memory? *Motivated forgetting* is a concept introduced by Freud (1957) as a defense mechanism against unpleasant memories. Through **repression**, or submerging painful memories away from consciousness, we may choose to avoid traumatic memories. Recent evidence suggests it is possible to prevent unwanted declarative memories from entering consciousness (Anderson & Green, 2001). So do people sometimes intentionally forget the past? Williams (1994) interviewed women who had documented histories of sexual victimization in childhood. A large proportion of the women (38%) did not recall the abuse that had been reported 17 years earlier. Women who were younger at the time of the abuse or molested by someone they knew were more likely to have no recall of the abuse. Of the more than 60% of victims who recalled the events, 10% reported they had, at some time in the past, forgotten about the abuse. Those with "recovered memories" tended to be younger at the time of the event and had received less support from their mothers (Williams, 1995). There were no differences in the accuracy of those with recovered memories from those who reporting always remembering.

Another study surveyed professional psychologists and found approximately 25% who reported childhood abuse. Of these, 40% reported a period of forgetting some or all of the abuse (Feldman-Summers & Pope, 1994). Both sexual and nonsexual abuse were subject to periods of forgetting, and the most frequently reported factor related to recall was being in therapy. This suggests that traumatic events can be "missing" from memory for some period of time and later accessed as a result of available cues or therapeutic intervention (Palm & Gibson, 1998). Some psychologists argued that recovered memories are more likely in some types of trauma, such as the betrayal of trust (Freyd, 1995). In the practice of therapy, clinicians became interested in pursuing repressed memories as explanations for their clients' difficulties as adults (Frederickson, 1992). Perhaps as a result, the 1990s brought an increasing number of reports of the recovery of previously repressed memories of childhood abuse.

However, Loftus and Ketchum (1994) argued that many ways of attempting to retrieve memories can cause them to be unwittingly created. As we saw with false memories from repeated suggestive questions, it may be possible to induce false memories of abuse (Loftus, 1993). By asking clients to imagine that abuse had occurred, repeatedly raising questions, and use of hypnosis, therapists may have unintentionally encouraged the creation of false memories of traumatic events (Loftus & Davis, 2006). The result can be unintended yet have tragic consequences. An example from a 1989 criminal case involved an adult woman coming forward with a 20-year-old "recovered memory" of her 8-year-old friend's rape and murder: She now recalled that the perpetrator was her own father (Morain, 1995). The father spent more than 6 years in jail before his conviction was overturned.

While some cases of recovered memories have been documented (Schooler, 2001; Schooler et al., 1997), they are extremely rare. One explanation for them is that how the person thinks about events at the time may be different from his or her views of events later in life (Geraerts et al., 2007). In addition, people who recovered their memories of abuse

Repression Mentally pushing away explicit recall of unpleasant memories.

through suggestive therapy also exhibit a heightened susceptibility to the construction of false memories (Geraerts et al., 2009). While some memories may indeed come to mind unexpectedly, more often, the key problem with traumatic memories is learning to live with them. Cases of posttraumatic stress disorder and the trauma of war experiences (Sargant & Slater, 1941) suggest memories we would like to forget more often haunt us (Rubin, Berntsen, & Bohni, 2008).

Amnesia

Perhaps the most eloquent descriptions of forgetting come from those who suffer from a neurological impairment, demonstrating both the loss of memory and its importance in defining us as individuals. Cases like that of H.M. show the consequences of the loss of hippocampal function, resulting in an inability to create new memories. While H.M.'s case was unique in terms of the destruction of the hippocampus in both hemispheres, a similar case of amnesia resulted from a stab wound. When a fencing foil entered his brain through the right nostril, taking a slightly oblique course to the left, patient N.A. also suffered a loss of the ability to encode new verbal information (Teuber et al., 1968). Other patients have been found to have explicit memory for events lasting no more than 1 minute. In one study, two patients (on three occasions each) readily consumed a second lunch when it was offered 10 to 30 minutes later, and usually began to consume a third meal 10 to 30 minutes after that. These findings suggest that memory for the recent past is important even for simple behaviors like eating (Rozin, Dow, Moscovitch, & Rajaram, 1998).

Amnesia also occurs after damage to the medial temporal lobe, often caused by encephalitis. However, one recent, very rare case resulted from trauma, which restricted blood flow (and so cut off oxygen) to the right temporal lobe. Scott Bolzan, a former NFL player, slipped in the bathroom and landed on the back of his head (Bolzan et al., 2011). He lost his memories of the 46 years of his life, including his teenage sons, his wife, and even his own parents. Bolzan can add new memories of life since the accident, but lost all memory for his life prior to the injury. However, he continues to have intelligence and reasoning, as well as language function. He retained some skills like bike riding, which are part of procedural memory. However, he could not remember how to start the car the first time he drove months later, though knew the meaning of road signs and lights. Simply telling him about the events of his life did not lead to recovery of his experiences from his own memory. Balzan also understands that he has a memory disorder, and retains the fact.

With Bolzan, as well as H.M., explicit memory was impaired, but implicit memory still functioned. One historical case of implicit learning involved a woman with Korsakoff's syndrome (see FIGURE 7-38). Korsakoff's syndrome is marked by the loss of explicit memory, usually as a result of chronic alcoholism. In 1911, physician Edouard Claparède hid a pin in his right hand before meeting her, which pricked her painfully when they shook hands. When he returned the next day, the patient did not recall having met him previously, but

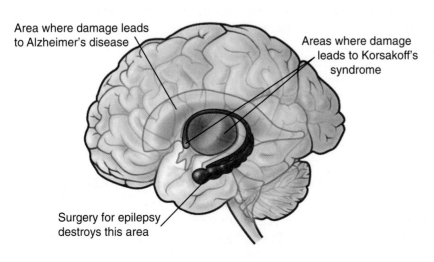

Area where damage leads to Alzheimer's disease

Areas where damage leads to Korsakoff's syndrome

Surgery for epilepsy destroys this area

FIGURE 7-38 Brain areas involved in damage to memory based on clinical cases.

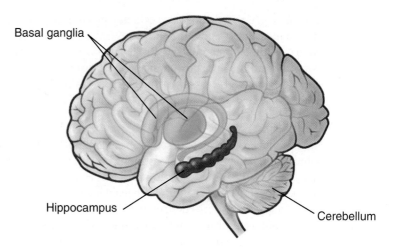

FIGURE 7-39 Brain areas involved in processing explicit (hippocampus) and implicit (cerebellum and basal ganglia) memories.

Basal ganglia

Hippocampus

Cerebellum

Alzheimer's disease A progressive memory disorder in which people lose access to explicit memory.

Dementia Clinical diagnosis of major memory loss with age or disease.

she refused to shake his hand, saying, "Sometimes pins are hidden in people's hands" (Schwartz & Resiberg, 1991). Patients with **Alzheimer's disease**, a progressive memory disorder, also show an ability to perform visual tasks in the occipital cortex involving implicit knowledge while showing no signs of explicit recall in the tasks (Golby et al., 2005). As a result, patients can continue to perform a routine task like bathing by following implicit cues while forgetting many of their explicit memories (such as recognizing family members).

Studies of malfunctions of memory, in particular forms of **dementia** or memory loss, have helped researchers understand how we encode, store, and retrieve memories. Cases like H.M.'s support the stage model of memory, in which explicit memories are recorded as sensory memory (the immediate initial stage), then short-term memory (or working memory), and only then into long-term memory. However, studies of patients with memory loss also show that an important type of memory—implicit memory—does not appear to rely on the same brain areas thought to support the stage model of memory.

The evidence from studies of patients who experience loss of explicit memory but retain intact implicit memory (including patient H.M.) suggest an alternate route for storing memories in the brain that bypasses the hippocampus. Procedural knowledge in memory, such as riding a bike or learning to type, can remain intact in these patients (Schacter, 1992). The reason is that motor movements involved in performing procedures are processed through the cerebellum and basal ganglia areas of the brain (see FIGURE 7-39). As a result, damage to the hippocampal area shows no impact on implicit memory for procedural knowledge. In some studies, patients were taught a new motor task successfully even though they always reported that they had never performed the task before (Schacter, 1992). This alternate route explains why memory appears to be divided between explicit and implicit knowledge.

CONCEPT LEARNING CHECK 7.7   *Learning from Case Studies of Amnesia*

Identify which type of forgetting is illustrated in these case examples.

A. Implicit memory

B. Amnesia

C. Dementia

1. _____ Mary suffers from Korsakoff's syndrome and can't encode any new experiences.

2. _____ Despite suffering from amnesia, Bill has learned how to type, even though he doesn't remember learning.

3. _____ Helen is able to function well at home, but she can no longer hold conversations on the phone about the past.

7.8 How to Improve Your Memory

The principles of memory reveal helpful strategies for improving retention.

◼ Identify principles that can improve memory.

Memory Principles Applied to Studying

From evidence about the encoding process, it is clear that active effort by the learner is required. The following guidelines group the principles of memory into active steps you can take to improve your recall.

Actively Construct Memory

Learning is not the same as reading; instead, you need to actively construct your memory for the material. Several principles help with constructing memory, including elaboration, generation, depth of processing, self-reference, self-explanation, and mnemonic devices. For all of these principles, you will want to ensure that you are *actively* processing the information you want to remember. Simply rereading, highlighting, and repeating it (such as replaying a lecture podcast) are *not* effective ways to help encode new material. *You* must be thinking about it in as many different ways as possible to construct your own view of the material. If you can rephrase the information in your own words, in ways that are relevant to you and tie in to what you already know, you will have prepared an excellent account to encode into long-term memory.

Our knowledge of the many types of memory organizations points out how critical it is to encoding and retrieval. Unlike computer disks, we can't afford endless searches through random lists of information. Human memory is built around organizing related information together, grouping meaningful units for easier retrieval. Judging from its importance in memory research, taking the time to organize the information you are attempting to learn is key to accomplishing this goal. One trick is to spend time after each class rewriting your notes, organizing clusters of information in hierarchies and related lists. This also helps to point out any missing connections between concepts and prepares you to ask questions at the next class session. You can't rely on your processing during the frantic note taking in lectures to lead to a thoughtful organization that suits your learning.

Schedule Study Sessions

A second set of related principles addresses how you should schedule study sessions. The spacing effect says that studying two different times for an hour each time is twice as effective as studying once for 2 hours. This explains why cramming your studying into one massive session before an exam is less effective than studying for shorter periods over the term. Rehearsing material a day later greatly promotes memory for the material when tested at a later time. You will save time and have better learning if you study regularly rather than all at once. In general, shorter practice sessions spaced widely apart produce the best effects for long-term memory. Now that you know how important it is to space out your learning sessions, you can build this principle into your study habits. In addition, try to avoid studying similar material back to back to avoid interference effects. Instead, switch to a less-related course after you finish one session. Finally, don't forget the lessons from forgetting: Sleep is critically important in forming new memories, and failing to sleep enough will limit how much of your new knowledge can be encoded into long-term memory. It's a hard lesson for busy college students, but sleep is your best friend when it comes to learning.

Test to Learn

Testing is also a critical part of learning. Asking questions, even ones you can't answer correctly, works to draw associations to the material you're learning. Repeated attempts to retrieve the information help you build up intermediate cues that aid recall. This even works for simple tasks like remembering where you parked your car today. When you are first out of sight of the car, ask yourself to remember where it is. This simple act of practicing recall can boost your ability to repeat this feat later. Surprisingly, testing even without feedback promotes the mindset and connections among ideas you will need for mastery of the material. We learn from testing as well as studying, so include self-testing in your study plans. And keep studying even when you know the answers. Overlearning works to practice the associations you've learned and strengthen them for later access.

Cue Retrieval

Retrieval problems can lead to frustration because you feel the knowledge is "in there," but you can't access it. The principles of retrieval cuing can help when you're drawing a blank. In the moment, think about related information and any mnemonic cues you used during studying to help you come across the information through an alternate route. Try reinstating the context of the time of initial learning. This includes your state of mind, mood, the physical setting, and related concepts in mind at the time of learning. Context is very important in guiding you towards the knowledge in memory. In addition, state-dependent and mood-dependent memory effects suggest you should also maintain a rested, calm mind while studying and testing.

Summary of Multiple Influences on Memory

Multiple influences color our psychological experience of memory. Biology plays a significant role, as demonstrated by the importance of sleep in forming new memories. Failing to sleep enough will limit how much new knowledge can be encoded into long-term memory. The consolidation of information into long-term memory takes some time for neuronal processes to work. Another source of biological evidence is the devastating impact of brain injury and disease on memory functions. Damage to some areas, such as the hippocampus, can destroy the possibility of encoding new memories.

Another source of influence on memory is our past experiences. When we experience similar things, we automatically group them together in memory: faces of family members or celebrities, words or pictures, are all associated together in memory based on how we experienced them. Our networks of memories provide access to information based on how things belong together. "Bread and butter" or "tofu and edamame" are connections formed in our memories as patterns of associations. Human memory is built around organizing related information together, grouping meaningful units as we experience them for easier retrieval.

Finally, the environment around us plays an important role in memory. It's easier to recall information in the same context, so you recognize schoolmates on campus that you may pass by at the mall. Retrieval is aided by reinstating the context at the time of initial learning. This assists in accessing information by invoking the same state of mind, a similar mood, the physical setting, or concepts in mind at the time of learning. Context is very important in guiding access to knowledge in memory. In addition, state-dependent and mood-dependent memory effects suggest your state of mind is part of this environment.

Knowing the multiple influences affecting memory, we can identify ways to take advantage of this knowledge and improve our memory for new information. Suggestions for how to improve your memory are summarized in **TABLE 7-3**.

TABLE 7-3 Techniques for Improving Memory

Technique	Description	Guideline	Example
Context effects	Cues from the learning context help to retrieve information	Reestablish the context to aid in recall.	"Let's see, the other types of memory were declarative and procedural, so implicit must be paired with . . ."
Depth of processing	The more deeply you think about the meaning, the better you will learn	Rephrase the point in your own words: How can you best describe the meaning?	"So to me, "procedural learning" is something you can't forget as long as you can do it."
Elaboration	Link the material to information you already have in your memory	Think of how the new information relates to concepts you know.	"So semantic nets organize a bunch of concepts."

(continues)

TABLE 7-3 Techniques for Improving Memory *(continued)*

Technique	Description	Guideline	Example
Forgetting curve	Learned information drops off quickly over time	Review the material again before a quiz to keep it accessible in memory.	"Since the quiz is tomorrow, I'll make time to go back over Chapter 8 tonight."
Generation	Make up a new idea or example on your own.	Tie the new information to clear examples	"Procedural knowledge is like riding a bike."
Mnemonic devices	Create memorable links between new concepts	Try to break down new terms into easy-to-remember pieces.	"Declarative knowledge is the kind you can 'declare' out loud."
Organization	Organize new information into related units to learn together	Outline new information to understand which parts fit together.	"Here are all the ways I can improve my studying."
Overlearning	Learning continues even after we think we know the information well	Continue to study the information even if you get it right on quizzes.	"I got them all right, but I'm going to go over them and explain why they're right."
Self-explanation	Create an explanation of why specific concepts work the way they do.	Talk your way through the material in your own words.	"So, the amygdala is close to the hippocampus, and emotion plays a role in memory!"
Self-reference effect	Link the material to thoughts about yourself	Remember a time that this concept happened to you.	"One of my 'flashbulb' memories is the inauguration of President Obama."
Spacing effect	Study periods spaced out over time results in the best learning	Study the material every day throughout the term.	"I'm going to study one topic in Chapter 7 every day this week."
Testing effects	Help your learning by giving yourself frequent practice recall tests.	After learning, practice recalling what you just learned.	"Let me try to recall the three stages of memory."
Visual imagery	Changing formats from verbal to visual can help to create complementary memories.	Think of a visual representation of the information.	"The sensory store trickles some information into short-term memory which trickles some information into long-term memory.

CONCEPT LEARNING CHECK 7.8   *Developing Helpful Study Habits*

Select three principles from Table 7-3 that have been shown to improve memory.

Describe how you could incorporate each principle into your study routine. Example: Organization. I can reorganize the material to group related concepts together and create an overall outline that captures the relationships among them.

Visual Overview Types of Knowledge in Memory

Different kinds of knowledge are organized in different ways in long-term memory.

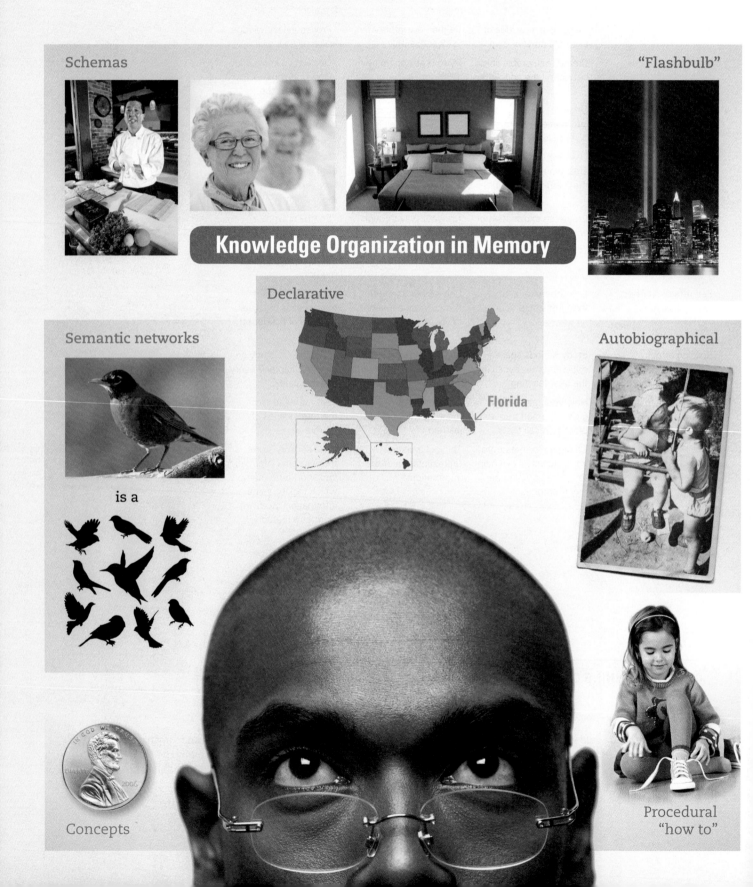

Schemas

"Flashbulb"

Knowledge Organization in Memory

Declarative

Semantic networks

Florida

Autobiographical

is a

Concepts

Procedural "how to"

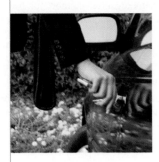

7.1 Overview: What Is Memory?

- Memory is the enduring consequence in the mind of our experiences with the world.
- It is an active process that interprets our experiences, not simply recording them.

- Memory is central to every other psychological process.

7.2 Constructing Memory

- Automatic processing occurs when information is encoded into memory without conscious awareness.
- Attention is needed to select from the information currently available and encode it into memory.
- Effortful processing is needed to ensure that information is successfully transferred into memory.
- *Levels of processing* refers to the notion that the more "deeply" the meaning is understood, the more likely it will be stored in memory.
- Elaboration is the process of drawing out the meaning of information and connecting it to related information already in memory.
- Self-reference effects show that we are most likely to remember things that are tied to ourselves in some way.

- Generation effects show that actively processing by "going beyond the information given," such as coming up with examples, enhances memory.
- Self-explanation facilitates memory through a deeper processing of why concepts work the way they do.
- Visual encoding makes use of our rich visual sense to make information more memorable.
- Mnemonics are tricks for making information more memorable through rhymes, acronyms, and other memory aids.

Hippocampus

7.3 The Three Stages of Memory

- There are three different memory stages for the conscious processing of memories.
- Sensory memory takes in sensory input in a rich display, but it fades in a fraction of a second.
- Short-term memory is information you are currently conscious of, and it fades in less than a minute or is displaced by new thoughts.
- Short-term memory is limited to around seven items at any one time, but "chunking" information can make this more efficient.
- Working memory refers to the same stage as short-term memory but highlights that work is needed to keep information in mind and that it supports cognitive tasks.

- Long-term memory is the permanent stage of memory that can hold an unlimited amount of information indefinitely.
- Memories are stored in the brain by long-term potentiation, which changes the interaction of neurons at the receptor sites to preserve information.
- Memories are stored in a distributed fashion all over the cortical areas of the brain and in the cerebellum.
- The hippocampus is the memory structure that helps to consolidate new information into long-term memory.

7.4 Organizing Information in Memory

- Knowledge in memory is organized into groupings based on content.
- Declarative memory is memory for information you can state explicitly.
- Semantic memory is a type of declarative memory that includes factual information.
- Concepts, concept hierarchies, and semantic networks capture the building blocks of information and their rich interconnections in memory.

- The schema organizes memory for events and captures the repetition of experiences like a "script."
- Episodic memory includes autobiographical experiences along with "flashbulb" memory events.
- Procedural memory includes information that is known implicitly and is "performed" through action.

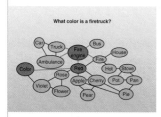

7.5 Retrieval from Memory

- Context provides the key to retrieving information from memory.
- Retrieval cues work by spreading activation from related concepts in memory.
- Adding context promotes retrieval by providing cues like the ones at encoding.

- Encoding specificity is the principle that matching context at encoding and retrieval maximizes recall.
- The act of practicing retrieval makes future retrievals more likely to be successful. So test often!

7.6 Reconstructing Memories

- Memory is a dynamic process that constructs both old and new information.
- Reconstruction involves creating a memory by filling in information from memory.
- Source monitoring involves knowledge about when, where, and how information was acquired.

- False memories include information encoded into memory that is inaccurate.
- The misinformation effect shows that incorrect information can be added to a memory at a later time.

7.7 Forgetting

- The forgetting curve shows that we lose a lot of knowledge immediately after learning.
- Repeated study sessions boost the baseline of long-term knowledge.

- Forgetting is useful because it limits our memory to information we expect to be useful later.
- Cases of memory loss inform us about the principles of successful memory.

7.8 How to Improve Your Memory

- The principles of memory reveal many helpful strategies for improving retention.

- Study habits can improve the likelihood of encoding and retrieving information when you need it.

7.1 Overview: What Is Memory?

1. Memory is:
A. an accurate record of what we experience.
B. the enduring consequences of our experiences.
C. our ability to recall facts.
D. the outcome of trying to learn.

7.2 Constructing Memory

2. The process by which we transform what we perceive, think, or feel into an enduring memory is called:
A. encoding.
B. remembering.
C. reconstructing.
D. storing.

3. Long-term retention of information is greatly enhanced by:
A. repetitive processing.
B. visual assessment.
C. elaborative encoding.
D. rhyme judgment.

4. When learning a new word, like *hippocampus*, you will remember it best if you:
A. think about what the word means.
B. think of another word that rhymes with it.
C. picture how the word looks.
D. write the word in large block letters.

7.3 The Three Stages of Memory

5. Memory storage is composed of sensory memory, short-term memory, and:
A. working memory.
B. long-term memory.
C. potentiated memory.
D. retrieval.

6. The process of keeping information in short-term memory by mentally repeating it is called:
A. maintenance rehearsal.
B. chunking.
C. memorizing.
D. mnemonic storage.

7. Short-term memory can hold:
A. a seven-digit telephone number but not a list of seven words.
B. approximately seven meaningful items.
C. information for no more than 3 minutes.
D. an unlimited amount of information.

8. When rats are given drugs that block long-term potentiation:
A. they develop stronger synaptic connections.
B. they lose their ability to encode information.
C. they get easily lost in familiar mazes.
D. neurotransmitter release is enhanced.

7.4 Organizing Information in Memory

9. Emile said that he vividly remembers the day he turned 21. This is an example of a(n):
A. explicit memory.
B. procedural memory.
C. implicit memory.
D. iconic memory.

10. Every year around the anniversary of her father's death, without realizing why, Judy experiences a feeling of sadness. This reaction is an example of a(n):
A. explicit memory.
B. implicit memory.
C. state-dependent retrieval cue.
D. emotional retrieval cue.

11. A network of associated facts and concepts that make up our general knowledge of the world is called:
A. semantic memory.
B. episodic memory.
C. explicit memory.
D. implicit memory.

7.5 Retrieval from Memory

12. Of the following, the best example of using retrieval context is:
A. learning the material so thoroughly that it comes right to mind.
B. sitting in your usual desk in your usual classroom when taking an exam.
C. using memory drugs to enhance neural processing.
D. drinking coffee while studying.

13. When Jorge studies for a test in his noisy dorm, he always has his favorite energy drink at hand. The encoding specificity principle would suggest that he should:
A. have some of the energy drink a few hours before the test.
B. have a sip of the energy drink right before going to sleep to enhance memory.
C. take a can of the energy drink with him to the test.
D. ask the instructor if he can use an iPod to listen to soothing music during the test.

7.5 Retrieval from Memory

14. A world-famous musician left his multimillion-dollar instrument in the trunk of a taxi. What might have caused him to forget something so important to him?

A. The lack of retrieval cues

B. Source memory

C. The novel context

D. Mood-dependent memory

7.6 Reconstructing Memories

15. Recall of when, where, and how information was acquired is called:

A. constructive memory.

B. retrospective memory.

C. source memory.

D. misinformation in memory.

16. When subjects in Loftus's experiment on misinformation saw a picture of a yield sign and then read a question about a stop sign, they were more likely than control subjects to report having seen:

A. a yield sign.

B. a stop sign.

C. both signs.

D. neither sign.

17. Defense attorneys often protest prosecutors' use of eyewitness testimony because:

A. source errors may cause an eyewitness to make a false identification.

B. eyewitnesses are more prone to forgetting.

C. poor eyesight in eyewitnesses tends to invalidate their testimony.

D. a confident eyewitness is usually right.

7.7 Forgetting

18. Research by Hermann Ebbinghaus using nonsense syllables demonstrated that:

A. memories of new information fade at a constant rate over time.

B. new memories remain strong for up to 4 weeks before they begin to fade.

C. most forgetting of new information happens soon after learning.

D. individuals remember much more than they think they do.

19. Information can be kept for hours, days, weeks, or years in the:

A. retrieval terminal.

B. hippocampus.

C. remembrance database.

D. long-term memory store.

20. Johan has difficulty remembering events in his life that occurred after his recent surgery; his neurosurgeon has diagnosed him as suffering from:

A. dementia.

B. long-term potentiation.

C. synaptic enhancement.

D. amnesia.

7.8 How to Improve Your Memory

21. Studies show that, following a heavy session of studying, you should:

A. exercise.

B. sleep.

C. switch to a different course topic to study.

D. avoid thinking about the material.

22. The following are all methods of elaborative encoding except for:

A. generation.

B. self-reference.

C. self-explanation.

D. highlighting.

23. For optimal results in terms of longest-term memory for the material, is it best to plan your study sessions so that they:

A. switch back and forth between class topics.

B. occur in one marathon session for each course.

C. occur in widely spaced out shorter sessions.

D. repeat the material over and over.

CHAPTER DISCUSSION QUESTIONS

1. You have an exam coming up. Remind yourself of helpful ways to prepare for it. What are the terms for these techniques?

2. Describe one of your flashbulb memories and explain why that memory is so firmly imprinted in your mind.

3. You are a juror in a case involving the robbery of a convenience store. An eyewitness identifies the accused. In considering this evidence, what should you bear in mind?

4. The head of your study group has asked you to obtain 10 items for tomorrow's meeting; unfortunately, you're not in a position to make a written list. The items are pens, a ruler, 3 × 5 cards, ice, sodas, a master key, a list of members, cookies, cups, and a carton to use as a waste basket. Discuss two methods you might use to remember the 10 items.

5. Imagine that a reliable, effective memory-enhancing drug were available for purchase. Describe some of the pros and cons of this drug.

CHAPTER PROJECTS

1. Read an article or book about the experiences of people who have memory disorders. Oliver Sacks has written several, including *The Man Who Mistook His Wife for a Hat*. What does the experience of the patients described tell you about normal memory functions? Are there any limits to the use of this type of data in learning about memory?

2. Several popular films have investigated short-term memory loss:

Memento (2003)
50 First Dates (2004)
Finding Nemo (2003)

Watch one of these commercial movies. Is the movie accurate in its depiction of how memory works?

CHAPTER KEY TERMS

Alzheimer's disease
Amnesia
Automatic processing
Category
Chunking
Concept
Conceptual hierarchy
Connectionist models
Consolidation
Cued recall
Decay theory
Declarative memory (explicit memory)
Dementia
Echoic memory
Elaboration
Encoding
Encoding specificity
Episodic memory
False memory

Flashbulb memory
Forgetting curve
Generation effect
Hippocampus
Hyperthymesia
Iconic memory
Incidental memory
Interference theory
Levels of processing
Link method
Long-term memory (LTM)
Long-term potentiation
Maintenance rehearsal
Memory
Method of loci
Misinformation effect
Mnemonic
Mood congruence
Overlearning
Priming

Procedural memory (implicit memory)
Reconstruction
Relearning
Repression
Schema
Self-reference effect
Semantic memory
Semantic network model
Sensory memory
Short-term memory (STM)
Source monitoring
Spacing effect
Spreading activation
Stage model of memory
Tip-of-the-tongue phenomenon
Working memory
Working memory span

ANSWERS TO CONCEPT LEARNING CHECKS

7.1 Defining Memory

1. A. Essay. Essays are the most difficult because you have to retrieve all of the information from memory, and there are very few cues offered to help.

2. B. Multiple-choice. These questions are easier because the information is presented to you, and you can match it to what you have in memory. All you need to do is recognize the right answer. Fill-in-the-blank questions also require recalling information, but having the surrounding information helps you retrieve the needed term.

3. C. Fill-in-the-blank. Memory retrieval can be difficult, but having some cues to help you find the information in memory is very helpful.

4. Recognizing information in memory is easier when you don't have to do the step of retrieval. You might conclude that retrieval is the hard part, and cues from the surrounding context or choices help a lot.

7.2 Applying Methods of Encoding

1. D. This fits the self-reference effect because effort is made to turn the concept into a personal example.

2. D. This fits self-reference encoding because the concept is being tied to specific events in the learner's own life.

3. F. This fits mnemonics because the learner is using the words' relationship to remember the concepts.

4. C. This fits depth of processing because they are capturing the deeper meaning of the material.

5. E. Self-explanation is the method that tries walking through examples to make sure you understand why every step occurs.

7.3 Movement of Information Through the Stages of Memory

Information flows from sensory memory to short-term memory to long-term memory. Sensory and short-term memory can drop information, but long-term memory does not.

A. Sensory memory.
B. Short-term memory.
C. Long-term memory.

7.4 Organizing Information in Memory

1. A pig has a curly tail. [A. Concepts]
2. The moment you found out you got into college. [E. Episodic memory]
3. Taking a seat in the waiting room at the dentist. [D. The schema]
4. A whale is a mammal, not a fish. [B. Concept hierarchies]
5. Name a vehicle that is red and has a siren: a fire truck. [C. Semantic networks]

7.5 Practicing Retrieval

1. Generating retrieval cues. [Thinking of related words will help by spreading activation to the word you're trying to recall.]
2. Adding context. [Matching the context of retrieval to the context of learning helps in accessing the word in memory.]
3. Retrieval practice. [Studies show practice with retrieval, even without feedback, helps with later retrieval; so practicing trying to retrieve the word will help when you try to access it again later.]

7.6 Introducing Error in Memory

1. A. [Reconstruction, because she is filling in the participants based on what usually happens.]
2. C. [Misinformation effect, because two dates were given in two separate communications, and the contradiction was not noted.]

3. B. [Source monitoring error, because the face was familiar from the poster, not from knowing the woman.]
4. D. [False memory, because the story is not true, but Colleen has invented some details to support it.]

7.7 Learning from Case Studies of Amnesia

1. B. [Amnesia refers to the inability to form new memories since an event.]
2. A. [Implicit memory can provide the ability to perform functions without explicit knowledge.]
3. C. [Dementia refers to the loss of explicit memories of the past.]

7.8 Developing Helpful Study Habits

Self-reference effect. I can think about an example of when a topic happened in my own life and work through it to illustrate the important properties of the concept.

Spacing effect. I can plan to study my calculus material every day the class meets, so I'll stretch the study sessions out over the week.

Testing effects. At the end of each study session, I can test myself on the key terms.

More examples are in Table 7-3.

ANSWERS TO CHAPTER REVIEW TEST

7.1 Overview: What Is Memory?

1. B. Rationale: Memory involves more than facts or what we try to learn, and it can be a distorted picture of our experiences; however, it captures what remains from our experiences.

7.2 Constructing Memory

2. A. Rationale: Unlike the two other stages of memory, *encoding* refers to taking information into memory.
3. C. Rationale: *Elaboration* refers to enhancing memory through meaning, unlike the other options listed.
4. A. Rationale: Unlike the other strategies listed, encoding based on meaning works best.

7.3 The Three Stages of Memory

5. B. Rationale: The two other stages of memory lead to the encoding of information into long-term memory.
6. A. Rationale: The only means of maintaining information in short-term memory that involves repetition is maintenance rehearsal.
7. B. Rationale: The capacity of short-term memory is reflected in the "magic 7 ± 2."
8. B. Rationale: The function of long-term potentiation is to make changes in the receptivity of neuronal connections, making it possible to store new knowledge in long-term memory.

7.4 Organizing Information in Memory

9. A. Rationale: The only option reflecting conscious awareness of the information is explicit memory.

10. B. Rationale: This option reflects the lack of conscious awareness of the information, and D is not a term covered in the chapter.
11. A. Rationale: This option reflects stated knowledge and is more specific than option C (explicit memory).

7.5 Retrieval from Memory

12. B. Rationale: This option reflects matching the context of learning to the context at testing.
13. C. Rationale: This option reflects matching the context of learning to the context at testing, the principle of encoding specificity.
14. A. Rationale: This option reflects the lack of potential cues to remind him of the instrument in the trunk, while there is no information to suggest C or D are relevant.

7.6 Reconstructing Memories

15. C. Rationale: This option reflects the definition of source memory.
16. A. Rationale: This option reflects the results of the study in which subjects were misled by information included in a follow-up question but didn't notice any contradiction.
17. A. Rationale: This option reflects the example of eyewitness error discussed in the text, and the other options are incorrect statements.

7.7 Forgetting

18. C. Rationale: This option reflects the major point about the forgetting curve.
19. D. Rationale: This option reflects the fact that only the long-term memory store holds information without decay.

20. D. Rationale: This option reflects the fact that only memories since the event are not recalled.

7.8 How to Improve Your Memory

21. B. Rationale: This option reflects the fact that sleep is needed to encode information into long-term memory. The alternatives are either not mentioned (A and D) or explicitly incorrect based on the text.

22. D. Rationale: This option reflects the fact that highlighting simply repeats rather than elaborates on the information, while the other alternatives add meaning to the information.

23. C. Rationale: This option reflects the spacing effect, while the other alternatives are explicitly incorrect based on the text.

REFERENCES

Alloway, T. P., & Alloway, R. G. (2010). Investigating the predictive roles of working memory and IQ in academic attainment. *Journal of Experimental Child Psychology, 80*(2), 606–621.

Anderson, M. C., & Green, C. (2001). Suppressing unwanted thoughts by executive control. *Nature, 410,* 366–369.

Atkinson, R. C., & Shiffrin, R. M. (1968). Human memory: A proposed system and its control processes. In K. W. Spence & J. T. Spence (Eds.), *The psychology of learning and motivation* (Vol. 2, pp. 89–195). New York: Academic Press.

Bachevalier, C., & Vargha-Khadem, F. (2005). The primate hippocampus: Ontogeny, early insult and memory. *Current Opinion in Neurobiology, 15*(2), 168–174.

Baddely, A. D. (2001). Is working memory still working? *American Psychologist, 56,* 849–864.

Baddeley, A. D., & Hitch, G. J. L. (1974). Working memory. In G. A. Bower (Ed.), *The psychology of learning and motivation: Advances in research and theory* (Vol. 8, pp. 47–89). New York: Academic Press.

Bahrick, H. P. (1984). Semantic memory content in permastore: Fifty years of memory for Spanish learned in school. *Journal of Experimental Psychology: General, 113,* 1–35.

Bargh, J. A., Chen, M., & Burrows, L. (1996). Automaticity of social behavior: Direct effects of trait construct and stereotype activation on action. *Journal of Personality and Social Psychology, 71*(2), 230–244.

Barrett, D. (1980). The first memory as a predictor of personality traits. *Journal of Individual Psychology, 36*(2), 136–149.

Bartlett, F. C. (1932). *Remembering: A study in experimental and social psychology.* Cambridge, UK: Cambridge University Press.

Bolzan, S., Bolzan, J., & Rother, C. (2011). *My life, deleted: A memoir.* New York: HarperOne.

Bousfeld, W. A. (1953). The occurrence of clustering in the recall of randomly arranged associates. *Journal of General Psychology, 49,* 229–240.

Bower, G. H. (1981). Mood and memory. *American Psychologist, 36*(2), 129–148.

Bower, G. H., Black, J. B., & Turner, T. J. (1979). Scripts in memory for texts. *Cognitive Psychology, 11*(2), 177–220.

Brewer, W. F. (1988). Memory for randomly sampled autobiographical events. In U. Neisser & E. Winograd (Ed.), *Remembering reconsidered: Ecological and traditional approaches to the study of memory* (pp. 21–90). Cambridge, MA: Cambridge University Press.

Brewer, W. F., & Treyens, J. C. (1981). Role of schemata in memory for places. *Cognitive Psychology, 13,* 207–230.

Brown, A. S. (1991). A review of the tip-of-the-tongue experience. *Psychological Bulletin, 109*(2), 204–223.

Bruce, V., & Le Voi, M. E. (1983). Recognizing faces [and discussion]. *Philosophical Transactions of the Royal Society of London. Series B, Biological Sciences, 302*(1110), 423–436.

Bruck, M., & Ceci, S. J. (1999). The suggestibility of children's memory. *Annual Review of Psychology, 50,* 419–439.

Carrier, M., & Pashler, H. (1992). The influence of retrieval on retention. *Memory & Cognition, 20*(6), 633–642.

Ceci, S. J., Crossman, A. M., Scullin, M. H., Gilstrap, L., & Huffman, M. L. (2002). Children's suggestibility research: Implications for the courtroom and the forensic interview. In H. L. Westcott, G. M. Davies, & R. H. C. Bull (Eds.), *Children's testimony: A handbook of psychological research and forensic practice* (pp. 117–130). West Sussex, England: John Wiley & Sons Ltd.

Ceci, S. J., Huffman, M. L. C., Smith, E., & Loftus, E. F. (1994). Repeatedly thinking about a non-event: Source misattribution among preschoolers. *Consciousness & Cognition, 3,* 388–407.

Cepada, N. J., Pashler, H., Vul, E., Wixted, J. T., & Rohrer, D. (2006). Distributed practice in verbal recall tasks: A review and quantitative synthesis. *Psychological Bulletin, 132*(3), 354–380.

Chi, M. T. H., Bassok, M., Lewis, M. W., Reimann, P., & Glaser, R. (1989). Self-explanations: How students study and use examples in learning to solve problems. *Cognitive Science, 13*(2), 145–182.

Chi, M. T. H., De Leeuw, N., M-H., & Lavancher, C. (1994). Eliciting self-explanations improves understanding. *Cognitive Science, 18*(3), 439–477.

Cohen, N. J., Eichenbaum, H., Deacedo, B. S., & Corkin, S. (1985). Different memory systems underlying acquisition of procedural and declarative knowledge. *Annals of the New York Academy of Sciences, 444,* 54–71.

Collins, A. M., & Loftus, E. F. (1975). A spreading activation theory of semantic processing. *Psychological Review, 82,* 407–428.

Conway, M., Cohen, G., & Stanhope, N. (1991). On the very long-term retention of knowledge acquired through formal education. *Journal of Experimental Psychology: General, 120,* 395–409.

Cowan, N. (2001). The magical number four in short-term memory: A reconsideration of mental storage capacity. *Behavioral and Brain Sciences, 24,* 87–185.

Craik, F. I. M, & Tulving, E. (1975). Depth of processing and the retention of words in episodic memory. *Journal of Experimental Psychology: General, 104,* 268–294.

Crombag, H. F. M., Wagenaar, W. A., & Van Koppen, P. J. (1996). Crashing memories and the problem of "source monitoring." *Applied Cognitive Psychology, 10,* 95–104.

Deese, J. (1959). On the prediction of occurrence of particular verbal intrusions in immediate recall. *Journal of Experimental Psychology, 58,* 17–22.

Dempster, F. N. (1988). The Spacing Effect: A case study in the failure to apply the results of psychological research. *American Psychologist, 43*(8), 627–634.

Dudai, Y. (2004). The neurobiology of consolidations, or, how stable is the engram? *Annual Review of Psychology, 55,* 51–86.

Ebbinghaus, H. (1885; reprinted in 1913). Memory: A contribution to experimental psychology. (Translation by H. Roger & C. Bussenius). New York: Teacher's College Press.

Ericsson, K. A., & Chase, W. G. (1982). Exceptional memory. *American Scientist, 70*(6), 607–615.

Ericsson, K. A., Krampe, R. T., & Tesch-Romer, C. (1993). The role of deliberate practice in the acquisition of expert performance. *Psychological Review, 100*(3), 363–406.

Feldman-Summers, S., & Pope, K. S. (1994). The experience of forgetting childhood abuse: A national survey of psychologists. *Journal of Consulting and Clinical Psychology, 62,* 636–639.

Fowler, R. L., & Barker, A. S. (1974). Effectiveness of highlighting for retention of text material. *Journal of Applied Psychology, 59*(3), 358–364.

Frederickson, R. (1992). *Repressed memory: A journey to recovery from sexual abuse.* New York: Fireside (Simon & Schuster).

Freud, S. (1957). Repression. In J. Strachey (Ed. & Trans.), *The standard edition of the complete psychological works of Sigmund Freud* (Vol. 14, pp. 146–158). London: Hogarth.

Freyd, J. J. (1995). *Betrayal trauma: The logic of forgetting childhood abuse.* Cambridge, MA: Harvard University Press.

Garven, S., Wood, J. M., Malpass, R. S., & Shaw, J. S., III. (1998). More than suggestion: The effect of interviewing techniques from the McMartin preschool case. *Journal of Applied Psychology, 83*(3), 347–359.

Geraerts, E., Schooler, J. W., Merckelbach, H., Jelicic, M., Hauer, B. J. A., & Ambadar, Z. (2007). The reality of recovered memories: Corroborating continuous and discontinuous memories of childhood sexual abuse. *Psychological Science, 18,* 564–567.

Gerarts, E., Lindsay, D. S., Merckelbach, H., Jelicic, M., Raymaekers, L., Arnold, M. M., & Schooler, J. W. (2009). Cognitive mechanisms underlying recovered-memory experiences of childhood sexual abuse. *Psychological Science, 20*(1), 92–98.

Gluck, M. A., & Myers, C. E. (1997). Psychobiological models of hippocampal function in learning and memory. *Annual Review of Psychology, 48,* 481–514.

Golby, A., Silverberg, G., Race, E., Gabrieli, S., O'Shea, J., Knierim, K., Stebbins, G., & Gabrieli, J. (2005). Memory encoding in Alzheimer's disease: An fMRI study of explicit and implicit memory. *Brain, 128*(4), 773–787.

Goodman, G. S., & Quas, J. A. (2008). Repeated interviews and children's memory: It's more than just how many. *Current Directions in Psychological Science, 17*(6), 386–390.

Goodwin, D., Powell, B., Bremer, D., Hoine, H., & Stern, J. (1969). Alcohol and recall: State-dependent effects in man. *Sciences, 163*(3873), 1358–1360.

Hayne, H., & Simcock, G. (2002). Breaking the barrier? Children fail to translate their preverbal memories into language. *Psychological Science, 13*(3), 225–231.

Hintzman, D. L. (1974). Theoretical implications of the spacing effect. In R. L. Solso (Ed.), *Theories in cognitive psychology: The Loyola Symposium* (pp. 77–99). Potomac, MD: Erlbaum.

Howe, M. L., & Courage, M. L. (1997). The emergence and early development of autobiographical memory. *Psychological Review, 104*(3), 499–523.

James, W. (1890). *The principles of psychology, Vol. 1 and 2.* New York: Dover Publications, 1950.

Jenkins, J. G., & Dallenbach, K. M. (1924). Oblivescence during sleep and waking. *American Journal of Psychology, 35,* 605–612.

Johnson, H. M., & Seifert, C. M. (1994). Sources of the continued influence effect: When misinformation in memory affects later inferences. *Journal of Experimental Psychology: Learning, Memory, and Cognition, 20*(6), 1420–1436.

Johnson, M. K., Hashtroudi, S., & Lindsay, D. S. (1993). Source monitoring. *Psychological Bulletin, 114*(1), 3–28.

Kandel, E. R., & Schwartz, J. H. (1982). Molecular biology of learning: Modulation of transmitter release. *Science, 218,* 433–443.

Lashley, K. S. (1950). In search of the engram. In the *Symposium of the Society for Experimental Biology (Vol. 4).* New York: Cambridge University Press.

Lewandowsky, S., Stritzke, W. G. K., Oberauer, K., & Morales, M. (2005). Memory for fact, fiction, and misinformation: The Iraq War 2003. *Psychological Science, 16,* 190–195.

Lindsay, D. S., & Johnson, M. K. (1991). Recognition memory and source monitoring. *Psychological Bulletin, 29*(3), 203–205.

Loftus, E. F. (1975). Leading questions and the eyewitness report. *Cognitive Psychology, 7,* 560–572.

Loftus, E. F. (1979). The malleability of human memory. *American Scientist, 67*(3), 312–320.

Loftus, E. F. (1980). *Memory: Surprising new insights into how we remember and why we forget.* Reading, MA: Addison-Wesley.

Loftus, E. F. (1993). The reality of repressed memories. *American Psychologist, 48,* 518–537.

Loftus, E. F. (1996). *Eyewitness testimony.* Cambridge, MA: Harvard University Press.

Loftus, E. F. (1997). Creating false memories. *Scientific American, 277,* 70–75.

Loftus, E. F., & Davis, D. (2006). Recovered memories. *Annual Review of Clinical Psychology, 2,* 469–498.

Loftus, E. F., & Ketchum, K. (1994). *The myth of repressed memory: False memories and the allegations of sexual abuse.* New York: St. Martin's Press.

Loftus, E. F., Miller, D. G., & Burns, H. J. (1978). Semantic integration of verbal information into a visual memory. *Journal of Experimental Psychology: Human Learning and Memory, 4*(1), 19–31.

Lynch, G., & Stabli, U. (1991). Possible contributions of long-term potentiation to the encoding and organization of memory. *Brain Research Reviews, 16,* 204–206.

Meyer, D. E., & Schvaneveldt, R. W. (1971). Facilitation in recognizing pairs of words: Evidence of a dependence between retrieval operations. *Journal of Experimental Psychology, 90,* 227–234.

Miller, G. A. (1956). The magical number seven, plus or minus two: some limits on our capacity for processing information. *Psychological Review, 63*(2), 81–97.

Milner, B. (1970). Memory and the temporal regions of the brain. In K. H. Pribram & D. E. Broadbent (Eds.), *Biology of memory.* New York: Academic Press.

Milner, B., Squire, L. R., & Kandel, E. R. (1998). Cognitive neuroscience and the study of memory. *Neuron, 20,* 445–468.

Morain, D. (1995). Recovered memory murder case unravels. *Los Angeles Times,* December 25, Ret. 11/11/2011, http://articles.latimes.com/1995-12-25/news/mn-17740_1_memories-cases-recovered.

Neisser, U., & Harsch, N. (1992). Phantom flashbulbs: False recollections of hearing the news about *Challenger.* In E. Winograd and U. Neisser (Eds.), *Affect and accuracy in recall: Studies of "flashbulb" memories* (pp. 9–31). New York: Cambridge University Press.

Newman, L. S., & Baumeister, R. F. (1996). Toward an explanation of the UFO abduction phenomenon: Hypnotic elaboration, extraterrestrial sadomasochism, and spurious memories. *Psychological Inquiry, 7*(2), 99–126.

Nickerson, R. S., & Adams, M. J. (1979). Long term memory for a common object. *Cognitive Psychology, 11,* 287–307.

Palm, K. M., & Gibson, P. (1998). Recovered memories of childhood sexual abuse: Clinicians' practices and beliefs. *Professional Psychology: Research and Practice, 29*(3), 257–261.

Parker, E. S., Cahill, L., & McGaugh, J. L. (2006). A case of unusual autobiographical remembering. *Neurocase, 12,* 35–49.

Penrod, S., & Cutler, B. (1995). Witness confidence and witness accuracy: Assessing their forensic relation. *Psychology, Public Policy, and Law, 1*(4), 817–845.

Poole, D. A., & Lindsay, D. S. (1998). Assessing the accuracy of young children's reports: Lessons from investigations of child sexual abuse. *Applied and Preventive Psychology, 7*(1), 1–26.

Powell, M. B., & Freckelton, I. (2008). The contribution to forensic psychology by professor Donald Thomson. *Psychiatry, Psychology and Law, 15*(3), 361–361.

Press, A., Hager, M., King, P., Namuth, T., Sherman, D., & Walters, S. (1985). The youngest witnesses. *Newsweek,* February 19, 72–74.

Raven, J. C. (1936). *Mental tests used in genetic studies: The performance of related individuals on tests mainly educative and mainly reproductive.* MSc Thesis, University of London.

Richland, L. E., Kornell, N., & Kao, L. S. (2009). The pretesting effect: Do unsuccessful retrieval attempts enhance learning? *Journal of Experimental Psychology: Applied, 15*(3), 243–257.

Roediger, H. L. III, & Karpicke, J. D. (2006). Test-enhanced learning: Taking memory tests improves long-term retention. *Psychological Science, 17*(3), 249–255.

Roediger, H. L., & McDermott, K. B. (1995). Creating false memories: Remembering words not presented in lists. *Journal of Experimental Psychology: Learning, Memory, and Cognition, 21*(4), 803–814.

Rogers, T. B., Kuiper, N. A., & Kirker, W. S. (1977). Self-reference and the encoding of personal information. *Journal of Personality and Social Psychology, 35,* 677–688.

Rozin, P., Dow, S., Moscovitch, M., & Rajaram, S. (1998). What causes humans to begin and end a meal? A role for memory for what has been eaten, as evidenced by a study of multiple meal eating in amnesic patients. *Psychological Science, 9*(5), 392–396.

Rubin, D. C., Berntsen, D., & Bohni, M. K. (2008). A memory-based model of posttraumatic stress disorder: Evaluating basic assumptions underlying the PTSD diagnosis. *Psychological Review, 115*(4), 985–1011.

Sachs, J. (1967). Recognition memory for syntactic and semantic aspects of connected discourse. *Perception and Psychophysics, 2,* 437–442.

Sargant, W., & Slater, E. (1941). Amnesic syndromes in war. *Proceedings of the Royal Society of Medicine, 34*(12), 757–764.

Schacter, D. L. (1992). Understanding implicit memory: A neuroscience approach. *American Psychologist, 47,* 559–569.

Schank, R. C. (1982). *Dynamic memory.* Cambridge: Cambridge University Press.

Schank, R. C., & Abelson, R. P. (1977). *Scripts, plans, goals, and understanding: An inquiry into human knowledge structures.* Hillsdale, NJ: Lawrence Erlbaum Assoc.

Schank, R. C., & Abelson,. P. (1995). Knowledge and memory: The real story. In R. S. Wyer, Jr. (Ed.), *Advances in knowledge and memory: The real story* (pp. 1–85). Hillsdale, NJ: Lawrence Erlbaum Associates.

Schooler, J. W. (2001). Discovering memories in the light of metaawareness. *Journal of Aggression, Maltreatment and Trauma, 4,* 105–136.

Schooler, J. W., Ambadar, Z., & Bendiksen, M. A. (1997). A cognitive corroborative case study approach for investigating discovered memories of sexual abuse. In J. D. Read & D. S. Lindsay (Eds.), *Recollections of trauma: Scientific research and clinical practices* (pp. 379–388). New York: Plenum.

Schwartz, B., & Reisberg, D. (1991). *Learning and memory.* New York: Norton.

Shepard, R. N. (1967). Recognition memory for words, sentences, and pictures. *Journal of Verbal Learning and Verbal Behavior, 6,* 156–163.

Slamecka, N. J., & Graf, P. (1978). The generation effect: Delineation of a phenomenon. *Journal of Experimental Psychology: Human Learning and Memory, 4*(6), 592–604.

Sperling, G. A. (1960). The information available in brief visual presentation. *Psychological Monographs: General and Applied, 74*(11), 1–29.

Standing, L. (1973). Learning 10,000 pictures. *Quarterly Journal of Experimental Psychology, 25,* 207–222.

Stickgold, R., Hobson, J. A., Fosse, R., & Fosse, M. (2001). Sleep, learning, and dreams: Off-line memory reprocessing. *Science, 294*(5544), 1052–1057.

Teuber, H. L., Milner, B., & Vaughan, H. G., Jr. (1968). Persistent anterograde amnesia after stab wound of the basal brain. *Neuropsychologia, 6*(3), 267–282.

Thompson-Cannino, J., & Cotton, R. (2009). *Picking Cotton: Our memoir of injustice and redemption.* New York: St. Martin's Griffin.

Tulving, E., & Thompson, D. M. (1973). Encoding specificity and retrieval processes in episodic memory. *Psychological Review, 80,* 352–373.

Usher, J., & Neisser, U. (1993). Childhood amnesia and the beginnings of memory for four early life events. *Journal of Experimental Psychology, 122*(2), 155–165.

von Restorff, H. (1933). Über die Wirkung von Bereichsbildungen im Spurenfeld. *Psychologische Forschung, 18,* 299–342.

Wade, K. A., Garry, M., Read, J. D., & Lindsay, D. S. (2002). A picture is worth a thousand lies: Using false photographs to create false childhood memories. *Psychonomic Bulletin & Review, 9,* 597–603.

Wade, S. E., & Trathen, W. (1989). Effect of self-selected study methods on learning. *Journal of Educational Psychology, 81*(1), 40–47.

Williams, L. M. (1994). Recall of childhood trauma: A prospective study of women's memories of child sexual abuse. *Journal of Consulting and Clinical Psychology, 62*(6), 1167–1176.

Williams, L. M. (1995). Recovered memories of abuse in women with documented child sexual victimization histories. *Journal of Traumatic Stress, 8*(4), 649–673.

Williams, M. D., & Hollan, J. (1981). The process of retrieval from very long-term memory. *Cognitive Science, 5,* 87–119.

Yaniv, I., & Meyer, D. E. (1987). Activation and metacognition of inaccessible stored information: Potential bases for incubation effects in problem solving. *Journal of Experimental Psychology: Learning, Memory, and Cognition, 13*(2), 187–205.

Chapter Overview ▼

8 Thinking and Language

Learning Objectives ▼

8.1 ■ Explain the dual processes of thinking.

8.2 ■ Compare and contrast the processes for problem solving.
■ Discuss how bias impacts problem solving.
■ Explain problem representation.

8.3 ■ Examine the pros and cons of heuristic use in decision making.

8.4 ■ Explain how presented knowledge may bias reasoning.
■ Demonstrate how beliefs impact reasoning.

8.5 ■ Define language and describe the unique characteristics of human language.
■ Describe the theories of language acquisition.

8.6 ■ Explain how language use reveals its impact on our thinking.
■ Describe the influence of biology and culture on how we think.

A friend mentioned he was visiting his cousin in California, Uma Thurman. Later, I told my colleague, Sam, who is a big fan. "Wow," said Sam, "Do you think you can get your friend to introduce me to her?" I looked over at Sam, a nice looking 30-year-old cognitive psychologist, and thought of Uma, a famous actor in films like the *Kill Bill* series, and the classic *Pulp Fiction*. With the skepticism apparent on my face, I promised to ask. The next day was April 1st, and I could not resist. I phoned Sam and left a message saying I had talked to my friend, and it was a go: "Uma is dying to meet you!" After a couple of hours, I called back to say, "April Fool's!" But Sam was already planning his big date, and called a few friends to share the good news. He has never really forgiven me for that April Fool's joke. Was it rational thinking for professor Sam to think a Hollywood star would be "dying to meet him"?

8.1   Overview: What Is Thinking?

Thinking involves dual processes that help us make sense of our experiences in the world.

- Explain the dual processes of thinking.

Thinking The internal mental processes that make sense of our experiences.

Cognition All types of thinking, including knowing, remembering, reasoning, deciding, and communicating.

Rational thinking Thinking marked by the use of deliberate reasoning.

Deliberation Slow, careful thinking aimed at considering all alternatives.

Is thinking "rational?" In psychology, **thinking** is defined by the many kinds of mental processes we perform as we experience the world. Within psychology, we use the term **cognition** to refer to thinking processes, including knowing, remembering, reasoning, deciding, and communicating. In Chapter 7, we discussed the variety of concepts in memory and the different ways concepts can be represented in memory. These concepts obviously form the core content of thinking, and their nature influences how we are able to refine, combine, and create new concepts through thinking. We are all very familiar with our internal thoughts, yet our awareness of the influences on our thinking may be somewhat limited. Our emotions, associations in memory, biological functions in the brain, and cultural experiences may affect our thinking but are not considered to be thinking processes. With so much on our minds, cognitive researchers have developed a rich set of theories to describe how thinking is accomplished. A central point is that our thinking is often far from a rational process.

People often believe that thinking should be logical, follow rules, and arrive at a "correct" answer or conclusion. **Rational thinking** is marked by the use of reason, or coming to conclusions when considering facts fully and carefully. This form of thinking is slow and deliberate, with the goal of avoiding errors and arriving at the best conclusion (Kuo et al., 2009). It takes a great deal of effort to consider all of the relevant information. For example, when you chose a college to attend, you may have felt the need to figure out all of the relevant factors, including the programs available at each college, the cost, the location, and so forth. In this type of slow **deliberation**, writing down all of the pros and cons of the options can be helpful, along with searching for information to help identify the best choices. This rational approach may seem like the "right" way to approach thinking; after all, one of the worst things someone can say is that we are being illogical. But consider how often you perform this type of careful thinking: Did you do it today or yesterday? We think constantly, yet we choose to do this deliberative thinking only sometimes.

Most of us believe that our thinking is of this deliberative style. However, more often, our thinking can be described as intuitive, quick, and easy. We try to make fast, efficient judgments because we need to make so many of them. When to cross the street at the intersection, what drink to order with a meal, and who to call next? We are constantly making decisions, and life is too short to always perform careful deliberation. Instead, we may rely on first impressions, instincts, or emotions to drive our choices without given them much thought. Sometimes, even though all of the evidence points toward a choice, we may have a "gut feeling" about what to do. This fast **intuition** (Kahneman et al., 1982) seems to describe a lot of our day-to-day thinking, from which route to take to which jam to buy. This type of thinking has been called "fast and frugal," because it helps us to arrive at a decision quickly while minimizing the effort we have to expend (Gigerenzer, 2007). We resort to "quick and dirty" thinking, or use our intuition, so we can move on to more important matters. However, this does leave us open to making errors in our thinking.

When you have a "gut instinct" but cannot consciously explain it, what does it reveal about your thinking? A study in cognitive neuroscience demonstrated the power of gut instincts (Bechara, Damasio, Tranel, & Damasio, 1997). In the study, people played the Iowa Gambling Task FIGURE 8-1. Four decks of virtual cards are presented on a screen in front of you, and you can select which deck to draw from. The decks pay off differently; some provide a small gain and others a steep loss. To win, you have to figure out the incentive value of the deck choices available to you. As you play, you gradually figure out which are the "good" decks, leading to wins, and which deck to avoid drawing from. After about 40 or 50 selections, people are fairly good at picking from only the good decks. But much sooner, after only 10 tries, people show a "stress" reaction (sweaty palms) as they reach for a bad deck, as measured by galvanic skin response FIGURE 8-2. This "gut-level" recognition that a deck is bad happened well before people fully understood or could explain why it was bad. Only after playing much longer did they get to the point where they could explain what was happening with the differing deck payoffs.

Interestingly, a part of the brain that processes emotion may play a big role in our ability to choose well. When clinical patients with orbitofrontal cortex (OFC) dysfunction play the card game, they continue to choose from the bad decks, sometimes even though they know consciously that they are losing money overall. It is as if they do not experience the same emotional reaction to bad events that other players do. These patients point out that our gut reactions to choices are important indicators of what is important to us in the world. Damasio called this a **somatic marker** through which the body reveals a response about an outcome. This physical response may then influence our decision-making processes, both unconsciously and consciously. As a result, our gut reactions may provide a better measure of how we should choose next.

These "**dual processes**" in thinking—slow, deliberative, conscious reasoning versus fast, automatic, and emotional reactions—describe the major ways we think across many tasks (Stanovich & West, 1998). What determines whether we will do one of these two types of thinking? First, people are more likely to rely on the fast and easy strategies if they are tired or pressed for time. When you are feeling stressed, you are much more likely to grab an easy answer (like a cheeseburger). Second, we are much more likely to use deliberative thought if the stakes are high (as in making a decision about a medical procedure) and the decision is infrequent, compared to decisions (like what to have for lunch) that we make over and over again. One mode of thinking is not "better" than the other; rather, giving each decision the appropriate type of effort is the key. Later in this chapter, we will illustrate this difference of slow and careful versus fast and easy, the dual modes of thought.

Intuition The "gut feeling" that leads to a fast and easy conclusion.

Somatic marker A visceral, physiological response that reveals underlying emotion about an event or decision.

Dual processes The two modes of thinking, one fast and easy, one slow and careful.

FIGURE 8-1 Four decks of cards are presented to participants, and they choose which deck to play next. The decks have differing payoffs, so participants learn over time which decks tend to provide better payoffs.
Source: Reproduced from Bechara, A., Damasio, H., Tranel, D., Damasio, A. R. (1997). Deciding advantageously before knowing the advantageous strategy. Science, 275(5304), 1293–1295.

FIGURE 8-2 Average numbers of cards selected from the bad decks versus the good decks, and the mean magnitudes of anticipatory skin conductance responses (SCRs) associated with the same cards.
Source: Reproduced from Bechara, A., Damasio, H., Tranel, D., Damasio, A. R. (1997). Deciding advantageously before knowing the advantageous strategy. Science, 275(5304), 1293–1295.

Metacognition Reflective thoughts about your own thinking processes.

When given a choice between two identical nylon stockings, people still managed to select one over the other and generate an explanation for their choice.

A final question in defining thinking is our awareness of our own thinking processes, also called **metacognition**. You might expect we would be experts on cognition, since we observe our own internal thoughts constantly. However, we are often unaware of the internal mental activities that give rise to our conscious experience of thinking. A physician once asked me, "Isn't thinking really just *random*?" Hopefully, it does not seem too random to him as he performs surgery, but more likely as he drives home and lets his thoughts flow freely. As we observe our own internal thoughts, we find that ideas come to mind spontaneously, new ideas interrupt others, and staying on track to arrive at conclusions can sometimes be very difficult. It is a problem for us to consider what processes are driving our thoughts, what is influencing our decisions, and why we want ice cream. Let us practice "thinking about your thinking": Now, for one minute, stop reading and reflect about your thinking.

What did you notice? You may have found that you had *some* awareness of what you were thinking, what brought ideas to mind, or what caused you to become distracted. However, your own thinking may take place outside of your conscious awareness. A clever example comes from research in which people are asked to say what they think about a decision even when, objectively, there is no real reason for the decision. In one study, people were asked to choose one of two identical nylon stockings and then explain their choice (Nisbett & Wilson, 1977). Logically, there is no reason to prefer one, and people tended to choose the one on the right (as most were right handed). However, people did choose one and then came up with a plausible reason for preferring it, such as, "It is more sheer." We are constantly influenced during thinking in ways we are not consciously aware of, and so we are often left to explain our thinking without key information. In fact, some studies show that trying to think about our own thinking processes can lead to decisions we are *less* happy with (Wilson & Schooler, 1991). So making good decisions may not depend on being aware of our thinking process but, rather, on choosing the right thinking process for a certain situation.

CONCEPT LEARNING CHECK 8.1 | *Defining Thinking*

Consider the dual processes of thinking discussed in this section.

1. Which process would you choose to use when deciding what college to attend? Why?

2. What process would you follow when deciding what to order for lunch today? Why?

8.2 Problem Solving

We solve problems through trial and error, deterministic algorithms, heuristic "guesses," and insight.

- Compare and contrast the processes for problem solving.
- Discuss how bias impacts problem solving.
- Explain problem representation.

Much of our thinking is focused on solving a specific problem; for example, how can I get this paper done before the deadline, or how can I find a ride to the airport? A **problem** is any given situation that differs from a desired goal state, and there is a *nonobvious* way to get from one to the other. Turning on the TV is not a problem when the remote control is in your hand; however, it is a problem when you cannot find the remote! To solve problems, you have to think about how to get from the current state to the **goal** (the situation you want to achieve), and getting there involves some novel thinking. For example, if your goal were to become president of your college student body, how would you go about doing so? Some goals have clear, practiced paths, and some require creative new plans. By studying problem solving, cognitive psychologists have identified key features of successful solutions.

> **Problem** A situation with a starting point, a goal state, and a nonobvious way to get to it.
>
> **Goal** A situation you would like to achieve.

Problem-Solving Methods

The experimental study of problem solving began with some classic demonstrations of thinking (Köhler, 1929). Consider a famous problem called the two string problem (Maier, 1931): The experiment was carried on in a large room in which two cords hung from the ceiling. As a participant, you soon learn that if you hold either cord in one hand, you cannot reach the other cord FIGURE 8-3. The goal is to tie the two cord ends together, and you can use anything in the room: poles, ring stands, clamps, pliers, extension cords, tables, and chairs. People think of solutions such as using the extension cord to lengthen one of the cords, using a pole as an arm extension to pull one string over, and anchoring one string in place with a chair while the other is brought over to it. A third of

FIGURE 8-3 In the two string problem, the participant is asked to tie the ends of two cords together; however, the cords are spaced far enough apart that you can't reach them using just your hands. What solutions can you think of?
Source: Data from Maier, N. R. F. (1931). Reasoning in humans: II. The solution and its appearance in consciousness. Journal of Comparative Psychology, 12, 181–194.

Trial and error Creating a solution, testing to see if it works, and then starting over if unsuccessful.

Generate and test Guess at the answer and see if it works on a trial-and-error basis.

Algorithm A well-defined process that is guaranteed to produce a solution.

Means-end analysis A problem-solving strategy that reduces differences between the current and the goal states.

Heuristic A mental shortcut, or rule of thumb, that may or may not lead to a correct solution.

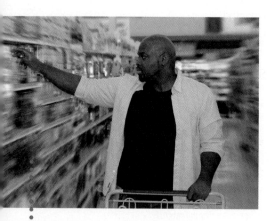

Shoppers often follow heuristic shortcuts, like "bigger boxes are better bargains," rather than computing the best value using math (an algorithm).

participants implement a pendulum, using the pliers as a weight and setting the weighted cord swinging so that it can be caught in position near the other cord. How do we solve problems like the two string problem?

There are a variety of methods to follow in trying to generate solutions to problems. Typically, we use a **trial and error** process in which we create a solution, test to see whether it worked, and then start over if unsuccessful. This method is also known as **generate and test**, because you generate a solution and then test to see whether it is correct. So, in creating your course schedule for next term, you might start by choosing four courses and then find that two of them conflict. Since that solution failed, you would try again to select courses and see if that new set works. Trial and error is a slow method that is likely to lead to failures. It would be a bad choice for something like guessing a locker combination because there are so many possibilities. However, trial and error might work when you need to recover a computer logon password you cannot recall: You may try your past passwords one at a time in hopes that you might come across the solution. When there is a small set of possible solutions, trial and error can work to solve a problem. Though most people start with this approach, it is not a helpful method for a problem like the two string problem because you are not likely to generate a solution.

Sometimes, you want to choose a well-defined process that is guaranteed to produce a solution, called an **algorithm**. For example, if your goal is to find out how much money you have, you would follow an algorithm to identify each money source and its amount and each debt owed, summing them carefully and determining the final correct figure. This requires deliberative thinking (and a pencil and paper, bank statements, a calculator, or a spreadsheet). However, if you are careful in performing the algorithm, you *will* arrive at the correct solution. A useful way to determine whether a process is an algorithm is to think about whether it could be programmed into a computer. If it can, it follows sequential steps that, when done correctly, will lead to the right solution. However, for many problems and for the two string problem, there are no known algorithms (or computer programs) that can devise a solution.

Another problem-solving method is to break problems into subparts. **Means-end analysis** compares differences between where you are now and your goal state (Newell & Simon, 1972). In using this strategy, you try to reduce the differences between the current state and the goal. For example, you may decide to eat a healthier diet. By identifying key differences in how you would like to eat, you can figure out ways to reduce these differences and get you closer to your goal. For example, you might decide to substitute a multigrain bagel for a donut because the bagel has more nutritional value. The means-ends approach may help you with the two string problem: The goal involves having both strings located at the same point in space at the same time. So you can reduce the difference between your current state and the goal state by fixing one of the strings at that meeting point. Thinking this way may break the problem down into the subpart of getting each string to that location (by tying it to a chair or swinging it into place).

Often, even when an algorithm is known, people prefer to take a "mental shortcut" to a solution. For example, suppose you are in the grocery store to buy a box of Cap'n Crunch cereal. There are three boxes available: a 12-ounce box for $2.88, a 17-ounce box for $3.58, and a 27.5-ounce box for $4.50. Which is the best deal? You can use an algorithm like arithmetic to divide the cost by the number of ounces to compare the cost per ounce of each box. This is a difficult and effortful algorithm requiring time, and you may make errors while standing in the aisle. Instead, you may decide to take a shortcut and use a **heuristic**, or mental shortcut that may or may not lead to a correct solution. An example of a heuristic people use in grocery shopping is to choose the largest-size package available because it usually provides the best price (Lave, 1988). By using this heuristic, you will usually get the best deal. However, there are times when it will fail; for example, a promotion may have a smaller-size box marked down to a lower price per ounce. With heuristics, you are using a shortcut method that minimizes the time and effort required to make a selection, and you are willing to settle for the mistakes that will sometimes occur.

The "rules of thumb" provided by heuristics are useful in our day-to-day thinking because they are fast, require little effort, and usually lead to the right answer. For something like grocery shopping, estimation heuristics are a good choice because the cost of an error is not too high. However, if you are building a bridge, you want to follow algorithms guaranteed to get to the correct solution! The main conclusion from psychological research is that people very often use heuristics in their thinking even when more accurate algorithms are available. The reason seems to be that heuristics often lead to good answers and require much less time and effort. For other problems, there are no known algorithms to guide your solution. For example, whom should you marry? Given the uncertainly about what will happen in your future and in the difficulty of predicting whether you will have a happy marriage, it is difficult to determine the best candidate. Your approach to a given problem may involve choosing from a variety of heuristics observed in problem solving, decision making, and reasoning (see **TABLE 8-1**).

New situations automatically bring past experiences to mind from memory. Consequently, we often rely on our past experiences to solve new problems. **Analogy** involves recalling a previous problem with a known solution to apply to a novel, or new, problem. An example is the "curved tube" problem shown in FIGURE 8-4 (Kaiser, McCloskey, & Proffitt, 1986). Once a ball travels through a curved tube, what path will it take when exiting the tube? Even children as young as 4 are able to solve this problem correctly by thinking by analogy: When you see water coming out of a garden hose, it travels in a straight line even if the hose is tangled and twisted. And, in the curved tube problem, this analogy can help you correctly choose the straight path solution. School-age students sometimes choose the curved path, perhaps confused by new knowledge about physics (such as centripetal and centrifugal forces). However, when they view a special-effects video showing a curved path, even these students recognize that it "looks funny" through analogy to their past experiences. While analogy should help to solve problems, studies show people often have difficulty recognizing when a new problem is similar to an old one (Gick & Holyoak, 1980). This is called **lack of transfer**.

Another problem-solving process is called **insight**, or the sudden appearance in consciousness of a solution. We have all experienced the flash of insight, sometimes with a feeling of "Aha!" Insight occurs when the representation of the problem is **restructured**, or changed to alter your perspective. Consider this problem (Davidson & Sternberg, 1984):

> A man has black socks and blue socks in a drawer mixed in a ratio of 4 to 5. It is dark, and so the man cannot see the colors of the socks he removes from the drawer. How many socks must he take out to make sure to have a pair of the same color?

To most people, this looks like a math problem; instead, think about what you do when you put on a pair of socks in the morning. As you do, you may feel insight dawn on you: If there are two colors, you need just three socks to make a pair. In one study, people

Analogy A problem-solving process that makes use of a previous solution.

Lack of transfer The failure to use a past analogy that offers a solution.

Insight The sudden appearance in consciousness of a solution.

Restructuring Changing the representation of a problem to remove unnecessary constraints.

TABLE 8-1 The Role of Information in Cognitive Biases

Information Source	Heuristic Leading to Bias	Correction Method for Bias
Problem Solving		
Irrelevant information	Unnecessary constraints	Change your representation of the problem
Past experience	Mental set	Approach it as if it is a completely novel task
Usual uses and habits	Functional fixedness	Imagine using an object in novel ways
Decision Making		
Schemas in memory	Representativeness	Ignore "what it looks like" and focus on statistics
Recall from memory	Availability	Recall additional possibilities from memory
Description provided	Framing	Restate the problem in neutral or opposite terms
Reasoning		
Initial belief formed	Confirmation bias	Look for contradictory evidence
Existing beliefs	Belief perseverance	Consider the possibility that your belief is wrong
Self-knowledge	Overconfidence	Consider what you don't (and can't) know

Bias A preexisting perspective applied to a problem or decision.

Representation An internal, mental description of a problem or information.

Irrelevant information Knowledge referred to in a problem that is not needed in its solution.

Unnecessary constraint An apparent requirement for a solution that is not really needed.

FIGURE 8-4 The curved tube problem (A), its correct solution (B), and the most common incorrect response (C).
Source: Reproduced from Kaiser, M. K., McCloskey, M., & Proffitt, D. R. (1986). Development of intuitive theories of motion: Curvilinear motion in the absence of external forces. Developmental Psychology, 22(1), 67–71.

A   B   C

were asked to solve math problems or insight problems, and to give a "close to solution?" rating every 15 seconds as they worked. On math problems, more people give higher ratings as time passes. For insight problems, ratings of closeness to solution do not go up during the work period, but stay low right up to the moment when solution occurs (Metcalfe & Wiebe, 1987). Then, suddenly, the ratings rise at once as they see the insightful solution. However, the feeling of insight may not necessarily include a solution. The insight may instead indicate you have found a new way of looking at the problem. Evidence from neuroimaging and event related potential (ERP) studies have identified neurological correlates of the feeling of "Aha!" Insight solutions are associated with a burst of high-frequency neural activity starting about 300 milliseconds *before* participants signaled they had arrived at a solution by pressing a button (Jung-Beeman et al., 2004; Kounios & Beeman, 2009). The location of the activity is in the right anterior temporal lobe FIGURE 8-5.

Biases in Problem Solving

A bias refers to holding a belief that affects your ability to think objectively. In problem solving, **bias** can occur when we approach a problem with past experiences and assumptions that alter our perspective. Often, these beliefs are helpful in finding solutions; however, they can lead to the inability to find solutions because they affect your mental **representation**, or internal description, of the problem. For example, the socks problem above is difficult because it includes **irrelevant information**, or details not needed, about the ratio of socks that makes the problem appear to be a math problem. Sometimes, it is important to reduce the information you have in your representation because it is not needed, or even distracting. In the nine-dot problem FIGURE 8-6 (Burnham & Davis, 1969), we perceive requirements for a solution that are actually **unnecessary constraints**. From the appearance of the rows and columns of dots, we assume the solution must fit inside the apparent "box" of dots. Now, if I tell you that the solution involves going "outside the box" formed by the dots, you may have an idea about how to solve it

FIGURE 8-5 A high-frequency EEG shows activity associated with problem solution. Panel A shows neural activity over time. The activity for "insight" begins just before the response (yellow R). Panel B shows frequency over time, with red areas where insight EEG power is greater than noninsight, beginning 0.3 seconds before the response. Panel C shows the topographic distribution of this neural activity located in the right anterior temporal lobe.

FIGURE 8-6 The nine-dot problem (left) asks the solver to draw four straight lines that go through the middle of all of the dots without taking the pencil off the paper. The solution (right) is possible only by going outside the perceived box of dots.
Source: Data from Jung-Beeman, M. Bowden, E. M., Haberman, J., Frymiare, J. L., Arambel-Liu, S., Greenblatt, R., Reber, P. J., & Kounios, J. (2004). Neural activity when people solve verbal problems with insight. PLoS Biology, 2, 502–505.

(though you will still need to work out a specific solution). The phrase "thinking outside the box," derived from the nine-dot problem (Kihn, 2005), has become synonymous with removing constraints, leading to more creative solutions. Creating an appropriate problem representation, or description of the problem elements, is critical to solving it.

Another type of bias in problem solving is the use of habits we learn from solving past problems. For example, after seeing a series of math problems involving ratios, you will have an even harder time figuring out the answer to the socks problem above. By finding the solution to a series of problems using a specific method first, you will have a harder time switching to a new method. In other words, you have become "stuck in a rut." Your **mental set**, a preexisting state of mind, habit, or attitude, can affect and mislead your attempt to solve a new problem (Luchins, 1942). Once you have latched onto a particular approach, it can be very difficult to consider alternatives, called **fixation**. People often become stuck on a dead end in their solution path, which may block the consideration of alternatives (Kaplan & Simon, 1990). In effect, your initial ideas can limit your effectiveness in solving problems (Smith, 1995).

A related obstacle to solution arises from our previous use of objects in specific ways. In the candle problem FIGURE 8-7 (Duncker, 1945), you are asked to affix a candle to a wall using only a box of tacks, a candle, and a book of matches. There is an object available in the problem that leads to an elegant solution; however, **functional fixedness**, the tendency to see an object as having only a familiar function, prevents us from seeing it (Maier, 1937). In a different version of the study, the objects are presented with the tacks dumped out of the box; now people are much more likely to see the box as a potential holder for the candle and tack it onto the wall for the solution. In order to get around functional fixedness, you need a fresh, unbiased view of the objects and their properties. And once again, to be creative, you need to think "outside the box"; this time, outside the box of tacks!

The biases in our problem solving may be obvious, but we often fail to notice them. When faced with a difficult problem, it often helps to take a fresh perspective toward the problem. Taking a break from the problem, doing something else, and returning with a different mindset can help to break through some problem-solving obstacles. **Incubation** is defined as a period of time in which a problem is set aside prior to further attempts to solve it. An early study suggested an incubation period produced better solution rates than working straight through for the same amount of time (Silveira, 1972). A meta-analysis of incubation studies found that tasks with open-ended solutions show more benefit from incubation (Sio & Ormerod, 2009). One possible explanation is that you are able to approach the problem after a break with a new perspective. It is also possible that you will be exposed to information during the incubation interval that might help you to solve the problem (Seifert et al., 1995). When in doubt, taking a break may be helpful in jump-starting you toward a solution.

Mental set An existing state of mind, habit, or attitude that affects new problem solving.

Fixation Getting stuck on an approach to a problem and failing to see alternative approaches.

Functional fixedness Seeing objects for use only in their intended roles.

Incubation A period of time in which a problem is set aside prior to further attempts to solve it.

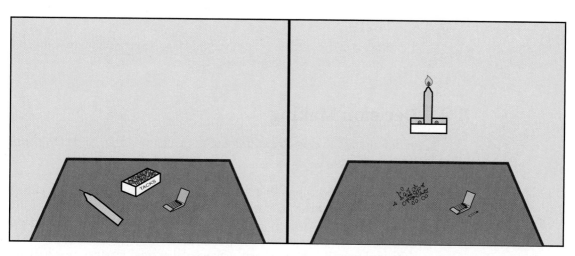

FIGURE 8-7 How can you affix the candle to the wall and light it?
Source: Data from Duncker, K. (1945). On problem solving. Psychological Monographs, 58*(270)*.

Deliberative practice
Working on skills just beyond your current level of comfort.

Decisions Thinking that requires a choice among alternatives.

Judgment Making an informed guess about something unknown or uncertain.

Uncertainty The state of not being determined, either because the event has not occurred or cannot be known logically.

Expertise

How much practice do you need to get better at problem solving? Studies of skill building over time, including chess experts, pianists, and athletes, found that approximately 10,000 hours of practice are needed to produce outstanding performance (Ericsson et al., 1993) FIGURE 8-8. A great deal of time and experience are needed to acquire a large enough knowledge base to excel (Chi, Glaser, & Farr, 1988). Experts have *more* knowledge, and their knowledge is *organized* around important patterns in the domain (Chase & Simon, 1973; Chi, Feltovich, & Glaser, 1981; Ericsson & Ward, 2007). For example, a chess expert can look at a board during play and see the styles of attack and the history of the game so far, while a novice may recognize only specific moves (de Groot, 1965). This knowledge enables experts to think in larger units, tackling problems in bigger steps. A most surprising conclusion from this research is that experts are made, not born. All performers, including the most naturally gifted or talented, need a minimum of approximately 10 years of intense practice before they can win at international levels in highly competitive domains. **Deliberative practice** (focusing on tasks just beyond your current level of competence and comfort) leads to success (Ericsson et. al, 1993). The good news is that *anyone* can be an expert: All it takes is 10 years!

FIGURE 8-8 The development of expert performance as related to age. Elite performers typically reach their peak career performance in the middle to late 20s for vigorous sports, and two decades later for chess, billiards, arts, and sciences.
Source: Reproduced from Ericsson, K. A., & Ward, P. (2007). Capturing the naturally occurring superior performance of experts in the laboratory. Current Directions in Psychological Science, 16*(6), 346–350.*

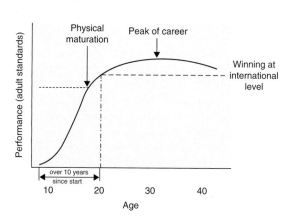

CONCEPT LEARNING CHECK 8.2   *Applying Methods of Problem Solving*

For each example, determine which type of problem solving strategy is illustrated.

A. Generate and test

B. Algorithm

C. Means-ends analysis

D. Analogy

1. _____ Let me try to think of a good name for our team. How about Sunday Strikers?

2. _____ I will try 1-1-1, then 1-1-2, then 1-1-3, and keep going until the locker opens.

3. _____ This chemistry lab reminds me of cooking, so I had better measure each portion carefully.

4. _____ I will get to my home in LA by first flying into town, then taking a taxi to the house.

8.3   Decision Making

Rather than following algorithms, our decisions are often guided by heuristics.

■ Examine the pros and cons of heuristic use in decision making.

In addition to solving problems, we are called upon to make **decisions** where we must choose among alternatives, or whether to take some action. **Judgment** refers to a type of decision making in which we project beyond what we already know and draw our "best guess" conclusion. Judgments take place under **uncertainty**: That is, we do not know definitively whether the defendant committed the crime, whether we will enjoy this first date, or whether it will rain tomorrow. However, we often must use whatever evidence we have to make our best estimate of what might be true, or most likely. In sum, the evidence suggests people often use heuristics, or shortcuts, in decision making that can lead to biases and errors. This main conclusion led to a 2002 Nobel Memorial Prize in Economics for Daniel Kahneman for his work with Amos Tversky (1937–1996).

Algorithms in Decision Making

Just as in problem solving, there are algorithms available to help you determine the best decision. For judgments, we can use **probability theory** to take into account all contingencies and their likelihoods and determine the best estimate of what will occur. For example, in judging whether to go camping on July 4, you could look up the weather on this date for the past 100 years to determine how many times it rained, providing a statistical estimate. Similarly, if you are deciding whether to drive or fly home for Thanksgiving, you can create a **decision tree** showing all of your choices (share ride, drive, bus, train, plane) and weigh each one based on its value to you (the cost, ease of scheduling, and risks; Hastie, 2001) FIGURE 8-9. Then, with all of the options given specific values, you can choose the best one. Algorithms using principles of probability and statistics provide methods for how we "should" make judgments—but do we use them?

Many people find it difficult and time consuming to use algorithms in their everyday lives (Arkes, 1991). Even when you are presented with this information, you may not

> **Probability theory** A statistical algorithm that takes into account all contingencies and their likelihoods to determine the best estimate of an uncertain event.
>
> **Decision tree** A decision-support tool that uses a tree-like graph of options, including chance event, resources, cost, and value.
>
> **Representativeness heuristic** Making a guess based on how much the situation "looks like" something known.

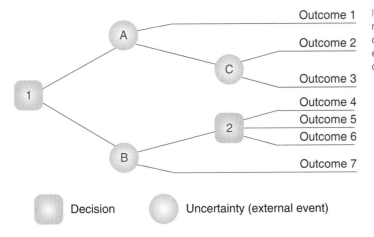

FIGURE 8-9 A decision tree is a method for analyzing the possible choices, along with uncontrollable events, to forsee potential outcomes of all possible choices.

Outcome 1
Outcome 2
Outcome 3
Outcome 4
Outcome 5
Outcome 6
Outcome 7

Decision   Uncertainty (external event)

use it. For example, the National Highway Traffic Safety Administration estimates that your chance of getting in a car accident increases by 300% if you are talking on your cellular phone. Will this information stop you from talking while driving? Using the algorithm to determine the answer, it is rational to stop calling or texting while driving! Yet you may still choose to do it. We must be influenced by other factors as well when we make decisions.

Heuristics in Decision Making

Just as with problem solving, people often use heuristics, or rules of thumb, to help us make decisions (Nisbett & Ross, 1980). For example, imagine you go to a class on environmental studies, and you know that 30% of its students are prelaw and 70% are environmental studies majors. You meet Chris, who is wearing a suit and carrying a leather briefcase FIGURE 8-10. Would you guess Chris is a lawyer? Most people would; however, since there are more environmental studies students in the class, that is, statistically, a better guess. Instead, we are influenced by the **representativeness heuristic**; that is, whether things "look like" what we expect (Kahneman & Tversky, 1972). If Chris looks more like a pre-law major, we make that assumption even though, statistically, it is not as likely. Most of the time, using the representativeness heuristic leads

FIGURE 8-10 Would you guess these are more likely to be future environmentalists or future lawyers?

Availability heuristic Using the ease of memory access as a measure of the likelihood of an event.

Framing effect A bias in decisions based on the description of the problem.

Loss aversion Preferring options that will avoid losing rather than maximize gains.

Choice overload The presence of too many options, causing problems in decisions.

We tend to overestimate how often events occur if they are readily available in memory; events covered by the press seem to us to occur more often than ones not receiving coverage.

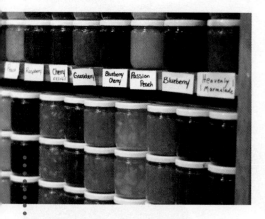

It seems decisions would improve if more options are made available. How many choices are enough, and can there be too many?

to a quick and easy decision that is often correct (Kunda & Nisbett, 1986). However, "judging a book by its cover" can lead to errors, and in important ways. Representativeness can lead to judgments based on stereotypes, in which assumptions are unfairly made based on gender, ethnicity, and socioeconomic status. First impressions and are just one small sample of someone's behavior are often inaccurate.

Another source of information used in decisions is what is already in your memory. When thinking about familiar things, this information comes readily to mind, allowing us to conclude it happens frequently. For example, you have likely heard of Michael Jackson, but perhaps not Johnny Hallyday, so you would be correct in guessing that Jackson has sold more records. The **availability heuristic** is the tendency to estimate the likelihood of an event in terms of how easily it can be recalled (Tversky & Kahneman, 1974). The effort in retrieving the information determines your judgment of how frequently it occurs. This heuristic can backfire: Has Johnny Hallyday sold more music than Jennifer Lopez? From the availability heuristic, you may incorrectly say Lopez has sold more. Another example is that people overestimate the frequency of death by car accident, tornados, and botulism while underestimating the frequency by diabetes, stroke, and asthma (Slovic et al., 1979). This may occur because media coverage more frequently reports the first set, leading to greater accessibility of examples in memory (Schwarz et al., 1991).

Decision making can also be biased by the way the choices are presented, known as the **framing effect** (Tversky & Kahneman, 1981). For example, would you prefer to purchase ground beef with a label saying "75% lean" or one saying "25% fat"? The fat content is the same, but the information "frame" led 82% of participants to choose the "75% lean" beef (Keren, 2007). A study with beachgoers during spring break showed that framing of information can have direct effects on behavior. People were approached on the beach and given a free coupon toward the purchase of condoms. One coupon boasted a "95% effectiveness" rate, while the other mentioned a "5% failure" rate. The safety information was the same, but the decision framing made a difference in how many coupons were redeemed. The "95% effective" coupons were much more likely to be used for purchases (Linville, Fischer, & Fischhoff, 1993). How we tell the story can impact people's understanding of the relevant information. In all cases, framing effects follow a simple pattern: People try to make choices that will minimize losses, called **loss aversion** (Tversky & Kahneman, 1991). People prefer to make a choice that involves the least risk and avoids any chance of loss.

How can we avoid making decision errors based on heuristics? One way to try to "debias" your thinking is to examine how any given information can help—or hurt—your decision making. We assume that information in front of us is relevant and informative about the situation. Imagine that it could be in error, or just not informative for making a good decision. One strategy is to either ignore or at least question the information you are given. Another strategy is to "change the frame" by thinking of risks or probabilities over time. For example, some drivers fail to wear seat belts every time because they know the probability of a fatal accident on any one trip is very small (1 in 3.5 million "person trips"). However, over 50 years of driving (around 40,000 trips), the probability is 0.01, and for a disabling accident, 0.33 (Slovic et al., 1978). People asked to think about this longer-term perspective were more likely to say they would buckle up every time.

In today's world, you may often face decisions in which *too much* information is available. **Choice overload** refers to having too many choices to handle in decision making. If you were buying a new jam, how many options would you like to choose from? Should the number of options matter? A field study showed that people might be happier when facing *fewer* choices! Iyengar and Lepper (2000) offered grocery shoppers the choice of either 24 new jam flavors or just 6. Shoppers stopped at a table for a taste and were given a $1 coupon. Would having more choices result in more jam purchases? The results showed people presented with more choices were *more* likely to taste jams but *less* likely to buy one! FIGURE 8-11 We may be overstating the appeal of variety when what we really prefer is the same strawberry jam every day.

In such cases, when we are faced with too many choices, we may be more likely to resort to heuristics. For example, in the supermarket, we could determine the best buy using math (Lave, 1988). But, we may instead choose the bigger "bargain" bottle

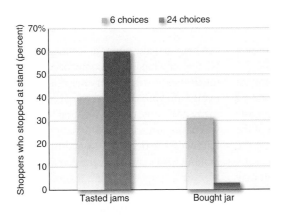

FIGURE 8-11 Percentage of customers who tasted vs. purchased jam based on number of choices presented. *Source: Data from Iyengar, S. S., & Lepper, M. R. (2000). When choice is demotivating: Can one desire too much of a good thing?* Journal of Personality and Social Psychology, 79*(6),* 995–1006.

or whichever is on sale this week. When we generate rules to handle frequent decisions, it saves us the time and effort of deciding. For example, you may have a rule about what you order to drink when in a restaurant. While we may believe "variety is the spice of life," we tend to choose our favorites when the time comes (Schwartz et al., 2002). And, we are influenced by factors such as what *other* people are ordering. One study found that groups of people ordering beer privately tended to all choose the same kind FIGURE 8-12; however, when they took turns ordering aloud (as in the usual restaurant situation), people chose different types of beer, apparently to avoid making the same choice as others (Ariely & Levav, 2000). This suggests we have a social expectation that variety in choice is good, and we feel compelled to follow it despite our personal preferences for our old favorite. It may be important to consider your gut reaction when making choices, and let emotion be your guide when the decision is one of personal preference.

FIGURE 8-12 When you order your drink privately, you may order differently than when you hear others' orders.

CRITICAL THINKING APPLICATION

What do experts recommend as strategies for making good decisions? When the decision is important, it is worthwhile to take extra care to consider all possible consequences, along with ways to increase your alternative choices. For example, imagine that you have several options for the upcoming summer break, including an internship in marketing in New York City, a summer job in a social service agency in your college town, or the job you had in your hometown last year, now accompanied by a substantial raise. Each alternative has many advantages and disadvantages, so which one is the best option for you?

Researchers have identified a variety of methods to help you weigh your options (Yates, 1990). One approach keeps things simple by selecting just one most important aspect to focus on within the decision, called the Single-Feature Model. For example, you may decide that your financial needs must take precedence, so no matter how tempting the other offers, living at home

and getting more pay takes priority. A second approach, called Elimination by Aspects (Tversky, 1972), involves looking at each alternative and ruling out ones that do not meet your minimum requirements. For example, you may decide you need to earn at least $250 each week and then rule out the social service alternative because it cannot provide that salary. Finally, you may, with the

(Continues)

help of a pencil and paper, consider each option on each of its features, rating them on a scale. So, the marketing job is in New York (+10 rating for location) and provides a good salary (+5 rating for salary) but will have expensive living costs (−10 on costs). Once you have rated each of the features for each of the options, you add up the ratings to see which alternative has a better score.

When you do a decision analysis, you may be surprised by the results: Even though, on paper, working at home is the "best" option, your emotions may make it difficult to give up the opportunity to be in New York or the rewards of helping others in the social service job. The exercise of writing down the pros and cons and considering what is most important to you can help to make your gut feelings more evident. No matter what the outcome, becoming aware of the desires you feel is very helpful in making and living with your decision (Naqvi et al., 2006). For many decisions, there is no "best" choice because we cannot foresee what will happen in the future following the decision. In addition, if you keep looking, you may discover other alternatives that are just as appealing (say, a summer course on film making in San Francisco). At some point, people choose to **satisfice** (Simon, 1955), or find a choice that is satisfactory given what is known. With the large number of decisions we face daily and the uncertainty about the future, we often have to decide when we have arrived at a "good enough" decision.

CONCEPT LEARNING CHECK 8.3   *Recognizing Heuristics in Decision Making*

For each heuristic below, give an example and identify how it makes difficult or time-consuming decisions easier.

1. Representativeness

2. Availability

3. Framing

4. Satisficing

8.4   Reasoning

Rather than always rational, our reasoning may be biased by what we think we know.

- Explain how presented knowledge may bias reasoning.
- Demonstrate how beliefs impact reasoning.

Satisfice Finding a satisfactory choice rather than the best one.

Reasoning Thinking through our knowledge and beliefs to reach a conclusion.

Inductive reasoning Generalizing from specific information to form a rule.

Deductive reasoning A logical task in which new assertions are derived from what is known.

Syllogism A simple deduction task with three statements or premises.

A third type of thinking is called **reasoning**, or evaluating information (including facts, assumptions, and beliefs) to draw a conclusion. In **inductive reasoning**, we move from some specific information to a more general conclusion. For example, you might see several stories about a pit bull attack and conclude that this type of dog is more aggressive than others. In inductive reasoning, you draw from specific instances to conclude in general terms, even though it may not always be correct. The use of stereotypes and schemas illustrate that people readily draw conclusions from a small amount of specific information. Alternatively, in **deductive reasoning**, you start with a general rule and apply it to a specific instance. If I know that "All state residents are charged in-state tuition" and you mention you are a state resident, I can conclude you are charged in-state tuition. Deductive reasoning involves drawing valid, new assertions from what is already known.

Algorithms in Reasoning

The rules of logic provide algorithms for drawing conclusions; unfortunately, studies in psychology show that people do not use the rules of logic very often (Wilkins, 1928). You may recognize logic problems called **syllogisms**; for example, "All As are Bs.

EXAMPLE 1

A. Some As are Bs;
All Bs are Cs:

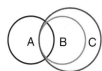

Therefore, all As are Cs:

Invalid

B. Some pets are dogs;
All dogs are mammals:

Therefore, all pets are mammals:

Invalid

EXAMPLE 2

A. All As are Bs;
Some Bs are Cs:

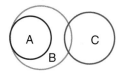

Therefore, some As are Cs:

Invalid

B. All dogs are mammals;
Some mammals are pets:

Therefore, some dogs are pets:

Valid?

FIGURE 8-13 Mental models for examples one and two show there are two different ways to interpret the given statements. For example 1, "some" can mean some or all; and in problem 2, not enough information is given to say whether A and C overlap. So, you have to keep both possibilities in mind to answer the question. In addition, in example 1, the content in 1B helps you see the right answer (what about geckos?), while in 2, the content in B (we know dogs are pets!) can mislead you.

All Bs are Cs. Does it follow that all As are Cs?" People are able to solve simple logic problems, but they make errors on the majority of problems (Revlis, 1975). Instead, people try to reason logically by creating a **mental model** (a spatial representation of the possibilities; Johnson-Laird, 2001). People construct models, like the ones shown in FIGURE 8-13, to help them think about the problem. These models help us to consider possibilities that may not be obvious without the diagram. For example, "some As are Bs" can means that some As are not Bs, or that *all* As are Bs, leading to a common logical error. Another factor in solving logic problems is that people are influenced by the **content**, or meaning, of the words used in the problem, even though they do not matter in logic. Consider the same problem in a concrete context: "All boys are children. All children are humans. Does it follow that all boys are humans?" People are more likely to get this version right because the content of the question—boys, children, and humans—is familiar, and they can judge its truth without using logic. Studies of deduction have demonstrated that people are very prone to judge statements on their content rather than on their logic (Johnson-Laird & Byrne, 2002).

To illustrate, a problem called the **Wason selection task** (Wason and Johnson-Laird, 1972) asked people to determine which of four cards have to be turned over to test a rule FIGURE 8-14. The rule is, "If a vowel is on one side, an even number is on the other side." This task is notoriously difficult; most people check the card that shows the rule is followed (card a), but they fail to check the card that would show if the rule was *not* followed (card d). However, a new version of the problem was created that showed much better success (Griggs & Cox, 1982). This time, FIGURE 8-15 the rule was, "If they are drinking beer, they must be over 21." Now, people recognize that they have to check the "underage card" (card d) to make sure no one is breaking the rule. When the problem is framed as "checking for cheaters," people were much more likely to check for cases that

Mental model A visual, spatial, or content-based representationof a problem or situation.

Content The surface meaning of the words in a problem.

Wason selection task A card game that requires checking for rule violations.

E   K   4   7

FIGURE 8-14 Which card or cards must you turn over to determine whether this rule is correct: "If a vowel is on one side, an even number is on the other side."
Source: Data from Wason, P. C., & Johnson-Laird, P. N. (1972).
Psychology of reasoning: Structure and content. *Cambridge, MA: Harvard University Press.*

FIGURE 8-15 Which card or cards must you turn over to determine whether this rule is correct: "If they are drinking beer, they must be over 21."
Source: Data from Cheng, P. N., & Holyoak, K. J. (1985). Pragmatic reasoning schemas. Cognitive Psychology, *17, 391–416.*

disconfirm the rule (Cheng & Holyoak, 1985). Content is highly influential in reasoning, so that there are some topics that people find very challenging to reason about and others about which they are able to be much more logical. Evolutionary theorists have argued that our ability to reason may have been affected by our long history of living in social groups and the resulting need to reason about interactions with others (Cosmides, 1989). This may have led to a survival advantage for those able to reason about social matters like catching cheaters.

Biases in Reasoning

The information that we have in memory is used to process new information. As a result, our thinking processes are also affected by the **confirmation bias**, in which it is easier to process and incorporate new information that is consistent with what we already know (Klayman, 1985). As a result, we tend to seek out information that confirms what we know rather than looking for new evidence that might prove us wrong. Consider a detective working on a crime case: She will look for witnesses to verify that the suspect was in the crime location, but may not look for witnesses to identify the suspect in other places at that time. We follow through on our beliefs by "piling on" new evidence consistent with them. In its extreme form, this can cause us to discount or ignore conflicting information when it is available. In a study with law students, their initial assessment of guilt following reading about a case also determined how likely they were to pursue further investigation of it (Rassin et al., 2010). The schemas that organize information in memory, lead us to predict and expect information in the world to match.

Cultural styles of reasoning may produce some variation in how people handle discrepant information. Consider whether you agree with these statements:

A. Nothing is identical to itself because everything is dynamic and changeable over time.

B. Contradictions like "good and bad" and "old and new" exist in the same object or event.

C. Nothing is ever isolated or independent, but instead, everything is related.

These principles capture aspects of dialectical thinking, which involves accepting contradiction among ideas FIGURE 8-16. Peng and Nisbett (1999) found differences in how people think about contradictory or dialectical ideas based on their cultural background. Specifically, they found evidence that when Chinese and American students were presented

Confirmation bias
Seeking out information consistent with what is believed to be true.

FIGURE 8-16 In dialectical thinking, opposing ideas are considered valid at the same time, and a synthesis is created.

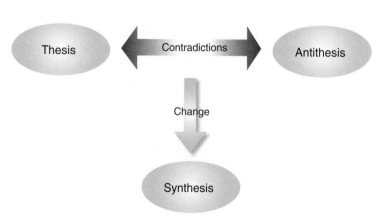

with contradictions from everyday social life, they differed in their responses. When given scenarios about conflicts between mothers and daughters, Americans tended to give responses that were one-sided (e.g., "Mothers should respect their daughters' independence"). Chinese students, in contrast, found merit and fault on both sides (e.g., "The mothers and daughters have failed to understand each other"). Of course, while both groups are capable of thinking dialectically and logically ("No statement can be both true or false"), they differed in how often they used specific styles of thinking. The style of thinking was more likely to be dialectical in nature, reflecting both "black and white," when from Chinese students. So cultural influences can alter our characteristic ways of reasoning.

Across cultures, when we hold beliefs, we try very hard to maintain them, even in the face of conflicting evidence. Once established, we have a tendency to reject evidence against our beliefs and favor evidence that supports them, called **belief perseverance**. In one study, students both for and against the death penalty were given "information from research studies" (Lord, Ross, & Lepper, 1979). Some of the reports provided evidence that the death penalty is an effective crime deterrent, and others offered evidence that it has no effect on crime rates. For example, one study reported was: "Palmer & Crandall (1977) compared murder rates in 10 pairs of neighboring states with different capital punishment laws. In 8 of the 10 pairs, murder rates were *higher* in the state *with* capital punishment. The research opposes the deterrent effect of the death penalty." The students interpreted this study differently based on their existing beliefs. A proponent of the death penalty concluded, "It seems that the researchers studied a carefully selected group of states and that they were careful in interpreting the results." An opponent of the death penalty viewed the same report and said, "There might be very different circumstances between the two sets of states, even though they were sharing a border." No matter what their opinion was, the students raised more doubts and criticism about the evidence that was *against* their existing belief and claimed the evidence in favor of their belief was stronger. If we only accept evidence that supports our beliefs and reject other information, our beliefs become impervious to evidence. We stop looking to see *whether* our beliefs are right and look for evidence *that* they are right. These reasoning errors can make it quite difficult to change our beliefs even when overwhelming evidence is presented.

Perhaps as a result of these processes, we are also very prone to show **overconfidence** about our beliefs, in which we overestimate how likely we are to be correct. In these studies, people are asked about facts and then asked to estimate how likely they are to be correct in their answers (e.g., "What is the capital of Bolivia? How sure are you of your answer?"). People consistently overestimate the odds of their being correct by about 15% (Koriat et al., 1980). People are also overconfident about how well they drive, how quickly they can get tasks done, and whether they are doing well on a test (Dunning et al., 2004). The problem may be that you know a lot about what you know; but, by definition, you *do not* know what you do not know. In fact, studies have shown that the *less* knowledge you have in a domain, the *more* likely you are to overestimate your success in it (Kruger & Dunning, 1999). These factors may at last explain why Sam was so ready to fall for my April Fool's joke about Uma Thurman. Sam has a healthy self-image, so why would Uma Thurman not want to date him? Sam was perhaps overconfident about his own ability to interest possible dates and failed to consider what other options Uma Thurman may have. Of course, perhaps Sam was right; so, I would like to apologize here to Sam, and to Uma!

In problem solving, decision making, and reasoning, we have seen repeated examples of how heuristic use may be fast and easy, often leading to good outcomes. However, heuristics can also be viewed as biases that lead you astray in your thinking. The heuristics and biases in this chapter are shown in Table 8-1, along with suggestions of ways to correct your thinking. Of course, noticing your own biases is not trivial; in fact, studies have shown that people can be unaware of their own cognitive biases. When judging your own possible bias, you tend to rely on introspection; however, for other people, you may think of other ways to assess their bias (Pronin, Lin, & Ross, 2002). Just as in overconfidence, you have more information about your internal thinking, and that may mislead you rather than help you recognize your limitations in thinking. Metacognition, or the ability to reflect on your own thinking, may be limited in recognizing the use of

Belief perseverance
Holding onto a belief in the face of evidence against it.

Overconfidence Being more certain about your beliefs than you should be.

heuristics and resulting biases. As an alternative, ask someone else what they think about your reasoning: Our peers may be able to provide more accurate assessments of how we are doing in our thinking processes.

CONCEPT LEARNING CHECK 8.4   *Practicing Reasoning*

Consider the need to reason about whether you are prepared for your upcoming test on this material. Suppose that, after studying, you decide you are ready for the exam. How might each of these factors influence the validity of your conclusion? And how might you correct for these influences?

1. Content effects

2. Confirmation bias

3. Belief perseverance

4. Overconfidence

8.5   Language

Learning a language provides evidence of special thinking skills.

- Define language and describe the unique characteristics of human language.
- Describe the theories of language acquisition.

Learning theorist B. F. Skinner famously referred to thinking as "sub-vocal speech" (McGuigan, 1970). He meant that we cannot know what is occurring inside the mind, but we can observe the communications it produces. **Language**, one form of communication, is a core and defining process of human thinking and it identifies the human species as different from all others. While many animals have elaborate and sophisticated communication systems ("It's me!" "Where are you guys?" "Look out for that owl!"), only human communication meets some definitions of a "language."

What Is a "Language"?

Why is this? A few key properties separate human language use from communications in other species. First, our language has **semanticity**, or meaning. While animals likely express a great variety of experiences and emotions through squeaks and growls, human language offers meaningful units that, in combination, convey meaning quite unlike their sounds. A high school graduate knows about 45,000 different words, and a college graduate at least twice that amount (Miller, 1991). Our language has a code for meaning that is extensive beyond the one hundred basic sounds we are capable of making. Another property is **generativity**, the capacity to use a finite set of words and rules for combining them to generate an endless variety of unique things to say. In fact, whenever you begin to suspect that every possible combination of words has already been expressed, someone invents something like "twittering." Finally, our language includes **displacement**, the ability to communicate about things that are not in our immediate surroundings. Imagine what a limitation it would be if we were unable to refer to objects, locations, and people not present, or to express abstract or imaginary ideas. Our language provides a new method of thinking that takes us far beyond the world in front of us.

Language Structure

There are at least seven thousand distinct languages worldwide, and tens of thousands of differing dialects. Each is based on the same structures, though they differ in which specific elements are included. The smallest units of speech are **phonemes**, the basic sounds of all languages. English has up to 45 distinct phonemes, such as *t*, *sh*, and *ch*. The smallest unit that carries meaning is called a **morpheme**. For example, *dog* is a morpheme, but *dof* is not, even though each contains three phonemes. Every **word** has one or more morphemes, including prefixes like *anti-* and suffixes like *-able*. Combining groups of words leads to

---

Language A form of thinking used to communicate with others and ourselves.

Semanticity Containing meaning or reference to things in the world.

Generativity The capacity to use a finite set to create endless variety of unique combinations.

Displacement The ability to refer to things not visible in our immediate surroundings.

Phonemes The basic sounds of human languages.

Morpheme The smallest unit of sounds that carries meaning.

Word A meaningful pattern of sound defined within a language.

phrases, and phrases are then combined into **sentences**. An organized sequence of words can convey facts, hypotheses, questions, requests, intentions, and thoughts.

The organization of words within a language, or **grammar**, involves two levels: the **surface structure**, or the ordering of a sequence of words in time, and the **deep structure**, or the composition of meaning within a phrase FIGURE 8-17. You may recall drawing sentence trees to learn proper grammar in school. These trees capture the difference between the surface structure, such as "The horse that raced past the barn fell," and the underlying deep structure meaning, "The horse (that raced past the barn) fell" (Frazier & Rayner, 1982). Linguists study how languages create meaning through the words and rules of combination they allow. Psycholinguists show how the language is used, how it impacts comprehension, and what is later recalled from memory. For example, consider this story:

> There is an interesting story about the telescope. In Holland, a man named Lippershey was an eye-glass maker. One day his children were playing with some lenses. They discovered that things seemed very close if two lenses were held about a foot apart. Lippershey began experimenting, and his "spyglass" attracted much attention. He sent a letter to Galileo, the great Italian scientist. Galileo at once realized the importance of the discovery and set about to build an instrument of his own. He used an old organ pipe with one lens curved out and the other in. On the first clear night he pointed the glass toward the sky. He was amazed to find the empty dark spaces filled with gleaming stars! Night after night Galileo climbed to a high tower, sweeping the sky with his telescope. One night he saw Jupiter, and to his great surprise discovered near it three bright stars.

Now, write down the story without looking back at the text. What do you recall? Sachs (1967) measured people's memory for specific sentences either right away, after they had read another 80 syllables of story, or after they had read another 160 syllables. The results are shown in FIGURE 8-18. He found that people could correctly identify the

Phrase Two or more words combined to convey meaning.

Sentence Organized sequence of words that conveys facts, hypotheses, questions, requests, intentions, and thoughts.

Grammar Rules within a language that determine whether a sentence is properly formed and complete.

Surface structure The ordering of a sequence of words in time.

Deep structure The meaning composed by a phrase or sentence.

FIGURE 8-17 A tree diagram maps out the words in a sentence, organizing them into the parts of language that reveal their "deep structure" or underlying meaning.

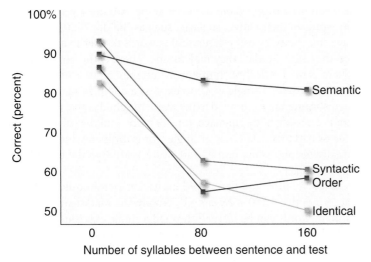

FIGURE 8-18 After reading a story, only semantics, or the meaning of the text (green), stays available in memory.
Source: Adapted from Sachs, J. (1967). Recognition memory for syntactic and semantic aspects of connected discourse. Perception and Psychophysics, 2, 437–442.

Gist The semantic meaning of a sentence.

Paraphrase A description of the same meaning using different elements.

Pragmatics The social context of language that adds to its meaning.

Extralinguistic factors Information outside of language that aids in comprehension.

Babbling The initial vocalizing performed by babies learning to speak.

Holophrastic The use of a single word to represent more complex ideas in early language learning.

semantic structure, order, syntactic structure, and the identical sentence if tested right away. However, after reading further, the only format recalled was the semantic structure. People preserve the semantics, or **gist**, of the information, but they "forget" other aspects of the language expression. After reading, you can recall a **paraphrase** or description of the meaning it contained, but you do not preserve other linguistic elements.

Of course, language is a social vehicle, and the **pragmatics**, or social context, of language is also critical to comprehension. Consider the question, "Can you pass the salt?" If you answer, "yes," you are answering the literal meaning of the question, but not the pragmatic meaning, which is, "Give me the salt!" Studies by Gibbs (1986) showed that you are actually faster to process the intended meaning ("Pass the salt!") than the literal meaning ("Are you able to pass the salt?") for these types of indirect requests. If you listen carefully to speech, you will see that we often use the pragmatics of the situation around us to guide our understanding. For example, when someone says, "Good job!" to you, they may be sincerely complimenting you, or insulting you by being sarcastic. Determining which meaning the speaker intends is part of communication, but it depends on **extralinguistic factors**—that is, information outside of the literal content of language that aids in comprehension.

Many extralinguistic factors play into our comprehension of meaning in communication. For example, the speaker's intonation ("Good job?") can suggest a question. Facial expressions also provide cues, where falling down laughing might suggest they were being sarcastic. Gestures such as shaking the head, pointing, or giving a "thumbs up" also play a critical role in deriving meaning from communication. For all of these reasons, the medium of communication makes an important difference in how easily we understand each other. Over a phone, by text or e-mail, or even video link, important cues about the other person can be degraded. Studies have found that, despite advances in technology, no medium produces better communication between people than face-to-face interaction (Baltes et al., 2002). Given the long history of human evolution, it makes sense that we came to rely on many cues from the speaker in interpreting the meaning behind communications.

Language Development

Stop to think for a moment about how long you have been in school and how many years of instruction have gone into the level of knowledge you have attained. Now think about this: Children of all cultures absorb the words and grammar of language without any instruction at all! Just by being exposed to language, children learn an average of nine words per day between ages 1 and 6 and average around 14,000 words by then. They also learn to use rules of grammar that are often too complicated even for adults to explain. While some children may learn to speak earlier than others, and some may struggle with language, the sequence of milestones in development is the same for all (Brown, 1973).

Newborns cry to communicate. In the second month of life, infants begin using their tongues to coo, making sounds like *oh* and *ah*. At about 4 months, babies begin **babbling**, vocalizing in ways that sound like human speech. These three stages are consistent regardless of the language heard (and occur even in babies that cannot hear). However, sounds not used in your own language (e.g., for Japanese speakers, the phoneme "r" is not present) are eventually dropped out of the babbling. Around 1 year, babies produce their first, short words in their native language, such as "ba" for "bottle." Even year-old toddlers display semanticity by using recognizable words to refer to specific meanings. However, when they say, "Bottle," they may mean, "There is the bottle," or "I want a bottle," or "Where is my bottle?" Such one-word utterances are called **holophrastic**, referring to this early use of a single word to express a complex idea (Braine, 1971). Though the linguistic utterance is limited to the word, the child is able to convey actions, desires, and emotions using body language, tone of voice, and the surrounding context (the dinner table or nap time). This use of single words for increasingly complex ideas ("bottle" eventually becomes "my bottle" and "want bottle") is the foundation of the child's growing vocabulary.

For the next few months, toddlers' word mastery increases quickly, from 5 at 12 months to 30 at 18 months to 250 at 2 years old (Woodward, Markman, & Fitzsimmons, 1994). Interestingly, words can be learned through a single exposure (as anyone who has ever uttered a bad word in front of a toddler already knows). What do babies talk about? They express their desires (people, toys, "more") and point out things that move (dogs, cars, birds). Around 2 years of age, their vocabulary explodes to hundreds of new words each year. Toddlers also begin **telegraphic speech**, in which they combine two- and three-word phrases ("More milk" for "I want more milk"). Exposure to enriched environments, including *Sesame Street* on TV, can increase vocabularies more rapidly (Rice et al., 1990). As they enter grade school, children's vocabulary continues to expand, and they construct longer and more complex sentences. They display generativity, constructing phrases of their own they have never heard said by others. They learn to correctly apply rules of grammar, such as using the past tense, plurals, and pronouns. For example, initially, children learn that you can add "-ed" to the end of a word to say it happened already, such as "added," "played," and "barked." They may **overregularize** the rule, adding "-ed" to words where the past tense does not require it, such as "runned," "drinked," and "falled" (Marcus, 1995). Eventually, the unusual past tenses ("ran," "drank," fell") are learned as well. The unique, rule-breaking variations are the most difficult to acquire, as any English as a Second Language learner will tell you. By speaking in the past tense, children display the property of displacement, or referring to events no longer in the immediate environment.

Later in grade school, children begin to understand that words can have double meanings. After visiting the petting zoo, 6-year-old Stephanie held up her chicken nugget at dinner and said, "Isn't it funny that 'chicken' sounds just like 'chicken'?" Young children find knock-knock jokes so funny because they are beginning to realize that one word can have two very different meanings ("Knock knock." "Who's there?" "Dewey." "Dewey who?" "Do we have to go to school today?") Later in grade school, children begin to understand abstract concepts, like "mammals," "freedom," and "abstract." Metaphors, analogies, and adages become more interpretable, such as, "The grass is always greener on the other side of the fence" (Vosniadou, 1987). These developmental milestones are quite consistent across gender, language, and cultures. What would happen if children were not exposed to a rich language environment as they learn? Would language develop if the child was not surrounded by other speakers? Of course, no one would attempt an experiment that would intentionally isolate a child from others' language.

But for some individuals, language isolation has occurred. A 13-year-old victim of lifelong child abuse, Genie was discovered in her home in November of 1970, strapped to a potty chair (Rymer, 1994). Her father and mother had isolated her in the basement, and she was rarely exposed to speech. After her rescue, she appeared unable to acquire language as completely as other children (Fromkin et al., 1974). Through cases where normal development did not occur, we have learned that early childhood is a **critical period** for learning language (Lennenberg, 1967). This critical period is a window of time required for successful language development to take place. Children not exposed to language by around age 7 gradually lose their potential for learning the complexities of language. Other evidence comes from studies of American Sign Language (ASL), a complete language using hand gestures to represent morphemes and letters. A study by Newport (1990) compared deaf children who learned American Sign Language from infancy (native speakers), *early* learners (first exposed to ASL at age 4 to 6), and *late* learners (first exposed after age 12). Late learners can still master words and order but never become as fluent in signing as native signers and have less crisp and more grammatically inconsistent forms FIGURE 8-19. Deaf children can sometimes be given cochlear implants that allow them to hear sounds, and their language learning then appears the same as in hearing children (Svirsky, 2000). The critical period for language learning also appears in second-language learning. If you learn another language before puberty, you will likely be able to speak it without an accent. As an adult, the initial language leaves its trace in new language learning (Oyama, 1976). Hakuta and colleagues (2003) have shown that later age at emigration predicts more difficulty in learning a second language.

Theories of Language Acquisition

How language acquisition takes place is a question hotly debated within psychology. **Behaviorist theories**, such as that of B. F. Skinner, argue there is nothing special about language learning; instead, it follows the same principles identified in general learning theories. In this view, the principles of association, imitation, and reinforcement are adequate to explain

Telegraphic speech Two- and three-word combinations with meaning.

Overregularize Applying a rule of grammar beyond its limits.

Critical period A sensitive time in development during which learning must occur.

Behaviorist theory The view that language is learned just like other things.

The American Sign Language sign for, "I love you."

FIGURE 8-19 This graph shows control over basic word order in ASL. There are effects of age of acquisition, but the scores on seven tests of ASL morphology (form) show consistent effects of age, with natives outscoring early learners, who in turn outscore late learners.
Source: Adapted from Newport, E. L. (1990). Maturational constraints on language learning. Cognitive Science, 14, 11–28.

Nativist theory The view that language is a special skill we are born with.

Interactionist theory The view that language combines inborn abilities with special environmental triggers.

how language acquisition occurs. **Nativist theories**, such as that of Noam Chomsky, argue that language learning is too remarkable to be explained by experience alone; instead, some built-in capacity must account for our language capacity. Chomsky (1972) argued that the human brain is biologically hardwired as a "language acquisition device" or "LAD." In other words, we are born with "programs" to help infants readily acquire language. As evidence, Chomsky argued that all people have language, and all languages have particular properties (like nouns and verbs) in common. Children all over the world learn to fluently speak the language they hear, at about the same age, and without much effort or instruction. Pinker (1995) argues that humans are genetically prepared for language, and evidence shows that humans are born with unique sensitivities to the sounds and structures of speech (MacWhinney, 1998).

Language is another example of multiple influences in thinking. Nature may prepare us to learn language remarkably quickly; however, without the external situation around us—hearing and interacting with others—language skills do not develop normally. **Interactionist theories** attempt to combine explanations of inborn tendencies with the special environmental triggers that enhance the development of language. Other aspects of social interaction, such as gestures, also assist in language learning (Goldin-Meadow, 2003). Social interaction is, after all, the purpose of learning language, and aspects of the social environment greatly impact it. In particular, being spoken to frequently by caregivers speeds the development of language (Richards, 1994). Even the dreaded "baby talk" that parents lapse into serves a purpose: Its high pitch and exaggerated intonation are preferred to normal speech by 4 month olds (Fernald, 1985). While we have developed ways of using language that are far removed from any specific recipient, such as writing textbooks and messages in bottles, at heart, language is social thought.

Language in Animals

Many animals are also social. So why is their communication, however rich and complex, not considered the equivalent of human language? What language capacities exist in animals? Researchers have studied communication in apes, dolphins, and even parrots to uncover what makes human language so special. However, the question has not been, "What are they saying to each other?" The question for psychologists has been, "Are any of them able to talk to *us*?"

Irene Pepperberg (2002) and colleagues spent more than 20 years teaching English to an African gray parrot named Alex. Because parrots can mimic sounds, they have the potential to produce spoken language sounding like human speech, unlike any other species. Alex knows more than 70 words, can count objects up to six, and can compare two objects ("smaller," "bigger") and choose objects based on multiple features ("What is blue and triangular?"). Alex can name an object placed in front of him ("block") and respond to questions about it ("red," "wood," and "square") with 80% accuracy. This is quite impressive, but imagine how annoying this performance would be in a friend. Alex learned from watching a human model be scolded or rewarded for his or her answers, and eye contact along with pointing were important parts of learning. While Alex was a well-trained bird (he died in 2007), his mastery of language left something to be desired.

Psychologist Irene Pepperberg and her research team worked with an African gray parrot named Alex on his speech sounds for over 20 years.

On the other hand, studies of communication among dolphins have demonstrated rudimentary semantics and syntax use (Hillix & Rumbaugh, 2004; Linden, 1993). Two bottlenose dolphins, Phoenix and Akeakamai, were trained to communicate with trainers through hand gestures and electronic whistles. When given commands of two to five words, such as "Right water left Frisbee fetch," the dolphins correctly took the Frisbee to the water on the right. Dolphins are good candidates for language capacity, as their brains are very large, and they normally live in a highly complex and very social environment. However, like Alex, their ability to learn human language seems more like behavior captured by learning theories rather than the spontaneous burst of untrained language learning in human toddlers. To answer whether any animal could learn human language, researchers turned to our nearest evolutionary relatives: The great apes.

Early researchers working with chimpanzees quickly realized they lacked the anatomy to produce speech sounds like ours. Premack (1971) was able to teach a chimp named Sarah to communicate by placing colored chips onto a magnetic board (though Sarah later bit off Premack's fingers, in another form of communication). American Sign Language use proved more successful, when Allen and Beatrice Gardner (1989) successfully taught four chimpanzees, including their star pupil, Washoe. She learned more than 132 signs and was able to combine signs into simple sentences. She also showed innovation in sign use, combining them in ways she had not seen expressed by others, such as calling a swan a "water bird" and describing a toy doll in a teacup as "Baby in my cup." Washoe also communicated with other chimps in sign language and taught her son 68 different signs. A gorilla named Koko, trained by Patterson and Linden (1981), holds the record with a 600-word vocabulary.

These smart animals clearly learned a lot, but how was their learning like human language learning? Sue Savage-Rumbaugh and colleagues (1998) set out to see if chimps could learn like humans do–through exposure to language in context rather than through instruction. Kanzi, a pygmy chimp, learned to talk by making hand signals, pointing to symbols on a board, and pressing symbols on a keyboard, and he can understand spoken English. Kanzi reacted appropriately to requests that varied, such as, "Turn on the light," "Show me the light," and "Bring me the light." Without seeing the speaker, Kanzi once heard, "Jeanie hid the pine needles in her shirt"; immediately, he walked up to Jeanie and searched her shirt. Clearly, apes are able to understand and produce communications at a level showing language properties like semanticity and generativity.

But how does this compare to human language learning? Savage-Rumbaugh performed a head-to-head test of Kanzi and a 2-year-old human named Alia. In tests over a 9-month period, the two were tested on more than 650 commands in spoken English. The sentences were designed to be new (not previously heard) and to combine objects in unusual ways (e.g., "Can you pour the ice water in the potty," and "Make the doggie bite the snake"). Both Kanzi (with 74% correct) and Alia (with 65% correct) showed they understood spoken language, semantics, and syntax, even though they were unable to produce it. Clearly, Kanzi mastered more language comprehension than most people ever thought possible for a chimp. However, his learning peaked there, while Alia, at 2, was just beginning her language "burst." While it is clear that animals may understand much more than they can say, it is also unlikely they are able to give speeches, write poetry, or think about particle physics. Language, and the deep thoughts it captures, appear to be a uniquely human capacity.

As social animals, dolphins have sophisticated communication skills and have learned to respond to complex signals from humans.

Koko, a gorilla, learned to communicate with trainers through American Sign Language.

CONCEPT LEARNING CHECK 8.5 | *Features of Language*

Consider the principles of semanticity, generativity, and displacement.

1. Identify examples of these three language capacities in other animal species.

2. Which of these principles is missing from animal language use?

8.6 Brain, Language, and Culture

Our language use reveals its impact on our thinking and the influence of biology and culture.

- Explain how language use reveals its impact on our thinking.
- Describe the influence of biology and culture on how we think.

Broca's area Part of the left frontal lobe that produces speech sounds.

Wernicke's area Part of the left temporal lobe that comprehends spoken words.

Linguistic relativity The notion that language shapes our ideas and not the other way around.

What is special about humans that allowed us to develop language and to think abstract thoughts? One answer can be determined from our "hardware," the specific functions supported in the brain that allow us to comprehend and produce spoken language. Early clues about brain function arose from clinical cases of brain injury. In 1865, Paul Broca noticed his medical patients sometimes suffered from an inability to speak. One man was called the Tan Man because he was only able to produce the word *tan*. He was able to comprehend what was spoken to him and even to sing familiar songs, but his production of spoken language was limited to that single word. The damaged area of the brain was in the left frontal lobe, called **Broca's area**. Another area located in the left temporal lobe, called **Wernicke's area**, produced different behavior when damaged by strokes. In these cases identified by Carl Wernicke in patients in 1874, words still flowed freely but made little sense, described as "word salad." The right ingredients—the individual words—were produced correctly, but the meaning in word combinations was lacking. These patients also had trouble comprehending speech.

As brain injury cases suggested, language processing in the brain has been found to occur mainly in the left hemisphere. In all right-handed people and even most left-handed people, these language-processing centers are located only in the left hemisphere FIGURE 8-20. Wernicke's area is active when hearing words, and Broca's area is active when speaking words. In addition to brain anatomy, the mouth, throat, and larynx allow us to systematically vary the sounds we create, and our faces express meaning, along with our gestures. Humans are gifted with the hardware that allows language to take place with minimal effort. In fact, the close ties between our use of language and the development of thinking raises the question of which came first, the thought or its description?

Linguistic relativity is the idea that language shapes our ideas and not the other way around. The language we speak may determine the ways we conceptualize the world

FIGURE 8-20 In this image, Broca's area for speech generation (in the left frontal lobe) is shown in blue, and Wernicke's area for speech comprehension (in the left temporal lobe) is shown in green.

Broca's area

Wernicke's area

(Whorf, 1956). For example, German contains a word, *Schadenfreude*, which is translated as "delighting in others' misfortune." Is this a concept you knew before you heard this word? If not, your thinking about this concept is relative, or dependent on, the language you speak. This notion, that language creates thought, is called the Sapir-Whorf hypothesis (Kay & Kempton, 2009). Of course, anyone who speaks more than one language knows it is possible to express the same idea in different languages. The idea here is that the *ways* of expression created by language may in turn influence how we think. Whorf's study of the Hopi led him to conclude that their language contained no words or grammatical forms that refer directly to past, present, or future. This suggested that people living in different cultures and speaking different languages may be thinking about time in different ways.

Imagine you had four pictures of a person at various ages. As an English speaker, you would almost certainly order the pictures chronologically left to right, with the oldest pictures to the right. Or you could arrange them "east to west," as do the Pompuraawan, a remote tribe in Australia. Their language does not have words such as *left* or *in front of*; instead, they use the cardinal directions, such as "my south arm." How a culture thinks spatially influences how they think about time (Boroditsky & Gaby, 2010). In one study, Mandarin Chinese and English speakers were examined because they differ in the spatial metaphors used to describe time (Boroditsky, 2001). In English, we think of a line extending horizontally to describe time, looking "forward" to events and putting past events "behind" us. In Mandarin, people speak about time on a vertical axis, with the past as *shang*, or up, and later events as *xia*, or down. In a laboratory study, native speakers were reminded of either horizontal or vertical space and then had to quickly answer temporal questions, such as, "May comes earlier than April, true or false?" English speakers answered more quickly with reminders of horizontal space, while Mandarin speakers were quicker with reminders of vertical space FIGURE 8-21. How we think also influences what we understand in language comprehension. If I tell you, "Next Wednesday's meeting has been advanced by two days," which day is the new meeting day? If you say "Friday,"

Image of Hopi woman from Whorf's study of language and culture.

FIGURE 8-21 English speakers think of time horizontally, so they performed better with a horizontal prime when making a time judgment. Mandarin speakers think of time vertically, so they performed worse with the horizontal prime on the same task. *Source: Data from Boroditsky, L. (2001). Does language shape thought? English and Mandarin speakers' conceptions of time.* Cognitive Psychology, *43(1), 1–22.*

you are thinking of time as a horizontal line stretching ahead of you, and advancing the meeting means moving it further into the future. However, if you thought "Monday," your thinking may use a metaphor of time as a horizontal river flowing past you. So, if something is "advanced" in time, it is moved closer toward you (McGlone & Harding, 1998).

Another place where language may drive the concepts we use is the topic of gender. Many languages, such as French, have gender marked in reference to objects; for example, *window* is preceded by the feminine *la* rather than the masculine *le*. German has three genders for things: masculine, feminine, and neutral, while English has one: neutral. Does "gendered" language affect the way we think, or is it a harmless practice to talk about "fresh*man*," "chair*man* of the board," and the "evolution of *man*"? Studies show that the use of masculine pronouns such as *he*, even when intended to be inclusive, lead people to think of males. For example, students were asked to write short stories starting with, "In a large co-ed institution, the average student will feel isolated in his courses." Sixty-five percent of the resulting stories focused on a male student (Moulton et al., 1978). The fact that gender is built into references in languages—some more than others—suggests that linguistic relativity is readily evident in our language use and thinking.

The complexity of the interactions between thought and language makes it a wonder that we ever understand each other at all. It suggests the study of second languages may be an important way to increase understanding across cultures. When we examine language and thinking in different cultures, we find evidence that they reflect the lived experiences that greatly vary across cultures. Given that the culture surrounding us influences our modes of thinking, thought may be subject to "cultural relativity." Individualism-collectivism describes the degree to which a culture relies on and has allegiance to the self (independence) or the group (interdependence; see **TABLE 8-2**). Those in Western cultures like Americans tend to focus on independence in their self-descriptions, while those in East Asian cultures identify interdependence as a value (Markus & Kitayama, 1991; Triandis et al., 1988). A worldwide study of 116,000 employees of IBM found the most independent people were from the United States, Australia, Great Britain, Canada, and the Netherlands, while the most interdependent people were from Venezuela, Colombia, Pakistan, Peru, and Taiwan (Hofstede, 1980). FIGURE 8-22 illustrates the difference between an individual view versus a collectivist view of the self. Which description fits how you think about yourself? When asked to complete the fragment, "I am . . .," will your responses be characteristics of yourself ("an athlete," "a risk taker"), or of your relationship to others ("a sister," "a son")? This difference between an individualist versus a collectivist view of oneself varies across the two types of cultures (Markus & Kitayama, 1991) FIGURE 8-23. And it varies even within people who happen to be bicultural. When Chinese Americans were "primed" by answering in Chinese, they focused on duties to others, fitting in, and harmonious interdependence FIGURE 8-24. When primed by writing in English, Chinese Americans focused on individual descriptors (Hong et al., 2001). The language we speak influences our thinking about ourselves—a core aspect of cognition—and the cultural values we hold.

Summary of Multiple Influences on Thinking and Language

The ways we think and how we use language are clearly subject to multiple influences from biology and culture. The functional specialization of brain areas plays an important role in the comprehension and production of language. It also reveals that our decisions

TABLE 8-2 Summary of Key Differences Between an Independent and an Interdependent Construal of Self

Feature Compared	Independent	Interdependent
Definition	Separate from social context	Connected with social context
Structure	Bounded, unitary, stable	Flexible, variable
Important features	Internal, private (abilities, thoughts, feelings)	External, public (statuses, roles, relationships)
Tasks	Be unique	Belong, fit-in
	Express self	Occupy one's proper place
	Realize internal attributes	Engage in appropriate action
	Promote own goals	Promote others' goals
	Be direct; "say what's on your mind"	Be indirect; "read other's mind"
Role of others	*Self-evaluation:* others important for social comparison, reflected appraisal	*Self-definition:* relationships with others in specific contexts define the self
Basis of self-esteem	Ability to express self, validate internal attributes	Ability to adjust, restrain self, maintain harmony with social context

Source: Data from Markus, H. R., & Kitayama, S. (1991). Culture and the self: Implications for cognition, emotion, and motivation. Psychological Review, 98(2), 224–253.

Siblings

Mother

Father

Individualistic Self

Collectivist Self

Friends

Coworkers

FIGURE 8-22 An identity focused on individualism defines the self independently from other people.

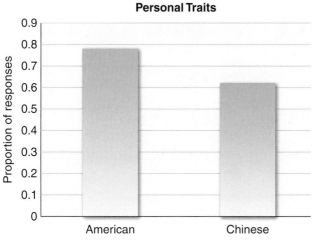

Personal Traits

Proportion of responses

American   Chinese

FIGURE 8-23 American students were more likely to report personal traits in their self-descriptions, while Chinese students reported more interdependent relationships to define themselves.
Source: Data from Markus, H. R., & Kitayama, S. (1991). Culture and the self: Implications for cognition, emotion, and motivation. Psychological Review, 98*(2), 224–253.*

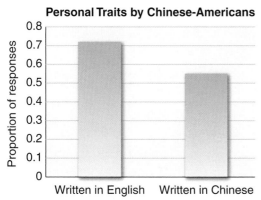

Personal Traits by Chinese-Americans

Proportion of responses

Written in English   Written in Chinese

FIGURE 8-24 People who held both Chinese and American identities (biculturals) were asked to complete the self-identity task writing in English or in Chinese. When primed by the language, they altered their descriptions to fit the cultural identity of the language in which they were writing.
Source: Data from Hong, Y., Ip, G., Chiu, C., Morris, M. W., & Menon, T. (2001). Cultural identity and dynamic construction of the self: Collective duties and individual rights in Chinese and American cultures. Social Cognition, 19*(3), 251–268.*

are influenced not just by the content stored in the cerebral cortex but also by the flow of emotion in the orbital-frontal cortex and limbic system. Biology plays a role in determining which of the dual thinking processes—the slow, deliberate reasoning or the fast, associative instinct—drives our decisions. The biology of our brains certainly produces a kind of thinking that appears to be unique to humans: the use of complex language. At the same time, thinking and language are greatly influenced by the cultural context we experience. Whether we consider our connectedness to other people when thinking about ourselves and whether we can see both sides of an issue are examples of how cultural background affects thinking. Languages and cultures go together, so that speaking in one well-known language may change not just the word you use but how you think about the world. Thinking and language provide another example of the importance of biological and sociocultural influences in psychology.

CONCEPT LEARNING CHECK 8.6 | *Multiple Influences on Language Use*

Identify the concept illustrated in each example, and explain how biology or culture affects the sample of language provided.

1. (Holding teacup) "Could dogs nurse the television?"

2. "To describe myself: I am a biker, I love cats, and I enjoy sudoku."

3. "On the one hand, Republicans have the right idea about cutting government spending, but on the other hand, they are wrong about the high costs of social welfare programs."

4. "G-g-go . . . go . . . go . . . h-h-home."

5. "That was a long time ago, I cannot go back there."

Visual Overview Types of Thinking Processes

Three main types of thinking—problem solving, decision making, and reasoning—are identified in the chapter. Each has a distinct set of methods and algorithms that can be used to think through the question, and each has specific heuristics (or short cuts in thinking) and biases (or errors) to watch out for.

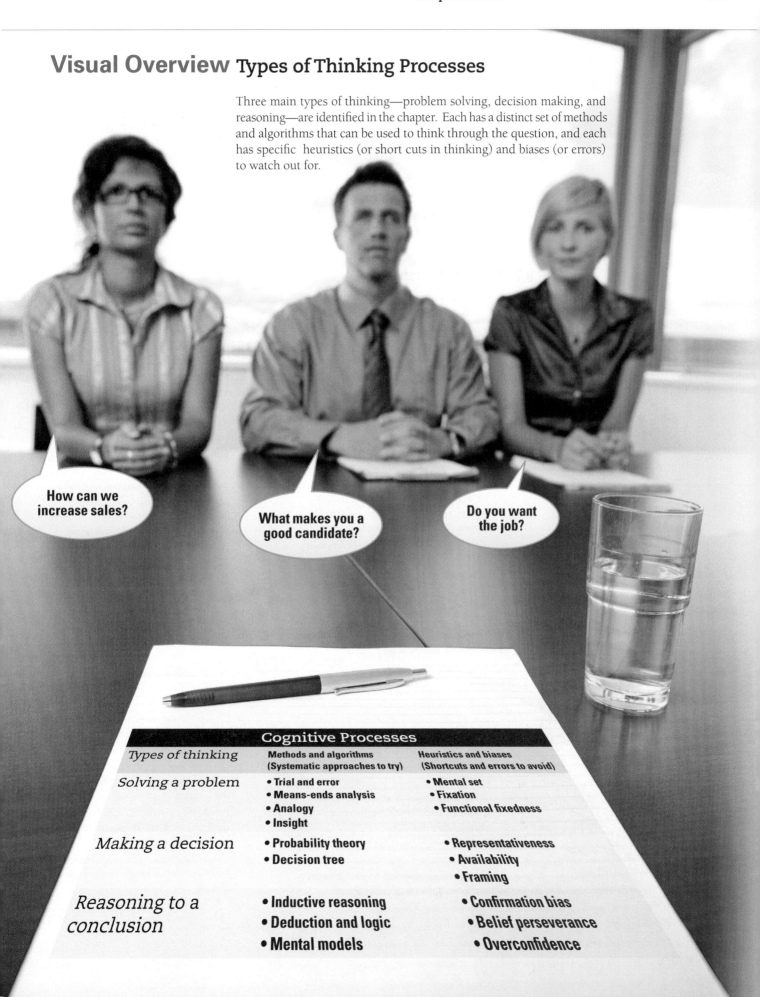

How can we increase sales?

What makes you a good candidate?

Do you want the job?

Cognitive Processes

Types of thinking	Methods and algorithms (Systematic approaches to try)	Heuristics and biases (Shortcuts and errors to avoid)
Solving a problem	• Trial and error • Means-ends analysis • Analogy • Insight	• Mental set • Fixation • Functional fixedness
Making a decision	• Probability theory • Decision tree	• Representativeness • Availability • Framing
Reasoning to a conclusion	• Inductive reasoning • Deduction and logic • Mental models	• Confirmation bias • Belief perseverance • Overconfidence

8.1 Overview: What Is Thinking?

- Thinking includes the internal processes of the mind that help us make sense of the world.
- Rational thinking is marked by the use of reason, or coming to conclusions when considering facts fully and carefully. This form of thinking has the goal of avoiding errors and arriving at the best conclusion.

- Intuition is using first impressions, instincts, or emotions to drive our choices without given them much thought.
- These dual processes in thinking—slow, deliberative, conscious reasoning versus fast, automatic, and efficient reactions—describe the major ways we think across many tasks.

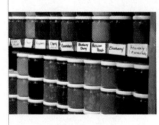

8.2 Problem Solving

- We solve problems through both deterministic algorithms and heuristic guesses.
- A problem is any given situation that differs from a desired goal state, and there is a *nonobvious* way to get from one to the other.
- An algorithm is a well-defined process that is guaranteed, eventually, to produce a solution. When one is available, and when the problem is important, this is a good choice for finding a solution.
- A heuristic is a mental shortcut in thinking that may or may not lead to a correct solution. The rules of thumb provided by heuristics are fast, require little effort, and usually lead to the right answer.
- Trial and error, means-ends analysis, analogy, and insight identify different approaches to solution.

- A bias is a tendency to hold on to one familiar perspective at the expense of (possibly equally valid) alternatives.
- Irrelevant information and unnecessary constraints can be distracting in a representation.
- Mental set is a preexisting state of mind, habit, or attitude, that can affect and mislead thinking.
- Fixation is when the solver sticks to an initial approach and cannot consider alternatives.
- Incubation helps by setting aside a problem for a break before further attempts to solve it.
- Ten thousand hours of practice are needed to produce expertise.
- Deliberative practice involves working on skills just beyond your current level.

8.3 Decision Making

- Rather than following algorithms, our decisions are often guided by heuristics.
- Making decisions involves choosing among alternatives or whether to take some action.
- Judgment is when we reach beyond what we already know and draw a conclusion.
- Probability theory is an algorithm that takes into account all contingencies and their likelihoods.
- A decision tree shows all choices and weighs each one based on its value.
- Heuristics are easy shortcuts that usually work but sometimes cause errors.

- The representativeness heuristic guides judgments based on what things "look like."
- The availability heuristic uses the ease of recall from memory to estimate the likelihood of an event.
- Decision making can also be biased by the way the choices are presented, known as the framing effect.
- People try to make choices that will minimize or avoid losses, called loss aversion.
- Choice overload refers to having too many choices to handle in decision making.

8.4 Reasoning

- Rather than always being rational, our reasoning may be biased by what we think we know.
- Reasoning is attempting to go beyond what we now know to draw a conclusion.
- Algorithms for reasoning are based on deduction and logic.
- Inductive reasoning draws more general conclusions from specific information.
- People are influenced by the content or meaning of the words used in a problem.

- Mental models are visual or graphical representations of the problem.
- In confirmation bias, we seek information that matches what we already know.
- Belief perseverance maintains beliefs even in the face of contradictory evidence.
- People show overconfidence by overestimating how likely we are to be correct.

8.5 Language

- Learning a language provides evidence of special thinking skills unique to humans.
- Language is a core and defining process of human thinking.
- A few key properties of human language are: semanticity, or meaning; generativity, the capacity to use a finite set of words to generate an endless variety of statements; and displacement, the ability to communicate about things that are not in the immediate surroundings.
- The structure of language includes phonemes, morphemes, words, phrases, and sentences.
- The organization of words within a language, or grammar, involves two levels:
  - the surface structure, or the ordering of a sequence of words in time.
  - the deep structure, or the composition of meaning within a phrase.
- People preserve the semantics, or gist, of the information, but they "forget" other aspects of the language expression.
- Pragmatics, or the social context, of language is also critical to comprehension.
- Extralinguistic factors outside of the literal content of language aid in comprehension, such as facial expressions and gestures.
- Children of all cultures absorb the words and grammar of language without any instruction.

- The sequence of milestones in language development is the same for all children.
- There is a critical period for learning language at around age 7, when we gradually lose the potential for learning language.
- Behaviorist theories argue there is nothing special about language and that it follows general learning theories.
- Nativist theories argue that language learning is built in or hardwired in the brain.
- Interactionist theories attempt to combine explanations of inborn tendencies with the special environmental triggers that enhance language learning.
- Studies of communication among dolphins and apes have demonstrated use of semantics and grammar.
- Chimpanzees have shown innovation in sign language use and can learn like humans do through exposure to language in context.
- However, animal learning of human languages peaks at the level attained by humans at age 2 or 3.
- Language and the complex thought it captures appear to be uniquely human capacities.

8.6 Brain, Language, and Culture

- The brain comprehends and produces language in two areas of left hemisphere: Broca's area for producing words and Wernicke's area in comprehension.

- Linguistic relativity is the idea that language shapes our ideas and not the other way around.

- Language reveals a culture's way of thinking, such as conceptions about time.

- People think similarly within cultures and differently from those in other cultures on topics like dialectical ideas and relationships to others.

- The ways we think and how we use language are clearly subject to multiple influences from biology and culture.

8.1 Overview: What Is Thinking?

1. Thinking marked by the use of reason, or coming to conclusions when considering facts fully and carefully, is called:
   A. rational.
   B. instinct.
   C. intuitive.
   D. metacognition.

8.2 Problem Solving

2. A step-by-step sequence of rules that always leads to the correct solution for a problem is called:
   A. an algorithm.
   B. a heuristic.
   C. representation.
   D. an analogy.

3. A mental shortcut in thinking that may or may not lead to a correct solution is called:
   A. an algorithm.
   B. a heuristic.
   C. representation.
   D. an analogy.

4. Jarrod approaches his problem by identifying the differences between the current state and the goal state he desires. He is likely to use using the problem-solving approach called:
   A. trial and error.
   B. means-ends analysis.
   C. analogy.
   D. insight.

5. Approaching a problem using the same strategies you always use reflect a bias called:
   A. mental set.
   B. mental models.
   C. analogy.
   D. insight.

6. You need to tighten a screw but have no screwdriver, so you pull a penny out of your pocket and use it to fix the faucet. What problem-solving bias have you just overcome?
   A. Means-end analysis
   B. Anchoring
   C. Brainstorming
   D. Functional fixedness

7. The process that helps by setting aside a problem for a break before further attempts to solve it is called:
   A. incubation.
   B. insight.
   C. intuition.
   D. means-ends analysis.

8. Studies found that expert performance at the highest levels requires:
   A. 1,000 hours of practice.
   B. 10,000 hours of practice.
   C. 100,000 hours of practice.
   D. true talent.

8.3 Decision Making

9. Simon is meek, tidy, quiet, and overly concerned with order and detail. People who meet him and guess that he is probably a bookkeeper are relying on:
   A. the confirmation bias.
   B. the representativeness heuristic.
   C. the availability heuristic.
   D. the framing effect.

10. People will accept a bet when they have a 10% chance of winning but are less likely to accept a bet in which they are told they have a 90% chance of losing. This is an example of which cognitive bias?
   A. The availability heuristic
   B. The representativeness heuristic
   C. The confirmation bias
   D. The framing effect

11. Selma estimates that breast cancer is the leading cause of death for women because it readily comes to mind. This example illustrates using:
   A. the framing heuristic.
   B. the availability heuristic.
   C. the representativeness heuristic.
   D. the confirmation bias.

12. Laying out all of the possible alternatives and their possible outcomes is a method for decision making called:
   A. logic.
   B. heuristics.
   C. trial and error.
   D. decision tree.

8.4 Reasoning

13. We often seek information that matches what we already know, called the:
   A. confirmation bias.
   B. belief perseverance.
   C. overconfidence.
   D. availability heuristic.

8.5 Language

14. The language property that separates human language use from other species is called:
   A. semanticity.
   B. generativity.
   C. displacement.
   D. grammar.

8.6 Brain, Language, and Culture

15. The area of the brain found to be involved in difficulties in producing spoken language, as in patients like the Tan Man, who could only say *tan*, is called:
   A. Broca's area.
   B. Wernicke's area.
   C. Chomsky's area.
   D. cerebellum.

CHAPTER DISCUSSION QUESTIONS

1. Identify one situation in which you think you would use rational thinking and one situation where you think you would use intuitive thinking. For each situation, evaluate the pros and cons of using the opposite style of thinking. For example, for your rational situation, what would happen if you used intuitive thinking instead?

2. Problem solving involves identifying a strategy to go from where you are to your goal. Think of a problem you have in your life and then examine how you would use the following problem-solving strategies to work toward your goal. Strategies: generate and test, algorithm, means-ends analysis, analogy.

3. Advertisers and marketing executives are very aware of the heuristics that we use in decision making. In fact, they often capitalize on our natural tendencies in the hope that we will decide to use their products. Find an example of a heuristic that is being used to sell a product in an advertising campaign. Identify the heuristic and then explain how it is being used in the advertising campaign.

4. Sections 8.5 and 8.6 review many of the factors that influence our ability to use language, including development, biology, and culture. Assess the role of each factor—development (8.5), biology (8.6), and culture (8.6)—in your own language skills. Would each factor have the same importance if you were to learn a new language now as it did when you learned your first language?

CHAPTER PROJECTS

1. Problem solving, decision making, and reasoning are three important aspects of thinking that are separate but related. Write a story in which the main character is confronted with at least three different situations, so one is best solved with problem solving, one with decision making, and one with reasoning. Highlight and number the beginning of each situation. Then, in a separate paragraph, identify whether the situation requires problem solving, decision making, or reasoning and how the character used a strategy from the book to continue toward the story's conclusion.

2. Imagine that you are the country's top language expert, and as such, the president has asked you to come and work on a very special project. Your job is to develop a plan to help infants learn to speak. As this language expert, develop a plan for the President, explaining how your strategy fits with our current understanding of how humans learn and develop language skills.

CHAPTER KEY TERMS

Algorithm
Analogy
Availability heuristic
Babbling
Behaviorist theory
Belief perseverance
Bias
Broca's area
Choice overload
Cognition
Confirmation bias
Constraints
Content
Critical period
Decisions
Decision tree
Deductive reasoning
Deep structure
Deliberation
Deliberative practice
Displacement
Dual processes
Extralinguistic factors
Fixation
Functional fixedness
Framing effect

Generate and test
Generativity
Gist
Goal
Grammar
Heuristic
Holophrastic
Incubation
Inductive reasoning
Insight
Interactionist theory
Intuition
Irrelevant information
Judgment
Lack of transfer
Language
Linguistic relativity
Loss aversion
Means-end analysis
Mental model
Mental set
Metacognition
Morpheme
Nativist theory
Overconfidence
Overregularize

Paraphrase
Phonemes
Phrase
Pragmatics
Probability theory
Problem
Rational thinking
Reasoning
Representation
Representativeness heuristic
Restructuring
Satisfice
Semanticity
Sentence
Somatic marker
Surface structure
Syllogism
Telegraphic speech
Thinking
Trial and error
Uncertainty
Unnecessary constraint
Wason selection task
Wernicke's area
Word

ANSWERS TO CONCEPT LEARNING CHECKS

8.1 Defining Thinking

1. Because the stakes are high (you only go to college once in your life), this calls for the slow, deliberation mode of thinking.

2. Lunch is something you decide daily, so using a quick, intuitive decision mode will not have serious consequences.

8.2 Applying Methods of Problem Solving

1. Let me try to think of a good name for our team. How about Sunday Strikers? [A. Generate and test]

2. I will try 1-1-1, then 1-1-2, then 1-1-3, and keep going until the locker opens. [B. Algorithm]

3. This chemistry lab reminds me of cooking, so I had better measure each portion carefully. [D. Analogy]

4. I will get to my home in LA by first flying into town, then taking a taxi to the house. [C. Means-ends analysis]

8.3 Recognizing Heuristics in Decision Making

1. You might use representativeness to decide that someone in a coffee shop near campus looks like another student. This provides stereotypical guesses that are often correct.

2. Which have you done more often, brushed your teeth or brushed your shoes? Ease of access in memory works most times to tell us what has happened more often.

3. How you "frame" a decision ("You don't want to go to the party, do you?" vs. "Let's go to the party!") can lead to the answer you want to hear.

4. Choosing shoes that fit and look okay may be a good decision compared to continuing to hunt for the perfect shoe. (Fashionistas may disagree!) Satisficing helps by letting you settle for a "good enough" answer to meet your needs.

8.4 Practicing Reasoning

1. Content effects may make the concepts easy to understand but unclear in another setting. So make sure you can generate your own example of each concept.

2. Confirmation bias may lead you to look for examples showing you do understand the materials but not to test yourself in ways that show you do not. So be sure to really test yourself and not just read over the information and affirm that you know it.

3. Belief perseverance may make it hard to see the evidence that you are not performing well. So use some objective measures of whether you have mastered the material, such as asking someone to verify your definitions of key terms.

4. Overconfidence may lead you to estimate a higher level of mastery than you have achieved. So continue studying even after you feel confident you know it.

8.5 Features of Language

1. Dolphins showed semanticity by demonstrating use of semantics and syntax; Washoe the chimpanzee showed generativity in that she created novel sentences.

2. No evidence is provided that the animals described referred to things outside their current view, which shows a lack of displacement.

8.6 Multiple Influences on Language Use

1. This "word salad" statement shows a lack of meaning, associated with damage to Wernicke's area.

2. This self-description is typical of an individualist view of oneself, often found in Western cultures.

3. This statement reflects dialectical thinking, in which opposing views are held at the same time, more common in Eastern cultures.

4. This speech difficulty is associated with damage to Broca's area.

5. This view of time as "behind us" reflects an English cultural model with time as horizontal.

ANSWERS TO CHAPTER REVIEW TEST

8.1 Overview: What Is Thinking?

1. A. Rational thinking requires slow, deliberative thought in contrast to quick intuitive judgments.

8.2 Problem Solving

2. A. The definition of an algorithm is that it always leads to a correct solution when executed properly.

3. B. A heuristic is a "rule of thumb" that leads to a fast answer, but is not always correct.

4. B. Means-ends analysis attempts to "reduce the differences" between your current situation and your goal.

5. A. Mental set is a specific way of approaching problems based on your past experience, potentially causing you to miss new ways.

6. D. You don't normally use a penny as a screwdriver, so you are considering a new function rather than the "fixed" function it usually serves.

7. A. Incubation involves taking a break in your solution attempts so you can take a fresh approach.

8. B. Experts practice for 10,000 hours before reaching elite levels of performance in many fields.

8.3 Decision Making

9. B. Representativeness involves making judgments based on what things look like.

10. D. Framing is the story told about the information that can bias you towards a given focus.

11. B. Availability involves judging how likely something is based on how easily it comes to mind.

12. D. The decision tree method for making decisions involves identifying all of the options and what they might lead to in the future.

8.4 Reasoning

13. A. Looking for what we expect to see is a bias that confirms what we know rather than challenges it.

8.5 Language

14. C. Animals communicate, but there is limited evidence that they refer to things not present in the current environment.

8.6 Brain, Language, and Culture

15. A. Broca's area is involved in producing speech, and the Tan Man could only repeat that word.

REFERENCES

Ariely, D., & Levav, J. (2000). Sequential choice in group settings: Taking the road less traveled and less enjoyed. *Journal of Consumer Research, 27*(3), 279–290.

Arkes, H. (1991). Costs and benefits of judgment errors: Implications for debiasing. *Psychological Bulletin, 110*(3), 486–498.

Baltes, B. B., Dickson, M. W., Sherman, M. P., Bauer, C. C., & LaGanke, J. S. (2002). Computer-mediated communication and group decision making: A meta-analysis. *Organizational Behavior and Human Decision Processes, 87*(1), 156–179.

Bechara, A., Damasio, H., Tranel, D., Damasio, A. R. (1997). Deciding advantageously before knowing the advantageous strategy. *Science, 275*(5304), 1293–1295.

Boroditsky, L. (2001). Does language shape thought? English and Mandarin speakers' conceptions of time. *Cognitive Psychology, 43*(1), 1–22.

Boroditsky, L., & Gaby, A. (2010). Remembrances of times east: Absolute spatial representations of time in an Australian Aboriginal community. *Psychological Science, 21*(11), 1635–1639.

Braine, M. D. S. (1971). On two types of models of the internalization of grammars. In D. I. Slobin (Ed.), *The ontogenesis of grammar: A theoretical symposium.* New York: Academic Press.

Brown, R. (1973). *A first language: The early stages.* Cambridge, MA: Cambridge University Press.

Burnham, C. A., & Davis, K. G. (1969). The nine-dot problem: Beyond perceptual organization. *Psychonomic Science, 17*(6), 321–323.

Chase, W. G., & Simon, H. A. (1973). Perception in chess. *Cognitive Psychology, 4*, 55–81.

Cheng, P. N., & Holyoak, K. J. (1985). Pragmatic reasoning schemas. *Cognitive Psychology, 17*, 391–416.

Chi, M. T. H., Feltovich, P., & Glaser, R. (1981). Categorization and representation of physics problems by experts and novices. *Cognitive Science, 5*(2), 121–152.

Chi, M. T. H., Glaser, R., & Farr, M. J. (1988). *The nature of expertise.* Englewood Cliffs, NJ: Lawrence Erlbaum Associates.

Chomsky, N. (1972). *Language and mind.* New York: Harcourt, Brace, Jovanovich.

Cosmides, L. (1989). The logic of social exchange: Has natural selection shaped how humans reason? *Cognition, 31*, 187–276.

Davidson, J. E., & Sternberg, R. J. (1984). The role of insight in intellectual giftedness. *Gifted Child Quarterly, 28*(2), 58–64.

de Groot, A. D. (1965). *Thought and choice in chess.* The Hague: Moulton.

Duncker, K. (1945). On problem solving. *Psychological Monographs, No. 58* (270).

Dunning, D., Heath, C., & Suls, J. M. (2004). Flawed self-assessment: Implications for health, education, and the workplace. *Psychological Science in the Public Interest, 5*(3), 69–106.

Ericsson, K. A., Krampe, R. T., & Tesch-Römer, C. (1993). The role of deliberate practice in the acquisition of expert performance. *Psychological Review, 100*(3), 363–406.

Ericsson, K. A., & Ward, P. (2007). Capturing the naturally occurring superior performance of experts in the laboratory. *Current Directions in Psychological Science, 16*(6), 346–350.

Fernald, A. (1985). Four-month-old infants prefer to listen to motherese. *Infant Behavior and Development, 8*(2), 181–195.

Frazier, L., & Rayner, K. (1982). Making and correcting errors during sentence comprehension: Eye movements in the analysis of structurally ambiguous sentences. *Cognitive Psychology, 14*(2), 178–210.

Fromkin, V., Krashen, S., Curtiss, S., Rigler, D., & Rigler, M. (1974). The development of language in Genie: A case of language acquisition beyond the critical period. *Brain and Language, 1*, 81–107.

Gardner, R. A., Gardner, B. I., & Van Cantfort, T. E. (Eds.). (1989). *Teaching sign language to chimpanzees.* Albany: State University of New York Press.

Gibbs, Jr., R. W. (1986). What makes some indirect speech acts conventional? *Journal of Memory and Language, 25*(2), 181–196.

Gick, M. L., & Holyoak, K. J. (1980). Analogical problems solving. *Cognitive Psychology, 12*, 306–355.

Gigerenzer, G. (2007). *Gut feelings: The intelligence of the unconscious.* New York: Viking.

Goldin-Meadow, S. (2003). *Hearing gesture: How our hands help us think.* Cambridge, MA: Harvard University Press.

Griggs, R. A., & Cox, J. R. (1982). The elusive thematic-materials effect in Wason's selection task. *British Journal of Psychology, 73*, 407–420.

Hakuta, K., Bialystok, E., & Wiley, E. (2003). Critical evidence: A test of the Critical-Period Hypothesis for second-language acquisition. *Psychological Science 14*(1), 31–38.

Hastie, R. (2001). Problems for judgment and decision making. *Annual Review of Psychology, 52*, 653–683.

Hillix, W. A., & Rumbaugh, D. M. (2004). *Animal bodies, human minds: Ape, dolphin, and parrot language skills.* New York: Kluwer.

Hofstede, G. (1980). *Culture's consequences: International differences in work-related values.* Newbury Park, CA: Sage.

Hong, Y., Ip, G., Chiu, C., Morris, M. W., & Menon, T. (2001). Cultural identity and dynamic construction of the self: Collective duties and individual rights in Chinese and American cultures. *Social Cognition, 19*(3), 251–268.

Iyengar, S. S., & Lepper, M. R. (2000). When choice is demotivating: Can one desire too much of a good thing? *Journal of Personality and Social Psychology, 79*(6), 995–1006.

Johnson-Laird, P. N. (2001). Mental models and deduction. *Trends in Cognitive Sciences, 5*(10), 434–442.

Johnson-Laird, P. N., & Byrne, R. M. J. (2002). Conditionals: A theory of meaning, pragmatics, and inference. *Psychological Review, 109*(4), 646–678.

Jung-Beeman, M. Bowden, E. M., Haberman, J., Frymiare, J. L., Arambel-Liu, S., Greenblatt, R., Reber, P. J., & Kounios, J. (2004). Neural activity when people solve verbal problems with insight. *PLoS Biology, 2*, 502–505.

Kahneman, D., Slovic, P., & Tversky, A. (Eds.). (1982). *Judgment under uncertainty: Heuristics and biases.* New York: Cambridge University Press.

Kahneman, D., & Tversky, A. (1972). Subjective probability: A judgment of representativeness. *Cognitive Psychology, 3*(3), 430–454.

Kaiser, M. K., McCloskey, M., & Proffitt, D. R. (1986). Development of intuitive theories of motion: Curvilinear motion in the absence of external forces. *Developmental Psychology, 22*(1), 67–71.

Kaplan, C. A., & Simon, H. A. (1990). In search of insight. *Cognitive Psychology, 22*(3), 374–419.

Kay, P., & Kempton, W. (2009). What is the Sapir-Whorf hypothesis? *American Anthropologist, 86*(1), 65–79.

Keren, G. (2007). Framing, intentions, and trust–choice incompatibility. *Organizational Behavior and Human Decision Processes, 103*(2), 238–255.

Kihn, M. (2005). "Outside the box": The inside story. *FastCompany, 95*, 40.

Klayman, J. (1995). Varieties of confirmation bias. *Psychology of Learning and Motivation, 32*, 385–418.

Köhler, W. (1929). *Gestalt psychology.* Oxford, England: Liveright.

Koriat, A., Lichtenstein, S., & Fischhoff, B. (1980). Reasons for confidence. *Journal of Experimental Psychology: Human Learning and Memory, 6*(2), 107–118.

Kounios, J., & Beeman, M. (2009). The aha! moment: The cognitive neuroscience of insight. *Current Directions in Psychological Science, 18*(4), 210–216.

Kruger, J., & Dunning, D. (1999). Unskilled and unaware of it: How difficulties in recognizing one's own incompetence lead to inflated self-assessments. *Journal of Personality and Social Psychology, 77*(6), 1121–1134.

Kunda, Z., & Nisbett, R. E. (1986). Prediction and the partial understanding of the law of large numbers. *Journal of Experimental Social Psychology, 22*(4), 339–354.

Kuo, W-J., Sjöström, T., Chen, Y-P., Wang, Y-H., & Huang, C-Y. (2009). Intuition and deliberation: Two systems for strategizing in the brain. *Science, 324*(5926), 519–522.

REFERENCES, *continued*

Lave, J. (1988). *Cognition in practice: Mind, mathematics, and culture in everyday life.* Cambridge: Cambridge University Press.

Lennenberg, E. H. (1967). *Biological foundations of language.* New York: Wiley.

Linden, E. (1993, March 22). Can animals think? *Time,* 52–61.

Linville, P. W., Fischer, G. W., & Fischhoff, B. (1993). AIDS risk perceptions and decision biases. The social psychology of HIV infection. In J. B. Pryor & G. D. Reeder (Eds.), *The social psychology of HIV infection* (pp. 5–38). Hillsdale, NJ, England: Lawrence Erlbaum Associates.

Lord, C. G., Ross, L., & Lepper, M. R. (1979). Biased assimilation and attitude polarization: The effects of prior theories on subsequently considered evidence. *Journal of Personality and Social Psychology, 37,* 2098-2109.

Luchins, A. S. (1942). Mechanization in problem solving—the effect of Einstellung. *Psychological Monographs,* No. 54(6). Washington, DC: American Psychological Association.

MacWhinney, B. (1998). Models of the emergence of language. *Annual Review of Psychology, 49,* 199–227.

Maier, N. R. F. (1931). Reasoning in humans: II. The solution and its appearance in consciousness. *Journal of Comparative Psychology, 12,* 181–194.

Maier, N. R. F. (1937). Reasoning in rats and human beings. *Psychological Review, 44*(5), 365–378.

Marcus, G. F. (1995). The acquisition of the English past tense in children and multilayered connectionist networks. *Cognition, 56*(3), 271–279.

Markus, H. R., & Kitayama, S. (1991). Culture and the self: Implications for cognition, emotion, and motivation. *Psychological Review, 98*(2), 224–253.

McGlone, M. S., & Harding, J. L. (1998). Back (or forward?) to the future: The role of perspective in temporal language comprehension. *Journal of Experimental Psychology: Learning, Memory, and Cognition, 24,* 1211–1223.

McGuigan, F. J. (1970). Covert oral behavior during the silent performance of language tasks. *Psychological Bulletin, 74*(5), 309–326.

Metcalfe, J., & Wiebe, D. (1987). Intuition in insight and non-insight problem solving. *Memory and Cognition, 15,* 238–246.

Miller, G. A. (1991). *The science of words.* New York: Freeman.

Moulton, J., Robinson, G. M., & Elias, C. (1978). Sex bias in language use: "Neutral" pronouns that aren't. *American Psychologist, 33*(11), 1032-1036.

Naqvi, N., Shiv, B., & Bechara, A. (2006). The role of emotion in decision making: A cognitive neuroscience perspective. *Current Directions in Psychological Science, 15*(5), 260–264.

Newell, A., & Simon, H. A. (1972). *Human problem solving.* Englewood Cliffs, NJ: Prentice-Hall.

Newport, E. L. (1990). Maturational constraints on language learning. *Cognitive Science, 14,* 11–28.

Nisbett, R. E., & Ross, L. (1980). *Human inference: Strategies and shortcomings of social judgment.* Englewood Cliffs, NJ: Prentice-Hall.

Nisbett, R. E., & Wilson, T. D. (1977). Telling more than we can know: Verbal reports on mental processes. *Psychological Review, 84*(3), 231–259.

Oyama, S. (1976). A sensitive period for the acquisition of a nonnative phonological system. *Journal of Psycholinguistic Research, 5,* 261–285.

Patterson, F. G. P., & Linden, E. (1981). *The education of Koko.* New York: Holt, Rinehart, & Winston.

Peng, K., & Nisbett, R. E. (1999). Culture, dialectives, and reasoning about contradiction. *American Psychologist, 54,* 741–754.

Pepperberg, I. M. (2002). *The Alex studies: Cognitive and communicative abilities of grey parrots.* Cambridge, MA: Harvard University Press.

Pinker, S. (1995). *The language instinct: How the mind creates language.* New York: Harper-Collins.

Premack, D. (1971). Language in the chimpanzee. *Science, 172,* 808–822.

Pronin, E., Lin, D. Y., & Ross, L. (2002). The bias blind spot: Perceptions of bias in self versus others. *Personality and Social Psychology Bulletin, 28*(3), 369–381.

Rassin, E., Eerland, A., & Kuipers, I. (2010). Let's find the evidence: An analogue study of confirmation bias in criminal investigations. *Journal of Investigative Psychology and Offender Profiling, 7,* 231–246.

Revlis, R. (1975). Two models of syllogistic reasoning. *Journal of Verbal Learning & Verbal Behavior, 14,* 180–195.

Rice, M. L., Huston, A. C., Truglio, R., & Wright, J. (1990). Words from "Sesame Street:" Learning vocabulary while viewing. *Developmental Psychology, 26,* 421–428.

Richards, B. J. (1994). Child-directed speech and influences on language acquisition: Methodology and interpretation. In C. Gallaway & B. Richards (Eds.), *Input and interaction in language acquisition* (pp. 74–106). New York: Cambridge University Press.

Rymer, R. (1994). *Genie: A scientific tragedy.* New York: Harper Perennial.

Sachs, J. (1967). Recognition memory for syntactic and semantic aspects of connected discourse. *Perception and Psychophysics, 2,* 437–442.

Savage-Rumbaugh, S., Shanker, S., & Taylor, T. J. (1998). *Apes, language, and the human mind.* New York: Oxford University Press.

Schwartz, B., Ward, A., Monterosso, J., Lyubomirsky, S., White, K., & Lehman, D. R. (2002). Maximizing versus satisficing: Happiness is a matter of choice. *Journal of Personality and Social Psychology, 83*(5), 1178–2119.

Schwarz, N., Bless, H., Strack, F., Klumpp, G., Rittenauer-Schatka, H., Simons, A. (1991). Ease of retrieval as information: Another look at the availability heuristic. *Journal of Personality and Social Psychology, 61*(2), 195–202.

Seifert, C. M., Meyer, D. E., Davidson, N., Patalano, A. L., & Yaniv, I. (1995). Demystification of cognitive insight: Opportunistic assimilation and the prepared-mind perspective. In R. J. Sternberg & J. E. Davidson (Eds.), *The nature of insight* (pp. 65–124). Cambridge, MA: MIT Press.

Silveira, J. (1972). *Incubation: The effect of interruption timing and length on problem solution and quality of problem processing.* Unpublished doctoral dissertation, University of Oregon.

Simon, H. (1955). A behavioral model of rational choice. *Quarterly Journal of Economics, 69*(1), 99–118.

Sio, U. N., & Ormerod, T. C. (2009). Does incubation enhance problem solving? A meta-analytic review. *Psychological Bulletin, 135*(1), 94–120.

Slovic, P., Fischhoff, B., & Lichtenstein, S. (1978). Accident probabilities and seat belt usage: A psychological perspective. *Accident Analysis and Prevention, 10,* 281–285.

Slovic, P., Fischhoff, B., & Lichtenstein, S. (1979). Rating the risks. *Environment, 21*(3), 14–20, 36–39.

Smith, S. M. (1995). Fixation, incubation, and insight in memory and creative thinking. In S. M. Smith, T. B. Ward, & R. A. Finke (Eds.), *The creative cognition approach* (pp. 135–155). Cambridge, MA: MIT Press.

Stanovich, K. E., & West, R. F. (1998). Individual differences in rational thought. *Journal of Experimental Psychology: General, 127,* 161–188.

Svirsky, M. A., Robbins, A. M., Kirk, K. I., Pisoni, D. B., & Miyamoto, R. T. (2000). Language development in profoundly deaf children with cochlear implants. *Psychological Science, 11*(2), 153–158.

Triandis, H., Bontempo, R., Villareal, M., Asai, M., & Lucca, N. (1988). Individualism and collectivism: Cross-cultural perspectives on self-ingroup relationships. *Journal of Personality and Social Psychology, 54,* 323–338.

Tversky, A. (1972). Elimination by aspects: A theory of choice. *Psychological Review, 79*(4), 281–299.

Tversky, A., & Kahneman, D. (1974). Judgment under uncertainty: Heuristics and biases. *Science, 185,* 1124–1131.

Tversky, A., & Kahneman, D. (1981). The framing of decisions and the psychology of choice. *Science, 211,* 453–458.

Tversky, A., & Kahneman, D. (1991). Loss aversion in riskless choice: A reference-dependent model. *Quarterly Journal of Economics, 106*(4) 1039–1061.

Vosniadou, S. (1987). Children and metaphors. *Child Development, 58*(3), 870–885.

Wason, P. C., & Johnson-Laird, P. N. (1972). *Psychology of reasoning: Structure and content.* Cambridge, MA: Harvard University Press.

Whorf, B. J. (1956). In J. B. Carroll (Ed.), *Language, thought and reality: Selected writings of Benjamin Lee Whorf.* Boston: MIT Press.

Wilkins, M. C. (1928). The effect of changed material on the ability to do formal syllogistic reasoning. *Archives of Psychology, 16,* 83.

Wilson, T. D., & Schooler, J. W. (1991). Thinking too much: Introspection can reduce the quality of preferences and decisions. *Journal of Personality and Social Psychology, 60*(2), 181–192.

Woodward, S. A., Markman, E. M., & Fitzsimmons, C. (1994). Rapid word learning in 13- to 18-month-olds. *Developmental Psychology, 30,* 538–553.

Yates, J. F. (1990). *Judgment and decision making.* Englewood Cliffs, NJ: Prentice Hall.

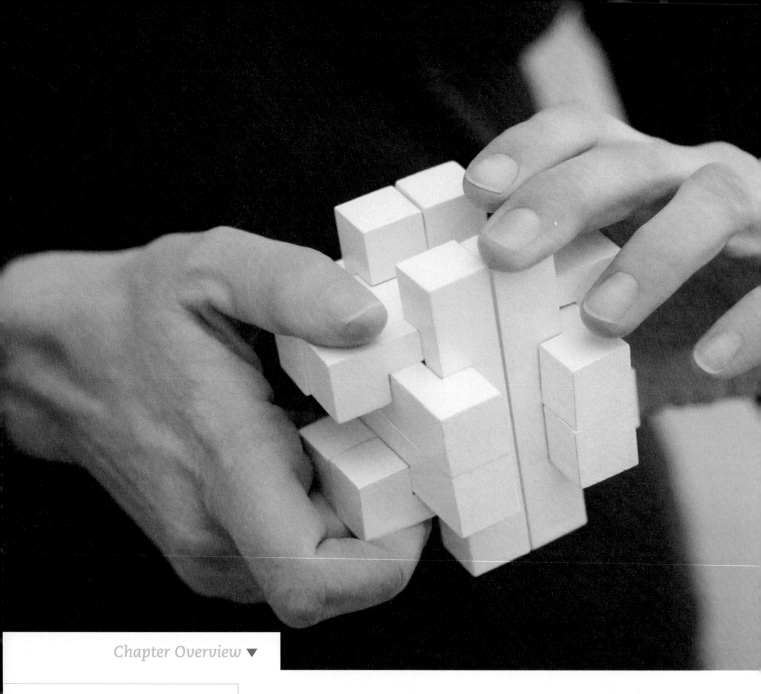

Chapter Overview ▼

9 Intelligence

Learning Objectives ▼

9.1
- Define intelligence from an adaptation perspective.
- Compare and contrast theories of intelligence.
- Explain how brain size and neural efficiency relate to intelligence.

9.2
- Examine the development of intelligence testing.
- Describe the principles of test construction.
- Discuss reliability and predictive validity of intelligence testing.

9.3
- Illustrate the varieties of intelligence including high intellectual ability and intellectual disability.

9.4
- Explain reasons for gender and ethnic gaps in standardized intelligence tests.
- Identify types of biases in intelligence testing.

9.5
- Describe the roles of genetics and environment, and their interaction, in determining intelligence.

Mrs. Nola looked angry as she told me my intelligence test results. I had produced the highest score in my second grade class, but I had missed one question: "Can you hear cabbage boiling in a pot?" I had answered, "No." She scolded me, "Of course the answer should be, 'Yes!' Anyone knows that! You can hear the water boiling away!" A tear fell as I watched her turn and walk away. I did not dare tell her what I was thinking: "Yes, you can hear it boiling, but you *cannot* know that it is *cabbage* in the pot!" Even to my 7-year-old mind, my answer seemed more intelligent than hers. (Not that I am holding a grudge!) Ever since that day, I have been suspicious of tests that claimed to measure how smart I was, how much potential I had in school, and how likely I was to succeed in life. It seemed patently unfair to judge my intelligence based on whether I had ever cooked cabbage. Are intelligence tests capable of measuring true intellectual ability? And if so, what is "intelligence"?

9.1 The Nature of Intelligence

While we may perceive a basic intellectual ability in others, there is little agreement about what that entails.

- Define intelligence from an adaptation perspective.
- Compare and contrast theories of intelligence.
- Explain how brain size and neural efficiency relate to intelligence.

We are often struck by the intelligence of individuals around us. They may quickly figure out a math problem you are struggling with, or come up with a surprising idea you have never thought about. The variation in intelligence among people seems like a fact of life: Some are particularly "gifted," while others struggle with mental tasks you find quite easy. Are these apparent differences in intelligence real? Or is it possible that we are all operating with the same basic mental capacity, and the differences we see are due to specific knowledge, training, or experience? Often, and with little evidence, we believe that someone who excels in the classroom will also be intelligent in other areas of life. What have psychologists learned about these common assumptions?

Defining Intelligence

What do we mean when we say someone is "intelligent?" When people are asked to define it, they give answers such as, "profits from experience," "reasons logically," "knows a lot about the world," "well-read and well-spoken," and "does well in school" (Sternberg et al., 1981). The word derives from *intellect*, meaning the capacity for thinking and acquiring knowledge, especially of a high or complex order. Most commonly, we think of intelligence as a general capacity to comprehend and reason, emphasizing cognition (Spearman, 1904). Though they differ in emphasis, psychologists define **intelligence** as a very general mental capability involving the ability to reason, plan, solve problems, think abstractly, comprehend complex ideas, learn quickly, and learn from experience (Gottfredson, 1997a). This emphasizes the role of learning appropriate behaviors in intelligence. To be smart, we both avoid doing things that lead to failure and figure out which things lead to success in life.

When we say someone excels in athletics, we mean that they are good at particular sports; but we would also expect them to be better than average at any physical task. For example, an NFL football player may not be great at basketball, but he would likely be better than the average person due to his strength and conditioning. Similarly, with intelligence, we expect a highly intelligent person to do well in school, perform at the top of her or his profession, and make good choices in her or his personal life. It is

Intelligence The capacity to learn from experience, acquire knowledge, adapt to the environment, and solve problems.

surprising (and makes for big new stories) when someone accomplishes a high level of achievement, such as becoming a state governor, yet displays poor judgment in financial or personal matters. We expect an intelligent person to be well rounded in mental prowess so that he or she does well in every task.

We also think of intelligence as a capacity that stays with an individual throughout life. We think that a smarter child is also going to be a smarter adult, and a straight-A college student is more likely to become a judge. In fact, people tend to maintain the same measured level of intelligence throughout their life span, with very little measurable change even in middle childhood and early adolescence (Moffitt et al., 1993). Correcting for education, there is no drop-off in test scores on vocabulary measures, but a small decline on performance tasks in the oldest group (Kaufman et al., 1989) FIGURE 9-1. However, all of us go through changes in mental capabilities as our neural systems continue to develop in adolescence and well into our twenties.

Because we view intelligence as the capacity to adapt appropriately, we expect this ability to be beneficial in whatever domain a person enters. So we expect a future doctor to have good grades in high school, run his or her personal and financial lives successfully, and succeed if they switch to law school instead. But is there flexibility in intelligence? Are "smart" people smart all of the time and in all things? Or is there more variation, so that exceptional intelligence is shown in some areas but not in every arena?

Myron Rolle, 23, is a professional football player for the Tennessee Titans. He graduated from Florida State as a pre-med major in 2½ years with a 3.75 GPA.

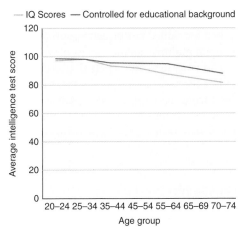

FIGURE 9-1 Scores from seven adult age groups (ranging from 20–24 to 70–74) in the WAIS-R intelligence test standardization sample, comprising a sample of 1480 men and women. *Source: Data from Kaufman, A. S., Reynolds, C. R., & McLean, J. E. (1989). Age and WAIS-R intelligence in a national sample of adults in the 20- to 74-year age range: A cross-sectional analysis witheducational level controlled. Intelligence, 13(3), 235–253.*

Theories of Intelligence

To answer these questions, psychologists have developed theories of intelligence. A central question is whether intelligence is best viewed as one core capacity or as a combination of different cognitive skills. For example, Albert Einstein is renowned as a physicist who invented the theory of relativity, Thurgood Marshall was a brilliant lawyer and Supreme Court justice, Marie Curie was the first person honored with two Nobel Prizes (in physics and chemistry), and Kenneth Wayne Jennings III holds the record for the longest winning streak (74 games) and highest money won (more than $3 million) on the game show *Jeopardy!*. Are these intellectual standouts demonstrating the same underlying "intelligence"? Psychologists have addressed this question by comparing how individuals perform on multiple tasks that vary in the type of cognitive skill required. Several different theories of intelligence have resulted (see **TABLE 9-1**).

Intelligence as a General Ability

Charles Spearman proposed that a **general intelligence (g)** capacity was the sole source of all mental abilities. Spearman gave individuals a variety of mental tasks to perform, including solving puzzles, running mazes, copying spatial designs, and forming verbal analogies (1904). While different people scored the highest on different tasks, Spearman noted that those who excelled at one task also tended to perform well on the others. So while some individuals may be more skilled in some tasks than in others, their performances in these tasks were moderately correlated. (Recall that a "moderate" correlation coefficient ranges from 0.3 to 0.7). This pattern of results led Spearman

General intelligence (g) Spearman's theory that all mental abilities reflect a single underlying capacity.

TABLE 9-1 Psychological Theories of Intelligence

Theorist	Major Concept	Key Points
Charles Spearman (1904)	General intelligence	A single, general intelligence capacity ("*g*") is the source of all mental abilities
Louis Thurstone (1938)	Primary mental abilities	Discovered a set of seven different factors related to varied task scores
Raymond Cattell (1963)	Fluid and crystalized	Discovered just two underlying abilities: fluid intelligence and crystallized intelligence
Robert Sternberg (1985)	Triarchic theory	Broadened Cattell's concept into three categories of intelligence: analytic, creative, and practical
Howard Gardner (1983)	Multiple intelligences	Proposed a theory of seven separate intelligence abilities operating independently
Mayer, Salovey, Caruso, & Sitarenios (2001)	Emotional intelligence	The ability to perceive, understand, integrate, and regulate emotions to promote personal growth

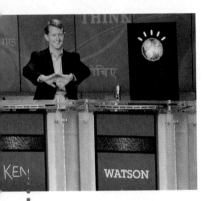

Ken Jennings III is the winningest game show participant in television history. In February, 2011, he played Jeopardy against an IBM computer program called "Watson" and lost.

Specific intelligences (s)
Spearman's theory of performance factors only involved in each particular task.

Primary mental abilities
Thurstone's theory of a set of seven different factors related to intelligence.

Fluid intelligence The ability to figure out relationships between new concepts within a given task.

Crystalized intelligence
The ability to draw upon previously learned knowledge and skills.

Intelligence test A measure intended to identify the relative mental ability of individuals.

to conclude that there is a single, general intelligence underlying performance in all intellectual tasks. So a single "intelligence" score could be determined that will predict how a person will perform on any mental task.

Of course, this correlation between tasks is not perfect. Spearman also proposed **specific intelligences (s)** that accounted for skilled performance, specific to each particular task. Any cognitive task draws upon multiple abilities, some of which are unique to the specific task (such a pressing a particular key) and others that also apply to other tasks (such as detecting a stimulus). More recent work has shown that the single g score predicts success in many areas of life, including work, physical health, and accidents (Gottfredson, 2004). Simply by knowing someone's g score, you can estimate to some degree how well that person will do on a wide variety of tasks involving intellectual and personal-life outcomes.

Intelligence as Multiple Abilities

While Spearman focused on how similar people's performances were across tasks, others focused on how performances differed. Why are some people really exceptional in math and only above average on language tasks? Louis Thurstone (1938) set out to determine how many different types of mental abilities might exist. Thurstone gave college students many different tests capturing differing aspects of intelligence. He then compared their performances to see which tasks were correlated; that is, where an individual scoring high on one (say, mental arithmetic) also scored high on the other (say, geometry). Thurstone's results showed a set of seven different types of tasks, which he called **primary mental abilities**. These include perceptual speed, verbal comprehension and fluency, number, spatial visualization, memory, and reasoning. To predict how people might perform on a task, you would need to know their abilities in all seven areas.

Raymond Cattell (1963) performed further analyses and found just two underlying abilities: **fluid intelligence**, the ability to determine relationships among new concepts, and **crystalized intelligence**, the ability to draw upon previously learned knowledge and skills. The tasks used in assessing intelligence were separable into those that rely on past learning and those that require on-the-spot processing in a novel problem context (Deary et al., 2010). An example of a test of fluid intelligence is Raven's Progressive Matrices (Raven, 2000). This test is designed to require no specific prior knowledge to perform well. Crystalized intelligence captures the facts you learned over time. Cattell further proposed that crystalized intelligence would continue to grow with age, while fluid intelligence would diminish at older ages (Cattell, 1987) FIGURE 9-2.

Analytical ability is the focus of **intelligence tests**, designed to measure intellectual ability. Both Spearman and Thurstone's work involved tasks focused on cognitive components or mental steps, such as comparing two items or solving computations. For example, consider this analogy problem: "Lawyer is to client as doctor is to . . ." To solve it, you must determine the meaning of each word, compare the relationship between

FIGURE 9-2 A theoretical depiction of intellectual abilities over the life span.
Source: Data from Intelligence: Its structure, growth and action *(p. 206) by R. B. Cattell, 1987, Amsterdam: North-Holland. Copyright 1987 by Elsevier Science Publishers.*

lawyer and *client*, map that relationship onto *doctor*, and then generate the matching word. Intelligence would be revealed on this problem by how quickly you could perform these cognitive operations and select the right answer on a multiple-choice test (*patient*; Sternberg, 1985). Analytic problems come with all the information needed to solve them and have only a single right answer, which can be reached by only a single method. These theories focused on clearly "cognitive" tasks in which a stimulus is presented and the subject thinks and then produces a written or verbal response. So the intelligence displayed involves a limited range of tasks, all very similar to "schoolwork." But what if the tasks were expanded to include a wider range of problems?

Practical problems, in contrast, require work on formulating the problem, gathering information, and using your prior experience (Neisser et al., 1996). Sternberg's (1985) **triarchic** (three-part) **theory of intelligence** extends the concept of intelligence to include not just the mental operations you perform (**analytic intelligence**) but also the ability to vary your approach to problems (**creative intelligence**) and manage your cognitive resources (**practical intelligence**) to get the job done. Creative intelligence includes the ability to decide which information is relevant, how the old connects to the new, how to combine ideas in novel ways, and to see the "big picture" when faced with a problem. The third component in Sternberg's theory is practical intelligence, the ability to assess the situation and do what is necessary to be successful. Key aspects are identifying what is expected of you, knowing your strengths and weaknesses, and working effectively within the time provided. The ability to solve the problem may not be sufficient to be successful; instead, you also need to be innovative in how you approach a task and be smart about how you work on the problem.

Expanding the Concept of Intelligence

Other theorists have expanded the notion of intelligence to include movements, audition, and even "reading" other people. Seeing the genius of a speed skater or surgeon, it seems logical to extend the notion of intelligence outside of academic tasks. Most prominently, Howard Gardner (Gardner, 1983) proposed a theory of **multiple intelligences** in which separate abilities operate independently. Gardner proposed eight types of intelligence, including linguistic, logical-mathematical, musical, spatial, bodily-kinesthetic, naturalist, interpersonal, and intrapersonal (Gardner & Hatch, 1989; see **TABLE 9-2**). To Gardner,

Triarchic theory of intelligence Sternberg's theory positing three underlying aspects of cognition: analytic, creative, and practical.

Analytic intelligence Sternberg's theory posited the ability to break problems down into component parts for analysis.

Creative intelligence Sternberg's theory suggests an underlying component of applying mental abilities to your experience in novel and helpful ways.

Practical intelligence Sternberg's theory proposed the ability to assess a situation and do what is necessary to be successful.

Multiple intelligences Gardner's theory proposed seven separate types of cognitive abilities operating independently.

TABLE 9-2 Gardner's Multiple Intelligences

Type of Intelligence	Exemplar	Core Components
Linguistic	Poet, journalist	Sensitivity to the sounds, rhythms, and meanings of words; sensitivity to the different functions of language
Logical—mathematical	Scientist, mathematician	Sensitivity to and capacity to discern logical or numerical patterns; ability to handle long chains of reasoning
Musical	Composer, violinist	Ability to produce and appreciate rhythm, pitch, and timbre; appreciation of the forms of musical expressiveness
Spatial	Navigator, sculptor	Capacity to perceive the visual-spatial world accurately and to perform transformations on initial perceptions

(continues)

TABLE 9-2 Gardner's Multiple Intelligences *(continued)*

Type of Intelligence	Exemplar	Core Components
Body—kinesthetic	Dancer, athlete	Ability to control bodily movements and to handle objects skillfully
Naturalist	Botanist, chef	Ability to make fine discriminations among the flora and fauna of the natural world or the patterns and designs of human artifacts
Interpersonal	Therapist, salesperson	Capacity to discern and respond appropriately to the moods, temperaments, motivations, and desires of other people
Intrapersonal	Person with detailed, accurate self-knowledge	Access to one's own feelings and the ability to discriminate among them and draw on them to guide behavior; knowledge of one's own strengths, weaknesses, desires, and intelligence

Source: H. Gardner & T. Hatch, Multiple intelligences go to school: Educational implications of the theory of multiple intelligences, Educational Researcher, 18(8) (1989), with adaptation based on personal communication from H. Gardner (1996).

Emotional intelligence
The ability to perceive, understand, integrate, and regulate emotions to be self-motivated and socially skilled.

individuals like Einstein, Marshall, Curie, and Jennings are "geniuses" in different ways, and a single conception of "intelligence" is not adequate to account for the varieties of intelligence they display (Gardner, 1993). More recently, Gardner has expanded this list to include spiritual or existential intelligence (Gardner, 2000).

Others have expanded the notion of intelligence to include **emotional intelligence**, or the ability to perceive, understand, integrate, and regulate emotions to promote personal growth (Mayer et al., 2001). You may have the ability to notice how others are feeling or to recognize your own emotions and use that information to guide your thoughts and behaviors (see **TABLE 9-3**) (Goleman, 1998). And it is helpful to regulate your emotions by doing things that can improve your mood. Further studies have found significant correlations between tests of emotional intelligence and general intelligence (*g*) (Schulte et al., 2004; Schutte et al., 1998). While general intelligence is important, purely intellectual ability must be managed well in order to produce desired outcomes.

TABLE 9-3 A Test of Emotional Intelligence

Take this test to determine your emotional intelligence (Schutte et al., 1998). Rate your response to each item on a five-point scale, where "1" means, "Strongly disagree," "2" is "Disagree," "3" is "Neutral," "4" is "Agree," and "5" is "Strongly agree."

1. I know when to speak about my personal problems to others _____
2. When I am faced with obstacles, I remember times I faced similar obstacles and overcame them _____
3. I expect that I will do well on most things I try _____
4. Other people find it easy to confide in me _____
5. I find it easy to understand the non-verbal messages of other people _____
6. Some of the major events of my life have led me to re-evaluate what is important and not important _____
7. When my mood changes, I see new possibilities _____
8. Emotions are one of the things that make my life worth living _____
9. I am aware of my emotions as I experience them _____
10. I expect good things to happen _____
11. I like to share my emotions with others _____
12. When I experience a positive emotion, I know how to make it last _____
13. I arrange events others enjoy _____
14. I seek out activities that make me happy _____
15. I am aware of the non-verbal messages I send to others _____

(continues)

TABLE 9-3 A Test of Emotional Intelligence *(continued)*

16. I present myself in a way that makes a good impression on others _____
17. When I am in a positive mood, solving problems is easy for me _____
18. By looking at their facial expressions, I recognize the emotions people are experiencing _____
19. I know why my emotions change _____
20. When I am in a positive mood, I am able to come up with new ideas _____
21. I have control over my emotions _____
22. I easily recognize my emotions as I experience them _____
23. I motivate myself by imagining a good outcome to tasks I take on _____
24. I compliment others when they have done something well _____
25. I am aware of the non-verbal messages other people send _____
26. When another person tells me about an important event in his or her life, I almost feel as though I have experienced this event myself _____
27. When I feel a change in emotions, I tend to come up with new ideas _____
28. When I am faced with a challenge, I don't give up because I believe I will succeed _____
29. I know what other people are feeling just by looking at them _____
30. I help other people feel better when they are down _____
31. I use good moods to help myself keep trying in the face of obstacles _____
32. I can tell how people are feeling by listening to the tone of their voice _____
33. It is not difficult for me to understand why people feel the way they do _____

Scoring: Sum the number of your scale points for each of the 33 items. A higher score suggests better emotional intelligence, and a lower score suggests lower emotional intelligence. For comparison, some average scores for female prisoners: 120.1; men: 124.8; women: 130.9; therapists: 134.9 (Schutte et al., 1998).

Source: Schutte. N. S., Malouff, J. M., Hall, L. E., Haggerty, D. J., Cooper, J. T., Golden, C. J., & Dornheim, L. (1998). Development and validation of a measure of emotional intelligence. Personality and Individual Differences, 25, *167–177.*

Creativity Novel thinking in which we redefine problems, see gaps in knowledge, generate ideas, and take reasonable risks in implementing them.

CRITICAL THINKING APPLICATION

Creativity may be a very different cognitive ability than intelligence. **Creativity** has been described as novel thinking in which we redefine problems, see gaps in knowledge, generate ideas, and take reasonable risks in implementing them (Sternberg, 2001; Treffinger et al., 2000; Weisberg, 1986). Creativity involves combining and connecting ideas in new ways (Finke, Ward, & Smith, 1992).

Consider this problem: Design a new application (app) for a cell phone. Take a minute now to think about what problems you might be able to solve with an app, what enjoyment it might provide, and what desirable features could be added to a phone though apps. When you have generated several ideas, choose one and write it out, including a drawing of what it might look like.

Now, should you consider your proposed app "creative"? One of the most widely accepted definitions of a creative outcome is one that is both "novel" and "useful" (Amabile, 1996). Does yours meet both criteria? Usually, people feel that it is not too difficult to think of an app that would be useful. Imagine an app that would find the closest public restroom in the vicinity of the phone—very useful! But what about

novelty? Is your idea one that may already exist among the thousands of apps already available on phones? Or is it one that no one is likely to have thought of yet?

While we think of intelligence as a set capacity that does not change much over a lifetime, studies have shown that creativity can be trained in any individual (Scott et al., 2004). What can you do to improve your creative skills? Here is a set of suggestions drawn from research on creativity:

Find the problem. Studies of successful artists found that they did not just "jump" into creating; instead, they stopped, considered, and developed their ideas about what the "problem" really was (Csikszentmihalyi & Getzels, 1988). What essence or emotion did they want to capture in their art? For the app design, think

(Continues)

CRITICAL THINKING APPLICATION (Continued)

through how you use your phone and about the bugs or problems of everyday life with which it could potentially be helpful. Before you can create a "genius" solution, you need to deeply understand and then capture the problem.

Generate as many ideas as possible. You only need one really good idea for a successful business. But, to find one, it is best to first generate as many ideas as possible! Then, you can select among them to find the best (Smith, 1998). To do so, you want to try a wide variety of techniques and approaches. For example, you might think about ways that people used their home phones in the 1960s and then think of what people carry in their purses or wallets as ways to generate more ideas.

Break your "set." Psychological studies show that people have a hard time thinking of a *second* idea. Once the first becomes established, you tend to like it, and this becomes your "mental set" (Bilalic et al., 2010). As a result, you may get "stuck" on that solution and fail to see alternatives. So try to produce variation among your ideas by taking a set-breaking attitude. What if you *could not* use your cell phone? What apps does that suggest? Or what if you could only use it underwater? Try to switch the ways in which you think about the problem so that you can get to varied ideas.

Combine two very different things. Some studies have shown the power of analogies in creating new ideas (Dahl & Moreau, 2002). For example, think about ways animals communicate and what that may suggest for cell phones. Or use conceptual combination (Finke et al., 1992), in which you put two very different ideas together. For example, how could your cell phone serve as a kitchen? These techniques help you consider "far-out" ideas that do not come readily to mind.

Take a break and incubate. A final approach is to take a step away from the problem and come back at a later time. This period in which you are not working on the problem, called "incubation," may help by exposing you to information that may help in your task (Seifert et al., 1995). At the least, you will come back refreshed with a new approach to your problem.

Creativity is linked to intelligence because, certainly, some intelligence is required for the purposeful act of creation (Sternberg, 2001). However, the fact that creative potential changes with training, such as music lessons, cooking experience, and creativity programs, means it is not a fixed capacity. Instead, every individual can become more creative by practicing techniques like the ones listed above.

Now, about that cell phone app design . . . Try it again, with these ideas in mind!

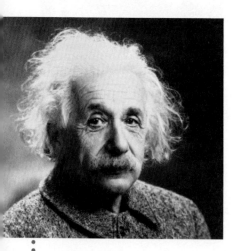

Many applications have been designed for cell phones. Can you create a new one, suggesting a novel and useful idea?

The Brain and Intelligence

Cognitive theories have not yet explained the nature of intelligence. Can we gain any evidence about intelligence from studies of the brain? The long-standing assumption has been that "size matters": Bigger brains have long been thought to relate to better mental functioning. For example, researchers preserved Albert Einstein's brain, hoping to find that the great theoretical physicist would show different features in the anatomy of his brain. On autopsy, they discovered that Einstein's brain was actually a bit smaller than that of other men his size. However, they did find that the area of the brain devoted to mathematical thinking was 15% wider than in other comparison samples (Witelson, Kigar, & Harvey, 1999) FIGURE 9-3. This area was also unusual in that it lacked a sulcus, or cleft, seen in all control brain samples. Visuospatial cognition, mathematical thought, and imagery of movement are associated with this inferior parietal lobe area. And as it happens, Einstein said he came up with visual images and then translated them into the language of mathematics (the theory of special relativity, for example, was triggered by his musings on what it would be like to ride through space on a beam of light).

What about for the rest of us? Is brain size related to intelligence? The clearest evidence is that, in healthy people, total brain volume (measured using structural MRI) is moderately correlated ($r = 0.35$) with intelligence test scores (Deary et al., 2010). But is this true for the entire brain, or are there specific areas of brain function most related to intelligence? Based on a review of existing fMRI studies, Jung and Haier (2007) proposed that the parietal and frontal brain regions, along with the association cortex, show the

Albert Einstein, physicist and Nobel prize winner.

FIGURE 9-3 Comparison of a male control brain (1, 2, 3) and the brain of Einstein (4, 5, 6). Notice the relatively larger posterior parietal area.

greatest relationship to scores on tests of intelligence. These regions are thought to be connected by a special neural tract to facilitate communication between them FIGURE 9-4. Keep in mind that studies are correlational in nature, so how the quantity of brain tissue relates to the quality of cognitive functions is unknown (Deary et al., 2010).

However, when it comes to intelligence, size may be less important than efficiency in brain functioning. Neural circuits that link areas and offer fast movement of signals between areas may be important to intelligence. Deary and colleagues (2010, using functional neuroimaging findings) suggest intelligent brains process information more efficiently (that is, use fewer neural resources when performing cognitive tasks) than do less intelligent brains. So the sheer size of the brain may be less important than the development of interconnections between brain areas supporting intelligence. So brains

FIGURE 9-4 The brain areas correlated with intelligence (Jung and Haier, 2007). The yellow areas show left-hemispheric correlations, and in green, right-hemispheric correlations. The arcuate fasciculus (shown in pink) is a white matter tract that connects the involved brain regions.

of more intelligent people may simply work faster than the brains of others. Supporting this idea, research has found that the speed with which people can perform simple tasks is correlated with intelligence (Deary, Der, & Ford, 2001). The tasks include determining which of two lines is longer (called inspection speed; Deary & Stough, 1996) or pressing (as quickly as possible) one of eight buttons that is currently lighted. People with higher conduction speed also had higher scores on an intelligence test FIGURE 9-5. Brains that are better wired to pass along signals faster may be responsible for some of the differences observed in intelligence.

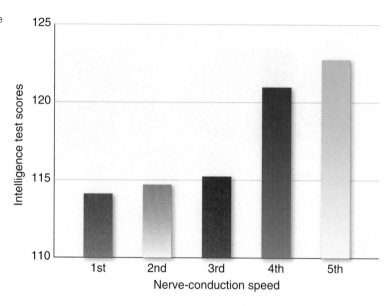

FIGURE 9-5 Performance by subjects ordered from slowest (1st) to fastest (5th)
Source: Adapted from Deary, I. J., Der, G., & Ford, G. (2001). Reaction times and intelligence differences: A population-based cohort study. Intelligence, 29*(5), 389–399.*

CONCEPT LEARNING CHECK 9.1   *Comparing Theories of Intelligence*

Several different theories have been proposed to account for the nature of intelligence. For each example below, identify the theory most related, and explain how it accounts for the example.

A. Spearman's *g*

B. Thurstone's primary abilities

C. Cattell's fluid and crystalized intelligence

D. Sternberg's triarchic theory of intelligence

E. Gardner's theory of multiple intelligences

F. Emotional intelligence

1. _____ Ben works part time as a bagger at the grocery store, where he excels in imagining how the individual items can be put together within the space of a paper bag to produce the best fit.

2. _____ Ellie is going on 80, and while she has slowed down some in her thinking, she can still quickly recall her knowledge of books from her years of work as a librarian.

3. _____ Thurman is undecided about his career direction, so while in college, he took the MCAT (premedical school exam), the LSAT (the prelaw exam), and the GRE (the graduate study exam). Thurman was hoping the tests would make his decision for him; however, he scored in the 95th percentile on all three exams.

4. _____ Katrina loves math and does really well in her math courses and on tests of mathematical ability. However, whenever the test involves verbal material, Katrina has difficulty reading and receives much lower scores.

5. _____ Sharan has a difficult time in her courses, but she excels in her entrepreneurship club and is able to come up with very creative ideas for products.

6. _____ Helaina is the "house mom" of her dorm: She loves meeting new people, learning about them, and connecting to them emotionally.

9.2 Measuring Intelligence

Tests are designed to measure intelligence, but what they measure is debatable.

- ■ Examine the development of intelligence testing.
- ■ Describe the principles of test construction.
- ■ Discuss reliability and predictive validity of intelligence testing.

Intelligence is one of the most debated topics within the field of psychology. One reason is that the stakes involved are extremely high. Many opportunities—such as attending top schools, selection for important jobs, and appointments to leadership positions—are reserved for the "most intelligent" candidates. Clearly, selecting intelligent candidates for medical school would make good use of human resources. But how do we determine who is most intelligent? Tests depend on underlying theories of the nature of intelligence, and as we have seen, there is little agreement on this question. As a result, intelligence is defined, practically speaking, as "whatever the tests test" (Boring, 1923). In this section, we will uncover the history of the intelligence test and explain the state of the art.

The Development of Intelligence Testing

Intelligence is a controversial topic because some people have tried to use intelligence tests for their own political agenda, claiming one group of people is superior to others. Sir Francis Galton (1822–1911), a cousin of naturalist Charles Darwin, noted that some families (including his own) in English society at the time seemed to have a wealth of intelligent individuals. This led him to suspect that intelligence was based on genetics. One of the problems with his reasoning is that most "intelligent" people he studied also happened to be well educated, while the less intelligent people he tested were often poor and not well educated. But which factor caused the other? Galton concluded that wealth and power were caused by intelligence, and one of his followers developed the idea of "eugenics," through which society could be improved by "weeding out" people who were not intelligent and encouraging those who were to have more children. It was suggested that some individuals of low intelligence should be sterilized, and such programs for developmentally disabled individuals ended as recently as 1981 in the United States (Sullivan, 2002).

Street scene in France, 1904, at the time of Binet's development of the first modern intelligence test.

Alfred Binet: Predicting School Achievement

The modern study of intelligence testing began with Alfred Binet (1857–1911), who was asked by the French Ministry of Education in 1904 to come up with a way to identify children who were "sub-normals." Binet and his colleague, Theodore Simon, collected a wide variety of tasks, including memory, math, vocabulary, and logical reasoning, focusing on schoolwork. He then tested many children on these tasks and found which ones predicted academic success. Binet selected 30 items of increasing difficulty for the test's final version. **TABLE 9-4** provides examples of the test items

TABLE 9-4 Items from Binet's Tests of Intelligence for Children

Year 3
1. Point to eyes, nose, and mouth
2. Repeat two digits
3. Identify objects in a picture
4. Repeat a sentence of six syllables

Year 7
1. Show right hand and left ear
2. Describe a picture
3. Carry out three commands given simultaneously
4. Count the value of six coins

Year 15
1. Repeat seven digits
2. Find three rhymes for a given word in one minute
3. Repeat a sentence of twenty-six syllables
4. Interpret a set of given facts

Source: Binet, A. & Simon T. (1916). The development of intelligence in children: The Binet-Simon Scale. E.S. Kite (Trans.), Training School at Vineland New Jersey, Department of Research No. 11. Baltimore, MD: Williams & Wilkins.

Standardized procedure
Protocol for testing that follows the same steps for all test takers.

Norm Comparison of many individuals on the same test so that relative performance can be determined.

Mental age The average level of intellectual development for a child of a particular age.

Scale A test designed to measure a particular skill from low to high.

Intelligence quotient (IQ) The ratio of a child's "mental age" score on the Stanford-Binet test divided by his or her chronological age.

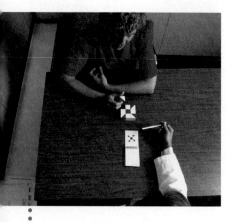

All over the world, children are given standardized intelligence tests every year.

test items representing average performance at different age levels. Binet also took care to conduct the tests in the same manner for each child: The test was administered to one student at a time by one examiner who posed tasks and questions. Testing required several hours, beginning with simpler problems and progressing until the student was unable to give correct answers. This **standardized procedure** ensured that every child had the same experience during testing and that the examiner would give the same instructions to all.

The problem Binet had to solve was, "What is the criterion, or standard, for 'intelligent' responses?" Suppose a child is tested on a problem like, "Can you hear cabbage boiling in a pot?" Is this a good question that reflects whether a child would benefit from school? How could we know? There must be some standard for comparison; otherwise, even a bright child may get the item wrong. Binet solved this by testing all of the items with students of differing ages. This allowed the establishment of **norms**, or the average performance across a large number of students. Then they could compare a single child's answers to those of others the same age. By doing so, they could calculate what Binet called a "**mental age**," or the average level of intellectual development for a child of a given age. A child with the mental age of 10 gives answers like other 10-year-olds on the scale. If they scored more similarly to 8-year-olds, their mental age would be 8 even though they were older, and if they were more advanced, their mental age would be higher than their chronological age (birth year). This allowed the placement of students into classes with others of similar schoolwork ability.

Binet's **scale** (called "scale" because it measures) worked very well at identifying students who scored similarly on the exam. But recall that the standard for comparison is the average from the students already in school FIGURE 9-6. All the first graders had been tested, and their average score now served as the norm for new students. By definition, they would score well on the test. If a student failed to score as well as current first graders, what can be concluded? What if, in 1904, the tested students who comprised the mental age group were mainly children from city families who did not need them to work? Later, rural families became able to send their children to school. These rural children may have had different experiences, such as little access to books or reading in their homes, more limited exposure to foods, industries, and travelers, and little practice at sitting quietly in a chair and answering questions. As a result, such a child may not achieve his or her mental age on Binet's normed scale. But the cause may not have been intelligence, but experience. No matter: Binet made no claims about what the test measured; instead, his scale provided a way to compare new children to those already in school. This circular reasoning in item development is an inherent feature of testing: You must begin with some way of deciding which items belong on the test.

Lewis Terman and the Stanford-Binet Intelligence Test

From Binet's work, intelligence testing in the same form has continued to this day. In 1916, Louis Terman at Stanford University translated and revised the scale and collected new norms. The Stanford-Binet Scale had its latest revision in 2004 (Roid & Barram, 2004). Terman also contributed an important concept, based on work by German psychologist William Stern, called the **intelligence quotient (IQ)**. Recall that Binet's mental age is based on test performance. By dividing the child's mental age by her or his chronological age, you can create a ratio reflecting the comparison. If mental age is greater than chronological, the ratio is greater than 1; if they are the same, the ratio is 1; and if the test score is lower

FIGURE 9-6 Determining whether an intelligence test item is a good one depends on having a criterion for comparison; however, this leads to a circular definition.

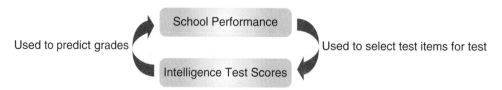

Used to predict grades   School Performance   Used to select test items for test

Intelligence Test Scores

than the age, the ratio is less than 1. Terman multiplied each ratio by 100 to increase the size of the number:

$$IQ = \frac{\text{Mental Age}}{\text{Chronological Age}} \times 100$$

Terman's formula indicated how mental age and chronological age are related. The average IQ for a population is set to 100. A score above 100 meant that you were smarter than average, and a score below 100 meant that you were less intelligent than the average student. This technique worked well for children, but not for adults: If you performed the same on the test when you were 20 and 21, your IQ would actually go down! Another problem is that a 9-year-old who scores the same as 10-year-olds has a higher IQ than a 10-year-old who scores the same as 11-year-olds. Current tests no longer use the IQ ratio, but people frequently refer to their scores on intelligence tests as their IQ. Scores on other intelligence tests are still designed to have 100 indicate the average score, reflecting Terman's legacy.

The Wechsler Intelligence Scales

As chief psychologist of New York City's Bellevue Psychiatric Hospital, David Wechsler (1896–1981) saw many patients passing through the system. He needed more efficient measures of adult intelligence that were easy to administer and required shorter testing time for his patients. In 1955, he published the first **Wechsler Adult Intelligence Scale (WAIS)**, revised in 1981 (WAIS-R), 1997 (WAIS-III), and 2008 (WAIS-IV). Wechsler identified two primary categories of intelligence, one for verbal and one for nonverbal performance. The verbal tests included information, comprehension, arithmetic, similarities, vocabulary, and digit span. Performance tests included block patterns, picture arrangement, object assembly, picture completion, and digit-to-symbol mapping. Examples of the types of items on the most recent update of the WAIS are shown in FIGURE 9-7.

Wechsler Adult Intelligence Scale (WAIS) An intelligence test written for adults and widely used in group assessment.

VERBAL

General information:
What is a ruby?

Comprehension:
Why do people keep money in a bank?

Arithmetic reasoning:
How many nickels are needed to make $2.15?

Vocabulary:
Tell me the meaning of deficit.

PERFORMANCE

Object assembly:
Arrange these blocks into this pattern.

Digit symbol substitution:

FIGURE 9-7 Example of the types of items found on the Wechsler Adult Intelligence Scale.
Source: Adapted from Thorndike, A. L., & Hagen, E. P. (1977). Measurement and evaluation in psychology and education. New York: Macmillan.

The verbal and performance subscales are used to determine the strengths and weaknesses of an individual and sometimes provide clues about neurological deficits with adult patients. They are also useful in identifying and planning interventions for language disabilities; for example, a patient may score high on the performance scales and lower on verbal scales. Because it is the most popular intelligence test used to test individuals, you will be likely to see it should you ever undergo intelligence testing as an adult. Military services, government jobs, and many employers use these fairly speedy assessments to screen individuals. For children in school, the WISC (Wechsler Intelligence Scale for Children) is the standard individual test given to students in public schools when evaluation is necessary. And if your child is headed for an elite preschool program, she or he will likely take a preschool test, the WPPSI, before she or he can read.

Group Intelligence Testing

More likely, you have already had a version of an intelligence test aimed at assessing your aptitude, or the likelihood of benefitting from further training. **Aptitude tests** are given to groups of people with paper and pencil or computerized administration. Group testing measures were developed by Robert Yerkes (1876–1956) for the armed services as an efficient way to screen recruits and identify appropriate jobs during wartime. During World War I, the U.S. Army gave Yerkes' test to 1.75 million recruits to screen out the unfit (those scoring low) and to identify candidates for officer training (those scoring high). Current military enlistment standards exclude any individual whose score is below about 85 (Gottfredson, 1998). Today, **group aptitude tests** are a rite of passage for those applying to colleges. The Scholastic Assessment Test (SAT) and the ACT (from American College Testing, Inc.) are often used as predictors of your ability to benefit from college training as aptitude tests. However, they also explicitly measure past achievement in school, such as knowledge of geometry. **Achievement tests** are intended to measure the *outcomes* of education; that is, what was learned, rather than how well you might learn in a new program of study. State and national testing programs use achievement tests at all grade levels to determine how well schools are doing at educating children to specific standards. Colleges have become increasingly reliant on group aptitude test scores in admissions, so "merit" for college education is defined based on test scores (Alon & Tienda, 2007).

Group standardized testing, allowing the comparison of individuals on a national and international basis, were devised in the 1930s as a way to "level the playing field" and ensure that those admitted to elite colleges were those students deserving of the opportunity (Lemann, 1999). However, the tests have also been criticized as providing unfair advantage to those who attend top preparatory schools (or simply better schools), putting those from other backgrounds at a disadvantage. For example, some individuals pay for coaching classes from companies that analyze the exams each year. The average gain from a preparatory class is around 50 points on the 400–1600 SAT scale (Powers & Rock, 1999). The main advantage from retaking tests is that the test taker is more familiar with the exam format. So investing in learning about the test in advance may pay off.

Some group tests are explicitly designed to survey knowledge needed for professional training, such as the MCAT (Medical College Admission Test). Others purport to measure aptitude for skills like management (the Graduate Management Admission Test, or GMAT). The Graduate Record Exam (GRE) is an aptitude test for postcollege study in any field. Increasingly, questions are being raised about its value in comparing applicants coming from diverse educational circumstances. Studies show that the best predictor of college success is grades, not test scores. Many qualities important for graduate study are more evident in transcripts and letters of recommendation. However, because these tests are offered, the test information is often used to compare individuals for admissions and scholarships.

Given the importance of aptitude tests in students' opportunities, it is fair to ask, "What do they measure?" To answer this, think back to the beginning of the intelligence test and Binet's work in the French classroom. There must be a criterion for comparison. Consider how a standardized exam like the GRE creates new questions: They add them onto the end of existing tests and then use the current test scores of these individuals to decide whether the item reflects ability. So a student scoring high on the exam should get the new item correct, and a student with a low score should get the item incorrect; if that happens, it is a useful item for future tests. The circular question of how to decide that an item is able to identify an "intelligent" or "high-aptitude" student remains.

Principles of Test Construction

Testing has come a long way since 1904. What are the principles involved in creating a successful test of intelligence?

Aptitude test A measure of the ability to benefit from further training.

Group aptitude test A test meant to assess your ability to benefit from further training or education, but are also affected by past achievements in school. (e.g., ACT)

Achievement test A measure of what is already known or learned, as the outcome of education.

Selecting Questions for Intelligence Tests

The most frequently used test, the Wechsler Adult Intelligence Scale, includes a wide variety of types of questions in order to tap intelligence in differing domains. The test includes questions that require specific background knowledge. For example, the verbal scale includes questions that require cultural knowledge ("On what continent is France?" and "Why are children required to go to school?"). It also tests for vocabulary and arithmetic, skills clearly developed during schooling. On the performance scale, a picture completion task requires putting images in order, such as the sequence of steps in catching a fish. Object assembly tasks involve putting pieces of a picture into a whole, such as recognizing a violin, and picture completion tasks involve figures such as windmills or horses. It is difficult to create test items that do not rely on some background knowledge.

Items like this point out a problem with test items related to experience. Better schools and exposure to specific cultural knowledge will make some people better able to answer these items. If your family just returned from a trip to France, you are much more likely to answer that question correctly, while if you have never been fishing or seen a violin, your limited experience puts you at a disadvantage. Consequently, there has been concern about whether intelligence tests are culture fair or may depend on a specific cultural exposure (Cattell, 1949). One test demonstrated that it is possible to select a culture, such as African Americans in the 1970s, and design a test where only that group would perform well (Williams, 1972). Raven's Progressive Matrices task (Raven, 2000) was designed to avoid all verbal references by relying on visual pattern matching as a test of intelligence. However, this results in a single type of measure, while other tasks may reveal other intellectual strengths.

Increasingly, tasks are added to tests attempt to tap intellectual processes without drawing upon past knowledge. An example is the digit symbol task, in which you are provided with a map between numbers and unique figures, and you must quickly map the figures into a new order on the test item. Other new tasks supplementing the most recent version of the WAIS include more object mapping tasks, such as balancing objects on a scale, and constructing block designs. One task, called cancellation, requires you to quickly follow instructions to mark only some objects on the page even though other, similar objects are present FIGURE 9-8. The intent of these new items is to allow the assessment of the ability to quickly reason in a new domain and minimize the need for recall of past knowledge.

Cross out all *except*:

Example:

Test item:

FIGURE 9-8 This sample test question illustrates an object mapping task called cancellation. *Source: Adapted from Vernon, P. A. (1983). Speed of information processing and general intelligence.* Intelligence, 7(1), 53–70.

Heavy emphasis is also placed on the capacity of working memory. It makes sense that working memory is important to intelligence because any complex task requires maintaining information in memory (Engle et al., 1999). For example, when you add the numbers 396 and 417, you need to keep the result of each computation in mind as you turn to the next column. If you are able to create and store intermediate results as you are working and recall them as needed, you can work further into a problem without losing

Working memory capacity The amount of information you can retain for a short period and report back correctly.

Standardization Conversion of scores from the number of correct answers to a relative performance score compared to others on the same test.

any information. To test **working memory capacity**, or the amount of information you can retain for a short interval of time, intelligence tests like the WAIS use the digit span test: You hear a sequence of digits and report back the entire string in order. The longer the string of consecutive digits you can listen to and report back correctly, the greater your working memory capacity.

Researchers have found that working memory capacity strongly predicts your performance on many intelligence tests, including abstract problem-solving and even social intelligence (Ackerman, 2005). However, new evidence has shown that it is possible to train your working memory skills, increasing your score on tests of fluid intelligence (Cattell, 1963). In these studies, individuals underwent training on the "*n*-back" task, which requires you to remember a series of stimuli. For example, you see a string of letters presented one at a time on a computer screen "C—A—G—T—?" and are asked to report the stimulus that appeared a certain number of trials (*n*) "back" (before the test question). So, if *n* = 3, you would report "C" (3 back), and if *n* = 2, you would report "A" (2 back). This requires that you keep the stimuli in memory so that you are prepared to answer whenever the test comes up. Jaeggi and colleagues (2008; 2011) found that practicing this kind of task for about 20 minutes each day for 20 days significantly improves performance on a standard test of fluid intelligence. And this improvement lasted for up to 3 months after training. Some people were able to work up to recalling as many as nine letters back! This is good news if your goal is to "train your brain" to perform at its best on reasoning problems.

But it does raise questions about the items on intelligence test: If practice can improve your intelligence scores, then is the test really measuring an underlying, unchanging intelligence? Or do these findings suggest that we can all improve our intelligence by practicing cognitive tasks? This raises a very different view of "whatever the tests test!"

Standardization

Intelligence scores are meaningful only in comparison to others who have taken the same test. Your height and weight have an independent or absolute value in the world, where the score is meaningful by itself. Your intelligence score, on the other hand, must be compared to others' in order to derive its meaning. For example, how many difficult problems should you have to solve in order to be considered "intelligent"? There is no absolute answer to this question. However, by comparing how many you solve to how many *others* solve, we can determine your relative success. Modern intelligence test scores, along with aptitude and achievement tests, are always converted from the number of correct answers you gave to your relative performance compared to others on the same test. This process is called **standardization**.

The range of measureable scores on intelligence tests is from around 20 to 145. Scores in the middle of this range are the most stable or accurate. But when measured, people's scores do not fall evenly across this range. Instead, the frequency of scores forms a bell-shaped curve FIGURE 9-9, with most people scoring near the center and fewer on the two ends of the range. This bell curve is also called the normal distribution (or normal curve) and refers to the common phenomenon of natural observations falling in a specific

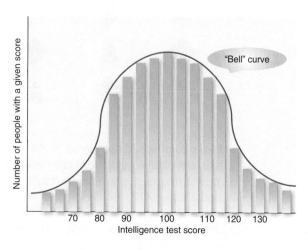

FIGURE 9-9 Intelligence scores fall in a normal distribution, centered around the average score of 100.

pattern around an average. For example, a graph showing the height of all students taking your course would show that the majority cluster around the average height of the group, with fewer at the more extreme points, and very few that are much shorter or much taller than the average. Many aspects of human performance are normally distributed; typically, performance on academic tests results in a normal curve, with most students clustered around the average score.

Recall that Terman set the average score at 100. Later tests (like Wechsler's) use this same average and compute intelligence scores as deviation IQ scores, representing the point on the normal distribution where a score falls. With the standard deviation of the distribution set at 15, a score of 115 would mean the person scored one standard deviation above the mean, and an 85 would indicate he or she scored one standard deviation below the mean. Because raw intelligence test scores are converted into this normal distribution, 68% of individuals score between 85 and 115, or one standard deviation away from the mean FIGURE 9-10. Two standard deviations reflect scores of 70 to 130, and more than 95% of test takers score within this range. That leaves less than 5% of people scoring lower than 70 or higher than 130. The extreme scores indicate these individuals are very different than the majority of people taking the test. So modern test scores are "normed" so as to reveal exactly where you fall on this normal distribution of intelligence scores. These norms are comparable to percentile scores, indicating the percentage of scores falling below a certain value. So the average test score of 100 is also the median score and the 50th percentile, where half of the group scores lower and half scores higher.

FIGURE 9-10 Test scores are converted to reflect how far they fall from the mean given the scores of others taking the test, called standardization.

Reliability

A well-designed measure is consistent, called **reliability**. Imagine you weigh yourself on a scale two times over the course of a day. If your weight was about the same each time, the scale would be said to have high **test-retest reliability**, in which repeating the measurement leads to the same outcome. You can imagine if the two weights were very different, you would not have much faith in that scale. So we can measure the reliability of intelligence tests by giving the test multiple times to the same person. What happens when this procedure is followed? Test-retest reliability of intelligence tests is very high. The standard error of measurement is about 3 points; so the odds are about 2 out of 3 that a repeated test will produce a score that ranges from 3 points above to 3 points below the first score. In general, correlations between scores for the same individual are around +0.95 (Kaufman, 2009). Whatever the test measures, it appears quite good at measuring the same thing again at a later time. In fact, there is good correlation between intelligence test scores at a young age and in later life. A single 45-minute test of general intelligence had a correlation of +0.63 for people tested at age 11 and then again at 79 years (Deary et al., 2003)! Individuals are not born with fixed, unchangeable levels of intelligence; however, scores do gradually stabilize during childhood and generally do not change much as an adult.

You also want to be sure that all the items in your test are measuring the same thing. For example, imagine a test with 15 calculus problems and one analogy question. All the

Reliability Consistency in measurement.

Test-retest reliability The likelihood of receiving a similar score when a test is repeated.

math questions may be measuring one set of knowledge, but the analogy question is measuring something else. If you were trying to measure math skill, this test would be said to have low within-test reliability because of the analogy item. Another way to ensure reliability is to consider within-test comparisons, called **split-half reliability**. Performance on one-half of the test (say, the even-numbered items) is compared against performance on the other half (the odd-numbered items). If the test were measuring one underlying ability, scores on one half would be highly correlated with the other. Intelligence tests are well designed to ensure this type of reliability. Items that do not produce similar results are removed from the test, and repeat testing on new people continues until the items are consistent across the test. Individuals rarely perform equally well on all the different kinds of items: One may do relatively better on verbal than on spatial items, for example, while another may show the opposite pattern. Nevertheless, subtests measuring different abilities tend to be positively correlated, so that people who score high on one such subtest are likely to be above average on others as well (Neisser et al., 1996).

Validity

The more important question about intelligence tests is their **validity**: Do they really get at what we mean when we say someone is "intelligent"? There are several different types of validity to consider. **Content validity** refers to the surface appearance of the items on the test and whether they reflect the underlying concept. For example, an intelligence test could include a question like, "Do you eat oatmeal in the morning?" This may actually relate to intelligence to some degree, in that people who eat healthy breakfasts are more likely to get good nutrition and perform better in school. So, indirectly, oatmeal may relate to intelligence. However, the content of the problem does not reflect what we think of as "intelligence." This brings us back to the "cabbage boiling" example in the chapter opener. This item lacks content validity because it does not reflect, on its surface, intellectual ability. Modern intelligence tests have moved away from items like these toward reasoning problems that look more like they tap what we intend on intelligence tests.

Another way to determine how well intelligence tests tap what we really mean when we say someone is "intelligent" is to assess their predictive ability. How do intelligence test scores relate to real-life outcomes? We imagine that intelligence is the key to success in all of our endeavors. Intelligence should enhance your ability to learn and adapt to new challenges in every area of life. So what outcomes are related to high scores on intelligence tests, called **predictive validity**? Intelligence test scores have a high correlation with school performance (Binet's original goal in creating his test). They are correlated at around $r = +0.50$ with school grades (Kline, 1991). This is very substantial considering all of the factors that vary in education (schools, curricula, teachers, study time, etc.). This means that the explained variance in grades is 25%; that is, the proportion of the variability in grades that is accounted for by intelligence test scores is one-quarter. As Neisser and colleagues concluded, "Wherever it has been studied, children with high scores on tests of intelligence tend to learn more of what is taught in school than their lower-scoring peers" (Neisser et al., 1996).

Your intelligence test score also predicts the number of years of education you will complete, your occupational status, and your income in adult life. Of course, this is a circular pattern: If you "test well," you will do well on the achievement tests that determine your access to educational opportunities, which lead to better jobs. Intelligence test scores are among the best predictors of how well employees perform in their jobs and are a much better predictor ($r = +0.53$) than job interviews ($r = +0.14$) or education ($r = +0.10$; Hunter & Hunter, 1984). Occupations also differ in the range of intelligence test scores, as shown in FIGURE 9-11 (Hauser, 2002).

Intelligence tests also predict success in other life outcomes. Gottfredson (1998) reviews evidence showing many social and personal outcomes in life, as well as job stability and likelihood of incarceration, are correlated with performance on intelligence tests FIGURE 9-12. For example, people who score highly on intelligence tests are more likely to achieve high-status jobs (Gottfredson, 2003). There is some evidence that even moderate differences in measured intelligence scores predict systematic differences in outcomes. Comparing those somewhat below average (between 76 and 90) and somewhat above average scores (between 111 and 125), men are more likely to be unemployed, and

Split-half reliability Performance on one-half of the test is compared against performance on the other half.

Validity The ability of a measure to capture what was intended.

Content validity Refers to the surface appearance of the items on the test and whether they reflect the concept of interest (also called face validity).

Predictive validity The ability of a test to identify those who will have high scores on other measures.

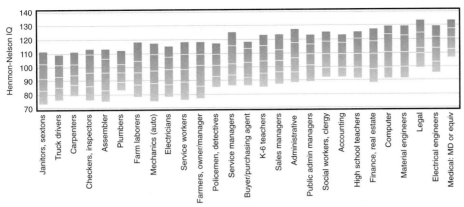

FIGURE 9-11 Henmon-Nelson IQ test scores for occupational groups. The horizontal lines represents the 25th to 75th percentiles, and the middle line is the mean.
Source: Adapted from Hauser, R. M. 2002. "Meritocracy, cognitive ability, and the sources of occupational success." CDE Working Paper 98-07 (rev). Center for Demography and Ecology, The University of Wisconsin-Madison, Madison, Wisconsin.

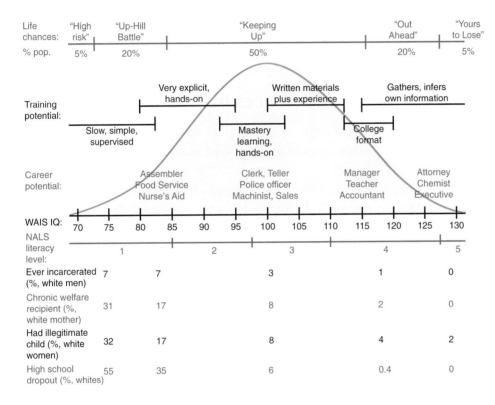

FIGURE 9-12 Career outcomes along parts of the intelligence test continuum.
Source: Reproduced from Gottfredson, L. S. (1997b). Why g matters: The complexity of everyday life. Intelligence, 24(1), 79–132.

women are more likely to become welfare recipients. People with scores somewhat below average are 88 times more likely to drop out of high school, seven times more likely to be jailed, and five times more likely to live in poverty than people of somewhat above-average scores (Gottfredson, 1998). In addition, below-average scorers are 50 percent more likely to be divorced.

Perhaps it is not surprising that higher-scoring individuals do better in school and enjoy more positive life outcomes compared to those who score lower and struggle with school, employment, and social and financial stability. However, these comparisons are between individuals that differ quite a bit on their test scores. The predictive ability of the tests arises from the extreme ends of the spectrum: Those with very high intelligence scores have much better outcomes than those with very low. When you consider just those who are admitted to college, the scores have a restricted range, meaning you are comparing those who score in only a small part of the distribution. Once people have achieved this higher score, differences in test scores among them may hold little predictive ability. In other words, the fact that your roommate's ACT score was five points higher than yours has no bearing on your future outcomes. Intelligence tests are most useful in determining, as Binet first set out to do in 1904, which children will struggle in school.

1. For each score, identify the meaning of the score by referring to Figure 9-10. What does each score tell you about that person's intelligence?

    A. John scored a 100 on his intelligence test.

    B. Susan scored a 115 on her intelligence test.

    C. Bill scored a 70 on his intelligence test.

    D. Kate scored a 170 on her intelligence test.

2. Which of these concepts is best developed in intelligence tests, and why?

    A. Reliability

    B. Validity

3. Explain the two types of validity described for intelligence tests: content and predictive.

9.3 Individual Differences in Intelligence

What identifies individuals scoring at the extremes of intelligence tests?

- Illustrate the varieties of intelligence including high intellectual ability and intellectual disability.

As a way to determine which students need additional assistance, intelligence tests perform a vital role in making sure all children receive the support they need to succeed in school. While intelligence tests work well for this purpose, their use has been extended to comparing individuals for selective admission to schools, eligibility for scholarships, hiring, and qualification for government support programs. When comparing the test scores of individuals, small differences in scores may not predict much in terms of differences in intellectual ability. However, very large differences—those falling more than two standard deviations from the average score—have been a focus of attention. In this section, we examine the characteristics of individuals who score very high and very low on intelligence tests.

Intellectual Disability

Intellectual disability
A limitation in intellectual functioning indicated by an intelligence test score of less than 70 along with problems in adaptive behavior.

Adaptive behavior
Cognitive, social, and practical skills used to assess intellectual disability in low-scoring individuals.

An intelligence test score lower than 70 is used to indicate a limitation in intellectual functioning, termed **intellectual disability** (Kaufman & Lichtenberger, 2006). According to the American Association on Intellectual and Developmental Disabilities (Shalock et al., 2010), intellectual disability involves significant limitations in reasoning, learning, and problem solving (previously described as "mental retardation") originating before the age of 18. Another important indicator of intellectual disability is **adaptive behavior**. This includes conceptual skills (e.g., language and literacy; concepts of money, time, and number; self-direction), social skills (e.g., interpersonal skills, social responsibility, self-esteem, social problem solving), and practical skills of daily living (e.g., personal care, occupational skills, health care, schedules or routines, safety). Because intelligence tests cannot identify difficulties in these areas, a new test for adaptive behavior has been developed (the Diagnostic Adaptive Behavior Scale) to provide diagnostic information about the areas of "significant limitation."

In a study in Atlanta, about 1 in 100 10-year-old children were diagnosed with intellectual disabilities (Yeargin-Allsopp et al., 1992). Other estimates suggest 3% of the population score below 70 on intelligence tests (Gottfredson, 1997a). Historically, intelligence test scores alone determined intellectual disability, and individuals were classified into four levels (see **TABLE 9-5**). Three-quarters are regarded as "mild" in disability, with intelligence scores falling between 50 and 70. Most can develop social and communication

TABLE 9-5 Level of Disability Based on Intelligence Score

Levels of Disability	Intelligence Score
Profound intellectual disability	Below 20
Severe intellectual disability	20–34
Moderate intellectual disability	35–49
Mild intellectual disability	50–69

skills, complete grade school without special help, and perform semiskilled jobs. The next level, with about 20% of individuals, is termed "moderate," with intelligence test scores below 50 and greater difficulty in learning social conventions. Less than 4% are termed "severe," with limited potential to learn to speak or coordinate motor movements. The most extreme cases (called "profound") are few in number (less than 2% of this group) but require complete custodial care.

Intellectual disability occurs from a wide range of causes, such as illness, injury, and physiological dysfunction. Infections of a pregnant mother (e.g., rubella), perinatal events (e.g., lack of oxygen during birth), childhood infections (e.g., meningitis or mumps), poisons such as lead, illicit drugs and alcohol or other toxins, metabolic disorders (e.g., Tay-Sachs disease), and premature birth are known to cause intellectual disability. For example, fetal alcohol syndrome is caused by repeated exposure of the fetus to alcohol in utero during development, especially in the first trimester when a woman may be unaware of her pregnancy. This exposure can delay development and produce significant functional problems in thinking, speech, movement, and social skills (Streissguth et al., 1991). Genetic problems also occur, along with more subtle physiological defects that are not diagnosed. About 1 out of 1,000 births results in **Down syndrome**, which involves the presence of an extra chromosome. Physical characteristics like poor muscle tone and slanting eyes are evident at birth, and intellectual disability occurs in the mild to moderate range. However, as standards for care have changed over time, the prognosis for development has also improved, and those with the syndrome are sometimes able to live independently.

Much more commonly, about 75% of cases with intellectual disability cannot be linked to any physical cause and are attributed to socioeconomic, cultural, or environmental factors in early childhood (Yeargin-Allsopp et al., 1997). Many factors can limit intellectual ability, such as poor nutrition, neglect, or the absence of stimulation from books or conversation in the home. Using intelligence testing, schoolchildren are identified as needing special education based on their scores; however, ethnic minorities are disproportionately selected (Mercer, 1973). This suggests there may be bias in identifying children as "learning disabled" (having a problem with reading or writing) versus "intellectually disabled." To intervene in this problem, a program called Head Start was created in the 1960s to prepare preschool children from poor families for school (Zigler & Berman, 1983). The evidence shows that Head Start was very successful in getting children ready for school and resulted in cognitive gains, less likelihood of repeating grades, and less need for remedial education (Darlington et al., 1980; Lee et al., 1990; Zigler & Muenchow, 1992). Some studies suggest a longer-term impact, including an increased probability of completing high school and attending college, and decreased probability of being charged or convicted of a crime (Garces et al., 2002; Reynolds, 2001). A review of studies found large short-term benefits on intelligence tests and long-term benefits on school achievement and social adjustment (Barnett, 1995). But other studies suggest gains did not persist after entering school (Lazar et al., 1982) or were only long-lasting for boys (Jordan et al., 1985). Without the support of an ongoing program, the continuing influence of negative aspects of environment may place these children at risk. While the Head Start program focused on early literacy and social skills, one of the researchers involved noted that children may benefit simply from receiving daily milk for breakfast while in the program FIGURE 9-13 (Zigler, 1984).

Down syndrome An extra chromosome causes physical characteristics like poor muscle tone and slanting eyes, and moderate to severe intellectual disability.

Individuals with Down syndrome may score in the moderate range of intellectual disability, but may lead somewhat independent lives.

FIGURE 9-13 It is difficult to separate the effects on student outcomes of a supportive preschool program from those of the enhanced nutrition provided by the program.

Health in general is a concern for those identified as intellectually disabled. Younger people with intellectual disability have poorer physical health (i.e., physical disabilities, coordination difficulties, hearing/visual problems, epilepsy, asthma, obesity, digestive problems, and language difficulties) compared to others (Taggart et al., 2010). In adults, after adjusting for age and socioeconomic status, men with low intelligence test scores were increasingly more likely to be suicidal than those with higher scores (Batty et al., 2011). These findings suggest that both biological and environmental factors may contribute to intellectual disabilities, and that lower intellectual functioning results in less ability to respond to physical and mental health needs. Psychopathology in young people with intellectual disability is "both substantial and persistent," and therefore there is an even greater need for effective mental interventions targeted toward young people diagnosed with intellectual disability (Einfeld et al., 2006).

Receiving a diagnosis of an intellectual disability is important for determining eligibility for special education services, home- and community-based services, and Social Security Administration benefits. In addition, intellectual disability is given specific treatment within the criminal justice system. For example, in 2002, the U.S. Supreme Court ruled that executing the mentally retarded violates the Eighth Amendment's ban on cruel and unusual punishment. Most importantly, the overarching reason for evaluating and classifying individuals with intellectual disabilities is to tailor support for each individual. With a set of strategies and services provided over a sustained period, individuals with disabilities can be successful. In fact, many students identified with intellectual disabilities in school appear to leave their disability behind once they leave school and have no further difficulties with life skills. Public schools are now required by law to prepare individualized education plans to aid in the development of every child, tailoring assistance to each child's needs.

High Intellectual Ability

At the opposite end of the distribution of intelligence test scores, individuals with remarkable abilities are frequently documented. But intelligence scores are not very useful in predicting success above a score of around 115. What can we learn about intellectual abilities by examining people who are at the extreme high end of intelligence?

Individuals who have an extraordinary talent in one area but are average or even deficient in most areas of cognitive functioning are described by **savant syndrome** (Miller, 1998; Treffert, 1989). Savants may show an ability to calculate the day of the week for any date in history, memorize long sequences of digits, or perform artistic feats of surprising skill. For example, Stephen Wiltshire was born in London to West Indian parents (Deutsch Smith, 2005). Aged 3, he was diagnosed as autistic. At the age of 5, Stephen was sent to Queensmill School in London, where it was noted that the only pastime he enjoyed was drawing. Unable to speak until the age of 9, he lived entirely in his own world. His particular talent is drawing lifelike and incredibly accurate representations of cities. Interestingly,

Savant syndrome
Individuals who are average (or even deficient) in most areas of cognitive functioning but display an extraordinary talent in one area.

savants have been identified in the areas of mental computation, memory, art, and music, corresponding to some of the multiple intelligences identified by Gardner (1983).

Also remarkable in his or her ability, a **prodigy** is defined as a child with a special skill or talent far exceeding the norm for his or her age. A famous example is Wolfgang Amadeus Mozart (1756–1791), who was an accomplished composer of complex music and a gifted performer who began a European tour at age 6. Feldman (1980) suggests that prodigies are not as unusual as we might think. From case studies, he concluded that prodigies appear in just a few fields, like music, math, and athletics, which may tap specific perceptual and motor abilities. Feldman's study also showed that the prodigies were "normal" in other areas of ability. Feldman concluded that prodigies do not develop in a vacuum; rather, a special environment surrounds them that helps them develop and reach an early potential in their one specific area. For example, golfer Tiger Woods was a child prodigy, introduced to golf before the age of 2 by his father Earl, who worked hard at developing Tiger's golf ability (Woods & McDaniel, 1997). A prodigy requires other people similarly devoted to her or his exceptional talent.

A third category of exceptional intellectual ability is defined solely by intelligence tests. Those scoring in the top ranges of tests (above 130) are considered to be "**gifted**," and many school programs and educational institutions have focused on developing their higher intellectual potential. As soon as he created the **Stanford-Binet Scale**, Lewis Terman (1925) began studying individuals who scored higher than 135. He collected more than 1,500 students, and these "Termites" (as they were called) were studied repeatedly over their lifetime (Shurkin, 1992). Unlike the stereotypes, Terman found that highly intelligent students were also more athletic, healthy, socially well adjusted, and emotionally stable. As a group, they succeeded in life, enjoying professional careers with many occupational and educational attainments, and successful family lives (Pyryt, 1993). Somewhat surprisingly, however, none of them ended up famous for their career successes.

While high intelligence test scores clearly indicated these students were "capable," it is not clear whether they were more capable than other students scoring below the "gifted" cutoff. This is important because many schools still use intelligence tests of young children as a means of identifying which students will most benefit from the specialized or higher-quality "enriched" instruction (Subotnik et al., 2007). Clearly, all students would benefit from such programs (Robinson et al., 2007; Robinson et al., 2000). But do gifted students benefit more than others would? There is little evidence to suggest that selective admission to gifted programs takes these students beyond where they would have gone on their own (for an exception, see Olszewski-Kubilius & Lee, 2004), or that the students who would make the most use of these extra educational resources are best identified by intelligence tests.

What about true **geniuses**, those whose accomplishments outlive them? Genius is rare and requires some history for recognition, so it is not possible to go beyond case studies of individuals. Simonton (2009) has studied cases over many years and has characterized commonalities among cases. Genius tends to occur in just one domain, though the individuals tend to have high intelligence scores as children and adolescents, and come from intellectually stimulating homes. Simonton estimates the variation in achievement may be about 30% to 40% genetic, but their achievements come through apprenticeship training and hard work over a long period of time (more than 10 years), as suggested in research on expertise. Geniuses also tend to have long careers, with peak achievement occurring somewhere around age 40 and continuing well into very late life (Del Banco, 2011). In keeping with some famous cases such as the painter van Gogh (Blumer, 2002), geniuses are roughly twice as likely as the general population to experience psychopathology, with depression being most common. Based on these exceptional individuals, it appears that high intelligence contributes to some examples of exceptional abilities; however, intelligence alone is not sufficient to account for them.

Practice during early childhood led Tiger Woods to a career excelling in golf.

Prodigy A child with a special skill or talent far exceeding the norm for his or her age.

Gifted A determination made by some schools and educational programs based on an intelligence test score of more than 130.

Stanford-Binet Scale A version of the intelligence test devised by Louis Terman and tested on many American schoolchildren.

Genius A noted, exceptional individual whose accomplishments outlive them.

During a relatively short period of 10 years, van Gogh completed over 900 paintings. He then began to alternate between fits of madness and lucidity and was sent to an asylum in Saint-Remy for treatment.

Match each concept to the individual description that best represents an extreme form of intelligence.

A. Savant

B. Prodigy

C. Gifted

D. Genius

1. _____ Mensa is a social club founded in England in 1946 by Roland Berrill, a barrister, and Dr. Lance Ware, a scientist and lawyer. They had the idea of forming a society for bright people, the only qualification for membership of which was a high intelligence test score. Only those scoring above 130, or in the top 2.2% of the population, are allowed to join.

2. _____ Carl Friedrich Gauss (1777–1855) was precocious as a toddler and made his first groundbreaking mathematical discoveries while still a teenager. He completed his magnum opus at the age of 21.

3. _____ Gottfried Mind (1768–1814) was called the Raphael of Cats for his art. He was described as "very weak, incapable of hard work, full of talent for drawing, a strange creature, drawing is his whole employment. He could with difficulty be made to write his name, and he had not the slightest idea of arithmetic."

4. _____ Leonardo di ser Piero da Vinci (1452–1519) was an Italian painter, sculptor, architect, musician, scientist, mathematician, engineer, inventor, anatomist, geologist, cartographer, botanist, and writer. He is widely considered to be one of the greatest painters of all time and perhaps the most diversely talented person ever to have lived.

9.4 Group Differences in Intelligence

Designed to compare individuals, intelligence test scores have sometimes been compared across groups of people.

- Explain reasons for gender and ethnic gaps in relation to standardized intelligence tests.
- Identify types of biases in intelligence testing.

Intelligence tests were created to identify children who needed extra assistance in schooling. By comparing an individual's score to the performance of a large group of people, standardization could be used to determine how an individual compares to the rest of a group. However, as soon as tests were created, comparisons were also made between men and women, between people from different countries, and between people of differing race and ethnicity. While not designed for this use, the meaning of these small differences between groups is one of the most hotly debated topics in psychology (Hunt & Carlson, 2007). Those with a political or personal agenda have sometimes used the evidence (sometimes inaccurately) to support their views. In this section, we will examine what is known from scientific studies about group differences.

Differences Within Groups and Differences Between Groups

When considering how different groups of people score on intelligence tests, it is important to keep in mind that there is always variation *within* a given group and that this variation is far greater than the variation *between* groups. Recall that 99% of the population scores between 60 and 140 (three standard deviations from the mean of 100); in addition, more than 68% of the population scores between 85 and 115. Any one person's score may fall from three points higher to three points lower when retested. Consequently, with most of us in the middle of the distribution, there is not a lot of room for comparing score differences among groups of people. In addition, the explained variance (differences among scores) attributable to differences between individuals far exceeds the variance related to group membership (Neisser et al., 1996). In other words, any two people will differ on their scores due to factors about that individual, and group membership (their gender, or ethnicity) is a very small factor in this. This point is conceded even by those arguing that group differences are important (Jensen, 1980).

Gender Group Differences

One consistent finding is that there are more males than females that score in the extreme ends of the distribution—that is, scoring either very high (above 130) or very low (below 70) on intelligence tests (Hedges & Nowell, 1995). So there is more variation among men in their intelligence test scores than there is among women. However, both appear in the groups scoring highest and lowest in the distribution, meaning the scores of the two groups completely overlap FIGURE 9-14 (Deary et al., 2003). There is absolutely *no* difference between the mean intelligence test scores for males and females. Is that surprising? The reason is because intelligence test scores are *designed* to produce the same average score for males as for females! When intelligence tests are developed, any test items that favor boys over girls or girls over boys are discarded. By selecting only items that males and females answered equally well, a gender-neutral test is created. This means that the test designers decided that there was no difference in intelligence among males and females; therefore, the measure of intelligence should have the same average score by gender.

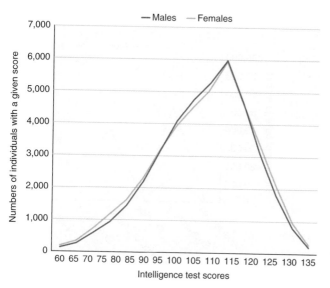

FIGURE 9-14 Percentages of boys and girls found within each 5-point band of IQ scores. Both boys and girls are represented in each score range, but the percentage of boys is higher in the extreme ends.
Source: Reproduced from Deary, I. J., Leaper, S. A., Murray, A. D., Staff, R. T., & Whalley, L. J. (2003). Cerebral white matter abnormalities and lifetime cognitive change: A 67-year follow up of the Scottish Mental Survey 1932. Psychology and Aging, 18, 140–148.

Though average levels of intelligence do not differ between men and women (by definition), there are gender differences on more specific types of intelligence tests (termed *gender gaps*). Males tend to do better on tests of mathematical abilities (Maccoby & Jacklin, 1974). On a task called mental rotation, your speed is measured as you match an object to its appearance from a different viewpoint FIGURE 9-15. Males outscore females by more than 1 standard deviation on this spatial task (Neisser et al., 1996). Women do better than men on verbal tasks, including spelling, writing, and pronouncing words (Halpern et al., 2007), though Hyde and Linn (1988) found only a "slight" female superiority. On school achievement tests, girls outscore boys on tests involving verbal abilities, and boys surpass girls (on average) in tests of math (after grade school; Eccles & Jacobs, 1986). So gender groups show small differences in the quality, or nature, of their intellectual performance as measured by tests. Of course, they differ in experience and opportunity, as reflected by the number of female psychological theorists mentioned in this chapter (none!).

Standard   Response (a)   Response (b)   Response (c)

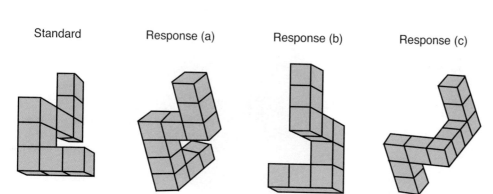

FIGURE 9-15 In a mental rotation task, a standard figure (left) is visually compared to three alternatives. Which is the same figure as the standard, but rotated? Answer: b.
Source: Shepard, R. N., & Metzler, J. (1971). Mental rotation of three-dimensional objects. Science, 171, 701–703.

Males and females also differ in their *interests*, as measured by the field of study they choose during college: Women are more likely to choose a major in the biological or social sciences FIGURE 9-16. Lawrence Summers (2005), then president of Harvard University, suggested that the underrepresentation of women in science and engineering could be due to a "different availability of aptitude at the high end." However, psychological studies of children's school performance have documented that the observed differences in career paths may be due to social variables rather than intellectual ability. Math grades in middle school and students' plans to take more math courses are related to students' own estimates of their math abilities, their perceptions of the value of math courses, and their levels of math anxiety (Eccles & Jacobs, 1986). The students' beliefs, in turn, are related most strongly to the beliefs of their *mothers* concerning the difficulty of mathematics for their children. Stereotypes about genders play a significant role in whether students decide to pursue mathematics very early in life—as early as second grade (Cvencek, Meltzoff, & Greenwald, 2011).

FIGURE 9-16 Women tend to earn more degrees in the social sciences, whereas men earn more in the physical sciences. *Source: Data from the National Survey of Recent College Graduates, National Science Foundation, 2008.*

Girls tend to perform less well on math tests beginning in middle school, perhaps due to social factors.

Ethnic Group Differences

In designing intelligence tests, gender is presumed to play no role in predicting test scores, so the tests are designed to produce the same average score for males as for females. No such assumptions are made about the relationship between ethnicity or race and intelligence. Historically, the groups tested during the development of intelligence tests were located in France and in Northern California, and the ethnicity of the individuals tested was predominantly white or European. These same tests have been given to individuals all over the world, and as more data became available, people began to compare the scores of groups based on race. It is important to recognize that "race" has no biological definition based on genetics (American Anthropological Association, 1994). Instead, race is a social categorization defined—and self-defined—by social conventions based on country or ethnic origin, as well as physical characteristics such as skin color FIGURE 9-17. Any category combines some people that may not feel an affiliation, such as "Asian American" including people with diverse familial backgrounds in China, Japan, Korea, Laos, Vietnam, the Philippines, India, and Pakistan.

FIGURE 9-17 Estimated population of the United States by race and ethnicity, 2009. *Source: Data from the US Census Bureau, 2009.*

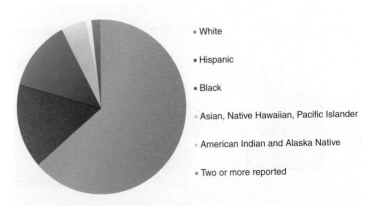

Because claims about ethnic differences have been used in racial discrimination in the past, any claims must be subject to very careful scrutiny (Neisser et al., 1996). Just as eugenicists argued that some races were superior to others, there are people today who claim that whites are "smarter" than blacks (Hermstein & Murray, 1994). To support their claim, they point out that the average intelligence test score for whites (100) is higher than the average score for blacks (85; Gottfredson, 1997a), called a **racial gap**. Rushton and Jensen (2005) recently stated that the difference in average scores remains as large today as it was 100 years ago. But on the most recent review of available data, this difference is smaller, with an estimate of 90.5 for black schoolchildren in 2002 (Dickens & Flynn, 2006). Because blacks have gained 4 to 7 IQ points on whites over the past 30 years, differences based on genetics are not likely to be responsible for the gap.

Environmental influences are social, cultural, physical, or family settings that affect an individual. Several lines of evidence support the role of environmental factors in lower scores for blacks. For example, one study followed children born to German mothers and American fathers working in the armed services in Germany after World War II (Eyferth, 1961). There was no difference between the intelligence test scores of children with white or black fathers. Other studies have attempted to compare intelligence test scores for blacks based on population genetics. African Americans average about 20 percent European genes, largely as a legacy of slavery. But the proportion of European genes ranges widely among individuals, from near zero to more than 80 percent. If the racial gap is mostly genetic, then blacks with more European genes ought to have higher scores on average. In fact, they do not: The proportion of European genes bears no relationship to measured intelligence among African-American children (Loehlin, Vandenberg, & Osborne, 1973; Loehlin, Willerman, & Horn, 1988). Finally, a study of black children adopted by white families (Scarr, Weinberg, & Waldman, 1993) found their intelligence test scores averaged 106, exceeding the national average for both blacks and whites.

Adoption studies identify another factor as significant in intelligence test scores—namely, socioeconomic status. When upper-middle-class families adopt poor children, they show a test score gain of 12 to 16 points. Because blacks are disproportionately represented in lower incomes, this factor may explain why average scores are lower. What about other groups? Hispanics' scores are typically between those of blacks and whites (Gottfredson, 1997a). Are there any groups scoring higher than whites? You might expect Asian Americans to score higher, based on their higher school grades and higher scores on achievement tests like the SAT and GRE (Neisser et al., 1996). However, in more than a dozen studies from the 1960s and 1970s, the average scores of Japanese and Chinese American children were around 97 or 98; none was over 100 (Flynn, 1991). One smaller group does have a higher average intelligence test score: Ashkenazi Jews average somewhere between 110 and 115. Across all of these groups; however, when you statistically control for factors like socioeconomic status and school quality, differences between group scores are not evident (Nisbett, 2009).

Bias in Intelligence Testing

While there are different types of intelligence tests, they all seem to measure the same underlying "intelligence," as shown by their high correlations. Some use words or numbers and require specific cultural knowledge (e.g., vocabulary), while others avoid this by using shapes or designs and simple, universal concepts (e.g., many/few, open/closed, up/down; Gottfredson, 1997a). Researchers and **psychometricians** (those who study the principles of psychological measurement) claim to produce a test that is fair and free of bias. Are they successful?

Cultural Bias in Intelligence Tests

Americans and other Westernized groups typically outperform members of traditional societies on intelligence tests, even those designed to be culture fair. But then, it is primarily Western science that has created the industry of intelligence testing, and the tests may provide an advantage to those from the same culture. For example, the 1937 Stanford-Binet test was used from 1937 to 1960 based on norms collected only with white children. How do cultural factors shape differences in intelligence test scores? Fagan and Holland (2002) tested blacks and whites on their knowledge and ability to learn and reason with words and concepts. The whites had substantially more existing knowledge of the various

Racial gap Differences on average test scores between groups associated by racial or ethnic definitions.

Environmental influence A factor in the social, cultural, physical, or family setting that may influence an individual.

Psychometrician A scientist who studies the principles of psychological measurement.

Though small differences are reported in group performance, environment is influential in the development of intelligence.

words and concepts, but when tested on their ability to learn new words, the blacks did just as well as the whites. When the tests used words and concepts known equally well to blacks and whites, on both comprehension and analogies, there were no differences. These data support the view that cultural differences in information and processes provided to children may account for group differences in intelligence scores (Fagan & Holland, 2007; Irvine & Berry, 1988).

If the children all live in the United States, where do cultural differences arise? The experience of individuals is different based on area of the country, schooling, socioeconomic status, gender, and race and ethnicity. Cultural environment includes how people live, what they value, and what they do with their time, which differs for each family. For example, in poorer black families, children are rarely asked "known-answer" questions (in which the asker already knows the right answer), such as, "What color is an elephant?" (Nisbett, 2009). These children may be confused by hearing this type of question at school (e.g., "Doesn't the teacher already know that elephants are gray?"). If the answer is obvious, then why is the question being asked? Even tests designed to avoid any cultural influences seem to be unsuccessful at doing so. For example, in one study, the Cattell Culture-Fair Intelligence Test was given to American, Nigerian, and Indian adolescents, and 59% of the items were found to be culturally biased (Nenty, 1986). Despite this fact, some researchers attempt to compare whole countries' average intelligence scores and draw conclusions about their economic prospects (Lynn & Vanhanen, 2006).

Even the ability to take intelligence tests depends on experience with formal schooling (Neisser, 1976). To college students, taking tests is second nature, and you are able to respond quickly to test items from long years of practice. If you hand your exam to a parent or grandparent, their lack of practice will make it more difficult for them to respond even if they know the answers. This is illustrated by researchers' stories of testing individuals from non-Western cultures without literacy experience. For example, Smith (1996) reported that his research team recruited native Mayans in Guatemala to participate in research on syllogism problems. The problems included fictional concepts (e.g., "sesamoid bones"), and the subjects were told to reason about categories. For example, "Fish have sesamoid bones. Birds have sesamoid bones. How likely are all animals to have sesamoid bones?" American college students answered the question easily, while one Mayan protested, "You are the one who knows about 'sesamoid bones,' so you tell *me* the answer." While the individual was capable of performing the reasoning, answering questions with made-up words was not a familiar task.

Stereotype Threat

Imagine that I ask you to take a math test right now. How do you feel you will do on it? Now, imagine I ask you to do so wearing either a bikini or a Speedo swim brief. Do you think you can perform at your best? In a study looking at how people feel when their body is "objectified" (they are made aware of others' perspectives on their body), students were asked to put on either a bulky sweater or a tiny swimsuit. Then, they took a math test wearing the outfit. Do you think this would make a difference in math test scores? After all, we have been discussing mathematical ability as a stable, reliable measure of intelligence. However, Fredrickson and colleagues (1998) found wearing a revealing swimsuit produced lower scores on a math test, but only for the female students FIGURE 9-18.

Achi Maya preserve traditional farming and building practices in rural Guatemala, but may score less well on tests involving school experience.

FIGURE 9-18 Math performance by experimental condition and gender. Means are corrected for guessing and past performance on standardized math tests.
Source: Reproduced from Fredrickson, B. L., Roberts, T-A., Noll, S. M., Quinn, D. M., & Twenge, J. M. (1998). That swimsuit becomes you: Sex differences in self-objectification, restrained eating, and math performance. Journal of Personality and Social Psychology, 75(1), 269–284.

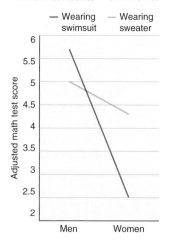

They argued that making women more aware of others' views about their bodies (by wearing the swimsuit) drew their attention and disrupted their intellectual performance.

In the same way, our knowledge of stereotypes about ourselves (e.g., "girls are not good at math," "boys are not good at language," and "Asians are good at math") may alter how we behave when we face a test. Knowing what people expect of you may change how much attention you pay to the task, how hard you work, and how confident you are in performing at your best. Because Asian American students are aware of the stereotype, reminding them of it before they take a difficult math test can improve their performance on the test (Walton & Cohen, 2003). On the other hand, sometimes stereotypes are negative and can cause people to perform more poorly. Claude Steele and Joshua Aronson (1995) discovered that black students are affected by negative stereotypes about the racial gap in intelligence test scores. In their study, African American college students were asked to take a test containing standardized questions. Some were told the test was "an exercise in problem solving," while others were told it was a "test diagnostic of verbal ability," and thus related to intelligence. The students performed worse (in comparison to their prior test scores) on the questions when they thought the test was related to intelligence FIGURE 9-19. This phenomenon, called **stereotype threat**, was demonstrated in another study in which black students asked to indicate their race before a math test (activating the stereotype) performed more poorly than they had on prior exams. The scores of white students were not affected by being asked to indicate their race.

Steele and Aronson (1995) argued that thinking about negative stereotypes related to a task that you are performing creates stereotype threat. This is defined as decrements in performance caused by knowledge of cultural stereotypes. The negative impact of race on standardized tests may be caused, at least in part, by the knowledge that you, as a black student, are expected to perform poorly. Stereotype threat has been demonstrated in a variety of tasks and groups. For example, when a math task is described as "diagnostic of intelligence," Latinos and Latinas perform more poorly than do whites (Gonzales, Blanton, & Williams, 2002). White men perform more poorly on a math

If female, how would you feel taking a math test in a bikini?

If male, would wearing this swimsuit affect your performance on a math test?

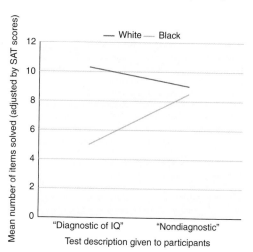

FIGURE 9-19 When African American students were told a test would be diagnostic of intelligence, they performed worse than their prior performance; however, white students showed no change. *Source: Reproduced from Steele, C. M., & Aronson, J. (1995). Stereotype threat and the intellectual test performance of African Americans.* Journal of Personality and Social Psychology, 69*(5), 797–811.*

test when they told that their performance will be compared to Asian American men (Aronson et al., 2005). And capturing another stereotype, whites perform more poorly than blacks on a sports task when it is described as measuring "natural athletic ability" (Stone, 2002). Stereotype threat is created by testing situations that raise concerns about your performance relative to that of others. When stereotypes lead others to believe that we are likely to perform poorly, we are more likely to do so. However, these effects can be reduced by reminding people of the positive characteristics of themselves or their group (Cohen et al., 2006).

Expectations

In addition to the test-taker's beliefs, expectancies, or expectations about performance, from other people may play a role in performance differences. In a groundbreaking study by Rosenthal and Jacobson (1968), the expectations teachers had for their students were manipulated. At the beginning of a school year, Rosenthal got permission from

When white students were told a test involved natural athletic ability, they performed worse.

Stereotype threat
Performance decrements caused by knowledge of cultural stereotypes.

grade school teachers to administer a special test to their students. He told them these new tests would predict the development of intelligence in schoolchildren. Then, he instituted a specific manipulation: "Do not let this influence you," he said, "But I thought you would like to know that in your classroom, these students scored particularly high on the test. Their intellects will bloom in the coming year." In fact, there was nothing special about the selected students: Rosenthal chose them at random among the students in the class. But their teachers now expected them to show some sort of intellectual leap during the year. And they did! By the end of the year, the selected students' grades improved, and their performance on conventional intelligence tests greatly improved! How did the manipulation succeed in causing real changes in the students' test performances?

The explanation is that the teachers who heard that some of their students were about to "bloom" must have treated them differently. Maybe they spent more time with them, encouraged them, or challenged them more than the other students. So, as a result of the expectancies planted by Rosenthal, the actual academic outcomes of these students were changed. This effect is called a self-fulfilling prophecy, meaning an event that happens *because* you have predicted it. Rosenthal's finding is one of the most important in psychology, and one that should be recalled by every teacher and parent: You will get what you expect from a child! If a teacher's expectations can affect academic performance and intelligence tests for the better, they can also change them for the worse. If teachers expect that some students are not as intelligent, perhaps because of their ethnicity, social class, or cultural background, they may end up treating them in ways that lead to worse outcomes. All children are encouraged by adults expecting the best from them!

Teachers' increased expections for some individual students resulted in actual gains on intelligence tests for those students.

CONCEPT LEARNING CHECK 9.4 | *Expecting to Be Smarter*

1. Based on the concept of stereotype threat, which of these situations is most relevant?

   A. A male taking a math test

   B. An Asian male taking a math test

   C. A female taking an intelligence test

   D. A Hispanic male taking an intelligence test

2. What was caused by the expectancies of the teachers in the Rosenthal study?

   A. They believed some students would "bloom" in class.

   B. Some students received higher grades.

   C. Some students improved on standardized intelligence tests.

3. Based on self-fulfilling prophecy, what should you tell yourself about your next psychology test?

9.5 Multiple Influences: The Roles of Genetics and Environment in Determining Intelligence

Both genes and environment contribute to intelligence, but the relationship is complex.

- Describe the roles of genetics and environment, and their interaction, in determining intelligence.

We have seen that intelligence as measured by tests is a fairly stable characteristic of a person over his or her life span. But are the underlying causes of differences in intelligence a result of nature ("in the genes") or of nurture (the environment)? Let us examine the available evidence.

Evidence for Heredity

The relationship between heredity and IQ is continually debated within the field. **Heritability** is the proportion of the variance (differences between individuals) that is due to genetic factors. Note that heritability describes differences *between* people and cannot be applied to a single individual. People vary in eye color and blood type, and the variance in these traits is accounted for by genetics. But for traits like the specific religion you practice or the language you use, there is no genetic influence: These traits are not "heritable" at all. Instead, environmental factors determine how people differ. In the middle are traits for which there is a moderate genetic influence on the variation observed. Even psychological traits, such as how religious you are, how proficient you are with language, and how liberal or conservative you are, may be partially heritable (Pinker, 2004). The scale for heritability goes from 0, or not influenced at all by genetics, to 1, meaning completely determined by genetics.

How can we determine whether genetics or heritability impacts intelligence? We can look at people that are biologically related and see if their intelligence test scores are also related. Estimates of heritability come from comparing the intelligence test scores of blood relatives, such as identical twins (who share all of their genes), fraternal twins and siblings (who share half of their genes), and less-related family members. If intelligence is heritable, then the relatives of a person with a high intelligence test score should exhibit a comparably high score. Bouchard and McGue (1981), in a review of 111 studies, concluded the mean correlation of scores between identical twins was 0.86, between siblings, 0.47, between half-siblings, 0.31, and between cousins, 0.15. This pattern is what you might expect if genetics played an important role in intelligence: The greater the genetic similarity between two individuals, the more similar their intelligence scores FIGURE 9-20.

Heritability The proportion of variance (differences between individuals) in an observable trait that is due to genetic factors.

Twin study Examining the heritability of traits by comparing identical twins (who share all of their genes) to fraternal twins (who share 50% of their genes).

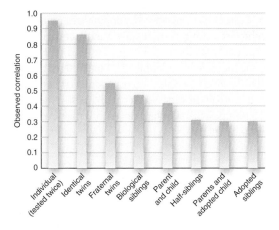

FIGURE 9-20 Correlations between individuals by family relationship.
Source: Data from Kaufman, A. S., & Lichtenberger, E. (2006). Assessing adolescent and adult intelligence *(3rd ed.). Hoboken, NJ: Wiley.*

Estimates of the heritability of intelligence range from 0.4 to 0.8 (Gottfredson, 1997a). This relationship is also seen in studies of brain structure in related siblings. Evidence from brain studies of twins shows a higher similarity in the patterns of cortical grey matter, made up of neuronal cell bodies. These studies suggest that genetic links in intelligence are caused by brain structure, which is determined by genetics. In FIGURE 9-21, the high heritability of grey matter is evident in identical compared to fraternal twins (Toga & Thompson, 2005). Genetic influences on brain structure may be the cause of the similarities in intelligence that arise from biological relatedness.

Evidence for Environmental Influence

If genetics alone determines intelligence, we would expect people within biologically related families to have very similar scores. But members of the same family can differ substantially in intelligence test scores (by an average of about 12 points). In fact, studies of twins and other blood relatives *also* show that environment has an effect on intelligence. These **twin studies** compare intelligence test scores for siblings that were raised together to pairs that were adopted by two different families. If two individuals are raised together, the correlation in intelligence test score is always higher than if they were raised or are living apart FIGURE 9-22. So the shared environment of being from the same family makes two people *more* similar in their intelligence test scores. And the scores of unrelated individuals living together are correlated at $r = +0.23$, while the scores of any two

FIGURE 9-21 "Heritable" means that the correlation is greater for identical twins than for fraternal twins. Results show similarities from genetics appear in frontal and temporal lobe regions.
Source: Data from Toga, A. W., & Thompson. P. M. (2005). Genetics of brain structure and intelligence. Annual Review of Neuroscience, *28, 1–23.*

Flynn effect The increase in intelligence test scores have (about three points per decade, across the globe) over generations taking the tests.

individuals at random are not correlated, showing a shared environment does affect intelligence scores. This data shows the importance of environment as well.

Studies of twins may overestimate heritability because we all share environment in important ways (for example, in the United States, we all attend school). That makes identical twins raised apart more similar because they share many elements of the environment *except* immediate family, but we count all similarity in twins raised apart as attributable to genes. To see this, imagine we all grew up in the same environment; then, all differences in intelligence would seem to be solely genetic. This is especially true for adoptive families, which Nisbett (2009) argues, "are all alike." Not only are they more affluent than average, they also tend to give children lots of cognitive stimulation and emphasize the importance of education. So, comparison data of those raised apart provide erroneously high estimates of heritability. Identical twins adopted into different families are raised with different parents, but in the United States, they attend the same suburban public schools, enjoy the same financial advantages, watch *Sesame Street*, and eat at McDonald's. The available evidence from intelligence test scores cannot separate out the contribution solely from genetics because some aspects of environment are always shared.

Generational Changes: The Flynn Effect

Another source of evidence that intelligence is not determined by heredity alone is that average intelligence scores appear to be changing over time. James Flynn noticed this trend, later termed the **Flynn effect**. Intelligence test scores have increased by about three points per decade, across the globe, for as long as there have been recorded tests (Flynn, 1984). Of course, the tests are repeatedly standardized over time, and this process resets the mean score to 100 again, so the increase is not apparent. But if 20 years have passed since the last time the test was standardized, people who now score 100 on the new version would probably average about 106 on the old (Neisser et al., 1996). If everyone alive today is smarter (by more than 15 points, a full standard deviation) than everyone alive in 1940, what does that tell us about the concept of intelligence, or at least its measurement?

FIGURE 9-22 Pairs of people living together are shown in blue bars, living apart in red; the difference indicates the impact of environmental factors.
Source: Data from Kaufman, A. S., & Lichtenberger, E. (2006). Assessing adolescent and adult intelligence (3rd ed.). Hoboken, NJ: Wiley.

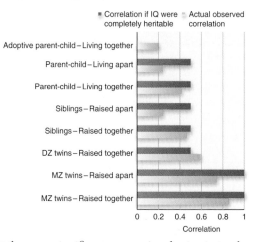

Flynn (1984) states that the fact that there are significant generational gains in intelligence means that the scores cannot be determined by genetics. The highest gains are on culturally loaded subtests with questions like, "How are dogs and rabbits similar?" Today, we are more likely to answer using abstract categories ("dogs and rabbits are mammals") than more concrete categories ("dogs and rabbits are pets"; Flynn, 2007). Our genes could not have changed enough over 60 years to create this difference in thinking; instead, it must result from environmental factors like education. As noted earlier, the difference between black and white average intelligence test scores has also changed over time, from 15 to less than 10 points. If intelligence changes within the population over a short period of time, environmental factors must be the cause.

Environmental Differences

What factors in the environment predict intelligence test scores? One clear factor is schooling: Intelligence is correlated at about $r = +0.60$ with the number of years spent in school (Neisser, 1996). In part, this may be because people with higher intelligence scores may enjoy taking classes and thus are more likely to stay in school. But education itself also has a causal effect on intelligence scores. Because of school year calendars, some children who are very close in chronological age just miss the deadline to enroll and have to wait until the next year to begin school. Children who make the deadline for entering school have higher intelligence scores than those who just missed it, even though they are nearly identical in age. So schooling, and not the extra year alone, accounts for the improvements in scores.

Another major influence from the environment is social and economic deprivation, experienced disproportionately by black and other minority families. When poor children are adopted by upper-middle-class families, they show a gain of 12 to 16 points on intelligence tests (Nisbett, 2009). Households without enough money to cover living expenses have children with lower intelligence test scores even when controlling for other factors, like education, race, and parenting (Brooks-Gunn & Duncan, 1997). Many other stressors follow with low socioeconomic status, such as poor nutrition, parental alcohol and drug use, younger age of parenting, less prenatal care, and lower birth weight. Lower-class children are also less likely to be breastfed, which offers a seven-point advantage in intelligence test scores if carried through for 8 months (Horwood et al., 2001). Moving households is also a source of instability: In inner-city schools, the turnover of children in a single classroom throughout an academic year can be as high as 100%. This means that, for the poor, improvements in childhood environment have great potential to bring about increases in intelligence. As Nisbett (2009) says, "If we want the poor to be smarter, we should just make them richer."

A. *Japanese family's possessions.* B. *Malian family's possessions.* C. *Mexican family's possessions.* D. *South African family's possessions.*

Nisbett (2009) also argues that parenting in upper-class homes is also very different: By the age of 3, children with parents employed professionally have heard 30 million words. With working-class parents, this drops to 20 million, and to as low as 10 million for black welfare mothers. Parents also speak differently to their children, with many more encouragements per reprimand (six) in professional homes, and a reversed ratio of two reprimands for each encouragement in lower-class families. When parents prepare their children to face the world they perceive around them, this may lead to very different ways of raising children, affecting their intellectual development.

Our unique, individual experiences may make the largest environmental contribution to intelligence. One of these factors may be birth order. You differ from your siblings because your family was very different before and after you joined it. For the first child, the average intelligence for the family combines two adults and one child; but, for a fourth child, the average now includes three other children. Research has shown that intelligence scores decrease as the number of children in the family increases and decrease based on order of birth (Zajonc, 1976). A recent study confirmed that this effect is likely explained through simple resource allocation: When there are more children, the resources will be more scarce for everyone compared with the firstborn (who gets all the attention with no competition); (Kristensen & Bjerkedal, 2007). Many other yet to be uncovered experiential factors may contribute to differences measured by intelligence tests.

Jenny Ferrill, of Danville, Ill., plays with her 2-year-old quintuplets at their home. The number of children in the family may affect intelligence by competition for adult interaction.

Summary of Multiple Influences on Intelligence

The evidence provided from empirical studies shows that genetic contributions are one cause of individual differences in intelligence test scores. But what does it mean to say that intelligence is heritable? We think of genes as causing traits like eye color. However, genes also produce traits that require certain environments, actions, or triggers to be expressed. (Plomin, DeFries, & Loehlin, 1977). For example, a trait like shyness might be caused by genes but only observed when someone is alone with strangers. Further, even if genes are critical, we may be able to alter their impact (e.g., we wear glasses to correct vision) and prevent poor outcomes. At the same time, environmental factors also contribute substantially to the development of intelligence (Mackenzie, 1984). Just what those factors are or how they influence development is also not yet clear (Neisser et al., 1996). Attendance at school is certainly important, for example, but *which* aspects of schooling are critical? Clearly, early childhood development requires adequate nutrition and care, and exposure to learning environments seems to benefit all children. But once the basic needs of children are met, it is still difficult to predict children's intellectual potential.

Studies have attempted to compare the contributions of genetics and the influence of environment. For example, intelligence test scores are roughly five points higher if a child has highly educated parents (van der Sluis et al., 2008). But is this due to genetics or to the environment that parents provide, or are both required to produce higher intelligence? The childhood home environment can influence the extent to which genetic factors and environmental factors contribute to the differences observed in children's cognitive ability (van der Sluis et al., 2008). Findings with adults suggest that genetics plays a role across types of environment, while for children, genes and environment interact to influence intelligence (Tucker et al., 2011). In particular, the impact of genetics is more readily observed in poorer environments, while children from more affluent homes do well regardless of their genetic makeup (Turkheimer et al., 2003).

In sum, it is clear that intelligence tests measure something, and that it is related to school performance. Genetics plays a role in influencing intellectual growth, and environment plays a role in providing a supportive base for development. But do not forget the importance of expectancies, as seen in the Rosenthal study of classroom teachers. A related factor not yet discussed is self-motivation: You can control your school performance through more practice. In studies of middle school students, those who hold a "fixed" theory of intelligence are mainly concerned with how smart they are and prefer tasks they can already do well (Blackwell et al., 2007). They avoid tasks on which they may make mistakes and not look smart. In contrast, people who believe in an "expandable" or "growth" theory of intelligence want to challenge themselves to increase their abilities, even if they fail at first. One researcher, Carol Dweck, recalled a young boy who was a ringleader of the troublemakers in his class. "When we started teaching this idea about the mind being malleable, he looked up with tears in his eyes, and he said, 'You mean, I don't have to be dumb?'" she said. "A fire was lit under him" (Trei, 2007).

Teaching children to believe in their own capacity to learn has benefits for education and intelligence

---

CONCEPT LEARNING CHECK 9.5   *Understanding the Evidence on the Heredity-Environment Question*

Heritability for traits in humans is estimated by comparing resemblances between twins. Fraternal (DZ) twins on average share half their genes, and so identical (MZ) twins on average are twice as similar genetically as DZ twins. A crude estimate of heritability, then, is approximately twice the difference in correlation between MZ and DZ twins. Refer to the data in Figure 9-20 to answer these questions:

1. How do identical twins differ from fraternal twins in the correlation between their intelligence test scores? Describe how the two correlations compare and what that says about heritability.

2. Environmental influence is shown by comparing twins raised together versus twins raised apart. How do identical twins' intelligence test scores differ based on whether they grow up together? Describe how the two correlations compare and what that says about heritability.

3. What do you conclude from this evidence?

Visual Overview Steps in Creating an Intelligence Test

Creating a new test of intelligence requires selecting test items, verifying them against a criterion group, establishing reliability and standardization, and determining whether the test has predictive validity.

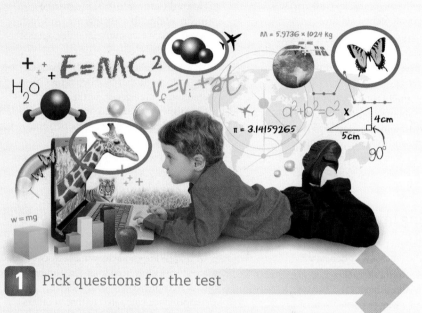

1 Pick questions for the test

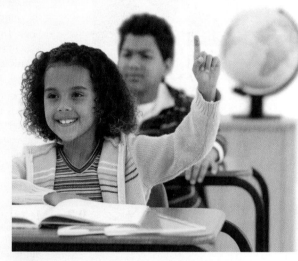

2 Test Against Criterion

Do "smart" students get it right, and "not smart" get it wrong? If so, include on test.

5 Validity

Does the test predict which students will succeed in life?

3 Establish Reliability

Test, retest, scores the same?

4 Standardization

Test with large numbers of people to refine, establish norms.

9.1 The Nature of Intelligence

- While we may perceive a basic intellectual ability in others, there is little agreement about what that entails.
- Charles Spearman (1904) proposed that a general intelligence capacity (called *g*) was the source of all mental abilities.
- Louis Thurstone's (1938) results showed a set of seven different factors related to task scores, which he called primary mental abilities.
- Raymond Cattell (1963) found just two underlying abilities: fluid intelligence, the ability to determine relationships within a given task, and crystalized intelligence, the ability to draw upon previously learned knowledge and skills.

- Sternberg's (2001) triarchic theory of intelligence placed intelligence within three categories: analytic, creative, and practical.
- Howard Gardner (1983) proposed a theory of multiple intelligences in which seven separate cognitive abilities operate independently.
- Mayer and colleagues (2001) expanded the concept further by examining emotional intelligence, or the ability to perceive, understand, integrate, and regulate emotions to promote personal growth.
- The speed with which people can perform simple tasks is predictive of intelligence.

9.2 Measuring Intelligence

- Tests are designed to measure intelligence, but what they measure is debatable.
- The modern study of intelligence testing began with Alfred Binet (1857–1911), who created a way to predict school achievement in all children through testing.
- Binet defined "mental age" as the average level of intellectual development for a child of a particular age.
- The intelligence quotient, or IQ, was defined by Terman as a child's mental age divided by his or her chronological age.
- David Wechsler (1896–1981) created more efficient measures of adult intelligence called the Wechsler Adult Intelligence Scale (WAIS).
- Most tests include a wide variety of types of questions in order to tap intelligence in differing domains.
- Working memory capacity strongly predicts a person's performance on a battery of intelligence tests that measure everything from abstract problem-solving to social intelligence.

- Modern intelligence test scores, along with aptitude and achievement tests, are always converted from the number of correct answers to your relative performance compared to that of others on the same test, called standardization.
- The "normal distribution" for intelligence tests refers to the "bell curve" shape of scores falling around an average of 100.
- Reliability refers to repeating the measurement and getting the same outcome.
- Content validity (also called face validity) is how well they get at what we really mean when we say someone is "intelligent."
- Predictive validity refers to how well test scores correlate with intelligence as displayed in the world.
- Intelligence test scores predict school performance, the number of years of education you will complete, occupational status, income, and how well employees perform in their jobs.

9.3 Individual Differences in Intelligence

- Intellectual disability is defined as an intelligence test score of less than 70 originating before the age of 18, and was historically classified into four levels: "mild," "moderate," "severe," with limited potential to learn to speak; and "profound," requiring complete care.
- The origins of intellectual disability include a wide range of physical causes, but about 75% of cases cannot be linked to any physical cause, and may be due to socioeconomic, cultural, or environmental factors in early childhood.
- Savants are individuals who are average (or even deficient) in most areas of

cognitive functioning but display an extraordinary talent in one area.
- A prodigy is defined as a child with a special skill or talent far exceeding the norm for his or her age.
- Terman's study found that high-scoring students were also more athletic, healthy, socially well adjusted, and emotionally stable; however, they did not become famous for their career successes.
- Geniuses are defined within domains rather than universally, are very productive, work hard over a long period of time (more than 10 years), and have long careers.

9.4 Group Differences in Intelligence

- Designed to compare individuals, intelligence test scores have sometimes been used to compare groups of people.
- There is always variation (differences between individuals) within a given group, and that variation far outweighs the differences between groups.
- There is absolutely *no* difference between the mean intelligence test scores for males and females, but there are more males than females that score in the extreme ends of the intelligence score distribution (above 130 or below 70).
- Women tend to do better than men on some verbal tasks, including spelling, writing, and pronouncing words.
- Boys surpass girls (on average) in tests of math (after grade school) and on spatial tasks.

- Historically, the groups used to develop intelligence tests were predominantly white or Eastern European.
- Tests find the average IQ score for whites (100) is higher than the average score for blacks (85). However, holding economic status and school quality constant, there is little difference between group IQ scores.
- Adoption studies suggest the differences in intelligence test score averages may be based on environmental factors.
- Our knowledge of stereotypes about us ("girls are not good at math," "boys are not good at language," and "Asians are good at math") may alter how we behave when we face a test.
- The teachers who heard that some of their students were about to "bloom" intellectually expected they would do so, treated them differently, and they did.

9.5 Multiple Influences: The Roles of Genetics and Environment in Determining Intelligence

- Both genes and environment contribute to intelligence, but the relationship is complex.
- If intelligence is heritable (that is, based on genetics alone), then the heritability, or the correlation of phenotype (the gene's behavioral expression) and genotype (squared), would be 1.0; but, estimates of the heritability of intelligence range from 0.4 to 0.8.
- Flynn effect: IQ scores have increased by about three points per decade, across the globe, for as long as there have been recorded tests.

- Intelligence is correlated at about $r = +0.6$ with the number of years spent in school.
- When poor children are adopted by upper-middle-class families, they show a gain of 12 to 16 points on intelligence tests.
- Genetics plays a role in influencing intellectual growth, and environment plays a role in providing a supportive base for intellectual development.

9.1 The Nature of Intelligence

1. A person who scores equally high on several different intelligence test measures, such as mathematical, verbal, musical, emotional, the ACT, and the Stanford-Binet, provides evidence for:
   A. general intelligence (*g*).
   B. Gardner's multiple intelligences.
   C. specific intelligence (*s*).
   D. savants.

2. Raymond Cattell's (1963) theory of intelligence identified just two abilities underlying intelligence: fluid intelligence, the ability to determine relationships within a given task, and:
   A. specific intelligence (*s*).
   B. crystalized intelligence.
   C. primary mental abilities.
   D. creative intelligence.

3. Sam's intelligence is described as "bodily kinesthetic." Which theory of intelligence is referred to here?
   A. general intelligence (*g*)
   B. Gardner's multiple intelligences
   C. Sternberg's triarchic theory
   D. Emotional intelligence

4. Sternberg's triarchic theory of intelligence includes creative intelligence, practical intelligence, and:
   A. analytical intelligence.
   B. emotional intelligence.
   C. logico-mathematical intelligence.
   D. spatial intelligence.

9.2 Measuring Intelligence

5. If your intelligence quotient is 100 as measured with the Stanford-Binet test, you have a "mental age" that is:
   A. determined to be above average.
   B. different than your chronological age.
   C. the same as your chronological age.
   D. determined to be below average.

6. According to providers of tests like the Wechsler, WAIS, GRE, SAT, and ACT, modern psychological tests of intelligence are now designed to provide all of the following *except*:
   A. standardization.
   B. validity.
   C. reliability.
   D. mental age.

7. Susan scores a 520 on the math GRE. She studies for 6 months and retakes it, to score a 520. This example suggests the GRE score is:
   A. standardized.
   B. reliable.
   C. valid.
   D. biased against women.

8. You take a test today that measures your willingness to help others. Next month, you take the same test and get the same score. This illustrates the technique used to measure:
   A. test-retest reliability.
   B. criterion validity.
   C. content validity.
   D. split-half reliability.

9. Intelligence tests are most accurate when used to predict:
   A. practical decision-making.
   B. academic performance.
   C. parenting skills.
   D. job success.

9.3 Individual Differences in Intelligence

10. Intellectual disability is defined as scoring below _____ on intelligence tests.
    A. 100
    B. 70
    C. 30
    D. 120

11. In addition to tests of intelligence, advocates for the intellectually disabled suggest measuring:
    A. literacy.
    B. cognition.
    C. adaptive behavior.
    D. mental health.

12. According to Simonton (2009), the cases of "genius" he studied show that:
    A. genius is a collective recognition, like a school of art.
    B. genius is universal, with excellence across many domains.
    C. geniuses are not very productive, often producing one great work.
    D. geniuses tend to have long careers, peaking around age 40.

9.4 Group Differences in Intelligence

13. In Rosenthal's study of school performance, he told teachers which of their students were "on the verge of blooming" intellectually. At the end of the year, his findings showed that:

A. teachers' expectations led to greater learning for those students.

B. his intelligence test was in fact able to identify conceptual "blooming" in children.

C. standardized tests were not a valid measure of student achievement.

D. students' actual learning was not related to their teacher's expectations.

14. A student is asked to report her gender at the top of a mathematics test. Based on "stereotype threat" research, doing this will very likely:

A. boost her performance on the test.

B. hinder her performance on the test.

C. have no effect on her performance.

D. lower her stress level.

9.5 Multiple Influences: The Roles of Genetics and Environment in Determining Intelligence

15. Factors that significantly impact intelligence test scores include all of these *except*:

A. academic achievement.

B. socioeconomic status.

C. gender.

D. genetics.

16. The highest correlation between two individuals' intelligence test scores is found when the two are:

A. fraternal twins raised together.

B. nonbiological siblings.

C. identical twins raised apart.

D. biological parent and child.

17. The Flynn effect refers to finding that the intelligence tests scores for every generation since 1920 have:

A. gone up steadily.

B. stayed at the average score of 100.

C. gone down due increases in poverty levels.

D. showed differences between ethnic groups.

CHAPTER DISCUSSION QUESTIONS

1. Imagine that you are a teacher for first-grade children who are just beginning to learn how to read, write, and do mathematical operations. Evaluate the pros and cons of at least three theories of intelligence in helping you understand how to teach your students. As with all classes of students, you should expect a wide range of strengths and weaknesses in the group.

2. IQ-like tests are sometimes used during the hiring process for different businesses, where the skills needed for the job are assessed in the test. Imagine that you are the person making hiring decisions for wait staff in a restaurant and you are using an IQ-like test to make your decisions. Differentiate the errors that you would make if your test was not reliable versus if it was not valid. What problems might you find in your wait staff if you hired based on a nonreliable test versus a nonvalid test?

3. We can see in Section 9.4 that environment plays a role for most all group differences in intelligence, lowering scores for some groups. Relate this difference in scores to differences in life outcomes. In other words, if someone is at risk for a lower IQ score due to environmental circumstances, what areas of his/her life are likely to be affected?

4. Section 9.5 reviews evidence for both heredity and environment in intelligence. Assess the role of heredity and environment in determining IQ scores. Do heredity and environment always have the same relative importance in determining IQ? In other words, does heredity play a bigger role for some groups versus others? Or is the role of heredity and environment always about the same for everyone?

CHAPTER PROJECT

1. Design your own intelligence text. What are example items that you feel truly capture what we mean by "intelligence"? Write ten example questions and answers. Then, give your exam to three people, and determine whether there are any differences in performance. What elements of your test were successful, and which were less so? Why is creating an intelligence test so difficult?

2. View a movie tackling the issues of life for a person with intellectual disability. Are there any aspects of the depiction that surprised you? What issues are raised about personal independence and the right of self-determination?

CHAPTER KEY TERMS

Achievement test	Emotional intelligence	Intellectual disability
Adaptive behavior	Environmental influence	Intelligence
Analytic intelligence	Fluid intelligence	Intelligence quotient (IQ)
Aptitude test	Flynn effect	Intelligence test
Content validity	General intelligence (*g*)	Mental age
Creative intelligence	Genius	Multiple intelligences
Creativity	Gifted	Norm
Crystalized intelligence	Group aptitude test	Practical intelligence
Down syndrome	Heritability	Predictive validity

Primary mental abilities
Prodigy
Psychometrician
Racial gap
Reliability
Savant syndrome
Scale

Specific intelligences (s)
Split-half reliability
Standardized procedure
Standardization
Stanford-Binet Scale
Stereotype threat
Test-retest reliability

Triarchic theory of intelligence
Twin study
Validity
Wechsler Adult Intelligence
    Scale (WAIS)
Working memory capacity

ANSWERS TO CONCEPT LEARNING CHECKS

9.1 Comparing Theories of Intelligence

1. Spatial intelligence is proposed as a separate ability in Gardner's multiple intelligences theory to account for individuals' exceptional performance on visual imagination tasks.

2. Cattell's theory distinguished fluid intelligence, or the processing of information, from crystalized intelligence, or the recall of knowledge and skills learned in the past. Ellie is able to make good use of her previous knowledge, but shows decreased functioning in fluid intelligence with age.

3. Spearman's theory of g, or general intelligence, says that there is a single underlying intellectual capacity that is reflected in all tests of cognition. His theory predicts that someone who scores high on one of these tests will likely score high on the others.

4. Thurstone's theory of primary abilities recognizes different specialized abilities that comprise intelligence. So Katrina might excel in math and do less well on tests of verbal comprehension and fluency.

5. Sharan shows great creativity. This skill is posited by Sternberg as one of the core intelligences in his triarchic theory of intelligence.

6. Helaina's ability to make interpersonal connections is an ability described in two different theories: Gardner's multiple intelligences theory includes interpersonal intelligence, and the theory of emotional intelligence describes a similar ability to "read" other people's emotions and make connections to them.

9.2 Understanding What Scores Mean

Question 1

A. A score of 100 is exactly at the average and median score of the population; 50% score higher and 50% score lower.

B. A score of 115 falls at one standard deviation above the mean; 84% of people score lower than Susan.

C. A score of 70 falls at two standard deviations below the mean; more than 97% of people score higher than Bill.

D. A score of 170 is very high, with less than 1 in 1,000 people scoring higher than Kate.

Question 2

A. Intelligence tests are much more refined in terms of reliability. The tests are very consistent across time, so

that the same person scores similarly when he or she retakes the test, and the test items are consistent across the test.

B. Validity is much more difficult to achieve with testing.

Question 3

Content validity asks whether the items appear on the surface to capture what is meant by "intelligence." Predictive validity is whether the test captures the intended outcomes the tests are designed to assess; for example, college success and career achievement.

9.3 Varieties of Intelligence

1. Mensa [C. Gifted]

2. Carl Friedrich Gauss [B. Prodigy]

3. Gottfried Mind [A. Savant]

4. Leonardo di ser Piero da Vinci [D. Genius]

9.4 Expecting to Be Smarter

1. Only item D reflects stereotype threat, because the concept only applies when the test taker expects the test to confirm a negative stereotype about him or her.

2. All three outcomes were caused by the teachers' expectancies, showing their beliefs actually created better intellectual development in the students.

3. You should expect that you will work hard and learn the concepts well and then do well on the test. Believing this will make it more likely to happen!

9.5 Understanding the Evidence on the Heredity-Environment Question

1. The correlation for identical twins (around +0.80) is larger than the correlation for fraternal twins (+.45). So the difference between these two correlations shows heritability.

2. The correlation for identical twins raised together is about +0.85, and raised apart, about +0.75. So intelligence is somewhat less correlated when raised apart. So the size of contribution from nongenetic factors is small.

3. The correlations are larger for biological relatedness, and being raised in different environments has a small effect.

ANSWERS TO CHAPTER REVIEW TEST

9.1 The Nature of Intelligence

1. A. Rationale: Spearman's theory holds that one major factor accounts for the display of intelligence across different tasks.

2. B. Rationale: Cattell posited fluid intelligence relating to processing new information, and crystalized intelligence reflected what is already stored in memory.

3. B. Rationale: Gardner's multiple intelligences theory included a variety of types of intelligence offered in no other theories.

4. A. Rationale: Sternberg's third component is the analytical ability posited in most theories.

9.2 Measuring Intelligence

5. C. Rationale: Your intelligence quotient is your mental age divided by your chronological age; for example, a 9-year-old who tests at the level of other 9-year-olds would have an IQ of 100.

6. D. Rationale: Mental age is no longer measured by modern tests.

7. B. Rationale: Reliability means scoring about the same when the same person takes the test at a different time.

8. A. Rationale: This illustrates taking the test and then retesting, so it is a measure of test-retest reliability.

9. B. Rationale: Intelligence tests are much like school tests, so it is not surprising that they predict who will do well on school tasks.

9.3 Individual Differences in Intelligence

10. B. Rationale: Individuals scoring lower than a 70 are two standard deviations below the average of 100, and so are a small proportion of the population.

11. C. Rationale: Rather than skill at tests, the ability to adapt to situations is critical for living independently.

12. D. Rationale: The body of work recognized as "genius" seems to require a long career within a field.

9.4 Group Differences in Intelligence

13. A. Rationale: The teachers were given false information about their students' test scores, but their belief in them caused the teachers to expect certain performance from those students, and they lived up to those expectations.

14. B. Rationale: A female knows that girls tend to score lower in math, so she may feel threatened by the test and perform worse than her best.

9.5 Multiple Influences: The Roles of Genetics and Environment in Determining Intelligence

15. C. Rationale: Intelligence tests are designed so that the average for both males and females is the same.

16. C. Rationale: Genetics play a large role in intelligence as measured by current tests.

17. A. Rationale: The increase in test scores every 10 years shows the population as a whole is getting "smarter" (or more educated) based on current intelligence tests.

REFERENCES

Ackerman, P. L., Beier, M. E., & Boyle, M. O. (2005). Working memory and intelligence: The same or different constructs? *Psychological Bulletin, 131*(1), 30–60.

Alon, S., & Tienda, M. (2007). Diversity, opportunity, and the shifting meritocracy in higher education. *American Sociological Review, 72*, 487–511.

Amabile, T. M. (1996). *Creativity in context: Update to the social psychology of creativity.* Boulder, CO: Westview Press.

American Anthropological Association. (1994). Statement on "race" and intelligence. http://www.aaanet.org/stmts/race.htm

Aronson, J., Fried, C. B., & Good, C. (2005). Reducing the effects of stereotype threat on African American college students by shaping theories of intelligence. *Journal of Experimental Social Psychology, 38*, 113–125.

Barnett, W. S. (1995). Long-term effects of early childhood programs on cognitive and school outcomes. *The Future of Children, 5*(3), Long-Term Outcomes of Early Childhood Programs, 25–50.

Batty, G. D., Whitley, E., Deary, I. J., Gale, C. R., Tynelius, P., & Rasmussen, F. (2011). Psychosis alters association between IQ and future risk of attempted suicide: Cohort study of 1,109,475 Swedish men. *British Medical Journal, 340*, 1348.

Bilalic, M., McLeod, P., & Gobet, F. (2010). The mechanism of the Einstellung (Set) Effect: A pervasive source of cognitive bias. *Current Directions in Psychological Science, 19*, 111–115.

Blackwell, L. S., Trzesniewski, K. H., & Dweck, C. S. (2007). Implicit theories of intelligence predict achievement across an adolescent transition: A longitudinal study and an intervention. *Child Development, 78*(1), 246–263.

Blumer, D. (2002). The illness of Vincent van Gogh. *American Journal of Psychiatry, 159*, 519–526.

Boring, E. G. (1923). Intelligence as the tests test it. *New Republic, 35*, 35–37.

Bouchard, T. J., & McGue, M. (1981). Familial studies of intelligence: A review. *Science, 212*(4498), 1055–1059.

Brooks-Gunn, J., & Duncan, G. J. (1997). The effects of poverty on children. *The Future of Children, 7*(2), 55–71.

Cattell, R. B. (1949). *The culture-free intelligence test.* Champaign, IL: Institute for Personality and Ability Testing.

Cattell, R. B. (1963). Theory of crystalized and fluid intelligence: A critical experiment. *Journal of Educational Psychology, 54*, 1–22.

Cattell, R. B. (1987). *Intelligence: Its structure, growth and action* (p. 206). Amsterdam: Elsevier Science Publishers.

Cohen G. L., Garcia, J., Apfel, N., & Master, A. (2006). Reducing the racial achievement gap: A social-psychological intervention. *Science, 313*(5791), 1307–1310.

Csikszentmihalyi, M., & Getzels, J. W. (1988). Creativity and problem finding in art. In F. Farley & R. Neperud (Eds.), *The foundations of aesthetics, art, and art education* (pp. 91–116). New York: Praeger.

Cvencek, D., Meltzoff, A. N., & Greenwald, A. G. (2011). Math–gender stereotypes in elementary school children. *Child Development,* 766–779.

Dahl, D. W., & Moreau, P. (2002). The influence and value of analogical thinking during new product ideation. *Journal of Marketing Research, 39*, 47–60.

Darlington, R. B., Royce, J. M., Snipper, A. S., Murray, H, W., & Lazar, I. (1980). Preschool programs and later school competence of children from low-income families. *Science, 208*(4440), 202–204.

Deary, I. J., Der, G., & Ford, G. (2001). Reaction times and intelligence differences: A population-based cohort study. *Intelligence, 29*(5), 389–399.

Deary, I. J., Leaper, S. A., Murray, A. D., Staff, R. T., & Whalley, L. J. (2003). Cerebral white matter abnormalities and lifetime cognitive change: A 67-year follow up of the Scottish Mental Survey 1932. *Psychology and Aging, 18*, 140–148.

Deary, I. J., Penke, L., & Johnson, W. (2010). The neuroscience of human intelligence differences. *Nature Reviews: Neuroscience, 11*, 201–211.

Deary, I. J., & Stough, C. (1996). Intelligence and inspection time: Achievements, prospects, and problems. *American Psychologist, 51*(6), 599–608.

Deary, I. J., Thorpe, G., Wilson, V., Starr, J. M., & Whalley, L. J. (2003). Population sex differences in IQ at age 11: The Scottish mental survey 1932. *Intelligence, 31*(6), 533–542.

Del Banco, N. (2011). *Lastingness: The art of old age.* New York: Grand Central Publishing.

Deutsch Smith, D. (2005). *Introduction to special education: Teaching in an age of opportunity.* New York: Allyn & Bacon/Longman.

Dickens, W. T., & Flynn, J. R. (2006). Black Americans reduce the racial gap: Evidence from standardization samples. *Psychological Science,17*(10), 913–920.

Eccles, J. S., & Jacobs, J. E. (1986). Social forces shape math attitudes and performance. *Signs, 11*(2), 367–380.

Einfeld, S. L., Piccinin, A. M., Mackinnon, A., Hofer, S. M., Taffe, J., Gray, K. M., Bontempo, D. E., Hoffman, L. R., Parmenter, P. T., & Tonge, B. J. (2006). Psychopathology in young people with intellectual disability. *Journal of the American Medical Association, 296*, 1981–1989.

Engle, R. W., Tuholski, S. W., Laughlin, J. E., Conway, A. R. A. (1999). Working memory, short-term memory, and general fluid intelligence: A latent-variable approach. *Journal of Experimental Psychology: General, 128*, 309–331.

Eyferth, K. (1961). Leistungen verschiedener Gruppen von Besatzungskindern in Hamburg-Wechsler Intelligenztest fur Kinder (HAWIK) [Performance of different groups of occupation children on the Hamburg-Wechsler Intelligence Test for Children]. *Archiv fur die gesamte Psychologie, 113*, 222–241.

Fagan, J. F., & Holland, C. R. (2002). Equal opportunity and racial differences in IQ. *Intelligence, 30*(4), 361–387.

Fagan, J. F., & Holland, C. (2007). Racial equality in intelligence: Predictions from a theory of intelligence as processing. *Intelligence, 35*(4), 319–334.

Feldman, D. H. (1980). *Beyond universals in cognitive development.* Norwood, NJ: Ablex.

Finke, R. A., Ward, T. B., & Smith, S. M. (1992). *Creative cognition: Theory, research, and applications.* Cambridge, MA: MIT Press.

Flynn, J. R. (1984). The mean IQ of Americans: Massive gains 1932 to 1978. *Psychological Bulletin, 95*(1), 29–51.

Flynn, J. R. (1991). Asian Americans: Achievement beyond IQ. Hillsdale, NJ: Lawrence Erlbaum Assoc.

Flynn, J. R. (2007). *What is intelligence?: Beyond the Flynn Effect.* Cambridge, MA: Cambridge University Press.

Fredrickson, B. L., Roberts, T-A., Noll, S. M., Quinn, D. M., & Twenge, J. M. (1998). That swimsuit becomes you: Sex differences in self-objectification, restrained eating, and math performance. *Journal of Personality and Social Psychology, 75*(1), 269–284.

Garces, E., Thomas, D., & Currie, J. (2002). Longer-term effects of Head Start, *American Economic Review, 92*(4), 999–1012.

Gardner, H. (1983). *Frames of mind: The theory of multiple intelligences.* New York: Basic Books.

Gardner, H. (1993). *Creating minds.* New York: Basic Books.

Gardner, H. (2000). A case against spiritual intelligence. *International Journal for the Psychology of Religion, 10*(1), 27–34.

Gardner, H., & Hatch, T. (1989). Multiple intelligences go to school: Educational implications of the theory of multiple intelligences. *Educational Researcher, 18*(8), 4–9.

Goleman, D. (1998). *Working with emotional intelligence.* New York: Bantam Books.

Gonzales, P. M., Blanton, H., & Williams, K. J. (2002). The effects of stereotype threat and double-minority status on the test performance of Latino women. *Personality and Social Psychology Bulletin, 28*(5), 659–670.

Gottfredson, L. S. (1997a). Mainstream science on intelligence: An editorial with 52 signatories, history, and bibliography. *Intelligence, 24,* 13–23.

Gottfredson, L. S. (1997b). Why g matters: The complexity of everyday life. *Intelligence, 24*(1), 79–132.

Gottfredson, L. S. (1998). The general intelligence factor. *Scientific American Presents, 9,* 24–29.

Gottfredson, L. S. (2003). The challenge and promise of cognitive career assessment. *Journal of Career Assessment, 11*(2), 115–135.

Gottfredson, L. S. (2004). Intelligence: Is it the epidemiologists' elusive "fundamental cause" of social class inequalities in health? *Journal of Personality and Social Psychology, 86*(1), 174–199.

Halpern, D. F., Benbow, C. P., Geary, D. C., Gur, R. C., Hyde, J. S., & Gernsbache, M. A. (2007). The science of sex differences in science and mathematics. *Psychological Science in the Public Interest, 8*(1), 1–51.

Hedges, L. V., & Nowell, A. (1995). Sex differences in mental test scores, variability, and numbers of high-scoring individuals. *Science, 269*(5220), 41–45.

Hermstein, R. J., & Murray, C. (1994). *The bell curve: Intelligence and class structure in American life.* New York: Free Press.

Horwood, L. J., Darlow, B. A., & Mogridge, N. (2001). Breast milk feeding and cognitive ability at 7–8 years. *Archives of Disease in Childhood: Fetal and Neonatal, 84*(1), F23–27.

Hunt, E., & Carlson, J. (2007). Considerations relating to the study of group differences in intelligence. *Perspectives on Psychological Science, 2,* 194–213.

Hunter, J. E., & Hunter, R. F. (1984). Validity and utility of alternative predictors of job performance. *Psychological Bulletin, 96*(1), 72–79.

Hyde, J. S., & Linn, M. C. (1988). Gender differences in verbal ability: A meta-analysis. *Psychological Bulletin, 104*(1), 53–69.

Irvine, S. H., & Berry, J. W. (Eds.). (1988). *Human abilities in culture.* Cambridge, MA: Cambridge University Press.

Jaeggi, S. M., Buschkuehl, M., Jonides, J., & Perrig, W. J. (2008). Improving fluid intelligence with training on working memory. *Proceedings of the National Academy of Sciences, 105*(19), 6829–6833.

Jaeggi, S. M., Buschkuehl, M., Jonides, J., & Shah, P. (2011). Short- and long-term benefits of cognitive training. *Proceedings of the National Academy of Sciences, 108*(25), 10081–10086.

Jensen, A. R. (1980). *Bias in mental testing.* New York: Free Press.

Jordan, T. J., Grallo, R., Deutsch, M., & Deutsch, C. P. (1985). Long-term effects of early enrichment: A 20-year perspective on persistence and change. *American Journal of Community Psychology, 13*(4), 393–415.

Jung, R. E., & Haier, R. J. (2007). The Parieto-Frontal Integration Theory (P-FIT) of intelligence: Converging neuroimaging evidence. *Behavioral and Brain Sciences, 30,* 135–154.

Kaufman, A. S. (2009). *IQ testing 101.* New York: Springer.

Kaufman, A. S., & Lichtenberger, E. (2006). *Assessing adolescent and adult intelligence* (3rd ed.). Hoboken, NJ: Wiley.

Kaufman, A. S., Reynolds, C. R., & McLean, J. E. (1989). Age and WAIS-R intelligence in a national sample of adults in the 20- to 74-year age range: A cross-sectional analysis with educational level controlled. *Intelligence, 13*(3), 235–253.

Kline, P. (1991). *Intelligence: The psychometric view.* New York: Rutledge, Chapman, & Hall.

Kristensen, P., & Bjerkedal, T. (2007). Explaining the relation between birth order and intelligence. *Science, 316*(5832), 1717.

Lazar, I., Darlington, R., Murray, H., Royce, J., & Snipper, A. (1982). Lasting effects of early education: A report from the Consortium for Longitudinal Studies. *Monographs of the Society for Research in Child Development* (Series No. 195), *47,* 2–3.

Lee, V. E., Brooks-Gunn, J., Schnur, E., & Liaw, F.-R. (1990). Are Head Start effects sustained? A longitudinal follow-up comparison of disadvantaged children attending Head Start, no preschool, and other preschool programs. *Child Development, 61,* 495–507.

Lemann, N. (1999). *The big test: The secret history of the American meritocracy.* New York: Farrar, Strauss, & Giroux.

Loehlin, J. C., Vandenberg, S. G., & Osborne, R. T. (1973). Blood group genes and Negro–White ability differences. *Behavior Genetics, 3,* 263–270.

Loehlin, J. C., Willerman, L., & Horn, J. M. (1988). Human behavior genetics. *Annual Review of Psychology, 39,* 101–133.

Lynn, R., & Vanhanen, T. (2006). *IQ and global inequality.* Augusta, GA: Washington Summit Publishers.

Maccoby, E. E., & Jacklin, C. N. (1974). *The psychology of sex differences.* Stanford, CA: Stanford University Press.

Mackenzie, B. (1984). Explaining Race Differences in IQ: The Logic, the Methodology, and the Evidence. *American Psychologist, 39*(2), 1214–1233.

Mayer, J. D., Salovey, P., Caruso, D. L., & Sitarenios, G. (2001). Emotional intelligence as a standard intelligence. *Emotion, 1,* 232–242.

Mercer, J. R. (1973). IQ: The lethal label. *Education Digest: Essential Readings Condensed for Quick Review, 38*(5), 17–20.

Miller, L. K. (1998). Defining the savant syndrome. *Journal of Developmental and Physical Disabilities, 10*(1), 73–83.

Moffitt, T. E., Caspi, A., Harkness, A. R., & Silva, P. A. (1993). The natural history of change in intellectual performance: Who changes? How much? Is it meaningful? *Journal of Child Psychology and Psychiatry, 3,* 455–506.

Neisser, U. (1976). General, academic, and artificial intelligence. In L. B. Resnick (Ed.), *The nature of intelligence* (pp. 135–144). Hillsdale, NJ: Erlbaum.

Neisser, U., Boodoo, G., Bouchard, T. J. Jr., Boykin, A. W., Brody, N., Ceci, S. J., Halpern, D. F., Loehlin, J. C., Perloff, R., Sternberg, R. J., & Urbina, S. (1996). Intelligence: Knowns and unknowns. *American Psychologist, 51*(2), 77–101.

Nenty, H. J. (1986). *Cross-Cultural bias analysis of Cattell Culture-Fair Intelligence Test.* 67th Annual Meeting of the American Educational Research Association, San Francisco, CA, April 16–20.

Nisbett, R. E. (2009). *Intelligence and how to get it: Why schools and cultures count.* New York: Norton.

Olszewski-Kubilius, P., & Lee, S. Y. (2004). Parent perceptions of the effects of the Saturday Enrichment Program on gifted students' talent development. *Roeper Review, 26,* 156–165.

Pinker, S. (2004). Why nature & nurture won't go away. *Dædalus, 133*(4), 5–17.

Plomin, R., DeFries, J. C., & Loehlin, J. C. (1977). Genotype–environment interaction and correlation in the analysis of human behavior. *Psychological Bulletin, 84*(2), 309–322.

Powers, D. E., & Rock, D. A. (1999). Effects of coaching on SAT I: Reasoning test scores. *Journal of Educational Measurement, 36*(2), 93–118.

Pyryt, M. C. (1993). Career development for the gifted and talented: Helping adolescents chart their futures. *Journal of Secondary Gifted Education, 5*(1), 18–21.

Raven, J. (2000). The Raven's Progressive Matrices: Change and stability over culture and time. *Cognitive Psychology, 41,* 1–48.

Reynolds, A. J., Temple, J. A., & Robertson, D. L. (2001). Long-term effects of an early childhood intervention on educational achievement and juvenile arrest: A 15-year follow-up of low-income children in public schools. *Journal of the American Medical Association, 285*(18), 2339–2346.

Robinson, A., Shore, B. M., & Enersen, D. (Eds.). (2007). *Best practices in gifted education.* Waco, TX: Prufrock Press.

Robinson, N. M., Zigler, E., & Gallagher, J. J. (2000). Two tails of the normal curve: Similarities and differences in the study of mental retardation and giftedness. *American Psychologist, 55,* 1413–1424.

Roid, G. H., & Barram, R. A. (2004). *Essentials of Stanford-Binet Intelligence Scales (SB5) assessment.* Hoboken, NJ: John Wiley & Sons.

Rosenthal, R., & Jacobson, L. (1968). *Pygmalion in the classroom: Teacher expectation and pupils' intellectual development.* New York: Holt, Rinehart, & Winston.

Rushton, J. P., & Jensen, A. R. (2005). Thirty years of research on race differences in cognitive ability. *Psychology, Public Policy, and Law, 11,* 235–294.

Schulte, M. J., Ree, M. J., & Carretta, T. R. (2004). Emotional intelligence: Not much more than *g* and personality. *Personality and Individual Differences, 37,* 1059–1068.

Schutte, N. S., Malouff, J. M., Hall, L. E., Haggerty, D. J., Cooper, J. T., Golden, C. J., & Dornheim, L. (1998). Development and validation of a measure of emotional intelligence. *Personality and Individual Differences, 25,* 167–177.

Scarr, S., Weinberg, R. A., & Waldman, I. D. (1993). IQ correlations in transracial adoptive families. *Intelligence, 17,* 541–555.

Scott, G., Leritz, L. E., & Mumford, M. D. (2004). The effectiveness of creativity training: A quantitative review. *Creativity Research Journal, 16*(4), 361–388.

Seifert, C. M., Meyer, D. E., Davidson, N., Patalano, A. L., & Yaniv, I. (1995). Demystification of cognitive insight: Opportunistic assimilation and the prepared-mind hypothesis. In R. J. Sternberg & J. E. Davidson (Eds.), *The nature of insight* (pp. 65–124). Cambridge, MA: MIT Press.

Shalock, R. L., Borthwirk-Duffy, S. A., Bradley, V. J., Buntinx, W. H. E., Coulter, D. L., Craig, E. M., Gomez, S. C., Lachapelle, Y., Luckasson, R., Reeve, A., Shogren, K. A., Snell, M. E., Spreat, S., Tassé, M. J., Thompson, J. R., Verdugo-Alonso, M. A., Wehmeyer, M. L., & Yeager, M. H. (2010). *Intellectual disability: Definition, classification, and systems of supports* (11th Ed.). Annapolis Junction, MD: AAIDD Publications.

Shepard, R. N., & Metzler, J. (1971). Mental rotation of three-dimensional objects. *Science, 171,* 701–703.

Shurkin, J. N. (1992). *Terman's kids: The groundbreaking study of how the gifted grow up.* New York: Little, Brown and Co.

Simonton, D. K. (2009). *Genius 101.* New York: Springer.

Smith, E. E. (1996). Personal communication.

Smith, G. F. (1998). Idea-generation techniques: A formulary of active ingredients. *Journal of Creative Behavior, 32*(2), 107–133.

Spearman, C. (1904). General intelligence objectively determined and measured. *American Journal of Psychology, 15,* 201–293.

Steele, C. M., & Aronson, J. (1995). Stereotype threat and the intellectual test performance of African Americans. *Journal of Personality and Social Psychology, 69*(5), 797–811.

Sternberg, R. J. (1985). *Beyond IQ: A triarchic theory of human intelligence.* New York: Cambridge University Press.

Sternberg, R. J. (2001). What is the common thread to creativity: Its dialectical relation to intelligence and wisdom. *American Psychologist, 56,* 360–362.

Sternberg, R. J., Conway, B. E., Ketron, J. L., & Bernstein, M. (1981). People's conceptions of intelligence. *Journal of Personality and Social Psychology, 41*(1), 37–55.

Stone, J. (2002). Battling doubt by avoiding practice: The effects of stereotype threat on self-handicapping in white athletes. *Personality and Social Psychology Bulletin, 28,* 1667–1678.

Streissguth, A. P., Aase, J. M., Clarren, S. K., Randels, S. P., LaDue, R. A., & Smith, D. F. (1991). Fetal alcohol syndrome in adolescents and adults. *Journal of the American Medical Association, 265,* 1961–1967.

Subotnik, R. F., Olszewski-Kubilius, P., & Worrell, F. C. (2011). Rethinking giftedness and gifted education: A proposed direction forward based on psychological science. *Psychological Science in the Public Interest, 12*(1) 3–54.

Sullivan, J. (2002). State will admit sterilization past. *Portland Oregonian,* November 15, 2002. (Mirrored in *Eugene Register-Guard,* November 16, 2002, at Google News.)

Summers, L. H. (2005). Archive of Remarks at the National Bureau of Economic Research Conference on Diversifying the Science & Engineering Workforce. Cambridge, MA. January 14, 2005.

Taggart, L., Taylor, D., McCrum-Gardner, E. (2010). Individual, life events, family and socio-economic factors associated with young people with intellectual disability and with and without behavioural/emotional problems. *Journal of Intellectual Disability, 14*(4), 267–288.

Terman, L. M. (1925). *Genetic studies of genius. Mental and physical traits of a thousand gifted children.* Oxford, UK: Stanford University Press.

Thorndike, A. L., & Hagen, E. P. (1977). *Measurement and evaluation in psychology and education.* New York, NY: Macmillan.

Thurstone, L. L. (1938). *Primary mental abilities.* Chicago: University of Chicago Press.

Toga, A. W., & Thompson. P. M. (2005). Genetics of brain structure and intelligence. *Annual Review of Neuroscience, 28,* 1–23.

Treffert, D. (1989). *Extraordinary people.* New York: Harper and Row.

Treffinger, D., Isaksen, S., & Dorval, B. (2000). *Creative problem solving: An introduction* (3rd ed.). Waco, TX: Prufrock Press.

Trei, L. (2007). New study yields instructive results on how mindset affects learning. *Stanford Report,* February 7. http://news.stanford.edu/news/2007/february7/dweck-020707.html

Tucker-Drob, E. M., Rhemtulla, M., Harden, K. P., Turkheimer, E., & Fask, D. (2011). Emergence of a gene x socioeconomic status interaction on infant mental ability between 10 months and 2 years. *Psychological Science, 22*(1), 125–133.

Turkheimer, E., Haley, A., Waldron, M., D'Onofrio, B., & Gottesman, I. I. (2003). Socioeconomic status modifies heritability of IQ in young children. *Psychological Science, 14*(6), 623–628.

van der Sluis, S., Willemsen, G., de Geus, E. J. C., Boomsma, D. I., & Posthuma, D. (2008). Gene–environment interaction in adults' IQ scores: Measures of past and present environment. *Behavior Genetics, 38*(4), 348–360.

Vernon, P. A. (1983). Speed of information processing and general intelligence. *Intelligence, 7*(1), 53–70.

Walton, G. M., & Cohen, G. L. (2003). Stereotype lift. *Journal of Experimental Social Psychology, 39*(5), 456–467.

Weisberg, R. W. (1986). *Creativity: Genius and other myths.* New York: Freeman.

Williams, R. L. (1972). *The BITCH-100: A culture-specific test.* American Psychological Association Annual Convention, Honolulu, HI.

Witelson, S. F., Kigar, D. L., & Harvey, T. (1999). The exceptional brain of Albert Einstein. *The Lancet, 353,* 2149–2153.

Woods, E., & McDaniel, P. (1997). *Training a Tiger: Raising a winner in golf and in life.* New York: HarperCollins Publishers.

Yeargin-Allsopp, M., Murphy, C. C., Cordero, J. F., Decouflé, P., & Hollowell, J. G. (1997). Reported biomedical causes and associated medical conditions for mental retardation among 10-year-old children, metropolitan Atlanta, 1985 to 1987. *Developmental Medicine and Child Neurology, 39*(3), 142–149.

Yeargin-Allsopp, M., Murphy, C. C., Oakley, G. P., & Sikes R. K. (1992). A multiple-source method for studying the prevalence of developmental disabilities in children: The Metropolitan Atlanta Developmental Disabilities Study. *Pediatrics, 89*(4 Pt 1), 624–630.

Zajonc, R. B. (1976). Family configuration and intelligence: Variations in scholastic aptitude scores parallel trends in family size and the spacing of children. *Science, 192,* 227–229.

Zigler, E. (1984). Personal communication.

Zigler, E., & Berman, W. (1983). Discerning the future of early childhood intervention. *American Psychologist, 38*(8), 894–906.

Zigler, E., & Muenchow, S. (1992). *Head Start: The inside story of America's most successful educational experiment.* New York: Basic Books.

Chapter Overview ▼

10 Motivation

On a rare visit to my hometown, I ran into a high school classmate, Terri. "What have you been doing in the last 10 years since graduation?" she asked. Terri had already filled me in on her life on a Montana ranch, working on a ski patrol in Aspen, and marriage with two children. When I answered, I surprised even myself by observing, "I have been in school since I last saw you!" Following 4 years of college, I was finishing my sixth year of a PhD program in psychology. I realized that I was 28 and had never been out of school! The end goal—becoming a professor—was not even within reach. Two years of postdoctoral study followed before I began my first full-time job at age 30. Terri's look of amazement matched my own: What motivates us to work for years toward long-term goals? It is no wonder that there are many theories developed to explain motivation. But as we shall see, no one theory has yet satisfactorily explained every aspect of motivation.

10.1 Motivational Theories

A variety of theories have been proposed to explain what moves us toward the fulfillment of a goal.

- Define the concept of motivation.
- Discuss the theories about what moves individuals toward the fulfillment of a goal.

Why did you get out of bed today? Sometimes, it is hard to see our true motivations because our daily lives are quite routine. So, for a moment, imagine your life without alarm clocks, cell phones, or schedules. If you had a day with unstructured time, what would you do first when you woke up? Biological requirements for maintaining your body would likely come first, such as thirst, urination, keeping warm or cool, and eating. The human body can live for only 3 minutes without oxygen, 3 days without water, and 3 weeks without food. But a human can live a lifetime without sex, even though it is required to propagate our species. Once beyond biological needs, you may soon want to talk to someone you care about or eventually feel the need to accomplish something during your day. How can we capture the many reasons for our decisions to act?

Motivation is described as an inner state that energizes people toward the fulfillment of a goal. Importantly, motivation is considered to arise internally, as an act of will, rather than an external force compelling you to take action (like pulling your hand back from a hot stove). Motivation is also related to an intention or outcome that you desire; so you are motivated to achieve some goal or state, such as being financially independent, or in a happy relationship. At the base level, a **motive** is the pursuit of pleasure in some form and the avoidance of pain or displeasure. Just about any goal can be termed a motive as long as it motivates a person to pursue it for any reason. Throughout the history of psychology, several theories of motivation have been proposed. Theories of motivation try to explain how and why we are energized to move toward specific goals.

Instinct Theories

Comparative psychology grew from the study of animal behavior. Understanding the built-in behaviors that occur in animals led to **instinct theories**, or motivation as inborn, programmed behaviors occurring in response to a cue (Weiner, 1972). An instinct can be triggered by internal cues (such as the menstrual cycle in mammals) as well as external (environmental) cues (e.g., the presence of a receptive partner for mating). Humans, too, have instincts, or behavior that arises across cultures, apparently without learning. For example, if a newborn is placed near a woman's breast, it will "root" around with its mouth, attempting to suck on the nipple. This is a basic behavior that appears to be inborn in all humans. Other instincts include smiling, fear of snakes and spiders,

Motivation An inner state that energizes people toward the fulfillment of a goal.

Motive The pursuit of pleasure and the avoidance of pain or displeasure.

Instinct theories Motivation from biologically programmed behaviors occurring in response to environmental cues.

and protecting your children. However, most of human behavior cannot be considered instinctual because it can be overridden even in the presence of a cue. For example, a basic motivation like eating when you are hungry can occur or not occur based on a willful decision. As a result, the theory of instincts that accounts for animal behaviors cannot explain our voluntary decisions about whether to take specific actions. The theory's greatest weakness is the fact that humans are motivated to do many things, particularly at higher levels of control (like earning a college degree!), that cannot be explained as simple instincts.

Evolutionary Theories

Evolutionary psychologists apply the theory of evolution to explain the psychology behind our behaviors (Buss, 1995). They believe there exist **universals** in human behavior—that is, behaviors that people perform regardless of their cultures. Further, these universal behaviors are the product of millions of years of human history and have little to do with the modern environment surrounding us today. Instead, the behaviors of early humans that led to their survival also led to children more likely to pursue the same behaviors. As a species, their behaviors thus **evolved** or were selected over generations to leave the ones best fit for that environment. For example, throughout the history of humans, food supplies tended to wax and wane. Some groups had to live through periods of scarcity during which little food was available. Some of these humans liked to overeat when food was available, preferring fatty and sweet foods that were stored as body fat. Then, when food was not available, these individuals had the advantage of stored body fat to help them through the lean times. So the question of why we overeat may relate back to our ancestors: Those who ate more were more likely to survive and, therefore, become the ancestors of today's ice cream lovers.

Evolutionary theories of motivation focus on motives that affect the success of the population over time. While we may think of these as primarily biological, such as acquiring food, human evolution is thought to reflect the increasing importance of social motives in the survival of an individual. The individual needed the group to provide safety, a partner to provide the opportunity to mate, a larger family to assist with raising the young, and the skills to cooperate and compete for resources within the group (Bernard et al., 2005). As a result, humans were selected based on their interest, desire, and success at solving problems within the social domain. The generations of humans who survived to raise children shaped the patterns of motivations we see in people today.

Considering the theory of evolution in psychology may seem a bit odd. However, it is important to remember how many generations of humans lived before our recorded history. More than 150,000 years ago, *Homo sapiens* lived in roving groups of 50 to 80 people and, around 90,000 years ago, lived on the African Savanna. About 60,000 years ago, *Homo sapiens* moved out around the world. They lived as hunters and gatherers for the last 50,000 years. Less than 10,000 years ago, they began farming, and modern settlements became possible. Large groups of people living in close proximity are a recent development in human history. The early environments in which humans lived and survived were very different from our own. For example, modern humans in Western cultures know more individuals at age 6 than most early humans would have encountered over their lifetimes! For humans in prehistory, much of their time was devoted to finding food on a daily basis by hunting and gathering; in today's world, grocery stores make this a minor effort each day. More recent developments playing a large role in our lives, such as the Internet and cell phones, are just a blip on the time scale of evolution. That leaves plenty of room for evolutionary factors that shaped human behaviors to impact the motivations of people today.

Drive Theories

A **drive** is defined as tension arising from within our physiological systems, which in turn motivates action (Hull, 1943). For example, over time, your cells need more water, so you become motivated to drink. As more time passes, the need for water causes a tension within your system. Eventually, you are driven to take action and satisfy the drive, releasing the tension. When our bodies need something, the states of tension caused are quite unpleasant (such as the feeling of being thirsty or hungry). The body attempts to

Evolutionary psychologist A researcher who applies the theory of evolution to explain the psychology behind behaviors.

Universals Behaviors that all people perform regardless of their cultures.

Evolved behaviors Behaviors selected over generations to best fit the environment.

Drive A tension arising from within physiological systems that motivates action.

Homeostasis The process of maintaining a stable or balanced physiological state over time.

Drive theory A theory that states of tension motivate us to take action to reduce them.

Arousal theory The theory that we are motivated to seek out a particular level of arousal.

Optimal arousal A level of activation that is sufficient but not overwhelming.

Yerkes-Dodson law of arousal The theory that performance is best at medium levels of arousal.

According to arousal theory, people may be motivated to increase their level of arousal through acts like skydiving.

maintain **homeostasis**, or a steady internal state. **Drive theory** says these states are what motivate us to take action to reduce those unpleasant feelings. Drives are usually thought of as biological needs, such as thirst, eating, and sex. Drive theory is helpful for explaining why we get hungry and eat, or why we scratch when we itch. For many people in the world today, satisfying the drives for food, water, and safety are daily occurrences; in the more developed world, we may devote much less effort toward the pursuit of drives.

Unconscious drives, such as the drive to stay alive and to be aggressive, self-destructive, or to die, have also been proposed by psychologists such as Sigmund Freud (1856–1939). However, drives cannot predict when specific behaviors will occur. In particular, people sometimes perform actions that *increase* feelings of tension. Skydiving, driving too fast, and watching scary movies all add to our feelings of unresolved tension, yet some people sometimes enjoy increasing the tension they feel.

Arousal Theories

If people sometimes choose to reduce tension and other times to increase it, perhaps we are attempting to manage the level of tension we experience. **Arousal theory** states that we are motivated to seek out a particular level of arousal, one that is stimulating but not overwhelming (Fiske & Maddi, 1961). If your arousal level is too low and you are bored, you may seek out environments, people, and situations that will increase your arousal. And if it is too high, you may decrease your arousal by practicing meditation, avoiding stimulation, or isolating yourself from others. Arousal theory suggests that tension is not a bad thing, but it should be regulated so that you have just the right amount, or **optimal arousal**.

The relationship between your level of arousal and your performance is described as curvilinear, according to the **Yerkes-Dodson law of arousal** FIGURE 10-1. Consider taking a standardized test before applying to college. If you considered the test to be routine, you might have had a very low level of anxiety or arousal about it and may not have performed your best (as quickly or accurately) during the hours of the exam. On the other hand, if you felt very anxious about the exam, your arousal may have been too high and interfered with your performance. This predicts that your best performance will occur when your arousal level is "optimal"—when you feel excited, but not too excited. For example, one experienced psychology instructor now runs up and down a flight of stairs just before his large lectures begin. After years of teaching, he does not feel the edge of tension about his performance, so he recreates the feeling by stimulating his level of arousal through exercise. Athletic teams do this, too, through "pumped up" pep talks just before games. Arousal theory may explain getting out of bed in the morning; as pleasant as it is to lie quietly for some time, eventually the boredom of the setting may cause you to initiate some other action. So, if your arousal is too low, you may try some more stimulating behavior to keep your arousal level within a target range. Arousal theory takes the environment around you into account in explaining why you are motivated to make changes. However, arousal theory is not very helpful in explaining long-term motivation. Why might you continue studying throughout college? It may relate to keeping your level of arousal at an

FIGURE 10-1 At both high and low levels of arousal, performance on a task is worse.

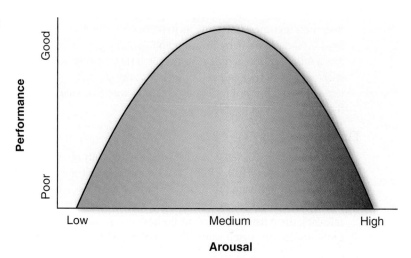

optimal level; however, it may more likely be caused by a desire to be successful, make money, gain power, or do something that you find rewarding.

Incentive Theories

Another view of motivation, known as **incentive theories**, focuses on the reward or payoff for behaviors. We quickly learn to perform behaviors that lead to desirable consequences. So perhaps the explanation for more complex behaviors involves incentives. **Incentives** are the rewards and punishments associated with different actions that lure people into taking action. This account of motivation says we can explain why you took a particular action by looking into the incentives that followed it. Incentives can have complex relationships with behaviors; for example, coming late to a party seems bad, but it may result in your skipping out on paying for the pizza. So incentives for taking action can be hidden or explicit and can work differently for different people (e.g., some people do not like ice cream; Atkinson, 1964).

Incentive theory says we are motivated to do things by two types of incentives: intrinsic and extrinsic. **Intrinsic incentives** involve internal feelings. These incentives motivate you to do things because they make you happy, make you feel good, or at least make you feel less bad. Donating change at the Salvation Army bucket leads to a warm feeling through knowing you are helping others, and holding a job that you love serves as its own reward. These behaviors reflect **intrinsic motivations**, or behaviors performed for an internal reward. **Extrinsic incentives** are external rewards or punishments that motivate you to perform a specific action. So, you may hold a job because you want the pay you receive, or you earn good grades because you want your parents' approval. **Extrinsic motivation** refers to the desire to gain external rewards for behavior. There is a reason we do not have to pay people to watch cartoons but do pay them to sell hotdogs. When we are not motivated by intrinsic motivations, external incentives are used to help motivate us. The world is organized around incentives, as are social relationships, and they often mix intrinsic and extrinsic rewards.

Are the effects of intrinsic and extrinsic incentives the same? That is, does paying people to do something (extrinsic incentive) have the same psychological effect as their doing it because they enjoy it (intrinsic incentive)? To answer this question, researchers brought college students into a lab for three test sessions (Deci, 1971). In all three sessions, the control group was given block puzzles to solve and then left alone while researchers watched to see how many more puzzles these students would solve on their own time. For the incentive group, the students were paid to complete each puzzle, but only during the second work session. During the third session, both groups were again tested without any incentives. The control group voluntarily spent time on the puzzles during the breaks between sessions, and there was no difference in how many they did across the three sessions. They appeared to do the puzzles because they enjoyed doing so. But the incentive group behaved differently: They spent a lot more time on the puzzles in the session for which they were paid, and a lot less time on them during the third session, when they were not paid FIGURE 10-2.

The results showed that paying people to do a task they already enjoyed (and did for free in the first session) made them lose interest in doing it for free. This effect is called the **overjustification effect**, in that the extrinsic reward provides a complete rationale for doing the task, so no intrinsic

Incentive theories
Motivation that focuses on the reward or payoff for behaviors.

Incentive The rewards and punishments associated with different actions.

Intrinsic incentives
Feelings of reward created within the individual.

Intrinsic motivation
The desire to perform behaviors for an internal reward.

Extrinsic incentives
Rewards (such as pay) given to motivate people to perform certain behaviors.

Extrinsic motivation The desire to gain external rewards for behavior.

Overjustification effect
When a task provides an extrinsic reward, no intrinsic motive is needed.

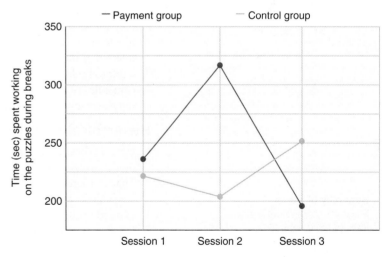

FIGURE 10-2 Students who were paid to solve puzzles during their free time (red) completed more puzzles in the second session (when paid), but fewer in the third session (when not paid), compared to the control group (blue).
Source: Data from Deci, E. L. (1971). Effects of externally mediated rewards on intrinsic motivation. Journal of Personality and Social Psychology, 18(1), 105–115.

motive is needed (Lepper et al., 1973). To say you were paid to do it *and* that you enjoyed doing it would be *over*justifying your behavior. Does being paid really undermine your intrinsic interest in a task? One study looked at the work of professional artists who completed pieces either on commission (paid for by an art patron) or for their own collection (for potential sale at a later time). Commissioned works were judged as "less creative" than noncommissioned work (Amabile, 1996).

Further, *more* external incentives do not necessarily improve performance. In a recent study, students were given a variety of tasks to complete, involving remembering strings of digits, performing motor skills, or creative games (Ariely et al., 2009). Different groups were given either small, medium, or large financial rewards based on their performance. For mechanical skills, for which no thinking was involved, higher rewards did lead to better performance. But if the task involved cognitive skill in even a rudimentary way, the larger reward led to poorer performance FIGURE 10-3. Increasing the incentives made performance *worse* on tasks that involved thinking.

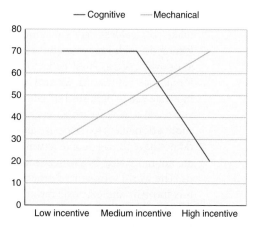

FIGURE 10-3 Results showing performance based on level of incentives for mechanical skills and cognitive skills. *Source: Data from Ariely, D., Gneezy, W., Lowenstein, G., & Mazar, N. (2009). Large stakes and big mistakes.* Review of Economic Studies, 76, *451–469.*

So extrinsic incentives have a complex relationship to our behavior. A meta-analysis of 111 randomized controlled studies concluded that "Financial incentives, if they are big enough, can influence discrete behavior at the individual level in the short run" (Kane et al., 2004). But the fundamental fact of motivation is that human beings cannot be compelled to change their behaviors, such as what and how much they eat, or whether they smoke or exercise. These behavior changes can be *initiated* by "extrinsic" motivators like rewards (Curry et al., 1991). But human nature is such that we do not necessarily internalize motivation based on rewards (Pink, 2009). The incentive approach does not work to build up the intrinsic motivation needed to sustain behavior change over time (Amabile, 1996). External incentives get people to perform a behavior but not necessarily to believe in—or understand—its value.

Hierarchical Theories

How do these differing accounts of motivation fit together? One important approach to motivation attempts to understand the needs and motivations of humans in terms of levels. That is, there are basic or primary needs, like hunger and thirst, that we fulfill before considering other types of needs. Abraham Maslow (1908–1970) identified a **hierarchy of needs** FIGURE 10-4 in which each level of need depends on satisfying the lower levels. So we focus first on physiological needs like hunger and thirst before considering the importance of safety, which is dealt with before addressing our need for love or belonging, and so on. Higher-level needs like esteem, including status, power, and respect, can only be addressed once the lower-level needs are satisfied.

At the highest level, once our biological and social needs are met, Maslow posited the idea of **self-actualization**, or the goal of fulfilling your potential, or "being all that you can be." Maslow is identified with the humanist tradition in psychology, which proposes that the greatest goal for humankind is for each individual to develop into his or her greatest potential. Maslow developed his theory by studying the lives of eminent people, who had often succeeded in reaching the pinnacle of self-actualization. While the needs Maslow proposed are intuitively appealing, there is little evidence in support of this

Hierarchy of needs
Maslow's theory that each level of need depends on satisfying lower levels.

Self-actualization
Maslow's concept that the highest need is to fulfill individual potential.

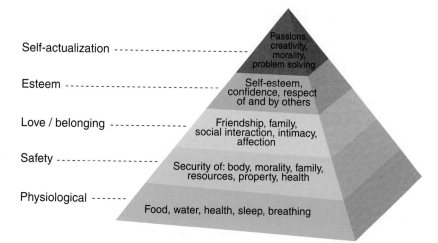

FIGURE 10-4 Maslow's hierarchy of needs shows basic needs as a foundation, with higher level needs built upon them.

Self-actualization — Passions, creativity, morality, problem solving

Esteem — Self-esteem, confidence, respect of and by others

Love / belonging — Friendship, family, social interaction, intimacy, affection

Safety — Security of: body, morality, family, resources, property, health

Physiological — Food, water, health, sleep, breathing

model. For example, in a cross-cultural study with participants from 39 countries, the fulfillment of "esteem" needs was considered more important only in Western cultures, where independence is stressed over interdependence (Oishi et al., 1999).

For many of us, our basic needs are met each day without much effort. But what if you live in a dangerous environment in which you must be concerned about walking home at night or being safe while you sleep? These needs would prevent you from working on your goals for relationships and self-actualization. Across the world, most people expend their effort in meeting basic needs for clean water, enough food, and a safe environment. Similarly, in some contexts, social goals of building relationships with family and maintaining social status might limit your search for self-actualization, requiring your service or duty to the family or group. Finally, consider an emergency situation, such as the impact of Hurricane Katrina. After the storm and flooding subsided, would you begin thinking about your basic physiological needs? Or would contacting your family members be your priority? Clearly, many factors, from biological to social to achievement needs, play into the psychology of motivation.

Natural disasters and emergencies can reveal psychological differences in our motivation to act.

CONCEPT LEARNING CHECK 10.1 — Theories of Motivation

Match each example to the theory that gives the best account of the motivation described.

A. Instinct

B. Evolution

C. Drive

D. Arousal

E. Incentive

F. Hierarchy of needs

1. _____ Harry finds his mind wandering after studying for hours in a carrel in the library. He heads to the local bar to find some action.

2. _____ Jamal dislikes his job, but he sticks with it because he needs the money.

3. _____ Karen eventually stops playing and leaves the soccer game in progress to head to the sidelines for some water.

4. _____ Even though she knows it is not a healthy choice, Rebecca loves the taste of fried foods.

5. _____ Tommy saw a spider and ran from it.

6. _____ Francesca has to work to provide for her family before she can attend college.

Explain

7. For each of these theories, explain whether they can account for motivational differences observed for people living in different environments, such as a modern Japanese high-rise apartment versus a remote desert hut.

A. Instinct

B. Evolution

C. Drive

D. Arousal

E. Incentive

F. Hierarchy of needs

10.2 Motivation of Hunger

Many biological and environmental factors affect the system that regulates hunger and eating.

- Illustrate the biology/physiology of hunger.
- Explain environmental influences on hunger.
- Describe the eating disorders and self-regulation.

Hunger provides an example of how a basic motivation can require a complex system for regulation. The human body has not just one system to regulate eating behavior but many. A great deal of research has examined why we eat, what we eat, and, increasingly, what to do when we eat too much.

The Physiology and Regulation of Hunger

Many biological factors contribute to the regulation of hunger and eating. These systems are located throughout the body, including the stomach and digestive organs, the brain, the endocrine system, the blood, and our genes. The hunger motivation ensures that we maintain a nourished body using feedback from all of these biological sources.

The Stomach

The first thing to think of is the stomach: Its growls seem to signal that food is needed, and when full, its stretching signals that you have had enough. To test the idea of the stomach as the regulator of hunger, an early study involved intentionally swallowing a balloon (Cannon & Washburn, 1912). The balloon was inflated with air to fill the stomach, and a recording device registered whenever the stomach contracted. Meanwhile, the subject (A. J. Washburn) pushed a button whenever he felt hungry FIGURE 10-5. Sure enough, the reports of feelings of hunger were directly related to the contractions of the empty stomach.

FIGURE 10-5 Cannon and Washburn's study showed that stomach contractions were the cause of feelings of hunger pangs.

It seemed the case was closed; however, patients who had their stomachs removed due to disease still reported feelings of hunger. In addition, an experiment with rats showed that they continued to eat even though their stomachs were surgically removed. So while hunger pangs in the stomach play a role in motivating you to eat, they are not the only mechanism that regulates our eating behavior.

The Brain

Early studies examined the role the brain plays in hunger and eating. The limbic system, located in the center of the brain, controls motivation, emotion, and memory FIGURE 10-6. The structure called the **hypothalamus**, located just below the thalamus, is the functional center of motivation in the brain. Studies of animals tested what happens to eating behavior when the hypothalamus was either destroyed or was stimulated by placing an electrode within it. The results showed two separate areas of the hypothalamus that activate and deactivate eating behavior.

One area of the hypothalamus, called the **lateral hypothalamus**, appears to be a "start eating" center. When it is activated, it "turns on" hunger, and the animal starts eating. When stimulated with a small amount of electricity through an electrode in this area,

Hypothalamus The functional center of motivation in the brain.

Lateral hypothalamus The "start eating" functional center in the brain.

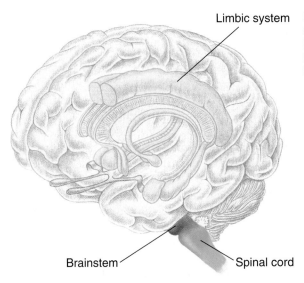

FIGURE 10-6 The limbic system including the amygdala, hippocampus, and hypothalamus, is responsible for motivated behavior, memory, and emotion.

Limbic system

Brainstem   Spinal cord

Ventromedial hypothalamus The functional "stop eating" center in the brain.

Endocrine system The network of glands throughout the body that manufacture and secrete hormones.

a rat will eat even after it is full (Teitelbaum & Epstein, 1962). However, if this area is destroyed by killing cells, the "start button" no longer works. Animals with lesions in this lateral (or side) area of the hypothalamus will not initiate eating on their own FIGURE 10-7.

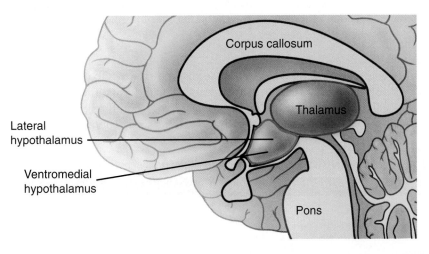

FIGURE 10-7 Two areas of the hypothalamus, the lateral and the ventromedial, are responsible for motivating the starting and stopping of eating.

Corpus callosum

Thalamus

Lateral hypothalamus

Ventromedial hypothalamus

Pons

Another area of the hypothalamus is called the **ventromedial hypothalamus**, located below and toward the center of the structure. This area appears to be a "stop eating" center, turning hunger off. When the ventromedial area of the hypothalamus is stimulated, a rat will not eat. It will act as if it is full even though it has not been fed. And, when this area is damaged, the rat appears to lose the ability to "shut off" its hunger. These rats consume endlessly, growing to more than three times their normal body weight FIGURE 10-8 (Wyrwicka & Dobrzecka, 1960). So there appear to be brain centers located in the hypothalamus that control the initiation and the cessation of eating.

FIGURE 10-8 When the ventromedial hypothalamus is destroyed, rats will continue eating to the point of tripling their body weight.

Hormones

But what signals these centers to make eating stop and start? The hypothalamus is a brain area that regulates the **endocrine system**, the network of glands throughout the body that manufacture and secrete hormones. The hypothalamus is the neural center

Hormones Chemicals that influence body growth, mood, and sexual characteristics.

Ghrelin A hormone secreted by the empty stomach to stimulate hunger.

Leptin A protein secreted by fat cells to signal adequate stores.

Metabolism The physiological processes used to convert energy from nutrients.

Basal metabolic rate The body's ability to use nutrients efficiently to maintain itself when at rest.

that communicates with the endocrine system to produce more or fewer hormones as needed. **Hormones** are chemicals that influence body growth, mood, eating, and sexual characteristics. Some hormones function as neurotransmitters, providing a connection between the brain and the endocrine system. TABLE 10-1 shows the major endocrine glands and the effects of the hormones they produce. In particular, digestive hormones in the stomach, gut, and pancreas work to control the processing of food and signal when more food is needed. In particular, a hormone called **ghrelin** is secreted by the empty stomach to stimulate hunger. Another, called *obestatin*, sends out a "fullness" signal. Other hormones also suppress hunger, including peptide *PYY* in the digestive tract, *orexin* from the hypothalamus, and **leptin**, a protein secreted by fat cells to signal that adequate fat stores already exist.

For those who have successfully lost weight, hormones may work against maintaining the loss: After losing weight, hormonal changes occur that increase appetite. In one study, participants' hormone levels and appetites were assessed after they ate breakfast (Sumithran et al., 2011). They then spent 10 weeks on a very-low-calorie (less than 550 calories a day) diet and lost an average of 14% of their body weight. The hormone, leptin, which tells the brain how much body fat is present fell by two-thirds immediately after the weight loss. When leptin falls, appetite increases, and subjects said they were hungrier than when they started the study. A year later, the subjects were gaining the weight back despite a maintenance diet (on average, half of what they had lost). And leptin levels were still one-third lower than they were at the start of the study. Other hormones that stimulate hunger, such as ghrelin and peptide *PYY*, were also changed in a way that increased subjects' appetites. After being overweight, that weight becomes the new "normal" that your body attempts to maintain.

Metabolism

Hormones impact the body through the regulation of the **metabolism** of the body, or the physiological processes used to convert energy from nutrients. The **basal metabolic rate** is the ability to use nutrients efficiently to maintain the body when at rest for functions like breathing and digesting. The body strives for a state of homeostasis, maintaining a

TABLE 10-1 Major Endocrine Glands and the Functions of the Hormones They Produce

Gland(s)	Produce Hormones that Regulate
Adrenals	Fight-or-flight responses Metabolism Sexual desire in women
Anterior pituitary	Testes and ovaries Breast milk production Metabolism Reactions to stress
Gut	Digestion
Hypothalamus	Release of pituitary hormones
Ovaries	Development of female sexual traits Ova production
Pancreas	Glucose metabolism
Parathyroid	Calcium levels
Posterior pituitary	Water conservation Breast milk excretion Uterus contraction
Testes	Development of male sexual traits Sperm production Sexual desire in men
Thyroid	Metabolism Growth and development

stable or balanced physiological state over time. Individuals vary in how much energy their bodies expend when at rest, with some at a faster rate of calorie burn and some requiring very few calories when not in motion. Regulation of metabolism is handled through the thyroid gland. About 65 to 70% of calories burned each day are used to keep up the routine body functions—heart, kidneys, and liver. About 10 to 15% are spent eating and assimilating food. And the rest are spent by the exercising of muscles. Your metabolic rate makes a difference in how much food you need to consume to provide enough energy to keep your body functioning. Each body has a weight that it naturally gravitates to, and researchers have found that all people, fat or thin, adjust their metabolism to maintain that weight (Leibel et al., 1995). This individual **set point** seems to maintain a particular range of body weight FIGURE 10-9. So, if food intake is sharply cut back, the metabolism slows to maintain the usual weight, and if too much food is taken in, metabolism increases to burn off extra calories (Keesey & Powley, 1986). The body responds to changes in weight by attempting to maintain its present weight, though some studies have not found evidence of metabolic adaptation to weight loss (Weinsier et al., 2000).

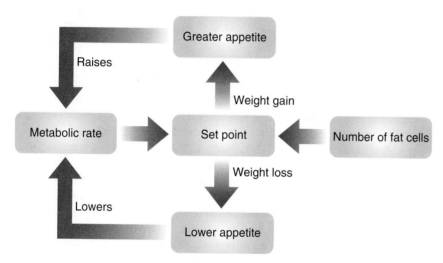

FIGURE 10-9 Set point theory suggests the body works to maintain a particular weight, so that when intake is reduced, metabolism slows to burn fewer calories.
Source: Data from Keesey, R. E., & Powley, T. L. (1986). The regulation of body weight. Annual Review of Psychology, *37, 109–133.*

Many obese people eat about the same amount as those of normal weight (Spitzer & Rodin, 1981). When pairs of individuals are matched by weight, height, age, and activity level, differences in metabolic rate are apparent (Rose & Williams, 1961). So one person may eat twice as many calories in a day as another but maintain the same weight due to differences in metabolism. If your metabolism is very efficient, it stores more calories as body fat in reserve, and over time, weight gain occurs. As mentioned earlier, leptin (a protein) is secreted by fat cells and acts as a signal to make the metabolism less efficient, burning more calories. While obese individuals still produce leptin, the receptors in the brain that respond to this signal appear to be deficient (Maffei et al., 1995). As a result, it can be difficult to lose or gain weight beyond a range in which your body comfortably operates. However, because changes in weight do occur, the tendency to maintain a set weight is sometimes called a **settling point** instead. The National Weight Control Registry (Wing & Hill, 1994) tracks individuals who have successfully lost more than 100 pounds, demonstrating that it is possible to change this system over time.

Glucose Monitoring

In addition to regulating endocrine mechanisms, the brain also controls the level of **glucose** (or sugar) in the bloodstream FIGURE 10-10. The brain automatically monitors the levels of glucose in the blood and changes the level of hormones produced by the endocrine system in response. After eating, the levels of glucose in the blood rise as the food is processed. This leads the hypothalamus to stimulate the endocrine system to process the glucose using the hormone **insulin**, secreted by the pancreas and used to convert glucose

Set point The tendency to maintain a particular range of body weight.

Settling point Tendency to maintain an approximate but changeable weight range.

Glucose The form of sugar that carries nutrients in the bloodstream.

Insulin A hormone secreted by the pancreas and used to convert glucose into energy for muscle use.

FIGURE 10-10 The hypothalamus coordinates the work of the endocrine system to use and store glucose throughout the body.
Source: Data from Campfield, L. A., Smith, F. J., Rosenbaum, M., & Hirsch, J. (1996). Human eating: Evidence for a physiological basis using a modified paradigm. Neuroscience and Biobehavioral Reviews, 20(1), 133–137.

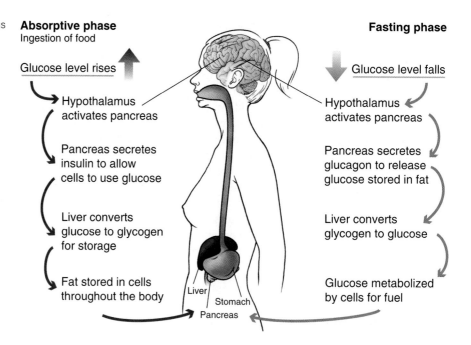

Diabetes A disease in which sugar in the blood is ineffectively used due to resistance to or an absence of insulin.

Adipose tissue Fat cells stored beneath the skin and throughout the abdomen.

into energy for muscle use. The inability to produce insulin, or resistance to it, leads to the disease called **diabetes**. Unused glucose is converted into glycogen, a form of animal starch, and stored in the liver. For longer-term storage, fat tissue (called **adipose tissue**) is stored beneath the skin and throughout the abdomen. Adipose tissue absorbs nutrients from blood and converts them to triglycerides (fats). In obese individuals, the size of the fat cells increases to hold more stored energy.

The result of these processes is that when blood sugar is low, people feel hungry and want food (Campfield et al., 1996). When food intake raises glucose levels, hunger is reduced FIGURE 10-11. However, this regulatory system takes time to operate. We can eat quickly, but it takes some time for the food in the stomach to be processed and for blood glucose to rise. As a result, it is easy to eat more than necessary to restore glucose levels or to wait too long to eat again and then feel extreme effects of deprivation. Foods also differ in how quickly they are converted into glucose. Simple sugars such as fruit juices have a high glucose index, meaning they are taken up quickly to affect sugar in the bloodstream, while complex carbohydrates take longer to process, leading to extended periods of glucose uptake. All of these biological processes work together to signal when to start or stop eating.

FIGURE 10-11 The cycle of consumption is started by detecting lowered glucose levels, and ended by raised glucose levels.

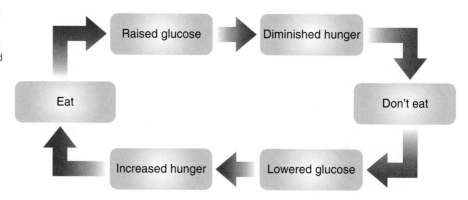

Genetics

Genetics also plays a major role in regulating hunger. Studies of twins demonstrate that adult body weight is more similar in identical twins than in fraternal twins (Stunkard et al., 1990) FIGURE 10-12. These correlations occur even when twins are raised apart and so experience different environments. Adoptive siblings do not resemble each other in weight even when they share a family environment, but they do resemble their biological

FIGURE 10-12 Identical twins have a more similar body weight than fraternal twins, even if they were not raised together.
Source: Data from Bulik, C. M., Wade, T. D., Heath, A. C., Martin, N. G., Stunkard, A. J., & Eaves, L. J. (2001). Relating body mass index to figural stimuli: population-based normative data for Caucasians. International Journal of Obesity and Related Metabolic Disorders, *25(10),* 1517–1524.

parents (Grilo & Pogue-Geile, 1991). The factor that puts children at greatest risk of being overweight is having obese parents (Agras et al., 2004). This provides strong evidence that the many physiological factors regulating hunger are influenced by genetic heritage (Schwartz et al., 2000).

This brings us back to evolutionary theories of motivation. The limbic system that controls motivation evolved in mammals that lived in very different environments than we do today. Then, food was often scarce and took a great deal of energy to acquire, and little storage was possible. So each day was consumed with efforts toward securing enough food to eat. The ability to store fat was an advantage through early human history, when food sources were sometimes unavailable (Assanand et al., 1998). Today, the average American consumes 150 cups of sugar a year. Such abundance of pure calories was never possible in the environment of early humans, and our system for regulating hunger never had to cope with too much food. As a result, the delicate biological machinery regulating our food consumption is faced with environmental challenges unlike any experienced in the history of human evolution. Perhaps it is not surprising that hunger, eating, and weight have become important health concerns today.

Environmental Influences

Apart from the many biological factors involved in the motivation to eat, a wealth of environmental factors plays a role as well. Imagine standing at a buffet: Which foods will you select for your plate? People have individual taste preferences, such as a "sweet tooth" or an addiction to hot sauce. But in all people, sweetness causes neural systems to actively generate a "liking" reaction, so sweet tastes are more desirable than other tastes (Pecina et al., 2003). We have a specific hunger for sodium if our bodies lack it, leading us to seek out salty foods. More typically, we seek out foods with tastes we enjoy and prefer those foods when available (Murphy, 1947). One strategy to test whether you are truly "hungry" is to ask whether you would eat something you do not enjoy. And deprivation can make foods seem more enticing. Dieting in which specific foods are not eaten can increase your desire for (and consumption of) the forbidden foods (Stirling & Yeomans, 2004). Culture also influences what we eat, so that certain familiar foods are desired, while foods regularly eaten in some cultures may seem unpalatable in others.

We are also sensitive to food cues in the environment. You may not have thought about eating a cupcake recently, but seeing them in the store may make you decide to try one again. Exposure to food cues leads to increased consumption, which forms the basis of modern advertising. But can exposure to food cues ever help to curb your appetite? A recent study asked some people to imagine placing 30 individual pieces of candy one by one into a bowl. Another group was told to imagine eating 30 pieces, concentrating on the taste, chewing, and swallowing of each one. Then, both groups were given real candies, and the amount they chose to eat was measured. Those who had imagined simply placing the candies in a bowl ate more than the control group; but, those who had imagined *eating* the candy ate less! This finding demonstrates the principle of habituation in which the first bite is delicious and the 20th bite is not as satisfying. Specifically imagining repeatedly eating a certain food can lead to a decrease in our desire for it (Morewedge et al., 2010).

Foods eaten in some cultures, like these grasshoppers, are unacceptable in others.

Unit bias Tendency to eat the amount provided as a serving.

Anorexia nervosa An eating disorder in which an individual feels he or she is overweight despite objective evidence.

Why doesn't habituation always work to curb eating? It does in most people and situations. But other factors can influence how much we continue to eat past the point of satisfying hunger. **Unit bias** refers to the fact that people eat more when offered larger servings (Geier et al., 2006). Even factors in the setting like the variety of food on display can influence eating, while exposure to the same food every day can diminish your intake. People ate a third more when offered sandwiches with four different fillings rather than one and more when given three flavors of yogurt (distinctive in taste, texture, and color) compared to just one of their favorite flavors (Rolls et al., 1981). The presence of others also affects eating: As the group size at the buffet increases, the meal size increases as well (Herman et al., 2003).

In addition, we often eat "mindlessly," watching television or socializing without being aware of how much we consume (Wansink & Sobel, 2007). We tend to report only a fraction of the food decisions we make, and we seem to be unaware (or unwilling to admit) that our environment influences these decisions. Environmental factors like package size, plate shape, lighting, seating, and music can influence consumption far more than we realize. The environment affects how much we eat by inhibiting our self-monitoring and by suggesting alternative norms for amounts of food we "should," or wish to, consume (Wansink, 2004). We also respond to external incentives around eating, such as eating what is served to you as a guest, a situation in which refusal may be viewed as insulting. And have you ever been admonished to finish the food on your plate? Avoiding the wasting of food, eating a complete meal, or demonstrating that the chef's work was excellent can lead to consuming more than is truly desired.

In American culture, there is pervasive exposure to food that is highly caloric, heavily marketed, and readily available. This creates a "toxic environment" for eating in which nutritious food is harder to find and more expensive than less healthy choices (Horgen & Brownell, 2002). These forces include the explosion of fast food outlets, increasingly large restaurant portion sizes, "all-you-can-eat" buffets, the proliferation of mini markets that sell high-calorie snacks and drinks, widespread food advertising, and contracts between schools, snack food, and soft drink companies to sell products in school cafeterias. And the prevalence of severely overweight children, 15%, has doubled during the past 20 years.

With these environmental factors surrounding eating, it is easy to see how hunger changes from "what the body needs" to "what the person wants." The attraction to eat something pleasurable becomes even larger when you are hungry or stressed, leading you to eat more. Individuals with high responses to stress (measured by cortisol reactivity) eat more after stressful tasks and eat significantly more sweet food on both stressful and nonstressful days (Epel et al., 2001). Stressors also lead to increases in negative mood and then greater food consumption. These results suggest that psychophysiological responses to stress lead to uncontrolled eating behavior for some people. Combined with the availability of food, the college environment appears to promote an average weight gain of 2.9 pounds during the first year on campus (Hoffman et al., 2006). Over time, these environments can impact both weight and health (Epel et al., 2001).

Hunger, Eating, and Weight

When any of these biological or environmental factors goes awry, there is the potential for difficulty in maintaining a healthy weight. Most commonly, the problem is obesity: Two-thirds of American adults and one-third of school-age children are either overweight or obese. These proportions increased by 50% for adults and 300% for children in the past 50 years (Arkowitz & Lilienfeld, 2009). Obesity is considered a medical problem because it often leads to diseases like diabetes, high blood pressure, and heart disease. But, as we have seen, many factors influence whether someone is overweight; so being overweight alone is not considered to be the result of an "eating disorder." Three specific eating disorders have been identified by the American Psychiatric Association based on research in psychology and psychiatry: anorexia nervosa, bulimia, and binge eating disorder.

Eating Disorders

Anorexia nervosa is an eating disorder in which individuals continue to feel they are overweight despite objective evidence that they are actually underweight. This disorder is defined as involving weight loss of at least 25%, restriction of intake, fear of becoming obese, and problems with body image. Disturbance of body image, or **body dysmorphia**, involves an overly self-critical attitude toward your own appearance and occurs in both men and women. For example, anorexics asked to estimate the size of their body parts by drawing on paper or making a belt consistently overestimated their true size (Pierloot & Houben, 1978). They may follow extreme diets in the attempt to control their weight or overdo their exercise regimens to gain a sense of control over their weight. With too little body fat, cessation of the menstrual cycle sometimes occurs. This disorder has appeared throughout history, as this description from the 17th century shows (Silverman, 1983):

> *Mr. Duke's daughter in St. Mary Axe, in the year 1684, and the Eighteenth year of her Age . . . fell into a total suppression of her monthly courses from a multitude of Cares and Passions of her mind. From which time her Appetite began to abate . . . She wholly neglected to care for herself for two years . . . (like a skeleton only covered with skin) . . .*
> —Richard Morton (1689) (cited in Bliss & Branch, 1960, pp. 9–11).

Anorexia typically develops in early adolescence, and approximately 2% of girls are affected. Boys make up only 10% of cases, though this number is growing. Anorexia is very difficult to treat, often involving longer-term in-hospital stays and relapses, with around 10% of cases resulting in death from heart problems caused by lack of proper nutrition.

A second type of eating disorder is called **bulimia nervosa** and refers to individuals that binge eat large amounts of food but maintain relatively normal weights by purging (vomiting) or using laxatives to avoid absorbing food. The diagnostic criteria for bulimia include episodes of binging followed by purging, an inability to stop voluntarily, depression with self-deprecating thoughts, and binges followed by dieting. Other health problems arise from this cycle of behavior, such as damage to the teeth or esophagus from repeated purging. It, too, can be a fatal disease. Some estimates show around 4% of college-age women show some symptoms of bulimia (Drewnowski et al., 1988).

Binge eating disorder is a pattern of frequently consuming unusually large amounts of food (Pull, 2004). Almost everyone overeats on occasion, but for some people, over-eating becomes a regular occurrence. Someone with binge eating disorder often eats in secrecy and does not compensate by purging or overexercising so is often overweight.

Perceptions of body weight can play a role in these eating disorders. In anorexics, perceptual distortions (body dysmorphia) prevent them from perceiving their shrinking size. For others, trying on small swimsuits in the mirror may be anxiety provoking. A recent study suggests that culture may play a role in the perceptions of weight and body image. Think about your ideal body at age 18. Which figure FIGURE 10-13 fits your ideal best? Now, which figure fits your real body at age 18? Most people find a mismatch, suggesting the ideal body is different from their own. But where did your idea of the "ideal body" come from?

Researchers asked both African American and white teenage girls to describe their "ideal" (Parker et al., 1995). White teens suggested someone blue-eyed, 5 feet 7 inches tall, weighing between 100 and 110 pounds, a rather narrow definition of beauty. African American teens, however, described personal qualities such as a sense of style, a nice personality, or "having a good head on one's shoulders." For a physical description, most

Body dysmorphia A disturbance of body image including an overly self-critical attitude.

Bulimia nervosa A disorder involving binge eating large amounts of food but maintaining relatively normal weight by purging.

Binge eating disorder An eating disorder marked by repeated overeating without the compensatory strategies found in bulimia.

To someone with anorexia, a thin appearance may be perceived as grossly overweight.

FIGURE 10-13 Which body image most resembles our culture's ideal? Which image most resembles your own body? *Source: Adapted from Bulik, C. M., Wade, T. D., Heath, A. C., Martin, N. G., Stunkard, A. J., & Eaves, L. J. (2001). Relating body mass index to figural stimuli: population-based normative data for Caucasians.* International Journal of Obesity and Related Metabolic Disorders, *25(10), 1517–1524.*

Nicole Richie (May 2007) was "outed" as pregnant based on the "baby bump" in this photo.

Obesity An excess level of fat in the body, at least 15% above ideal weight for a given height.

Body mass index (BMI) A ratio of height and weight that includes comparison to others.

responded that fuller hips, large thighs, and a small waist were desirable. Close to 90% of the white teens were dissatisfied with their weight, versus 30% of the black respondents. For white girls, weight seemed a central aspect of their self-image, promoting unrealistic expectations. However, other research suggests this is changing, and an increase in anorexia and bulimia is occurring among African American women of all socioeconomic levels (Crago et al., 1996). Other studies have found strong correlations between levels of eating disturbance, self-esteem, and body dissatisfaction in male homosexuals (Williamson & Hartley, 1998), suggesting this may also be a vulnerable population.

Perceptions of body image are clearly influenced by values that vary from one culture to another (Striegel-Moore & Builk, 2007). In Western cultures, unrealistic images of beauty are propagated through movies, television, and print advertisements (Bulik et al., 2001). Do these images impact our views of ourselves and others? One study demonstrated that viewing ideal images can make you more critical of the real people in your life. Men and women saw slides depicting either opposite-sex nudes or abstract art. Then they were asked how attractive they found their current romantic partner, and how "in love" they were with this partner. Women were unaffected; however, men were more dissatisfied with their current partner after looking at the nudes (Kenrick, Gutierres, & Goldberg, 1989). People tend to perform social comparison, so that considering the appearance of others around us may influence how we view ourselves (Suls et al., 2002) and our partners.

Another consequence of an overemphasis on low body fat manifests as poor reproductive health. Infertility and cessation of menses occur with lower weights, and while doctors recommend gaining 20 pounds during a pregnancy, this can be frightening to those concerned about being overweight. This also may negatively affect attitudes about breastfeeding. While we see media reports on "body after baby," showing celebrities who get back into shape quickly following birth, a slower-paced recovery to normal weight is more typical.

Obesity

The most common problem with hunger motivation is overeating, resulting in excess body weight. Obesity itself is not considered an eating disorder because excess weight can arise from multiple influences. Sometimes there is a problem with a biological mechanism, such as genetics, a too-slow metabolism, a problem in the response to sugar in the blood, or a disease of the endocrine system such as Cushing's disease, caused by high levels of cortisone in the blood. For other people, excess weight is caused by physical inactivity, overeating, or "disordered eating," in which specific foods are eaten to excess. Other times, obesity results from situational factors, such as the "freshman 15" (which turns out to be more often 5 pounds of extra weight in first-year students) resulting from the variety and availability of residence hall food combined with the stress of college study (Holm-Denoma et al., 2008). Obesity is a problem that must be considered in the context of the multiple influences of biology and environment.

Obesity is defined as an excess level of fat in the body, when someone is at least 15% above ideal weight for a given height. A ratio of weight to height called the **body mass index (BMI)** is used to classify degrees of obesity as a function of excess weight FIGURE 10-14

FIGURE 10-14 The body mass index (BMI) shows the categories of weight based on the larger population.
Source: Data from the CDC/Division of Nutrition, Physical Activity, and Obesity, National Center for Chronic Disease Prevention and Health Promotion.

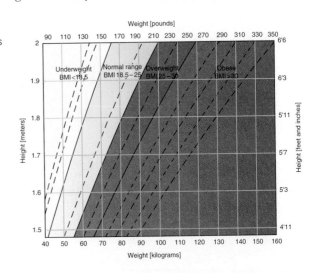

(Eknoyan, 2008; Keys et al., 1972). The index requires only height and weight and provides comparison based on the general population. Currently, Western cultures are experiencing an epidemic of obesity at rates never seen before, and weight increases are spreading across the globe. With abundantly available processed foods high in sugar and fat and a decline in physical exercise or exertion at work and school, more people than ever before in history are currently well above their ideal weight (NIH, NHLBI Obesity Education Initiative, 1998).

Why does this matter? Obesity is a leading preventable cause of disease and one of the most serious public health problems of today (Barness et al., 2007) FIGURE 10-15. For example, in women, a BMI above 32 has been associated with a doubled mortality rate

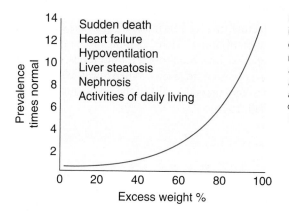

FIGURE 10-15 Prevalence increases exponentially when excess weight is 60% or more above desirable weight. *Source: Reproduced from Kral, J. G. (1985). Morbid obesity and related health risks.* Annals of Internal Medicine, 103*(6)*, 1043–1104.

(Manson et al., 1995). In addition, excess weight increases the risk of heart disease, diabetes, and stroke FIGURE 10-16. Research shows that as BMI approaches the "overweight" and "obese" categories, risk of cancers (endometrial, breast, and colon), hypertension (high blood pressure), high cholesterol, liver and gallbladder diseases, sleep apnea and respiratory problems, osteoarthritis, and infertility also greatly increase (Kral, 1985). In addition, these diseases often combine to create metabolic syndrome, a combination of type 2 diabetes, high blood pressure, high blood cholesterol, and high triglyceride levels (Haslam & James, 2005).

Clearly, from the evolutionary perspective, human bodies are not suited to carrying so much extra fat. In some times and places, obesity was widely perceived as a symbol of wealth and fertility and still is in some areas (Haslam & James, 2005). When food is scarce, extra body weight is viewed as attractive; in some areas, young girls are encouraged to overeat to gain excess weight as a sign of beauty. In Mauritania, women are fighting back against force-feeding, but up to one-third of the country's women risk their health by putting on weight to conform to a cultural aesthetic standard (IRIN, 2009). But when food is plentiful, thin is "in"; in fact, social class differences are associated with weight, presumably because nutritious food is more expensive.

In addition to health risks, there are many psychological, social, and economic consequences to being overweight. Obesity is stigmatized in much of the world. Being overweight leads to negative stereotypes such as laziness, slothfulness, and lower class status. The obese are often discriminated against in employment, salary determinations, and housing. For example, one study found weight discrimination in employment is greater than bias about ethnicity and gender (Roehling et al., 2007). And the obese may have difficulty in romantic relationships and friendships and have been found to suffer bullying during grade school (Lumeng et al., 2010).

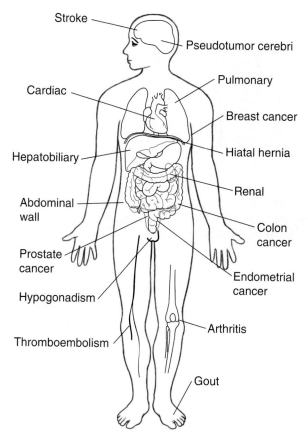

FIGURE 10-16 Organ systems with complications and conditions associated with obesity.

While there is a wealth of information available on weight loss, there is no magic solution. Studies suggest several strategies. First, decide to make permanent changes in eating habits (rather than dieting) so that weight loss is more likely to be permanent. Track your food intake to keep aware of how much you are eating (Lichtman et al., 1992). New recommendations for preventing weight gain have increased from 30 minutes of moderate-intensity activity daily to 45 to 60 minutes per day (Saris et al., 2003). Intrinsic sources of motivation (e.g., interest and enjoyment in exercise) play a more important role than extrinsic rewards in longer-term weight management (Teixeira et al., 2006). It helps to want to change for your own sake, such as to feel healthier and enjoy life, rather than simply wanting to look good in someone else's eyes.

A Comparison: Motivation of Thirst

We have just seen the many factors involved in motivating when and what we eat. In contrast, consider the motivation of "thirst." Here, a simple mechanism detects when fluid in the body is low (the hypothalamus monitors cell fluid levels, and the pituitary gland and kidneys monitor blood plasma fluid levels). When low levels are detected, we feel thirst, take in fluid, and as water enters the cells of the body, our feelings of thirst subside FIGURE 10-17 (Blass & Hall, 1976).

When you see someone drinking from a large water bottle, do you think of their behavior as driven by psychology?

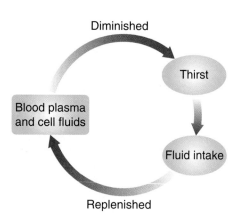

FIGURE 10-17 Compared to the complex mechanisms responsible for hunger, the motivation for thirst involves a much simpler mechanism based on cell and blood plasma hydration.
Source: Data from Blass, E. M., & Hall, W. G. (1976). Drinking termination: Interactions among hydrational, orogastric, and behavioral controls in rats. Psychological Review, 83(5), 356–374.

When you see someone drinking water, no one thinks, "Look at her drinking all of that water! What a hog!" No one pays you less because you drink a lot of water or sees you as a less desirable mate, nor do you hate yourself for doing it. What if our motivation to eat were more like the system that controls thirst? With the notable exception of alcohol, no one consumes too much by drinking. Imagine that as your goal for hunger: That you eat what your body needs as it needs it.

CONCEPT LEARNING CHECK 10.2   *Eating Disorder or Disordered Eating?*

For each concept, explain the behavior and whether it is considered an eating disorder:

1. Bulimia

2. Binge eating disorder

3. Obesity

4. Anorexia

CRITICAL THINKING APPLICATION

Imagine that I place a marshmallow in front of you (and imagine you enjoy eating them). I leave you alone with the marshmallow, and you can eat it any time you wish; however, if you wait until I return to eat it, I will give you an extra marshmallow. Left alone, how long will you resist the temptation to eat the marshmallow in front of you? In a study of 5-year-olds, this task turned out to be an excellent measure of **self-regulation**, or the ability to control behavior through intentional strategies (Mischel et al., 1972). Some of the children went ahead and ate the marshmallow right away. Some focused their attention on the marshmallow and were led to eat it a short time later. But the children who managed to distract themselves from the reward, by looking or turning away, singing, or talking to themselves about other things, lasted the longest without eating and thereby won the second reward.

This ability to postpone rewards, called the **delay of gratification**, is viewed as a sign of maturity. Can you work for a long time toward a goal without a taste of the reward? Getting a college degree, an MD, or a PhD, as in the opening story, may be one of the longest delays of gratification in life. Most often, we overemphasize the present rather than the future. It tastes good now, and that feels more important than the upcoming swimsuit season. Resisting temptation is often considered an act of willpower in which you resolve not to give in. One theory suggests that willpower requires effort, and exerting that effort requires energy (Baumeister et al., 1998). Since energy is a limited resource, you may run out of it; however, after some time, it is replenished. But if you use up your energy on other things, you will have less energy available for self-control.

The prediction from this theory is that using your willpower in one situation will reduce the probability of successfully using it again later. In one study, participants came into a lab filled with the smell of fresh-baked chocolate chip cookies (Baumeister et al., 2007). A plate containing both cookies and radishes was presented. They were assigned at random to taste only one food (either the cookies or the radishes). In a control condition, no food (and no cookie smell) was presented. They were left alone in the room to taste the food for 5 minutes. Next, the participants worked on a puzzle, and the time they spent on it was measured. In fact, the puzzle was unsolvable, and eventually, all of them gave up on it. But would their use of self-control make a difference in how long they kept trying? The cookie participants were allowed to smell and then eat then cookies. However, the radish participants had to see and smell the cookies but taste only the radishes. Did exercising their self-control by not eating the cookies affect how much willpower they applied to the puzzle?

The results in **TABLE 10-2** show that it did. The group eating the chocolate chip cookies worked about as long (on average) as the control participants. However, the group eating the radishes kept working half as long on the frustrating puzzle task. This suggests that using their willpower to avoid eating the cookies took a toll on them, making them less able to sustain their effort on the puzzle. The self-control of behavior—doing what you think is best rather than what you feel you really want—takes effort. It is also influenced by situational factors, like stress and exhaustion. You may notice that you tend to eat more junk food around exam times or miss your exercise when you are feeling tired. Just as a muscle gets tired from exertion, using your self-control can cause difficulty doing so again in the short term, even on unrelated tasks. Bouncing back depends on, of all things, your blood glucose level. Laboratory tests showed that initial acts of self-control decrease self-control on later tasks, but consuming a glucose drink restored it (Baumeister et al., 2007). So exerting

Self-regulation The ability to control behavior through intentional strategies.

Delay of gratification The ability to postpone rewards until a later time.

TABLE 10-2 Persistence on Unsolvable Puzzles (Experiment 1)

Condition	Time (min)	Attempts
Radish	8.4	19.4
Chocolate	18.9	34.3
No food control	20.9	32.8

Note: Standard deviations for Column 1, top to bottom, are 4.67, 6.86, and 7.30. For Column 2, SDs = 8.12, 20.16, and 13.38.
Source: Baumeister, R. F., Vohs, K. D., & Tice, D. M. (2007). The strength model of self-control. Current Directions in Psychological Science, 16(6), 351–355.

(Continues)

CRITICAL THINKING APPLICATION *(Continued)*

your self-control requires a certain amount of glucose in your system. This provides another reason to keep your blood sugar levels constant by eating healthy meals and snacks throughout the day.

How can you improve your self-regulation? Studies of dieters found that people eat more while watching television because they are distracted from monitoring their behavior. Binge eating may even be motivated by the desire to escape from self-awareness (Heatherton & Baumeister, 1991). Those with high standards for themselves and sensitivity to opinions of others feel anxious when they fall short. To escape such negative pressures and feelings, binge eaters narrow their attention to the immediate stimulus (the food) and avoid thinking more broadly about themselves. Other behaviors can also help us escape from feelings of negative self-awareness; for example, drinking alcohol provides the feeling of escape, but also makes it especially hard to regulate how much you drink. Fortunately, you can find harmless means of escape through other behaviors. In particular, exercise (even a single session!) has been shown to be an effective way to narrow focus and improve your mood while providing benefits to your health (Yeung, 1996).

Recommendations for improving your self-control include:

- Set realistic goals.
- Think in terms of "health*ier*" rather than perfection.
- Keep a record of your behavior to raise your awareness.

- Keep trying to align your behavior with your goals in "baby steps."
- Save your self-control resources by managing your exposure.

If self-control takes effort, it can help to use care in exposing yourself to situations in which you will have to exert it. For example, if you know you will be attending a party with lots of fattening food, you might consider eating a healthy meal beforehand so that you are not as tempted to eat the treats at the party. Controlling your home environment by keeping only healthy foods around will mean you will not have to exercise control to avoid eating the cookies in the kitchen. By choosing environments that support your goals, you can avoid having to exercise self-control in the moment (stay out of bakeries and donut shops!).

The good news is that what seems challenging now and requires a great deal of willpower will become easier as you successfully practice the behavior. For example, if you are currently drinking a lot of soda, choosing not to do so requires exercising your self-control. However, the more you do not drink it, the easier it will be to choose not to drink it the next time. This is another reason to keep records of your behavior: After some time passes, you can look back and see what your behavior was like and see how you were able to make changes successfully. Taking even "baby steps," like cutting back on soft drinks, makes a big difference in your health over time.

10.3 Sexual Motivation

The motivation for sex is present in all animals and is necessary to ensure their reproduction.

- Examine the physiology of human sexual response.
- Compare and contrast gender norms in sexual motivation.
- Discuss evolutionary theories of mating.
- Describe the biological and environmental factors in sexual orientation.

Mating Male-to-female intercourse for the purpose of reproduction.

While biology plays a central role in **mating** (male-to-female intercourse for the purpose of reproduction) in animals, psychological forces motivate human sexual desire and behavior. Giving and receiving pleasure and feeling and expressing love and value with another person are important motivators for human sexual behavior. But in humans, *sex* refers to many behaviors in addition to intercourse, including manual or oral sex with a partner, same-sex partners, individual masturbation, or even erotic dreams and fantasies. So it is important to understand the basic biology of human sexual response.

Physiology of Sexual Response

William H. Masters and Virginia E. Johnson initiated research on sexual response in the 1960s (Masters & Johnson, 1966). Until the publication of their work, societal attitudes about sex required secrecy. As a result, there was little scientific information available about what happens physically during sexual activities. To study sexual responses in the laboratory, Masters and Johnson came up with elaborate methods for their studies. In addition to physiological measures like respiration and heart rate, they created devices to measure erection, vaginal lubrication, and orgasmic contraction. They brought individuals into the lab and observed them as they masturbated or performed intercourse in a variety of positions. At the time, it was challenging to find volunteers for the studies; while men were willing, some women were recruited based on their experience with prostitution.

In their initial studies, the team observed more than 10,000 complete sexual responses. Masters and Johnson found certain predictable consistencies across individuals. While we may differ in what kinds of stimulation are most exciting to us, our physical responses to stimulation are very similar. Masters and Johnson described four phases of physiological responses during sex, called the **human sexual response cycle**: excitement, plateau, orgasm, and resolution **TABLE 10-3**. During the **excitement phase**, as arousal begins, blood circulates into all the erectile structures in the body (e.g., penis, clitoris, nipples), a process called **vasocongestion**. A sex flush, or reddening of the skin, can occur, along with an increase in heart rate and breathing. Males experience an erection, while females display vaginal lubrication and swelling of the clitoris, labia, and uterus. In both men and women, the breasts, nipples, and areola enlarge slightly with excitement.

In the **plateau phase**, there is a leveling off of excitement, as arousal remains elevated and deepens. The penis can produce a few drops of fluid at this stage. In females, the glans of the clitoris retracts under the clitoral hood, becoming less available for stimulation. As a result, most women do not receive enough stimulation from intercourse alone to result in orgasm. In the **orgasmic phase**, the climax of arousal occurs. Short in duration (around 15 seconds), the pelvic muscles contract at a rate of less than a second between 3 and 15 times, and in males, ejaculation occurs. What does an orgasm feel like? Men and women report similar experiences, including sensations throughout the genitals and pelvic area. Male and female descriptions of orgasms are very similar, including pleasure and satisfaction, emotional intimacy, ecstasy, relaxation, and sensations like flooding, flushing, and throbbing (Mah & Binik, 2005).

However, as seen in FIGURE 10-18, the response cycle does differ between genders. Most importantly, the female response cycle takes longer in the excitement and plateau stages. And they differ in the final **resolution phase**, in which excitement levels return to base rate. After orgasm, men experience a return to baseline levels of excitement and require some time before another orgasm is possible, called a **refractory period**. In women,

Masters and Johnson were married during their research studies of sexuality, but later divorced.

Human sexual response cycle Phases of excitement, plateau, orgasm, and resolution that complete a sexual act.

Excitement phase Sexual arousal begins with blood circulation into all the erectile structures in the body.

Vasocongestion Blood circulates into all the erectile structures in the body (e.g., penis, clitoris, nipples).

Plateau phase The second stage of the sexual response cycle, during which there is a leveling off of excitement.

Orgasmic phase The climax of arousal during which orgasm and ejaculation occur.

Resolution phase Final stage of the sexual response cycle, during which excitement levels return to base rate.

Refractory period Period of time following orgasm during which males cannot achieve another.

TABLE 10-3 The Human Sexual Response Cycle for Males and Females

Phase	Arousal Level	Characteristics
Excitement phase	Increasing	Vasocongestion, increased heart rate and breathing, penile erection, vaginal lubrication and swelling of the clitoris, labia, and uterus. Slight enlargement of the breasts, nipples, and areola.
Plateau phase	High	Arousal remains elevated, seminal fluid released from penis. In females, the glans of the clitoris retracts under the clitoral hood.
Orgasmic phase	Highest	Orgasm occurs (~15 seconds), pelvic muscles contract at a rate of less than a second between 3 and 15 times, and in males, ejaculation occurs.
Resolution phase	Decreasing	Arousal returns to base rate. Males require some time before another orgasm is possible, called a refractory period.

Source: Data from Masters, W. H., & Johnson, V. E. (1966). Human sexual response. Oxford, England: Little, Brown.

FIGURE 10-18 Differences by gender in the response cycle.
Source: Data from Masters, W. H., & Johnson, V. E. (1966). Human sexual response. Oxford, England: Little, Brown.

further stimulation can cause another orgasm before excitement tapers off. Or, if orgasm is not reached (as is frequent from intercourse alone), a longer resolution phase may occur.

This research changed our basic knowledge of how the body responds during sex. The work was important in medicine and psychology because it offered identification of problems in sexual responses (**sexual disorders**) that were undiagnosable in the past. A great deal of research since that time has identified the importance of sex hormones in causing responses. **Testosterone**, the male sex hormone, stimulates production of sperm and is responsible for the development of sex organs in males, In addition, testosterone levels in the blood have been shown to correlate with sexual desire in men and must also be present in women in order for them to feel sexual interest (Meston & Frohlich, 2000). Now, treatment involving replacing hormones could help individuals with sexual disorders. Another hormone, **oxytocin**, is released during orgasm in both genders and leads to sensations of emotional well-being. And dopamine, the neurotransmitter associated with the pleasure response, increases during sex to convey qualitative or interpretive information about its rewarding value (Becker et al., 2001). This suggests the purpose of orgasm goes beyond pleasure to lead to bonding between two people experiencing sex together.

Sexual disorder Problems occurring in the sexual response cycle.

Testosterone The male sex hormone that stimulates production of sperm and sex organs in males and sex drive in males and females.

Oxytocin "Feel-good" hormone released after orgasm.

Sex norms Typical behaviors observed across people.

Gender Norms in Sexual Motivation

Sex norms, or typical behaviors for males and females, may arise from both evolutionary pressures and from cultural learning. For example, adults experience intercourse two to three times per week on average; of course, this includes many individuals who are not sexually active and those who experience it daily. It is very difficult to define "normal" sexual behavior because your own preferences define what is normal for you.

Nevertheless, one common observation is that men seem to desire sex more than women (Baumeister et al., 2001). Masturbation rates show that males are much more likely to experience orgasms than are females, start at an earlier age, and do so more often (Peplau, 2003). While almost all boys learn to masturbate for pleasure FIGURE 10-19, about half of girls do so as teenagers. What is happening to sexual impulses in young girls? One idea is that boys experience sexual arousal very directly through erections (Ramsey, 1943). But because sexual arousal is more diffuse in female bodies, girls learn to associate arousal with more general stimuli, developing "crushes" and placing boy band posters on their

FIGURE 10-19 Percentage of boys reporting masturbation to orgasm.
Source: Data from Ramsey, G. V. (1943). The sexual development of boys. American Journal of Psychology, 56*(2), 217–233.*

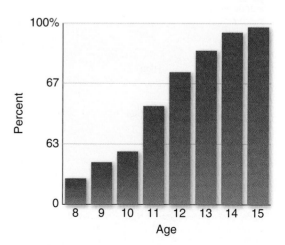

bedroom walls. Freud (1915) described this as **sublimation**, in which sexual urges are disguised by pursuing more acceptable behaviors.

Even as adults, however, the observed norm is that men think about and desire sex more often than women, rate the strength of their drive higher, initiate sex with their partners more frequently, and desire more frequent sex than women (Peplau, 2003). Considering only heterosexual intercourse, 98% of men reach orgasm, while 75% of married women and 62% of single women do so. Years ago, newspaper advice columnist Ann Landers asked her female readers, "Would you rather cuddle or have sex?" Of the 90,000 women who responded, 72% preferred cuddling to intercourse, while the vast majority of men responding far preferred sexual activity with their partners (Angier, 1985).

Men and women also appear to differ in the age of **sexual peak**, or highest point of interest and engagement in sex over the lifetime. One of the earliest studies of men's self-reported sexual behavior found that frequency of orgasm is highest in the teens and 20s, peaking at 30 and then declining. For males, sexual performance in terms of strength and number of erections decreases with age past the 20s. Women, on the other hand, report more frequent orgasms beginning at 30 and continuing into their 40s (Kinsey et al., 1953). In one study, people over 35 were asked to estimate the age of males' and females' sexual peaks, highest frequency of sexual activity, highest rate of sexual satisfaction, and highest rate of sexual desire (Barr et al., 2002). Women report greatest interest in their 30s, and men in their 20s FIGURE 10-20. Why is the sexual peak so differently timed?

> **Sublimation** The notion that sexual urges may be disguised by pursuing more acceptable behaviors.
>
> **Sexual peak** The highest point of interest and engagement in sex.

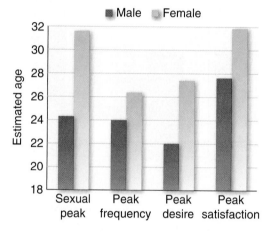

FIGURE 10-20 Reported age at sexual peak overall and for each dimension of sexuality (Barr, 2002).
Source: Data from Barr, A., Bryan, A., & Kenrick, D. T. (2002). Sexual peak: Socially shared cognitions about desire, frequency, and satisfaction in men and women. Personal Relationships, *9, 287–299.*

Another difference in sex norms by gender is in the number of different sexual partners. Ideally, how many partners should a person have over his or her lifetime? Is the number different for men than for women? A study by the National Center for Health Statistics, a branch of the Centers for Disease Control and Prevention, examined this for 1999 to 2002. Twenty-five percent of women and 17% of men reported having no more than one partner of the other sex in their lifetime, while 9% of women and 29% of men reported having more than 15 partners FIGURE 10-21. (The median number of partners for women was four and for men, seven.) The survey found only about 11% of never-married adults had never experienced intercourse (Fryar et al., 2007).

FIGURE 10-21 Average number of sexual partners reported over the lifetime by gender.
Source: Data from Fryar, C. D., Hirsch, R., Porter, K. S., Kottiri, B., Brody, D. J., & Louis, T. (2007, June 28). Drug use and sexual behaviors reported by adults: United States, 1999–2002. Advance Data from Vital and Health Statistics, No. 384, 1–16. http://www.cdc.gov/nchs/data/ad/ad384.pdf

NBA Hall of Famer Wilt Chamberlain said he had sex with 20,000 women. In his 1991 biography, A View from Above, Chamberlain devoted an entire chapter to sex. He wrote, "At my age, that equals out to having sex with 1.2 women a day, every day since I was 15 years old."

Another sex norm is that men are more likely to seek casual sex with an acquaintance. A classic study took place on a college campus in which researchers hired "attractive" male and female assistants (Clark & Hatfield, 1989). Individuals of the opposite sex were approached, and the assistant stopped them to say, "I've been noticing you around campus. I find you very attractive." This was followed by one of three straightforward requests: "Would you go out with me tonight?" "Would you come over to my apartment tonight?" or "Would you go to bed with me tonight?" Men and women responded to the request for a date about equally; in one study, 50% of both sexes agreed. But a noticeable difference was found for the sex request. In two experiments, around 70% of the men agreed to the request for sex, compared to not one of the women FIGURE 10-22. In fact, a common response among these men was along the lines of, "Why do we have to wait until later?" Recent research suggests many factors play into women's rejection of the offer (Conley, 2011). Women are more likely to be concerned about sexual assault. And men can almost be guaranteed a pleasurable sexual encounter with an attractive partner, while women experience orgasm only 35% as often in first-time sexual encounters. So maybe women accept fewer casual sexual relations because they are more relaxed, and thus more receptive, when they are with partners they know and trust.

Reproductive strategies The preferences males and females show in their mating behavior.

Paternal uncertainty Historically, men could not be sure whether a child was their genetic offspring.

FIGURE 10-22 Results from a study inviting males and females for a date vs. sexual activity. *Source: Data from Clark, R. D., III, & Hatfield, E. (1989). Gender differences in receptivity to sexual offers.* Journal of Psychology and Human Sexuality, 2, *39–55.*

These sex norms suggest men prefer having sex more strongly, earlier in life, more frequently, and with more partners than do women. Cases in which men risk their families and jobs by engaging in sex outside of marriage appear regularly in the headlines, suggesting that sex remains a powerful motive for men throughout their lives.

Evolutionary Theories of Mating

What might explain these behavioral differences between genders? Evolutionary theory suggests differences in sex norms fit well with gender differences in **reproductive strategies** (Buss, 1994, 1995). These are the preferences males and females show in their mating behavior. First, note that evolutionary theory attempts to account for sexual behavior within the species, and not differences among individuals. Its focus is on the survival of the species and what the best strategies are for procreation, considered in just the same way as for other animals. This account does not say that any behavior is "right" or appropriate; however, it does suggest that different strategies for mating lead to reproductive advantages. Individuals benefit if they successfully mate, produce children, and have those children survive to adulthood. That way, their own genetic contribution is most likely to be passed down to future generations. The "winning" strategies are "naturally selected" over time by their success and so are increasingly likely to occur.

First, consider the case of male reproductive strategy. For males, the cost of procreation is small, limited to the acts of intercourse, and there is no waiting period until they can father more children. So men would benefit from following a strategy of impregnating many different women while minimizing investment in them or their children. That is, the male strategy is "quantity." By having a number of mates, an individual male could produce more surviving children than if he devoted himself to raising children with only one mate. An additional complication is that until very recently, men had no way of knowing whether a child was their genetic offspring (called **paternal uncertainty**); so, rather

Monica Lewinsky, a White House intern, alleged nine sexual encounters occurred between her and President Clinton from 1995 to 1997 in or near the Oval Office.

than investing in each child, they are more likely to be successful by attempting to father as many children as possible.

For females, on the other hand, the costs of reproduction are much higher. First, pregnancies and giving birth are dangerous. A much greater investment of resources is needed to carry, breastfeed, and care for the limited number of offspring a woman can produce over her lifespan. As a result, women should be more selective in their reproductive choices, because each child matters much more to her success in passing on her genes. The female strategy is "quality." Choosing high-status mates could enhance a woman's reproductive potential by raising her own social status, providing material and nutritional benefits, and providing access to social and economic resources. This is especially important given that our species produces the slowest-maturing offspring among all animals—for some of us, maturation takes more than 20 years!

Because their reproductive investments differ, males and females may use different reproductive strategies, called **parental investment theory**. Evolutionary theory does not suggest that any individual person is consciously thinking about these strategies. Instead, the theory argues that some people happened to behave in these ways, and as a result, their genes were more likely to be passed on. So, over generations, these different strategies provided an advantage and were then passed on to their children FIGURE 10-23. Over many generations, these reproductive strategies would give some people and their offspring a selective advantage and so occur more often in the population as a whole. This rather cold view of reproduction ignores all of the psychological aspects of relationships between individuals and focuses on which strategies are successful in transferring genes to the next generation.

Parental investment theory
The required investment in offspring differs between genders, resulting in differing strategies.

Fertile A female able to conceive and bear children.

Status High economic and social status within the group is a desirable quality in male mates.

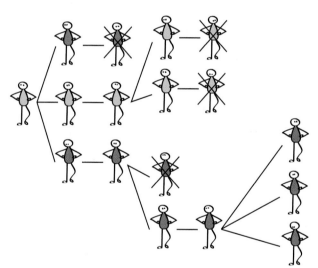

FIGURE 10-23 Variation in features of individuals, and in their preferences for mates, occur. Some of these lead to reproduction and success of offspring, and so are passed on to later generations. Some are not as successful, and are therefore not passed on to surviving generations.

Businessman Donald Trump and his third wife, Melania. "I continue to stay young, right? I produce children, I stay young," said the 59-year-old Trump. Their baby is Trump's fifth child and his wife's first.

Interestingly, differences in reproductive strategies by gender fit well with the sex norms observed (Buss, 1994). Based on their smaller investment in offspring, men should want to have more sex, more often, with more partners, and earlier in life. Women, on the other hand, should be more selective about their mates, waiting to find ones that can provide resources to support them and their children. Further, it would also explain why women would experience a sexual peak later in life, motivating them to continue reproducing throughout the lifespan (which was much shorter throughout human evolutionary history). So the differences in sex norms by gender fit well with this evolutionary account of differences in reproductive strategies.

In addition, strategy differences predict which types of partners should be most attractive to men and women (Buss, 1995). Men should look for mates that are **fertile**, or able to conceive and bear children. This is a problem because, in humans, it is not obvious when a woman is fertile. Women are sexually responsive throughout their menstrual cycles, while other female animals are capable of sexual responses only during periods when they are fertile. So men should look for signs related to fertility, such as youthfulness and good health. Women, on the other hand, should look for mates that can support them and their offspring by providing resources. This is referred to as **status**, since having a

Anna Nicole Smith married elderly oil billionaire J. Howard Marshall in 1994 when she was 26 and Marshall was 89. Thirteen months later, Marshall died, and after Smith's own death, his fortune was inherited by her infant daughter from another man.

high economic and social status within the group suggests you can command resources and help from others. Women benefit from a high-status, committed mate.

Both men and women spend a great deal of time and energy advertising themselves as potential mates and evaluating the desirability of other people as mates. Is there any evidence that they do so with these different qualities as their focus? One study examined mate preferences by setting up a "dating game" (Kenrick & Keefe, 1992). The task was to read profiles of various possible partners and rate them for suitability. The study manipulated the reported status and physical attractiveness of the potential dates. The results showed that men were affected by the physical attractiveness of the women targets but not affected by their status. In contrast, just the opposite pattern emerged for the women subjects: They were affected by the status of the male targets but relatively unaffected by their physical attractiveness.

Consistent with the idea that men marry "beauty" and women marry "status," a survey of 16 different cultures showed that men tend to marry younger women, and women tend to marry older men (Buss & Schmitt, 1993). As shown in FIGURE 10-24, women always preferred older partners, and men younger, across every culture sampled. Why is this the case, and could it have been different? The evolutionary argument that says men may have evolved preferences for beauty because women's fertility is relatively time bounded. Essentially, choosing women without gray hair or wrinkled skin and with high energy and symmetrical features (showing no sign of disease) would help ensure they are young and healthy and, therefore, fertile.

FIGURE 10-24 Cross-cultural comparisons found men always preferred younger wives, and women always preferred older husbands.
Source: Data from Buss, D. M., & Schmitt, D. P. (1993). Sexual strategies theory: An evolutionary perspective on human mating. Psychological Review, 100(2). 204–232.

Hourglass shape   Rectangle shape

Women's shapes can vary from a low waist-to-hip ratio (left) to a high waist-to-hip ratio, resulting in a straighter body profile.

Buss (1989) argues that these preferences evolved because some men preferred these traits in mates and so were more likely to have fertile mates and more children. Over thousands of generations, this selection pressure fashioned a psychological mechanism that inclines males to seek youthful females. In the same way, over millions of years, women who preferred men with higher status and commitment had children who survived. Today's women are descendants of females who were good at evaluating the resources and commitment of potential mates.

Do reproductive strategies affect men's preferences about female figures? Are men really seeking fertile mates? To answer these questions, Singh (1993, 1994) tested two possible preferences.

Body weight is a poor predictor of fertility, as being too thin can cause a failure to menstruate, while weight must be very high to affect fertility. So choosing thinner women does not help to find the most fertile mates. However, a low **waist-to-hip ratio (WHR)** is a better predictor of fertility. If a woman's waist size is much smaller than her hip size—an "hourglass" figure—she has a low WHR. For example, a 22-inch waist and 36-inch hips is a WHR of 0.6—an hourglass shape—while a waist of 30 inches and hips of 36 inches is a WHR of 0.83. The smaller the WHR, the more "hourglass" the figure, and the more healthy and fertile the woman. In the old days, this shape was referred to as "birthin' hips" and today as a "Kim Kardashian" look.

Do men prefer women with less body weight or a smaller WHR? For the study, Singh provided drawings that increased in weight by row, but showed the same WHRs across the rows FIGURE 10-25. In the study, men were asked which figure they viewed as most attractive. Men preferred a low waist-to-hip ratio regardless of body weight, as shown by their preference for the models on the far left, no matter which weight (row) they preferred. Males consistently rated low-WHR models more attractive, independent of the body weight shown. The figures with the low WHR were even judged to be younger! These findings suggest that a cultural bias toward thin women does not predict male judgments of attractiveness. Instead, men are sensitive to the waist-to-hip ratio, a predictor of fertility. Evolutionary theory argues that this preference for a low WHR was selected during generations of human reproduction. (Of course, note that having a thick waist might also indicate that a potential mate is already pregnant!)

Celebrity Kim Kardashian became famous for her disproportionately wide hips, exemplifying the low waist-to-hip ratio preference.

I
WHR 0.7 (U7)   0.8 (U8)   0.9 (U9)   1.0 (U10)

II
WHR 0.7 (N7)   0.8 (N8)   0.9 (N9)   1.0 (N10)

III
WHR 0.7 (O7)   0.8 (O8)   0.9 (O9)   1.0 (O10)

FIGURE 10-25 Men chose which figure they preferred in a woman. While the figures weigh more in row 3, each row shows variants in waist-to-hip ratios.
Source: Reproduced from Singh, D. (1993). Adaptive significance of waist-to-hip ratio and female physical attractiveness. Journal of Personality and Social Psychology, 65, *293–307.*

Of course, mate preferences may reflect both evolutionary and cultural influences. Women's greater interest in commitment and status is supported by many cultural messages about desirable mates. Children are socialized by their cultures to value certain types of potential mates. Many other preferences may arise from cultural values that differ from those predicted by evolutionary theory, such as body weight, height, and a sense of humor. How we select potential partners and what we value about relationships are different questions than sexual motivation alone.

Sexual Orientation

The evolutionary approach focuses on mating in **heterosexuals**, or those who desire sex with members of the opposite sex. But **sexual orientation** refers more broadly to the gender a person prefers for emotional, romantic, and sexual intimacy. Orientation includes the gender of people you date, fall in love with, choose to partner with in life, and your self-identification of preference even if you never engage in any sexual activity with others. Individuals of all orientations share similar attractions, emotions, attitudes, and experiences about relationships.

Alfred Kinsey (1894–1956) conducted the first surveys of adult men and women that included questions about same-sex behaviors (Kinsey et al., 1948, 1953). Kinsey defined a **continuum of sexual orientation**, from exclusively heterosexual (opposite-sex partners) to exclusively **homosexual** (same-sex partners). In Kinsey's results, most people fell in

Waist-to-hip ratio (WHR) A woman's waist size divided by hip size gives an index of figure shape.

Heterosexual A person who desires emotional and sexual intimacy with members of the opposite sex.

Sexual orientation The gender preferred for emotional sexual intimacy—same sex, opposite sex, or bisexual.

Continuum of sexual orientation Most people report falling somewhere in the range from exclusively heterosexual to exclusively homosexual.

Homosexual A person who desires emotional and sexual intimacy with members of the same sex.

Alfred Kinsey founded the Institute of Sex Research in 1947.

the middle zones of the continuum. They acknowledged some experiences (including fantasies, dreams, emotions, and behaviors) with both same- and opposite-sex partners. So individuals may be characterized as predominantly heterosexual or homosexual, or anywhere in between FIGURE 10-26. **Bisexual** refers to those with more than incidental involvement with both male and female partners.

While the challenges and cultural messages may be very different for homosexuals, there are far more similarities than differences between homosexual and heterosexual relationships. Most gays and lesbians form close, enduring relationships that are happy and functional and enjoy similar family and social support networks. In fact, overall satisfaction in a relationship is about the same for homosexuals as for heterosexuals (Gottman et al., 2003). Freed from the gender roles of "husband" and "wife," homosexual relationships can balance power and responsibility more flexibly. Homosexuals can legally marry in a growing number U.S. states or file legal domestic partnerships. Many gay and lesbian couples feel the same desire as other couples to have and nurture children. And studies show that the children of homosexuals are as well-adjusted as children of heterosexuals and are no more likely to be homosexual (Fitzgerald, 1999).

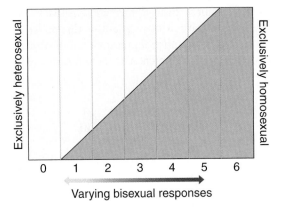

FIGURE 10-26 Kinsey characterized orientation as falling along a continuum from solely heterosexual to exclusively homosexual, with most people falling in between.

Bisexual A person with more than incidental involvement with both male and female partners.

Coming out Sharing one's same-sex orientation with others or the public.

Does someone *choose* who they will be attracted to? Can you change your sexual orientation? One way to think about this question is to examine your own experience (Rochlin, 1982). When did you first decide to be heterosexual or homosexual? What do you think caused your sexual orientation? How do you know you would not enjoy sex with other types of partners? Just like most heterosexuals, most homosexuals feel they did not have to be told their orientation; rather, it became clear to them through the relationships and emotions they experienced as they matured. However, because of strong cultural biases, homosexuals are likely to experience many challenges during their development, including prejudice, the need to come to terms with their identity, and the need to share their orientation with others, called "**coming out**" (Rhoads, 1995).

However, the question of what factors may cause sexual orientation has been hotly debated, and historically, there was much interest in attempting to change sexual orientation. What evidence exists about how sexual orientation originates?

Biological Factors

Biologically speaking, male and female heterosexuals and homosexuals are highly similar. Only a few small biological differences have been identified. Three biological factors have been correlated with sexual orientation: brain structure and function, prenatal hormones, and genetic influences. One study has identified a possible relationship in an area of the brain within the hypothalamus. Called the third interstitial nucleus, this area is related to emotions and sexual urges. It is larger in men than in women; however, it was found to be larger in straight men than in gay men, and about the same size in gay men as in women (LeVay, 1991). More recent studies have found the degree of symmetry between the hemispheres and connections between them are also different in gay and heterosexual individuals (Savic & Lindstrom, 2008). These imaging results also show similar patterns in gay men and straight women and in straight men and gay women.

Mourners at a prayer vigil for murder victim Matthew Shepherd. This event prompted legislation to expand the definition of hate crime to include persecution based on sexual orientation.

Another biological factor affecting sexual development is the presence of hormones in the prenatal period. In fact, whether an individual develops male genitals depends on the presence of testosterone during the first 2 months of prenatal development (by default, all fetuses are initially female). Sexual differentiation in the brain starts in the second half of pregnancy (Garcia-Falgueras & Swaab, 2010). **Estrogen** is the hormone central to female sexual development and fertility, and overexposure to synthetic estrogen during pregnancy has been related to later bisexuality and homosexuality (Meyer-Bahlburg et al., 1995). This suggests hormonal exposure in the womb correlates with differences in orientation.

Another factor may be the number of older brothers you have! Mothers who carry male fetuses may develop antibodies to male hormones. When they are carrying later boys, these antibodies may interfere with hormonal development. In men, sexual orientation correlates with the number of older brothers, with each additional older brother increasing the odds of homosexuality by approximately 33% (Blanchard & Klassen, 1997). However, no such relationship in sibling births has been found in females (Blanchard et al., 1998).

Genetic explanations would mean sexual orientation is determined at conception. Twin studies of gays and lesbians show that the concordance rate, or likelihood of one twin having a characteristic if the other has it, is around 20 to 40% for homosexuality (Långström et al., 2008). As the genetic similarity increases, the similarity of orientation also increases, independently of environment (Pillard & Bailey, 1998) FIGURE 10-27. Sibling, twin, and adoptee concordance rates are compatible with the hypothesis that genes account for at least half of the variance in sexual orientation. The role of genes in determining orientation is now widely accepted, but specific mechanisms and how they influence orientation are not yet known.

Estrogen The hormone central to female sexual development and fertility.

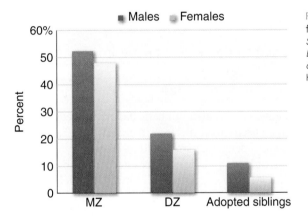

FIGURE 10-27 Concordance rates for homosexuality.
Source: Data from Pillard, R. C., & Bailey J. M. (1998). Human sexual orientation has a heritable component. Human Biology, 70(2), 347–365.

Environmental Factors

Theories of environmental causes of sexual orientation have abounded, yet *none* have received scientific support. For example, domineering mothers and absent fathers, sex play experiences or molestation during childhood, and homosexual parents have all been posited but rejected by numerous studies. In fact, no exclusively environmental factor has ever been shown to relate to differences in sexual orientation. This is a powerful statement given the many studies that have attempted to find differences in experiences that might account for orientation.

Another possibility is that an interaction of biology and environment may play a role in orientation. One such account (Bem, 2000) suggests we are born not with a specific orientation but with many personality predispositions. Our tendencies to be aggressive, shy, or agreeable seem to be built in. As a result, children are attracted to certain types of activities and playmates. For some, it is play behavior that fits within gender norms, like roughhousing in boys and dolls with girls. For most children in the grade school years, gender segregation is evident on the playground and in social groups, as well as in the activities they choose to pursue. As a result, they spend most of their time with others of the same gender (following the "cootie" theory of grade schoolers). Because they are rarely exposed to the opposite gender, they later become interested in them as "exotic," leading to sexual attraction in adolescence. Bem called this theory **"exotic becomes erotic"** (Bem, 1996).

"Exotic becomes erotic" Bem's theory that typical gender preferences lead to less exposure to the opposite sex and, thus, later attraction.

Some children's personalities may lead them to choose activities and playmates of the opposite gender. Then, their early play experiences are with the opposite sex, and they may feel they are very different from others of their own gender. They may then see children of their own gender as strange and exotic, eventually leading to feelings of arousal toward their own gender. In fact, there is little evidence that differences in play preferences are involved in sexual orientation. Bem's theory suggests we find someone attractive simply because that person is so different from us; but in fact, similarity is often the basis of attraction. In summary, we know very little about what environmental factors may affect sexual orientation or about how our experiences affect our sexual preferences and activities as adults. While the motivation for sex is powerful, we have much to learn about what drives our sexual behavior.

CONCEPT LEARNING CHECK 10.3 | *Evolution and Gender Differences*

Explain the evolutionary account of gender differences in sexual behavior.

1. Why do males and females differ in their reproductive strategies?

2. What do men look for in a mate?

3. What do women look for in a mate?

4. How does a preference, such as males preferring younger mates, become prevalent in the population?

10.4 Social Motivations

After our basic biological needs are satisfied, we move up the hierarchy to higher-level social and achievement needs.

- Define the social motivations and give examples of each.

Abraham Maslow (1943) suggested that, after our basic biological needs are met, we can begin to pursue the higher-level needs in the hierarchy of motivations. Safety has received little research attention outside of dangerous work settings. However, more research has addressed the need to belong and love and the need for esteem for oneself and from others. Finally, research on self-fulfillment suggests how motivation to achieve may fit into Maslow's description of self-actualization.

Motivation to Belong

First among the social motives is the **need to belong**. We may want to feel a part of a relationship or group in the form of friendship, romantic relationship, closeness to family, religious or professional groups, shared activities, or even starting a family of our own. Humans are social animals, and the need to belong is a fundamental human motive (Baumeister & Leary, 1995). Humans have a pervasive drive to form and maintain lasting, positive, and significant interpersonal relationships. This requires frequent interactions with the same individuals over time.

Wanting to belong with others would obviously be a competitive advantage for survival in the physical world; in the social world, belonging may provide considerable assistance. Deprivation of good relationships has been linked to a variety of negative consequences. People who lack belongingness suffer higher levels of mental and physical illness and are more prone to behavioral problems ranging from traffic accidents to criminality (Baumeister & Leary, 1995). Social isolation is strongly related to unhappiness; in fact, it is about the only objective factor that shows a substantial (negative) correlation with feelings of well-being (Baumeister, 1991).

People seem widely and strongly inclined to form social relationships quite easily, even in the absence of any special set of circumstances. If you ask couples how they met, you will find many circumstances quite unremarkable, even though the outcome of their meeting was very meaningful. Friendships seem to arise spontaneously and readily, and people invest a great deal of time and effort in others. For example, first-year college

Need to belong Motivation to feel a part of relationships or groups of people.

Groups often encourage feelings of belonging by sharing identifiable signs. Are you wearing anything right now that signals your belonging to a group?

students interact with whomever is in their immediate proximity and form long-term friendships with a subset of those people (Marmaros & Sacerdote, 2006). And people are just as reluctant to break social bonds as they are eager to form them. In fact, the tendency to respond with distress and protest to the end of a relationship is nearly universal across different ages and genders (Davis et al., 2003).

Clearly, we were meant to be together. Being accepted, included, or welcomed leads to a variety of positive emotions (e.g., happiness, elation, contentment, and calm), whereas being rejected, excluded, or ignored leads to strong negative feelings (e.g., anxiety, depression, grief, jealousy, and loneliness; Baumeister, 1991). The near universality of distress associated with divorce and bereavement is consistent with the belongingness hypothesis; indeed, there is little evidence that significant social bonds can ever be broken without suffering or distress. Moreover, changes in belongingness status are an important cause of emotions. In fact, one of the basic functions of emotion may be to regulate our behavior in forming and maintaining our social bonds (Baumeister & Leary, 1995).

As evidence, we are finely tuned to be highly sensitive to signs of **social rejection**, or exclusion from contact by others. Anyone who has lived through middle and high school knows well the experience of acceptance and rejection from peers and how deeply it affects us. In fact, recent studies show the pain of social rejection is quite similar to physical pain. One set of studies had people play a computer game of ball tossing, and some were systematically left out of the cooperative game (Eisenberger et al., 2003). When excluded from the game, compared to when included, participants showed increased activity in two neural regions that are frequently associated with the unpleasantness of physical pain—the dorsal anterior cingulate cortex and the anterior insula. Those who showed greater activity reported feeling more upset by the rejection episode. Thus, neural responses to social exclusion recruited some of the same neural regions that are involved in physical pain, supporting the commonsense notion that rejection really does "hurt."

Real-world experiences of social rejection have also shown activation of the same regions of the brain that are involved in the sensory experience of physical pain (Kross et al., 2010). This study recruited people who had gone through a romantic breakup during the past 6 months, leading to intense feelings of rejection and pain. Participants underwent fMRI (functional magnetic resonance imaging) scans while they looked at photos of their ex or else a friend and thought about their experiences. They were also measured while a device caused tolerable pain on their arms. These were compared to scans of other people's brain responses to physical pain and activated the same regions of the brain. We are motivated to maintain good relationships and try to repair them when problems arise because breakups and rejections really hurt. Other research shows that taking acetaminophen, a physical pain reliever, diminishes the pain of hurt feelings and social exclusion (DeWall et al., 2010) FIGURE 10-28. If the experience of not belonging feels as important as physical pain, our motivation to maintain ties with others must be very strong indeed.

Social rejection Exclusion from contact by others causes emotional pain.

FIGURE 10-28 Changes in neural activity (during social exclusion or inclusion) were observed in two brain areas: (a) dorsal anterior cingulate cortex (dACC) and (b) right anterior insula. Participants took either acetaminophen or a placebo. The change in intensity of neural activity (shown in color bar) was greater for those who took placebo. Taking acetaminophen reduced social pain.

Motivation to Achieve

Esteem motivation Desire to feel appreciation from others.

Achievement motivation A desire to accomplish difficult jobs in an area with a standard of excellence.

Maslow (1943) suggested the next level of motivation was desire for **esteem**, or appreciation from others. What fuels the drive to succeed, excel, and advance in the world and to have others recognize our accomplishments? **Achievement motivation** is a desire to accomplish difficult tasks in an area with a standard of excellence (Murray, 1938). To determine your inner need for achievement, an indirect test called the **thematic apperception test (TAT)** measures your fantasies about the outcomes of situations (Morgan & Murray, 1935). A participant looks at a drawing and creates a story about it FIGURE 10-29. For example, what is the person thinking about in the image, what will they do next, and what will happen to them? Murray (1938) found that people projected their own desires onto characters, and the stories they created showed systematic differences that revealed their own motivations. This method worked better than asking people about their motivations because they did not worry about what the experimenter wanted to hear. Instead, they mentioned the ideas they themselves were most interested in through the content of the stories they created.

By scoring TAT responses systematically, McClelland and colleagues (1953, 1976) identified which people were high in their **need for achievement**, or desire to succeed at challenging tasks. This measure was shown to relate to how hard people work, how persistent they are at tasks, and how innovative they are. Individuals with a high need for achievement also get better grades in school, are more successful in their careers, and are more "upwardly mobile." People who are motivated to succeed set high but realistic goals so that they are challenged yet can succeed. But what about the process of achievement? How are we affected by successes and setbacks along the way to a goal?

FIGURE 10-29 Thematic apperception test card showing an image. What do you think the woman in the image is thinking? This test draws out people's implicit motivations.

Thematic apperception test (TAT) An indirect test measuring your fantasies about the outcomes of situations, reflecting your motivations.

Need for achievement Desire to succeed at challenging tasks.

Achievement gap The difference in U.S. school test scores and grades for white compared to African American children.

It is clear that cultures differ in their expectations for achievement, and family, social, and school pressures may influence your desire to accomplish goals in the world. Parental attitudes and practices provide the foundation for children's development of beliefs about school achievement and thus are critical determinants of children's school experiences (Taylor et al., 2004). For example, one stereotype in American culture is that Asian-Americans are more driven to perform well academically. Research has concluded that Asian Americans perceive and have experienced restrictions in upward mobility unrelated to education. Consequently, education has assumed greater importance within the culture as a means of escaping limited options (Sue & Okazaki, 1990). For groups defined by gender, race, ethnicity, or socioeconomic status, an **achievement gap** appears on measures such as standardized test scores, grade point averages, dropout rates, and college enrollment and completion rates (Ladson-Billings, 2006). The possible reasons for differences in achievement for whites and ethnic minorities are under debate. However, a meta-analysis showed that the most accurate predictor of student achievement is the ways in which the family is involved in a child's education (Henderson et al., 1994; Lee & Bowen, 2006).

Within educational psychology, two modes of achievement have been identified that predict different outcomes from learning: mastery versus performance orientation (Ames, 1992; Ames & Archer, 1988). Mastery orientation is a desire to become proficient in a skill to the best of your ability. With this goal, you are concerned not about external evaluation but with your own sense of your ability to perform well at the target task. Mastery orientation is associated with deeper engagement with the task and greater perseverance in the face of setbacks. Performance orientation, on the other hand, is the desire to achieve on external indicators of success, such as grades. If your sense of satisfaction is highly influenced by your grade, you may be defining your achievement in terms of this external standard for success. Performance orientation is associated with higher anxiety because you feel less control over whether you can be successful, since an external judge decides whether your achievement is adequate. In addition, performance orientation can make the actual learning seem secondary to doing well on tests, rather than focusing on the goal of learning the material well.

Another key factor in achieving your goals is your mindset (Dweck, 2006). **Mindsets** are beliefs about yourself and your abilities, such as intelligence, talents, and personality. Are these fixed traits, things you cannot change? Or are they things you can, with effort, develop and improve throughout your life? People with a **fixed mindset** believe that their traits are predetermined, and nothing can change that. People with this mindset worry about their traits and whether they are adequate. On the other hand, a **growth mindset** sees these qualities develop through dedication and effort.

Does how you think about your achievements make a difference in your success? Dweck (2006) and her research team studied the effect of praise. Fifth grade students were given a series of puzzles easy enough so they all did fairly well. Half were praised for their intelligence: "You must be smart at this." The other half were praised for their *effort*: "You must have worked really hard." Then the students were allowed to choose the next test: a more difficult one that they would learn a lot from, or another just like the first. Of those praised for their effort, 90% chose the *harder* set of puzzles. Of those praised for their intelligence, a majority chose the *easy* test. They had chosen to avoid the risk of embarrassment. Next, all of the students were given a difficult test, which all failed. A final round of tests was as easy as the first round. The results showed those who had been praised for their effort improved by about 30%. Those who had been told they were smart did worse than they had at the very beginning—by about 20%.

The ability to repeatedly respond to failure by exerting more effort (instead of giving up) is the key to achievement. People with **persistence** rebound well from failures and can sustain their motivation through long periods of delayed gratification. Specific brain circuitry has been identified in the orbital and medial prefrontal cortex (Gusnard et al., 2003). This area monitors the reward center of the brain, and like a switch, it intervenes when there is no immediate reward. When it switches on, it is telling the rest of the brain that the reward is coming later, so do not stop trying. The brain has to learn that frustrating events can be worked through without reward. As a result, a person who grows up getting rewards infrequently will have persistence, because he or she will keep going even when rewards are not yet in sight.

Motivation for Self-actualization

Maslow's hierarchy points to the self as the ultimate motivation. Self-actualization involves working toward becoming the best version of yourself you can be—specifically, "The full use and exploitation of talents, capacities, and potentialities" (Maslow, 1970, p. 50). Achieving this is the ultimate motivation, that of fulfilling your human potential. For most, life goals include spirituality, community, family, career, lifestyle, and other interests. Maslow suggests that we strive to become the best version of ourselves out of an inner motivation. So we work to achieve our full potential, increasing our complexity, independence, and social responsibility (Bozarth & Brodley, 1991). Self-actualization theory says we know what is good for us, and we are motivated to achieve it.

However, there is plenty of evidence that people pursue behaviors that are damaging to themselves, including smoking, procrastinating, and overeating. Why do we have difficulty reaching our full potential given our motivation to self-actualize? Work in **humanistic psychology** explains potential causes of problems in developing self-actualization (Rogers, 1951). Taking a motivational view, we can look at studies of health behavior that attempt to help people stop smoking, lose weight, and stop drinking. People's lack of interest in or reluctance to participate in health and wellness programs is the "No. 1 obstacle" to changing health behaviors (National Business Group on Health, 2010).

The good news is that people do not need to depend on external rewards for their behavior. Instead, we can identify internal incentives for behaviors and, as a result, be less dependent on external rewards. This process involves integrating new behaviors within your own internal values. Through integration, the regulation of behavior is taken into your core sense of self. As a result, the behavior becomes "self-determined." Decades of studies have demonstrated that self-determination is the key factor in long-term motivation. **Self-determination theory** (Deci & Ryan, 1985) points to three factors that promote internalization. First, a meaningful rationale must be provided because people want to know why the behavior change is important. Second, it is important to acknowledge people's feelings about the behavior change. Third, as much as possible, choices should be provided about the behavior.

Mindset A belief about yourself and your abilities, such as intelligence, talents, and personality.

Fixed mindset The belief that your traits are predetermined and nothing can change them.

Growth mindset Belief that your qualities and capacities develop through effort.

Persistence The ability to repeatedly respond to failure by exerting more effort.

Humanistic psychology Theories of motivation emphasizing the goal to develop to the highest potential for each individual.

Self-determination theory Motivation involves integrating new behaviors into your internal values.

Choice appears to be the key to intrinsic motivation. Imagine being assigned a movie to watch or choosing one for yourself. Even if it is the same movie, the mere act of choosing makes your experience of it much more personal. In building intrinsic motivation, the key is in the personal: It must mean something to *you* (Ryan, et al., 1983). For example, losing weight for a partner's sake is much less likely to be successful than when you decide to do so for your own health reasons (Teixeira et al., 2006). So making choices based on your own internal values will help to integrate your desired behavior with your goals. Based on these findings about motivation, some suggestions for making improvements (or self-actualizing) your behaviors include:

- Make choices in novel ways: It is easy to be "stuck in a rut" in which you do the same thing every time you are in a given situation. Try going out to eat someplace new rather than the old favorite, or switch your usual beverage to something you have never tried. If you add to your behavioral repertoire, it may be easier to make good choices and avoid problem areas.
- Link the present with long-term goals: It is important to keep the goal state in mind, knowing that you do not have to enjoy the process to relish the rewards. Walking every day may seem a small step, but after 6 months, the benefits from it will be very rewarding. So keep the long-term goal in mind to help you initiate the first steps.
- Make use of higher-level thinking processes: We are sensitive to cues in the environment that can alter our intentions, like advertisements, habits, and cultural customs. So take a moment to step back and think about why you are making a choice. Is it relevant to your long-term goals or motivated by something specific in your environment? Try to be vigilant about the factors affecting your choices, and think through which ones are positive for you.
- Practice self-regulation: We all perform self-regulation of a variety of important behaviors; otherwise, we would be unable to meet even our basic needs. But while we may feel we cannot regulate some behaviors—we fail to exercise, eat poorly, or drink too much alcohol—the truth is that we *are* regulating it already. To move it in the direction you desire, try to think in terms of baby steps: Have one less drink than you want, or eat one less treat per day. By practicing your regulation, you will get better at moving in the desired direction.

Changing your intentions is the first step in changing behavior, and it leads directly to success. A meta-analysis of 47 experiments found that changes in behavioral intentions do lead to significant behavior changes (Webb & Sheeran, 2006). By taking advantage of what you know about motivation, you can guide your own behavior toward your goals. Self-actualization is, by definition, a motivation that continues throughout life, encouraging us to strive to become better people. It represents the best of human nature through its motivation to continually improve ourselves.

CONCEPT LEARNING CHECK 10.4   *Fostering Achievement*

Based on information you just read in this section, answer the following question.

1. What can you do to foster your own need for achievement?

10.5 Motivation and Work

For most adults, the workplace provides a setting that tests our motivation.

- Explain the relationship between human motivation and work.

Industrial and organizational psychology Field of study addressing the psychology of work.

For most people, basic motivations drive their everyday behavior. Across the world, many people travel great distances every day for clean water and spend the majority of their day earning money for food, housing, and other basic needs. Fewer people enjoy the luxury of combining their need to earn a living with their higher-level motivations to belong, achieve, and find self-fulfillment. The subfield of **industrial and organizational** psychology addresses the psychology of "work," including motivation at work, the personality qualities and skills ideally suited to differing occupations, hiring and evaluation procedures, maximizing performance at work, and organizing workplaces to help achieve the best outcomes. These psychologists use their knowledge of psychological principles to provide consultation to employers. Hiring, salary, and promotion practices must follow legal guidelines from the Civil Rights Act, the Americans with Disabilities Act, and other legislation surrounding issues like harassment in the workplace. In addition to laboratory studies, research in this field often tests theories in actual workplaces to determine the best practices for motivating employees within work organizations.

One of the earliest studies in the field attempted to determine what factors lead to improved motivation. The study took place in the late 1920s at a large electric company in which parts were assembled. A special testing room and a control room were set up to allow the comparison of the effects of specific interventions on worker productivity. In the test room, the management tried changing to very bright lighting, changing to very dim lighting, adding rest periods, shortening the work day, shortening the work week, interviewing the employees, and adding financial incentives to see what worked best. The surprising finding was that the test room workers performed better for *every* intervention tested. Apparently, the increased interest shown toward the workers in the test room was, by itself, enough to improve their motivation. This phenomenon was called the **Hawthorne effect** after the plant in the study (Mayo, 1933). Hawthorne effects may last anywhere from a few days to years, depending on the situation (Roethlisberger & Dickson, 1939). It demonstrates that people are motivated not just by financial rewards but also by their own higher motivations and needs. Industrial and organizational psychologists have been examining workplaces ever since to identify how to make workplaces more rewarding to employees.

Personnel Psychology

Personnel psychology focuses on selection, training, and evaluation of employees (Schuler, Farr, & Smith, 1993). As in personality psychology, industrial psychologists have sought to measure individuals' interests and aptitudes and identify guidelines for career selection. One such test is the Strong Interest Inventory (Donnay et al., 2011). This survey compiled responses from individuals in many varied types of occupations. Then, when a new individual takes the survey, the responses are compared to determine the best fit to workers in each career field. For example, someone who is interested in interacting with a wide variety of people, from intellectuals to the sports-minded to fun-loving friends, may find "military officers" as a match because officers regularly deal with a broad range of types. The test places you in a work category with others who report sharing the same interests and aptitudes, suggesting you may enjoy the same jobs. Studies show that people flourish when there is a good fit between their personality type and the characteristics required by the job (Holland, 1996) **TABLE 10-4**. Career centers and coaches offer similar tests to help determine which professions are a "best match" for an individual.

The Hawthorne study of plant workers found that any increase of interest toward the workers led to improved motivation.

Hawthorne effect
Improvement in a test group (compared to a control group) caused by the increased interest shown toward them.

Personnel psychology Field focusing on the selection, training, and evaluation of employees.

TABLE 10-4 Types of Personalities and Complementary Jobs

Personality Type	Preferences	Description	Occupation Type	Jobs
Realistic	Machines, tools, objects	Practical, frank	Concrete, mechanical	Carpenter, driver
Investigative	Gaining knowledge	Asocial, intellectual	Analytic, problem solving	Psychology, scientist
Artistic	Literature, music, art	Unconventional, creative	Innovative, imaginative	Musician, designer
Social	Interpersonal, emotional	Nurturant, agreeable	Working with others	Counselor, clergy
Enterprising	Directing or persuading	Energetic, gregarious	Selling, leading	Lawyer, manager
Conventional	Orderly routines	Careful, conforming	Meet goals and standards	Editor, accountant

Source: Reproduced from Holland, J. L. (1996). Exploring careers with a typology: What we have learned and some new directions. American Psychologist, 51(4), 397–406.

Other types of tests examine your cognitive abilities, integrity, job knowledge, physical ability, and personality, as well as your background and experiences. A meta-analysis of procedures for selecting employees analyzed later job and training performance (Schmidt & Hunter, 1998). General mental ability was an important predictor of eventual success in all types of jobs. Other selection methods also predicted success on the job. Work sample tests are hands-on simulations of the job performed by applicants, such as a welding test. Consulting and technology firms sometimes pose difficult puzzles in interviews to assess how the candidate reasons about problems (Poundstone, 2004). Integrity tests screen for behaviors like drinking or drugs, fighting, stealing, and absenteeism. And structured interviews provide a fixed procedure and ordering of questions, along with standards for scoring; as a result, they provide much better prediction than open-ended interviews. Virtually every major organization in the United States uses interviews to select personnel; however, interviews have been shown to be poor at assessing abilities (Arvey & Campion, 1982).

How do employers know what to look for in a potential employee? **Job analysis** is one of the most widely used techniques (McCormick et al., 1972). This method determines the tasks that a worker is responsible for, as well as the knowledge, skills, and abilities needed in the job. Then recruiting can take place with those qualities in mind. This approach led to the Job Diagnostic Survey, designed to determine whether (and how) jobs might be redesigned to improve employee motivation and productivity (Hackman & Oldham, 1975). However, one of the best indicators of whether a person and a job are a good match is a **realistic job preview**. This involves having the potential employee sample the work experience to determine his or her interest in the job and whether the job requirements are a good match for the candidate. Job previews tend to lower initial expectations from the potential employee and increase self-selection, organizational commitment, job satisfaction, performance, and job survival (Premack & Wanous, 1985). Internships, paid and unpaid, are one route to preview jobs and can lead to employment prospects.

And how do potential employees know what to look for in a job? This is quite challenging for those entering their first full-time jobs as professionals after graduation from college. While the liberal arts prepare students to read, write, analyze, and discuss, they provide little information about the world of work. The biggest knowledge gap for students is what kinds of jobs exist in the world outside of college and how to gain access to them. To learn more about the working world during college, visit your campus career center early and look at the opportunities it offers to explore jobs, including informational interviews and internships. And when the time comes to search for jobs, as you might expect, job-search behavior is significantly and positively related to finding employment (Kanfer et al., 2001). Effort put into the search and the intensity of your effort do pay off in the likelihood of success.

Just like many other areas of human interaction, hiring is subject to biases in perception. Interviewers tend to believe in their own intuitive abilities to find good candidates in the absence of evidence, called the **interviewer illusion** (Nisbett, 1987). As a result, they can be resistant to using testing or other decision aids to help in selecting employees (Highhouse, 2008). In a study in which managers viewed resumes and photos, both gender and attractiveness affected their ratings of candidates (Marlowe et al., 1996). The extent of the bias was generally smaller for the most experienced managers, but less-attractive female applicants were routinely at a disadvantage regardless of managerial experience. Racial bias is a key issue in hiring discrimination, while black hiring officers were found to hire a greater proportion of blacks who apply (Stoll et al., 2004). Homosexuals were also found to be discriminated against in a survey study (Crow et al., 1998), as were overweight people in a laboratory study (Pingitore et al., 1994). Those hiring, managing, and evaluating workers have an obligation to avoid bias in these processes.

Most people feel their work provides more than economic benefits. As evidence, 65 to 95% of the workforce across Western countries state they would continue to work even if they had enough money to live comfortably for the rest of their lives (Harpaz, 1988). People attach a broader social and psychological significance to their work lives; after all, we spend a third of our days in full-time employment and often socialize with coworkers outside of work. A study of the meaning of work across countries measured the centrality of work to life, economic and self-expressive goals, and the sense of social obligation (England, 1990). Patterns identified included a "balanced" worker, one for whom work

---

Job analysis Determination of the tasks, knowledge, skills, and abilities needed in a job.

Realistic job preview A potential employee samples the work experience to determine his or her interest in a job.

Interviewer illusion Belief in one's own intuitive abilities to find good candidates in the absence of evidence.

is central to life and includes economic and expressive goals; a duty-oriented worker who feels obligation and is very satisfied with his or her work; an economic worker who focuses on pay and security; and the "alienated" worker, who does not feel invested in any of these goals. These patterns led to differences in the effort made by workers and, thus, to outcomes on the job.

What makes people feel most engaged and interested in their work? Early research focused on **job burnout**, defined as a prolonged response to chronic emotional and interpersonal stress on the job (Maslach et al., 2001). Extensive research has established that stressful jobs lead to exhaustion, cynicism, and lack of effectiveness. More recently, research has focused on **engagement**, or feelings of involvement and interest in work. One study asked employees whether they "have the opportunity to do what they do best every day." Only one in five employees strongly agreed with this statement; but, if they did, their work units showed substantially higher performance (Harter, Schmidt, & Hayes, 2002). When employees feel engaged, businesses are more successful, employees use their talents, and there is lower turnover in the staff. So why is not every employer concerned about engagement at work? The incentive theory, with the premise that we work for the paycheck, has been pervasive in business. Increasingly, however, organizations are working to help employees structure their jobs in ways that help them feel more engaged in their work as a way of improving retention.

Balancing the characteristics of jobs can improve engagement and result in feelings of **flow** (Csikszentmihalyi, 1990). This state of mind arises during activities you greatly enjoy, when attention is focused on the task in front of you, and the challenge of the task is met by your own expertise. Work sessions feel seamless, and "time flies" when you are working in a state of flow. This requires changing the nature of a job over time in order to keep up with the changing development of the employee. This quality is hard to capture in performance evaluations for raises, promotions, and layoffs. Evaluation often focuses on what can be counted (number of sales, number of products completed) or on qualitative judgments of managers (global ratings of success in the job; Landy & Farr, 1980). With subjective judgments, there is potential for bias from a supervisor. An alternative approach, called **360-degree feedback**, solicits evaluation (sometimes anonymously) from everyone who interacts with an employee, including customers, peers, subordinates, and supervisors (Ghorpade, 2000) FIGURE 10-30. By 1996, this approach had become standard among Fortune 500 companies.

Job burnout A prolonged response to chronic emotional and interpersonal stress on the job.

Engagement Feelings of involvement and interest in work.

Flow A state of mind arising during activities when the challenge of the task is met by expertise.

360-degree feedback Evaluation method that solicits input from everyone who interacts with an employee.

FIGURE 10-30 360-degree feedback seeks information from all of those who interact with an employee to evaluate their performance and identify goals for improvement.

Organizational Psychology

Rather than studying individuals, **organizational psychology** examines how the structure of jobs and the workplace affects the success of group efforts. Policy decisions, working teams, and management style all affect how work gets accomplished and the ultimate success of organizations.

One important factor in work organization is management. Better performance in top management teams occurs when there is more positive than negative communication among teams (Losada & Heaphy, 2004). The most profitable, productive, and

Organizational psychology Field examining how the structure of jobs and the workplace affects the success of group efforts.

effective teams had a ratio of five positive statements for each negative statement during their work interactions. The lowest-performing teams had a ratio of three negative for every positive statement. This same "five positive to one negative" ratio was discovered by Gottman (1994) in studies of successful marriages. The best predictor of whether a marriage will last was a large majority of positive communications. "Toxic" workplaces—and people—are ones whose negative communications wear down your initiative to make changes. Recent work in organizational psychology has identified the "positive organization" as a way to implement ideas from positive psychology into the workplace (Bakker & Schaufeli, 2008).

A surprising trend in the modern workplace is the increased presence of incivility in the workplace, defined as interpersonal mistreatment such as disrespect, condescension, and degradation (Andersson & Pearson, 1999). Almost 70% of workers reported some experience with workplace incivility, from as many as one-third of the most powerful individuals within organizations (Cortina et al., 2001). For example, do you think it is appropriate to use curse words during heated discussions? Can you imagine being called a "bitch" on the job? Surprisingly, this is becoming more common in less formal workplaces. While women reported more occurrences of incivility at work, it has been found to have negative impacts on job satisfaction for all (Cortina et al., 2001). Another problem is **sexual harassment** on the job, a situation in which unwelcome sexual comments or advances are imposed in the workplace. On average, 58% of women report having experienced potentially harassing behaviors, and 24% report having experienced sexual harassment at work (Ilies et al., 2003). These results suggest that sexual harassment is more prevalent in organizations with relatively large power differentials between organizational levels. Training managers to improve interactions and team-building skills can help to set standards for interactions in the workplace.

Organizational psychologists are also interested in the factors that affect workplaces on a broader scale. For example, societal factors such as gender norms may affect how an organization works. Of the 21 million professional jobs in the United States., women hold 53%. But of the 8 million better-paying jobs (averaging more than $40,000 in 1998), women hold only 28% (Doyle, 2000). These jobs include physicians, lawyers, engineers, computer and natural scientists, and college instructors FIGURE 10-31. Women in these professions also have lower compensation, on average, because they work fewer hours and are in lower-paying positions. Valian (1999) argues that cultural values and assumptions

Sexual harassment
Unwelcome sexual comments or advances imposed in the workplace.

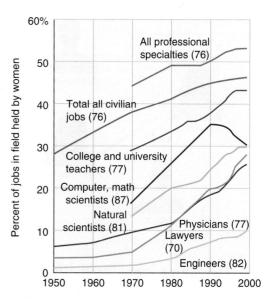

FIGURE 10-31 The percent of women in major professions by year, with data from the 1950–1980 census and 5-year moving averages. The figures in parentheses indicate women's earnings as a percent of men's in 1998 dollars.
Source: Data from U.S. Bureau of the Census and Bureau of Labor Statistics.

are the cause of the resulting pay differences. Women are expected to carry more of the family and homemaking responsibilities, resulting in less availability for work. And when comparing candidates for positions, gender stereotypes about success favor males. While women are catching up in higher education, in which the percentage gaining PhDs in some fields outstrips men, those in professorships are still disproportionately male. This suggests that factors beyond any individual affect the experience of work in organizations.

Gender stereotyping also results in differences in perception on the job. While many women are advancing in business, there appears to be a "glass ceiling," a situation in which women find it harder to break through to the top ranks of a field, such as chief executive officer, director, or dean (Lynness & Thompson, 1997). In this study, financial services executives in comparable jobs had less authority, received fewer stock options, and had less international mobility if they were female. Women at the highest executive levels reported more obstacles than lower-level women and had lower satisfaction with future career opportunities. In 1987, Ann B. Hopkins was the only female among 88 candidates for partnership at Price Waterhouse, Inc. Though noted as an outstanding performer, she was not accepted as a partner. A colleague explained that, in order to improve her chances, she should "walk more femininely, talk more femininely, dress more femininely, wear make-up, have her hair styled, and wear jewelry." Hopkins brought a gender discrimination lawsuit against her employer, which eventually reached the Supreme Court. The court ruled that gender-based stereotyping had influenced perceptions of her behavior, and she won the case (Fiske et al., 1991).

The problem with differences in treatment or pay is that people want to perceive their outcomes as fair. **Equity theory** posits that people want their effort and pay to be fair compared to others' (Adams, 1962). Relative to other workers, if you work harder or produce more, you expect to be paid more. Even monkeys have a sense of equity. In a study by Brosnan & Dewahl (2003), monkeys (brown capuchins) performed tasks for rewards (like grapes). If another monkey received the same reward with less or no effort, the monkeys objected vociferously. This suggests there may be an evolutionary origin for our aversion to inequity.

A field study at an insurance firm demonstrated that people adjust their work to match their perceptions of equity. In the study, more than 200 employees were temporarily relocated to other offices (Greenberg, 1988). They were assigned at random to offices that belonged to others that were higher, the same, or lower in rank at the company. The number of cases processed and decision quality were measured before, during, and after this relocation period. The results showed that those placed in better offices actually worked harder to produce better work, while those placed in lower offices felt undercompensated and lowered their performance FIGURE 10-32. Perceptions of unfair treatment can interfere with work performance.

Equity theory The notion that people want their effort and pay to be fair compared to that of others.

FIGURE 10-32 Insurance workers' performance over time, including a middle period during which some were assigned to better, or worse, offices than their peers. Perceptions of unfair treatment undermined work performance. *Source: Modified from Greenberg, J. (1988). Equity and workplace status: A field experiment.* Journal of Applied Psychology, 73*(4), 606–613.*

A great deal of research in organizational psychology has asked what causes exceptional group or team performance. Group work is central to many jobs, so understanding what leads to well-functioning groups could greatly improve productivity. The face-to-face group is preferred in most workplaces, yet studies of performance show that it can lead to group **process loss**, or time spent coordinating discussion rather than working on the task itself (Hill, 1982). As a result, for many tasks, summing the work of individuals working alone results in better performance than asking a group to work together. Interventions that structure group interactions to minimize process loss have been shown to improve effectiveness for certain kinds of groups and tasks (Hackman, 1987). There is

Process loss Time a group spends coordinating discussion rather than working on the task itself.

less evidence that interventions around group composition affect the success of groups. Interventions that focus directly and primarily on the quality of relationships among members usually succeed in changing attitudes and sometimes behavior but have no consistent effects on group performance (Hackman, 1987). Nevertheless, some evidence suggests that using personality tests to set up work teams with specific characteristics can be effective (Bell, 2007). Some of the first research in the field was on group compatibility (Schutz, 1955) and suggested that groups that are happy together are more productive.

Leadership provided by managers is a key component to a well-functioning workplace. The focus of many leadership theories is on traits, such as intelligence and originality (Yukl & Van Fleet, 1992). But on the job, the main function of a leader is the development and shaping of team processes and the monitoring and management of ongoing team performance (Kozlowski & Bell, 2003). One experimenter worked with intact management teams from a Fortune 500 high-technology company (Korsgaard et al., 1995). Some team leaders showed high consideration by listening to members' input. As a result, their groups had higher perceptions of fairness and higher commitment to the recommendations that were reached, and attachment and trust in the leader increased. If team leaders showed low consideration by listening but not commenting on input from the team, member attachment and trust in the leader decreased. Even though the members of these groups had a history of working together, leaders who actively listened to team members and incorporated their ideas into a final recommendation significantly affected the quality of decisions made. This has considerable ramifications for the impact of leader behavior in an ongoing work context: Listen to employees and incorporate their input!

Career Directions

As a college student, you may soon face the problem of career and work: How can you best determine which career direction or job possibilities are your best options? The average American changes jobs 10 times between the ages of 18 and 42 (Bureau of Labor Statistics, 2006). In addition, people in a wide range of work contexts are not only looking for a job or paid employment; instead, they may also be looking for a career or a related sequence of jobs with increasing responsibilities and compensation. Finally, some people may look for a "calling." A **calling** is defined as an occupation that an individual (1) feels drawn to pursue, (2) expects to be intrinsically enjoyable and meaningful, and (3) sees as a central part of his or her identity (Berg et al., 2010). The example at the beginning of the chapter fits this description: Becoming a professor was not just a career choice but also a choice of identity. The short-term sacrifices on the path to becoming a professor are worth it for someone who would rather be in a bookstore on Friday night!

In a survey across types of workers, about a third identified their work as a "job," another third as a "career," and another third as a "calling" (Wrzesniewski et al., 1997). So there is a range of possibilities in careers, and you can choose the approach that is the best fit for you:

- If you approach work as a job, you focus primarily on the financial rewards. The nature of the work itself may hold less interest for you. What is important is the money, which is motivating for you. If a job with more pay comes your way, you will likely move on. And you find the remuneration very satisfying.

- If you approach work as a career, you are likely interested in advancement. You may want to climb the career ladder as far as possible or be among the most highly regarded professionals in your field. You are motivated by the status, prestige, and power that come with the job and by becoming one of the top performers as well as part of a group.

- If you approach your work as a calling, you focus on the work itself. You are less interested in financial gain or career advancement, preferring instead to find a sense of fulfillment from the work. You are less concerned about financial payoff and greatly desire the identity the career provides.

Experiencing work as a calling is associated with a series of psychological benefits, including increased life, health, and job satisfaction (Wrzesniewski et al., 1997). Callings inspire feelings of passion—strong emotional inclinations toward work-related

Calling Choice of occupation you feel drawn to pursue for intrinsic meaning and identity.

activities that individuals find interesting, important, and worthy of their time and energy. One of America's largest job-search companies (Monster.com) urges job seekers to "find your calling." Today, individuals are exposed to—and can consider—many more occupational choices than in the past (Twenge, 2006). A calling can be much more motivating than a job because the rewards are personal as well as financial.

However, the world of work is structured in a way that restricts your ability to pursue all of the occupations that may "call" to you. You may feel called toward different occupations or may choose less satisfying but more financially lucrative or socially desirable occupations (Iyengar et al., 2006). Or you may feel shut out of your desired options through lack of skills or opportunities to succeed (Twenge, 2006). Finally, you may discover callings in other fields after you have chosen your occupation, making it difficult or impossible to pursue these other callings. For others, a job may become a "calling" as the challenges and rewards from success lead you to invest in a career. Many people find their careers through happenstance, a connection through a relative or friend, and end up feeling very invested because they devote themselves to it.

There are steps you can take to "craft" your current job into your calling (Berg et al., 2010). In this study, some workers described taking active steps to alter their jobs and leisure activities to pursue their unanswered callings. Two core dimensions are enjoyment and meaning or a sense of purpose and personal growth. Participants reported using three techniques to create opportunities for their unanswered callings: task emphasizing, job expanding, and role reframing **TABLE 10-5**. In addition, they crafted their leisure pursuits to meet their achievement needs outside of work.

TABLE 10-5 Crafting Techniques

Technique	Explanation	Illustration
Job Crafting		
Task emphasizing *(highlighting assigned tasks to pursue an unanswered calling)*	Changing the nature of an assigned task to incorporate aspects of an unanswered calling	"I still get to help families in my job . . . like when I run events here in the library, I make sure to talk with students and parents not just about media stuff, which is my job, but also about them as people. . . . So I feel like there are parallels there . . . [because] I'm doing something valuable and something good." (Fannie)
	Dedicating additional time, energy, or attention to an assigned task that is related to an unanswered calling	"I try to use the technology [involved in my job] as much as possible . . . I have a Smart Board in my room. I'm on the technology district committee, and the technology committee for our school. I really like being on those committees. I'm excited that I'm going to start to be able to use more technology in the classroom." (Amy)
Job expanding *(adding tasks to pursue an unanswered calling)*	Taking on short-term or temporary tasks to incorporate aspects of an unanswered calling	"We had a request into the office for someone to speak at a university a couple months ago, and so I volunteered. . . . It gave me a chance to talk with a whole group of college students about what we do, and why, and how we're effective. I really enjoyed it and it was really exciting and fun for me." (Paula)
	Increasing the number of tasks continually expected of individual to incorporate aspects of an unanswered calling	"I think I've become kind of the go-to person on a junior level for just anything that has to do with communications or writing, someone who's not at the management level. So I work with a lot of the other Associates when they have ideas or questions about writing and things like that. . . . It makes me feel like I'm important. . . . It's not exactly the writing that I want to do in my life, but I think it's helped me understand the nuances of word choice and how to message things, and I enjoy it." (Emma)

(continues)

TABLE 10-5 Crafting Techniques *(continued)*

Technique	Explanation	Illustration
Role reframing *(altering one's perception of a role to pursue an unanswered calling)*	Establishing a cognitive connection to align the conventional social purpose of a job responsibility with an unanswered calling	"I think the question for me has always been 'How can I grow and how can I make a contribution?' . . . and therapy felt that way for me. I mean, I thought I could make a contribution in other people's lives, and I knew that in hearing their stories and being intimate, on that sort of intellectual level with them, would make a contribution to their lives. And it seems to me that teaching is really about the whole of the student and the faculty member. It's about their interaction, and about how what you're talking about in class might relate to what you are living in your life. It's not therapy in the sense that you don't intrude on the privacy of folks, but I really think if education doesn't help you live more joyfully and creatively and love better, then it's not worth much." (Craig)
	Broadening the conventional social purpose of a job responsibility to incorporate an unanswered calling	"I often liken teaching to being a musician because of when I'm in front of a classroom, I put on my performance face. I can be talking in a rather soft voice like this to you outside a classroom, and as soon as I enter that classroom, [Guitarist Gary] the performer is on. And it's the same way with music; you kind of put on your stage face. . . . It's entertaining education: edu-tainment. And I'm doing that all the time. I'm trying to make class time interesting and fun and entertaining because research on education demonstrates when people are in a good mood, they tend to learn better and learn more. . . . I remember when I was performing and I had my rock band and my other bands, the high which I got from playing in front of people was very similar to the high which I get from performing teaching in front of people." (Gary)
Leisure Crafting		
Vicarious experiencing	Seeking fulfillment through others' participation in an unanswered calling	"Whenever we do go to a concert or musical theatre . . . I will fantasize a little bit and daydream about if I was the one up there singing, or I was the one up there playing the piano. . . . I really don't think I have the talent to really do anything very important from the musical end, but I'm happy that I still have it in my life for my own enjoyment." (Mary)
Hobby participating	Pursuing leisure and volunteer activities related to an unanswered calling	"I'm not going to retire from either. As long as I can hold a guitar in my hands, I'm going to be playing. And as long as I can stand in front of a class and teach, and somebody lets me, I'm going to be doing that. . . . Music more so. I can see somebody getting too old to teach. But I can't imagine somebody, or at least I can't imagine myself, ever getting too old to at least once in a while, pick up my instrument and play it. Because it's just a different world. It's a totally different world." (Abe)

Source: Reproduced from Berg, J. M., Grant, A. M., & Johnson, V. (2010). When callings are calling: Crafting work and leisure in pursuit of unanswered occupational callings. Organization Science, 21(5), 973–994.

Working with fewer external incentives may actually increase your sense of self-determination. Many people are choosing jobs not for the financial benefits but for the achievements they can experience through them. Programs like Teach for America and the Peace Corps work well because people join in order to enjoy the sense of contributing and "doing good" in the world and are willing to work for very low pay compared to other jobs. Field studies show that doing good on the job, when combined with intrinsic motivation, results in better performance and increased persistence (Grant, 2008).

People have different reasons for the career choices they make. None are "good" or "bad," but the key is the match to what you value. Are you willing to delay gratification through a long training period, sacrifice a normal lifestyle, and do what it takes to become a medical doctor? Or are you better suited to a career path that puts you into the action sooner and allows you to learn through the challenges along the way? Take some time to reflect about what motivates and inspires you and how you plan to approach your work. Talk to your parents and others who work to hear about their motivations and their satisfaction with their jobs.

Many resources are available to help with the important career decisions ahead. A place to start is your campus career center, which typically offers help with job searches and interview preparation. There are many online resources, books, and articles about career selection and guides to help you think about careers. You can even find counselors at your school or professional career coaches that can help you identify a path. The best advice is to start considering your options now and attempt to gain experience in a variety of workplaces to discover what best serves to motivate you.

Summary of Multiple Influences on Motivation

As we saw from the discussions of motivation based on physiological needs, humans have elaborate systems for controlling behavior. Like other animals, we have sophisticated biological systems that monitor and regulate basic behaviors like eating and sex. At the same time, these same behaviors are influenced by social factors, environmental contexts, and cultural conventions.

For example, we examined the elaborate system that regulates the motivation of hunger. From physiology, stomach receptors and hormones motivate eating when the stomach is empty and suppress it when full. "Start" and "stop" eating areas in the hypothalamus control the initiation of eating based on signals from sugar in the bloodstream. The hypothalamus also communicates with glands throughout the digestive system through hormones to coordinate eating. A longer-term monitoring system, the metabolism, affects the maintenance of weight as a set or settling point. And genetics plays a major role in the long-term outcome of these mechanisms.

To this, many additional environmental factors join in to affect whether eating takes place. Food preferences, availability, cues from the environment like advertisements, and moods affect what and how much we eat. In addition, the social setting can lead to eating more when we are joined by others. Our cultural practices also tell us which food to savor and which to avoid. Even our cultural depictions of "ideal" others can affect how we feel about our own and others' bodies and, therefore, how we choose to eat (or not to eat).

These environmental and biological factors combine to stimulate eating. As a result, there are many ways in which the hunger motivation can lead us astray. When obesity or eating disorders occur, it is tempting to think they share the same cause. However, each of the influences described can lead to changes in eating behavior, so the underlying cause(s) can be different for each person. Causes of increased weight may involve disruptions of processes in genetics, the brain, the endocrine system, the stomach, and behaviors responsive to the environment. The number of processes involved suggests there may be many different causes for the same symptom of excess weight.

The same argument holds for higher-level motivations: Why are some people driven by a need for achievement while others are content to do "well enough?" The roots of our higher-level motivation may lie in early parenting relationships, experiences in childhood, "self-talk" about what is needed to accomplish goals, environmental influences like education, competition with others, and physiological influences like arousal. These motivations present complex pictures of the influence of biological and environmental factors.

Motivation clearly illustrates how the expression of a specific behavior can be caused by biological and environmental factors, some of which are outside of our awareness. This makes understanding and changing our behavior a challenging task!

CONCEPT LEARNING CHECK 10.5 | *What "Works" at Work?*

Complete this true or false quiz and explain why each answer is correct.

1. Interviews provide good evidence of the best person to hire.   T   F

2. Most people say their work is their true "calling."   T   F

3. General mental ability is a good predictor of success in any job.   T   F

4. Gender makes no difference in career outcomes.   T   F

5. Productive work teams communicate more positives than negatives.   T   F

Visual Overview Motivation: Sources of Hunger

The motivation to eat has characteristic influences in our physical bodies (shown in blue) and in our environment (shown in green).

Are You Hungry?

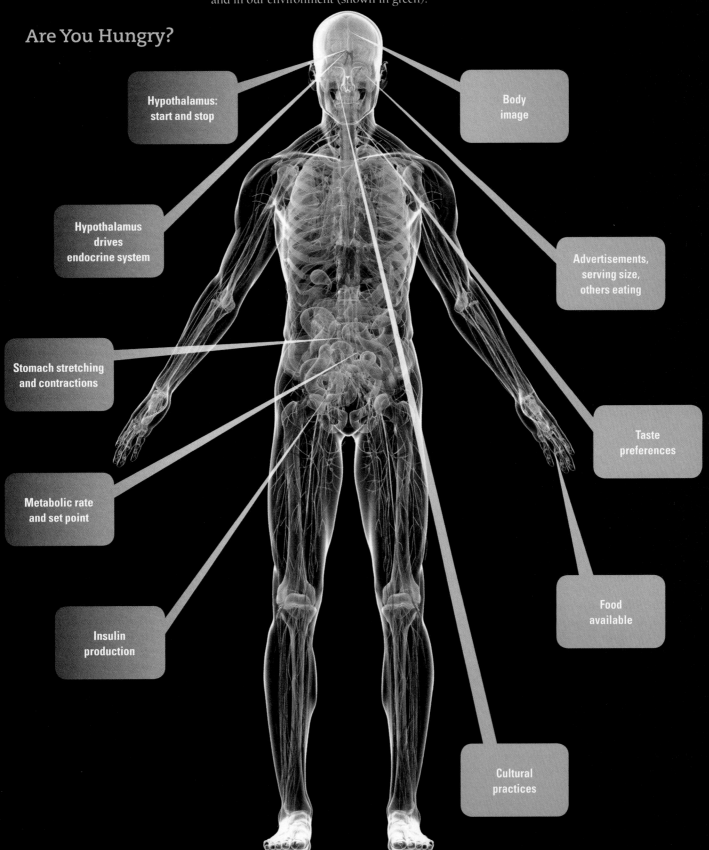

Hypothalamus: start and stop

Body image

Hypothalamus drives endocrine system

Advertisements, serving size, others eating

Stomach stretching and contractions

Taste preferences

Metabolic rate and set point

Insulin production

Food available

Cultural practices

10.1 Motivational Theories

- Motivation is described as an inner state that energizes people toward the fulfillment of a goal.
- Understanding built-in behaviors led to instinct theories, or motivation as programmed behavior occurring in response to environmental cues.
- Evolutionary psychologists apply the theory of evolution to explain behaviors.
- A drive is defined as tension arising from within our physiological systems, which in turn motivates action.

- Arousal theory states that we are motivated to seek out an optimal level of arousal.
- Incentive theories focus on the reward or payoff for behaviors.
- Maslow posited that the needs and motivations of humans form levels, called the hierarchy of needs.

10.2 Motivation of Hunger

- Our physiological system attempts to manage our hunger and keep our energy stores in a steady state.
- Hunger pangs in the stomach play a role, but are not our only motivation for eating.
- The structure called the hypothalamus is the functional center of motivation in the brain.
- The hypothalamus also regulates the endocrine system, the network of glands throughout the body that manufacture and secrete hormones.
- Another source of regulation for hunger occurs through the metabolism of the body, or the physiological processes used to convert energy from nutrients.
- When the level of glucose (or sugar) in the bloodstream is low, people feel hungry, and when food raises the glucose levels, hunger is reduced.
- Genetics also plays a major role in metabolism, set point, and body type.

- A wealth of environmental factors play a role in motivating us to eat.
- Anorexia nervosa is an eating disorder in which someone feels he or she is overweight despite objective evidence.
- Binge eating disorder and bulimia nervosa refer to individuals who binge eat large amounts of food. In bulimia, relatively normal weight is maintained by purging.
- Perceptions of body image are influenced by personal, social, and cultural values that may vary from one culture to another.
- Obesity, defined as an excess level of fat in the body, at least 15% above ideal weight for a given height, is a leading preventable cause of disease and one of today's most serious public health problems.

Hourglass shape

Rectangle shape

10.3 Sexual Motivation

- The motivation for sex is present in all animals, necessary to ensure their reproduction.
- Masters and Johnson described four phases of physiological responses during sex called the human sexual response cycle: excitement, plateau, orgasm, and resolution.

- The male sex hormone testosterone has been shown to correlate with sexual desire, and another hormone called oxytocin is released during orgasm, leading to sensations of emotional well-being.
- Differences between genders may follow from different reproductive strategies, called parental investment theory.

- Sexual orientation refers to the gender preferred for emotional and sexual intimacy.
- Kinsey defined a continuum of sexual orientation, from exclusively heterosexual (opposite sex) to bisexual to exclusively homosexual (same sex).

- No theories of environmental causes of sexual orientation have ever received scientific support.

10.4 Social Motivations

- Maslow suggested that, after our basic biological needs are satisfied, we move up the hierarchy to social and achievement needs.
- We all want to feel a part of a relationship or group, called the need to belong.
- Motivated people set high but realistic goals so that they are challenged, yet can succeed.
- Mindsets, or beliefs about yourself and your abilities, oriented toward growth

help to develop skills through dedication and effort.
- Self-actualization involves working toward the full use and exploitation of your talents, capacities, and potentials.
- Decades of studies have demonstrated that self-determination, or choice, is the key factor in long-term motivation.

10.5 Motivation and Work

- The subfield of industrial and organizational psychology addresses the psychology of work.
- The Hawthorne effect occurs when increased interest directed toward a worker results in improved performance.
- Interviewers tend to believe in their own intuitive abilities to find good candidates in the absence of evidence, called the interviewer illusion.
- Race, gender, sexual orientation, obesity, and attractiveness have been shown to influence the selection and hiring of employees.

- There is more positive than negative communication within effective teams, in a ratio of five positive to one negative.
- Gender norms still affect career choices and compensation in the workplace.
- A calling is defined as an occupation that an individual (1) feels drawn to pursue, (2) expects to be intrinsically enjoyable and meaningful, and (3) sees as a central part of his or her identity.
- Motivation clearly illustrates how the expression of a specific behavior can be caused by biological and environmental factors, some outside of our awareness.

10.1 Motivational Theories

1. The fact that Jack enjoys racing on dirt bikes but not sky diving supports the _____ theory of motivation.
   A. instinct
   B. arousal
   C. drive
   D. incentive

2. Patrick ate a large breakfast. When he arrived for class, a friend offered him a muffin. Even though Patrick was still quite full, he wanted to make his friend happy, so he ate it anyway. Patrick's behavior can best be explained by the _____ theory of motivation.
   A. self-awareness
   B. instinct
   C. drive
   D. incentive

3. According to Maslow's hierarchy of needs, which of these is the most primary need?
   A. Safety
   B. Intimacy
   C. Self-actualization
   D. Belonging

4. Tevin's dad paid him a dollar for every "A" grade he brought home in high school. Now that Tevin is in college, his grades have started to drop. This suggests Tevin's high school study efforts were motivated:
   A. instinctually.
   B. extrinsically.
   C. as needed.
   D. intrinsically.

10.2 Motivation of Hunger

5. Because the _____ regulates the glands, it could be considered to be the connection between the brain and the endocrine (hormonal) system.
   A. hypothalamus
   B. hippocampus
   C. thalamus
   D. amygdala

6. Several motivations, such as hunger and sex, are accomplished through hormones (such as testosterone) secreted directly into the bloodstream through the _____ system.
   A. endocrine
   B. autonomic nervous
   C. limbic
   D. peripheral nervous

7. If a rat has a brain tumor that results in a disruption of "start eating" behavior, which of the following areas is the most likely location of the tumor?
   A. Hypothalamus
   B. Thalamus
   C. Cerebellum
   D. Brainstem

8. Patients diagnosed with anorexia nervosa have been shown to have:
   A. bouts with bulimia.
   B. failed at diets repeatedly.
   C. distorted body images.
   D. lived in a modern culture.

10.3 Sexual Motivation

9. Masters and Johnson studied female and male sexual responses. Which of these statements expresses their main findings about sexual response?
   A. Female sexual satisfaction depends on penis size.
   B. There is no refractory period.
   C. Men have greater orgasmic capabilities than women.
   D. The sexual response cycle is the same in men and women.

10. Evolutionary theory predicts that, due to differences in parental investment, women should seek mates who are:
   A. physically attractive.
   B. intelligent.
   C. muscular.
   D. high in status.

11. Evolutionary theory predicts that, due to differences in parental investment, men should seek mates who:
   A. are physically attractive.
   B. are of normal weight.
   C. have a low waist-to-hip ratio.
   D. are high in status.

12. The correlations in homosexual orientation between identical twins compared to fraternal twins and other siblings suggest that sexual orientation:
   A. is influenced more by environment.
   B. is influenced more by genetics.
   C. is affected equally by both.
   D. is not known to be related to either environment or genetics.

10.4 Social Motivations

13. Sarah and Alice meet at a student group meeting. They begin talking and eventually become friends. Even though Sarah is not always nice to Alice, they continue to be friends. This best demonstrates the human:
  A. need for belonging.
  B. need for self-actualization.
  C. need for achievement.
  D. need for power.

14. Patrice really enjoys solving difficult equations. Whenever she has free time, she plops down and does some calculations. She is then asked to be in a study in which she gets paid $5 for every equation she solves. According to results from Deci's puzzle experiment on intrinsic and extrinsic motivation, Patrice will now be likely to:

  A. enjoy doing calculations just as much.
  B. like doing calculations even more.
  C. get less satisfaction out of doing calculations on her own.
  D. refuse to participate in any more research studies.

15. At the top of Maslow's hierarchy of needs, he proposed that we all share the deep motivation to:
  A. make the most of our potential.
  B. form a significant relationship.
  C. provide for ourselves and loved ones.
  D. receive the respect of others around us.

10.5 Motivation and Work

16. The Hawthorne effect, first observed with workers in a special "test" room versus a control room, showed that:
  A. better pay increased production.
  B. none of the interventions applied to the test room led to increased production.
  C. all interventions applied to the test room led to increased production.
  D. improving the brightness in the room led to increased production.

17. The best predictor of later job success is:
  A. the need to belong.
  B. general mental ability.
  C. an outgoing personality.
  D. the need to achieve.

18. The study of insurance workers assigned at random to offices of others of higher, the same, and lower status on the corporate structure showed that people:
  A. benefit from changed surroundings.
  B. will work harder for more money.
  C. are sensitive to equity in compensation.
  D. dislike changes in leadership.

CHAPTER DISCUSSION QUESTIONS

1. Section 10.1 defines motivation as an inner state that energizes people toward the fulfillment of a goal. However, you will find that each theory of motivation (instinct, evolutionary, drive, arousal, incentive, and hierarchical) places a different emphasis on the role of the internal state. Evaluate each theory of motivation by how strong an influence it places on internal states in driving goal fulfillment.

2. Compare and contrast the physiological factors and environmental factors involved in feeling hungry. Are some factors more powerful than others? Should you expect individual differences in how much each factor influences a person's eating patterns?

3. Think of a common theme about sex and relationships that you have seen depicted in movies or television shows. Relate the information in this chapter about sexual motivation to the theme you have selected. Does the information in the chapter support the ideas in movies and television? Why or why not?

4. Assess the relationship between the higher motivations discussed in section 10.4 (belonging, achievement, self-actualization) and work motivation. How might your higher motivations influence your success in getting hired, maintaining a job, and getting promoted?

CHAPTER PROJECTS

1. How would your life be different without one of your motivations? Review hunger, sexual, and the higher motivations and pick one that is particularly interesting to you. Then, create a scenario that illustrates how your life would be different without that motivation. How would it change your daily life? How would it change your long-term life planning?

2. Advertisers and marketers use information about our motivations when they create advertising campaigns. Find video (e.g., YouTube) clips of commercials for a particular product and identify which motivations are being targeted in the ads. In your evaluation of the commercials, make sure that you refer to specific knowledge of motivation discussed in the chapter.

CHAPTER KEY TERMS

360-degree feedback
Achievement gap
Achievement motivation
Adipose tissue
Anorexia nervosa
Arousal theory
Basal metabolic rate
Binge eating disorder
Bisexual
Body dysmorphia
Body mass index (BMI)
Bulimia nervosa
Calling
Coming out
Continuum of sexual orientation
Delay of gratification
Diabetes
Drive
Drive theory
Endocrine system
Engagement
Equity theory
Esteem motivation
Estrogen
Evolutionary psychologist
Evolved behaviors
Excitement phase
"Exotic becomes erotic"
Extrinsic incentives
Extrinsic motivation
Fertile
Fixed mindset
Flow
Ghrelin
Glucose

Growth mindset
Hawthorne effect
Heterosexual
Hierarchy of needs
Homeostasis
Homosexual
Hormones
Humanistic psychology
Human sexual response cycle
Hypothalamus
Incentive
Incentive theories
Industrial and organizational psychology
Instinct theories
Insulin
Interviewer illusion
Intrinsic incentives
Intrinsic motivation
Job analysis
Job burnout
Lateral hypothalamus
Leptin
Mating
Metabolism
Mindset
Motivation
Motive
Need for achievement
Need to belong
Obesity
Optimal arousal
Organizational psychology
Orgasmic phase
Overjustification effect

Oxytocin
Parental investment theory
Paternal uncertainty
Persistence
Personnel psychology
Plateau phase
Process loss
Realistic job preview
Refractory period
Reproductive strategies
Resolution phase
Self-actualization
Self-determination theory
Self-regulation
Set point
Settling point
Sex norms
Sexual disorder
Sexual harassment
Sexual orientation
Sexual peak
Social rejection
Status
Sublimation
Testosterone
Thematic apperception test (TAT)
Unit bias
Universals
Vasocongestion
Ventromedial hypothalamus
Waist-to-hip ratio (WHR)
Yerkes-Dodson law of arousal

ANSWERS TO CONCEPT LEARNING CHECKS

10.1 Theories of Motivation

1. D. He is seeking increased arousal.

2. E. He is motivated by pay.

3. C. The biological drive to drink overrides the social game.

4. B. Preferred tastes for sweet and fat may have helped human ancestors survive in environments in which food was scarce.

5. A. Some inborn fears and reflexes occur when certain stimuli are presented.

6. F. Meeting physiological needs by gaining resources comes before higher-level needs in hierarchy theory.

7. Instinct, evolutionary, and drive theories posit the same motivations for everyone. However, satisfying drives may be more effortful for some people. Arousal theory takes the situation into account, so it would predict different motivations for people in different environments. Incentive theory is very sensitive to the features of the environment that reward behavior; so someone in Japan may work longer hours because there are more goods available to buy with the financial incentives they received for work.

Finally, the hierarchy of needs theory is designed to take differences in situations into account. People that have their basic needs met (such as the Japan example) are free to pursue their higher-level motivations.

10.2 Eating Disorder or Disordered Eating?

1. Bulimia. [Binging by overeating followed by purging the body through vomiting or laxatives; eating disorder.]

2. Binge eating disorder. [Binging by overeating large quantities not followed by purging but compulsively performed in secret; eating disorder.]

3. Obesity. [Gaining weight to more than 15% of the ideal body weight for your height; not an eating disorder.]

4. Anorexia. [Losing at least 25% of your weight with restriction of eating and fear of becoming obese; eating disorder.]

10.3 Evolution and Gender Differences

1. They differ in strategy because they differ in parental investment. Strictly speaking, males need only donate sperm, and they may have a large number of offspring. Females must invest in pregnancy and birth, then nursing

and raising the child and can produce fewer children over their lifetime.

2. Based on cues that predict fertility, males would be attracted based on youth, health, and low waist-to-hip ratio signals.

3. Based on cues that predict status, females would be attracted to older males, high social status, and high material wealth signals, as these help to support her.

4. First, within a population, there are some males who prefer younger mates, some who prefer older, and some the same. Over generations, the successful males are ones who chose younger mates and thus were able to reproduce and pass their genes on to the next generation. As a result, the preference for younger mates spreads so more men have that tendency in progressive generations.

10.4 Fostering Achievement

1. Following Dweck's work, you can focus on your process toward achievement rather than ability. So rewarding yourself for hours of study is more beneficial than rewarding yourself for the outcome of the grade. This reflects a growth mindset. Belief in hard work and effort to accomplish goals ("You worked really well today; You put so much effort into learning the material!") is more effective than encouragement based on ability ("You are a smart person; You always do badly at math."), which reflects an unchanging and fixed mindset.

Following self-determination theory, you can work to integrate your externally rewarded behavior into your personal values. Identify intrinsic motivations in your behavior that will sustain it when the external reward is no longer available.

10.5 What "Works" at Work?

1. F. The interviewer illusion shows people believe they can learn the most from interviews, but only structured interviews show benefits.

2. F. Only a third of those surveyed said their work was their calling.

3. T. Intelligence is the strongest factor related to job success across fields.

4. F. Women are less likely to end up in higher-paying fields and jobs.

5. T. The ratio is five positive statements for each negative.

ANSWERS TO CHAPTER REVIEW TEST

10.1 Motivational Theories

1. B. Rationale: Arousal theory says we seek the optimum level of arousal, not the highest level.

2. D. Rationale: Since he is not hungry, he is eating for an external reason, the incentive of making his friend happy.

3. A. Rationale: Safety is the most basic need listed, and Maslow proposed basic needs come first.

4. B. Rationale: The extrinsic incentive of money was motivating him, and without it, he does not continue the behavior.

10.2 Motivation of Hunger

5. A. Rationale: The hypothalamus is the brain structure involved in motivation.

6. A. Rationale: The endocrine system releases hormones.

7. A. Rationale: The hypothalamus region, specifically the lateral hypothalamus.

8. C. Rationale: They are overly self-critical about their bodies.

10.3 Sexual Motivation

9. D. Rationale: Males and females go through similar response cycles (with some differences).

10. D. Rationale: High status commands more resources and help from others, which benefits her.

11. C. Rationale: Males should be concerned with fertility, which is predicted by waist-to-hip ratio.

12. B. Rationale: The more related, the more concordance of orientation, and there is little evidence about environmental influences.

10.4 Social Motivations

13. A. Rationale: We need to belong and avoid rejection when possible.

14. C. Rationale: Once paid for an activity, people find it not as enjoyable to do for fun.

15. A. Rationale: Maximizing our potential is Maslow's self-actualization.

10.5 Motivation and Work

16. C. Rationale: All of the interventions showed improvement due to increased interest in the workers.

17. B. Rationale: General intelligence was found to be the best predictor; need to achieve may be a mismatch in some jobs.

18. C. Rationale: People worked harder in nicer offices and less in less nice offices, showing they were sensitive to the "perks" that come with jobs.

REFERENCES

Adams, J. S. (1963). Toward an understanding of inequity. *Journal of Abnormal and Social Psychology, 67,* 422–436.

Agras, W. S., Hammer, L. D., McNicholas, F., & Kraemer, H. C. (2004). Risk factors for childhood overweight: A prospective study from birth to 9.5 years. *Journal of Pediatrics, 145*(1), 20–25.

Amabile, T. M. (1996). Motivational synergy: Toward new conceptualizations of intrinsic and extrinsic motivation in the workplace. *Human Resource Management Review, 3*(30), 185–201.

Ames, C. (1992). Classrooms: Goals, structures, and student motivation. *Journal of Educational Psychology, 84*(3), 261–327.

Ames, C., & Archer, J. (1988). Goals in the classroom: Students' learning strategies and motivation processes. *Journal of Educational Psychology, 80*(3), 260–267.

Andersson, L. M., & Pearson, C. M. (1999). Tit for tat? The spiraling effect of incivility in the workplace. *Academy of Management Review, 24,* 452–471.

Angier, N. (1985, January 28). Finding trouble in paradise: Do women really prefer cuddling over "the act"? *Time, 125,* 76.

Ariely, D., Gneezy, W., Lowenstein, G., & Mazar, N. (2009). Large stakes and big mistakes. *Review of Economic Studies, 76,* 451–469.

Arkowitz, H., & Lilienfeld, S. O. (2009). Environment and weight. *Scientific American Mind, 20,* 68–69.

Arvey, R. D., & Campion, J. E. (1982). The employment interview: A summary and review of recent research. *Personnel Psychology, 35,* 281–322.

Assanand, S., Pinel, J. P. J., & Lehman, D. R. (1998). Personal theories of hunger and eating. *Journal of Applied Social Psychology, 28,* 998–1015.

Atkinson, J. W. (1964). *An introduction to motivation.* New York: Van Nostrand.

Bakker, A. B., & Schaufeli, W. B. (2008). Positive organizational behavior: Engaged employees in flourishing organizations. *Journal of Organizational Behavior, Special Issue: Contexts of Positive Organizational Behavior, 29*(2), 147–154.

Barness, L. A., Opitz, J. M., & Gilbert-Barness, E. (2007). Obesity: Genetic, molecular, and environmental aspects. *American Journal of Medical Genetics, 143A*(24), 3016–3034.

Barr, A., Bryan, A., & Kenrick, D. T. (2002). Sexual peak: Socially shared cognitions about desire, frequency, and satisfaction in men and women. *Personal Relationships, 9,* 287–299.

Baumeister, R. F. (1991). The need to belong: Desire for interpersonal attachments as a fundamental human motivation. *Psychological Bulletin, 117*(3), 497–529.

Baumeister, R. F., Bratslavsky, E., Muraven, M., & Tice, D. M. (1998). Is the active self a limited resource? *Journal of Personality and Social Psychology, 74,* 1252–1265.

Baumeister, R. F., Catanese, K. R., & Vohs, K. D. (2001). Is there a gender difference in strength of sex drive? Theoretical views, conceptual distinctions, and a review of relevant evidence. *Personality and Social Psychology Review, 5*(3), 242–273.

Baumeister, R. F., & Leary, M. R. (1995). The need to belong: Desire for interpersonal attachments as a fundamental human motivation. *Psychological Bulletin, 117,* 497–529.

Baumeister, R. F., Vohs, K. D., & Tice, D. M. (2007). The strength model of self-control. *Current Directions in Psychological Science, 16*(6), 351–355.

Becker, J. B., Rudick, C. N., & Jenkins, W. J. (2001). The role of dopamine in the nucleus accumbens and striatum during sexual behavior in the female rat. *Journal of Neuroscience, 21*(9), 3236–3241.

Bell, S. T. (2007). Deep-level composition variables as predictors of team performance: A meta-analysis. *Journal of Applied Psychology, 92*(3), 595–615.

Bem, D. J. (1996). Exotic becomes erotic: A developmental theory of sexual orientation. *Psychological Review, 103*(2), 320–335.

Bem, D. J. (2000). Exotic becomes erotic: Interpreting the biological correlates of sexual orientation. *Archives of Sexual Behavior, 29*(6), 531–548.

Berg, J. M., Grant, A. M., & Johnson, V. (2010). When callings are calling: Crafting work and leisure in pursuit of unanswered occupational callings. *Organization Science, 21*(5), 973–994.

Bernard, L. C., Mills, M., Swenson, L., & Walsh, R. P. (2005). An evolutionary theory of human motivation. *Genetic, Social, and General Psychology Monographs, 131,* 129–184.

Blanchard, R., & Klassen, P. (1997). H-Y antigen and homosexuality in men. *Journal of Theoretical Biology, 185*(3), 373–378.

Blanchard, R., Zucker, K. J., Siegelman, M., Dickey, R., & Klassen, P. (1998). The relation of birth order to sexual orientation in men and women. *Journal of Biosocial Science, 30,* 511–519.

Blass, E. M., & Hall, W. G. (1976). Drinking termination: Interactions among hydrational, orogastric, and behavioral controls in rats. *Psychological Review, 83*(5), 356–374.

Bliss, E. L., & Branch, C. H. H. (1960). *Anorexia Nervosa: Its history, psychology and biology.* New York: Paul B. Hoeber.

Bozarth, J. D., & Brodley, B. T. (1991). Actualization: A functional concept in client-centered therapy. *Journal of Social Behavior & Personality, 6*(5), 45–59.

Brosnan, S. F., & de Waal, F. B. M. (2003). Monkeys reject unequal pay. *Nature, 425*(6955), 279–299.

Bulik, C. M., Wade, T. D., Heath, A. C., Martin, N. G., Stunkard, A. J., & Eaves, L. J. (2001). Relating body mass index to figural stimuli: Population-based normative data for Caucasians. *International Journal of Obesity and Related Metabolic Disorders, 25*(10), 1517–1524.

Buss, D. M. (1989). Sex differences in human mate selection: Evolutionary hypotheses tested in 37 cultures. *Behavior and Brain Sciences, 12,* 1–49.

Buss, D. M. (1994). The strategies of human mating: People worldwide are attracted to the same qualities in the opposite sex. *American Scientist, 82,* 238–249.

Buss, D. M. (1995). Evolutionary psychology: A new paradigm for psychological science. *Psychological Inquiry, 6,* 1–30.

Buss, D. M., & Schmitt, D. P. (1993). Sexual strategies theory: An evolutionary perspective on human mating. *Psychological Review, 100*(2), 204–232.

Campfield, L. A., Smith, F. J., Rosenbaum, M., & Hirsch, J. (1996). Human eating: Evidence for a physiological basis using a modified paradigm. *Neuroscience and Biobehavioral Reviews, 20*(1), 133–137.

Cannon, W. B., & Washburn, A. L. (1912). An explanation of hunger. *American Journal of Physiology, 29,* 441–454.

Clark, R. D., III, & Hatfield, E. (1989). Gender differences in receptivity to sexual offers. *Journal of Psychology and Human Sexuality, 2,* 39–55.

Conley, T. D. (2011). Perceived proposer personality characteristics and gender differences in acceptance of casual sex offers. *Journal of Personality and Social Psychology, 100*(2), 309–329.

Cortina, L. M., Magley, V. J., Williams, J. H., & Langhout, R. D. (2001). Incivility in the workplace: Incidence and impact. *Journal of Occupational Health Psychology, 6*(1), 64–80.

Crago, M., Shisslak, C. M., & Estes, L. S. (1996). Eating disturbances among American minority groups: A review. *International Journal of Eating Disorders, 19,* 239–248.

Crow, S. M., Fok, L. Y., & Hartman, S. J. (1998). Who is at greatest risk of work-related discrimination—Women, blacks, or homosexuals? *Employee Responsibilities and Rights Journal, 11*(1), 15–26.

Csikszentmihalyi, M. (1990). *Flow: The psychology of optimal experience.* New York: Harper & Row.

Curry, S. J., Wagner, E. H., & Grothaus, L. C. (1991). Evaluation of intrinsic and extrinsic motivation interventions with a self-help smoking cessation program. *Journal of Consulting and Clinical Psychology, 59,* 318–324.

Davis, D., Shaver, P. R., & Vernon, M. L. (2003). Physical, emotional, and behavioral reactions to breaking up: The roles of gender, age, emotional involvement, and attachment style. *Personality and Social Psychology Bulletin, 29*(7), 871–884.

Deci, E. L. (1971). Effects of externally mediated rewards on intrinsic motivation. *Journal of Personality and Social Psychology, 18*(1), 105–115.

Deci, E. L., & Ryan, R. M. (1985). *Intrinsic motivation and self-determination in human behavior.* New York: Plenum Press.

DeWall, C. N., MacDonald, G., Webster, G. D., Masten, C. L., Baumeister, R. F., Powell, C., Combs, D., Schurtz, D. R., Stillman, T. F., Tice, D. M., & Eisenberger, N. J. (2010). Acetaminophen reduces social pain: Behavioral and neural evidence. *Psychological Science, 21*(7), 931–937.

Donnay, D. A. C., Morris, M. L., Schaubhut, N. A., Thompson, R. C., Grutter, J., & Hammer, A. L. (2011). *Strong Interest Inventory (r)* [Newly Revised]. Mountain View, CA: CPP.

Doyle, R. (2000). Women and the professions. *Scientific American,* April, 30–31.

Drewnowski, A., Yee, D. K., & Krahn, D. D. (1988). Bulimia in college women: Incidence and recovery rates. *American Journal of Psychiatry, 145*(6), 753–755.

Dweck, C. (2006). *Mindset: The new psychology of success.* New York: Random House.

Eisenberger, N. I., Lieberman, M. D., & Williams, K. D. (2003). Does rejection hurt? An fMRI study of social exclusion. *Science, 302,* 290–292.

Eknoyan, G. (2008). Adolphe Quetelet (1796–1874)—the average man and indices of obesity. *Nephrology, Dialysis, & Transplantation, 23*(1), 47–51.

England, G. W. (1990). The patterning of work meanings which are coterminous with work outcome levels for individuals in Japan, Germany and the USA. *Applied Psychology, 39*(1), 29–45.

Epel, E., Lapidus, R., McEwen, B., & Brownell, K. (2001). Stress may add bite to appetite in women: A laboratory study of stress-induced cortisol and eating behavior. *Psychoneuroendocrinology, 26*(1), 37–49.

Fiske, D. W., & Maddi, S. R. (1961). *The function of varied experience.* Homewood, IL: Dorsey.

Fiske, S. T., Bershoff, D. N., Borgida, E., Deaux, K., & Heilman, M. E. (1991). Social science research on trial: Use of sex stereotyping research in *Price Waterhouse v. Hopkins. American Psychologist, 46*(10), 1049–1060.

Fitzgerald, B. (1999). Children of lesbian and gay parents: A review of the literature. *Marriage and Family Review, 29,* 57–75.

Freud, S. (1915). Instincts and their vicissitudes. Reprinted in J. Strachey (Ed.) (1957), The standard edition of the complete psychological works of Sigmund Freud, volume XIV (1914–1916): On the history of the Psycho-Analytic movement, papers on metapsychology and other works, pp. 109–140. London: The Hogarth Press and the Institute of Psycho-analysis.

Fryar, C. D., Hirsch, R., Porter, K. S., Kottiri, B., Brody, D. J., & Louis, T. (2007, June 28). Drug use and sexual behaviors reported by adults: United States, 1999–2002. *Advance Data from Vital and Health Statistics,* No. 384, 1–16. http://www.cdc.gov/nchs/data/ad/ad384.pdf

Garcia-Falgueras, A., & Swaab, D. F. (2010). Sexual hormones and the brain: An essential alliance for sexual identity and sexual orientation. In S. Loche, M. Cappa, L. Ghizzoni, M. Maghnie, & M. O. Savage (Eds.), *Pediatric neuroendocrinology: Endocrine development, Vol. 17* (pp. 22–35). Basel: Karger.

Geier, A. B., Rozin, P., & Doros, G. (2006). Unit bias: A new heuristic that helps explain the effects of portion size on food intake. *Psychological Science, 17,* 521–525.

Ghorpade, J. (2000). Managing five paradoxes of 360-degree feedback. *Academy of Management Executive, 14*(1), 140–150.

Gottman, J. M. (1994). *Why marriages succeed or fail.* New York: Simon & Schuster.

Gottman, J. M., Levenson, R. W., Gross, J., Frederickson, B., McCoy, K., Rosenthal, L., Ruef, A., & Yoshimoto, D. (2003). Correlates of gay and lesbian couples' relationship satisfaction and relationship dissolution. *Journal of Homosexuality, 45*(1), 23–43.

Grant, A. M. (2008). Does intrinsic motivation fuel the prosocial fire? Motivational synergy in predicting persistence, performance, and productivity. *Journal of Applied Psychology, 93*(1), 48–58.

Greenberg, J. (1988). Equity and workplace status: A field experiment. *Journal of Applied Psychology, 73*(4), 606–613.

Griebel, T. (2006). Self-portrayal in a simulated life: Projecting personality and values in The Sims 2. *International Journal of Computer Game Research, 6*(1).

Grilo, C. M., & Pogue-Geile, M. F. (1991). The nature of environmental influences on weight and obesity: A behavior genetics analysis. *Psychological Bulletin, 110,* 520–537.

Gusnard, D. A., Ollinger, J. M., Sulman, G. L., Cloninger, C. R., Price, J. L., Van Essen, D. C., & Raichle, M. E. (2003). Persistence and brain circuitry. *Proceedings of the National Academy of Sciences, 100*(6), 3479–3484.

Hackman, J. R. (1987). The design of work teams. In J. W. Lorsch (Ed.), *Handbook of organizational behavior* (pp. 315–342). Englewood Cliffs, NJ: Prentice-Hall.

Hackman, J. R., & Oldham, G. R. (1975). Development of the Job Diagnostic Survey. *Journal of Applied Psychology, 60*(2), 159–170.

Harpaz, I. (1988). Variables affecting non-financial employment commitment. *Applied Psychology, 33,* 235–247.

Harter, J. K., Schmidt, F. L., & Hayes, T. L. (2002). Business-unit-level relationship between employee satisfaction, employee engagement, and business outcomes: A meta-analysis. *Journal of Applied Psychology, 87*(2), 268–279.

Haslam, D. W., & James, W. P. (2005). Obesity. *Lancet, 366*(9492), 1197–1209.

Heatherton, T. F., & Baumeister, R. F. (1991). Binge eating as escape from self-awareness. *Psychological Bulletin, 110*(1), 86–108.

Henderson, A. T., Berla, N., & The National Committee for Citizens in Education. (1994). *A new generation of evidence: The family is critical to student achievement.* Columbia, MD: National Committee for Citizens in Education.

Herman, C. P., Roth, D. A., & Polivy, J. (2003). Effects of the presence of others on food intake: A normative interpretation. *Psychological Bulletin, 129,* 873–886.

Highhouse, S. (2008). Stubborn reliance on intuition and subjectivity in employee selection. *Industrial and Organizational Psychology, 1,* 333–342.

Hill, G. W. (1982). Group versus individual performance: Are N+1 heads better than one? *Psychology Bulletin, 91,* 517–539.

Hoffman, D. J., Policastro, P., Quick, V., & Lee, S. K. (2006). Changes in body weight and fat mass of men and women in the first year of college: A study of the "freshman 15." *Journal of American College Health, 55*(1), 41–45.

Holland, J. L. (1996). Exploring careers with a typology: What we have learned and some new directions. *American Psychologist, 51*(4), 397–406.

Holm-Denoma, J., Joiner, T., Vohs, K., & Heatherton, T. (2008). The "freshman fifteen" (the freshman five actually): Predictors and possible explanations. *Health Psychology, 27,* S3–S9.

Horgen, K. B., & Brownell, K. D. (2002). Confronting the toxic environment: Environmental and public health actions in a world crisis. In T. A. Wadden & A. J. Stunkard (Eds.), *Handbook of obesity treatment* (pp. 95–106). New York: Guilford Press.

Hull, C. L. (1943). *Principles of behavior.* New York: Appleton-Century-Crofts.

Ilies, R., Hauserman, N., Schwochau, S., & Stibal, J. (2003). Reported incidence rates of work-related sexual harassment in the United States: Using meta-analysis to explain reported rate disparities. *Personnel Psychology, 56,* 607–631.

Integrated Regional Information Networks (IRIN). (2009, June 26). *Mauritania: Force-feeding on decline, but more dangerous.* http://www.unhcr.org/refworld /docid/4a4885d540.html

Iyengar, S. S., Wells, R. E., & Schwartz, B. (2006). Doing better but feeling worse: Looking for the "best" job undermines satisfaction. *Psychological Science, 17*(2), 143–150.

Kane, R. L., Johnson, P. E., Town, R. J., & Butler, M. (2004). A structured review of the effect of economic incentives on consumers' preventive behavior. *American Journal of Preventive Medicine, 27*(4), 327–352.

Kanfer, R., Wanberg, C. R., & Kantrowitz, T. M.. (2001). Job search and employment: A personality–motivational analysis and meta-analytic review. *Journal of Applied Psychology, 86*(5), 837–855.

Keesey, R. E., & Powley, T. L. (1986). The regulation of body weight. *Annual Review of Psychology, 37,* 109–133.

Kenrick, D. T., Gutierres, S. E., & Goldberg, L. L. (1989). Influence of popular erotica on judgments of strangers and mates. *Journal of Experimental and Social Psychology, 25,* 159–167.

Kenrick, D. T., & Keefe, R. C. (1992). Age preferences in mates reflect sex differences in reproductive strategies. *Behavioral and Brain Sciences, 15,* 75–133.

Keys, A., Fidanza, F., Karvonen, M. J., Kimura, N., & Taylor, H. L. (1972). Indices of relative weight and obesity. *Journal of Chronic Disease, 25*(6), 329–343.

Kinsey, A. C., Pomeroy, W. B., & Martin, C. E. (1948). *Sexual behavior in the human male.* Philadelphia: Saunders.

Kinsey, A. C., Pomeroy, W. B., Martin, C. E., & Gebhard, P. H. (1953). *Sexual behavior in the human female.* Philadelphia: Saunders.

Korsgaard, M. A., Schweiger, D. M., & Sapienza, H. J. (1995). Building commitment, attachment, and trust in strategic decision-making teams: The role of procedural justice. *Academy of Management Journal, 38*(1), 60–84.

Kozlowski, S. W. J., & Bell, B. S. (2003). Work groups and teams in organizations. In W. C. Borman, D. R. Ilgen, & R. J. Klimoski (Eds.), *Handbook of psychology (Vol. 12): Industrial and organizational psychology* (pp. 333–375). New York: Wiley.

Kral, J. G. (1985). Morbid obesity and related health risks. *Annals of Internal Medicine, 103*(6), 1043–1104.

Kross, E., Berman M. G., Mischel, W., Smith, E. E., & Wager, T. D. (2010). Social rejection shares somatosensory representations with physical pain. *Proceedings of the National Academy of Sciences, 108*(15), 6270–6275.

Ladson-Billings, G. (2006). From the achievement gap to the education debt: Understanding achievement in U.S. schools. *Educational Research, 35*(7), 3–12.

Landy, F. J., & Farr, J. L. (1980). Performance rating. *Psychological Bulletin, 87*(1), 72–107.

Långström, N., Rahman, Q., Carlström, E., & Lichtenstein, P. (2008). Genetic and environmental effects on same-sex sexual behavior: A population study of twins in Sweden. *Archives of Sexual Behavior, 39*(1), 75–80.

Lee, J.-S., & Bowen, N. K. (2006). Parental involvement, cultural capital and the achievement gap among elementary school children. *American Educational Research Journal, 43*(2), 193–218.

Leibel, R. L., Rosenbaum, M., & Hirsch, J. (1995). Changes in energy expenditure resulting from altered body weight. *New England Journal of Medicine, 332,* 621–628.

Lepper, M. R., Greene, D., & Nisbett, R. E. (1973). Undermining children's intrinsic interest with extrinsic reward: A test of the "overjustification hypothesis." *Journal of Personality and Social Psychology, 28*(1), 129–137.

LeVay, S. (1991). A difference in hypothalamic structure between heterosexual and homosexual men. *Science, 253*(5023), 1034–1037.

Lichtman, S. W., Pisarska, K., Berman, E. R., Pestone, M., Dowling, H., Offenbacher, E., Weisel, H., Heshka, S., Matthews, D. E., & Heymsfield, S. B. (1992). Discrepancy between self-reported and actual caloric intake and exercise in obese subjects. *New England Journal of Medicine, 327*(27), 1893–1898.

Losada, M., & Heaphy, E. (2004). The role of positivity and connectivity in the performance of business teams—A nonlinear dynamics model. *American Behavioral Scientist, 47,* 740–765.

Lumeng, J. C., Forrest, P., Appugliese, D. P., Kaciroti, N., Corwyn, R. F., & Bradley, R. H. (2010). Weight status as a predictor of being bullied in third through sixth grades. *Pediatrics, 125*(6), e1301–e1307.

Lynness, K. S., & Thompson, D. E. (1997). Above the glass ceiling? A comparison of matched samples of female and male executives. *Journal of Applied Psychology, 82*(3), 359–375.

Maffei, M., Halaas, J., Ravussin, E., Praley, R. E., Lee, G. H., Zhang, Y., Fei, H., Kinm, S., Lallone, R., & Ranganathan, S. (1995). Leptin levels in human and rodent: Measurement of plasma leptin and ob RNA in obese and weight-reduced subjects. *Nature Medicine, 11,* 1155–1161.

Mah, K., & Binik, Y. M. (2005). Are orgasms in the mind or the body? Psychosocial versus physiological correlates of orgasmic pleasure and satisfaction. *Journal of Sex & Marital Therapy, 31,* 187–200.

Manson, J. E., Willett, W. C., Stampfer, M. J., Colditz, G. A., Hunter, D. J., Hankinson, S. E., Hennekens, C. H., & Speizer, F. E. (1995). Body weight and mortality among women. *New England Journal of Medicine, 333*(11), 677–685.

Marlowe, C. M., Schneider, S. L., & Nelson, C. E. (1996). Gender and attractiveness biases in hiring decisions: Are more experienced managers less biased? *Journal of Applied Psychology, 81*(1), 11–21.

Marmaros, D., & Sacerdote, B. (2006). How do friendships form? *Quarterly Journal of Economics, 121*(1), 79–119.

Maslach, C., Wilmar, B., Schaufeli, W. B., & Leiter, M. P. (2001). Job burnout. *Annual Review of Psychology, 52,* 397–422.

Maslow, A. H. (1943). A theory of human motivation. *Psychological Review, 50*(4), 370–396.

Maslow, A. H. (1970). *Motivation and personality* (2nd Ed.). New York: Harper & Row.

Masters, W. H., & Johnson, V. E. (1966). *Human sexual response.* Oxford, UK: Little, Brown.

Mayo, E. (1933). *The human problems of industrial civilization.* New York: Macmillan.

McClelland, D. C., Atkinson, J. W., Clark, R. A., & Lowell, E. L. (1953). *The achievement motive.* New York: Appleton-Century.

McClelland, D. C., Atkinson, J. W., Clark, R. A., & Lowell, E. L. (1976). *The achievement motive.* Oxford, UK: Irvington.

McCormick, E. J., Jeanneret, P. R., & Mecham, R. C. (1972). A study of job characteristics and job dimensions as based on the position analysis questionnaire (PAQ) [Monograph]. *Journal of Applied Psychology, 56,* 347–368.

Meston, C. M., & Frohlich, P. F. (2000). The neurobiology of sexual function. *Archives of General Psychiatry, 57,* 1012–1030.

Meyer-Bahlburg, H. F. L., Ehrhardt, A. A., Rosen, L. R., Gruen, R. S., Veridiano, N. P., Vann, F. H., & Neuwalder, H. F. (1995). Prenatal estrogens and the development of homosexual orientation. *Developmental Psychology, Special issue: Sexual Orientation and Human Development, 31*(1), 12–21.

Mischel, W., Ebbesen, E. B., & Raskoff Zeiss, A. (1972). Cognitive and attentional mechanisms in delay of gratification. *Journal of Personality and Social Psychology, 21*(2), 204–218.

Morewedge, C. K., Huh, Y. E., & Vosgerau, J. (2010). Thought for food: Imagined consumption reduces actual consumption. *Science, 330*(6010), 1530–1533.

Morgan, C. D., & Murray, H. A. (1935). A method for investigating fantasies. *Archives of Neurology and Psychiatry, 34,* 289–306.

Murphy, G. (1947). *Personality: A biosocial approach to origins and structures.* New York: Harper.

Murray, H. A. (1938). *Explorations in personality.* New York: Oxford University Press.

National Business Group on Health (15th Annual) and the Towers Watson. (2010). *Survey on Purchasing Value in Health Care, with 507 employers of 1,000 or more employees that collectively employ 11.5 million workers.* http://www.businessgrouphealth.org/pressrelease.cfm?ID=151

NIH, NHLBI Obesity Education Initiative. (1998). *Clinical guidelines on the identification, evaluation, and treatment of overweight and obesity in adults.* http://www.nhlbi.nih.gov/guidelines/obesity/ob_gdlns.pdf

Nisbett, R. E. (1987). Lay personality theory: Its nature, origin, and utility. In N. E. Grunberg, R. E. Nisbett, J. Singer (Eds.), *A distinctive approach to psychological research: The influence of Stanley Schacter* (pp. 87–117). Hillsdale, NJ: Erlbaum.

Oishi, S., Diener, E. F., Lucas, R. E., & Suh, E. M. (1999). Cross-cultural variations in predictors of life satisfaction: Perspectives from needs and values. *Personality and Social Psychology Bulletin, 25*(8), 980–990.

Parker, S., Nichter, M., Nichte, M., Vuckovic, N., Sims, C., & Ritenbaugh, C. (1995). Body image and weight concerns among African American and White adolescent females: Differences that make a difference. *Human Organization, 54*(2), 103–114.

Pecina, S., Cagniard, B., Berridge, K. C., Aldridge, J. W., & Zhuang, X. (2003). Hyperdopaminergic mutant mice have higher "wanting" but not "liking" for sweet rewards. *Journal of Neuroscience, 23*(28), 9395–9402.

Peplau, L. A. (2003). Human sexuality: How do men and women differ? *Psychological Science, 12*(2), 37–40.

Pierloot, R. A., & Houben, M. E. (1978). Estimation of body dimensions in anorexia nervosa. *Psychological Medicine, 8,* 317–324.

Pillard, R. C., & Bailey, J. M. (1998). Human sexual orientation has a heritable component. *Human Biology, 70*(2), 347–365.

Pingitore, R., Dugoni, B. L., Tindale, R. S., & Spring, B. (1994). Bias against overweight job applicants in a simulated employment interview. *Journal of Applied Psychology, 79*(6), 909–917.

Pink, D. H. (2009). *Drive: The surprising truth about what motivates us.* New York: Riverhead Books.

Poundstone, W. (2004). *How would you move Mount Fuji?: Microsoft's cult of the puzzle—How the world's smartest companies select the most creative thinkers.* New York: Little, Brown.

Premack, S. L., & Wanous, J. P. (1985). A meta-analysis of realistic job preview experiments. *Journal of Applied Psychology, 70*(4), 706–719.

Pull, C. B. (2004). Binge eating disorder. *Current Opinion in Psychiatry, 17*(1), 43–48.

Ramsey, G. V. (1943). The sexual development of boys. *American Journal of Psychology, 56*(2), 217–233.

Rhoads, R. A. (1995). Learning from the coming-out experiences of college males. *Journal of College Student Development, 36*(1), 67–74.

Rochlin, M. (1982). *The language of sex: The heterosexual questionnaire, Changing Men.* Waterloo, ON: University of Waterloo.

Roehling, M. V., Roehling, P. V., & Pichler, S. (2007). The relationship between body weight and perceived weight-related employment discrimination: The role of sex and race. *Journal of Vocational Behavior, 71*(2), 300–318.

Roethlisberger, F. J., & Dickson, W. J. (1939). *Management and the worker: An account of a research program conducted by the Western Electric Company, Hawthorne Works, Chicago.* Cambridge, MA: Harvard University Press.

Rogers, C. R. (1951). *Client-centered therapy: Its current practice, implications, and theory.* Oxford, England: Houghton Mifflin.

Rolls, B. J., Rolls, E. T., Rowe, E. A., & Sweeney, K. (1981). Sensory specific satiety in man. *Physiology & Behavior, 27*(1), 137–142.

Rose, G. A., & Williams, R. T. (1961). Metabolic studies of large and small eaters. *British Journal of Nutrition, 15,* 1–9.

Ryan, R. M., Mims, V., & Koestner, R. (1983). Relation of reward contingency and interpersonal context to intrinsic motivation: A review and test using cognitive evaluation theory. *Journal of Personality and Social Psychology, 45*(4), 736–750.

Saris, W. H. M., Blair, S. N., Van Baak, M. A., Eaton, S. B., Davies, P. S. W., Di Pietro, L., Fogelholm, M., Rissanen, A., Schoeller, D., Swinburn, B., Tremblay, A., Westerterp, K. R., & Wyatt, H. (2003). How much physical activity is enough to prevent unhealthy weight gain? Outcome of the IASO 1st Stock Conference and consensus statement. *Obesity Reviews, 4,* S101–S114.

Savic, I., & Lindstrom, P. (2008). PET and MRI show differences in cerebral asymmetry and functional connectivity between homo- and heterosexual subjects. *Proceedings of the National Academy of Sciences of the United States of America, 105*(27), 9403–9408.

Schmidt, F. L., & Hunter, J. E. (1998). The validity and utility of selection methods in personnel psychology: Practical and theoretical implications of 85 years of research findings. *Psychological Bulletin, 124*(2), 262–274.

Schuler, H., Farr, J. L., & Smith, M. (1993). *Personnel selection and assessment: Individual and organizational perspectives.* Hillsdale, NJ: Erlbaum.

Schutz, W. C. (1955). What makes groups productive? *Human Relations, 8,* 429–465.

Schwartz, M. W., Woods, S. C., Porte, D. Jr., Seeley, R. J., & Baskin, D. G. (2000). Central nervous system control of food intake. *Nature, 404*(6778), 661–671.

Silverman, J. A. (1983). Richard Morton, 1637–1698, limner of anorexia nervosa: His life and times, a tercentenary essay. *Journal of the American Medical Association, 250*(20), 2830–2832.

Singh, D. (1993). Adaptive significance of waist-to-hip ratio and female physical attractiveness. *Journal of Personality and Social Psychology, 65,* 293–307.

Singh, D. (1994). Is thin really beautiful and good? Relationship between waist-to-hip ratio (WHR) and female attractiveness. *Personality & Individual Differences, 16*(1), 123–132.

Spitzer, L., & Rodin, J. (1981). Human eating behavior: A critical review of studies in normal and overweight individuals. *Appetite, 2,* 293–329.

Stirling, L. J., & Yeomans, M. R. (2004). Effect of exposure to a forbidden food on eating in restrained and unrestrained women. *International Journal of Eating Disorders, 35*(1), 59–68.

Stoll, M. A., Raphael, S., & Holzer, H. J. (2004). Black job applicants and the hiring officer's race. *Industrial and Labor Relations Review, 57*(2), 267–287.

Striegel-Moore, R. H., & Bulik, C. M. (2007). Risk factors for eating disorders. American Psychologist, *Special Issue: Eating Disorders, 62*(3), 181–198.

Stunkard, A. J., Harris, J. R., Pedersen, J. L., & McClearn, G. E. (1990). The body-mass index of twins who have been reared apart. *New England Journal of Medicine, 332,* 1483–1487.

Sue, S., & Okazaki, S. (1990). Asian-American educational achievements: A phenomenon in search of an explanation. *American Psychologist, 45*(8), 913–920.

Suls, J., Martin, R., & Wheeler, L. (2002). Social comparison: Why, with whom, and with what effect? *Current Directions in Psychological Science, 11*(5), 159–163.

Sumithran, P., Prendergast, L. A., Delbridge, E., Purcell, K., Shulkes, A., Kriketos, A., & Proietto, J. (2011). Long-term persistence of hormonal adaptations to weight loss. *New England Journal of Medicine, 365,* 1597–1604.

Taylor, L. C., Clayton, J. D., Rowley, S. J. (2004). Academic socialization: Understanding parental influences on children's school-related development in the early years. *Review of General Psychology, 8*(3), 163–178.

Teitelbaum, P., & Epstein, A. N. (1962). The lateral hypothalamus syndrome: Recovery of feeding and drinking after lateral hypothalamic lesions. *Psychological Review, 69*(2), 74–79.

Teixeira, P. J., Going, S. B., Houtkooper, L. B., Cussler, E. C., Metcalfe, L. L., Blew, R. M., Sardinha, L. B., & Lohman, T. G. (2006). Exercise motivation, eating, and body image variables as predictors of weight control. *Medicine & Science in Sports & Exercise: Applied Sciences: Psychobiology and Behavioral Strategies, 38*(1), 179–188.

Twenge, J. M. (2006). *Generation "Me:" Why today's young Americans are more confident, assertive, entitled—and more miserable than ever before.* New York: Free Press.

Valian, V. (1999). *Why so slow? The advancement of women.* Cambridge: MIT Press.

Wansink, B. (2004). Environmental factors that increase the food intake and consumption volume of unknowing consumers. *Annual Review of Nutrition, 24,* 455–479.

Wansink, B., & Sobel, J. (2007). Mindless eating: The 200 daily food decisions we overlook. *Environment and Behavior, 39*(1), 106–123.

Webb, T. L., & Sheeran, P. (2006). Does changing behavioral intentions engender behavior change? A meta-analysis of the experimental evidence. *Psychological Bulletin, 132*(2), 249–268.

Weiner, B. (1972). *Theories of motivation: From mechanism to cognition.* Oxford, UK: Markham.

Weinsier, R. L., Nagy, T. R., Hunter, G. R., Darnell, B. E., Hensrud, D. D., & Weiss, H. L. (2000). Do adaptive changes in metabolic rate favor weight regain in weight-reduced individuals? An examination of the set-point theory. *American Journal of Clinical Nutrition, 72*(5), 1088–1094.

Williamson, I., & Hartley, P. (1998). British research into the increased vulnerability of young gay men to eating disturbance and body dissatisfaction. *European Eating Disorders Review, 6*(3), 160–170.

Wing, R. R., & Hill, J. O. (1994). Successful weight loss maintenance. *Annual Review of Nutrition, 21,* 323–341.

Wrzesniewski, A., McCauley, C., Rozin, P., & Schwartz, B. (1997). Jobs, careers, and callings: People's relations to their work. *Journal of Research in Personality, 31,* 21–33.

Wyrwicka, W., & Dobrzecka, C. (1960). Relationship between feeding and satiation centers of the hypothalamus. *Science, 132,* 805–806.

Yeung, R. R. (1996). The acute effects of exercise on mood state. *Journal of Psychosomatic Research, 40*(2), 123–141.

Yukl, G., & Van Fleet, D. D. (1992). Theory and research on leadership in organizations. In M. Dunnette & L. Hough (Eds.), *Handbook of I/O psychology* (Vol. 3, pp. 147–198). Palo Alto, CA: Consulting Psychologists Press.

Chapter Overview ▼

11 Emotion, Stress, and Health

wack! Thud! Plonk! Bam! Crash! Those were the sounds I heard at 3 a.m. My first groggy thought was a grumpy, "What's Bailey knocked over this time?!" I always thought cats were supposed to be stealthy, but mine didn't get that memo, especially Bailey, who seems to intentionally topple mugs and flick pens onto the floor in order to get my attention. But this crash was different. This crash grabbed my attention and shook most of the house. I opened my eyes and I saw both my cats, Barnum and Bailey, on the bed. I looked at them; they looked at me. Then, as we all realized at the same time that it must be something else, they darted from the bedroom as I stumbled to the front of the house.

What I saw through the window stopped me in my tracks. A man with a bat in his hand was slamming his body against the screen door to my front porch. He had already torn off the screen and moved his attention to the door. I didn't know what to do: Save the cats, scare away the intruder, call the police, cry? Then, for a brief second, I caught the invader's eye. I gave my most menacing grimace and he fled.

I was simultaneously terrified and angry as I called the police. When the police arrived about 20 minutes later, I was still shaking. Unless you count my recent ride on the Daredevil roller coaster, it was the most frightened I can remember being. I was exhausted. It was 5:30 a.m. and in an hour I needed to leave for work, but I was drained and wanted to go back to sleep. I had experienced a flood of emotions that had swept over me, leaving me exhausted.

What are emotions and where do they come from? Many emotions are linked to stress. What are the effects of stress on your body? What explains where I found the strength to try to protect my cats and house instead of cowering under the covers?

When thinking about emotions, it's important to consider the vast array of experiences that are part of emotion. We think of an emotion as a feeling, but really it's more than that. Emotion is a class of subjective reactions brought on by an event, including four types: physiological (my heart beat faster when I saw the intruder), behavioral (I ran to the door and scowled at the intruder), cognitive (I perceived the noise as harmless at first, and then dangerous), and affective (I was afraid).

Emotion A class of subjective feelings elicited by stimuli that have high significance to an individual.

Fight-or-flight response A reaction to danger in which the sympathetic nervous system prepares the organs for vigorous activity.

11.1 The Role of Physiology and Evolution in Emotion

Biological processes are involved in emotion.

- Define how bodily processes are involved in emotion.
- Define how physiological processes are involved in emotion.
- Discuss the evolutionary basis of emotion.

The Role of Physiology in Emotion

There are many physiological reactions that occur with emotions. Your sympathetic nervous system prepares you to fight, freeze, or flee. This **fight-or-flight response**

FIGURE 11-1 is a reaction to danger in which the sympathetic nervous system prepares the organs for vigorous activity. Once stimulated, your autonomic nervous system signals the adrenal glands to release stress hormones like **corticosteroids**, which are hormones produced in the adrenal cortex in reaction to stress, and **catecholamines**, which are stress hormones released by the adrenal glands FIGURE 11-2. Your muscles tense, blood pressure increases, heart rate quickens, endorphins release. In this state, your pupils dilate, your attention focuses, and your digestive functioning slows to a crawl (which explains butterflies in the stomach).

Corticosteroids
Hormones produced in the adrenal cortex in reaction to stress.

Catecholamines Stress hormones released by the adrenal glands.

Yerkes Dodson law
A theory that performance is best at medium levels of arousal.

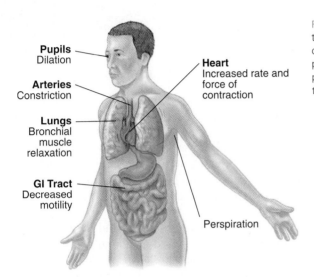

Pupils Dilation

Arteries Constriction

Lungs Bronchial muscle relaxation

GI Tract Decreased motility

Heart Increased rate and force of contraction

Perspiration

FIGURE 11-1 Stress can activate the hypothalamus, which can cause increased heart rate, perspiration, and dilation of pupils. This is the first stage of the stress response: alarm.

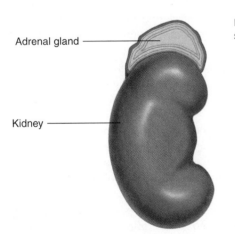

Adrenal gland

Kidney

FIGURE 11-2 The adrenal glands sit on top of the kidneys.

When the parasympathetic nervous system takes over, things slow down. You may feel sleepy or relaxed after an anxiety-producing situation. The parasympathetic nervous system helps you to recover, digest, and rest.

Is arousal always bad? Not really. A little bit of stress or arousal can be helpful. According to the **Yerkes Dodson law**, optimal levels of arousal may be helpful, while too little arousal can be problematic. For example, during an exam, being sleepy can be a problem, on the other hand, too much arousal can lead to test anxiety and cause you to freeze up. As you can see in FIGURE 11-3, the Yerkes Dodson law looks like an upside down U, with optimal outcomes occurring at moderate levels of arousal for most behaviors (Teigen, 1994). However, the more complicated a behavior, the lower the best arousal level. This is also true for new behaviors or ones that require careful judgment or creativity. If you are playing chess, you might need complete silence and zero distractions. On the other hand, simple, instinctual, and well-rehearsed tasks, like washing the dishes or folding laundry, might have higher optimal arousal levels.

Dilated pupils are a sign of the fight-or-flight response.

FIGURE 11-3 According to the Yerkes Dodson law, optimal levels of arousal occur in the moderate range.

Activities such as video games may have a high level of optimal arousal.

Polygraph A machine that uses physiological measurements to detect lies.

Galvanic skin response (GSR) A measurement of the conductivity of your skin.

Anthropomorphism Assigning human emotions or behaviors to nonhumans.

The Yerkes Dodson law may explain why you can do so well playing video games with music blaring and sensory overload coming from the screen and your friends screaming "Jump! Jump!" at you. Each person has a level of arousal that works best for her or him—an optimal level of arousal. Too much arousal causes problems, and too little leaves you disengaged.

Knowing the physiological elements of emotions and the nervous system can be handy. One way that this knowledge is used is in a **polygraph**, a machine that uses biological measurement to detect lies FIGURE 11-4. From *poly*, meaning many, and *graph*, meaning write, a polygraph will test autonomic nervous system arousal in multiple ways including pulse, blood pressure, breathing, fidgeting, and **galvanic skin response (GSR)**, which is a measurement of the conductivity of your skin. Why skin conductivity? Well, when you have a sympathetic nervous system spike, the tips of your fingers begin to release tiny beads of sweat. This sweat makes your skin more conductive, and electricity can pass along the skin more quickly. These sweat glands are activated by the sympathetic nervous system and deactivated by the parasympathetic nervous system. Because of this relationship, skin conductivity is a handy measure of your stress response.

One idea behind the polygraph is that lies produce different stress patterns from nondeceptive responses. Polygraphs assume that lying leaves distinctive physiological cues. Once a baseline of arousal is established by answering a series of questions, the polygrapher will ask questions and look for spikes of sympathetic nervous system activity.

An alternative way to use a polygraph is the guilty knowledge test (GKT). A GKT is used to determine if the subject has "guilty knowledge" about a situation, such as a crime. In the guilty knowledge test, the subject is asked about key elements of a case, knowledge that only someone that knows intimate details of the case would know. People tend to respond physiologically to things that are familiar, so the autonomic nervous system will answer the questions for them. The polygrapher will ask a series of multiple-choice questions and look for sympathetic nervous system reactions to the correct answer, which indicate guilty knowledge of the situation. For example, a polygrapher might say "The gun was left on the desk. The gun was left on the floor. The gun was left in the bathroom. The gun was left under the bed." If the gun was left under the bed and the subject knows that, the polygrapher would notice a sympathetic nervous system reaction when he or she read that question.

The use of polygraphs is controversial and admissible in court in a minority of states in the United States. There are arguments about the validity of the tests in the scientific community, with some experts suggesting that the

FIGURE 11-4 A polygraph uses physiological measurement to detect lies.

tests are accurate (Grubin, 2010), while others suggest that the science behind the tests is weak (National Research Council, 2003).

The Role of Evolution in Emotion

Evolution suggests that certain traits are more likely to be passed along if they make reproduction or survival more likely. If you know about this theory, you may not be surprised to learn that Charles Darwin FIGURE 11-5 had a theory that emotions were evolved behaviors. In his classic text, *The Expression of Emotions in Man and Animals* FIGURE 11-6 (Darwin, 2009; Feinstein, Adolphs, Damasio, & Tranel, 2011), Darwin suggested that emotions were innate and evolved adaptive responses. People who had the ability to create and understand the emotions on the faces of others had a reproductive advantage because they can, for example, instill fear or anticipate aggression.

Look at the photos in FIGURE 11-7. Can you tell what emotions these animals are experiencing? Bared teeth might represent anger. Dogs growl and bare their teeth. Cats hiss and bare their teeth. You may have even bared your teeth in anger at a driver who cut you off in traffic. Showing your teeth is a way of communicating, "See these teeth? I could bite you with them!" Hopefully it won't come to biting, but animals that can communicate and understand nonverbal signals are at an advantage. However, seeing emotional expressions in the faces of nonhuman animals can easily lead to **anthropomorphism**, assigning human emotions or behaviors to nonhumans. Thinking that golden retrievers and dolphins are cheerful because their faces look like they are smiling or that King Charles spaniels have a yearning sadness because they have huge pools of eyes may say more about humans than it does about the animals. Anthropomorphism may also explain why I describe my cat Bailey as manipulative because of his pen-flicking behavior.

FIGURE 11-5 Charles Darwin had a theory that emotions were evolved behaviors.

FIGURE 11-6 "Fear" from Charles Darwin's *The Expression of Emotions in Man and Animals* (1872).

FIGURE 11-7 Can you tell what emotions these animals are experiencing?

CONCEPT LEARNING CHECK 11.1 | *Bodily Processes and Emotion*

Match the term to the situation or statement that explains it.

A. Fight-or-flight response

B. Galvanic skin response

C. Anthropomorphism

D. Yerkes Dodson law

1. _____ It is really hard to concentrate on studying neuroscience when I have had too much caffeine.

2. _____ We think that dolphins look happy because they look like they are smiling.

3. _____ After my friends yelled "SURPRISE!," I noticed my heart was racing.

4. _____ Carol attached small pads to the fingertips of the suspect in order to measure conductivity.

5. _____ A physiological process that might cause us to freeze when we are confronted with danger.

Explain

6. Explain, using the Yerkes Dodson law, why it might be easier to clean your room when it's noisy in your house than when it's quiet.

Showing your teeth is a way your face expresses anger.

Doesn't this horse look happy? Anthropomorphism refers to assigning human emotions or behaviors to nonhumans.

11.2 The Role of Behavior and Cognition in Emotion

Thoughts and behaviors can have an impact on emotion.

- Explain the impact that thoughts and behaviors have on emotion.
- Explain the connection between behavior and emotion.

Your emotional experience is made up of more than physiological reactions. How you interpret those reactions also influences how you feel. For example, people who tend toward **catastrophic thinking** will distort the scale and impact of a stressful event and may interpret an event as more threatening than others would. Indeed, our emotional experience incorporates our evaluation of an event.

But can you have an emotional response that isn't prompted by a thought? Absolutely. Robert Zajonc (pronounced ZI-yence; rhymes with science; Zajonc, 1980) suggested that thoughts and emotional responses are not always tied together. Sometimes you can have an emotional response without a thought tied to it. One morning, while at the beach, I was enjoying breakfast and reading the newspaper. In the background, I heard a song and started to feel very, very sad. I had no idea why. Later on when I was headed to the shore, it hit me: That was the song I played to soothe my dog when he was very sick. Since then, I'd never been able to hear that song without feeling very sad. In this case, the sadness was linked to the song, but there was no thought that accompanied it.

Why is this so? There are multiple influences on how emotions are processed. Some emotions are the result of a neural shortcut. Rather than being processed in the cortex, visual and auditory sensations can hop on neural pathways from your eyes and ears to the **amygdala**, a cluster of neurons in the temporal lobe linked to emotions such as anger and fear FIGURE 11-8. This means that things you see or hear can activate the amygdala. The amygdala, in turn, can influence your thoughts and feelings (LeDoux, 1998). This gives biological support to the idea that thoughts and simple feelings can sometimes be disconnected.

The Role of Behavior in Emotion

Your friend returns from class and you know instantly that she's had a bad day. How do you know? You can tell by the look on her face. Facial expressions send social signals.

People don't usually express their emotion in facial expressions unless others are around (Buck, Losow, Murphy & Costanzo, 1992). Facial expressions convey different

FIGURE 11-8 Some emotions take a shortcut and pass from the eyes and ears directly to the amygdala.

meanings depending on the circumstances. People often use facial expressions to lie about their feelings as well as to express them.

Darwin suggested that facial expressions were evolved behaviors to communicate information. For this to be true, other people have to be able to recognize those facial expressions. To test this theory, Paul Ekman FIGURE 11-9; (Ekman, Friesen, O'Sullivan, & Chan, et al., 1987) showed photographs of people displaying emotions. He took these photographs (like the ones in FIGURE 11-10) to several countries: Argentina, Brazil,

FIGURE 11-9 Paul Ekman researched basic emotions.

FIGURE 11-10 Ekman used photos like these in his research.

Catastrophic thinking A cognitive distortion of the scale and impact of a stressful event.

Amygdala A cluster of neurons in the temporal lobe linked to emotions such as anger and fear.

Chile, Japan, New Guinea, and the United States. He discovered that people from those countries were pretty good at recognizing the emotions of anger, fear, disgust, happiness, sadness, and surprise. Because they are thought to be universally expressed, anger, fear, disgust, happiness, sadness, and surprise are known as **basic emotions**—feeling states thought to be expressed in a common way. In fact, many of these facial expressions occur in children blind from birth (Galati, Miceli, & Sini, 2001). Since then, Ekman and others have proposed additional nominees for basic emotions, as you can see listed in **TABLE 11-1** (Ekman, 1999).

Facial expressions do vary a bit from culture to culture (Mesquita & Frijda, 1992), which could explain why people are better at identifying emotional expression from faces from their own culture than those of people from other cultures FIGURE 11-11.

Basic emotions Feeling states that are thought to be expressed in a universal way.

Facial feedback hypothesis A theory that suggests that the position of the facial muscles influences emotional expression.

Facial Feedback and Emotion

While some researchers debated about which came first, the emotion or the physiological response, others debated what seemed like an obvious order—the emotion or the facial expression. After all, aren't facial expressions just a reaction to your emotions? Well, the **facial feedback hypothesis** suggests that an emotion is regulated, in part, by the feedback

Facial expressions can also send social signals.

TABLE 11-1 Additional Basic Emotions

| Amusement |
| Contempt |
| Contentment |
| Embarrassment |
| Excitement |
| Guilt |
| Pride in achievement |
| Relief |
| Satisfaction |
| Sensory pleasure |
| Shame |

Source: Adapted from T. Dalgleish, & M. J. Power (Eds.), Handbook of cognition and emotion (pp. 45–60). New York: John Wiley & Sons Ltd.

FIGURE 11-11 Percent of people from different countries who were able to correctly identify facial expressions. *Source: Adapted from Ekman, P., & Friesen, W. V. (2003). Unmasking the Face: A Guide to Recognizing Emotions From Facial Expressions. Malor Books.*

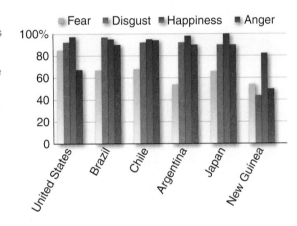

your brain gets from the way your face is arranged (Kraut, 1982). This would mean that frowning can make you sad and smiling can make you feel happy.

According to facial feedback, the way you hold your face can produce emotions. You are sad because you cry. To test this hypothesis, researchers (Strack, Martin, & Stepper, 1988) asked participants to look at cartoons while holding a pen in one of three positions: between their teeth, between their lips, or in their hand FIGURE 11-12. The idea was that holding a pen between your teeth forces you to smile and a frown results from lip holding. Those who were asked to hold the pen between their teeth rated the cartoons the funniest, and those who held the pen between their lips rated them the least funny.

Facial expressions of emotion are sometimes blunted when we are alone.

FIGURE 11-12 Holding a pencil between the teeth (A) forces a smile, while between the lips (B) produces a frown.

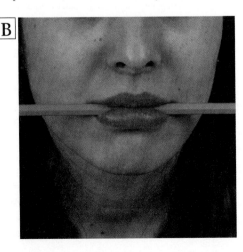

Some theorists suggest that facial feedback alone influences emotion. Other theories suggest that facial muscles act in a way to control blood flow to your brain. Smiles, the theory proposes, cool the brain, while frowns increase brain temperature (McIntosh, Peter, Stephen, & Emerick, 1997).

CONCEPT LEARNING CHECK 11.2 | *Behavior and Cognition and Emotion*

Indicate if the statement is true or false.

1. You can have an emotion without a thought.

2. The amygdala is a cluster of neurons linked to sadness.

3. Sensory signals can take a neural shortcut from the eyes to the brain in order to create emotions.

4. Thinking about things differently can impact emotions.

Fill in the blank with the correct term.

5. Children born without the ability to see will often smile when they are happy. Some researchers say that this is evidence that happiness is a _____ emotion.

6. The _____ suggests that smiling more can make you feel happier.

Explain

7. Some people use botulinum toxin to temporarily reduce the wrinkles in the face by making them unable to move some of their facial muscles. Explain the impact of this procedure on their emotional experience, according to the facial feedback hypothesis.

11.3 Theories of Emotion

Psychologists have various theories of emotion.

- Identify and discuss the main theories of emotion.

But which comes first—the thoughts, the physiological reactions, or the feelings? Or do they all flood in at the same time? Different theories of emotion offer different angles on how emotions arise. In general, theories will highlight the multiple influences of biology and sociocultural influences on emotion. The **biopsychosocial model** recognizes three equally important aspects of human mental processes and behaviors: biological (including brain chemistry), psychological (thoughts, emotions, and behaviors), and social (cultural and societal influences).

Common-Sense Theory

If you ask most people where emotions come from, you are likely to get a common description. Common sense might suggest that the perception of an event would elicit an emotion, which would then cause your body to react FIGURE 11-13. Thinking back to the story of the attempted break-in, this would mean that first I saw the intruder, then I recognized him as something dangerous, and finally I was afraid. That feeling set off the typical physiological fear response, such as a pounding heart and sweating.

James-Lange Peripheral Feedback Theory

The James-Lange theory of emotion, created by William James and Carl Lange (James, 1948), suggests exactly the opposite. According to the **James-Lange theory**, our emotional experience is really just an interpretation of the specific physiological recipe for that emotion: "We feel sad because we cry." As we experience that unique combination of biological events, we experience that emotional reaction. In other words, perception of a stimulus causes bodily arousal, which leads to an emotion FIGURE 11-14.

Biopsychosocial model
A theory that recognizes three equally important aspects of human mental processes and behaviors: biological (including brain chemistry), psychological (thoughts, emotions, and behaviors), and social (cultural and societal influences).

James-Lange theory
A concept of emotion that suggests that emotions are composed of our awareness of biological reactions to stimuli.

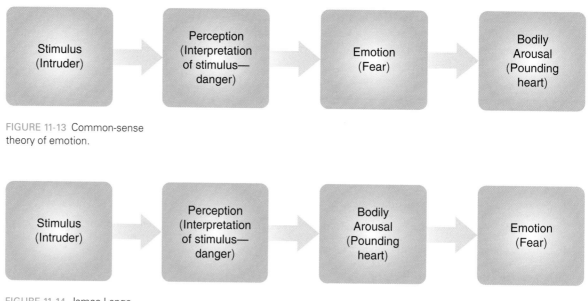

FIGURE 11-13 Common-sense theory of emotion.

FIGURE 11-14 James-Lange peripheral feedback theory.

This means that after seeing the intruder, I perceived him as something threatening. This perception generated a specific combination of body responses—an increase in blood pressure and heart rate, sweating—that was interpreted as fear. The experience of emotion is, according to this theory, an awareness of the physiological responses to emotion-arousing stimuli.

Cannon-Bard Simultaneous Trigger Theory

The James-Lange theory has one (huge) problem, according to physiologist Walter Cannon. If emotions were observations of unique bodily reactions, then that would mean you'd need a unique combination of physiological reactions for every emotion: one set of reactions for fear, one for sadness, one for love. The problem is that this doesn't seem to be the case—at least, not in any way we can measure. If you hook a person up to a machine that measures different physiological responses, like heart rate and blood pressure, it's hard to distinguish between the physiological responses that come with different emotions. Does a pounding heart mean the person is in love, or afraid, or excited, or angry? And what about emotion mash-ups, like when you are both frightened and angry at the same time? All that psychologists have been able to determine is a general level of sympathetic nervous system arousal. In fact, this general arousal was all the emotions seemed to have in common, according to some researchers (Cacioppo, Berntson, Klein, & Poehlmann, 1997). Perhaps physiological arousal and affect, or feelings, were two different components of emotions that arose simultaneously. That's the idea behind the Cannon-Bard theory of emotion.

Cannon-Bard theory
A theory of emotion that suggests that events cause emotions by triggering biological and psychological experience of emotions at the same time.

The **Cannon-Bard theory** of emotion suggests that perception of a stimulus causes bodily arousal and emotion at the same time. Emotion-arousing stimuli simultaneously trigger physiological responses and subjective experience of emotion FIGURE 11-15. This would mean that once I saw the intruder, two things happened at the same time: My heart started to race and I felt an emotional experience of fear.

Schacter-Singer Two-Factor Theory of Emotion

Schacter and Singer (1962) proposed a cognition-plus-feedback theory of emotion. They suggested that perceiving and thinking about a stimulus influence the kind of emotion that is felt. The degree of body arousal can also influence the intensity of the emotion. Schacter and Singer (1962) suggested that our bodily reaction (physiology) as well as our thoughts, influenced by our interpretations, previous experiences, and memories, create

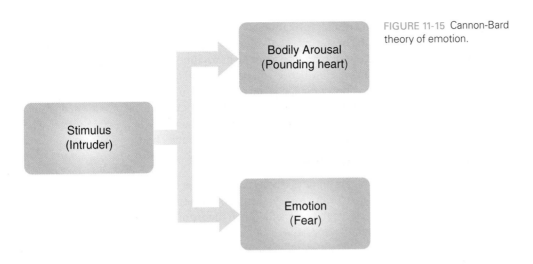

FIGURE 11-15 Cannon-Bard theory of emotion.

the emotion. Remember the story about the break-in? At first I heard the CRASH. Since my previous experience with crashes meant that my cat had knocked over something, my interpretation of that event didn't trigger the emotion of fear. In fact, my first reaction was anger since I thought the crash was Bailey's fault.

The **Schacter-Singer two-factor theory** of emotion suggests that feelings are a combination of bodily arousal and how we interpret that arousal. This theory suggests that all emotions are physiologically similar—basically just sympathetic nervous system arousal—and what distinguishes them is the label we place on that emotion. Emotion = arousal + labels FIGURE 11-16.

In 1962, Schacter and Singer attempted to test their two-factor theory of emotion. They created a fake vitamin called Suproxin that was supposed to improve vision. Suproxin was simply a shot of adrenalin that would have caused a temporary spike of blood pressure, heart rate, and breathing rate, with most of the effects subsiding in 10 to 15 minutes. Over several days, they brought nearly 200 subjects to their lab and randomly divided them into two groups. One group would be informed of the possible side effects of Suproxin. They were told that their hands might shake and their hearts might beat faster. The other group was not informed of any possible side effects; they were told only that the shot was harmless. After being informed (or not), the subjects were put in a variety of situations that might elicit emotion. For example, one group was subjected to an insulting and intrusively personal questionnaire. In that group was a member of the research team, disguised as a participant in the experiment, who was becoming increasingly agitated and vocal about how annoying the questionnaire was. The questions, too, became increasingly obnoxious, ending in, "With how many men (other than your father) has your mother had extra marital relationships? A. 4 and under; B. 5–9; C. 10 and over." You'll notice that the lowest number is "4 and under." By this time in the experiment, the disguised research team member sitting next to the study participant

Schacter-Singer two-factor theory A theory of emotion that suggests that feelings are a combination of body arousal and how we think about that arousal.

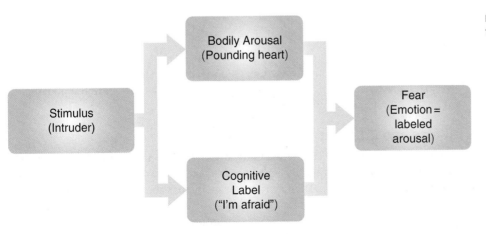

FIGURE 11-16 Schacter-Singer two-factor theory of emotion.

Disguised research team members faked anger to test the two-factor theory of emotion.

Cognitive-mediational theory of emotion
A theory that feelings are caused by what we think caused our thoughts.

rips up the questionnaire and storms out. Soon after, the participant is asked to rate how irritated or annoyed he or she felt. The "informed" group reported feeling less annoyed while the "uniformed" group reported feeling more annoyed. Why? Well, according to the Schacter-Singer two-factor theory, you need arousal and a label for emotion. While both groups were provided with adequate arousal, the informed group already had an explanation for their arousal—the side effects of the Suproxin. The uninformed group, on the other hand, was left to itself to surmise the source of their extra arousal. The uninformed group labeled its arousal as irritation from the obnoxious survey.

Cognitive-Mediational Theory of Emotion

Some emotion researchers emphasize physiological reactions, while others emphasize cognitive labels attached to emotions, and still others emphasize certain behaviors, such as facial expressions. The **cognitive-mediational theory of emotion** suggests that feelings are caused by our cognitive appraisal. Different cognitive appraisals explain why similar situations can create different emotions in different people. It may even explain why a situation may create the emotional mash-up of anger and fear that I felt during my porch invasion, since I had multiple explanations for my feelings. The cognitive-mediational theory also creates an intervention point. Changing your appraisal of the situation can change your emotion.

Lazarus (Lazarus, 1991b) suggested that cognitive appraisals could happen outside of awareness and without a thought, or a thought that occurs so quickly that you don't know you had it. Incidents can create situation–feeling pairings, so that when a situation happens again, the feeling is generated automatically. Remember the story about the song that suddenly made me sad? The music was paired to a sad situation, so now every time I hear it, I feel sad.

CONCEPT LEARNING CHECK 11.3 | *Theories of Emotion*

For each theory, identify the components.

1. James-Lange: Each emotion has a _____.

2. Cannon-Bard: This theory suggests that a stimulus that leads to emotions triggers both _____ and _____ at the same time.

3. Schacter and Singer: This theory suggests that emotion is caused by _____ plus a _____.

11.4 Expressing Emotion

Special factors and situations have the potential to influence how and when emotions are expressed.

■ Examine and explain the special factors and situations that can influence the expression of emotions.

You will recall that emotions involve four components: physiological, behavioral, cognitive, and affective. However, many special factors and situations have the potential to influence how and when emotions are expressed.

Culture and Emotion

Emotion is influenced by culture. Not only does culture determine what makes people feel angry, sad, lonely, happy, ashamed, or disgusted, it can also affect the behavioral component of the emotion. **Display rules** are guidelines about how you should express emotions. In some cultures, for example, it's considered impolite not to cover your mouth while you laugh FIGURE 11-17. Also, people in cultures that favor individualistic behavior are more comfortable with public displays of negative emotions, like anger (Matsumoto,

FIGURE 11-17 In some cultures, display rules suggest that it is polite to cover your mouth when you are laughing.

Yoo, & Fontaine, 2008). Individualistic cultures, like the United States, may have more instances of couples fighting in public, for example.

While growing up, we learn an emotional script that outlines how we are expected to behave and show emotion in different situations. These norms reflect not only how people react, but when.

Gender and Emotion

Display rules also govern how men and women express their emotions. Some suggest that men tend to show their feelings less often and less intensely (Plant, Hyde, Keltner, & Devine, 2000), except for power presentations like anger (LaFrance & Banaji, 1992). This doesn't, however, mean that men feel emotions less than women do. Women may report more emotions because of social and cultural norms of display rules (Grossman & Wood, 1993). Women may be more likely to pick up on emotional cues than men (Klein et al., 2004) and may score higher on tests of **emotional intelligence**, the capacity to understand and manage feelings.

Fear

Except for the occasional horror movie or haunted house, most of us don't like to experience fear. Fear is an emotion that lets us know that something dangerous is about to happen or is happening. Sometimes, we need to tolerate fear in order to get things done. However, what if nothing scared you—if you were immune to fear? What would happen if you could remove the part of your brain that's linked to the fear response? Would your life be better if you had no reaction to fear? That's what patient SM feels (or rather doesn't feel). Lesions and scars created by lipoid protenosis, also known as Urbach-Wiethe disease, destroyed her amygdala, and as a result she experiences no fear (Feinstein et al., 2011).

What's more, SM can't recognize fear in the faces of others. The part of the brain that's most involved in fear is the amygdala. The amygdala is the brain area most involved in the processing, memory, and emotional reactions to fear. It lights up on an MRI when you see something that makes you feel fearful. In fact, even thinking about something scary can trigger the amygdala. It seems that the brain areas that are responsible for our sensation of fear are also linked to our recognition of fear responses in others.

Anger and Aggression

Early views of anger regarded this emotion as a reaction to a goal blocked or unattained. Known as the **frustration-aggression hypothesis**, this theory suggests that **frustration** occurs when a goal is blocked and leads to anger and **aggression**, which are words or physical acts a person does to cause harm. A blocked goal, however, can produce more than just aggression. Embarrassment, guilt, and nervousness can all be reactions to a thwarted goal. What makes anger different? In anger, you see someone else as responsible for blocking your goal. Anger assumes that the other person had control over his or her actions, and, for some reason, acted without considering your needs. Lazarus (Lazarus, 1991a) defined anger as an emotional reaction to a perceived "demeaning offence against me and mine."

You may remember that anger is one of the basic six emotions. But anger is also governed by display rules. People who think that venting their anger is useful because it provides **catharsis** or releases pent-up emotions and prevents the anger from exploding are more likely to express their anger. The display rules for anger in their family may even encourage them to show their anger when they are frustrated. Research, unfortunately, doesn't support the theory that venting anger is healthy or useful. Venting anger actually makes people more angry rather than less (Lohr, Olatunji, Baumeister, & Bushman, 2007). While venting may make you feel a little better at first, in the long run it may make matters worse.

If venting your anger only makes it worse, what can you do? Sometimes the best thing you can do is to wait it out. Anger often passes if you don't feed it by rehearsing

Display rules Guidelines about how one should express emotions.

Emotional intelligence The capacity to understand and manage your own feelings as well as the feelings of others.

Frustration-aggression hypothesis Early theory of anger suggesting that anger is a reaction to a goal blocked or unattained.

Frustration Anxiety felt when attempts to reach a goal are hindered.

Aggression Words or physical acts a person does in order to cause harm.

Catharsis A release of pent-up emotions.

The amygdala regulates our own fear response and also helps us to recognize fear in the faces of others.

in your head or out loud to other people what made you angry. Exercising or listening to calming (not angry) music can also help. Once the anger dissipates a bit, it might be time to discuss what angered you. Controlled displays of anger can be more beneficial than the scorched-earth approach of hostile venting and retaliation (even though that may feel good at first).

Love

Love is an emotion featured in books, music, movies, poems . . . well, nearly everywhere. Love is a complex emotion and concept. Robert Sternberg (Sternberg, 1986) proposed what he called a **triangular theory of love** FIGURE 11-18. His theory suggested that all interpersonal relationships are composed of one or more of three components:

1. Intimacy: close feelings; sharing private and personal thoughts and emotions;
2. Passion: physical attraction; and
3. Commitment: a pledge to maintain the connection into the future.

These ingredients of relationships can be combined in different amounts to create eight different kinds of love, according to Sternberg.

1. Nonlove represents an absence of all three. Nonlove may describe how you feel about people you pass on the street or have no connection with.
2. Friendship/liking involves intimacy only, no commitment or passion. You may have close feelings and share important details about your life.
3. Infatuation involves passion only but lacks any sharing or commitment. Infatuation can burn bright and hot but can easily vanish.
4. Empty love involves commitment only, no passion and no intimacy. There is commitment to maintaining the relationship. When couples "stay together for the children" or a marriage is arranged for them, it can result in empty love.
5. Romantic love consists of intimacy and passion, but no commitment. Often a couple early in a relationship experiences romantic love before they have made a long-term commitment to each other.

> **Triangular theory of love** Sternberg's theory that relationships are composed of three components: intimacy, passion, commitment.

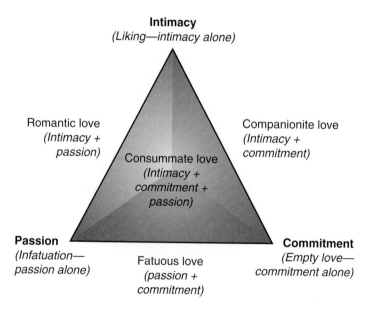

FIGURE 11-18 The triangular theory of love.

6. Companionate love consists of intimacy combined with commitment, without passion. Long-term best friends, family, and even couples for whom passion has faded are examples of companionate love.

7. Fatuous love involves passion and commitment but not intimacy. *Fatuous* (meaning foolish) suggests that the commitment without any intimacy is a problem with this kind of love. People who get married after knowing each other for only a few hours could be accused of fatuous love.

8. Consummate love is love that consists of all three forms: intimacy, passion, and commitment.

Neuropsychologists have something to say about love, too. Oxytocin, sometimes called the "cuddle chemical," is involved in attachment. Oxytocin is a pituitary hormone and is released during breastfeeding and sexual intercourse and may work as a physiological mark for empathy (Barraza & Zak, 2009). Other chemicals involved in love and passion include estrogen, testosterone, dopamine, and serotonin.

CONCEPT LEARNING CHECK 11.4 | *Expressing Emotion*

Match the components to the kind of love indicated.

A. Intimacy

B. Passion

C. Commitment

1. _____ Companionate

2. _____ Consummate

3. _____ Empty

4. _____ Fatuous

5. _____ Friendship

6. _____ Infatuation

7. _____ Nonlove

8. _____ Romantic

Explain

9. People who think that venting their anger is useful because it provides _____ or releases pent-up emotions and prevents the anger from exploding are more likely to express their anger.

10. Describe the research on venting anger and describe some alternative solutions.

11.5 Stress

Various factors lead to stress; stress has multiple effects.

- Examine the various factors that lead to stress.
- Discuss the physical and psychological effects of stress.

Stress A response that occurs from events seen as a challenge.

Stressors Anything perceived as a challenge.

Acute stressors Brief events that require a period of coping.

Chronic stressors Long-lasting events that require adaption.

Cope To reduce the impact of an event.

Stress is a response that occurs from events seen as a challenge (Lazarus & Folkman, 1984). We all have experienced stress when late for an appointment, during relationship problems, in quarreling with a roommate, or from lack of money. When studying stress, some psychologists emphasize exposure to events that are linked to the stress reaction, or **stressors**. Anything perceived as a challenge can be a stressor. Some stressors can be acute. **Acute stressors** are brief events that require a period of coping, like figuring out a new way to get to the airport because of road construction. **Chronic stressors** are long-lasting events that require you to adapt, such as starting college or adjusting to life in a new city.

What Is Stress?

"Stressed out," "freaking out"—these are some terms people use to describe how they feel when they question whether they can **cope**, meaning to reduce the impact of an event or handle what's in front of them. If you are stressed out over midterms, then you wonder if you can do all the things you need to do in order to be successful—read, organize your notes, and prepare for the exam. Psychologists have examined the components and implications of stress in our lives.

Sources of Stress

Researchers Holmes and Rahe realized that different stressors require different amounts of life change and coping (Holmes & Rahe, 1967). To measure the impact of life change, they created the Social Readjustment Rating Scale. The Holmes and Rahe Social Readjustment Rating Scale is a scale of stressful events. Different events such as the ones in TABLE 11-2

TABLE 11-2 Items from the Social Readjustment Rating Scale

Shown below are sample items from the Social Readjustment Rating Scale. Users of the complete scale simply add up the values for the listed life events that have occurred within the past year. Totals are categorized using specific ranges for: no significant problems, mild, moderate, or major life crisis.

Item	Life Event Value
Death of Spouse	100
Divorce	73
Death of close family member	63
Personal injury or illness	53
Marriage	50
Marital reconciliation	45
Pregnancy	40
Sex difficulties	39
Death of close friend	37
Begin or end school	26
Trouble with boss	23
Change in work hours or conditions	20
Change in schools	20
Change in recreation	19
Change in social activities	18
Change in sleeping habits	15
Total: _____	

For those using the complete scale, the 37% who had scores in the mild range suffered from illness, compared with 61% of those in the moderate range and 79% of those in the major range.

Source: Reproduced from Holmes, T. H., & Rahe, R. H. (1967). The social readjustment rating scale, Journal of Psychosomatic Research, 11(2), 213–218. doi:10.1016/0022-3999(67)90010-4

were assigned different numbers of life change units, with higher numbers indicating more adjustment needed and therefore more stress. After adding up all the numbers, the Social Readjustment Scale indicates how likely it is that the stressors will lead to health difficulties.

Students often have different stressors than the ones listed in the original scale. Inspired by Holmes and Rahe, other researchers (Mullen, 1981) have created a scale for young college students that reflect the kinds of stressors most common for them (see **TABLE 11-3** for some examples).

TABLE 11-3 Items from the Student Stress Scale

Item	Stress Rating
Divorce between parents	65 points
Failed important course	47
Serious argument with close friend	40
Change of major	39
Trouble with parents	39
New girl or boyfriend	38
Increased workload at school	37
First quarter/semester in college	36
Serious argument with instructor	30
Lower grades than expected	29
Too many missed classes	25
Change of college	24
Dropped more than one class	23

Source: Adapted from Mullen, K. D. & Costello, G. (1981). Health awareness through self-discovery: A workbook. Minneapolis: Burgess Publishing.

Rude people, traffic jams, and lost keys can be a hassle. Daily hassles can build up over time to be as much of a stressor as a major life event.

Daily hassles (microstressors) Minor irritations that produce stress.

While Holmes and Rahe focused on major life events as bringing about stress, other researchers (DeLongis, Coyne, Dakof, Folkman, & Lazarus, 1982) focused on small events that can build up over time. Called **daily hassles** or **microstressors**, these small events can affect you even more than a rare major life event. Researchers suggested that things like rude people and traffic jams affect us more due to the seemingly unending aggravation and annoyance triggered by these hassles **TABLE 11-4**.

Cognition and Stress

But stress isn't just an event. Something can be stressful to one person but not to someone else. Whether something creates a stress reaction also depends on how it is perceived. The ways in which we see, or appraise, a situation can help to determine if it is stressful for us. We appraise not only the threat but also our ability to handle such a threat. These appraisals are subjective in nature. A move to a new city can be a negative stress for one person, while another might experience it as a positive event and not at all stressful.

TABLE 11-4 Examples of Daily Hassles

- Misplacing keys
- Arguments
- Traffic jams
- Time pressures
- Lack of sleep
- Fear of crime
- Shopping
- Bureaucracy
- Waiting
- Loneliness
- Waiting in line
- Pollution
- Gossip
- Relatives
- Excess noise
- Inconsiderate people
- Difficult neighbors
- Car breakdown
- Meal preparation
- Job dissatisfaction
- Office politics

The stress reaction depends, in part, on how you experience and appraise an event and how you think you can and will handle the event. If you think you have all of the resources you need to overcome the event, then you may not see it as stressful. If you have only some of the resources, you may perceive the event as a challenge and feel moderate stress if you can overcome the event with some effort. You feel lots of stress if you think you don't have the resources to overcome the event. This means that you assess not only the event, but also your potential ways of dealing with the event.

Choice as a Stress

Choice also causes stress. You might think that having choices in your life makes things great. Variety is the spice of life, isn't it? If you've ordered an expensive coffee from a specialty coffee shop lately, you've likely been flooded by beverage possibilities (up to 87,000 combinations of syrups and toppings). Even if you like all your options, choosing (approaching) something means not choosing (avoiding) something else. Making a choice can cause a situation involving incompatible goals or a **conflict**. With choices come four kinds of conflict, each with the potential to cause stress (Lewin, 1935).

An **approach-approach conflict** is a situation in which a decision must be made between two incompatible choices that both have positive features. An approach-approach conflict carries the smallest amount of stress since you like both options. However, you may have some regret since you can't choose both.

The flipside occurs in an avoidance-avoidance conflict. An **avoidance-avoidance conflict** is a situation in which a decision must be made between two undesirable choices. Since you have to choose between two things that are unlikable, you might have a problem deciding and experience more stress than you'd expect with an approach-approach conflict.

In an **approach-avoidance conflict**, a decision must be made about a goal that has both positive and negative features. Sometimes people get stuck in the decision-making process and can't stop thinking about what to do (Emmons & King, 1988). Working through approach-avoidance conflicts requires that you calm down, understand the relative benefits of each choice, gather information, and maybe even outsource the decision to someone you trust. Sometimes the decision process feels bigger than the actual decision itself.

Most of the time, we are confronted with many choices, each with positive and negative consequences, as in the **multiple-approach-avoidance conflict**. If you have ever gotten choice paralysis over deciding what to do over a vacation or spring break, you've experienced the multiple-approach-avoidance conflict. Should you go to the beach, a theme park, the mountains? Welcome to the multiple-approach-avoidance conflict. The conflict, unfortunately, doesn't always dissolve once your choice has been made. This can sometimes result in a postdecision remorse, like buyers' remorse, if your final choice doesn't end up being as rosy as you imagined.

Conflict A situation that involves incompatible objectives.

Approach-approach conflict A situation in which a decision must be made between two incompatible choices that both have positive features.

Avoidance-avoidance conflict A situation in which a decision must be made between two undesirable choices.

Approach-avoidance conflict A situation in which a decision must be made about a goal that has both positive and negative features.

Multiple-approach-avoidance conflict A situation in which a decision must be made between many choices, each with positive and negative consequences.

Acculturative stress The anxiety felt in response to challenges from new cultural expectations.

Culture and Stress

Adjusting to anything new can cause stress, including being part of a new culture. **Acculturative stress** is the anxiety felt in response to challenges from new cultural

Aerobic activity has been shown to reduce the negative impact of stress.

General adaptation syndrome (GAS) Selye's term for the body's stress response that occurs in three stages: alarm, resistance, and exhaustion.

Psychosomatic diseases Disorders in which a real medical syndrome is exacerbated by psychological factors. Also known as psychophysiological illness.

Type A personality A style characterized by difficulty relaxing, impatience, and anger when delayed.

Type B personality A style characterized by being relaxed about time, slow to anger, and relative ease at relaxing.

Coronary heart disease A medical condition that results in narrowing of the vessels that supply blood to the heart.

Immune system Processes the body uses to protect against disease.

Lymphocytes A type of cell involved in the immune system that works to attack foreign substances.

expectations. Knowing and understanding the nuances of display rules, a new language, and unfamiliar customs can be exhausting.

There is also stress associated with not being a member of a dominant group. In a study of around 500 African-Americans in California, 95% of them reported racial discrimination in the previous 12 months (Klonoff, Landrine, & Ullman, 1999). Similar outcomes have been uncovered for other minority groups, including Hispanics, Asian-Americans (Jackson, Williams, & Torres, 1997), bisexuals, and homosexuals (Stotzer, 2010). In fact, even expecting to be discriminated against can be stressful (Flores et al., 2008).

Effects of Stress

Stress has two main fronts: physical and psychological. Stress is a biological and psychological reaction to a provocative event. An early theory of how humans react to stress was created by Walter Cannon. Cannon (1939) suggested that when your body identifies a danger it prepares to fight, freeze, or flee. More commonly known as the fight-or-flight response, your sympathetic nervous system is activated. Over time, chronic activation of your sympathetic nervous system can cause wear and tear on your body.

Stress is also a process. Stressors, according to Hans Selye (Selye, 1936) produce a predictable pattern of reactions. After studying people who experienced stress, Selye described the **general adaptation syndrome (GAS)**, a process by which any organism organizes itself against stress. The GAS begins with resistance as the organism gathers the resources needed to confront the event. If the event is defeated—great. If not, the organism moves on to the next phase, alarm, in which more resources are gathered. The last phase is exhaustion, when the resources are depleted, and illness may occur. An example of exhaustion from an unresolved stressor can be seen in burnout.

Stress and Health

"You'll worry yourself sick" is something my mom used to say to me as a kid. The connection between stress and illness is well established. Links between stress and ulcers (Sharma, Ghosh, & Sharma, 2004) as well as headaches (Martin, Lae, & Reece, 2007) have been made in the literature. When there is a link between an illness and stress, it's thought of as a psychosomatic illness. A **psychosomatic disease** is a disorder in which a real medical syndrome is exacerbated by psychological factors. While it is common to think that a psychosomatic illness is all in your head, stressors can create or worsen real illness. Headaches, for example can be made worse when under stress.

Personality, stress, and illness interact. Back in the 1960s, cardiologists uncovered a link between reactions to stress and cardiac disease (Friedman & Rosenman, 1974). This led to the discovery of two personality types.

Type A personalities tend to be competitive, hostile, and impatient. They are the type of people who not only will walk up an escalator but be gruff when they are passing you. The type A personality is so aware of time that even the slightest delays in a schedule will cause them a lot of anxiety. They also escalate to anger pretty quickly.

On the other hand, **Type B personalities** are relaxed and patient. Seemingly unflappable, the Type B personalities are more resistant to time pressure, more cooperative, easy going, and patient. Researchers discovered that Type A personalities have a greater likelihood for **coronary heart disease**, a medical condition that results in narrowing of the vessels that supply blood to the heart.

If you are watching the clock as you read this chapter, it's not time to worry—it seems that the dangerous mix of ingredients in the Type A personality is anger and hostility (Smith & Ruiz, 2002).

Stress and the Immune System

Stress can impact the body and the immune system. The **immune system** consists of processes the body uses to protect against disease. Your immune system defends against external invasions such as bacteria and viruses, in part by employing **lymphocytes**, cells that attack foreign substances FIGURE 11-19. Without the immune system, you would be vulnerable to illness and disease.

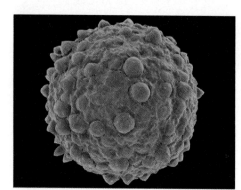

FIGURE 11-19 Lymphocytes are cells involved in immune functioning.

Hormones such as endorphins and corticosteroids flow into your body during stress and can weaken the immune response. Called **immunosuppression**, stress makes the immune system work less efficiently—in essence, stressing your immune system. Constantly alerting your immune system can, over time, reduce your ability to react and defend against the foreign substances, which invade your body and can lead to more increased illness (Glaser, Rice, Sheridan, & Fertel, 1987).

Coping with and Managing Stress

While stress causes discomfort and even leads to illness, stress also leads to motivation to reduce the stress. The things that you do to get rid of the stress are called coping. While stress is the response to the event you see as a challenge, **coping** is the way that you manage the stress.

Coping with the stress doesn't always lead to resolving the cause of the stress. Some forms of coping might involve escaping or avoiding the stressful situation altogether, or simply hunkering down and bearing the stress. Under stress, some people engage in behaviors that are unhealthy, known as **negative coping**. This can include blaming themselves for the events, blaming others, and self-indulgent behaviors like overeating and excessive computer use or **Internet addiction**. Negative coping can just make matters worse.

Others shut down under stress and do not attempt to respond or cope. **Learned helplessness** occurs when an animal fails to take action to escape a noxious stimulus. The same appears to be true for people. When in a situation in which you feel you have no control, you may tolerate it rather than fight (Peterson, Maier, & Seligman, 1993).

There are also several constructive ways to cope with stress, which rely on the way you think and what you do in the environment. Coping can be directed inward to alter your perception of stress, or outward, targeted at the problem causing the stress. Researchers have divided the way you cope into two different classes: changing the actual stressor and changing your emotional reaction to the event.

Emotion-focused coping directs coping at the response to the event. This can be cognitive (varying the way you think about the event) or behavioral (things that you do, like distract yourself). At best, cognitive and behavioral approaches can lead to reappraisal of the stressful situation and help you to see the situation in a new light. At worst, emotion-focused coping can result in drug and alcohol abuse.

You are more likely to employ emotion-focused responses when you think there is not much that you can do to change the actual stressor (Lazarus & Folkman, 1984). A **problem-focused coping** strategy, on the other hand, directs the coping toward the situation itself. You tend to use problem-focused coping if you think you can influence the situation.

Employing **constructive coping**, healthy efforts to reduce the impact of stress, is the best thing you can do to combat stress and make a preemptive strike to keep the effects of stress at bay. Exercise, including **aerobic exercise**, physical activity that increases the capacity of the heart and lungs, has been shown to reduce stress, as do getting adequate sleep, eating healthy foods, and meditation. Interestingly, these are the very things that people stop doing when they begin to feel stress.

Interventions

Because of the important link between stress, health, and psychology, many professionals will employ the use of these techniques to help promote health and prevent and treat illnesses. **Health psychology** is a branch of psychology that is concerned with how psychological factors impact wellness, illness, and medical treatment. **Behavioral medicine**, for example is an interdisciplinary field concerned with health and illness that combines knowledge of the social and medical sciences to improve health and combat illness. Practitioners who utilize behavioral medicine will often intervene with psychological techniques like biofeedback to reduce their stress. In **biofeedback**, a person becomes aware of physiological functions, such as heartbeat or galvanic skin response, and attempts to influence those functions. If you are aware of your heart rate, for example, you can use relaxation or meditation techniques to reduce your heart rate and activate your parasympathetic nervous system.

Immunosuppression Weakening the immune response.

Coping Efforts to reduce the impact of stressors.

Negative coping Engaging in behaviors that are unhealthy and can make matters worse.

Internet addiction Excessive use of computer systems that causes impairment in social, occupational, or school functioning.

Learned helplessness When an animal fails to take action to escape a noxious stimulus.

Emotion-focused coping A reaction to stress that involves managing the feelings that arise from the situation.

Problem-focused coping A reaction to stress that involves the management of the event causing the stress.

Constructive coping Healthy efforts to reduce the impact of stressors.

Aerobic exercise Physical activity that increases the capability of the heart and lungs.

Health psychology A branch of psychology that is concerned with how psychological factors impact wellness, illness, and medical treatments.

Behavioral medicine An interdisciplinary field concerned with health and illness that combines knowledge of social and medical sciences.

Biofeedback A procedure through which a person becomes aware of physiological functions in order to influence the physiological functions.

| CONCEPT LEARNING CHECK **11.5** | *Sources and Effects of Stress* |

Match each numbered example below with the proper category.

A. Type A

B. Major life event

C. Daily hassle

D. Constructive coping

E. Negative coping

1. _____ Aerobic activity

2. _____ Blaming others

3. _____ Divorce

4. _____ Getting enough sleep

5. _____ Hostility

6. _____ Internet addiction

7. _____ Lost keys

8. _____ Moving

9. _____ Time urgency

10. _____ Traffic

Explain

11. The most important factors in the Type A behavior pattern are _____ and _____.

12. Describe a way that the Type A behavior pattern could influence illness.

11.6 Positive Psychology

Positive psychology emphasizes the constructive features of human strength and healthful living rather than pathology.

- Illustrate how positive psychology emphasizes the constructive features of human strength and healthful living rather than pathology.

Since well before Freud, psychology has been criticized for focusing too much on what's wrong with people—the negative inside of them. Some suggest that psychology was born of misery. After all, most of the theories of personality were derived from meticulous studies of patient populations, and psychologists' views of people come from those who sought relief from suffering. But this clearly must provide a distorted view of humanity. It would be like drawing a medical atlas only from people who visited the emergency room. When I was a graduate student in clinical psychology, some students joked that "normal" people were "undiagnosed clients." Positive psychology turns that idea on its head. **Positive psychology** is a branch of psychology that studies human strengths. Positive psychology focuses on what's good about individuals and the qualities that bring out the best in humanity. Because of this imbalance between illness and health, some suggest that maybe now we know enough about illness and disease and we should try to focus on strengths like happiness, hardiness, and optimism rather than deficits.

Happiness

Happiness consists of positive emotions and **subjective well-being**, or feeling good about your life. Researchers have discovered that happy people are more likely to be solution-focused and are also more likely to be helpful, called the **feel-good, do-good phenomenon**—happy people are helpful people.

Positive psychology
A branch of psychology that studies human strengths.

Subjective well-being
A feeling of satisfaction with life and happiness.

Feel-good, do-good phenomenon The theory that people are more likely to be helpful if they are happy.

Happiness can be a moving target. How happy you feel now depends, in part, on how you've felt in the past. If you get a raise at work or more vacation time, you will feel happier, but you can easily adjust to the new norm. The **adaption-level phenomenon** is the ability to adapt to a new situation so that the new situation becomes the norm and you may end up wanting more. It's easy to get used to the new normal.

Our happiness also depends on how we feel in comparison to others (Lyubomirsky, Tucker, & Kasri, 2001). If you feel worse off than your comparison group, it can affect how happy you feel. **Relative deprivation** is your opinion that you are worse off than your comparison group. If you earned a B on a paper, you might feel worse if your friends all earned As than you would if they earned Cs. Relative deprivation may be more important than absolute deprivation since we normally focus our attention to those around us such as our comparison groups.

Seeking money doesn't make you happier. In fact, those who seek and value love and friendship report being happier than those who seek money (Sheldon & Kasser, 2001). Positive emotions not only make you happier but are related to a longer life, too. Researchers read the autobiographies of 180 nuns (Danner, Snowdon, & Friesen, 2001) and counted the number of positive emotional states like gratitude, love, happiness, and hope. The nuns who wrote more about positive emotions lived longer (up to 9 more years) than the nuns whose stories contained fewer positive feelings, despite having lived together for most of their lives and experiencing similar events. There are lots of reasons positive emotions could be protective. Positive emotions can counteract stresses to the immune response created by ongoing stress. What's more, they could lead to greater problem solving and less helplessness.

Age, gender, amount of schooling, attractiveness, or having kids doesn't predict how happy you are. What does? Having good friends, work you like, and health behaviors predict happiness more than anything else TABLE 11-5.

There are multiple effects on happiness.

Adaptation-level phenomenon The ability to adapt to new situations so that the new situation becomes the norm.

Relative deprivation The opinion that a person is worse off than a comparison group.

Hardiness A personality style characterized by commitment, challenge, and control.

Hardiness

You may recall Seligman's studies of dogs' responses to a series of shocks. What often isn't reported is that there were some dogs who never learned to be helpless—hardy doggies that never gave up. Also found in people, hardiness acts as a buffer against stress. **Hardiness** is a personality style characterized by commitment, challenge, and control.

1. Challenge: seeing problems as challenges to be vanquished

2. Commitment: to self, friends, family, and values

3. Control: a perception of control over life and work

Hardiness is associated with lower stress levels and fewer illnesses (Eschleman, Bowling, & Alarcon, 2010) and greater job satisfaction (Maddi, 2006). It's the polar opposite of learned helplessness, a behavioral reaction to negative events over which a

TABLE 11-5 Summary of Research on Happiness

Weak Predictors of Happiness	Moderate Predictors of Happiness	Strong Predictors of Happiness
Money	Health	Love
Age	Social activity	Supportive relationships
Intelligence	Religious affiliation	Fulfilling work
Attractiveness		

Source: Adapted from Doherty, A. M., & Kelly, B. D. (2010). Social and psychological correlates of happiness in 17 European countries. Irish Journal of Psychological Medicine, 27(3), 130–134.

An optimistic explanatory style has little to do with seeing a glass half full or half empty and more to do with how you explain negative events that happen to you.

Social support The help provided by others.

Explanatory style Reflects what you think caused an event. Explanatory style can be either optimistic or pessimistic.

Internal locus of control The idea that your reinforcers and punishments are under your own control.

External locus of control The idea that reinforcers and punishments are outside of your control.

Pessimistic explanatory style A way of explaining negative events by using internal, stable, and global attributions.

Locus of control Your idea of the source of reinforcement and punishment.

Optimistic explanatory style A way of explaining negative events by using external, unstable, and specific attributions.

person has or perceives him- or herself to have no control. While those who feel helpless tend to freeze in the face of adversity, hardy individuals employ problem-focused coping and easily accept **social support** or help from others when they are stressed (Eschleman, Bowling, & Alarcon, 2010)

Optimism

In their experiments on learned helplessness, Peterson and Seligman discovered three cognitive components of helplessness and reformulated the helplessness approach by examining explanatory style.

Your **explanatory style** reflects what you think caused or explains an event. By nature, you tend to be more consistent about the ways you explain negative events than positive events (Peterson et al., 1982). A negative event, on the other hand, requires an explanation so that you can prevent it from happening in the future.

Peterson and his colleagues (1982; **TABLE 11-6**) suggested that our responses to negative events tend to revolve around three questions about the event itself:

1. Is the event *internal* or *external*? In other words, who or what caused the event? Was it your fault or did someone else cause the event to occur? In an **internal locus of control**, you believe that any good or bad things that happen to you are the result of your own actions. **External locus of control**, on the other hand, is the idea that reinforcers and punishments are outside of your control.

2. Is the event *stable* or *unstable*? In other words, is the cause of the negative event here to stay or does it come and go?

3. Is the event *global* or *specific*? That is, does the event affect other things in your life, or does it have a relatively localized impact?

The way you answer these questions or explain such events to yourself determines your explanatory style, or your characteristic way of interpreting the cause of events. Those whose explanatory style reflects *internal*, *stable*, and *global* explanations will have a **pessimistic explanatory style** and be more prone to helplessness. When negative events occur, they tend to fold. If you've lost your keys and have a pessimistic explanatory style, you are likely to have thoughts that reflect *internal* blame, or **locus of control**; ("It's my fault that I lost my keys"), *stable* ("I'm an idiot, I'm always doing things like this"), and *global* ("this is exactly why I shouldn't get an expensive cell phone, I'd lose that, too").

However, a person with an **optimistic explanatory style** will often attribute the negative event to an outside, or *external*, factor ("I was distracted"), that the event is a temporary, or *unstable*, occurrence ("because my phone was ringing"), whose impact has a limited, or *specific*, effect ("it will likely never happen again"; Table 11-6).

People with an optimistic explanatory style tend to be happier and healthier. Optimists tend to have longer life spans (Zuckerman, 2001), recover more quickly from illnesses (Affleck, Tennen, & Apter, 2001), and have overall better health (Seligman, 2006). While some people tend to have that style automatically, it's also something that can be learned.

TABLE 11-6 Explanatory Styles for Negative Events

Explanatory Style	Internality	Stability	Globality
Optimism	External	Unstable	Specific
Pessimism	Internal	Stable	Global

Source: Adapted from Peterson, C., Semmel, A., Baeyer, C., Abramson, L. Y., Metalsky, G. I., & Seligman, M. E. P. (1982). The attributional style questionnaire. Cognitive Therapy and Research, 6(3), 287–299. doi:10.1007 /BF01173577

Summary of Multiple Influences on Emotion, Stress, and Health

After the break-in, the rest of the day went smoothly. What caused my emotions that morning? My reaction was the result a combination of biological, social, and cognitive factors.

My heart racing, my high blood pressure, and other sympathetic nervous system actions were fully present that morning. Darwin and other evolutionary theorists would suggest that my ability to create an angry face and the intruder's ability to recognize it could be an adaptive response. Cognition was involved as well. Theories that emphasize cognitive factors would suggest that my initial reaction of thinking the noise came from my cat was driven by previous experiences. The emotion that flowed from that thought was one of annoyance. After I thought it might be something dangerous, my body reacted with alarm.

The result of the incident was certainly stressful. Instead of emotion-focused coping, I called the police, a problem-focused solution. Later, as I told my students the story of what happened, some asked me if I planned to move to another neighborhood or get a guard dog. My first thought was, Oh, I'm sure it was a fluke, it will never happen again—revealing my optimistic explanatory style. There are multiple influences on emotion, stress, and health.

Calling the police in response to a break-in, is an example of a problem-focused solution.

CONCEPT LEARNING CHECK 11.6 | *Positive Psychology*

For each type of explanatory style, select the correct components.

A. Optimistic explanatory style

B. Pessimistic explanatory style

1. _____ External locus of control for negative events

2. _____ Internal locus of control for negative events

3. _____ Negative events have a global impact

4. _____ Negative events have a local impact

5. _____ See negative events as a temporary occurrence

6. _____ See negative events as having a lasting impact

Explain

7. One aspect of positive psychology is the research on hardiness. Hardiness is a personality style characterized by _____, _____, and _____.

8. Identify some of the benefits of hardiness.

CRITICAL THINKING APPLICATION

College students are subjected to a growing amount of stress. Lots of reading, assignments, financial stress, and worries about future jobs and college loans can create significant stress. Stress is even worse around midterms and final exams!

Evaluate

1. Given what you know about stress, health, and positive psychology, design an intervention for college students that would reduce the dangerous impact of stress.

2. When people begin to feel stress, they often stop doing exactly the things that will decrease their stress. People turn to alcohol, stop sleeping, stop hanging out with their friends, and stop exercising. Why do you think this is and what can be done to increase the healthy activities?

Visual Overview Theories of Emotion

In this chapter we have reviewed several theories that explain the nature and origin of our emotional responses. This overview summarizes five theories of emotions and how each might explain the fear of encountering an intruder.

Common-Sense Theory

James-Lange Theory
Emotions occur after arousal.

Cannon-Bard Theory
Arousal and emotion occur at the same time.

Schacter and Singer Two-Factor Theory
Emotions occur with a combination of arousal and a label for the arousal.

Facial Feedback Theory
Facial expressions lead to arousal and emotion.

11.1 The Role of Physiology and Evolution in Emotion

- Bodily processes are involved in emotion.
- The fight-or-flight response is a reaction to danger that prepares you to fight, freeze, or flee.
- The sympathetic nervous system releases stress hormones like corticosteroids and catecholamines.
- According to the Yerkes Dodson law, optimal levels of arousal are helpful, while too little arousal or too much arousal can be problematic.
- A polygraph will use biological data in order to detect lies.
- Polygraphs have been controversial.
- Charles Darwin suggested that there was an evolutionary base for the emotional response.

11.2 The Role of Behavior and Cognition in Emotion

- Thoughts can have an impact on emotion.
- Emotional responses can occur in the absence of cognition.
- Sensory input from your eyes and ears can often take a neural shortcut to the amygdala and trigger an emotional response.
- Behavior and emotion are interconnected.
- Paul Ekman researched basic emotions, feeling states that are expressed in common ways.
- The original list of basic emotions includes anger, fear, disgust, happiness, sadness, and surprise.
- The facial feedback hypothesis suggests that how we feel is regulated, in part, by the signal your brain gets from the way your face is arranged.

11.3 Theories of Emotion

- Psychologists have various theories of emotion.
- The James-Lange theory of emotion suggests the emotional experience is an interpretation of the specific physiological recipe for that emotion.
- The Cannon-Bard theory of emotion suggests that perception of a stimulus causes bodily arousal and emotion at the same time.
- The Schacter-Singer Two-Factor theory of emotion suggests that feelings are a combination of body arousal and how we think about that arousal.
- The cognitive-mediational theory of emotion suggests that feelings are influenced by what we think caused our thoughts.

11.4 Expressing Emotion

- Special factors and situations have the potential to influence how and when emotions are expressed.
- Display rules are guidelines about how you should express emotions.
- The amygdala processes stimuli related to fear.
- The frustration-aggression hypothesis suggests that when a goal is blocked, it can lead to anger and aggression.
- Research does not support the catharsis theory of anger.
- Sternberg created a triangular theory of love, suggesting that all interpersonal relationships contain some combination of intimacy, passion, and commitment.

11.5 Stress

- Various factors lead to stress, and stress can have multiple effects on your life.
- Stress is a response that occurs from events seen as a challenge.
- Stress can be ongoing, or acute.
- Coping refers to the reduction of the impact of a stressor.
- Stress can come from major life events or from daily hassles.
- The way you think about things can increase or decrease stress
- Choices in your life can cause conflict and stress.
- Culture can cause stress.
- There is a link between stress and illness.
- Type A personalities tend to be competitive, hostile, and impatient and have a higher risk for coronary heart disease.
- Stress can lead to immunosuppression and increased illness.
- Under stress, some people engage in negative coping strategies that can make matters worse.
- Emotion-focused coping directs coping at the way you feel about the event, while problem-focused coping directs coping towards the event itself.
- Practitioners use information about the interaction between psychology and health and illness through biofeedback, behavioral medicine, and health psychology.

11.6 Positive Psychology

- Positive psychology emphasizes the constructive features of human strength and healthful living rather than pathology.
- Happiness is related to feeling good about your life. Happiness is related to many positive outcomes.
- Hardiness is a personality style characterized by commitment, openness to challenge, and a sense of control.
- Those with an optimistic explanatory style tend to be happier and healthier.

11.1 The Role of Physiology and Evolution in Emotion

1. "Optimal levels of arousal produce the best reaction" is the basis of the:
   A. parasympathetic nervous system
   B. flight-or-fight response
   C. galvanic skin response
   D. Yerkes Dodson law

2. Polygraphs use a number of measurements to detect sympathetic nervous system arousal, including _____, a measurement of skin conductivity.
   A. corticosteroids
   B. catecholamines
   C. GSR

11.2 The Role of Behavior and Cognition in Emotion

3. According to Robert Zajonc, sometimes you can have an emotional response without a conscious thought. Physiological evidence to support this comes from the idea that:
   A. sometimes sights and smells take a neural shortcut to the amygdala.
   B. the brain is not activated during emotions.
   C. sometimes sights and smells take longer to process into emotions.

4. Susan is being recorded while she watches a funny movie. According to the research, you should expect that Susan's face is:
   A. more expressive because she watched the movie alone.
   B. just as expressive as when watching alone or with other people.
   C. less expressive because she watched the movie alone.

5. According to Ekman, a basic emotion is an emotion that is:
   A. necessary in order to get along in a group.
   B. conveyed in the same way across cultures.
   C. used to create other emotions.
   D. important to express every day.

6. If someone says, "Smile, you'll feel better," there might be some truth in it, due to what we know about:
   A. the facial feedback hypothesis
   B. basic emotions
   C. catastrophic thinking

11.3 Theories of Emotion

7. The _____ theory states that emotions are the result of purely physiological events.
   A. James-Lange
   B. common-sense
   C. Schacter-Singer
   D. cognitive-mediational

8. The central idea behind the Cannon-Bard theory of emotion rests on the idea that
   A. emotions are cognitive responses to events.
   B. what distinguishes feelings is the label we place on that emotion.
   C. an emotional experience is an interpretation of the specific physiological recipe for that type of arousal.
   D. the perception of a stimulus causes bodily arousal and emotion at the same time.

9. According to the Schacter-Singer two-factor theory of emotion:
   A. emotions are cognitive responses to events.
   B. what distinguishes feelings is the label we place on that type of arousal.
   C. an emotional experience is an interpretation of the specific physiological recipe for that emotion.
   D. the perception of a stimulus causes bodily arousal and emotion at the same time.

11.4 Expressing Emotion

10. When people cover their mouths when they laugh, this is governed by:
    A. display rules
    B. anthropomorphism
    C. the amygdala
    D. the facial feedback hypothesis

11. When a person is afraid, the _____ is activated.
    A. MRI
    B. amygdala
    C. GSR
    D. parasympathetic nervous system

11.5 Stress

12. Long-lasting events, such as adjusting to a new job in a different country, are thought of as:
- **A.** acute stressors
- **B.** coping mechanisms
- **C.** chronic stressors
- **D.** conflicts

11.6 Positive Psychology

14. Which of the following is the strongest predictor of happiness, according to recent research?
- **A.** age
- **B.** intelligence
- **C.** attractiveness
- **D.** fulfilling work

13. If you just won the lottery and had to choose between a $10,000 lump-sum payment or $1,000 a month for 10 months, you might experience what kind of conflict?
- **A.** approach-approach conflict
- **B.** avoidance-avoidance conflict
- **C.** approach-avoidance conflict
- **D.** nonapproach conflict

15. Those who tend to explain negative events as being external, temporary, and with limited impact have:
- **A.** an optimistic explanatory style
- **B.** a pessimistic explanatory style
- **C.** learned helplessness
- **D.** Type A behavior pattern

CHAPTER DISCUSSION QUESTIONS

1. Compare the strengths of the various theories of emotion.

2. What are the strengths and limitations of using a polygraph?

3. What are the strengths and weaknesses of using daily hassles as an assessment of stress?

4. Identify the dangers of venting anger. What factors do you think influence how people express their anger?

5. Discuss the general adaptation syndrome in relationship to stressful life events. What are some ways in which you can identify healthy coping mechanisms in those who experience stress before they reach the exhaustion phase?

CHAPTER PROJECTS

1. Use the two-factor theory of emotion to design an intervention to help someone with test anxiety.

2. The critical factor in the Type A personality is hostility. Use your knowledge of emotion, stress, and health to design

a frustration-aggression reduction program to help those with Type A personality.

CHAPTER KEY TERMS

Acculturative stress
Acute stressors
Adaptation-level phenomenon
Aerobic exercise
Aggression
Amygdala
Anthropomorphism
Approach-approach conflict
Approach-avoidance conflict
Avoidance-avoidance conflict
Basic emotions
Behavioral medicine
Biofeedback
Biopsychosocial model
Cannon-Bard theory
Catastrophic thinking
Catecholamines
Catharsis
Chronic stressors

Cognitive-mediational theory
    of emotion
Conflict
Constructive coping
Cope
Coping
Coronary heart disease
Corticosteroids
Daily hassles (microstressors)
Display rules
Emotional intelligence
Emotion-focused coping
Emotion
Explanatory style
External locus of control
Facial feedback hypothesis
Feel-good, do-good phenomenon
Fight-or-flight response
Frustration

Frustration-aggression hypothesis
Galvanic skin response (GSR)
General adaptation syndrome
    (GAS)
Hardiness
Health psychology
Immune system
Immunosuppression
Internal locus of control
Internet addiction
James-Lange theory
Learned helplessness
Locus of control
Lymphocytes
Multiple-approach-avoidance
    conflict
Negative coping
Optimistic explanatory style
Pessimistic explanatory style

Polygraph
Positive psychology
Problem-focused coping
Psychosomatic diseases
Relative deprivation

Schacter-Singer two-factor theory
Social support
Stress
Stressors
Subjective well-being

Triangular theory of love
Type A personality
Type B personality
Yerkes Dodson law

ANSWERS TO CONCEPT LEARNING CHECKS

11.1 Bodily Processes and Emotion

1. D. The Yerkes Dodson law suggests that moderate amounts of arousal are best.

2. C. Anthropomorphism is assigning human emotions to nonhumans.

3. A. The fight-or-flight response is a reaction to danger in which the sympathetic nervous system prepares the organs for vigorous activity.

4. B. The galvanic skin response is a measure of skin conductivity that is associated with stress.

5. A. The fight-or-flight response is a reaction to danger in which the sympathetic nervous system prepares the organs for vigorous activity. It sometimes leads to freezing.

6. The Yerkes Dodson law suggests that moderate amounts of arousal are best. For easy tasks, more arousal can be tolerated than for tedious tasks.

11.2 Behavior and Cognition and Emotion

1. You can have an emotion without a thought. [T]

2. The amygdala is a cluster of neurons linked to sadness. [F]

3. Sensory signals can take a neural shortcut from the eyes to the brain in order to create emotions. [T]

4. Thinking about things differently can impact emotions. [T]

5. Children born without the ability to see will often smile when they are happy. Some researchers say that this is evidence that happiness is a **basic** emotion.

6. The **facial feedback hypothesis** suggests that smiling more can make you feel happier.

7. According to the facial feedback hypothesis, how you feel an emotion is regulated, in part, by the feedback your brain gets from the way your face is arranged. If you can't arrange your face in certain ways, it might blunt your emotional experience.

11.3 Theories of Emotion

1. James-Lange: Each emotion has a **specific physiological recipe is derived from this theory of emotion**.

2. Cannon-Bard: This theory suggests that a stimulus that leads to emotions triggers both **physiological** and **emotional experiences** at the same time.

3. Schacter and Singer: This theory suggests that emotion is caused by **arousal** plus a **cognitive label**.

11.4 Expressing Emotion

1. Companionate [intimacy + commitment]

2. Consummate [intimacy + passion + commitment]

3. Empty [commitment]

4. Fatuous [passion + commitment]

5. Friendship [intimacy]

6. Infatuation [passion]

7. Nonlove [none]

8. Romantic [intimacy + passion]

9. People who think that venting their anger is useful because it provides **catharsis** or releases pent-up emotions and prevents the anger from exploding are more likely to express their anger.

10. Some alternative solutions to venting anger include waiting, exercising, listening to calming music, and solution-focused coping.

11.5 Sources and Effects of Stress

1. Aerobic activity [D]

2. Blaming others [E]

3. Divorce [B]

4. Getting enough sleep [D]

5. Hostility [A]

6. Internet addiction [E]

7. Lost keys [C]

8. Moving [B]

9. Time urgency [A]

10. Traffic [C]

11. The most important factors in the Type A behavior pattern are **anger** and **hostility**.

12. The anger and hostility can lead to increased stress. Hormones such as endorphins and corticosteroids flow into your body during stress and can weaken the immune response, which can lead to increased illness.

11.6 Positive Psychology

1. External locus of control for negative events [A]

2. Internal locus of control for negative events [B]

3. Negative events have a global impact [B]

4. Negative events have a local impact [A]

5. See negative events as a temporary occurrence [A]

6. See negative events as having a lasting impact [B]

7. Hardiness is a personality style characterized by **commitment**, **challenge**, and **control**.

8. Hardiness is associated with greater job satisfaction, lower stress levels, fewer illnesses, and increased optimism.

11.1 The Role of Physiology and Evolution in Emotion

1. D. Rationale: The Yerkes Dodson law suggests that optional arousal is best, while too much or too little can hinder performance.

2. C. Rationale: GSR or galvanic skin response is a measurement of the conductivity of skin.

11.2 The Role of Behavior and Cognition in Emotion

3. A. Rationale: Sights and smells take a neural shortcut to the amygdala, which can process the stimulation as fear.

4. C. Rationale: People don't usually express their emotions in facial expressions as much unless others are around.

5. B. Rationale: A basic emotion is a feeling state thought to be expressed in a common way across cultures.

6. A. Rationale: According to facial feedback, emotion is regulated, in part, by the way your face is arranged.

11.3 Theories of Emotion

7. A. Rationale: According to the James-Lange theory of emotion, our emotional experiences are an interpretation of the specific physiological recipe for that emotion.

8. D. Rationale: The Cannon-Bard theory of emotion suggests that perception of a stimulus causes bodily arousal and emotion at the same time.

9. B. Rationale: According to the Schacter-Singer two-factor theory of emotion, what distinguishes feelings is the label we place on a type of arousal.

11.4 Expressing Emotion

10. A. Rationale: Display rules are guidelines about how you should express emotions.

11. B. Rationale: The amygdala is the part of the brain that's involved with fear.

11.5 Stress

12. C. Rationale: Chronic stressors are long-lasting events that require you to adapt.

13. A. Rationale: In an approach-approach conflict, a decision must be made between two incompatible choices that both have positive features.

11.6 Positive Psychology

14. D. Rationale: According to the research, age, intelligence, and attractiveness are weak predictors of happiness, while having fulfilling work is a strong predictor.

15. A. Rationale: A person with an optimistic explanatory style will often attribute the negative event to an outside factor that is a temporary occurrence whose impact has a limited effect.

REFERENCES

Affleck, G., Tennen, H., & Apter, A. (2001). Optimism, pessimism, and daily life with chronic illness. In E. C. Chang (Ed.), *Optimism & pessimism: Implications for theory, research, and practice* (pp. 147–168). Washington, DC: American Psychological Association.

Barraza, J. A., & Zak, P. J. (2009). Empathy toward strangers triggers oxytocin release and subsequent generosity. In O. Vilarroya, S. Altran, A. Navarro, K. Ochsner, & A. Tobeña (Eds.), *Values, empathy, and fairness across social barriers* (Annals of the New York Academy of Sciences Vol. 1167, pp. 182–189). New York: New York Academy of Sciences.

Buck, R., Losow, J. I., Murphy, M. M., & Costanzo, P. (1992). Social facilitation and inhibition of emotional expression and communication. *Journal of Personality and Social Psychology, 63,* 962–968. doi:10.1037/0022-3514.63.6.962

Caccioppo, J. T., Berntson, G. G., Klein, D. J., & Poehlmann, K. M. (1997). Psychophysiology of emotion across the life span. *Annual review of Gerontology and Geriatrics, 17,* 27–74.

Cannon, W. B. (1939). *The wisdom of the body.* W.W. Norton & Company, Inc.

Danner, D. D., Snowdon, D. A., & Friesen, W. V. (2001). Positive emotions in early life and longevity: Findings from the nun study. *Journal of Personality and Social Psychology, 80,* 804–813. doi:10.1037/0022-3514.80.5.804

Darwin, C. (2009). *The expression of the emotions in man and animals, anniversary edition* (4th ed.). New York: Oxford University Press.

DeLongis, A., Coyne, J. C., Dakof, G., Folkman, S., & Lazarus, R. S. (1982). Relationship of daily hassles, uplifts, and major life events to health status. *Health Psychology, 1,* 119–136. doi:10.1037/0278-6133.1.2.119

Ekman, P. (1999). Basic emotions. In T. Dalgleish & M. J. Power (Eds.), *Handbook of cognition and emotion* (pp. 45–60). New York: John Wiley & Sons.

Ekman, P., Friesen, W. V., O'Sullivan, M., & Chan, A., et al. (1987). Universals and cultural differences in the judgments of facial expressions of emotion. *Journal of Personality and Social Psychology, 53*(4), 712–717. doi:10.1037 /0022-3514.53.4.712

Emmons, R. A., & King, L. A. (1988). Conflict among personal strivings: Immediate and long-term implications for psychological and physical well-being. *Journal of Personality and Social Psychology, 54*(6), 1040–1048. doi:10.1037/0022-3514.54.6.1040

Eschleman, K. J., Bowling, N. A., & Alarcon, G. M. (2010). A meta-analytic examination of hardiness. *International Journal of Stress Management, 17*(4), 277–307. doi:10.1037/a0020476

Feinstein, J. S., Adolphs, R., Damasio, A., & Tranel, D. (2011). The human amygdala and the induction and experience of fear. *Current Biology, 21*(1), 34–38. doi:10.1016/j.cub.2010.11.042

Flores, E., Tschann, J. M., Dimas, J. M., Bachen, E. A., Pasch, L. A., & de Groat, C. L. (2008). Perceived discrimination, perceived stress, and mental and physical health among Mexican-origin adults. *Hispanic Journal of Behavioral Sciences, 30*(4), 401–424. doi:10.1177/0739986308323056

Friedman, M., & Rosenman, R. (1974). *Type A behaviour and your heart.* New York: Knopf.

Galati, D., Miceli, R., & Sini, B. (2001). Judging and coding facial expression of emotions in congenitally blind children. *International Journal of Behavioral Development, 25*(3), 268–278. doi:10.1080/01650250042000393

Glaser, R., Rice, J., Sheridan, J., & Fertel, R. (1987). Stress-related immune suppression: Health implications. *Brain, Behavior, and Immunity, 1*(1), 7–20. doi:10.1016/0889-1591(87)90002-X

Grossman, M., & Wood, W. (1993). Sex differences in intensity of emotional experience: A social role interpretation. *Journal of Personality and Social Psychology, 65*(5), 1010–1022. doi:10.1037/0022-3514.65.5.1010

Grubin, D. (2010). The polygraph and forensic psychiatry. *Journal of the American Academy of Psychiatry and the Law, 38*(4), 446–451.

Holmes, T. H., & Rahe, R. H. (1967). The Social Readjustment Rating Scale. *Journal of Psychosomatic Research, 11*(2), 213–218. doi:10.1016 /0022-3999(67)90010-4

Jackson, J., Williams, D., Torres, M. (1997). *Perception of discrimination: The stress process and physical and psychological health.* Washington, DC: National Institute for Mental Health.

James, W. (1948). What is emotion? 1884. In W. Dennis (Ed.), *Readings in the history of psychology* (pp. 290–303). East Norwalk, CT: Appleton-Century-Crofts. doi:10.1037/11304-033

Klein, S., Smolka, M. N., Wrase, J., Grusser, S. M., Mann, K., Braus, D. F., & Heinz, A. (2004). The influence of gender and emotional valence of visual cues on fMRI activation in humans: Erratum. *Pharmacopsychiatry, 37*(3). doi:10.1055/s-2004-827166

Klonoff, E. A., Landrine, H., & Ullman, J. B. (1999). Racial discrimination and psychiatric symptoms among Blacks. *Cultural Diversity and Ethnic Minority Psychology, 5*(4), 329–339. doi:10.1037/1099-9809.5.4.329

Kraut, R. E. (1982). Social presence, facial feedback, and emotion. *Journal of Personality and Social Psychology, 42*(5), 853–863. doi:10.1037/0022-3514.42.5.853

LaFrance, M., & Banaji, M. (1992). Toward a reconsideration of the gender–emotion relationship. In M. S. Clark (Ed.), *Emotion and social behavior* (Review of personality and social psychology, Vol. 14, pp. 178–201). Thousand Oaks, CA: Sage.

Lazarus, R. S. (1991a). *Emotion and adaptation.* New York: Oxford University Press.

Lazarus, R. S. (1991b). Progress on a cognitive-motivational-relational theory of emotion. *American Psychologist, 46*(8), 819–834. doi:10.1037/0003-066X.46.8.819

Lazarus, R. S., & Folkman, S. (1984). *Stress, appraisal, and coping.* New York: Springer Publishing Company.

LeDoux, J. (1998). *The emotional brain: The mysterious underpinnings of emotional life.* New York: Simon & Schuster.

Lewin, K. (1935). *A dynamic theory of personality.* New York: McGraw-Hill.

Lohr, J. M., Olatunji, B. O., Baumeister, R. F., & Bushman, B. J. (2007). The psychology of anger venting and empirically supported alternatives that do no harm. *The Scientific Review of Mental Health Practice: Objective Investigations of Controversial and Unorthodox Claims in Clinical Psychology, Psychiatry, and Social Work, 5*(1), 53–64.

Lyubomirsky, S., Tucker, K. L., & Kasri, F. (2001). Responses to hedonically conflicting social comparisons: Comparing happy and unhappy people. *European Journal of Social Psychology, 31*(5), 511–535. doi:10.1002/ejsp.82

Maddi, S. R. (2006). Hardiness: The courage to be resilient. In J. C. Thomas, D. L. Segal, & M. Hersen (Eds.), *Comprehensive handbook of personality and psychopathology, Vol. 1: Personality and everyday functioning* (pp. 306–321). Hoboken, NJ: John Wiley & Sons.

Martin, P. R., Lae, L., & Reece, J. (2007). Stress as a trigger for headaches: Relationship between exposure and sensitivity. *Anxiety, Stress & Coping: An International Journal, 20*(4), 393–407. doi:10.1080/10615800701628843

Matsumoto, D., Yoo, S. H., & Fontaine, J. (2008). Mapping expressive differences around the world: The relationship between emotional display rules and individualism versus collectivism. *Journal of Cross-Cultural Psychology, 39*(1), 55–74. doi:10.1177/0022022107311854

McIntosh, D., Peter, R. B. Z., Stephen, S. V., & Emerick, W. (1997). Facial movement, breathing, temperature, and affect: Implications of the vascular theory of emotional efference. *Cognition & Emotion, 11*(2), 171–196. doi:10.1080/026999397379980

Mesquita, B., & Frijda, N. H. (1992). Cultural variations in emotions: A review. *Psychological Bulletin, 112*(2), 179–204. doi:10.1037/0033-2909.112.2.179

Mullen, K. D. (1981). *Health awareness through self-discovery: A workbook.* New York: Burgess Publishing.

National Research Council. (2003). *The polygraph and lie detection.* Committee to Review the Scientific Evidence on the Polygraph. Division of Behavioral and Social Sciences and Education. Washington, DC: National Academies Press.

Peterson, C., & Park, N. (2007). Explanatory style and emotion regulation. In J. J. Gross (Ed.), *Handbook of emotion regulation* (pp. 159–179). New York: Guilford Press.

Peterson, C., Maier, S. F., & Seligman, M. E. P. (1993). *Learned helplessness: A theory for the age of personal control.* New York: Oxford University Press.

Peterson, C., Semmel, A., Baeyer, C., Abramson, L. Y., Metalsky, G. I., & Seligman, M. E. P. (1982). The attributional style questionnaire. *Cognitive Therapy and Research, 6*(3), 287–299. doi:10.1007/BF01173577

Plant, E. A., Hyde, J. S., Keltner, D., & Devine, P. G. (2000). The gender stereotyping of emotions. *Psychology of Women Quarterly, 24*(1), 81–92. doi:10.1111/j.1471-6402.2000.tb01024.x

Schacter, S., & Singer, J. (1962). Cognitive, social, and physiological determinants of emotional state. *Psychological Review, 69*(5), 379–399. doi:10.1037/h0046234

Seligman, M. E. P. (2006). *Learned optimism: How to change your mind and your life.* New York: Vintage.

Selye, H. (1936). A syndrome produced by diverse nocuous agents. *Nature, 138.* doi:10.1038/138032a0

Sharma, S., Ghosh, S. N., & Sharma, M. (2004). Life events stress, emotional vital signs and peptic ulcer. *Psychological Studies, 49*(2–3), 167–176.

Sheldon, K. M., & Kasser, T. (2001). Goals, congruence, and positive well-being: New empirical support for humanistic theories. *Journal of Humanistic Psychology, 41*(1), 30–50. doi:10.1177/0022167801411004

Smith, T. W., & Ruiz, J. M. (2002). Psychosocial influences on the development and course of coronary heart disease: Current status and implications for research and practice. *Journal of Consulting and Clinical Psychology, Behavioral Medicine and Clinical Health Psychology, 70*(3), 548–568. doi:10.1037/0022-006X.70.3.548

Sternberg, R. J. (1986). A triangular theory of love. *Psychological Review, 93*(2), 119–135. doi:10.1037/0033-295X.93.2.119

Stotzer, R. L. (2010). Seeking solace in West Hollywood: Sexual orientation-based hate crimes in Los Angeles County. *Journal of Homosexuality, 57*(8), 987–1003. doi:10.1080/00918369.2010.503506

Strack, F., Martin, L. L., & Stepper, S. (1988). Inhibiting and facilitating conditions of the human smile: A nonobtrusive test of the facial feedback hypothesis. *Journal of Personality and Social Psychology, 54*(5), 768–777. doi:10.1037/0022-3514.54.5.768

Teigen, K. H. (1994). Yerkes-Dodson: A law for all seasons. *Theory & Psychology, 4*(4), 525–547. doi:10.1177/0959354394044004

Zajonc, R. B. (1980). Feeling and thinking: Preferences need no inferences. *American Psychologist, 35*(2), 151–175. doi:10.1037/0003-066X.35.2.151

Zuckerman, M. (2001). Optimism and pessimism: Biological foundations. In E. C. Chang (Ed.), *Optimism & pessimism: Implications for theory, research, and practice* (pp. 169–188). Washington, DC: American Psychological Association

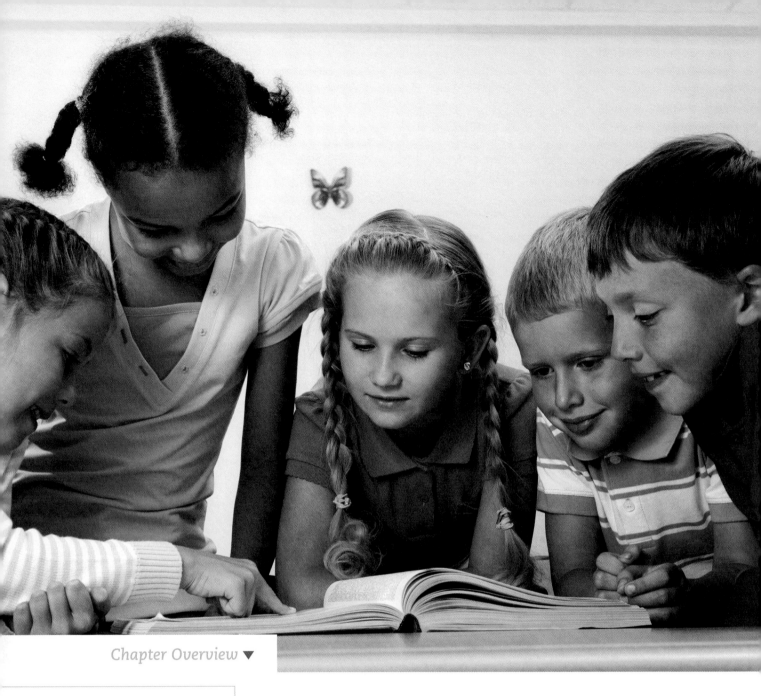

Chapter Overview ▼

12 Development Throughout the Life Span

Learning Objectives ▼

12.1 ■ Describe the development of the field and explain the prenatal and newborn stages of human development.

12.2 ■ Discuss physical development in infants and newborns.
■ Examine Piaget's stage theory in relation to early cognitive development.
■ Illustrate the importance of attachment in psychosocial development.

12.3 ■ Discuss the impact of sexual development in adolescence and changes in moral reasoning in adolescents and young adults.
■ Examine the life stages within Erikson's theory of psychosocial development.

12.4 ■ Illustrate the physical, cognitive, and social aspects of aging.

12.5 ■ Describe the multiple influences of nature and nurture in human development.

What is the first question ever asked about *you*? It was not your name, nor where you are from, nor which of your parents you most resemble. I guarantee that is was, "What is it?" As soon as we know there *is* a baby, we ask whether it is a boy or a girl. Why should the answer matter? How does knowing gender make us feel more connected to this new person? With modern ultrasound techniques, you can have a color photograph of your baby nestled in the womb as early as 4 weeks from conception. My own pregnancy was a miraculous surprise, and at my advanced age of 40, considered "high risk." I anxiously awaited the ultrasound pictures, wanting reassurance that my baby was healthy and developing normally. When I left, I was given my first picture of my baby-to-be. And there, labeled clearly in capital letters, was the answer: "BOY," along with an arrow pointing to the evidence. Before I knew he would survive, or how much I would love him, I knew he was a boy, and that changed everything: his name, his baby blankets, the wall color in his room, the toys that filled our house, the friends he made, his experience in school, and the activities (mostly involving superheroes) we spend our days pursuing. Why does gender matter so much?

12.1 The Beginnings of Development

Developmental psychology studies the changes we experience throughout life beginning at conception.

■ Describe the development of the field and explain the prenatal and newborn stages of human development.

The field of developmental psychology studies the changes we experience from the beginning to the end of our lives. When you think about yourself now and in your earliest memories, how are you the same and different? Many factors play a role in development; of course, there is biological growth, but there are also influences from your surrounding environment. Where you were born, who your parents are, what culture surrounded you, and your gender all play important roles in creating the person you are now. In this chapter, we will examine development in three areas (physical, cognitive, and social) from before birth, in infancy and childhood, through adolescence, adulthood, and advanced age.

What Is Development?

The notion of "childhood" is a relatively recent invention. It is only in modern societies (with good medical care) that parents have the luxury of assuming their babies will live to adulthood. For example, in the 1700s in rural areas of Europe, about one-third of children died before age 15. As one mother in 1772 wrote, after losing her eighth child after only 10 hours: ". . . one cannot grieve after her too much and I have just now other things to think of . . ." (Hyde, 1976). With many demands, affection was limited for children who may not live long. In addition, historically, children were often put to work as soon as possible to help support the family. From the 1700s to mid-1800s, coal mines and trades employed boys and girls from age 5. This practice still takes place today, as an estimated 150 million children aged 5 to 14 are engaged in child labor, or one in six children in the world (Basu & Tzannatos, 2003). Conditions like these led to a growing cry for reform by 1890, and child labor laws established free and compulsory education in western Europe and the United States (Nardinelli, 1990). The industrial revolution provided an economic base to "indulge" children because it became economically feasible to have children who did not work. The legacy of child labor is seen today in the practice of summer vacations from U.S. schools, required initially because children worked in the fields during the growing seasons. The changing socioeconomic conditions led to a growing attention to the processes of childhood development.

Development is one of the most challenging areas within psychology because its focus is on how the individual *changes over time*. How have you changed from your first year of high school to this year? If we repeatedly measured aspects of your life over time, we would be conducting a longitudinal study. This type of study compares the same person to him- or herself at different points in time. Alternatively, we can try to understand change by comparing people entering college to others entering high school. This approach, called a cross-sectional study, compares different groups of people at different ages. The problem is that there may be cohort effects; that is, life may be different for those entering high school now than it was for you way back then TABLE 12-1 (McBride & Nief, 2011).

Psychologists try to identify the "universal" features of development over time. These are features that hold true for everyone, no matter what culture they are raised in, what gender they are, or any other differences among individuals. However, culture plays a critical role in human development. Newborn humans are helpless compared to many other animals (e.g., horses or turtles). We are not able to protect ourselves from predators or to feed ourselves for many years. The human cortex does the bulk of the work to support our decisions, and that requires about 8 years to develop. In the meantime, survival depends on our relationships with others. Humans may take more than 20 years to fully "leave the nest," while the average robin accomplishes this over one summer. In modern society, some milestones, like the age of first marriage, are now increasingly delayed to over 28 for men and 26 for women in the United States (U.S. Census Bureau, 2009). One consequence of our long maturation phase is that there is plenty of time for culture to play a major role in our development.

Prenatal Development

Maturation refers to biological growth that occurs continuously over time. From the moment of conception, when a sperm cell meets an egg cell and they combine, growth begins.

> **Maturation** Biological growth occurring in a continuous fashion over time.

TABLE 12-1   *The Mindset List* for the Classes of 2010 and 2015

Here are some ideas in the mindset of students entering college as the class of '10, and a comparison to the class of '15 when they entered college

2010	2015
1. A stained blue dress is famous to their generation.	1. They have always had to wear bike helmets.
2. They have known only two presidents.	2. They have always wanted to be like Shaq or Kobe.
3. They had headphones in the back seat of the minivan.	3. Women have never been too old to have children.
4. Faux fur has always been a necessary element of style.	4. No state has ever failed to observe Martin Luther King Day.
5. They grew up pushing their own miniature shopping carts in the supermarket.	5. Women have always been kissing women on television.
6. "Boogers" candy has always been a favorite for grossing out parents.	6. Unlike older siblings, they spent bedtime on their backs as infants.
7. "So" as in "Sooooo New York," has always been a drawn-out adjective modifying a proper noun.	7. Music has always been available via free downloads.
8. "Outing" has always been a threat.	8. They pressured their parents to take them to Taco Bell or Burger King to get free pogs.
9. They have always "dissed" what they don't like.	9. They've broken up with their significant others via texting, Facebook, or MySpace.
10. They grew up with virtual pets to feed, water, and play games with, lest they die.	10. When they were 3, their parents battled other parents in toy stores to buy them a "Tickle Me Elmo" while they lasted.

Source: Created using data from the Beloit College Mindset Lists, administered by Tom McBride and Ron Nief. http://www.beloit.edu/mindset

Each cell contains 23 pairs of chromosomes, one of each pair from your father and one from your mother. Each chromosome is made up of more than 2,000 genes for a total of 50,000 genes within each cell. These genes make all the proteins in the body, which promote development and growth and carry out all body functions. So, is development dictated by genotype, your unique genetic pattern of DNA? Genotypes provide a "blueprint" for your body's development; however, genes are expressed flexibly, so that they may be turned on and off and may require specific environmental cues in order to act (Panning & Taatjes, 2008). As a result, your phenotype (your observed characteristics) may or may not reflect the underlying genetic code. For example, you may be born with the genotype to make you 6 feet tall; however, if nutrition is inadequate, your actual height (the expressed phenotype) may be much shorter. Another example is a trait like extraversion, or how sociable and outgoing you tend to be. Your genotype may plan a very extraverted personality; but, based on environment (being an only child, home day care, limited interactions with other children), you may develop a less outgoing nature as a toddler. So genetics provide a *predisposition* or potential for a characteristic, but expressing it may require contributions from the environment (Parens, 2004). Genetic factors may also affect development much later in life, becoming active at puberty, during periods of stress, or in old age.

Because people vary in so many ways, it is tempting to think that all of these variations are driven by genetic differences. However, keep in mind that our genetic code overlaps 96% with that of chimpanzees (Britten, 2002). Even so, heredity does influence the observed behaviors of individuals. For example, identical twins have more similar personalities than fraternal twins, whether or not they are raised together (Bouchard et al., 1990). So two people with the same DNA who are raised in very different families, neighborhoods, and classrooms still show similar personalities as adults. This suggests that our characteristic ways of thinking, feeling, and behaving are related to the specific combination of DNA determined at conception. Genes matter!

Genetics influence **prenatal** (before birth) development by directing the growth of the fertilized egg. The initial stage, called the **zygote**, lasts only between 1 and 2 weeks. If genes or chromosomes are missing or extra copies are present, or if mutations occur, then needed proteins may be absent or made in excess. As a result, abnormal development and growth of the zygote may result. Sometimes abnormalities are inherited, and sometimes they occur spontaneously, without reason. As a result, fewer than half of zygotes conceived will survive (James, 2000). Once implanted in the uterus, the zygote enters the **embryo** stage for between 2 and 8 weeks. In the embryo, the heart begins beating. By 2 months, sexual differentiation occurs: Males, who have an XY chromosome pattern, begin producing testis differentiating factor, causing the development of male sex organs. If this factor is not present at this time, the same tissue develops into female genitalia by default. About 126 male embryos are formed for every 100 female embryos, but male embryos have lower chances of survival, with 105 males born for every 100 females (Davis et al., 1998).

Sometimes, errors occur in genetic replication of the sex chromosomes or in the processing of sex hormones (androgen and testosterone) and enzymes. As a result, some babies are born with physical characteristics of both genders, such as a chromosomally male (XY) baby with female external genitalia. Sometimes called "intersex" or "hermaphrodite," the condition is now called a *disorder of sex development*. Imagine discovering as an adult that your genetics indicate you are a different gender! Women in sports are sometimes required to undergo gender screening because higher-than-normal levels of the male hormone testosterone may be an advantage. For example, Caster Semenya won the women's 800-meter final at the 2009 World Championships in Berlin FIGURE 12-1. Her appearance (and her amazing performance) raised questions about her gender. Following genetic and gynecological screening, Semenya was allowed to keep her medal (O'Reilly, 2010). Perhaps this is why the ultrasound technician was quick to label my son: Sometimes, that first question of life, "What is it?" may have a less certain answer.

From around 9 weeks until birth, the now identifiably human **fetus** continues to develop FIGURE 12-2. But exposure to toxic agents from the environment, called **teratogens**,

Prenatal stage Development taking place in the mother's womb before birth.

Zygote An initial stage in development as the fertilized egg grows through cell division and attaches to the uterine wall.

Embryo Prenatal stage following zygote lasting 2 to 8 weeks; in this stage, the heart begins beating.

Fetus The unborn child from around 9 weeks until birth.

Teratogens Toxic agents from the environment, such as disease, poisons, or drugs, that can harm the fetus.

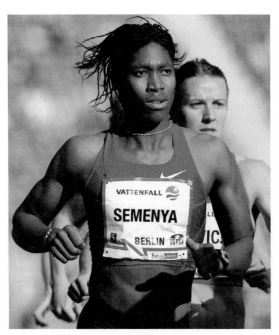

FIGURE 12-1 Caster Semenya, winner of the 800-meter gold medal in Berlin, 2009.

FIGURE 12-2 Stages in fetal development before birth.

is a dangerous problem for fetal development. Mothers who take in toxic substances like cigarettes, some prescribed medications, or street drugs place their babies at greater risk. Infections or disease (like measles), along with x-ray radiation, can negatively impact the fetus. Heavy alcohol use causes more than 40,000 children in the United States to be born with **fetal alcohol syndrome**, resulting in irreversible brain abnormalities (Burd, 2004). *Any* alcohol consumed by a pregnant woman can adversely affect the developing child. Lack of vitamins and minerals (such as folic acid) in the mother's diet can cause problems in the physical development of the fetus (Milunsky et al., 1989). In addition, diseases like HIV/AIDS can be passed from mother to fetus. If a pregnant woman is infected with HIV, she has a 20 to 50% chance of transmitting the virus to her baby during pregnancy, labor and delivery, or breastfeeding (De Cock et al., 2000). The best thing a pregnant woman can do to increase the likelihood of a healthy baby is to take care of her body during pregnancy: Do not smoke, avoid secondhand smoke, avoid alcohol and all illicit drugs, eat a healthy diet and take prenatal vitamins, exercise and get plenty of rest, and get early and regular prenatal care. Clearly, the biological vulnerability of the fetus makes planning for a pregnancy vital to its health; if unplanned, the mother may be unaware of the pregnancy during the earliest weeks of development.

Experiences in the womb also contribute to the developing person. The fetus learns the sound of its mother's voice and prefers it to the sounds of other voices (DeCasper, 1994). In addition, mothers' mental states during pregnancy appear to change the infant's reactivity to stress (Rice et al., 2010). Mothers diagnosed prenatally with anxiety and depression were more likely to have children with behavior problems at 1.5 years (Barker et al., 2011). In one study, exposure to hormones in the womb was found to correlate with development of cognitive abilities (Brosnan, 2008). In this study, ring fingers that were longer than index fingers, a sign of high prenatal testosterone exposure, were correlated with higher scores on standardized math tests. Girls with lower prenatal testosterone exposure (revealed by a shorter ring finger) had higher literacy SAT scores. (Check your own fingers: If you have a longer ring finger, your right brain may be more developed!)

The fetus is not just *growing* before birth but also increasing in **differentiation**; that is, its structures and functions are becoming more specific to perform given tasks. By around 6 months, the fetus has developed enough that it may survive on its own if born prematurely, called the **age of viability** FIGURE 12-3. A full-term birth is typically 37 weeks of prenatal development. Birth itself carries risks: The death rate of mothers from childbirth in the United States has gone from 1 in 100 before 1800 to 1 in 10,000 today. And child survival still depends on the survival of mothers. In a recent study in West Africa, children were more than four times more likely to die by age 5 if their mothers died (Strassman, 2011).

Fetal alcohol syndrome
Irreversible brain abnormalities caused by the mother's consumption of alcohol during pregnancy.

Differentiation Growth in complexity over time, with structures and functions becoming more specific for given tasks.

Age of viability By around 6 months, the fetus has developed enough that it may survive if born prematurely.

FIGURE 12-3 Stages in fetal development before birth.

Prenatal development illustrates the importance of both biological and environmental influences, and in the final section of this chapter, we will return to this theme.

The Newborn

Most animals enter the world with many "built-in" abilities to help them survive. For example, ducks and geese instinctively follow their mothers through *imprinting*. Newborn humans are also equipped with reflexes present for the first few months of life. Babies have a "rooting" instinct, in which a touch on the cheek causes them to turn and open their mouths. If you touch their lips, they try to suck. And when they feel a touch on the back of their mouths, they swallow. These instincts are obviously helpful in ensuring that newborns are able to breastfeed immediately after birth. The grasp reflex involves grabbing onto anything placed in the baby's palm, and the Moro reflex is a "startle" response to loud noises or the sudden loss of support: The baby throws its arms and legs outward, and then pulls them back together. With these physical actions, a baby may rescue itself by clinging onto a parent. These reflexes are tested at birth as signs of healthy neurological development (Majnemer et al., 1992).

Infants show considerable variability in their natural reactions to stimulation from the environment. A child may be fearful and cry with moderately stimulating play; another enjoys vigorous play and seeks out exciting events. Individual differences in **temperament**, or emotional, motor, and attentional reactions to stimulation, are evident in the first few weeks of life (Carey & McDevitt, 1978; Rothbart, 1981, 1986). Temperament appears to be biologically based (Rothbart et al., 2007). Some babies are called *difficult* because they are irritable, intense, and unpredictable, while *easy* babies are cheerful, relaxed, and more predictable. A third group is considered *slow to warm up* because they resist or withdraw from novel stimulation or new people. These observed differences in behavior may be due to underlying differences in the tuning of physiological systems, so that some infants are more aroused by stimulation than others (Kagan & Snidman, 2004).

The visual system is not well developed at birth, and infants see best at a distance of around 8 inches (Salapatek et al., 1976). This happens to be about how far they are from their mother's face while breastfeeding. But newborns have inborn visual preferences that are particularly helpful. What pattern do you suppose babies like to look at the most? In one study, 2- to 5-day-old infants were shown pairs of disks, including some with bright colors and complex patterns FIGURE 12-4 (Fantz, 1961). Their *preferential looking*—which of the two images they looked at more—was measured. The pattern babies preferred was the depiction of a human face! But perhaps they simply liked the more complex pattern in faces. To find out, another study compared a disk with a face to one with the same graphics scrambled out of order (Johnson et al., 1991). While the complex figure was interesting to them, infants spent more time following the image of the face.

In fact, babies are so attentive to faces that they can make surprising distinctions between them. In one study, faces (without hair or makeup) were shown to 9-month-old babies (Leinbach & Fagot, 1993). When they saw a series of female faces, they grew bored and stopped looking as long at each picture (they "habituated" to them). But when a male face appeared, they suddenly became interested and spent more time looking. The same behavioral pattern occurred when a series of male faces was interrupted by a female face. How do babies recognize gender? Looking at the facial profiles in FIGURE 12-5, can you

Temperament Individual differences in infants' emotional, motor, and attentional reactivity to stimulation.

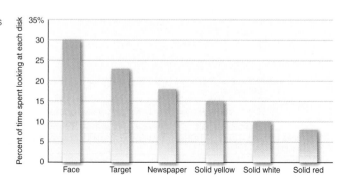

FIGURE 12-4 Babies were shown disks with different patterns. Based on eye and head movements, babies were most interested in the face design. *Source: Data from Fantz, R. L. (1961). The origin of form perception.* Scientific American, 204*(5), 1961, 66–72.*

FIGURE 12-5 Male and female profiles tend to differ in fullness of the lower face area.

spot any difference between male and female faces? It turns out that the lower facial area tends to be more full in females, sometimes called a "muzzle" effect (Bruce, 1990). Male faces (on average) have more protuberant noses and brows. A fuller lower face is associated with children and young animals, and this "baby face" feature seems to protect them from aggression from others (Berry & McArthur, 1985).

Babies are not only more interested in faces; they also come prepared to mimic them. Within 72 hours of birth, newborns imitate gestures, such as pursing their lips or sticking out their tongues (Meltzoff & Moore, 1983, 1989). Imitation may serve a purpose by connecting the newborn infant to the caregiver, helping to form social bonds. By around 2 months old, they develop the social skill of smiling with intention (Anisfeld, 1982). Imitation of behavior has been shown to promote affiliation toward humans by other primates as well (Paukner et al., 2009). Like vision, newborns' hearing is also underdeveloped at birth, but infants have been found to like listening to higher-pitched voices (Trainor & Zacharias, 1998). As a result, a "baby talk" voice (called **motherese**—high in pitch, rhythmic, and simple) is better at attracting responses from babies. These inborn patterns of attention are very helpful in focusing attention on social interactions, a very adaptive behavior in evolutionary terms. Clearly, the natural tendencies for infants to be "in tune" with parents provide an advantage, making them more likely to be cared for and, therefore, to survive.

Motherese "Baby talk" that is high in pitch, rhythmic, and simple and may better attract responses from babies.

CONCEPT LEARNING CHECK 12.1 | *Before and After Birth*

1. During the longest stage of prenatal development, the soon-to-be baby is called a _____.

2. A research study method that, for example, follows moms and babies from the prenatal period through the first year of life is called _____.

3. Dangerous external agents that affect babies during the prenatal period are called _____.

4. Newborns arrive with built-in reflexes that help them immediately _____.

5. A newborn's favorite visual pattern is _____.

12.2 Infancy and Childhood

Experiences in infancy set a foundation for social relationships, while children's thinking is qualitatively different from that of adults.

- Discuss physical development in infants and newborns.
- Examine Piaget's stage theory in relation to early cognitive development.
- Illustrate the importance of attachment in psychosocial development.

From the moment of birth through sexual maturity, we develop from 7-pound weaklings into strapping youths able to fend for ourselves if need be. A look back at childhood photos will show you how strikingly you changed from year to year compared to changes over a year as an adult. But in addition to physical changes, many changes take place in our cognitive and social development through infancy and childhood.

Physical Development

Physical growth occurs at a faster rate in the young, with another spurt in adolescence. After the first year, the head becomes proportionally smaller FIGURE 12-6. In humans, infant cranial capacity is only 23% of adult capacity; at age 2.5, cranial capacity is 75%; and at age 5, the brain has reached 90% of adult size. But the biological processes of growth are also affected by experience in the world. When rats were raised (for 4–10 weeks) in enriched playgrounds with stimulating toys, they developed heavier and thicker cerebral cortexes (Rosenzweig et al., 1972). While the number of neurons did not change, their size grew, and their synapses (the points at which two cells meet) were 50% larger. Stimulating environments produce larger, more interconnected brains.

Young children also appear to have greater **plasticity** in their neural functions. Plasticity is the capacity of the brain to adapt to the "dings, dents, and major insults" that alter it (Stein et al., 1995). After damage, other areas of the brain can change to compensate for the loss. This is because synaptic connections are created more quickly in younger brains. In one 6-year-old child, epilepsy required surgical removal of the cortex over her entire right hemisphere. Five years later, the only sign of its absence was the limited use of her left arm, and she loves math, music, and art, skills usually involving the right side of the brain (Nash, 2001). Younger people are also less likely to have linguistic deficits than people whose brains are injured when older (Chapman & McKinnon, 2000). The maturing brain also increases its speed of processing. Between the ages of 8 and 12, the children get much faster at performing a mental task, such as adding two numbers together or searching for information in memory (Kail, 1991).

In addition to continuous maturation or growth, development can take place as an orderly progression of *stages*, or discrete, qualitative "jumps" over time. Developmental psychologists have been struck by the regularity in the occurrence of stages of development. Consider the task of learning to walk FIGURE 12-7. Typically, 2-day-old babies spend

Plasticity The capacity of the brain and neurons to adapt to damage that alters them.

FIGURE 12-6 The head alone comprises about one-quarter of body size at birth, and a large proportion through 5 years of age.

Newborn   2 years   5 years   Adult

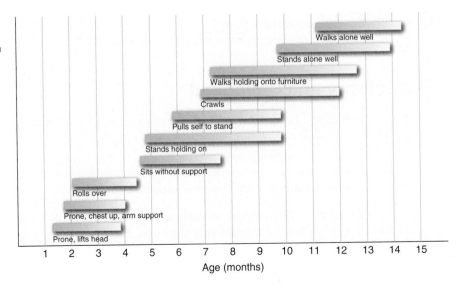

FIGURE 12-7 Children move through an orderly sequence of stages in motor development in the first year.

Walks alone well
Stands alone well
Walks holding onto furniture
Crawls
Pulls self to stand
Stands holding on
Sits without support
Rolls over
Prone, chest up, arm support
Prone, lifts head

1   2   3   4   5   6   7   8   9   10   11   12   13   14   15
Age (months)

most of their time curled in a fetal position. Three months later, they learn to roll over. At about 6 months, they are sitting up by themselves, and by 9 months, they are crawling. At 12 months, they can stand alone and will begin to walk by themselves. Do you think there are babies that can walk but cannot sit up? In fact, babies seem to go through the exact same progression of different stages in a fixed sequence as they learn to walk.

Developmental **norms** are milestones that identify *when* certain behaviors usually occur in normal development **TABLE 12-2**. Normative stages include motor skills (run, keep balance, use hands to eat and draw), language skills (gestures and communication), cognitive skills (learning, remembering, reasoning), and social skills (cooperating, responding to others). Doctors use norms to identify children that may have disruptions (such as hearing loss) or delays in their development. For example, autism spectrum disorders can be detected from videotapes of first birthday parties based on observed behaviors (Osterling & Dawson, 1994). The striking differences involve the number of sensorimotor actions performed by the children; normal children are much more active with objects in their environment. Early intervention in children with autism and other disorders can be highly beneficial to their development (Dawson et al., 2010). Keep in mind, however, that though each milestone is associated with age, the actual age when a given child reaches that milestone can vary quite a bit. Every child is unique!

> **Norm** Behavioral milestone that identifies when certain behaviors usually occur in normal development.

TABLE 12-2 Developmental Norms by Age

	Motor Skills	Sensory and Thinking Skills	Language and Social Skills
By 3 months of age does your child:	• Lift head when held at your shoulder • Lift head and chest when lying on his stomach • Turn head from side to side when lying on his stomach • Follow a moving object or person with his eyes • Often hold hands open or loosely fisted • Grasp rattle when given to her • Wiggle and kick with arms and legs	• Turn head toward bright colors and lights • Turn toward the sound of a human voice • Recognize bottle or breast • Respond to your shaking a rattle or bell	• Make cooing, gurgling sounds • Smile when smiled at • Communicate hunger, fear, discomfort (through crying or facial expression) • Usually quiet down at the sound of a soothing voice or when held • Anticipate being lifted • React to "peek-a-boo" games
By 6 months of age does your child:	• Hold head steady when sitting with your help • Reach for and grasp objects • Play with his toes • Help hold the bottle during feeding • Explore by mouthing and banging objects • Move toys from one hand to another • Shake a rattle • Pull up to a sitting position on her own if you grasp her hands • Sit with only a little support • Sit in a high chair • Roll over • Bounce when held in a standing position	• Open his mouth for the spoon • Imitate familiar actions you perform	• Babble, making almost sing-song sounds • Know familiar faces • Laugh and squeal with delight • Scream if annoyed • Smile at herself in a mirror
By 12 months of age does your child:	• Drink from a cup with help • Feed herself finger food like raisins or bread crumbs • Grasp small objects by using her thumb and index or forefinger • Use his first finger to poke or point • Put small blocks in and take them out of a container • Knock two blocks together • Sit well without support • Crawl on hands and knees	• Copy sounds and actions you make • Respond to music with body motion • Try to accomplish simple goals (seeing and then crawling to a toy) • Look for an object she watched fall out of sight (such as a spoon that falls under the table)	• Babble, but it sometimes "sounds like" talking • Say his first word • Recognize family members' names • Try to "talk" with you • Respond to another's distress by showing distress or crying • Show affection to familiar adults • Show mild to severe anxiety at separation from parent • Show apprehension about strangers • Raise her arms when she wants to be picked up

(continues)

TABLE 12-2 Developmental Norms by Age *(continued)*

	Motor Skills	Sensory and Thinking Skills	Language and Social Skills
	• Pull himself to stand or take steps holding onto furniture • Stand alone momentarily • Walk with one hand held • Cooperate with dressing by offering a foot or an arm		• Understand simple commands
By 18 months of age does your child:	• Like to pull, push, and dump things • Pull off hat, socks, and mittens • Turn pages in a book • Stack two blocks • Carry a stuffed animal or doll • Scribble with crayons • Walk without help • Run stiffly, with eyes on the ground	• Identify an object in a picture book • Laugh at silly actions (as in wearing a bowl as a hat) • Look for objects that are out of sight • Put a round lid on a round pot • Follow simple one-step directions • Solve problems by trial and error	• Say 8–10 words you can understand • Look at a person who is talking to him • Ask specifically for her mother or father • Use "hi," "bye," and "please," with reminders • Protest when frustrated • Ask for something by pointing or by using one word • Direct another's attention to an object or action • Become anxious when separated from parent(s) • Seek attention • Bring toys to share with parent • Act out a familiar activity in play (as in pretending to take a bath) • Play alone on the floor with toys • Compete with other children for toys • Recognize herself in the mirror or in pictures • Seem selfish at times
By 2 years of age does your child:	• Drink from a straw • Feed himself with a spoon • Help in washing hands • Put arms in sleeves with help • Build a tower of three or four blocks • Toss or roll a large ball • Open cabinets, drawers, boxes • Operate a mechanical toy • Bend over to pick up a toy and not fall • Walk up steps with help • Take steps backward	• Like to take things apart • Explore surroundings • Point to five or six parts of a doll when asked	• Have a vocabulary of several hundred words • Use two- or three-word sentences • Say names of toys • Ask for information about an object (asks, "Shoe?" while pointing to shoe box) • Hum or try to sing • Listen to short rhymes • Like to imitate parents • Sometimes get angry and have temper tantrums • Act shy around strangers • Comfort a distressed friend or parent • Take turns in play with other children • Treat a doll or stuffed animal as though it were alive • Apply pretend action to others (as in pretending to feed a doll) • Show awareness of parental approval or disapproval for her actions • Refer to self by name and use "me" and "mine" • Verbalize his desires and feelings ("I want cookie") • Laugh at silly labeling of objects and events (as in calling a nose an ear) • Enjoy looking at one book over and over • Point to eyes, ears, or nose when you ask

Source: Reprinted with permission from the National Network for Child Care (NNCC). Powell, J., & Smith, C. A. (1994). The 1st year. In Developmental milestones: A guide for parents. Manhattan, KS: Kansas State University Cooperative Extension Service.

Stage theory predicts that babies must crawl before they walk. Crawling appears to be required before progressing to other neuromuscular stages. However, crawling may also depend upon the culture in which a baby is raised. In Papua New Guinea, Au mothers and siblings carry infants about 85% of the time during the first year of life (Johnson, 2004). When they are put down, babies are propped up in a seated position. These babies go through a "scooting" stage in which they learn to pull themselves forward while sitting. As a result, they "skip" the crawling stage and learn to walk without ever learning to crawl. These children do not experience any problems from this different stage sequence, and babies in a number of other traditional societies are raised in this way. Anthropologist David Tracer contends the crawling stage is a recent invention that emerged only within the past century or two, after humans began living in houses with flooring that avoids exposure to dirt and germs (Wong, 2009). This example points out the importance of examining differences in development across cultures rather than assuming a universal truth for all.

In some cultures, babies and toddlers are carried by adults or siblings most of the time, resulting in different stages of motor development.

Cognitive Development

What is a baby thinking? This question is difficult to answer because young children cannot tell us what they are thinking and cannot control much of their movements. Early work on cognitive development focused on what could be observed about infants' natural behaviors. Jean Piaget (1896–1980) was a child prodigy who published his first scientific article (on albino sparrows) at age 10! Always good at meticulous scientific observation, he later applied his skills to watching the development of his own three children and trying out informal experiments with them (Gardner, 1981). From his observations, he created a theory of development that captured the field of developmental psychology (Piaget, 1928, 1932, 1951, 1952).

Piaget's Stage Theory

Piaget's theory of cognitive development focused on the formation of concepts, or mental frameworks for organizing and categorizing information. These concepts change through two processes: (1) **assimilation**, or using current concepts to understand new information, and (2) **accommodation**, or changing concepts to fit new information.

Imagine a child with a concept of a "fish." Now she sees a picture of a dolphin. It looks a lot like a fish, so the child assimilates dolphins into her category of "fish." But then her parent says, "No, dolphins are not fish, they are a different kind of water animal." Now her existing concepts cannot incorporate this new knowledge, so she accommodates by creating a new category, "water animals." Piaget sees thinking as the constant interplay of these two processes to form more and more complex concepts. Piaget then identified four different stages of thinking during development, each marked by specific qualities of thinking TABLE 12-3. Piaget proposed all humans go through an orderly sequence of stages in cognitive development, and he identified *when* the stages take place.

Assimilation Using current concepts in memory to understand new information.

Accommodation Changing concepts in memory to fit new information.

TABLE 12-3 Piaget's Stages of Development

Stage	Age	Group	Description
Sensorimotor	0–2 years	Babies and toddlers	Explores the world through sensory and motor contact
Preoperational	2–6 years	Preschool and kindergarteners	Uses symbols (words and images) but not yet logic
Concrete operational	7–12 years	Grade school years	Thinks logically about concrete objects
Formal operational	12 and on	Teens and adults	Reasons abstractly and thinks hypothetically

Source: Data from Piaget, J. (1928). The child's conception of the world. London: Routledge and Kegan Paul.

For a baby under 8 months, objects not in view seem to leave their attention, showing a lack of "object permanence."

Sensorimotor Stage

In this first stage, think of babies and toddlers as they approach the world: For them, it is all about learning to grasp and manipulate objects (a bottle, a rattle, a toy) and move through the world (to crawl, walk, and run). As a result, they are focused on developing their sensory and motor processes to coordinate their movements and their eyes with their hands. Piaget called this the **sensorimotor stage** and identified a specific behavior that changes during this stage, called **object permanence**. With babies younger than 8 months, "out of sight is out of mind." They seem to forget about objects they can no longer see and do not seem to search for them if removed. By around 9 months, babies will look for a hidden object, suggesting they are now thinking about it even when it is no longer in view. Now they love playing peek-a-boo, because they now know that objects that appear hidden are really still there. Object permanence is a key sign that a child is moving out of the sensorimotor period and into the preoperational stage.

Preoperational Stage

When you think about Piaget's **preoperational stage**, think of "*preschoolers.*" They have solved the problems of moving around their environment and can recall and think about objects that are not present. They are also rapidly learning language, using verbal symbols to represent concepts. However, preschoolers are still focused on what they perceive. Piaget identified **conservation** as a mental ability that points out the limitations of preoperational thinking. Conservation is the principle that an object maintains the same mass, volume, or number, even if it is displaced across space: A stack of pennies is the same even if spread out across the table **TABLE 12-4**. Children in the preoperational stage are overwhelmed by what things look like. This explains a preschooler's concern with sharing a cupcake: It has to *look* like two identical halves, and if one ends up spread across the plate, it looks "bigger" to them! Until around age 7, the child lacks the concept of conservation and may be misled by superficial changes in appearance.

Preschool children also believe that others know, think, and feel the same way they do, called **egocentrism**. For example, a 3-year-old child calls to his mother downstairs, "Mommy, what is this?" Preoperational preschoolers have not developed the ability to perceive things from another person's viewpoint. For example, imagine a story in which the momma bear leaves home, and a monkey comes in the window and eats a cake. When the momma bear returns, who will she blame for the missing cake? Preoperational children

Sensorimotor stage
Piaget's stage for babies and toddlers who are focused on developing their sensory and motor processes.

Object permanence
Babies remembering objects they can no longer see in front of them.

Preoperational stage
Piaget's stage for preschoolers, marked by an intense focus on what they perceive.

Conservation The knowledge that physical properties of an object stay the same even though there may be superficial changes in appearance.

Egocentrism In preschool children, the belief that others know, think, and feel the same way they do.

TABLE 12-4 Conservation Tasks

Principle	Scenario 1	Scenario 2	Interpretation
Conservation of Liquid	Two identical glasses filled with colored fluid	One glass unchanged and the other changed to a tall, thin glass, so the fluid level appears much higher	The child sees two identical glasses with the same amount of liquid. One glass is then emptied into a tall, thin glass. The child is asked, "Which glass holds more liquid?" Preoperational children will say the taller glass holds more.
Conservation of Mass	Two identical balls of colored clay	One ball unchanged and the other spread out into a longer, thinner shape	The child sees two balls of clay the same size. One ball is then flattened out so it is longer. The child is asked, "Which piece has more clay?" Preoperational children will say the longer piece has more clay.
Conservation of Number	Two rows of eight flowers each	One row unchanged and the other spread apart between flowers to make a longer row	The child see two rows of flowers with the same number in each row. One row is spread out so that it is spread across the table. The child is asked, "Which row has more flowers?" Preoperational children will say the spread out row has more flowers.

cannot yet distinguish between what *they* know and what *others* know, so they answer, "The monkey!" (Wimmer & Perner, 1983). Egocentrism and lack of conservation demonstrate that the preoperational child is able to think from only one perspective at a time.

Concrete Operational Stage

Around 7 years of age, children advance into the **concrete operational stage**. They have achieved conservation and are no longer fooled by appearances. At the same time, they usually enter grade school and receive some training in learning to think logically. But while they are able to learn concrete concepts like arithmetic, they are still limited in their reasoning. What does it mean that "the Earth is round?" FIGURE 12-8. One study examined how children's conceptions of the Earth's shape changed from preschool to fifth grade (Vosniadou & Brewer, 1992). This concept is difficult because you must combine the notion of the round planet with the powerful perceptual sense that the Earth you are standing upon is flat. One research project created a flight simulator that took children on a ride around the Earth, showing the flat Earth on takeoff and landing. Even after the trip, children reported that they believed the Earth is flat (Johnson et al., 1999). The ability to combine two dimensions at once, such as a local view and a distant view of Earth, is finally accomplished toward the end of the concrete operational stage. But even more advanced reasoning is identified with the final stage of Piaget's theory, the formal operational stage.

Formal Operational Stage

Piaget's **formal operational stage** begins at about age 12 and is characterized by reasoning on a logical or hypothetical level. Before this stage, children use trial and error to solve problems; with formal operations, they can use logical methods like experimentation. For example, can you design an experiment that would identify whether cell phones cause brain tumors? Or explain the consequences if people were able to fly? Thinking in an orderly fashion and conceiving novel causes and consequences represents the highest level of cognitive development. Of course, most adults do not always function at this formal level. As discussed earlier, people often use heuristic "rules" to take shortcuts in reasoning. But children around the time of puberty are finally cognitively *capable* of learning the formal methods of thinking, and formal schooling helps to develop these skills.

Challenges to Piaget's Stage Theory

After Piaget, researchers finally came up with new ways of asking babies about what they are thinking. The key was developing ways to measure it. For example, one study placed a mobile (a toy with objects hanging from it) suspended over a crib and connected it with a string to the right foot of a baby. Just 3 months old, the babies quickly learned to jiggle just their right foot to make the mobile move (Rouvee-Collier et al., 1980). Further, though the babies forgot about the kicking after about 8 days, they were able to recall it up to 4 weeks later if given a brief refresher training. This far exceeds the cognitive development Piaget described for the sensorimotor period.

Another innovative technique to assess infant thinking is based on habituation, or loss of response to a stimulus over time (Bornstein, 1989). Babies shown a picture of a red turtle will initially look at it closely; but if a similar picture is presented again, the infant shows a lack of interest by looking away, a lowered heartbeat, or decreasing their sucking on a pacifier. Now, if a picture of a blue bird is presented, the baby will

> **Concrete operational stage** Piaget's stage when grade schoolers have achieved conservation and are no longer fooled by appearances.
>
> **Formal operational stage** Piaget's final stage (around age 12) characterized by reasoning on a logical or hypothetical level.

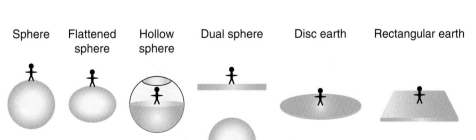

Sphere Flattened sphere Hollow sphere Dual sphere Disc earth Rectangular earth

FIGURE 12-8 The notion that the flat surface you stand on is actually a giant globe is difficult to grasp, and children go through stages in its understanding.
Source: Reproduced from Vosniadou, S., & Brewer, W. F. (1992). Mental models of the earth: A study of conceptual change in childhood. Cognitive Psychology, 24, 535–585.

FIGURE 12-9 Based on behaviors that indicate surprise, researchers can determine babies' cognitive expectations.

look at it much longer, showing it is perceived as novel. So the habituation procedure involves first making the baby "bored" by showing similar things and then seeing if he notices a new item as different. A longer looking time or *preferential looking* (judged by observers who cannot see what the baby is looking at) reveals the baby is surprised by the new stimulus (Fantz, 1961).

Piaget claimed that, after about 9 months, babies will search for hidden objects, suggesting the infant achieved *object permanence*. But new studies using looking times showed that infants as young as 5 months thought the hidden object was still there. How do we know? They showed surprise! For example, if a bunny is shown to an infant, then a screen comes down to hide it, and then the screen rises to show *no* bunny, the infants look longer than when the bunny is still there FIGURE 12-9. Based upon observations of the surprise reactions, babies expected object permanence at a much younger age—they just could not show it by reaching out for the object themselves (Baillargeon et al., 1985; Wynn, 1992). By depending only on the baby's motor behaviors, Piaget underestimated the cognitive abilities of babies.

Now that we know how to ask them, what do babies really think? In one study, 4-month-old babies watched a stick moving across a stage with an obstruction across its middle (Kellman & Spelke, 1983) FIGURE 12-10. The two ends they could see always moved together. When the obstruction was removed, some saw a complete stick left behind, and these babies showed habituation—it was what they expected. But for other babies, when the obstruction was removed, two *separate* sticks were revealed. Then, the babies looked 30 seconds longer at the two stick pieces. So, 10-week-old babies expect that objects are unitary (parts that move together are parts of the same object). Other studies showed babies were surprised when a block stayed suspended in midair or a car seemed to pass through a solid object (Baillargeon, 2008; Talbot, 2006). Nine-month-old babies also show a sense of number, distinguishing between two and three objects, or two versus three repetitions of actions (McCrink & Wynn, 2004). Babies know a lot more about the world than we thought!

Piaget's notion of egocentrism has also been expanded to reflect the **theory of mind**, or the child's conception of what he or she and others know (Wellman, 1990). Three-year-olds have some understanding of their own and others' minds, knowing that they can have a dream while someone else did not, or hide objects so someone else cannot see them (Flavell, Shipstead, & Croft, 1978). Two-year-olds can predict actions and emotions; for example, if Pat looks for her friend in one location and cannot find him, they understand that she will be sad and will look for him somewhere else. But not until age 3 can children predict where Pat might look based on what *Pat* believes. The child's theory of mind—including differences between what he or she knows and what other people know—develops throughout the preschool years (Wellman, 1990). The idea of

Theory of mind The child's conception of what he or she and others know, and that these can differ.

FIGURE 12-10 With a block in front, the stick moving behind it is assumed to be a single object. When it is revealed to be two separate sticks, babies are surprised! *Source: Reproduced from Kellman, P. J., & Spelke, E. S. (1983). Perception of partly occluded objects in infancy. Cognitive Psychology, 15(4), 483–524.*

false beliefs does not arise until age 4 or 5. For example, 3-year-olds are presented with a candy box and see pencils inside. They say that other kids will also think pencils are in the box. They will also say they had *always* thought there were pencils in the box (Gopnik & Astington, 1988). Four-year-olds "get" the trick the experimenter is playing, and they predict that *other* children will also be tricked.

Other theorists, such as Lev Vygotksy (1896–1934), proposed that cognition also requires social processes during learning (Wertsch, 1985). A mental skill like retracing your steps to find a lost item may be learned by internalizing information in a social interaction. For example, you lose your jacket, and your mom asks you, "Were you wearing it when you came home?" By seeing another's strategies, we internalize new ways of thinking. Vygotsky also proposed a **zone of proximal development** that predicts *what* children will learn next. This zone is the range between what the child can already do and what he or she is ready to accomplish. For example, once a child can count, he or she is ready to learn about zero. This notion of just-right-sized steps in learning is very important in the design of modern school curricula.

Given this new evidence about development, was Piaget wrong? Yes, in that babies know more than he suspected, and that cognition develops more gradually and continuously than he proposed. For example, a child may grasp conservation of number before displaying conservation of mass. And a child may be able to recognize someone else's emotions before becoming able to understand another's beliefs. However, Piaget was accurate in that children do seem to progress through his four stages of thinking in the same order and at about the ages he predicted they would. So Piaget was pretty close!

Social Development

Human infants, like the young of most mammals, are dependent on their parents to help them survive and thrive in the world. One of the primary bonds across species is the mother–infant bond. In evolutionary terms, it is in a mother's best interest to foster the well-being of her child and for the child to attract and hold the interest of its mother. **Attachment** refers to this deep, emotional bond that an infant develops with its caregiver. But what motivates the infant to bond?

The Power of Touch

In a paper called "The Nature of Love," Harry Harlow (1906–1981) set out to determine why infants bond. Using rhesus monkeys, his studies tested a theory called the primary drives theory (Harlow, 1958). Attachment may happen just because you associate the satisfaction of primary drives (hunger, thirst) with the person who satisfies them. In other words, you, like my dog, may become emotionally attached to whoever feeds you. To test this theory, Harlow constructed surrogate "mothers" from wood, rubber, terry cloth, and wire. The "mothers" had a working nursing device to provide milk and a light bulb within the body to provide warmth. But one "mother" was covered by a wire form, and the other by softer sponge rubber covered by terry cloth FIGURE 12-11. Infant monkeys were placed

Zone of proximal development Children's readiness to learn the next step from what they already know.

Attachment A deep, emotional bond that an infant develops with its caregiver.

FIGURE 12-11 Two surrogate monkey "moms," one made of wire and one of terry cloth.

in cages containing both of these mothers. In half the cages, the cloth mother provided the milk, and in the other half, the wire mother did. Infant monkeys lived alone in one of these cages for the first 5 months of their lives, and the amount of time they spent in direct contact with each surrogate "mother" was recorded.

Not surprisingly, the monkeys preferred the softer, terry cloth mom. But Harlow's study showed that the source of milk had very little impact on the amount of time spent with each surrogate. *All* of the monkeys spent nearly *all* of their time clinging to the soft mother, regardless of whether the wire mother or the cloth mother provided milk FIGURE 12-12. Even the monkeys feeding from the wire surrogate left the cloth surrogate as briefly as possible to nurse and quickly returned to the terry cloth "mom" FIGURE 12-13. Harlow called this need **contact comfort**, or the need for touch as a primary drive in monkeys. Further studies showed that when the monkeys were faced with threatening objects, like a noisy robot, they raced to their cloth "mother" for comfort and protection. When left in the cage without the soft surrogate, they would

Contact comfort The need for touch as a primary drive in monkeys and humans.

FIGURE 12-12 Baby monkey clings to its terry cloth "mom."

FIGURE 12-13 Monkeys held onto their soft "mom" even when driven to nurse from the wire "mom."

FIGURE 12-14 Motherless monkeys showed signs of emotional devastation, raising ethical questions about the studies.

freeze in fear or cry, crouch, and suck their thumbs FIGURE 12-14. With their soft "mom" present, they were more likely to investigate the robot from this secure base. Harlow's findings identified the attachment bond as psychological (contact) rather than biological (food). From his studies, Harlow concluded that contact comfort was the primary need in infants and that the ability to nurse was not as important.

At the time (in 1958), this idea went against the prevailing culture in the United States. Harlow was stating that the source of the bond between baby and mother was not milk but the frequent and intimate body contact between them. He suggested that fathers and other caregivers could serve this contact need just as well as mothers. Later studies supported the idea that increased contact with fathers had benefits for the father and child (Keller et al., 1985; Lamb, 1977). In fact, fathers who were allowed to hold their babies at birth were more likely to touch them when observed while playing at 3 months (Rödholm, 1981). Cultures vary in the practice of contact between fathers and infants and in the rates of breast versus bottle feeding. However, the benefits of child–caregiver touch are readily observed across cultures and childrearing practices (Johnson, 2004; Jung & Fouts, 2011). For example, mothers given free infant carriers rather than infant seats were found to be more responsive to their babies' vocalizations at 3.5 months (Anisfeld et al., 1990). In short, babies need as much contact comfort as possible! Note that this fits with an evolutionary perspective: An infant that is clinging to its mother is much less likely to be hurt or left behind in an emergency. Contact comfort also serves to keep infants safe by keeping them close to their protectors.

Harlow's research was also controversial because of the use of monkeys as subjects and their experiences in the studies. The surrogate mothers were not real parents, and monkeys reared in these conditions had difficulty in social settings once they rejoined social groups. Some monkeys were left alone without even surrogate "mothers," and their emotional suffering was readily apparent. However, Harlow's studies also had important benefits for the lives of many children. The "power of touch" was soon implemented in institutional care settings in which orphans had in the past received little attention beyond feeding. Now, infants are intentionally held and touched as much as possible by staff and volunteers. For example, premature infants' medical care often limits their interaction with others FIGURE 12-15; by introducing "kangaroo care," even premature babies benefit from skin-to-skin contact FIGURE 12-16 (Feldman & Eidelman, 1998; Feldman et al., 2003).

What motivates the caregiver to bond with a child? Biology plays an important role in creating the bond between mother and child. Oxytocin, the hormone linked to close relationships and sexual intercourse, also plays a role in parenting. Mothers with higher levels of oxytocin in their blood before and after giving birth are more strongly attached to their babies (Levine et al., 2007). Attachment is observed in mothers who focused their gaze mostly on the child, exhibited positive energy, maintained constant affectionate touch, and used a "motherese" speech pattern. For fathers, close contact with their children has been shown to lead to decreases in levels of testosterone, the male hormone related to sex and aggression (Gettler et al., 2011). In a longitudinal study, fathers reporting 3 hours or more of daily childcare had lower testosterone levels at follow-up compared with fathers not involved in care. Biological responses to infants help parents to focus attention on their newborns and to build bonds with their children that are of great importance to their relationships in infancy and throughout life. Clearly, these bonds have value in promoting the survival of the babies.

Attachment Theory

John Bowlby (1969, 1973, 1980) developed a theory about the formation of attachment bonds and suggested there is a *sensitive period* for them. This means attachment relationships develop more readily when the child is between 6 months to 24 months of age. After the sensitive period, a first attachment relationship can develop, but with greater difficulty. This sensitive period coincides with a period during which the baby shows an increasing tendency to approach familiar caregivers and to avoid unfamiliar adults FIGURE 12-17. This **stranger anxiety** refers to the fear reaction infants develop around 12 months of age. A related fear, called separation anxiety, is expressed when babies are separated from mother or father, and is observed across cultures FIGURE 12-18 (Kagan, 1976; Werner, 1988). It may reflect improving memory and conceptual development in the baby (Kagan, 1976), and it coincides with the timing of Piaget's (1932) object permanence. All children go through this normal stage of separation anxiety during development.

However, developmental psychologists also noticed that children *differ* in their level of attachment to their caregiver. As a result of their experiences, some children are more attached than are other children. Mary Ainsworth (1913–1999) created a test of Bowlby's theory of attachment in a laboratory (Ainsworth & Bell, 1970; Ainsworth et al., 1978; Bell & Ainsworth, 1972). First, a child and its mother are left alone together in a playroom. In the **strange situation procedure**, the mother then leaves the child alone, and a friendly

FIGURE 12-15 Premature birth often requires medical interventions that limit the ability to hold and nurse the infant.

FIGURE 12-16 Parents are now encouraged to have regular skin-to-skin contact with their babies.

FIGURE 12-17 Babies demonstrate a "stranger anxiety" with fearful crying that peaks around 12 months.

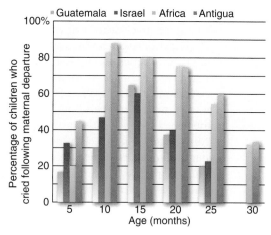

FIGURE 12-18
Anxiety when separated from mother is observed across cultures.
Source: Adapted from Kagan, J. (1976). Emergent themes in human development. American Scientist, 64, 186–196.

stranger enters and tries to interact with the child. Finally, the mother returns to rejoin them. How do the babies react?

Sixty percent of infants tested at 1 year of age showed a *secure attachment* to their mother **TABLE 12-5** (Ainsworth, 1979). "Secure" describes an attachment in which the child seems happy with the parent present, distressed when the parent leaves, and delighted by the parent's return. Just like the monkeys with the Harlow "soft moms," securely attached babies are comfortable when their mothers are near, and they use her as a *secure base* for venturing out and exploring the world. When she is gone, the child is upset, and when she returns, the child greets her with excitement. With secure attachment, the infant feels her caregiver will meet her needs. Secure attachment is more likely to occur when the mother is available and appropriately responsive to her child (Ainsworth, 1979).

When children have a secure attachment at 1 year, they grow up to feel happier and have more successful peer relationships (Pastor, 1981; Waters et al., 1979). Securely attached children have been shown to be more positive about others when they become adolescents and have better adult relationships (Allen et al., 2003). They seem to face the world with an ongoing confidence that the world is a safe place, a result of the *basic trust* they felt toward their caregiver (Erikson, 1959, 1968). Our early attachment experiences

Stranger anxiety A fear reaction of infants to new people usually peaking around 12 months.

Strange situation procedure A test in which the mother leaves her child alone in the playroom, and a friendly stranger tries to interact with the child. Finally, the mother rejoins them.

TABLE 12-5 Attachment Styles

Attachment Pattern	Child	Caregiver
Secure	• Caregiver is a "secure base" during exploration • Protests caregiver's departure • Seeks caregiver and is comforted on return • May be comforted by stranger, but prefers caregiver	• Responds appropriately to needs • Behaves contingently with the child's requests
Avoidant	• Little or no distress on departure • Little or no visible response to caregiver's return • Ignoring, or turning away if picked up • Treats the stranger the same as the caregiver	• Little or no response to distressed child • Discourages crying and encourages independence
Ambivalent/anxious	• Clinging before separation occurs • Distressed on separation • Ambivalent, angry on return • Seeks contact but resists when it is achieved	• Inconsistent responses • Responds to increased attachment behavior from the infant
Disorganized	• Freezing or rocking • Lack of coherent attachment strategy	• Frightened or frightening behavior, abuse toward the child

Source: Data from Ainsworth, M. D. S., Blehar, M., Waters, E., & Wall, S. (1978). Patterns of attachment: Psychological studies of the strange situation. Hillsdale, NJ: Erlbaum.

appear to form a basis of our other close relationships, even as adults (Waters & Cummings, 2000; Waters et al., 2000). As adults, our styles in relationships tend to mirror the same pattern of attachment we experienced in our primary relationship (Hazan & Shaver, 1987; Shaver & Mikulincer, 2007). About 30% of people report changing attachment styles in adulthood, most notably those who had insecure attachments to parents early in life (Davila & Cobb, 2003). Of course, many other factors influence our intimate relationships.

Children thrive under attentive care giving. But that does not always mean their mother, their father, a relative, or even one single person must be involved. In the Efe of Zaire, multiple caregivers are involved with each child (Field, 1996). In this culture, women work together to care for all young children, taking turns holding and nursing newborns. As a result, the child forms strong attachments to multiple adults in the community. It appears that there are many ways of providing for an infant to produce the outcome of a healthy, secure child (Werner, 1988). Similarly, children raised on Israeli kibbutzim, a communal arrangement in which children live separately from their parents, appear to form satisfactory bonds for secure attachment (Sagi et al., 1994). However, secure attachments were more frequent when the children also slept at home with their parents. The important factor is not *who* gives the care, but that someone does.

Disruption of Attachment

What happens when secure attachment is disrupted? Some babies learn they cannot rely upon the caregiver and act this out in the strange situation task mentioned earlier by showing *insecure attachment* (see **TABLE 12-5**). Some of these children seem to alternately seek out and then avoid their mothers, called *ambivalent/anxious attachment*. For example, the baby clings to the parent when she or he tries to leave, cries during separation, but reacts with anger to their reunion. For these children, there is no secure base, and they respond with anxiety. Others show *avoidant attachment*, with none of the typical signs of interest in or consolation from their mothers. They treated the stranger in the same way as their caregivers. What causes these differences in attachment style?

Ainsworth's studies of families in their homes demonstrated that a secure attachment relationship depends on the quality of caregiving the infant receives. Consistent and *responsive* caregiving—noticing and responding to the child—leads to a more secure attachment (Ainsworth et al., 1978; Ainsworth, 1979). Disrupted attachment results when parents are inattentive or respond only some of the time. Problems with attachment also affect other outcomes; for example, those with secure attachment are less likely to have behavioral problems in preschool (Erickson et al., 1985). Intervention programs have been successful at teaching mothers to be more sensitive to their babies' signals (Velderman, 2006).

Is there evidence for a sensitive period in forming attachments? We know from studies of other animals that bonding is sometimes limited to a specific time window, called a **critical period**. For example, the imprinting of baby ducks (in which they focus on following their mother) has a critical period of 13 to 16 hours shortly after hatching; if missed, imprinting will not occur. Because it would be highly unethical to intentionally disrupt human attachment, the only available information comes from cases of neglected infants. This sometimes occurs because of institutional care before adoption or from extreme neglect in the home. One such child, Genie (a pseudonym), was discovered when she was 13 years old. Since infancy, her parents had locked her alone in a small room. When she was discovered, she was unable to stand, was not toilet trained, and could understand only her name. During the first 7 months after her rescue, Genie learned to walk (PBS, 1997). Over time, her cognitive abilities improved, reaching normal levels on some perceptual tasks. While Genie did improve her skills, she did not fully develop language. She did form attachments to her caregivers and to a psychologist studying her language use (Curtiss, 1977). Though her father was convicted of child abuse, Genie was eventually returned to live with her mother. As this case shows, the consequences of missing the attachment bond in infancy can be extreme.

Critical period A period during development where specific abilities must occur.

Family Relationships

Studies of parenting have identified differences in terms of how parents establish control over their children. The authoritarian parenting style focuses on obedience without question: "Because I said so!" This parenting pattern tends to produce children with low

Authoritative parenting style A balance between obedience from the child and willingness to explain and make exceptions.

self-esteem. Permissive parents go to an opposite extreme, allowing the children to impose their own control on their behavior: "What do you want to do?" As a result of a lack of boundaries, their children are often impulsive and more immature than other children. Finally, the **authoritative parenting style** falls in the middle of these extremes: They have rules to be followed, but these parents are willing to explain the reasons behind them and to allow occasional exceptions to them. Children reporting high levels of self-confidence tend to have authoritative parents (Baumrind, 1996). This pattern has been observed across cultures throughout the world (Sorkhabi, 2005).

Within families, each parent is experienced differently by each child (Ricciuti & Scarr, 1990). Children may perceive unequal treatment from their parents, termed *differential parenting*. If children receive equal affection from their parents (in comparison to siblings), they have higher self-esteem, more secure attachment styles, and less romantic relationship distress (Rauer & Volling, 2007). However, if parents "played favorites," their children felt more negative about themselves, whether or not they were the favored child. The early within-family experiences of childhood appear critical to building healthy self-esteem, and these first relationships continue to influence us throughout life (Bronfenbrenner, 1986).

Sibling relationships also contribute to development (Brody, 2004). Interactions with older siblings can improve language and cognitive development and the understanding of other people's emotions and perspectives. However, aggressive older siblings can lead to younger children performing poorly in school and having fewer positive peer experiences (Bank, Patterson, & Reid, 1996). These risks are greater for children living in disadvantaged neighborhoods (with high unemployment rates and pervasive poverty; Brody et al., 2003). However, older siblings can also provide a buffer to younger siblings from the negative effects of family disruption (Jenkins, 1992). And parents' experiences with older children also tend to improve their parenting of younger children (Whiteman & Buchanan, 2002).

A major concern for many parents is the effect of daycare on their child's development. Many families in which parents work outside the home worry that their children will be harmed by having other caregivers for long periods. No research has shown a relationship between working mothers and outcomes of development (Goldberg et al., 2008). Studies *have* found that high-quality daycare, with warm, supportive interactions with adults in a safe and stimulating environment, produces better outcomes (Scarr, 1997; Phillips et al., 2000). Lower socioeconomic status is associated with problems in daycare, along with less stimulation and fewer educational opportunities (Burchinal et al., 1989). But, daycare can even be a protective factor in families of lower socioeconomic status, enhancing academic achievement in elementary school (Burchinal et al., 2009). For at-risk children, more hours of daycare have a compensatory effect, but children from middle-income households did less well with more hours of outside care.

A longitudinal study found that children who had spent more time in daycare showed increased aggressive behavior, but only through grade 3 (NICHD, 2005). A consistent finding is that more hours of childcare are correlated with problem behaviors, even into mid-adolescence (Vandell et al., 2010). However, across 40 years of childcare research, studies show the quality and type of care are related to gains in cognitive, academic, and language functioning in young children and that benefits extend for more than 10 years after leaving daycare (Vandell et al., 2010). These long-lasting (albeit small) benefits occurred for middle-class and affluent children as well as for those who are economically disadvantaged (Ziegler & Styfco, 2004). More research on the impact of daycare and how the features of care affect different children is needed. At this point, the evidence suggests daycare can benefit all children if it is of moderately high quality and if the hours of care are not excessive.

A rite of passage for many children is the divorce of their parents. When divorce occurs, it is often accompanied by a history of family strife and other changes, such as an absent father, working mother, and change in homes (Johnston et al., 1989). As a result, it can be difficult to discern the causal factors in adjustment (Kelly, 2000). Surrounding the time of divorce, family conflicts increase, including custody and financial issues, and continue postdivorce. Parental discipline can become less consistent (Hetherington et al., 1985). In the midst of change, children can respond with anger, grief, guilt, and depression. Some feel better off, some adjust quickly, and some show long-term negative effects, such as poorer grades (Amato, 2000; Amato & Keith, 1991a;

Kelly & Emery, 2003). Children with divorced parents score significantly lower on measures of academic achievement, conduct, psychological adjustment, self-concept, and social relations (Amato, 2001). A review of studies of the economic impact of divorce suggests that families are better off if they stay together (Hetherington, 1999). A meta-analysis of studies showed consequences for the children such as fewer years of education, early parenting, and an increased likelihood of becoming divorced themselves (Amato & Keith, 1991b; Kiernan & Hobcraft, 1997).

Peers

One of the first self-identifications children make is their gender: They learn to think of themselves as male or female by age 4 (Martin & Ruble, 2004). They then use this knowledge to self-segregate by gender to form peer groups. One study found a 10-to-1 ratio in same-sex versus opposite-sex play partners in kindergarteners (Laosa & Brophy, 1972). Throughout childhood, differences in the activities of boys and girls have been observed across human and primate societies. For example, from age 3, girls spend more time working, whereas boys spend more time in play; boys engage in more rough-and-tumble play, while girls engage in more infant contact and grooming (real and play; Edwards, 1993). **Gender roles**—our expectations about how males and females should act—are learned through culture. Gender differences in "play-mothering" (i.e., carrying sticks like mother chimpanzees carrying infants) have been observed in chimpanzees and appear to be supported by cultural practices within a group FIGURE 12-19 (Kahlenberg & Wrangham, 2010). Gender differences in observed behavior occur early in development, well before the biological influences from reproductive maturation in puberty (McIntyre & Pope Edwards, 2009).

Peer relationships in childhood can be important bonds even for very young children like preschoolers. Children who had been together for 3 to 4 years but then transferred to new schools showed increases in desire for physical contact, negative statements and affect, fussiness, and illness, as well as changes in eating and sleeping patterns (Field, 1984). In addition, the children's drawings of themselves showed agitation and disorganization, with distorted facial and body parts and sad faces FIGURE 12-20. While we think of peer relationships as critical in adolescence, children are learning from their peers from a very young age and developing bonds, even though the friendships are much shorter in duration.

Gender roles Our expectations about how males and females should act are learned through culture.

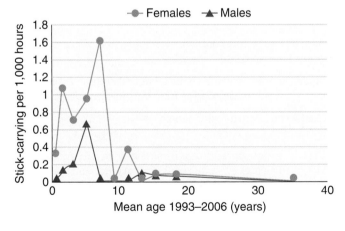

FIGURE 12-19 Age and sex differences in the rate of stick carrying as "dolls" in chimpanzees.
Source: Reproduced from Kahlenberg, S. M., & Wrangham, R. W., (2010). Sex differences in chimpanzees' use of sticks as play objects resemble those of children. Current Biology, *20(24), R1067–R1068.*

FIGURE 12-20 A 4-year-old boy created this self-portrait just before moving to a new preschool (Field, 1984).
Courtesy of Tiffany Field.

Peer relationships can sometimes be marked by bullying, either as an aggressor or as a victim. Bullying may be physical or verbal—hitting or kicking, teasing or taunting—or may involve indirect actions such as manipulating others or purposefully excluding other children from activities (Rivers & Smith, 1994). Both children and adults underestimate the prevalence of and harm from bullying (Whitney & Smith, 1993). A study of fourth to sixth graders in the rural South indicated that 1 in 4 students had been bullied with some regularity within the past 3 months and that 1 in 10 had been bullied at least once a week (Limber et al., 1997). Children who are chronic victims of bullying experience more physical and psychological problems than their peers, and they tend not to grow out of the role of victim (Olweus, 1993). These negative interactions can have devastating long-term effects on self-esteem (Seals & Young, 2003). One 11-year-old boy, Jaheem Herrera, told his mother he was being bullied. He used to say "Mom they keep telling me this . . . this gay word, this gay, gay, gay. I'm tired of hearing it; they're telling me the same thing over and over" (Simon, 2009). Jaheem took his own life to escape the constant harassment. Increasingly, children are able to exert bullying behavior using the Internet, and **cyberbullying**, or online harassment, which has been documented in primary schools as well as secondary schools (DeHue et al., 2008). Schools are making efforts to intervene, and schoolwide programs about bullying have been shown to reduce reported incidents (Olweus, 1996).

Cyberbullying Aggressive and hostile acts toward others through Internet media.

A child's development of social relationships is influenced by multiple factors, from the initial family environment, extended family, caregivers, and peers to biological influences such as the evolutionary tendencies that promote taking care of infants. Other biological factors like temperament may alter how social bonds are formed, and environmental factors like daycare and school may influence the child's sense of social ties. Environmental and biological influences combine to create a unique experience in each child's social development.

CONCEPT LEARNING CHECK 12.2 | *Stages of Cognitive Development*

Match the concept to the examples.

A. Sensorimotor stage

1. _____ Helen is looking at a large picture book while her Dad is seated at a desk in the next room. "What is this at the top of the page, Dad?" she asks.

B. Preoperational stage

2. _____ Harold grabs his cup, moves it away from the table, and drops it. His mom puts it back on the table. Harold grabs his cup, moves it away from the table, and drops it.

C. Concrete operational stage

3. _____ Jordana gets upset when her twin sister dumps her bag of Halloween candy. Jordana's neatly piled stack looks much smaller than her sister's spread-out pile.

D. Formal operational stage

4. _____ Jorges is not sure which of the three syrups he likes best on his pancakes. So he tries out each one separately first, then he tries every pair of syrups together, and then combines all three at a time. He finally settles on his favorite flavor and color.

12.3 Adolescence and Young Adulthood

Adolescence is an important period in which puberty, brain development, and social interactions produce rapid changes in the individual.

- Discuss the impact of sexual development in adolescence and changes in moral reasoning in adolescents and young adults.
- Examine the life stages within Erikson's theory of psychosocial development.

For 12-year-olds, childhood is behind them. Ahead lies adolescence, the dawn of a new era in development, stretching from the teen years through age 20. Many cultures mark this turning point in development. For example, Jewish families hold bar mitzvah and bat mitzvah for 13-years-olds, Hispanic and South American families celebrate the quinceañera for girls at 15, and many African cultures have a ceremonial rite of passage between childhood and full inclusion into a tribe or social group. This next stage of development toward adulthood is characterized by great changes in physical, cognitive, and social development. In the United States, the early 20s mark a time of many transitions, as students complete college, enter long-term relationships, select a career direction, and leave the family home. In *emerging adulthood* (Arnett, 2006), many questions of how you will choose to live your life are addressed for the first time.

Physical Development

The causal factor leading to these big changes in development is *puberty*, or the sexual maturation that occurs as a result of rising hormone levels; specifically, testosterone in boys and estrogen and progesterone in girls. The hormones cause biological changes that signal reproductive maturity. **Primary sexual characteristics**, the reproductive organs and external genitalia, undergo development. **Secondary sexual characteristics** (pubic hair, breast development in girls and facial hair and lowered voice in boys) announce puberty, along with a spurt in height and changes to the body's overall shape. For girls, the first menstrual period, called **menarche** (me-NAR-kee) occurs (on average) at age 12, indicating the capacity to become pregnant. For boys, the first ejaculation occurs around age 14, followed a year later by the development of mature sperm cells, called **spermarche** (sperm-AR-kee; Hirsch et al., 1985). These are notable changes, but the physical changes continue on into adulthood as the body matures under hormonal influences. These changes can be difficult to adjust to, especially if puberty occurs earlier or later than average. The average age is also lower for both boys and girls than in the past (12.5 for girls in the United States; Anderson et al., 2003) due to improvements in nutrition (Gilger et al., 1991).

What are the psychological effects of these physical changes caused by hormones? For girls, their appearance can become a dominant concern, while boys experience puberty as a more positive change (Petersen et al., 1991). Sexuality is imposed on all adolescents in terms of interest, curiosity, and readiness for sexual reponse. U.S. surveys show 48% of teenage boys and 43% of teenage girls are sexually active (Brener et al., 2002). Though teen pregnancy rates are now in decline, approximately 80% of pregnancies under age 18 are unplanned. Regardless of the outcome—abortion, early marriage, single parenthood—early pregnancies change lives dramatically. Yet in one study, the majority of college students surveyed stated they had not used contraception in their first sexual experience (Darling et al., 1992). This suggests the rapid pace of physical development in adolescence far outpaces development in cognitive and social areas.

As it happens, the physical maturation of the brain goes through its own growth spurt during adolescence FIGURE 12-21 (Lenroot & Giedd, 2006). Because the brain reaches 90% of adult size by age 6, it was thought that the brain was also fully matured. In fact, our brains

Primary sexual characteristics The reproductive organs and external genitalia.

Secondary sexual characteristics Physical changes, including pubic hair, breast development in girls, facial hair and lowered voice in boys, along with a spurt in height and changes to the body's overall shape, that occur during puberty.

Menarche The occurrence of a first menstrual period, indicating the capacity to become pregnant.

Spermarche For boys, the first ejaculation occurs around age 14, followed a year later by the development of mature sperm cells.

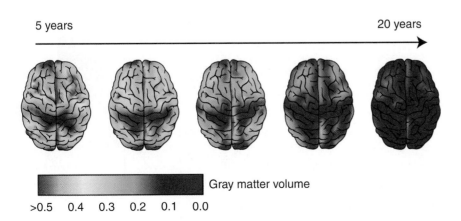

5 years   20 years

Gray matter volume

>0.5   0.4   0.3   0.2   0.1   0.0

FIGURE 12-21 Gray matter volume in the cortex (shown in purple) increases with maturation from 5 to 20 years of age. *Source: Reproduced from Lenroot, R. K., & Giedd, J. N. (2006). Brain development in children and adolescents: insights from anatomical magnetic resonance imaging.* Neuroscience & Biobehavioral Review, 30(6), 718–729.

Neural pruning
Winnowing down the number of neural connections in the brain, associated with adolescence.

undergo a massive reorganization between our 12th and 25th years (Casey et al., 2008) FIGURE 12-22. The infant brain has relatively few connections between neurons. Early brain development involves tremendous growth in the number of connections made between neurons. Over time, the neural connections become more and more dense. Then, in adolescence, a new type of physical development takes place in the brain: winnowing down the number of neural connections, called **neural pruning** (Blakemore, 2008). The brain differentiates useful connections from useless connections: The most heavily used synapses grow richer and stronger, and the connections that do not get used are lost and literally disappear. So the neural connections in the brain become increasingly complex and differentiated in their purpose in the adolescent years. As a result, the cortex becomes thinner but more efficient. In addition, the speed of processing in the brain grows to be a hundred times faster due to increased myelination (or covering) of neural axons, allowing speedier transfer of information along neural pathways (Silveri et al., 2006).

The teenage brain is driven by emotion, and cognitive control takes longer to develop. Physical changes in the brain during adolescence start in the rear brain areas and the limbic system and move slowly toward the frontal lobes. This means that more basic functions, such as emotion, vision, and movement, improve in processing speed first. The amygdala areas respond to negative or fearful stimuli more intensely during adolescence (Guyer et al., 2008), and brain areas involved in rewards are activated more in teens (Somerville et al., 2011). Later, stronger links are added between the hippocampus and the frontal lobe areas that control behavior (Asato et al., 2010). This means emotional reactivity increases *before* the development of control provided by the frontal areas FIGURE 12-23. As a result, adolescents' capacity for cognitive control has not fully matured (Somerville

FIGURE 12-22 In the first panel, the interconnections between neurons at birth are sparse; by age 12, the interconnections are quite dense; in the teen years, the connections are "pruned" to maintain only those often used.

FIGURE 12-23 Adolescents show a larger magnitude of activation in response to happy faces relative to both children and adults.
Source: Reproduced from Somerville, L. H., Hare, T., & Casey, B. J. (2011). Frontostriatal maturation predicts cognitive control failure to appetitive cues in adolescents. Journal of Cognitive Neuroscience, 23(9), 2123–2134.

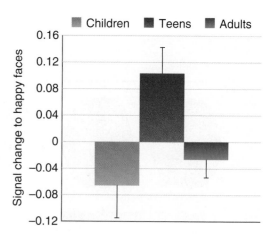

et al., 2011). By the end of adolescence, there is gradual improvement in the ability to control or inhibit behavior, to weigh decisions, and to consider more information at one time (Spear, 2007; 2000).

The consequence of neural development is that thinking is *qualitatively* different during adolescence. That is, teenagers think in a different way than adults. Immaturity in behavior, such as taking risks like speeding or stealing and overdoing drinking or using drugs, may be a consequence of lagging brain development (Ernst & Mueller, 2008). One study tested people in a video task in which their eye movements and brain activity were measured (Hwang et al., 2010). The game involved watching a video screen and looking away from the direction of a light that appeared without warning. This is difficult because the light attracts your attention, and the ability to avoid looking at it requires control from frontal areas of the brain. Young children (age 10) can do it about half of the time, and teens score around 75%. But brain scans show teens make less use of the brain regions responsible for catching errors and staying focused. By age 20, those areas were accessed automatically, and performance improved to that of adults. While it is tempting to think of uncontrolled impulses as the "problem of adolescence," some argue that neural changes during this period are actually helpful. Because teens are less controlled and focused, they may be more flexible in noticing and responding to new situations, just at the time when they are moving from the family into a larger world (Casey et al., 2008).

Cognitive Development

Now able to think and reason logically in the last of Piaget's stages, formal operations, adolescents can let loose their minds on problems of interest. Piaget (1932) pointed out that the ability to reason about abstractions provides an opportunity for the growth of moral reasoning. Building on this notion, Lawrence Kohlberg (1981, 1984) argued that adolescence is a prime time for developing a sense of morality. To investigate this topic, he presented simple scenarios to people and asked their response. Consider this classic example (Kohlberg, 1969): A woman suffering from cancer was near death, and the one drug that might save her was only available from its inventor. The drug was expensive to make, but the inventor was charging 10 times what it cost him. The woman's husband tried unsuccessfully to borrow the money. He then went to the inventor and asked for a discount and offered to pay more over time. But he was told, "No." Finally, the desperate husband broke into the inventor's warehouse to steal the drug for his sick wife. Should the husband have broken into the store to steal the drug for his wife? Why or why not?

In Kohlberg's view, it is not important what someone thinks the husband should *do*. Kohlberg (1969) believed that the *justification* someone offers is what is significant. He collected responses from people of all ages and devised a theory with three levels of moral thinking, each divided into two stages as shown in **TABLE 12-6**. A *preconventional* level of moral reasoning judges the morality of an action based on its consequences, particularly to oneself. An action is morally wrong if you will be punished. A *conventional* level of moral reasoning determines right and wrong based on social roles and society's laws. Good intentions are taken into account, but the law is the law. Finally, the *postconventional level* of moral reasoning considers that social contracts, laws, and rules can bend to uphold individual and universal rights.

Studies have shown that people do pass through the first two stages of moral reasoning in order, just as Kohlberg specified (Colby et al., 1983; Thoma & Rest, 1999). Before adolescence, most children are preconventional, and during adolescence, they begin to reason in conventional terms. Surprisingly, as far as studies can tell, few adolescents and adults reason using postconventional arguments. Only educated adults from middle-class, urban areas were found to display postconventional reasoning (Snarey et al., 1985). This may indicate that postconventional reasoning is a cultural value, and cultures with different values would not develop this same type of moral justification. For example, Americans focus on how events will affect them personally, while South Asians speak in terms of interpersonal concerns (Miller, 1994). In addition, Kohlberg developed his theory using only male subjects. Women may address moral issues with more compassion for individuals and less emphasis on abstractions (Gilligan, 1982).

TABLE 12-6 Examples of Kohlberg's Stages of Moral Reasoning

Stage one (*obedience*):	"Heinz should not steal the medicine because he will consequently be put in prison which will mean he is a bad person."
Stage two (*self-interest*):	"Heinz should not steal the medicine because prison is an awful place, and he would more likely languish in a jail cell than over his wife's death."
Stage three (*conformity*):	"Heinz should not steal the drug because stealing is bad and he is not a criminal."
Stage four (*law-and-order*):	"Heinz should steal the drug for his wife but also take the prescribed punishment for the crime as well as paying the druggist what he is owed. Criminals cannot just run around without regard for the law; actions have consequences."
Stage five (*human rights*):	"Heinz should steal the medicine because everyone has a right to choose life, regardless of the law."
Stage six (*universal human ethics*):	"Heinz should steal the medicine, because saving a human life is a more fundamental value than the property rights of another person."

Source: Data from Kohlberg, L. (1984). The psychology of moral development: The nature and validity of moral stages. *San Francisco: Harper & Row.*

Another theory focuses on moral *feelings* rather than thoughts. Like our thinking, our moral reasoning may involve a faster, emotional response and a slower, more deliberate justification for our behavior. For example, a 7-year-old boy dove from a dock to rescue a toddler that had fallen into deep water. He said he "didn't think at all," but panicked at the sight of the girl in danger. Afterward, he talked about how it was the right thing to do; but in the moment, he simply felt an emotion and acted upon it. The *social intuitionist* account of morality (Haidt, 2001, 2008) explains our decisions based on the feelings evoked rather than justifications for actions. Consider this dilemma: A runaway trolley is headed down a track. Five people will be killed unless you flip a switch to divert the trolley onto a backup track. But if you do so, a man standing on that track will certainly die. Will you do it? Most people say, "yes," because more people will be saved. But if the scenario is changed so that you have to physically push the stranger onto the track to stop the trolley, most people say, "no!" The reason seems to be that the second scenario evokes an emotional response (Greene & Haidt, 2002), which is evident in the brain during imaging (Greene et al., 2001). It is difficult emotionally to be the one to directly cause death. Another view of morality is that how we justify our actions or even how we feel about them is less important; instead, morality may depend on what we choose to *do*.

Social Development

Erik Erikson's (1902–1994) **theory of psychosocial development** identifies a series of stages in life as we develop from childhood through old age **TABLE 12-7** (Erikson, 1959, 1968). For adolescents, Erikson defined the central task to be the forming of an **identity**, or a distinct, individualized sense of self. Erikson called this process the "*identity crisis*," in which teenagers explore alternative ways of living and describing themselves to the world. In the adolescent years, you break free from your relationship with your parents, going from spending most of your free time with family to spending most of it without them. In one study, the amount of time adolescents were with their family went down from 35 to 14% of waking hours (Larson et al., 1996). In addition, teenagers reported feeling more negatively when around their family, but this improved in the 9th and 10th grade for boys and the 11th and 12th grades for girls. Parents and teenagers tend to disagree, and their arguments place a strain on the entire family (Silverberg & Steinberg, 1990).

An evolutionary perspective suggests the reasons for these family strains lie in the problem of having sexually mature offspring living within the family group. In many primate species, such as gibbons and chimpanzees, individuals depart from their group at

Theory of psychosocial development Erikson's stage theory of important issues to resolve across the life span.

Identity formation The process of developing a distinct, individualized personality.

TABLE 12-7 Erikson's Stages of Psychosocial Development

Virtue	Crisis	Age	Description
Hope	Trust vs. Mistrust	Infants, birth to 12–18 months	Infants achieve a sense of safety when their basic needs are met
Will	Autonomy vs. Self-doubt	Toddlers, 18 months to 3 years	Children learn to exercise their will to make things happen
Purpose	Initiative vs. Guilt	Preschool, 3 to 6 years	Children learn to initiate activities, gaining self-confidence
Competence	Industry vs. Inferiority	Childhood, 6 to 12 years	Children learn to systematically explore and develop their abilities
Fidelity	Identity vs. Role confusion	Adolescence, 12 to 18 years	Adolescents create their own values and goals
Love	Intimacy vs. Isolation	Young adults, 18 to 25 years	Young adults learn to merge their identity with another
Care	Generativity vs. Stagnation	Middle adulthood, 25 to 50 years	Middle adults focus concern on the world and their contributions
Wisdom	Ego Integrity vs. Despair	Later adults, 50 years onwards	Later adults must come to terms with their previous choices

Source: Adapted from Erikson, E. H. (1959). Identity and the life cycle. *New York: International Universities Press.*

puberty (Steinberg, 1989), presumably to form new families. In modern humans, the age of marriage is much later, and children may remain living in the home for longer periods and return after college. Living as an adult with your parents poses problems for a sense of autonomy. In more traditional cultures, with less emphasis on independence, there is less tension between adolescents and parents (Arnett, 1999; Schlegel & Barry, 1991). Cultural values may direct an individual toward independence or toward interdependence with others (Greenfield et al., 2003).

Another important aspect of social development is *gender identity*. From the moment of birth, gender is an important social label that influences the way adults interact with you, the peers you choose, and the activities you do. Are men and women as different as society treats them, or are they more alike? Throughout human history, and in varied cultures, gender differences are assumed to operate due to differences in reproduction. Evolutionary theory stresses the roles taken within the family in a hunter-gatherer society, in which childcare is the responsibility of women. Across cultures, the type of work performed outside the home and educational opportunities provided differ greatly for women and men. However, research into the *psychological* differences between males and females has found they are actually quite similar (Maccoby & Jacklin, 1974). Cross-cultural studies (including nonindustrial societies) suggest that both biological differences and social roles contribute to observed differences by gender (Wood & Eagly, 2002). There are some differences that appear regularly across cultures: Males appear to be more aggressive and have better mathematical and spatial abilities, while females have better verbal skills (Maccoby & Jacklin, 1974). Societal expectations for careers and child rearing reinforce stereotypes that even parents and teachers are unable to ignore (Fagot et al., 1985; Stern & Karraker, 1989). Each individual is left to work out his or her place within the sometimes-conflicting views of gender within a culture.

An important marker of adolescent social development is increasing emphasis on peer relationships. Moving away from gender segregation, adolescents seek out friendships with the opposite sex, distinguishing between friends and romantic partners (Furman & Shaffer, 1999). Peer groups provide a reference to compare and evaluate a developing identity. A study of pairs of friends in grades 7 to 11 showed an influence of closest friends on the likelihood of binge drinking or engaging in sexual activity (Jaccard et al., 2005).

Peer relationships are marked by conformity of behavior, or *peer pressure*, peaking in the ninth grade (Gavin & Furman, 1989; Ge et al., 2007). Peers can influence both negatively (increasing likelihood of drug use) and positively (improving grades; Lansford et al., 2003). For those excluded from peer groups, loneliness, low self-esteem, and depression may occur (Steinberg & Morris, 2001). Teens with warmer (and more demanding) parents are somewhat less likely to follow the influence of peers (Mounts & Steinberg, 1995).

What makes some adolescents able to thrive despite conditions of neglect, abuse, and trauma? This phenomenon is called **resilience**, or good developmental outcomes despite high risks, competence under stress, or recovery from trauma (Masten, 2001; Masten & Obradovic, 2006; Werner, 1995). Studies in younger children suggest resilience may be partly heritable (Kim-Cohen et al., 2004; Moffitt et al., 2006). When children overcome the odds to do well in adolescence and later life, they often have personal qualities like an engaging personality, good communication and problem-solving skills, and a belief that their own actions can make a difference in their lives. In fact, the surprising finding is that resilience is so "ordinary;" that is, so many adolescents go through events that might derail their development, yet they somehow recover and thrive (Masten, 2001). Schools can foster resilience by taking a whole-school approach, building on strengths and connections between families, teachers, and social services (Smith et al., 2004).

Resilience Good developmental outcomes despite high risks, competence under stress, or recovery from trauma.

CONCEPT LEARNING CHECK 12.3 | *Defining Adolescence*

Define these important concepts from adolescent development.

1. Menarche and spermarche

2. Neural pruning

3. Conventional morality

4. Social intuitionist

5. Identity crisis

CRITICAL THINKING APPLICATION

"When I was 16, four friends jumped into my car one night, and we headed to a local 'lovers' lane.' I drove up next to a parked car with steamy windows, and we all began to sing "Love to Love You Baby" by Donna Summer. After a few minutes, the dome light in the other car went on, and a handgun was clearly visible. I peeled out and drove like mad, with the other car in pursuit. After running a yellow light and barely missing a passing police car, I finally stopped for help. Our pursuer drove off, and the officer agreed not to give us a ticket if we went down to the station to report what had happened. There we were, under age, in the middle of the night, trying to explain why the evening's events had seemed like a good idea at the time. What was I thinking?"

Teenagers are known for their risky choices. But studies of risk perception and appraisal cannot explain why teenagers engage in more risky behaviors than adults given that they appear to recognize risks (Steinberg, 2006). Several factors may be involved:

1. Changes in reward sensitivity occurring at puberty. Adolescents seek more novelty and require higher levels of stimulation to achieve the same subjective feelings of excitement. It is not that adolescents cannot perceive the higher risk of activities like smoking, drugs, and drinking, but they have a higher need for the stimulation risk taking provides. They weigh the benefits of the risky behavior (such as unprotected sex) more heavily (Steinberg, 2007).

2. An "illusion of unique invulnerability." People often fail to use effective contraception methods because they engage in a systematic distortion of their likelihood of being involved in an unwanted pregnancy relative to others (Burger & Burns, 1988).

(Continues)

3. Delayed development of the brain's prefrontal cortical areas. The prefrontal cortex is the seat of inhibition of behavior yet has a relatively slow development compared to other parts of the brain. The higher-level, self-regulatory capabilities involved in impulse control and planning continue to mature into adulthood (Keating, 2004; Silveri et al., 2006). In fact, maturation in the brain goes on through age 25 (Crews et al., 2007).

These factors are biologically driven, normative, and unlikely to be remediable by education (Steinberg, 2006). So what should we conclude about the appropriate age for rights and responsibilities to be assigned to adolescents? Some researchers argue that the evidence of neural changes in adolescence should be considered in establishing public policies (Steinberg, 2009). What do you think? Examine each of the factors below, consider the legal age for the rights by law, and decide on what age you feel is most appropriate for each.

Right/Responsibility	Legal Age	Appropriate Age
A. Driver's license	16(MI)	
B. Purchasing cigarettes	18(MN)	
C. Voting	18(Federal)	
D. Gun ownership	18(Federal)	
E. Purchasing alcohol	21(NY)	
F. Enlistment in military service	18(Federal)	
G. Eligibility for the death penalty	18(Federal)	

12.4 Adulthood and Aging

Adulthood is marked by important developmental stages, including determining one's purpose and a partner in life and, later, coming to terms with the choices made.

■ Illustrate the physical, cognitive, and social aspects of aging.

The many choices in life, combined with the realities of financial and social needs, can be overwhelming. But there is no one right way to develop, no single right path to finding the future of your dreams. One metaphor imagines starting at the top of a mountain, with crossing pathways circling down (Bee, 1987). You make your way down, altering your path at every intersection, finding harder and easier routes and better or less-preferred spots. Every individual takes a unique route down the mountain, but we all pass through the same elevations as we travel through development. While we all begin in the same spot, our experiences of development can be quite different and yet equally satisfying.

Physical Development

By our mid-20s, humans are finally physically mature, and all of our systems are fully developed. Unfortunately, it is all downhill from here! The passage of time results in changes to physical abilities we may take for granted when younger. During the 1960s, Vietnam war protester Jerry Rubin gave a rallying cry, "Don't trust anyone over 30!" All too soon, we join the ranks of adults in their 30s and 40s and begin noticing physical changes, including wrinkles, stooped posture, thinning white or graying hair, and "shrinkage," with men losing an inch in height and women two. After age 20, a 1% loss in muscle mass occurs each year.

Aging gracefully becomes increasingly difficult for some people in cultures where a youthful appearance is highly valued. Jocelyn Wildenstein reportedly underwent dozens of plastic surgeries in a misguided attempt to win back her husband (CBS News, 2011). She is reported to have undergone a brow lift, facelift, lip-plumping injections,

Jocelyn Wildenstein reportedly sought plastic surgery to halt the aging process, attempting to minimize features such as wrinkles, thinning lips, and sagging skin.

Menopause The cessation of menstrual periods in women, usually occurring around age 50.

Grandmother hypothesis Evolutionary theory that older females aid in the reproductive success of their families by helping to raise grandchildren.

chin augmentation, fat grafting and/or cheek implants, upper and lower eyelid surgery, and canthopexy, a procedure that elevates the eyes to give them a catlike appearance. There have been reports of social parties in which the guests are given injections of Botox to "freeze" facial muscles and hide wrinkles (Cooper, 2002). After spending the adolescent years attempting to look older, adults struggle with looking younger. Appearance counts heavily in old age as well, with elderly persons who appear more youthful enjoying more optimism, social ties, and work opportunities. People who look older than their actual age are not as healthy and are even likely to die earlier (Kligman & Graham, 1986).

Reproductive Life

Delaying parenthood until after age 22 is associated with positive health benefits, and, for women, maximum health benefits are predicted for a first birth at age 30 (Mirowsky, 2002). But reproductive ability also diminishes with age, particularly for females. Even with assistive technology, women over 40 can have a difficult time becoming pregnant. Around age 50, women experience **menopause**, or the cessation of menstrual periods. In men, sperm continue to be produced throughout the life span, but the number and motility of sperm decrease. While modern medicine has extended pregnancy to later ages, physical limits to reproductive life eventually weigh in. What happens after the possibility of reproduction ends? In evolutionary terms, this period of life appears to be a relatively recent invention in human history. Once people started living longer lives and had completed their own reproduction, they became available to help others in the family. It has been argued that the presence of grandparents aids in raising the young, called the **grandmother hypothesis** (e.g., Shanley et al., 2007). Grandmaternal investment, in the form of help from extended family, may have allowed women to successfully raise more babies closer together in age. This pattern of grandparental care is not apparent among other primates (Hawkes et al., 1998).

However, new evidence suggests that nonreproducing members of a group may be a drain on resources. A meta-analysis of published studies over several centuries in 17 patrilineal societies showed that paternal grandparents who lived with their grandchildren did not have a beneficial effect on the grandchildren's survival (Strassmann & Garrard, 2011), though maternal grandparents did. An ongoing, 25-year study of the Dogon people of Mali, West Africa, a traditional, agricultural society, showed resources are scarce and mortality is high. Like many human groups in the past, Dogon society is patrilineal, with a tight-knit web of kinship established through fathers. Dogon women give birth to nine children, on average, over their lifetimes. Their children were 52% less likely to die if their paternal grandparents were dead. This is because the paternal grandparents are likely to live with the child and compete for scarce resources (Strassman, 2011). In some circumstances, having a village to raise a child is too expensive.

Life Expectancy

In 2008, there were 506 million people in the world over 65; in 2040, there will be 1.4 billion (Kinsella & He, 2009). For the first time in modern history, older adults will outnumber children younger than age 14. As we age, strength, speed, and endurance grow weaker. Slowly, our sensory detectors start to fail, making us less sensitive to light, sound, and smell. Around age 50, the ability to focus light on the retina fails, and reading glasses are needed. The loss of sensory acuity is viewed as responsible for increasing physical deterioration in other areas, called the common cause hypothesis (Baltes & Lindenberger, 1997). However, health and physical abilities are affected more by behavior than by the mere passing of time: Physical exercise aids brain cells by increasing oxygen and nutrient circulation (Pereira et al., 2007). Exercise also aids the creation of new neurons in the hippocampus, important to building new memories.

Life expectancy in countries with modern medical care now exceeds 80, far past the time frame designed by evolution. Women have longer lives than men, and in the highest age group, women outnumber men 5 to 1. Later age of parental death is associated with better functional performance and cognitive ability in their children, suggesting that living longer may be heritable (Vaillant & Mukamal, 2001). While advanced age shows continued deterioration of physical skills, other qualities of life in this age group remain vital. In particular, those with a positive view toward their own aging live more than 7 years longer than others and have higher rates of engagement in healthy behaviors (Levy et al., 2002). In a longitudinal Dutch study of older men, greater optimism was related to lower rates of death (Giltay et al., 2004). Having a sense of usefulness to others (Gruenewald et al., 2007) also leads to a longer life.

Death and Dying

Successful aging receives far less attention than physical health (Depp et al., 2010). Rowe and Kahn (1987) define successful aging as: (a) freedom from disability and disease; (b) high cognitive and physical functioning; and (c) social engagement (in terms of involvement in both social and productive activities). Recent clinical trials found positive effects for a variety of interventions, such as physical exercise, dietary restriction, cognitive stimulation, social interventions, and stress reduction (Depp et al., 2010). All of these may enhance cognitive and emotional health in older people.

While people may fear senility, or the widespread loss of cognitive function, it occurs in less than 5% of people. These individuals experience the loss of brain cells leading to **dementia**, or progressive loss of cognitive function due to aging or disease. Strokes, tumors, and other diseases can cause the deterioration of the brain in old age. Alzheimer's disease is caused by the disruption of the neurotransmitter acetylcholine and is diagnosed in about 3% of elderly patients. Alzheimer's has a genetic component, shown by an identical twin's 60% likelihood of also getting the disease, with 30% for a fraternal twin (Plomin & Crabbe, 2000).

Dementia Progressive loss of cognitive function due to aging or disease.

Current medical thinking defines death as an active physical process occurring over time. In psychological terms, the process of dying also involves reactions that unfold over time (Kübler-Ross, 1969) **TABLE 12-8**. Through interviews with terminally ill patients, five stages of dying were identified: denial, anger, bargaining, depression, and acceptance. Kübler-Ross's theory was the first to qualitatively describe systematic observations; however, this stage theory has not been supported by other research (Schulz & Aderman, 1974). A dying person may experience many changes in attitude over time and events. Surprisingly, it is those in middle adulthood who fear death most (Bengston et al., 1977), while those who feel they have achieved their goals in life fear death less (Neimeyer & Chapman, 1980/1981). This fits well with Erikson's (1959) life-span theory suggesting the need to resolve the final conflict—ego integrity vs. despair—in development over the lifespan.

Cognitive Development

As physical systems decline with age, cognitive processes show similar impairment. With age, we have more trouble assimilating new information, cannot recall information from memory as accurately, and are slower to learn associations through classical conditioning. In addition, mental processing speed begins to slow down, so it takes longer to recall information, react to signals, and perform mental computations (Salthouse, 2011).

TABLE 12-8 Stages of Coping with Death and Dying

1. Denial	The first reaction is to refuse to believe death will occur: "There must be some mistake here."
2. Anger	The second stage is resentment against those who are healthy, caregivers, or the cause of death: "Why did this have to happen to me?"
3. Bargaining	In the third stage, people try to make a deal to stay alive: "If I get better, I will exercise every day!"
4. Depression	A time of mourning for oneself and all of the losses death will bring: "I'll never see my grandchildren."
5. Acceptance	The final stage involves understanding death as inevitable, and accepting it with equanimity.

Source: Adapted from Kubler-Ross, E. (1969). On death and dying. New York: Scribner. Reprinted 1997.

Age-related declines in many cognitive variables have been reported with correlations ranging from –0.30 to –0.50 FIGURE 12-24 (Salthouse, 2011). All adults, not just those at advanced ages, show a decline in performance on tasks requiring *fluid intelligence*, or reasoning about new information. However, *crystalized intelligence*, or reasoning using knowledge already existing in memory, shows *no* decline with advancing age (Cattell, 1963). Old people do know better!

Lehman (1962, 1966a, 1966b) showed a pattern of decreasing performance on achievement tests with age (c.f. Simonton, 1988) FIGURE 12-25. The inverted-U-shaped curve—a steep increase, a relatively early peak, and a gradual decline with age—shows up across disciplines and historical periods, and across measures of achievement, including counts of products (number of published articles, paintings, inventions, or musical recordings) and quality of products (highly cited articles or Nobel Prizes) (Salthouse, 2011). Similar results have been obtained in within-individual comparisons (Simonton, 1988); specifically, fields such as lyric poetry, pure mathematics, and theoretical physics, which may focus on novel problem solving, tend to have earlier peaks and more rapid declines than do fields with more reliance on accumulated knowledge (e.g., novel writing, history, philosophy). To illustrate, Simonton (1997) noted that the peak age for greatest career success is 26.5 for mathematicians, but 38.5 for historians.

Individual minds may also be differently resilient when damage occurs. *Cognitive reserve* refers to the brain's ability to adapt to damage by recruiting alternate brain regions to perform tasks (Stern, 2009). Higher education levels, participating in mentally demanding occupations and cognitively stimulating activities, along with lifestyle factors, contribute to cognitive reserve (Fratiglioni & Wang 2004). In fMRI studies, older adults appear to make more use of *both* hemispheres during tasks compared to younger people (Eyler et al., 2011; Hedden & Gabrieli, 2004). Cognitive aging can be impacted by adopting strategies for

FIGURE 12-24 Knowledge gained from experience (accumulated) shows less change over time than scores on tests of solving novel problems.
Source: Reproduced from Salthouse, T. (2011). Consequences of age-related cognitive declines. Annual Review of Psychology, 63, *5.1–5.26.*

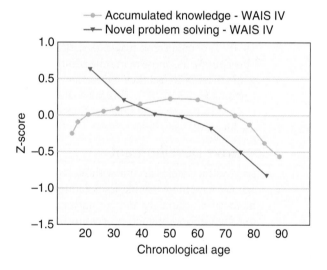

FIGURE 12-25 Scores on achievement tests show an inverted U shape, with increases in the early adult years followed by steady declines with age.
Source: Data from Lehman, H. C. (1962). More about age and achievement. Gerontologist, 2, *141–148.*

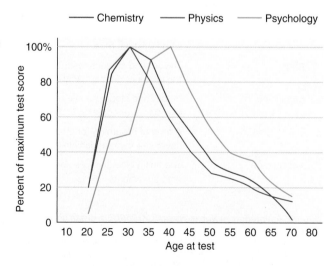

performing tasks. Commercial "brain-training" games appear (based on longitudinal data) to show a relationship between cognitive stimulation and reduced risk of dementia (Wilson et al., 2002). However, Salthouse (2006) questioned the "use-it-or-lose-it" hypothesis because there is little evidence that the rate of cognitive aging is affected by such interventions.

Surprisingly, these slowdowns in cognitive systems and achievements with age do not show up as changes in perceived performance in real-world settings (Salthouse, 2011). This is because in most work settings, you seldom need to perform at peak ability, you use more accumulated knowledge than novel reasoning FIGURE 12-26, and you can be successful in ways not limited to cognition. So the elderly corporate board member is called upon to bring to bear his experience, not to reason quickly about new problems. In addition, older adults may use methods to accommodate for cognitive declines, such as organizers, notes, and calendars. For example, prospective memory tasks—remembering to perform an action at a later time, such as take a pill or let the dog in—are harder with advanced age (Henry et al., 2004). However, planning reminders may help to implement intentions (Patalano & Seifert, 1997). For example, patients who planned when they would take a walk helped cut their recovery time in half (Orbell & Sheeran, 2000). With age, we appear to be increasingly likely to use strategies that help us perform tasks. While the expectation is that cognitive declines will make for poorer performance with age, the wisdom of experience can compensate quite well (Baltes & Baltes, 1990).

Social Development

Erikson's (1959) theory of development noted many important stages in adulthood, focusing on love, caring, and wisdom (see **TABLE 12-7**). Successfully resolving earlier conflicts in life is thought to lead to better later-life outcomes. Whether the final stages end in "ego integrity" and satisfaction with your choices or "despair" and regret depends upon how you resolve developmental crises throughout your life (Erikson, 1959).

Continuity or Change

Now that you are an adult, we can ask the question, "How much are you like the infant, child, and adolescent you once were?" Do people change a great deal as they develop, or is a shy child likely to become a shy adult? Let us consider the evidence from studies of personality traits such as openness, conscientiousness, extraversion, agreeableness, and neuroticism. Across time and age, personality traits are largely consistent (Fraley & Roberts, 2005; Roberts & Mroczek, 2008) FIGURE 12-27. A cross-sectional study comparing personality traits like extroversion over age groups found consistent patterns across nationalities, including Turkey, Germany, Spain, Britain, and Czechoslovakia (McCrae et al., 1997; Schmitt et al., 2007) FIGURE 12-28. Individual differences in personality traits show some continuity from early childhood on and are essentially fixed by age 30 (McCrae & Costa, 1994). However, there is also evidence that people can change over time: With increased age, people show increased self-confidence, warmth, self-control, and emotional stability (Roberts et al., 2006).

But is maturation the cause, or is it simply "getting older"? Life experiences in young adulthood may be the most likely reason for changes in personality with age. In young

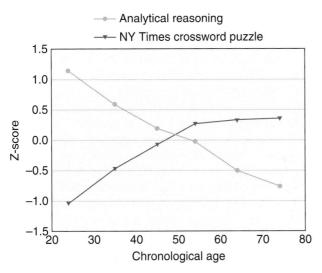

FIGURE 12-26 Reasoning test scores decline with advanced age, but practical skills like crossword solutions remain high. *Source: Reproduced from Salthouse, T. (2011). Consequences of age-related cognitive declines. Annual Review of Psychology, 63, 5.1–5.26.*

FIGURE 12-27 Change in personality traits over time for six trait domains (assuming cumulative change over time). Extraversion is broken into social vitality and social dominance. *Source: Data from Roberts, B. W., & Mroczek, D. (2008). Personality trait change in adulthood.* Current Directions in Psychological Science, *17(1), 31–35.*

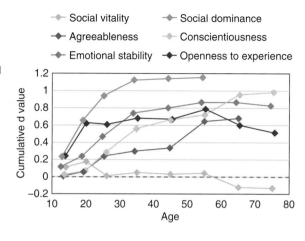

FIGURE 12-28 Mean levels of extraversion in five cultures by age group. Total scores (T) are based on the mean and standard deviation of all respondents over age 21 within each culture. *Source: Reproduced from McCrae, R. R., Costa, P. T., Jr., Ostendorf, F., Angleitner, A., Hřebíčková, M., Avia, M. D., Sanz, J., Sánchez-Bernardos, M. L., Kusdil, M. E., Woodfield, R., Saunders, P. R., & Smith, P. B. (2000). Nature over nurture: Temperament, personality, and life span development.* Journal of *Personality and Social Psychology, 78(1), 173–186.*

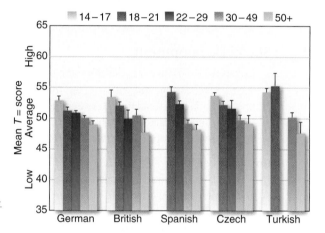

adulthood, there are many life tasks most people experience for the first time, such as finding a romantic partner, starting a family, and establishing a career. Perhaps as a result of growing responsibilities, we develop increased conscientiousness and emotional stability. This pattern is supported across cultures and ethnic groups (Helson et al., 2002). Changes in social roles also occur with age; for example, you move from child to parent to grandparent. A first job may bring expectations about showing up on time, working hard and extra hours, and being agreeable with coworkers. Other people may encourage you to change by punishing or rewarding your behavior, such as providing raises or social rejection. Personality may be further shaped by the social expectations experienced in these adult roles (Roberts & Mroczek, 2008).

In addition, personality traits continue to change in middle adulthood and old age (Roberts et al., 2006). As they age, people decrease on social vitality (a facet of extraversion), openness, agreeableness, and neuroticism. Older people tend to be a little less sociable but also less worried about life. Your chronological age may be less important than the life experiences you encounter at different stages of life. Erikson's theory proposes stages tied to age, but each involves specific types of first experiences that challenge the individual (Erikson, 1959). The task of finding a life partner often occurs in young adulthood, a period of accomplishment follows in middle adulthood, and later, concern about the impact of your efforts is more likely to arise (the generativity vs. stagnation crisis). In older adulthood, resolving the questions of "what it all means" and whether you are satisfied with your life choices fits with having lived the majority of your life span. Because these stages are not as tied to chronological age as they are to experience, the notion of "psychological age" may be a better metric for stages of development (Roberts et al., 2006).

Relationships

One of the most profound developmental tasks is selecting a life partner, an individual who remains with you through time and circumstance. More than 90% of heterosexuals marry at some point in their lives. Satisfaction in marriage is high at first (O'Leary & Smith, 1991) and hits a low point when adolescent children are in the home, rising again once they leave the "empty nest" (White & Edwards, 1990). Many factors influence the quality of marriages, such as loyalty, emotional security, sexual intimacy, respect, and communication (Levenson et al., 1993). Men are happier in marriage than women, and research has pointed out a specific trouble point: Following the birth of children, couples report greater marital stress. Once children enter the family, women feel overextended with work outside the home and unequal responsibilities for childcare (Erel & Burman, 1995). Devoting attention to sharing the workload has the potential to head off problems within marriages.

One clinical psychologist working with couples began bringing them into the laboratory to record them as they argued just as they would at home (Gottman, 1994, 1998). After observing more than 2,000 couples, he reported a very clear finding: Couples that stayed together maintained a ratio of five positive comments for every one negative comment. Imagine smiles, hugs, compliments, and laughs sprinkled with occasional sarcasm and criticism. By managing the tone of the conversations, couples that lasted kept the relationship on a positive track. The best predictor of which couples ended up divorcing was any expression of "contempt:" When one member of the couple reached the point at which he or she had no respect for the other, the damage was more likely to be irreparable.

Divorce is one of the most difficult transitions encountered in life. In the middle 1800s, only 4% of marriages ended in divorce; today, about half of all first marriages in the United States end in divorce (Raley & Bumpass, 2003). Following divorce, there is greater risk of health problems, drinking and drug use, and depression. However, most people make a recovery within 2 years after divorce (Hetherington et al., 1985). The majority of those who divorce go on to remarry, and on average, their experience with marriage is as satisfying (Huyck, 1982). When a spouse dies, both physical and psychological difficulties can follow (Strobe & Strobe, 1983). Because women tend to marry older men and are more likely to live longer, many women experience the loss of a husband in later life. There are perhaps 10 times as many women as men who have lost their spouses. Friends who have also experienced loss are particularly helpful in recovery (Utz et al., 2002).

Ages and Stages of Adulthood

When asked about critical points in their lives, people mention graduation, first jobs, getting married, having children, moving to a new home, health changes, and world events like wars (Ryff, 1989). For certain milestones, people are sensitive to a **social clock**, or norms for ages at which these events occur. People who are out of sync with these expectations experience more stress than those who are "on time" (Neugarten, 1979). Work and career goals also include expectations for age of achievements and limitations on beginning training in some professions. For example, federal air traffic controllers must begin training by age 30 and retire by 59. Because opportunities often depend on chance encounters (Bandura, 1998), the pressure to make choices and move ahead can grow throughout adulthood.

An additional task in this phase of life is identifying a "purpose" in life, or something personally meaningful to pursue (Damon, 2004). For many people, motivation in their career or work fills the majority of their hours, and jobs with better matches to personal goals are viewed as more fulfilling. During middle adulthood, climbing the professional ladder or accomplishing financial goals becomes a central focus in order to to support a family, desired lifestyle, or future retirement. An additional demand arises in middle age: Elderly parents often need care from their children, both in social support and financial contributions (Brody, 1985). Cultures differ in the expectations for caring for elderly parents, with black families expressing higher expectations for support (Lee et al., 1998) and Chinese-American families mandating that children care for elderly parents (Dai & Dimond, 1998).

In later adulthood, people find increasing satisfaction by "giving back," termed **generativity** by Erikson (1959). Contributing to the development of the next generation, making a mark upon the world, and "making a difference" are all motivations cited by adults who feel their own life goals are largely satisfied. In fact, life satisfaction ratings are similar across age ranges, suggesting that around 75 to 80% of people feel satisfied with their lives (Inglehart, 1990) FIGURE 12-29. This is a surprising finding because it provides no evidence for a turbulent "midlife crisis" taking place in the 40s; in fact, rates of divorce, job change, and suicide do not increase in midlife (Wethington, 2000). Another surprise

Social clock Cultural norms for appropriate ages to seek out life events like marriage.

Generativity Erikson's stage of life focusing on contributing to the development of the next generation and "making a difference."

FIGURE 12-29 Levels of life satisfaction show little difference based on age.
Source: Data from Inglehart, R. (1990). Culture shift in advanced industrial society. *Princeton, NJ: Princeton University Press.*

is that satisfaction does not decrease in later life. Life satisfaction may relate more to the state of your relationships and your experiences at work than to your chronological age.

The psychological effects of aging also include a changing sense of time itself and the value of the present compared to the future (Charles & Carstensen, 2009). Young people are forging new connections to others and looking for new opportunities, while older adults become more selective about how and with whom they spend their time (Lang & Carstensen, 2002). Perhaps with less time remaining, using the present is more important. When not in distress over health or other events, older adults in everyday life enjoy social and emotional functioning that is equal to or better than that of younger adults (Scheibe & Carstensen, 2010). So in many ways, in the later years of life, we take advantage of the expertise we accumulate through living our lives.

CONCEPT LEARNING CHECK 12.4   *Is There a "Right Time" for Everything?*

Answer each question in a few sentences.

1. Explain an evolutionary view of why the end of human life occured at around age 40 in early human history.

2. Describe the kinds of cognitive tasks in which older people have an advantage in performance and those that are more challenging for them.

3. Identify the "social clock" and explain where you personally are on the typical timeline of life events.

12.5 Nature and Nurture

The question of whether nature (biological influences) or nurture (environmental influences) is more important in development has changed to reflect that multiple influences create psychological outcomes.

■ Describe the multiple influences of nature and nurture in patterns of development.

One of the ongoing questions about development is the relative importance of nature (biological influences including genetics, hormones, and evolutionary tendencies) to that of nurture (environmental influences such as family life, schooling, culture, and experiences). What creates the person you grow up to be? Which influences play a greater role in determining the outcomes of development?

Learning theorist John B. Watson claimed that nurture could change the future of any child: "Give me a dozen healthy infants, well-formed, and my own specified world to bring them up in and I will guarantee to take any one at random and train him to become any type of specialist I might select—doctor, lawyer, artist, merchant-chief and, yes, even beggar-man and thief, regardless of his talents, penchants, tendencies, abilities, vocations, and race of his ancestors" (Watson, 1930, p. 82). Watson believed that learning from the environment was the primary determinant in development. And much of the evidence about development points to environmental factors (caregivers, peers, rich environments) as important influences in development.

At the same time, some environmental variables that would seem to be very important in development have been found to have little effect. For example, why are children from the same family so different (Pinker, 2002; Hoffman, 1991)? The shared environment of family life has clear influences on development, yet it appears to have little impact on personality. Studies of adoptive families show that people growing up together, whether related or not, do not resemble each other much in their personalities (Plomin et al., 1998). Does it really not matter whether you are raised by your specific family or by wolves in developing your characteristic ways of thinking, acting, and feeling? Why does sharing our earliest relationships within a family have so little impact on our individual ways of approaching the world? Is every environment "nonshared," so that even growing up in the same family is a very different experience for each sibling?

Nature weighs in on development early: The temperaments of newborns—how emotionally excitable they are, whether they seek or avoid extra stimulation—is heritable (McCrae et al., 2000; Rothbart, 2006). No matter what learning takes place later, that basic response to stimulation remains in place throughout life. The emotional reactivity of newborns relates to their temperament as young adults (Larsen & Diener, 1987). Studies of twins show many similarities influenced by genetics, including intelligence, extraversion, neuroticism, abilities, interests, and even fears (Bouchard et al., 1990). Genetic predispositions affect our likelihood of developing diseases, pursuing behaviors like drinking, and reactions to stress. Increasingly, evidence from behavioral genetics suggests that virtually all individual differences, when reliably measured, are moderately to substantially heritable (Bouchard & McGue, 2003). For much of the history of developmental psychology, the importance of nature was underweighted, and it remains so today.

An example comes from a tragic case study of twin boys born in Canada in 1966 (Colapinto, 2001). After the accidental destruction of one twin's penis, medical experts advised his parents to raise him instead as a girl. This idea was consistent with theories at the time that gender is a socially constructed identity (Cerulo, 1997): "If you treat her as a girl, she will become a girl." Did it work? The psychiatrist following the case reported that the mother said her daughter, by 4 1/2 years of age, was much neater than her brother, and in contrast with him, disliked to be dirty: "She likes for me to wipe her face. She doesn't like to be dirty, and yet my son is quite different. I can't wash his face for anything. . . . She seems to be daintier. Maybe it's because I encourage it" (Money, 1975). The development of different gender identities in the identical twins was reported as a great success (Money, 1975).

However, other researchers later uncovered the truth about the case: "Brenda" never accepted himself as a girl (Diamond & Sigmundson, 1997). When his mother told him the truth at age 14, he immediately changed his name to "David," and assumed his male identity. As an adult, David Reimer commented, "There's . . . there's no way of knowing whether you're a boy or girl 'cause nobody tells you. You don't wake up one morning and say, 'Oh I'm . . . I'm . . . I'm a boy today.' You know! You know! It's . . . it's . . . it's in you. Nobody has to tell you *who* you are" (*NOVA*, 2001). The traumatic effects of this experiment in gender assignment were followed by a drug overdose by his brother, and David's own suicide. His experience strongly suggests that gender is not simply socially defined but is determined by multiple influences on development.

So what influences determine gender identity? In David Reimer's case, he was likely affected by the presence of normal male hormones during prenatal development. Recall that sexual differentiation of the genitals takes places in the first 2 months of pregnancy. Later, during the second half of pregnancy, sexual differentiation also takes place in brain functions. Both of these periods require the presence of specific hormones in order for male and female development to occur. Since David was a boy at birth, his prenatal experience was inconsistent with being raised as a girl. In fact, genital and brain development occur *independently* of each other during the prenatal period, potentially giving rise to mismatches. Some children, adolescents, and adults experience *transsexuality*, or the perception of their true gender identity as different from their biologically determined

David Reimer was born a normal boy, but after a surgical accident, was raised as a girl from age 2. Though socially identified as a girl, he never accepted it, and assumed his male gender identity when he was told the truth at age 14.

sexual identity (Swaab, 2007). We are born with a biological predisposition that is fixed by genetics and hormones, so that certain sexual and gender behaviors are likely to be expressed (Diamond, 1995). But *which* patterns are expressed also depends upon the societal and cultural gender roles that are imposed upon us and the degrees of tolerance our culture allows (Diamond, 1979). A child also asks herself, "Who am I like, and who am I not like?" An identification with gender in society comes from general observation of roles and expectations and from comparing yourself with your parents and your peers (Diamond, 2000). So nature and nurture can work together, or sometimes at cross-purposes, to influence the development of a child's gender identity.

In addition, nature and nurture can *interact* to create patterns of development, such as individual differences in intellectual ability. These differences appear to be greatly influenced by environment, particularly for lower-socioeconomic-status (SES) families. Children from families without economic and social resources (like access to good schools) tend to score lower on tests of intelligence. Further studies show that biology *does* play a role in intelligence test scores for some children, but only for those raised in high-SES homes. For the low-SES children, genetics does not predict their intelligence test scores, while their disadvantaged homes provide a good predictor of their cognitive ability (Tucker-Drob et al., 2011). How can this be? In the study, 750 pairs of twins were measured on cognitive tests at 10 months and at 2 years old. At age 10 months, genes did not account for any variation in mental ability for any of the children. However, genetic influences emerged over the course of development: At age 2, genes accounted for nearly 50% of the variation in intelligence scores of children raised in high-SES homes. But genes *still* did not explain any differences in mental ability for children raised in low-SES homes; rather, their poor environments predicted their intelligence test outcomes. A gene-by-environment *interaction* occurs: Genes do matter for intelligence, but only for those children whose basic needs are already being supported by their environment.

Poor-socioeconomic homes limit children's opportunities to engage with environments that support cognitive growth. As a result, possible genetic influences are limited in their expression. In particular, SES disadvantages are likely to make it harder to elicit responsive care and stimulation from caregivers. Later in childhood, disadvantage limits opportunities to seek out educational and social experiences that fit with their own (potentially genetically influenced) interests (such as music, educational toys, or preschool programs; Scarr & McCartney, 1983). From this data, it appears that the role of genetics depends on *reciprocal* interactions between the child and his or her environment (Bronfenbrenner & Ceci, 1994; Dickens & Flynn, 2001). Some environments provide fertile ground for biological factors to play out. Like seeds planted in rich soil versus dry sand, the right environment is required to allow biological processes to unfold.

Further, people are not just passively affected by the biological and environmental contributions to their development. For example, children create their own development based on the reactions they elicit from others, and these reactions in turn affect the child's development (Lerner, 1982). For example, a toddler who is impulsive may be socially rejected by his peers, leading to longer-term patterns of aggression toward others (Olson, 1992). Some children are more affected—both for better and for worse—by their experiences growing up (Belsky et al., 2007). And finally, even as children, we choose and, to some extent, create the environments that influence us (Scarr & McCartney, 1983). Biological factors such as sensitivity to stimulation can affect our choice of environments, including the activities and peers we choose (Scarr, 1996). Based on temperamental differences, an "easy" baby may readily learn from social interactions, while a "difficult" baby may shut his eyes to avoid too much stimulation and miss learning social cues. Individuals may actively seek out environments that foster the expression of their genetic tendencies. Alternatively, one may choose environments that inhibit genetic tendencies; for example, while higher testosterone levels in males can produce aggression (Olweus et al., 1980), some men choose to avoid its expression (Lore & Schultz, 1993). Both nature and nurture affect our development, but our choices in life can inhibit, alter, or enhance their effects.

Summary of Multiple Influences on Development

Throughout this chapter, we have seen multiple influences affecting the development of individuals throughout the life span. Biology determines our natures at birth, and we come into the world with temperamental differences that bias our reactions to it. Biology is also a major determinant of behavior during adolescence as hormonal changes in puberty alter our physical, cognitive, and emotional growth. At the same time, the environment causes key differences among us during development: how we bond with our caregivers, who we associate with as peers, and the opportunities and events of later life that help shape us as individuals. And these influences interact, so that certain environments are required for some genetic traits to be displayed, and biological tendencies can be altered through context.

Consider the question of gender differences, with which we began this chapter. Evolutionary theory would argue that we would see the largest gender differences surrounding the behaviors that have to do with reproduction, since the mating strategies for males and females differ. Yet there are few real "gender differences" observed in human sexual behaviors and attitudes. In a meta-analysis, Petersen and Hyde (2010) reviewed 834 studies with more than one million subjects. Most of the gender differences they found were small in size, with the exception of a few, such as masturbation, pornography use, and attitudes toward casual sex. Importantly, in studies of more gender-equal societies, even these differences were small. So differences in behavior tied to biological influences like gender are affected by the context of the social environment. Gender differences in sexuality are not immutable, and are altered by environmental influences. Biology creates gender, but our social environment influences what it means to be a "girl" or a "boy." This can be readily seen by comparing the lives of men and women across cultures; for example, in some countries, whether you are allowed to drive a car, hold a job, or go to school may depend on your gender, but not for biological reasons.

The complexity of development ensures that both nature and nurture contribute to our developing self. We also actively select environments that suit our biological tendencies; we attend or skip parties, we seek or avoid relationships, we study hard or drop out of school. While we are subject to the biological and environmental influences surrounding us, we also drive the changes that take place as we develop. Though we share many experiences with others, each person's development occurs in a context that is unique, following a biological and environmental path that is different from all others.

CONCEPT LEARNING CHECK **12.5**   *Nature or Nurture?*

Explain how nature and nurture each may affect development in this example case.

Adam grew up in Evanston, Illinois, where his father is a professor and his mother is a product researcher. He learned how to program and opened his own profitable web page on college sports. He was accepted to enter Harvard University this fall.

1. Genetics

2. Socioeconomic status

3. Activity preferences and experiences (e.g., enjoying reading)

Visual Overview Stages of Development Across the Lifespan

Each stage of development has characteristic changes in our physical, cognitive, and social well-being.

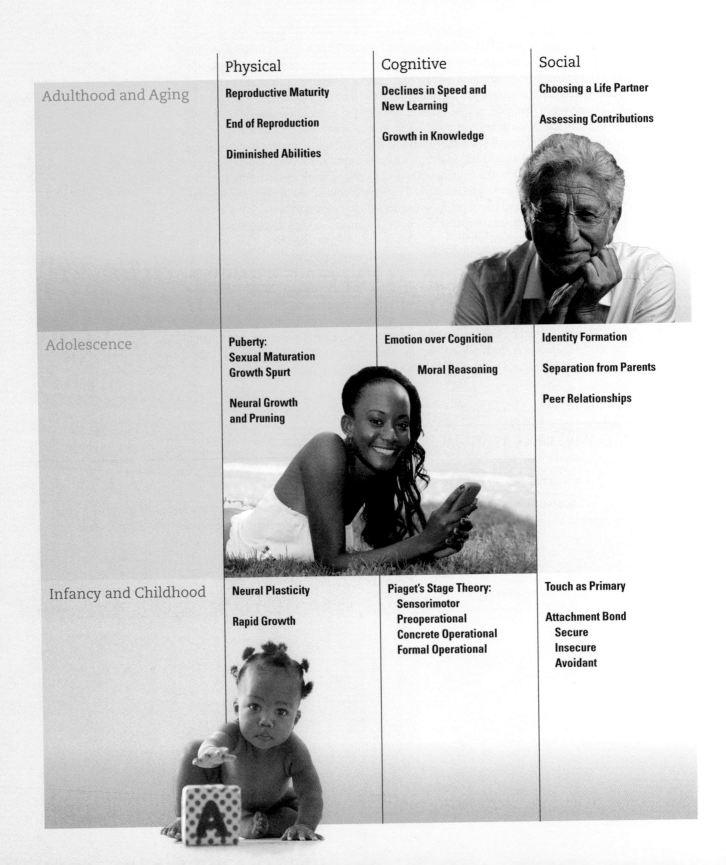

	Physical	**Cognitive**	**Social**
Adulthood and Aging	Reproductive Maturity End of Reproduction Diminished Abilities	Declines in Speed and New Learning Growth in Knowledge	Choosing a Life Partner Assessing Contributions
Adolescence	Puberty: Sexual Maturation Growth Spurt Neural Growth and Pruning	Emotion over Cognition Moral Reasoning	Identity Formation Separation from Parents Peer Relationships
Infancy and Childhood	Neural Plasticity Rapid Growth	Piaget's Stage Theory: Sensorimotor Preoperational Concrete Operational Formal Operational	Touch as Primary Attachment Bond Secure Insecure Avoidant

12.1 The Beginnings of Development

- Culture plays an important role in our development across the life span.
- Genetics provides a predisposition for a characteristic, but expressing it may require contributions from the environment.
- Exposure to toxic agents from the environment, called teratogens, is a dangerous problem.

- Newborns are *not* "blank slates;" instead, they are prepared with inborn abilities.
- Biologically based individual differences in temperament are already evident in the newborn, along with reflexes and visual preferences.

12.2 Infancy and Childhood

- Physical growth occurs at a faster rate in the young, with another spurt in adolescence.
- Young children appear to have greater *plasticity* in their neural functions.
- The formation of concepts proceeds through assimilation and accommodation of new information.
- Babies and toddlers learn to grasp and manipulate objects, and to move through the world in the sensorimotor stage.
- Preschool children are focused on what they perceive and are egocentric in believing that others know, think, and feel the same way they do in the preoperational stage.
- Conservation tasks show children in grade school (the concrete operational stage) are no longer overwhelmed by what things look like.
- Piaget's final stage, formal operations, is characterized by reasoning on a logical or hypothetical level.

- New methods of testing such as habituation uncovered surprising abilities in young babies.
- Harlow's studies identified contact comfort, or the need for touch, as a primary drive.
- *Attachment* refers to the deep, emotional bond that an infant develops with its caregiver. Ainsworth's strange situation task showed that most infants showed a *secure attachment* to their mothers.
- Some babies seem to feel they cannot rely upon the caregiver and act this out in the strange situation task by showing insecure or avoidant attachment.
- Differences in parenting style have been identified in how parents establish control over their children.
- Peer relationships can sometimes be marked by bullying, either as an aggressor or as a victim.

12.3 Adolescence and Young Adulthood

- Big changes in development result from *puberty*, or the sexual maturation that occurs as a result of rising hormone levels in preteen years.
- The physical maturation of the brain goes through a similar growth spurt in adolescence and then goes through neural pruning.
- The teenage brain is driven by emotion, and cognitive control takes longer to develop.

- Kohlberg's theory of moral reasoning identifies a progression in justifications for actions from concern about consequences to following laws to individual and universal rights.
- Erik Erikson's theory of psychosocial development identifies a series of stages in life, including establishing your own identity as an adolescent.

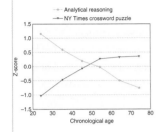

12.4 Adulthood and Aging

- By their mid-20s, humans are finally physically mature, and deterioration begins.
- Reproductive ability also diminishes with age, particularly for females.
- Human life spans now exceed the time frame designed by evolution.
- A small percentage of people experience the loss of brain cells leading to dementia.
- Cognitive declines occur with advanced age, with more trouble assimilating new information, recalling information, and learning new associations.
- Erikson's (1959) final stage involves reconciling with your life choices.

- Across time and age, personality traits are largely consistent from early childhood on and are essentially fixed by age 30, but change still occurs in middle adulthood and old age.
- One of the most profound developmental tasks is selecting a life partner, an individual who remains with you through time and circumstance.
- In later adulthood, people find increasing satisfaction by "giving back," termed *generativity* by Erikson.

12.5 Nature and Nurture

- We are born with a biological predisposition that is fixed by genetics and hormone levels, but societal and cultural roles also influence us.
- Individuals may actively select and create environments that foster or inhibit the expression of their genetic tendencies.

- The complexity of development ensures that both nature and nurture contribute to our sense of self.

12.1 The Beginnings of Development

1. A study that follows a person through different ages as he or she develops is called a(n) _____ study.
 A. cross-sectional
 B. longitudinal
 C. cohort
 D. experimental

2. The longest stage of prenatal development is the _____ stage.
 A. zygote
 B. fetus
 C. embryo
 D. newborn

3. In a study of visual preferences, researchers presented newborns with head-shaped forms that depicted a properly featured face, a scrambled face, or a blank, featureless face. The infants' visual tracking behavior indicated:
 A. a preference for the scrambled face.
 B. a preference for the properly featured face.
 C. no preferences among the three stimuli.
 D. a preference for the blank, featureless face.

12.2 Infancy and Childhood

4. After a child's pet kitten runs away, his parents buy him a puppy. The child finds out that puppies are different from kittens and then acts differently with the puppy. This best illustrates Piaget's concept of:
 A. assimilation.
 B. accommodation.
 C. egocentrism.
 D. conservation.

5. A child who is reading a book upstairs calls to his mother who is downstairs, "Mommy, what is this a picture of?" This illustrates that the child is:
 A. egocentric.
 B. concrete operational.
 C. experiencing separation anxiety.
 D. babbling.

6. A child returns from Halloween trick-or-treating and promptly dumps a bag of candy in a pile on the kitchen table. She then spreads it out at and it looks like more, but she knows it is the same amount of candy. You can conclude she:
 A. is in the preoperational stage of development.
 B. is no longer egocentric in her thinking.
 C. has a good understanding of conservation of mass.
 D. is at least 7 years old.

7. In a classic series of experiments on attachment by Harlow, newborn monkeys were placed in cages that contained "surrogate mothers." How did the monkeys react to these "moms"?
 A. They developed as normally as if they were with their real mothers.
 B. They became attached to the one that provided milk.
 C. They became attached to the one that was soft and cuddly.
 D. They became attached to both kinds of "mothers."

8. In the context of parent–child relationships, *attachment* refers to:
 A. a deep emotional bond between infant and primary caretaker.
 B. the fondness that a child sometimes has for inanimate objects like "blankies."
 C. clinging behavior that is characteristic of insecure relationships.
 D. an instinctive tendency for babies to follow their mothers.

9. How do children with secure attachment behave in the strange situation procedure when their mother returns after leaving them earlier?
 A. They are indifferent.
 B. They actively ignore her.
 C. They react with anger.
 D. They appear delighted.

12.3 Adolescence and Young Adulthood

10. According to Kohlberg, postconventional moral thought:
 A. violates a person's conscience.
 B. reflects norms set by sources of authority.
 C. is based on satisfying self-interests.
 D. is based on abstract principles like justice.

11. According to Erikson, the central task in adolescence is resolving the _____ crisis.
 A. intimacy
 B. identity
 C. autonomy
 D. trust

12. Making "riskier" decisions during adolescence may be correlated with:
 A. lack of peer contact.
 B. differential parenting.
 C. slower frontal lobe development.
 D. delays in reaching puberty.

12.4 Adulthood and Aging

13. The most likely cause of changes in personality with increased age is:
- **A.** life experiences.
- **B.** further maturation.
- **C.** dementia.
- **D.** changes in physical abilities.

14. Older adults tend to have declines in cognitive processes but show little decline in:
- **A.** crystalized intelligence.
- **B.** memory recall.
- **C.** fluid intelligence.
- **D.** speed of processing.

12.5 Nature and Nurture

16. The case study of identical twin boys, one of whom suffered the loss of his penis and was raised as a girl, suggests that in this case, the medical specialist underweighted the importance of _____ to gender identity.
- **A.** biology
- **B.** socialization
- **C.** both nature and nurture
- **D.** attachment

15. People's ratings of satisfaction with their lives are:
- **A.** higher in adolescence.
- **B.** higher in older adults.
- **C.** lower in adolescence.
- **D.** about the same across the life span.

CHAPTER DISCUSSION QUESTIONS

1. Consider what you have learned about brain development across the life span. What do the stages in brain development suggest about the ability of the person to recuperate from damage (physical injury, surgery, or tumors) to the brain?

2. Consider the parenting style you experienced from your parents or caregivers. Would you identify it as authoritative, authoritarian, or permissive? What style would you choose to use should you become a parent?

3. Section 12.2 reviews the major areas of development in infancy and childhood (physical, cognitive, and social). Evaluate each of these areas of development in terms of

their long-term impact on an adult's life. Is there one area that you consider to be most important? Least? Explain.

4. Adolescence is widely considered to be a difficult period of human development. Consider the areas of development and judge the contribution of each to the difficulty of adolescent development. Explain your reasoning for each (physical, cognitive, and social).

5. After reviewing the areas of development (physical, cognitive, and social) as they relate to adulthood and aging, analyze each area for choices a person can make that will create more enjoyable adult lives. Explain your reasoning.

CHAPTER PROJECTS

1. What does a "life well lived" mean to you? Think about a possible life path for yourself. What type of career might you pursue that will give you a sense of mastery and purpose, as well as meeting your financial needs? What types of relationships will be a priority to you, and who will you live with? How will you impact the world around you and contribute to the development of others?

2. Demonstrate the interdependence of the areas of development (physical, cognitive, and social) by imagining a person's behavior with one area missing. Create three scenarios, each with a different area of development lacking. You may focus on a specific age or imagine how a later age would be affected by the lack of an area during an earlier age (e.g., how a lack of cognitive development during infancy would affect the behavior of an adolescent).

CHAPTER KEY TERMS

Accommodation	**Conservation**	**Egocentrism**
Age of viability	**Contact comfort**	**Embryo**
Assimilation	**Critical period**	**Fetal alcohol syndrome**
Attachment	**Cyberbullying**	**Fetus**
Authoritative parenting style	**Dementia**	**Formal operational stage**
Concrete operational stage	**Differentiation**	**Gender roles**

Generativity
Grandmother hypothesis
Identity formation
Maturation
Menarche
Menopause
Motherese
Neural pruning
Norm
Object permanence

Plasticity
Prenatal stage
Preoperational stage
Primary sexual characteristics
Resilience
Secondary sexual characteristics
Sensorimotor stage
Social clock
Spermarche
Stranger anxiety

Strange situation procedure
Temperament
Teratogens
Theory of mind
Theory of psychosocial
  development
Zone of proximal development
Zygote

ANSWERS TO CONCEPT LEARNING CHECK

12.1 Before and After Birth

1. Fetus

2. Longitudinal

3. Teratogens

4. Feed

5. Faces

12.2 Stages of Cognitive Development

1. B. Helen is showing egocentric behavior by assuming her father can see the page in the same direction as she can. That identifies the preoperational stage.

2. A. The sensorimotor stage involves learning to control movements, and repeating is great practice.

3. B. Jordana shows she does not yet have conservation of mass; therefore, she is in the preoperational stage.

4. D. Jorges shows systematic reasoning in his careful approach to the problem, suggesting formal operations.

12.3 Defining Adolescence

1. *Menarche* is a girl's first menstrual period, and *spermarche* is a boy's first production of mature sperm cells.

2. *Neural pruning* refers to the stage of brain development in adolescence when the number of connections between neurons is cut down to preserve only those most frequently used.

3. *Conventional morality* refers to justifications of moral decisions based on social roles or laws.

4. The *social intuitionist* refers to making moral judgments using emotion rather than reasoning.

5. *Identity crisis* refers to the stage of developing your own sense of personal identity.

12.4 Is There a "Right Time" for Everything?

1. Once humans reach the end of their reproductive life span (at age 40 for females), they may help with raising grandchildren but would also compete for limited resources within the family group.

2. Any task involving a knowledge base of expertise would show those of advanced age as highly competent, while tasks involving speedy responses or recall from memory would show poorer performance.

3. The social clock provides a timeline of typical ages when life events like marriage are expected to take place. Your place on this timeline is individual, and you may alter it as you wish, with biological constraints like reproduction in mind.

12.5 Nature or Nurture?

1. Genetics may play a role in Adam's intelligence. Both of his parents have professions requiring intelligence, which is partly heritable.

2. Adam grew up in an affluent town where his parents were both employed in high-paying professions. They likely provided opportunities for learning in the home which helped with his school performance.

3. Adam pursued his interests in programming to create a successful business, contributing to his preparation for college.

12.1 The Beginnings of Development

1. B. Rationale: Following the same person over time allows comparison at different life stages.

2. B. Rationale: This stage lasts from 9 weeks until birth at 37 weeks.

3. B. Rationale: Even newborns prefer looking at faces.

12.2 Infancy and Childhood

4. B. Rationale: The boy had to change his concepts in memory to fit in the new "dog" information.

5. A. Rationale: The child thinks his mother can see the same things he is seeing.

6. C. Rationale: She recognizes that appearances may change, but the amount does not.

7. C. Rationale: Harlow named this *contact comfort*.

8. A. Rationale: Attachment is defined as the first bond in life.

9. D. Rationale: Securely bonded children are thrilled to have Mom back again.

12.3 Adolescence and Young Adulthood

10. D. Rationale: This stage goes beyond rules or law.

11. B. Rationale: Adolescents are forming their personalities in this crisis.

12. C. Rationale: The emotional areas of the brain develop faster than the control areas in the frontal lobe.

12.4 Adulthood and Aging

13. A. Rationale: People change at different points and in different ways, likely due to experience.

14. A. Rationale: Using past knowledge allows older adults to continue to function well.

15. D. Rationale: People rate themselves equally satisfied in all age groups.

12.5 Nature and Nurture

16. A. Rationale: Prenatal hormones were normal in this case, and the resulting gender identity was male.

REFERENCES

Ainsworth, M. D. S., & Bell, S. M. (1970). Attachment, exploration, and separation: Illustrated by the behavior of one-year-olds in a strange situation. *Child Development, 41*(1), 49–67.

Ainsworth, M. D. S., Blehar, M., Waters, E., & Wall, S. (1978). *Patterns of attachment: Psychological studies of the strange situation.* Hillsdale, NJ: Erlbaum.

Ainsworth, M. S. (1979). Infant–mother attachment. *American Psychologist, 34*(10), 932–937.

Allen, J. P., McElhaney, K. B., Land, D. J., Kuperminc, G. P., Moore, C. W., O'Beirne-Kelly, H., & Liebman Kilmer, S. (2003). A secure base in adolescence: Markers of attachment security in the mother–adolescent relationship. *Child Development, 74*(1), 292–307.

Amato, P. R. (2000). The consequences of divorce for adults and children. *Journal of Marriage and Family, 62*(4), 1269–1287.

Amato, P. R. (2001). Children of divorce in the 1990s: An update of the Amato and Keith (1991) meta-analysis. *Journal of Family Psychology, 15*(3), 355–370.

Amato, P. R., & Keith, B. (1991a). Parental divorce and well-being. *Journal of Marriage and the Family, 53,* 43–58.

Amato, P. R., & Keith, B. (1991b). Parental divorce and the well-being of children: A meta-analysis. *Psychological Bulletin, 110*(1), 26–46.

Anderson, S. E., Dallal, G. E., Must, A. (2003). Relative weight and race influence average age at menarche: Results from two nationally representative surveys of US girls studied 25 years apart. *Pediatrics, 111*(4 Pt 1), 844–850.

Anisfeld, E. (1982). The onset of social smiling in preterm and full-term infants from two ethnic backgrounds. *Infant Behavior and Development, 5*(2–4), 387–395.

Anisfeld, E., Casper, V., Nozyce, M., & Cunningham N. (1990). Does infant carrying promote attachment? An experimental study of the effects of increased physical contact on the development of attachment. *Child Development, 61*(5), 1617–1627.

Arnett, J. J. (1999). Adolescent storm and stress, reconsidered. *American Psychologist, 54*(5), 317–326.

Arnett, J. J. (2006). Emerging adulthood: Understanding the new way of coming of age. In J. J. Arnett & J. L. Tanner (Eds.), *Emerging adults in America: Coming of age in the 21st century* (pp. 3–19). Washington, DC: American Psychological Association.

Asato, M. R., Terwilliger, R., Woo, J., & Luna, B. (2010). White matter development in adolescence: A DTI study. *Cerebral Cortex, 20*(9), 2122–2131.

Baillargeon, R. (1994). How do infants learn about the physical world? *Current Directions in Psychological Science, 5,* 133–140.

Baillargeon, R. (2008). Innate ideas revisited: For a principle of persistence in infants' physical reasoning. *Perspectives on Psychological Science, 3*(1), 2–13.

Baillargeon, R., Spelke, E. S., & Wasserman, S. (1985). Object permanence in five-month-old infants. *Cognition, 20*(3), 191–208.

Baltes, P. B., & Baltes, M. M. (1990). Selective optimization with compensation. In P. B. Baltes & M. M. Baltes (Eds.), *Successful aging: Perspectives from the behavioral sciences* (pp. 1–34). New York: Cambridge University Press.

Baltes, P. B., & Lindenberger, U. (1997). Emergence of a powerful connection between sensory and cognitive functions across the adult life span: A new window to the study of cognitive aging? *Psychology and Aging, 12*(1), 12–21.

Bandura, A. (1998). Exploration of fortuitous determinant of life paths. *Psychological Inquiry, 9*(2), 95–115.

Bank, L., Patterson, G. R., & Reid, J. B. (1996). Negative sibling interaction patterns as predictors of later adjustment problems in adolescent and young adult males. In G. H. Brody (Ed.), *Sibling relationships: Their causes and consequences* (pp. 197–229). Norwood, NJ: Ablex.

Barker, E. D., Jaffee, S. R., Uher, R., & Maughan, B. (2011). The contribution of prenatal and postnatal maternal anxiety and depression to child maladjustment. *Depression and Anxiety, 28*(8), 696–702.

Basu, K., & Tzannatos, Z. (2003). The global child labor problem: What do we know and what can we do? *World Bank Economic Review, 17*(2). 147–173.

Baumrind, D. (1996). The discipline controversy revisited. *Family Relations, 45*(4), 405–414.

Bee, H. L. (1987). *The journey of adulthood.* New York: Macmillan.

Bell, S. M., & Ainsworth, M. D. S. (1972). Infant crying and maternal responsiveness. *Child Development, 43*(4), 1171–1190.

Belsky, J., Bakermans-Kranenburg, M. J., & van Ijzendoorn, M. H. (2007). For better and for worse: Differential susceptibility to environmental influences. *Current Directions in Psychological Science,16,* 300–304.

Bengston, V. L., Cuellar, J. B., & Ragan, P. K. (1977). Stratum contrasts and similarities in attitudes toward death. *Journal of Gerontology, 32*(1), 76–88.

Berry, D. S., & McArthur, L. Z. (1985). Some components and consequences of a babyface. *Journal of Personality and Social Psychology, 48*(2), 312–323.

Blakemore, S.-J. (2008). The social brain in adolescence. *Nature Reviews Neuroscience, 9,* 267–277.

Bornstein, M. H. (1989). Information processing (habituation) in infancy and stability in cognitive development. *Human Development, 32,* 129–136.

Bouchard, T. J., Lykken, D. T., McGue, M., Segal, N. L., & Tellegen, A. (1990). Sources of human psychological differences: The Minnesota Study of Twins Reared Apart. *Science, 250*(4978), 223–228.

Bouchard, T. J. Jr., & McGue, M. (2003). Genetic and environmental influences on human psychological differences. *Journal of Neurobiology, Special Issue: Special Issue on Genes and Behavior,* 4–45.

Bowlby, J. (1969). *Attachment and loss: Vol. I. Attachment.* New York: Basic Books.

Bowlby, J. (1973). *Attachment and loss: Vol. 2. Separation: Anxiety and anger.* New York: Basic Books.

Bowlby, J. (1980). *Attachment and loss: Vol. 3. Loss.* New York: Basic Books.

Brener N. D., Kann, L., McManus, T., Kinchen, S. A., Sundberg, E. C., & Ross, J. G. (2002). Reliability of the 1999 Youth Risk Behavior Survey Questionnaire. *Journal of Adolescent Health, 31*(4), 336–342.

Britten, R. J. (2002). Divergence between samples of chimpanzee and human DNA sequences is 5%, counting intels. *Proceedings of the National Academy of Sciences, 99,* 13633–13635.

Brody, E. M. (1985). Parent care as a normative family stress. *The Gerontologist, 25*(1), 19–29.

Brody, G. H. (2004). Siblings' direct and indirect contributions to child development. *Current Directions in Psychological Science, 13*(3), 124–126.

Brody, G. H., Ge, X., Kim, S. Y., Murry, V. M., Simons, R. L., Gibbons, E. X., Gerrard, M., & Conger, R. (2003). Neighborhood disadvantage moderates associations of parenting and older sibling problem attitudes and behavior with conduct disorders in African American children. *Journal of Consulting and Clinical Psychology, 71,* 211–222.

Bronfenbrenner, U. (1986). Ecology of the family as a context for human development: Research perspectives. *Developmental Psychology, 22*(6), 723–742.

Bronfenbrenner, U., & Ceci, S. J. (1994). Nature-nurture reconceptualized in developmental perspective: A bioecological model. *Psychological Review, 101*(4), 568–586.

Brosnan, M. J. (2008). Digit ratio as an indicator of numeracy relative to literacy in 7-year-old British schoolchildren. *British Journal of Psychology, 99*(1), 75–85.

Bruce V. (1990). Perceiving and recognizing faces. *Mind & Language, 5*(4), 342–364.

Burchinal, M., Lee, M., & Ramey, C. (1989). Type of day-care and preschool intellectual development in disadvantaged children. *Child Development, 60*(1), 128–137.

Burchinal, M., Vandergrift, N., Pianta, R., & Mashburn, A., (2009). Threshold analysis of association between child care quality and child outcomes for low-income children in pre-kindergarten programs. *Early Childhood Research Quarterly, 25,* 166–176.

Burd, L. (2004). Fetal alcohol syndrome. *American Journal of Medical Genetics, 127,* 1–2.

Burger, J. M., & Burns, L. (1988). The illusion of unique invulnerability and the use of effective contraception. *Personality and Social Psychology Bulletin,14*(2), 264–270.

Carey, W. B., & McDevitt, S. C. (1978). Revision of the Infant Temperament Questionnaire. *Pediatrics, 61,* 735–739.

Casey, B. J., Jones, R. M., & Hare, T. A. (2008). *The adolescent brain. Annals of the New York Academy of Sciences, 1124 The Year in Cognitive Neuroscience*, 111–126.

Cattell, R. B. (1963). Theory of crystalized and fluid intelligence: A critical experiment. *Journal of Educational Psychology, 54*, 1–22.

CBS News. (2011). Celebrity plastic surgery disasters? http://www.cbsnews.com/2300-204_162-10006001-7.html

Cerulo, K. A. (1997). Identity construction: New issues, new directions. *Annual Review of Sociology, 23*, 385–409.

Chapman, S. B., & McKinnon, L. (2000). Discussion of developmental plasticity: Factors affecting cognitive outcome after pediatric traumatic brain injury. *Journal of Communication Disorders, 33*(4), 333–344.

Charles, S. T., & Carstensen, L. L. (2009). Social and emotional aging. *Annual Review of Psychology, 6*, 383–409.

Colapinto, J. (2001). *As nature made him: The boy who was raised as a girl.* New York: Harper Perennial. Revised in 2006.

Colby, A., Kohlberg, L., Gibbs, J., Lieberman, M., Fischer K., & Saltzstein, H. D. (1983). A longitudinal study of moral judgment. *Monographs of the Society for Research in Child Development, 48*(1/2), 1–124.

Cooper, R. R. (2002). Botox parties. *New York Times*, December 15. Retrieved from http://www.nytimes.com/2002/12/15/magazine/the-year-in-ideas-botox-parties.html?scp=1&sq=2002+botox+parties&st=nyt&pagewanted=print

Crews, F., He, J., & Hodge, C. (2007). Adolescent cortical development: A critical period of vulnerability for addiction. *Pharmacology, Biochemistry, and Behavior, 86*(2), 189–199.

Curtiss, S. (1977). *Genie: A linguistic study of a modern-day "wild child."* New York: Academic Press.

Dai, Y. T., & Dimond, M. F. (1998). Filial piety. A cross-cultural comparison and its implications for the well-being of older parents. *Journal of Gerontological Nursing, 24*(3),13–18.

Damon, W. (2004). What is positive youth development? *Annals of the American Academy of Political and Social Science, 591*(1), 13–24.

Darling, C. A., Davidson, J. K., & Passarello, L. C. (1992). The mystique of first intercourse among college youth: The role of partners, contraceptive practices, and psychological reactions. *Journal of Youth and Adolescence, 21*(1), 97–117.

Davila, J., & Cobb, R. W. (2003). Predicting change in self-reported and interviewer-assessed adult attachment: Tests of the individual difference and life stress models of attachment change. *Personality and Social Psychology Bulletin, 29*(7), 859–870.

Davis, D. L., Gottlieb, M. B., & Stampnitzky, J. R. (1998). Reduced ratio of male to female births in several industrial countries: A sentinel health indicator? *Journal of the American Medical Association, 279*(13), 1018–1023.

Dawson, G., Rogers, S., Munson, J., Smith, M., Winter, J., Greenson, J., Donaldson, A., Varley, J. (2010). Randomized, controlled trial of an intervention for toddlers with autism: The Early Start Denver model. *Pediatrics, 125*(1), e17–e23.

DeCasper, A. J., Lecanuet, J.-P., Busnel, M.-C., Granier-Deferre, C., & Maugeais, R. (1994). Fetal reactions to recurrent maternal speech. *Infant Behavior and Development, 17*(2), 159–164.

De Cock, K. M., Fowler, M. G., Mercier, E., de Vincenzi, I., Saba, J., Hoff, E., Alnwick, D. J., Rogers, M., & Shaffer, N. (2000). Prevention of mother-to-child HIV transmission in resource-poor countries: Translating research into policy and practice. *Journal of the American Medical Association, 283*(9), 1175–1182.

Dehue, F., Bolman, C., & Völlink, T. (2008). Cyberbullying: Youngsters' experiences and parental perception. *CyberPsychology & Behavior, 11*(2), 217–223.

Depp, C., Vahia, I. V., & Jeste, D. (2010). Successful aging: Focus on cognitive and emotional health. *Annual Review of Clinical Psychology, 6*, 527–550.

Diamond, M. (1979). Sexual identity and sex roles. In V. Bullough (Ed.), *The frontiers of sex research* (pp. 33–56). Buffalo, NY: Prometheus.

Diamond, M. (1995). Biological aspects of sexual orientation and identity. In L. Diamant & R. McAnulty (Eds.), *The psychology of sexual orientation, behavior and identity: A handbook* (pp. 45–80). Westport, CT: Greenwood Press.

Diamond, M. (2000). Sex and gender: Same or different? *Feminism Psychology, 10*(1), 46–54.

Diamond, M., & Sigmundson, K. (1997). Sex reassignment at birth: Long-term review and clinical implications. *Archives of Pediatrics & Adolescent Medicine, 151*(3), 298–304.

Dickens, W. T., & Flynn, J. R. (2001). Heritability estimates versus large environmental effects: The IQ paradox resolved. *Psychological Review, 108*(2), 346–369.

Edwards, C. P. (1993). Behavioral sex differences in children of diverse cultures: The case of nurturance to infants. In M. E. Pereira & L. A. Fairbanks (Eds.), *Juvenile primates: Life history, development, and behavior* (pp. 327–338). New York/Oxford: Oxford University Press.

Erel, O., & Burman, B. (1995). Interrelatedness of marital relations and parent–child relations: A meta-analytic review. *Psychological Bulletin, 118*(1), 108–132.

Erickson, M. E, Sroufe, L. A., & Egeland, B. (1985). The relationship between quality of attachment and behavior problems in preschool in a high-risk sample. *Monographs of the Society for Research in Child Development, 50*(1 & 2), 147–166.

Erikson, E. H. (1959). *Identity and the life cycle.* New York: International Universities Press.

Erikson, E. H. (1968). *Identity, youth and crisis.* New York: Norton.

Ernst, M., & Mueller, S. C. (2008). The adolescent brain: Insights from functional neuroimaging research. *Developmental Neurobiology, 68*(6), 729–743.

Eyler, L. T., Serzai, A., Kaup, A. R., & Jeste, D. V. (2011). A review of functional brain imaging correlates of successful cognitive aging. *Biological Psychiatry, 70*(2), 115–122.

Fagot, B. I., Hagan, R., Leinbach M. D., & Kronsberg, S. (1985). Differential reactions to assertive and communicative acts of toddler boys and girls. *Child Development, 56*(6), 1499–1505.

Fantz, R. L. (1961). The origin of form perception. *Scientific American, 204*(5), 66–72.

Feldman, R., & Eidelman, A. (1998). Intervention programs for premature infants: How and do they affect development? *Clinics in Perinatology, 25*(3), 613–629.

Feldman, R., Weller, A., Sirota, L., & Eidelman, A. (2003). Testing a family intervention hypothesis: The contribution of mother–infant skin-to-skin contact (kangaroo care) to family interaction, proximity, and touch. *Journal of Family Psychology, 17*(1), 94–107.

Field, T. (1984). Peer separation of children attending new schools. *Developmental Psychology, 20*, 786–792.

Field, T. (1996). Attachment and separation in young children. *Annual Review of Psychology, 47*, 541–561.

Flavell, J. H., Shipstead, S. G., & Croft, K. (1978). Young children's knowledge about visual perception: Hiding objects from others. *Child Development, 49*(4), 1208–1211.

Fraley, C., & Roberts, B. W. (2005). Patterns of continuity: A dynamic model for conceptualizing the stability of individual differences in psychological constructs across the life course. *Psychological Review, 112*, 60–74.

Fratiglioni, L., Wang, H.-X., et al. (2004). Brain reserve hypothesis in dementia. *Journal of Alzheimer's Disease, 12*(1), 11–22.

Furman, W., & Shaffer, L. A. (1999). A story of adolescence: The emergence of other-sex relationships. *Journal of Youth and Adolescence, 28*(4), 513–522.

Gardner, H. (1981). *The quest for mind.* Chicago: University of Chicago Press.

Gavin, L. A., & Furman, W. (1989). Age differences in adolescents' perceptions of their peer groups. *Developmental Psychology, 25*(5), 827–834.

Ge, X., Natsuaki, M. N., Neiderhiser, J. M., & Reiss, D. (2007). Genetic and environmental influences on pubertal timing: Results from two national sibling studies. *Journal of Research on Adolescence, 17*(4), 767–788.

Gettler, L. T., McDade, T. W., Feranil, A. B., & Kuzawa, C. W. (2011). Longitudinal evidence that fatherhood decreases testosterone in human males. *Proceedings of the National Academy of Sciences*, published ahead of print September 12, 2011, doi:10.1073/pnas.1105403108

Gilger, J. W., Geary, D. C., & Eisele, L. M. (1991). Reliability and validity of retrospective self-reports of the age of pubertal onset using twin, sibling, and college student data. *Adolescence, 26*, 41–53.

Gilligan, C. (1982). *In a different voice: Psychological theory and women's development.* Cambridge, MA: Harvard University Press.

Giltay, E. J., Geleijnse, J. M., Zitman, F. G., Hoekstra, T., & Schouten, E. G. (2004). Dispositional optimism and all-cause and cardiovascular mortality in a prospective cohort of elderly Dutch men and women. *Archives of General Psychiatry, 61,* 1126–1135.

Goldberg, W. A., Prause, J., Lucas-Thmpson, R., & Himsel, A. (2008). Maternal employment and children's achievement in context: A meta-analysis of four decades of research. *Psychological Bulletin, 134*(1), 77–108.

Gopnik, A., & Astington, J. W. (1988). Children's understanding of representational change and its relation to the understanding of false belief and the appearance–reality distinction. *Child Development, 59*(1), 26–37.

Gottman, J. M. (1994). *What predicts divorce? The relationship between marital processes and martial outcomes.* Hillsdale, NJ: Lawrence Erlbaum.

Gottman, J. M. (1998). Psychology and the study of marital processes. *Annual Review of Psychology, 49,* 169–197.

Greene, J. D., Sommerville, R. B., Nystrom, L. E., Darley, J. M., & Cohen, J. D. (2001). An fMRI investigation of emotional engagement in moral judgment. *Science, 293*(5537), 2105–2108.

Greene, J. & Haidt, J. (2002). How (and where) does moral judgment work? *Trends in Cognitive Sciences, 6*(12), 517–523.

Greenfield, P. M., Keller, H., Fuligni, A., & Maynard, A. (2003). Cultural pathways through universal development. *Annual Review of Psychology, 54,* 461–490.

Gruenewald, T. L., Karlamanglia, A. S., Greendale, G. A., Singer, B. H., & Seeman, T. E. (2007). Feelings of usefulness to others, disability, and mortality in older adults: The MacArthur Study of Successful Aging. *Journal of Gerontology B, 62*(1), P28–P37.

Guyer, A. E., Monk, C. S., McClure-Tone, E. B., Nelson, E. E., Roberson-Nay, R., Adler, A. D., Fromm, S. J., Leibenluft, E., Pine, D. S., & Ernst, M. (2008). A developmental examination of amygdala response to facial expressions. *Journal of Cognitive Neuroscience, 20*(9), 1565–1582.

Haidt, J. (2001). The emotional dog and its rational tail: A social intuitionist approach to moral judgment. *Psychological Review, 108*(4), 814–834.

Haidt, J. (2008). Morality. *Perspectives on Psychological Science, 3*(1), 65–72.

Harlow, H. F. (1958). The nature of love. *American Psychologist, 13,* 673–685.

Hawkes, K., O'Connell, J. F., Blurton Jones, N. G., Alvarez, H., & Charnov, E. L. (1998). Grandmothering, menopause and the evolution of human life histories. *Proceedings of the National Academy of Sciences USA, 95,* 1336–1339.

Hazan, C., & Shaver, P. (1987). Romantic love conceptualized as an attachment process. *Journal of Personality and Social Psychology, 52*(3), 511–524.

Hedden, T., & Gabrieli, J. D. E. (2004). Insights into the ageing mind: A view from cognitive neuroscience. *Nature Reviews Neuroscience, 5,* 87–96.

Helson, R., Jones, C., & Kwan, V. S. (2002). Personality change over 40 years of adulthood: Hierarchical linear modeling analyses of two longitudinal samples. *Journal of Personality and Social Psychology, 83*(3), 752–766.

Henry, J. D., MacLeod, M. S., Phillips, L. H., & Crawford, J. R. (2004). A meta-analytic review of prospective memory and aging. *Psychology and Aging, 19*(1), 27–39.

Hetherington, E. M. (1999). Should we stay together for the sake of the children? In E. M. Hetherington (Ed.), *Coping with divorce, single parenting, and remarriage: A risk and resiliency perspective* (pp. 93–116). Mahwah, NJ: Erlbaum.

Hetherington, E. M., Cox, M., & Cox, R. (1985). Long-term effects of divorce and remarriage on the adjustment of children. *Journal of the American Academy of Child Psychiatry, 24,* 518–530.

Hirsch, M., Lunenfeld, B., Modan, M., Ovadia, J., & Shemesh, J. (1985). Spermarche: The age of onset of sperm emission. *Journal of Adolescent Health Care, 6*(1), 35–39.

Hoffman, L. W. (1991). The influence of the family environment on personality: Accounting for sibling differences. *Psychological Bulletin, 110*(2), 187–203.

Huyck, M. H. (1982). From gregariousness to intimacy: Marriage and friendship over the adult years. In T. M. Field, A. Huston, H. C. Quay, L. Troll, & G. E. Finlay (Eds.), *Review of human development* (pp. 471–484). New York: Wiley.

Hwang, K., Velanova, K., & Luna, B. (2010). Strengthening of top-down frontal cognitive control networks underlying the development of inhibitory control: A functional magnetic resonance imaging effective connectivity study. *Journal of Neuroscience, 30*(46), 15535–15545.

Hyde, M. (1976). *The Thrales of Streatham Park.* Cambridge, MA: Harvard University Press.

Inglehart, R. (1990). *Culture shift in advanced industrial society.* Princeton, NJ: Princeton University Press.

Jaccard, J., Blanton, H., & Dodge, T. (2005). Peer influences on risk behavior: An analysis of the effects of a close friend. *Developmental Psychology, 41*(1), 135–147.

James, W. H. (2000). Reproductive physiology: Why are boys more likely to be preterm than girls? Plus other related conundrums in human reproduction: Opinion. *Human Reproduction, 15*(10), 2108–2122.

Jenkins, J. (1992). Sibling relationships in disharmonious homes: Potential difficulties and protective effects. In F. Boer & J. Dunn (Eds.), *Children's sibling relationships: Developmental and clinical issues* (pp. 125–138). Hillsdale, NJ: Erlbaum.

Johnson, A., Moher, T., Ohlsson, S., & Gillingham, M. (1999). The round earth project—collaborative VR for conceptual learning. *IEEE Computer Graphics, 19*(6), 60–69.

Johnson, D. (2004). Will baby crawl? National Science Foundation Discoveries, July 21. http://www.nsf.gov/discoveries/disc_summ.jsp?cntn_id= 103153&org=NSF

Johnson, M. H., Dziurawiec, S., Ellis, H. D., & Morton, J. (1991). Newborns' preferential tracking of faces and its subsequent decline. *Cognition, 40,* 1–19.

Johnston, J. R., Kline, M., & Tschann, J. M. (1989). Ongoing postdivorce conflict: Effects on children of joint custody and frequent access. *American Journal of Orthopsychiatry, 59,* 576–592.

Jung, M.-J., & Fouts, H. N. (2011). Multiple caregivers' touch interactions with young children among the Bofi foragers in Central Africa. *International Journal of Psychology, 46*(1), 24–32.

Kagan, J. (1976). Emergent themes in human development. *American Scientist, 64,* 186–196.

Kagan, J., & Snidman, N. C. (2004). *The long shadow of temperament.* Cambridge, MA: Belknap Press.

Kahlenberg, S. M., & Wrangham, R. W. (2010). Sex differences in chimpanzees' use of sticks as play objects resemble those of children. *Current Biology, 20*(24), R1067–R1068.

Kail, R. (1991). Developmental changes in speed of processing during childhood and adolescence. *Psychological Bulletin, 109,* 490–501.

Keating, D. (2004). Cognitive and brain development. In R. Lerner & I. Steinberg (Eds.), *Handbook of adolescent psychology* (2nd ed., pp. 45–84). New York: Wiley.

Keller, W. D., Hildebrandt, K. A., & Richards, M. E. (1985). Effects of extended father–infant contact during the newborn period. *Infant Behavior & Development, 8*(3), 337–350.

Kelly, J. B. (2000). Children's adjustment in conflicted marriage and divorce: A decade review of research. *Journal of the American Academy of Child & Adolescent Psychiatry, 39*(8), 963–973.

Kelly, J. B., & Emery, R. E. (2003). Children's adjustment following divorce: Risk and resilience perspectives. *Family Relations, 52*(4), 352–362.

Keller, W. D., Hildebrandt, K. A., & Richards, M. E. (1985). Effects of extended father–infant contact during the newborn period. *Infant Behavior & Development, 8*(3), 337–350.

Kellman, P. J., & Spelke, E. S. (1983). Perception of partly occluded objects in infancy. *Cognitive Psychology, 15*(4), 483–524.

Kiernan, K. E., & Hobcraft, J. (1997). Parental divorce during childhood: Age at first intercourse, partnership and parenthood. *Population Studies, 51*(1), 41–55.

Kim-Cohen, J., Moffitt, T. E., Caspi, A., & Taylor, A. (2004). Genetic and environmental processes in young children's resilience and vulnerability to socioeconomic deprivation. *Child Development, 75*(3), 651–668.

Kinsella, K., & He, W. (2009). An aging world: 2008 (International Population Reports). Washington, DC, National Institute on Aging, Census Bureau. Retrieved from http://www.census.gov/prod/2009pubs/p95-09-1.pdf, 06.07.2010.

Kligman, A. M., & Graham, J. A. (1986). The psychology of appearance in the elderly. *Dermatologic Clinics, 4*(3), 501–507.

Kohlberg, L. (1969). Stage and sequence: The cognitive developmental approach to socialization. In D. A. Goslin (Ed.), *Handbook of socialization theory and research.* Chicago: Rand McNally.

Kohlberg, L. (1981). *Essays on moral development.* San Francisco: Harper & Row.

Kohlberg, L. (1984). *The psychology of moral development: The nature and validity of moral stages.* San Francisco: Harper & Row.

Kübler-Ross, E. (1969). *On death and dying.* New York: Scribner. Reprinted 1997.

Lamb, M. E., (1977). Father–infant and mother–infant interaction in the first year of life. *Child Development, 48*(1), 167–181.

Lang, F. R., & Carstensen, L. L. (2002). Time counts: Future time perspective, goals, and social relationships. *Psychology and Aging, 17*(1), 125–139.

Lansford, J. E., Michael, M., Criss, M. M., Pettit, G. S., Dodge, K. A., & Bates, J. E. (2003). Friendship quality, peer group affiliation, and peer antisocial behavior as moderators of the link between negative parenting and adolescent externalizing behavior. *Journal of Research on Adolescence, 13*(2), 161–184.

Laosa, L. M., & Brophy, J. E. (1972). Effects of sex and birth order on sex role development and intelligence among kindergarten children. *Developmental Psychology, 6,* 409–415.

Larsen, R. J., & Diener, E. (1987). Affect intensity as an individual difference characteristic: A review. *Journal of Research in Personality, 21*(1), 1–39.

Larson, R. W., Richards, M. H., Moneta, G., Holmbeck, G., & Duckett, E. (1996). Changes in adolescents' daily interactions with their families from ages 10 to 18: Disengagement and transformation. *Developmental Psychology, 32*(4), 744–754.

Lee, G. R., Peek. C. W., & Coward, R. T. (1998). Race differences in filial responsibility expectations among older parents. *Journal of Marriage and Family, 60*(2), 404–412.

Lehman, H. C. (1962). More about age and achievement. *Gerontologist, 2,* 141–148.

Lehman, H. C. (1966a). The most creative years of engineers and other technologists. *Journal of Genetic Psychology, 108,* 263–270.

Lehman, H. C. (1966b). The psychologist's most creative years. *American Psychologist, 21,* 363–369.

Leinbach, M. D., & Fagot, B. I. (1993). Categorical habituation to male and female faces: Gender schematic processing in infancy. *Infant Behavior and Development, 16*(3), 317–332.

Lenroot, R. K., & Giedd, J. N. (2006). Brain development in children and adolescents: Insights from anatomical magnetic resonance imaging. *Neuroscience Biobehavior Review, 30*(6), 718–729.

Lerner, R. M. (1982). Children and adolescents as producers of their own development. *Developmental Review, 2,* 342–370.

Levenson, R. W., Carstensen, L. L., & Gottman, J. M. (1993). Long-term marriage: Age, gender, and satisfaction. *Psychology and Aging, 8*(2), 301–313.

Levine, A., Zagoory-Sharon, O., Feldman, R., & Weller, A. (2007). Oxytocin during pregnancy and early postpartum: Individual patterns and maternal–fetal attachment. *Peptides, 28*(6), 1162–1169.

Levy, B. R., Slade, M. D., Kunkel, S. R., & Kasl, S. V. (2002). Longevity increased by positive self-perceptions of aging. *Journal of Personality and Social Psychology, 83*(2), 261–270.

Limber, S. P., Cunningham, P., Florx, V., Ivey, J., Nation, M., Chai, S., & Melton, G. (1997). *Bullying among school children: Preliminary findings from a school-based intervention program.* Fifth International Family Violence Research Conference, Durham, NH, June/July.

Lore, R. K., & Schultz, L. A. (1993). Control of human aggression: A comparative perspective. *American Psychologist, 48*(1), 16–25.

Maccoby, E. E., & Jacklin, C. N. (1974). *The psychology of sex differences.* Stanford, CA: Stanford University Press.

Majnemer, A., Brownstein, A., Kadanoff, R., & Shevell M. I. (1992). A comparison of neurobehavioral performance of healthy term and low-risk preterm infants at term. *Developmental Medicine & Child Neurology, 34*(5), 417–424.

Martin, C. L., & Ruble, D. (2004). Children's search for gender cues—cognitive perspectives on gender development. *Current Directions in Psychological Science, 13,* 67–70.

Masten, A. S. (2001). Ordinary magic: Resilience processes in development. *American Psychologist, 56*(3), 227–238.

Masten, A. S., & Obradovic, J. (2006). Competence and resilience in development. *Annals of the New York Academy of Sciences, 1094,* 13–27.

McBride, T., & Nief, R., (2011). *The Mindset Lists of American history: From typewriters to text messages, what ten generations of Americans think is normal.* New York: John Wiley & Sons.

McCrae, R. R., & Costa, P. T. (1994). The stability of personality: Observations and evaluations. *Current Directions in Psychological Science, 3*(6), 173–175.

McCrae, R. R., & Costa, P. T., Jr. (1997). Personality trait structure as a human universal. *American Psychologist, 52*(5), 509–516.

McCrae, R. R., Costa, P. T., Jr., Ostendorf, F., Angleitner, A., Hrebícková, M., Avia, M. D., Sanz, J., Sánchez-Bernardos, M. L., Kusdil, M. E., Woodfield, R., Saunders, P. R., & Smith, P. B. (2000). Nature over nurture: Temperament, personality, and life span development. *Journal of Personality and Social Psychology, 78*(1), 173–186.

McCrink, K., & Wynn, K. (2004). Large-number addition and subtraction by 9-month-old infants. *Psychological Science, 15*(11), 776–781.

McIntyre, M. H., & Pope Edwards, C. (2009). The early development of gender differences. *Annual Review of Anthropology, 38,* 83–97.

Meltzoff, A. N., & Moore, M. K. (1983). Imitation of facial and manual gestures by human neonates. *Child Development, 54,* 702–709.

Meltzoff, A. N., & Moore, M. K. (1989). Imitation in newborn infants: Exploring the range of gestures imitated and the underlying mechanisms. *Developmental Psychology, 25,* 954–962.

Miller, J. G. (1994). Cultural diversity in the morality of caring: Individually oriented versus duty-based interpersonal moral codes. *Cross-Cultural Research: The Journal of Comparative Social Science, 28,* 3–39.

Milunsky, A., Jick, H., Jick, S. S., Bruel, C. L., MacLaughlin, D. S., Rothman, K. J., & Willett, W. (1989). Multivitamin/folic acid supplementation in early pregnancy reduces the prevalence of neural tube defects. *Journal of the American Medical Association, 262*(20), 2847–2852.

Mirowsky, J. (2002). Parenthood and health: The pivotal and optimal age at first birth. *Social Forces, 81*(1), 315–349.

Moffitt, T. E., Caspi, A., & Rutter, M. (2006). Measured gene-environment interactions in psychopathology: Concepts, research strategies, and implications for research, intervention, and public understanding of genetics. *Perspectives on Psychological Science, 1*(1), 5–27.

Money, J. (1975). Ablatio penis: Normal male infant sex-reassignment as a girl. *Archives of Sexual Behavior, 4,* 65–71.

Mounts, N. S., & Steinberg, L. (1995). An ecological analysis of peer influence on adolescent grade point average and drug use. *Developmental Psychology, 31*(6), 915–922.

Nardinelli, C. (1990). *Child labor and the industrial revolution.* Bloomington: Indiana University Press.

Nash, J. M. (2001). Fertile minds. *Time,* June 24.

Neimeyer, R. A., & Chapman, K. M. (1980/1981). Self-ideal discrepancy and fear of death: The test of an existential hypothesis. *Omega, 11,* 233–239.

Neugarten, B. L. (1979). Time, age, and the life cycle. *American Journal of Psychiatry, 136,* 887–894.

NICHD Early Child Care Network. (2005). *Child care and child development: Results from the NICHD Study of Early Child Care and Youth Development.* New York: Guilford.

NOVA. (2001). (TV series). Sex: Unknown (transcript). 2001-10-30.

O'Leary, K. D., & Smith, D. A. (1991). Marital interactions. *Annual Review of Psychology, 42,* 191–212.

Olson, S. L. (1992). Development of conduct problems and peer rejection in preschool children: A social systems analysis. *Journal of Abnormal Child Psychology, 20*(3), 327–350.

Olweus, D. (1993). Victimization by peers: Antecedents and long-term outcomes. In K. H. Rubin & J. B. Asendorf (Eds.), *Social withdrawal, inhibitions, and shyness* (pp. 315–341). Hillsdale, NJ: Erlbaum.

Olweus, D. (1996). Bullying at school: Knowledge base and an effective intervention program. *Annals of the New York Academy of Sciences, 794, Understanding Aggressive Behavior in Children,* 265–276.

Olweus, D., Mattson, A., Schalling, D., & Low, H. (1980). Testosterone, aggression, physical, and personality dimensions in normal adolescent males. *Psychosomatic Medicine, 42,* 253–269.

Orbell, S., & Sheeran, P. (2000). Motivational and volitional processes in action initiation: A field study of the role of implementation intentions. *Journal of Applied Social Psychology, 30,* 780–797.

O'Reilly, I. (2010, February 15). Tension over sex testing in sport. BBC NEWS, http://news.bbc.co.uk/go/pr/fr/-/2/hi/in_depth/8511176.stm

Osterling, J., & Dawson, G. (1994). Early recognition of children with autism: A study of first birthday home videotapes. *Journal of Autism and Developmental Disorders, 24*(3), 247–257.

Panning, B., & Taatjes, D. J. (2008). Transcriptional regulation: It takes a village. *Molecular Cell, 31*(5), 622–629.

Parens, E. (2004), Genetic differences and human identities: On why talking about behavioral genetics is important and difficult. *Hastings Center Report Supplement 34,* S1–S36.

Pastor, D. (1981). The quality of mother–infant attachment and its relationship to toddlers' initial sociability with peers. *Developmental Psychology, 17*(3), 326–335.

Patalano, A. L., & Seifert, C. M. (1997). Opportunistic planning: Being reminded of pending goals. *Cognitive Psychology, 34,* 1–36.

Paukner, A., Suomi, S. J., Visalberghi, E., & Ferrari, P. F. (2009). Capuchin monkeys display affiliation toward humans who imitate them. *Science, 325*(5942), 880–883.

PBS. (1997, March 4). Secret of the wild child. *NOVA.*

Pereira, A. C., Huddleston, D. E., Brickman, A. M., Sosunov, A. A., Hen, R., McKhann, G. M., Sloan, R., Gage, F. H., Broan, T. R., & Small, S. A. (2007). An *in vivo* correlate of exercise-induced neurogenesis in the adult dentate gyrus. *Proceedings of the National Academy of Sciences, 104*(13), 5638–5643.

Petersen, A. C., Sarigiani, P. A., & Kennedy, R. E. (1991). Adolescent depression: Why more girls? *Journal of Youth and Adolescence, 20*(2), 247–271.

Petersen, J. L., & Hyde, J. S. (2010). A meta-analytic review of research on gender differences in sexuality, 1993–2007. *Psychological Bulletin, 136*(1), 21–38.

Phillips, D., Mekos, D., Scarr, S., McCartney, K., & Abbott-Shim, M. (2000). Within and beyond the classroom door: Assessing quality in child care centers. *Early Childhood Research Quarterly, 15*(4), 475–496.

Piaget, J. (1928). *The child's conception of the world.* London: Routledge and Kegan Paul.

Piaget, J. (1932). *The moral judgment of the child.* London: Kegan Paul, Trench, Trubner.

Piaget, J. (1951). *The psychology of intelligence.* London: Routledge and Kegan Paul.

Piaget, J. (1952). *The origins of intelligence in children.* New York: International University Press. (Original work published 1936.)

Pinker, S. (2002). *The blank slate: The modern denial of human nature.* New York: Penguin.

Plomin, R., & Crabbe, J. (2000). DNA. *Psychological Bulletin, 126*(6), 806–828.

Plomin, R., Corley, R., Caspi, A., Fulker, D. W., & De Fries, J. C. (1998). Adoption results for self-reported personality: Not much nature or nurture? *Journal of Personality and Social Psychology, 75,* 211–218.

Raley, R. K., & Bumpass, L. (2003). The topography of the divorce plateau: Levels and trends in union stability in the United States after 1980. *Demographic Research, 8*(8), 245–260.

Rauer, A. J., & Volling, B. L. (2007). Differential parenting and sibling jealousy: Developmental correlates of young adults' romantic relationships. *Personal Relationships, 14*(4), 495–511.

Ricciuti, A. E., & Scarr, S. (1990). Interaction of early biological and family risk factors in predicting cognitive development. *Journal of Applied Developmental Psychology, 11*(1), 1–12.

Rice, F., Harold, G. T., Boivin, J., van den Bree, M., Hay, D. F., & Thapar, A. (2010). The links between prenatal stress and offspring development and psychopathology: Disentangling environmental and inherited influences. *Psychological Medicine, 40,* 335–345.

Rivers, I., & Smith, P. K. (1994). Types of bullying behavior and their correlates. *Aggressive Behavior, 20,* 259–368.

Roberts, B. W., & Mroczek, D. (2008). Personality trait change in adulthood. *Current Directions in Psychological Science, 17*(1), 31–35.

Roberts, B. W., Walton, K. E., & Viechtbauer, W. (2006). Patterns of mean-level change in personality traits across the life course: A meta-analysis of longitudinal studies. *Psychological Bulletin, 132*(1), 1–25.

Rödholm, M. (1981). Effects of father–infant postpartum contact on their interaction 3 months after birth. *Early Human Development, 5*(1), 79–85.

Rosenzweig, M. R., Bennett, E. L., & Diamond, M. C. (1972). Brain changes in response to experience. *Scientific American, 226*(2), 22–29.

Rothbart, M. K. (1981). Measurement of temperament infancy. *Child Development, 52*(2), 569–578.

Rothbart, M. K. (1986). Longitudinal observation of infant temperament. *Developmental Psychology, 22*(3), 356–365.

Rothbart, M. K., & Bates, J. E. (2006). Temperament. In N. Eisenberg, W. Damon, & R. M. Lerner (Eds.), *Handbook of child psychology: Vol. 3, Social, emotional, and personality development* (6th ed., pp. 99–166). New York: Wiley.

Rothbart, M. K., Sheese, B. E., & Posner, M. I. (2007). Executive attention and effortful control: Linking temperament, brain networks, and genes. *Child Development Perspectives, 1*(1), 2–7.

Rouvee-Collier, C. K., Sullivan, M. W., Enright, M., Lucas, D., & Fagen, J. W. (1980). Reactivation of infant memory. *Science, 208*(4448), 1159–1161.

Rowe, J. W., & Kahn, R. L. (1997). Successful aging. *Gerontologist, 37*(4), 433–440.

Ryff, C. D. (1989). Happiness is everything, or is it? Explorations on the meaning of psychological well-being. *Journal of Personality and Social Psychology, 57*(6), 1069–1081.

Sagi, A., van Ijzendoorn, M. H., Aviezer, O., Donnell, F., & Mayseless, O. (1994). Sleeping out of home in a kibbutz communal arrangement: It makes a difference for infant–mother attachment. *Child Development, 65*(4), 992–1004,

Salapatek, P., Bechtold, G., & Bushnell, E. W. (1976). Infant visual acuity as a function of viewing distance. *Child Development, 47*(3), 860–863.

Salthouse, T. A. (2006). Mental exercise and mental aging: Evaluating the validity of the "Use It or Lose It" hypothesis. *Perspectives on Psychological Science, 1*(1), 68–87.

Salthouse, T. (2011). Consequences of age-related cognitive declines. *Annual Review of Psychology, 63,* 5.1–5.26.

Scarr, S. (1992). Developmental theories for the 1990s: Development and individual differences. *Child Development, 63*(1), 1–19.

Scarr, S. (1996). How people make their own environments: Implications for parents and policy makers. *Psychology, Public Policy, and Law, 2*(2), 204–228.

Scarr, S. (1997). Why child care has little impact on most children's development. *Current Directions in Psychological Science, 6*(5), 143–148

Scarr, S., & McCartney, K. (1983). How people make their own environments: A theory of genotype x environment effects. *Child Development, 54,* 424–435.

Scheibe, S., & Carstensen, L. L. (2010). Emotional aging: Recent findings and future trends. *Journal of Gerontology, 65B*(2), 135–144.

Schlegel, A., & Barry, H., III. (1991). *Adolescence: An anthropological inquiry.* New York: Free Press.

Schmitt, D. P., Allik, J., McCrae, R. R., & Benet-Martínez, V. (2007). The geographic distribution of Big Five personality traits: Patterns and profiles of human self-description across 56 nations. *Journal of Cross-Cultural Psychology, 38*(2), 173–212.

Seals, D., & Young, J. (2003). Bullying and victimization: Prevalence and relationship to gender, grade level, ethnicity, self-esteem, and depression. *Adolescence, 38,* 735–747.

Chapter Review

Shanley, D. P., Sear, R., Mace, R., & Kirkwood, T. B. I. (2007). Testing evolutionary theories of menopause. *Proceedings of the Royal Society of London B: Biological Sciences, 274,* 2943–2949.

Shaver, P. R., & Mikulincer, M. (2007). Adult attachment strategies and the regulation of emotion. In J. J. Gross (Ed.), *Handbook of emotion regulation* (pp. 446–465). New York: Guilford.

Silveri, M., Rohan, M. L., Pimentel, P. J., Gruber, S. A., Rosso, I. M., & Yurgelun-Todd, D. A. (2006). Sex differences in the relationship between white matter microstructure and impulsivity in adolescents. *Magnetic Resonance Imaging, 24*(7), 833–841.

Silverberg, S. B., & Steinberg, L. (1997). Psychological well-being of parents with early adolescent children. *Developmental Psychology, 26*(4), 658–666.

Simon, M. (2009, April 23). My bullied son's last day on earth. CNN U.S. http://articles.cnn.com/2009-04-23/us/bullying.suicide_1_bullies-gay-tired?_s=PM:US

Simonton, D. K. (1988). Age and outstanding achievement: What do we know after a century of research? *Psychological Bulletin, 104*(2), 251–267.

Simonton, D. K. (1997). Creative productivity: A predictive and explanatory model of career trajectories and landmarks. *Psychological Review, 104*(1), 66–89.

Smith, E. P., Boutte, G. S., Zigler, E., & Finn-Stevenson, M. (2004). Opportunities for schools to promote resilience in children and youth. In L. I. Maton, C. J. Schellenbach, B. J. Leadbeater, A. L. Solarz, (Eds.), *Investing in children, youth, families, and communities: Strengths-based research and policy* (pp. 213–231). Washington, DC: American Psychological Association.

Snarey, J. R., Reimer, J., & Kohlberg, L. (1985). Development of social-moral reasoning among Kibbutz adolescents: A longitudinal cross-cultural study. *Developmental Psychology, 21*(1), 3–17.

Somerville, L. H., Hare, T., & Casey, B. J. (2011). Frontostriatal maturation predicts cognitive control failure to appetitive cues in adolescents. *Journal of Cognitive Neuroscience, 23*(9), 2123–2134.

Sorkhabi, N. (2005). Applicability of Baumrind's parent typology to collective cultures: Analysis of cultural explanations of parent socialization effects. *International Journal of Behavioral Development, 29*(6), 552–563.

Spear, L. P. (2000). The adolescent brain and age-related behavioral manifestations. *Neuroscience Biobehavioral Review, 24,* 417–463.

Spear, L. P. (2007). The developing brain and adolescent-typical behavior patterns: An evolutionary approach. In D. Romer and E. Walker (Eds.), *Adolescent psychopathology and the developing brain.* New York: Oxford University Press.

Stein, D. G., Brailowsky, S., & Will, B. (1995). *Brain repair.* New York: Oxford University Press.

Steinberg, L. (1989). Pubertal maturation and parent–adolescent distance: An evolutionary perspective. In L. Steinberg, G. R. Adams, R. Montemayor, & T. P. Gullotta (Eds.), *Biology of adolescent behavior and development, advances in adolescent development: An annual book series, Vol. 1* (pp. 71–97). Thousand Oaks, CA: Sage.

Steinberg, L. (2006). Risk taking in adolescence: What changes, and why? *Annals of the New York Academy of Sciences, 1021*(1), 51–58.

Steinberg, L. (2007). Risk taking in adolescence: New perspectives from brain and behavioral science. *Current Directions in Psychological Science, 16*(2), 55–59.

Steinberg, L. (2009). Should the science of adolescent brain development inform public policy? *American Psychologist, 64*(8), 739–750.

Steinberg, L., & Morris, A. S. (2001). Adolescent development. *Annual Review of Psychology, 52,* 83–110.

Stern, M., & Karraker, K. H. (1989). Sex stereotyping of infants: A review of gender labeling studies. *Sex Roles, 20*(9–10), 501–522.

Stern, Y. (2009). Cognitive reserve. *Neuropsychologia, 47*(10), 2015–2028.

Strassmann, B. I. (2011). Cooperation and competition in a cliff-dwelling people. *Proceedings of the National Academy of Sciences, 108*(2), 10894–10901.

Strassmann, B. I., & Garrard, W. M. (2011). Alternatives to the grandmother hypothesis: A meta-analysis of the association between grandparental and grandchild survival in patrilineal populations. *Human Nature, 22,* 201–222.

Strobe, M. S., & Strobe, W. (1983). Who suffers more? Sex differences in health risks of the widowed. *Psychological Bulletin, 93,* 279–301.

Swaab, D. F. (2007). Sexual differentiation of the brain and behavior. *Best Practice & Research Clinical Endocrinology & Metabolism, 21*(3), 431–444.

Talbot, M. (2006, September 4). The baby lab. *New Yorker, 82*(27), 91–101.

Thoma, S. J., & Rest, J. R. (1999). The relationship between moral decision making and patterns of consolidation and transition in moral judgment development. *Developmental Psychology, 35*(2), 323–334.

Trainor, L. J., & Zacharias, C. A. (1998). Infants prefer higher-pitched singing. *Infant Behavior and Development, 21*(4), 799–805.

Tucker-Drob, E. M., Rhemtulla, M., Harden, K. P., Turkheimer, E., & Fask, D. (2011). Emergence of a gene x socioeconomic status interaction on infant mental ability between 10 months and 2 years. *Psychological Science, 22*(1), 125–133.

U.S. Census Bureau. (2009). Median age at first marriage for women and men. Retrieved from http://factfinder.census.gov/servlet/GRTSelectServlet?ds_name=ACS_2009_1YR_G00_, 5/21/2011.

Utz, R. L., Carr, D., Nesse, R., & Wortman, C. B. (2002). The effect of widowhood on older adults' social participation: An evaluation of activity, disengagement, and continuity theories. *The Gerontologist, 42*(4), 522–533.

Vaillant, G. E., & Mukamal, K. (2001). Successful aging. *American Journal of Psychiatry, 158,* 839–847.

Vandell, D. L., Belsky, J., Burchinal, M., Steinberg, L., Vandergrift, N., & NICHD Early Child Care Research Network. (2010). Do effects of early child care extend to age 15 years? Results from the NICHD study of early child care and youth development. *Child Development, 81*(3), 737–756.

Velderman, M. K., Bakermans-Kranenburg, M. J., Juffer, F., & van Ijzendoorn, M. H. (2006). Effects of attachment-based interventions on maternal sensitivity and infant attachment: Differential susceptibility of highly reactive infants. *Journal of Family Psychology, 20*(2), 266–274.

Vosniadou, S., & Brewer, W. F. (1992). Mental models of the earth: A study of conceptual change in childhood. *Cognitive Psychology, 24,* 535–585.

Waters, E., & Cummings, M. (2000). A secure base from which to explore close relationships. *Child Development, 71*(1), 164–172.

Waters, E., Merrick, S., Treboux, D., Crowell, J., & Albersheim, L. (2000). Attachment security in infancy and early adulthood: A twenty-year longitudinal study. *Child Development, 71*(3), 684–689.

Waters, E., Wippman, J., & Sroufe, L. A. (1979). Attachment, positive affect, and competence in the peer group: Two studies in construct validation. *Child Development, 50,* 821–829.

Watson, J. B. (1930). *Behaviorism* (revised edition). Chicago: University of Chicago Press.

Wellman, H. M. (1990). *The child's theory of mind.* Cambridge: MIT Press.

Werner, E. E. (1988). A cross-cultural perspective on infancy research and social issues. *Journal of Cross-Cultural Psychology, 19*(1), 96–113.

Werner, E. E. (1995). Resilience in development. *Current Directions in Psychological Science, 4*(3), 81–85.

Wertsch, J. V. (1985). *Vygotsky and the social formation of mind.* Cambridge, MA: Harvard University Press.

Wethington, E. (2000). Expecting stress: Americans and the "midlife crisis." *Motivation and Emotion, 24*(2), 85–103.

White, L. & Edwards, J. N. (1990). Emptying the nest and parental well-being: An analysis of National Panel Data. *American Sociological Review, 55*(2), 235–242.

Whiteman, S. D., & Buchanan, C. M. (2002). Mothers' and children's expectations for adolescence: The impact of perceptions of an older sibling's experience. *Journal of Family Psychology, 16,* 157–171.

Whitney, I., & Smith, P. K. (1993). A survey of the nature and extent of bullying in junior/middle and secondary schools. *Educational Research, 35,* 3–25.

Wilson, R. S., Mendes de Leon, C. F., Barnes, L. L., Schneider, J. A., Bienias, J. L., Evans, D. A., & Bennett, D. A. (2002). Participation in cognitively stimulating activities and risk of incident Alzheimer disease. *Journal of the American Medical Association, 287*(6), 742–748.

Wimmer, H., & Perner, J. (1983). Beliefs about beliefs: Representation and constraining function of wrong beliefs in young children's understanding of deception. *Cognition, 13*(1), 103–128.

Wong, K. (2009). Hitching a ride. *Scientific American,* July, 20–23.

Wood, W., & Eagly, A. H. (2002). A cross-cultural analysis of the behavior of women and men: Implications for the origins of sex differences. *Psychological Bulletin, 128*(5), 699–727.

Wynn, K. (1992). Children's acquisition of the number words and the counting system. *Cognitive Psychology, 24*(2), 220–251.

Ziegler, E., & Styfco, S. (2004). *The Head Start debates.* Baltimore, MD: Brookes.

Chapter Overview ▼

13 Personality

Learning Objectives ▼

13.1 ▪ Describe the characteristics of a well-crafted personality theory.

13.2 ▪ Compare and contrast the psychoanalytic theories of Freud, Jung, and Adler.

13.3 ▪ Illustrate the humanistic perspective of personality using Rogers's Person-Centered Perspective and Maslow's Theory of Self-actualization.

13.4 ▪ Discuss the factors involved in the trait perspective.

13.5 ▪ Analyze the social cognitive theories of Bandura as compared to those of Mischel.

13.6 ▪ Explain the different biological perspectives and theories of how physiological processes determine personality.

13.7 ▪ Identify the different tools to understand personality and how they are used.

13.8 ▪ Describe how culture and belief systems can shape and be shaped by personality.

I turned out to be a really good morning to play hooky from work. That morning, my neighbor Stephanie, who had graciously agreed to help me renovate the bathroom of my 1920s bungalow, dragged me to a home improvement store. That bathroom had not been refreshed since the previous owner swathed the entire room with gloomy grays and dingy tans. We had just returned from looking at sinks when I got a call. It was Sharon, another psychologist at Oxford College. "*Do not come into work,*" she commanded.

"Oh . . . okay?" I responded inquisitively.

Sharon then explained how a group of students had managed to wrangle an animal to the third floor of my 19th-century Victorian brick office building as a prank.

"Apparently," I later explained to Stephanie, "the building is not fit to enter. The students . . . well, the students stole a zebra as a prank." I blurted out like it was all one word, hoping she would not ask for details.

"A *zebra*?" she enunciated. "Are they *sure* it was a *zebra*?" She contorted her face to be sure that I understood that either she did not hear me correctly or I must have been mistaken.

I paused for a moment. "What else looks like a zebra?"

"Goodness, what *kind* of person would steal a *zebra* and walk it up three flights of stairs as a prank?"

I slipped into professor mode and answered her question with a question (Socratic style). "What kind of person?" I began. "I suppose that depends on who you ask."

Stephanie was right. It probably takes a special kind of person to coax an animal up three flights of stairs . . . but what kind of person? What, in general, motivates us to do what we do?

13.1 Defining Personality

Psychologists define personality in many ways.

- Describe the characteristics of a well-crafted personality theory.

Personality An individual's pattern of thinking, feeling, and behaving.

Disposition The way a person behaves across different situations as well as over time.

Personality theory A system used to describe and explain the genesis and development of an individual's pattern of thinking, feeling, and behaving.

Personality is your pattern of thinking, feeling, and behaving. It is the enduring nature of who you are. It describes not only what you like but also why you like what you like. Personality theorists try to explain a person's **disposition**, which is the way a person behaves across different situations as well as over time. Personality psychologists are interested not just in describing personality but also in understanding where personality comes from and how it develops over time. **Personality theory** is a system used to describe and explain the genesis and development of an individual's pattern of thinking, feeling, and behaving.

According to Magnavita (2002), a well-crafted personality theory will possess several characteristics:

1. Clinical utility. Is the theory helpful to mental health practitioners to understand and treat psychological conditions?

2. Practical utility. Can the theory be applied to everyday situations?

3. Predictive value. Can the theory predict future behavior?

4. Insight into human nature. Does the theory provide useful information on what it means to be human?

5. Ability to provide self-understanding. Does the theory offer an individual some degree of insight into his or her own personality?

6. Ability to understand complex human behavior. Does the theory help explain nuances in our behavior?

As convenient as it might be, people do not come with instruction manuals, so different theories have emerged about the nature and components of personality. In this chapter, we will examine the major grand or all-encompassing theories of personalities, including the psychoanalytic perspective, the humanistic perspective, the trait perspective, the social cognitive perspective, and the biological perspective. And maybe, just maybe, we will figure out what kind of person would kidnap a zebra and hold it hostage as a prank.

CONCEPT LEARNING CHECK 13.1 | *Describing Personality Theories*

Please match the goals of a useful personality theory to the examples below.

A. Clinical utility

B. Practical utility of the theory

C. Predictive value

D. Insight into human nature

E. Self-understanding

F. Describes complex human behavior

1. _____ A theory of personality suggests that people are basically good.

2. _____ Understanding a theory well can help a therapist design a treatment for a client.

3. _____ Understanding a person's personality can help you to know why you do what you do.

4. _____ A theory helps you to understand what it means to be human.

5. _____ A theory helps you to know how a friend will react to being asked to be part of a flash mob.

13.2 The Psychoanalytic Perspective

According to the psychoanalytic perspective, unconscious processes determine your personality.

- Compare and contrast the psychoanalytic theories of Freud, Jung, and Adler.

The Nature of the Psychoanalytic Perspective

The **psychoanalytic theories** (sometimes referred to as psychodynamic, dynamic, or Freudian) are a family of personality theories originated by Sigmund Freud FIGURE 13-1 that focus on unconscious motivation. The notion is that the psyche, or personality, moves energy around to where the energy is needed. The movement of energy is why the theory is called dynamic.

Like many personality theories, the psychoanalytic tradition was developed alongside a psychotherapy technique. The psychoanalytic theorists have assumptions about the formation and development of personality as well as treatment techniques known as psychoanalysis.

FIGURE 13-1 Dr. Sigmund Freud.

Psychoanalytic theories A family of theories originated by Freud that focuses on unconscious motivation.

Psychoanalysis A type of therapy in which unconscious conflicts and motivation are uncovered, explored, and redirected.

Catharsis A release of emotions.

Unconscious According to Freud, thoughts, memories, feelings, and wishes that reside outside of awareness.

Conscious mind According to Freud, a part of the mind that is aware of current thoughts and experiences.

Preconscious According to Freud, the part of your mind that contains material just outside of awareness that is easy to pull into awareness.

Id According to Freud, the part of the personality that operates on the pleasure principle, always looking to reduce tension that comes from basic physiological drives.

Pleasure principle According to Freud, the drive to reduce tension.

The tension reduction of a rollercoaster is fun for your id.

Your id tries to reduce tension by creating images of the things that it wants.

Psychoanalysis is a type of therapy, based on the psychoanalytic technique, in which unconscious conflicts or motivations are uncovered, explored, and redirected.

Not all psychoanalytic perspectives are Freudian. They all, however, do share some assumptions about the nature of human personality, including the presence of the unconscious. In this section, we will discuss three: those of Sigmund Freud, Carl Jung, and Alfred Adler.

Freud's Psychoanalytic Theory

Sigmund Freud, the founder of psychoanalysis, is often considered to be the founder of the first well-organized grand theory of personality. Trained in neurology, his early work focused on using hypnosis to bring about a release of emotions, or **catharsis**. Freud's research in this area led to one of his first publications, *Studies on Hysteria* (Breuer & Freud, 1895). Later, he abandoned the use of hypnosis and shifted to examining the **unconscious**, or the thoughts, memories, feelings, and wishes that reside outside of awareness.

Structure of Personality

Freud describes the landscape of the mind as having several realms, some in awareness and some outside of it. The components of awareness include the **conscious mind**, which encompasses your current thoughts and experiences. As you are reading this text, for example, the words are in your conscious mind. Sometimes, however, you have memories that you can pull into your consciousness fairly easily. Until I mentioned it, you might not have had in your consciousness what you had for lunch yesterday. It was in your preconscious, but it now resides in your consciousness. The **preconscious**, according to Freud, is the part of your mind that contains material just outside of awareness that is easy to pull into awareness. The majority of our mind, however, is in the vast unconscious. The unconscious contains thoughts, memories, feelings, and wishes that reside outside of awareness, including instincts, drives, and memories that may have been repressed or forgotten. As you can see in FIGURE 13-2, most of personality resides outside of your awareness in your unconscious mind. Many people compare the massiveness of the unconscious to an iceberg: You might only see the tip, but there is much lurking beneath.

Freud suggested that there are three main structures within our psyche: the id, ego, and superego. The **id**, according to Freud, is the part of the personality that operates on the **pleasure principle**, meaning the id is always looking to reduce the tension that comes from basic physiological drives. The id is not especially smart, but it knows what it likes, and what it likes is reduction of tension. What kind of tension? All kinds. As a human, you have all sorts of physiological needs and drives. When these needs are unmet, tension builds up. Being thirsty creates tension; sipping a tart lemonade will reduce that tension. Being hungry creates tension; munching on a juicy chicken sandwich will reduce that tension. When the tension is reduced, the id feels satisfied, sometimes referred to as gratification. When the id feels tension, the first thing it does is to create an image of the thing that it wants. This can satisfy the id in the short run, but thinking of a moist four-layer chocolate cake will not make you less hungry. The need becomes stronger, and you

FIGURE 13-2 According to the psychoanalytic perspective, your personality is like an iceberg—there is a lot more to it than what you can perceive.

might not be able to think of anything else. Think of a time when you drank so much water that you really needed to use the restroom but you were not in a place where you could do so. After awhile, all you can think about is going to the restroom. Freud says that this is due to your id.

The main driving force of the id is that pleasure principle—the drive to reduce tension at all costs. The physical and physiological needs that motivate the id keep us alive, causing us to eat, drink, and perpetuate the species by having sex. Freud grouped these drives into a cluster of instincts called eros, or the life instinct. **Eros** is the id instinct that reduces tension associated with basic biological drives. A type of eros is **libido**, or the energy linked with sexuality.

Life instincts are not all that motivate the id; there is another way the id seeks the pleasure principle. Remember the id is not very smart, but it knows what it likes. Freud also suggested that the id has a death instinct, an unconscious desire to be dead—the ultimate state of tension reduction called **thanatos**. According to Freud, thanatos is a way in which we reduce tensions that are aggressive and destructive.

What stops you from satisfying your id instincts in inappropriate ways? Let us say I am thirsty in class and a student is gulping a refreshing root beer. What prevents me from stopping mid-sentence, snatching the beverage from my student's hand, and downing the entire can? According to Freud, my good behavior is due, in part, to the ego and the reality principle. The **ego** is the part of the personality responsible for interacting with conscious reality. Rather than the pleasure principle, the ego is governed by the reality principle. The **reality principle** suggests that the ego will defer pleasure until a reasonable way to satisfy id instincts is available.

But the ego has another master, the superego. While not fully developed until age 2 or 3, the **superego** is the internalization of your parental and societal values. The superego is governed by the **perfection principle**. Also known as the ego ideal, the perfection principle is the image of the perfect person, or ego, that inspires the superego. The superego makes us feel proud when we do well, but it can also cause us to feel shame and guilt when we do not measure up to expectations. While the id's demands are generated from biological needs, the superego's demands come from societal pressures. As you can imagine, sometimes these demands can clash, forcing the ego to compromise.

Personality Development

Freud noticed that the tension-reduction pleasure principle did not always manifest itself in the same way throughout life. In fact, as people grow and develop, the area of the body involved in tension reduction shifts. He named these developmental phases **psychosexual stages**, developmental periods in which tension reduction focuses on different areas of the body (oral, anal, phallic, latency, genital) **TABLE 13-1**. For example, think about the job description of a newborn child. It does not do much. Nevertheless, biological needs still build tension in its body. It gets hungry, gassy, and thirsty. The main area of the body where tension reduction is centered is the mouth. Biting, sucking, chewing, and crying are ways tension is reduced. Freud decided to name the stages of development after the part of the body where tension reduction is centered.

But the tension reduction does not stay in the mouth forever. Imagine a child having the urge to defecate. As an infant, the child would just go—like exhaling. Defecation is not really something children think about much. Then somewhere around 18 months,

Some people smoke even though they know it's not good for them. Freud might suggest that this motivation is generated from thanatos, the death instinct.

Eros An id instinct that reduces tension associated with basic biological drives.

Libido According to Freud, the energy linked with sexuality.

Thanatos According to Freud, ways in which we reduce tensions that are aggressive and destructive; also known as the death instinct.

Ego According to Freud, the part of the personality responsible for interacting with conscious reality.

TABLE 13-1 Freud's Stages of Development

Age	Stage
0–18 months	Oral
18–38 months	Anal
3–6 years	Phallic
6 years–puberty	Latency
Puberty–Adulthood	Genital

Guilt is a feeling that comes from the internalization of parental and societal values. The superego creates these feelings to encourage us to behave in an ideal way, according to Freud.

In the oral stage, tension reduction is centered in the mouth.

The Oedipus complex is the psychoanalytic explanation of why boys end up identifying with Dad rather than Mom.

Reality principle According to Freud, the main focus of the ego that suggests that the ego will defer pleasure until a reasonable way to satisfy id instincts is available.

Superego According to Freud, the part of the personality governed by the perfection principle.

Perfection principle The image of the perfect person, or ego, that inspires the superego; also know as the ego ideal.

Psychosexual stages According to Freud, childhood developmental stages in which tension reduction is focused on different areas of the body (oral, anal, phallic, latency, genital).

Oedipal complex According to Freud, a boy's unconscious desire for his mother that results in identification with his father.

it is as if someone taps them on the shoulder and says, "Hey, you know that thing you used to do that you never thought about? Today is a new day. You have to go at a certain time and in a certain place." What happens if you do not? Well, for the first time in your very short life, you are something that you have never been before—bad. Being a good boy or good girl involves delay of gratification (reduction of tension) and an internalization of your parental and societal values concerning how to relieve yourself appropriately. After all, getting along with others really requires that you avoid defecation around other people.

The anal stage starts at around 18 months and goes until about age 3, where the tension reduction is focused on the genitals during the phallic stage. Masturbation is common in this stage. In the latent stage from age 5 to around age 12, sexual impulses are suppressed. The genital stage starts around puberty when sexual impulses return.

Something else occurs during the phallic stage for boys, the Oedipal complex. According to Freud, the **Oedipal complex** is a boy's unconscious desire for his mother that results in copying the behavior of or identification with his father. The Oedipal complex gets its name from the Greek story of Oedipus, who inadvertently murdered his dad and married his own mother. I know you might be thinking that this sounds very odd, but stick with me. The Oedipal crisis was a way to solve a dilemma that Freud noticed and needed to explain. Why is it that as boys grow up, they come to identify with their fathers right after puberty but cling so closely to their moms before that?

Back in the 1800s, women had the responsibility of raising children, and children were drawn to their mothers. After all, mothers are the id's ticket to most tension reduction, and children crave attention, affection, and love from her. Some boys even say they want to grow up and marry their mom. There is at least one wrinkle in this plan—Dad. Freud suggested that the id becomes jealous of Dad because he, too, receives attention from Mom. The child sees Dad as competition and a threat. The ego uses a defense mechanism to protect the ego from this danger and satisfy the id instinct of wanting Mom. The ego identifies with the aggressor. By identifying with Dad, the ego is no longer in danger from the aggressor and is safe. Plus there is a bonus. Since Dad is married to Mom, by identifying with Dad, the child will be connected to Mom as well. The Oedipal crisis happens unconsciously. Freud believed that the Oedipal crisis resulted in boys' identification with Dad.

There are some after effects of the psychosexual stages. Freud suggested that too much or too little tension reduction at a certain stage can lead to fixation at that stage. **Fixation** is a habit of obtaining tension reduction from a certain stage of psychosexual development. For example, a child who always gets a bottle during the oral stage may become fixated at that stage later. That means that during adulthood, he or she may seek oral tension reduction when under stress. If you talk a lot, eat, or chew your pencil when you are stressed, you may have an oral fixation. Fixation is not bad; it just describes where you go to seek a reduction of tension—it is a way of explaining one aspect of your personality. Fixation can occur at any stage. For example, too much tension reduction during the anal stage can lead to an anal-retentive personality. Those who are perfectionistic or exceptionally clean are attempting to control their world in the same way they receive pleasure from the tension reduction of controlling their bowels.

Defense Mechanisms

Remember, the ego has two masters: the id and the superego. It has to meet the demands of the id and the prohibitions of the superego. Often, to satisfy the id, the superego, and the realities of life, the ego has to compromise. One way the ego does this is through **defense mechanisms**, which are unconscious arrangements that the ego uses to satisfy id instincts indirectly **TABLE 13-2**.

These compromises often take the form of defense mechanisms that have been described by Sigmund Freud and his daughter, Anna Freud (Freud, 1967) **FIGURE 13-3**. All defense mechanisms occur unconsciously, not on purpose.

Not all defense mechanisms are problematic. In sublimation, a person unconsciously redirects an id instinct in a socially acceptable fashion, basically performing an id instinct in a superego way. A person who has an id instinct to beat up another person may unconsciously transform that into a desire to be a boxer, or a person with a hostile

TABLE 13-2 Freudian Defense Mechanisms

Defense Mechanism	Description
Denial	A psychoanalytic defense mechanism in which a person fails to accept a reality
Displacement	A psychoanalytic defense mechanism in which an impulse is unconsciously directed to a substitute object or person
Identification	According to Freud, the unconscious process of copying the behavior of a person
Projection	A defense mechanism in which a person unconsciously attributes their threatening impulses to another person
Rationalization	A defense mechanism in which an irrational behavior is unconsciously explained as acceptable in order to reduce anxiety
Reaction formation	A defense mechanism where a person will unconsciously replace a feeling
Regression	A defense mechanism in which a person reverts to an earlier age of functioning
Repression	A defense mechanism in which a person unconsciously forces a threatening experience from their awareness
Sublimation	A defense mechanism in which a person unconsciously redirects an id instinct in a socially acceptable way

Tongue piercings are an example of an oral fixation, according to some psychoanalytic theorists.

Fixation According to Freud, a habit of obtaining tension reduction from an earlier stage of psychosexual development.

Defense mechanism According to the psychoanalytic perspective, a compromise that the ego uses to satisfy an id instinct indirectly.

Neo-Freudian Psychoanalytic theories inspired by Sigmund Freud.

Personal unconscious According to Jung, the part of one's personality that stores material currently outside of awareness.

Collective unconscious According to Jung, the part of the personality that stores shared experiences and ideas from previous generations.

unconscious impulse to cut other people may long to be a surgeon. All positive activities, according to Freud, are sublimations of negative id impulses.

Jung's Analytical Psychology

Freud's work inspired other psychologists to develop other theories of personality. Carl Jung, FIGURE 13-4 for example, was an early **neo-Freudian**, meaning a theorist inspired by Sigmund Freud. Jung called his version of psychoanalytic theory "analytical psychology." It divided the psyche into three realms: the ego was the conscious mind, what you are aware of at any given moment; the **personal unconscious**, which contains information that can be made conscious; and the **collective unconscious**, which includes all personal unconsciousness from everyone who has ever lived. One way to think about the contents of the psyche as Jung described it is with a computer metaphor: The conscious is what is on your screen at that moment, the personal unconscious is what might be on your hard drive, and the collective unconscious is the Internet.

FIGURE 13-3 Sigmund Freud and his daughter, Anna.

The collective unconscious contains a collection of thoughts known as **archetypes**. Examples of archetypes include the great mother, the shadow, the persona, the hero, the wise old man, and the trickster. These figures are universal symbols: a great mother is not necessarily a woman or a man or even a mother. The **great mother** archetype symbolizes a person or thing that loves to nurture without wanting anything in return. You probably know someone to whom you go when you have had a bad day and they will make you soup and listen to your story. A great mother is a bottomless supply of support and love.

Another archetype is the shadow, your dark side, which is part of your daily life and awareness. Why are you reading your textbook? Maybe, for some of you, before you opened the book you considered other things that you would rather do, like play a game, talk to friends, surf the Internet. But you are reading. Why? What would happen if you did not read for class . . . ever? Some people imagine that they would not do well on the next exam or the one after that. If you did not read for class . . . why attend? That might lead to you failing one or several classes, maybe losing your job, or who knows what else?

Sublimation suggests that even the most noble actions may be rooted in id instincts.

Archetypes According to Jung, a universal thought form that exists in the collective unconscious.

Great mother An archetype described by Jung that symbolizes a person or thing that provides nurture without wanting anything in return.

Shadow An archetype described by Jung that represents the worst possible version of a person.

Persona An archetype that represents the public self.

Hero An archetype that represents someone who saves the day.

Wise old man An archetype that represents wisdom.

Trickster An archetype that represents someone who pretends to be something that he or she is not.

Freud (front row, left) inspired many theorists including Carl Jung (front row, right).

The shadow is the archetype that describes what you might become if you give in to your negative impulses.

FIGURE 13-4 Dr. Carl Gustav Jung.

What might happen next would be the first step in a spiral downward to the worst possible version of you. Like Freud, Jung believed you have a dark side, one that you are well aware of: the shadow. The **shadow** is the archetype that describes your view of what you think you would become if you gave in to your negative impulses. Sometimes those impulses drive you to be a better person. The only problem is that the more successful you become, the darker and more destructive your shadow becomes. Jung also suggested that sometimes you might have negative, unexplained reactions to people because they remind you of your shadow. While this may lead to empathy, you might avoid telling them, "I'm sorry I've been so mean to you; you seem to remind me of the worst possible version of myself." You will not make a friend that way. Monsters, snakes, witches, warlocks, and villains in fiction are all symbols of the shadow archetype.

The **persona** is the archetype that represents your public face. It is like a mask that you wear to the outside world. You may have different personas at work, school, home, or around your friends and family. These various personas can also cause problems if they clash. When I was a college student, I worked as a server at a gourmet pizza restaurant in the mall. I had my peppy pizza server persona, which was very different than my cool peacemaking resident advisor persona. When students who lived in my residence hall came to visit, the personas clashed, which led to very bad tips.

The **hero** is the archetype of someone who saves the day. The hero often fights other archetypes such as the shadow or the trickster in stories with help from the great mother or wise old man. Stories like "Little Red Riding Hood" or "Hansel and Gretel" often feature the hero battling against the shadow or other archetypes. The **wise old man** is a source of unending wisdom. Like the great mother archetype, the wise old man does not need to be a man, or old, just wise. Yoda and Dumbledore are examples of the wise old man archetype. The **trickster** is an archetype that represents someone who pretends to be something that he or she is not.

Jung suggested that personality operated by three fundamental principles: the principle of opposites, the principle of equivalence, and the principle of entropy. The **principle of opposites** states that every wish unconsciously proposes its opposite. As you carefully take a cake out of the oven and work as carefully as you can to place it on the table gingerly, unconsciously you would love to smash it. The second principle is the **principle of equivalence**. The principle of equivalence extends from the principle of opposites. It suggests that the energy devoted to do one thing will equally be devoted to the opposite activity. Denying negative feelings can be a problem since it feeds your shadow archetype. The last principle is a principle of entropy. The **principle of entropy** suggests that opposites tend to come together over time. The principle of entropy explains why people tend to mellow as they get older. As you can see, Jung suggested that we are a dichotomy, always wanting to do two things. The principle of entropy suggests that over time, we can resolve this dichotomy. The process of trying to resolve and rise above the dichotomy of who we are is called **transcendence**.

Perhaps the most widely known of Jung's theories is his theory of preferences for the internal or external world. **Introverts** prefer their internal world to the external world. Introverts may be reserved when interacting socially. **Extroverts**, on the other hand, prefer the external world to the internal world. While some extroverts tend to be outgoing and sociable, the active ingredient for introversion and extroversion is actually energy. Determining if you are an introvert or an extrovert has more to do with where you seek your energy—how you recharge yourself. After a bad day, extroverts tend to recharge themselves by being around others. An extrovert who has had a bad day might want to go hang out with friends and feel better, while an introvert might rather be alone.

Adler's Individual Psychology

The psychologist Alfred Adler FIGURE 13-5 believed the major drive of personality to be striving for superiority (Ansbacher & Ansbacher, 1964). **Striving for superiority**, or compensation, according to Adler, is an attempt to overcome feelings of inferiority by being a better person. Adler called his theory of personality "individual psychology." Adler suggested that when we are young, we have a sense that we are less than or inferior to others for the simple reason that we are. When you are a child, there are always people who can do things you cannot. Maybe they can reach things or stay up late or dodge that big red ball on the playground. As kids, we are constantly bombarded by inabilities. Adler called this idea **inferiority** or organ inferiority: At a basic level, we all feel inferior. Adler believed we spend the rest

FIGURE 13-5 Dr. Alfred Adler.

of our lives striving for superiority in order to make up for those feelings of inferiority. The way in which you strive for superiority in order to overcome feelings of inferiority is called your style of life, or **lifestyle**. Adler thought that those who strive for superiority by beating down others had an **unhealthy lifestyle** or mistaken lifestyle. If you try to be the best version of yourself by working together with others toward common goals, you are exhibiting a **healthy lifestyle**.

Social interests separate healthy from unhealthy styles of life. I had a friend who gained some weight after having a baby. She was having trouble losing the weight when she told me about a "brilliant idea" that she had. She started baking cakes and cookies for her friends. The idea was that she would cause her friends to gain weight so that, in comparison, she would look slimmer. I was not sure how to respond to her. According to Adler, however, her way of striving for superiority would be mistaken.

Evaluating the Psychoanalytic Perspective—Is Freud in Error?

Ask people what they think of Freud and the neo-Freudian theorists and you are likely to see a person make a face and say something like, "That fraud?" People tend to have negative views of both Freud as a person and his theories. Strangely, however, when you listen to the way that people tend to describe personality characteristics, you hear Freudian language and theory everywhere. It is hard to go even a week without stumbling over one of Freud's terms: *repressive, denial, unconscious.* Freud has become part of our culture.

Freud is often criticized for his views of women as well. It is important to remember that Freud's views reflect the ideas of society at the time that he lived; every personality theory does to some degree. *Studies on Hysteria*, for example, was published in 1895—only 2 years before the first European country allowed women to vote, and some 25 years before women were allowed to vote in the United States.

Another criticism is leveled at Freud because many of his theories were derived from case studies of his patients. This makes the evidence difficult to generalize to everyone and hardly objective. Many of his theories are not scientifically sound because they defy the **principle of falsifiability**. In order to be scientific, a theory must be testable and able to be disproved. It is difficult to disprove the existence of the ego and superego since, by definition, they are outside of your awareness.

Despite this, modern psychodynamic researchers (e.g., Betan, Heim, Zittel, Conklin, & Westen, 2005) have tested Freud's theories, and many have withstood the rigor of modern techniques. For example, his core theories that suggest that early experience impacts later behavior and the theory of unconscious motivation have amassed supportive evidence.

While psychoanalytic theory has its critics, no one person or one theory has had as much influence on psychology as has Sigmund Freud.

Principle of opposites According to Jung, the theory that every wish also represents the opposite of the same wish.

Principle of equivalence According to Jung, the energy devoted to do one thing will be equally devoted to the opposite activity.

Principle of entropy Jung's theory that opposites tend to come together over time.

Transcendence According to Jung, the process of resolving the dichotomy of who we are as people.

As children, we are constantly bombarded by inabilities; these form the basis of our inferiority, according to Adler.

Introvert A personality type that prefers the internal world to the external world; also known as introversion.

Extrovert A personality type that prefers the external world to the internal world; also known as extroversion.

Striving for superiority According to Adler, an attempt to overcome feelings of inferiority by being a better person; also known as compensation.

Inferiority According to Adler, feelings of inadequacy; also known as organ inferiority.

Lifestyle According to Adler, the way in which you strive for superiority in order to make up for feelings of inferiority.

CONCEPT LEARNING CHECK **13.2** | *Comparing the Psychoanalytic Perspectives*

There are five psychosexual stages. For each stage listed below, circle the number that corresponds to that stage's order in personality development.

1. Anal   1 2 3 4 5

2. Genital   1 2 3 4 5

3. Latency   1 2 3 4 5

4. Oral   1 2 3 4 5

5. Phallic   1 2 3 4 5

Explain

6. All psychoanalytic theories have unconscious processes as a primary motivation of behavior. How are the primary unconscious motivations different in Freud, Jung, and Adler's theories?

13.3 The Humanistic Perspective

According to the humanistic perspective, your personality is influenced by an innate capacity for personal growth.

- Illustrate the humanistic perspective of personality using Rogers's Person-Centered Perspective and Maslow's Theory of Self-actualization.

While Freud saw people as basically selfish and needing to be tamed by society's influence on the superego, humanists saw people as inherently good. Humanists believe that all humans, indeed all living things, have an **actualizing tendency** or a need for **self-actualization**, that is, a desire to be the best version of themselves possible. Like a plant turns toward the sunlight and grows, you have an innate drive to be the best you that you can be given your environment. It is just your nature. **Humanism** or the phenomenological approach is a family of personality theories that emphasizes growth, potential, and self-actualization.

Because of this actualizing tendency, you know, internally and maybe even unconsciously, what is best for you. You also have an understanding of your **self**, or an awareness of your own personal characteristics and maybe even your level of functioning. According to the **humanistic psychology**, if you are in touch with yourself, you will make the best choices for yourself. It is like you have an internal global positioning system, or GPS, that points you in the correct direction for your best growth. Because a person's way of being the best version of him- or herself is unique, humanists believe that it is important to examine humans on an individual level. Like the saying "In order to understand people, you need to walk a mile in their shoes," humanists believe that in order to understand a person, you need to understand the world from his or her perspective.

Rogers's Person-Centered Perspective

Carl Rogers FIGURE 13-6 (Rogers, 1989) suggested that besides food, water, and shelter, humans have a need for **positive regard**, a sense of being loved and respected. At some point, we also develop **positive self-regard**, which is a kind of grow-your-own version of positive regard. You develop positive self-regard through the positive regard you get from others.

The ideal way to obtain positive regard that grows into positive self-regard is through **unconditional positive regard**—that is, a sense of respect and love that is not linked to specific behaviors. Unconditional positive regard would allow you to love and respect yourself and get in touch with the internal sense of what is best for you. All of this works out just fine unless positive regard is given with strings attached. If you feel

All living things, according to humanists, have an actualizing tendency.

A GPS gives you guidance. Our actualizing tendency, according to humanists, guides you to the best version of you.

like you must act a certain way in order to be loved and respected, you are receiving **conditional positive regard**, or love and respect only when you act in ways that others want. This leads to the performance of particular behaviors in order to be loved and respected. It is important to note that parents, teachers, and friends often deliver conditional regard unintentionally and not usually out of some desire to control you. Most people deliver conditional regard because it is a pretty good way of getting you to do what they want and what they think is best for you. It becomes problematic, however, because conditional regard can cause you to shift from doing things because of your own internal GPS reasons to an external reason (in order to get that respect and love), and as a result you are no longer listening to your own internal GPS to guide you. You dampen that voice inside of you.

FIGURE 13-6 Dr. Carl Rogers.

Rogers suggested that the internal GPS that guides you by means of the actualizing tendency is your **real self**. However, the way you see yourself is your **self-image**. Through conditional regard, you develop an idea of what you "should become" to get maximum worthy feelings from others. You develop an internal idea of an **ideal self**, which would possibly meet all the conditions of worth we discern from others. The difference between your real self and the artificial ideal self is **incongruency**. The more incongruency you have, the more miserable you are.

Rogers believed that a **fully functioning person** is one who is open to experience, is accurate in his or her perceptions of the world, and accurately perceives his or her own feelings and motives. The person lives in the here and now, trusts him- or herself to do what is right, feels free to make independent choices, and contributes to the actualization of others. Rogers believed that in order to help people regain connection with their internal GPS, therapists should be genuine and honest and have empathy and genuine respect for clients.

Maslow's Theory of Self-actualization

At its essence, Abraham Maslow's (Maslow, 1987) theory is a simple one—some needs take precedence over others. If you are both very thirsty and chilly and have a choice to address one need over the other, people will tend to choose to drink water before putting on a parka. According to Maslow, there is a **hierarchy of needs**, meaning an order of importance of motivations from basic physiological needs to self-fulfillment needs. Maslow's hierarchy of needs consists of five levels, which you can see in FIGURE 13-7. Biological needs and safety needs are at the bottom, forming the base of the pyramid, and esteem and self-actualization needs are at the top. The higher-level needs are less important because we can survive without them. From bottom to top, the levels of the pyramid are:

1. Physiological needs: biological drives and survival
2. Safety and security needs: stability and well-being
3. Love and belonging needs: relationships and sense of purpose
4. Esteem needs: being valued by others
5. Actualization needs: being the best version of yourself possible

Maslow described most of the needs as deficit needs or **D needs**, meaning that you really feel that need when you are running low on it. If your need is being met, you are not aware that the need exists. Lacking D needs will stunt your personal growth. Actualization, on the other hand, is a being need or **B need** because we grow toward it. Unlike hunger that goes away once you have enough food, self-actualization continues to grow the more energy you put toward it.

Unhealthy (mistaken) lifestyle Adler's description of those who strive for superiority by competing with others.

Healthy lifestyle According to Adler, attempts to compensate for feelings of inferiority in a socially useful way.

Principle of falsifiability The notion that a theory must be able to be disproved in order to be testable and scientific.

Actualizing tendency According to the humanists, the instinctual desire to be the best version of yourself possible.

Self-actualization The motivation to be the best version of yourself possible.

Humanism A theoretical orientation that emphasizes growth, potential, and self-actualization; also known as the phenomenological approach.

Self A person's awareness of his or her own characteristics.

Humanistic psychology A family of personality theories that emphasize human growth, potential, and self-actualization.

Positive regard A communication of love and respect.

Positive self-regard Respect for your own decisions.

Unconditional positive regard According to Rogers, a sense of respect and love that is not linked to specific behaviors.

Conditional positive regard According to Rogers, the idea that respect comes only when certain circumstances are met.

Real self According to Rogers, your internal idea of who you should be.

Self-image How you see yourself.

Ideal self According to Rogers, a version of yourself that could please other people.

Incongruency According to Rogers, the difference between your ideal self and your actual self.

Fully functioning person According to Jung, a person who has a developed real self.

Hierarchy of needs According to Maslow, the order of importance of motivations, from basic physiological needs to self-fulfillment needs.

D (deficit) needs According to Maslow, needs other than self-actualization needs.

B (being) needs According to Maslow, self-actualization needs.

Peak experience According to Maslow, "transient moments of self-actualization" that are associated with feelings of harmony, interconnectedness, and joy.

FIGURE 13-7 Maslow's need hierarchy.

Self-actualization — Passions, creativity, morality, problem solving

Esteem — Self-esteem, confidence, respect of and by others

Love/belonging — Friendship, family, social interaction, intimacy, affection

Safety — Security of: body, morality, family, resources, property, health

Physiological — Food, water, health, sleep, breathing

Maslow suggested that maybe only a small percentage of the population will make it to this level. Many self-actualized people have some things in common. They see the journey as being more important that the result, enjoy being alone, and accept others for who they are. Self-actualized people are known to have an efficient perception of reality and the presence of **peak experiences**, which Maslow defined as "transient moments of self-actualization" that are associated with feelings of harmony, interconnectedness, and joy (Maslow, 1987).

Evaluating the Humanistic Perspectives

Despite the positive view that the humanistic theory holds of humans, not all humans hold humanistic theory in such high regard. As with Freudian theory, it is difficult to muster scientific evidence for humanist theory. Much of the evidence for the theory comes from case studies of the healthiest of people. And many believe the humanistic approach to be so overly confident regarding the nature of personality as to be impractical.

Still, humanistic ideas have found their way into our everyday language: living authentically and awareness are part of our understanding of ourselves and others. In addition, humanist influences have formed our understanding of therapy and have influenced other research trends such as positive psychology.

CONCEPT LEARNING CHECK 13.3   *Illustrating the Humanistic Perspective*

For each stage listed below, circle the number that corresponds to that need's level in the hierarchy.

1. Actualization needs: being the best version of yourself possible   1 2 3 4 5

2. Physiological needs: biological drives and survival   1 2 3 4 5

3. Love and belonging needs: relationships and sense of purpose   1 2 3 4 5

4. Esteem needs: being valued by others   1 2 3 4 5

5. Safety and security needs: stability and well-being   1 2 3 4 5

Explain

6. Give an example to illustrate the following:

    A. Unconditional positive regard

    B. Conditional regard

13.4 Trait Perspectives

According to the trait perspective, your personality has stable characteristics of behavior.

■ Discuss the factors involved in the trait perspective.

"Have you met Marsha? What she like?" I overheard one student ask another.

"Well, she's a bit shy, but she's funny once you get to know her . . . oh . . . and she's got great taste in clothes, too."

We use traits to describe personality all the time. One way to think of a **trait** is as a stable quality that differentiates one individual from another individual. And the **trait theory** of personality focuses on identifying the traits that summarize and predict a person's behavior. Raymond Cattell (Cattell, 1964) and other trait theorists make a distinction between traits you can observe, or **surface traits**, and **source traits**, which are universal, enduring behavioral characteristics, the underpinnings that produce the traits that we see.

Factor Analysis

One of the things that trait theorists focus on is the number of traits that you can use to describe a person's personality. Sure, you could just use every word possible in the English language to describe a person, but at nearly 14,000 traits, it be would tedious to describe a person's personality in about as many words as are in this chapter. Psychologists needed a simpler, more elegant solution. With the hundreds and hundreds of traits that are in our language, how do psychologists determine which are the most important? One tool they have to whittle down the choices is factor analysis. **Factor analysis** is a statistical technique that is used to find clusters of related items. Factor analysis reveals the core quality, or factor, that lies under many variables. A person may be outgoing, talkative, sociable, and enjoy parties, but the underlying trait that links these qualities may be extroversion. Since one of the main goals of science is parsimony—meaning simpler is better—explaining personality using the fewest traits possible is best.

The Big Five Factors

Factor analysis of trait terms of the English language yielded the five-factor model of personality, also known as the **Big Five** (McCrae & Costa, 1987). The five-factor model of personality is a trait theory concept suggesting that the five most essential personality traits are openness to experience, conscientiousness, extroversion, agreeableness, and neuroticism. A great way to remember the five factors is the acronym OCEAN **TABLE 13-3**.

Trait A stable characteristic of behavior.

Trait theory A theory of personality that focuses on identifying and measuring characteristics of behavior.

Surface trait An enduring behavior that is easily observed.

Source trait A universal, enduring behavioral characteristic.

Factor analysis A statistical technique used to find clusters of related items.

Big Five A trait theory concept suggesting that the five most essential personality traits are openness to experience, conscientiousness, extroversion, agreeableness, and neuroticism; also known as the five-factor model of personality.

TABLE 13-3 The Big Five

Trait	Low Scorers	High Scorers
Openness	Conforming Favors predictability Real-world	Autonomous Favors change Creative
Conscientiousness	Chaotic Cavalier Hasty	Prepared Meticulous Methodical
Extroversion	Timid Restrained Distant	Outgoing Boisterous Demonstrative
Agreeableness	Unfeeling Skeptical Unhelpful	Soft-hearted Unquestioning Accommodating
Neuroticism	Still Confident Smug	Nervous Unconfident Self-absorbed

Source: Adapted from McCrae & Costa (1986).

Openness to experience
A personality trait that is part of the Big Five that describes how much affection a person has for newness.

Conscientiousness A Big Five trait that describes how trustworthy a person might be.

Extroversion A trait that describes that an individual is energized by the external world rather than by the internal world.

Agreeableness A personality trait that is part of the Big Five that describes how trusting a person is.

Neuroticism A personality trait that describes how emotional the person might be.

Theoretical approach to traits Deriving traits from another theory of personality.

Lexical approach to traits An approach that uses language to determining the most important traits of personality.

Openness to experience is affection for the new. People who score high on openness are curious and imaginative. People who score low on openness might be seen as conventional. If, whenever you go to a restaurant, you always order exactly the same thing, you might score low on openness to experience. **Conscientiousness** describes how trustworthy a person might be. People who score high on conscientiousness are seen as organized, reliable, and punctual. Those low on conscientiousness are seen as unreliable. **Extroversion** describes where you get your energy. This is similar to Jung's concept of extroversion and introversion. People who score high on extroversion are seen as social, active, and talkative. People who score low on extroversion, otherwise known as introverts, are reserved and quiet. **Agreeableness** describes how trusting the person might be. People who score extremely high on agreeableness are serious, trusting, helpful, and forgiving. They may also be seen as gullible, perhaps agreeing to cash checks for stranded royalty who send emails. Those low on agreeableness and are seen as cynical and suspicious and are always looking for ways they may get tricked: "Don't eat the bread at a buffet, that's how they trick you into eating less!" **Neuroticism** describes how emotional the person might be. People who score high on neuroticism are seen as worrying and nervous and excitable. He or she may call you and yell, "Oh my gosh, the *worst* thing happened to me today," when it may be a minor event. Those with extremely low scores on neuroticism can be seen as cold and stoic.

The Revised NEO Personality Inventory consists of 240 items that measure the factors in the Big Five (Piedmont, 1998).

Assessing Traits

Some personality researchers derived traits using a theoretical approach. A **theoretical approach to traits** means that the traits come from another theory of personality. An example might be how Jung's theory gave rise to the trait of extroversion in the Big Five—a trait perspective approach. Using a theoretical approach has some problems. Any deficits in the original theory will be duplicated in the trait version of the theory.

Some personality psychologists use a **lexical**, or language, approach to determining the most important traits. Important personality characteristics are embedded within the language, according to this theory. The more a word is used to describe people, the more central the concept. The more frequently the word appears, the more likely that that trait is important. Frequency reflects not just the number of times a word is used but also the number of synonyms a word might have. In addition to frequency, cross-cultural universality is another important lexical quality. The more often different languages invoke a certain trait, the more likely it is that these words are reflecting a similar understanding of the same underlying trait.

Evaluating the Trait Perspective

While we no doubt can describe people in terms of traits (be it three or five or sixteen or more), researchers do have criticisms of this approach to personality. Some psychologists wonder if the trait approach to personality is even really a theory of personality. While it does a good job of describing and perhaps predicting behavior, the trait approach falls flat at explaining where the traits originated or what happens

---

CONCEPT LEARNING CHECK 13.4   *Identifying the Big Five Traits*

Match each personality description to one of the Big Five personality trait categories below. Remember that people can score from high to low in each of the five trait categories.

BIG FIVE TRAIT	PERSONALITY DESCRIPTION
A. Openness	1. _____ Becomes anxious easily
B. Consciousness	2. _____ Prefers time alone to recharge
C. Extroversion	3. _____ Is nearly always on time
D. Agreeableness	4. _____ Loves trying new foods
E. Neuroticism	5. _____ Suspicious and cautious

if the situation changes. Also, unlike the humanistic and psychodynamic approaches, the trait approach does not describe any underlying motivation behind behavior or any developmental patterns over time—how personality is formed or how or why or if personality changes over time.

13.5 The Social Cognitive Perspective

According to the social cognitive perspective, an interaction among traits, thoughts, and the environment determines your personality.

- Analyze the social cognitive theories of Bandura as compared to those of Mischel.

Earlier, we discussed learning theory and **behaviorism**, the study of learning based on directly observable actions. Behaviorists believe that your personality is the result of reinforcement and punishment. One of the problems of the behavioral perspective is that people think. While it is true that we learn from our environment, we also have subjective thoughts about what we learn, as well as the consequences. According to the **social cognitive perspective**, your personality is not just your history of reinforcements and punishments; it is based on the interplay among traits, thoughts, and the environment.

If I invited you to listen to a dull 3-hour lecture and offered to pay you $1,000 to attend the lecture, you might jump at the chance. Classic behaviorism has no problem explaining that! But what if you had just won $100,000 in a game show? You might not be as excited about the opportunity. The subjective nature of your interpretation of your environment, what you think you can do, and what you expect from your environment and yourself are subjective, and these expectations can have a big impact when folded into the ideas of behaviorism. The social cognitive theories of personality take the subjective nature of cognition into consideration.

Bandura's Social Cognitive Theory

Earlier, we discussed Albert Bandura's FIGURE 13-8 theory of observational learning. **Observational learning** acknowledges that behavior can change simply from watching others, or **models**. A model is a person who performs specific behaviors that others observe. If you have ever driven on the highway and suddenly slowed down to the speed limit because someone else has been pulled over by a police officer for speeding, you have participated in observational learning. Slowing down is strange because the likelihood of being pulled over for speeding has just decreased, but your behavior has changed. Why? Bandura would explain your behavior as witnessing someone (a model) being punished for the exact behavior you are exhibiting (speeding). This vicarious punishment acts to change your behavior.

Bandura had another important theory about personality: You change your environment; the environment changes you. This is the central notion in Bandura's idea of reciprocal determinism. **Reciprocal determinism** is a concept that suggests that behavior, environment, and cognitions are interrelated, as you can see in FIGURE 13-9. A key cognitive factor in reciprocal determinism is self-efficacy, or your perception of your ability to perform a certain task. Feeling like you can do something well increases the likelihood that you will do that behavior. It is also likely that you will seek out environments in which you can show yourself or other people your ability to do things well. If you think you are good dancer, you will seek out environments in which you can show your moves. On the other hand, if you think your singing skills are best left in the shower, you will likely avoid the karaoke bars.

Behaviorism The study of learning based on directly observable actions in the absence of mental processes.

Social cognitive perspective A personality theory that focuses on the interplay among traits, thoughts, and environmental contexts.

Observational learning Acquiring new behaviors by watching a model.

Model One who performs specific behaviors that others observe.

Reciprocal determinism Bandura's concept that suggests that behavior, environment, and thoughts are interrelated.

FIGURE 13-8 Dr. Albert Bandura.

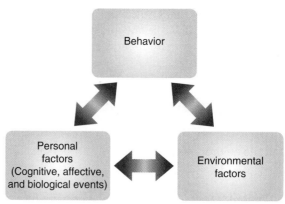

FIGURE 13-9 Reciprocal determinism.

Self-efficacy is subjective and specific. You might, for example have rather high self-efficacy for puzzles and dismal self-efficacy for learning a new dance. The higher your self-efficacy, the more likely you are going to try to excel and exhibit your prowess.

In addition to self-efficacy, Bandura also emphasized a key behavioral factor in reciprocal determinism: **self-regulation**, or the ability to control or adjust our own behavior. Personality, to a large extent, involves understanding what we can do and being able to put those beliefs in motion.

Mischel's Social Cognitive Theory

One of the important assumptions of personality theory is that personality is an enduring characteristic. But what if it is not? What if personality is not consistent across different situations and across time? That is exactly what Walter Mischel discovered. A person's behavior, when carefully scrutinized, depends on situational cues rather than being consistent across situations (Mischel, 1996).

This introduces what some call the **consistency paradox**. Most people believe their personality is the same all the time, but it is not, according to Michel. Although most believe that people behave consistently, there is actually low cross-situational consistency (Mischel & Peake, 1982). Mischel's approach does not predict that behavior will be consistent across situations. It argues that your behavior in a given situation depends on situational cues and expectations to be rewarded or punished. Consistency, Mischel suggests, occurs only when the same behavior is reinforced in a variety of situations or the person is unable to determine what situation she or he is in. **Cognitive person variables** are individual traits that shape the way you act in different situations.

Cognitive person variables affect your way of seeing the world and the way you navigate through life. Examples of cognitive person variables include your values, expectations, and competencies. Many of the factors included in cognitive person variables make up the collection of your beliefs about yourself—your **self-concept**.

Locus of control is a cognitive person variable that summarizes your idea of the source of reinforcement and punishment (Rotter, 1966). Locus of control can either be internal or external. In an **internal locus of control**, you believe that any good or bad things that happen to you are the result of your own actions. **External locus of control**, on the other hand, is the idea that reinforcers and punishments are outside of your control. For example, if you believe that how well you do on the exam is based mostly on how difficult the exam is, that will change how much and how hard you will study in school. What you try to achieve in the world, according to the cognitive theory of personality, depends on what you believe you can do, or your **self-efficacy**. If you believe that you cannot do well on an exam because the professor does not like you, then the reinforcement for studying is out of your control, and you believe that you cannot do well. How you behave in that situation depends more on those factors than your individual personality. Mischel believes that if you are looking for consistency in personality or traits, you are looking in the wrong place. Consistency depends on the situations we seek out.

Self-regulation The ability to control or adjust our own behavior.

Consistency paradox The idea that people believe that personality is stable, although research says that it is not.

Cognitive person variables Individual traits that affect the way you see the world.

Self-concept The collection of all your beliefs about yourself.

Locus of control A cognitive person variable that summarizes your idea of the source of reinforcement and punishment.

Internal locus of control The idea that reinforcers and punishments are under your own control.

External locus of control The idea that reinforcers and punishments are outside of your control.

Self-efficacy Your perception about your ability to do a certain task.

Evaluating the Social Cognitive Perspective

The behavioral and social cognitive approaches are rooted in a scientific view of personality. The social cognitive approach is powered by learning theory but goes beyond learning theory and behavioral approaches by incorporating situational and person factors into understanding personality. Nevertheless, some suggest that cognitive variables such as a tendency to expect bad things to happen can be vague and difficult to study scientifically. Pure behaviorists wonder if the introduction of vague cognitive variables raises more questions than it answers.

While the social cognitive perspective extends the behavioral perspective, it may retain some of the main weaknesses of the behavioral approach, such as reducing human personality to simply what we do. Although they take into account subjective thoughts, social cognitive theories are harder to test scientifically than pure behavioral ones.

CONCEPT LEARNING CHECK 13.5 | *Comparing Social Cognitive Perspectives*

Fill in the blank with the correct term or word.

1. Sarah thinks no matter how hard she studies, she will get bad grades. Sarah has a(n) _____ locus of control.

2. _____ is a theorist that suggested that we learn by modeling the behaviors of others.

3. Mischel believed that behavior is _____ across time.

Explain

4. Leah is an expert cheerleader and loves to be the center of attention. Sketch out how Bandura would explain why she is a cheerleader based on his idea of reciprocal determinism.

13.6 The Biological Perspective

According to the biological perspective, physiological processes determine your personality.

■ Explain the different biological perspectives and theories of how physiological processes determine personality.

Biological underpinnings of personality are certainly not new. Some of the earliest theories of personality were biologically based. For example, the ancient Greeks had a theory of personality that was biologically rooted. They felt that those who had certain temperaments must have an abundance of certain humors. The four humors—blood, black bile, yellow bile, and phlegm—were thought to be fluids in the body that at various levels could create differences in personality (Strathern, 2005) FIGURE 13-10. Too much blood, for example, was associated with an aggressive personality. Too much phlegm, on the other hand, was associated with a dopey or phlegmatic personality. Intervention into disordered personality was created by balancing out these different fluids through diet, exercise, and more gruesome types of manipulations like bloodletting. It is no wonder they thought that too much phlegm was associated with a sluggish personality: Think about what happens when you are sick, with so much phlegm that it is coming out of your nose. They thought that maybe you blew out the extra phlegm, and when the phlegm levels returned to normal, your energy level increased.

Even Freud's personality theory may have been, in part, a biological model. Some suggest that Freud was trying to explain the different levels of energy and how it transferred and flowed throughout the body (Peterson, 2010). Some believe that Freud was actually describing a physiological theory of personality.

More modern biological theories focus on brain structures and physiological mechanisms that may result in changes in personality. The biological perspective on personality suggests that individual differences are based in biological differences. Brain anatomy and biochemistry are involved in personality, and differences in observed traits such

FIGURE 13-10 The four humors—blood, black bile, yellow bile, and phlegm.

as introversion or extroversion or impulsivity and sensation seeking are all based upon biological factors, according to the biological perspective.

There is a good deal of evidence that suggests that parts of the brain, for example, are associated with personality. You may recall Phineas Gage, whose damaged frontal lobe caused dramatic differences in his personality. We also know from psychosurgery such as lobotomy that changes in personality can occur after surgery on the brain. You can also see differences in personalities from comparing PET scans and MRIs of individuals who score as high or low on traits such as sensation seeking (Freeman & Beer, 2010).

Eysenck's Theory

Temperament According to the biological perspective, inborn biological traits.

Hans Eysenck FIGURE 13-11 suggested that differences in **temperament**, or inborn biological traits, determine individual differences in personality. According to Eysenck's three-factor model of personality, the three most important dimensions of personality are neuroticism (N), extroversion (E), and psychoticism (P) (Zuckerman, Kuhlman, Joireman, Teta, & Kraft, 1993).

Eysenck believed that extroversion was influenced by variations in arousal in the cortex (Eysenck & Eysenck, 1985). This arousal theory maintained that the introvert's arousal "engine" idled higher, suggesting introverts need less external stimulation to feel comfortable. Extroverts, on the other hand, have lower baseline levels of cortical arousal and thus seek out stimulation. According to this theory, pursuing or shunning arousing situations

FIGURE 13-11 Dr. Hans Eysenck.

(such as social situations or noise) is a tactic for maintaining optimal levels of arousal. For example, researchers had subjects choose the level of background noise they preferred while working on a matching task. Introverts chose noise levels that were much lower than those of extroverts, and each group performed best under its preferred noise level (Geen, 1984).

While the biological perspective suggested that the introversion-extroversion dimension is driven by cortical arousal, Eysenck suggested that neuroticism, or emotional stability, is based on how easily the sympathetic nervous system is activated. Those who trip the sympathetic nervous system easily have low activation thresholds and have a harder time inhibiting their feelings. This means that minor events can make them stressed. Those with low levels of neuroticism, on the other hand, have higher activation thresholds and take longer to experience negative feelings and are harder to unnerve.

Psychoticism is a trait that combines the attributes of the Big Five traits of openness and agreeableness. Those who score high on psychoticism can be inflexible, creative, sometimes inconsiderate, quick to anger, and reckless. The physiological basis suggested by Eysenck for psychoticism is testosterone, with higher levels of psychoticism associated with higher levels of testosterone (Eysenck & Eysenck, 1985).

Genetics and Personality

If personality is largely biological, as Eysenck and others suggest, it would stand to reason that the biologically derived traits should share characteristics of other biological processes, such as genetic links. There is research that supports this contention FIGURE 13-12. **Behavioral genetics** is an interdisciplinary field that examines the influences of heredity and environment on behavior. Genetic factors, according to researchers, make up about half of individual differences on many traits (Jang, Livesley, & Vernon, 1996).

Psychoticism A personality trait that describes how inflexible, creative, or reckless a person is.

Behavioral genetics An interdisciplinary field that examines the influences of heredity and environment on behavior.

Sociobiology A theory that your behaviors and personality can be explained through the ideas of evolution.

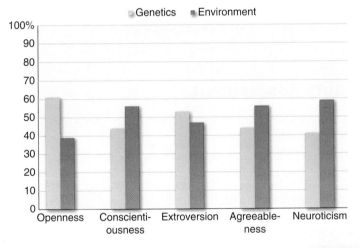

FIGURE 13-12 Heritability estimates for personality traits. *Source: Data from Jang, K. L., Livesley, W. J., & Vernon, P. A. (1996). Heritability of the big five personality dimensions and their facets: a twin study.* Journal of Personality, *64(3), 577–591.*

Evolutionary Theories of Personality

Evolutionary theories of personality are extensions of biological theories. If biology is the root of all our traits, then the patterns of behavior could also be passed down from generation to generation. Temperament would be under the influence of heritability and evolutionary forces, and certain behaviors may increase the likelihood of passing along your genes to future offspring.

The evolutionary theory of **sociobiology**, developed by E. O. Wilson FIGURE 13-13, suggests that our social behavior is under evolutionary pressure and that personality and social behavior are products of natural selection (Wilson, 2004). Wilson developed this theory by examining mating strategies of nonhuman animals, and these were extended to explain mating strategies of humans.

FIGURE 13-13 E. O. Wilson.

Evaluating the Biological Perspective

Biological theories of personality are compelling and can be combined with other theories of personality, such as the trait perspective. Given what we know about the brain, it is hard to ignore that biological processes are at the root of who we are. Another strength of the biological approach is an emphasis on a scientific explanation of personality.

Despite the strengths of the biological approach, there are still some criticisms of this approach. Biological approaches tend to ignore hard-to-evaluate concepts like thoughts or motivations. Doing so ignores the multiple influences that culture and society have on our personalities. Can what it means to be human be reduced to brain functioning alone? It is easy to oversimplify personality as brain and hormonal functioning alone. Some suggest that because of this, biological theories are not complete theories of personality. In addition, biological theories, much like the trait approach, do not provide any background for the development of personality.

CONCEPT LEARNING CHECK 13.6 | *Understanding the Biological Perspective*

Fill in the blanks with the correct response.

1. According to Eysenck, the three most important dimensions of personality are _____, _____, and _____.

2. According to the biological perspective, the arousal "engine" of extroverts idles _____.

3. _____ is the theory that personality traits are influenced by evolution.

Explain

4. Explain Eysenck's theory of the differences between introverts and extroverts.

13.7 Personality Assessment

Psychologists use a number of different tools to understand and describe an individual's personality.

- Identify the different tools to understand personality and how they are used.

Psychological test A measure used to assess or describe mental functioning.

Personality inventory A test used to measure an individual's pattern of thinking, feeling, and behaving.

Graphology A technique in which handwriting is analyzed in order to describe personality.

Intrapsychic conflict Differences between the desires of the id, ego, and superego.

Projective test A personality instrument in the psychoanalytic perspective that uses interpretation of ambiguous stimuli to uncover unconscious conflicts.

Projective hypothesis A theory that suggests that reactions to ambiguous material reveal intrapsychic conflicts.

How can you gauge or describe a person's personality? One way is through a psychological test. A **psychological test** is a measure used to assess or describe mental functioning. A **personality inventory** is a special type of psychological test that is used to measure an individual's pattern of thinking, feeling, and behaving. The way that psychologists measure or assess personality depends on their approach to personality. For example, if you believed that the way a person formed the letters as they wrote said something about his or her personality, you would employ **graphology**, a technique in which handwriting is analyzed in order to assess personality. Graphology, unfortunately, is not a good predictor of personality (Dazzi & Pedrabissi, 2009). For a personality test to be useful, it must be valid and reliable.

In the psychoanalytic realm, psychologists are interested in revealing **intrapsychic conflicts**, meaning the differences between the desires of the id, ego, and superego. Psychologists do this by using **projective tests**, a kind of personality instrument that uses the interpretation of ambiguous stimuli to uncover unconscious conflicts. Projective tests operate by means of the **projective hypothesis**, which suggests that when you see ambiguous material, you describe it in a way that reveals the interplay of your id, ego, and superego desires. Projective tests get their name from the defense mechanism of projection. You will recall that projection is a defense mechanism in which a person unconsciously attributes his or her own threatening impulses to another person. In projective tests, a person will unconsciously attribute his or her intrapsychic conflicts onto the test material. Examples of projective tests include free association tasks, the Rorschach inkblot test, and the thematic apperception test (TAT).

Let's say Geoff is on his way to take a **free association** test, which is a test in which you say the first thing that comes to your mind in response to a target word. On the drive, Geoff accidently hits a white rat on the way to the psychologist's office. His id is thrilled by the tension reduction of the act, but his superego is horrified at his carelessness. While at the psychologist's office, the therapist introduces a free association task. "I'm going to say a word and I want you to say the first word that pops into your head." The therapist may also time how long it takes Geoff to react. "Let's get started. White." Well, Geoff's id wants to shout, "White fluffy rat that I killed!" The super ego interjects unconsciously, "What ever you do, don't mention the rat; you don't want the psychologist to know how careless you are!" Geoff is in the middle of an intrapsychic battle. The stronger the fight between id and superego, the longer it takes to resolve the conflict. Eventually Geoff responds, "I can't think of anything."

Another projective test, which may be familiar from the movies, is the **Rorschach inkblot test** FIGURE 13-14. In this test, unconscious conflicts are revealed by the client's interpretation of and reactions to ambiguous patterns of ink. The Rorschach inkblot test, developed by Herman Rorschach in 1921, consists of 10 inkblots. The cards are presented one at a time, and the person tested reports what he or she sees and where it is on the card. Scoring of the Rorschach is complex and uses various criteria dependent on the scoring method used such as Exner's (Exner, 1993). Most scoring systems include the kinds and placement of objects reported in the cards.

FIGURE 13-14 A woman takes the Rorschach inkblot test. She will respond with what images she sees in the card.

The **thematic apperception test (TAT)** FIGURE 13-15, is a projective personality instrument in which unconscious conflicts are revealed by the interpretation of stories told in reaction to a series of ambiguous images. Most of the images in the TAT show people interacting with each other. As with other projective instruments, the kinds of stories told will reveal intrapsychic and unconscious conflicts. If all the stories are about people fighting and never talking again, for example, this may reflect the way the subject handles fights in his or her life.

All projective tests involve subjective scoring by the examiner. While they can reveal a great deal of complex information about a person and can be useful in a therapeutic setting, they can be time consuming to administer and require extensive training. Some scientists question the validity and reliability of projective tests (Lilienfield, 2005) since the scoring is subjective and the same test can produce inconsistent results even from the same person.

FIGURE 13-15 The thematic apperception test.

If it is traits you are after, then self-report inventories are useful. **Self-report inventories** are tests in which a person will directly answer questions about her or his behaviors, thoughts, or feelings. Unlike projective tests, self-report inventories are often **empirically derived**, meaning they are created by using a large number of test questions and are whittled down to a smaller number that best reflect the characteristic being tested. Examples of self-report inventories include the Minnesota Multiphasic Personality Inventory, the California Personality Inventory, and the Sixteen Personality Factor Questionnaire.

The **Minnesota Multiphasic Personality Inventory (MMPI)** is an empirically derived personality test that assesses a range of characteristics. The MMPI is an objective personality instrument. Unlike projective tests like the TAT or Rorschach, the

Graphology claims to understand personality through analyzing handwriting.

Free association A psychoanalytic technique in which people will report the first things that occur to them. Used to uncover unconscious conflicts.

Rorschach inkblot test A projective test in which someone's unconscious conflicts are revealed by his or her interpretation of and reactions to ambiguous patterns of ink.

Thematic apperception test (TAT) A projective personality instrument in which unconscious conflicts are revealed by the interpretation of stories told in reaction to a series of ambiguous images.

Self-report inventory A type of test in which a person will directly answer questions about his or her behaviors, thoughts, or feelings.

Empirically derived test A type of instrument that starts with a large number of test questions in order to select the ones that best reflect the characteristics being tested.

Minnesota Multiphasic Personality Inventory (MMPI) An empirically derived personality test that assesses a range of characteristics.

Objective A scoring system where the results are the same no matter who scores it.

California Personality Inventory (CPI) A type of personality test designed to measure characteristics important to daily life.

Sixteen Personality Factor Questionnaire (16PF) A personality inventory with results that are closely related to the Big Five.

results of an MMPI are **objective**, meaning the results are the same no matter who scores it; in fact, most MMPIs are computer scored, although hand-sorting options are available. The newest incarnation of the MMPI is the MMPI II-RF (for restructured form); it consists of 567 true–false items that determine 4 validity scores and 10 clinical scales (Butcher, 2011).

Not all personality tests are used in clinical work. The **California Personality Inventory (CPI)** is a type of personality test designed to measure characteristics important to daily life. Unlike the MMPI, which has more of a focus on psychopathology, the CPI describes personality in terms of individual strengths and challenges (Furnham & Henderson, 1982). The **Sixteen Personality Factor Questionnaire (16PF)** is a multiple-choice personality inventory that contains 185 multiple-choice items. Results of the 16PF reveal 16 primary factors or traits and 5 global factors that are closely related to the Big Five (Gregory, 2011).

CONCEPT LEARNING CHECK 13.7   *Identifying Personality Assessments*

Indicate whether the personality test is an empirical or projective test.

A. Empirical test   **1**. _____ MMPI

B. Projective test   **2**. _____ Rorschach inkblot test

3. _____ Sixteen personality factor questionnaire

4. _____ Thematic apperception test

5. _____ Word association

13.8 Culture and Personality

Culture and belief systems can shape and be shaped by personality.

■ Describe how culture and belief systems can shape and be shaped by personality.

Terror management theory A theory that suggests that because of our awareness of death, we battle anxiety by boosting our self-esteem and cultural connections.

Self-esteem Your self-worth.

Collectivist culture A culture that places an emphasis on interreliance rather than self-reliance.

Individualist culture A culture that places an emphasis on each person's rights rather than on the society.

Allocentrism A personality trait with an interreliant focus in which people tend to see themselves as part of a community.

Ideocentrism A personality trait with an interreliant focus.

Some researchers are starting to investigate how aspects of personality may be responsible for strengthening cultural beliefs. **Terror management theory**, for example, suggests that because we are self-aware, we know about the possibility of death. Whenever we are confronted with things that could cause death, we feel anxiety, fear, and unconscious terror (Greenberg & Kosloff, 2008). In order to combat this anxiety, we attempt to boost our **self-esteem**, or self-worth, by connecting with things that we feel are immortal and long lasting, like a cultural worldview. The theorists suggest that this explains surges in school sprit after a tragedy in a high school. The more you are confronted with your own mortality, the more you may emphasize your culture.

Culture can also shape personality. **Collectivist cultures** tend to emphasize interreliance (Sivadas, Bruvold, & Nelson, 2008). Members of collectivist cultures often have an interdependent understanding of the self and view themselves as part of a whole. In contrast, **individualist cultures** place an emphasis on each person's rights and place society in the background. Independent understanding of self is emphasized, and members of individualist cultures view themselves as independent units. As a result, collectivist cultures tend to generate members who have the trait of **allocentrism**, a personality trait with an interreliant focus, in which people tend to see themselves as part of a community. Individualistic cultures tend to create **ideocentrism**, a personality trait with an individual focus in which people tend to see themselves as self-reliant entities. A focus on self-esteem, for example, promotes your belief in yourself and is probably more prevalent in individualist cultures.

Summary of Multiple Influences on Personality

I never did find out who kidnapped the zebra and deposited him in Seney Hall. What caused the students to do it? No doubt there were multiple influences that affected their decision and multiple influences for their personality. Freud and the other psychoanalytic theorists might argue that intrapsychic conflict, the Shadow, or a need for superiority possessed the zebra-nappers that day. In contrast, the humanists might have suggested that a pull into incongruency drove the decision. Trait theories would point to extroversion and openness to experience. Biologically oriented theorists might point to sensation seeking or other temperament explanations. Some personality theorists may even take an eclectic approach. An **eclectic approach** blends several theories to explain or influence behavior. All personality approaches recognize the multiple influences of individual biology and individual characteristics, be they an individual preference for certain defense mechanisms, learned traits, or a tendency to be mischievous.

Eclectic approach Blending several theories together to explain or influence behavior.

CONCEPT LEARNING CHECK **13.8** | *Examining Culture and Personality*

Indicate whether each statement is true or false.

1. _____ People with the trait of allocentrism tend to see themselves as self-reliant.

2. _____ Those from collectivist cultures tend to emphasize interreliance.

3. _____ Terror management theory suggests that fear of culture is the main source of anxiety for people.

4. _____ Collectivist cultures encourage the trait of ideocentrism.

5. _____ Individualist cultures encourage the trait of allocentrism.

Explain

6. Describe how culture has influenced your personality.

CRITICAL THINKING APPLICATION

As far as I am concerned, everyone should get to watch *one* television show without being judged, no matter how ridiculous the show. Be it people losing weight, swapping spouses, strangers living together, or trying to survive on an island, reality TV has been an entertainment fixture for quite some time. People watch reality TV, in part, to get a glimpse into, as one show puts it, "what happens . . . when people stop being polite . . . and start getting real." But how much of an actual glimpse into human personality is reality TV? Certainly the situations that are created are extraordinary, but do extraordinary situations breed extraordinary personality?

Evaluate

1. How would different families of personality theories explain the behavior on reality TV?

2. Compare and contrast the role of personality and environmental influences that could lead someone to say, "I'm not here to make friends," a common reality TV phrase, but something people rarely say in real life.

3. As reality TV continues to be popular, what kinds of behaviors from reality TV have started to be modeled in the real world? What are the possible effects of this?

Visual Overview The major theories of personality, theorists, and concepts.

What kind of person would kidnap a zebra? Different theories of personality might offer different explanations. This overview summarizes the major theories of personality.

Adler

According to the psychoanalytic theory, unconscious processes determine your personality.

Freud

- Sublimation
- Rationalization
- Displacement
- Reaction formation
- Ego
- Fixation
- Reality principle
- Id
- Regression
- Catharsis
- Thanatos
- Oedipal complex
- Repression
- Sublimation
- Superego
- Defense mechanisms
- Projection
- Denial
- Psychosexual stages

- Great mother
- Principle of entropy
- Collective unconscious
- Hero
- Persona
- Principle of equivalence
- Transcendence
- Wise old man

Jung

- Inferiority
- Striving for superiority
- Compensation

Rogers
- Unconditional positive regard
- Fully functioning person
- Conditional positive regard
- Ideal self
- Incongruence

Maslow
- Hierarchy of needs
- D-needs
- B-needs

According to the humanistic perspective, an innate capacity for personal growth influences your personality.

Bandura
- Self-efficacy
- Observational learning
- Reciprocal determinism

Mischel
- Consistency paradox

According to the social cognitive perspective, your personality is determined by an integration of traits, thoughts, and the environment.

Eysenck
- Three-factor model of personality

Wilson
- Sociobiology

McCrae & Costa
- Big Five

According to the biological perspective, physiological processes determine your personality.

According to the trait perspective, your personality consists of stable characteristics of behavior.

13.1 Defining Personality

- Psychologists define personality in many ways.
- Personality is your pattern of thinking, feeling, and behaving.

- A good personality theory has clinical utility, practical utility, and predictive value, gives insight into human nature, can provide self-understanding, and helps describe complex behavior.

13.2 The Psychoanalytic Perspective

- According to the psychoanalytic perspective, unconscious processes determine your personality.
- According to Freud, your personality has conscious, preconscious, and unconscious components.
- The structures of your personality include the id, ego, and superego, according to Freud.
- As people grow and develop, the way they processes tension shifts, resulting in different stages of psychosexual development.
- The Oedipal complex describes a boy's unconscious desire for his mother, which results in identification with his father.

- Defense mechanisms describe unconscious compromises among the id, ego, and superego.
- Jung's theory of personality includes the conscious mind, the personal unconscious, and the collective unconscious as the basic structures of personality.
- Your collective unconscious contains a collection of archetypes, or universal thought forms, including the great mother, the shadow, the persona, wise old man, trickster, and the hero.
- Adler's theory of personality suggested that the major drive of personality is striving for superiority.
- Although there are many criticisms of psychodynamic theory, it remains a major force in psychology.

13.3 The Humanistic Perspective

- According to the humanistic perspective, your personality is influenced by an innate capacity for personal growth.
- Rogers suggested that providing unconditional positive regard would lead to growth, while conditional regard would lead to the development of an artificial ideal self and incongruency.
- Maslow suggested that a need hierarchy exists, meaning an order of importance

for motivations from basic physiological needs to self-fulfillment needs.
- Self-actualized people, according to Maslow, have the basic needs fulfilled.
- Humanistic theories are difficult to test; however, they have influenced psychotherapy and the positive psychology movement.

13.4 Trait Perspectives

- According to the trait perspective, your personality has stable characteristics of behavior.
- Factor analysis is a statistical technique used to find clusters of related items and is a major tool of the trait perspective.
- Factor analysis has yielded the five-factor model of personality, which suggests

that the five most essential personality traits are openness to experience, conscientiousness, extroversion, agreeableness, and neuroticism.
- While the trait approach is based on research, some psychologists do not think it is as comprehensive a theory as the psychodynamic or humanistic approaches.

13.5 The Social Cognitive Perspective

- According to the social cognitive perspective, an interaction among traits, thoughts, and the environment determines your personality.
- Bandura suggests that behavior can change simply from watching others.
- Reciprocal determinism is a concept that suggests that behavior, environment, and cognitions are interrelated.

- Mischel hypothesized that personality may not be as consistent as once thought.
- The social cognitive perspective of personality has the strength of a well-researched theory but may not add additional value to a traditional behavioral view of personality.

13.6 The Biological Perspective

- According to the biological perspective, physiological processes determine your personality.
- Brain structures and hormones may affect temperament and determine individual differences in personality.
- Behavioral genetics is a field that examines the influences of heredity and environment on behavior.

- Genetic factors make up about half of the individual differences on many traits.
- Temperament may be under the influence of heritability and evolutionary forces.
- Biological theories are compelling but can oversimplify complex behavior, and there are many alternative explanations for the same behavior.

13.7 Personality Assessment

- Psychologists use a number of different tools to understand personality.
- Projective tests measure intrapsychic conflicts.

- Empirically derived tests are derived through research methods.

13.8 Culture and Personality

- Culture and belief systems can shape and be shaped by personality.
- Terror management theory suggests that because of our awareness of death, we

battle anxiety by boosting our self-esteem and cultural connections.
- Collectivist and individualist cultures can influence the expression of personality.

13.1 Defining Personality

1. Your pattern of thinking, feeling, and behaving is called your:
   A. persona.
   B. personality.
   C. conscious mind.
   D. ego ideal.

13.2 The Psychoanalytic Perspective

2. If a person starts to talk in baby talk when under stress, Freud might suggest he or she is using the defense mechanism known as:
   A. regression.
   B. sublimation.
   C. denial.
   D. reaction formation.

3. Which structure of the personality, according to Freud, represents moral values?
   A. Id
   B. Ego
   C. Superego
   D. Collective unconscious

4. The id, according to Freud, was driven by aggressive and sexual instincts. This corresponds to Jung's archetype called:
   A. wise old man.
   B. great mother.
   C. shadow.
   D. persona.

5. People on reality TV shows who win by tearing down the other contestants may have a _____ style of life.
   A. healthy
   B. mistaken
   C. compensation
   D. thanatos

13.3 The Humanistic Perspective

6. If parents say to their kids, "We love you when you obey us," they may communicate:
   A. conditional positive regard.
   B. unconditional positive regard.
   C. incongruency.
   D. deficit needs.

7. What is the result from lacking in a D need, according to the humanists?
   A. Stunting of personal growth
   B. Encouragement of growth
   C. Self-actualization
   D. Denial of the need

13.4 Trait Perspectives

8. Veena orders scrambled eggs for breakfast no matter what. According to the Big Five, Veena would score _____ on the trait of _____.
   A. high; conscientiousness
   B. high; openness to experience
   C. low; openness to experience
   D. low; conscientiousness

13.5 The Social Cognitive Perspective

9. Mischel's work on cross-situational consistency suggested that personality is:
   A. inconsistent.
   B. based on modeling.
   C. based on observing others.
   D. biologically based.

13.6 The Biological Perspective

10. Those who link personality to biology point to research that suggests that extroverts seek stimulation because their typical arousal level is relatively:
    A. low.
    B. high.
    C. unstable.
    D. unaffected by external factors.

11. Inborn traits, according to biological theorists, are called:
    A. sociobiology.
    B. factor analysis.
    C. genes.
    D. temperament.

13.7 Personality Assessment

12. Psychologists use projective tests in order to assess:
  A. self-actualization.
  B. conscious motivation.
  C. unconscious motivation.
  D. happiness.

13. If Aubree is taking the thematic apperception test, which of the following will she do?
  A. Tell stories about a series of cards presented to her.
  B. Explain what she sees in a series of inkblots.
  C. Draw a picture of her family doing something.
  D. Take a paper-and-pencil test with true/false answers.

13.8 Culture and Personality

14. Which of the following traits is more helpful in individualistic cultures than in collectivist cultures?
  A. The trait of allocentrism
  B. The trait of ideocentrism
  C. Source traits
  D. Surface traits

15. According to terror management theory, being confronted with death creates anxiety. To confront this anxiety, you attempt to boost:
  A. self-esteem.
  B. allocentrism.
  C. ideocentrism.
  D. introversion.

CHAPTER DISCUSSION QUESTIONS

1. Tempers erupt during the holiday season when the passengers of an airline have been told that it has been overbooked. Craig's response illustrates displacement, while Scott's response illustrates regression. Describe the scene at the airport by giving an example of Craig's and Scott's reactions. Which response do you think will be more effective in getting them what they each want? Why?

2. A good theory of personality can help explain psychopathology. How does psychopathology arise according to Freud? Rogers?

3. How does a person's personality, according to the Big Five, shape the kind of music or clothes a person buys?

4. What are some challenges and practical solutions for parenting using unconditional positive regard?

5. Walter Mischel determined that personality is not always consistent. Are his findings in line with your experience of other people? How consistent or inconsistent do you feel your personality is? Why?

6. Considering the many theories of personality, how changeable or unchangeable do you think someone's personality is?

CHAPTER PROJECTS

1. Use Jung and the Big Five to describe the personality of a popular TV character.

2. Create a grid of well-known characters from TV, movies, and books that show extremes of each of the Big Five dimensions. You should have 10 characters total.

CHAPTER KEY TERMS

Actualizing tendency
Agreeableness
Allocentrism
Archetypes
B (being) needs
Behavioral genetics
Behaviorism
Big Five
California Personality
  Inventory (CPI)
Catharsis
Cognitive person variable
Collective unconscious
Collectivist culture
Conditional positive regard
Conscientiousness
Conscious mind
Consistency paradox
D (deficit) needs
Defense mechanism
Denial

Displacement
Disposition
Eclectic approach
Ego
Empirically derived test
Eros
External locus of control
Extroversion
Extrovert
Factor analysis
Fixation
Free association
Fully functioning person
Graphology
Great mother
Healthy lifestyle
Hero
Hierarchy of needs
Humanism
Humanistic psychology
Id

Ideal self
Identification
Ideocentrism
Incongruency
Individualist culture
Inferiority
Internal locus of control
Intrapsychic conflict
Introvert
Lexical approach to traits
Libido
Lifestyle
Locus of control
Minnesota Multiphasic
  Personality Inventory (MMPI)
Model
Neo-Freudian
Neuroticism
Objective
Observational learning
Oedipal complex

Openness to experience
Peak experience
Perfection principle
Persona
Personality
Personality inventory
Personality theory
Personal unconscious
Pleasure principle
Positive regard
Positive self-regard
Preconscious
Principle of entropy
Principle of equivalence
Principle of falsifiability
Principle of opposites
Projection
Projective hypothesis
Projective test
Psychoanalysis
Psychoanalytic theories
Psychological test

Psychosexual stages
Psychoticism
Rationalization
Reaction formation
Reality principle
Real self
Reciprocal determinism
Regression
Repression
Rorschach inkblot test
Self
Self-actualization
Self-concept
Self-efficacy
Self-esteem
Self-image
Self-regulation
Self-report inventory
Shadow
Sixteen Personality Factor
   Questionnaire (16PF)
Social cognitive perspective

Sociobiology
Source trait
Striving for superiority
Sublimation
Superego
Surface trait
Temperament
Terror management theory
Thanatos
Thematic apperception
   test (TAT)
Theoretical approach to traits
Trait theory
Trait
Transcendence
Trickster
Unconditional positive regard
Unconscious
Unhealthy (mistaken) lifestyle
Wise old man

ANSWERS TO CONCEPT LEARNING CHECKS

13.1 Describing Personality Theories

1. D. Insight into human nature
2. A. Clinical utility
3. E. Self-understanding
4. D. Insight into human nature
5. C. Predictive value

13.2 Comparing the Psychoanalytic Perspectives

1. Anal [2]
2. Genital [5]
3. Latency [4]
4. Oral [1]
5. Phallic [3]
6. Sample answer: Freud: intrapsychic conflict among the id, ego, and superego. Jung: unconscious operations of the principle of opposites, the principle of equivalence, and the principle of entropy. Adler: unconscious striving for perfection

13.3 Illustrating the Humanistic Perspective

1. Actualization needs: being the best version of yourself possible [5]
2. Physiological needs: biological drives and survival [1]
3. Love and belonging needs: relationships and sense of purpose [3]
4. Esteem needs: being valued by others [4]
5. Safety and security needs: stability and well-being [2]
6. A: Answers should indicate respect despite the person's behavior, such as "I don't agree with your decision to spend your allowance all in one place, but I still love and respect you."

   B: Answers should indicate respect but with strings, such as, "No daughter of mine will act that way!"

13.4 Identifying the Big Five Traits

1. Neuroticism [E]
2. Extroversion [C]
3. Consciousness [B]
4. Openness [A]
5. Agreeableness [D]

13.5 Comparing Social Cognitive Perspectives

1. Sarah thinks no matter how hard she studies, she will get bad grades. Sarah has an **external** locus of control.
2. **Bandura** is a theorist that suggested that we learn by modeling the behaviors of others.
3. Michel believed that behavior is **inconsistent** across time.
4. Behavior: Cheers

   Environment: Seeks out situations where she can get attention

   Personal factors: Ability to be a good cheerleader

13.6 Understanding the Biological Perspective

1. According to Eysenck, the three most important dimensions of personality are **neuroticism**, **extroversion**, and **psychoticism**.
2. According to the biological perspective, the arousal "engine" of extroverts idles **lower**.
3. **Sociobiology** is the theory that personality traits are influenced by evolution.
4. The introversion-extroversion dimension is driven by cortical arousal. Those who trip the sympathetic nervous system easily have low activation thresholds and have a harder time inhibiting their feelings. This means that minor events can make them stressed.

13.7 Identifying Personality Assessments

1. MMPI [Empirical]
2. Rorschach inkblot test [Projective]
3. Sixteen personality factor questionnaire [Empirical]
4. Thematic apperception test [Projective]
5. Word association [Projective]

13.8 Examining Culture and Personality

1. People with the trait of allocentrism tend to see themselves as self-reliant. [F]
2. Those from collectivist cultures tend to emphasize interreliance. [T]
3. Terror management theory suggests that fear of culture is the main source of anxiety for people. [F]
4. Collectivist cultures encourages the trait of ideocentrism. [F]
5. Individualist cultures encourage the trait of allocentrism. [T]

ANSWERS TO CHAPTER REVIEW TEST

13.1 Defining Personality

1. B. Rationale: Your personality is your pattern of thinking, feeling, and behaving.

13.2 The Psychoanalytic Perspective

2. A. Rationale: Regression is the defense mechanism in which a person reverts to an earlier age of functioning.
3. C. Rationale: According to Freud, the superego is the personality governed by the perfection principle.
4. C. Rationale: The shadow is the archetype that describes your view of what you would become if you gave in to your negative impulses.
5. B. Rationale: Those who strive for superiority by beating down others have a unhealthy, or mistaken style of life, according to Adler.

13.3 The Humanistic Perspective

6. A. Rationale: Communicating love and respect only when you act in ways that others want.
7. A. Rationale: Lacking a D need or deficit need.

13.4 Trait Perspectives

8. C. Rationale: Openness to experiences is an affection for the new. People who score low are conventional and love routines.

13.5 The Social Cognitive Perspective

9. A. Rationale: Mischel's theory revealed low cross-situational consistency.

13.6 The Biological Perspective

10. B. Rationale: Eysenck's arousal theory suggested that the introvert's arousal engine idled higher, suggesting introverts need less external stimulation to feel comfortable.
11. D. Rationale: Temperament is your inborn personality.

13.7 Personality Assessment

12. C. Rationale: Projective tests are a kind of personality instrument that uses the interpretation of ambiguous stimuli to uncover unconscious conflicts.
13. A. Rationale: The thematic apperception test is a projective personality instrument in which unconscious conflicts are revealed by the interpretation of stories told in reaction to a series of ambiguous images.

13.8 Culture and Personality

14. B. Rationale: Ideocentrism is a personality trait with an individual focus in which people see themselves as self-reliant entities.
15. A. Rationale: According to terror management theory, boosting self-esteem by connecting with things we feel are immortal can reduce anxiety.

REFERENCES

Ansbacher, H., & Ansbacher, R. R. (1964). *Individual psychology of Alfred Adler.* New York: Harper Perennial.

Betan, E., Heim, A. K., Zittel Conklin, C., & Westen, D. (2005). Countertransference phenomena and personality pathology in clinical practice: An empirical investigation. *American Journal of Psychiatry, 162*(5), 890.

Breuer, J., & Freud, S. (1895). *Studies on hysteria.* New York: Basic Books.

Butcher, J. N. (2011). Departures from MMPI–2 empirical traditions: The fake bad scale, restructured clinical scales, and the MMPI–2–RF. *A beginner's guide to the MMPI-2* (3rd ed., pp. 175–194). Washington, DC: American Psychological Association.

Cattell, R. B. (1964). *Personality & social psychology: Collected papers of Raymond B. Catell.* San Diego, CA: Robert R. Knapp.

Dazzi, C., & Pedrabissi, L. (2009). Graphology and personality: An empirical study on validity of handwriting analysis. *Psychological Reports, 105*(3, Pt2), 1255–1268.

Freud, A. (1967). *The ego and the mechanisms of defense.* New York: International Universities Press.

Eysenck, H. J. & Eysenck, J. H. (1975). *Manual of the Eysenck Personality Questionnaire.* London: Hodder and Stoughton.

Freeman, H. D., & Beer, J. S. (2010). Frontal lobe activation mediates the relation between sensation seeking and cortisol increases. *Journal of Personality, 78*(5), 1497–1528. doi:10.1111/j.1467-6494.2010.00659.x

Furnham, A., & Henderson, M. (1982). A content analysis of four personality inventories. *Journal of Clinical Psychology, 38*(4), 818–825. doi:10.1002/1097-4679(198210)38:4<818::AID-JCLP2270380422>3.0.CO;2-Y

Geen, R. G. (1984). Preferred stimulation levels in introverts and extroverts: Effects on arousal and performance. *Journal of Personality and Social Psychology, 46*(6), 1303–1312. doi:10.1037/0022-3514.46.6.1303

Greenberg, J., & Kosloff, S. (2008). Terror management theory: Implications for understanding prejudice, stereotyping, intergroup conflict, and political attitudes. *Social and Personality Psychology Compass, 2*(5), 1881–1894. doi:10.1111/j.1751-9004.2008.00144.x

Gregory, R. J. (2011). *Psychological testing: History, principles, and applications* (6th ed.). Boston: Allyn & Bacon.

Jang, K. L., Livesley, W. J., & Vernon, P. A. (1996). Heritability of the big five personality dimensions and their facets: A twin study. *Journal of Personality, 64*(3), 577–591.

Lilienfeld, S., Wood, J., & Garb, H. (2001). What's wrong with this picture? *Scientific American 284*(5), 80–87

Magnavita, J. J. (2002). *Theories of personality: Contemporary approaches to the science of personality.* New York: John Wiley and Sons.

Maslow, A. H. (1987). *Motivation and personality* (3rd ed.). New York: HarperCollins.

McCrae, R. R., & Costa, P. T. (1987). Validation of the five-factor model of personality across instruments and observers. *Journal of Personality and Social Psychology, 52*(1), 81–90. doi:10.1037/0022-3514.52.1.81

Mischel, W. (1996). *Personality and assessment.* London: Psychology Press.

Mischel, W., & Peake, P. K. (1982). Analyzing the construction of consistency in personality. *Nebraska Symposium on Motivation,* 233–262.

Peterson, C. (2010). Psychological approaches to mental illness. In T. L. Scheid & T. N. Brown (Eds.), *A handbook for the study of mental health: Social contexts, theories, and systems* (2nd ed., pp. 89–105). New York: Cambridge University Press.

Piedmont, R. L. (1998). *The revised NEO Personality Inventory: Clinical and research applications* (The Plenum series in social/clinical psychology, 1st ed.). New York: Springer.

Rogers, C. (1989). *The Carl Rogers reader* (1st ed.). Boston: Mariner Books.

Rotter, J. B. (1966). Generalized expectancies of internal versus external control of reinforcements. *Psychological Monographs, 80*(609), 1–28.

Sivadas, E., Bruvold, N. T., & Nelson, M. R. (2008). A reduced version of the horizontal and vertical individualism and collectivism scale: A four-country assessment. *Journal of Business Research, 61*(3), 201–210. doi:10.1016/j.jbusres.2007.06.016

Strathern, P. (2005). *A brief history of medicine: From Hippocrates' four humours to Crick and Watson's double helix.* Philadelphia: Running Press.

Wilson, E. O. (2004). *On human nature: Revised edition.* Boston: Harvard University Press.

Zuckerman, M., Kuhlman, D. M., Joireman, J., Teta, P., & Kraft, M. (1993). A comparison of three structural models for personality: The big three, the big five, and the alternative five. *Journal of Personality and Social Psychology, 65*(4), 757–768. doi:10.1037/0022-3514.65.4.757

14 Psychological Disorders

Learning Objectives ▼

14.1 ■ Define psychological disorders as determined by the American Psychiatric Association (APA) and explain the criteria for abnormal behavior using the *Diagnostic and Statistical Manual of Mental Disorders*.

14.2 ■ Distinguish between different types of anxiety, compulsiveness, and stress disorders; identify signs and symptoms of anxiety disorders.
　　　 ■ Categorize the types of anxiety disorders according to diagnostic criteria.
　　　 ■ Explain biological, behavioral, and cognitive perspectives of anxiety disorders.

14.3 ■ Understand personality, behavioral, cognitive, and unconscious factors involved in the development of somatic symptom and related disorders.

14.4 ■ Identify the signs and symptoms of dissociative disorders.

14.5 ■ Examine types of mood disorders based upon APA guidelines using D-SIGECAPS
　　　 ■ Be able to differentiate between a unipolar and bipolar mood disorder.

14.6 ■ Recognize signs and symptoms of psychotic disorders.

14.7 ■ List and describe the personality disorders as described in the *DSM-5*

Balloons. Not two or three, but dozens of them. I wasn't sure what to think. There she was, in my waiting room, with what must have been three dozen balloons of all different colors tied with brightly colored ribbons.

As a clinical psychologist, I've learned to watch for certain behaviors in my therapy waiting room. Most clients are anxious: They might sip nervously from a cup of water, or thumb through a magazine. Some bring props, photo albums, diaries, or lists. None had brought balloons.

I led her back to my office. Anyone else might have jumped right in and asked, "So, what's with the balloons?" But as a psychologist, you learn to let these things unfold in their own time. She was disheveled, her face worn with age, and she had sadness in her eyes. She waited, as many clients do on their first visit, for my cue. "So what brings you here today?" I began.

She explained to me that a year ago, on this very day, her 8-year-old son had died. She described his long, protracted illness. She told me how much he loved balloons. She and a few dozen others, who had also lost loved ones, were on their way to the park. There they would write notes to the people they had lost, tie the notes to the balloons, and set them free, one by one. It was sad, and beautiful, and yes, a little strange.

14.1 Overview: Understanding Psychological Disorders

Psychologists use a number of different tools to diagnose and understand psychological disorders.

- Define psychological disorders as determined by the American Psychiatric Association (APA) and explain the criteria for abnormal behavior using the *Diagnostic and Statistical Manual of Mental Disorders.*

If a person lines up fries before eating them, it might be unusual, but it's not likely to be a disorder.

What causes people to behave in unusual or disturbing ways? To what extent do outside influences (nurture) combine with biological forces (nature) to affect behavior? Does the person described above have a psychological disorder or a very healthy way of dealing with her grief? Psychologists understand a **psychological disorder** to be any behavior or mental process that causes a person to suffer or worry or produce harm to his or her social or work life. The science of understanding and diagnosing these psychological disorders is called **psychopathology**. In their quest to understand the nature of psychological disorders, psychologists use several tools to identify, study, and discover the origins of disordered behavior. These tools include diagnostic manuals, statistics, and biopsychosocial models. By the end of this chapter, you will have examined some of these tools and how psychologists combine their use to understand psychological disorders. You will also use these tools to define and identify psychological disorders.

Defining Psychological Disorders

Not all abnormal or unusual behavior qualifies as a psychological disorder. Lining up French fries in rows before eating them may be unusual behavior. However, it probably does not indicate a psychological disorder. There are two widely used approaches to understanding and defining psychological disorders: the medical model and the biopsychosocial approach.

The *DSM*, or Medical Model

Over several years, mental health professionals developed a system for categorizing and describing disordered behavior. This system is presented in the *Diagnostic and Statistical Manual of Mental Disorders,* or *DSM,* published by the American

Psychiatric Association. The *DSM* is researched, written, and reviewed by scientists, doctors, psychiatrists, and psychologists. Because so many members of the medical community help develop the *DSM*, it reflects the **medical model**, or approach, to the study of psychological disorders. The *DSM* is used by most mental health professionals in the United States to research and form clinical diagnoses.

As its name suggests, the *DSM* has two functions. First, it acts as a diagnostic manual, listing the symptoms that must be present in order to identify or diagnose a condition or disorder. Second, the *DSM* serves as a statistical manual, supplying important **epidemiological**, or statistical, information about the disorders. Epidemiological information can include the usual first age when a person might expect to have symptoms or the percentage of the population with a certain disorder, also known as prevalence FIGURE 14-1.

The current edition of the *DSM* is *DSM-5*. *DSM-5* reflects the most recent advances in our understanding and treatment of psychological disorders.

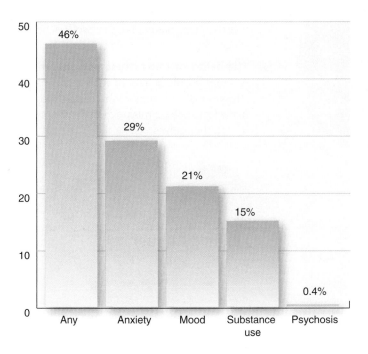

FIGURE 14-1 Prevalence of psychological disorders among U.S. adult population.
Source: Data from Kessler, R. C., Berglund, P., Demler, O., Jin, R., Merikangas, K. R., & Walters, E. E. (2005). Lifetime prevalence and age-of-onset distributions of DSM-IV disorders in the national comorbidity survey replication. Archives of General Psychiatry, 62(6), 593–602. oi:10.1001/archpsyc.62.6.593

The Biopsychosocial Approach

More recently, psychologists have developed a more holistic approach to understanding the influences that affect mental and emotional development and functioning. The **biopsychosocial approach** to psychopathology recognizes three equally important aspects of human mental processes and behavior: biological, psychological, and social. The biological aspect explores the essential influence of brain chemistry on disordered behavior. The psychological aspect explores the role played by thoughts, emotions, and behaviors in psychological disorders. The social aspect explores societal influences and whether a disorder causes problems when viewed within a social context FIGURE 14-2.

Criteria of Abnormal Behavior

Distinguishing between disordered behavior and abnormal behavior isn't easy. A psychologist might spend a great deal of time observing and listening to a patient before forming a diagnosis. In forming a diagnosis, psychologists must rely on professional, generally agreed-upon standards about the nature and symptoms of psychological disorders. As mentioned earlier, most psychologists consult the *DSM* for diagnostic and statistical information on disordered behavior.

According to the *DSM*, any one of three criteria must be satisfied in order to diagnose abnormal or unusual behavior as a psychological disorder:

1. **The behavior must be deviant.** Deviant means departing from existing and accepted standards. The behavior may be a departure from commonly accepted cultural

Psychological disorder A psychological condition that varies from the norm, is usually maladaptive, and may cause personal distress.

Psychopathology The science of diagnosing and understanding psychological disorders.

Medical model A theory that suggests that psychological disorders are illnesses that require treatment.

Epidemiology A science that examines the frequency of medical conditions.

Biopsychosocial approach A theory that recognizes three equally important aspects of human mental processes and behavior: biological (including brain chemistry), psychological (thoughts, emotions, and behaviors), and social (cultural and societal influences).

Psychological Influences

Social Influences

Biological Influences

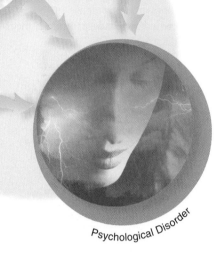

Psychological Disorder

FIGURE 14-2 The biopsychosocial approach stresses the importance of examining all three factors that might contribute to a psychological disorder.

standards of behavior. The behavior may represent a deviation from the statistical standards outlined in the *DSM*. Betty didn't violate any cultural standards by bringing balloons to a psychologist's office. She did, however, violate some statistical ones. By itself, though, statistical infrequency is not a compelling standard. This would mean that only conformity is normal and nonconformity is at best, abnormal, and at worst, disordered.

2. **The behavior must be maladaptive.** Much of our behavior is adaptive. We eat, we drink, we sleep. All of these things are adaptive because they help us to survive. If something is maladaptive it means that it decreases, or impairs, our ability to function. The *DSM* considers how much impairment a person has in his or her work, school, and social life.

3. **The behavior must cause personal distress.** At times people behave in ways that cause them stress or make them miserable. These people may not want to behave this way, but they seem unable to stop themselves FIGURE 14-3.

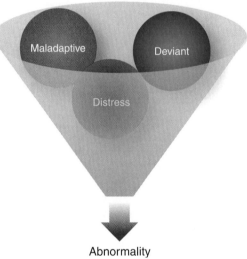

FIGURE 14-3 A person who is suffering from a psychological disorder exhibits behavior that is maladaptive, deviant, or causes him or her significant distress.

Someone whose behavior varies from the norm does not necessarily have a disorder.

Classifying and Labeling Psychological Disorders

The previous *DSM* (*DSM-IV-TR*) took a multiaxial approach TABLE 14-1 for diagnosis that consisted of five separate categories of information for psychologists to consider as part of a diagnosis. *DSM-5* has some important differences from *DSM-IV*. Some disorders have new names or new categories and the multiaxial system has been abandoned. TABLE 14-2 should help you understand some of the important differences between *DSM-IV-TR* and *DSM-5*.

TABLE 14-1 Sample *DSM-IV-TR* Multiaxial Approach

Axis I	Clinical disorders
Axis II	Personality disorders
Axis III	General medical conditions
Axis IV	Psychosocial stressors
Axis V	Global assessment of functioning (GAF)

TABLE 14-2 Major Differences between *DSM-IV-TR* and *DSM-5*

DSM-IV-TR	DSM-5
Uses a multiaxial system to categorize different parts of the diagnosis.	Uses a non-axial system. Individual disorders are rated for serenity.
Mood disorders are all in a single chapter that includes both depressive and bipolar disorders.	Depressive disorders and bipolar disorders are in separate chapters.
All disorders with components of anxiety are in one chapter titled "Anxiety Disorders."	Disorders with significant components of anxiety are spread across three chapters: "Anxiety Disorders," "Obsessive-Compulsive and Related Disorders," and "Trauma- and Stressor-Related Disorders."
Disorders usually first diagnosed in infancy, childhood, and adolescence are in a separate chapter.	Disorders usually first diagnosed in infancy, childhood, and adolescence are now integrated into the other disorder chapters.
The disorder hypochondriasis emphasizes the idea that a person is interpreting everyday aches and pains as an illness.	The new disorder called illness anxiety disorder has more of an emphasis on feelings of contracting an illness and less on unexplained symptoms.
Body dysmorphic disorder is considered a somatoform disorder.	Body dysmorphic disorder is grouped with obsessive-compulsive and related disorders
No diagnosis describes individuals with hoarding behaviors.	Hording disorder has been added to the list of obsessive-compulsive and related disorders.
Somatization disorder is a condition characterized by a long history of many vague physical complaints.	Somatic symptom disorder has been added as a disorder in which a person experiences disruptive and persistent thoughts, feelings, and behaviors that accompany illness symptoms.
Binge-eating disorder is described in a category of disorders to be considered.	Binge-eating disorder has been added as an eating disorder where a person may have uncontrollable periods of overeating.
Gambling disorder is grouped with impulse-control disorders.	Gambling disorder is grouped with addictive disorders.
Gender identity disorder is in the chapter, "Sexual and Gender Identity Disorders."	Gender identity disorder renamed gender dysphoria and is now in a separate chapter.
Autistic disorder, Asperger's disorder, and childhood disintegrative disorder are considered separate conditions.	Autism spectrum disorder describes a range of conditions. Severity of the disorder depends on how much support a person might require.
Mental retardation	Mental retardation has been renamed intellectual developmental disorder
Includes different subtypes of schizophrenia such as paranoid and catatonic.	Subtypes of schizophrenia have been removed.

DSM-5 was published in May of 2013. This table summarizes some of the differences between DSM-IV-TR and DSM-5.

Advantages and Disadvantages of Classification Systems

Diagnostic and labeling systems present both strengths and weaknesses. A system such as the *DSM* serves as useful shorthand for mental health professionals as they communicate with each other. In addition, since the *DSM* is based on statistical data, it has predictive value. A psychologist who knows that a person is depressed, for example, can expect certain symptoms to cluster together. A person who is depressed is likely to experience not just sadness, but also problems sleeping, feeling inappropriately guilty, and thoughts about death.

Labels, however, are seldom perfect. For example, depression presents itself somewhat differently in each individual who experiences it. When mental health professionals label disorders—and the people who suffer from them—they risk making an error that can have important consequences. In a classic study, psychologist David Rosenhan had "pseudopatients" present themselves at psychiatric hospitals with complaints of hallucinations. All were diagnosed and admitted. Beyond their complaints of hallucination, the pseudopatients behaved normally. Nevertheless, their normal everyday behavior was diagnosed as abnormal (Rosenhan, 1973) FIGURE 14-4. Critics of the medical model (Szasz, 2010) use the study as evidence of the subjective nature of diagnostic judgements and the negative effects of labeling psychological conditions as diseases. Supporters of the medical model point out that there are no biological tests for most psychological conditions and that, because of that, it is important to rely on self-report from clients. It would be unusual for someone to report having hallucinations when they don't have them. The Rosenhan studies resulted in more detailed criteria in later editions of the *DSM*.

TABLE 14-3 *DSM-5 Key Diagnostic Categories*

Category	Examples
Neurodevelopmental Disorders	Autism Spectrum Disorder Attention Deficit-Hyperactivity Disorder
Schizophrenia Spectrum and Other Psychotic Disorders	Schizophrenia Brief Psychotic Disorder
Bipolar and Related Disorders	Bipolar I Disorder Cyclothymic Disorder
Depressive Disorders	Major Depressive Disorder Persistent Depressive Disorder (Dysthymia)
Anxiety Disorders	Specific Phobia Social Anxiety Disorder (Social Phobia) Generalized Anxiety Disorder
Obsessive-Compulsive and Related Disorders	Obsessive-Compulsive Disorder Body Dysmorphic Disorder Hoarding Disorder
Trauma- and Stressor-Related Disorders	Posttraumatic Stress Disorder Adjustment Disorder
Dissociative Disorders	Dissociative Identity Disorder Dissociative Amnesia
Somatic Symptom and Related Disorders	Somatic Symptom Disorder Illness Anxiety Disorder Conversion Disorder (Functional Neurological Symptom Disorder)
Feeding and Eating Disorder	Anorexia Nervosa Bulimia Nervosa Binge Eating Disorder
Elimination Disorders	Enuresis
Sleep-Wake Disorders	Insomnia Disorder Obstructive Sleep Apnea Hypopnea Syndrome
Sexual Dysfunctions	Premature (Early) Ejaculation Female Orgasmic Disorder
Gender Dysphoria	Gender Dysphoria
Disruptive, Impulse-Control, and Conduct Disorders	Pyromania Kleptomania
Substance-Related and Addictive Disorders	Alcohol Use Disorder Caffeine Intoxication
Neurocognitive Disorders	Major Neurocognitive Disorder due to Alzheimer's Disease
Personality Disorders	Antisocial Personality Disorder Dependent Personality Disorder
Paraphilic Disorders	Voyeuristic Disorder Frotteuristic Disorder

Etiology of Psychological Disorders

Clara is a 42-year-old mother of two. She is in the waiting room of her local university counseling center. She clutches her stuffed animal tightly. She's terrified of who is about to enter the room—Giggles, a clown who has been hired to help her with her fear of clowns. When Giggles enters, she hyperventilates and is filled with panic. "No . . . please . . . no. I can't do this," she says over and over. It is obvious that Clara has a specific phobia of clowns. But where did this fear come from and how is it treated?

Etiology Cause of a disorder.

The *DSM* does not identify the **etiology**, or cause, of a disorder. Nor does the *DSM* recommend treatment. Clinicians use their theoretical orientations to determine the etiology. The etiology of a disorder also helps to determine the treatment for a disorder. This is true for a variety of conditions. For example, we used to think that ulcers were caused by stress and spicy food. The treatment would be to check your temper and stay away from meatball subs. Current evidence suggests a possible bacterial etiology for ulcers (*Helicobacter pylori*), which is why some people are prescribed amoxicillin, an antibiotic, as a treatment for ulcers.

Why do some clinicians treat a disorder one way, while others choose a different treatment? Most psychological disorders can be successfully treated in various ways because the disorders have complex etiological roots. The answer to the question "Are psychological disorders caused by biology (nature) or the environment (nurture)?" is "yes"—they are caused by both.

Two important theories explain the interaction of nature and nurture: the diathesis-stress hypothesis and the reciprocal gene environment model. The **diathesis-stress hypothesis** suggests that a condition may have a biological root or cause (diathesis) that is brought out by an environmental stressor. For example, up to 30% of the population will have a photic sneeze reflex, meaning that they sneeze when looking at bright lights (Whitman & Packer, 1993). The diathesis is the sneezing response and the stressor or environmental condition is the bright lights. This means that under similar situations, some people will never sneeze while other people always will. There is evidence that supports the same diathesis-stress connection for many psychological conditions (Praag, Kloet, and Os, 2004) FIGURE 14-5.

Another theory picks up where the diathesis-stress hypothesis ends. The **reciprocal-gene environment model** suggests that while there may be biological propensities for certain conditions, these biological propensities can themselves cause stress that will feed back and make things worse (Rutter, Moffitt, & Caspi, 2006). For example, let's say that you have a tendency to become forgetful during stress. During exams and other high stress periods, you begin to be forgetful and misplace your books. Being unable to find your books causes even more stress and more forgetting, leading to a vicious cycle FIGURE 14-6.

Diathesis-stress hypothesis A hypothesis that suggests a condition can have a biological root or cause that is triggered by an environmental stressor.

Reciprocal-gene environment model A model that suggests that established biological tendencies toward a condition can themselves cause stress, which in turn aggravates the condition, and then begins the cycle again.

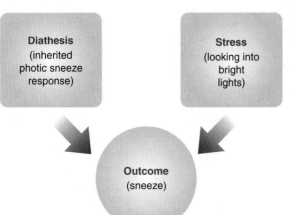

FIGURE 14-5 Example of the diathesis-stress hypothesis.

FIGURE 14-6 The reciprocal gene-environment model suggests a feedback loop between stress and diathesis.

Because of the multiple biological and environmental causes of disorders, clinicians may intervene at various points. Different kinds of medications can intervene at different points on the nervous system. Similarly, different psychological interventions can attack the environmental elements of the condition. A clinician may use one therapy or several. When they use several, the treatment is called "eclectic."

CONCEPT LEARNING CHECK 14.1   *Identifying Psychological Disorders*

Consider each behavior according to the three criteria of psychological disorders. Then decide whether the behavior is disordered or not.

Betty brought balloons to her first appointment with her therapist.

Ben throws a tantrum almost every day whenever he doesn't get his way. Ben is 22.

Sam throws a tantrum almost every day whenever he doesn't get his way. Sam is 2.

Clara is afraid of clowns. She wants to take her children to the circus, but she's afraid she'll see a clown. She avoids toy aisles in department stores for the same reason.

Maria is very afraid of snakes. She enjoys hiking, but won't go in the reptile house at the zoo.

Is it deviant?					
Does it cause the person distress?					
Is it maladaptive?					
Is it a disorder?					

14.2 Anxiety, Compulsiveness, and Stress Disorders

Anxiety disorders are marked by feelings of nervousness, distress, apprehension, and often disruptive attempts to diminish anxiety.

- Distinguish between different types of anxiety, compulsiveness, and stress disorders; identify signs and symptoms of anxiety disorders.
- Categorize the types of anxiety disorders according to diagnostic criteria.
- Explain biological, behavioral, and cognitive perspectives of anxiety disorders.

Generalized anxiety disorder is marked by worry.

Everyone feels anxious every now and then: the feeling you might have before an important exam or interview, the worry you have if you are running late for an appointment. Anxiety is part of our everyday lives. For most of us, anxiety can even be adaptive. It can help motivate us to do our best or to be prepared. People with **anxiety disorders**, on the other hand, have feelings of nervousness, distress, and apprehension, and often have disruptive ways of diminishing their anxiety. Three disorder categories in the *DSM* have prominent features of anxiety: anxiety disorders, obsessive-compulsive and related disorders, and the trauma- and stressor-related disorders. In this chapter we will refer to these conditions collectively as anxiety disorders. Like all psychological disorders, anxiety disorders are diagnosed only when a person has significant distress or impairment FIGURE 14-7.

Generalized Anxiety Disorder

Generalized anxiety disorder (GAD) is marked by unexplained, excessive worry that is not linked to anything in particular. People with GAD also find that their worry is

FIGURE 14-7 Prevalence of anxiety disorders among U.S. adult population.
Source: Data from Kessler, R. C., Berglund, P., Demler, O., Jin, R., Merikangas, K. R., & Walters, E. E. (2005). Lifetime prevalence and age-of-onset distributions of DSM-IV disorders in the national comorbidity survey replication. Archives of General Psychiatry, *62(6), 593–602. oi:10.1001/archpsyc.62.6.593*

Anxiety disorder A psychological condition marked by nervousness, distress, apprehension, and disruptive attempts to reduce anxiety.

Generalized anxiety disorder (GAD) A psychological condition characterized by unexplained, excessive worry that has an unspecific cause.

Panic attack A period of intense fear or discomfort that is linked with specific physical and psychological symptoms.

Panic disorder The presence of frequent, recurrent panic attacks, along with the fear of panic attacks.

Agoraphobia The fear of having a panic attack, which causes a person to avoid places and situations where having a panic attack would be particularly embarrassing or dangerous.

difficult to control (APA, 2003). Their worry and dread seem to have a life of their own. Sometimes the anxiety is described as "free floating," meaning that it will float and stick to any thought the person might have and infect it with worry. In addition to worry, GAD is associated with restlessness, fatigue, concentration difficulties, irritability, muscle tension, and sleep disturbances. For a diagnosis, symptoms must have been experienced on more days than not, for a period of six months or longer. Evidence from several countries suggests a lifetime prevalence of around 3% (Andrews, Sanderson, Slade, & Issakidis, 2000; Kessler et al., 2005).

Panic Disorder

A **panic attack** is a period of intense fear or discomfort in which four or more of the following symptoms are present: pounding heart, sweating, shaking, feelings of choking, chest pain or discomfort, abdominal distress, feeling faint, feelings of unreality, fear of losing control, fear of dying, numbness, and chills or hot flashes. A panic attack can begin quickly, often out of nowhere, and it peaks in intensity within 10 minutes. A panic attack itself is not a disorder, but if panic attacks happen frequently and there is constant fear of having another panic attack, it is considered **panic disorder**. About 4% of adults in the United States suffer from panic disorder, and it is twice as common among women as among men (Halbreich, 2003).

Imagine you were told that at some point today you would experience a panic attack. What would you do? Would you go about your normal day? Would you stay close to home?

People who fear having a panic attack will sometimes stick close to home or travel away from home only with a friend who could help them if they did have a panic attack. They avoid places and situations where having a panic attack would be particularly embarrassing or where it might be very difficult to get help, like riding on a bus or train. Psychologists refer to this as **agoraphobia**. Some people think that agoraphobia means fear of crowds or open places (after all, it translates to "fear of the marketplace"). However, what people with agoraphobia fear is the potential embarrassment or helplessness they might experience while having a panic attack, not the crowds or open places themselves FIGURE 14-8.

A panic attack is a period of intense fear and discomfort.

FIGURE 14-8 Because crowded shopping centers wouldn't be a good place to have a panic attack, people with agoraphobia avoid them.

Phobia A psychological symptom in which fear is unreasonably great or it interferes with a person's life.

Social anxiety disorder An anxiety disorder characterized by performance anxiety in nearly all types of social situations.

Social phobia An anxiety disorder characterized by fear of public embarrassment or humiliation.

Snakes are a common specific phobia.

Phobic Disorders

Everyone is frightened of something. Maybe it's heights, or snakes, or even killer bees. **Phobias** are diagnosed when the fear is unreasonably great or it interferes with your life in some way. Psychologists distinguish between two broad categories of phobias: specific phobias and social phobias.

Specific phobias are fears of certain objects or certain situations. Seeing or anticipating the object or situation almost invariably produces a phobic response. Specific phobias come in different flavors, including phobias of animals, heights, blood and injured tissue, and storms FIGURE 14-9.

While specific phobias are fears of objects or situations, **social anxiety disorder**, also known as **social phobia**, involves a different kind of fear—that of embarrassment or humiliation. The fears in a social phobia are usually of things that are public—speaking in public, eating in public, or maybe even writing in public. The fear of humiliation produces the anxiety response, and the anxiety increases the fear of humiliation, making things even worse.

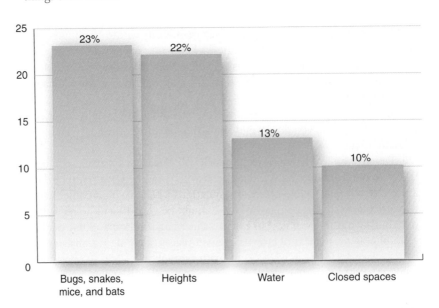

FIGURE 14-9 Prevalence of the most common specific phobias among U.S. adult population.
Source: Data from Eaton, W. W., Dryman, A., & Weissman, M. M. Panic and Phobia. In Psychiatric Disorders in America: The Epidemiologic Catchment Area Study, ed. L. N. Robins and D. A. Regier, 155–179. Simon and Schuster, 1991.

Many people have a mild fear of public speaking. It isn't the act of speaking that people fear; it's the possibility of making a public mistake—stammering, saying the wrong thing, becoming paralyzed or "freezing up." Thinking about these possibilities—that is, thinking about the fear itself—generates anxiety. Greater anxiety, in turn, increases one's chances of making a public mistake. Often social phobias create such vicious cycles FIGURE 14-10. Some people fear performing, or suffer performance anxiety, in nearly all types of social situations. Like all disorders, it's appropriate to diagnose a person with a specific or social phobia only if it causes significant distress or impairment TABLE 14-4, FIGURE 14-11.

Obsessive-Compulsive Disorder

Let's say you have arrived at the post office. You get out of your car and close the door. You hit the button on your car key, and "chirp-chirp," the doors are locked. Now you head into the store. A moment later you think to yourself, "Did I lock the car?" It is easy to do it so automatically; perhaps you just thought you locked it. "Better safe than sorry," you think to yourself. You might push the button again, or maybe even unlock and

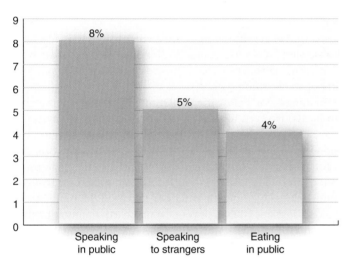

FIGURE 14-10 Prevalence of social phobias among U.S. adult population.
Source: Data from Eaton, W. W., Dryman, A., & Weissman, M. M. Panic and Phobia. In Psychiatric Disorders in America: The Epidemiologic Catchment Area Study, ed. L. N. Robins and D. A. Regier, 155–179. Simon and Schuster, 1991.

Public speaking is a common social phobia.

TABLE 14-4 Thirteen Unusual Phobias

Arachibutyrophobia	Fear of peanut butter sticking to the roof of your mouth
Limnophobia	Fear of lakes
Catoptrophobia	Fear of mirrors
Peladophobia	Fear of bald people
Anthrophobia	Fear of flowers
Automatonophobia	Fear of ventriloquist's dummies
Belonephobia	Fear of pins and needles
Chiraptophobia	Fear of being touched
Xanthophobia	Fear of the color yellow
Homichlophobia	Fear of fog
Logophobia	Fear of words
Trichopathophobia	Fear of hair
Triskaidekaphobia	Fear of the number 13

Did you lock your car today?

Obsessive-compulsive disorder A psychological disorder associated with obsessions, or obsessions linked to compulsions.

Obsession A thought that is unwanted, intrusive, and distressing.

Compulsions A condition in which a person feels compelled to perform behaviors or mental actions in response to an obsession.

The fear of fire caused by an unattended flame is an example of a fear associated with obsession.

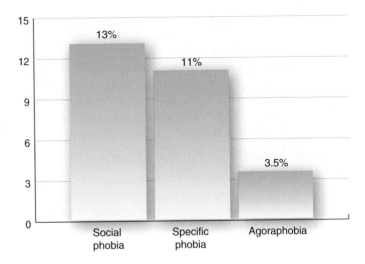

FIGURE 14-11 Prevalence of phobias among U.S. adult population.
Source: Data from Eaton, W. W., Dryman, A., & Weissman, M. M. Panic and Phobia. In Psychiatric Disorders in America: The Epidemiologic Catchment Area Study, ed. L. N. Robins and D. A. Regier, 155–179. Simon and Schuster, 1991.

lock it again. Now you are reassured, and your anxiety goes down. For the person with obsessive-compulsive disorder, or OCD, that would just be the beginning. For that person, the obsession is a disquieting thought or impulse: He or she has left the car unlocked and something terrible will come from that.

In order to be diagnosed with **obsessive-compulsive disorder**, a person must have an obsession or have an obsession linked to a compulsion. About 80% of people with OCD have both. As you will learn, a person can have an obsession without a compulsion, but not a compulsion without an obsession.

Each of us likes certain things. For a close friend of mine, it is tennis. He watches every tennis game he can locate. He even records games and watches them over and over again. Some would say he's obsessed with tennis. Psychologists might disagree. For psychologists, an **obsession** is an unwanted thought that the person finds intrusive and distressing FIGURE 14-12. An obsession is something that you find disquieting to think about, such as hurting your own child, or thinking you've forgotten something that will cause harm to others. These distressing thoughts enter our minds all the time. Maybe you've left a candle unattended. Perhaps you've left your car unlocked. For most people, these thoughts are easy to dismiss. For others, the doubt takes root and then takes over.

Compulsions, on the other hand, are behaviors or mental actions that a person feels compelled to perform in response to an obsession. This is why you can have an obsession by itself, but a compulsion must be linked with an obsession. Some compulsions are directly linked to a companion obsession, like hand washing after being exposed to dirt. Other compulsions are meant to neutralize or undo the obsessions through a thought or mental act such as counting or praying FIGURE 14-13.

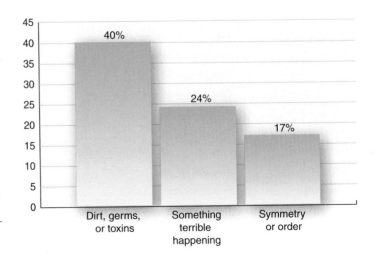

FIGURE 14-12 Percentage of common obsessions among U.S. adult population who have obsessive-compulsive disorder.
Source: Data from Rapoport. J. L. (1989, March). The biology of obsessions and compulsions. Scientific American, pp. 83–98.

FIGURE 14-13 Percentage of common compulsions among U.S. adult population who have obsessive-compulsive disorder.
Source: Data from Rapoport. J. L. (1989, March). The biology of obsessions and compulsions. Scientific American, *pp. 83–98.*

Hand washing is a common compulsion.

Posttraumatic Stress Disorder

Posttraumatic stress disorder, or PTSD, is a trauma- and stressor-related disorder triggered by a traumatic event that involves reexperiencing the trauma, increased arousal, and symptoms of numbing and avoidance. In order to be diagnosed with PTSD, a person needs to have experienced a trauma; after all, it is called **posttraumatic stress disorder**. The *DSM* is very particular about what constitutes a trauma. Saying something embarrassing in front of your entire class—not a trauma. Showing up at a party with exactly the same outfit as someone else—not a trauma. In order to meet the criteria for a trauma, an event has to cause actual or threatened injury or sexual violence.

However, not all individuals who experience a trauma go on to develop PTSD. In fact, most don't. The criteria for PTSD fall into four broad clusters:

1. **Intrusions.** People with PTSD will reexperience the traumatic event. They may have flashbacks, dreams, and distress at reminders of the trauma, or even a sense that they are reliving the event.

2. **Avoidance.** Often people with PTSD will avoid activities, thoughts, or conversations about the traumatic event.

3. **Increased arousal and reactivity.** They may have difficulty sleeping or problems with concentration. They also sometimes may be irritable or startle easily.

4. **Alterations in cognition and mood.** In addition, they may forget important details of the trauma, and sometimes exhibit depressive-type symptoms such as flat moods, detachment from others, or an inability to experience pleasure. Some even will have distorted thoughts about the cause of the trauma or negative beliefs about themselves or others after the trauma.

Posttraumatic stress disorder Associated with a traumatic event, this disorder involves re-experiencing the trauma, increased arousal, and symptoms of numbing and avoidance.

Etiology of Anxiety, Compulsiveness, and Stress Disorders

Biological Perspective

Quite a few biological factors have been implicated in the development of anxiety disorders. Some suggest that we are biologically "programmed" to have certain fears. Others point to abnormalities in brain structures or neurotransmitters. There are several cues that a biological predisposition to anxiety disorders might be present. There is some evidence that OCD is genetic; it tends to run in families (Grabe et al., 2006).

Natural Selection

Psychological disorders can be considered part of a continuum. On one side is everyday behavior, in the middle are atypical or "subclinical" behaviors, and at the other extreme are true psychological disorders. We can think about anxiety disorders as maladaptive or disruptive versions of adaptive behaviors. Remember that natural selection makes some behaviors—even fear—useful for survival: Some snakes are venomous, some heights are dangerous, and some dogs bite.

The idea of preparedness suggests that our evolutionary history makes us more prone to some fears than others, producing rapid fear responses that are hard to reduce (Seligman, 1971). This may explain why many people have phobias of things they rarely encounter, such as scorpions, as opposed to electrical outlets or cars that are, statistically speaking, far more common and dangerous (Mineka & Öhman, 2002).

Traumas include witnessing harm or injury.

The Brain

Many brain structures are involved in anxiety disorders FIGURE 14-14. The anterior cingulate cortex, especially active in OCD, checks for errors (Ursu, Stenger, Shear, Jones, & Carter, 2003). Evidence also indicates that people with panic disorders are more likely to have limbic system structures that are more easily activated and trigger fear (Shin et al., 2005). This would predispose certain individuals to respond with fear to stressful events and perhaps to develop "anxiety disorders." Another theory suggests that abnormalities in the limbic system, frontal lobes, and basal ganglia may interfere with the signal your brain sends to let you know you've finished a task. This would cause people with OCD to feel that they need to complete the task again (Szechtman & Woody, 2004).

Brain chemicals also play a part in anxiety disorders. Several biological theories focus on GABA (gamma-aminobutyric acid), an inhibitory neurotransmitter that reduces synaptic activity. Think of GABA as the "brakes" of the nervous system. Some theorists think that low GABA can result in a more active nervous system. Medications, such as benzodiazepines, that increase the activity of GABA in the synapse seem to improve anxiety disorder systems (Stahl, 2009). This suggests that GABA plays a key role in anxiety disorders. In addition to GABA, the neurotransmitter serotonin has also been implicated in OCD, PTSD, and generalized anxiety disorder (Stahl, 2009) FIGURE 14-15.

Learning Perspective

Biology by itself explains much, but not all, of the story. Even if someone has a biological disposition to a disorder, that disposition may not explain why he or she acquires a social phobia at age 35. The learning perspective suggests that disorders are learned behaviors. Anxiety disorders may be acquired and maintained through learning.

FIGURE 14-14 Limbic system structures such as the hypothalamus and thalamus may be involved with OCD.

Cerebral cortex (gray matter)

Corpus callosum

Thalamus

Lateral ventricles

Basal ganglia

Hypothalamus

Third ventricle

FIGURE 14-15 Neurotransmitters such as GABA have been implicated in OCD.

Conditioning

Up to 40% of people with phobias can remember a particular event that led to their disorder (Mineka & Zinbarg, 2006). Using what we know about classical conditioning, theorists of the **learning perspective** suggest that these precipitating events became associated with what became the phobia. The learning model suggests that someone may acquire a phobic response to a previously neutral stimulus when that stimulus is paired with a frightening experience. This is known as phobia acquisition. The phobia is then maintained by avoidance of the newly acquired conditioned stimulus. This is known as phobia maintenance. In other words, anxiety disorders are acquired through classical conditioning and maintained through operant conditioning. This is referred to as the two-process conditioning model.

1. **Phobia acquisition.** Clara has a childhood experience in which she was severely frightened by a clown.

2. **Phobia maintenance.** Imagining she might see a clown increases her fear. Avoiding clowns reduces her fear. Even avoidance, one aspect of her fear response, reinforces and maintains her fear of clowns.

Learning perspective
A theory that suggests that anxiety disorders are learned behaviors.

Observational Learning

We can also develop anxiety from watching others. A father who has a phobia of storms and who forces his children to turn out all the lights in their home and unplug all the appliances probably sends his children the message that storms are dangerous and should be feared. Evidence suggests that wild monkeys can transmit their fear of snakes to their young (Mineka, Keir, & Price, 1980). When we react to something fearfully, we can effectively communicate its potential danger to others.

Cognitive Factors

Cognition means thinking. Cognitive theorists emphasize the idea that maladaptive thoughts can be linked to anxiety.

The theory of anxiety sensitivity (Schmidt, Lerew, & Jackson, 1997) suggests that anxious people are highly sensitive to internal sensations associated with anxiety and tend to misinterpret harm, focus on threat, and are more likely to recall information that is threatening. In addition, when presented with ambiguous situations, anxious people viewed them as threatening (Eysenck, Mogg, May, Richards, & Mathews, 1991) FIGURE 14-16.

FIGURE 14-16 Anxious people attributed harmful meanings to the middle statement. Non-anxious people attributed benign meanings to the same statement *Source: Adapted from Eysenck, M. W., Mogg, K., May, J., Richards, A., & Mathews, A. (1991). Bias in interpretation of ambiguous sentences related to threat in anxiety. Journal of Abnormal Psychology, 100(2), 144–150. doi:10.1037/0021-843X.100.2.144*

CONCEPT LEARNING CHECK 14.2 *Identifying Anxiety, Compulsiveness, and Stress Disorders*

1. As a child, Clara had a terrible experience in which a clown frightened her. Now, as an adult, if she even imagines seeing a clown, she grows extremely nervous, frightened, and distressed. What kind of anxiety order does Clara seem to have?

2. Manuel has been worrying "all the time" and says that it's not about anything in particular. He finds it difficult to control his worry and feels restless, tired, and irritable. He's also having problems sleeping. Manuel most likely has which disorder?

3. Marty, 27, reports a long-standing fear of speaking in public. When asked to speak in front of a large group of people he becomes extremely anxious and thinks he'll be embarrassed. Because of this fear, he has passed on promotions and other opportunities to advance in his career. On one occasion when he was forced to speak, he became so anxious that he started shaking and panicking. Marty most likely has which disorder?

Somatic symptom and related disorders Psychological disorders characterized by having symptoms of physical illness that are not fully explained by a medical condition.

Malingering A condition involving an external motivation for illness, such as avoiding a test.

Factitious disorder A psychological disorder in which a person plays the sick role for the emotional gain, sometimes called Münchausen syndrome.

Somatic symptom disorder A type of somatic symptom disorder in which a person experiences disruptive and persistent thoughts, feelings, and behaviors that accompany illness symptoms.

14.3 Somatic Symptom and Related Disorders

The essential features of somatic symptom disorders are symptoms of a physical illness that are unexplained by a general medical condition.

■ Understand personality, behavioral, cognitive, and unconscious factors involved in the development of somatic symptom and related disorders.

Imagine you are a physician at a clinic and a patient—let's call him Jack—comes in with a stomachache. You've run about a dozen tests and you still can't, for the life of you, figure out why his stomach hurts. In fact, biologically, as much as you can figure, Jack's stomach is fine. It really *shouldn't* hurt. What might you have on your hands?

One of the possibilities is in the *DSM* chapter of somatic symptom and related disorders. All somatic symptom disorders share the essential feature of symptoms of a physical illness that are not well explained by a medical condition.

When considering whether someone has a **somatic symptom or related disorder**, a few other conditions need to be eliminated. First, symptoms cannot be entirely explained by a physical illness. Also, somatic symptom disorders can't involve any sort of external motivation for being sick, such as getting out of a test or hoping to cash in on a lawsuit, which is called **malingering**. Also absent is an emotional gain such as the motivation to play the sick role as you might expect in **factitious disorders**, which are sometimes called Münchausen syndrome, hospital addiction syndrome, or hospital hopper syndrome.

People with somatic symptom disorders feel sick even when they are completely healthy. A person with a somatic symptom disorder may convince his doctor to run diagnostic tests to discover what's wrong, but the doctors never can find any physical cause for all of the complaints. Often, there is some psychological connection to the beginning or worsening of the illness of a person with a somatic symptom disorder.

TABLE 14-5 describes the somatic symptom disorders listed in the *DSM-5*, but we will focus on just three: somatic symptom disorder, conversion disorder, and illness anxiety disorder.

Somatic Symptom Disorder

In **somatic symptom disorder**, a person experiences illness symptoms that are overly distressing and persistent. Although these symptoms may be due to a medical condition the thoughts and behaviors the person experiences are out of proportion to the actual illness and cause distress and impairment in his or her daily life.

In somatic symptom disorder, the focus is on the disruptive and persistent thoughts, feelings, and behaviors that accompany illness symptoms.

TABLE 14-5 Somatic Symptom and Related Disorders

Disorder	Description
Somatic symptom disorder	Disruptive and persistent thoughts, feelings, and behaviors that accompany illness symptoms.
Conversion disorder (functional neurological symptom disorder)	Symptoms that suggest neurological damage, such as numbness with no reason for the symptoms.
Illness anxiety disorder	Fear of having or getting an illness based on the misreading of normal body functions. Formerly known as hypochondriasis.
Factitious disorder	A psychological disorder in which a person plays the sick role for the emotional gain, sometimes called Münchausen syndrome.

Source: Adapted from American Psychiatric Association. Diagnostic and Statistical Manual of Mental Disorders: *DSM-5. American Psychiatric Publishing, 2013.*

Conversion Disorder

In **conversion disorder** (also known as functional neurological symptom disorder), a psychological worry or concern is transformed (converted) into a physical symptom. For most conversion disorders, the symptoms suggest a neurological disorder such as partial paralysis, numbness, muscle weakness, or even blindness.

Often a clue that the symptoms are a conversion disorder will lie in the way the symptoms are presented. People with numbness caused by conversion disorder, for example, will often complain of numbness only in their hands (called glove anesthesia), which is impossible given the physiology of the arm. People with numbness resulting from neurological damage, on the other hand, lose all sensation in their entire arms and hands. This makes sense because the nerves in the arm provide sensory input along the entire limb.

Another clue to conversion disorders is the blitheness patients have about their symptoms. You might expect that if you suddenly went blind or had numbness in your arms you might be extremely bothered. However, people with conversion disorder seem strangely blasé about their condition (sometimes called "la belle indifference").

Like many somatic symptom disorders, the onset or exacerbation of the symptoms is linked to some sort of event in the person's life. When matters get worse, the symptoms do too. Only 1.5% of people who seek medical treatment meet the criteria for conversion disorder (Fink, 2004).

Physical symptoms can sometimes be somatic symptom disorders.

Illness Anxiety Disorder (Hypochondriasis)

We all know someone who we think is a hypochondriac. He or she always has the latest sickness. This week it's Lyme disease, next week it might be the H1N1 influenza. This is somewhat like the *DSM-5* disorder of hpochondriasis. The person with illness anxiety disorder is worried about contracting an illness. Sometimes the person is convinced that he or she has a specific disease process unfolding despite being fine. A person with illness anxiety disorder interprets normal body symptoms as evidence of disease. He or she may even have invasive medical procedures to find out what he or she might have. These tests, as you can imagine, all come back normal. Often, these investigative medical procedures themselves produce lingering symptoms that the person will interpret as part of the very illness the tests disproved. For a diagnosis of illness anxiety disorder the symptoms need to persist despite medical evidence to the contrary and go on for at least 6 months.

Like all disorders, illness anxiety disorder has to cause distress or impairment in functioning. Research suggests that 4.7% of adults who seek medical treatment meet *DSM-5* criteria for hypochondriasis (Fink, 2004).

Conversion disorder A disorder in which a worry or concern is transformed into a physical symptom.

Illness anxiety disorder A disorder characterized by a specific disease process that progresses in a person in which there is no physiological cause.

Etiology of Somatic Symptom and Related Disorders

As you might expect, somatic symptom disorders can have multiple causes. Some speculate that vulnerabilities such as hypersensitivity to physical sensations and a history of illnesses may combine with stressors such as emotional conflicts to produce somatic symptom disorders. Your patient Jack, for example, may have always been sensitive to physical sensations. You find out from chatting with him that he recently lost his job, girlfriend, and dog. Now he has persistent nausea. He's been tested over and over and there's no biological reason for it. Jack quite possibly is suffering from a somatic symptom disorder.

Personality and Cognitive Perspectives

There may be personality and cognitive patterns involved with somatic symptom disorders. Some research has suggested that those with somatic symptom disorders are more highly susceptible to hypnosis compared to people without somatic symptom disorders (Roelofs et al., 2002). This leads researchers to believe that people with somatic symptom disorders are highly susceptible to even the idea that they may have an illness.

Numbness in just the hand can be a sign of a conversion disorder.

In addition to such personality factors, there are some cognitive and learning factors that might be involved in somatic symptom disorders. Even though people with most somatic symptom disorders are not producing the illness to play the sick role, people around them may unintentionally reinforce them for being sick. In this way they may have inadvertently learned that being sick brings them greater attention. Also, people with somatic symptom disorders more often associate normal physical sensations with catastrophic events and exaggerate and distort the meaning of the sensations, like thinking the pain of a normal stomachache is something terrible like stomach cancer.

There are some researchers who believe that somatic symptom disorders are actually more like anxiety disorders about health concerns. What adds to this theory is that people with illness anxiety disorder often have a family history of anxiety disorders (Deacon & Abramowitz, 2008).

CONCEPT LEARNING CHECK 14.3   *Identifying Somatic Symptom and Related Disorders*

1. James, a 22-year-old man, was referred to your clinic for evaluation of his complaints. He's convinced that he has stomach cancer despite being told that it is very unlikely. He has cramps when he overeats and reports that his tongue "just doesn't look right." Despite medical evidence to the contrary, James has continued to believe that he has stomach cancer. What is the most likely diagnosis?

2. Martha was robbed at gunpoint about 3 months ago. Luckily she wasn't hurt and the police were able to recover her purse and capture the assailant. About a week before Martha had to identify the man who robbed her, Martha suddenly lost her sight. She didn't seem that concerned about it. What's the most likely diagnosis?

14.4 Dissociative Disorders

Dissociative disorders involve a sudden loss of the integration of consciousness, memory, for events and experiences in a person's life.

- Identify the signs and symptoms of dissociative disorders.

Dissociation A split of consciousness or attention into two or more separate streams.

Dissociative disorders A disorder characterized by the sudden loss of the integration of consciousness or memory, or a change in personal identity.

Dissociative amnesia A condition characterized by extreme memory lapses or forgetting important personal information; usually associated with a traumatic emotional experience.

Dissociation means a split of your consciousness or attention into separate streams. We all dissociate now and then. Maybe you are doing a presentation and thinking about lunch at the same time. Perhaps you are reading psychology and wondering how much longer the text will be. These are all forms of normal dissociation that can occur frequently (Kihlstrom, Glisky, & Angiulo, 1994). Some people call it "multitasking" since many people can engage in one activity automatically and still be aware of the things they need to do to conduct the other behavior.

Dissociation only becomes problematic when the streams become too separate, disjointed, and fragmented, and there is a loss of the integration of the personality. This is what is seen in the **dissociative disorders**. Dissociative disorders involve a sudden loss of the integration of consciousness or memory, or a change in a person's identity. The streams become so distinct that there is a disruption in the personality and a disconnection or even amnesia during the experience. Sometimes the streams may even take on a life of their own.

Dissociative disorders can occur when a stressful event becomes tremendously overwhelming and the individuals escape by diverting awareness from the painful memories, thoughts, and emotions. Sometimes in dissociated states, individuals escape from conflicts by giving up consistency and rejecting a part of themselves.

All of the dissociative disorders described in *DSM-5* are listed in **TABLE 14-6**. We will focus on three forms of dissociative disorders—dissociative amnesia, dissociative fugue, and dissociative identity disorder.

Dissociative Amnesia and Fugue

Imagine waking up one day and having no idea where you are. You are dazed, confused, and unsure of anything. A moment later, you also realize you aren't even sure who you are. Frightening. In **dissociative amnesia**, individuals forget important personal infor-

TABLE 14-6 Dissociative Disorders

Dissociative Disorder	Description
Depersonalization/derealization disorder	Periods of detachment from self or surroundings, which may be experienced as "unreal" (lacking in control of or "outside of" self), while retaining awareness that this is only a feeling and not a reality.
Dissociative amnesia	Noticeable memory impairment resulting from emotional trauma.
Dissociative identity disorder	The alternation of two or more distinct identities with impaired recall among the alters.

Source: Adapted from American Psychiatric Association. Diagnostic and Statistical Manual of Mental Disorders: *DSM-5. American Psychiatric Publishing, 2013.*

mation—much more than you would expect with normal forgetfulness. They may not remember their own identity, including their birthday, address, or their name, even though they have not had any sort of head trauma.

Some researchers suggest that this can be triggered by a severe emotional event such as physical abuse, war, or even relationship difficulties (Mclewin & Muller, 2006). A few years ago, after a man was distraught after discovering his wife of 13 years had been cheating on him, he woke up to find that he couldn't recall the last 13 years of his life.

Some with dissociative amnesia forget all the details of their lives. Often they are found wandering the street confused and bewildered. Luckily, it is fairly self-limiting, and episodes usually last less than a week. Their entire memory soon returns, often in fits and spurts, to full function

Others with symptoms of dissociative amnesia lose their memory, but not all parts of their identity. This is called **dissociative fugue**, which is a type of dissociative amnesia. In addition to experiencing amnesia, they may travel away from home and live in a new location. It's like dissociative amnesia—with travel ("fugue" means flight). People with dissociative fugue forget who they are and often will travel great distances and assume new identities that are similar to their old identity. Unlike in dissociative amnesia, people in such fugue states will often recover their memory all at once and have amnesia about the fugue period. As rare as the disorder is—(the prevalence of dissociative fugue has been estimated at 0.2% (APA, 2000)—it is even more rare for it to occur twice in the same individual. Details of the fugue state are difficult to come by since those in the fugue state don't realize they are in one.

Dissociative Identity Disorder

Recall that dissociation is a splitting of your consciousness and attention. Sometimes this split becomes so extreme that an identity can take on a life of its own. This is the case in **dissociative identity disorder (DID)**. You may know DID under its older name, multiple personality disorder. DID is a much better name since it highlights the importance of dissociation in the disorder. In DID, two or more distinct identities (sometimes called alters) exist inside of one person, each with his or her own unique characteristics. Dramatic differences have been reported in the personalities of the alters. Alters with different genders, food preferences, and eyeglass prescriptions have been reported (Miller, Blackburn, Scholes, White, & Mamalis, 1991).

The primary, or host, personality will be in control of the person most of the time. Often memories of the behaviors of the alters are shrouded by amnesia. Shifts between alters can often be initiated by stressful circumstances (Sar, Akyüz, & Dogan, 2007).

DID is very rare, but it used to be even more so. Until around 1980 only 300 cases had been reported; since then thousands more have been identified (Spanos, 1999). For some, this shift in the numbers indicates that we are much better at diagnosing the people who have DID and that those who need treatment are able to get the help they need. For others, this dramatic increase raises even more suspicion about the existence of the condition.

Dissociative fugue A disorder in which a person forgets who he or she is, often traveling great distances and assuming new identities that resemble his or her original identity.

Dissociative identity disorder (DID) A dissociative disorder in which two or more distinct identities, each with unique characteristics, exist within one person.

Forgetfulness in dissociative amnesia is greater than normal forgetfulness.

Etiology of Dissociative Disorders

One theory of the cause of dissociative disorders is that the dissociative experience helps to separate and disconnect a person from the awareness of a disturbing experience (Dorahy, 2001). In this way, the dissociation acts as a mechanism to help the person to cope.

Others believe that the behavior seen in dissociative disorders is reinforced attention-seeking behavior (Lilienfeld et al., 1999). These theories do not suggest that the conditions are faked, but rather that the behaviors help them to make sense of the many incompatible and contradictory emotions that can be experienced during and after a trauma. The new identities become real to the patient and they behave accordingly.

CONCEPT LEARNING CHECK 14.4   *Identifying Dissociative Disorders*

1. A 24-year-old man is brought to the hospital emergency room because he was found wandering the street. He reports feeling "confused" and says that he isn't sure where he is. The last thing he remembers is coming home to a fire in his house. After examination you discover no head trauma or any kind of injury that would account for his loss of memory. What is the most likely diagnosis?

14.5 Mood Disorders

Mood disorders are marked by fluctuations in emotional states and can include problematic social functioning, thinking, behaviors, and physical symptoms.

- Examine types of mood disorders based upon APA guidelines using D-SIGECAPS.
- Be able to differentiate between a unipolar and bipolar mood disorder.

We've all had our ups and downs. When something great happens, it's uplifting and our mood soars. When something terrible occurs we might feel down in the dumps. The peaks, valleys, potency, and length of our moods are predictable in relation to the things that happen to us. For people with mood disorders, however, extremes in their emotional state can create distress and impairment in their social and work life.

Moods are long-lasting, nonspecific emotional states. Mood disorders are marked by turbulent emotional states and can include problematic social functioning, thinking, behaviors, and physical symptoms.

Mood disorders are pretty common. Researchers indicate up to 20.8% of adults have suffered from mood disorders (Kessler et al., 2005). There are two disorder chapters in the *DSM-5* that focus on mood: "Depressive Disorders" and "Bipolar and Related Disorders." We will refer to the disorders in both of these chapters as mood disorders. TABLE 14-7 summarizes the mood disorders described in *DSM-5*. We will focus on two of these: major depressive disorder and bipolar disorder.

> **Moods** Long-lasting, non-specific emotional states.

Major Depressive Disorder

I'm sure you've had a time in your life when things just weren't going right. Maybe after

TABLE 14-7 Mood Disorders

Depressive Disorders	Description
Major depressive disorder	Two or more weeks of a low mood or anhedonia and a at least four other behavioral, cognitive, or emotional symptoms
Persistent depressive disorder (dysthymic disorder)	A chronic depressed mood that a person experiences for at least 2 years
Bipolar and Related Disorders	**Description**
Bipolar I disorder	Cycling between mania and either hypomania or depression
Bipolar II disorder	Cycling between hypomania and depression
Cyclothymic disorder	A chronic mood syndrome where a person cycles between symptoms of hypomania and symptoms of dysthymia. A person must experience these symptoms for at least 2 years

Source: Adapted from American Psychiatric Association. Diagnostic and Statistical Manual of Mental Disorders: DSM-5. *American Psychiatric Publishing, 2013.*

a breakup or when you'd moved to a new city. You might have felt normal sadness. How can you tell normal sadness from major depressive disorder? Partly due to the severity and length of the symptoms you experience.

Depression is more than just a sad mood. It's a syndrome that carries a number of behavioral, cognitive, and emotional features. It's most commonly associated with a sad or low mood, but it also may carry with it a reduced capacity to feel pleasure (sometimes called **anhedonia**), hopelessness, loss of energy, disrupted sleep patterns, weight and appetite changes, difficulty in concentration, and thoughts of death (APA, 2013).

Because it's so common, depression is often called the common cold of mental illness. Depression is the most common mental health problem seen in a physician's office. In addition, nearly a third of college students will encounter mild depression at some point in their undergraduate career (Seligman, 2006).

It's not just common; it has quite an impact as well. Depression has been ranked as the fourth leading cause of disability worldwide and it is expected to rise to second by 2020 (Murray & Lopez, 1997).

There are nine symptoms that could signal depression. You need to have five or more symptoms most of the day, nearly every day, for at least 2 weeks, for these symptoms to be considered chronic and severe enough to be major depressive disorder. One way psychologists remember the symptoms is the acronym D-SIGECAPS, as you can see in **TABLE 14-8**.

Depression is thought to be self-limiting, lasting between 6 and 18 months even without treatment. This isn't to suggest that it's a good idea to just wait it out. With no help or treatment of any sort, about 80% of people will relapse into another depressive episode (Mueller et al., 1999). Luckily, the relapse rate for treated depression is much lower, so it makes sense to treat depression and treat it early. However, despite the myriad of effective treatments, only one-third of people seek any sort of treatment for their depression, and some of those who seek treatment delay as long as 8 years before they get any sort of help (Wang et al., 2005).

Depression and Bipolar Disorders

As you have learned, the central feature of major depressive disorder is a major depressive episode (five of those nine D-SIGECAPS). However, a major depressive episode isn't the only kind of mood episode that psychologists describe. Some individuals have symptoms that are the polar opposite. Instead of feeling down and blue, their mood is abnormally elevated, and their mood is so good they do things that get them into trouble.

Think about the best mood you've ever had . . . then double it. Some people even describe their mood as "better than good." This is called a manic episode. In addition to this elevated, expansive, or sometimes irritable mood, the person has three of the following symptoms most days, for at least a week.

Symptoms of **mania** include:
- inflated self-esteem
- decreased need for sleep

Anhedonia A reduced capacity to feel pleasure.

Mania A condition associated with an elevated, expansive, or sometimes irritable mood.

Although sadness is a symptom of major depressive disorder, one can meet the criteria for depression without being sad.

TABLE 14-8 Major Symptoms of Depression

Letter	Symptom	Description
D	Depressed mood	Sadness
S	Sleep	Change in sleep, maybe insomnia, or hypersomnia (lots of sleep without feeling rested)
I	Lack of Interest	Lack of interest in normally pleasurable activities
G	Guilt	Inappropriate guilt or feelings of worthlessness
E	Energy	Lack of energy
C	Concentration	Problems in concentration or indecisiveness
A	Appetite	Change in appetite
P	Psychomotor agitation/ retardation	Moving more slowly than is normal (psychomotor retardation) or more fidgety than normal (psychomotor agitation)
S	Suicidality	Thoughts of death or suicide

Excessive involvement in risky behaviors, such as excessive shopping, can be a sign of mania.

- feeling a pressure to keep talking
- a flight of ideas, or the feeling that your thoughts are racing
- increase in goal-directed behavior
- excessive involvement in pleasurable activities that have a high possibility for painful consequences (like unrestrained shopping sprees)

I'm sure that in that list you could find three symptoms that you might like to have (I'll sign up for a decreased need for sleep). You'll recall that in order for something to be a disorder it has to cause distress and/or impairment. Some people can have symptoms of mania and do not get themselves into trouble. In this case you would experience **hypomania** ("hypo" meaning under—like a hypodermic needle that goes under the dermis). In hypomania, a person shows symptoms of an elevated mood and other signs of mania, but these symptoms don't interfere with daily life. In fact, the symptoms can be helpful. Hypomania alone is not a disorder, but hypomania can occur in combination with other mood episodes, like depression and mania as part of bipolar disorder.

A diagnosis of **bipolar disorder** requires at least one manic episode. Often in the months and years following the manic episode, people with bipolar disorder will have depressive episodes, hypomanic episodes, or even additional manic episodes. In these cases, the mood episodes that follow the manic episodes are all considered to be part of the bipolar disorder.

Bipolar disorders are far less common than their unipolar (depressive only) counterparts, with only about 2 in 100 people in the United States having had the diagnosis (Kessler et al., 2005).

Etiology of Mood Disorders

Remember that the diathesis-stress hypothesis suggests that most disorders include a biological vulnerability as well as environmental factors that can put these vulnerabilities in motion. This is believed to be true of mood disorders as well.

The Biological Perspective

There is a good deal of evidence that the biological perspective can explain many parts of the mood disorders. There is evidence, for example, of genetic, neurochemical, and neuroanatomical factors for depression.

Genetic Vulnerability

Mood disorders seem to have a genetic link. Depression, for example, certainly runs in families (Sullivan, Neale, & Kendler, 2000), and while the genetic commonality is stronger for depressive disorders, bipolar disorder runs in families too. For example, if you have a parent or sibling with bipolar disorder, your chance of having it too is up to 20 times higher than if your relatives didn't have bipolar disorder (MacKinnon, Jamison, & DePaulo, 1997) FIGURE 14-17.

Hypomania A condition in which a person has symptoms of mania but avoids getting into trouble.

Bipolar disorder A mood disorder in which a person may alternate between a sad, depressive mood and elevated, irritable, or manic episodes.

FIGURE 14-17 The risk of bipolar disorder increases with genetic relatedness.
Source: Adapted from Gottesman, I. I. (1990). Schizophrenia Genesis: The Origins of Madness (1st ed.). New York: W. H. Freeman.

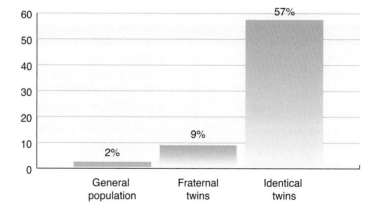

Suicide

One of the most upsetting and troubling symptoms of depression are the thoughts of death, or suicidality, that often accompany the disorder. These thoughts and emotions are part of the constellation of symptoms that come with depression. When the symptoms of depression fade with treatment, the symptoms of suicidality and hopelessness fade too.

Despite this, suicide remains a significant problem. More than half a million people in the United States each year will make a suicide attempt that is so severe that it results in hospitalization, and more than 1 million people each year will actually kill themselves. The completed suicide rates only tell part of the story, since suicide attempts outnumber completed suicides by a ratio of 20 to 1 (Sudock, 2005).

Suicide is the second leading cause of death among college students (Rawe & Kingsburry, 2006). The National Suicide Prevention Lifeline (http://www.suicidepreventionlifeline.org/) offers assistance to those in crisis and stories of attempt survivors.

Neurochemical and Neuroanatomical Factors

You'll remember that neurotransmitters help the nervous system to communicate. The **monoamine hypothesis of depression** suggests that depressive symptoms are brought on by a malfunction of certain types of neurotransmitters, specifically norepinephrine (NE), serotonin (5HT), and dopamine (DA) neurons (also known as monoamines). These neurotransmitters connect to important areas in the brain's limbic system. Lower activity in the limbic system has been implicated in the symptoms of depression. What's more, medications that boost the effectiveness of these neurotransmitters help those with depression get better (Stahl, 2008a).

Monoamine hypothesis of depression A hypothesis that suggests that depressive symptoms are brought on by a malfunction of certain types of neurotransmitters.

The Social-Cognitive Perspective

The learned helplessness model suggests that when people feel they don't have any control over the good things that happen to them, they are more likely to become depressed. This theory comes from research done in animals: When the animals were exposed to uncontrollable negative stimuli, like a mild shock, and were unable to escape it, they learned to be helpless. When they were in a position to escape the bad event—they didn't (Peterson, Maier, & Seligman, 1995).

An expansion of this idea is seen with cognitive distortions. The idea is that some people have thoughts about themselves, the world, or other people that are not accurate; they are distortions of reality. However inaccurate, these thoughts can shape their actions and emotions. They may, for example, filter out the positive things in their life and remember more disappointing moments instead. What results is a belief that they are worthless and defective.

CONCEPT LEARNING CHECK 14.5   *Identifying Mood Disorders*

1. After a recent move Sean "has lost a considerable amount of weight and has periods when he cries." He misses his old friends. He feels exhausted most of the day has trouble sleeping. What's the most likely diagnosis?

2. A few months later Sean returns to his therapist with some new symptoms. He says he's feeling much better, in fact he reports feeling "better than good." He says he has been focusing on his work for about 15 hours a day. He sleeps only for about 2 hours, but says that he still feels rested. Despite all his work he hasn't been that productive. His supervisor says that Sean's presentations are sloppy, and it seems as if Sean feels a pressure to keep talking. Sean says his thoughts are racing around in his head. Because of his lack of productivity, Sean has been put on probation at work. Given the new symptoms, what is the most likely diagnosis?

3. A 36-year-old-woman says that for the past 2 months she has been feeling irritable and has lost interest in most of her usual activities. She says that she also has trouble concentrating at work, doesn't sleep well at night, and has lost about 10 pounds. What's the most likely diagnosis?

14.6 Psychotic Disorders

Psychotic disorders involve a loss of contact with reality.

■ Recognize signs and symptoms of psychotic disorders.

Schizophrenia A psychological disorder characterized by disordered thinking, delusions, hallucinations, and disordered behavior and emotions.

Delusions Beliefs that most people would think are incredible or impossible.

Bizarre delusions False and impossible beliefs.

Non-bizarre delusions False beliefs that are possible but highly unlikely.

The devastating impact of **schizophrenia** is clear. The experience can be terrifying and disruptive and is characterized by disordered thinking, delusions, hallucinations, irrational thoughts, and disturbed emotions and actions. In the United States, nearly 2.5 million people have schizophrenia and nearly a third of those require inpatient assistance (Kessler & Wang, 2008).

Schizophrenia has more than just a devastating emotional impact; it also has a very significant financial impact. If you add up all the financial costs of treating schizophrenia, it makes up around 3% of the entire U.S. healthcare budget and nearly 75% of all U.S. mental health care expenses (Knapp, Mangalore, & Simon, 2004).

Schizophrenia is chronic. Up to 80% of those hospitalized with their first episode of schizophrenia will return to the hospital with another episode eventually (Eaton et al., 1992). Luckily, up to 30% of those diagnosed will get much better with treatment (Wiersma, Nienhuis, Slooff, & Giel, 1998).

Psychotic symptoms appear in a number of psychological disorders like anxiety or mood disorders. When psychotic symptoms appear as the central feature of the disorder, it might suggest a psychotic disorder such as schizophrenia. **TABLE 14-9** summarizes the psychotic disorders described by the *DSM-5*. Our discussion will focus on just one: schizophrenia.

Symptoms of Psychotic Disorders

Symptoms of psychosis include disordered thinking, delusions, and hallucinations, as well as disordered behavior and emotions.

Disorganized Thinking

The way we speak is often a sign of the way we think. Therefore, the disorganized speaking often found in people with psychosis is a clue to the disordered thoughts these individuals have. Disorganized speaking patterns can range from rapidly switching from one unrelated topic to the next (as in "loose associations") to totally incomprehensible word patterns ("incoherence" or "word salad").

Delusions and Hallucinations

Delusions are false beliefs. These are beliefs that most anyone would believe are false. They come in two types: bizarre and non-bizarre. **Bizarre delusions** are beliefs that are totally impossible. **Non-bizarre delusions** are very, very unlikely, but possible. For example, if I told you that I thought that the nightly local newscast is a way to communicate my daily whereabouts to a government agency, although this is unlikely, it is possible (involving microphones, codes, and such). On the other hand, saying that I believed my organs were turning into straw would be a bizarre delusion, since that is impossible.

TABLE 14-9 Psychotic Disorders

Psychotic Disorder	Description
Schizophrenia	A disorder that lasts for at least 6 months and includes at least 1 month of active-phase symptoms (i.e., two [or more] of the following: delusions, hallucinations, disorganized speech, grossly disorganized or catatonic behavior, negative symptoms)
Delusional disorder	Only delusions for at least 30 days
Brief psychotic disorder	Symptoms of psychosis lasting at least 1 day and no more than 30 days

Source: Adapted from American Psychiatric Association. Diagnostic and Statistical Manual of Mental Disorders: *DSM-5. American Psychiatric Publishing, 2013.*

CRITICAL THINKING APPLICATION

A few years ago in a small Connecticut city, a man named Scott left his office and began his drive home. He was 25 years old, single, and in good health. In fact, he had never suffered from more than a cold or a bad case of food poisoning. With no history of seizure disorder, Scott had a seizure while driving. Unable to control his muscles or his car, he lost control of the vehicle, killing one person and injuring several others.

When people who hear this story are asked if they think Scott should be punished, most say no, because they believe the accident wasn't his fault. Some may suggest that his driving privileges should be suspended until he is seizure-free. Almost everyone agrees, however, that putting him in jail wouldn't prevent or deter another similar accident.

Strangely, when this story is told so that Scott's "seizures" are instead called "hallucina-tions," people take a harsher view of Scott's role. They suggest that Scott should be committed to a mental institution or arrested and tried for the death and destruction he caused.

If we think about it, most of us would agree that seizures and hallucinations share some biological and physiological characteristics. Nevertheless, we tend to feel very differently about behavior that results from one condition versus another. Why?

Evaluate

1. Do attitudes about mental health affect how we treat, punish, or choose not to treat mental illnesses as opposed to other illnesses? Explain.

2. How might stigmas and biases about mental illness be reflected in our language and in our laws?

Hallucinations, on the other hand, are sensory perceptions with no sensory input. People who experience hallucinations may see things that aren't there or hear things that no one else hears. Hallucinations can come from all five senses. Most, however, are auditory or visual.

Catatonia

Another example of a symptom of psychosis is catatonia. Catatonia is a problem with movement. It comes in two types. One is **agitated catatonia**, in which the person has uncontrollable movements. They may flap their arms or spin in circles. It can also be exhibited as **stuporous catatonia**, where the person is immobile and nonreactive. They may even exhibit waxy flexibility (you can move their arms and they stay in that position).

Deficits of Behavior

The symptoms that were already mentioned are called **positive symptoms**. They are referred to as positive, not because they are good, but because they are in addition to typical behavior. For example, most people do not have hallucinations, so this would be an addition to expected behavior. Positive symptoms are distinct from **negative symptoms**, which are deficits in behavior—things that are expected but are sometimes absent in psychosis. They all begin with the letter A. Negative symptoms include avolition (lack of will), alogia (lack of elaborative speech), and affective flattening (flat moods).

Identifying Schizophrenia

Diagnosing schizophrenia is more complicated than just identifying psychosis. For a firm diagnosis, the symptoms must be present for a minimum amount of time and cause distress and impairment. In addition, it is important to know that people with schizophrenia don't always exhibit these symptoms of psychosis and often have long stretches with no symptoms whatsoever.

Hallucinations Sensory perceptions with no sensory input. The perceptions may affect any or all of the five senses.

Agitated catatonia A symptom of schizophrenia that is characterized by excessive motor activity and periods of inexhaustibility.

Stuporous catatonia A symptom of schizophrenia that is characterized by restricted motor activity such as periods of immobility and muscle rigidity.

Positive symptoms of psychosis Symptoms, such as hallucinations or delusions, that are present in addition to expected behavior.

Negative symptoms of psychosis Symptoms of psychosis that involve behavior deficits, or expected behaviors that are absent.

This waxing and waning of symptoms can occur with other conditions. Think back to the last time you had a cold. You probably had a time when you were sneezing and coughing and felt horrible. Then maybe you started to feel better, but still had some leftover ickyness. You could consider the time you were feeling bad and the symptoms were really the worst to be the active phase of your illness. The other is a residual (leftover) phase.

A diagnosis of schizophrenia is much the same. Continuous signs of the disorder must last for at least 6 months. At least 1 month must be an active phase. At this point the person will show symptoms of psychosis most of the day, nearly every day. This is often followed by several months of a residual phase. The residual period sometimes consists of positive symptoms with less severe impact, or maybe just negative symptoms. Some can have it worse and have several months of an active phase.

Etiology of Psychotic Disorders

Schizophrenia most likely is the result of many things. Like most every psychological disorder, there is evidence of both a biological underpinning and non-biological influences.

Genetic Vulnerability

Genes play a significant role in schizophrenia. The more closely a person is related to someone with schizophrenia, the greater his or her likelihood for having the disorder. You may remember that there is a 1 in 100 chance of a person being diagnosed with schizophrenia. This changes to 1 in 10 with a parent or sibling with the disorder and 1 in 2 if the sibling is identical. This holds true no matter if the individuals grow up in the same household or apart (Plomin, DeFries, McClearn, & McGuffin, 2000; Gottesman, 1990).

Brain Abnormalities

There are several differences in the brains of individuals diagnosed with schizophrenia. Brain scans reveal that people with schizophrenia have larger ventricles—fluid-filled cavities—in their brain than do people without this disorder (Galderisi, 2000) FIGURE 14-18. Other researchers found that the hippocampus and areas within the cerebral cortex were a bit smaller than would be expected (Lui et al., 2009). Although these structural differences are convincing, they are not enough to explain the vast behavioral and emotional differences in those with schizophrenia.

The **dopamine hypothesis of schizophrenia** suggests that the neurotransmitter dopamine plays a key role in the disorder. Current theories suggest that a complex imbalance

> **Dopamine hypothesis of schizophrenia** A hypothesis that suggests that the neurotransmitter dopamine plays a key role in schizophrenia.

FIGURE 14-18 Enlarged brain ventricles are often present in people with schizophrenia.

might lead to the symptoms of schizophrenia as well as the side effects of medications used to balance out dopamine in the brain (Conklin & Iacono, 2002). For example, there may be too much dopamine in the mesolimbic system, which is involved in emotion and thinking. Too much dopamine in this area could explain the delusions, hallucinations, and distorted thinking often found in people suffering from psychosis. On the other hand, low dopamine levels in the prefrontal area have been implicated in the organization of behavior, attention, and motivation (Stahl, 2008b).

Neurodevelopment in the Uterus

Neurodevelopment refers to the growth and maturation of the nervous system. The neuro-developmental hypothesis of schizophrenia proposes that the nervous system differences found in schizophrenia are due, in part, to factors that occur during the growth of the nervous system before birth (McGrath, Féron, Burne, Mackay-Sim, & Eyles, 2003). These factors can be genetic (like having a family member with schizophrenia), environmental (like maternal malnutrition, infection, or incompatible blood types), or both (Fatemi & Folsom, 2009).

Psychological Factors

Biology doesn't tell the whole story. It never does. There is strong evidence that psycho-social influences may interact with genetic vulnerability in producing schizophrenia. Extremely poor parenting and the failure of developing adequate psychosocial and coping skills can increase the stress that could set schizophrenia into motion (Walker & Diforio, 1997). Other sources of stress can include being raised in an abusive family, experiencing disturbed patterns of communication in the family, and early trauma.

CONCEPT LEARNING CHECK 14.6   *Classifying Signs and Symptoms of Schizophrenia*

Decide whether each of the following symptoms is a positive or a negative symptom of schizophrenia. Place a check mark in the appropriate column.

Positive and Negative Symptoms of Schizophrenia

Symptom	Positive	Negative
Avolition		
Visual hallucinations		
Delusions		
Anhedonia		
Stuporous catatonia		
Flattened affect		
Inability to experience pleasure		
Auditory hallucinations		
Alogia		

14.7 Personality Disorders

Personality disorders involve extreme, inflexible global personality traits that are both chronic and pervasive.

- List and describe the personality disorders as described in the *DSM-5*

Personality disorder
A psychological condition, that involves extreme, inflexible global personality traits that are chronic and pervasive.

Ego syntonic A psychological symptom that does not cause a person distress.

Ego dystonic A psychological symptom that causes a person distress.

For something to be a **personality disorder**, it has to be a disruptive pattern that is both chronic and pervasive. Chronic means it doesn't come and go; it ends up being the main way they interact with people all the time. The personality disorders also begin early and are often identifiable by the time a person reaches early adulthood.

In addition to being long lasting, the disorder is pervasive, meaning that it creeps into every nook and cranny of a person's life. Personality disorders are self-defeating and rigid and often very resistant to change.

You might think that a behavior pattern so disruptive and so impairing would be something the person doesn't like. Most of the time this is true, but often people with personality disorders don't find their own behavior disagreeable. Some types of personality disorders are **ego syntonic**, meaning that they do not bother the person. Think of a friend of yours who has a shirt with a hole in it. You might find it unthinkable to leave the house with an obvious problem with your clothing, but to that person, it is not a big deal. He might not think twice about it. It's the same with behaviors sometimes. When behaviors are ego **syn**tonic, they are similar to how they see themselves (like the word synonym, meaning words that are similar). Most of the disorders, however, are **ego dystonic**, meaning they are dissimilar to how they see themselves. Ego dystonic disorders are easier to treat since clients are usually more motivated to change things they don't like about themselves. If the behavior is ego syntonic, treatment can be rough-going or even futile.

Personality disorders affect about 1% of the population (Kessler & Wang, 2008) **TABLE 14-10** lists the ten personality disorders described in the *DSM-5*. We will focus on three: antisocial personality disorder, paranoid personality disorder, and borderline personality disorder.

Antisocial Personality Disorder

I'm sure you've been tempted to do something you know you shouldn't do. I know I have. Taking something that doesn't belong to you or sneaking gummy worms into a movie

TABLE 14-10 Personality Disorders

Disorder	Key Themes
Paranoid personality disorder	Distrust and suspiciousness
Schizoid personality disorder	Apathy and detachment from others, including family members
Antisocial personality disorder	Breaking rules and harming others without remorse
Borderline personality disorder	Instability in relationships, mood, and ever-changing view of self
Histrionic personality disorder	Always needs attention from others
Narcissistic personality disorder	Inflated sense of self-importance and extreme preoccupation with themselves
Avoidant personality disorder	Extreme reaction to the criticism of others
Dependent personality disorder	Insatiable need for care from others
Obsessive-compulsive personality disorder	Fixation with rules and lists that interferes with them getting things done

Source: Adapted from American Psychiatric Association. Diagnostic and Statistical Manual of Mental Disorders: *DSM-5. American Psychiatric Publishing, 2013.*

theater that has a sign that reads "No outside food allowed" are things that might cross our minds at times, but most of us stop ourselves before we act on these impulses. We might feel guilty for even entertaining the thought. We follow the rules and hope others will too. But let's say you didn't care to follow the rules and you gave into every impulse you had and didn't care about the consequences or who you hurt or cheated even if it was your best friend or your parents.

That's similar to what you might expect in **antisocial personality disorder**, a personality disorder where a person breaks the rules of society often with no remorse or anxiety. For a diagnosis of antisocial personality disorder, in addition to conduct difficulties, before age 15 you would expect three or more symptoms including law-breaking, frequent lying, impulsivity, aggressiveness, disregard for the safety of others, irresponsibility, and lack of remorse or even rationalizing having hurt others.

Antisocial personality disorder is more often found in men (with a prevalence of 3%) than in women (1%) (APA, 2000).

Antisocial personality disorder A personality disorder in which a person breaks societal rules, often without remorse or anxiety.

Etiology of Antisocial Personality Disorder

Scientists have been trying to determine the cause or causes of antisocial personality disorder. Some have wondered about the role of biology. Is there a criminal mind? Are there really natural born killers? Certainly, biology does play a role. In fact, the prefrontal cortex—the part of the cerebral cortex that controls impulses and aids in ethical behavior and moral decision making—has been found to be different in people who have been diagnosed with antisocial personality disorder (Kiehl, 2006).

There is even some evidence that those individuals with antisocial personality disorder crave higher levels of sensation to maintain the normal feelings we all have. They are chaos junkies, so to speak. They are easily susceptible to boredom and pick activities that will give them a quick fix (Gabbard, 2005).

Dr. James Fallon, a neuroscientist at the University of California, Irvine, discovered a specific area of the brain, the orbital cortex, that he feels is involved in the impulse control lacking in people with antisocial personality disorder (Fallon, 2006). His research has even been able to identify low activity in this area using brain scans, after studying brain scans in many people with antisocial personality disorder. This was exciting stuff—a link to a test for antisocial personality disorder FIGURE 14-19.

FIGURE 14-19 Dr. Fallon studies brain images in people with antisocial personality disorder.

There is a twist. After being encouraged to check into his family background, Fallon discovered that one of his ancestors allegedly murdered his own mother. It didn't stop there. There were seven alleged murders in that line of his family, including the notorious Lizzy Borden, who in August of 1892 allegedly killed her father and stepmother with an axe (she was acquitted of the murder).

Fallon was shocked. He studied the brain scans of all the members of his immediate family to see if they too had the low activity in the orbital frontal cortex. He discovered that none of them had the underactivity you might expect for antisocial personality disorder. None except for one—Fallon himself. He had exactly the orbital frontal profile shared by all of the people with antisocial personality disorder who were also murderers he had been studying, as well as all the known high-risk violence-related genes.

As you are no doubt well aware by now, biology doesn't determine everything—the environment plays a critical role, and in Fallon's case his entire upbringing was filled with love and support from his entire extended family. Many factors during childhood, such as lack of warmth, neglect, and harsh punishment, are also important for the development of antisocial personality disorder (Johnson, Cohen, Chen, Kasen, & Brook, 2006).

Paranoid Personality Disorder

Individuals with paranoid personality disorder have a long history of seeing malicious intent in the actions of others. This suspiciousness and mistrust does not subside no matter how long they know you.

A diagnosis of this disorder includes four symptoms that should pervade every part of their lives. They expect to be exploited or harmed by others and are preoccupied with the trustworthiness of their friends. In addition, they think that information they give about themselves will be used against them, and they read hidden meaning into harmless remarks. What's more, they are unforgiving of insults, are quick to counterattack, and often doubt the fidelity of their romantic partners.

As you can imagine, they are always on guard and it causes significant impairment in their work lives and social lives.

Etiology of Paranoid Personality Disorder

The cause of **paranoid personality disorder** remains a mystery. Paranoid personality disorder tends to run in families (Kendler et al., 2006). Other researchers suggest that paranoid personality disorder could be acquired through learning. In this way paranoid behaviors once could have been adaptive responses to stressful situations (Bradley, Conklin, & Westen, 2007).

Borderline Personality Disorder

Individuals with **borderline personality disorder** have a long history of instability in their lives. This instability extends to their relationships, self-image, and moods. Borderline personality disorder is a troubling and difficult disorder in which the individual often has difficulty in controlling his or her impulses.

Instability can cause disruptions in relationships and changes in goals, work, and friends. The instability can leave one feeling worried and with little sense of who he or she is as a person. This can lead to frequent fights and hot tempers, and fears of abandonment. **TABLE 14-11** outlines the symptoms of borderline personality disorder.

Although borderline personality disorder is not very common (about 2% of the general population), the severity of symptoms makes it overrepresented in treatment populations. About one in every ten people in outpatient mental health settings are diagnosed with borderline personality disorder, and about two of every ten people among psychiatric inpatients (Kessler & Wang, 2008).

Etiology of Borderline Personality Disorder

As with other disorders, researchers have found several possible causes for this one. Some suggest that serotonin might be related to reduced impulse control. Studies of twins with borderline personality disorder provide strong evidence that there might be a genetic component to the disorder (Siever & Koenigsberg, 2000). Other studies have suggested that the amygdala, responsible for regulating emotions, could be involved. In people with borderline personality disorder, this area is overactive and the brain areas responsible for controlling emotional responses are underactive (Meyer-Lindenberg, 2008).

Biology is only part of the story. Many people with borderline personality disorder have reported significant abuse, neglect, instability, and psychopathology in their backgrounds. Often these abuses are reflected in their earliest memories (Bradley et al., 2007). One study reported that up to 70% of people with borderline personality disorder had been sexually abused (Zanarini, 2000).

Paranoid personality disorder A disorder characterized by a long and unwavering history of attributing malicious intent to others.

Borderline personality disorder A personality disorder marked by a history of instability in a person's self-image, ability to control impulses, relationships, and moods.

TABLE 14-11 Borderline Personality Disorder

People with borderline personality disorder have an unstable view of themselves, their friends, and they experience rapidly shifting moods. These three core symptoms characterize their world. Additional symptoms include—

1. Trying to prevent important others from abandoning them
2. Stormy relationships with others in which the other person is alternately idealized and condemned
3. Shallow understanding of themselves
4. Recklessness that can get them into trouble
5. Physical self-harm that may include cutting or suicide attempts
6. Feelings of emptiness
7. Intense anger

Source: Adapted from American Psychiatric Association. Diagnostic and Statistical Manual of Mental Disorders: *DSM-5. American Psychiatric Publishing, 2013.*

Summary of Multiple Influences on Psychological Disorders

I never heard from Betty again. Odds are that the behaviors she exhibited, despite being unusual, were not indicative of a psychological condition. What creates a psychological disorder? The etiology of psychological disorders is certainly not singular. The diathesis-stress and reciprocal gene environment model, for example, suggest that biological forces such as natural selection, brain anatomy, and biochemical activity may be involved. Also, environmental factors like learning and exposure to stressful events also have an impact. In addition, sociocultural forces like family background, and how a person interprets what happens in his or her life may also increase the likelihood of developing a psychological condition. Multiple influences are at play in how disorders start and are maintained.

CONCEPT LEARNING CHECK 14.7 | *Categorizing Personality Disorders*

1. Alex, age 40, has long-standing difficulty maintaining relationships because of her frequent shifts in moods. She also has the following symptoms: a history of unstable friendships, frequent mood shifts, indecisiveness, and a fear of being left alone. Alex seems to suffer from which disorder?

Visual Overview Distinguishing Psychological Disorders

Well-trained psychologists can identify specific disorders and apply appropriate treatments. As you study psychological disorders, you might find it challenging to keep them straight. Two of these disorders—dissociative identity disorder and schizophrenia—are easily confused. When you compare their symptoms, however, you'll see that there is little resemblance.

Anxiety disorders are marked by feelings of nervousness, distress, and apprehension. They are often disruptive attempts to diminish anxiety (*Section 14.2*).

Somatic symptom disorders are symptoms of a physical illness that are not fully explained by a medical condition (*Section 14.3*).

Mood disorders are marked by turbulent emotional states and can include problematic social functioning, thinking, behaviors, and physical symptoms. Mood disorders include major depressive disorder and bipolar disorder (*Section 14.5*).

Dissociative identity disorders involve a loss of the integration of consciousness, loss of memory, or a change in the identity of a person. In dissociative identity disorder (formerly called multiple personality disorder), at least two personalities take control of an individual's behavior (*Section 14.4*).
Core symptoms:
- Two or more identities or personalities within one person
- Amnesia between different identities

Are people with multiple personalities schizophrenic? Students sometimes confuse dissociative identity disorder with schizophrenia.

Personality disorders involve extreme, inflexible, global personality traits that are chronic and pervasive. People suffering from these disorders may break societal rules, often with no remorse or anxiety (*Section 14.7*).

Psychotic disorders encompass a number of psychological conditions that include symptoms of psychosis (*Section 14.6*).
Core symptoms:
- Hallucinations
- Disorganized speech
- Catatonic behavior
- Negative symptoms (affective flattening, alogia, or avolition)

14.1 Overview: Understanding Psychological Disorders

- Psychopathology is the science of diagnosing and understanding psychological disorders.
- Psychologists use a number of different tools to diagnose and understand psychological disorders.
- The *Diagnostic and Statistical Manual of Mental Disorders* (*DSM-5*) is the manual that mental health professionals use to describe mental disorders.

- For most disorders in the *DSM-5*, the behavior must be deviant, maladaptive, or cause personal distress.
- The biopsychosocial approach to psychopathology recognizes three important aspects of human behavior: biological, psychological, and social.
- Classifying and labeling psychological disorders has both advantages and disadvantages.

14.2 Anxiety, Compulsiveness, and Stress Disorders

- Anxiety conditions include anxiety disorders, bipolar and related disorders, and trauma- and stressor-related disorders.
- Anxiety disorders are marked by feelings of nervousness, distress, and apprehension, and disruptive attempts to diminish anxiety.

- Anxiety disorders include generalized anxiety disorder, agoraphobia without a history of panic disorder, panic disorder with agoraphobia, panic disorder without agoraphobia, specific phobia, social phobia, obsessive-compulsive disorder, and posttraumatic stress disorder.
- Both biology and environment are important in explaining the cause of anxiety disorders.

14.3 Somatic Symptom and Related Disorders

- The essential features of somatic symptom disorders are symptoms of a physical illness that are not entirely explained by a general medical condition.
- Somatic symptom and related disorders include somatic symptom disorder, conversion disorder, and illness anxiety disorder (hypochondriasis).
- In somatic symptom disorder, a person has disruptive and persistent thoughts, feelings, and behaviors that accompany illness symptoms.

- In conversion disorder, a psychological worry or concern is transformed (converted) into a physical symptom.
- In illness anxiety disorder, a person is worried about having or contracting an illness despite being physically fine.
- Biological vulnerabilities and stressors such as emotional conflicts likely bring on somatic symptom disorders.

14.4 Dissociative Disorders

- Dissociative disorders involve a sudden loss of the integration of consciousness, memory, or a change in the identity of a person.
- Dissociative disorders include dissociative amnesia, dissociative fugue, and dissociative identity disorder.
- The core symptom of dissociative amnesia is loss of personal memory.
- In dissociative fugue, amnesia is exacerbated by travel away from home and the creation of a new identity.

- Dissociative identity disorder is diagnosed when two or more distinct identities exist within one individual.
- Theories of the etiology of dissociative disorders include the symptoms helping to separate and disconnect a person from a disturbing experience. Other researchers believe the symptoms to be reinforced attention-seeking behavior.

14.5 Mood Disorders

- Mood disorders are marked by tumultuous emotional states and can include problematic social functioning, thinking, behaviors, and physical symptoms.
- Mood disorders include the depressive disorders and the bipolar and related disorders.
- Symptoms of depression include a sad mood, anhedonia, hopelessness, loss of energy, disrupted sleep patterns, weight and appetite changes, difficulty in concentration, and thoughts of death.
- Symptoms of mania include inflated self-esteem, decreased need for sleep, a pressure to keep talking, a flight of ideas, increase in goal-directed behavior, and excessive involvement in pleasurable activities that have a high possibility for painful consequences.

- When a major depressive episode occurs alone, it is diagnosed as a major depressive disorder.
- When a major depressive episode alternates with a manic episode, it is diagnosed as a bipolar disorder.
- Mood disorders are caused by both biological and environmental factors.
- The monoamine hypothesis of depression suggests that depressive symptoms are brought on by a malfunction of norepinephrine, serotonin, and dopamine.
- The learned helplessness model of depression suggests that when people feel they don't have any control over the good things that happen to them, they are more likely to be depressed.

14.6 Psychotic Disorders

- Psychotic disorders encompass a number of psychological conditions that include symptoms of psychosis.
- The dopamine hypothesis of schizophrenia suggests that the neurotransmitter dopamine plays a key role in the disorder.
- The neurodevelopmental hypothesis proposes that the nervous system

differences found in schizophrenia are due, in part, to factors that occur during the growth of the nervous system before birth.
- There is strong evidence that psychosocial influences may interact with genetic vulnerability in producing schizophrenia.

14.7 Personality Disorders

- Personality disorders involve extreme, inflexible global personality traits that are both chronic and pervasive.
- Personality disorders include antisocial personality disorder, paranoid personality disorder, and borderline personality disorder.
- Antisocial personality disorder is a personality disorder in which a person breaks the rules of society often with no remorse or anxiety.

- Individuals with paranoid personality disorder have a long history of seeing malicious intent in the actions of others.
- Individuals with borderline personality disorder have a long history of instability in their lives. This instability extends to their relationships, self-image, and moods.

14.1 Overview: Understanding Psychological Disorders

1. Using the multiaxial system of *DSM-IV-TR*, conditions such as schizophrenia and anxiety disorders are coded on:
   A. Axis I.
   B. Axis II.
   C. Axis III.
   D. Axis IV.

2. The *DSM-5* contains:
   A. the etiology of mental disorders.
   B. treatments of mental disorders.
   C. criteria for diagnosing mental disorders.
   D. theoretical approaches to psychopathology.

3. Using the multiaxial system of *DSM-IV-TR*, conditions such as paranoid personality disorder and borderline personality disorder are coded on:
   A. Axis I.
   B. Axis II.
   C. Axis III.
   D. Axis IV.

14.2 Anxiety, Compulsiveness, and Stress Disorders

4. In the diathesis-stress model, "diathesis" refers to:
   A. biological predisposition.
   B. environmental stressor.
   C. ways to treat the disorders.
   D. the main cause of a disorder.

5. Which of the following best describes an obsession?
   A. A behavior or mental act that a person feels compelled to perform
   B. An unwanted thought that a person finds intrusive and distressing
   C. Something a person enjoys doing and talking about constantly
   D. Continually reliving a traumatic event

14.3 Somatic Symptom and Related Disorders

6. Pam has completely lost her sense of taste during the past year, but doctors cannot explain her loss of sensory function. This is most likely an example of what kind of disorder?
   A. Somatic symptom
   B. Mood
   C. Psychotic
   D. Personality

7. When might symptoms of conversion disorder typically emerge?
   A. Soon after a stressful event
   B. Several months after a physical injury
   C. Several years after a traumatic incident
   D. Soon after an episode of unconsciousness

14.4 Dissociative Disorders

8. Which of the following disorders usually involves travel and the creation of a new identity?
   A. Dissociative identity disorder
   B. Borderline personality disorder
   C. Schizophrenia
   D. Dissociative fugue

9. What is the diagnosis when two or more distinct identities exist within one individual?
   A. Schizophrenia
   B. Bipolar disorder
   C. Dissociative identity disorder
   D. Conversion disorder

14.5 Mood Disorders

10. One of the symptoms of a mood disorder is anhedonia, which means:
    A. a depressed mood.
    B. lack of feeling pleasure.
    C. feelings of worthlessness.
    D. change in appetite.

11. What is the main difference between mania and hypomania?
    A. Hypomanic symptoms are more serious than manic symptoms.
    B. Hypomanic symptoms are less serious than manic symptoms.
    C. Hypomanic symptoms include symptoms of anxiety.
    D. Hypomanic symptoms include symptoms of hyperactivity.

14.6 Psychotic Disorders

12. A psychologist sees from a patient's chart that he is experiencing alogia. Based on this information the psychologist can expect that the patient will answer her questions with:
- **A.** short answers.
- **B.** long, rambling answers.
- **C.** tangential or unrelated answers.
- **D.** a different answer depending on which personality is answering.

13. The neurodevelopmental hypothesis of schizophrenia suggests that this disorder is due in part to:
- **A.** a brain injury.
- **B.** malnutrition in early adulthood.
- **C.** factors that occur before birth.
- **D.** suffering or witnessing trauma.

14.7 Personality Disorders

14. Impulsive suicidal behavior is sometimes a symptom of:
- **A.** borderline personality disorder.
- **B.** generalized anxiety disorder.
- **C.** social phobia.
- **D.** paranoid personality disorder.

15. The core symptom of antisocial personality disorder is:
- **A.** shyness.
- **B.** failure to comply with social norms.
- **C.** dislike for other people.
- **D.** anxiety around strangers.

CHAPTER DISCUSSION QUESTIONS

1. What are some of the benefits of a diagnostic system like the *DSM-5*?

2. What are the various contributions of nature and nurture in the development of different psychological disorders?

3. What are the main criticisms of the *DSM*?

4. Why do you suppose the rates of psychological conditions are higher for women than for men?

5. What are some of the ways we can mediate the factors that cause psychological disorders and boost the factors that are protective?

6. Given the risks of labeling people, do you think the *DSM* does more harm than good? What are some alternatives to diagnostic labels for mental health professionals?

CHAPTER PROJECTS

1. While watching TV, YouTube, or movies, notice the differences between the way the media describe psychopathology and the way mental health professionals do.

2. Read an autobiography by a person with a psychological disorder and see if you can describe the constellation of symptoms as they would be listed in the *DSM*.

CHAPTER KEY TERMS

Agitated catatonia
Agoraphobia
Anhedonia
Antisocial personality disorder
Anxiety disorder
Biopsychosocial approach
Bipolar disorder
Bizarre delusions
Borderline personality disorder
Compulsions
Conversion disorder
Delusions
Diathesis-stress hypothesis
Dissociation
Dissociative amnesia
Dissociative disorders
Dissociative fugue
Dissociative identity disorder (DID)
Dopamine hypothesis of
    schizophrenia
Ego dystonic

Ego syntonic
Epidemiology
Etiology
Factitious disorder
Generalized anxiety disorder
    (GAD)
Hallucinations
Hypomania
Illness anxiety disorder
    (Hypochondriasis)
Learning perspective
Malingering
Mania
Medical model
Monoamine hypothesis of
    depression
Moods
Negative symptoms of psychosis
Non-bizarre delusions
Obsession
Obsessive-compulsive disorder

Panic attack
Panic disorder
Paranoid personality disorder
Personality disorder
Phobia
Positive symptoms of psychosis
Posttraumatic stress disorder
Psychological disorder
Psychopathology
Psychophysiological disorder
Reciprocal-gene environment
    model
Schizophrenia
Social anxiety disorder
Social phobia
Somatic symptom disorder
Somatic symptom and related
    disorders
Stuporous catatonia

ANSWERS TO CONCEPT LEARNING CHECKS

14.1 Identifying Psychological Disorders

Consider each described behavior according to the three criteria of psychological disorders. Then decide whether the behavior is disordered or not.

Behavior Description	Is it deviant?	Does it cause the person distress?	Is it maladaptive?	Is it a disorder?
Betty brought balloons to her first appointment with her therapist.	Yes			No
Ben throws a tantrum almost every day whenever he doesn't get his way. Ben is 22.	Yes	Yes	Yes	Possibly
Sam throws a tantrum almost every day whenever he doesn't get his way. Sam is 2.		Yes		No
Clara is afraid of clowns. She wants to take her children to the circus, but she's afraid she'll see a clown. She avoids toy aisles in department stores for the same reason.	Yes	Yes	Yes	Yes
Maria is very afraid of snakes. She enjoys hiking, but won't go in the reptile house at the zoo.		Yes		No

14.2 Identifying Anxiety, Compulsiveness, and Stress Disorders

1. As a child, Clara had a terrible experience in which a clown frightened her. Now, as an adult, if she even imagines seeing a clown, she grows extremely nervous, frightened, and distressed. What kind of anxiety order does Clara seem to have? [Specific phobia]

2. Manuel has been worrying "all the time" and says that it's not about anything in particular. He finds it difficult to control his worry and feels restless, tired, and irritable. He's also having problems sleeping. Manuel most likely has which disorder? [Generalized anxiety disorder]

3. Marty, 27, reports a long-standing fear of speaking in public. When asked to speak in front of a large group of people he becomes extremely anxious and thinks he'll be embarrassed. Because of this fear, he has passed on promotions and other opportunities to advance in his career. On one occasion where he was forced to speak, he became so anxious that he started shaking and panicking. Marty most likely has which disorder? [Social phobia]

14.3 Identifying Somatic Symptom and Related Disorders

1. James, a 22-year-old-man, was referred to your clinic for evaluation of his complaints. He's convinced that he has stomach cancer despite being told it is very unlikely. He has cramps when he overeats and reports that his tongue "just doesn't look right." Despite medical evidence to the contrary, James has continued to believe that he has stomach cancer. What is the most likely diagnosis? [Illness anxiety disorder or hypochondriasis]

2. Martha was robbed at gunpoint about 3 months ago. Luckily she wasn't hurt and the police were able to recover her purse and capture the assailant. About a week before Martha had to identify the man who robbed her, Martha suddenly lost her sight. She didn't seem that concerned about it. What's the most likely diagnosis? [Conversion disorder]

14.4 Identifying Dissociative Disorders

1. A 24-year-old-man is brought to the hospital emergency room because he was found wandering the street. He reports feeling "confused" and says he isn't sure where he is. The last thing he remembers is coming home to a fire in his house. After examination you discover no head trauma or any kind of injury that would account for his loss of memory. What is the most likely diagnosis? [Dissociative amnesia]

14.5 Identifying Mood Disorders

1. After a recent move Sean "has lost a considerable amount of weight and has periods where he cries." He misses his old friends. He feels exhausted most of the day, and has trouble sleeping. What's the most likely diagnosis? [Major depressive disorder]

2. A few months later Sean returns to his therapist with some new symptoms. He says he's feeling much better, in fact he reports feeling "better than good." He says he has been focusing on his work for about 15 hours a day. He sleeps only for about 2 hours, but says that he still feels rested. Despite all his work he hasn't been that productive. His supervisor says that Sean's presentations are sloppy, and it seems as if Sean feels a pressure to keep talking. Sean says his thoughts are racing around in his head. Because of his lack of productivity, Sean has been put on probation at work. Given the new symptoms, what is the most likely diagnosis? [Bipolar disorder]

3. A 36-year-old-woman says that for the past 2 months she has been feeling irritable and has lost interest in most of her usual activities. She says that she also has trouble concentrating at work, doesn't sleep well at night and has lost about 10 pounds. What's the most likely diagnosis? [Major depressive disorder]

14.6 Classifying Signs and Symptoms of Schizophrenia

Positive and Negative Symptoms of Schizophrenia

Avolition: Negative

Visual hallucinations: Positive

Delusions: Positive

Anhedonia: Negative

Stuperous catatonia: Positive

Flattened affect: Negative

Inability to experience pleasure: Negative

Auditory hallucinations: Positive

Alogia: Negative

14.7 Categorizing Personality Disorders

1. Alex, age 40, has long-standing difficulty maintaining relationships because of her frequent shifts in moods. She also has the following symptoms: a history of unstable friendships, frequent mood shifts, indecisiveness, and a fear of being left alone. Alex seems to suffer from which disorder? [Borderline personality disorder]

14.1 Overview: Understanding Psychological Disorders

1. **A.** Rationale: In *DSM-IV-TR* Axis I conditions are clinical disorders such as schizophrenia and anxiety disorders. Axis II conditions are personality disorders. Axis III conditions are general medical conditions, and Axis IV would list the current psychosocial stressors.

2. **C.** Rationale: The *DSM* is the classification system used by most mental health professionals in the United States. It contains the criteria for diagnosing mental disorders. It does not, however, contain any suggestions for treatment or any causes of the disorder.

3. **B.** Rationale: Psychological conditions that are coded on Axis II of the *DSM-IV-TR* involve extreme, inflexible global personality traits that are both chronic and pervasive.

4. **A.** Rationale: A diathesis is a biological root or cause of a disorder.

14.2 Anxiety, Compulsiveness, and Stress Disorders

5. **B.** Rationale: An obsession is an unwanted thought that the person finds intrusive and distressing.

14.3 Somatic Symptom and Related Disorders

6. **A.** Rationale: Somatic symptom disorders are psychological disorders where individuals have symptoms of a physical illness that are not well explained by a general medical condition.

7. **A.** Rationale: A conversion disorder is a condition in which a worry or concern is transformed into a physical symptom. They usually appear soon after a stressful event.

14.4 Dissociative Disorders

8. **D.** Rationale: In dissociative fugue a person forgets who they are and often will travel great distances and assume a new identity that resembles their original identity.

9. **C.** Rationale: In dissociative identity disorder a person has two or more distinct identities within one individual. A split of consciousness is typical in dissociative disorders but would not be expected in psychotic disorders such as schizophrenia, mood disorders like bipolar, or the conversion disorders.

14.5 Mood Disorders

10. **B.** Rationale: A symptom of depression and sometimes of psychosis, anhedonia is a reduced capacity to feel pleasure.

11. **B.** Rationale: Hypomania is a condition in which a person has symptoms of mania but avoids getting into trouble. Therefore hypomania would be less serious than mania.

12. **A.** Rationale: Alogia is the lack of elaborative speech. Someone with alogia is likely to have brief and simple answers to any questions asked.

14.6 Psychotic Disorders

13. **C.** Rationale: The neurodevelopmental hypothesis of schizophrenia suggests that the disorder might be related to factors that occur during the growth and development of the nervous system.

14.7 Personality Disorders

14. **A.** Rationale: Individuals with borderline personality disorder have a long history of instability in their lives. This instability can even extend to impulsive suicidal behavior, which is one of the symptoms of borderline personality disorder.

15. **B.** Rationale: In antisocial personality disorder a person breaks societal rules, often without remorse or anxiety. It isn't so much that they don't like people, but that they break rules without considering others.

REFERENCES

Andrews, G., Sanderson, K., Slade, T., & Issakidis, C. (2000). Why does the burden of disease persist? Relating the burden of anxiety and depression to effectiveness of treatment. *Bulletin of the World Health Organization, 78*, 446–454.

APA. (2013). *Diagnostic and statistical manual of mental disorders: DSM-5.* (4th ed.). Washington, DC: American Psychiatric Association.

Beck, A. T., & Clark, D. A. (1997). An information processing model of anxiety: Automatic and strategic processes. *Behaviour Research and Therapy, 35*(1), 49–58.

Bijl, R. V., de Graaf, R., Hiripi, E., Kessler, R. C., Kohn, R., Offord, D. R., Ustun, T. B., et al. (2003). The prevalence of treated and untreated mental disorders in five countries. *Health Affairs, 22*(3), 122–133. doi:10.1377/hlthaff.22.3.122

Bradley, R., Conklin, C. Z., & Westen, D. (2007). Borderline personality disorder. *Personality disorders: Toward the DSM-V*, 167–201.

Burns, D. D. (1999). *The Feeling Good Handbook* (Rev Sub.). Plume. CDC-injury-national suicide statistics at a glance: Suicide rates by race/ethnicity and sex 10+. (n.d.). Retrieved from http://www.cdc.gov/violenceprevention/suicide/statistics/rates02.html

Conklin, H. M., & Iacono, W. G. (2002). Schizophrenia: A neurodevelopmental perspective. *Current Directions in Psychological Science (Wiley-Blackwell), 11*(1), 33.

Deacon, B., & Abramowitz, J. S. (2008). Is hypochondriasis related to obsessive-compulsive disorder, panic disorder, or both? An empirical evaluation. *Journal of Cognitive Psychotherapy, 22*(2), 115–127. doi:10.1891/0889-8391.22.2.115

Dorahy, M. J. (2001). Dissociative identity disorder and memory dysfunction: The current state of experimental research and its future directions. *Clinical Psychology Review, 21*(5), 771–795.

Eaton, W. W., Mortensen, P. B., Herrman, H., Freeman, H., Bilker, W., Burgess, P., & Wooff, K. (1992). Long-term course of hospitalization for schizophrenia: Part I. Risk for rehospitalization. *Schizophrenia Bulletin, 18*(2), 217–228.

Eysenck, M. W., Mogg, K., May, J., Richards, A., & Mathews, A. (1991). Bias in interpretation of ambiguous sentences related to threat in anxiety. *Journal of Abnormal Psychology, 100*(2), 144–150. doi:10.1037/0021-843X.100.2.144

Fallon, J. H. (2006). Neuroanatomical background to understanding the brain of the young psychopath. *Ohio State Journal of Criminal Law, 3*(34), 341–367.

Fatemi, S. H., & Folsom, T. D. (2009). The neurodevelopmental hypothesis of schizophrenia, revisited. *Schizophr Bull, 35*(3), 528–548. doi:10.1093/schbul/sbn187

Fink, P. (2004). The prevalence of somatoform disorders among internal medical inpatients. *Journal of Psychosomatic Research, 56*(4), 413–418. doi:10.1016/S0022-3999(03)00624-X

Gabbard, G. O. (2005). Mind, brain, and personality disorders. *Am J Psychiatry, 162*(4), 648–655. doi:10.1176/appi.ajp.162.4.648

Galderisi, S. (2000). Qualitative MRI findings in patients with schizophrenia: A controlled study. *Psychiatry Research: Neuroimaging, 98*(2), 117–126. doi:10.1016/S0925-4927(00)00047-0

Gottesman, I. I. (1990). *Schizophrenia genesis: The origins of madness* (1st ed.). New York: W. H. Freeman.

Grabe, H. J., Ruhrmann, S., Ettelt, S., Buhtz, F., Hochrein, A., Schulze-Rauschenbach, S., Meyer, K., et al. (2006). Familiality of obsessive-compulsive disorder in nonclinical and clinical subjects. *The American Journal of Psychiatry, 163*(11), 1986–1992.

Johnson, J. G., Cohen, P., Chen, H., Kasen, S., & Brook, J. S. (2006). Parenting behaviors associated with risk for offspring personality disorder during adulthood. *Arch Gen Psychiatry, 63*(5), 579–587. doi:10.1001/archpsyc.63.5.579

Kendler, K. S., Czajkowski, N., Tambs, K., Torgersen, S., Aggen, S., C. Neale, M., & Reichborn-Kjennnerun, T. (2006). Dimensional representations of DSM-IV cluster A personality disorders in a population-based sample of Norwegian twins: A Multivariate Study. *Psychological Medicine, 36*(11), 1583–1591. doi:10.1017/S0033291706008609

Kessler, R. C., Berglund, P., Demler, O., Jin, R., Merikangas, K. R., & Walters, E. E. (2005). Lifetime prevalence and age-of-onset distributions of *DSM-IV* disorders in the national comorbidity survey replication. *Archives of General Psychiatry, 62*(6), 593–602. doi:10.1001/archpsyc.62.6.593

Kessler, R. C., & Wang, P. S. (2008). The descriptive epidemiology of commonly occurring mental disorders in the United States. *Annual Review of Public Health, 29*(1), 115–129. doi:10.1146/annurev.publhealth.29.020907.090847

Kiehl, K. A. (2006). A cognitive neuroscience perspective on psychopathy: Evidence for paralimbic system dysfunction. *Psychiatry research, 142*(2–3), 107–128. doi:10.1016/j.psychres.2005.09.013

Kihlstrom, J. F., Glisky, M. L., & Angiulo, M. J. (1994). Dissociative tendencies and dissociative disorders. *Journal of Abnormal Psychology, 103*(1), 117–124.

Knapp, M., Mangalore, R., & Simon, J. (2004). The global costs of schizophrenia. *Schizophrenia Bulletin, 30*, 279–293.

Lilienfeld, S. O., Lynn, S. J., Kirsch, I., Chaves, J. F., Sarbin, T. R., Ganaway, G. K., Powell, R. A., et al. (1999). Dissociative identity disorder and the sociocognitive model: Recalling the lessons of the past. *Psychological Bulletin, 125*, 507–523.

Lui, S., Deng, W., Huang, X., Jiang, L., Ma, X., Chen, H., Zhang, T., et al. (2009). Association of cerebral deficits with clinical symptoms in antipsychotic-naive first-episode schizophrenia: An optimized voxel-based morphometry and resting state functional connectivity study. *Am J Psychiatry, 166*(2), 196–205. doi:10.1176/appi.ajp.2008.08020183

MacKinnon, D. F., Jamison, K. R., & DePaulo, J. R. (1997). Genetics of manic depressive illness. *Annual review of neuroscience, 20*(1), 355–373.

McGrath, J. J., Féron, F. P., Burne, T. H. J., Mackay-Sim, A., & Eyles, D. W. (2003). The neurodevelopmental hypothesis of schizophrenia: A review of recent developments. *Annals of Medicine, 35*(2), 86–93.

Mclewin, L., & Muller, R. (2006). Childhood trauma, imaginary companions, and the development of pathological dissociation. *Aggression and Violent Behavior, 11*(5), 531–545. doi:10.1016/j.avb.2006.02.001

Meyer-Lindenberg, A. (2008). Psychology: Trust me on this. *Science, 321*(5890), 778–780. doi:10.1126/science.1162908

Miller, S. D., Blackburn, T., Scholes, G., White, G. L., & Mamalis, N. (1991). Optical differences in multiple personality disorder. A second look. *The Journal of Nervous and Mental Disease, 179*(3), 132–135.

Mineka, S., Keir, R., & Price, V. (1980). Fear of snakes in wild- and laboratory-reared rhesus monkeys (*Macaca mulatta*). *Animal Learning & Behavior, 8*(4), 653–663.

Mineka, S., & Öhman, A. (2002). Phobias and preparedness: The selective, automatic, and encapsulated nature of fear. *Biological Psychiatry, 52*(10), 927–937. doi:10.1016/S0006-3223(02)01669-4

Mineka, S., & Zinbarg, R. (2006). A contemporary learning theory perspective on the etiology of anxiety disorders: It's not what you thought it was. *The American Psychologist, 61*(1), 10–26. doi:10.1037/0003-066X.61.1.10

Mueller, T. I., Leon, A. C., Keller, M. B., Solomon, D. A., Endicott, J., Coryell, W., Warshaw, M., et al. (1999). Recurrence after recovery from major depressive disorder during 15 years of observational follow-up. *Am J Psychiatry, 156*(7), 1000–1006.

Murray, C. J., & Lopez, A. D. (1997). Alternative projections of mortality and disability by cause 1990–2020: Global burden of disease study. *Lancet, 349*(9064), 1498–1504. doi:10.1016/S0140-6736(96)07492-2

Patterson, J. M., & Turnbull, A. P. (1993). *Cognitive coping, families, and disability.* Baltimore, MD: Paul H. Brookes Publishing Co.

Peterson, C., Maier, S. F., & Seligman, M. E. P. (1995). *Learned helplessness: A theory for the age of personal control.* New York: Oxford University Press.

Plomin, R., DeFries, J. C., McClearn, G. E., & McGuffin, P. (2000). *Behavioral genetics* (4th ed.). New York: Worth Publishers.

Praag, H., Kloet, E., & Os, J. (2004). *Stress, the brain and depression* (1st ed.). Cambridge, UK: Cambridge University Press.

Rapoport. J. L. (1989, March). The biology of obsessions and compulsions. *Scientific American*, 83–98.

Roelofs, K., Hoogduin, K. A., Keijsers, G. P., Näring, G. W., Moene, F. C., & Sandijck, P. (2002). Hypnotic susceptibility in patients with conversion disorder. *Journal of Abnormal Psychology, 111*(2), 390–395.

Rosenhan, D. L. (1973). On being sane in insane places. *Science, 179*(70), 250–258.

Sar, V., Akyüz, G., & Dogan, O. (2007). Prevalence of dissociative disorders among women in the general population. *Psychiatry Research, 149*(1–3), 169–176. doi:10.1016/j.psychres.2006.01.005

Schmidt, N. B., Lerew, D. R., & Jackson, R. J. (1997). The role of anxiety sensitivity in the pathogenesis of panic: Prospective evaluation of spontaneous panic attacks during acute stress. *Journal of Abnormal Psychology, 106*(3), 355–364.

Seligman, M. E. (1971). Phobias and preparedness. *Behavior Therapy, 2*(3), 307–320. doi:10.1016/S0005-7894(71)80064-3

Seligman, M. E. P. (2006). *Learned optimism: How to change your mind and your life*. New York: Vintage Books.

Shin, L. M., Wright, C. I., Cannistraro, P. A., Wedig, M. M., McMullin, K., Martis, B., Macklin, M. L., et al. (2005). A functional magnetic resonance imaging study of amygdala and medial prefrontal cortex responses to overtly presented fearful faces in posttraumatic stress disorder. *Archives of General Psychiatry, 62*(3), 273–281.

Siever, L. J., & Koenigsberg, H. W. (2000). The frustrating no-mans-land of borderline personality disorder. In *Cerebrum, the dana forum on brain science* (Vol. 2).

Spanos, N. P. (1999). Multiple identities and false memories: A socio-cognitive perspective. *Journal of Psychology and Christianity*, (Spring). Retrieved from http://search.ebscohost.com.proxy.library.emory.edu/login.aspx?direct=true&db=33h&AN=33h-3EB969FB-74DE95B3&site=ehost-live

Stahl, S. (2009). *The prescriber's guide* (3rd ed.). Cambridge, UK: Cambridge University Press.

Stahl, S. M. (2008a). *Stahl's essential psychopharmacology: Neuroscientific basis and practical applications* (3rd ed.). Cambridge, UK: Cambridge University Press.

Stahl, S. M. (2008b). *Antipsychotics and mood stabilizers: Stahl's essential psychopharmacology*, (3rd ed.). Cambridge, UK: Cambridge University Press.

Sullivan, P. F., Neale, M. C., & Kendler, K. S. (2000). Genetic epidemiology of major depression: Review and meta-analysis. *Am J Psychiatry, 157*(10), 1552–1562. doi:10.1176/appi.ajp.157.10.1552

Szechtman, H., & Woody, E. (2004). Obsessive-compulsive disorder as a disturbance of security motivation. *Psychological Review, 111*(1), 111–127. doi:10.1037/0033-295X.111.1.111

Ursu, S., Stenger, V. A., Shear, M. K., Jones, M. R., & Carter, C. S. (2003). Overactive action monitoring in obsessive-compulsive disorder: Evidence from functional magnetic resonance imaging. *Psychological Science: A Journal Of The American Psychological Society / APS, 14*(4), 347–353.

Villalta-Gil, V., Vilaplana, M., Ochoa, S., Dolz, M., Usall, J., Haro, J. M., et al. (2006). Four symptom dimensions in outpatients with schizophrenia. *Comprehensive Psychiatry, 47*, 384–388.

Walker, E. F., & Diforio, D. (1997). Schizophrenia: A neural diathesis-stress model. *Psychological Review, 104*(4), 667–685.

Wang, P. S., Berglund, P., Olfson, M., Pincus, H. A., Wells, K. B., & Kessler, R. C. (2005). Failure and delay in initial treatment contact after first onset of mental disorders in the National Comorbidity Survey Replication. *Archives of General Psychiatry, 62*(6), 603–613. doi:10.1001/archpsyc.62.6.603

Whitman, B. W., & Packer, R. J. (1993). The photic sneeze reflex: Literature review and discussion. *Neurology, 43*(5), 868–871.

Wiersma, D., Nienhuis, F. J., Slooff, C. J., & Giel, R. (1998). Natural course of schizophrenic disorders: A 15-year follow-up of a Dutch incidence cohort. *Schizophr Bull, 24*(1), 75–85.

Zanarini, M. C. (2000). Childhood experiences associated with the development of borderline personality disorder. *Psychiatric Clinics of North America, 23*(1), 89–101. doi:10.1016/S0193-953X(05)70145-3

World Health Organization. (2009). World health organization mental health surveys. Cambridge, UK: Cambridge University Press.

15 Therapies for Psychological Disorders

Learning Objectives ▼

15.1
- Compare and contrast the roles of psychiatrists, counseling psychologists, and clinical psychologists.
- Discuss the settings used by mental health practitioners.

15.2
- Define psychodynamic therapy.
- Illustrate the techniques used in psychodynamic therapy.
- Compare and contrast traditional psychoanalytic therapy and short-term psychodynamic therapy.

15.3
- Describe the role of genuineness, acceptance, and empathy in client-centered approaches.

15.4
- Explain the ways in which behavioral therapies attempt to change maladaptive associations, discourage maladaptive behaviors, or encourage more adaptive ones.
- Compare and contrast classical conditioning and operant conditioning.

15.5
- Discuss Beck's cognitive therapy and Ellis's rational emotive therapy as they relate to cognitive therapy.

15.6
- Illustrate how family systems therapy focuses on how individuals function in their relationships through communication patterns.

15.7
- Explain the focus on changing physiological problems that lead to psychological conditions in biomedical therapies.
- Compare and contrast the major classes of antidepressant drugs, the major drug treatments for anxiety, and antipsychotic medications.
- Discuss other nondrug medical treatments for psychological conditions.

15.8
- Describe how clinical trials test treatments for psychological conditions.
- Discuss types of research that have provided evidence of the efficacy of treatments for psychological disorders.

I must have looked terrified. There I was, staring out the window at the wing of the airplane, doing my best to interpret the signals and noises around me. I always chose the window seat over the wing. It is the safest part of the airliner, or so I was told, and it had the added benefit of being a front-row seat to all the commotion on the ever-wobbling wings. Every sound, every noise, every bump was a prelude to disaster—or so I imagined. This time was going to be different. In the palm of my hand was the miracle pill that would rescue me from my anxiety. I had recently received a prescription for a medication to help me with my phobia of flying.

Even as a psychology student, I always thought "fear of flying" was an odd term. It really was not the flying that scared me—it was the potential to suddenly *not* be flying that was the problem. On the plane, my brain would go into overtime analyzing hints of possible problems. I would scrutinize the flight attendants' faces for any sign of nervousness, analyze the whirr and flailing of little flaps on the wing as they went up and down, and usually could convince myself, briefly, that it was some sort of visual warning to the other planes to stay way. My anxiety usually got the best of me.

I took the pill wondering how in the world something so small could help with such great anxiety. I expected it to make me feel dopey or sleepy like Xanax or Valium might. But it did not. In fact, it did not do anything at all. The next moment, as the engine started, I noticed that I was searching my body for anxiety. None was there. It was as if my brain had signaled, "cue stomach for anxiety," and my stomach simply refused to obey. Something was different. But would it last?

The **etiology**, or cause, of a disorder informs the disorder's treatment. Tension headaches, for example, are caused by inflammation. Reducing the inflammation with aspirin can be a good treatment. Because there are multiple influences on the creation of psychological conditions, there are many ways to intervene. Treatments can be behavioral, biological, sociocultural, or a mix of all of these. In this chapter, we will describe the professionals who use these techniques as well as many treatments that mental health practitioners employ to help those with psychological conditions. By the end of the chapter, you will have learned how each of these treatments is used, and you may realize that it took more than that one tiny pill to get me through the flight.

Etiology Cause of a disorder.

15.1 Mental Health Practitioners and Settings

There are various kinds of mental health practitioners who help clients in a variety of settings.

- Compare and contrast the roles of psychiatrists, counseling psychologists, and clinical psychologists.
- Discuss the settings used by mental health practitioners.

Generally, when people experience a lot of stress, a significant event, depression, or other symptoms, they employ their own ways of coping. Often things get better. Sometimes they do not. When regular coping mechanisms offer little relief, or a new, objective approach is desired, people often seek professional help. How do people decide to get help? To what settings and what kind of person do they turn?

Naturally, some people are uneasy about seeking treatment the first time. People new to therapy sometimes think that the professional will think they are weak. Others seeking treatment wonder if they will be in therapy forever. These are common and understandable concerns. Unfortunately, such concerns can delay help. The median delay for seeking treatment is about 6 years for bipolar disorder, 8 years for depression, and up to 10 years for panic disorders (Wang et al., 2005). Fortunately, many do seek treatment, and in the United States, about 15% of the population seek mental health treatment, mostly for depression and anxiety (Narrow, Regier, Rae, Manderscheid, & Locke, 1993).

Often people will say that they are going to a therapist, counselor, or a psychotherapist, which could refer to any number of mental health practitioners with various approaches to mental health concerns. There are many kinds of mental health professionals. In this section, we will discuss three: psychiatrists, counseling psychologists, and clinical psychologists.

Psychiatrists

Psychiatry is a branch of medicine that treats mental and behavioral conditions. The first 2 years of medical training focus on the biomedical clinical sciences, followed by training in clinical specialties. Students earn professional doctoral degrees such as doctor of medicine (MD) or doctor of osteopathic medicine (DO). After medical school, those interested in psychiatry practice as psychiatric residents for another 4 years of in-depth training. Psychiatrists spend the majority of their time treating severe psychological conditions and may prescribe psychotropic mediation or order and interpret laboratory tests.

Counseling and Clinical Psychologists

It can be confusing that some psychologists call themselves counseling psychologists while others are known as clinical psychologists. After all, counseling and clinical psychologists often do similar tasks and may even work together. A peek into the history of these two fields reveals their similarities and differences.

Counseling Psychologists

A **counseling psychologist** is a mental health professional who helps people experiencing difficulty adjusting to life stressors to achieve greater well-being. *Counsel* comes from the Latin *consulere*, which means to consult or seek advice. Historically, counseling psychologists delivered occupational advice to help people choose careers best suited to their abilities and interests. Since then, counseling psychologists have expanded their role by providing psychotherapy. Many counseling psychologists focus on everyday people by helping them adjust to changes in their lives.

Clinical Psychologists

Clinical psychologists are mental health practitioners who research, evaluate, and treat psychological conditions. *Clinical* gets its name from Greek *kline*, which means bed, as in recline, since most medical clinical work was done at the bedside. Historically, clinical psychologists have focused on psychopathology. Clinical psychologists began by providing testing services and added psychotherapy, previously practiced only by psychiatrists, to their portfolio.

Clinical psychology training programs vary in their emphasis on the different roles of clinical psychologists. Clinical training programs can be based on a scientist-practitioner model, a practitioner-scholar model, or a clinical researcher model. The **scientist-practitioner model**, also called the Boulder model, is a balanced program in which students learn clinical skills as well as research skills. However, not everyone who is interested in clinical psychology wants to generate new research. Some are interested only in treatment. An alternative model for clinical psychologists is a program that focuses more on treatment than on generating research. This model emphasizes work with clients

Psychiatry A branch of medicine that treats mental and behavioral conditions.

Counseling psychologist A mental health professional who helps people experiencing difficulty adjusting to life stressors to achieve greater well-being.

Clinical psychologist A mental health practitioner who researches, evaluates, and treats psychological conditions.

Scientist-practitioner model Also called the Boulder model, a balanced program in which psychologists learn about clinical skills as well as research skills.

Practitioner-scholar model
Also called the Vail model, a program in which psychologists emphasize clinical training over generating new research in order to understand, synthesize, and apply existing research.

Clinical researcher model A type of psychology program that emphasizes clinical psychology research over direct work with clients.

Psychopharmacology Treatment of psychological conditions using medication.

Mental hospital A medical center that treats psychological conditions.

Outpatient Treatment settings that are outside of a hospital.

and shifts the focus from generating new research to understanding, synthesizing, and applying existing research. The **practitioner-scholar model**, otherwise known as the Vail model, along with a professional doctorate in psychology (doctor of psychology, or PsyD) is well suited for individuals who want to focus on treatment. Still others who are interested in psychology focus on generating new research and less on working directly with clients. Research is the basis of the **clinical researcher model**, a training program that emphasizes clinical psychology research over direct work with clients FIGURE 15-1.

In addition to coursework, doctoral students in psychology undertake 2 to 3 years of supervised training and complete scholarly work such as a dissertation in PhD programs or an extensive literature review in PsyD programs.

Practitioner-scholar model	Scientist-practitioner model	Clinical researcher model
• more clinical work	• balance of clinical work and research	• more research

Clinical ⟵————————————⟶ Research

FIGURE 15-1 Types of psychological training programs.

Recently, some psychologists with advanced training in **psychopharmacology**, treatment of psychological conditions using medication, have been licensed to prescribe medicine. New Mexico granted properly trained psychologists prescriptive authority in 2002, and Louisiana followed by granting medical psychologists prescriptive authority.

Master's-Level Therapists

So far we have discussed mental health practitioners at the doctoral level. However, there are also many mental health practitioners who are trained at the master's level. These include social workers, pastoral counselors, licensed professional counselors, and marriage and family therapists.

Settings for Mental Health Practitioners

Mental health practitioners work in many settings. Some work in modern **mental hospitals**, medical centers that treat psychological conditions. Many more work in **outpatient** settings, which are outside of hospitals.

Mental hospitals have come a long way since their beginning. The first mental hospitals, called asylums, opened in Europe around 850. The Bethlem Royal Hospital in London FIGURE 15-2, for example, was an early mental hospital for those suffering from mental conditions. It also housed the poor and people being punished for crimes. Those hospitalized were sometimes subjected to torture and deprivation. It would not be until the late 1700s when more humane mental hospitals would be built (Porter, 2003).

A psychiatrist's work with clients may include writing prescriptions to treat psychological conditions.

FIGURE 15-2 The first Bethlem Royal Hospital was built in the 14th century. Known as "Bedlam," this was the first hospital specializing in the treatment of psychiatric conditions.

By the mid-19th century, there were many state-funded mental hospitals in the United States. Led in part by Dorothea Dix FIGURE 15-3 and others, the new facilities were established to provide more humane treatment to those suffering from psychological conditions (Gollaher, 1995). By the mid-1950s, however, large state facilities fell into disrepair from lack of funding, which resulted in too many patients and too few well-trained staff members. Mental hospitals again became notorious for poor treatment. In reaction to the poorly funded large hospitals, many patients were discharged from the hospitals and a community-based system was established for those suffering from psychological conditions. Community mental health services include housing with oversight by either full- or part-time mental health professions in assisted-living facilities or half-way houses. **Deinstitutionalization** is the process of replacing inpatient psychiatric care with community outpatient services. While offering more freedom for clients and costing less than care in large hospitals, deinstitutionalization released many people with severe conditions, few work skills, and limited access to the level of care required for their condition. Many former patients became homeless or ended up in prison FIGURE 15-4. The inpatient population plummeted from 555,000 in the mid-1950s to around 70,000 by 2000 FIGURE 15-5 as the imprisoned and homeless populations grew.

Even in the mid-1940s in the United States, patients in mental hospitals were subjected to inadequate conditions.

The Role of Psychotherapy

Psychotherapy, or talk therapy, has probably been around as long as language itself and is often misunderstood. In therapy, many believe, the cure comes from complaining. It is understandable that people who have never been in therapy may be unaware of the therapeutic process or of the variety of procedures used in the different styles of psychotherapy. Theories of personality explain the nature of humans, and, in many cases, offer ways to treat psychological conditions. An understanding of the sources and motivation of behavior leads to therapeutic **insight**, which is central to therapies such as psychodynamic, humanistic, and systems approaches, while it is less important to behavioral and cognitive approaches. Psychotherapies that use insight as part of treatment are referred to as **insight therapies**. In the next sections, we will discuss therapy treatments from five established therapies: psychodynamic, humanistic, behavioral, cognitive, and systems approaches.

Before we begin, a note about terminology: You will recall that there are several different kinds of mental health care practitioners—psychiatrists, clinical psychologists, and counseling psychologists, to name a few. There are also many terms for those who receive services. Some mental health practitioners call the people with whom they work *clients*, some call them *patients*, and others use the term *consumer*. In this chapter, we will use the terms *therapist* and *client* or *patient* as general terms for those who provide and those who receive therapeutic services.

FIGURE 15-3 Dorothea Dix (1802–1887) was a leader in promoting ethical treatment for those in psychiatric hospitals. She was responsible for the founding of dozens of mental institutions in the United States.

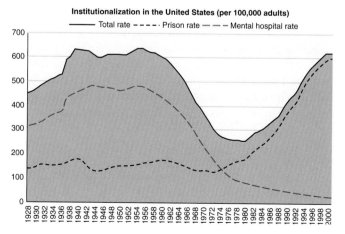

Institutionalization in the United States (per 100,000 adults)

— Total rate - - - · Prison rate — — Mental hospital rate

FIGURE 15-4 As the population in mental hospitals declined through deinstitutionalization, the prison population increased dramatically. *Source: Data from Harcourt, B. E. An institutionalization effect: The impact of mental hospitalization and imprisonment on homicide in the United States, 1934–2001 (March 1, 2007). Journal of Legal Studies, Vol. 40, 2011; University of Chicago Law & Economics, Olin Working Paper No. 335; University of Chicago, Public Law Working Paper No. 155. Available at SSRN: http://ssrn.com/abstract=970341*

Deinstitutionalization The process of replacing inpatient psychiatric care with community outpatient services.

Insight An understanding of the motivation of behavior.

Insight therapies A family of psychotherapies that focus on the unconscious motivations of behavior.

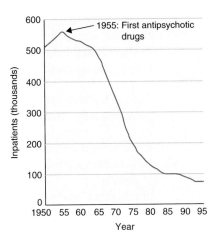

FIGURE 15-5 In 1955 the first antipsychotic medications were in wide use. By 1955, the number of patients in mental hospitals had been reduced remarkably.
Source: Data from Deinstitutionalization—Special Reports\The New Asylums\FRONTLINE\PBS, Out of the shadows: Confronting America's mental illness crisis by E. F. Torrey, M.D. (New York: John Wiley & Sons, 1997).

CONCEPT LEARNING CHECK 15.1   *Comparing the Roles and Settings of Mental Health Practitioners*

1. Compare some of the results, both positive and negative, of deinstitutionalization.

2. Compare and contrast the roles of psychiatrists, counseling psychologists, and clinical psychologists.

Psychodynamic therapies
A family of psychotherapies that have at their core the exploration of intrapsychic conflict and the role of insight to bring about therapeutic change.

15.2 Psychodynamic Therapy

Psychodynamic treatments are based on settling unconscious conflicts that are created in childhood.

- Define psychodynamic therapy.
- Illustrate the techniques used in psychodynamic therapy.
- Compare and contrast traditional psychoanalytic therapy and short-term psychodynamic therapy.

Modern psychotherapy emerged from the personality theories and treatments of Sigmund Freud (1856–1939) FIGURE 15-6. Earlier physicians had relied on other devices and techniques, including hypnosis and even machines designed to rock patients into passivity FIGURE 15-7 to treat psychological conditions. **Psychodynamic therapies** are a family of treatments that have at their core the exploration of unconscious internal conflict. They use insight to bring about therapeutic change.

According to Freud, unresolved unconscious conflicts from childhood cause difficulties in adulthood. These difficulties include unhealthy defense mechanisms, anxiety, and problematic ways of guarding against the wishes of the id. Unhealthy defense mechanisms need to be dismantled because they are not successful at reducing anxiety and they cause problems in everyday life. For example, a person may sabotage healthy relationships because he or she feels unlovable, all at the unconscious level.

In order to be healthy, clients must come to understand their unconscious conflicts and gain the ability to make informed, mature decisions about fears and desires created in the formative childhood years. Insight into these internal workings requires an emotional appreciation and not simply a cognitive understanding. After all, someone can intellectually understand an unconscious conflict but not really appreciate its potentially overwhelming emotional force.

Techniques of Psychodynamic Therapy

Psychodynamic techniques use several tools to help clients bring unconscious conflicts into awareness and gain insight, including interpretation, analysis of dreams, transference, and resistance, as well as free association.

FIGURE 15-6 Dr. Sigmund Freud in 1885.

FIGURE 15-7 The Darwin-Coxe machine was used to swing patients until they were quiet.

In order to explore the unconscious and discover what is causing the symptoms in consciousness, the therapist must find a way to bring unconscious processes into consciousness. Free association is one way to explore the unconscious. **Free association** is a psychodynamic therapy technique that reveals unconscious conflicts by interpreting spontaneous responses to given words. Free association provides evidence about unconscious conflicts that can be interpreted by the therapist.

Evidence of unconscious conflicts can also be revealed through **dream analysis**—the interpretation of dreams. According to the psychodynamic theory of dreams, dreams contain both a surface or **manifest content**, as well as a deeper unconscious or **latent content**. Through therapy, the latent content can be revealed.

A goal of psychodynamic therapy is to bring into awareness problematic intrapsychic conflicts. Awareness allows the client to work through unresolved conflicts in a more adaptive way. Since the conflicts are unconscious, the therapist must take care to reveal them in a way that is useful or helpful to the client. Because the therapist is trained in psychodynamic techniques and is not entangled in the intrapsychic conflicts of the client, the therapist can see patterns in the evidence, or material revealed by the client. Using the material gathered, the therapist may develop an understanding of the landscape of the client's unconscious world. Making carefully timed **interpretations**, or explanations of the client's unconscious motivations, in order to improve psychological functioning is an important part of therapy. Interpretations can help clients to understand their own unconscious worlds.

But the therapist's work is more complex than simply revealing the interpretation. If it is revealed too quickly or in the wrong way, the client may reject it. A client may reject an interpretation no matter how it is revealed. Interpretations, especially controversial ones, can be met with unconscious or conscious **resistance**. Resistance is a client's employment of a defense mechanism during therapy. **Defense mechanisms** are unconscious arrangements that the ego uses to satisfy id instincts indirectly. In fact, the closer to the conflict, the greater the resistance can be. Resistance can show up in subtle ways. Coming late to a session or revealing important information so late in a session that there is little time to actually address it are all examples of resistance because they block the therapeutic process.

Sometimes, unconsciously, clients will act out the kinds of relationships they have in their lives and shift the fears or wishes of past important relationships into the therapeutic relationship. This shift is called **transference**. Analysis of transference provides the therapist with additional material for interpretation. Interpreting transference gives the client insight into his or her relationships. One way the therapist can encourage transference is to be as neutral as possible so that he or she can use the therapeutic relationship itself as a tool to help the client. For example, a few years ago, I needed to rebook a client for a later appointment in the same week. About 2 weeks before the event, I let my client know about the change. He responded angrily, "You are just like my dad. You are never there when I need you." I knew that he was not really upset with me but with his father. The unconscious feelings about being disappointed by

Free association A psychoanalytic therapy technique that reveals intrapsychic conflicts by interpreting spontaneous responses to given words.

Dream analysis A psychoanalytic technique that reveals intrapsychic conflicts through interpretations of dreams.

Manifest content In the psychoanalytic theory, the dream as the dreamer reports it.

Interpretation A psychoanalytic technique in which a therapist will reveal explanations of the client's unconscious motivations in order to improve psychological functioning.

Latent content In the psychoanalytic theory, the true, underlying, undisguised meaning of a dream.

Resistance In psychoanalysis, a client's employment of a defense mechanism during therapy.

Defense mechanism Unconscious arrangements that the ego uses to satisfy id instincts indirectly.

Transference In psychoanalysis, a type of displacement in which the client will unconsciously act out relationships with the therapist.

important people in his life bubbled to the surface, and we had a chance to discuss that in the session.

Types of Psychodynamic Therapy

There are several categories of psychodynamic therapies. We will discuss two: classical psychoanalysis and short-term psychodynamic therapy.

Psychoanalysis

Although not broadly practiced, classical psychoanalysis is performed in much the same way as Freud developed it. Psychoanalytic therapy, or **psychoanalysis**, is based on Freud's traditional approach to psychotherapy. The client lies on a comfortable couch while the therapist sits out of view and encourages free association FIGURE 15-8. This creates a comfortable environment in which free association can take place without the client having to look at the therapist directly. Much like it is easier to tell someone something while looking down, relaxing on a sofa in an inviting environment with only your thoughts is a better environment for psychotherapy, according to the psychoanalytic approach. Psychoanalysis is intense, with hour-long sessions taking place three to five times a week for years. Psychoanalysis is prohibitively expensive and time consuming for most people. However, it does have a track record of helping those with complex psychological conditions (Leichsenring & Rabung, 2008).

The couch of Sigmund Freud.

Psychoanalysis A type of therapy based on Freud's theory of personality.

Short-term psychodynamic therapy A type of solution-focused psychoanalytic treatment.

Short-Term Psychodynamic Therapy

Short-term psychodynamic therapy is a type of solution-focused psychoanalytic treatment rooted in Freud's classical psychoanalysis. The client–therapist relationship is much more casual in short-term psychodynamic therapy. While still exploring intrapsychic dynamics, the therapist and client sit face to face in chairs FIGURE 15-9. Psychodynamic therapy is much more goal oriented, lasting from 12 to 50 weekly sessions. Short-term psychodynamic therapy is more active and directive than psychoanalysis, with the goal of figuring out a client's current problems rather than restructuring his or her personality. Because of its duration, short-term psychodynamic therapy is much more affordable but not necessarily appropriate for in-depth personality change as might be required, for personality disorders, for example (Knekt et al., 2008).

FIGURE 15-8 In classic psychoanalysis, the therapist is out of view of the client.

FIGURE 15-9 In short-term psychodynamic therapy, client and therapist sit face to face in a more casual and goal-oriented approach.

CONCEPT LEARNING CHECK 15.2   *Understanding Psychodynamic Therapies*

1. Psychoanalytic therapy is considered an insight-oriented therapy. What kind of insight does this therapy provide?

2. Compare and contrast traditional psychoanalytic therapy and short-term psychodynamic therapy.

15.3 Humanistic Therapy

Humanistic therapy focuses on the therapeutic environment to release an individual's ability to improve his or her own life.

■ Describe the role of genuineness, acceptance, and empathy in client-centered approaches.

As a personality theory, **humanism** is based on the idea that all humans have an **actualizing tendency**, that is, an instinctual desire to be the best possible version of themselves. As such, therapies based on the humanistic perspective attempt to activate this natural actualizing tendency by fostering self-acceptance and self-awareness. Humanistic therapies do this by encouraging clients to understand and be accountable for their own behavior and use the therapeutic relationship to lead the client toward therapeutic change. For example, **client-centered therapy**, a humanistic psychotherapy based on a nondirective, genuine, and accepting environment, features humanistic therapeutic techniques.

Carl Rogers and Client-Centered Therapy

Carl Rogers FIGURE 15-10 established client-centered therapy based on humanistic personality theory. In nondirective client-centered therapy, the therapist's major role is to clarify and to provide the proper therapeutic environment, working as an equal with the client. Client-centered therapists create the environment for therapeutic change by providing feedback to the client, with minimal advice giving, instruction, or interpretation. An important part of client-centered therapy is **active listening**, a communication method in which the listener responds in ways that demonstrate understanding of what another person says. Using these techniques, the therapist helps clients deeply explore their emotions and approaches to life. The therapeutic relationship leads the client toward personality change. Client-centered approaches are powered by the active ingredients of genuineness, acceptance, and empathy (Rogers, 1989).

Genuineness refers to authenticity in the relationship. In client-centered therapy, the therapist is encouraged to behave in exactly the way she or he feels, revealing his or her inner experiences to the client. In that way, client-centered therapy encourages therapists to be transparent in their relationships with their clients. In order to be genuine, the therapist is encouraged to focus more on the "here and now" rather than past experience (the "there and then"). As clients sense genuineness in the therapist, they will offer more genuineness themselves. Genuineness encourages clients to become more aware of their experiences and to become better able to know and express what is going on in the moment. Instead of recalling and discussing past feelings, humanistic therapies explore emotions in real time as they occur.

Acceptance, or communication of respect, is also important for client-centered therapy. Rogers suggests that the client is more likely to be able to change if the therapist grants the client the respect that all humans should receive. This respect should be communicated as **unconditional positive regard**, or a sense of respect and love that is not linked to specific behaviors and does not have to be earned. Respect from the therapist will increase self-respect and self-acceptance in the client and, according to Rogers, lead to greater self-understanding.

Empathy refers to the therapist's attempt to understand the client's inner world. The client-centered approach is rooted in the idea of phenomenology, which emphasizes each individual's unique perspective. **Phenomenology** is the idea that in order to understand someone, it is important to understand what it feels like to be that person and to see the world from his or her perspective.

By exposing clients to an atmosphere of genuineness, acceptance, and empathy, the therapeutic environment helps clients to understand hidden aspects of themselves, relate more directly to others, better tolerate the nuances of situations, and emphasize conscious over unconscious processes. The relationship encourages clients to focus on growth and to appreciate and be accountable for their own behavior.

Humanism A theoretical orientation that emphasizes growth, potential, and self-actualization.

Actualizing tendency According to the humanists, the instinctual desire to be the best version of yourself possible.

Client-centered therapy A humanistic psychotherapy based on a nondirective, genuine, and accepting environment.

Active listening A communication method in which the listener responds in ways that demonstrate understanding of what another person says.

Genuineness According to the client-centered approach, authenticity in a relationship.

Acceptance Communication of respect.

Unconditional positive regard According to Rogers, a sense of respect and love that is not linked to specific behaviors.

Empathy An attempt to understand the client's inner world.

Phenomenology The idea that, in order to understand a person, it is important to understand the world from that person's perspective; also known as phenomenological approach.

FIGURE 15-10 Dr. Carl Rogers.

Many therapies have been influenced by client-centered approaches, including positive psychotherapy, which helps clients recognize strengths and relish positive experiences (Joseph & Linley, 2006). Positive psychotherapy is an applied version of **positive psychology**, a branch of psychology that studies human strengths.

CONCEPT LEARNING CHECK 15.3   *Describing the Elements of Humanistic Therapy*

1. Humanistic therapists seem to focus more on the therapeutic environment than the actual psychotherapy. Why do you suppose the client-centered approach focuses so much on the environment?

Positive psychology
A branch of psychology that studies human strengths.

Behavior therapy A family of therapies that use learning theory to change behavior.

Symptom substitution
The emergence of a replacement symptom of a psychological condition if the root cause is not resolved.

Social skills training
A type of behavior therapy intended to improve interaction with others.

Classical conditioning
Learning in which a neutral stimulus becomes associated with an unlearned stimulus and the response it automatically elicits.

Counterconditioning
A behavioral technique in which a response to a stimulus is replaced by a new response.

Bell-and-pad treatment
A classical conditioning treatment used to treat nighttime bedwetting.

15.4 Behavior Therapy

Behavioral therapies attempt to modify clients' maladaptive actions.

- Explain the ways in which behavioral therapies attempt to change maladaptive associations, discourage maladaptive behaviors, or encourage more adaptive ones.
- Compare and contrast classical conditioning and operant conditioning.

Behavior therapies use learning theory to change behavior. Behavior therapies for psychological conditions assume that psychological disorders are the result of maladaptive behavior patterns: Change the behaviors and you can change the emotions, too. Behavioral therapists question the role of insight in producing change. Symptoms, behavioral therapists believe, are not a sign of the problem—they are the only problem. On the other hand, insight-oriented therapists believe that if you just get rid of a symptom, it will return in another way, in what is called **symptom substitution**. Symptom substitution is like a game of whack-a-mole, with new symptoms emerging if the root cause of the condition is not found. Behaviorists disagree, arguing that knowing why you do something does not necessarily stop the behavior. Knowing that you should not eat three cupcakes a day might not stop you from doing it. So behavior therapies focus on current symptoms by discouraging maladaptive behaviors and encouraging constructive ones.

Sometimes behavior therapy will treat a specific sign related to the complaint. Lack of social skills, for example, can lead to nervousness and, in extreme cases, social isolation. Since social skills are attained through learning, according to behaviorists, behavior therapy uses social skills training to increase social ease. **Social skills training** is a type of behavior therapy intended to improve interaction with others, and it has been used to treat many issues, including social anxiety (Spence, Donovan, & Brechman-Toussaint, 2000) and autism (Leaf, Dotson, Oppenheim-Leaf, Sherman, & Sheldon, 2011).

More often, behavioral therapies are used as a way to change associations, discourage maladaptive behaviors, or encourage more adaptive ones. Behavioral therapists use classical conditioning and operant conditioning techniques to achieve therapeutic change.

Classical Conditioning Techniques

Classical conditioning focuses on the basic physiological responses to various experiences, also known as stimuli. Classical conditioning is a type of associative learning in which two things are paired together. Sometimes people make maladaptive or accidental associations that lead to problematic behaviors or reactions. Behavioral therapists attempt to decouple these associations by using **counterconditioning**, a behavioral technique in which a response to a stimulus is replaced by a new response. Classical conditioning techniques attempt to extinguish behaviors in various ways. The **bell-and-pad treatment** FIGURE 15-11 is a classical conditioning treatment used to treat nighttime bedwetting. A moisture sensor in the bed (pad) is activated by bedwetting. When the moisture sensor is activated, an alarm (bell) awakens the person. An association of relaxation of the bladder with waking up prevents bedwetting. Having a full bladder (a conditioned stimulus) triggers waking up (a conditioned response) since the sensation has been linked to the bell that would awaken you FIGURE 15-12. Bell-and-pad treatments have been shown to be very effective, with few people needing additional treatments (Gim, Lillystone, & Caldwell, 2009).

The bell-and-pad treatment can be an effective behavioral treatment for bedwetting.

FIGURE 15-11 A bell-and-pad device uses classical conditioning techniques as a treatment for bedwetting.

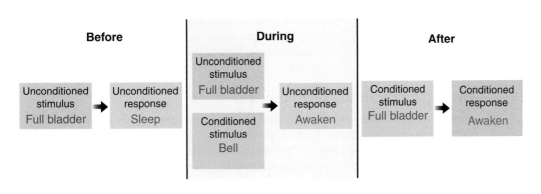

FIGURE 15-12 Classical conditioning helps to associate a full bladder with waking up.

Anxiety can be countered by using relaxation as a substitute. Since anxiety is produced by the sympathetic nervous system, which prepares the body to fight, flee, or freeze, and relaxation by the parasympathetic nervous system that conserves the bodily functions and energy, these two states cannot exist at the same time. Mary Cover Jones (1924) developed **exposure therapy**. This behavior therapy technique involves repeatedly presenting the client with a distressing object in order to reduce anxiety. Repetitive exposure leads to less anxiety and reduces the fear response over time (Deacon & Abramowitz, 2004). A common type of exposure therapy is **systematic desensitization**, in which a client practices relaxation while facing progressively more fear-inducing stimuli.

Systematic desensitization has three components:

1. Constructing a hierarchy of fears such as the one in **TABLE 15-1**

2. Training the client in progressive relaxation

3. Alternately exposing the client through the fear hierarchy and relaxing until the fear response is extinguished so that it no longer occurs.

Exposure therapies, including systematic desensitization, can be done **en vivo**, meaning actual exposure to the thing that causes anxiety; using imagination, in which the person will create a mental image of the feared object; or by using computers, as

Exposure therapy A behavior therapy technique that involves repeatedly presenting the client with a distressing object in order to reduce anxiety.

Systematic desensitization Treatment for phobia in which a client practices relaxation during progressively more fear-inducing stimuli.

En vivo A type of exposure therapy in which the actual feared object is used.

TABLE 15-1 Hierarchy of Fears for Flying

Anticipated Distress Level	Description
100	Strapping yourself into the airplane seat
90	Finding your seat on the airplane
80	Boarding the airplane
70	Waiting at the gate for your flight
60	Finding your gate
50	Arriving at the airport

FIGURE 15-13 Virtual reality exposure therapy is a form of behavior therapy in which the soldier is subjected to simulations of the event that caused the PTSD symptoms.

in virtual reality exposure therapy FIGURE 15-13. **Virtual reality exposure therapy** is a behavior therapy technique involving the repetitive presentation of a simulated distressing object or situation in order to reduce anxiety. Virtual reality therapy has been used for posttraumatic stress disorder and for flight anxiety (Krijn, Emmelkamp, Olafsson, & Biemond, 2004).

Aversive conditioning involves pairing an unpleasant stimulus with an undesired behavior in order to reduce the target behavior. Painting an unpleasant-tasting liquid on the fingernails of people who bite their nails to reduce the nail biting, for example (Vargas & Adesso, 1976), is using aversive conditioning. Although aversive conditioning has been shown to be beneficial in the short run, its use has been limited because of the availability of more effective treatments such as operant conditioning techniques (Nakatani et al., 2009).

Operant Conditioning Techniques

Operant conditioning involves training emitted behaviors to make them more likely to occur again. Techniques seek to increase the occurrence of certain behaviors and reduce the occurrence of others. Operant techniques include positive reinforcement, or a consequence that creates a pleasant state, making behavior more likely to occur again, of adaptive behaviors and nonreinforcement and sometimes punishment of behaviors that are maladaptive, or undesired. Often, desired or adaptive behaviors are encouraged through **shaping**, in which a part of a behavior is reinforced initially, and then increasing the goal to more complex behaviors later on. Sometimes what is called a token economy is used for reinforcement. In this type of behavior therapy, involving positive reinforcement of specific behaviors, tokens or points can be swapped for privileges or other reinforcements.

Painting a bad-tasting liquid on the fingernails can be an example of aversive conditioning.

CONCEPT LEARNING CHECK 15.4   *Designing a Behavioral Treatment Plan*

1. Create a systematic desensitization behavioral treatment plan for a person who has a fear of flying.

15.5 Cognitive Therapies

Cognitive therapies attempt to modify clients' maladaptive thoughts.

■ Discuss Beck's cognitive therapy and Ellis's rational emotive therapy as they relate to cognitive therapy.

Cognitive and rational emotive therapists may ask clients to fill out forms in order to analyze their thoughts.

Cognitive therapy is a type of treatment emphasizing the link between thoughts and emotions. Cognitive therapies suggest that thoughts are the etiology, or cause, of psychological conditions. The goal of cognitive therapy is to understand these maladaptive thinking patterns and develop healthier ways of thinking: change the way you think and you can change the way you feel. While this may sound like using the power of positive thinking, it is not the same thing. Therapists use specific techniques to recognize patterns of maladaptive thoughts and apply intervention strategies to reshape ways of thinking. The two most common types of cognitive therapy are Beck's cognitive therapy and Ellis's rational emotive therapy.

Aaron Beck and Cognitive Therapy

Aaron Beck, who was trained as a psychoanalyst, noticed that his clients' language changed over the course of therapy (Beck, Rush, Shaw, & Emery, 1987). Reflecting on this observation, he wondered if a therapist could change clients' thoughts more directly using language. As in all forms of cognitive therapy, the basis of Beck's model is that psychological conditions, like depression, result from thoughts. People who are depressed tend to have a pessimistic explanatory style, and when bad things occur, they tend to blame themselves. They are also more likely to discount positive events (Beck et al., 1987). In therapy, the goal is to identify any negative self-talk and examine it fully. Rather than just thinking positively, the therapist encourages clients to notice and test their maladaptive or distorted beliefs through questioning techniques and homework. Cognitive behavior therapy is a type of treatment that emphasizes the link between thoughts, emotions, and behavior. In therapy, a cognitive therapist will give clients tools that can help them address distortions in their thinking. **TABLE 15-2** gives examples of common cognitive distortions.

TABLE 15-2 Examples of Maladaptive Beliefs in Cognitive Therapy

All or nothing thinking	Seeing things in inflexible extremes such as good or bad
Overgeneralization	Seeing one negative event as an ongoing pattern
Disqualifying the positive	Filtering out the positive aspects of a situation
Jumping to conclusions	Assuming something negative without enough evidence
Magnification or minimization	Amplifying the significance of something negative or lessening the significance of something positive
Emotional reasoning	An assumption that negative emotions mean that negative things are really happening
Labeling	Instead of describing a mistake you negatively brand yourself as "loser" or an "idiot"

Virtual reality exposure therapy A behavioral therapy technique that involves the repetitive presentation of a simulated distressing object or situation in order to reduce anxiety.

Aversive conditioning A behavioral technique that pairs an unpleasant stimulus with an undesired behavior in order to reduce the target behavior.

Shaping Reinforcing part of a behavior initially and then increasing the goal to more complex behaviors.

Cognitive therapy A type of treatment that emphasizes the link between thoughts and emotions; also known as cognitive behavior therapy.

Rational emotive therapy A type of active and directive therapy that emphasizes the link between thoughts and emotions.

Albert Ellis and Rational Emotive Therapy

Like Beck, Albert Ellis was also trained as a psychoanalyst, but Ellis's approach to cognitive therapy is different from Beck's. Ellis's **rational emotive therapy** is a type of active and directive therapy that emphasizes the link between thoughts and emotions.

Ellis rejected the notion that the past is important to a person's current condition. In fact, he believed that you affect your future more than the past affects you. Your current problems are based on the idea that you teach yourself false notions of yourself, the world, or other people over and over again (Ellis, 2001). How do we do this? Ellis says that we use self-talk to focus on irrational or unrealistic expectations, leading to unwanted feelings. Statements like "I am worthless" are illogical overgeneralizations associated with anxiety and depression. Ellis also emphasizes the importance of action. Like cognitive therapy, rational emotive therapy involves homework in which clients practice their new ways of thinking.

CONCEPT LEARNING CHECK 15.5   *Comparing Cognitive Therapies*

1. Compare and contrast the cognitive therapy approaches of Aaron Beck and Albert Ellis.

Family and couples therapy attempt to change the way that individuals in a group relate to one another.

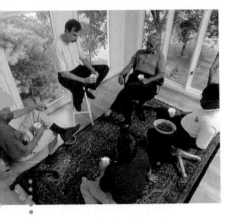

Both therapy and support groups treat clients in a collective setting.

15.6 Family Systems and Group Therapy

Family systems and group therapy focus on how individuals function in their relationships to evaluate and improve communication and interpersonal connections.

■ Illustrate how family systems therapy focuses on how individuals function in their relationships through communication patterns.

Some psychotherapies focus on the individual in treatment. Other therapies take into account the relationships that people have in their lives. For example, family systems and group therapy approaches both recognize the influence of other people in an individual's life.

Systems Approaches

Family therapy is a type of psychotherapy that treats the immediate social system, the family, to improve individuals' psychological functioning. Family therapy, also known as family system therapy or couples therapy, is an approach to psychotherapy that attempts to change the way individuals in a group (such as a family or couple) relate to each other (Becvar, 1998). Systems approaches emphasize the importance of relationships.

No psychological condition is an individual issue, according to this approach. Systems approaches suggest that even when an individual has a psychological condition, something in his or her system is involved in establishing, maintaining, or exacerbating the current psychological state. Systems therapists recognize this and use the system as an important intervention point in treatment. Families, couples, and friends may participate in the therapy session. Systems approaches also note that people will often play roles in certain social structures, such as being first born in a family.

The systems approach is **eclectic**, meaning it integrates a broad range of intervention strategies and therapies, including psychodynamic, humanistic, behavioral, and cognitive ones. Systems approaches also utilize communication skills training and relationship education in an effort to open up the lines of communication. Rather than examining intrapsychic conflicts or assigning blame in the system, the intervention focuses on patterns of communication, exploring the ways of communication within the system. Sometimes the intervention involves examining intergenerational patterns, using **genograms** or family trees to understand common roles that people play in the system.

Group Therapy

Group therapy can use some of the same intervention techniques as family systems approaches, except the clients in the group have similar concerns. **Group therapy** is a technique that treats multiple clients in a collective setting, often under the direction of one or several therapists (Yalom & Leszcz, 2005). One type of group therapy is the **support group**, in which members meet without a therapist to provide social support for each other.

Group therapy has both strengths and weaknesses. It is much less expensive than individual therapy since the members share the cost of the therapist. In addition, the group experience can reveal patterns of problematic relationships that may not show themselves in individual settings. However, while members of the group do save money because they share therapist, they compete for the therapist's time. Confidentiality is harder to control in group settings as well. Groups are helpful for some concerns but not appropriate for all conditions.

Primary Theoretical Orientations for Psychologists

Eclectic (36%)	Psychodynamic (29%)	Cognitive behavioral (19%)	Other (10%)	Humanistic (6%)	Family systems (3%)

Primary theoretical orientations for psychologists.
Source: Adapted from Norcross, J. C., Hedges, M., & Castle, P. H. (2002). Psychologists conducting psychotherapy in 2001: A study of the Division 29 membership. Psychotherapy: Theory, Research, Practice, Training, 39(1), 97–102. doi:10.1037/0033-3204.39.1.97

1. The systems approach is eclectic, meaning it integrates a broad range of intervention strategies, including psychodynamic, humanistic, behavioral and cognitive ones. Illustrate how a group therapy approach can be combined with a humanistic approach.

15.7 Biomedical Therapies

Biomedical therapies focus on changing physiological problems that lead to psychological conditions using drug treatments as well as surgical interventions.

- Explain the focus on changing physiological problems that lead to psychological conditions in biomedical therapies.
- Compare and contrast the major classes of antidepressant drugs, the major drug treatments for anxiety, and antipsychotic medications.
- Discuss other nondrug medical treatments for psychological conditions.

Psychotherapy is not the only technique used to help with psychological conditions. **Biomedical therapies** are a family of therapies that use surgery, medication, or other physiological interventions for the treatment of psychological conditions. In this section, we will focus on drug treatments, including medications for depression, bipolar and anxiety disorders, and psychosis; as well as more invasive medical procedures such as electroconvulsive therapy, transcranial magnetic stimulation, and deep brain stimulation.

Drug Treatments

Psychotropic medications are drugs used to treat psychological conditions. Most biomedical therapies are pharmaceutical or drug treatments. **Psychopharmacologists** are researchers and practitioners who study and often prescribe psychiatric medications. Psychopharmacologists include physicians, nurse practitioners, doctors of nursing practice, pharmacists, medical psychologists, and prescribing psychologists with extensive knowledge of medicines that treat psychological conditions. Psychopharmacologists assume that psychological conditions are, in part, the result of physiological problems, including neurotransmitter abnormalities. Neurotransmitters are chemical messengers that transmit information from one neuron to another. Drug treatments have reduced patients' hospitalizations and relieved their suffering from the symptoms of psychological disorders.

All prescription medications undergo extensive review in the United States by the Food and Drug Administration (FDA). In order for a medication to be approved for use, its developers have to provide evidence that the medication is both safe and effective. "Safe" does not mean that the medication is without risk. In general, a medication is considered "safe" if the benefits of the medicine outweigh the risks. For example, some medications have significant or dangerous adverse effects such as nausea or seizures. Similarly, "effective" does not mean that the medication cures or removes all symptoms of the condition. A medication is considered "effective" if the medication's treatment effects outperform a placebo, a substance without an active ingredient. In fact, many placebos can have treatment effects as well as side effects. When a placebo helps a condition, it is considered to be a **placebo effect**, a treatment result in response to a physiologically ineffective treatment. People have reported side effects such as nausea, sweating, rash, and fever, while using placebos (Hróbjartsson & Norup, 2003).

After a medication has been approved by the FDA to be used as a treatment for a condition, the developer of the medication is granted a patent for the medication. Medicines normally have both a generic name (often related to the molecule or how it works) as well as a brand name that is used in marketing the medication. Brand names are usually written with the first letter capitalized, while the generic name is lowercase. For example, if you have been to the supermarket in search of something to help your headache, you may have chosen Tylenol® (a brand name) or a supermarket version of acetaminophen (generic). Once the patent for the medication runs out, other companies can produce

Family therapy A type of psychotherapy that treats the immediate social system, i.e., the family, to improve individuals' psychological functioning.

Eclectic approach A therapy technique that integrates ideas from several theories.

Genogram Family tree.

Group therapy A psychotherapeutic technique that treats multiple clients in a collective setting.

Support group A type of group therapy in which members meet without a therapist to provide social support.

Biomedical therapies A family of therapies that focuses on surgery, medication, or other physiological interventions for the treatment of psychological conditions.

Psychotropic medication A drug used to treat psychological conditions.

Psychopharmacologists Researchers and practitioners who study and often prescribe psychiatric medications.

Placebo A substance without an active ingredient.

Placebo effect Treatment result in response to a physiologically ineffective treatment.

generic versions of the medication. While these generic medications are usually much less expensive because their manufacturers do not have to recoup any development costs for the medication, they contain the same active ingredients as the brand-name medication. Some brand-name medications also contain inactive ingredients that might help them work better, but in general, generic medications are quite similar to brand-name medications (Howland, 2009).

Antidepressant Drugs

> **Antidepressant medication**
> A type of drug used to reduce the symptoms of depressive mood disorders.

An **antidepressant medication** is a type of drug used to reduce the symptoms of depressive mood disorders. There are dozens of different antidepressants on the market today. They are all designed to affect neurotransmitters, the chemical messengers in the brain. The monoamine hypothesis of depression is the theory that depression is related to problems in a family of neurotransmitters called monoamines (Preston, O'Neal, & Talaga, 2010). The monoamines include serotonin (abbreviated 5-HT), norepinephrine (NE), and dopamine (DA). Some theories suggest that excessive reuptake of monoamines is a problem related to the symptoms of depression. This means that the transport proteins reabsorb the monoamines too aggressively and take too many of the monoamines out of the synaptic gap, leaving too few of the monoamines to bind to the receptor site and deliver the message that the next neuron should fire. Other biomedical theories of depression suggest that neurons are not releasing enough monoamines, so the "fire" message is not delivered as quickly as it should be. Another theory suggests that the enzyme responsible for cleaning up the synaptic gap, monoamine oxidase (MAO), is overactive. Overactive MAO metabolizes, or breaks down, the monoamines too quickly. This leaves too few monoamines available to bind with neurons to deliver the "fire" message. A different theory suggests that the receptor site that receives the neurotransmitter is abnormal in some way and needs extra stimulation in order to send the message to the receiving neuron. In all of these theories, monoamine malfunction results in symptoms of depression.

Whatever the case, increasing the availability or efficiency of monoamines does reduce the symptoms of depression. Two out of three people who are depressed will benefit from antidepressant medications (Gitlin, 2002). While many medications are indicated for treatment of depression, these medications can also be used to treat other conditions. Prozac, for example, is useful in alleviating the symptoms of both depression and anxiety (Stahl, 2008). Because medications can treat more than one condition, medications are categorized into functional classes according to what they do rather than the specific conditions that they treat. Functional classes that have an antidepressant effect include monoamine oxidase inhibitors (MAOIs), selective serotonin reuptake inhibitors (SSRIs), and serotonin-norepinephrine reuptake inhibitors (SNRIs).

Monoamine Oxidase Inhibitors

Some of the oldest medications for use in depression are monoamine oxidase inhibitors, or MAOIs. As the name suggests, MAOIs **TABLE 15-3** work by preventing the enzyme monoamine oxidase from doing its job of metabolizing, or destroying, the family of neurotransmitters known as monoamines: serotonin, norepinephrine, and dopamine (Preston et al., 2010). MAOIs typically take about 4 to 6 weeks to start working and have side effects including dizziness, diarrhea, insomnia, and weight gain (Stahl, 2009). One notable side effect of MAOIs is what some call the "cheese effect," or hypertensive crisis. Because MAO helps to regulate blood pressure, destroying MAO makes it difficult to control blood pressure under certain situations. One of these situations occurs when you ingest tyrine, a naturally occurring substance in many foods **TABLE 15-4** and

A pepperoni pizza can be a problematic choice for those on MAOIs.

TABLE 15-3 Commonly Prescribed Monoamine Oxidase Inhibitors (MAOIs)

phenelzine (Nardil)
tranylcypromine (Parnate)
selegiline (Emsam)

TABLE 15-4 Foods to Avoid with Monoamine Oxidase Inhibitors (MAOIs)

All tap beers	
Matured or aged cheese	
Casseroles made with aged cheeses	
Fermented or dry sausage like pepperoni, salami, or summer sausage	
Improperly stored meat, fish, or poultry	
Fava or broad bean pods	
Soy sauce or other soybean condiments	

Source: Adapted from Gardner, Shulman, Walker, & Tailor (1996).

medicines. Ingesting too much tyrine from, for example, eating pepperoni pizza and taking cough medicine if you are not feeling well can lead to a sudden spike of your blood pressure, giving you a terrible headache or even a stroke. Because many people need to stay on MAOIs for several years, adherence to a tyrine-free diet can be challenging. For this reason, MAOIs are not usually the first medicine that prescribers choose, even though they decrease symptoms in up to 75% of patients with depression (Stein, Kupfer, & Schatzberg, 2005).

Selective Serotonin Reuptake Inhibitors

Another way to keep monoamines in the synaptic gap is to prevent them from being reabsorbed. That is what SSRIs do. **Selective serotonin reuptake inhibitors (SSRIs)** TABLE 15-5 are a class of medications that increase the efficiency of serotonin binding in the nervous system. Like their name suggests, SSRIs work by blocking the reabsorption of the neurotransmitter serotonin to the presynaptic neurons FIGURE 15-14. Doing this causes

Selective serotonin reuptake inhibitor (SSRI) A class of medications that increase the efficiency of serotonin binding in the nervous system.

TABLE 15-5 Commonly Prescribed Selective Serotonin Reuptake Inhibitors (SSRIs)

citalopram (Celexa)
escitalopram (Lexapro)
paroxetine (Paxil)
sertraline (Zoloft)

serotonin to build up in the synaptic gap and increases the likelihood that serotonin will bind with the receptor sites on the postsynaptic neuron. Serotonin is normally removed from the synapse by reuptake sites on the presynaptic neuron. SSRIs block the serotonin reuptake sites, allowing serotonin to remain active in the synapse longer.

FIGURE 15-14 SSRIs are a class of antidepressants used in the treatment of depression and anxiety disorders. They block the reabsorption of serotonin to the presynaptic cell and therefore increase the availability of serotonin in the synapse. Here serotonin is represented as green beads that have been blocked from reentering the presynaptic cell by the SSRI (red), at left.

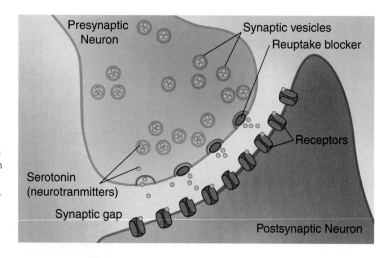

SSRIs are well tolerated, meaning that people do not have as many side effects on SSRIs as they might on other medications. Fewer side effects increases the likelihood that clients who are depressed will take them. In addition, SSRIs are not toxic in overdose and are available as generics, which makes them less expensive than some of the newer drugs. Side effects of SSRIs include high rates of sexual dysfunction, decreased appetite, nausea, diarrhea, insomnia, and headaches.

Vilazodone (Viibryd) is a new SSRI that works on both the presynaptic and post-synaptic neurons. You will recall that the monoamine hypothesis of depression suggests that problems of depression can happen both upstream (on the sending neuron) as well as downstream (on the receiving neuron). Vilazodone targets serotonin by blocking reabsorption (like an SSRI) and by antagonizing, or stimulating, the receiving neuron by pretending to be a type of serotonin. Vilazodone has a lower rate of sexual dysfunction than SSRIs (de Paulis, 2007).

Serotonin-Norepinephrine Reuptake Inhibitors

Some antidepressants work in more than one way. Serotonin-norepinephrine reuptake inhibitors (SNRIs) are medicines used to treat depression that keep both serotonin and nor-epinephrine in the synapse longer **TABLE 15-6**. This gives them the benefits of SSRIs while also treating depression in an additional way by targeting norepinephrine. Unfortunately, SNRIs also have additional side effects, including nervousness, insomnia, and increase in blood pressure (Stahl, 2009).

TABLE 15-6 Commonly Prescribed Serotonin-Norepinephrine Reuptake Inhibitors (SNRIs)

venlafaxine (Effexor)
desvenlafaxine (Pristiq)
duloxetine (Cymbalta)

Some SNRIs offer different kinds of action on serotonin and norepinephrine. Venlafaxine, for example, inhibits the reuptake only of serotonin in low doses, meaning it works just like an SSRI. At moderate doses, venlafaxine inhibits more serotonin and starts to block norepinephrine as well. At high doses, venlafaxine blocks reuptake of serotonin, norepinephrine, and dopamine (Stahl, 2008).

Taking an Antidepressant

When taking an antidepressant, it is important to follow the prescriber's directions very carefully. It is also important not to stop taking the medication, even if you start to feel better. Antidepressants are not taken like you might take an aspirin for a headache. Normally, prescribers will suggest that a person remain on a medication for a few months to a few years (Preston et al., 2010). Many times, when people stop taking the medicine too quickly, they will have headaches and feel dizzy, tired, and irritable. This is because they are experiencing a discontinuation syndrome. It is not that they are hooked on the medicine—antidepressants are not associated with dependency. Taking an antidepressant to treat depression decreases the severity of the depression and reduces the likelihood of a **relapse**, meaning a recurrence of the condition. If a person has had several episodes of depression, the guidelines suggest that it is better to stay on the medication than go on and off the medication. If one antidepressant does not work, your prescriber may recommend trying a different one. Among patients whose depression is not helped by one antidepressant, about 25% improve when their prescriber changes their medication (Rush, 2007).

Antianxiety Drugs

An **antianxiety medication** is a type of drug used to reduce the symptoms of agitation and nervousness. Nervousness and tension are present in a number of different anxiety disorders, including flight anxiety. The most common antianxiety medications are benzodiazepines, SSRIs, and SNRIs.

Benzodiazepines **TABLE 15-7** are the most commonly used antianxiety medications. Sometimes known as tranquilizers, benzodiazepines are fast-acting and effective (Stahl, 2009). While some caution against their use because of the risk that patients will develop **tolerance**, a reduction in a person's sensitivity to a drug over time, others suggest they are not as risky as once believed (Ballenger, 2000).

Benzodiazepines work on the neurotransmitter GABA. **Gamma-aminobutyric acid (GABA)** is an all-purpose inhibitory neurotransmitter. By affecting GABA, benzodiazepines reduce central nervous system arousal, dampening the anxiety response.

In addition to benzodiazepines, SSRIs and SNRIs are also effective antianxiety medications. Just as when they are used for depression, SSRIs and SNRIs take a few weeks to start working and may need to be taken in larger doses than when used as an antidepressant.

You are already familiar with the advantages and disadvantages of using SSRIs and SNRIs, but benzodiazepines present some different challenges. Long-term use of benzodiazepines is associated with both tolerance and **dependence**. In addition, many people report having memory problems and feeling tired and dizzy when they take benzodiazepines.

Mood-Stabilizing Drugs

Mood stabilizers **TABLE 15-8** are a family of medications used to treat the symptoms of bipolar mood disorders. True mood-stabilizing drugs will treat both the manic/hypomanic phase as well as the depressive phase of a bipolar condition (Stahl, 2008a). The gold standard medication to treat bipolar mood disorders is **lithium** (Stahl, 2008a). Unfortunately, lithium is associated with some serious potential side effects. Although it is more like an antimanic medication than a true mood stabilizer, Depakote (divalproex) is more widely prescribed than lithium (Thase & Denko, 2008).

Relapse A recurrence of a condition or disorder.

Antianxiety medication A type of drug used to reduce the symptoms of agitation and nervousness.

Tolerance A reduction in a person's sensitivity to a drug over time.

Gamma-aminobutyric acid (GABA) The nervous system's primary inhibitory neurotransmitter.

Dependence When a person's drug use has led to distress or impairment and unsuccessful efforts to reduce drug use.

Mood stabilizers A family of medications used to treat bipolar mood disorders.

Lithium A medication used to treat bipolar mood disorders.

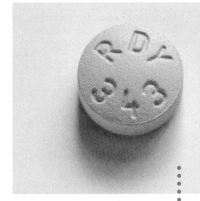

Citalopram (Celexa) is an antidepressant and antianxiety medication which acts as a selective serotonin reuptake inhibitor (SSRI), increasing the amount of the neurotransmitter in the synaptic gap.

TABLE 15-7 Commonly Prescribed Benzodiazepines

alprazolam (Xanax)
diazepam (Valium)

TABLE 15-8 Commonly Prescribed Mood Stabilizers

Lithium
divalproex (Depakote)

Australian medical scientist Dr. John Cade first used lithium as a treatment for psychological conditions in the 1940s. He discovered the treatment almost by mistake after delivering the medicine to a group of mice. He thought that the lithium calmed them, although it actually made them sick. Luckily, the lithium treatment did help his patients, and lithium is an effective treatment (Gim et al., 2009). It does, however, have some limitations. Lithium has a narrow therapeutic window. If lithium levels are too low, the medication will not be helpful, but if they are too high, thyroid and kidney damage can result. Lithium's mechanism of action is on the neurotransmitter glutamate (Grandjean & Aubry, 2009). Glutamate is an all-purpose excitatory neurotransmitter, the "gas" or "accelerator" of the nervous system. By stabilizing glutamate, lithium treats the manic and depressive phases of bipolar disorder. Valproate is helpful for those who do not respond well to lithium (Davis, Bartolucci, & Petty, 2005).

While medicines like lithium combat the symptoms of both mania and depression, other medicines, such as the anticonvulsant lamotrigine (Lamictal), target only manic symptoms. They often need to be combined with an antidepressant for the depressive phase of the condition. Lamotragine helps with rapid cycling (Calabrese et al., 2000). Lamotragine does not have the same side-effect profile as lithium. It has a broader therapeutic window but has its own unwanted side effects, including, in rare cases, a terrible rash (Stahl, 2009).

Antipsychotic Drugs

Antipsychotic medications TABLE 15-9 are a type of drug used to reduce the symptoms of psychosis as seen in schizophrenia. Symptoms of psychosis can include positive symptoms such as **hallucinations**, sensory experiences with no sensory input, and **delusions**—beliefs that most people would think are incredible or impossible. Psychosis can also include deficits of behavior, or **negative symptoms**, such as **anhedonia**, or lack of pleasurable experiences, **avolition**, or lack of will, and **alogia**, or lack of elaborative speech. Antipsychotic medications diminish psychosis in about 70% of patients (Sadock & Sadock, 2010) in just a few weeks (Emsley, Rabinowitz, & Medori, 2006).

The dopamine hypothesis of psychosis suggests that symptoms of psychosis are associated with low amounts of dopamine. Some of the early medications used to treat psychosis targeted this neurotransmitter. By blocking dopamine, they reduced dopamine activity in brain areas in which it was thought to be overactive. Since they were used so regularly, medications such as haloperidol (Haldol) were known as typical antipsychotics. Typical antipsychotics were beneficial at targeting the positive symptoms of psychosis, like hallucinations and delusions. The impact of these drugs on the lives of people experiencing these symptoms is powerful. Many have seen dramatic improvement in just a few weeks of treatment.

Adverse effects of typical antipsychotics include debilitating symptoms such as **tardive dyskinesia**, a neurological condition involving involuntary, repetitive movements caused by typical antipsychotics' effects on dopamine. Tardive dyskinesia is estimated to occur in one in five people who take the typical antipsychotics (Miyamoto, Lieberman,

Antipsychotic medication A type of drug used to reduce the symptoms of thought disorders.

Hallucination Sensory experience with no sensory input.

Delusion A belief that most people would think is incredible or implausible.

Negative symptoms of psychosis Symptoms of psychosis that involve behavior deficits, or expected behaviors that are absent.

Anhedonia A reduced capacity to experience pleasure.

Avolition Lack of will.

Alogia Lack of elaborative speech.

Tardive dyskinesia A neurological condition involving involuntary, repetitive movements.

TABLE 15-9 Commonly Prescribed Antipsychotic Medications

Typical Antipsychotics	Atypical Antipsychotics
haloperidol (Haldol)	risperidone (Risperdal)
	aripiprazole (Abilify)

Fleishhacker, Aoba, & Marder, 2006). While reducing dopamine in places in which its concentration may be too high, typical antipsychotics may also reduce dopamine levels in places in which it is in the normal range, resulting in adverse effects such as tardive dyskinesia. The name of this condition literally means "late to arrive" (like tardy) and "abnormal" (like dysfunction) "movements" (like kinetics), because tardive dyskinesia is associated with abnormal movements like lip smacking, blinking, puckering, and grimacing. Although it can be controlled with medication, the condition is considered permanent.

Another disadvantage of typical antipsychotics is that the treatment effects seem to focus only on the positive symptoms of psychosis. Although those are important symptoms, the negative symptoms of psychosis, including flat affect, avolition, and alogia, also have a great impact on the lives of people who experience them.

More recently, newer medications have been discovered that reduce both the positive and negative symptoms of psychosis. Since these new medications were not the ones normally given, they were called atypical antipsychotics. Atypical antipsychotics (or second-generation antipsychotics) target dopamine as well as other neurotransmitters. Atypical antipsychotic medications, also listed in Table 15-9, are drugs that reduce both the positive and negative symptoms of psychosis. Atypical antipsychotics have an additional benefit of producing lower rates of tardive dyskinesia than typical antipsychotics (Stahl, 2009). Atypical antipsychotics do cause weight gain and higher rates of diabetes than the earlier medications (Stahl, 2009).

Risperdal is a second-generation antipsychotic.

Medical Procedures

Medicines are not the only medical treatment for psychological conditions. Medical treatments also include electroconvulsive therapy and medical devices such as transcranial magnetic stimulation and deep brain stimulation.

Electroconvulsive Therapy

Electroconvulsive therapy (ECT), sometimes referred to as shock therapy, is a biological treatment in which seizures are induced in anesthetized patients FIGURE 15-15. Back in the 1930, Ladislas von Meduna noticed that very few people who had epilepsy also had schizophrenia (Dukakis & Tye, 2007). Von Meduna hypothesized that epilepsy and schizophrenia were not able to exist in the same body. Perhaps, he surmised, seizures were curative of schizophrenia. If schizophrenia and epilepsy are incompatible, maybe seizures could treat psychological conditions. Although von Meduna's hypothesis proved false, the connection he saw between seizures and the absence of schizophrenia led to an effective treatment for the condition.

> **Electroconvulsive therapy (ECT)** A biological treatment in which seizures are induced in anesthetized patients.

When most people think about ECT, they think of a barbaric procedure. ECT procedures in the movies are very different than modern electroconvulsive therapy. Improvements in techniques make it a different kind of intervention than you might think. Around 100,000 people receive ECT annually in the United States. While most often used to treat depression, ECT has been effective for treating mania and catatonia as well (Glass, 2001).

The ECT procedure begins with a patient receiving a muscle relaxant and a general anesthetic so that the patient will be unconscious during the procedure. Then a short burst of electrical current is sent through electrodes placed on one or both sides of the patient's temple. The electrical current creates a seizure that lasts between 30 and 60 seconds. Often 6 to 10 sessions are used to treat depression.

FIGURE 15-15 Patient undergoing ECT in which seizures are electrically induced in anesthetized patients for therapeutic effect.

Unlike antidepressant medications that can often take months to work, ECT relieves symptoms after only a few days. In fact, about 80% of depressed patients who receive ECT improve (Glass, 2001). Unfortunately, ECT has a high relapse rate. About half of people treated with ECT will have a recurrence of their depression within just 6 months (Glass, 2001). Additional ECT treatments or the addition of antidepressants can stave off these new depressive episodes. Side effects include memory loss about the treatment. Research suggests that ECT does not produce any brain damage (Eschweiler et al., 2007).

Despite the benefits of ECT, it is still a rare procedure, prescribed by only 8% of all psychiatrists. Although the side effects are relatively minor, such as memory loss around the time of the procedure, some researchers think the low usage rates of the procedure are due to the misunderstandings and fears that people have about ECT.

How ECT works is still a mystery. Some theories suggest that ECT lowers activity in brain areas that might be involved in depression (Nobler et al., 2001), while others suggest that ECT stimulates **neurogenesis**, or new nerve growth, that may be the source of the symptom relief.

Other Medical Procedures

There are other medical procedures that can help with psychological conditions. **Psychosurgery**, or treatment of mental and behavioral conditions using an invasive biological procedure, has come a long way since early treatments. Previously, medical procedures were limited to drilling holes in the head to release spirits or less specific surgical procedures such as **lobotomy**, a surgery that involves destruction of nerves in the prefrontal cortex in order to improve symptoms of psychological conditions FIGURE 15-16.

FIGURE 15-16 Frontal lobotomies used to be performed to intentionally damage the regions involved in emotion in an attempt to cure or improve individuals with severe aggression. This was performed by drilling holes into the skull. After the holes were drilled, needles were placed into the frontal lobe and rocked back and forth to sever neuronal connections. In this image you can see inactive (dark) regions in the frontal lobe near the top of the image.

One example of newer medical procedures is **transcranial magnetic stimulation (TMS)** FIGURE 15-17. This procedure uses magnetic fields generated by electromagnetic coils to activate or deactivate nerve cells in specific areas of the brain. Depressed moods seem to improve when TMS is applied. TMS has a benefit over ECT in that TMS causes no memory loss or seizures. About 50% of those who have received TMS procedures show an improvement in their symptoms (Schutter, 2009). Another procedure is **deep brain stimulation (DBS)**, in which a small electrode connected to a pulse generator stimulates the overexcited junction between the limbic system and the frontal lobe FIGURE 15-18. In addition, some patients with chronic depression have found relief through a chest implant that stimulates the vagus nerve, which sends signals to the brain's mood related limbic system (Conway et al., 2011).

FIGURE 15-17 Using a high-power magnet, transcranial magnetic stimulation (TMS) excites neurons in the brain, triggering activity.

FIGURE 15-18 Electrodes for deep brain stimulation treatment.

CONCEPT LEARNING CHECK 15.7   *Explaining the Use of Medicines for Psychological Conditions*

1. A friend of yours has just returned from a psychiatrist and is confused. Even though your friend went with a presenting problem of anxiety, the doctor prescribed him Prozac, an antidepressant. Explain why this is not an unusual choice.

15.8 Evaluating Therapies for Psychological Disorders

Researchers use clinical trials to test treatments for psychological conditions and have found psychotherapy to be an effective treatment.

- Describe how clinical trials test treatments for psychological conditions.
- Discuss types of research that have provided evidence of the efficacy of treatments for psychological disorders.

Before we discuss the effectiveness of therapies for psychological conditions, it is important to understand the natural progression of a disorder. Many psychological conditions are self-limiting, meaning they go away all by themselves. This is true for some nonpsychological conditions, too. The average length of the common cold, for example, is about 10 days. In contrast, the average of an episode of major depressive disorder is between 6 months and 2 years (Katon & Schulberg, 1992). After that point, many people experience a **spontaneous remission**, or a reduction of symptoms of a condition even in the absence of treatment. People who are depressed, for example, do not stay depressed in exactly the same way for the rest of their lives. Although some people with psychological conditions do remain impaired for significant amounts of time, there is also a propensity for symptoms to change over time. This change is called **regression toward the mean** and refers to a tendency for those with severe symptoms to move to more moderate symptoms. What is more, many people with psychological conditions experience a placebo effect with treatment. "Placebo effect" refers to a client's response to nontreatment disguised as treatment, such as receiving a sugar pill while being told it is a therapeutic drug. Clients will sometimes improve by being on a waiting list for psychotherapy or even receiving a sugar pill (Kirsch, Moore, Scoboria, & Nicholls, 2002).

Effectiveness of Therapies for Psychological Disorders

How can psychologists and other mental health care practitioners tell if therapy is working? The scientific method is a powerful tool in evaluating the effectiveness of both psychotherapy and biomedical therapies. People who measure the effectiveness of therapies often use a **clinical trial**, which employs the scientific method to test a treatment for a disorder or condition. In a clinical trial meant to test a treatment for depression, for example, researchers ideally would like to study everyone who is depressed. But since that would be impossible, researchers instead use a convenience sample made up of people who volunteer to be part of their study. Then, the researchers randomly assign these participants into two groups—the "treatment" group gets the intervention (a type of psychotherapy or perhaps a drug that is being tested), and the "no treatment" group gets no treatment (they may be assigned to a waiting list for psychotherapy or receive a placebo instead of the drug being tested). Other than receiving or not receiving the intervention being tested, the two groups are treated in exactly the same way. Before the intervention takes place, researchers measure the severity of the participants' conditions. For our depression example, they might use a standard depression survey such as the Beck Depression Inventory (Beck & Aaron, 1988). Then, at regular intervals, they retake the measurements. If the participants' final depression scores were different, the researchers would conclude that the change was due to the administration of the **dependent variable**, which would be receiving the particular therapy. This technique distributes any nontreatment artifacts, such as regression to the mean, spontaneous remission, or the placebo effect, into both groups randomly since all of the participants have an equal chance of getting the intervention.

Often researchers replicate studies like the one described and compare the interventions to other drugs or other therapies. After a while, researchers know a lot about a particular intervention. At that point, researchers can statistically combine the individual studies to get a broad view of the intervention using a meta-analysis. A **meta-analysis** is a statistical technique that pools the results of several research studies so that practitioners can make the best decisions for their clients. **Evidence-based practice** involves selecting therapy treatments using information gained through research. For example, a meta-analysis (Davidson & Parker, 2001) of a sometimes-controversial therapeutic technique, **eye movement desensitization reprocessing (EMDR)**, a therapy technique involving bilateral stimulation in order to process distressing memories, revealed that EMDR is an

Neurogenesis New nerve growth.

Psychosurgery Treatment of mental and behavioral conditions using an invasive biological procedure.

Lobotomy A surgery that involves destruction of nerves in the prefrontal cortex in order to improve symptoms of psychological conditions.

Transcranial magnetic stimulation (TMS) A procedure that uses electromagnetic coils to activate nerve cells in the brain.

Deep brain stimulation (DBS) A surgical treatment in which a medical device is used to send electrical impulses to parts of the nervous system.

Spontaneous remission Reduction of symptoms of a condition in the absence of treatment.

Regression toward the mean The inclination for extreme scores to move toward the average over time.

Clinical trial The use of the scientific method to test a treatment for a disorder or condition.

Dependent variable The measurement collected to determine if there was any effect of the independent variable in an experiment.

Meta-analysis A statistical technique that pools the results of several research studies.

Evidence-based practice Selecting therapy treatments using information gained through research.

Eye movement desensitization reprocessing (EMDR) A therapy technique involving bilateral stimulation in order to process distressing memories.

effective treatment for PTSD, but perhaps not in the way originally thought. Through meta-analysis and subsequent research, it was determined that it was the exposure and not the bilateral stimulation that appeared to be the most important part of the intervention.

Effectiveness of Different Therapies

So what have we discovered through research techniques like clinical trials and meta-analyses? Psychotherapy is effective. Half of all people who enter therapy show improvement by the second month, and by 9 months, three out of four show significant improvement (McNeilly & Howard, 1991). In fact, according to a classic meta-analysis, those in the treatment group show a greater improvement than 80% of those untreated (Smith & Glass, 1977). Treatment effects are good for medication, too, and patients fare even better when the two are combined. What researchers have not found is one therapy that is best for everyone when comparing psychodynamic, humanistic, behavioral, cognitive, or drug treatments (Nathan, Stuart, & Dolan, 2000). Smith and Glass's (1977) meta-analysis of 400 clinical trials showed that no one therapy was best overall. However, there were some winners for particular kinds of conditions: Behavioral and cognitive behavioral therapies were the best treatment for panic disorder and obsessive compulsive disorder, and cognitive behavioral therapy was best for depression TABLE 15-10.

TABLE 15-10 Empirically Supported Therapies for Psychological Conditions

Problem	Strong Research Support*	Modest Research Support**
Bipolar disorder		• Cognitive therapy
Depression	• Cognitive therapy • Behavioral therapy	• Short-term psychodynamic therapy
Generalized anxiety disorder	• Behavioral therapy • Cognitive therapy	
Insomnia	• Cognitive behavioral therapy • Relaxation training	• Biofeedback
Obsessive-compulsive disorder	• Behavioral therapy • Cognitive therapy	
Panic disorder	• Cognitive behavioral therapy	• Relaxation • Psychoanalytic treatment
PTSD	• Exposure therapy • Eye movement desensitization reprocessing	
Schizophrenia	• Social skills training • Cognitive behavioral therapy	
Social phobia	• Cognitive therapy • Behavioral therapy	
Specific phobias	• Exposure therapies	

*Research support for a given treatment is labeled "strong" if criteria are met for what Chambless et al. (1998) termed "well-established" treatments. To meet this standard, well-designed studies conducted by independent investigators must converge to support a treatment's efficacy.

**Research support is labeled "modest" if criteria are met for what Chambless et al. (1998) termed "probably efficacious treatments". To meet this standard, one well-designed study or two or more adequately designed studies must support a treatment's efficacy.

Source: Data from the American Psychological Association, Division 12, Society of Clinical Psychology.

Common Factors That Increase Effectiveness

There appear to be some crosscutting factors related to the effectiveness of psychotherapy treatments. Across all therapy techniques, the better the quality of the therapeutic relationship, the better the outcomes. Similar to what the humanistic psychologists Carl Rogers suggested, genuineness and warmth are important therapeutic characteristics, and they appear to have a treatment effect of their own (Lambert & Barley, 2001). In addition to therapist factors, client factors are important, too. For example, clients' outcomes are better when they have greater access to support in their environments and when they are motivated (Lambert & Barley, 2001).

Culture, Cultural Values, and Psychotherapy

Cultures can vary on the amount of stigma associated with seeking treatments for psychological conditions. The more stigma associated with seeking help, the fewer choices for help, and the less likely those who suffer will look for assistance. Although psychotherapy is relatively accepted in the United States, this is not the case all over the world. China, for example, has relatively few therapists that are as extensively trained as those in the United States (Gao et al., 2010).

Psychotherapy treatments also reflect the values of a particular culture. Cultures that place an emphasis on interreliance rather than self-reliance, or **collectivist cultures**, for example, often discourage public emotional displays and focusing on the self too much (Lee, 2006). Other cultures place an emphasis on the family, and sharing problems outside of the family is discouraged (La Roche & Maxie, 2003). A focus away from the self can run counter to many insight-oriented therapies, such as self-exploration, emotional expression, and self-disclosure.

Collectivist culture A culture that places an emphasis on interreliance rather than self-reliance.

Understanding cultural nuances can be important in psychotherapy. Professional associations such as the American Psychological Association, the Association for Psychological Science, the American Psychiatric Association, and many state psychological licensing boards require training in cultural differences that could potentially influence the therapeutic relationship and emphasize awareness of the influences and challenges that are faced. Despite additional training, some clients prefer therapists who are culturally similar to them (Sanchez & Atkinson, 1983).

CRITICAL THINKING APPLICATION

Treatments for psychological conditions can be effective in relieving stress and helping those with psychological disorders. Professional organizations, client advocate groups, and government agencies all give advice about how to choose a therapist. This information is subject to bias toward the particular group, so sorting through the information can be confusing to those unfamiliar with psychology. Finding the right therapist and therapy is important, and those seeking help should be encouraged to ask questions and to find the best person and treatment for them.

Using the Internet, search the websites of agencies such as the American Psychiatric Association, PsychCentral, and the American Psychological Association, construct a guide for a person seeking therapy. In your guide, be sure to fold in information about the cross-cutting themes of effective therapies that are mentioned in this chapter. Your guide should encourage those seeking therapy to ask direct questions about how long the therapists have been seeing clients, their areas of expertise, the types of treatments they use, and what licenses they hold. In addition, it is important to talk about finances, fees, and if health insurance is accepted.

It will also be important to note in your guide that there are licensing boards to report a therapist if you feel the therapist is engaging in unethical behavior. A person can stop treatment with a psychotherapist at any time.

Summary of Multiple Influences on Therapies for Psychological Disorders

Ideally, psychological conditions are treated on multiple levels as seen in FIGURE 15-19. For example, many research studies have shown that depression responds better when treated with both medication and psychotherapy (Zuckerbrot, 2007). Two are better than one alone. It results in a faster recovery and a lower chance of relapse than when the depression is treated with only one intervention.

For example, cognitive therapy with a systems approach might examine family dynamics that have contributed to the problem. Learned behaviors may intersect with

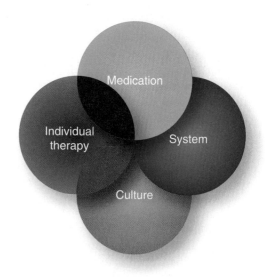

FIGURE 15-19 Interventions for psychological conditions can occur on multiple levels.

the larger social environment. Some psychologists are examining large-scale interventions that target the social issues that may set the stage for psychological conditions or may prevent those suffering from seeking treatment. In fact, many college residence halls focus on prevention in this way. Targeting society may well be the best way to attack psychological conditions, since it will allow a psychological condition to be targeted on many levels.

The medicine I took for my flight quelled my anxiety for the first few hours. Ultimately, my nearly 6,000-mile flight from Chicago to Istanbul, Turkey, meant that a behavioral exposure technique for my anxiety would also be at work due to the length of the flight. I landed exhausted but relaxed, jetlagged, and with a huge reduction of my fear of flying. To this day, I am still not convinced that it was the medication that got rid of my flight anxiety. There were probably multiple influences on my treatment. Sure, the medicine helped biologically by reducing my central nervous system activity, but I also realized that I may have had an unconscious worry about not being in control (psychodynamic). I had to trust what I felt would be best for me to take care of myself in that situation (humanistic) and even question my irrational thoughts and fears (cognitive) while I listened to relaxing music, although I was feeling frightened (behavioral). Ultimately, there were multiple influences on my treatment of my flight anxiety. I fly all the time now with only the slightest hint of anxiety, but I still prefer the window seat.

CONCEPT LEARNING CHECK 15.8 | *Summarizing the Factors of Effective Psychotherapy*

1. Summarize some of the crosscutting factors thought to increase likelihood of effective psychotherapy.

Visual Overview

Visual Overview · Common Medications Used to Treat Psychological Disorders

Those who prescribe medication to treat psychological conditions choose from a number of medicines. This overview summarizes the common classes of psychotropic medications, the conditions they treat, as well as examples of each class of medicine.

Rx Patient _____ Date _____

MAOI (Monoamine Oxidase Inhibitors)

Uses include treatments for major depressive disorder

Examples include:
phenelzine (Nardil)
tranylcypromine (Parnate)
emsam (Selegiline)

Rx Patient _____ Date _____

Lithium

Uses include treatments for both mania and depression in bipolar disorder

Rx Patient _____ Date _____

Benzodiazepines

Uses include treatments for anxiety disorders

Examples include:
diazepam (Valium)
alprazolam (Xanax)

Rx Patient _____ Date _____

SNRI (Serotonin Norepinephrine Reuptake Inhibitors)

Uses include treatments for mood disorders like depression, anxiety disorders like generalized anxiety disorder

Examples include:
venlafaxine (Effexor)
duloxetine (Cymbalta)
desvenlafaxine (Pristiq)

Rx Patient _____ Date _____

Anticonvulsants

Uses include treatments for the manic phase of bipolar disorder.

Examples include:
lamotrigine (Lamictal)

Rx Patient _____ Date _____

Antipsychotics

Uses include treatments for psychotic disorders like schizophrenia. Some antipsychotics are used to boost the effectiveness of an SSRI in the treatment of depression.

Examples include:
Typical antipsychotic:
haloperidol (Haldol)

Atypical antipsychotics:
risperdal (Risperidone)
aripiprazole (Abilify)

Signature _____
Federal I. D. Control Number _____

_____, M.D.

Rx Patient _____ Date _____

SSRI (Selective Serotonin Reuptake Inhibitors)

Uses include treatments for mood disorders like major depressive disorder, anxiety disorders like PTSD

Examples include:
citalopram (Celexa)
escitalopram (Lexapro)
paroxetine (Paxil)
sertraline (Zoloft)
vilazodone (Viibryd)

_____, M.D.

_____ ature _____
_____ I. D. Control Number _____

_____, M.D.

Signature _____
Federal I. D. Control Number _____

15.1 Mental Health Practitioners and Settings

- Despite effective treatment, many people wait years to get help for psychological conditions.
- There are a number of mental health practitioners with various approaches to mental health concerns.
- Psychiatrists are medical doctors with a clinical specialty in treating psychological conditions.

- Clinical and counseling psychologists both study and treat individuals with psychological concerns.
- Although much improved, historically, mental hospitals have had a stormy history in providing adequate care for those in need of psychological treatment.

15.2 Psychodynamic Therapy

- Modern psychodynamic therapy emerged out of the personality theories and treatments of Sigmund Freud.
- Psychodynamic treatments are based on settling unconscious conflicts that are created in childhood.
- Psychodynamic therapists use many tools, including free association, dream analysis,

carefully timed interpretations and analysis of transference, and resistance for treatments.
- There are several types of psychodynamic therapies, including classical psychoanalysis and short-term psychodynamic therapy.

15.3 Humanistic Therapy

- Humanistic therapy is based on the idea that all humans have an actualizing tendency.
- Carl Rogers pioneered client-centered therapy based on humanistic personality theory.

- Client-centered therapists create the proper conditions so that therapeutic change will occur in their clients.
- Client-centered approaches are powered by genuineness, acceptance, and empathy.

15.4 Behavior Therapy

- Behavior therapies for psychological conditions are based on the assumption that psychological disorders are the result of maladaptive behavior patterns.
- Behavioral therapies attempt to change maladaptive associations, discourage maladaptive behaviors, or encourage more adaptive ones.
- Behavioral therapies use classical conditioning techniques to decouple

problematic associations using counterconditioning techniques to attempt to extinguish the behaviors.
- Classical conditioning techniques include exposure therapies, aversive conditioning, and systematic desensitization.
- Operant conditioning techniques attempt to increase the occurrence of behaviors and reduce the occurrence of others using positive reinforcement.

15.5 Cognitive Therapies

- Cognitive therapies suggest that the causes of psychological conditions are the results of maladaptive thoughts.
- Cognitive therapists use various techniques to recognize patterns of maladaptive thinking and construct

intervention strategies to reshape ways of thinking.
- The two most common types of cognitive therapy are Beck's cognitive therapy and Ellis's rational emotive therapy.

15.6 Family Systems and Group Therapy

- Family systems therapy focuses on how individuals function in their relationships.

- The focus of interventions for systems approaches is on communication patterns.

15.7 Biomedical Therapies

- Biomedical therapies focus on changing physiological problems that lead to psychological conditions using drug treatments as well as surgical interventions.

- Most antidepressants are constructed by the monoamine hypothesis of depression, suggesting that depression is related to problems in a family of neurotransmitters that includes serotonin, norepinephrine, and dopamine.

- Monoamine oxidase inhibitors (MAOIs) work by preventing the enzyme monoamine oxidase from metabolizing the neurotransmitters serotonin, norepinephrine, and dopamine in the synaptic gap.

- Selective serotonin reuptake inhibitors (SSRIs) increase the efficiency of serotonin by blocking the reabsorption of the neurotransmitter serotonin into the presynaptic neurons.

- Serotonin-norepinephrine reuptake inhibitors (SNRIs) are medicines that keep both serotonin and norepinephrine in the synapse longer.

- Antianxiety medications reduce the symptoms of agitation and nervousness.

- Benzodiazepines work by affecting gamma-aminobutyric acid (GABA) in the nervous system.

- Mood stabilizers are a family of medications used to treat bipolar mood disorders.

- Lithium is a medication that will stabilize the manic and depressive phases of bipolar disorder.

- Anticonvulsants such as lamotrigine and valproate are helpful antimanic medications for those who do not respond well to lithium.

- Antipsychotic medications reduce the symptoms of thought disorders like schizophrenia.

- Older medications such as the typical antipsychotics improve the positive symptoms of psychosis (including hallucinations and delusions) but have limited impact on the negative symptoms of psychosis (i.e., affective flattening and avolition).

- Typical antipsychotics can have disruptive side effects including tardive dyskinesia.

- Newer atypical antipsychotics have a lower rate of tardive dyskinesia and offer relief for both positive and negative symptoms of psychosis but are associated with higher rates of weight gain and diabetes.

- In addition to medications, other medical treatments for psychological conditions include electroconvulsive therapy, transcranial magnetic stimulation, and deep brain stimulation.

15.8 Evaluating Therapies for Psychological Disorders

- Clinical researchers utilize clinical trials to test treatments for psychological conditions.

- Research has provided evidence of the efficacy of treatments for psychological disorders.

- Researchers did not find one kind of therapy that was better than others, except for specific treatments for specific disorders.

- Research has found some crosscutting factors for effective psychotherapy treatments, including therapist factors such as genuineness and warmth and client factors such as access to supportive environments and client motivation.

- Combining psychotherapy and drug therapy can be more effective than one alone.

15.1 Mental Health Practitioners and Settings

1. Your friend just returned from a visit with a mental health practitioner. He said the person had a DO degree after her name and gave your friend a prescription for a medication for anxiety. Your friend cannot remember the kind of practitioner. Based on this information, the practitioner was most likely a:
   A. psychiatrist.
   B. counseling psychologist.
   C. clinical psychologist.
   D. psychiatric nurse.

15.2 Psychodynamic Therapy

2. If a client comes in 20 minutes late to every session soon after the therapist has uncovered an important issue, this could be a sign of:
   A. insight.
   B. free association.
   C. resistance.
   D. transference.

3. Which type of therapy is most like the one that Freud would have practiced?
   A. Transference therapy
   B. Short-term psychodynamic therapy
   C. Psychodynamic therapy
   D. Psychoanalysis

15.3 Humanistic Therapy

4. Client-centered approaches are rooted in:
   A. creating an environment of genuineness, acceptance, and empathy.
   B. examining intrapsychic conflicts.
   C. increasing the occurrence of adaptive behaviors.
   D. challenging maladaptive cognitions.

5. What emotions do humanists explore most often?
   A. The emotions that arise naturally in therapy
   B. The emotions generated from projective tests, such as the Rorschach inkblot test
   C. Emotions that occur from early memories
   D. Emotions that the client recalls from dreams

15.4 Behavior Therapy

6. In the bell-and-pad treatment, the bell serves as a(n):
   A. unconditioned stimulus.
   B. unconditioned response.
   C. conditioned stimulus.
   D. conditioned response.

7. In systematic desensitization, each step of the hierarchy of fears is associated with:
   A. an aversive stimulus.
   B. relaxation.
   C. the feared outcome.
   D. a substitute symptom.

15.5 Cognitive Therapies

8. In cognitive therapy, clients are taught to identify negative thoughts and then:
   A. relax.
   B. question them.
   C. stop thinking the thought.
   D. think more positive thoughts.

9. Beck's cognitive therapy (CT) differs from Ellis's rational emotive therapy [RET] in that:
   A. RET has homework and CT does not.
   B. RET is more directive and CT is more guiding.
   C. RET suggests that psychological conditions are caused by maladaptive thoughts and CT suggests that psychological conditions are caused by maladaptive behaviors.
   D. Ellis was trained as a psychoanalyst while Beck was trained as a behaviorist.

15.6 Family Systems and Group Therapy

10. Systems approaches will sometimes use genograms in order to:
    A. uncover the source of blame in the family.
    B. examine patterns of intrapsychic conflicts in the family.
    C. explain and examine the common roles that people play in the family.
    D. interpret dreams.

15.7 Biomedical Therapies

11. SSRIs work by:
    A. blocking the reabsorption of serotonin.
    B. binding to receptor sites.
    C. encouraging the release of more serotonin.
    D. inhibiting the removal of serotonin by the enzyme MAO.

12. If a client takes the antipsychotic Haldol, which of the following symptoms is it most likely to help?
    A. A flat affect
    B. Auditory hallucination
    C. Lack of elaborative speech
    D. Lack of pleasurable experiences

13. Which of the following is considered an advantage of a benzodiazepine like Xanax?
    A. Benzodiazepines have a low risk for abuse.
    B. Benzodiazepines are an effective treatment for depression.
    C. Benzodiazepines work quickly.
    D. Benzodiazepines have an action on the neurotransmitter serotonin.

15.8 Evaluating Therapies for Psychological Disorders

14. If a client comes in with lots of anxiety it is likely that, on its own, the anxiety will decrease because of the phenomenon of:
    A. resistance.
    B. regression toward the mean.
    C. counterconditioning.
    D. transference.

15. Your friend Emily said that she is looking for a therapist to help with some personal struggles. Without knowing her specific condition, which type of psychotherapist would be best for her, according to the research?
    A. Psychodynamic
    B. Humanistic
    C. Behavioral
    D. Cognitive
    E. They are all equally effective.

CHAPTER DISCUSSION QUESTIONS

1. Section 15.1 describes three main types of mental health practitioners: psychiatrists, counseling psychologists, and clinical psychologists. Compare and contrast the assistance you would receive from each type of mental health practitioner. Are there some situations where one type of practitioner might be more appropriate than another?

2. Imagine that you are suffering from test anxiety and that you are researching a different therapy approaches that might help you overcome your anxiety. Review psychodynamic, humanistic, behavioral, cognitive, and family and group therapy techniques. Then, rank each theory in terms of how effective you think it would be in helping you with your test anxiety. Explain the order of your rankings.

3. Review all the approaches to therapy from Section 15.2–7 and evaluate how comfortable you would be accepting each form of therapy for yourself. Once you've gone through all the therapies, look at your ratings for biological versus nonbiological therapies. Do you see a preference for biological or nonbiological? What are the reasons for your preference?

4. Section 15.8 explains how to evaluate the effectiveness of different forms of therapy, but also highlights some other factors that may improve a person's mental state such as a placebo effect. Differentiate those factors other than therapy that may influence a person's psychological status.

CHAPTER PROJECTS

1. Imagine that you have a friend who has come to you for advice about choosing a type of therapy for depression. Formulate a guide for your friend to help him or her understand the pros and cons of each type of therapy.

2. Identify a common problem among college students that might require psychological therapy. Then, act out a therapy session to work through the problem using at least four different approaches to therapy. Develop a script for each therapy session. Use a video camera to record the sessions. To complete the project, write a summary of the results of each session and your conclusions about what worked and what might have been done differently.

CHAPTER KEY TERMS

Acceptance
Active listening
Actualizing tendency
Alogia
Anhedonia
Antianxiety medication
Antidepressant medication
Antipsychotic medication
Aversive conditioning
Avolition
Behavior therapy
Bell-and-pad treatment
Biomedical therapies
Classical conditioning
Client-centered therapy
Clinical psychologist
Clinical researcher model
Clinical trial
Cognitive therapy
Collectivist culture
Counseling psychologist
Counterconditioning
Deep brain stimulation (DBS)
Defense mechanism
Deinstitutionalization
Delusions
Dependence
Dependent variable
Dream analysis
Eclectic approach
Electroconvulsive therapy (ECT)

Empathy
En vivo
Etiology
Evidence-based practice
Exposure therapy
Eye movement desensitization reprocessing (EMDR)
Family therapy
Free association
Gamma-aminobutyric acid (GABA)
Genogram
Genuineness
Group therapy
Hallucination
Humanism
Insight
Insight therapies
Interpretation
Latent content
Lithium
Lobotomy
Manifest content
Mental hospital
Meta-analysis
Mood stabilizers
Negative symptoms of psychosis
Neurogenesis
Outpatient
Phenomenology
Placebo
Placebo effect

Positive psychology
Practitioner-scholar model
Psychiatry
Psychoanalysis
Psychodynamic therapies
Psychopharmacologist
Psychopharmacology
Psychosurgery
Psychotropic medication
Rational emotive therapy
Regression toward the mean
Relapse
Resistance
Scientist-practitioner model
Selective serotonin reuptake inhibitor (SSRI)
Shaping
Short-term psychodynamic therapy
Social skills training
Spontaneous remission
Support group
Symptom substitution
Systematic desensitization
Tardive dyskinesia
Tolerance
Transcranial magnetic stimulation (TMS)
Transference
Unconditional positive regard
Virtual reality exposure therapy

ANSWERS TO CONCEPT LEARNING CHECKS

15.1 Comparing the Roles and Settings of Mental Health Care Practitioners

1. Deinstitutionalization created more freedom and choices for treatment, but it also created more homelessness and a population that did not receive the treatment it needed.

2. Psychiatrists typically use medicine to treat psychological disorders and counseling and clinical psychologists employ psychotherapy. Clinical and counseling psychologists are more similar than different in the way they research and treat psychological conditions.

15.2 Understanding Psychodynamic Therapies

1. Psychoanalytic therapies provide insight into problematic intrapsychic conflicts.

2. Traditional psychoanalytic therapy is long term and more formal, whereas short-term psychodynamic therapy is time limited and more casual in focus.

15.3 Describing the Elements of Humanistic Therapy

Humanistic therapies attempt to active the actualizing tendency or the instinctual desire to be the best possible version of oneself. By providing the correct environment, the therapist releases this the potential in the client.

15.4 Designing a Behavioral Treatment Plan

The behavioral treatment plan should include relaxation training, a hierarchy of fears, and paired exposure with relaxation.

15.5 Comparing Cognitive Therapies

Both Beck and Ellis emphasize the importance of action and maladaptive thoughts. Ellis's approach is more directive and active, while Beck's approach is to encourage clients to test out their beliefs.

15.6 Describing an Eclectic Systems Approach

1. The components of the client-centered approaches are genuineness, acceptance, and empathy. The therapist would help the members of the group to practice those components in the group.

15.7 Explaining the Use of Medications for Psychological Conditions

Although called an antidepressant, Prozac is an SSRI that can also be used for chronic anxiety.

15.8 Summarizing the Factors of Effective Psychotherapy

The better the quality of the therapeutic relationship, the better the outcomes such as genuineness and warmth. Client factors are important, too, such as supportive environments and client motivation.

ANSWERS TO CHAPTER REVIEW TEST

15.1 Mental Health Practitioners and Settings

1. A. Rationale: Psychiatrists are practitioners with professional medical doctorates (like MD or DO). Psychiatrists will sometimes treat psychological conditions using medication.

15.2 Psychodynamic Therapy

2. C. Rationale: Resistance is a client's employment of a defense mechanism during therapy.

3. D. Rationale: Psychoanalysis is a type of therapy based on Freud's theory of personality.

15.3 Humanistic Therapy

4. A. Rationale: Client-centered approaches are powered by the creation of an environment of genuineness, acceptance, and empathy.

5. A. Rationale: Instead of recalling and discussing emotions, humanists discuss the ones that occur during real time in therapy.

15.4 Behavior Therapy

6. A. Rationale: The bell would naturally wake you up, and this is an unconditioned stimulus that generates an unconditioned response of waking.

7. B. Rationale: Systematic desensitization is a treatment for phobia in which a client practices relaxation during progressively more fear-inducing stimuli.

15.5 Cognitive Therapies

8. B. Rationale: Rather than just thinking positively, the therapist encourages the client to notice and test out maladaptive beliefs through questioning techniques and homework.

9. B. Rationale: RET and CT are similar, except RET takes a more active and directive approach as compared to CT.

15.6 Family Systems and Group Therapy

10. C. Rationale: Systems approaches also note that people will often play roles in certain systems. These patterns can sometimes be revealed in genograms, or family trees.

15.7 Biomedical Therapies

11. A. Rationale: Selective serotonin reuptake inhibitors are a class of medications that increase the efficiency of serotonin by binding to the reuptake sites.

12. B. Rationale: Hallucinations are positive symptoms of psychosis.

13. C. Rationale: Benzodiazepine are fast-acting medicines for the treatment of anxiety. They have an action on the neurotransmitter GABA and have a high risk for abuse.

15.8 Evaluating Therapies for Psychological Disorders

14. B. Rationale: Regression toward the mean is the inclination for extreme scores to move toward the average over time.

15. E. Rationale: Without knowing the specific condition, the research suggests that all the interventions are about equally effective.

REFERENCES

Ballenger, J. C. (2000). Anxiety and depression: Optimizing treatments. *Primary Care Companion to the Journal of Clinical Psychiatry, 2*(3), 71.

Beck, R. A., & Aaron, T. (1988). Psychometric properties of the Beck Depression Inventory: Twenty-five years of evaluation. *Clinical Psychology Review, 8*(1), 77–100.

Beck, A. T., Rush, A. J., Shaw, B. F., & Emery, G. (1987). *Cognitive therapy of depression* (1st ed.). New York: Guilford.

Becvar, R. J. (1998). *Systems theory and family therapy: A primer* (2nd ed.). Lanham, MD: University Press of America.

Calabrese, J. R., Suppes, T., Bowden, C. L., Sachs, G. S., Swann, A. C., McElroy, S. L., et al. (2000). A double-blind, placebo-controlled, prophylaxis study of lamotrigine in rapid-cycling bipolar disorder. Lamictal 614 Study Group. *Journal of Clinical Psychiatry, 61*(11), 841–850.

Conway, C. R., Sheline, Y. I., Chibnall, J. T., Bucholz, R. D., Price, J. L., Gangwani, S., & Mintun, M. A. (2011). VNS-induced cerebral blood flow in depression. Brain blood-flow change with acute vagus nerve stimulation in treatment-refractory major depressive disorder. *Brain Stimulation.* doi:10.1016/j.brs.2011.03.001

Davidson, P. R., & Parker, K. C. (2001). Eye movement desensitization and reprocessing (EMDR): A meta-analysis. *Journal of Consulting and Clinical Psychology, 69*(2), 305–316.

Davis, L. L., Bartolucci, A., & Petty, F. (2005). Divalproex in the treatment of bipolar depression: A placebo-controlled study. *Journal of Affective Disorders, 85*(3), 259–266.

Deacon, B. J., & Abramowitz, J. S. (2004). Cognitive and behavioral treatments for anxiety disorders: A review of meta-analytic findings. *Journal of Clinical Psychology, 60*(4), 429–441.

Dukakis, K., & Tye, L. (2007). *Shock: The healing power of electroconvulsive therapy.* New York: Penguin.

Ellis, A. (2001). *Overcoming destructive beliefs, feelings, and behaviors: New directions for rational emotive behavior therapy.* Amherst, NY: Prometheus Books.

Emsley, R., Rabinowitz, J., & Medori, R. (2006). Time course for antipsychotic treatment response in first-episode schizophrenia. *American Journal of Psychiatry, 163*(4), 743–745. doi:10.1176/appi.ajp.163.4.743

Eschweiler, G. W., Vonthein, R., Bode, R., Huell, M., Conca, A., Peters, O., et al. (2007). Clinical efficacy and cognitive side effects of bifrontal versus right unilateral electroconvulsive therapy (ECT): A short-term randomised controlled trial in pharmaco-resistant major depression. *Journal of Affective Disorders, 101*(1–3), 149–157.

Gao, X., Jackson, T., Chen, H., Liu, Y., Wang, R., Qian, M., & Huang, X. (2010). There is a long way to go: A nationwide survey of professional training for mental health practitioners in China. *Health Policy, 95*(1), 74–81.

Gim, C. S. Y., Lillystone, D., & Caldwell, P. H. Y. (2009). Efficacy of the bell and pad alarm therapy for nocturnal enuresis. *Journal of Paediatrics and Child Health, 45,* 405–408.

Gitlin, M. J. (2002). Pharmacological treatment of depression. Handbook of depression. In I. Gotlib, & C. Hammen, (Eds.), *Handbook of depression,* (pp. 360–382). New York, NY: Guilford Press.

Glass, R. M. (2001). Electroconvulsive therapy. *JAMA: The Journal of the American Medical Association, 285*(10), 1346–1348. doi:10.1001/jama.285.10.1346

Gollaher, D. L. (1995). *Voice for the mad: The life of Dorothea Dix* (1st ed.). New York: Free Press.

Grandjean, E. M., & Aubry, J.-M. (2009). Lithium: Updated human knowledge using an evidence-based approach: Part I: Clinical efficacy in bipolar disorder. *CNS Drugs, 23,* 225–240.

Howland, R. H. (2009). What makes a generic medication generic? *Journal of Psychosocial Nursing and Mental Health Services, 47*(12), 17–20. doi:10.3928/02793695-20091103-99

Hróbjartsson, A., & Norup, M. (2003). The use of placebo interventions in medical practice—A national questionnaire survey of Danish clinicians. *Evaluation & the Health Professions, 26*(2), 153–165. doi:10.1177/0163278703026002002

Jones, M. (1924). A laboratory study of fear: The case of Peter. *Pedagogical Seminary, 31,* 308–315.

Joseph, S., & Linley, P. A. (2006). *Positive therapy: A meta-theory for positive psychological practice* (1st ed.). London: Routledge.

Katon, W., & Schulberg, H. (1992). Epidemiology of depression in primary care. *General Hospital Psychiatry, 14*(4), 237–247. doi:10.1016/0163-8343(92)90094-Q

Kirsch, I., Moore, T. J., Scoboria, A., & Nicholls, S. S. (2002). The emperor's new drugs: An analysis of antidepressant medication data submitted to the US Food and Drug Administration. *Prevention & Treatment, 5*(1), 23a.

Knekt, P., Lindfors, O., Harkanen, T., Valikoski, M., Virtala, E., Laaksonen, M. A., Marttunen, M., et al. (2008). Randomized trial on the effectiveness of long- and short-term psychodynamic psychotherapy and solution-focused therapy on psychiatric symptoms during a 3-year follow-up. *Psychological Medicine, 38*(05), 689–703. doi:10.1017/S003329170700164X

Krijn, M., Emmelkamp, P. M. G., Olafsson, R. P., & Biemond, R. (2004). Virtual reality exposure therapy of anxiety disorders: A review. *Clinical Psychology Review, 24*(3), 259–281. doi:10.1016/j.cpr.2004.04.001

Lambert, M. J., & Barley, D. E. (2001). Research summary on the therapeutic relationship and psychotherapy outcome. *Psychotherapy: Theory, Research, Practice, Training, 38*(4), 357–361. doi:10.1037/0033-3204.38.4.357

La Roche, M. J., & Maxie, A. (2003). Ten considerations in addressing cultural differences in psychotherapy. *Professional Psychology: Research and Practice, 34*(2), 180–186. doi:10.1037/0735-7028.34.2.180

Leaf, J. B., Dotson, W. H., Oppenheim-Leaf, M. L., Sherman, J. A., & Sheldon, J. B. (2011). A programmatic description of a social skills group for young children with autism. *Topics in Early Childhood Special Education.* doi:10.1177/0271121411405855

Lee, C. C. (2006). *Multicultural issues in counseling: New approaches to diversity* (3rd ed.). Alexandria, VA: American Counseling Association.

Leichsenring, F., & Rabung, S. (2008). Effectiveness of long-term psychodynamic psychotherapy: A meta-analysis. *JAMA: The Journal of the American Medical Association, 300*(13), 1551–1565. doi:10.1001/jama.300.13.1551

McNeilly, C. L., & Howard, K. L. (1991). The effects of psychotherapy: A re-evaluation based on dosage. *Psychotherapy Research, 1,* 74–78.

Miyamoto, S., Lieberman, J., Fleishhacker, W., Aoba, A., & Marder, S. (2003). Antipsychotic drugs. In J. Tasman, J. Kay, & J. Lieberman (Eds.), *Psychiatry* (2nd ed.). New York: Wiley.

Nakatani, Y., Matsumoto, Y., Mori, Y., Hirashima, D., Nishino, H., Arikawa, K., & Mizunami, M. (2009). Why the carrot is more effective than the stick: Different dynamics of punishment memory and reward memory and its possible biological basis. *Neurobiology of Learning and Memory, 92*(3), 370–380. doi:10.1016/j.nlm.2009.05.003

Narrow, W. E., Regier, D. A., Rae, D. S., Manderscheid, R. W., et al. (1993). Use of services by persons with mental and addictive disorders: Findings from the National Institute of Mental Health Epidemiologic Catchment Area Program. *Archives of General Psychiatry, 50*(2), 95–107.

Nathan, P. E., Stuart, S. P., & Dolan, S. L. (2000). Research on psychotherapy efficacy and effectiveness: Between Scylla and Charybdis? *Psychological Bulletin, 126*(6), 964.

Nobler, M. S., Oquendo, M. A., Kegeles, L. S., Malone, K. M., Campbell, C., Sackeim, H. A., & Mann, J. J. (2001). Decreased regional brain metabolism after ECT. *American Journal of Psychiatry, 158*(2), 305.

Norcross, J. C., Hedges, M., & Castle, P. H. (2002). Psychologists conducting psychotherapy in 2001: A study of the Division 29 membership. *Psychotherapy: Theory, Research, Practice, Training, 39*(1), 97–102. doi:10.1037/0033-3204.39.1.97

de Paulis, T. (2007). Drug evaluation: Vilazodone—a combined SSRI and 5-HT1A partial agonist for the treatment of depression. *IDrugs: The Investigational Drugs Journal, 10*(3), 193–201.

Porter, R. (2003). *Madness: A brief history* (1st ed.). Oxford, UK: Oxford University Press.

Preston, J. D., O'Neal, J. H., & Talaga, M. C. (2010). *Handbook of clinical psycho-pharmacology for therapists* (6th ed.). Oakland, CA: New Harbinger.

Rogers, C. (1989). *The Carl Rogers reader* (1st ed.). New York: Mariner Books.

Rush, A. J. (2007). STAR*D: What have we learned? *American Journal of Psychiatry, 164*(2), 201–204.

Sadock, B. J., & Sadock, V. A. (2010). *Kaplan and Sadock's pocket handbook of clinical psychiatry* (5th ed.). Philadelphia: Lippincott Williams & Wilkins.

Sanchez, A. R., & Atkinson, D. R. (1983). Mexican-American cultural commitment, preference for counselor ethnicity, and willingness to use counseling. *Journal of Counseling Psychology, 30*(2), 215–220. doi:10.1037/0022-0167.30.2.215

Schutter, D. J. L. G. (2009). Antidepressant efficacy of high-frequency transcranial magnetic stimulation over the left dorsolateral prefrontal cortex in double-blind sham-controlled designs: A meta-analysis. *Psychological Medicine, 39*(01), 65–75. doi:10.1017/S0033291708003462

Smith, M. L., & Glass, G. V. (1977). Meta-analysis of psychotherapy outcome studies. *American Psychologist, 32*(9), 752.

Spence, S. H., Donovan, C., & Brechman-Toussaint, M. (2000). The treatment of childhood social phobia: The effectiveness of a social skills training-based, cognitive-behavioural intervention, with and without parental involvement. *Journal of Child Psychology and Psychiatry and Allied Disciplines, 41*(06), 713–726.

Stahl, S. M. (2008). *Stahl's essential psychopharmacology: Neuroscientific basis and practical applications* (3rd ed.). New York: Cambridge University Press.

Stahl, S. (2009). *The prescriber's guide* (3rd ed.). New York: Cambridge University Press.

Stein, D. J., Kupfer, D. J., & Schatzberg, A. F. (2005). *The American Psychiatric Publishing textbook of mood disorders* (1st ed.). Arlington, VA: American Psychiatric Publishing.

Thase, M. E., & Denko, T. (2008). Pharmacotherapy of mood disorders. *Annual Review of Clinical Psychology, 4,* 53–91. doi:10.1146/annurev.clinpsy.2.022305.095301

Vargas, J. M., & Adesso, V. J. (1976). A comparison of aversion therapies for nailbiting behavior. *Behavior Therapy, 7*(3), 322–329. doi:10.1016/S0005-7894(76)80058-5

Wang, P. S., Berglund, P., Olfson, M., Pincus, H. A., Wells, K. B., & Kessler, R. C. (2005). Failure and delay in initial treatment contact after first onset of mental disorders in the National Comorbidity Survey Replication. *Archives of General Psychiatry, 62*(6), 603–613. doi:10.1001/archpsyc.62.6.603

Yalom, I. D., & Leszcz, M. (2005). *Theory and practice of group psychotherapy* (5th ed.). New York: Basic Books.

Zuckerbrot, R. A. (2007). Combined fluoxetine plus cognitive behavioural therapy is more effective than monotherapy or placebo for adolescents with depression. *Evidence-Based Mental Health, 10*(3), 1393–1403. doi:10.1136/ebmh.10.3.84

Chapter Overview ▼

16 Social Psychology

Learning Objectives ▼

16.1
- Define social psychology.
- Compare and contrast social cognition, social influence, and social norms.
- Describe the core social motives.

16.2
- Illustrate social categorization.
- Discuss how stereotypes and subjectivity impact personal perception.

16.3
- Explain the various types of attribution.

16.4
- Describe the components of attitudes.
- Illustrate the different ways to influence attitudes.

16.5
- Differentiate between conformity, obedience, and compliance.

16.6
- Describe the biological, psychological, and sociocultural aspects of prejudice, aggression, and attraction.

16.7
- Discuss the pros and cons of group influence on an individual.

Throughout my life, I have encountered my share of wounding acts of discrimination, along with the lesser nicks of mostly harmless and even humorous assumptions that others have made. The range of these experiences has been vast. Once, upon reading my name, "Dr. Carter," on my credit card, a man asked me if that was my "rap name." Another time, when I was wearing a tuxedo at my friend's wedding, a man handed me his coat because he thought that I was a member of the hotel staff. On a different occasion, when I arrived to pick up a rented academic robe before a college graduation ceremony, a kind woman told me, "When you see Dr. Carter, please tell him to hang the regalia up to ease out the wrinkles." My youthful appearance, my race, or a mixture of both had motivated the assumptions these people made about who I was. But none of these experiences prepared me for the assumptions of a 5-year-old girl at a cupcake shop.

You see, most days when I have exercised, and many days when I have not, I treat myself to a cupcake at a local bakery within walking distance of my house. It is a quirky place with mismatched tables and chairs, walls lined with built-in bookshelves, and stacks and stacks of used books for sale. Some wall space is reserved for posters of local bands and other announcements. In the front of the establishment are the gems: dozens of puffy, fluffy cupcakes in a kaleidoscope of colors, encrusted with crunchy candy bits. They occupy a once-revolving 5-foot-tall glass case. It is one of those local places full of Southern charm, where they come to expect you. The owners delight in coming up with surprises for regulars.

"Hey, what will it be today?" one of the bakers said with a slight smile, because I nearly always order exactly the same item.

"Oh . . . hmm . . . I . . . think I'll have . . . one cupcake to go, please," I said, doing my best to make it sound like I gave it some thought.

"I thought so," she replied. "I actually saved something special for you in the back. Wait right here, Hun." She popped to the back of the shop and was quickly replaced by a little girl who must have been 5 years old and who was dressed like a fairy princess.

"Hi," she said, "My mom is gone to get you a special cupcake. Are you a president?"

"Hello," I responded, and then I did not know how to answer. Thinking I must have misunderstood, I said, "I'm sorry, I don't understand. Am I a what?"

"Are you a president?"

"Oh . . . no." I laughed. "Are *you* a president?"

"No, silly; black people can be a president, like him." She pointed to a poster of Barack Obama. Then it suddenly hit me: She must have thought that all black people were presidents.

For the rest of the day, I wondered what led to the little girl's assumptions about me and people who she thought were similar to me. What kinds of experiences influenced her assumptions?

16.1 Social Thought and Behavior

The way people think about others influences the way they relate to them.

- Define social psychology.
- Compare and contrast social cognition, social influence, and social norms.
- Describe the core social motives.

Think about the many roles you play. In any given day, your **role** might be a student, a customer, a son or daughter, a parent, and an employee, each with its own set of customary behaviors based on your position. Your assumptions and thoughts about how these **social roles** function is called a **schema**. Schemas are sets of thoughts and presumptions and they help define the roles you play.

The roles you play involve multiple tasks, and for the most part, you slide easily from one role to another. Take ordering a cupcake in a bakery, for example. This activity involves taking on the role of a customer, holding certain expectations, and performing tasks associated with that role: You locate the bakery; you expect to be greeted by a polite, knowledgeable employee; you make your selection, and the employee wraps it and presents it to you as you pay for it. Ordering a cupcake follows an expected pattern, like a script for a play. The ability to perform various roles helps make life easier, because knowing these roles and their scripts can reduce the uncertainty of otherwise complex social situations. When everyone has a role to play, everyone generally knows what is expected.

Schemas, then, are like cognitive shorthand, internalized scripts, based on assumptions about the behaviors that occur in social situations. Schemas are efficient. They enable you to walk into new situations and figure out pretty quickly what to do. You can, for example, walk into an unfamiliar restaurant and determine the roles and expectations with minimal effort. Schemas and roles can also lead you to make mistakes in unfamiliar or uncommon social situations. For example, assumptions about one's expected behavior at a wedding, a funeral, or a large family gathering can vary drastically according to social and cultural norms or expectations. Finally, both schemas and roles can reveal the complex backstory of how humans sort out social situations. In this chapter, we will examine how you think, feel, and behave in relation to the social roles and social influences you encounter.

Psychology studies mental processes and behavior. As we have discussed in other chapters, many things can influence your thoughts and behavior. Some of the most prevalent influences are those that involve other people. Other people—even imagined others—can have a huge impact on your behavior. The presence of other people can cause you to work harder or even pull back on your effort. Your thoughts about other people can influence how you treat them. **Social psychology** is the branch of psychology that focuses on how people's thoughts, feelings, and behavior influence and are influenced by others. It also examines the ways we explain the behavior of others, make social connections, and form or justify our own attitudes and opinions. As a social science, social psychology applies the scientific method of formulating and testing theories—in this case, theories about how people think and behave in relation to others. As we will see, several of the more famous of these social scientific experiments offer unique insights into what it means to be human in a social context.

Role A set of customary behaviors based on your position.

Social roles Assumptions about the way people should behave given their status.

Schema A structured set of thoughts and presumptions.

Social psychology The branch of psychology that focuses on how the way people think, feel, and behave influences and is influenced by others.

Group Collection of people who have something in common.

Groups

Groups are collections of people who have something in common. They can be as small as two people or as large as several million. The concept of the group is fundamental to social psychology, which examines the person as part of a group as well as the group's influence on the person. We will examine various aspects of groups later in the chapter; however, two important areas related to the study of groups are social cognition and social influence. **Social cognition** refers to the way our thoughts and assumptions about other people help shape our attitudes and behaviors toward them. **Social influence** refers to the way other people and events directly influence and change our attitudes and behavior. These two areas of study offer two different ways of thinking about, observing, and sometimes predicting attitudes and social behavior.

People in groups rely on their expectations of each other. **Social norms** are the expectations we have for the behaviors of others and ourselves, helping to define what we expect people to do and how we might expect them to behave. Social norms associated with specific circumstances, like that of a teacher in a classroom, are called social roles. Sometimes roles and norms are clearly spelled out and expectations are well defined, both for the people in a particular social role and for those who may find themselves part of the environment, even temporarily. For example, if all employees of a department store wear red shirts and tan pants, then you might expect that everyone dressed that way works there. The role of the salespeople is defined, so it is considered okay for customers to approach them and ask about the location of items in the store. If you are a customer unfortunate enough to have chosen to wear a red shirt and tan pants that day, then strangers are likely to approach you to ask for assistance. Those strangers might be confused to discover that you do not work there.

Roles can also carry with them power differences and social status. Managers in a department store may direct the sales associates, for example. Often, the higher the status someone has, the more power, money, and decision-making power he or she possesses within the group.

Core Social Motives

Several things direct and influence behavior. For example, more often than not, people are motivated to belong and to be correct. These principles can direct how we operate in the social world.

Susan Fiske (Fiske, 2003) classified five core social motives—belonging, understanding, controlling, enhancing self, and trusting, or BUC(k)ET.

1. Belonging. People are motivated to join together and to create relationships.
2. Understanding. People are motivated to make sense of the world. This helps people to predict their own behavior and the behavior of others.
3. Controlling. People are motivated to exert power over the things that happen.
4. Enhancing self. People are motivated to feel and be perceived as worthy.
5. Trusting. People are motivated to see the world in a positive light.

For example, in an effort to enhance self, people like to see their own behavior as typical. That is, most people tend to believe that they are correct and figure that others would respond to situations or information in the same ways that they would. The habit of seeing our own behavior as typical is called the **false consensus effect**. A similar shortcut in our thinking is the **availability heuristic**: The more quickly we can think of an example of something, the more likely we suppose it must be true. We can easily identify examples of our own behavior and opinions, so according to the availability heuristic, we see our own opinions and thoughts as common opinions and thoughts. These core social motives influence our social interactions.

Social cognition Thoughts people use to understand their social world.

Social influence The way behavior is shaped.

Social norm An expectation about customary behaviors based on a person's position.

Groups can be as small as two and as large as millions.

Social norms are the expectations we have for the behaviors of others.

CONCEPT LEARNING CHECK 16.1   *Describing Social Roles*

1. Describe some typical roles involved in ordering a meal at a fine restaurant. List the social roles and briefly describe the behavioral expectations associated with each role.

16.2 Person Perception

Person perception includes the way people categorize and react to others.

- Illustrate social categorization.
- Discuss how stereotypes and subjectivity impact personal perception.

How do we form opinions about others? Psychologists call this issue **person perception**. Person perception includes **social categorization**, or the way we sort or tag people into various types, often depending on physical appearance, stereotype, and our personal and cultural beliefs about people. Person perception also includes biases that affect our opinions about others, the information we use to form them, and their accuracy.

We often pay particularly close attention to negative behaviors, called a negativity bias. When we catch a glimpse of something negative about a person, we are more likely to assume that the negative behavior is a snapshot into the person's personality (Baumeister et al., 2001; Taylor, Peplau, & Sears, 2005). This happens, in part, because negative stimuli grab our attention more than positive stimuli do (Smith et al., 2003). On a recent trip, I saw a man shuffle luggage in the overhead bin to make room for his bags. Frustrated and in a rush, he took out another passenger's bag and left it in the aisle. The owner of the bags reminded him to return it, barking, "You can't leave my bag there! Put it back!"

I then overheard the owner of the bag say to the passenger sitting next to him, "I can't imagine what his wife must go through every day." He was assuming that the other passenger's behavior was typical of his behavior at all times. Negative information affects our first impressions much more strongly than the good things we notice about others (Carney, Colvin, & Hall, 2007).

Social Categorization

Social categorization involves the mental sorting of people into groups. We form opinions of others almost instantly, sometimes with only the smallest slices of information to go on. Without even being fully aware of it, we automatically tag the people we see as members of one or several groups (Seger, Smith, & Mackie, 2009). We mentally tag people into lots of categories, including race, gender, age, or in terms of their role. At the grocery store, when we look around, we see categories of people: customers waiting in line, clerks, and baggers. Categorization reflects the core social motive to understand our world. We tend to minimize behaviors that make individuals unique and focus attention on the behaviors that are linked to their category or role.

First impressions can determine how we tag or assess others. We do not pay attention to everything about other people. Instead, we use environmental cues to determine what aspects of other people to focus on. Unusual features especially grab our attention, and small, unimportant details can too: "Why is that person holding her hand *that* way?" We try our best to ascribe meaning to the behavior of others.

Sometimes we interpret the same behavior differently depending on the context. If we see a person painting her nails at a bus stop, we might see her as tidy, careful, and concerned about her appearance. If a representative at a ticket counter is painting her nails, we might see her as inattentive and careless. We may assume that this single example of her behavior represents the kind of person she is.

Physical Appearance

Person perception initially involves using physical appearance to assess others. We first notice nonverbal cues about people: how they walk, gesture, dress, facial expressions. These behaviors deliver a lot of information (Ambady & Rosenthal, 1993). People even judge personality traits based upon how a person looks. We glean information about their level of comfort or even mood (Ambady, Hallahan, & Conner, 1999). Instead of simply looking at someone, we examine, analyze, and do our best to explain why they look the way they look. The results of our analysis can go a long way in determining how we might interact with and respond to the person.

False consensus effect The habit of seeing our own behavior as typical.

Availability heuristic A thinking shortcut in which the more quickly a person can think of an example of something, the more likely he or she supposes it must be true.

Person perception Involves the way we form opinions about others.

Social categorization Mental sorting of people into groups.

People focus on unusual features in order to predict behavior or personality.

How you interpret behavior depends on the context. You might see this woman as being tidy and careful.

If you are waiting in line for assistance, you might see this woman as being inattentive and careless.

Person perception suggests that people categorize others based, in part, on physical appearance. Would you choose a seat next to this person if you were looking for someone quiet to sit next to on the bus?

It can take less than 1/10 of a second to determine whether or not you trust this man. Person perception suggests you can make a decision like this outside of your awareness.

For example, on a train, you might notice a person's posture, dress, gender, or age to determine what kind of music you think he might like. You may use physical cues to determine whom you would like to sit next to.

We do this incredibly quickly. One study suggested that it takes only about 1/10 of a second to determine how much we trust a person just based on the way he or she looks (Willis & Todorov, 2006).

Stereotypes

In order to make decisions about unfamiliar people, we sometimes employ sweeping generalizations. **Stereotypes** are overgeneralized beliefs—positive or negative—about a group and its members. Stereotypes highlight physical characteristics such as age, gender, or ethnicity, and suggest that people who look alike are alike. You might get ideas about the type of person you think someone is likely to be based on the way someone dresses, how her hair looks, or even the way her name sounds. Stereotypes help sort people into categories that are familiar to us. Although it is easier to think about people in categories than as completely unique individuals, relying on stereotypes can skew the way we see new people, how we perceive their behavior, and our expectations of them.

How do we learn stereotypes? Some researchers believe it is through behavior. People are rewarded for believing certain things. Stereotypes may also be molded through culture as people learn to believe accepted "truths" about groups of people. As we will discus later in the chapter, stereotypes can make up so much of our daily experiences that they affect our behavior without our awareness. Stereotypes develop as early as 6 years of age (Baron & Banaji, 2006).

Although stereotypes can be useful as shortcuts, they may create problems, too. A stereotype can emphasize differences between categorized groups and can create an "us versus them" mentality. Stereotypes can easily become entrenched: If you group together all the people in a given category, it is easy to search for evidence that supports the stereotype and to ignore all the evidence that might not. This minimizes differences within the stereotyped group, making group "members" seem more similar than they really are. What is more, stereotypes can affect initial impressions, which can be long lasting. Acting on initial impressions may cause you to prejudge a person's intentions and actions and can lead to **prejudice** toward the individual. Sometimes people are so convinced that a stereotype is true that when they encounter a person who does not fit the stereotype, they assign that person to a special category rather than changing the stereotype or their belief in it.

Despite these problems, the biological and evolutionary perspective would suggest that stereotypes are essential shortcuts to person perception. If we took the time needed to process individual characteristics to form an impression and decide on the appropriate behavior, this would significantly compromise our chances of survival. For example, automatically categorizing an individual as an "out-group" member may trigger the fight-or-flight response needed for survival.

Subjectivity

How we view other people can be subjective, meaning that our thoughts about them change depending on the situation and our personal feelings. We do not gather and interpret the same information about others in every situation. For example, if you expect to interact with a person only once, like whom you choose to sit next to on a bus, you may focus on very different aspects of their behavior than if you expect to see them every day, like what information you notice about a professor on the first day of a 15-week course. The situation and even our moods affect what information we gather and how we view it.

Culture and Person Perception

Just as situations and subjectivity can impact person perception, culture can also influence the categories and explanations for behaviors we assign to others. Research has demonstrated that those in **individualist cultures**, cultures that place an emphasis on each person rather than on the society, tend to explain a person's behavior as being the result of a person's personality. People in **collectivist cultures**, which are cultures that tend to emphasize the society, are more likely to explain behavior on situational factors (Knowles, Morris, Chiu, & Hong, 2001).

CONCEPT LEARNING CHECK 16.2 | *Person Perception and Musical Tastes*

CONCEPT LEARNING CHECK 16.2 | *Person Perception and Musical Tastes*

Look at the photos below and see if you can match the image with the kinds of music you think they might like.

 A

 B

 C

 D

1. _____ Rock

2. _____ Country

3. _____ Punk

4. _____ Classical

Explain

5. Using the theory of person perception, physical appearance, and social categorization, explain what led you to these assumptions.

16.3 Attribution: The Person or the Situation?

Attributions are the way we explain behavior and can be influenced by assumptions.

- Explain the various types of attribution.

If it is not clear why a person looks or behaves a certain way, we tend to fill in the blanks with our own ideas of his or her motivation. Sometimes we might focus on an environmental trigger, such as being in a hurry, and other times we rely on a personality explanation, such as that the person is a bully. An **attribution** is a mental explanation of events or behavior. **Attribution theory** is the theory that behavior is explained by situational or personal factors. **Internal attributions** explain behavior based on personality characteristics, while **external attributions** focus on environmental explanations.

Determining an attribution helps us make sense of behavior and predict future behaviors. The problem with attributions is they are often biased. Some common ways that our attributions can be biased include the actor-observer bias, the self-serving bias, and cultural influences on attribution tendencies.

Fundamental Attribution Error

In general, people tend to overestimate the influence of personality characteristics over environmental or situational characteristics when describing the causes of behavior. This tendency is called the **fundamental attribution error**. When we try to explain why someone does something, we tend to think that the behavior is linked to the "kind" of person they are.

Actor-Observer Bias

The fundamental attribution error does not always seem to show up. The way we tend to explain the behavior of other people is very different from the way we tend to explain our own behavior. We are likely to emphasize situational factors when we explain our

Stereotype Overgeneralized beliefs about a group and its members.

Prejudice Negative stereotypes or attitudes about members of a particular group.

Individualist cultures Cultures that place an emphasis on each person's right rather than on the society.

Collectivist cultures A type of culture that prioritizes the group over the individual.

Attribution Our mental explanations of events or behaviors.

Attribution theory The theory that behavior is explained by situational or personal factors.

Internal attribution An explanation of behavior based on personality characteristics.

External attribution An explanation of behavior that focuses on environmental explanations.

Fundamental attribution error An inclination to overestimate the impact of internal characteristics in explaining the behavior of others and underestimate the same characteristics in explaining your own behavior.

Actor A person who exhibits a behavior.

Actor-observer bias The likelihood of assigning an external and situational explanation to your own behavior while assigning internal, personal factors to the behavior of others.

own behavior, but when we explain the behavior of others, we emphasize personality. In a given situation, the **actor** is the person who exhibits a behavior, while the observer is the person who witnesses the behavior. The actor-observer bias is rooted in the idea that we rarely have much information about why someone else behaves in a certain way. Situational factors that motivate a behavior are especially elusive to outside observers, so we tend to attribute others' behavior to personality factors.

When we think about our own behavior, it is just the opposite. We see our own behavior from our own perspective, not as it appears to someone else. We are focused on interacting with our environment as we act, so we attribute our behavior to the situational factors of our environment. Also, we tend to assume that we would choose the best option, while we do not necessarily assume that about others. For example, we think that other people speed because they are aggressive and reckless drivers. But when we speed, it is because someone else caused us to be late. The **actor-observer bias** is our tendency to assign an external and situational explanation to our own behavior while assigning internal, personal factors to the behavior of others (Malle, 2006).

Defensive Attribution

It is common for us to blame others for their own misfortunes. That way, in our minds, it seems less likely that such misfortunes could happen to us. **Defensive attributions** involve blaming people for the bad things that happen to them in order to protect our own feelings and sense of fairness. An example of a defensive attribution is **blaming the victim**, which means attributing the cause of an unfortunate circumstance to the person experiencing it. Defensive attributions help people to feel that the world is fair. The **just-world hypothesis** suggests that we believe that people get what they deserve and deserve what they get. The just-world hypothesis may be linked to the core social motive of controlling, that is, our wish to control our outcomes and manage our world. People feel that they should be rewarded for doing good things and punished for doing bad things. This gives us a feeling of control over the good things that could happen. After all, no one wants to live in a world in which good people do not get what they deserve. It is much more comforting and reassuring to think that if bad things happen to someone, that person must be doing something wrong.

Self-Serving Bias

There is one exception to the actor-observer bias—when things go well. People tend to take credit when things go well and tend not to when they do not. This is called a **self-serving bias**, which is the tendency to see yourself in a positive light. The actor-observer and self-serving biases primarily protect people's self-esteem and the core social motive of enhancing the self (Trafimow, Armendariz, & Madson, 2004).

Is this person impatient or is the situation hard to tolerate? According to the actor-observer bias you tend to assign external and situational explanations to your own behavior and personality explanations to the behavior of others.

CONCEPT LEARNING CHECK 16.3   *Explaining Attributional Biases*

The way we explain our own behavior and the behavior of others is not always an accurate reflection of reality. Fill in each of the following assumptions and behaviors with an appropriate key term. Note what each theory says about why people distort their own and others' behavior.

1. Despite the fact she did not study much for the second exam, Nicole was convinced that the second physics exam was tricky. After all, she studied so hard for the first exam and got a great grade.

2. Wayne suggested the reason his friend's car was broken into was because his friend was careless about where he parked his car. This is strange, because when the same thing happened to Wayne, he said it was because of an increase in neighborhood crime.

3. Anita figured that her roommate's parents must have been doing something wrong if the Internal Revenue Service was auditing them.

16.4 Attitudes and Social Judgments

Attitudes contain affective, behavioral, and cognitive components and can be shaped to relieve the discomfort people feel when the components are not in harmony.

- Describe the components of attitudes.
- Illustrate the different ways to influence attitudes.

An **attitude** is a tendency to judge people, objects, or issues in a certain way. Some of our attitudes are front and center in our minds. Others fly under the radar, implicit; we may be unaware of their influences on our actions. Attitudes can be shaped by culture, experience, situations, and even pressure from others or the need to be consistent. We have attitudes about all sorts of things. Psychologists are concerned with how attitudes are created and changed. Attitudes can impact our interactions with people as well as ourselves: When we find that we have attitudes or behaviors that are inconsistent, we work hard to make them consistent.

Components of Attitudes

You might think that people would generally behave in ways consistent with their attitudes. Psychologists have found that the relationship between attitudes and behavior is sometimes complex. Attitude involves **a**ffects (emotions), **b**ehaviors (actions), and **c**ognitions (thoughts—ABC) FIGURE 16-1. When affects, behaviors, and cognitions are in harmony, it is easy to understand a person's motivation. For example, Edwin hates bananas (affective component); he thinks bananas give him indigestion (cognitive); so he will not eat them (behavioral).

However, sometimes social norms are not consistent with your attitudinal affects, behaviors, or cognitions. This disrupts the usual correspondence among these elements and creates internal tension or **conflict** (Ajzen, 2005). If Edwin's roommate is nice enough to surprise him with banana pancakes for breakfast, he might eat them even though he hates bananas.

Examining our behavior can help us learn about our attitudes. According to **self-perception theory** (Bem, 1967), we are not fully aware of our attitudes. In many cases, we infer our attitudes and preferences based on our behavior. This is interesting because we assume that our attitudes determine our behavior, not the other way around. For the most part, however, the theory applies to attitudes that could be considered trivial, such as a preference for a certain color or a type of food. Attitudes can also be shaped by a change in behavior (Webb & Sheeran, 2006). Nevertheless, cognitions are likely to predict behaviors, especially when the person holds an especially strong attitude, is very aware of the attitude, or discusses the attitude often (Ajzen, 2005).

People are less likely to help if they believe the victim is the cause of the misfortune. If this person dropped his papers because he was texting while walking up the stairs we might be less likely to offer assistance.

Defensive attribution Blaming people for bad things that happen to them in order to protect your own feelings.

Blaming the victim The tendency to attribute the cause of an unfortunate circumstance to the person experiencing it.

Just-world hypothesis A belief that people get what they deserve and deserve what they get.

Self-serving bias The tendency to see yourself in a positive light.

Attitude A tendency to judge people, objects, or issues in a certain way.

Conflict A situation that involves incompatible objectives.

Self-perception theory The theory that suggests that people discover their attitudes while observing their own behavior.

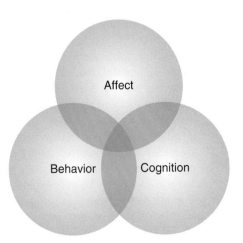

FIGURE 16-1 Attitudes consist of affects, behaviors, and cognitions.

Cognitive dissonance theory
The theory that we try to decrease our discomfort when holding two competing ideas at the same time by changing either our ideas or our behaviors.

Cognitive dissonance
Discomfort that you experience from holding two competing ideas at the same time.

Persuasion Convincing another person.

Central route to persuasion
A constructive response to an argument that focuses solely on the argument's merits.

Peripheral route to persuasion Influence based on small, noncore factors.

FIGURE 16-2 American social psychologist Leon Festinger (1919–1989).

If you are convinced by how a salesperson looks, you are employing the peripheral route to persuasion.

Relieving Cognitive Dissonance

You will recall that understanding is a core social motive. It is important for people to see behavior and attitudes as consistent, which makes understanding easier. According to **cognitive dissonance theory** (Festinger, 1957), when we hold two or more conflicting ideas, we try to decrease the discomfort this causes by changing our ideas and/or our behaviors. **Cognitive dissonance** is the discomfort that you experience from holding two or more ideas that oppose one another. Dissonance theory focuses on the differences in the components of a person's attitudes and/or behavior. At times, we sense a conflict—or dissonance—between two or more ideas or between our ideas and our behavior. When this happens, according to the theory, we will change our ideas or behavior enough to resolve the conflict. Often we do this in imperceptible ways, such as modifying our opinion about something or someone. But if we lock ourselves into a decision with no obvious escape, we may need to perform mental acrobatics to relieve the dissonance we experience. This has been the case with doomsday groups who have predicted the end of the world more than a few times. Social psychologist Leon Festinger FIGURE 16-2 (Festinger, Riecken, & Schachter, 2011) embedded himself in a doomsday group to try to understand their attitudes and actions. As the doomsday date approached, members gave away their possessions in preparation for what they fervently believed would be the end of the world. When the world did not end, there was a great amount of cognitive dissonance to be relieved. They were faced with two starkly conflicting thoughts or cognitions. Cognition one: They believed fervently (causing them to behave somewhat recklessly) that the world would end on a particular date. Cognition two: The world did not end on that date. How could the group's members resolve their cognitive dissonance? One way might have been to dismiss the group's leader as a fool or a charlatan. But this would have meant admitting they had been foolish and taken advantage of. Instead, many of the group's members latched on to a third cognition that resolved the dissonance of the first two: They decided that their fervent belief had actually *delayed* the end of the world. Armed with this explanation, they became even more entrenched in their belief that the end was near.

Influencing Attitudes: Persuasion

It seems as though there is always someone trying to change our attitudes. After all, we are inundated with as many as 3,000 advertisements per day (Huston et al., 1992). **Persuasion** is convincing another person to do or believe something. Attempts to sway opinions are not solely the realm of fast food restaurants and soda producers. Family, friends, and teachers do this all the time. Luckily, we are not changed by every attempt. Psychologists are interested in what kinds of messages do change our attitudes.

Persuasion can be more or less effective depending on how people examine the evidence that a would-be persuader offers. Using the **central route to persuasion** means that we examine the logical links of the persuader's argument. For example, you might choose a toothbrush based on how well the toothbrush cleans. People focus solely on the argument's merits and then we decide on a constructive response.

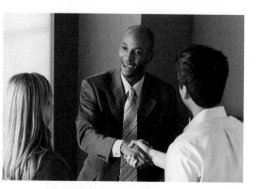

But we do not always do that. Often, people use a **peripheral route to persuasion** in which their attitudes are influenced not by the merits of the persuader's argument but by insignificant, noncore factors—for example, if you buy a toothbrush not because it cleans better but because it has a comic book character on it that you really like. When people are swayed by surface aspects, such as how much they like the person delivering the message, they are following a peripheral route to persuasion.

Several things can increase the likelihood that others will be persuaded to change their attitudes. Persuasion can be more or less successful based upon the source, the message, or the audience. Source factors that can increase persuasion include authority, likability, expertise, credibility, and similarity. Message variables include clarity, organization, and directness (direct attempts to persuade are less likely to change behavior than indirect messages). Audience factors include mood. Being in a good mood makes us easier to persuade—which is why buttering someone up with compliments is often a strategy of persuasion. In addition to these general techniques, there are other strategies for persuasion, including the foot-in-the-door technique and behavioral techniques.

The Foot-in-the-Door Technique

It is easier to persuade someone to comply with a small request than with a larger one. But once someone agrees to a small request, it is more likely that he or she will go along with a larger and more unreasonable request. This is called the **foot-in-the-door technique**, and it is commonly used as a way to secure agreement. The larger request may have been declined were it not preceded by the smaller request.

Self-perception theory can explain the mechanism behind this technique. When we comply with the small request, our attitude shifts. In order to maintain consistency with our previous attitude, we agree to the larger request. If you were willing to do a small thing, then it is likely you are willing to do the larger things (Meineri & Guéguen, 2008). Complying with a small request makes people believe they must be committed to the issue.

By contrast, the **door-in-the-face technique** starts off with an unreasonable request that will most likely be turned down, followed by a second, more reasonable request that is more likely to be accepted. The door-in-the-face technique secures agreement because the person who turned down the extreme request does not want to appear unreasonable in the face of a compromise over a smaller request.

> **Foot-in-the-door technique**
> A practice by which agreement to a small request makes agreement to a more unreasonable request more likely.
>
> **Door-in-the-face technique**
> A practice by which rejecting an unreasonable request will lead to a more reasonable request that is more likely to be accepted.

Role Playing Affects Attitudes

Even playing a role will increase your chances of preferring something. Self-perception theory suggests that the more work you put into something, even if playing a role, and pretending to like it, the more likely you are to have a shift or prefer that thing. In some ways, you convince yourself that you must possess that attitude if you went through that effort.

Attitudes can also be strengthened when a person goes through discomfort on behalf of an attitude. This discomfort means either that the cause is important or that you like to be uncomfortable. If you have gone through so much, it must be worth it.

Culture and Attitudes

Since attitudes are learned, culture can have a tremendous influence on the norms governing our attitudes. Some of the things that you might have strong attitudes about—being an organ donor, for example—are culturally influenced and may be drastically different in different parts of the world. Individualist cultures tend to emphasize the importance of being a unique individual, while collectivist cultures may emphasize their allegiance to certain groups (Hoshimo-Browne et al., 2005).

The fact that we experience dissonance and self-doubt when we act in a way that is not in harmony with our attitudes is also influenced by culture. In individualistic cultures, dissonance is more likely to be caused by acting in a way that is different from a belief, such as when a person spanks a child for fighting at school. In collectivist cultures, however, dissonance is more likely to happen in a situation that creates doubt in a person's standing and character in the community rather than how a person might define him- or herself (Kitayama, Snibbe, Markus, & Suzuki, 2004).

CONCEPT LEARNING CHECK 16.4   *Explaining Persuasion*

Think back to the last time you purchased something because you were persuaded by an advertisement. Use some of the following terms to explain what influenced your behaviors.

- Affect

- Behavior

- Cognition

- Self-perception theory

(Continues)

- Cognitive dissonance

- Persuasion

- Central route to persuasion

- Peripheral route to persuasion

- Foot-in-the-door technique

Conformity Changing your thoughts or behavior to align with those of another.

Obedience Behavior that is in response to the orders of another.

Compliance Shifting behavior because of a request.

16.5 Conformity and Obedience

Affects, behaviors, and cognitions can be shaped by conformity and obedience.

■   Differentiate between conformity, obedience, and compliance.

There are many good reasons to change your behavior. You might do so because of a request from another person, in order to go along with a group, or because of a direct order from another person. There are many good reasons to follow rules, orders, and instructions. Following rules, even unwritten ones, makes getting along more easily, and sometimes not doing so means suffering painful consequences. Not cutting in line at a store, for example, is usually driven by the social pressure of the other people waiting. **Conformity** involves changing your thoughts or behavior to align with someone else's, while **obedience** involves a change in your behavior in response to the orders of another. **Compliance** involves shifting your behavior because of requests. What factors make these shifts in behavior likely to happen and what kinds of orders people obey are the kinds of questions that interest social psychologists.

Conformity

Conformity involves aligning your thoughts or behavior with those of another. When we conform, we alter what we do or believe in order to align with a person or a group. The need to conform can be, in part, due to social pressures and norms (**normative social influence**). Normative social influence is linked to the core social motive of belonging. Internally, those who conform may feel more accepted. They may determine the best thing to do based on the actions of other people. You will recall that a basic core principle of social psychology is to be correct. Often, people will conform in order to be correct, which, in turn, can increase self-esteem. Conformity in order to be correct is called **informational social influence**. Informational social influence helps us to enhance the self. Two classic experiments studied the power of roles and conformity: the Asch line experiment (Asch, 1956) and the Stanford Prison experiment (Zimbardo, 2008).

Social psychologist Solomon Asch conducted an experiment to determine if people would conform when they knew for sure that their conforming behavior was wrong. After all, social psychology would predict that people, all other things being equal, like being right. Which would win over—the pressure to be correct or the pressure to conform?

Subjects in the experiment were asked to perform the simple task of identifying which of three lines was the same length as a target line (such as the lines in FIGURE 16-3). One line was exactly the same length as the target line and the other two were entirely different. Five people were shown the line. After the lines were displayed, each subject stated his answer. One by one, everyone agreed. This was repeated twice more with exactly the same results. The third time, something was different. Even though it was obvious that A was the correct answer, the first person responded with a confident "C." The second: "C." How could this be? Well, the experiment was rigged. The only true participant, or test subject, was the last person to answer. The others were all "confederates," or accomplices who worked for the researcher. Would the desire to be correct win over the desire to conform? Subjects gave the obviously incorrect answer some 35% of the time, with 75% conforming at least once.

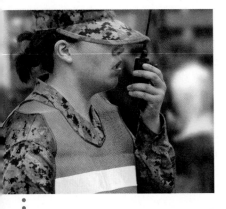

Obedience involves a change in behavior in response to the orders of another.

Social pressure to conform is known as normative social influence.

FIGURE 16-3 Lines like these were used in the Asch experiment. The reference line is on the left and the lines on the right were the three comparison lines.

A B C

Exhibit 1   Exhibit 2

The Power of the Situation: The Stanford Prison Experiment

To examine the power of roles and conformity, psychologist Philip Zimbardo FIGURE 16-4 recruited 24 male participants from Stanford University to be part of a study. They were randomly assigned to play the roles of either prisoners or guards in a simulated prison in the basement of a building on campus for 2 weeks. The guards wore uniforms and were outfitted with clubs. The prisoners were referred to by serial numbers. Before long, people fell into their roles, perhaps too well. The guards became offensive and insulting to the prisoners, who soon became passive and helpless. The entire situation got so out of hand that they abandoned the experiment before the end of the first week.

Obedience

Obedience is behavior that is in response to the orders of another who is perceived to have some form of power or authority. Perhaps the simplest way to get someone to do something is to just ask. Why do people comply with requests? There are several reasons: to obtain a reward, such as points or expertise; to gain information; coercion (when a person forces or intimidates someone else); and personal relationships (such as a friend who needs to be taken to the airport). Legitimate authorities, such as a boss at work, have the right to ask us to do things. Helplessness, too, can be a factor, such as when a small child asks for help in tying her shoes or someone asks you to reach something in a grocery store. But would people comply with a request out of "blind obedience"? That is what Stanley Milgram wanted to know.

Milgram's Experiment

It was a simple enough question. Would people blindly obey the directions of an authority? This question was on the minds of psychologists all over the world. At the time, World War II had just ended and the atrocities committed in Adolph Hitler's concentration camps were becoming widely known. Many people suggested that even though horrible things were done by officials and guards "just following orders," surely decent people would not and could not follow orders that would harm another person just because they were told to.

Psychology professor Stanley Milgram FIGURE 16-5 (Milgram, 1963) had a plan to test this assumption. He recruited everyday people from mailings and flyers to be part of a study FIGURE 16-6. Milgram's team recruited 40 men who were told that the

Normative social influence The need to conform due to social pressures.

Informational social influence Sway that comes from believing another person.

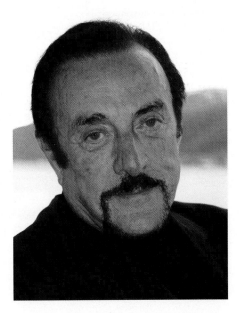

FIGURE 16-4 Philip Zimbardo's famous prison study examined the power of the situation in creating roles and social norms.

FIGURE 16-5 Milgram and his shock generator.

Public Announcement

WE WILL PAY YOU $4.00 FOR ONE HOUR OF YOUR TIME

Persons Needed for a Study of Memory

*We will pay five hundred New Haven men to help us complete a scientific study of memory and learning. The study is being done at Yale University.

*Each person who participates will be paid $4.00 (plus 50¢ carfare) for approximately 1 hour's time. We need you for only one hour: there are no further obligations. You may choose the time you would like to come (evenings, weekdays, or weekends).

No special training, education, or experience is needed. We want:

Factory workers	Businessmen	Construction workers
City Employees	Clerks	Salespeople
Laborers	Professional people	White-collar workers
Barbers	Telephone workers	Others

All persons must be between the ages of 20 and 50. High school and college students cannot be used.

*If you meet these qualifications, fill out the coupon below and mail it now to Professor Stanley Milgram, Department of Psychology, Yale University, New Haven. You will be notified later of the specific time and place of the study. We reserve the right to decline any application.

*You will be paid $4.00 (plus 50¢ carfare) as soon as you arrive at the laboratory.

- -

TO: PROF. STANLEY MILGRAM, DEPARTMENT OF PSYCHOLOGY, YALE UNIVERSITY, NEW HAVEN, CONN. I want to take part in this study of memory and learning. I am between the ages of 20 and 50. I will be paid $4.00 (plus 50¢ carfare) if I participate.

NAME (Please Print) ....

ADDRESS ....

TELEPHONE NO. .... Best time to call you ....

AGE .... OCCUPATION .... SEX ....

CAN YOU COME:

WEEKDAYS .... EVENINGS .... WEEKENDS ....

FIGURE 16-6 Public recruiting announcement used for the Milgram experiment.

study would test the effect of punishment on learning. Two participants were called into the room together. They chose slips of paper to determine the roles. One read "Learner" and the other "Teacher." In actuality, the drawing was rigged and the person who answered the flyer always ended up being the teacher.

In fact, much of the study was not what it appeared to be. The other participant was a confederate of the experimenter's, an adult male who was hired to behave in certain ways while pretending to be just another person who had responded to the flyer. Together, the experimenter and teacher walked the learner into an adjoining room, where he was strapped into a chair with wires and belts to hold him in place. This chair would deliver the shocks that were part of the learning experiment. The teacher also received a 75-volt test shock so he could feel what he would soon dole out. The experimenter and teacher walked back to the main room. A huge, scary-looking machine with switches and knobs with various voltages and labels sat on the table. The experimenter and teacher were together in the same room, and the learner was in an adjacent room FIGURE 16-7. The learner was to remember word pairs; the teacher was to deliver a shock if the learner responded incorrectly. The teacher could stop delivering the shocks whenever he wanted and could leave the experiment at any point.

When the outline of the experiment was described to 20 psychiatrists, they all said that surely the teacher would stop delivering the shocks as soon as the learner requested that he stop. No one would deliver the highest shock. It turned out that the experts severely underestimated the power of the situation on obedience.

When the shock was "delivered," the machine really did nothing. The learner responded based on a predetermined script. Early shocks produced responses like "ouch." Soon, the learner's responses escalated to pleading for the teacher to stop, around 300 volts; then begging to withdraw from the experiment, and falling eerily silent at where the dial read "450 volts." The experimenter provided only mild encouragement such as: "The experiment requires that you continue," and "Please continue." And continue they did. Of the 40 people tested, 2 out of 3 people provided shocks to the very end of the scale, and 100% delivered shocks well beyond what the experts predicted. In the years that followed, Milgram and others replicated the study in various forms with more than 1,000 participants: males, females, varying age and situations. But they came to the same conclusions. The Milgram experiment was repeated at various times and in various countries, and the proportion of "teachers" who continued to shock the "learners" all the way to the top of the scale was always the same—between 61 and 66% (Blass, 1999; Milgram, 2009). The situation is a powerful factor in determining blind obedience.

Milgram did try different variations of the study that decreased the amount of obedience. Situations that decreased obedience included teaming with others who also refused to obey; the learner being in the same room as the teacher; the teacher being alone in the room; or if two experimenters gave different commands. From Milgram's study and others, we have an idea of the kinds of things than can increase and decrease blind obedience to authority, as you can see in TABLE 16-1.

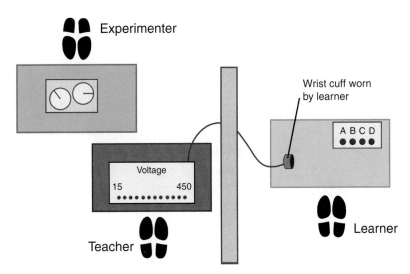

FIGURE 16-7 The Milgram experiment consisted of an experimenter and learner who were both part of the study, and a teacher.

While the participants in the experiment seemed to have no long-term effects from participating in the study, it begs the question about whether the study went too far. The experimenters subjected the teachers to a good deal of anxiety. Many of the teachers felt guilty about having "shocked" strangers and regretted their actions even after discovering no one was hurt. Certainly given the current guidelines for ethical behavior in research, the experiment could not be replicated in its original form.

TABLE 16-1 Factors that Increase and Decrease Conformity

Increase	Decrease
A unanimous group	Seeing others behaving independently
Giving your responses in the open	Low prestige of the person giving orders
Having a difficult task	Disinterest in the approval of others in the group
Having an ambiguous task	High self-confidence
Doubt of your ability	Knowledge of ethics
Attraction to the group	
Possessing low self-esteem	
Having a low amount of leadership potential	
Being in a large group	

Source: Data from Asch, S. E. (1956). Studies of independence and conformity: I. A minority of one against a unanimous majority. Psychological monographs; Deutsch, M., & Gerard, H. B. (1955). A study of normative and informational social influences upon individual judgment. The Journal of Abnormal and Social Psychology, *51(3), 629; Hofling, C. K., Brotzman, E., Dalrymple, S., Graves, N. & Bierce, C. (1966). An experimental study of nurse-physican relationships.* Journal of Nervous and Mental Disease, 143, *171–180.*

CRITICAL THINKING APPLICATION

Consider the Milgram experiment. Remember, the participants believed they are actually hurting the subjects.

Evaluate

1. Use the core motives of social psychology to explain the behavior of the participants.
2. Using what you know about social psychology, relate the concepts of social psychology to bullying and hazing.
3. Many people who hear about the Milgram experiment suggest they would have behaved differently. How can you explain this response using social psychology?

CONCEPT LEARNING CHECK 16.5   *Distinguishing Conformity, Obedience, and Compliance*

First, match the terms to the definitions of conformity, obedience, and compliance and then distinguish between conformity, obedience, and compliance in the following situations.

A. Compliance

B. Conformity

C. Obedience

Definitions

1. _____ A change in behavior in response to the orders of another.

2. _____ Changing thoughts or behavior to align with another.

3. _____ Shifting your behavior because of a request.

Situations

1. _____ You buy white earphones instead of black because all your friends own white earphones.

2. _____ A professor assigns a deadline for a paper, so you finish the paper by that day.

3. _____ A friend asks you to pick her up from the airport.

4. _____ Your boss at work requests that you change the paper in the photocopier.

5. _____ You consider having a milkshake at dinner, but since all your friends are just having water, you order water, too.

16.6 Social Interactions

The way we relate to each other can reveal our assumptions and influences prejudice, aggression, and attraction.

- Describe the biological, psychological, and sociocultural aspects of prejudice, aggression, and attraction.

Studying social interactions can help us understand how we prejudge people as well as the impact of aggression and attraction on social interactions. Studying and understanding prejudice can help us attempt to diminish the impact of prejudice.

Prejudice

Like all attitudes, prejudice contains three components: an affective, or emotional component (like or dislike toward the group), a behavioral component (acts toward or against a group), and a cognitive component (set of beliefs about the group). Prejudicial affects, beliefs, and behaviors can be strongly resistant to change.

Prejudice is universal. You may have prejudicial attitudes toward or against certain kinds of computers, food, music, areas of the country, body types, or racial groups. Prejudice can be overt or subtle. It can be so ingrained in the culture, it can be difficult to see—especially when it is your own. Prejudice is easier to spot in other people than in yourself.

Prejudice is the way people apply characteristics of and judgments about a group to an individual. Often these characteristics and judgments are negative. Discrimination goes a step further than prejudice. **Discrimination** involves the tendency to act differently toward a member of a particular group.

How prevalent is prejudice? It depends on whom you ask. A recent poll by CNN (2006) revealed that 18% of whites saw racial bias as a serious problem in the United States. The same poll showed that 49% of blacks saw racial bias as a problem FIGURE 16-8.

What reduces prejudice? Exposure alone does not necessarily help (Brewer & Brown, 1998). Rather, working together in a setting in which people are equal, in an environment that fosters friendships, and in which an authority encourages this setting does tend to improve relationships of people with different backgrounds (Pettigrew & Tropp, 2006).

Aggression

Aggression consists of words or physical acts a person does in order to cause harm. There are several types of aggression. **Instrumental aggression**, for example, is aggression that

Discrimination The tendency to act differently toward members of a particular group.

Aggression Words or physical acts that a person does in order to cause harm.

Instrumental aggression Words or physical acts a person does to cause harm in an ultimate goal to obtain something.

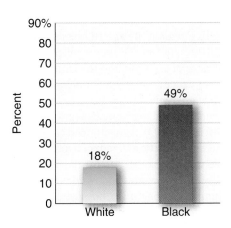

FIGURE 16-8 Prevalence of perceived racial bias based on race of respondent.
Source: Data from CNN poll, December 12, 2006.

is used to obtain something, like a child who hits another child to obtain a toy truck. **Hostile aggression** is a desire to inflict harm, as seen in bullying.

Biology of Aggression

Biological theories of aggression highlight areas of the brain and brain chemicals associated with aggression. Twin studies have suggested that about 34% of the factors associated with aggression, such as levels of certain hormones and neurotransmitters, could be biological (Brendgen, Vitaro, Boivin, Dionne, & Pérusse, 2006). For example, since a large percentage of people arrested for aggressive crime are men, and since men have higher levels of the sex hormone **testosterone**, research has pointed to the role of testosterone as a chemical associated with aggressive behavior. Newer research has also implicated low levels of **serotonin**, a neurotransmitter involved in sleep, mood, and appetite, as playing a role in aggression. Diminished serotonin is linked to problems in controlling behavior (Seo, Patrick, & Kennealy, 2008).

Certain brain areas are also important in aggression. The **amygdala**, a cluster of neurons in the temporal lobe linked to emotions such as anger and fear, and other areas of the limbic system have been associated with aggressive behavior. For example, damage to limbic system structures can produce aggression even when the person is not threatened (Siever, 2008).

Psychological and Sociocultural Aspects of Aggression

Psychological and social factors are also involved in aggression. Some psychologists point toward observational learning as a way we learn aggression. The Bobo experiments (Bandura, Ross, & Ross, 1961) were designed to find out whether watching aggression could make people more or less aggressive. After all, psychoanalytic theory might suggest that observing aggression could be **cathartic**, involving a release of pent-up emotions, and lead to less aggression in a person. Bandura's experiment involved a room full of toys, including an inflatable Bobo doll. A group of children watched as an adult played in the room with the plastic doll, hitting it, flinging it in the air, and kicking it. Another group of kids did not watch the adult play. Then, one by one, kids were set free to play in the room. Would watching aggression mean the kids would play more or less aggressively? Bandura and his team of researchers watched the kids play and counted only the aggressive acts that were not modeled by the adult. The kicks, punches and flings that the kids saw the adult modeling would not be counted. The children could choose to play however they liked. The result? The kids who watched the aggressive model exhibited more aggressive acts, including attraction to playing with toy guns, than the kids who did not watch the model.

Sociocultural theories of aggression suggest that societal and cultural factors can be important aspects of aggression. After all, crime is much higher in countries that have considerable gaps between poor and rich (Kennedy, Kawachi, Prothrow-Stith, Lochner, & Gupta, 1998). In addition, in cultures of honor, in which reputation is a core part of personality, insults more often result in aggression (Cohen, 2001; Cohen, Nisbett, Bowdle, & Schwarz, 1996).

Hostile aggression Aggression simply to inflict harm.

Testosterone A sex hormone that stimulates production of sperm and development of sex organs in males, and sex drive in males and females.

Serotonin A neurotransmitter involved in sleep, mood, and appetite.

Amygdala A cluster of neurons in the temporal lobe linked to emotions such as anger and fear.

Cathartic An experience that involves the release of pent-up emotions.

Media Impact: The Impact of TV, Movies, Music, and Videogames

It is no surprise that TV shows are full of aggression. By age 18, the average American has seen 40,000 murders (Huston et al., 1992). In fact, TV shows greatly exaggerate the amount of violence compared to actual rates of aggression in the United States. What are missing from the shows are the consequences of the violent behavior, which may unintentionally communicate that violence has limited impact.

Unfortunately, there is a wealth of evidence that exposure to aggressive TV, movies, and music increases aggression (Anderson et al., 2003). As mentioned earlier, it was once thought that viewing aggressive acts would be cathartic and reduce aggression in people, but it appears to do the opposite. People who are exposed to media violence are more aggressive than those who are not exposed to the aggression (Anderson & Bushman, 2001; Villani, 2001). Videogames fare similarly. In one study, boys who were allowed to play aggressive videogames displayed much more physical and verbal aggression than those who were not (Irwin & Gross, 1995).

Factors in Attraction

You will recall that one of the core principles of social psychology is that people like being correct and consistent and like to boost their self-esteem. The same formula attracts us to our friends and romantic interests. We like people who like us and who are competent, physically attractive, and similar to us. Furthermore we seek out these rewards while expending as little effort and cost as possible.

Competence

Surrounding yourself with competent people makes you feel good about who wants to be around you—as long as they are not overly competent. Too much competence can create discomfort. Having flaws, if you are very confident, helps to temper the high levels of confidence (Helmreich, Aronson, & LeFan, 1970).

Proximity

Proximity plays a central role in forming supportive contacts. Festinger (Festinger, 1951) examined friendship patterns among military veterans and their wives living in two student housing projects at the Massachusetts Institute of Technology. People who lived closer to each other were much more likely to become friends than were those whose apartments were farther apart. The exact location of people's apartments also had an effect on what kind of friendships were formed. For example, within the buildings, friendships were highly dependent on whether residents' apartments were centrally located or toward the end of the floor. An explanation for the importance of proximity may be familiarity. All other things being equal, people seem to like objects and people to which they have been exposed to before—this is called the **mere exposure effect** (Moreland & Zajonc, 1982). We tend to prefer things the more we are around them. Through repeated exposure to a person, you may grow to like him or her, and there is a greater chance that the person will become a supportive contact in your interpersonal world.

Mere exposure effect
Repeated exposure to a stimulus leads to preferring that stimulus.

Physical Attractiveness

Another important factor in the early stages of forming supportive contacts is appearance or physical attractiveness (Eagly, Ashmore, Makhijani, & Longo, 1991). Numerous studies have found a strong association between people's perception of others' attractiveness and their positive evaluation of those others as people whom they would like to meet (Dijkstra, Cillessen, Lindenberg, & Veenstra, 2010). In a study of roommates (Carli, Ganley, & Pierce-Otay, 1991), those who perceived their roommates to be attractive were more satisfied with roommate relations. People seem to respond generally favorably to more attractive individuals. Physically attractive people are believed to be nicer people (Lorenzo, Biesanz, & Human, 2010), more skillful verbal communicators (Rosenblat, 2008), and more exciting, sociable, interesting, sensitive, outgoing, nurturing, kind, and modest. People who participated in these studies predicted that physically attractive people would enjoy more satisfying lives, have more social and professional success, and benefit from happier marriages and prestige than less attractive people (Dion, Berscheid, & Walster, 1972). These perceptions may indicate to others that attractive individuals are better able to provide the benefits derived from friendships.

Even though we tend to think that highly attractive people are healthier, happier, and more successful than less attractive people, looks can be deceiving. High levels of attractiveness are not really related to levels of happiness or self-esteem (Major, 1984).

What is attractive? Ignoring the fads that come and go, women who are more youthful looking, and men who are healthy and dominant looking (Cunningham, 1986; Cunningham, Barbee, & Pike, 1990) are considered attractive, and the more average and symmetrical the faces appear, the better (Alley & Cunningham, 1991).

Similarity

Another major determinant of creating contacts is similarity. People tend to gravitate to those who are like themselves. Research suggests that individuals prefer people who are similar to themselves in intelligence, ability, ethnicity, socioeconomic status, and even size. Johnson (Johnson, 1989) discovered that having similar values, interests, and background were strong predictors of friendship in his sample of 50 pairs of friends. Attitudinal similarity may be one of the more powerful factors. When students were told the attitudes of hypothetical strangers, there was a strong and direct relationship between attitude similarity and the students' reports of liking the strangers (Byrne, 1971). Research showed that attitude similarity was a very strong predictor of how much students reported liking each other, even determining seating choice in a classroom (Mackinnon, Jordan, & Wilson, 2011). Some of this similarity is real; however, some may be only perceived similarity, since attitudes and beliefs may bend toward each other over time. There is evidence that similar people are drawn together across cultures and types of relationships (Berscheid & Reis, 1998).

Similarity is an important factor for attraction.

According to the **matching hypothesis**, people are paired to equally attractive partners. People who have similar attitudes may be drawn to each other. Perhaps this is due to our chronic desire to feel validated. Some believe that we overexaggerate similarity to people we like. Despite this, couples are likely to possess similar attitudes, values, and similar levels of attractiveness (Bleske-Rechek, Remiker, & Baker, 2009).

Reciprocity

Reciprocity is an important aspect of human relationships. If someone does something for you, you are more likely to do something for him or her. This principle even extends to liking. Knowing a person thinks you are attractive can also make that person more attractive to you. In addition, people tend to react positively to those who react positively to them (Greitemeyer, 2010). This principle is **reciprocity of liking**. When people like us, they treat us in ways that we appreciate, they smile at us, their eyes brighten when we enter the room, and they cheerfully say hello when we call. It is rewarding when people like us.

> **Matching hypothesis** The belief that people are paired to equally attractive partners.
>
> **Reciprocity of liking** Reacting positively to those who react positively to you.

CONCEPT LEARNING CHECK 16.6 | *Designing for Friendships*

1. A local university that is designing a residential education program has asked you to act as a consultant. You are in charge of helping to design the resident experience. What kinds of features would you include in the living spaces and educational programs to increase friendships and reduce prejudice in the community?

16.7 Group Influence on the Individual

Groups can have a powerful influence on how much an individual will help and on the decision-making and efforts of individuals.

■ Discuss the pros and cons of group influence on an individual.

Think about how you might describe yourself to someone you do not know. You probably would describe yourself as being part of several groups. The groups you belong to are really important. They are linked to your identity, provide a boost of self-esteem, and can be the source of important friendships. Be it your college alma matter, your favorite sports team, or a club, feeling good about the groups you belong to makes you feel good about yourself as well.

In-group bias Accepting the attitudes of your own team.

Out-group homogeneity The tendency for members of an out-group to seem similar to each other.

Sometimes people offer assistance for personal gain and not as an act of altruism.

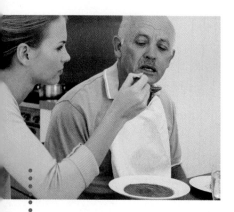

There are many reasons for prosocial behavior including the social responsibility norm, the assumption that assistance should be offered to those in need.

Any group we consider ourselves to be included in—"us"—is the in-group. The in-group consists of people who share similar attitudes and identity. We think of people who are not in our group as "them," or the out-group, a social group to which we do not belong. The in-group is special. Once we find ourselves in a group, we immediately treat the members in the group differently. We start to prefer those in our group. **In-group bias** is accepting the attitudes of your own team. We also tend to see the out-group members as being more alike than those in the in-group: "They are all alike." **Out-group homogeneity**, or the idea that members of the out-group are similar to each other, may be the basis of stereotypes and may also lead to discrimination.

According to social identity theory, in-groups raise our self-esteem because we see the members of the group as special. We can sometimes regard those who are not part of the group as inferior. When this is applied toward ethnic groups, it can result in **ethnocentrism**, which involves believing that your own group is superior to others and that it should be the standard by which other cultures are judged. Ethnocentrism can be the basis of prejudice or negative stereotypes and attitudes about members of a particular group.

There are a lot of benefits to being part of a group, and people are highly motivated to be accepted as members of groups. Once you become a member of a group, the group has a great deal of influence over your behavior, perhaps more than you realize. The social power of groups can affect many things, including how much we help or do not help, those in need, as well as the decisions we make while in a group.

Altruism

It is amazing how much we help each other in a given day. Sometimes we help for external reasons, such as to gain favor from another person; sometimes we do so because of internal motivation. We may help because of our attitudes toward helping those in need; we may see ourselves in or identify with those who need help; or we may feel responsible to help, if we can, because of our ethical standards. There are times when we even help for no reason at all.

How do psychologists think about helpful behavior, otherwise known as prosocial behavior? Why is our behavior sometimes governed by **altruism**, which involves being unselfish and helpful to other people? In part, it is because of the **social-responsibility norm**, the assumption that assistance should be given to those in need. We also help those who have helped us. According to the **reciprocity norm**, we are more likely to offer assistance to people who have helped us in the past. Psychologists are interested in why people risk their own safety for the safety of others, as well as why they sometimes refuse to help when someone is in obvious need.

According to Latane and Darley (1970), the decision to offer assistance happens in five distinct stages. Deciding not to help can happen at any point. First, you have to notice the situation and decide if help is needed. If you determine that help is needed, you then must take personal responsibility to assist. Then, you decide what kind of assistance is needed. Finally, you offer your assistance. For example, let us say you notice that someone has dropped a jar full of change in the parking lot. You first assess whether you should help (are they with someone else?). Then you decide what kind of help that person needs (just some help picking up the change) and you offer assistance if you think you can help.

Another theory of helping suggests that we feel distress when we see someone who needs help. Helping reduces that distress. However, offering help can come at a price. We offer to help when the cost of offering is less than enduring the distress of seeing the person in need (Dovidio, Piliavin, Gaertner, Schroeder, & Clark, 1991).

In addition to these models, there are also social forces that have an impact on helping.

Bystander Intervention

Imagine you are on the street, walking home, and you find yourself in a situation in which you need help. Would you prefer that you have just one stranger around who might provide assistance, or would you prefer three dozen? Before you answer, consider the story of a woman in a similar situation that launched dozens of research investigations into bystander intervention.

Kitty Genovese was attacked and stabbed one night as she returned home from work (Rosenthal, 2008). The attack happened in her neighborhood, over a grueling

30-minute timespan. Her neighbors heard her screams, most likely. Some said that up to 38 people reported hearing the screams and cries for help, yet no one even picked up the phone to call the police during the attack. Reports said that about 20 minutes after she died, the police were finally called, and that they arrived about 2 minutes after the phone call. After the call was made, it was, of course, too late. It turns out that the situation was stacked against Kitty due to the psychology of bystander intervention.

Psychologists interested in helping behavior are especially interested in whether a bystander will offer assistance. One factor determining whether bystanders decide to help is **diffusion of responsibility**, which occurs when the responsibility to help is spread across a crowd. If you are the only person around, then you have to assume responsibility to help. If you and another person are present, then each of you might think that the other person will help. If there are 38 people present, then you have 37 other people who could assume the responsibility, 37 others you could blame if help was not called, and 37 people to share in the guilt if nothing is done. The more people who are around, the less likely it is that a bystander will offer assistance (Fischer et al., 2011). How can this be? It would seem that if more people were around, it would be more likely that someone would help. Do groups make us heartless and uncaring? No. Groups lead us to assume that someone else has already offered their help. The **bystander effect** is a phenomenon in which people in groups are less likely to offer assistance than they would be by themselves.

To test the bystander effect and diffusion of responsibility, psychologists had participants fill out a questionnaire in a room. Some were tested alone; others were tested with one other person and some with two others. As they were diligently filling out the questionnaires, the room filled with ominous smoke. When the participants were by themselves, three out of four reported the smoke. However, as the number of bystanders increased to three, it dropped to one out of three reporting the smoke. In general, when alone, 75% of people will offer to help. It drops to just over half (53%) when in a group (Latane & Nida, 1981).

Besides diffusion of responsibility, there are other factors that increase and decrease bystander helping **TABLE 16-2**. Some argue that seeing others not helping makes it easier to assume that the situation is not urgent, and that this assumption reduces the likelihood of helping. Seeing others not react can lead us to believe that everything is okay. "See something, say something" campaigns are meant to create a sense of responsibility and to call people to action in order to reduce diffusion of responsibility.

Effects of Group Interaction

People tend to clump together and form groups. People live in cities and form sports teams, work groups, and even Internet chat groups. Humans seem to have a fondness for bonding. These groups, whether virtual or physical, are influenced by the people in them, and being a member of the group influences the individuals, too. Almost instantly, people begin to imitate the behaviors of the individuals in the group, look for a group leader, and tend to prefer their group's members over nonmembers.

You probably belong to dozens of groups—sports groups, classroom groups, maybe a sorority, fraternity, or even a secret society. Some groups last a lifetime. I will always feel like a member of the Spring Valley High School Class of 1985 (Go Vikings!). Other groups are quick to form and vanish nearly as instantly, like the one made up of the three people I stood next to for 4 minutes waiting for the campus shuttle.

Catherine (Kitty) Genovese.

Ethnocentrism Believing that your own group is superior to others and should be the standard by which other cultures are judged.

Altruism Being unselfish and helpful toward other people.

Social-responsibility norm The assumption that assistance should be given to those in need.

Reciprocity norm An assumption that you should behave positively toward those who have helped you.

Diffusion of responsibility The tendency for the responsibility to help is spread across a crowd.

TABLE 16-2 Factors that Increase and Decrease Bystander Assistance

Increase	Decrease
We know the victim	Rushed
In-group member requires assistance	Situation is ambiguous
Good mood	Might be injured
The person is dependent on others (like a child)	Out-group member needs help
	We perceive that the victim is responsible for needing help

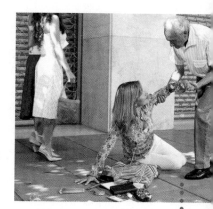

People are less likely to offer help if they believe that help has already been offered.

Bystander effect A phenomenon in which people are less likely to offer assistance to someone in need while in groups than they are by themselves.

Group polarization The likelihood that the attitudes of members of a team will become more similar over time.

Groupthink When a group's ideals become so important that alternative ideas are dismissed.

We can form in-group and out-group preferences almost instantly and prefer members of our in-group without even meeting them. In a study by Tajfel, Billig, Bundy, and Flament (1971), a group of about 50 students were shown slides of paintings by two different artists. They were asked to view the slides and indicate their preferences. The participants thought they were being placed into groups according to their preferences, but actually they were randomly assigned into one of the two groups. Then the subjects, newly aware of their group status, were asked to allocate money to the other participants. The researchers discovered that the subjects tended to favor their own group—quite a bit, as you can see in FIGURE 16-9. The study revealed a strong in-group bias, in which they were more accepting of the members of their own group.

FIGURE 16-9 Even when placed into random groups people were more likely to assign money to their own group members (blue) than to members of other groups (red).
Source: Tajfel, H., Billig, M. G., Bundy, R. P., & Flament, C. (1971). Social categorization and intergroup behavior. European Journal of Social Psychology, 1(2), 149–178.

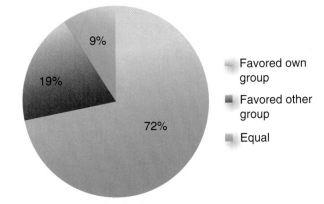

- Favored own group — 72%
- Favored other group — 19%
- Equal — 9%

Decision Making

Making decisions is not always easy. Making decisions in a group can be even more difficult. A lot of important decisions happen in groups. From serious ones like jury decisions to more light-hearted ones like where to have a family reunion or a birthday party, group decision making is much more complicated than making a decision by yourself. Since groups can influence the individual and individuals can influence the group, group decision making happens in complex ways, especially when groupthink and group polarization occur.

Group Polarization

Groups sometimes make riskier decisions than individuals might. The nature of the group may help determine how group decisions differ from individual ones. When individuals themselves are risk averse, they tend to be even more conservative when they are in a group. When individuals are prone toward risk taking, they take even more risks when together in a group. Basically, the group amplifies the individual members' inclinations. This tendency is called **group polarization**, which is the likelihood that the attitudes of members of a team will become more similar over time. How does this happen? Some believe that since people gather ideas from others, and they tend to listen to information that supports their thoughts, their groups can help them feel even more secure in their initial attitude.

People also compare their ideas as they share them. In order to be seen in the best light, they may change their views to match those in the group and increase a sense of belonging. While discussing ideas, they may form a membership with the group (in-group) and conform to their idea of the will of the group. Groups do not always cause polarization or risky (or conservative) shifts. Polarization tends to occur more often when the group consists of people who share particular feelings. The less the group's members share particular attitudes, the less likely group polarization will occur.

Groupthink

Sometimes groups begin to overestimate their moral position, become more closed off to new people and ideas, and pressure their members to conform. These are signs of **groupthink**, when a group's ideas become so important to the group that alternative ideas are dismissed. With groupthink, the members are so focused on being good members of the group that they are not focusing on making the best decisions.

In groupthink the members are so focused on being a good group member they aren't focused on making the best decisions.

When a team feels very optimistic and almost infallible, it can often form groupthink. When that happens, opposing views are shot down and decisions are made without concern for minority opinions. Everyone is on the same page on the surface, though in actuality, some members may find the decisions troubling. Groupthink is more likely in tight-knit groups with dynamic leaders. In order to prevent groupthink, the group's leader should show an ability to listen to criticism, and criticism should be actively encouraged. Since the leader may be highly influential, the leader should hide his or her thoughts until the individual members have expressed ideas and criticism. Smaller groups should be formed that can generate ideas and criticism. Bringing in members of other teams can bring fresh ideas. A devil's advocate should be appointed to give voice to alternative opinions (Packer, 2009).

Individual Influence

Individuals do have some power. Individuals in a minority who are stalwart in their positions have greater success in changing the views of the majority than do individuals who are wishy-washy (Moscovici, 1985). Their position may lead those in the majority to reconsider their views. Conformity to the minority position occurs through informational pressure rather than normative pressure. A consistent and confident message may get the minority view heard.

Social Loafing

Having more people involved in an activity can be useful. It might appear that the more people there are to help, the less each person has to do. However, when there is no way to assess how much each person has contributed, people tend to put forth less effort than they normally might. **Social loafing** is the tendency to put forth less effort in a group than one would on one's own. Social loafing seems to be affected by an individual's understanding of how essential his or her individual effort is to the overall task. It also depends on how much the individual wants the group to succeed. If people feel that their contributions are not really essential and that no one will know whether they helped, they tend to pull back on their efforts. The larger the group, the more this can be a problem.

What helps alleviate social loafing? Anything that can both strengthen the importance of group success and increase the uniqueness of an individual's contribution. Social loafing, as you may imagine, is greater when people work with people they do not know rather than with people they do know. Also, the more difficult and rewarding the group task, the less social loafing there likely will be.

Social loafing can be decreased by forming close relations in the group and by providing consequences for or criticism of loafers (Aggarwal & O'Brien, 2008). There is a cultural aspect to social loafing, too: It is more likely in individualistic cultures and less likely among collectivist cultures. In fact, in collectivist cultures, working in a group more often generates greater effort (Earley, 1993).

Social Facilitation

While groups can decrease individuals' efforts, being around people can at times increase performance. Maybe you have had the experience of working harder or improving your performance when you are with others. **Social facilitation** is the tendency to work harder when others are around (Bond & Titus, 1983). Having others around can be encouraging (Zajonc, 1965), as in a boot camp–type exercise setting, as well as motivating, especially for tasks that are not overly complex, like folding pizza boxes. Norman Triplett (1898) demonstrated that the pressure of others changed individual behavior. He found that in a bike race, the racers were speedier when other racers were nearby than when they were racing against the clock. Added social pressure helped the racers.

Deindividuation

Crowds can affect your individualism. Being in a crowd can even strip away your individuality. **Deindividuation** is a merging of the self with a group in order to feel anonymous. At times, people may behave differently when they are in a large crowd than when they are alone. During Mardi Gras, people dress up in costumes. Both locals and visitors behave quite differently than they do in their everyday lives. Normally, what we do is influenced by social roles and our attitudes, but when we are in an anonymous group, the

Is everyone here pulling as hard as they can? Probably not. When individual effort can't be measured it can lead to social loafing, a tendency to put forth less effort in a group.

Social loafing The tendency to work less in a group than by yourself.

Social facilitation The tendency to work harder when others are around.

Deindividuation A merging of the self with a group in order to feel anonymous.

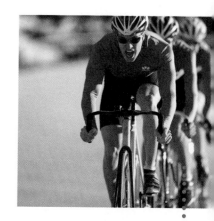

According to social facilitation, having others around can be motivating.

Being in a crowd can cause deindividuation and diminish self-control and individual responsibility.

group can diminish our sense of control and responsibility. Social psychologists call this deindividuation. As the crowd gets larger, we feel more anonymous and tend to behave in the way the group does rather than being influenced by our own attitudes. It is not just crowds that make us feel anonymous. Disguises and darkness can also create this feeling.

What causes this? Some believe that deindividuation causes people to become less connected to their own attitudes. Others suggest that identification with the crowd and conformity to the new norms become powerful forces, and those who are part of the group are conforming to the new norm (Li, 2010).

Summary of Multiple Influences on Social Psychology

The baker returned with a cupcake in the shape of a puppy face. It had molded chocolate toffee ears and a nose made from a licorice jellybean. It was a wonderful gift, and the baker said it gave her joy to do something nice for me. "It's on the house, Hun, enjoy it."

We are most human, for better or for worse, around others. Studying social psychology reveals a lot about what it means to be human—maybe more so than any other branch of psychology. So too are there multiple influences on the way our social interactions change us and on the ways we change those around us. Biology can set the scene and, for example, can impact our perception and aggression. Social settings bring out discrimination, selfless acts, and blind obedience in all of us. As society changes, we do too, which helps explain why a little girl assumed I was a president.

CONCEPT LEARNING CHECK 16.7 | *Preventing Groupthink*

1. You have been selected to be the leader of a community group to look over a local park. You have to make a decision about the installation of a controversial outdoor sculpture that has been donated to the city. The citizens in your group are long-standing residents of the houses that surround the park. What steps can you take to ensure that group's decision does not fall prey to groupthink?

Visual Overview The Core Social Motives

As you have seen in this chapter, people both influence and are influenced by, their social environments. Susan Fiske (2003) summarized the influences into five core social motives: BUC(k)ET. Remembering these core social influences is a good way to understand how we operate in our social world.

BELONGING

People are motivated to join together and create relationships.

UNDERSTANDING

People are motivated to make sense of the world. This helps people to predict their own behavior and the behavior of others.

CONTROLLING

People are motivated to exert power over the things that happen to them.

K

ENHANCING SELF

People are motivated to feel and be perceived as worthy.

TRUSTING

People are motivated to see the world in a positive light.

16.1 Social Thought and Behavior

- Social psychology is a branch of psychology that examines how the ways that people think, feel, and behave influence and are influenced by others.

- Social roles and social norms are expectations about customary behaviors based on a person's position.
- People strive to belong, control, enhance themselves, and understand.

16.2 Person Perception

- Person perception is concerned with the way people form opinions about others. One aspect of person perception is social categorization.

- People use physical appearance and stereotypes in order to categorize others.

16.3 Attribution: The Person or the Situation?

- An attribution is a mental explanation for events or behavior.
- Internal attributions explain behavior based on personality.
- External attribution focuses on environmental and situational explanations of behavior.

- The actor-observer discrepancy is the likelihood of assigning an external and situational explanation to one's own behavior while assigning an internal and personal factor to the behavior of others.
- The self-serving bias is the tendency to see oneself in a positive light.

16.4 Attitudes and Social Judgments

- An attitude is a tendency to judge people, objects, or issues in a certain way.
- Attitudes consist of affects, behaviors, and cognitions.
- When the components of an attitude are in harmony, it is easy to predict the other components.
- Cognitive dissonance is the discomfort that people experience from holding two competing ideas at the same time.

- Attitudes can be influenced by persuasion.
- When people use logic to change their attitudes, they are employing the central route to persuasion.
- The peripheral route to persuasion occurs when attitudes are influenced by noncore factors.
- Attitudes can be altered by role playing.

16.5 Conformity and Obedience

- Conformity involves a change in thoughts or behavior to align with another person or group.
- Obedience involves a change in behavior in response to the orders of another.
- Compliance involves shifting behavior because of a request.

- People conform in response to social pressure or norms (normative social influence) as well as to the need to be correct (informational social influence).
- The Asch, Zimbardo, and Milgram studies demonstrated the power of the situation in conformity and obedience.

16.6 Social Interactions

- Prejudice involves stereotyped attitudes about a member of a group.
- Discrimination is the tendency to act differently toward a member of a group.
- Aggression consists of words or physical acts a person does to cause harm to another and can be due to a desire to obtain something (as in instrumental aggression) or simply to inflict harm (hostile aggression).

- Aggression has multiple influences, including biological, psychological, and sociocultural.
- There are multiple influences to attraction, including competence, proximity, physical attractiveness, similarity, and reciprocity.

16.7 Group Influence on the Individual

- Groups can influence an individual.
- When in a group, we treat those in the group differently than those outside of a group.
- Prosocial behavior involves helping another and can be influenced by the presence of others.
- Diffusion of responsibility can cause a bystander effect in which people are less likely to offer assistance to someone in need while in a group than when they are by themselves.
- Groups can also affect decision making and can cause the individuals in the group to shift attitudes so they are more similar over time.

- When a group is involved in groupthink, its members overestimate the moral position of the group, become more closed off to ideas, and are pressured to conform.
- When there is no way to assess how much each person has contributed to a group, people tend to work less, according to the theory of social loafing.
- Social facilitation occurs when having others around increases a person's performance.
- Deindividuation is a merging of the self with a group and can diminish a person's sense of control and responsibility.

16.1 Social Thought and Behavior

1. Ryan was surprised to discover that his roommate did not like apple pie with cheddar cheese on it. Ryan loved it that way and figured everyone else did as well. Which of the following explains why he thought most people preferred apple pie with cheese?
   A. False consensus effect
   B. Social cognition
   C. Social influence
   D. Social norms

16.2 Person Perception

2. An overgeneralized belief about a person is known as:
   A. social categorization.
   B. stereotype.
   C. groupthink.
   D. person perception.

16.3 Attribution: The Person or the Situation?

3. Marina suggested that the reason her friend's car stereo was stolen was because he must have carelessly left the car unlocked. Marina is using a(n) _____ for the event.
   A. internal attribution
   B. external attribution
   C. self-serving bias
   D. social influence

4. According to the _____, people tend to believe that bad things happen to bad people and good things happen to good people.
   A. actor-observer discrepancy
   B. defensive attribution
   C. just-world hypothesis
   D. self-serving bias

16.4 Attitudes and Social Judgments

5. Which of the following theories suggests that people discover their attitudes while observing their own behavior?
   A. Self-serving bias
   B. Cognitive dissonance theory
   C. Actor-observer discrepancy
   D. Self-perception theory

6. If you buy a product because you find the person selling it attractive, your decision is being driven by:
   A. social norms.
   B. the central route to persuasion.
   C. a peripheral route to persuasion.
   D. the foot-in-the-door technique.

16.5 Conformity and Obedience

7. The senior partner in the law firm tells Taylor, a junior partner, to revise the brief before she leaves that evening, and she does. The act of doing so represents:
   A. conformity.
   B. obedience.
   C. central route to persuasion.
   D. normative social influence.

8. Carla changed her vote from guilty to not guilty simply because the rest of the jury voted that way. Which concept explains why?
   A. Normative social influence
   B. Informational social influence
   C. Compliance
   D. Obedience

16.6 Social Interactions

9. Five-year-old Drake hit his sister Cassie in order to take the ball she was playing with. The act of hitting Cassie to get the ball is an example of:
   A. discrimination.
   B. obedience.
   C. instrumental aggression.
   D. hostile aggression.

10. Nick is surprised that a couple he knows is getting married. "I think she can do better, she's so much more attractive than he is," he thinks. Nick is using which principle to determine the couple's compatibility?
    A. Mere exposure effect
    B. Matching hypothesis
    C. False conscious effect
    D. Self-perception theory

16.7 Group Influence on the Individual

11. Thinking that everyone in the South listens to country music is an example of:
    A. out-group homogeneity.
    B. out-group bias.
    C. ethnocentrism.
    D. in-group bias.

12. Darla helped her neighbor clean her gutters because earlier in the summer, the same neighbor helped her clean out the garage. This helping behavior demonstrates:
    A. social facilitation.
    B. altruism.
    C. social responsibility norm.
    D. reciprocity norm.

13. Individuals with a minority decision within a group will need to sway the larger group to the minority opinion using:
    A. informational social influence.
    B. normative social influence.
    C. social facilitation.
    D. groupthink.

14. Barbara likes exercising in boot camp with other people because she feels she works much harder than when she works out alone. Her extra effort is due to:
    A. diffusion of responsibility.
    B. bystander effect.
    C. deindividuation.
    D. social facilitation.

15. Although they were helping Trey get his truck unstuck from the mud, not everyone was pushing as hard as he could. The factor that explains this is:
    A. group polarization.
    B. groupthink.
    C. social loafing.
    D. deindividuation.

CHAPTER DISCUSSION QUESTIONS

1. Recognizing that they are all important, select the one social motive that you consider most important to you. Then, select the one that you consider least important to you. Explain your answers.

2. Section 16.2 outlines some of the reasons people develop stereotypes. Examine these reasons for stereotype development, and then consider if they could also be used to reverse a person's stereotypes. In other words, how might you use your knowledge of stereotypes to undo a stereotype?

3. Cognitive dissonance theory states that if we hold two conflicting beliefs, we will change our beliefs to decrease the discomfort of the conflict. Relate this theory to an experience from your own life. Is there a time when you have changed your opinion because you realized that your beliefs were in conflict? What were the original conflicting beliefs? What change in belief(s) reduced the discomfort of the conflict? Did you keep the new beliefs or find yourself wanting to return to the old beliefs?

4. Consider the difference between conformity (you shifting your thoughts to align with someone else's) versus obedience (changing because someone tells you to). Now consider a situation in which you might change your thoughts or behavior. Is there a difference in how you would evaluate your change if you did it to align with someone (conformity) versus if someone told you to change (obedience)? What positive or negative self-evaluations might go along with realizing you were conforming versus obedient?

5. Imagine that you are the manager of a group working on a team project. Review the different elements of group influences on the individual in Section 16.7 and identify the top three that would help you do a good job. Explain why you chose each group influence and how understanding it would make you a better manager.

CHAPTER PROJECTS

1. Imagine that you have a sibling who is about to start high school and is very nervous about making friends and getting along with his/her teachers. Use your knowledge of social psychology to prepare a guidebook of advice for your sibling. You may organize your book however you would like, but make sure it includes specific examples from the chapter along with specific scenarios in which social psychology would be helpful.

2. Think of a historical event about which you know something about the behavior and decisions of individuals from the event. Then, use the concepts from this chapter to interpret the behaviors and decisions of these individuals. Of course, you may not have all of the details of each person's behavior, so go with what you know and feel free to speculate a bit if necessary. How might your knowledge of social psychology change the interpretation of a person's behavior?

CHAPTER KEY TERMS

Actor	**Discrimination**	**Peripheral route to persuasion**
Actor-observer bias	**Door-in-the-face technique**	**Person perception**
Aggression	**Ethnocentrism**	**Persuasion**
Altruism	**External attribution**	**Prejudice**
Amygdala	**False consensus effect**	**Reciprocity norm**
Attitude	**Foot-in-the-door technique**	**Reciprocity of liking**
Attribution	**Fundamental attribution error**	**Role**
Attribution theory	**Group**	**Schema**
Availability heuristic	**Group polarization**	**Self-perception theory**
Blaming the victim	**Groupthink**	**Self-serving bias**
Bystander effect	**Hostile aggression**	**Serotonin**
Cathartic	**In-group bias**	**Social categorization**
Central route to persuasion	**Individualist cultures**	**Social cognition**
Cognitive dissonance	**Informational social influence**	**Social facilitation**
Cognitive dissonance theory	**Instrumental aggression**	**Social influence**
Collectivist cultures	**Internal attribution**	**Social loafing**
Compliance	**Just-world hypothesis**	**Social norm**
Conflict	**Matching hypothesis**	**Social psychology**
Conformity	**Mere exposure effect**	**Social-responsibility norm**
Defensive attribution	**Normative social influence**	**Social roles**
Deindividuation	**Obedience**	**Stereotype**
Diffusion of responsibility	**Out-group homogeneity**	**Testosterone**

ANSWERS TO CONCEPT LEARNING CHECKS

16.1 Describing Social Roles

Host: Seats customers, hands them a menu

Server: Greets customers, requests drink order, brings food, brings check

Customer: Gives food order, pays check, leaves tip

16.2 Person Perception and Musical Tastes

Typical answers would be:

1. D. Rock
2. A. Country
3. C. Punk
4. B. Classical

Would you be surprised if you were wrong? What influenced your answers?

16.3 Explaining Attributional Biases

1. Actor-observer bias. [The actor-observer bias suggests that people tend to assign an external and situational explanation to their own behavior while assigning internal, personal factors to the behavior of others.]

2. Self-serving bias. [The self-serving bias reflects the belief that good things happen because of ability and bad things occur because of external factors.]

3. Just-world hypothesis. [The just-world hypothesis suggests that we believe that people get what they deserve and deserve what they get. If Belinda's roommate's parents were going through an audit, they must have deserved the circumstance.]

16.4 Explaining Persuasion

Include as many key terms as you can.

16.5 Distinguishing Conformity, Obedience, and Compliance

1. C. Obedience—changing behavior in response to the orders of another

2. B. Conformity—changing thoughts or behavior to align with another

3. A. Compliance—shifting your behavior because of a request

1. You buy white earphones instead of black because all your friends own white earphones [conformity].

2. A professor assigns a deadline for a paper, so you finish the paper by that day [obedience].

3. A friend asks you to pick her up from the airport [compliance].

4. Your boss at work requests that you change the paper in the photocopier [obedience].

5. You consider having an expensive drink at dinner, but since all your friends are just having water, you order water, too [conformity].

16.6 Designing for Friendships

Example: Friendships could be increased by making sure that residents are near each other (proximity) and that they are aware of ways in which they are alike (similarity). Prejudice could be decreased by having residents of differing backgrounds work together on difficult tasks in which friendships are encouraged.

16.7 Preventing Groupthink

1. The leader should listen to and actively encourage criticism.

2. The leader should hide his or her thoughts until everyone has expressed ideas and criticism.

3. Small groups should be formed to generate new ideas.

4. A devil's advocate should be appointed to give voice to alternative opinions.

ANSWERS TO CHAPTER REVIEW TEST

16.1 Social Thought and Behavior

1. A. Rationale: The false consensus effect is the habit of seeing your own behavior as typical.

16.2 Person Perception

2. B. Rationale: A stereotype is an overgeneralized belief about a group and its members.

16.3 Attribution: The Person or the Situation?

3. A. Rationale: An internal attribution emphasizes the role of personality characteristics regarding an event.

4. C. Rationale: According to the just-world hypothesis, people get what they deserve and deserve what they get.

16.4 Attitudes and Social Judgments

5. D. Rationale: According to self-perception theory, people infer their attitudes from their behavior.

6. C. Rationale: The peripheral route to persuasion occurs when a person uses insignificant, noncore factors to make a decision—in this case, source attractiveness.

16.5 Conformity and Obedience

7. B. Rationale: Obedience involves a change in your behavior in response to the orders of another.

8. A. Rationale: Normative social influence involves social pressure to conform to a group's norms—in this case, the belief that the defendant in a trial was not guilty.

16.6 Social Interactions

9. C. Rationale: Instrumental aggression is aggression used to obtain something. Hostile aggression is aggression simply to inflict harm.

10. B. Rationale: According to the matching hypothesis, people are paired to equally attractive partners.

16.7 Group Influence on the Individual

11. A. Rationale: Out-group homogeneity suggests that members of an out-group are similar.

12. D. Rationale: The reciprocity norm suggests that when someone helps us, we are more likely to help that person in return.

13. A. Rationale: Informational social influence involves conformity due to evidence.

14. D. Rationale: Social facilitation is the tendency to work harder when others are around.

15. C. Rationale: Social loafing is the tendency to work less in a group than by yourself.

REFERENCES

Aggarwal, P., & O'Brien, C. L. (2008). Social loafing on group projects. *Journal of Marketing Education, 30*(3), 255.

Ajzen, I. (2005). *Attitudes, personality and behavior.* New York: McGraw-Hill International.

Alley, T. R., & Cunningham, M. R. (1991). Averaged faces are attractive, but very attractive faces are not average. *Psychological Science, 2*(2), 123–125.

Ambady, N., Hallahan, M., & Conner, B. (1999). Accuracy of judgments of sexual orientation from thin slices of behavior. *Journal of Personality and Social Psychology, 77*(3), 538–547. doi:10.1037/0022-3514.77.3.538

Ambady, N., & Rosenthal, R. (1993). Half a minute: Predicting teacher evaluations from thin slices of nonverbal behavior and physical attractiveness. *Journal of Personality and Social Psychology, 64*(3), 431–441. doi:10.1037/0022-3514.64.3.431

Anderson, C. A., Berkowitz, L., Donnerstein, E., Huesmann, L. R., Johnson, J. D., Linz, D., Malamuth, N. M., et al. (2003). The influence of media violence on youth. *Psychological Science in the Public Interest, 4*(3), 81.

Anderson, C. A., & Bushman, B. J. (2001). Effects of violent video games on aggressive behavior, aggressive cognition, aggressive affect, physiological arousal, and prosocial behavior: A meta-analytic review of the scientific literature. *Psychological Science, 12*(5), 353–359.

Asch, S. E. (1956). Studies of independence and conformity: I. A minority of one against a unanimous majority. *Psychological monographs, 70*(9), 1–70. doi: 10.1037/h0093718

Bandura, A., Ross, D., & Ross, S. A. (1961). Transmission of aggression through imitation of aggressive models. *Journal of Abnormal and Social Psychology, 63*(3), 575–582. doi:10.1037/h0045925

Baron, A. S., & Banaji, M. R. (2006). The development of implicit attitudes. Evidence of race evaluations from ages 6 and 10 and adulthood. *Psychological Science, 17*(1), 53–58. doi:10.1111/j.1467-9280.2005.01664.x

Baumeister, R. F., Bratslavsky, E., Finkenauer, C., & Vohs, K. D. (2001). Bad is stronger than good. *Review of General Psychology, 5,* 323–370.

Bem, D. J. (1967). Self-perception: An alternative interpretation of cognitive dissonance phenomena. *Psychological Review, 74*(3), 183.

Berscheid, E., & Reis, H. T. (1998). Attraction and close relationships. *Handbook of Social Psychology, 2,* 193–281.

Blass, T. (1999). The Milgram paradigm after 35 years: Some things we now know about obedience to authority. *Journal of Applied Social Psychology, 29*(5), 955–978.

Bleske-Rechek, A., Remiker, M. W., & Baker, J. P. (2009). Similar from the start: Assortment in young adult dating couples and its link to relationship stability over time. *Individual Differences Research, 7*(3), 142–158.

Bond, C. F., & Titus, L. J. (1983). Social facilitation: A meta-analysis of 241 studies. *Psychological Bulletin, 94*(2), 265–292. doi:10.1037/0033-2909.94.2.265

Brendgen, M., Vitaro, F., Boivin, M., Dionne, G., & Pérusse, D. (2006). Examining genetic and environmental effects on reactive versus proactive aggression. *Developmental Psychology, 42*(6), 1299–1312. doi:10.1037/0012-1649.42.6.1299

Brewer, M. B., & Brown, R. J. (1998). *Intergroup relations.* New York: McGraw-Hill.

Byrne, D. (1971). *The attraction paradigm (Personality and Psychopathology, Vol. 11,* 1st ed.). Academic Press.

Carli, L. L., Ganley, R., & Pierce-Otay, A. (1991). Similarity and satisfaction in roommate relationships. *Personality and Social Psychology Bulletin, 17*(4), 419.

Carney, D. R., Colvin, C. R., & Hall, J. A. (2007). A thin slice perspective on the accuracy of first impressions. *Journal of Research in Personality, 41*(5), 1054–1072. doi:16/j.jrp.2007.01.004

CNN (2006, December 12). Poll: Most Americans see lingering racism—in others. CNN.COM. Retrieved from http://edition.cnn.com/2006/US/12/12/racism.poll/index.html

Cohen, D. (2001). Cultural variation: Considerations and implications. *Psychological Bulletin, 127*(4), 451.

Cohen, D., Nisbett, R. E., Bowdle, B. F., & Schwarz, N. (1996). Insult, aggression, and the Southern culture of honor: An "experimental ethnography." *Journal of Personality and Social Psychology, 70*(5), 945.

Cunningham, M. R. (1986). Measuring the physical in physical attractiveness: Quasi-experiments on the sociobiology of female facial beauty. *Journal of Personality and Social Psychology, 50*(5), 925.

Cunningham, M. R., Barbee, A. P., & Pike, C. L. (1990). What do women want? Facialmetric assessment of multiple motives in the perception of male facial physical attractiveness. *Journal of Personality and Social Psychology, 59*(1), 61–72. doi:10.1037/0022-3514.59.1.61

Dijkstra, J. K., Cillessen, A. H. N., Lindenberg, S., & Veenstra, R. (2010). Same-gender and cross-gender likeability: Associations with popularity and status enhancement: The TRAILS study. *Journal of Early Adolescence, 30*(6), 773–802. doi:10.1177/0272431609350926

Dion, K., Berscheid, E., & Walster, E. (1972). What is beautiful is good. *Journal of Personality and Social Psychology, 24*(3), 285.

Dovidio, J. F., Piliavin, J. A., Gaertner, S. L., Schroeder, D. A., & Clark III, R. D. (1991). The arousal: Cost-reward model and the process of intervention: A review of the evidence. In M. Clark (Ed.), *Prosocial behavior. Review of personality and social psychology* (Vol. 12, pp. 86–118). Newbury Park, CA: Sage.

Eagly, A. H., Ashmore, R. D., Makhijani, M. G., & Longo, L. C. (1991). What is beautiful is good, but . . .: A meta-analytic review of research on the physical attractiveness stereotype. *Psychological Bulletin, 110*(1), 109.

Earley, P. C. (1993). East meets West meets Mideast: Further explorations of collectivistic and individualistic work groups. *Academy of Management Journal, 36*(2), 319–348. doi:10.2307/256525

Festinger, L. (1951). Architecture and group membership. *Journal of Social Issues, 7*(1–2), 152–163. doi:10.1111/j.1540-4560.1951.tb02229.x

Festinger, L. (1957). *A theory of cognitive dissonance.* Palo Alto, CA: Stanford University Press.

Festinger, L., Riecken, H., & Schachter, S. (2011). *When prophecy fails.* Eastford, CT: Martino Fine Books.

Fischer, P., Krueger, J. I., Greitemeyer, T., Vogrincic, C., Kastenmüller, A., Frey, D., Heene, M., et al. (2011). The bystander effect: A meta-analytic review on bystander intervention in dangerous and non-dangerous emergencies. *Psychological Bulletin, 137*(4), 517–537. doi:10.1037/a0023304

Fiske, S. T. (2003). Five core social motives, plus or minus five. *Motivated Social Perception, 9*, 233–246.

Greitemeyer, T. (2010). Effects of reciprocity on attraction: The role of a partner's physical attractiveness. *Personal Relationships, 17*(2), 317–330.

Helmreich, R., Aronson, E., & LeFan, J. (1970). To err is humanizing sometimes: Effects of self-esteem, competence, and a pratfall on interpersonal attraction. *Journal of Personality and Social Psychology, 16*(2), 259–264. doi:10.1037/h0029848.

Hoshino-Browne, E., Zamana, A., Spencer, S., Zanna, M., Kitayama S. & Lackenbauer, S. (2005). On the cultural guises of cognitive dissonance: The case of easterners and westerners. *Journal of Personal and Social Psychology, 89*(3), 294–310.

Huston, A. C., Zuckerman, D., Wilcox, B. L., Donnerstein, E., Fairchild, H., Feshbach, N. D., Katz, P. A., et al. (1992). *Big world, small screen: The role of television in American society.* Lincoln, NE: University of Nebraska Press.

Irwin, A. R., & Gross, A. M. (1995). Cognitive tempo, violent video games, and aggressive behavior in young boys. *Journal of Family Violence, 10*(3), 337–350.

Johnson, M. A. (1989). Variables associated with friendship in an adult population. *Journal of Social Psychology, 129*(3), 379–390.

Kennedy, B. P., Kawachi, I., Prothrow-Stith, D., Lochner, K., & Gupta, V. (1998). Social capital, income inequality, and firearm violent crime. *Social Science & Medicine, 47*(1), 7–17. doi:16/S0277-9536(98)00097-5

Kitayama, S., Snibbe, A. C., Markus, H. R., & Suzuki, T. (2004). Is there any "free" choice? Self and dissonance in two cultures. *Psychological Science, 15*(8), 527–533.

Knowles, E. D., Morris, M. W., Chiu, C. Y., & Hong, Y. Y. (2001). Culture and the process of person perception: Evidence for automaticity among East Asians in correcting for situational influences on behavior. *Personality and Social Psychology Bulletin, 27*(10), 1344–1356. doi:10.1177/01461672012710010

Latane, B., & Darley, J. M. (1970). *The unresponsive bystander: Why doesn't he help?* New York: Appleton-Century Crofts.

Latane, B., & Nida, S. (1981). Ten years of research on group size and helping. *Psychological Bulletin, 89*(2), 308–324. doi:10.1037/0033-2909.89.2.308

Lorenzo, G. L., Biesanz, J. C., & Human, L. J. (2010). What is beautiful is good and more accurately understood. *Psychological Science, 21*(12), 1777–1782. doi:10.1177/0956797610388048

Mackinnon, S. P., Jordan, C. H., & Wilson, A. E. (2011). Birds of a feather sit together: Physical similarity predicts seating choice. *Personality and Social Psychology Bulletin, 37*(7), 879–892. doi:10.1177/0146167211402094

Major, B., Carrington, P. I., & Carnevale, P. J. D. (1984). Physical attractiveness and self-esteem. *Personality and Social Psychology Bulletin, 10*(1), 43–50. doi:10.1177/0146167284101004

Malle, B. F. (2006). The actor-observer asymmetry in attribution: A (surprising) meta-analysis. *Psychological Bulletin, 132*(6), 895–919. doi:10.1037/0033-2909.132.6.895

Meineri, S., & Guéguen, N. (2008). An application of the foot-in-the-door strategy in the environmental field. *European Journal of Social Sciences, 7*(1), 71–74.

Milgram, S. (1963). Behavioral study of obedience. *Journal of Abnormal and Social Psychology, 67*(4), 371–378. doi:10.1037/h0040525

Milgram, S. (2009). *Obedience to authority: An experimental view* (Reprint.). New York: Harper Perennial Modern Classics.

Moreland, R. L., & Zajonc, R. B. (1982). Exposure effects in person perception: Familiarity, similarity, and attraction. *Journal of Experimental Social Psychology, 18*(5), 395–415.

Moscovici, S. (1985). Innovation and minority influence. In S. Moscovici, G. Mugny, & E. Van Avermaet (Eds.), *Perspectives on minority influence* (pp. 9–52). Cambridge, UK: Cambridge University Press..

Packer, D. J. (2009). Avoiding groupthink. *Psychological Science, 20*(5), 546–548. doi:10.1111/j.1467-9280.2009.02333.x

Pettigrew, T. F., & Tropp, L. R. (2006). A meta-analytic test of intergroup contact theory. *Journal of Personality and Social Psychology, 90*(5), 751.

Rosenblat, T. S. (2008). The beauty premium: Physical attractiveness and gender in dictator games. *Negotiation Journal, 24*(4), 465–481. doi:10.1111/j.1571-9979.2008.00198.x

Rosenthal, A. M. (2008). *Thirty-eight witnesses: The Kitty Genovese case.* Brooklyn, NY: Melville House.

Seger, C. R., Smith, E. R., & Mackie, D. M. (2009). Subtle activation of a social categorization triggers group-level emotions. *Journal of Experimental Social Psychology, 45*(3), 460–467. doi:16/j.jesp.2008.12.004

Seo, D., Patrick, C. J., & Kennealy, P. J. (2008). Role of serotonin and dopamine system interactions in the neurobiology of impulsive aggression and its comorbidity with other clinical disorders. *Aggression and Violent Behavior, 13*(5), 383–395.

Siever, L. J. (2008). Neurobiology of aggression and violence. *American Journal of Psychiatry, 165*(4), 429–442. doi:10.1176/appi.ajp.2008.07111774

Smith, N. K., Cacioppo, J. T., Larsen, J. T., & Chartrand, T. L. (2003). May I have your attention, please: Electrocortical responses to positive and negative stimuli. *Neuropsychologia, 41,* 171–183.

Taylor, S. E., Peplau, L. A., & Sears, D. O. (2005). *Social psychology* (12th ed.). Upper Saddle River, NJ: Prentice Hall.

Tajfel, H., Billig, M. G., Bundy, R. P., & Flament, C. (1971). Social categorization and intergroup behavior. *European Journal of Social Psychology, 1*(2), 149–178.

Trafimow, D., Armendariz, M. L., & Madson, L. (2004). A test of whether attributions provide for self-enhancement or self-defense. *Journal of Social Psychology, 144*(5), 453–464.

Triplett, N. (1898). The dynamogenic factors in pacemaking and competition. *American Journal of Psychology, 9*(4), 507–533.

Villani, S. (2001). Impact of media on children and adolescents: A 10-year review of the research. *Journal of the American Academy of Child & Adolescent Psychiatry, 40*(4), 392–401.

Webb, T. L., & Sheeran, P. (2006). Does changing behavioral intentions engender behavior change? A meta-analysis of the experimental evidence. *Psychological Bulletin, 132*(2), 249–268. doi:10.1037/0033-2909.132.2.249

Willis, J., & Todorov, A. (2006). First impressions: Making up your mind after a 100-ms exposure to a face. *Psychological Science, 17*(7), 592–598. doi:10.1111/j.1467-9280.2006.01750.x

Zajonc, R. B. (1965). Social facilitation. *Science, 149*(3681), 269–274.

Zimbardo, P. (2008). *The Lucifer effect: Understanding how good people turn evil.* New York: Random House.

Glossary

360-degree feedback Evaluation method that solicits input from everyone who interacts with an employee.

Absolute refractory period The point after an action potential when the neuron cannot produce another action potential no matter the intensity of the stimulation.

Absolute threshold The lowest amount of physical energy that can be detected reliably 50 percent of the time using a given sense organ.

Acceptance Communication of respect.

Accommodation Movement in an eye's muscles as we focus our vision on near or far objects provides a monocular depth cue; Changing concepts in memory to fit new information.

Acculturative stress The anxiety felt in response to challenges from new cultural expectations.

Acetylcholine Neurotransmitter that is involved in memory and muscle functions.

Achievement gap The difference in U.S. school test scores and grades for white compared to African American children.

Achievement motivation A desire to accomplish difficult jobs in an area with a standard of excellence.

Achievement test A measure of what is already known or learned, as the outcome of education.

Acquisition Gaining new knowledge or behavior to use in the future.

Action potential The electrical message or neural impulse that flows along a neuron's axon.

Activation-synthesis model of dreaming A theory of dreams that suggests that dreams are interpreted brain activity.

Active listening A communication method in which the listener responds in ways that demonstrate understanding of what another person says.

Actor A person who exhibits a behavior.

Actor-observer bias The likelihood of assigning an external and situational explanation to your own behavior while assigning internal, personal factors to the behavior of others.

Actualizing tendency According to the humanists, the instinctual desire to be the best version of yourself possible.

Acute insomnia Short-term inability to fall or stay asleep.

Acute stressor Brief event that requires a period of coping.

Adaptation A process by which a characteristic increases in a population because it makes reproduction or survival more likely.

Adaptation-level phenomenon The ability to adapt to new situations so that the new situation becomes the norm.

Adaptive behavior Cognitive, social, and practical skills used to assess intellectual disability in low-scoring individuals.

Adaptive theory of sleep A theory of sleep that suggests that our sleep-wake patterns are shaped by an evolved biological process.

Adipose tissue Fat cells stored beneath the skin and throughout the abdomen.

Adoption study A method that allows researchers to test hypotheses concerning the contributions of genetic and environmental factors by examining characteristics between children and their biological and non-biological parents.

Adrenal cortex The outer layer of the adrenal gland that secretes hormones during stress.

Adrenal glands Important glands of the endocrine system consisting of the adrenal cortex and the adrenal medulla.

Adrenal medulla The interior layer of the adrenal gland that secretes epinephrine and norepinephrine.

Aerobic exercise Physical activity that increases the capability of the heart and lungs.

Afferent nerve fibers Neurons that move information toward the brain and spinal cord.

Afterimage The appearance of an illusion of color (e.g., red) on a white surface after viewing its complementary color (e.g., green) for a prolonged period.

Age of viability By around 6 months, the fetus has developed enough that it may survive if born prematurely.

Aggression Words or physical acts a person does in order to cause harm.

Agitated catatonia A symptom of schizophrenia that is characterized by excessive motor activity and periods of inexhaustibility.

Agonist A substance that mimics or increases the effect of a neurotransmitter.

Agoraphobia The fear of having a panic attack, which causes a person to avoid places and situations where having a panic attack would be particularly embarrassing or dangerous.

Agreeableness A personality trait that is part of the Big Five that describes how trusting a person is.

Alcohol A type of depressant drug that is associated with reduced inhibition, slurred speech, and impairments in balance.

Algorithm A well-defined process that is guaranteed to produce a solution.

All-or-nothing law The concept that either a neuron fires or it doesn't. There is no partial firing.

Allocentrism A personality trait with an interreliant focus in which people tend to see themselves as part of a community.

Alogia Lack of elaborative speech.

Alpha waves A type of brain wave linked to relaxed wakefulness.

Altruism Being unselfish and helpful toward other people.

Alzheimer's disease A progressive memory disorder in which people lose access to explicit memory.

Ames room An illusion created by adding physical distortions to make a room appear to have a normal rectangular shape so that its contents appear to violate size constancy.

Amnesia The loss of memory in clinical patients.

Amphetamines A class of stimulant drugs that activates the central nervous system.

Amygdala A cluster of neurons in the temporal lobe linked to emotions such as anger and fear.

Analogy A problem-solving process that makes use of a previous solution.

Analytic intelligence Sternberg's theory posited the ability to break problems down into component parts for analysis.

Anecdotal evidence A type of information that relies on unscientific observation.

Anhedonia A reduced capacity to experience pleasure.

Anorexia nervosa An eating disorder in which an individual feels he or she is overweight despite objective evidence.

Antagonist A substance that blocks the action of a neurotransmitter.

Anthropomorphism Assigning human emotions or behaviors to nonhumans.

Antianxiety medication A type of drug used to reduce the symptoms of agitation and nervousness.

Antidepressant medication A type of drug used to reduce the symptoms of depressive mood disorders.

Antipsychotic medication A type of drug used to reduce the symptoms of thought disorders.

Antisocial personality disorder A personality disorder in which a person breaks societal rules, often without remorse or anxiety.

Anxiety disorders A psychological condition marked by nervousness, distress, apprehension, and disruptive attempts to reduce anxiety.

Aphasia An inability to understand or produce language based on damage to the language areas of the brain.

Applied research A type of research concerned with solving everyday problems.

Approach-approach conflict A situation in which a decision must be made between two incompatible choices that both have positive features.

Approach-avoidance conflict A situation in which a decision must be made about a goal that has both positive and negative features.

Aptitude test A measure of the ability to benefit from further training.

Archetypes According to Jung, a universal thought form that exists in the collective unconscious.

Arousal theory The theory that we are motivated to seek out a particular level of arousal.

Assimilation Using current concepts in memory to understand new information.

Association areas Areas of the cerebral cortex involved in integration of information.

Ataxia Loss of coordination of muscle movements.

Attachment A deep, emotional bond that an infant develops with its caregiver.

Attention Awareness of the sensations and perceptions that are a focus of thinking at any given time.

Attentional blink Difficulty in detecting new information after a information is presented.

Attitude A tendency to judge people, objects, or issues in a certain way.

Attribution Our mental explanations of events or behaviors.

Attribution theory The theory that behavior is explained by situational or personal factors.

Authoritative parenting style A balance between obedience from the child and willingness to explain and make exceptions.

Automatic processing Information made available without conscious effort.

Autonomic nervous system Part of the peripheral nervous system that interfaces with the heart, intestines, and other organs.

Availability heuristic A thinking shortcut in which the more quickly a person can think of an example of something, the more likely he or she supposes it must be true.

Aversive conditioning A behavioral technique that pairs an unpleasant stimulus with an undesired behavior in order to reduce the target behavior.

Avoidance-avoidance conflict A situation in which a decision must be made between two undesirable choices.

Avoidance learning Learning to stay away from stimuli that predict negative events.

Avolition Lack of will.

Axon The part of the neuron that carries the nerve impulse away from the soma.

Axon terminal The part of the neuron that discharges and recycles neurotransmitters; also called the terminal button.

B (being) needs According to Maslow, self-actualization needs.

Babbling The initial vocalizing performed by babies learning to speak.

Barbiturates A type of depressant drug that reduces stress and induces sleep.

Basal metabolic rate The body's ability to use nutrients efficiently to maintain itself when at rest.

Basic emotions Feeling states that are thought to be expressed in a universal way.

Basic research A type of research concerned with expanding knowledge, even if the knowledge has no practical application.

Basilar membrane A neural pathway within the cochlea that registers the movement of fluid through tiny hair cells on its surface.

Behavior modification An operant conditioning program designed to achieve a goal.

Behavior therapy A family of therapies that use learning theory to change behavior.

Behavioral contract The learner signs a written specification of an operant conditioning program.

Behavioral genetics An interdisciplinary field that examines the influences of heredity and environment on behavior.

Behavioral medicine An interdisciplinary field concerned with health and illness that combines knowledge of social and medical sciences.

Behaviorism The study of learning based on directly observable actions in the absence of mental processes.

Behaviorist theory The view that language is learned just like other things.

Belief perseverance Holding onto a belief in the face of evidence against it.

Bell-and-pad treatment A classical conditioning treatment used to treat nighttime bedwetting.

Between-subjects design A research plan in which different individuals take part in differing aspects of the study and the different groups are compared.

Bias A preexisting perspective applied to a problem or decision.

Big Five A trait theory concept suggesting that the five most essential personality traits are openness to experience, conscientiousness, extroversion, agreeableness, and neuroticism; also known as the five-factor model of personality.

Bimodal distribution A pattern of scores with two distinct clusters with different modes (frequently occurring scores).

Binge eating disorder An eating disorder marked by repeated overeating without the compensatory strategies found in bulimia.

Binocular cues Ways to determine depth of field that require having two eyes.

Biofeedback A procedure through which a person becomes aware of physiological functions in order to influence the physiological functions.

Biological preparedness Built-in tendencies to learn some associations more easily.

Biological psychology The branch of psychology that studies the connection of bodily systems and behavior.

Biomedical therapies A family of therapies that focuses on surgery, medication, or other physiological interventions for the treatment of psychological conditions.

Biopsychosocial model A theory that recognizes three equally important aspects of human mental processes and behaviors: biological (including brain chemistry), psychological (thoughts, emotions, and behaviors), and social (cultural and societal influences).

Bipolar cells Cells that process incoming information from the rods and cones in the retina.

Bipolar disorder A mood disorder in which a person may alternate between a sad, depressive mood and elevated, irritable, or manic episodes.

Bisexual A person with more than incidental involvement with both male and female partners.

Bizarre delusions False and impossible beliefs.

Blaming the victim The tendency to attribute the cause of an unfortunate circumstance to the person experiencing it.

Blind spot The small area of the retina where the optic nerve leaves the eyeball.

Body dysmorphia A disturbance of body image including an overly self-critical attitude.

Body mass index (BMI) A ratio of height and weight that includes comparison to others.

Borderline personality disorder A personality disorder marked by a history of instability in a person's self-image, ability to control impulses, relationships, and moods.

Bottom-up processing The stimulus-driven process of sensation that registers external physical energy and translates it into neural encoding.

Brainstem The part of the brain between the cerebral cortex and the spinal cord responsible for survival functions.

Broca's area Part of the left frontal lobe that produces speech sounds.

Bulimia nervosa A disorder involving binge eating large amounts of food but maintaining relatively normal weight by purging.

Bystander effect A phenomenon in which people are less likely to offer assistance to someone in need while in groups than they are by themselves.

Caffeine A type of stimulant drug that is associated with increased central nervous system activity.

California Personality Inventory (CPI) A type of personality test designed to measure characteristics important to daily life.

Calling Choice of occupation you feel drawn to pursue for intrinsic meaning and identity.

Cannon-Bard theory A theory of emotion that suggests that events cause emotions by triggering biological and psychological experience of emotions at the same time.

Case study The extensive examination of the experience of a single individual or group.

Cataplexy An abrupt and temporary weakness often following a strong emotional experience.

Catastrophic thinking A cognitive distortion of the scale and impact of a stressful event.

Catecholamines Stress hormones released by the adrenal glands.

Category A cluster of similar concepts.

Catharsis A release of pent-up emotions.

Cathartic An experience that involves the release of pent-up emotions.

Cell body The part of a nerve cell that keeps the entire cell alive; also called the soma.

Central nervous system A division of the nervous system that is comprised of the brain and spinal cord.

Central route to persuasion A constructive response to an argument that focuses solely on the argument's merits.

Central tendency The "typical value" of a group of scores, described by the mean, mode, or median.

Cerebellum A part of the hindbrain involved in the development and coordination of movement.

Cerebral cortex The part of the brain involved in complex cognitive functioning.

Cerebral hemispheres One of the two regions of the cerebral cortex.

Cerebrospinal fluid (CSF) Clear liquid created in the ventricular system that supports and protects the central nervous system.

Cerebrum The cerebrum is the largest part of the forebrain and consists of a left and right hemispheres and four lobes.

Change blindness A change occurs between two viewings of a scene, but it is not noticed.

Chemical senses The two external senses that involve the detection of chemical molecules either dissolved in water (taste) or floating in the air (smell).

Choice overload The presence of too many options, causing problems in decisions.

Chromosome Cellular organelle that contains genes.

Chronic stressors Long-lasting events that require adaption.

Chunking Grouping separate elements into a related unit in memory.

Circadian rhythm A biological process that occurs on a daily cycle.

Classical conditioning Learning in which a neutral stimulus becomes associated with an unlearned stimulus and the response it automatically elicits.

Client-centered therapy A humanistic psychotherapy based on a nondirective, genuine, and accepting environment.

Clinical psychologist A mental health practitioner who researches, evaluates, and treats psychological conditions.

Clinical researcher model A type of psychology program that emphasizes clinical psychology research over direct work with clients.

Clinical trial The use of the scientific method to test a treatment for a disorder or condition.

Cocaine A stimulant drug made from the coca plant.

Cochlea The semicircular canal of fluid-filled tubes that captures movements of the oval window to transduce vibrations into neural firing.

Cocktail party phenomenon Hearing your name mentioned despite not attending to its source.

Cognition All types of thinking, including knowing, remembering, reasoning, deciding, and communicating.

Cognitive The explanations of behavior based on changes in knowledge within the mind.

Cognitive dissonance Discomfort that you experience from holding two competing ideas at the same time.

Cognitive dissonance theory The theory that we try to decrease our discomfort when holding two competing ideas at the same time by changing either our ideas or our behaviors.

Cognitive map A mental representation of a physical path to a goal location.

Cognitive-mediational theory of emotion A theory that feelings are caused by what we think caused our thoughts.

Cognitive neuroscience The methodological study of brain action linked to thought, perception, and language.

Cognitive neuroscientist A scientist who studies brain action as it is linked to thought, perception, and language.

Cognitive person variables Individual traits that affect the way you see the world.

Cognitive therapy A type of treatment that emphasizes the link between thoughts and emotions; also known as cognitive behavior therapy.

Cohort effect A difference observed between age groups that may be due to differences in their experiences in addition to age.

Collective unconscious According to Jung, the part of the personality that stores shared experiences and ideas from previous generations.

Collectivist culture A type of culture that prioritizes the group over the individual.

Colorblindness A condition marked by difficulty in distinguishing among some shades of red, green, or, more rarely, blue.

Coming out Sharing one's same-sex orientation with others or the public.

Comparative study A research project that compares similarities and differences between human and animal behavior.

Compliance Shifting behavior because of a request.

Compulsions A condition in which a person feels compelled to perform behaviors or mental actions in response to an obsession.

Computed tomography scans (CT scans) A neuroscience imaging technique that uses computer-enhanced X-rays that are helpful at examining brain structures. Also called CT scans.

Concept A "building block" or basic unit of knowledge.

Conceptual hierarchy Organization of related concepts into levels of categories.

Concrete operational stage Piaget's stage when grade schoolers have achieved conservation and are no longer fooled by appearances.

Conditional positive regard According to Rogers, the idea that respect comes only when certain circumstances are met.

Conditioned response A physiological behavior that is associated with a learned stimulus.

Conditioned stimulus A learned signal that predicts another stimulus is about to occur.

Conditioning Training, or learning as displayed by an animal's or human's behavior.

Cone cells Cone-shaped cells on the retina that recognize colors.

Confirmation bias Seeking out information consistent with what is believed to be true.

Conflict A situation that involves incompatible objectives.

Conformity Changing your thoughts or behavior to align with those of another.

Confounding variable An alternative factor that might account for observed differences in the dependent measure.

Connectionist models Memory theories that capture the distributed interconnections between concepts.

Conscientiousness A Big Five trait that describes how trustworthy a person might be.

Conscious mind According to Freud, a part of the mind that is aware of current thoughts and experiences.

Consciousness A state of awareness of the internal and the external world.

Conservation The knowledge that physical properties of an object stay the same even though there may be superficial changes in appearance.

Consistency paradox The idea that people believe that personality is stable, although research says that it is not.

Consolidation The stabilization of information in long-term memory through structural changes in the brain.

Constancy The assumption that objects in the physical world do not change spontaneously, but maintain their size, shape, color, and brightness over time.

Constructive coping Healthy efforts to reduce the impact of stressors.

Contact comfort The need for touch as a primary drive in monkeys and humans.

Content The surface meaning of the words in a problem.

Content validity Refers to the surface appearance of the items on the test and whether they reflect the concept of interest (also called face validity).

Continuous positive airway pressure (CPAP) A treatment for insomnia utilizing a small machine and mask to keep the airway open.

Continuous reinforcement Following every behavior with a consequence.

Continuum of sexual orientation Most people report falling somewhere in the range from exclusively heterosexual to exclusively homosexual.

Control group In an experiment, the group that receives no extra treatment or experience.

Convenience sample A group of participants who are readily available for a study.

Convergence A cue to depth based on the muscle movement of your eyes as they work to coordinate focus on objects in front of you.

Conversion disorder A disorder in which a worry or concern is transformed into a physical symptom.

Cope To reduce the impact of an event.

Coping Efforts to reduce the impact of stressors.

Coronary heart disease A medical condition that results in narrowing of the vessels that supply blood to the heart.

Corpus callosum A dense network of fibers that connects the left and right cerebral hemispheres.

Correlation A measure of the degree to which different factors are associated with one another.

Correlation coefficient An index, called r, of the degree of relationship between two variables, ranging from −1.00 to +1.00.

Cortical localization The observation that certain areas of the brain are responsible for specific processes.

Corticosteroids Hormones produced in the adrenal cortex in reaction to stress.

Counseling psychologist A mental health professional who helps people experiencing difficulty adjusting to life stressors to achieve greater well-being.

Counterconditioning A behavioral technique in which a response to a stimulus is replaced by a new response.

Creative intelligence Sternberg's theory suggests an underlying component of applying mental abilities to your experience in novel and helpful ways.

Creativity Novel thinking in which we redefine problems, see gaps in knowledge, generate ideas, and take reasonable risks in implementing them.

Critical period A sensitive time in development during which learning must occur.

Critical thinking Identification and evaluation of evidence to guide thoughts and decision making.

Cross-cultural psychology A branch of psychology concerned with the impact that shared attitudes, customs, and behaviors have on individual behavior and mental processes.

Cross-sectional study Comparing people at different ages with different people in the age groups.

Crystalized intelligence The ability to draw upon previously learned knowledge and skills.

Cued recall Retrieving information from related pieces of information.

Cyberbullying Aggressive and hostile acts toward others through Internet media.

D (deficit) needs According to Maslow, needs other than self-actualization needs.

Daily hassles (microstressors) Minor irritations that produce stress.

Dark adaptation The increased sensitivity experienced when your eyes adjust to lower levels of available light.

Debriefing The process by which any deception used by researchers is fully disclosed to participants at the end of a study.

Decay theory The notion that information fades from memory on its own.

Deception To actively provide information to the participant that is untrue.

Decision Thinking that requires a choice among alternatives.

Decision tree A decision-support tool that uses a tree-like graph of options, including chance event, resources, cost, and value.

Deductive reasoning A logical task in which new assertions are derived from what is known.

Deep brain stimulation (DBS) A surgical treatment in which a medical device is used to send electrical impulses to parts of the nervous system.

Deep structure The meaning composed by a phrase or sentence.

Defense mechanism According to the psychoanalytic perspective, a compromise that the ego uses to satisfy an id instinct indirectly.

Defensive attribution Blaming people for bad things that happen to them in order to protect your own feelings.

Deindividuation A merging of the self with a group in order to feel anonymous.

Deinstitutionalization The process of replacing inpatient psychiatric care with community outpatient services.

Delay of gratification The ability to postpone rewards until a later time.

Deliberation Slow, careful thinking aimed at considering all alternatives.

Deliberative practice Working on skills just beyond your current level of comfort.

Delta waves A type of brain wave pattern linked to Stage 4 sleep.

Delusion A belief that most people would think is incredible or implausible.

Dementia Progressive loss of cognitive function due to aging or disease.

Dendrite Nerve cell structure that receives information from other cells.

Denial A psychoanalytic defense mechanism in which a person fails to accept a reality.

Dependence When a person's drug use has led to distress or impairment and unsuccessful efforts to reduce drug use.

Dependent variable The measurement collected to determine if there was any effect of the independent variable in an experiment.

Depolarize The process by which an axon becomes more positive.

Depressants A class of drugs that reduces the activity in the nervous system.

Depth perception The detection of the distance of a stimulus from the body.

Diabetes A disease in which sugar in the blood is ineffectively used due to resistance to or an absence of insulin.

Diathesis-stress hypothesis A hypothesis that suggests a condition can have a biological root or cause that is triggered by an environmental stressor.

Difference threshold The smallest difference in sensation that is reliably detectable.

Differentiation Growth in complexity over time, with structures and functions becoming more specific for given tasks.

Diffusion of responsibility The tendency for the responsibility to help is spread across a crowd.

Discrimination Learning to see the difference between two similar stimuli; The tendency to act differently toward members of a particular group.

Displacement The ability to refer to things not visible in our immediate surroundings.

Display rules Guidelines about how one should express emotions.

Disposition The way a person behaves across different situations as well as over time.

Dissociation A split of consciousness or attention into two or more separate streams.

Dissociation theory of hypnosis A theory of hypnosis that suggests that the hypnotic state produces a split in consciousness and separates the executive control system from the rest of the brain.

Dissociative amnesia A condition characterized by extreme memory lapses or forgetting important personal information; usually associated with a traumatic emotional experience.

Dissociative disorder A disorder characterized by the sudden loss of the integration of consciousness or memory, or a change in personal identity.

Dissociative fugue A disorder in which a person forgets who he or she is, often traveling great distances and assuming new identities that resemble his or her original identity.

Dissociative identity disorder (DID) A dissociative disorder in which two or more distinct identities, each with unique characteristics, exist within one person.

Distinctive features The essential physical properties that uniquely identify an object.

Divided attention The process of attending to two or more tasks to perform them at the same time.

Dizygotic (DZ) twins Twins who are formed from two fertilized eggs; also known as fraternal twins.

Dominant gene A unit of heredity whose influence is exerted over other genes.

Door-in-the-face technique A practice by which rejecting an unreasonable request will lead to a more reasonable request that is more likely to be accepted.

Dopamine Neurotransmitter that is involved in movement and reward systems.

Dopamine hypothesis of schizophrenia A hypothesis that suggests that the neurotransmitter dopamine plays a key role in schizophrenia.

Double-blind procedure A method in which both the experimenter and participant are not informed about the subject's assignment to a treatment within a study.

Down syndrome An extra chromosome causes physical characteristics like poor muscle tone and slanting eyes, and moderate to severe intellectual disability.

Dream An array of sensory events experienced during sleep.

Dream analysis A psychoanalytic technique that reveals intrapsychic conflicts through interpretations of dreams.

Drive A tension arising from within physiological systems that motivates action.

Drive theory A theory that states of tension motivate us to take action to reduce them.

Drug abuse A condition in which a person uses psychoactive substances that results in distress or impairment in their social, work, or school functioning.

Drug addiction A situation in which taking a psychoactive substance leads to habitual use and craving even though the use causes distress or impairment.

Drug dependence A situation in which a person's drug use has led to distress or impairment including drug tolerance, significant withdrawal symptoms, and unsuccessful efforts to reduce drug use.

Drug rebound effect A situation in which stopping the use of a drug can have the reverse effect of the action of the drug.

Dual processes The two modes of thinking, one fast and easy, one slow and careful.

Dual processing The ability to attend to and manage several stimuli at once, some automatically (out of consciousness) and some intentionally in your awareness.

Dyssomnia A condition that affects the quantity, quality, or timing of sleep.

Echoic memory Sensory memory for the sound reaching your ears.

Eclarative memory Memory for knowledge of which we are consciously aware; also called explicit memory.

Eclectic approach Blending several theories together to explain or influence behavior.

Eclectic model An approach that pulls together multiple ways of examining a particular problem or question

Ecstasy (MDMA) A stimulant-hallucinogenic drug that can induce euphoria and diminish anxiety.

Efferent nerve fibers A type of neuron that carries impulses away from the central nervous system.

Ego According to Freud, the part of the personality responsible for interacting with conscious reality.

Ego dystonic A psychological symptom that causes a person distress.

Ego syntonic A psychological symptom that does not cause a person distress.

Egocentrism In preschool children, the belief that others know, think, and feel the same way they do.

Elaboration Tying new information to that already stored in memory.

Electrical stimulation of the brain A technique used to stimulate neural networks in the nervous system. Also known as deep brain stimulation.

Electroconvulsive therapy (ECT) A biological treatment in which seizures are induced in anesthetized patients.

Electroencephalogram (EEG) A device that measures and illustrates the electrical activity in the brain.

Embryo Prenatal stage following zygote lasting 2 to 8 weeks; in this stage, the heart begins beating.

Emotion A class of subjective feelings elicited by stimuli that have high significance to an individual.

Emotion-focused coping A reaction to stress that involves managing the feelings that arise from the situation.

Emotional intelligence The ability to perceive, understand, integrate, and regulate emotions to be self-motivated and socially skilled.

Empathy An attempt to understand the client's inner world.

Empirical Research studies that gain information by carefully collecting observations, or data.

Empirical evidence A type of information that is capable of being confirmed or invalidated by systematic observation.

Empirically derived test A type of instrument that starts with a large number of test questions in order to select the ones that best reflect the characteristics being tested.

Empiricism The theory of knowledge that assumes that knowledge should be based on observation.

En vivo A type of exposure therapy in which the actual feared object is used.

Encoding The process of taking new information and storing it in short- and long-term memory.

Encoding specificity The principle that cues present at encoding will be the best cues for retrieval.

Endocrine system The network of glands throughout the body that manufacture and secrete hormones.

Endorphins Chemicals linked to pain perception and reward.

Engagement Feelings of involvement and interest in work.

Environmental influence A factor in the social, cultural, physical, or family setting that may influence an individual.

Epidemiology A science that examines the frequency of medical conditions.

Episodic memory Recall of your own personal, autobiographical experiences.

Equity theory The notion that people want their effort and pay to be fair compared to that of others.

Eros An id instinct that reduces tension associated with basic biological drives.

Escape learning An acquired behavior performed to avoid a noxious stimulus.

Esteem motivation Desire to feel appreciation from others.

Estrogen A sex hormone produced primarily by the ovaries that is central to female sexual development and fertility.

Ethnocentrism Believing that your own group is superior to others and should be the standard by which other cultures are judged.

Etiology Cause of a disorder.

Evidence-based practice Selecting therapy treatments using information gained through research.

Evolutionary psychologist Researcher who applies the theory of evolution to explain the psychology behind behaviors.

Evolutionary psychology A branch of psychology that examines the impact of natural selection on behavioral and mental processes.

Evolved behaviors Behaviors selected over generations to best fit the environment.

Excitatory postsynaptic potential (EPSP) A voltage change caused by the binding of neurotransmitters that causes a positive voltage shift in the resting potential of the postsynaptic neuron triggering the neuron to fire.

Excitement phase Sexual arousal begins with blood circulation into all the erectile structures in the body.

Executive control system An assortment of brain processes that plan and initiate actions.

Experiment A method by which one or more independent factors is manipulated by an experimenter, and the result is measured through one or more dependent variables.

Experimental group In an experiment, the group that receives some treatment or experience.

Experimenter bias The introduction of inaccuracy of measurements due to the researcher's expectations.

Explanatory style Reflects what you think caused an event. Explanatory style can be either optimistic or pessimistic.

Exposure therapy A behavior therapy technique that involves repeatedly presenting the client with a distressing object in order to reduce anxiety.

"Exotic becomes erotic" Bem's theory that typical gender preferences lead to less exposure to the opposite sex and, thus, later attraction.

External attribution An explanation of behavior that focuses on environmental explanations.

External locus of control The idea that reinforcers and punishments are outside of your control.

Extinction The tendency to stop responding to the conditioned stimulus when repeatedly presented without the unconditioned stimulus.

Extinguish To stop the display of a given behavior.

Extralinguistic factors Information outside of language that aids in comprehension.

Extrasensory perception (ESP or psi) Detecting information without knowing its sensory source.

Extrinsic incentives Rewards (such as pay) given to motivate people to perform certain behaviors.

Extrinsic motivation Behavior is repeated only when external reinforcement is provided.

Extroversion A trait that describes that an individual is energized by the external world rather than by the internal world.

Extrovert A personality type that prefers the external world to the internal world; also known as extroversion.

Eye movement desensitization reprocessing (EMDR) A therapy technique involving bilateral stimulation in order to process distressing memories.

Facial feedback hypothesis A theory that suggests that the position of the facial muscles influences emotional expression.

Factitious disorder A psychological disorder in which a person plays the sick role for the emotional gain, sometimes called Münchausen syndrome.

Factor analysis A statistical technique used to find clusters of related items.

Family study A method that allows researchers to test hypotheses concerning the contribution of genetic and environmental factors by examining biological relatives.

Family therapy A type of psychotherapy that treats the immediate social system, i.e., the family, to improve individuals' psychological functioning.

False consensus effect The habit of seeing our own behavior as typical.

False memory Inaccurate information incorporated into memory.

Feature detectors Individual cells in the visual cortex that respond only to certain types of visual patterns, such as lines, circles, or angles.

Feel-good, do-good phenomenon The theory that people are more likely to be helpful if they are happy.

Fertile A female able to conceive and bear children.

Fetal alcohol syndrome Irreversible brain abnormalities caused by the mother's consumption of alcohol during pregnancy.

Fetus The unborn child from around 9 weeks until birth.

Fight-or-flight response A reaction to danger in which the sympathetic nervous system prepares the organs for vigorous activity.

Fitness The contribution an individual makes to the gene pool of the next generation.

Fixation According to Freud, a habit of obtaining tension reduction from an earlier stage of psychosexual development; Getting stuck on an approach to a problem and failing to see alternative approaches.

Fixed-interval schedule Providing reinforcement for the first behavior after a set amount of time passes.

Fixed mindset The belief that your traits are predetermined and nothing can change them.

Fixed-ratio schedule Providing reinforcement after a set number of repeated behaviors.

Flashbulb memory An emotional or vivid event that appears to be well remembered.

Flooding A therapy to treat phobias based on intense exposure to the feared stimulus.

Flow A state of mind arising during activities when the challenge of the task is met by expertise.

Flynn effect The increase in intelligence test scores have (about three points per decade, across the globe) over generations taking the tests.

Foot-in-the-door technique A practice by which agreement to a small request makes agreement to a more unreasonable request more likely.

Forebrain The largest part of the brain, consisting of a number of structures including the cerebrum, the thalamus, and the limbic system.

Forgetting curve Graph showing that much information is immediately lost from memory after study.

Formal operational stage Piaget's final stage (around age 12) characterized by reasoning on a logical or hypothetical level.

Fovea The focal point of the retina where image processing is sharpest due to more cone cells.

Framing effect A bias in decisions based on the description of the problem.

Free association A psychoanalytic technique in which people will report the first things that occur to them. Used to uncover unconscious conflicts.

Frequency The wavelength of sound or light waves (the time distance between peaks).

Frequency theory The notion that the firing rate of neurons is determined directly by the frequency (length of time between sound waves) of the sound.

Frontal lobe The front part of the cerebral cortex involved in planning, organization, and personality.

Frustration Anxiety felt when attempts to reach a goal are hindered.

Frustration-aggression hypothesis Early theory of anger suggesting that anger is a reaction to a goal blocked or unattained.

Fully functioning person According to Jung, a person who has a developed real self.

Functional fixedness Seeing objects for use only in their intended roles.

Functional magnetic resonance imaging (fMRI) Neuroscience imaging technique used to measure changes in blood flow.

Functional plasticity The capacity to change areas of the brain that are responsible for activities.

Functionalism A school of psychology concerned with the purposes of behavior and mental processes.

Fundamental attribution error An inclination to overestimate the impact of internal characteristics in explaining the behavior of others and underestimate the same characteristics in explaining your own behavior.

Galvanic skin response (GSR) A measurement of the conductivity of your skin.

Gamma-aminobutric acid (GABA) The nervous system's primary inhibitory neurotransmitter.

Ganglion cells More complex cells that process patterns of receptor activation within the retina.

Gate-control theory The notion that interneurons in the spinal cord act as a gate to block some sensory signals from going to the brain.

Geon A simple three-dimensional form that, in combination, can create any shape.

Gender roles Our expectations about how males and females should act are learned through culture.

Gene A segment of DNA.

General adaptation syndrome (GAS) Selye's term for the body's stress response that occurs in three stages: alarm, resistance, and exhaustion.

General intelligence (g) Spearman's theory that all mental abilities reflect a single underlying capacity.

Generalizability How well a study's findings can be applied to other people and circumstances.

Generalization Learning to respond to stimuli similar to the one experienced.

Generalized anxiety disorder (GAD) A psychological condition characterized by unexplained, excessive worry that has an unspecific cause.

Generate and test Guess at the answer and see if it works on a trial-and-error basis.

Generation effect Memory is better for information that we create ourselves.

Generativity The capacity to use a finite set to create endless variety of unique combinations; Erikson's stage of life focusing on contributing to the development of the next generation and "making a difference."

Genius A noted, exceptional individual whose accomplishments outlive them.

Genogram Family tree.

Genome The sum of an organism's hereditary information.

Genotype An individual's genetic makeup.

Genuineness According to the client-centered approach, authenticity in a relationship.

Gestalt The "whole," reflecting the belief that the whole emerges in perception and is more than simply "the sum of its parts."

Ghrelin A hormone secreted by the empty stomach to stimulate hunger.

Gifted A determination made by some schools and educational programs based on an intelligence test score of more than 130.

Gist The semantic meaning of a sentence.

Glia cells Cells in the nervous system that provide support and protection for neurons.

Glucose The form of sugar that carries nutrients in the bloodstream.

Glutamate An excitatory neurotransmitter.

Goal A situation you would like to achieve.

Gonads An organ that secretes sex hormones.

Grammar Rules within a language that determine whether a sentence is properly formed and complete.

Grandmother hypothesis Evolutionary theory that older females aid in the reproductive success of their families by helping to raise grandchildren.

Graphology A technique in which handwriting is analyzed in order to describe personality.

Great mother An archetype described by Jung that symbolizes a person or thing that provides nurture without wanting anything in return.

Group Collection of people who have something in common.

Group aptitude test A test meant to assess your ability to benefit from further training or education, but are also affected by past achievements in school. (e.g., ACT)

Group polarization The likelihood that the attitudes of members of a team will become more similar over time.

Group therapy A psychotherapeutic technique that treats multiple clients in a collective setting.

Groupthink When a group's ideals become so important that alternative ideas are dismissed.

Growth mindset Belief that your qualities and capacities develop through effort.

Gustatory The sense of taste.

Hair cell receptors Sound receptors in the cochlea that transduce fluid movement into neural impulses.

Hallucination Sensory perception with no sensory input. The perception may affect any or all of the five senses.

Hallucinogens A type of drug that distort conscious experiences.

Hardiness A personality style characterized by commitment, challenge, and control.

Hawthorne effect Improvement in a test group (compared to a control group) caused by the increased interest shown toward them.

Health psychology A branch of psychology that is concerned with how psychological factors impact wellness, illness, and medical treatments.

Healthy lifestyle According to Adler, attempts to compensate for feelings of inferiority in a socially useful way.

Heritability How much of a characteristic can be linked to genetics as opposed to the environment.

Hero An archetype that represents someone who saves the day.

Heterosexual A person who desires emotional and sexual intimacy with members of the opposite sex.

Heterozygous condition A circumstance where genes are different for a given trait.

Heuristic A mental shortcut, or rule of thumb, that may or may not lead to a correct solution.

Hidden observer In the dissociation theory of hypnosis, the executive control system that witnesses without being involved.

Hierarchy of needs According to Maslow, the order of importance of motivations, from basic physiological needs to self-fulfillment needs.

Higher-order conditioning Learning to associate a neutral stimulus with an already-learned conditioned stimulus and conditioned response.

Hindbrain A region of the brain that includes the cerebellum, the pons, and the medulla. It supports vital bodily processes.

Hippocampus Part of the limbic system that is involved in processing new memories.

Holophrastic The use of a single word to represent more complex ideas in early language learning.

Homosexual A person who desires emotional and sexual intimacy with members of the same sex.

Homozygous condition A circumstance where both genes are the same for a given trait.

Hormone A chemical messenger that is produced by endocrine glands and influences body growth, mood, and sexual characteristics.

Hostile aggression Aggression simply to inflict harm.

Human sexual response cycle Phases of excitement, plateau, orgasm, and resolution that complete a sexual act.

Humanism A theoretical orientation that emphasizes growth, potential, and self-actualization; also known as the phenomenological approach.

Humanistic perspective A branch of psychology that emphasizes growth, potential, and self-actualization.

Humanistic psychology Theories of motivation emphasizing the goal to develop to the highest potential for each individual.

Hypermnesia Elevated memory recall by means of hypnosis.

Hyperthymesia Recalling past autobiographical events to an excessive degree and accuracy.

Hypnagogic hallucinations Sensory experiences that occur between being awake and asleep.

Hypnosis A trancelike state in which the subject readily accepts the hypnotist's suggestion of changes in consciousness or sensations.

Hypocretin A hormone that is linked to wakefulness.

Hypomania A condition in which a person has symptoms of mania but avoids getting into trouble.

Hypothalamus The functional center of motivation in the brain.

Hypothesis A clear statement or prediction that can be shown to be true or false in an experiment.

Iconic memory Sensory memory for visual information taken in.

Id According to Freud, the part of the personality that operates on the pleasure principle, always looking to reduce tension that comes from basic physiological drives.

Ideal self According to Rogers, a version of yourself that could please other people.

Identification According to Freud, the unconscious process of copying the behavior of a person.

Identity formation The process of developing a distinct, individualized personality.

Ideocentrism A personality trait with an interreliant focus.

Illness anxiety disorder (Hypochondriasis) A disorder characterized by a specific disease process that progresses in a person in which there is no physiological cause.

Illusion A visual image that creates a misperception of the world.

Immune system Processes the body uses to protect against disease.

Immunosuppression Weakening the immune response.

Impossible figure An image that can't be resolved into a single consistent interpretation.

In-group bias Accepting the attitudes of your own team.

Inattentional blindness Failing to process an object clearly present in a scene.

Incentive The rewards and punishments associated with different actions.

Incentive theories Motivation that focuses on the reward or payoff for behaviors.

Incidental memory Explicit knowledge you did not intentionally encode.

Inclusive fitness (kinship selection) Also known as kin selection, the contributions to the next generation's gene pool of both an individual and his or her relatives.

Incongruency According to Rogers, the difference between your ideal self and your actual self.

Incubation A period of time in which a problem is set aside prior to further attempts to solve it.

Independent variable The factor that an experimenter manipulates to create different experiences for participants.

Individualist culture A culture that places an emphasis on each person's rights rather than on the society.

Inductive reasoning Generalizing from specific information to form a rule.

Industrial and organizational psychology Field of study addressing the psychology of work.

Inferential statistic A numerical test to determine what conclusions can be drawn from observed data.

Inferiority According to Adler, feelings of inadequacy; also known as organ inferiority.

Informational social influence Sway that comes from believing another person.

Informed consent The process through which an experimenter describes the nature of study participation to the potential volunteer, including his or her right to stop at any time.

Inhalants Drugs whose vapors are breathed in to produce their intoxicating effect.

Inhibitory postsynaptic potential (IPSP) A voltage change caused by the binding of neurotransmitters that causes a negative voltage shift in the resting potential of the postsynaptic neuron preventing the neuron from firing.

Insight An understanding of the motivation of behavior.

Insight therapies A family of psycho-therapies that focus on the unconscious motivations of behavior.

Insomnia A condition in which a person is unable to fall or stay asleep.

Instinct theories Motivation from biologically programmed behaviors occurring in response to environmental cues.

Instinctual drift The tendency for new behaviors to revert to ones familiar to that species.

Instrumental aggression Words or physical acts a person does to cause harm in an ultimate goal to obtain something.

Insulin A hormone secreted by the pancreas and used to convert glucose into energy for muscle use.

Intellectual disability A limitation in intellectual functioning indicated by an intelligence test score of less than 70 along with problems in adaptive behavior.

Intelligence The capacity to learn from experience, acquire knowledge, adapt to the environment, and solve problems.

Intelligence quotient (IQ) The ratio of a child's "mental age" score on the Stanford-Binet test divided by his or her chronological age.

Intelligence test A measure intended to identify the relative mental ability of individuals.

Interaction between variables When the effect of one independent variable on the dependent variable depends upon the level of another independent variable.

Interactionist theory The view that language combines inborn abilities with special environmental triggers.

Interference theory New knowledge can disrupt recently learned memories.

Intermittent reinforcement Following behavior with a consequence sometimes, but not every time.

Internal attribution An explanation of behavior based on personality characteristics.

Internal locus of control The idea that reinforcers and punishments are under your own control.

Internet addiction Excessive use of computer systems that causes impairment in social, occupational, or school functioning.

Internet-mediated research Using the World Wide Web to collect data from remote participants.

Interneuron A neuron that communicates only with other neurons.

Interpretation A psychoanalytic technique in which a therapist will reveal explanations of the client's unconcious motivations in order to improve psycho-logical functioning.

Interval schedule Reinforcement is provided after time passes, and then a behavior is repeated.

Interviewer illusion Belief in one's own intuitive abilities to find good candidates in the absence of evidence.

Intrapsychic conflict Differences between the desires of the id, ego, and superego.

Intrinsic incentives Feelings of reward created within the individual.

Intrinsic motivation The desire to perform behaviors for an internal reward.

Introspection Examination of one's own mental and emotional processes.

Introvert A personality type that prefers the internal world to the external world; also known as introversion.

Intuition The "gut feeling" that leads to a fast and easy conclusion.

Irrelevant information Knowledge referred to in a problem that is not needed in its solution.

Isomorphic A representation taking on the same shape or form as the object itself.

James-Lange theory A concept of emotion that suggests that emotions are composed of our awareness of biological reactions to stimuli.

Job analysis Determination of the tasks, knowledge, skills, and abilities needed in a job.

Job burnout A prolonged response to chronic emotional and interpersonal stress on the job.

Journal A publication containing articles written by scientists that are reviewed before publication by a group of peers.

Judgment Making an informed guess about something unknown or uncertain.

Just noticeable difference (jnd) The smallest amount of change between two stimuli that a person can detect at least half of the time.

Just-world hypothesis A belief that people get what they deserve and deserve what they get.

K-complex An EEG waveform that is characteristic of Stage 2 sleep.

Kinetic depth effect The movement of a three-dimensional object reveals its shape.

Lack of transfer The failure to use a past analogy that offers a solution.

Language A form of thinking used to communicate with others and ourselves.

Latent content In psychoanalytic theory, the true, underlying, undisguised meaning of a dream.

Latent learning Knowledge that is not displayed in behavior until reinforcement is provided.

Lateral hypothalamus The "start eating" functional center in the brain.

Lateralization of function The concept that each hemisphere of the cerebral cortex is primarily responsible for certain activities.

Law of Effect Behaviors that lead to positive outcomes are likely to be repeated.

Laws of perceptual grouping Simple organizational principles that help to interpret image elements, including similarity, proximity, continuity, and closure.

Learned helplessness When an animal fails to take action to escape a noxious stimulus.

Learning A lasting change in knowledge or behavior based on experience.

Learning perspective A theory that suggests that anxiety disorders are learned behaviors.

Leptin A protein secreted by fat cells to signal adequate stores.

Lesion A natural or intentional destruction of brain tissue.

Levels of analysis Various ways of examining the same psychological phenomenon.

Levels of processing The depth of thinking with new information affects the likelihood of remembering it.

Lexical approach to traits An approach that uses language to determining the most important traits of personality.

Libido According to Freud, the energy linked with sexuality.

Lifestyle According to Adler, the way in which you strive for superiority in order to make up for feelings of inferiority.

Limbic system A group of structures surrounding the brainstem that governs emotions such as anger, happiness, and fear, and stores and retrieves new memories.

Linguistic relativity The notion that language shapes our ideas and not the other way around.

Link method Forming links between concepts to make them more memorable.

Lithium A medication used to treat bipolar mood disorders.

Lobotomy A surgery that involves destruction of nerves in the prefrontal cortex in order to improve symptoms of psychological conditions.

Locus of contro A cognitive person variable that summarizes your idea of the source of reinforcement and punishment.

Long-term memory (LTM) The enduring stage of memory that is unlimited in capacity and duration.

Long-term potentiation The process of changes in neuronal receptivity that encodes information into memory.

Longitudinal study Following a person through development by studying him or her at different points in time.

Loss aversion Preferring options that will avoid losing rather than maximize gains.

Lymphocytes A type of cell involved in the immune system that works to attack foreign substances.

Lysergic acid diethylamide (LSD) A synthetic psychedelic hallucinogenic drug that produces altered states of consciousness.

Magnetic resonance imaging (MRI) A non-invasive neuroscience imaging technique that uses magnets and radio equipment to produce detailed images.

Maintenance rehearsal Reactivating information in short-term memory to keep it in mind.

Malingering A condition involving an external motivation for illness, such as avoiding a test.

Mania A condition associated with an elevated, expansive, or sometimes irritable mood.

Manifest content In psychoanalytic theory, the dream as the dreamer reports it.

Marijuana A drug that has both painkilling as well as stimulating effects on the nervous system.

Matching hypothesis The belief that people are paired to equally attractive partners.

Mating Male-to-female intercourse for the purpose of reproduction.

Maturation Biological growth occurring in a continuous fashion over time.

Mean The arithmetic average, or the sum of all scores in a sample divided by the number of scores.

Means-end analysis A problem-solving strategy that reduces differences between the current and the goal states.

Mechanism of action MOA A description of the way a drug functions.

Median The score at the middle of a distribution of scores from a sample.

Medical model A theory that suggests that psychological disorders are illnesses that require treatment.

Meditation A mental practice that regulates attention and awareness.

Medulla Part of the hindbrain that is involved in breathing, heartbeat, and other essential functions.

Melatonin A hormone manufactured by the pineal gland that promotes sleepiness.

Memory The enduring consequence in the mind of our experiences with the world.

Menarche The occurrence of a first menstrual period, indicating the capacity to become pregnant.

Menopause The cessation of menstrual periods in women, usually occurring around age 50.

Mental age The average level of intellectual development for a child of a particular age.

Mental hospital A medical center that treats psychological conditions.

Mental model A visual, spatial, or content-based representation of a problem or situation.

Mental set An existing state of mind, habit, or attitude that affects new problem solving.

Mere exposure effect Repeated exposure to a stimulus leads to preferring that stimulus.

Meta-analysis A study that examines the results of many earlier studies on a topic and compares their findings to draw conclusions.

Metabolism The physiological processes used to convert energy from nutrients.

Metacognition Reflective thoughts about your own thinking processes.

Methamphetamine A stimulant drug that is associated with increased nervous system activity and elevated libido and self-esteem.

Method of loci Mnemonic for remembering items by placing them on a familiar path.

Midbrain Part of the brainstem involved in control of sensory processes.

Mind Mental processes and our subjective experiences.

Mindset A belief about yourself and your abilities, such as intelligence, talents, and personality.

Minnesota Multiphasic Personality Inventory (MMPI) An empirically derived personality test that assesses a range of characteristics.

Mirror neuron A type of neuron that fires when an individual watches an action and when performing the action.

Misinformation effect Adding new, incorrect information to a memory after the event.

Mnemonic Encoding "trick" that ties to-be-remembered information to something familiar.

Mode The most frequently observed score in a data sample.

Model One who performs specific behaviors that others observe.

Modeling Performing specific behaviors that others observe.

Mood Long-lasting, nonspecific emotional state.

Mood congruence Matching emotional mood as a cue at encoding and retrieval to improve memory.

Mood stabilizers A family of medications used to treat bipolar mood disorders.

Monoamine hypothesis of depression A hypothesis that suggests that depressive symptoms are brought on by a malfunction of certain types of neurotransmitters.

Monocular cues Ways of determining the distance of an object that require a single eye.

Monozygotic (MZ) twins Twins from a single fertilized egg; also known as identical twins.

Morpheme The smallest unit of sounds that carries meaning.

Motherese "Baby talk" that is high in pitch, rhythmic, and simple and may better attract responses from babies.

Motion parallax The interpretation that objects close to you are moving past you faster than objects farther away.

Motivation An inner state that energizes people toward the fulfillment of a goal.

Motive The pursuit of pleasure and the avoidance of pain or displeasure.

Motor cortex A region of the cerebral cortex involved in planning, controlling, and executing motor functions.

Motor neuron A type of neuron that interfaces with muscles and glands.

Müller-Lyer illusion Two lines of the same length appear to be different if one has inward "arrowhead" extensions compared to outward extensions.

Multiple-approach-avoidance conflict A situation in which a decision must be made between many choices, each with positive and negative consequences.

Multiple intelligences Gardner's theory proposed seven separate types of cognitive abilities operating independently.

Myelin sheath A fatty substance that insulates the axon and enables efficient transmission.

Narcolepsy A condition characterized by daytime sleepiness and sudden lapses into sleep during the day.

Nativist theory The view that language is a special skill we are born with.

Natural selection Varying success in reproduction resulting from the interaction of an organism with the environment.

Naturalistic observation Observing human behavior as it occurs in a real-world setting.

Need for achievement Desire to succeed at challenging tasks.

Need to belong Motivation to feel a part of relationships or groups of people.

Negative coping Engaging in behaviors that are unhealthy and can make matters worse.

Negative correlation An association between two variables where higher scores on one go with lower scores on the other.

Negative reinforcement A consequence that takes away an unpleasant state, making behavior more likely to occur.

Negative symptoms of psychosis Symptoms of psychosis that involve behavior deficits, or expected behaviors that are absent.

Neo-Freudian Psychoanalytic theories inspired by Sigmund Freud.

Neodissociation theory of hypnosis A theory of hypnosis that suggests that hypnosis causes subjects to divide their consciousness voluntarily.

Nerves Bundles of neurons.

Nervous system A collection of organs including neurons and supportive systems.

Neural pruning The destruction of certain neurons to increase the processing speed of the nervous system.

Neurogenesis The process of the development of new neurons.

Neuron A nerve cell.

Neuroscience The study of the brain and nervous system; also called biological psychology.

Neuroticism A personality trait that describes how emotional the person might be.

Neurotransmitter Chemical messenger that transmits information from one neuron to another.

Neutral stimulus An event or signal that causes no reflexive, automatic response.

Nicotine A type of drug that targets the nicotinic receptors. Found in tobacco.

Nightmare A type of dream that is frightening and often will wake up the dreamer.

Non-bizarre delusions False beliefs that are possible but highly unlikely.

Norepinephrine A neurotransmitter responsible for learning and memory.

Norm Behavioral milestone that identifies when certain behaviors usually occur in normal development; Comparison of many individuals on the same test so that relative performance can be determined.

Normal distribution The inverted bell-shaped frequency distribution that often occurs for psychological tests and variables such as height.

Normative social influence The need to conform due to social pressures.

nREM sleep Stages of sleep in which dreams are unlikely to occur and that are not associated with rapid eye movement.

Obedience Behavior that is in response to the orders of another.

Obesity An excess level of fat in the body, at least 15% above ideal weight for a given height.

Object permanence Babies remembering objects they can no longer see in front of them.

Objective A scoring system where the results are the same no matter who scores it.

Observational learning Acquiring new behaviors from watching a model.

Obsession A thought that is unwanted, intrusive, and distressing.

Obsessive-compulsive disorder A psychological disorder associated with obsessions, or obsessions linked to compulsions.

Occipital lobe An area in the back of the cerebral cortex. Its visual cortex processes image information.

Oedipal complex According to Freud, a boy's unconscious desire for his mother that results in identification with his father.

Olfaction The sense of smell.

Olfactory bulb The processing center for smell located at the base of the brain.

Openness to experience A personality trait that is part of the Big Five that describes how much affection a person has for newness.

Operant A behavior freely initiated or displayed, which can be conditioned.

Operant conditioning Training emitted behaviors to make them more likely to occur again.

Operational definition The concrete implementation of a psychological concept within a study.

Opiates A psychoactive substance made from opium that relieves pain and reduces the activity of the nervous system.

Opponent process theory The theory that opposing, or complementary, colors (yellow/blue, white/black, and red/green) are produced by differences in firing rates by complex cells within the retina.

Optic chiasm The place in the front of the brain where the neural tracts following from the optic nerve of each eye cross over so that some tracts lead to both the right and left hemispheres.

Optic nerve The bundle of neural fibers collecting sensation in the retina that passes out of the eyeball in a pathway to the brain.

Optimal arousal A level of activation that is sufficient but not overwhelming.

Optimistic explanatory style A way of explaining negative events by using external, unstable, and specific attributions.

Organizational psychology Field examining how the structure of jobs and the workplace affects the success of group efforts.

Orgasmic phase The climax of arousal during which orgasm and ejaculation occur.

Out-group homogeneity The tendency for members of an out-group to seem similar to each other.

Outpatient Treatment settings that are outside of a hospital.

Oval window Membrane in the ear that collects sound waves and translates them into fluid movement in the cochlea.

Overconfidence Being more certain about your beliefs than you should be.

Overjustification effect When a task provides an extrinsic reward, no intrinsic motive is needed.

Overlearning Continuing learning even when recall appears successful.

Overregularize Applying a rule of grammar beyond its limits.

Oxytocin "Feel-good" hormone released after orgasm.

Pacinian corpuscles Tiny pressure receptors located in the fatty layer beneath the skin.

Panic attack A period of intense fear or discomfort that is linked with specific physical and psychological symptoms.

Panic disorder The presence of frequent, recurrent panic attacks, along with the fear of panic attacks.

Papillae Visible bumps on the tongue.

Parallel processing Analyzing information in groups or "columns" of cells in the cortex at the same time in order to understand an overall pattern.

Paranoid personality disorder A disorder characterized by a long and unwavering history of attributing malicious intent to others.

Paraphrase A description of the same meaning using different elements.

Parapsychology The study of paranormal or extrasensory phenomena.

Parasomnia Abnormal behaviors associated with sleep.

Parasympathetic nervous system A component of the autonomic nervous system that conserves bodily functions and energy.

Parental investment theory The required investment in offspring differs between genders, resulting in differing strategies.

Parietal lobe An area of the cerebral cortex located behind the frontal lobe. Its somatosensory cortex processes body sensation information.

Participant A volunteer who agrees to take part in research studies, also called a subject.

Paternal uncertainty Historically, men could not be sure whether a child was their genetic offspring.

Peak experience According to Maslow, "transient moment of self-actualization" that is associated with feelings of harmony, interconnectedness, and joy.

Perception The process of organizing sensory information to form a meaningful interpretation.

Perceptual asymmetry Because of imbalances between the left and right cerebral hemispheres, visual or auditory processing happens at different speeds depending on whether sensory input is coming from the left or right side of the body.

Perceptual set The influence of recent processing as a framework for continuing perception.

Perfection principle The image of the perfect person, or ego, that inspires the superego; also know as the ego ideal.

Peripheral nervous system A division of the nervous system excluding the brain and spinal cord.

Peripheral route to persuasion Influence based on small, noncore factors.

Persistence The ability to repeatedly respond to failure by exerting more effort.

Person perception Involves the way we form opinions about others.

Persona An archetype that represents the public self.

Personal unconscious According to Jung, the part of one's personality that stores material currently outside of awareness.

Personality An individual's pattern of thinking, feeling, and behaving.

Personality disorder A psychological condition, coded on Axis II of the DSM, that involves extreme, inflexible global personality traits that are chronic and pervasive.

Personality inventory A test used to measure an individual's pattern of thinking, feeling, and behaving.

Personality theory A system used to describe and explain the genesis and development of an individual's pattern of thinking, feeling, and behaving.

Personnel psychology Field focusing on the selection, training, and evaluation of employees.

Persuasion Convincing another person.

Pessimistic explanatory style A way of explaining negative events by using internal, stable, and global attributions.

Phenomenology The idea that, in order to understand a person, it is important to understand the world from that person's perspective; also known as phenomenological approach.

Phenotype Expression of genetic influences.

Pheromone A characteristic biochemical odor emitted by an individual.

Phi phenomenon A series of static images viewed in sequence are interpreted as a moving image.

Philosophy The study of knowledge and existence.

Phobia A psychological symptom in which fear is unreasonably great or it interferes with a person's life.

Phonemes The basic sounds of human languages.

Photoreceptors The rod and cone cells in the retina that register the presence of light waves.

Phrase Two or more words combined to convey meaning.

Phrenology A procedure that uses bumps on an individual's head to determine and predict personality characteristics.

Physical dependence A condition in which a drug must be taken continually to avoid symptoms of withdrawal.

Physiology A branch of biology that studies internal biological processes.

Pituitary gland The endocrine system's master gland.

Place theory The notion that the pitch of a sound is determined by the location of the stimulation on the basilar membrane inside the ear.

Placebo A substance without an active ingredient.

Placebo effect Feeling benefit or improvement from a treatment known to have no effect.

Plasticity The ability of the nervous system to adapt by creating new neural pathways.

Plateau phase The second stage of the sexual response cycle, during which there is a leveling off of excitement.

Pleasure principle According to Freud, the drive to reduce tension.

Polygenic Characteristics that multiple genes shape.

Polygraph A machine that uses physiological measurements to detect lies.

Pons Part of the hindbrain that is involved in relaying information from the cortex, as well as in sleep and arousal.

Ponzo illusion The misjudgment based on linear perspective that identical objects placed within converging lines appears to be of different sizes.

Population The larger group about whom a study would like to draw conclusions.

Positive correlation An association between two variables where higher scores on one go with higher scores on the other.

Positive psychology A branch of psychology that emphasizes the constructive features of human strength and healthy living rather than pathology.

Positive regard A communication of love and respect.

Positive reinforcement A consequence that creates a pleasant state, making behavior more likely to occur.

Positive self-regard Respect for your own decisions.

Positive symptoms of psychosis Symptoms that are present in addition to typical psychotic behavior.

Positron emission tomography (PET) A neuroscience imaging technique that uses radioactive glucose to indicate areas of activity.

Posthypnotic suggestion A behavior or thinking pattern that comes out after hypnosis.

Postsynaptic neuron A neuron that receives a signal from another neuron.

Postsynaptic potential (PSP) Changes in the dendrite of the receiving neuron as the result of its binding with neurotransmitters.

Posttraumatic stress disorder Associated with a traumatic event, this disorder involves re-experiencing the trauma, increased arousal, and symptoms of numbing and avoidance.

Practical intelligence Sternberg's theory proposed the ability to assess a situation and do what is necessary to be successful.

Practitioner-scholar model Also called the Vail model, a program in which psychologists emphasize clinical training over generating new research in order to

understand, synthesize, and apply existing research.

Pragmatics The social context of language that adds to its meaning.

Preconscious According to Freud, the part of your mind that contains material just outside of awareness that is easy to pull into awareness.

Predictive validity The ability of a test to identify those who will have high scores on other measures.

Prejudice Negative stereotypes or attitudes about members of a particular group.

Prenatal stage Development taking place in the mother's womb before birth.

Preoperational stage Piaget's stage for preschoolers, marked by an intense focus on what they perceive.

Presynaptic neuron A neuron that sends a signal to another neuron.

Primary insomnia Difficulty falling asleep, staying asleep, or waking up too early that is not associated with another medical or psychological condition.

Primary mental abilities Thurstone's theory of a set of seven different factors related to intelligence.

Primary reinforcer A reward that provides basic needs.

Primary sexual characteristics The reproductive organs and external genitalia.

Priming The activation of information in memory from a related cue.

Principle of entropy Jung's theory that opposites tend to come together over time.

Principle of equivalence According to Jung, the energy devoted to do one thing will be equally devoted to the opposite activity.

Principle of falsifiability The notion that a theory must be able to be disproved in order to be testable and scientific.

Principle of opposites According to Jung, the theory that every wish also represents the opposite of the same wish.

Probability theory A statistical algorithm that takes into account all contingencies and their likelihoods to determine the best estimate of an uncertain event.

Problem A situation with a starting point, a goal state, and a nonobvious way to get to it.

Problem-focused coping A reaction to stress that involves the management of the event causing the stress.

Procedural memory Implicit, nonstated memory for how to do things; also called implicit memory.

Process loss Time a group spends coordinating discussion rather than working on the task itself.

Prodigy A child with a special skill or talent far exceeding the norm for his or her age.

Progressive relaxation A method for reducing stress by contracting and then releasing groups of muscles.

Projection A defense mechanism in which a person unconsciously attributes their threatening impulses to another person.

Projective hypothesis A theory that suggests that reactions to ambiguous material reveal intrapsychic conflicts.

Projective test A personality instrument in the psychoanalytic perspective that uses interpretation of ambiguous stimuli to uncover unconscious conflicts.

Prosocial behavior Actions that help others at a cost to oneself.

Pseudoscience Information that appears scientific but is based on unsound scientific principles.

Psychiatry A branch of medicine that treats mental and behavioral conditions.

Psychoactive drug A chemical that alters consciousness.

Psychoanalysis A type of therapy in which unconscious conflicts and motivation are uncovered, explored, and redirected.

Psychoanalytic theory A family of theories originated by Freud that focuses on unconscious motivation.

Psychoanalytic theory of dreams A theory of dreams that suggest that dreams are unconscious wishes and/or conflicts.

Psychodynamic therapies A family of psychotherapies that have at their core the exploration of intrapsychic conflict and the role of insight to bring about therapeutic change.

Psychological dependence A situation in which a person's use of a substance leads to cravings, with distress and impairment in the absence of physiological dependence.

Psychological disorder A psychological condition that varies from the norm, is usually maladaptive, and may cause personal distress.

Psychological science Research conducted on topics in the field of psychology.

Psychological test A measure used to assess or describe mental functioning.

Psychology The scientific study of behavior and mental processes.

Psychometrician A scientist who studies the principles of psychological measurement.

Psychopathology The science of diagnosing and understanding psychological disorders.

Psychopharmacologist Researcher and practitioner who studies and often prescribes psychiatric medications.

Psychopharmacology Treatment of psychological conditions using medication.

Psychophysiological disorder A disorder in which a real medical syndrome is exacerbated by psychological factors.

Psychosexual stages According to Freud, childhood developmental stages in which tension reduction is focused on different areas of the body (oral, anal, phallic, latency, genital).

Psychosomatic diseases Disorders in which a real medical syndrome is exacerbated by psychological factors. Also known as psychophysiological illness.

Psychosurgery Treatment of mental and behavioral conditions using an invasive biological procedure.

Psychoticism A personality trait that describes how inflexible, creative, or reckless a person is.

Psychotropic medication A drug used to treat psychological conditions.

Punishment by application Attempting to extinguish a behavior by applying a negative consequence.

Punishment by removal Attempting to extinguish a behavior by removing a positive state.

Racial gap Differences on average test scores between groups associated by racial or ethnic definitions.

Random assignment Assigning participants to receive a given treatment or control condition by chance so that each has an equal likelihood of appearing in a given group.

Random sampling Selecting which members of a population will participate in a study through a systematic method that gives every person an equal chance of selection.

Range A measure of variation in a data sample determined by subtracting the lowest score from the highest score.

Rapid eye movement (REM) sleep A period of sleep that is characterized by rapid eye movements and dreams.

Ratio schedules Reinforcement is provided after behaviors are repeated a number of times.

Rational emotive therapy A type of active and directive therapy that emphasizes the link between thoughts and emotions.

Rational thinking Thinking marked by the use of deliberate reasoning.

Rationalization A defense mechanism in which an irrational behavior is unconsciously explained as acceptable in order to reduce anxiety.

Reaction formation A defense mechanism where a person will unconsciously replace a feeling.

Reactivity Unintentionally altering people's natural behavior by attempting to measure it.

Real self According to Rogers, your internal idea of who you should be.

Realistic job preview A potential employee samples the work experience to determine his or her interest in a job.

Reality principle According to Freud, the main focus of the ego that suggests that the ego will defer pleasure until a reasonable way to satisfy id instincts is available.

Reasoning Thinking through our knowledge and beliefs to reach a conclusion.

Receptor site An area on the dendrite that receives neurotransmitters.

Recessive gene A unit of heredity whose influence is exerted only when paired with an identical gene.

Reciprocal determinism Bandura's concept that suggests that behavior, environment, and thoughts are interrelated.

Reciprocity norm An assumption that you should behave positively toward those who have helped you.

Reciprocity of liking Reacting positively to those who react positively to you.

Reconstruction Creating a memory of what likely occurred based on information you can recall.

Reflex An involuntary motor response.

Refractory period Period of time following orgasm during which males cannot achieve another.

Regression A defense mechanism in which a person reverts to an earlier age of functioning.

Regression toward the mean The inclination for extreme scores to move toward the average over time.

Reinforce To strengthen behavior, making it more likely to occur again.

Reinforcer A consequence (either positive or negative) following a behavior that makes it more likely to occur again.

Relapse A recurrence of a condition or disorder.

Relative deprivation The opinion that a person is worse off than a comparison group.

Relearning A measure of forgetting and learning that is based on how easy it is to learn information again at a later time.

Reliability The consistency of the results when similar studies are performed.

REM rebound After periods of loss of sleep, the tendency to increase the length of REM.

REM sleep behavior disorder A type of REM parasomnia in which a person will act out a dream.

Replicable Results from a research study that appear the same when the study is repeated.

Repolarize The process by which a neuron's axon will return to the resting potential.

Representation An internal, mental description of a problem or information.

Representativeness heuristic Making a guess based on how much the situation "looks like" something known.

Repression A defense mechanism in which a person unconsciously forces a threatening experience from their awareness.

Reproductive strategies The preferences males and females show in their mating behavior.

Resilience Good developmental outcomes despite high risks, competence under stress, or recovery from trauma.

Resistance In psychoanalysis, a client's employment of a defense mechanism during therapy.

Resolution phase Final stage of the sexual response cycle, during which excitement levels return to base rate.

Resting potentia An inactive neuron's negative charge.

Restorative theory of sleep The view that sleep is needed in order to maintain mental and physical operations.

Restructuring Changing the representation of a problem to remove unnecessary constraints.

Reticular formation A network of nerve fibers involved in sleep and wakefulness. Also called the reticular activating system (RAS).

Retina The layer of sensory receptor cells lining the back wall of the eye.

Retinal disparity Two slightly different images falling on each retina because of their distance from one another on the face.

Reuptake The reabsorption of neurotransmitters back into a presynaptic neuron.

Reversible figure An image that can be understood with two different interpretations.

Rod cells Rod-shaped cells in the retina that register degrees of lightness and darkness.

Role A set of customary behaviors based on your position.

Rorschach inkblot test A projective test in which someone's unconscious conflicts are revealed by his or her interpretation of and reactions to ambiguous patterns of ink.

Sample The subgroup of individuals included in a study to represent a larger population.

Sampling bias The selection of a sample of individuals from within a population that fails to capture an accurate representation of the larger group.

Satisfice Finding a satisfactory choice rather than the best one.

Savant syndrome Individuals who are average (or even deficient) in most areas of cognitive functioning but display an extraordinary talent in one area.

Scale A test designed to measure a particular skill from low to high.

Scatterplot Graph showing the points observed from scores on two variables.

Schacter-Singer two-factor theory A theory of emotion that suggests that feelings are a combination of body arousal and how we think about that arousal.

Schedule of reinforcement A plan for applying consequences following a behavior.

Schema A structured set of thoughts and presumptions.

Schizophrenia A psychological disorder characterized by disordered thinking, delusions, hallucinations, and disordered behavior and emotions.

Science The operation of general laws, especially as obtained and tested through the scientific method.

Scientific method A systematic approach to organizing the collection of data and drawing conclusions from a research study.

Scientist-practitioner model Also called the Boulder model, a balanced program in which psychologists learn about clinical skills as well as research skills.

Secondary insomnia Lack of sleep associated with another medical or psychological condition.

Secondary reinforcer (conditioned reinforcer) A reward that can be exchanged for ones meeting basic needs.

Secondary sexual characteristics Physical changes, including pubic hair, breast development in girls, facial hair and lowered voice in boys, along with a spurt in height and changes to the body's overall shape, that occur during puberty.

Selective attention The ability to focus thought or perception while filtering extraneous stimulation.

Selective serotonin reuptake inhibitors (SSRI) A class of medications that increases the efficiency of serotonin binding in the nervous system.

Self A person's awareness of his or her own characteristics.

Self-actualization Maslow's concept that the highest need is to fulfill individual potential.

Self-concept The collection of all your beliefs about yourself.

Self-determination theory Motivation involves integrating new behaviors into your internal values.

Self-efficacy Your perception about your ability to do a certain task.

Self-esteem Your self-worth.

Self-image How you see yourself.

Self-perception theory The theory that suggests that people discover their attitudes while observing their own behavior.

Self-reference effect Associating information with oneself to aid in retrieval.

Self-regulation The ability to control behavior through intentional strategies.

Self-report inventory A type of test in which a person will directly answer questions about his or her behaviors, thoughts, or feelings.

Self-serving bias The tendency to see yourself in a positive light.

Semantic memory Memory for the meaning of material.

Semantic network model Organization of information that captures meaningful relationships between concepts.

Semanticity Containing meaning or reference to things in the world.

Sensation The process of registering the stimulation of sensory receptors by an external physical stimulus.

Sensorimotor stage Piaget's stage for babies and toddlers who are focused on developing their sensory and motor processes.

Sensory adaptation A change in responsiveness to the same stimulation in a sensory organ over time.

Sensory memory The brief flash of input information through the senses.

Sensory neuron A Neuron that is responsible for carrying external stimuli to the central nervous system for processing.

Sensory receptor Specialized cells in each sense organ that react to only particular kinds of external physical stimulation.

Sentence Organized sequence of words that conveys facts, hypotheses, questions, requests, intentions, and thoughts.

Serotonin A neurotransmitter involved in sleep, mood, and appetite.

Set point The tendency to maintain a particular range of body weight.

Settling point Tendency to maintain an approximate but changeable weight range.

Sex norms Typical behaviors observed across people.

Sexual disorder Problems occurring in the sexual response cycle.

Sexual harassment Unwelcome sexual comments or advances imposed in the workplace.

Sexual orientation The gender preferred for emotional sexual intimacy—same sex, opposite sex, or bisexual.

Sexual peak The highest point of interest and engagement in sex.

Shadow An archetype described by Jung that represents the worst possible version of a person.

Shaping Reinforcing part of a behavior initially and then increasing the goal to more complex behaviors.

Short-term memory (STM) The memory stage consisting of whatever information is in consciousness.

Short-term psychodynamic therapy A type of solution-focused psychoanalytic treatment.

Signal detection theory A sensory testing method that takes into account both the actual stimulus intensity and your readiness to respond.

Sixteen Personality Factor Questionnaire (16PF) A personality inventory with results that are closely related to the Big Five.

Skinner box (operant chamber) A testing apparatus with a response mechanism that also delivers reinforcement.

Sleep A natural loss of consciousness that is associated with reduced motor and sensory activity.

Sleep apnea A sleep disorder characterized by abrupt gaps in breathing during sleep, causing momentary wakefulness; also called obstructive sleep apnea.

Sleep debt The difference between how much you should sleep and your actual amount of sleep.

Sleep disorder A condition in which the amount or quality of sleep is disturbed, resulting in distress or impairment.

Sleep eating A type of nREM parasomnia associated with preparing and consuming food while still asleep.

Sleep hygiene Sleep habits.

Sleep paralysis A sleep condition characterized by a temporary inability to move upon wakening.

Sleep spindle A type of brain wave pattern associated with Stage 2 sleep and the consolidation of new memories.

Sleep terror A type of nREM parasomnia characterized by observed panic and terror while asleep, often associated with amnesia about the situation. Also called night terror.

Sleepsex A type of nREM parasomnia associated with engaging in sexual activity while asleep. Also called sexsomnia.

Sleepthink Generic thought about the day during sleep.

Sleepwalking A type of nREM parasomnia in which a person will leave his or her bed and perform activities while still asleep.

Social anxiety disorder An anxiety disorder characterized by performance anxiety in nearly all types of social situations.

Social categorization Mental sorting of people into groups.

Social clock Cultural norms for appropriate ages to seek out life events like marriage.

Social cognition Thoughts people use to understand their social world.

Social cognitive perspective A personality theory that focuses on the interplay among traits, thoughts, and environmental contexts.

Social desirability bias Participants may alter their responses if they perceive them as depicting them negatively.

Social facilitation The tendency to work harder when others are around.

Social influence The way behavior is shaped.

Social loafing The tendency to work less in a group than by yourself.

Social norm An expectation about customary behaviors based on a person's position.

Social phobia An anxiety disorder characterized by fear of public embarrassment or humiliation.

Social psychology The branch of psychology that focuses on how the way people think, feel, and behave influences and is influenced by others.

Social rejection Exclusion from contact by others causes emotional pain.

Social-responsibility norm The assumption that assistance should be given to those in need.

Social roles Assumptions about the way people should behave given their status.

Social skills training A type of behavior therapy intended to improve interaction with others.

Social support The help provided by others.

Sociobiology A theory that your behaviors and personality can be explained through the ideas of evolution.

Sociocultural perspective A school of psychology that emphasizes the way that social and cultural elements in the world (or environment) influence behavior and mental processes.

Soma The part of the neuron that keeps the cell alive and contains the genetic material for the cell.

Somatic marker A visceral, physiological response that reveals underlying emotion about an event or decision.

Somatic nervous system The division of the peripheral nervous system that connects to voluntary muscle movement and communicates sensory information.

Somatic symptom disorder A type of disorder in which a person experiences disruptive and persistent thoughts, feelings, and behaviors that accompany illness symptoms.

Somatic symptom and related disorders Psychological disorders characterized by having symptoms of physical illness that cannot be explained by a general medical condition.

Somatosensory cortex An area of the parietal lobe that processes body sensation information.

Source monitoring Memory for the circumstances of acquiring information.

Source trait A universal, enduring behavioral characteristic.

Spacing effect Learning is improved if study effort is distributed over time.

Specific intelligences (s) Spearman's theory of performance factors only involved in each particular task.

Spermarche For boys, the first ejaculation occurs around age 14, followed a year later by the development of mature sperm cells.

Spinal cord A collection of neurons that run from the base of the brain down the back.

Spinal reflex An involuntary motor response coordinated by the spinal cord.

Split brain The result of severing the corpus callosum, so that the hemispheres of the cerebral cortex cannot communicate through the nerves that would usually connect them.

Split-brain surgery An operation that involves severing the corpus callosum. Also called a corpus callostomy.

Split-half reliability Performance on one-half of the test is compared against performance on the other half.

Spontaneous recovery The reappearance of an extinguished conditioned response.

Spontaneous remission Reduction of symptoms of a condition in the absence of treatment.

Spreading activation The links between concepts in memory help to access one given another.

Stage 1 A phase of sleep between relaxed wakefulness and being asleep.

Stage model of memory Atkinson and Shiffrins's three stages of memory—sensory, short-term, and long-term memory.

Standard deviation A statistical measure tracking how each score in a sample differs from the mean.

Standardization Conversion of scores from the number of correct answers to a relative performance score compared to others on the same test.

Standardized procedure Protocol for testing that follows the same steps for all test takers.

Stanford-Binet Scale A version of the intelligence test devised by Louis Terman and tested on many American schoolchildren.

Statistic A numerical summary of the results of data collection.

Statistically significant When the probability (p) of an observed difference occurring is determined to be less than 5% (p <0.05).

Status High economic and social status within the group is a desirable quality in male mates.

Stereotype Overgeneralized beliefs about a group and its members.

Stereotype threat Performance decrements caused by knowledge of cultural stereotypes.

Stimulant-induced psychosis Symptoms of hallucinations and delusions that are caused by medication that activates the nervous system.

Stimulants A class of psychoactive substances that increases activity in the nervous system.

Stimulus Physical energy in the world registered by a sensory organ, including light, sound, and smell.

Stimulus control therapy A treatment for insomnia that includes associating bedtime with sleep to reestablish a consistent sleep-wake schedule.

Stimulus threshold The point at which the neuron responds by changing its voltage.

Strange situation procedure A test in which the mother leaves her child alone in the playroom, and a friendly stranger tries to interact with the child. Finally, the mother rejoins them.

Stranger anxiety A fear reaction of infants to new people usually peaking around 12 months.

Stress A response that occurs from events seen as a challenge.

Stressors Anything perceived as a challenge.

Striving for superiority According to Adler, an attempt to overcome feelings of inferiority by being a better person; also known as compensation.

Structural plasticity The brain's ability to change in response to the environment.

Structuralism The school of psychology that studies human experience by breaking it down into smaller pieces.

Stuporous catatonia A symptom of schizophrenia that is characterized by restricted motor activity such as periods of immobility and muscle rigidity.

Subjective well-being A feeling of satisfaction with life and happiness.

Sublimation A defense mechanism in which a person unconsciously redirects an id instinct in a socially acceptable way.

Subliminal perception Sensation registered "below threshold," without conscious awareness of its occurrence.

Substantia nigra A midbrain structure that is responsible for initiation of movement.

Superego According to Freud, the part of the personality governed by the perfection principle.

Support group A type of group therapy in which members meet without a therapist to provide social support.

Suprachiasmatic nucleus A part of the hypothalamus that controls daily rhythms for sleep and wakefulness.

Surface structure The ordering of a sequence of words in time.

Surface trait An enduring behavior that is easily observed.

Survey A study method in which individuals are asked to respond to a set of questions designed by an experimenter.

Syllogism A simple deduction task with three statements or premises.

Sympathetic nervous system A branch of the autonomic nervous system that prepares the organs for vigorous activity.

Symptom substitution The emergence of a replacement symptom of a psychological condition if the root cause is not resolved.

Synapse An area that includes three structures; the terminal button of the sending neuron, the synaptic gap, and the dendrite of the receiving neuron.

Synaptic cleft The small space between the axon terminal of a sending neuron and the dendrite of the receiving neuron.

Synaptic pruning The destruction of less active synapses to organize an improve efficiency of the neural connections.

Synaptic transmission The process by which one neuron communicates with another by using neurotransmitters.

Synaptic vesicle A sac that contains neurotransmitters in the axon terminal.

Systematic desensitization Treatment for phobia in which a client practices relaxation during progressively more fear-inducing stimuli.

Tardive dyskinesia A neurological condition involving involuntary, repetitive movements.

Taste aversion Learning to dislike foods that were followed by nausea.

Telegraphic speech Two- and three-word combinations with meaning.

Temperament According to the biological perspective, inborn biological traits.

Temporal lobes An area of the cerebral cortex near the temples. Includes primary auditory cortex, and language centers.

Teratogens Toxic agents from the environment, such as disease, poisons, or drugs, that can harm the fetus.

Terror management theory A theory that suggests that because of our awareness of death, we battle anxiety by boosting our self-esteem and cultural connections.

Test-retest reliability The likelihood of receiving a similar score when a test is repeated.

Testosterone A sex hormone produced by the testes, adrenal cortex, and ovaries that is important in the male sex characteristics of the male body.

Tetrahydrocannabinol (THC) A psychoactive substance that is the active ingredient in marijuana.

Thalamus A forebrain structure that is a major relay station for sensory information.

Thanatos According to Freud, ways in which we reduce tensions that are aggressive and destructive, also known as the death instinct.

Thematic apperception test (TAT) A projective personality instrument in which unconscious conflicts are revealed by the interpretation of stories told in reaction to a series of ambiguous images.

Theoretical approach to traits Deriving traits from another theory of personality.

Theory An overarching conceptualization about how variables may cause behavior.

Theory of mind The child's conception of what he or she and others know, and that these can differ.

Theory of psychosocial development Erikson's stage theory of important issues to resolve across the life span.

Theta An EEG pattern that is associated with relaxed wakefulness.

Thinking The internal mental processes that make sense of our experiences.

Threshold The point at which a neuron will respond to an action potential.

Tip-of-the-tongue phenomenon The feeling of knowing a word but being unable to recall it from long-term memory.

Token economies Situations in which easy-to-use secondary reinforcers are traded in for a meaningful reward.

Tolerance A reduction in a person's sensitivity to a drug over time.

Top-down processing Perception through the use of information in memory to organize incoming sensations.

Trait A stable characteristic of behavior.

Trait theory A theory of personality that focuses on identifying and measuring characteristics of behavior.

Tranquilizers A type of drug used for sedation and reducing anxiety.

Transcendence According to Jung, the process of resolving the dichotomy of who we are as people.

Transcranial magnetic stimulation (TMS) A procedure that uses electromagnetic coils to activate nerve cells in the brain.

Transduction The process in which physical energy in the world is translated into an electrochemical signal—neurons firing—that represents sensation in the brain.

Transference In psychoanalysis, a type of displacement in which the client will unconsciously act out relationships with the therapist.

Trial and error Creating a solution, testing to see if it works, and then starting over if unsuccessful.

Triangular theory of love Sternberg's theory that relationships are composed of three components: intimacy, passion, commitment.

Triarchic theory of intelligence Sternberg's theory positing three underlying aspects of cognition: analytic, creative, and practical.

Trichromatic theory The notion that color vision relies on sensory receptors in the retina that process only red, blue, and green.

Trickster An archetype that represents someone who pretends to be something that he or she is not.

Twin study Examining the heritability of traits by comparing identical twins (who share all of their genes) to fraternal twins (who share 50% of their genes).

Type A personality A style characterized by difficulty relaxing, impatience, and anger when delayed.

Type B personality A style characterized by being relaxed about time, slow to anger, and relative ease at relaxing.

Uncertainty The state of not being determined, either because the event has not occurred or cannot be known logically.

Unconditional positive regard According to Rogers, a sense of respect and love that is not linked to specific behaviors.

Unconditioned response A physiological behavior that is involuntarily elicited by a stimulus.

Unconditioned stimulus An unlearned signal that leads to an automatic, reflexive response.

Unconscious According to Freud, thoughts, memories, feelings, and wishes that reside outside of awareness.

Unhealthy (mistaken) lifestyle Adler's description of those who strive for superiority by competing with others.

Unit bias Tendency to eat the amount provided as a serving.

Universals Behaviors that all people perform regardless of their cultures.

Unnecessary constraint An apparent requirement for a solution that is not really needed.

Validity The degree to which a research experiment captures what it claims to study.

Variable A factor that is manipulated or measured, or controlled, during an experiment.

Variable-interval schedule Providing reinforcement for the first behavior after a set average amount of time has passed.

Variable-ratio schedule Providing reinforcement after an average number of repeated behaviors.

Variance The variability between scores observed on a given dependent variable.

Vasocongestion Blood circulates into all the erectile structures in the body (e.g., penis, clitoris, nipples).

Ventromedial hypothalamus The functional "stop eating" center in the brain.

Virtual reality exposure therapy A behavioral therapy technique that involves the repetitive presentation of a simulated distressing object or situation in order to reduce anxiety.

Waist-to-hip ratio (WHR) A woman's waist size divided by hip size gives an index of figure shape.

Wason selection task A card game that requires checking for rule violations.

Wavelength The distance between peaks of incoming light waves that determines their color.

Weber's Law As the stimulus becomes stronger or larger, so does the just noticeable difference between it and other similar stimuli.

Wechsler Adult Intelligence Scale (WAIS) An intelligence test written for adults and widely used in group assessment.

Wernicke's area Part of the left temporal lobe that comprehends spoken words.

Wise old man An archetype that represents wisdom.

Withdrawal symptoms Distress and cravings associated with the rapid discontinuation of certain psychoactive substances.

Within-subjects design A research plan in which each subject takes part in every aspect of the study.

Word A meaningful pattern of sound defined within a language.

Working memory Synonym for short-term memory that reflects its role in thinking.

Working memory capacity The amount of information you can retain for a short period and report back correctly.

Working memory span The amount of different pieces of information (such as digits) that can be held in conscious memory for a short time and reported back correctly.

Yerkes-Dodson law of arousal The theory that performance is best at medium levels of arousal.

Zone of proximal development Children's readiness to learn the next step from what they already know.

Zygote An initial stage in development as the fertilized egg grows through cell division and attaches to the uterine wall.

Index

Credits

Chapter 6 Visual Overview
Page 215 © George Bailey/ShutterStock, Inc.; **page 215 (top right)** © Annettee Shaff/ShutterStock, Inc.; **page 215 (top middle)** © Jaimie Duplass/ShutterStock, Inc.; **page 215 (top left)** © kaczor58/ShutterStock, Inc.; **page 215 (middle left)** © Ignite Lab/ShutterStock, Inc.; **page 215 (bottom right)** © Jagodka/ShutterStock, Inc.; **page 215 (bottom left)** © Eric Isselée/ShutterStock, Inc.

Chapter 7
Opener © Junial Enterprises/ShutterStock, Inc.; **page 225** © Junial Enterprises/ShutterStock, Inc.; **second opener** © Hemera/Thinkstock; **7-17A** © Volina/ShutterStock, Inc.; **7-17B** © Jack Hollingsworth/Valueline/Thinkstock; **7-18A** © Ablestock.com/Thinkstock; **7-18B** © Hemera Technologies/Photos.com/Thinkstock; **7-18C** © Ryan McVay/Photodisc/Thinkstock; **7-18D** © iStockphoto/Thinkstock; **7-18E** © Jupiterimages/Polka Dot/Thinkstock; **7-18F** © Ablestock.com/Thinkstock; **7-19A** © iStockphoto/Thinkstock; **7-19B** © Jupiterimages/Comstock/Thinkstock; **7-19C** © Jupiterimages/Comstock/Thinkstock; **7-19D** © iStockphoto/Thinkstock; **7-19E** © atoss/ShutterStock, Inc.; **page 244 (left)** © Cheryl E. Davis/ShutterStock, Inc.; **page 244 (middle left)** © Four Oaks/ShutterStock, Inc.; **page 244 (middle right)** © photodisc; **page 244 (right)** © Olga Popova/ShutterStock, Inc.; **7-21A** Courtesy of Helene C. Stikkel/U.S. Department of Defense; **7-21B** © Stockbyte/Thinkstock; **7-21C** © Donald Miralle/Lifesize/Thinkstock; **7-22** © terekhov igor/ShutterStock, Inc.; **7-23A** © Design Pics/The Irish Image Collection/Valueline/Thinkstock; **7-23B** © Creatas Images/Thinkstock; **7-24** © Gulnara Samoilova/PA Photos/Landov; **7-29** © Jason Newman; **7-32** © Chuck Burton/AP Photos; **7-33** © Burlington Police Department/AP Photos.

Chapter 7 Visual Overview
Page 266 (middle) © George Doyle/Stockbyte/Thinkstock; **Autobiographical (top)** © Elzbieta Sekowska/ShutterStock, Inc.; **Autobiographical (bottom)** © Brian Goodman/ShutterStock, Inc.; **Concepts** © Sascha Burkard/ShutterStock, Inc.; **Declarative** © Volina/ShutterStock, Inc.; **Flashbulb** © Joshua Haviv/ShutterStock, Inc.; **Schemas (left)** © Golden Pixels LLC/ShutterStock, Inc.; **Schemas (middle)** © Yuri Arcurs/ShutterStock, Inc.; **Schemas (right)** © Paul Matthew Photography/ShutterStock, Inc.; **Semantic networks (top)** © gregg williams/ShutterStock, Inc.; **Semantic networks (bottom)** © Bipsun/ShutterStock, Inc.

Chapter 8
Opener © Petr Vaclavek/ShutterStock, Inc.; **page 277** © Petr Vaclavek/ShutterStock, Inc.; **second opener** © Luca Bruno/AP Photos; **8-1** Screen grab of the Iowa Gambling Task. Permission given by test's author, Dr. Antoine Bechara; **page 280** © Vladimir Kozieiev/ShutterStock, Inc.; **page 282** © Kenneth V. Pilon/ShutterStock, Inc.;

8-05 From "Neural Activity When People Solve Verbal Problems With Insight," by M. Jung-Beeman, E.M. Bowden, J. Haberman, J.L. Frymiare, S. Arambel-Liu, R. Greenblatt, et al., 2004, PLoS Biology, 2, pp. 502 and 505. 284; **8-10** © Andresr/ShutterStock, Inc.; **page 288 (middle)** © Martin Haas/ShutterStock, Inc.; **page 288 (bottom)** © Matthew Jacques/ShutterStock, Inc.; **8-12** © Shots Studio/ShutterStock, Inc.; **page 297** © Matt Antonino/ShutterStock, Inc.; **page 298** © AP Photos; **page 299 (top)** © Lucie Danninger/ShutterStock, Inc.; **page 299 (middle)** © The Gorilla Foundation/AP Photos; **page 301** © The Protected Art Archive/Alamy Images; **8-22A** © Photos.com; **8-22B** © szefei/ShutterStock, Inc.; **8-22C** © Dmitriy Shironosov/Dreamstime.com; **8-22D** © Photos.com; **8-22E** © EDHAR/ShutterStock, Inc.

Chapter 8 Visual Overview
© StockLite/ShutterStock, Inc.

Chapter 9
Opener © Steven Puetzer/Getty Images; **page 317** © Steven Puetzer/Getty Images; **second opener** © Martin Dohrn/Photo Researchers, Inc.; **page 319** © Left Eyed Photography/ShutterStock, Inc.; **page 320** © Seth Wenig/AP Photos; **page 324 (top)** © bannosuke/ShutterStock, Inc.; **page 324 (bottom)** © Photo Researchers, Inc.; **9-3** Reprinted from The Lancet, 353, Witelson, S. F., Kigar, D. L., & Harvey, T., The Exceptional Brain of Albert Einstein, 2149-2153, Copyright 1999, with permission from Elsevier; **page 327** © Mary Evans Picture Library/Alamy Images; **page 328** © Will & Deni McIntyre/Photo Researchers, Inc.; **page 337** © Tomasz Markowski/ShutterStock, Inc.; **page 339 (bottom)** © Michael Ventura/Alamy Images; **page 339 (top)** © photogolfer/ShutterStock, Inc.; **9-13** © Teresa Kasprzycka/ShutterStock, Inc.; **page 342** © Dmitriy Shironosov/ShutterStock, Inc.; **page 343** © Darrin Henry/ShutterStock, Inc.; **page 344** © guatebrian/Alamy Images; **page 345 (top)** © haveseen/ShutterStock, Inc.; **page 345 (middle)** © Nicholas Piccillo/ShutterStock, Inc.; **page 345 (bottom)** © S. Pytel/ShutterStock, Inc.; **page 346** © Orange Line Media/ShutterStock, Inc.; **9-21A** Courtesy, Dr. Arthur W. Toga and Dr. Paul M. Thomson, Laboratory of Neuro Imaging at UCLA. http://www.loni.ucla.edu; **9-21B** Courtesy, Dr. Arthur W. Toga and Dr. Paul M. Thomson, Laboratory of Neuro Imaging at UCLA. http://www.loni.ucla.edu; **page 349 (A)** © Peter Menzel/Photo Researchers, Inc.; **page 349 (B)** © Peter Menzel/Photo Researchers, Inc.; **page 349 (C)** © Peter Menzel/Photo Researchers, Inc.; **page 349 (D)** © Peter Menzel/Photo Researchers, Inc.; **page 350 (top)** © Robin Scholz/AP Photos; **page 350 (middle)** © Hasan Shaheed/ShutterStock, Inc.; **page 351 (1)** © Angela Waye/ShutterStock, Inc.; **page 351 (2)** © Stockbyte/Thinkstock; **page 351 (3 bottom)** © Brad Wynnyk/ShutterStock, Inc.; **page 351 (3 top)** © Brad Wynnyk/ShutterStock, Inc.; **page 351 (4)** © marekuliasz/ShutterStock, Inc.; **351 (5)** © Zurijeta/ShutterStock, Inc.

Chapter 10
Opener © Ljupco Smokovski/ShutterStock, Inc.; **page 361** © Ljupco Smokovski/ShutterStock, Inc.; **second opener** © tomas del amo/ShutterStock, Inc.; **page 364** © Germanskydiver/ShutterStock, Inc.; **page 367** © Martin Haas/ShutterStock, Inc.; **10-8** © OAK RIDGE NATIONAL LABORATORY/US DEPARTMENT OF ENERGY/Photo Researchers, Inc.; **page 373** © Nailia Schwarz/ShutterStock, Inc.; **page 375** © Baloncici/ShutterStock, Inc.; **page 376** © MAXA/Landov; **page 378** © David Mzareulyan/ShutterStock, Inc.; **page 380** © COOK/AP Photos; **page 383** © AP Photos; page 384 © AP Photos; **page 385** © Charles Sykes/AP Photos; **page 386 (top)** © Danny Moloshok/AP Photos; **page 387** © Donald Traill/AP Photos; **page 388 (top)** © Science Source/Photo Researchers, Inc.; **page 388 (bottom)** © Ed Andrieski/AP Photos; **10-26** © The Kinsey Institute; **page 391** © Heather Renee/ShutterStock, Inc.; **10-28A** Courtesy of Carrie Masten; **10-28B** Courtesy of Carrie Masten; **10-29** © Lew Merrim/Science Photo Library; **page 395** © Natalia Bratslavsky/ShutterStock, Inc.

Chapter 10 Visual Overview
© Sebastian Kaulitzki/ShutterStock, Inc.

Chapter 11
Opener © MaxFX/ShutterStock, Inc.; **page 147** © MaxFX/ShutterStock, Inc.; **second opener** © sculpies/ShutterStock, Inc.; **page 419** © Tim Mainiero/ShutterStock, Inc.; **11-4** © pefostudio5/ShutterStock, Inc.; **page 420** © Sanzhar Murzin/ShutterStock, Inc.; **11-5** © National Library of Medicine; **11-6** © SPL/Photo Researchers, Inc.; **11-7A** © Jenny Solomon/ShutterStock, Inc.; **11-7B** © Joy Brown/ShutterStock, Inc.; **11-7C** © Vikulin/ShutterStock, Inc.; **11-8** © Claus Lunau/Bonnier Publications/Photo Researchers, Inc.; **11-9** © Volker Steger/Photo Researchers, Inc.; **page 422 (top)** © Alexander Khokhlov/ShutterStock, Inc.; **page 422 (bottom)** © Studio 37/ShutterStock, Inc.; **page 424 (top)** © abd/ShutterStock, Inc.; **page 424 (bottom)** © Robert Adrian Hillman/ShutterStock, Inc.; **11-10A** © Yuri Arcurs/ShutterStock, Inc.; **11-10B** © iStockphoto/Thinkstock; **11-10C** © Lifesize/Thinkstock; **11-10D** © rebirth3d/ShutterStock, Inc.; **11-10E** © Kurhan/ShutterStock, Inc.; **11-10F** © Four Oaks/ShutterStock, Inc.; **11-17** © Elena Elisseeva/ShutterStock, Inc.; **page 428** © wavebreakmedia ltd/ShutterStock, Inc.; **page 429** © Arman Zhenikeyev/ShutterStock, Inc.; **page 433 (left)** © Lee Morris/ShutterStock, Inc.; **page 433 (middle)** © AbleStock; **page 433 (right)** © Poulsons Photography/ShutterStock, Inc.; **page 436** © Benis Arapovic/ShutterStock, Inc.; **11-19** © Hemera/Thinkstock; **page 439** © Yuri Arcurs/ShutterStock, Inc.; **page 440** © Elena Elisseeva/ShutterStock, Inc.; **page 441** © Christophe Testi/ShutterStock, Inc.

Chapter 11 Visual Overview
© sculpies/ShutterStock, Inc.

Chapter 12
Opener © Dmitriy Shironosov/Shutter-Stock, Inc.; **page 451** © Dmitriy Shiro-nosov/ShutterStock, Inc.; **second opener** © Darren Brode/ShutterStock, Inc.; **12-1** © Michael Sohn/AP Photos; **12-2** © lelik759/ShutterStock, Inc.; **12-5A** © Rui Vale de Sousa/ShutterStock, Inc.; **12-5B** © Olinchuk/ShutterStock, Inc.; **12-5C** © Stepanov/ShutterStock, Inc.; **12-5D** © Valua Vitaly/ShutterStock, Inc.; **page 461** © Charlie Edward/ShutterStock, Inc.; **12-11** © Photo Researchers, Inc.; **12-13** © Photo Researchers, Inc.; **12-12** © Photo Researchers, Inc.; **12-14** © Photo Re-searchers, Inc.; **12-16** © Iakov Filimonov/ShutterStock, Inc.; **12-17** © Ruslan Kudrin/ShutterStock, Inc.; **12-15** © Steve Lovegrove/ShutterStock, Inc.; **page 462 (top)** © Doug Goodman/Photo Research-ers, Inc.; **page 462 (bottom)** © Doug Good-man/Photo Researchers, Inc.; **page 480** © Jason LaVeris/FilmMagic/Getty Images; **page 487** © Reuters/Landov.

Chapter 12 Visual Overview
Page 490 (top) © Angelo Giampiccolo/ShutterStock, Inc.; **page 490 (middle)** © Samuel Borges/ShutterStock, Inc.; page 490 (bottom) © Monkey Business Images/ShutterStock, Inc.

Chapter 13
Opener © vipflash/ShutterStock, Inc.; **page 505** © vipflash/ShutterStock, Inc.; **second opener** © Pascal Janssen/Shut-terStock, Inc.; **13-1** Library of Congress, Prints & Photographs Division, [reproduc-tion number LC-USZ62-1234]; **page 508 (middle)** © Edwin Verin/ShutterStock, Inc.; **page 508 (bottom)** © ElenaGaak/ShutterStock, Inc.; **13-2** © Jurgen Ziewe/ShutterStock, Inc.; **page 509 (top)** © Ta-tiana Morozova/ShutterStock, Inc.; **page 509 (bottom)** © siamionau pavel/Shutter-Stock, Inc.; **page 510 (top)** © Melissa King/ShutterStock, Inc.; **page 510 (middle)** © iofoto/ShutterStock, Inc.; **13-3** © Mary Evans/Photo Researchers, Inc.; **page 511 (middle)** © Serg Shalimoff/ShutterStock, Inc.; **page 511 (bottom)** © Ingrid W./Shut-terStock, Inc.; **13-4** © National Library of Medicine; **page 512 (top)** © Science Source/Photo Researchers, Inc.; **page 512 (bottom)** © Adam Michal Ziaja/Shutter-Stock, Inc.; **page 513** © Chris Knapton/Photo Researchers, Inc.; **13-5** © SPL/Photo Researchers, Inc.; **page 514 (top)** © Alli-son Achauer/ShutterStock, Inc.; **page 514 (bottom)** © kaczor58/ShutterStock, Inc.; **13-8** Courtesy of Dr. Albert Bandura; **13-10** © Mary Evans Picture Library/Alamy Images; **13-11** Courtesy of The HJ Eysenck Memorial Fund; **13-13** © SPL/Photo Researchers, Inc.; **13-14** © Will & Deni McIntyre/Photo Researchers, Inc.; **13-15** © Lewis J. Merrim/Photo Researchers, Inc.; **page 525** © viviamo/ShutterStock, Inc.

Chapter 13 Visual Overview
Page 528 (top left) Library of Congress, Prints & Photographs Division, [reproduc-tion number LC-USZ62-1234]; **page 528 (top right)** © National Library of Medicine;

page 528 (middle) © Pascal Janssen/Shut-terStock, Inc.; **page 528 (middle right)** © SPL/Photo Researchers, Inc.; **page 528 (bottom right)** © SPL/Photo Researchers, Inc.

Chapter 14
Opener © Emilia Dotcheva/ShutterStock, Inc.; **page 537** © Emilia Dotcheva/Shut-terStock, Inc.; second opener © Able-Stock; **page 538** © Ingram Publishing/age fotostock; **page 540** © Oleg Seleznev/Dreamstime.com; **14-2A** © LiquidLibrary; **14-2B** © Rubberball Productions; **14-2C** © Monkey Business Images/ShutterStock, Inc.; **14-2D** © Matthew Gough/Shutter-Stock, Inc.; **14-2E** © LiquidLibrary; **14-2F** © Selahattin Bayram/ShutterStock, Inc.; **14-2G** © Mads Abildgaard/ShutterStock, Inc.; **14-4** Courtesy of Library of Con-gress, Prints & Photographs Division, [LC-USZ62-104691]; **page 544** © Jason Stitt/ShutterStock, Inc.; **page 544 (middle right)** © Diedie/ShutterStock, Inc.; **page 544 (middle)** © Vatikaki/ShutterStock, Inc.; **page 544 (right)** © Sim Kay Seng/ShutterStock, Inc.; **page 545** © Geotrac/Dreamstime.com; **page 546** © Mircea BEZERGHEANU/ShutterStock, Inc.; **14-8** © Sculpies/Dreamstime.com; **page 547** © Jonathan Souza/Dreamstime.com; **page 548 (top)** © sommthink/ShutterStock, Inc.; **page 548 (bottom)** © Valeev/Shut-terStock, Inc.; **page 549 (top)** © Muriel Lasure/ShutterStock, Inc.; **page 549 (bottom)** © Kileman/Dreamstime.com; **page 552** © Pixtal/age fotostock; **page 553 (top)** © Robert Kneschke/Shutter-Stock, Inc.; **page 553 (bottom)** © Jose Gil/Dreamstime.com; **page 555** © Lyn Baxter/Dreamstime.com; **page 557** © DNF-Style Photography/ShutterStock, Inc.; **page 558** © Andrey Kiselev/Dreamstime.com; **14-18** © Mikhail Basov/Dreamstime.com; **14-19** © Daniel Anderson and courtesy of Dr. James Fallon.

Chapter 14 Visual Overview
Page 568 (top right) © AbleStock; **page 568 (top right background)** © AbleStock; **Anxiety disorders** © Geotrac/Dream-stime.com; **Somatoform disorders** © Pixtal/age fotostock; **Dissociative identity disorder** © Bryoni Castelijn/Shutter-Stock, Inc.; **Mood disorders** © AbleStock; **Psychotic disorders** © dundanim/Shut-terStock, Inc.; **Personality disorders** © Martin Novak/ShutterStock, Inc.

Chapter 15
Opener © iStockphoto/Thinkstock; **page 579** © iStockphoto/Thinkstock; **second opener** © Anteromite/ShutterStock, Inc.; **page 582** © Arena Creative/ShutterStock, Inc.; **15-2** © Middle Temple Library/Photo Researchers, Inc.; **page 583** © Jerry Cooke/Photo Researchers, Inc.; **15-3** © National Library of Medicine; **15-6** Courtesy of Library of Congress, Prints & Photographs Division, [reproduction number LC-USZ62-1234]; **15-7** © Library of Congress/Photo Researchers, Inc.; **15-8** © Creatas/Thinkstock; **page 586** © Geraint Lewis/Alamy Images; **15-9** © Rob Marmion/

ShutterStock, Inc.; **page 588** © Jupiterim-ages/Brand X Pictures/Thinkstock; **15-11A** Courtesy of Malem Medical, http://www.malem.co.uk; **page 590 (middle)** © Piotr Marcincki/ShutterStock, Inc.; **page 590 (bottom)** © mast3r/ShutterStock, Inc.; **15-13** © US Army/Photo Researchers, Inc.; **page 592 (top)** © Garo/Phanie/Photo Researchers, Inc.; **page 592 (middle)** © Will & Deni McIntyre/Photo Research-ers, Inc.; **page 594** © Mike Flippo/Shut-terStock, Inc.; **Table 15-4A** © .shock/ShutterStock, Inc.; **Table 15-4B** © Knud Nielsen/ShutterStock, Inc.; **Table 15-4C** © Lilyana Vynogradova/ShutterStock, Inc.; **Table 15-4D** © SunnyS/ShutterStock, Inc.; **Table 15-4E** © Maxim Tupikov/ShutterStock, Inc.; **Table 15-4F** © nito/ShutterStock, Inc.; **Table 15-4G** © Gregory Gerber/ShutterStock, Inc.; **page 597** © Chris Gallagher/Photo Researchers, Inc.; **page 599** © Robert Brook/Photo Research-ers, Inc.; **15-15** © Will & Deni McIntyre/Photo Researchers, Inc.; **15-16** © Living Art Enterprises, LLC/Photo Researchers, Inc.; **15-17** © Richard T. Nowitz/Photo Researchers, Inc.; **15-18** © Medical Body Scans/Photo Researchers, Inc.

Chapter 15 Visual Overview
© iStockphoto/Thinkstock

Chapter 16
Opener © William Perugini/ShutterStock, Inc.; **page 615** © William Perugini/Shut-terStock, Inc.; **second opener** © Creatas/Thinkstock; **page 618 (top)** © Design Pics/Colleen Cahill/Valueline/Thinkstock; **page 618 (bottom)** © DigitalVision/Thinkstock; **page 619 (top)** © Jupiterimages/Polka Dot/Thinkstock; **page 619 (bottom)** © AISPIX by Image Source/ShutterStock, Inc.; **page 620 (bottom)** © iStockphoto/Thinkstock; **page 620 (middle)** © Comstock/Think-stock; **page 620 (top)** © Stockbyte/Think-stock; **page 621 (A)** © Pinkcandy/Shut-terStock, Inc.; **page 621 (B)** © Stephen Coburn/ShutterStock, Inc.; **page 621 (C)** © Gina Smith/ShutterStock, Inc.; **page 621 (D)** © Nejron Photo/ShutterStock, Inc.; **page 622** © iStockphoto/Thinkstock; **page 623** © Creatas/Thinkstock; **16-02** © Estate of Francis Bello/Photo Research-ers, Inc.; **page 624 (left)** © iStockphoto/Thinkstock; **page 624 (right)** © Jupiterim-ages/Comstock/Thinkstock; **page 626 (middle)** © Hemera/Thinkstock ; **page 626 (bottom)** © DigitalVision/Thinkstock; **16-4** © Philip G. Zimbardo, Inc.; **page 633** © Jack Hollingsworth/DigitalVision/Think-stock; **page 634 (middle)** © Comstock/Thinkstock; **page 634 (bottom)** © Jupi-terimages/Pixland/Thinkstock; **page 635 (top)** © AP Photos; **page 635 (bottom)** © Michael Blann/DigitalVision/Thinkstock; **page 636** © Jupiterimages/BananaStock/Thinkstock; **page 637 (top)** © iStockphoto/Thinkstock; **page 637 (bottom)** © Ryan McVay/DigitalVision/Thinkstock; **page 638** © Ryan McVay/Photodisc/Thinkstock.

Chapter 16 Visual Overview
© ZargonDesign/iStockphoto.

Critical Thinking Applications

Page 21 © Bobby Deal/RealDealPhoto/ShutterStock, Inc.; **page 62** © Christophe Testi/ShutterStock, Inc.; **page 101** © OtnaYdur/ShutterStock, Inc.; **page 129** © Karin Hildebrand Lau/ShutterStock, Inc.; **page 163** ©kuppa/ShutterStock, Inc.; **page 209** © Kuzma/ShutterStock, Inc.; **page 256** © iStockphoto/Thinkstock; **page 286** © Phil Date/ShutterStock, Inc.; **page 323** © Andresr/ShutterStock, Inc.; **page 379** © Katrina Brown/ShutterStock, Inc.; **page 441** © wavebreakmedia ltd/ShutterStock, Inc.; **page 478** © AbleStock; **page 527** © Stockbroker/Alamy Images; **page 561** © Tctomm/Dreamstime.com; © Ambrophoto/ShutterStock, Inc.; **page 629** © L.Watcharapol/ShutterStock, Inc.

Visual Summary

1.1 © Ladman/ShutterStock, Inc.; **1.2** © Photos.com/Thinkstock; **1.3** © Digital Vision/Thinkstock; **1.4** © Pat Sullivan/AP Photos; **2.1** © Yuri Arcurs/ShutterStock, Inc.; **2.2** © Denis Vrublevski/ShutterStock, Inc.; **2.3** © Denis Vrublevski/ShutterStock, Inc.; **2.4** © Ersin Kurtdal/ShutterStock, Inc.; **2.5** © Ragne Kabanova/ShutterStock, Inc.; **3.1** © Sebastian Kaulitzki/ShutterStock, Inc.; **4.2** © Republican Party/AP Photos; **4.4** © Juriah Mosin/ShutterStock, Inc.; **4.5** © AbleStock; **5.1** © Konstantin Sutyagin/ShutterStock, Inc.; **5.2** © Angela Waye/ShutterStock, Inc.; **5.3** © benicce/ShutterStock, Inc.; **5.4** © Sinisa Botas/ShutterStock, Inc.; **5.5** © Yuri Arcurs/ShutterStock, Inc.; **5.6** © ifong/ShutterStock, Inc.; **6.1** © mypokcik/ShutterStock, Inc.; **6.2** © Golden Pixels LLC/ShutterStock, Inc.; **6.3** © Irina Silvestrova/ShutterStock, Inc.; **6.4** © sextoacto/ShutterStock, Inc.; **7.1** © Hemera/Thinkstock; **7.4** © terekhov igor/ShutterStock, Inc.; **7.6** © Jason Newman; **7.8** © Junial Enterprises/ShutterStock, Inc.; **8.1** © Vladimir Kozieiev/ShutterStock, Inc.; **8.3** © Matthew Jacques/ShutterStock, Inc.; **8.5** © Lucie Danninger/ShutterStock, Inc.; **8.6A** © Photos.com; **8.6B** © szefel/ShutterStock, Inc.; **8.6C** © Dmitriy Shironosov/Dreamstime.com; **8.6D** © Photos.com; **8.6E** © EDHAR/ShutterStock, Inc.; **9.1** © Left Eyed Photography/ShutterStock, Inc.; **9.4** © Dmitriy Shironosov/ShutterStock, Inc.; **9.5** Data from Kaufman, A. S., & Lichtenberger, E. (2006). Assessing adolescent and adult intelligence (3rd ed.). Hoboken, NJ: Wiley; **10.1** © Germanskydiver/ShutterStock, Inc.; **10.2** © David Mzareulyan/ShutterStock, Inc.; **10.4** © Heather Renee/ShutterStock, Inc.; **10.5** © Natalia Bratslavsky/ShutterStock, Inc.; **11.1** © Tim Mainiero/ShutterStock, Inc.; **11.2** © abd/ShutterStock, Inc.; **11.3** © wavebreakmedia ltd/ShutterStock, Inc.; **11.4** © Arman Zhenikeyev/ShutterStock, Inc.; **11.5** © Poulsons Photography/ShutterStock, Inc.; **11.6** © Yuri Arcurs/ShutterStock, Inc.; **12.1** © Darren Brode/ShutterStock, Inc.; **12.2** © Charlie Edward/ShutterStock, Inc.; **12.4** Reproduced from Salthouse, T. (2011). Consequences of age-related cognitive declines. Annual Review of Psychology, 63, 5.1-5.26; **12.5** © Dmitriy Shironosov/ShutterStock, Inc.; **13.1** © Pascal Janssen/ShutterStock, Inc.; **13.2** Library of Congress, Prints & Photographs Division, [reproduction number LC-USZ62-1234]; **13.4** © Melissa King/ShutterStock, Inc.; **13.6** © Mary Evans Picture Library/Alamy Images; **13.7** © viviamo/ShutterStock, Inc.; **13.8** © iofoto/ShutterStock, Inc.; **14.1** © Ingram Publishing/age fotostock; **14.2** © Jason Stitt/ShutterStock, Inc.; **14.3** © Jose Gil/Dreamstime.com; **14.4** © Lyn Baxter/Dreamstime.com; **14.5** © Andrey Kiselev/Dreamstime.com; **14.6** © Mikhail Basov/Dreamstime.com; **14.7** © Petro Feketa/Dreamstime.com; **15.1** © National Library of Medicine; **15.2** Courtesy of Library of Congress, Prints & Photographs Division, [reproduction number LC-USZ62-1234]; **15.4** © Piotr Marcincki/ShutterStock, Inc.; **15.5** © mast3r/ShutterStock, Inc.; **15.6** © Garo/Phanie/Photo Researchers, Inc.; **16.2** © Jupiterimages/Polka Dot/Thinkstock; **16.3** © iStockphoto/Thinkstock; **16.4** © iStockphoto/Thinkstock; **16.5** © DigitalVision/Thinkstock; **16.6** © Jack Hollingsworth/DigitalVision/Thinkstock; **16.7** © Ryan McVay/Photodisc/Thinkstock.

End Sheets
Multiple Perspectives

Behavioral © Yco/ShutterStock, Inc.; **Cognitive** © Karuka/ShutterStock, Inc.; **Evolutionary** © iStockphoto/Thinkstock; **Humanistic** © Robert J. Daveant/ShutterStock, Inc.; **Positive psychology** © BananaStock/Thinkstock; **Psychoanalytic** © Dubova/ShutterStock, Inc.; **Sociocultural** © Hemera/Thinkstock.

Transduction from Physical Energy to Neural Signals

Middle © Robert Kneschke/ShutterStock; Inc.; **Overlay** © johnwoodcock/iStockphoto

Motivation: Sources of Hunger

© Sebastian Kaulitzki/ShutterStock, Inc.

The major theories of personality, theorists, and concepts.

Top right Library of Congress, Prints & Photographs Division, [reproduction number LC-USZ62-1234]; **Top left** © National Library of Medicine; **Middle** © Pascal Janssen/ShutterStock, Inc.; **Middle right** © SPL/Photo Researchers, Inc.; **Bottom left** © SPL/Photo Researchers, Inc.

Unless otherwise indicated, all photographs and illustrations are under copyright of Jones & Bartlett Learning, or have been provided by the authors.

Visual Overview Motivation: Sources of Hunger

The motivation to eat has characteristic influences in our physical bodies (shown in blue) and in our environment (shown in green).

Are You Hungry?

Hypothalamus: start and stop

Body image

Hypothalamus: drives endocrine system

Advertisements, serving size, others eating

Stomach stretching and contractions

Metabolic rate and set point

Taste preferences

Insulin production

Food available

Cultural practices

Adobo-Marinated Pork Tenderloin with Grilled-Pineapple Salsa

Tender, flavorful pork, complemented by the heat and grilled ingredients of the salsa, creates an outstanding combination.

- 1 cup fresh lime juice
- 2 teaspoons black pepper
- 2 teaspoons dried oregano
- 2 teaspoons ground cumin
- 1½ teaspoons salt
- 6 garlic cloves, crushed
- 2 pounds pork tenderloin
- 1½ teaspoons olive oil
- Cooking spray
- ¼ cup coarsely chopped fresh cilantro
- 2 tablespoons finely chopped green onions
- Grilled-Pineapple Salsa

1. Combine first 6 ingredients in a 2-quart baking dish. Trim fat from pork. Place pork in dish, turning to coat; cover and marinate in refrigerator 1 hour, turning pork occasionally.

2. Prepare grill.

3. Remove pork from dish; discard marinade. Brush pork with oil. Insert a meat thermometer into thickest portion of pork. Place on a grill rack coated with cooking spray, and grill 25 minutes or until thermometer registers 160° (slightly pink). Cut into ¼-inch-thick slices. Sprinkle with cilantro and green onions. Serve with Grilled-Pineapple Salsa. Yield: 8 servings (serving size: 3 ounces pork and ⅓ cup salsa).

CALORIES 194 (26% from fat); FAT 5.6g (sat 1.6g, mono 2.6g, poly 0.7g); PROTEIN 25.5g; CARB 10.5g; FIBER 1.5g; CHOL 79mg; IRON 2.8mg; SODIUM 306mg; CALC 42mg

GRILLED-PINEAPPLE SALSA:

- 1 fresh cored, peeled pineapple, cut into 1-inch slices
- 1 red bell pepper
- 1 yellow bell pepper
- Cooking spray
- ½ cup finely chopped red onion
- ½ cup chopped fresh cilantro
- 3 tablespoons fresh lime juice
- 1 tablespoon brown sugar
- 1½ teaspoons minced crystallized ginger
- 2 jalapeño peppers, seeded and minced
- 1 drained canned chipotle chile in adobo sauce, minced

1. Preheat grill.

2. Place first 3 ingredients on a grill rack coated with cooking spray; grill 3 minutes on each side. Discard stems and seeds from bell peppers; dice pineapple and bell peppers. Combine pineapple, bell pepper, onion, and remaining ingredients; toss gently. Yield: 3 cups (serving size: ⅓ cup).

CALORIES 36 (10% from fat); FAT 0.4g (sat 0g, mono 0.1g, poly 0.1g); PROTEIN 0.6g; CARB 8.7g; FIBER 1.1g; CHOL 0mg; IRON 0.7mg; SODIUM 11mg; CALC 13mg

How to Trim Pork Tenderloin

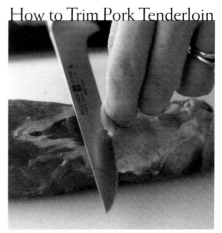

When preparing the pork tenderloin, remove the silver skin, which is the thin, shiny membrane that runs along the surface of the meat. Leaving the silver skin on can cause the tenderloin to toughen and lose shape during grilling. Stretching the membrane with one hand so it's tight, use your other hand to slip the tip of the knife underneath the silvery skin. Slowly slice back and forth, angling the sharp edge of the blade up, rather than down, through the meat. Continue this process until all the silver skin is removed, then discard.

Squash-Stuffed Cannelloni with Roasted-Shallot Sauce

Prepare the filling up to one day in advance. You'll need about 4 pounds butternut squash to get 10 cups. For a vegetarian version, use vegetable broth in place of chicken broth; sauté the shallots and garlic in oil, omitting the bacon.

FILLING:

10 cups (½-inch) cubed peeled butternut squash
¼ cup chopped shallots
 2 tablespoons chopped fresh sage
Cooking spray
 1 tablespoon butter, melted
½ cup fat-free sour cream
¼ cup half-and-half
¼ teaspoon salt
¼ teaspoon freshly ground black pepper

SAUCE:

 3 slices applewood smoked bacon, chopped
½ pound shallots, peeled and halved
 2 garlic cloves, crushed
½ cup dry white wine
 1 (14-ounce) can fat-free, less-sodium chicken broth
 2 tablespoons half-and-half
¼ teaspoon salt
¼ teaspoon freshly ground black pepper

REMAINING INGREDIENTS:

16 cooked lasagna noodles
¾ cup (3 ounces) shredded fontina cheese
¼ cup chopped blanched hazelnuts, toasted
Sage leaves (optional)

1. Preheat oven to 400°.

2. To prepare filling, combine first 3 ingredients in a bowl. Place mixture on a jelly-roll pan coated with cooking spray. Drizzle with butter; toss to coat. Bake at 400° for 25 minutes or until lightly browned, stirring occasionally. Place squash mixture in a large bowl; mash with a potato masher. Stir in sour cream and next 3 ingredients.

3. To prepare sauce, cook bacon in an ovenproof Dutch oven over medium-high heat until crisp. Remove bacon from pan, reserving 2 teaspoons drippings in pan; set bacon aside. Add halved shallots and garlic to drippings in pan; sauté 5 minutes or until browned. Bake at 400° for 25 minutes, stirring occasionally. Place pan on stovetop over medium-high heat. Add wine, scraping pan to loosen browned bits. Add broth; bring to a boil. Reduce heat; simmer 5 minutes. Remove from heat; stir in 2 tablespoons half-and-half, ¼ teaspoon salt, and ¼ teaspoon pepper.

4. Spread ¼ cup filling over each noodle, leaving a ½-inch border on each short end. Beginning with a short end, roll up noodles jelly-roll fashion. Place rolls, seam sides down, in a 13 x 9–inch baking pan coated with cooking spray. Pour sauce over noodles; sprinkle evenly with cheese. Bake at 400° for 25 minutes or until cheese is golden. Sprinkle with bacon and hazelnuts. Yield: 8 servings (serving size: 2 cannelloni).

CALORIES 349 (29% from fat); FAT 11.4g (sat 5g, mono 4.5g, poly 1g); PROTEIN 12.2g; CARB 51.8g; FIBER 7.8g; CHOL 26mg; IRON 3mg; SODIUM 414mg; CALC 206mg

Chili and Cheddar Farfalle Casserole

1   (7-ounce) can chipotle chiles in adobo sauce
1   tablespoon butter
1   cup chopped red bell pepper
½   cup diced Canadian bacon (about 2 ounces)
1   cup thinly sliced green onions
2   tablespoons all-purpose flour
1   teaspoon chili powder
½   teaspoon salt
½   teaspoon ground cumin
2¼   cups 2% reduced-fat milk
2   cups (8 ounces) shredded reduced-fat sharp Cheddar cheese, divided
2   tablespoons chopped fresh cilantro
8   cups hot cooked farfalle (about 6 cups uncooked bow tie pasta) or other short pasta
Cooking spray

1. Preheat oven to 400°.
2. Remove 1 teaspoon adobo sauce and 1 chile from canned chiles; mince chile. Place remaining sauce and chiles in a zip-top plastic bag; freeze for another use.
3. Melt butter in a large Dutch oven over medium-high heat. Add bell pepper and bacon; sauté 4 minutes. Add onions; sauté 1 minute. Stir in adobo sauce, minced chile, flour, chili powder, salt, and cumin; cook 1 minute. Gradually add milk, and cook until thick and bubbly (about 4 minutes), stirring constantly with a whisk. Remove from heat.

Gradually add 1½ cups cheese and cilantro, stirring until cheese melts. Add pasta to pan; toss well.
4. Spoon pasta mixture into an 11 x 7–inch baking dish coated with cooking spray. Sprinkle ½ cup cheese over pasta mixture. Bake at 400° for 15 minutes or until browned. Yield: 6 servings (serving size: 1⅓ cups).

CALORIES 369 (30% from fat); FAT 12.4g (sat 7.4g, mono 1.6g, poly 1g); PROTEIN 23.2g; CARB 43g; FIBER 3.1g; CHOL 44mg; IRON 1.6mg; SODIUM 758mg; CALC 472mg

Frittata with Smoked Cheese and Pancetta

Similar to a French omelet, a frittata is an Italian version that resembles a crustless quiche.

Cooking spray
1½   cups frozen Southern-style hash brown potatoes (such as Ore-Ida)
½   cup chopped onion
⅓   cup chopped pancetta (about 2 ounces)
½   teaspoon salt
½   teaspoon hot pepper sauce (such as Tabasco)
⅛   teaspoon black pepper
4   large eggs
4   large egg whites
¼   cup (1 ounce) shredded smoked mozzarella cheese
2   tablespoons chopped green onions
Green onion strips (optional)

1. Preheat broiler.
2. Heat a 10-inch ovenproof nonstick skillet over medium-high heat. Coat pan with cooking spray. Add potatoes, onion, and pancetta; sauté 8 minutes or until potatoes are golden brown. Remove from pan. Wipe pan clean with paper towels; recoat with cooking spray. Combine salt, hot pepper sauce, black pepper, eggs, and egg whites in a medium bowl, stirring with a whisk. Stir in potato mixture, cheese, and chopped green onions.
3. Heat pan over medium heat. Pour in egg mixture. Reduce heat to medium-low; cook 3 minutes or until bottom is lightly browned, lifting edges and tilting pan as eggs cook to allow uncooked portion to flow underneath cooked portion.
4. Broil 2 minutes or until top is lightly browned and set. Garnish with green onion strips, if desired. Yield: 4 servings (serving size: 1 wedge).

CALORIES 198 (50% from fat); FAT 11.1g (sat 4.5g, mono 1.9g, poly 0.7g); PROTEIN 14.9g; CARB 8.9g; FIBER 0.8g; CHOL 225mg; IRON 1mg; SODIUM 701mg; CALC 86mg

Spaghetti Carbonara

Carbonara (kar-boh-NAH-rah) literally translates as the "charcoal maker's wife." Word has it that the charcoal sellers from Abruzzo introduced this dish to the city of Rome. For a simple, tasty supper, you can't go wrong with this recipe. And if you have leftover ham it's even better, as chopped ham replaces the bacon in this version of the classic Italian dish. To speed up the prep even more, leave the water for the pasta covered so it will come to a boil faster.

  8 ounces uncooked spaghetti
  1 cup chopped cooked ham
  ⅓ cup (1½ ounces) grated Parmigiano-
      Reggiano or Parmesan cheese
  ¼ cup reduced-fat sour cream
  ½ teaspoon salt
  2 large eggs, lightly beaten
  1 garlic clove, minced
  ¼ teaspoon coarsely ground black pepper

1. Cook pasta according to package directions, omitting salt and fat. Drain pasta in a colander over a bowl, reserving ½ cup liquid.
2. Heat a large nonstick skillet over medium heat. Add ham, and cook 2 minutes or until thoroughly heated. Add pasta, and stir well. Combine cheese and next 4 ingredients, stirring with a whisk. Add reserved pasta liquid to egg mixture, stirring with a whisk. Pour egg mixture over pasta mixture; stir well. Cook over low heat 5 minutes or until sauce thickens, stirring constantly (do not boil). Sprinkle with pepper. Serve immediately. Yield: 4 servings (serving size: 1 cup).

CALORIES 352 (25% from fat); FAT 9.6g; (sat 4.6g, mono 2.2g, poly 0.9g); PROTEIN 21g; CARB 45g; FIBER 1.4g; CHOL 139mg; IRON 1.7mg; SODIUM 748mg; CALC 179mg

Creamy Ham Casseroles

These creamy casseroles get a double hit of cheese with Cheddar and cream cheese. Best of all, this recipe makes enough for two separate meals.

  4½ cups uncooked medium egg noodles
  2   quarts boiling water
  2   cups broccoli florets
  1   cup fat-free milk
  1   (10¾-ounce) can condensed reduced-fat,
       reduced-sodium cream of mushroom soup,
       undiluted
  2   cups (8 ounces) reduced-fat shredded
       Cheddar cheese, divided
  1   (6-ounce) tub light cream cheese with chives
       and onion, softened
  2   cups chopped lean ham
  1   cup chopped carrot
  Cooking spray
  1   cup fat-free herb-flavored croutons, crushed

1. Cook noodles in 2 quarts boiling water for 2 minutes. Add broccoli; cook 3 minutes. Drain.
2. Combine milk, soup, 1 cup Cheddar cheese, and cream cheese in a large bowl; stir well with a whisk. Add noodle mixture, ham, and carrot, and stir well. Divide noodle mixture evenly between 2 (8-inch) square baking dishes coated with cooking spray.
3. Combine remaining 1 cup Cheddar cheese and crouton crumbs; toss well. Sprinkle crumb mixture evenly over casseroles. Wrap unbaked casseroles with heavy-duty foil. Freeze up to 3 months.
4. Preheat oven to 350°.
5. Place frozen casseroles on a baking sheet. Bake, covered, at 350° for 1 hour. Uncover and bake an additional 15 minutes. Yield: 2 casseroles, 4 servings per casserole (serving size: 1 cup).

CALORIES 342 (38% from fat); FAT 14.6g; (sat 7.9g, mono 2g, poly 0.8g); PROTEIN 25.1g; CARB 27.6g; FIBER 1.8g; CHOL 80mg; IRON 1.5mg; SODIUM 395mg; CALC 308mg

Creamy Ham Casseroles

Sage Risotto with Fresh Mozzarella
and Prosciutto

Sage Risotto with Fresh Mozzarella and Prosciutto

Ever since northern Italians first stirred Arborio rice into a gooey risotto, cooks there have cast any remotely creamy grain-based dish as a risotto. This dish sticks more closely to the original than some more recent versions. You may substitute basil for sage, if desired.

    2   (14-ounce) cans fat-free, less-sodium chicken broth
    1   tablespoon butter
    1   cup finely chopped leek (about 2 small leeks)
    2   garlic cloves, minced
 1¼   cups Arborio rice
    ¼   teaspoon salt
    ½   cup dry white wine
 1½   to 2 tablespoons finely chopped fresh sage
    1   cup (4 ounces) finely chopped fresh mozzarella cheese
    2   ounces prosciutto, chopped (about ⅓ cup)
    ¼   teaspoon freshly ground black pepper
        Sage sprigs (optional)

1. Bring broth to a simmer (do not boil). Keep warm over low heat.
2. Melt butter in a medium sauté pan over medium heat. Add leek and garlic, and cook 3 minutes, stirring frequently. Add rice and salt; cook 1 minute, stirring constantly. Stir in wine; cook 2 minutes or until liquid is nearly absorbed, stirring constantly. Add broth, ½ cup at a time, stirring frequently until each portion is absorbed before adding the next (about 20 minutes total). Stir in chopped sage, and cook 2 minutes. Remove from heat; stir in mozzarella. Spoon 1 cup risotto into each of 4 bowls; top each serving with about 1½ tablespoons prosciutto. Sprinkle with black pepper. Garnish with sage sprigs, if desired. Yield: 4 servings.

CALORIES 443 (25% from fat); FAT 12.3g (sat 7g, mono 3g, poly 1g); PROTEIN 18.8g; CARB 59.6g; FIBER 1.4g; CHOL 43mg; IRON 1.3mg; SODIUM 863mg; CALC 193mg

Penne with Sausage, Eggplant, and Feta

Meaty breakfast sausage, earthy eggplant, and zesty feta complement each other in this hearty pasta dish. Buy precrumbled feta cheese to save time.

 4½   cups cubed peeled eggplant (about 1 pound)
    ½   pound bulk pork breakfast sausage
    4   garlic cloves, minced
    2   tablespoons tomato paste
    1   teaspoon dried oregano
    ¼   teaspoon freshly ground black pepper
    1   (14.5-ounce) can diced tomatoes, undrained
    6   cups hot cooked penne (about 10 ounces uncooked tube-shaped pasta)
    ½   cup (2 ounces) crumbled feta cheese
    ¼   cup chopped fresh parsley

1. Cook eggplant, sausage, and garlic in a large nonstick skillet over medium-high heat 5 minutes or until sausage is browned and eggplant is tender. Add tomato paste and next 3 ingredients; cook over medium heat 5 minutes, stirring occasionally.
2. Place pasta in a large bowl. Add tomato mixture, cheese, and parsley; toss well. Yield: 4 servings (serving size: 2 cups).

CALORIES 535 (32% from fat); FAT 18.9g (sat 7.6g, mono 7.5g, poly 2.1g); PROTEIN 25.5g; CARB 67.5g; FIBER 4.6g; CHOL 57mg; IRON 4.5mg; SODIUM 884mg; CALC 141mg

Cajun Sausage and Rice Skillet

For convenience, we used premeasured boil-in-bag rice. You can substitute 3 cups instant long-grain rice for the boil-in-bag rice. Round out this hearty Cajun meal with a crisp green salad.

2 teaspoons canola oil
1 cup presliced mushrooms
1 cup chopped onion
1½ tablespoons salt-free Cajun seasoning
8 ounces andouille sausage, sliced
3 (3½-ounce) bags boil-in-bag long-grain rice
1 (32-ounce) container fat-free, less-sodium chicken broth
1 (15-ounce) can kidney beans, rinsed and drained
¼ teaspoon salt

1. Heat oil in a large nonstick skillet over medium-high heat. Add sliced mushrooms and next 3 ingredients, and sauté 5 minutes.
2. Remove uncooked rice from bags; add to pan. Stir in broth, beans, and salt. Bring mixture to a boil; cover, reduce heat, and simmer 10 minutes or until rice is tender. Yield: 6 servings (serving size: about 1⅔ cups).

CALORIES 351 (22% from fat); FAT 8.5g (sat 2.8g, mono 0.9g, poly 0.6g); PROTEIN 15.1g; CARB 52.8g; FIBER 4.1g; CHOL 27mg; IRON 2.8mg; SODIUM 929mg; CALC 16mg

Red Beans and Rice

This traditional Louisiana Creole fare is the ultimate in thriftiness and convenience. The long cooking time coaxes the spiciness from the sausage into the beans. Be sure to add the salt to the dish after it has cooked and just before serving. Adding salt to dried beans too early will slow the cooking process and make the beans less tender. Served over rice with a side of slaw, this southern classic is hard to beat.

3 cups water
1 cup dried red kidney beans
1 cup chopped onion
1 cup chopped green bell pepper
¾ cup chopped celery
1 teaspoon dried thyme
1 teaspoon paprika
¾ teaspoon ground red pepper
½ teaspoon black pepper
½ (14-ounce) package turkey, pork, and beef smoked sausage (such as Healthy Choice), thinly sliced
1 bay leaf
5 garlic cloves, minced
½ teaspoon salt
3 cups hot cooked long-grain rice
¼ cup chopped green onions

1. Combine first 12 ingredients in a 2-quart electric slow cooker. Cover and cook on HIGH 5 hours. Discard bay leaf; stir in salt. Serve over rice in individual bowls; sprinkle evenly with green onions. Yield: 4 servings (serving size: 1 cup bean mixture, ¾ cup rice, and 1 tablespoon green onions).

CALORIES 413 (5% from fat); FAT 2.5g (sat 0.7g, mono 0.2g, poly 0.5g); PROTEIN 21.1g; CARB 76.3g; FIBER 10.1g; CHOL 18mg; IRON 6mg; SODIUM 749mg; CALC 102mg

poultry

Sautéed Chicken Breasts with Sherry-Vinegar
Sauce, page 192

Old-Fashioned Chicken Potpie

CRUST:

- 1 cup all-purpose flour
- 3 tablespoons ice water
- 1 teaspoon cider vinegar
- ¼ teaspoon salt
- ¼ cup vegetable shortening

FILLING:

- 3 cups fat-free, less-sodium chicken broth, divided
- 2⅓ cups cubed red potato (about 1 pound)
- 1 cup (¼-inch-thick) slices carrot
- 2 teaspoons butter
- ½ cup chopped shallots or onion
- ½ cup all-purpose flour
- 1 cup frozen petite green peas
- ¾ teaspoon salt
- ¼ teaspoon dried thyme
- Dash of black pepper
- 2 cups diced cooked chicken

REMAINING INGREDIENTS:

- Cooking spray
- 2 teaspoons 1% low-fat milk

1. To prepare crust, lightly spoon 1 cup flour into a dry measuring cup, and level with a knife. Combine ¼ cup flour, ice water, and vinegar in a small bowl. Combine ¾ cup flour and ¼ teaspoon salt in a large bowl; cut in shortening with a pastry blender or 2 knives until mixture resembles coarse meal. Add vinegar mixture; stir just until moist. Gently press mixture into a 5-inch circle on heavy-duty plastic wrap; cover with additional plastic wrap. Chill 15 minutes. Roll dough, still covered, into a 10-inch circle. Place dough in refrigerator.

2. Preheat oven to 400°.

3. To prepare filling, bring 2½ cups broth to a boil in a medium saucepan. Add potato and carrot; cook 10 minutes. Drain mixture in a colander over a bowl, reserving cooking liquid.

4. Melt butter in a large nonstick skillet over medium heat. Add shallots; cook 3 minutes. Lightly spoon ½ cup flour into a dry measuring cup; level with a knife. Combine ½ cup flour and remaining ½ cup broth, and stir with a whisk. Add to skillet. Stir in potato mixture, reserved cooking liquid, peas, ¾ teaspoon salt, thyme, and pepper. Cook 10 minutes until thickened; stir in chicken. Remove from heat, and cool slightly. Spoon chicken mixture into a 10-inch deep-dish pie plate coated with cooking spray. Remove 1 sheet of plastic wrap from dough. Place dough on top of chicken mixture,

pressing to edge of dish. Remove top sheet of plastic wrap. Cut 5 slits in top of crust to allow steam to escape. Gently brush crust with milk. Bake at 400° for 45 minutes or until golden. Let stand 10 minutes. Yield: 6 servings (servings size: about 1 cup).

CALORIES 362 (29% from fat); FAT 11.5g (sat 4.5g, mono 3g, poly 2.9g); PROTEIN 22.1g; CARB 41.3g; FIBER 3.6g; CHOL 43mg; IRON 3mg; SODIUM 764mg; CALC 38mg

Creamed Chicken

This recipe comes together in a flash, and the peas add a nice touch of color. If you can't find roasted skinless, boneless chicken breast, buy a whole roasted chicken, and substitute 2¼ cups chopped cooked breast meat. Add the leftover chicken to soup, pasta, or a salad later in the week.

- ½ cup all-purpose flour
- 2¼ cups whole milk
- 1 cup frozen green peas, thawed
- 2 teaspoons chopped fresh sage
- 1 teaspoon butter
- 1 (10-ounce) package roasted skinless, boneless chicken breast (such as Perdue Short Cuts), chopped
- 1 tablespoon fresh lemon juice
- ¼ teaspoon freshly ground black pepper
- Sage sprigs (optional)

1. Lightly spoon flour into a dry measuring cup, and level with a knife. Combine flour and ½ cup milk in a large saucepan over medium heat, stirring with a whisk until smooth. Stir in 1¾ cups milk. Cook 4 minutes or until thick, stirring constantly with a whisk.

2. Stir in peas, sage, butter, and chicken. Cook 2 minutes or until thoroughly heated. Remove from heat; stir in juice and pepper. Garnish with sage sprigs, if desired. Yield: 4 servings (serving size: about ¾ cup).

CALORIES 232 (23% from fat); FAT 6g (sat 3.6g, mono 1.8g, poly 0.4g); PROTEIN 20.9g; CARB 25.4g; FIBER 2.1g; CHOL 53mg; IRON 2.2mg; SODIUM 1,001mg; CALC 164mg

Old-Fashioned Chicken Potpie

Chicken Tetrazzini

Chicken Tetrazzini

1 tablespoon butter
Cooking spray
1 cup finely chopped onion
⅔ cup finely chopped celery
1 teaspoon freshly ground black pepper
¾ teaspoon salt
3 (8-ounce) packages presliced mushrooms
½ cup dry sherry
⅔ cup all-purpose flour
3 (14-ounce) cans fat-free, less-sodium chicken broth
2¼ cups (9 ounces) shredded fresh Parmesan cheese, divided
½ cup (4 ounces) block-style ⅓-less-fat cream cheese
7 cups hot cooked vermicelli (about 1 pound uncooked pasta)
4 cups chopped cooked chicken breast (about 1½ pounds)
1 (1-ounce) slice white bread

1. Preheat oven to 350°.

2. Melt butter in a large stockpot coated with cooking spray over medium-high heat. Add onion, celery, pepper, salt, and mushrooms, and sauté 4 minutes or until mushrooms are tender. Add sherry; cook 1 minute.

3. Lightly spoon flour into dry measuring cups; level with a knife. Gradually add flour to pan; cook 3 minutes, stirring constantly with a whisk (mixture will be thick). Gradually add broth, stirring constantly. Bring to a boil. Reduce heat; simmer 5 minutes, stirring frequently. Remove from heat.

4. Add 1¾ cups Parmesan cheese and cream cheese, stirring with a whisk until cream cheese melts. Add pasta and chicken, and stir until blended. Divide pasta mixture between 2 (8-inch square) baking dishes coated with cooking spray.

5. Place bread in a food processor, and pulse 10 times or until coarse crumbs form. Combine breadcrumbs and remaining ½ cup Parmesan cheese, and sprinkle evenly over pasta mixture.

6. Bake at 350° for 30 minutes or until lightly browned. Remove from oven; let stand 15 minutes. Yield: 2 casseroles, 6 servings each (serving size: about 1⅓ cups).

CALORIES 380 (29% from fat); FAT 12.2g (sat 6.6g, mono 3.4g, poly 0.7g); PROTEIN 33g; CARB 32.7g; FIBER 2g; CHOL 66mg; IRON 2.8mg; SODIUM 964mg; CALC 319mg

Hot Chicken and Chips Retro

This recipe has a nostalgic appeal that hearkens back to the 1950s and '60s. If you make it ahead, don't add the potato chips until it's time to bake the casserole, or they'll become soggy.

4 cups chopped roasted skinless, boneless chicken breast (about 4 breasts)
¼ cup chopped green onions
¼ cup chopped red bell pepper
2 tablespoons finely chopped fresh flat-leaf parsley
1 (8-ounce) can sliced water chestnuts, drained and chopped
½ cup low-fat mayonnaise
¼ cup reduced-fat sour cream
2 tablespoons fresh lemon juice
2 teaspoons Dijon mustard
½ teaspoon salt
½ teaspoon freshly ground black pepper
Cooking spray
¾ cup (3 ounces) shredded Swiss cheese
¾ cup crushed baked potato chips (about 2 ounces)

1. Preheat oven to 400°.

2. Combine chicken and next 4 ingredients in a large bowl; stir well. Combine low-fat mayonnaise and next 5 ingredients in a small bowl, stirring with a whisk. Add mayonnaise mixture to chicken mixture; stir well to combine. Spoon chicken mixture into an 11 x 7–inch baking dish coated with cooking spray; sprinkle with cheese. Top cheese evenly with chips. Bake at 400° for 13 minutes or until filling is bubbly and chips are golden. Yield: 6 servings.

CALORIES 321 (31% from fat); FAT 10.9g (sat 4.1g, mono 2.6g, poly 1g); PROTEIN 34.3g; CARB 20.4g; FIBER 2.6g; CHOL 96mg; IRON 11.4mg; SODIUM 606mg; CALC 175mg

North African Chicken and Couscous

Couscous, cumin, and cilantro are common elements in North African cuisine, as is the combination of savory and sweet. This dish makes a quick weeknight meal.

  2 cups water
1½ cups uncooked couscous
 ½ cup golden raisins
 ½ cup thawed orange juice concentrate, undiluted
 ⅓ cup lemon juice
 2 tablespoons water
 2 tablespoons olive oil
 2 teaspoons ground cumin
 ½ teaspoon salt
 ¼ teaspoon black pepper
 3 cups chopped ready-to-eat roasted skinless, boneless chicken breast (about 3 breasts)
 2 cups chopped peeled cucumber
 1 cup chopped red bell pepper
 ¼ cup thinly sliced green onions
 ½ cup chopped fresh cilantro
Sliced green onions (optional)

1. Bring water to a boil in a medium saucepan, and gradually stir in couscous and raisins. Remove from heat. Cover; let stand 5 minutes. Fluff with a fork.
2. Combine orange juice and next 6 ingredients; stir well with a whisk.
3. Combine couscous mixture, juice mixture, chicken, and next 4 ingredients in a large bowl, and toss well. Garnish with green onions, if desired. Yield: 6 servings (serving size: 2 cups).

CALORIES 332 (18% from fat); FAT 6.6g (sat 1.2g, mono 3g, poly 0.9g); PROTEIN 19.6g; CARB 51.2g; FIBER 3.3g; CHOL 35mg; IRON 2.8mg; SODIUM 498mg; CALC 51mg

Asparagus and Chicken Carbonara

Pasta carbonara is traditionally made with raw egg yolks and whipping cream. This lighter version achieves the same texture with egg substitute and fat-free evaporated milk. Serve this dish immediately; if it stands, the sauce can become too thick.

 8 ounces uncooked spaghetti
 2 cups (1-inch) slices asparagus (about ¾ pound)
 ½ cup egg substitute
 ½ cup evaporated fat-free milk
 2 teaspoons olive oil
 ½ cup chopped onion
 ¼ cup dry vermouth
 2 cups chopped skinless, boneless rotisserie chicken breast
 ½ cup (2 ounces) grated fresh Parmesan cheese
 3 tablespoons finely chopped fresh flat-leaf parsley
 ¾ teaspoon salt
 ½ teaspoon freshly ground black pepper
 4 bacon slices, cooked and crumbled

1. Cook pasta in boiling water 10 minutes or until al dente; add asparagus during final 2 minutes of cooking. Drain pasta mixture in a colander over a bowl, reserving ⅓ cup cooking liquid. Combine reserved cooking liquid, egg substitute, and milk, stirring with a whisk.
2. Heat a large nonstick skillet over medium-high heat. Add olive oil and onion to pan, and sauté 2 minutes. Add vermouth; cook 1 minute. Stir in pasta mixture. Remove from heat; stir in milk mixture, chicken, and cheese. Place pan over medium heat, and cook 4 minutes or until slightly thick, stirring frequently. Remove from heat; stir in parsley, salt, pepper, and bacon. Serve immediately. Yield: 5 servings (serving size: about 1¼ cups).

CALORIES 416 (23% from fat); FAT 10.8g (sat 3.7g, mono 4.4g, poly 2g); PROTEIN 34.7g; CARB 41.9g; FIBER 3.1g; CHOL 60mg; IRON 3.4mg; SODIUM 700mg; CALC 236mg

Asparagus and Chicken Carbonara

Three-Cheese Chicken Penne Florentine

Fresh spinach, chicken, and a combination of cheeses make this updated version of macaroni and cheese comforting enough for the last days of winter yet fresh enough for the first days of spring.

1 teaspoon olive oil
Cooking spray
3 cups thinly sliced mushrooms
1 cup chopped onion
1 cup chopped red bell pepper
3 cups chopped fresh spinach
1 tablespoon chopped fresh or 1 teaspoon dried oregano
¼ teaspoon freshly ground black pepper
1 (16-ounce) carton 2% low-fat cottage cheese
4 cups hot cooked penne (about 8 ounces uncooked tube-shaped pasta)
2 cups shredded roasted skinless, boneless chicken breast
1 cup (4 ounces) reduced-fat shredded sharp Cheddar cheese, divided
½ cup (2 ounces) grated fresh Parmesan cheese, divided
½ cup 2% reduced-fat milk
1 (10¾-ounce) can condensed reduced-fat, reduced-sodium cream of chicken soup, undiluted

1. Preheat oven to 425°.
2. Heat oil in a large nonstick skillet coated with cooking spray over medium-high heat. Add mushrooms, onion, and bell pepper; sauté 4 minutes or until tender. Add spinach, oregano, and black pepper; sauté 3 minutes or just until spinach wilts.
3. Place cottage cheese in a food processor; process until very smooth. Combine spinach mixture, cottage cheese, pasta, chicken, ¾ cup Cheddar cheese, ¼ cup Parmesan cheese, milk, and soup in a large bowl.
4. Spoon mixture into a 2-quart baking dish coated with cooking spray. Sprinkle with remaining ¼ cup Cheddar cheese and remaining ¼ cup Parmesan cheese. Bake at 425° for 25 minutes or until lightly browned and bubbly. Yield: 8 servings (serving size: about 1 cup).

CALORIES 345 (25% from fat); FAT 9.7g (sat 5.1g, mono 3.1g, poly 1g); PROTEIN 31.7g; CARB 32.9g; FIBER 2.1g; CHOL 56mg; IRON 2mg; SODIUM 532mg; CALC 275mg

Creamy Chicken and Mushroom Crêpes

Crêpes are paper-thin wrappers for sweet or savory fillings, and they are rolled up or folded over. Savory crêpes, such as these tasty rolls, are filled with meat, cheese, or vegetables and are often topped with a cream sauce. For convenience, buy prepackaged crêpes in the supermarket; look for them in refrigerated cases or in the produce department. Buy a prepackaged rotisserie chicken as well, and use the breast meat for this recipe. You'll have some leftover chicken you can use for another meal.

1 teaspoon butter
1 cup vertically sliced onion
1 garlic clove, minced
3 cups thinly sliced baby portobello mushroom caps (about 6 ounces)
¾ teaspoon salt
¼ teaspoon freshly ground black pepper
½ cup dry white wine
¾ cup fat-free, less-sodium chicken broth
2 teaspoons chopped fresh thyme
¼ cup crème fraîche
2 cups shredded roasted skinless, boneless chicken breast
6 (9-inch) packaged French crêpes (such as Melissa's)
Thyme sprigs (optional)

1. Melt butter in a large nonstick skillet over medium-high heat. Add onion and garlic; sauté 2 minutes or until onion begins to brown. Add mushrooms, salt, and pepper; cook 3 minutes or until liquid evaporates and mushrooms are tender, stirring frequently. Add wine, and cook 3 minutes or until liquid almost evaporates, stirring frequently. Add broth and chopped thyme; cook 2 minutes. Remove from heat; add crème fraîche, stirring until well blended. Add chicken, tossing to coat.
2. Place 1 crêpe on each of 6 plates. Spoon about ⅓ cup mushroom mixture into center of each crêpe; roll up. Garnish with thyme sprigs, if desired. Serve immediately. Yield: 6 servings (serving size: 1 filled crêpe).

CALORIES 272 (30% from fat); FAT 9.1g (sat 5g, mono 2.8g, poly 0.9g); PROTEIN 19.4g; CARB 27.5g; FIBER 0.8g; CHOL 66mg; IRON 2.1mg; SODIUM 643mg; CALC 66mg

Chicken Quesadillas with Fruit Salsa and Avocado Cream

Cooking spray
1⅓ cups shredded carrot
1 cup thinly sliced green onions
1 cup (4 ounces) shredded Monterey Jack cheese with jalapeño peppers
8 (8-inch) fat-free flour tortillas
2 cups chopped ready-to-eat roasted skinless, boneless chicken breast (such as Tyson; about 2 breasts)
½ cup fresh cilantro leaves
Fruit Salsa
Avocado Cream
Cilantro sprigs (optional)

1. Heat a large nonstick skillet over medium-high heat. Coat pan with cooking spray. Add carrot and onions; sauté 5 minutes or until tender. Sprinkle 2 tablespoons cheese over each of 4 tortillas, and top evenly with carrot mixture. Top each tortilla with ½ cup chicken, 2 tablespoons cilantro, 2 tablespoons cheese, and a tortilla.

2. Heat pan over medium heat. Coat pan with cooking spray. Add 1 quesadilla; cook 2 minutes on each side or until quesadilla is browned. Repeat with remaining quesadillas. Cut each quesadilla into 6 wedges. Arrange 4 quesadilla wedges on each of 6 plates. Top each serving with ⅔ cup Fruit Salsa, about 3 tablespoons Avocado Cream, and cilantro sprigs, if desired. Yield: 6 servings.

CALORIES 408 (28% from fat); FAT 12.5g (sat 4.9g, mono 5.4g, poly 1.2g); PROTEIN 20.6g; CARB 55.8g; FIBER 5.6g; CHOL 38mg; IRON 2.2mg; SODIUM 888mg; CALC 218mg

FRUIT SALSA:

Combine 2 cups coarsely chopped peeled ripe papaya or mango, 1½ cups coarsely chopped peeled kiwifruit, ¾ cup fresh corn kernels, ½ cup chopped red onion, ½ cup minced fresh cilantro, 3 tablespoons fresh lime juice, 1 tablespoon minced seeded jalapeño pepper, and ¼ teaspoon salt in a small bowl; cover and chill. Yield: 4 cups.

AVOCADO CREAM:

Place 1 peeled medium avocado (pitted and cut into chunks), ½ cup fat-free sour cream, and 2 tablespoons fresh lime juice in a blender; process until smooth. Spoon pureed mixture into a small bowl; stir in 2 tablespoons minced fresh cilantro. Cover and chill. Yield: 1⅓ cups.

Cuban Chicken Pizza

Bring a little of Havana to your home tonight. This dish receives five stars for convenience and taste. Toasting the corn in a skillet brings out its natural sweetness and adds a smoky note of flavor.

4   (8-inch) fat-free flour tortillas
Cooking spray
1   (11-ounce) can no salt–added whole-kernel corn, drained
½   teaspoon cumin seeds
2   cups diced roasted chicken breast
1   (15-ounce) can black beans, rinsed and drained
1   garlic clove, minced
2   tablespoons fresh lime juice
¾   cup (3 ounces) shredded Monterey Jack cheese with jalapeño peppers
4   teaspoons chopped fresh cilantro

1. Preheat oven to 350°.
2. Place flour tortillas on a baking sheet coated with cooking spray. Bake at 350° for 10 minutes or until edges are light brown. Remove from oven; stack and press down to flatten. Set aside.
3. Heat a large nonstick skillet over medium-high heat; coat pan with cooking spray. Add corn to pan, and cook 1 minute or until lightly charred. Add cumin seeds; cook 5 seconds, stirring constantly. Add chicken, black beans, and garlic; cook 2 minutes or until thoroughly heated. Remove from heat; stir in lime juice.
4. Place tortillas on baking sheet. Spoon ¾ cup bean mixture onto each tortilla; top each with 3 tablespoons cheese. Bake at 350° for 2 minutes or until cheese melts. Sprinkle each pizza with 1 teaspoon cilantro. Yield: 4 servings (serving size: 1 pizza).

CALORIES 460 (20% from fat); FAT 10.2g (sat 4.8g, mono 2.9g, poly 1.7g); PROTEIN 37.7g; CARB 54.3g; FIBER 8.4g; CHOL 78mg; IRON 3.6mg; SODIUM 760mg; CALC 210mg

Garlic Chicken Pizza

The combination of three cheeses and shredded chicken makes this an exceptionally hearty pizza.

 2 tablespoons red wine vinegar
 1½ tablespoons Dijon mustard
 4 garlic cloves, minced
 1 (16-ounce) Italian cheese-flavored pizza crust (such as Boboli)
 1½ cups shredded cooked chicken breast (about 8 ounces)
 1 cup chopped plum tomato
 1 cup chopped mushrooms
 ¾ cup (3 ounces) shredded part-skim mozzarella cheese
 ¼ cup (1 ounce) crumbled feta cheese
 ¼ cup (1 ounce) finely shredded fresh Parmesan cheese
 ¼ cup chopped green onions

1. Preheat oven to 400°.
2. Combine first 3 ingredients, stirring well with a whisk. Place crust on a baking sheet; brush vinegar mixture over crust. Top with chicken, tomato, and mushrooms; sprinkle with cheeses and green onions.
3. Bake at 400° for 15 minutes or until mozzarella and Parmesan cheeses melt. Yield: 8 servings (serving size: 1 slice).

CALORIES 263 (27% from fat); FAT 7.8g (sat 3.6g, mono 2.8g, poly 0.9g); PROTEIN 19.9g; CARB 27.1g; FIBER 0.5g; CHOL 36mg; IRON 2.1mg; SODIUM 563mg; CALC 296mg

About Pizza Crust

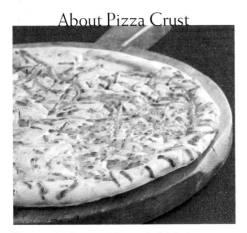

Homemade pizza crust is wonderful, but on a weeknight, there's rarely time to make it from scratch. Instead, take advantage of the convenience of a prebaked pizza crust. Because you control the toppings, you can create a low-fat pizza that provides not only great taste but is also packed with nutrients. Plus, you can have a pizza on the table in less time than it takes to have one delivered.

Oven-Fried Chicken Fingers with Honey-Mustard Dipping Sauce

These chicken fingers will have all your loved ones—especially kids—begging for an encore. The crunchy coating of the lightly breaded chicken and the sweet and slightly tangy zing of the dipping sauce are a perfect pairing. With this recipe in your repertoire, you'll spend less time at the drive-through and keep your family healthier, too.

SAUCE:
 ¼ cup honey
 ¼ cup spicy brown mustard
CHICKEN:
 1½ pounds chicken breast tenders (about 16 pieces)
 1 cup low-fat buttermilk
 1 cup coarsely crushed cornflakes
 ½ cup seasoned breadcrumbs
 2 tablespoons instant minced onion
 2 teaspoons paprika
 ½ teaspoon dried thyme
 ½ teaspoon black pepper
 1 tablespoon canola oil

1. To prepare sauce, combine honey and mustard in a small bowl; cover and chill.
2. To prepare chicken, combine chicken and buttermilk in a shallow dish; cover and chill 15 minutes. Drain chicken, discarding liquid.
3. Preheat oven to 400°.
4. Combine cornflakes and next 5 ingredients in a large zip-top plastic bag; add 4 chicken pieces to bag. Seal and shake to coat. Repeat procedure with remaining chicken. Spread oil evenly on a jelly-roll pan; arrange chicken in a single layer on pan. Bake at 400° for 5 minutes on each side or until done. Serve with sauce. Yield: 4 servings (serving size: 4 chicken tenders and 1 tablespoon sauce).

CALORIES 231 (13% from fat); FAT 3.4g (sat 0.6g, mono 1.4g, poly 1g); PROTEIN 22.6g; CARB 26g; FIBER 1.7g; CHOL 50mg; IRON 3.2mg; SODIUM 393mg; CALC 44mg

Chicken Strips with Blue Cheese Dressing

Kids of all ages will love this fast, easy recipe. Serve the chicken alongside crunchy carrot and celery sticks to tame the heat. If you don't like blue cheese dressing, substitute commercial fat-free ranch dressing.

CHICKEN:
½ cup low-fat buttermilk
½ teaspoon hot sauce
½ cup all-purpose flour
½ teaspoon paprika
½ teaspoon ground red pepper
½ teaspoon freshly ground black pepper
¼ teaspoon salt
1 pound chicken breast tenders
1 tablespoon canola oil

DRESSING:
½ cup fat-free mayonnaise
¼ cup (1 ounce) crumbled blue cheese
1 tablespoon red wine vinegar
1 teaspoon bottled minced garlic
¼ teaspoon salt
¼ teaspoon freshly ground black pepper

1. To prepare chicken, combine buttermilk and hot sauce in a shallow dish. Combine flour and next 4 ingredients in a shallow dish. Dip chicken in buttermilk mixture; dredge in flour mixture.

2. Heat oil in a large nonstick skillet over medium-high heat. Add chicken; cook 4 minutes on each side or until done. Remove from pan. Set aside, and keep warm.

3. While chicken cooks, prepare dressing. Combine mayonnaise and next 5 ingredients in a small bowl. Serve with chicken strips. Yield: 4 servings (serving size: about 3 tenders and 2 tablespoons dressing).

CALORIES 281 (28% from fat); FAT 8.7g (sat 2.6g, mono 3.2g, poly 1.5g); PROTEIN 30.8g; CARB 18.4g; FIBER 1.3g; CHOL 77mg; IRON 1.9mg; SODIUM 771mg; CALC 101mg

Herbed Chicken Parmesan

Dredging ordinary chicken breast tenders in a breadcrumb mixture transforms them into a golden-brown, tried-and-true dinner delight. Topped with ruby red tomato-basil pasta sauce and smothered in iconic Parmesan and provolone cheeses, they'll become a staple at your family table. We recommend serving rice-shaped orzo pasta with this saucy entrée, but you can use spaghetti or angel hair pasta instead. Round out the menu with roasted lemon-garlic broccoli—and don't forget the wine.

1⅓ cups (1½ ounces) shredded fresh Parmesan cheese, divided
¼ cup dry breadcrumbs
1 tablespoon minced fresh flat-leaf parsley
½ teaspoon dried basil
¼ teaspoon salt, divided
1 large egg white, lightly beaten
1 pound chicken breast tenders
1 tablespoon butter
1½ cups bottled fat-free tomato-basil pasta sauce
2 teaspoons balsamic vinegar
¼ teaspoon black pepper
⅓ cup (1½ ounces) shredded provolone cheese

1. Preheat broiler.

2. Combine 2 tablespoons Parmesan, breadcrumbs, parsley, basil, and ⅛ teaspoon salt in a shallow dish. Place egg white in a shallow dish. Dip each chicken tender in egg white; dredge in breadcrumb mixture. Melt butter in a large nonstick skillet over medium-high heat. Add chicken; cook 3 minutes on each side or until done. Set aside.

3. Combine ⅛ teaspoon salt, pasta sauce, vinegar, and pepper in a microwave-safe bowl. Cover with plastic wrap; vent. Microwave mixture at HIGH 2 minutes or until thoroughly heated. Pour sauce over chicken in pan. Sprinkle evenly with remaining Parmesan and provolone cheese. Wrap handle of pan with foil; broil 2 minutes or until cheese melts. Yield: 4 servings.

CALORIES 308 (30% from fat); FAT 10.4g (sat 5.7g, mono 3g, poly 0.6g); PROTEIN 35.9g; CARB 16.2g; FIBER 1.8g; CHOL 88mg; IRON 2.3mg; SODIUM 808mg; CALC 249mg

Herbed Chicken Parmesan

Chicken and Chucka
Soba with Peanut Sauce

Chicken and Chucka Soba with Peanut Sauce

This dish is great served at room temperature or cold; add a touch of warm water to loosen the noodles if serving cold. Serve with steamed broccoli for a complete meal.

> 5 ounces uncooked Japanese curly noodles (*chucka soba*)
> 2 teaspoons dark sesame oil, divided
> 1 pound chicken breast tenders
> 1½ cups red bell pepper strips
> ½ cup fat-free, less-sodium chicken broth
> ⅓ cup hoisin sauce
> ¼ cup creamy peanut butter
> 2 tablespoons rice vinegar
> 2 tablespoons ketchup
> ¼ teaspoon crushed red pepper
> 1 tablespoon bottled ground fresh ginger (such as Spice World)
> 1 teaspoon bottled minced garlic
> ½ cup chopped green onions, divided

1. Cook noodles according to package directions; drain.

2. Heat 1 teaspoon oil in a large nonstick skillet over medium-high heat. Add chicken; sauté 4 minutes. Add bell pepper; sauté 3 minutes. Remove from heat. Combine chicken mixture and noodles in a large bowl.

3. Combine broth and next 5 ingredients in a bowl; stir well with a whisk.

4. Heat 1 teaspoon oil in pan over medium heat. Add ginger and garlic; cook 15 seconds. Stir in broth mixture, and cook 30 seconds, stirring constantly. Add broth mixture and ¼ cup green onions to noodle mixture; toss well. Sprinkle with ¼ cup green onions. Yield: 5 servings (serving size: 1 cup).

CALORIES 353 (28% from fat); FAT 10.9g (sat 2g, mono 4.3g, poly 3.1g); PROTEIN 28.5g; CARB 36g; FIBER 2.3g; CHOL 53mg; IRON 1.5mg; SODIUM 663mg; CALC 21mg

Italian Chicken with Chickpeas

Onion and bell pepper add fresh flavor to canned tomatoes and chickpeas in this simple one-dish meal. If you want, add a little more Italian flair with fresh chopped basil and oregano. This dish reheats well the next day for lunch.

> 1 pound chicken breast tenders
> ¼ teaspoon salt
> ¼ teaspoon black pepper
> 1 tablespoon olive oil
> 1⅓ cups sliced onion
> 1 cup green bell pepper strips
> ½ teaspoon bottled minced garlic
> 1 (15½-ounce) can chickpeas (garbanzo beans), drained
> 1 (14.5-ounce) can organic diced tomatoes with basil, garlic, and oregano, undrained

1. Sprinkle chicken with salt and black pepper. Heat oil in a large nonstick skillet over medium-high heat. Add chicken to pan; cook 2 minutes on each side or until browned. Add onion and bell pepper; sauté 4 minutes. Reduce heat to medium. Add garlic, chickpeas, and tomatoes; cover and cook 8 minutes or until thoroughly heated and chicken is done. Yield: 3 servings (serving size: 2 cups).

CALORIES 369 (22% from fat); FAT 9.1g (sat 1.3g, mono 4.6g, poly 2.2g); PROTEIN 40.9g; CARB 28.3g; FIBER 6.4g; CHOL 88mg; IRON 3.6mg; SODIUM 831mg; CALC 68mg

About Chucka Soba

Japanese curly noodles, made from wheat flour, are long and wavy with a delicate texture and mild flavor. Their Japanese name, chucka soba, translates to "Chinese noodle." Parboiled *chucka soba* are often used to make *yakisoba*, or "fried noodles." However they're used, these noodles are a staple in quick-and-easy cuisine. Find them in the Asian section of your supermarket.

Parmesan Chicken and Rice

Parmesan Chicken and Rice

Rice and broth are added to sautéed chicken, onion, garlic, and mushrooms for a simple entrée that requires only one pan.

- 1 tablespoon olive oil
- ½ cup chopped onion
- 1 teaspoon bottled minced garlic
- ½ teaspoon dried thyme
- 1 (8-ounce) package presliced mushrooms
- ¾ pound skinless, boneless chicken breast, cut into bite-sized pieces
- ½ cup dry white wine
- ½ teaspoon salt
- ¼ teaspoon freshly ground black pepper
- 1 cup uncooked instant rice
- 1 cup fat-free, less-sodium chicken broth
- ½ cup (2 ounces) grated fresh Parmesan cheese
- ¼ cup chopped fresh parsley

1. Heat oil in a large nonstick skillet over medium-high heat. Add chopped onion, garlic, thyme, and mushrooms, and sauté 5 minutes or until onion is tender. Add chicken; sauté 4 minutes or until chicken is lightly browned. Add wine, salt, and pepper; cook 3 minutes or until liquid almost evaporates.
2. Stir in rice and broth. Bring to a boil; cover, reduce heat, and simmer 5 minutes or until liquid is absorbed. Stir in cheese and chopped parsley. Yield: 4 servings (serving size: about 1 cup).

CALORIES 395 (18% from fat); FAT 8g (sat 2.8g, mono 3.7g, poly 0.8g); PROTEIN 29.9g; CARB 44.4g; FIBER 2g; CHOL 57mg; IRON 4.1mg; SODIUM 656mg; CALC 171mg

About Instant and Regular Rice

Instant rice, also called precooked rice, is rice that has been partially or completely cooked and dried; it takes only a few minutes to prepare. For instant rice, the ratio of rice to liquid is 1 to 1. One cup instant rice plus 1 cup liquid yields 2 cups cooked rice. For regular rice, 1 cup uncooked rice will yield about 3 cups cooked rice. As a general rule of thumb when cooking regular rice, use 2 cups of water per 1 cup of uncooked rice.

Creamy Chicken and Rice Casserole

When you're craving a homestyle dinner, nothing beats a casserole with creamy rice; tender chicken; and a buttery, crunchy topping. Whether you assemble it ahead or the day you plan to cook it, this comfort-food casserole is a breeze to prepare.

- 1 (6.9-ounce) package ⅓-less-salt chicken-flavored rice-and-vermicelli mix with chicken broth and herbs
- 1 tablespoon butter
- 2½ cups hot water
- Cooking spray
- 1½ pounds skinless, boneless chicken breast halves, cut into bite-sized pieces
- 1 cup presliced mushrooms
- ½ teaspoon garlic powder
- ¾ cup fat-free sour cream
- ¼ teaspoon black pepper
- 1 (10¾-ounce) can condensed reduced-fat, reduced-sodium cream of mushroom soup, undiluted
- ¼ cup crushed multigrain crackers (about 6 crackers)
- 1 tablespoon butter, melted
- ½ teaspoon poppy seeds

1. Cook rice mix in a large nonstick skillet according to package directions, using 1 tablespoon butter and 2½ cups hot water. Remove mixture from pan; set aside. Wipe pan with a paper towel.
2. Heat pan over medium-high heat; coat pan with cooking spray. Add chicken, mushrooms, and garlic powder; sauté 6 minutes or until chicken is done. Combine rice mixture, chicken mixture, sour cream, pepper, and soup in a bowl; stir well. Spoon mixture into a 2-quart baking dish coated with cooking spray. Cover and refrigerate overnight, or freeze (thaw frozen casserole overnight in refrigerator before baking).
3. Uncover and let casserole stand at room temperature 30 minutes. Combine cracker crumbs, 1 tablespoon melted butter, and poppy seeds; stir well, and sprinkle over chicken mixture.
4. Preheat oven to 350°.
5. Bake at 350° for 35 minutes or until thoroughly heated. Yield: 6 servings (serving size: 1⅓ cups).

CALORIES 334 (18% from fat); FAT 6.8g (sat 3.4g, mono 1g, poly 1.3g); PROTEIN 32.2g; CARB 30g; FIBER 0.2g; CHOL 78mg; IRON 2mg; SODIUM 670mg; CALC 19mg

Mediterranean Chicken with Potatoes

4 teaspoons minced garlic, divided
1 tablespoon olive oil
1 teaspoon salt, divided
¼ teaspoon dried thyme
½ teaspoon black pepper, divided
12 small red potatoes, halved (about 1½ pounds)
Cooking spray
2 pounds skinless, boneless chicken breast, cut into bite-sized pieces
1 cup vertically sliced red onion
¾ cup dry white wine
¾ cup fat-free, less-sodium chicken broth
½ cup chopped pepperoncini peppers
¼ cup pitted kalamata olives, halved
2 cups chopped plum tomato
2 tablespoons chopped fresh basil
1 (14-ounce) can artichoke hearts, drained and quartered
½ cup (2 ounces) grated fresh Parmesan cheese
Thyme sprigs (optional)

1. Preheat oven to 400°.
2. Combine 2 teaspoons garlic, oil, ¼ teaspoon salt, thyme, ¼ teaspoon black pepper, and potatoes on a jelly-roll pan coated with cooking spray. Bake at 400° for 30 minutes or until tender.
3. Heat a large Dutch oven over medium-high heat. Coat pan with cooking spray. Sprinkle chicken with ½ teaspoon salt and remaining ¼ teaspoon black pepper. Add half of chicken to pan; sauté 5 minutes or until browned. Remove chicken from pan. Repeat procedure with remaining chicken; remove from pan.
4. Add onion to pan; sauté 5 minutes. Stir in wine, scraping pan to loosen browned bits. Bring wine to a boil; cook until reduced to ⅓ cup (about 2 minutes). Add potatoes, chicken, broth, pepperoncini peppers, and olives; cook 3 minutes, stirring occasionally. Stir in remaining 2 teaspoons garlic, remaining ¼ teaspoon salt, tomato, basil, and artichokes, and cook 3 minutes or until thoroughly heated. Sprinkle with cheese. Garnish with thyme sprigs, if desired. Yield: 8 servings (serving size: 1¼ cups).

CALORIES 331 (20% from fat); FAT 7.3g (sat 2.1g, mono 3.7g, poly 0.9g); PROTEIN 33.5g; CARB 32.5g; FIBER 3.6g; CHOL 71mg; IRON 2.9mg; SODIUM 897mg; CALC 124mg

Curried Chicken Penne with Fresh Mango Chutney

The sweetness of the mango and the coconut milk tempers the heat of the curry, resulting in a complex, delicious dish. Though the chutney takes some time to make from scratch, the end result is worth the effort.

CHUTNEY:
2 cups diced peeled ripe mango (about 2 mangoes)
1 cup finely chopped onion
½ cup water
2 tablespoons brown sugar
1 tablespoon curry powder
1 tablespoon fresh lime juice
½ teaspoon black pepper
½ teaspoon chopped peeled fresh ginger
¼ teaspoon salt

CHICKEN:
1 teaspoon olive oil
2 garlic cloves, minced
1 pound skinless, boneless chicken breast, cut into 1-inch pieces
1 cup light coconut milk
2 tablespoons sugar
1½ teaspoons red curry paste
1 to 2 teaspoons Thai fish sauce
1 teaspoon salt
2 cups broccoli florets
2 cups cauliflower florets
4 cups hot cooked penne rigate (about 2 cups uncooked tube-shaped pasta)
2 tablespoons chopped green onions (optional)

1. To prepare chutney, combine first 9 ingredients in a medium saucepan; bring to a boil. Reduce heat, and simmer 15 minutes or until most of liquid evaporates and mixture is thick, stirring occasionally.
2. To prepare chicken, heat oil in a large nonstick skillet over medium-high heat. Add garlic and chicken; sauté 5 minutes. Combine coconut milk and next 4 ingredients, stirring with a whisk. Add coconut mixture to pan; bring to a simmer. Add broccoli and cauliflower; cover and cook 7 minutes or until vegetables are crisp-tender, stirring occasionally. Add chutney and pasta; toss well. Sprinkle with green onions, if desired. Yield: 6 servings (serving size: about 1⅓ cups).

CALORIES 216 (18% from fat); FAT 4.3g (sat 1.8g, mono 0.9g, poly 0.4g); PROTEIN 20g; CARB 25.9g; FIBER 3.6g; CHOL 44mg; IRON 1.9mg; SODIUM 724mg; CALC 52mg

Thai-Style Stir-Fried Chicken

Once the chicken and vegetables are prepped, the cooking goes quickly. Have all the ingredients close at hand to whip up this sweet-hot dinner on a busy evening. It will be a beautiful Thai-inspired presentation that you and your dinner guests won't soon forget.

¼   cup rice vinegar
2   tablespoons brown sugar
2   tablespoons fresh lime juice
2   teaspoons red curry paste
⅛   teaspoon crushed red pepper
1   pound skinless, boneless chicken breast, cut into bite-sized pieces
1½ tablespoons vegetable oil, divided
1   cup chopped onion
1   cup chopped carrot
1   (8-ounce) package presliced mushrooms
½   cup light coconut milk
1   tablespoon fish sauce
½   teaspoon salt
1   cup fresh bean sprouts
¼   cup chopped fresh cilantro

1. Combine first 5 ingredients in a large zip-top plastic bag. Add chicken; seal and marinate in refrigerator 30 minutes, turning once.

2. Remove chicken from bag, reserving marinade. Heat 1 tablespoon oil in a large nonstick skillet or stir-fry pan over medium-high heat. Add chicken, and stir-fry 4 minutes. Remove chicken from pan; keep warm. Add remaining 1½ teaspoons oil to pan. Add onion and carrot; stir-fry 2 minutes. Add mushrooms; stir-fry 3 minutes. Add reserved marinade, scraping pan to loosen browned bits. Add coconut milk and fish sauce; bring to a boil. Reduce heat, and simmer 1 minute. Stir in chicken and salt; cook 1 minute. Top with sprouts and cilantro. Yield: 4 servings (serving size: 1 cup chicken mixture, ¼ cup sprouts, and 1 tablespoon cilantro).

CALORIES 271 (28% from fat); FAT 8.4g (sat 2.2g, mono 1.6g, poly 3.4g); PROTEIN 29.7g; CARB 19.6g; FIBER 2.9g; CHOL 66mg; IRON 2.2mg; SODIUM 767mg; CALC 43mg

Chicken Saté with Peanut Sauce

Chicken Saté with Peanut Sauce

You can broil these chicken skewers instead of grilling them. In fact, traditional Indonesian saté skewers are often broiled. Place on a broiler pan coated with cooking spray; broil 8 to 10 minutes, turning once. Serve the zesty peanut sauce in condiment bowls on individual serving plates.

SATÉ:

1½ pounds skinless, boneless chicken breast, cut into 8 strips
1 tablespoon light brown sugar
2½ tablespoons low-sodium soy sauce
2 teaspoons bottled ground fresh ginger (such as Spice World)
1 teaspoon grated lime rind
¼ teaspoon crushed red pepper
2 garlic cloves, minced

SAUCE:

1 tablespoon light brown sugar
1½ tablespoons low-sodium soy sauce
2 tablespoons natural-style, reduced-fat creamy peanut butter (such as Smucker's)
1 tablespoon fresh lime juice
¼ teaspoon crushed red pepper
1 garlic clove, minced

REMAINING INGREDIENTS:

Cooking spray
Wide rice noodles (optional)

1. Prepare grill.
2. To prepare saté, combine chicken and next 6 ingredients in a medium bowl. Let stand 10 minutes.
3. To prepare sauce, combine 1 tablespoon brown sugar and next 5 ingredients in a medium bowl, stirring until sugar dissolves.
4. Thread chicken strips onto each of 8 (8-inch) skewers. Place chicken on grill rack coated with cooking spray; grill 5 minutes on each side or until done. Serve chicken with sauce. Serve with wide rice noodles, if desired. Yield: 4 servings (serving size: 2 skewers and 1 tablespoon sauce).
NOTE: If using wooden skewers, soak them in water 30 minutes before grilling.

CALORIES 269 (17% from fat); FAT 5.2g (sat 1.2g, mono 0.5g, poly 0.5g); PROTEIN 42.4g; CARB 11.4g; FIBER 0.9g; CHOL 99mg; IRON 2mg; SODIUM 709mg; CALC 32mg

Mediterranean Chicken and Vegetable Kebabs

Serve these Mediterranean-inspired kebabs over couscous tossed with a bit of salt, cherry tomatoes, and chopped fresh mint.

½ cup fresh lemon juice
3 tablespoons fresh chopped or 1 tablespoon dried oregano
3 tablespoons olive oil
2 garlic cloves, minced
1½ pounds skinless, boneless chicken breast, cut into 32 (1½-inch) cubes
24 (½-inch-thick) slices zucchini (about 4 medium)
1 fennel bulb, cut into 16 wedges
16 garlic cloves, peeled
½ teaspoon salt
¼ teaspoon black pepper
Cooking spray
Couscous (optional)

1. Combine first 7 ingredients in a zip-top plastic bag; seal and shake well. Marinate in refrigerator at least 1 hour. Remove chicken and vegetables from bag, and discard marinade.
2. Prepare grill.
3. Cook 16 garlic cloves in boiling water 3 minutes; drain and cool.
4. Thread 4 chicken cubes, 3 zucchini slices, 2 fennel wedges, and 2 garlic cloves alternately onto each of 8 (12-inch) skewers. Sprinkle with salt and pepper. Place kebabs on grill rack coated with cooking spray. Grill 8 minutes or until chicken is done, turning kebabs once. Serve with couscous, if desired. Yield: 4 servings (serving size: 2 kebabs).
NOTE: If using wooden skewers, soak them in water 30 minutes before grilling.

CALORIES 335 (34% from fat); FAT 12.6g (sat 2g, mono 8g, poly 1.6g); PROTEIN 41.8g; CARB 13.9g; FIBER 2.9g; CHOL 99mg; IRON 2.2mg; SODIUM 441mg; CALC 98mg

Grilled Chicken Tostadas

Fried tortillas usually form the shells for tostadas, but grilling the tortillas lowers the fat. Prepared salsa, canned beans, and preshredded coleslaw make this recipe simple to prepare.

1½ pounds skinless, boneless chicken breast halves
1 tablespoon fresh lime juice
1 tablespoon 40%-less-sodium taco seasoning (such as Old El Paso)
½ teaspoon sugar
Cooking spray
6 (8-inch) flour tortillas
6 cups packaged coleslaw
1 (7-ounce) can green salsa
4 cups chopped tomato
¼ cup sliced ripe olives, chopped
1¼ cups fat-free refried beans
½ cup (2 ounces) crumbled feta cheese
6 tablespoons reduced-fat sour cream
¼ cup fresh cilantro leaves
¼ cup unsalted pumpkinseed kernels, toasted (optional)

1. Prepare grill, or heat a grill pan over medium-high heat.
2. Brush chicken with lime juice; sprinkle with taco seasoning and sugar. Place chicken on grill rack or grill pan coated with cooking spray; grill 4 minutes on each side or until done. Cool slightly. Cut chicken into ¼-inch strips; set aside. Place tortillas on grill rack or grill pan coated with cooking spray; grill 30 seconds on each side or until golden brown.
3. Combine coleslaw and salsa; toss to coat. Combine tomato and olives; toss gently.
4. Spread about 3 tablespoons beans over each tortilla; divide chicken evenly among tortillas. Top each serving with about ⅔ cup slaw mixture, ⅔ cup tomato mixture, 4 teaspoons cheese, 1 tablespoon sour cream, and 2 teaspoons cilantro. Sprinkle each serving with 2 teaspoons pumpkinseeds, if desired. Yield: 6 servings (serving size: 1 tostada).

CALORIES 361 (23% from fat); FAT 9.2g (sat 3.6g, mono 1.5g, poly 1.2g); PROTEIN 28.7g; CARB 43g; FIBER 6.8g; CHOL 65mg; IRON 3.7mg; SODIUM 844mg; CALC 221mg

Grilled Herb-Coated Chicken Breasts

¾ cup Herbed Lemon-Buttermilk Dressing
4 (4-ounce) skinless, boneless chicken breast halves
½ teaspoon salt
½ teaspoon freshly ground black pepper
2 tablespoons finely chopped fresh parsley
2 tablespoons finely chopped fresh chives
1 teaspoon canola oil
1 teaspoon honey
Cooking spray

1. Combine Herbed Lemon-Buttermilk Dressing and chicken in a large zip-top plastic bag. Seal and marinate in refrigerator 1 hour or up to 8 hours, turning bag occasionally.
2. Prepare grill.
3. Remove chicken from marinade; discard marinade. Sprinkle chicken with salt and pepper. Combine parsley, chives, oil, and honey, stirring well. Spoon herb mixture over tops of chicken. Place chicken, herb side down, on a grill rack coated with cooking spray, and grill 8 minutes on each side or until done. Yield: 4 servings (serving size: 1 chicken breast half).

(Totals include Herbed Lemon-Buttermilk Dressing) CALORIES 169 (24% from fat); FAT 4.6g (sat 0.9g, mono 1g, poly 0.7g); PROTEIN 26.9g; CARB 3.4g; FIBER 0.3g; CHOL 68mg; IRON 1mg; SODIUM 481mg; CALC 37mg

HERBED LEMON-BUTTERMILK DRESSING:

¾ cup fat-free buttermilk
⅓ cup low-fat mayonnaise
1 tablespoon grated lemon rind
1 tablespoon chopped onion
2 teaspoons fresh lemon juice
2 teaspoons Dijon mustard
1 teaspoon finely chopped fresh chives
1 teaspoon finely chopped fresh basil
1 teaspoon finely chopped fresh thyme
½ teaspoon coarsely ground black pepper
¼ teaspoon salt
1 garlic clove, minced

1. Combine all ingredients, stirring with a whisk until well blended. Yield: 1¼ cups (serving size: 1 tablespoon).
NOTE: Refrigerate dressing in an airtight container up to five days; stir well before using.

CALORIES 18 (65% from fat); FAT 1.3g (sat 0.3g, mono 0g, poly 0g); PROTEIN 0.4g; CARB 1g; FIBER 0.1g; CHOL 1mg; IRON 0mg; SODIUM 77mg; CALC 13mg

Lemon and Oregano–Rubbed Grilled Chicken

Pound the chicken breasts with a meat mallet or rolling pin until they're thin; the increased surface allows you to use even more of the flavorful rub. Using the pounding technique on the chicken not only tenderizes the meat but also shortens the cooking time and gives the appearance of a heartier portion.

4 (6-ounce) skinless, boneless chicken breast halves
5 teaspoons grated lemon rind
1 tablespoon olive oil
1½ teaspoons dried oregano
¾ teaspoon kosher salt
½ teaspoon freshly ground black pepper
¼ teaspoon water
2 garlic cloves, minced
Cooking spray
4 lemon wedges
2 tablespoons chopped fresh parsley

1. Prepare grill.
2. Place each chicken breast half between 2 sheets of heavy-duty plastic wrap; pound to ¼-inch thickness using a meat mallet or rolling pin.
3. Combine lemon rind and next 6 ingredient; rub evenly over both sides of chicken. Place chicken on a grill rack coated with cooking spray, and grill 3 minutes on each side or until done. Remove from heat. Squeeze 1 lemon wedge evenly over each chicken breast half. Sprinkle parsley evenly over chicken. Yield: 4 servings (serving size: 1 chicken breast half).

CALORIES 226 (22% from fat); FAT 5.6g (sat 1g, mono 3g, poly 0.8g); PROTEIN 39.6g; CARB 2.2g; FIBER 0.7g; CHOL 99mg; IRON 1.8mg; SODIUM 465mg; CALC 38mg

Tandoori Chicken

Although it's not cooked in a tandoor oven, this entrée has all the flavors of the traditional Indian dish, thanks to a long marinating time. Serve with tabbouleh and pita chips.

- ¾ cup coarsely chopped onion
- 1 teaspoon coarsely chopped peeled fresh ginger
- 2 garlic cloves, peeled
- ½ cup plain low-fat yogurt
- 1 tablespoon fresh lemon juice
- 1 teaspoon paprika
- 1 teaspoon ground cumin
- 1 teaspoon ground coriander seeds
- ½ teaspoon salt
- ½ teaspoon chili powder
- ¼ teaspoon black pepper
- Dash of ground nutmeg
- 4 (6-ounce) skinless, boneless chicken breast halves
- Cooking spray

1. Place first 3 ingredients in a food processor; process until finely chopped. Add yogurt and next 8 ingredients; pulse 4 times or until blended.
2. Make 3 (¼-inch-deep) diagonal cuts across top of each chicken breast half. Combine chicken and yogurt mixture in a large zip-top plastic bag. Seal and marinate in refrigerator 8 hours or overnight, turning occasionally.
3. Prepare grill or preheat broiler.
4. Remove chicken breast halves from bag; discard marinade. Place chicken on grill rack or broiler pan coated with cooking spray; cook 6 minutes on each side or until done. Yield: 4 servings (serving size: 1 chicken breast half).

CALORIES 208 (11% from fat); FAT 2.5g (sat 0.7g, mono 0.6g, poly 0.5g); PROTEIN 40.4g; CARB 3.5g; FIBER 0.5g; CHOL 100mg; IRON 1.5mg; SODIUM 272mg; CALC 55mg

Chicken with Provençal Sauce

Capturing every morsel of chicken flavor is the secret to this quick-to-prepare dinner favorite. The tiny browned bits that remain in the skillet after the chicken is cooked are the key. Use the chicken broth to loosen these bits so that you don't leave any behind. Garlic, herbs, and fresh lemon juice are added for extra flavor. A final pat of butter marries these flavors into a slightly thickened sauce that is so intense that a couple of tablespoons is all that's needed to finish the dish.

- 4 (6-ounce) skinless, boneless chicken breast halves
- ¼ teaspoon salt
- ¼ teaspoon freshly ground black pepper
- 1½ tablespoons olive oil
- 1 garlic clove, minced
- 1 cup fat-free, less-sodium chicken broth
- 1½ teaspoons dried herbes de Provence
- 1 teaspoon fresh lemon juice
- 1 teaspoon butter
- Thyme sprigs (optional)

1. Place each chicken breast half between 2 sheets of heavy-duty plastic wrap; pound to ½-inch thickness using a meat mallet or rolling pin. Sprinkle chicken evenly with salt and pepper.
2. Heat oil in a large nonstick skillet over medium heat. Add chicken; cook 6 minutes on each side or until done. Remove chicken from pan; keep warm.
3. Add garlic to pan; cook 1 minute, stirring constantly. Add broth and herbes de Provence; bring to a boil, scraping pan to loosen browned bits. Cook until broth mixture is reduced to ½ cup (about 3 minutes). Remove from heat; add lemon juice and butter, stirring until butter melts. Serve sauce over chicken. Garnish with thyme sprigs, if desired. Yield: 4 servings (serving size: 1 chicken breast half and about 2 tablespoons sauce).

CALORIES 248 (30% from fat); FAT 8.2g (sat 1.8g, mono 4.5g, poly 1g); PROTEIN 40.2g; CARB 1g; FIBER 0.3g; CHOL 101mg; IRON 1.5mg; SODIUM 376mg; CALC 32mg

Chicken with Provençal Sauce

Raspberry-Balsamic Glazed Chicken

This is your "go-to" recipe when time is short and your guests are about to arrive. While this tasty, quick-and-easy dish is perfect as is, consider substituting other varieties of fruit preserves, such as apricot, blackberry, or peach. Pair it with brown rice and vegetables, and you have a great meal.

1 teaspoon vegetable oil
Cooking spray
½ cup chopped red onion
1½ teaspoons minced fresh
  or ½ teaspoon dried thyme
½ teaspoon salt, divided
4 (6-ounce) skinless, boneless chicken
  breast halves
⅓ cup seedless raspberry preserves
2 tablespoons balsamic vinegar
¼ teaspoon black pepper

1. Heat oil in a large nonstick skillet coated with cooking spray over medium-high heat. Add onion; sauté 5 minutes. Combine thyme and ¼ teaspoon salt; sprinkle over chicken. Add chicken to pan; sauté 6 minutes on each side or until done. Remove chicken from pan; keep warm.
2. Reduce heat to medium-low. Add remaining ¼ teaspoon salt, preserves, vinegar, and pepper, stirring constantly until preserves melt. Spoon raspberry sauce over chicken. Yield: 4 servings (serving size: 1 chicken breast half and 2 tablespoons sauce).

CALORIES 277 (11% from fat); FAT 3.3g (sat 0.7g, mono 1g, poly 1g); PROTEIN 39.5g; CARB 20.6g; FIBER 0.3g; CHOL 99mg; IRON 1.4mg; SODIUM 113mg; CALC 27mg

Sautéed Chicken Breasts with Sherry-Vinegar Sauce

(pictured on page 167)

4 (6-ounce) skinless, boneless chicken breast
  halves
½ teaspoon salt
¼ teaspoon black pepper
1 teaspoon butter
1 teaspoon olive oil
½ cup minced shallots
¾ cup fat-free, less-sodium chicken broth
3 tablespoons sherry vinegar
2 tablespoons whipping cream
1 tablespoon chopped fresh parsley

1. Sprinkle chicken with salt and pepper. Heat butter and oil in a large nonstick skillet over medium-high heat. Add chicken; cook 4 minutes on each side or until done. Remove from pan; keep warm. Add shallots to pan; sauté 1 minute. Stir in chicken broth and vinegar, and cook 4 minutes or until liquid is reduced by half. Add whipping cream; cook 1 minute. Serve sauce with chicken. Sprinkle with parsley. Yield: 4 servings (serving size: 1 chicken breast half and 1 tablespoon sauce).

CALORIES 194 (29% from fat); FAT 6.3g (sat 2.9g, mono 2.2g, poly 0.6g); PROTEIN 27.4g; CARB 5.6g; FIBER 0.4g; CHOL 78mg; IRON 1.3mg; SODIUM 457mg; CALC 33mg

About Nonstick Skillets

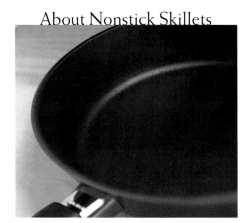

Nonstick skillets are a staple in the *Cooking Light* Test Kitchens. They are generally used for quick sautéing and for stir-frying meats, seafood, and vegetables. While nonstick coatings are durable, you can prolong their life by not overheating them, especially when they are empty. These pans' coatings are made of fluoropolymer substances that are damaged by excess heat, so stay away from the high setting on the cooktop dial. Also, if the recipe calls for cooking spray, coat the pan after it has heated.

Chicken with Roasted Red Pepper Sauce

If you love hot and spicy dishes, then this fiery recipe will heat things up. To curb some of the heat, you can always cut back on the chipotle chile or add some soothing sour cream. Try serving this dish with hearty chunks of bread or flour tortillas to soak up the sauce, if desired.

2 bacon slices
4 (6-ounce) skinless, boneless chicken breast halves
¼ teaspoon salt
¼ teaspoon black pepper
½ cup chopped red onion
½ teaspoon ground coriander
3 garlic cloves, minced
1 drained canned chipotle chile in adobo sauce, diced
1 cup salsa
1 (7.5-ounce) bottle roasted red bell peppers, drained and sliced
Chopped fresh cilantro (optional)

1. Cook bacon in a large nonstick skillet over medium-high heat until crisp. Remove bacon from pan; crumble and set aside. Sprinkle chicken with salt and black pepper. Add chicken to bacon drippings in pan; sauté 2 minutes on each side. Remove chicken from pan. Add onion, coriander, garlic, and chile to pan; sauté 3 minutes. Stir in salsa and bell peppers. Return chicken to pan. Cover and cook over medium heat 12 minutes or until chicken is done. Sprinkle with crumbled bacon, and garnish with cilantro, if desired. Yield: 4 servings (serving size: 1 chicken breast half and ½ cup sauce).

CALORIES 259 (15% from fat); FAT 4.2g (sat 1g, mono 1.1g, poly 0.6g); PROTEIN 41.4g; CARB 10.8g; FIBER 0.8g; CHOL 102mg; IRON 1.7mg; SODIUM 982mg; CALC 49mg

Chicken with Lemon-Caper Sauce

Measure ingredients for this recipe ahead, and then enjoy a glass of wine with company before the meal. You can have this dinner on the table in 15 to 20 minutes. It'll be so yummy that your guests will clean their plates. You may want to consider doubling the sauce to serve over noodles or rice.

- ¼ teaspoon salt, divided
- ¼ teaspoon black pepper, divided
- 4 (6-ounce) skinless, boneless chicken breast halves
- 1 tablespoon olive oil
- Cooking spray
- ⅓ cup extradry vermouth
- 3 tablespoons fresh lemon juice
- 1½ tablespoons capers
- 1 tablespoon chopped fresh parsley
- Hot cooked spaghetti (optional)

1. Sprinkle ⅛ teaspoon salt and ⅛ teaspoon pepper over chicken. Heat oil in a large nonstick skillet coated with cooking spray over medium-high heat. Add chicken; cook 6 minutes on each side or until done. Remove from pan. Set aside; keep warm.

2. Add remaining ⅛ teaspoon salt, remaining ⅛ teaspoon pepper, vermouth, lemon juice, and capers to pan, scraping pan to loosen browned bits. Cook until reduced to ¼ cup (about 2 minutes). Stir in chopped parsley. Spoon sauce over chicken. Serve over spaghetti, if desired. Yield: 4 servings (serving size: 1 chicken breast half and 1 tablespoon sauce).

CALORIES 222 (22% from fat); FAT 5.5g (sat 1g, mono 3g, poly 0.8g); PROTEIN 39.6g; CARB 1.5g; FIBER 0.1g; CHOL 99mg; IRON 1.5mg; SODIUM 377mg; CALC 25mg

Chicken Marsala

- 4 tablespoons butter, divided
- Cooking spray
- 1 (8-ounce) package presliced mushrooms
- 2 tablespoons finely chopped shallots
- 1 tablespoon minced fresh garlic
- 4 (6-ounce) skinless, boneless chicken breast halves
- ¼ teaspoon salt, divided
- ¼ teaspoon black pepper, divided
- 3 tablespoons all-purpose flour
- ¾ cup fat-free, less-sodium chicken broth
- ½ cup dry Marsala wine
- ½ cup frozen green peas
- 2 tablespoons half-and-half
- 4 cups hot cooked fettuccine (about 8 ounces uncooked pasta)

1. Place 3 tablespoons butter in a small glass measuring cup. Microwave at MEDIUM-HIGH 45 seconds or until butter melts. Let stand 1 minute. Skim foam from surface; discard. Pour melted butter through a fine sieve over a small bowl; discard milk solids. Set clarified butter aside.

2. Heat a large nonstick skillet over medium-high heat. Coat pan with cooking spray. Add mushrooms, shallots, and garlic. Cook 3 minutes or until moisture evaporates; remove mushroom mixture from pan. Set aside.

3. Place each chicken breast half between 2 sheets of heavy-duty plastic wrap, and pound to ¼-inch thickness using a meat mallet or rolling pin. Sprinkle both sides of chicken with ⅛ teaspoon salt and ⅛ teaspoon pepper. Place flour in a shallow dish; dredge chicken breast halves in flour.

4. Add clarified butter to pan, and place over medium-high heat. Add chicken; cook 3 minutes on each side or until lightly browned. Remove chicken from pan. Return mushroom mixture to pan; add broth and Marsala, scraping pan to loosen browned bits. Bring mixture to a boil, reduce heat, and simmer 5 minutes or until reduced to 1 cup. Stir in peas; cook 1 minute. Add remaining 1 tablespoon butter, remaining ⅛ teaspoon salt, remaining ⅛ teaspoon pepper, and half-and-half, stirring until butter melts. Return chicken to pan; cook until thoroughly heated and chicken is done. Serve chicken and sauce over pasta. Yield: 4 servings (serving size: 1 chicken breast half, 1 cup pasta, and ¼ cup sauce).

CALORIES 585 (24% from fat); FAT 15.3g (sat 8.4g, mono 4.1g, poly 1g); PROTEIN 51.4g; CARB 55g; FIBER 3.7g; CHOL 133mg; IRON 4.4mg; SODIUM 469mg; CALC 57mg

Chicken Marsala

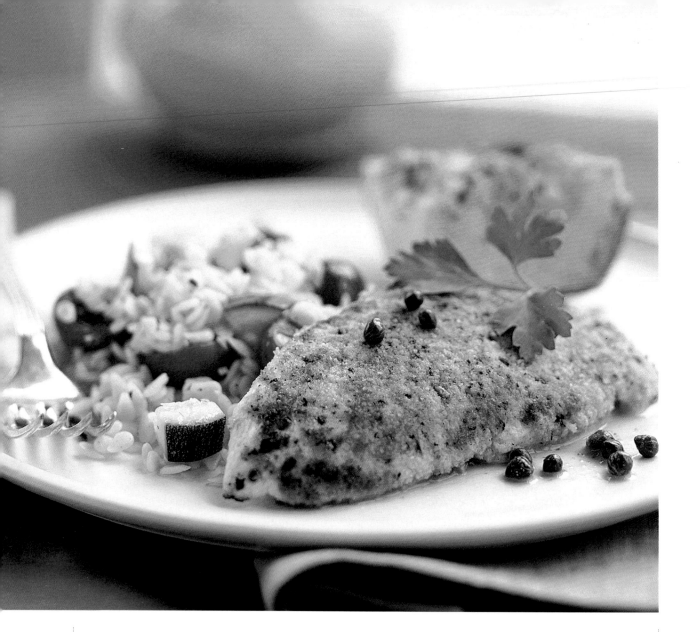

Chicken Scallopini

Pounding the chicken breast halves cuts the cooking time in half while leaving the chicken moist and tender. Orzo sautéed with zucchini and cherry tomatoes makes a great side dish, but you may also substitute rice in place of the orzo.

4   (6-ounce) skinless, boneless chicken breast halves
2   teaspoons fresh lemon juice
¼   teaspoon salt
¼   teaspoon black pepper
⅓   cup Italian-seasoned breadcrumbs
Cooking spray
½   cup fat-free, less-sodium chicken broth
¼   cup dry white wine
4   teaspoons capers
1   tablespoon butter
Flat-leaf parsley (optional)

1. Place each chicken breast half between 2 sheets of heavy-duty plastic wrap, and pound to ¼-inch thickness using a meat mallet or rolling pin. Brush chicken with lemon juice, and sprinkle with salt and pepper. Dredge chicken in breadcrumbs.

2. Heat a large nonstick skillet over medium-high heat. Coat pan with cooking spray. Add chicken to pan, and cook 3 minutes on each side or until done. Remove from pan; keep warm.

3. Add broth and wine to pan; cook 30 seconds, stirring constantly. Remove from heat. Stir in capers and butter. Garnish with parsley, if desired. Yield: 4 servings (serving size: 1 chicken breast half and 1 tablespoon sauce).

CALORIES 206 (20% from fat); FAT 4.6g (sat 2.2g, mono 1.3g, poly 0.5g); PROTEIN 29.2g; CARB 7.7g; FIBER 0.6g; CHOL 76mg; IRON 1.6mg; SODIUM 657mg; CALC 27mg

Breast of Chicken Oaxaca

This decadent dish is from the restaurant Casa del Sol in Ciudad Juárez, Mexico, just across the border from El Paso. Asadero cheese, also called Oaxaca or Chihuahua cheese, is a good melting cheese similar to Monterey Jack and is how this recipe gets its name. We sautéed the chicken breasts in a small amount of oil instead of frying them, and we used reduced-fat sour cream in the chipotle sauce in place of heavy cream.

CHIPOTLE SAUCE:
¼ cup hot water
½ teaspoon chicken-flavored bouillon granules
4 canned chipotle chiles in adobo sauce
¾ cup reduced-fat sour cream
1 tablespoon lime juice

CHICKEN:
1 peeled avocado, cut into 6 wedges
1 tablespoon lime juice
6 (6-ounce) skinless, boneless chicken breast halves
¾ cup (3 ounces) shredded asadero or Monterey Jack cheese
¼ teaspoon salt
⅛ teaspoon white pepper
2 tablespoons all-purpose flour
3 large egg whites, lightly beaten
1 cup seasoned breadcrumbs
1 tablespoon vegetable oil
Cooking spray

REMAINING INGREDIENTS:
8 cups hot cooked linguine (about 1 pound uncooked pasta)
¼ cup sliced ripe olives
2 tablespoons cilantro

1. To prepare chipotle sauce, combine first 3 ingredients in a blender; process until smooth. Pour sauce into a bowl; stir in sour cream and 1 tablespoon lime juice.

2. To prepare chicken, toss avocado with 1 tablespoon lime juice. Cut a horizontal slit through thickest portion of each breast half to form a pocket. Stuff 1 avocado slice and 2 tablespoons cheese into each pocket. Sprinkle chicken with salt and pepper, and dredge chicken in flour. Dip chicken in egg whites; dredge in breadcrumbs.

3. Heat oil in a large nonstick skillet coated with cooking spray over medium-high heat. Add chicken, and sauté 6 to 7 minutes on each side or until done.

4. Toss pasta with olives and cilantro. Place 1⅓ cups pasta on each of 6 plates. Top each serving with 1 chicken breast and about 3 tablespoons chipotle sauce. Yield: 6 servings.

CALORIES 702 (24% from fat); FAT 18.5g (sat 7.1g, mono 5.5g, poly 2.4g); PROTEIN 54.4g; CARB 77.8g; FIBER 5.4g; CHOL 125mg; IRON 5.4mg; SODIUM 919mg; CALC 220mg

Bell Pepper Chicken with Feta Orzo

With a nod to some traditional Greek ingredients, this easy meal showcases juicy chicken breasts, bell peppers sautéed in olive oil and oregano, and orzo simply seasoned with feta.

4 ounces uncooked orzo (rice-shaped pasta; about ½ cup)
4 teaspoons olive oil, divided
4 (6-ounce) skinless, boneless chicken breast halves
½ teaspoon salt
¼ teaspoon black pepper
⅛ teaspoon ground red pepper
1 cup red bell pepper strips
1 cup green bell pepper strips
1 teaspoon dried oregano
2 garlic cloves, minced
1½ tablespoons fresh lemon juice
¾ cup (3 ounces) crumbled feta cheese

1. Cook orzo according to package directions, omitting salt and fat.

2. While orzo cooks, heat 2 teaspoons olive oil in a large nonstick skillet over medium-high heat. Sprinkle chicken with salt, black pepper, and red pepper. Add chicken to pan, and cook 4 minutes on each side or until done. Remove chicken from pan, and keep warm.

3. Add remaining 2 teaspoons olive oil and bell peppers to pan; sauté 2 minutes. Add oregano and garlic, and sauté 1 minute. Remove from heat; stir in lemon juice.

4. Combine orzo and feta; serve with chicken and bell pepper mixture. Yield: 4 servings (serving size: 1 breast half, ½ cup orzo mixture, and ⅓ cup bell pepper mixture).

CALORIES 404 (26% from fat); FAT 11.7g (sat 4.5g, mono 4.8g, poly 1g); PROTEIN 46.8g; CARB 26.3g; FIBER 2g; CHOL 118mg; IRON 2.8mg; SODIUM 644mg; CALC 143mg

Chicken with Pecan Cream
and Mushrooms

Chicken with Pecan Cream and Mushrooms

A simple chicken sauté gets an elegant makeover. You can also serve it with rice or orzo to soak up the sauce. The sauce is also great made with almonds.

¾ cup coarsely chopped pecans, toasted
1 cup water
1¼ teaspoons salt, divided
6 (6-ounce) skinless, boneless chicken breast halves
1 teaspoon freshly ground black pepper
Cooking spray
¼ cup finely chopped shallots
1 (8-ounce) package presliced mushrooms
4 cups cooked egg noodles
Chopped fresh parsley (optional)

1. Place pecans in a food processor; process until smooth (about 1 minute), scraping sides of bowl once. With processor on, add water and ¾ teaspoon salt; process until smooth, scraping sides of bowl once.
2. Sprinkle chicken with remaining ½ teaspoon salt and pepper.
3. Heat a large nonstick skillet over medium-high heat. Coat pan with cooking spray. Add chicken, and sauté 3 minutes on each side or until done. Remove chicken from pan, and keep warm.
4. Add shallots and mushrooms to pan; sauté 3 minutes or until mushrooms are tender. Stir in pecan cream; bring to a boil. Cook 1½ minutes. Place ⅔ cup noodles on each of 6 plates. Slice chicken; top each serving with 1 chicken breast half and ⅓ cup sauce. Garnish with parsley, if desired. Yield: 6 servings.

CALORIES 446 (29% from fat); FAT 14.5g (sat 1.8g, mono 7g, poly 4.2g); PROTEIN 47.1g; CARB 31.1g; FIBER 3.2g; CHOL 134mg; IRON 3.6mg; SODIUM 605mg; CALC 47mg

Broiled Chicken Breasts with Vegetable Sauté

If your idea of the perfect chicken dish is one that looks and tastes impressive but is simple to prepare and cook, then this recipe is a keeper. It's a terrific entrée to serve any night of the week or for a weekend dinner party. It serves up beautifully—and colorfully—alongside a simple salad and crusty French bread.

1 teaspoon garlic powder
½ teaspoon salt, divided
¼ teaspoon black pepper, divided
4 (6-ounce) skinless, boneless chicken breast halves
Cooking spray
1 tablespoon olive oil
1 (8-ounce) package presliced mushrooms
1 small zucchini, quartered lengthwise and sliced (about 5 ounces)
4 garlic cloves, minced
1 cup chopped plum tomato
½ cup chopped red onion
½ cup chopped fresh basil
4 teaspoons balsamic vinegar
¼ cup (1 ounce) grated fresh Parmesan cheese

1. Preheat broiler.
2. Combine garlic powder, ¼ teaspoon salt, and ⅛ teaspoon pepper in a small bowl; sprinkle chicken with garlic powder mixture. Place chicken on a broiler pan coated with cooking spray, and broil 6 minutes on each side or until done. Remove chicken from pan; keep warm.
3. Heat olive oil in a large nonstick skillet over medium-high heat. Add remaining ¼ teaspoon salt, mushrooms, zucchini, and minced garlic; sauté 2 minutes. Add remaining ⅛ teaspoon pepper, tomato, onion, basil, and vinegar, and sauté 3 minutes. Serve vegetable mixture over chicken; sprinkle with cheese. Yield: 4 servings (serving size: 1 chicken breast half, ½ cup vegetables, and 1 tablespoon cheese).

CALORIES 284 (23% from fat); FAT 7.3g (sat 2g, mono 3.5g, poly 1.1g); PROTEIN 44.4g; CARB 9.4g; FIBER 2.2g; CHOL 103mg; IRON 2.2mg; SODIUM 488mg; CALC 106mg

Chicken Fricassee

Chicken Fricassee sounds upscale. In reality, it's the ultimate comfort food—a creamy dish of succulent chicken and tender vegetables smothered in a rich brown gravy that's best when spooned over mashed potatoes, rice, or even grits. Bone-in chicken pieces are essential, as the bones contribute depth of flavor to the overall dish. Braising—slow simmering in moist heat in a covered skillet—is the key to a good fricassee with tender chicken and thickened juices. First, the chicken is pan-fried in a little butter until brown and crisp. After the vegetables have cooked a bit, the chicken is added back to the pan with broth, wine, or a combination of the two. The pan is covered, and the chicken simmers in moist heat until it becomes tender and the juices thicken.

    3   tablespoons all-purpose flour
    1   teaspoon paprika
    1   teaspoon poultry seasoning
    ½   teaspoon salt
    ½   teaspoon black pepper
    4   (8-ounce) bone-in chicken breast halves, skinned
    2   teaspoons butter
 1 ½   cups chopped onion
    ½   cup chopped celery
    3   garlic cloves, minced
    1   cup fat-free, less-sodium chicken broth
    ⅓   cup dry white wine
    2   cups (3-inch) julienne-cut carrot
    ¼   cup chopped fresh parsley
        Hot cooked long-grain rice (optional)

1. Combine first 5 ingredients in a large zip-top plastic bag. Add chicken; toss well to coat. Remove chicken from bag; reserve flour mixture. Melt butter in a large nonstick skillet over medium heat. Add chicken, breast sides down; sauté 5 minutes or until chicken is browned. Remove chicken from pan; keep warm.

2. Add onion, celery, and garlic to pan; sauté 5 to 7 minutes, stirring occasionally. Stir in reserved flour mixture, and cook 1 minute. Add broth and wine; bring to a boil. Add carrot. Return chicken to pan, breast sides up. Cover, reduce heat, and simmer 25 minutes or until chicken is done. Sprinkle with chopped parsley. Serve over rice, if desired. Yield: 4 servings (serving size: 1 chicken breast half and ¾ cup sauce).

CALORIES 265 (14% from fat); FAT 4.1g (sat 1.9g, mono 0.5g, poly 0.6g); PROTEIN 37g; CARB 19g; FIBER 3.4g; CHOL 91mg; IRON 2.4mg; SODIUM 600mg; CALC 71mg

Rum-Marinated Chicken Breasts with Pineapple Relish

The skin helps keep chicken moist while grilling and can be easily removed before serving or at the table.

CHICKEN:
    ½   cup dark rum
    ¼   cup barbecue sauce
    3   tablespoons fresh lime juice
    1   tablespoon Caribbean hot sauce (such as Pickapeppa Sauce)
    1   teaspoon sea or kosher salt
    2   teaspoons canola oil
    4   (8-ounce) bone-in chicken breast halves
RELISH:
    1   small pineapple, peeled, cored, and cut into ½-inch-thick rings (about 12 ounces)
        Cooking spray
    ½   cup finely chopped red bell pepper
    1   teaspoon grated lime rind
    2   tablespoons fresh lime juice
    1   teaspoon dark rum
    ¼   teaspoon Caribbean hot sauce
    ⅛   teaspoon sea or kosher salt
    8   lime slices

1. To prepare chicken, combine first 6 ingredients in large zip-top plastic bag. Add chicken to bag; seal. Marinate in refrigerator 1 to 2 hours, turning bag occasionally. Remove chicken from bag, reserving marinade; set chicken aside. Let marinade stand at room temperature 10 minutes. Strain through a sieve into a bowl; discard solids. Set marinade aside.

2. Prepare grill.

3. To prepare relish, place pineapple on a grill rack coated with cooking spray; grill 3 minutes on each side or until soft and browned around the edge. Cool slightly; chop. Combine pineapple, bell pepper, and next 5 ingredients; set aside.

4. Place chicken on grill rack coated with cooking spray; grill 30 minutes or until done, turning occasionally. Remove and discard skin.

5. Bring reserved marinade to a boil in a small saucepan; cook 1 minute. Drizzle cooked marinade over chicken. Serve chicken with relish and lime wedges. Yield: 4 servings (serving size: 1 chicken breast half, ½ cup relish, 2 tablespoons sauce, and 2 lime slices).

CALORIES 289 (14% from fat); FAT 4.5g (sat 0.5g, mono 2.2g, poly 0.9g); PROTEIN 29.6g; CARB 15.6g; FIBER 1.9g; CHOL 72mg; IRON 1.5mg; SODIUM 971mg; CALC 28mg

Rum-Marinated Chicken
Breasts with Pineapple Relish

Chicken Barbecue

Chicken Barbecue

This weeknight favorite takes its cue from the classic cola-can chicken, where a whole chicken is smoked over an open can of cola to yield flavorful, succulent meat. In the slow-cooker version, we use chicken breasts and add the cola directly to the sauce—the result is just as yummy. Make sure to use regular cola for this recipe. Diet cola won't cook down to the same syrupy consistency. Corn on the cob and a green salad complete the meal.

1½ cups sliced onion
½ lemon, sliced and seeded
6 chicken breast halves (about 2¼ pounds), skinned
1 (18-ounce) bottle barbecue sauce
½ cup cola
½ cup all-purpose flour
½ cup water
Freshly ground black pepper (optional)

1. Place onion and lemon in a 4-quart electric slow cooker, and top with chicken. Combine barbecue sauce and cola; pour over chicken. Cover and cook on HIGH 1 hour. Reduce heat to LOW, and cook 4 hours or until chicken is tender. Remove chicken and lemon slices from cooker with a slotted spoon, reserving cooking liquid in cooker. Set chicken aside; keep warm. Discard lemon slices. Increase heat to HIGH.
2. Lightly spoon flour into a dry measuring cup; level with a knife. Place flour in a small bowl; gradually add water, stirring with a whisk until well blended. Stir flour mixture into cooking liquid in cooker. Cook, uncovered, 10 minutes or until thick, stirring occasionally. Serve sauce over chicken. Sprinkle with pepper, if desired. Yield: 6 servings (serving size: 1 chicken breast half and ⅔ cup sauce).

CALORIES 244 (11% from fat); FAT 3g (sat 0.6g, mono 1g, poly 0.9g); PROTEIN 28.4g; CARB 24.3g; FIBER 1.7g; CHOL 64mg; IRON 2.1mg; SODIUM 767mg; CALC 36mg

Provençale Chicken Supper

This rustic dish takes its cue from the typical fare served in Provence, a region in the southeastern part of France that is known for dishes highlighting fresh local ingredients such as garlic, tomatoes, olive oil, olives, and sweet bell peppers. For a hearty weeknight meal, serve this dish with crusty bread to soak up the juices.

4 chicken breast halves (about 1½ pounds), skinned
2 teaspoons dried basil
¼ teaspoon salt, divided
¼ teaspoon black pepper, divided
1 cup diced yellow bell pepper
1 (16-ounce) can navy beans, rinsed and drained
1 (14½-ounce) can pasta-style tomatoes, undrained
Basil leaves (optional)

1. Place chicken in a 4½-quart electric slow cooker; sprinkle with dried basil, ⅛ teaspoon salt, and ⅛ teaspoon black pepper.
2. Combine remaining ⅛ teaspoon salt, remaining ⅛ teaspoon black pepper, bell pepper, beans, and tomatoes in a bowl; stir well. Spoon over chicken. Cover and cook on HIGH 1 hour. Reduce heat to LOW, and cook 5 hours. Spoon bean mixture into 4 shallow bowls; top each with 1 chicken breast half. Garnish with basil leaves, if desired. Yield: 4 servings (serving size: 1 chicken breast half and about ¾ cup bean mixture).

CALORIES 253 (6% from fat); FAT 1.8g (sat 0.5g, mono 0.4g, poly 0.5g); PROTEIN 32.4g; CARB 26.8g; FIBER 6g; CHOL 64mg; IRON 3mg; SODIUM 866mg; CALC 82mg

Moroccan Chicken Thighs

This Moroccan-inspired chicken dish is best served over a bed of fluffy, yellow couscous. Couscous, which is central to Moroccan cuisine, is often cooked with spices, vegetables, nuts, and raisins and topped with rich stews and roasted meats. Morocco, the culinary star of North Africa, is the doorway between Europe and Africa. Unlike the herb-based cooking to the north, Moroccan cooking features rich spices, including cumin, coriander, saffron, chiles, dried ginger, cinnamon, and paprika.

2   teaspoons olive oil
1½ pounds skinless, boneless chicken thighs, trimmed and cut into bite-sized pieces
½   cup chopped fresh cilantro
½   cup quartered dried Calimyrna figs (about 2 ounces)
¼   cup chopped green olives
3   tablespoons sweet Marsala or Madeira
2   tablespoons honey
2   tablespoons balsamic vinegar
1   tablespoon bottled minced garlic
½   teaspoon ground coriander
½   teaspoon ground cumin
¼   teaspoon ground cardamom
Cilantro sprigs (optional)
Couscous (optional)

1. Heat oil in a large nonstick skillet over medium-high heat. Add chicken; cook 5 minutes or until browned, stirring frequently. Stir in chopped cilantro and next 9 ingredients; reduce heat to medium, and cook 8 minutes or until chicken is done, stirring occasionally. Garnish with cilantro sprigs and serve with couscous, if desired. Yield: 4 servings (serving size: ¾ cup).

CALORIES 389 (39% from fat); FAT 16.7g (sat 4g, mono 7.2g, poly 3.3g); PROTEIN 31.6g; CARB 27.6g; FIBER 3g; CHOL 112mg; IRON 2.7mg; SODIUM 183mg; CALC 72mg

Grilled Chicken Kebabs

The dark meat of chicken thighs stands up to the strong flavors of the marinade. If you have any leftover dressing, serve it as a dipping sauce.

1 cup Pomegranate-Orange Dressing, divided
2 pounds skinless, boneless chicken thighs, trimmed and cut into bite-sized pieces
2 large oranges
¼ teaspoon salt
¼ teaspoon black pepper
Cooking spray
¼ cup chopped fresh mint

1. Combine ½ cup Pomegranate-Orange Dressing and chicken in a large zip-top plastic bag. Seal and marinate in refrigerator 30 minutes, turning bag occasionally.
2. Prepare grill.
3. Cut each orange into 8 wedges; cut each wedge crosswise into 3 pieces.
4. Remove chicken from marinade; discard marinade. Thread chicken and orange alternately onto 16 (10-inch) skewers. Sprinkle with salt and pepper. Place kebabs on a grill rack coated with cooking spray; grill 5 minutes on each side or until chicken is done, basting occasionally with remaining ½ cup Pomegranate-Orange Dressing. Sprinkle with mint. Yield: 8 servings (serving size: 2 kebabs).
NOTE: If using wooden skewers, soak them in water 30 minutes before grilling.

(Totals include Pomegranate-Orange Dressing) CALORIES 205 (35% from fat); FAT 8g (sat 1.6g, mono 4.1g, poly 1.4g); PROTEIN 22.7g; CARB 9g; FIBER 0.7g; CHOL 94mg; IRON 1.6mg; SODIUM 320mg; CALC 35mg

POMEGRANATE-ORANGE DRESSING:

1 cup fresh orange juice
2½ tablespoons balsamic vinegar
2 tablespoons fresh lemon juice
2 tablespoons pomegranate molasses
2 teaspoons grated orange rind
2 teaspoons minced rosemary
1 teaspoon salt
1 teaspoon brown sugar
½ teaspoon ground cumin
½ teaspoon ground black pepper
¼ teaspoon ground red pepper
4 garlic cloves, minced
¼ cup extravirgin olive oil

1. Combine all ingredients except oil, stirring with a whisk. Gradually add oil, stirring constantly with a whisk until well combined. Yield: about 1½ cups (serving size: 1 tablespoon).
NOTE: Refrigerate dressing in an airtight container up to five days; stir well before using.

CALORIES 39 (55% from fat); FAT 2.4g (sat 0.3g, mono 1.8g, poly 0.2g); PROTEIN 0.1g; CARB 4.1g; FIBER 0.1g; CHOL 0mg; IRON 0.3mg; SODIUM 99mg; CALC 9mg

Quick Coq au Vin

This quick take on the classic long-simmered French dish is composed of succulent chicken, meaty mushrooms, salty bacon, and herbs—all cooked in dry red wine. Cooking uncovered over medium-high heat reduces the liquid and concentrates its flavors in a fraction of the time required for the traditional dish.

¼ cup all-purpose flour
1 teaspoon dried thyme
½ teaspoon salt
6 (6-ounce) skinless, boneless chicken thighs
1 tablespoon olive oil
6 cups quartered cremini mushrooms
2 cups (¼-inch-thick) slices carrot
⅓ cup (¼-inch-thick) slices Canadian bacon
1 cup dry red wine
1 cup fat-free, less-sodium chicken broth
1 tablespoon tomato paste
Thyme sprigs (optional)

1. Combine flour, thyme, and salt in a zip-top plastic bag; add chicken. Seal and shake to coat. Remove chicken from bag, shaking off excess flour mixture.
2. Heat oil in a large nonstick skillet over medium-high heat. Add chicken, and cook 8 minutes or until browned, turning frequently. Remove chicken from pan.
3. Add cremini mushrooms, carrot, and bacon to pan; sauté 2 minutes. Stir in wine, chicken broth, and tomato paste, and cook 9 minutes. Return chicken to pan; cook 8 minutes or until chicken is done. Garnish with thyme, if desired. Yield: 6 servings (serving size: about 1¼ cups).

CALORIES 293 (30% from fat); FAT 9.7g (sat 2.2g, mono 4g, poly 2g); PROTEIN 38.3g; CARB 12.4g; FIBER 2g; CHOL 145mg; IRON 2.8mg; SODIUM 579mg; CALC 50mg

Jamaican Chicken Thighs

When seasoned with classic island spices, chicken thighs become a Caribbean-accented meal. Serve alongside peaches tossed with lime juice and cilantro.

    2   teaspoons garlic powder
    1   teaspoon onion powder
    ½   teaspoon ground ginger
    ½   teaspoon dried thyme
    ½   teaspoon ground allspice
    ¼   teaspoon salt
    ¼   teaspoon ground nutmeg
    ¼   teaspoon ground red pepper
    ⅛   teaspoon freshly ground black pepper
    8   skinless, boneless chicken thighs (about
        1½ pounds)
    Cooking spray

1. Combine first 9 ingredients in a small bowl. Rub spice mixture evenly over chicken.
2. Heat a large nonstick skillet over medium-high heat; coat pan with cooking spray. Add chicken, and cook 5 minutes on each side or until done. Yield: 4 servings (serving size: 2 thighs).

CALORIES 213 (29% from fat); FAT 6.8g (sat 1.7g, mono 2.1g, poly 1.7g); PROTEIN 33.8g; CARB 2.2g; FIBER 0.6g; CHOL 141mg; IRON 2mg; SODIUM 293mg; CALC 25mg

Pan-Seared Chicken with Artichokes and Pasta

Since you cook everything in one pan, the larger the pan, the better. Slightly undercook the cavatappi; it will finish cooking when you add it to the chicken mixture.

    1   (6-ounce) jar marinated artichoke heart
        quarters, undrained
    8   skinless, boneless chicken thighs (about
        1½ pounds)
    ¼   teaspoon salt
    ¼   teaspoon black pepper
    Cooking spray
    ½   cup sliced green onions
    1   garlic clove, minced
    ½   cup dry white wine
    4   cups hot cooked cavatappi (about 2½ cups
        uncooked spiral tube-shaped pasta) or fusilli
        (short twisted spaghetti)
    1   tablespoon chopped pitted kalamata olives
    1   (14.5-ounce) canned diced tomatoes, drained
    2   tablespoons shredded fresh Parmesan cheese

1. Drain artichokes in a colander over a bowl, reserving marinade.
2. Sprinkle chicken with salt and pepper; coat with cooking spray. Heat a large nonstick skillet over medium-high heat. Add chicken; sauté 3 minutes on each side. Add onions and garlic; sauté 1 minute. Stir in reserved artichoke marinade and wine, scraping pan to loosen browned bits. Bring to a boil; reduce heat, and stir in artichokes, pasta, olives, and tomatoes. Cook 2 minutes or until thoroughly heated. Sprinkle with cheese. Yield: 4 servings (serving size: 2 thighs and about 1¾ cups pasta mixture).

CALORIES 436 (29% from fat); FAT 14g (sat 3.4g, mono 4.6g, poly 4.4g); PROTEIN 34.4g; CARB 39g; FIBER 1.9g; CHOL 115mg; IRON 3.9mg; SODIUM 594mg; CALC 96mg

One-Dish Rosemary Chicken and White Beans

Chicken thighs have a slightly higher fat content than breasts, but in a healthy, balanced meal like this, it's nothing to worry about. Plus, thighs are juicier and a bit cheaper than breasts. A spinach salad tossed with slivered red onions and drizzled with red wine vinaigrette complements this dish nicely.

    2   teaspoons olive oil
    1½   teaspoons dried rosemary
    ¼   teaspoon salt
    ¼   teaspoon black pepper
    8   skinless, boneless chicken thighs (about
         1½ pounds)
    1   (15-ounce) can navy beans, drained
    1   (14.5-ounce) can stewed tomatoes, undrained
    ¼   cup chopped pitted kalamata olives
    Rosemary sprigs (optional)

1. Heat oil in a large skillet over medium-high heat. Combine rosemary, salt, and pepper; sprinkle evenly over 1 side of chicken. Place chicken in pan, seasoned side down; cook 3 minutes. Reduce heat to medium; turn chicken. Add beans and tomatoes; cover and simmer 10 minutes or until chicken is done. Stir in olives. Garnish with fresh rosemary sprigs, if desired. Yield: 4 servings (serving size: 2 thighs and ¾ cup bean mixture).

CALORIES 391 (41% from fat); FAT 17.7g (sat 4.3g, mono 8.3g, poly 3.5g); PROTEIN 36.1g; CARB 19.6g; FIBER 5.1g; CHOL 112mg; IRON 4.1mg; SODIUM 894mg; CALC 86mg

Pan-Seared Chicken with
Artichokes and Pasta

Chicken with Prosciutto and
Tomatoes over Polenta

Chicken with Prosciutto and Tomatoes over Polenta

When it comes to great chicken flavor, thighs rule. Cheap and tasty, chicken thighs can go fancy or simple. And they can be quick and easy, too. Just prepare the polenta while the chicken cooks, and you've got dinner tonight in no time.

    4   bone-in chicken thighs (about 1⅛ pounds), skinned
    1   tablespoon chopped fresh or 1 teaspoon dried rubbed sage
    ¼   teaspoon salt, divided
    ¼   teaspoon freshly ground black pepper
    ½   cup all-purpose flour
    2   teaspoons olive oil
    ½   cup dry white wine
    ⅔   cup yellow cornmeal
    2   cups water
    1   cup chopped seeded peeled tomato
    1   teaspoon fresh lemon juice
    2   very thin slices prosciutto or ham, cut into thin strips (about ¼ cup)
    Sage sprigs (optional)

1. Sprinkle chicken with chopped sage, ⅛ teaspoon salt, and pepper. Place flour in a shallow dish. Dredge chicken in flour. Heat oil in a nonstick skillet over medium-high heat. Add chicken; cook 4 minutes on each side. Add wine; cover, reduce heat, and simmer 20 minutes or until a meat thermometer registers 180°.

2. Place cornmeal and remaining ⅛ teaspoon salt in a 1-quart casserole. Gradually add water, stirring until blended. Cover. Microwave at HIGH 12 minutes, stirring every 3 minutes. Let stand, covered, 5 minutes.

3. Remove chicken from pan. Add tomato to pan; cook 1 minute. Stir in lemon juice and prosciutto. Spoon polenta onto plates, and top with chicken. Serve with tomato sauce. Garnish with sage sprigs, if desired. Yield: 2 servings (serving size: 2 thighs, ½ cup polenta, and ½ cup sauce).

CALORIES 594 (30% from fat); FAT 20g (sat 4.9g, mono 8.4g, poly 3.8g); PROTEIN 41.2g; CARB 64.2g; FIBER 4.6g; CHOL 116mg; IRON 5.2mg; SODIUM 656mg; CALC 41mg

Chicken with Figs and Lemon

Lemon, dried figs, Dijon mustard, and garlic infuse saucy chicken thighs in this Mediterranean-inspired dish. Squeeze a fresh lemon and mince the garlic yourself to add the freshest flavors, and then save time with canned broth and a package of Alfredo sauce mix. This balance of quality produce enhanced with convenience products takes quick and easy cooking to a new level. Serve over a bed of couscous and add another hint of freshness with a sprig of fresh thyme.

    8   chicken thighs (about 2¼ pounds), skinned
    1   cup fat-free, less-sodium chicken broth
    ½   teaspoon grated lemon rind
    3   tablespoons fresh lemon juice
    1   (1.25-ounce) package creamy garlic Alfredo pasta sauce mix (such as McCormick)
    3   tablespoons Dijon mustard
    4   garlic cloves, minced, or 4 teaspoons bottled minced garlic
    1   cup sliced onion
    1   cup dried Calimyrna figs, halved
    Thyme sprigs (optional)

1. Brown chicken thighs in a skillet over medium-high heat 5 to 6 minutes, turning once.

2. Combine broth and next 5 ingredients in a 4½-quart electric slow cooker; stir mixture until well blended. Add onion, fig halves, and chicken, pushing chicken pieces down into broth mixture.

3. Cover and cook on LOW 6 to 8 hours or until chicken and figs are tender. Serve with sauce. Garnish with thyme, if desired. Yield: 4 servings (serving size: 2 thighs and ¾ cup sauce).

CALORIES 431 (33% from fat); FAT 15.9g (sat 5.3g, mono 4.8g, poly 3g); PROTEIN 34.1g; CARB 38.9g; FIBER 5.4g; CHOL 119mg; IRON 3.3mg; SODIUM 819mg; CALC 107mg

Chicken and Leeks Braised in Wine

Once cut diagonally into 2-inch pieces, the leeks soften and develop a delicate flavor but remain intact for a nice presentation.

Cooking spray
 8 bone-in chicken thighs, skinned
    (about 2 pounds)
 ¾ teaspoon salt, divided
 ½ teaspoon freshly ground black pepper,
    divided
 4 leeks (about 2¼ pounds), cut diagonally
    into 2-inch pieces
 1 teaspoon ground coriander
 1 (3-inch) cinnamon stick
 2 cups riesling or other slightly sweet white
    wine
 1 teaspoon sugar
 2 bay leaves
 2 oregano sprigs
 2 garlic cloves, peeled
 1 (5 x 1–inch) orange rind strip
 3 cups chopped seeded peeled tomato
 1 tablespoon chopped fresh oregano
Parsley sprigs (optional)

1. Heat a large nonstick skillet over medium-high heat. Coat pan with cooking spray. Sprinkle chicken with ½ teaspoon salt and ¼ teaspoon pepper. Add chicken to pan; sauté 4 minutes on each side. Remove from pan. Add leeks to pan; sauté 4 minutes or until browned, turning once. Remove from pan.
2. Add coriander and cinnamon to pan; cook 30 seconds. Add wine and next 5 ingredients, and bring to a boil. Cover, reduce heat, and simmer 3 minutes. Add leeks. Cover and cook 5 minutes. Add chicken. Cover and cook 8 minutes.
3. Add tomato; bring to a boil. Reduce heat, and cook, uncovered, 10 minutes or until chicken is done, stirring frequently. Remove cinnamon stick, bay leaves, and rind.
4. Stir in remaining ¼ teaspoon salt, remaining ¼ teaspoon pepper, and chopped oregano. Garnish each serving with parsley sprigs, if desired. Yield: 4 servings (serving size: 2 thighs, about 2 leek pieces, and ½ cup sauce).

CALORIES 357 (17% from fat); FAT 6.6g (sat 1.5g, mono 1.8g, poly 1.9g); PROTEIN 30.9g; CARB 46.7g; FIBER 6.8g; CHOL 107mg; IRON 8.2mg; SODIUM 624mg; CALC 199mg

Chicken in Wine Cream Sauce

If you wish to impress guests, this delicious recipe is the way to go. It's just like something you'd find in a fancy restaurant—only it's easy to make and adaptable to whatever ingredients you have on hand, such as brown rice or a commercial wild rice blend.

 2 teaspoons dried oregano
 2 teaspoons dried basil
 1½ teaspoons dried rosemary
 1 teaspoon garlic powder
 ½ teaspoon salt
 ½ teaspoon black pepper
 ¼ teaspoon paprika
 1 tablespoon plus 1 teaspoon olive oil, divided
 8 bone-in chicken thighs, skinned
Cooking spray
 ⅓ cup all-purpose flour
2¼ cups 1% low-fat milk
 1 cup dry white wine
 2 cups sliced mushrooms
 ¼ cup tub-style light cream cheese
 2 cups hot cooked wild rice
Oregano sprigs (optional)

1. Combine first 7 ingredients and 2 teaspoons olive oil in a small bowl; rub over chicken. Heat remaining 2 teaspoons oil in a large skillet coated with cooking spray over medium-high heat. Add chicken; cook 5 minutes on each side or until browned. Remove chicken from pan, and set aside.
2. Lightly spoon flour into a dry measuring cup; level with a knife. Place flour in a bowl; gradually add milk and wine, stirring with a whisk until blended. Add mixture to pan, scraping pan to loosen browned bits; bring to a simmer. Return chicken to pan; cover, reduce heat, and simmer 30 minutes or until chicken is done. Add mushrooms; cover and simmer 5 minutes. Remove chicken from pan; cover and set aside.
3. Add cheese to pan; cook, stirring constantly with a whisk, 5 minutes or until cheese melts. Place ½ cup rice on each of 4 plates. Top each with 2 chicken thighs and 1 cup sauce. Garnish with oregano sprigs, if desired. Yield: 4 servings.

CALORIES 444 (29% from fat); FAT 14.5g (sat 4.4g, mono 6.2g, poly 2.2g); PROTEIN 39.1g; CARB 39g; FIBER 2.5g; CHOL 128mg; IRON 4mg; SODIUM 568mg; CALC 246mg

Chicken with Green Olives

This North African dish is also served in southern Spain and Italy. Traditionally, it's made as a stew because the region's farm-raised chickens require long cooking for tenderness. This version calls for flavorful chicken thighs that cook quickly.

1 tablespoon olive oil
8 bone-in chicken thighs (about 2¼ pounds), skinned
¾ teaspoon black pepper, divided
¼ teaspoon salt
2 cups chopped onion
1 tablespoon minced fresh garlic
2 teaspoons minced peeled fresh ginger
1 teaspoon ground cumin
1 teaspoon paprika
½ teaspoon ground turmeric
Dash of ground red pepper
1 (3-inch) cinnamon stick
1 bay leaf
2 cups fat-free, less-sodium chicken broth
⅔ cup pitted green olives
2 tablespoons fresh lemon juice
¼ cup chopped fresh cilantro
3 cups hot cooked couscous

1. Heat olive oil in a large nonstick skillet over medium-high heat. Sprinkle chicken with ¼ teaspoon black pepper and ¼ teaspoon salt. Add chicken to pan; cook 10 minutes, browning on all sides. Remove chicken from pan; reduce heat to medium.

2. Add remaining ½ teaspoon black pepper, onion, and next 8 ingredients; cook 5 minutes, stirring occasionally. Add broth; bring to a boil. Return chicken to pan, and reduce heat. Simmer, uncovered, 15 minutes or until chicken is done. Discard cinnamon stick and bay leaf.

3. While chicken cooks, place olives in a small saucepan, and cover with water. Bring to a boil, and drain. Repeat procedure. Add olives and lemon juice to chicken mixture, and sprinkle with cilantro. Serve over couscous. Yield: 4 servings (serving size: 2 chicken thighs, ½ cup sauce, and ¾ cup couscous).

CALORIES 486 (37% from fat); FAT 19.8g (sat 4.5g, mono 9.8g, poly 3.6g); PROTEIN 37.1g; CARB 39.3g; FIBER 4g; CHOL 109mg; IRON 2.8mg; SODIUM 890mg; CALC 65mg

Saucy Italian-Style Chicken Thighs

Look in your pantry and you'll probably find most of the ingredients needed for this simple and delicious dish. Chicken thighs bring rich flavor and also make for an inexpensive meal. Serve with a slice of crusty bread or over brown rice, spinach fettuccine, or mashed potatoes to soak up the sauce.

12 chicken thighs (about 3 pounds), skinned
1 (14.5-ounce) can Italian-style diced tomatoes, undrained
1 (6-ounce) can tomato paste
½ cup chopped onion
1 tablespoon bottled minced garlic
1 teaspoon dried Italian seasoning
¼ teaspoon salt
¼ teaspoon black pepper

1. Place chicken in a 4-quart electric slow cooker. Combine tomatoes and next 6 ingredients; stir well. Pour sauce over chicken. Cover and cook on HIGH 1 hour. Reduce heat to LOW, and cook 4 to 5 hours or until chicken is tender. Yield: 6 servings (serving size: 2 thighs and about ¾ cup sauce).

CALORIES 202 (24% from fat); FAT 5.4g (sat 1.4g, mono 1.6g, poly 1.4g); PROTEIN 27.8g; CARB 9.6g; FIBER 2.1g; CHOL 109mg; IRON 2.3mg; SODIUM 526mg; CALC 35mg

Secrets to Rich Tomato Sauce

You don't always have to start from scratch to achieve homemade flavor. Combining Italian-style diced tomatoes with tomato paste yields a simple tomato sauce that, after simmering for hours, develops an intensely rich flavor that is anything but commercial.

Colonel Benjamin's Curry Chicken

Enjoy the intoxicating aromas of Indian cuisine with this century-old recipe. The spices meld well with the flavor from the chicken thighs in this traditional Indian chicken dish from the kitchen of Colonel Benjamin, a retiree from the Indian Army. This dish is a must for curry-lovers.

1 teaspoon salt
1 teaspoon ground coriander
1 teaspoon ground cumin
1 teaspoon chili powder
1 teaspoon grated peeled fresh ginger
¼ teaspoon ground turmeric
1 teaspoon canola oil
4 cups finely chopped onion
2 garlic cloves, minced
3½ cups coarsely chopped peeled tomato (about 1½ pounds)
2 tablespoons fresh lemon juice
12 bone-in chicken thighs (about 3 pounds), skinned
½ teaspoon salt
1½ pounds peeled baking potato, cut into 1-inch pieces
2 tablespoons chopped fresh cilantro
3 cups hot cooked rice
Cilantro sprigs

1. Combine first 6 ingredients.
2. Heat oil in a Dutch oven over medium-high heat. Add onion and garlic, and cook 15 minutes, stirring frequently. Add cumin mixture, tomato, and lemon juice. Reduce heat to medium, and cook 10 minutes, stirring occasionally.
3. Sprinkle chicken with ½ teaspoon salt. Add chicken and potato to pan; stir in chopped cilantro. Bring to a boil; cover, reduce heat, and simmer 50 minutes or until chicken is done. Serve over rice, and garnish with cilantro sprigs. Yield: 6 servings (serving size: 2 thighs, 1 cup potato curry, and ½ cup rice).

CALORIES 479 (24% from fat); FAT 12.6g (sat 3.3g, mono 4.8g, poly 3g); PROTEIN 32.7g; CARB 58.5g; FIBER 4.5g; CHOL 97mg; IRON 3.6mg; SODIUM 704mg; CALC 69mg

Colonel Benjamin's
Curry Chicken

Polynesian Chicken

Polynesian Chicken

Sweet pineapple, crispy water chestnuts, and crunchy chow mein noodles join to create a lively combination of textures in this island-inspired dish.

  3 chicken breast halves (about 18 ounces), skinned
  6 chicken thighs (about 1¾ pounds), skinned
  ¼ teaspoon salt
  ¼ teaspoon black pepper
  Cooking spray
  1 (8¼-ounce) can pineapple slices in heavy syrup, undrained
  1 (8-ounce) can sliced water chestnuts, drained
  1 cup fat-free, less-sodium chicken broth
  ¼ teaspoon ground ginger
  1 garlic clove, minced
  ¼ cup low-sodium soy sauce
  ¼ cup cornstarch
  1 tablespoon white vinegar
  ½ cup diagonally sliced green onions
  6 cups hot cooked rice
  6 tablespoons chow mein noodles

1. Sprinkle chicken evenly with salt and pepper. Heat a large nonstick skillet over medium-high heat; coat pan with cooking spray. Add half of chicken pieces; cook 3 minutes on each side or until browned. Repeat procedure with remaining chicken pieces. Place chicken in a 5-quart electric slow cooker.
2. Drain pineapple, reserving syrup. Quarter pineapple slices; arrange pineapple and water chestnuts over chicken. Combine reserved pineapple syrup, chicken broth, ginger, and garlic; pour over chicken.
3. Cover and cook on LOW 8 to 9 hours or until chicken is tender. Remove chicken from cooker with a slotted spoon; keep warm. Reserve cooking liquid in cooker. Increase heat to HIGH.
4. Combine soy sauce, cornstarch, and vinegar in a small bowl, stirring with a whisk until well blended. Stir cornstarch mixture and green onions into cooking liquid in cooker. Cook, uncovered, 10 minutes or until slightly thick, stirring frequently. Serve chicken and sauce over rice on individual plates; top with chow mein noodles. Yield: 6 servings (serving size: 1 chicken breast half or 2 thighs, 1 cup rice, ½ cup sauce, and 1 tablespoon chow mein noodles).

CALORIES 526 (15% from fat); FAT 8.5g (sat 2.2g, mono 3g, poly 2.2g); PROTEIN 34.4g; CARB 74.2g; FIBER 2.6g; CHOL 88mg; IRON 4.4mg; SODIUM 705mg; CALC 34mg

Jerk-Style Chicken

"Jerk" is a Jamaican cooking term used when chicken or pork is rubbed with a sweet-hot paste made from spices, herbs, and peppers and then cooked slowly over a fire of green pimiento wood. We achieved similar flavor results with the aid of a blender and grill.

  1 teaspoon grated lime rind
  ¼ cup fresh lime juice
  2 tablespoons olive oil
  1 to 2 tablespoons finely chopped jalapeño pepper
  1 tablespoon ground allspice
  1 tablespoon brown sugar
  1 teaspoon salt
  1 teaspoon coarsely ground black pepper
  1 teaspoon dried thyme
  1 teaspoon ground cinnamon
  ½ teaspoon ground nutmeg
  3 garlic cloves
  ½ cup chopped onion
  6 skinless, boneless chicken thighs (about 1⅛ pounds)
  3 (6-ounce) skinless, boneless chicken breast halves
  Cooking spray
  Hot cooked long-grain rice (optional)
  Parsley sprigs (optional)
  Lime slices (optional)

1. Combine first 12 ingredients in a blender; process until well blended. Pour mixture into a large heavy-duty zip-top plastic bag; add onion and chicken. Seal bag; marinate in refrigerator 1 to 2 hours, turning bag occasionally.
2. Prepare grill.
3. Remove chicken from bag; discard marinade. Place chicken on grill rack coated with cooking spray. Grill chicken, covered, 5 minutes on each side or until done. Serve over hot cooked rice, and garnish with parsley and lime slices, if desired. Yield: 6 servings (serving size: 2 thighs or 1 breast half).

CALORIES 303 (37% from fat); FAT 12.6g (sat 3.2g, mono 5.5g, poly 2.6g); PROTEIN 41.9g; CARB 2.9g; FIBER 0.7g; CHOL 130mg; IRON 2mg; SODIUM 325mg; CALC 32mg

Arroz con Pollo

Arroz con Pollo

Literally translated as "rice and chicken," *Arroz con Pollo* is a Spanish and Mexican dish that usually includes chicken, rice, tomatoes, green bell peppers, and seasonings. Sometimes saffron is also added. We use turmeric to color the rice yellow; other versions use annatto seeds or saffron.

6 chicken drumsticks (about 1½ pounds), skinned
6 bone-in chicken thighs (about 2 pounds), skinned
1½ teaspoons dried oregano, divided
½ teaspoon salt
¼ teaspoon freshly ground black pepper
1 tablespoon vegetable oil
2 tablespoons fresh lime juice
1 cup chopped onion
½ cup chopped green bell pepper
2 garlic cloves, minced
1 teaspoon ground turmeric
¾ teaspoon ground cumin
1½ cups uncooked Arborio rice
½ cup diced ham
2¼ cups fat-free, less-sodium chicken broth
1 (14.5-ounce) can diced tomatoes, undrained
½ cup frozen petite green peas, thawed
½ cup chopped pimiento-stuffed green olives

1. Sprinkle chicken with 1 teaspoon oregano, salt, and black pepper. Heat oil in a Dutch oven over medium-high heat. Add chicken; cook 8 minutes, browning on all sides. Remove chicken from pan; drizzle with lime juice. Cover; keep warm.
2. Add onion, bell pepper, and garlic to pan. Cover, reduce heat to low, and cook 10 minutes or until tender. Stir in remaining ½ teaspoon oregano, turmeric, and cumin, and sauté 1 minute. Stir in rice and ham; cook 1 minute. Increase heat to medium. Add broth and tomatoes; bring to a boil. Add chicken, nestling into rice mixture. Cover, reduce heat, and simmer 18 minutes or until liquid is almost absorbed and chicken is done. Stir in peas; cover and cook 3 minutes. Remove from heat, and let stand, uncovered, 5 minutes. Sprinkle with olives. Yield: 6 servings (serving size: 1 drumstick, 1 thigh, and 1 cup rice mixture).

CALORIES 405 (33% from fat); FAT 14.7g (sat 3.5g, mono 6g, poly 3.6g); PROTEIN 38.8g; CARB 28.2g; FIBER 2.9g; CHOL 119mg; IRON 2.9mg; SODIUM 853mg; CALC 53mg

Easy Bistro Chicken

Cozy up to a blazing fire on a cold winter's night with this comfort food classic. You'll find it's reminiscent of a cacciatore. Italian for "hunter," cacciatore is a stew-like dish flavored with onions, herbs, mushrooms, tomatoes, and sometimes wine.

2 tablespoons olive oil, divided
4 (8-ounce) bone-in chicken breast halves, skinned
4 bone-in chicken thighs (about 1½ pounds), skinned
4 chicken drumsticks (about 1 pound), skinned
2 cups chopped onion
4 garlic cloves, minced
1 cup chopped celery
½ cup chopped fresh basil
½ cup chopped fresh flat-leaf parsley
½ cup red wine vinegar
¼ cup sliced green olives
¼ cup capers
1 tablespoon sugar
Dash of ground red pepper
2 bay leaves
1 (28-ounce) can Italian-style tomatoes, undrained and chopped
8 cups hot cooked macaroni or cavatappi
Flat-leaf parsley sprigs (optional)

1. Heat 1½ teaspoons oil in a large nonstick skillet over medium-high heat. Add chicken breast halves to pan; sauté 2 minutes on each side or until lightly browned. Remove from pan. Add 1½ teaspoons oil and remaining chicken pieces; sauté 2 minutes on each side or until lightly browned. Remove chicken from pan.
2. Heat remaining 1 tablespoon oil in pan. Add onion and garlic; sauté 5 minutes. Add celery; sauté 5 minutes. Add basil and next 8 ingredients. Return chicken to pan; bring to a boil. Cover, reduce heat, and simmer 20 minutes.
3. Uncover and simmer 25 minutes or until chicken is tender. Discard bay leaves. Serve with pasta. Garnish with parsley sprigs, if desired. Yield: 8 servings (serving size: 1 chicken breast half or 1 thigh and 1 drumstick, ½ cup sauce, and 1 cup pasta).

CALORIES 485 (21% from fat); FAT 11.5g (sat 2.5g, mono 5.4g, poly 2.3g); PROTEIN 41.9g; CARB 50.3g; FIBER 4g; CHOL 101mg; IRON 6.2mg; SODIUM 471mg; CALC 90mg

Grilled Lemon-Herb Chicken

If your grill is large enough, cook two chickens at the same time to feed a larger group or just to have more leftovers for quick lunches. Or, if you don't want to use a whole bird, use chicken pieces, and grill for a shorter amount of time. Refrigerate any leftover chicken up to three days.

  1 (5-pound) roasting chicken
  3 tablespoons fresh lemon juice
  2 tablespoons chopped fresh parsley
  1 tablespoon chopped fresh thyme
  1 teaspoon salt
 ½ teaspoon freshly ground black pepper
Cooking spray
Lemon wedges (optional)
Parsley sprigs (optional)
Thyme sprigs (optional)

1. Remove and discard giblets and neck from chicken. Rinse chicken with cold water, and pat dry. Trim excess fat. Place chicken, breast side down, on a cutting surface. Cut chicken in half lengthwise along backbone (do not cut through breastbone). Turn chicken over. Starting at neck cavity, loosen skin from breast and drumsticks by inserting fingers, gently pushing between skin and meat.
2. Combine juice and next 4 ingredients; rub mixture under loosened skin and over breast and drumsticks. Gently press skin to secure. Place chicken in a large zip-top plastic bag. Seal and marinate in refrigerator 30 minutes.
3. Prepare grill.
4. Place chicken, skin side up, on a grill rack coated with cooking spray. Grill 55 minutes or until a thermometer inserted into meaty part of thigh registers 180°. Remove chicken from grill; cover and let stand 10 minutes. Remove and discard skin. Garnish with lemon wedges, parsley sprigs, and thyme sprigs, if desired. Yield: 5 servings (serving size: about 4 ounces).

CALORIES 203 (27% from fat); FAT 6.2g (sat 1.7g, mono 2.2g, poly 1.4g); PROTEIN 33.5g; CARB 1.1g; FIBER 0.2g; CHOL 100mg; IRON 1.5mg; SODIUM 565mg; CALC 21mg

Chicken, Date, and Apricot Tagine

For centuries, nomads in Morocco and North Africa have used portable cone-topped clay cookers called tagines to make their traditional stews. Updated versions of these classic stews are made in Dutch ovens. The recipes, which are basically slow-cooked meats with fruit and vegetables, are actually called tagines as well. Serve over hot cooked couscous for the ultimate one-dish meal.

   1 (3-pound) broiler-fryer chicken
   1 tablespoon olive oil
   1 cup chopped onion
   1 teaspoon ground turmeric
   1 teaspoon ground cumin
  ½ teaspoon ground ginger
  ½ teaspoon ground cinnamon
 ⅛ teaspoon ground red pepper
   5 garlic cloves, minced
1½ cups fat-free, less-sodium chicken broth
 ⅓ cup sliced whole pitted dates
 ⅓ cup sliced dried apricots
   2 teaspoons (1-inch) julienne-cut lemon rind
  ½ teaspoon salt
 ⅓ cup chopped fresh parsley
 ⅓ cup lemon sections, peeled and chopped
   2 tablespoons chopped fresh cilantro
   3 cups hot cooked couscous

1. Skin and cut chicken into 2 drumsticks, 2 thighs, 2 breast halves, and 2 wings. Reserve chicken wings for another use. Discard back and giblets.
2. Heat oil in a Dutch oven over medium-high heat. Add chicken; cook 5 minutes on each side or until browned. Add onion and next 6 ingredients; cook 4 minutes, stirring occasionally. Add broth, dates, apricots, rind, and salt. Bring to a boil; cover, reduce heat, and simmer 30 minutes or until chicken is tender. Remove from heat; stir in parsley, lemon sections, and cilantro. Serve over couscous. Yield: 4 servings (serving size: 1 breast half or 1 thigh and 1 drumstick, ¾ cup fruit mixture, and ¾ cup couscous).

CALORIES 473 (17% from fat); FAT 8.7g (sat 1.7g, mono 4g, poly 1.7g); PROTEIN 42.9g; CARB 55.6g; FIBER 5.4g; CHOL 113mg; IRON 4mg; SODIUM 648mg; CALC 77mg

Chicken, Date, and
Apricot Tagine

Sunday Roasted Chicken with Giblet Gravy

1   (6-pound) roasting chicken
2   (14-ounce) cans fat-free, less-sodium chicken broth, divided
1   carrot, cut into 2-inch pieces
1   celery stalk, cut into 2-inch pieces
1   onion, quartered
2   large garlic cloves, unpeeled and halved
2   bay leaves
1   teaspoon kosher salt
1   tablespoon dried thyme
1   tablespoon dried rubbed sage
¼   cup all-purpose flour
¼   teaspoon black pepper

1. Remove giblets and neck from chicken, discarding liver. Cut off wing tips, and combine with giblets, neck, 3 cups broth, carrot, celery, onion, garlic, and bay leaves in a saucepan. Bring to a boil; partially cover, reduce heat, and simmer 45 minutes. Strain broth mixture through a sieve into a bowl, reserving broth and giblets. Mince giblets; add to strained broth, and set aside. Discard remaining solids.
2. Preheat oven to 375°.
3. Rinse chicken with cold water, and pat dry. Trim excess fat. Starting at neck cavity, loosen skin from breast and drumsticks by inserting fingers, gently pushing between skin and meat. Combine salt, thyme, and sage in a small bowl. Rub thyme mixture under loosened skin and over breast and drumsticks. Gently press skin to secure. Tie legs with string.
4. Place chicken, breast side up, on rack of a broiler pan or roasting pan. Insert a meat thermometer into meaty part of thigh, making sure not to touch bone. Bake at 375° for 1 hour and 30 minutes or until thermometer registers 180° and juices run clear. Cover chicken loosely with foil; let stand 10 minutes for chicken to reabsorb juices. Discard skin. Remove rack from pan. Add ½ cup broth to drippings in pan, scraping pan to loosen browned bits. Place a zip-top plastic bag inside a 2-cup measure. Pour drippings into bag; let stand 10 minutes (fat will rise to the top). Seal bag; carefully snip off 1 corner of bag; drain liquid into saucepan, stopping before fat layer reaches opening. Discard fat.
5. Add reserved giblet mixture to broth mixture in saucepan.
6. Combine remaining ½ cup broth and flour in a bowl. Add flour mixture to saucepan; bring to a boil. Reduce heat; cook 10 minutes, stirring constantly. Stir in pepper. Serve with chicken. Yield: 8 servings (serving size: 4 ounces chicken and ⅓ cup gravy).

CALORIES 217 (20% from fat); FAT 4.8g (sat 1.2g, mono 1.5g, poly 1.2g); PROTEIN 37.3g; CARB 4.1g; FIBER 1g; CHOL 113mg; IRON 2.4mg; SODIUM 651mg; CALC 29mg

Grilled Cornish Hens with Apricot-Mustard Glaze

Serve the hens with grilled fennel bulb quarters and couscous. Preserves are chunkier than jelly and thus adhere better to the Cornish hens; peach preserves are a tasty alternative to the apricot preserves used in this recipe.

½   cup apricot preserves
¼   cup stone-ground mustard
2   tablespoons chopped fresh flat-leaf parsley
2   tablespoons chopped fresh mint
2   teaspoons Champagne vinegar or white wine vinegar
2   (18-ounce) Cornish hens, skinned and quartered
¼   teaspoon kosher salt
½   teaspoon freshly ground black pepper
Cooking spray

1. Combine first 5 ingredients, stirring with a whisk.
2. Sprinkle hens with salt and pepper. Place ¼ cup apricot mixture in a large zip-top plastic bag. Add hens; seal and marinate in refrigerator 1 hour, turning bag occasionally.
3. Prepare grill.
4. Remove hens from bag; discard marinade. Place hens on a grill rack coated with cooking spray; grill 12 minutes or until thermometer registers 180°, turning hens occasionally and basting frequently with remaining apricot mixture. Yield: 2 servings (serving size: 1 hen).

CALORIES 417 (15% from fat); FAT 7g (sat 1.7g, mono 2.2g, poly 1.6g); PROTEIN 41.7g; CARB 44.6g; FIBER 3.7g; CHOL 180mg; IRON 2.3mg; SODIUM 608mg; CALC 70mg

Grilled Cornish Hens with
Apricot-Mustard Glaze

Turkey Tetrazzini

By using just a few convenience products, such as pre-sliced mushrooms, frozen peas, and canned soup, you can get made-from-scratch flavor fast. A splash of sherry, freshly grated Parmesan cheese, and a crunchy breadcrumb topping elevate everyday fare to new heights. Make this dish ahead and refrigerate. Bake just before you're ready to serve.

    10 ounces uncooked vermicelli
    2   teaspoons vegetable oil
    1   pound turkey breast cutlets
    ¾   teaspoon onion powder, divided
    ½   teaspoon salt, divided
    ¼   teaspoon black pepper, divided
    2   tablespoons dry sherry
    2   (8-ounce) packages presliced mushrooms
    ¾   cup frozen green peas, thawed
    ¾   cup fat-free milk
    ⅔   cup fat-free sour cream
    ⅓   cup (about 1½ ounces) grated fresh
        Parmesan cheese
    1   (10¾-ounce) can reduced-fat cream of
        chicken soup (such as Healthy Choice)
    Cooking spray
    ⅓   cup dry breadcrumbs
    2   tablespoons butter, melted

1. Preheat oven to 450°.
2. Cook pasta according to package directions, omitting salt and fat. Drain.
3. Heat oil in a large nonstick skillet over medium-high heat. Sprinkle turkey with ½ teaspoon onion powder, ¼ teaspoon salt, and ⅛ teaspoon pepper. Add turkey to pan; cook 2 minutes on each side or until done. Remove turkey from pan.
4. Add ¼ teaspoon onion powder, sherry, and mushrooms to pan. Cover mixture, and cook 4 minutes or until mushrooms are tender.
5. Combine peas and next 4 ingredients in a large bowl. Chop turkey. Add ¼ teaspoon salt, ⅛ teaspoon pepper, pasta, turkey, and mushroom mixture to soup mixture, tossing gently to combine. Spoon mixture into a 13 x 9–inch baking dish coated with cooking spray.
6. Combine breadcrumbs and butter in a small dish, tossing to combine. Sprinkle breadcrumb mixture over pasta mixture. Bake at 450° for 12 minutes or until bubbly and thoroughly heated. Yield: 6 servings (serving size: about 1⅔ cups).

CALORIES 459 (29% from fat); FAT 14.8g (sat 5.9g, mono 4.4g, poly 2.8g); PROTEIN 30.5g; CARB 48.1g; FIBER 3.1g; CHOL 69mg; IRON 4mg; SODIUM 716mg; CALC 199mg

Slow-Cooked Lemon-Pepper Turkey Breast

With only four ingredients, this juicy turkey-and-gravy feast is hard to beat. Prepare and serve it as the centerpiece to a grand meal, and save the oven for all of those side dishes. A turkey sandwich with a side of grapes makes a terrific leftover meal.

    1   (5-pound) bone-in turkey breast,
        skinned and cut in half
    2   teaspoons lemon pepper
    2   tablespoons all-purpose flour
    3   tablespoons water

1. Sprinkle turkey evenly with lemon pepper. Place turkey breast halves, meaty sides down, in a 5-quart electric slow cooker. Cover and cook on HIGH 1 hour. Reduce heat to LOW; cook 5 hours or until turkey is tender. Remove turkey to a platter, reserving cooking liquid in cooker. Set turkey aside, and keep warm.
2. Combine flour and water in a medium saucepan, stirring with a whisk until well blended. Gradually add reserved cooking liquid, stirring constantly. Bring to a boil over medium-high heat, stirring constantly. Reduce heat, and simmer 4 minutes or until thick, stirring occasionally. Serve turkey with gravy. Yield: 9 servings (serving size: 6 ounces turkey and 2 tablespoons gravy).

CALORIES 227 (5% from fat); FAT 1.3g (sat 0.4g, mono 0.2g, poly 0.4g); PROTEIN 49.2g; CARB 1.3g; FIBER 0.1g; CHOL 123mg; IRON 2.4mg; SODIUM 124mg; CALC 20mg

Preparing for Slow Cooking

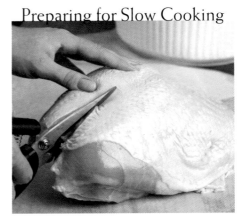

When using a slow cooker, you should cut any piece of meat or poultry that's over 3 pounds in half to ensure thorough cooking. Use kitchen shears to halve the turkey breast, or ask your butcher to halve it at the store. Or buy two 2½-pound turkey breast halves instead. Be sure to remove the skin before cooking.

Slow-Cooked Lemon-Pepper
Turkey Breast

Turkey Thighs with Olives and Dried Cherries

The sophisticated combination of earthy, spicy, and sweet flavors in this entrée will wow your dinner guests. Turkey thighs are easy to find, but you also can use skinless chicken thighs, if you prefer. Serve with mashed potatoes or couscous for a rustic yet impressive meal.

  1 cup thinly sliced leek (about 1 large)
  1 cup ruby port or other sweet red wine
  ¾ cup dried cherries
  ¾ cup pitted kalamata olives
  ⅓ cup fresh orange juice (about 1 orange)
  1 teaspoon paprika
  1 teaspoon crushed red pepper
  4 thyme sprigs
  1 (3-inch) cinnamon stick
1½ teaspoons salt, divided
3½ pounds turkey thighs, skinned
  1 tablespoon ground cumin

1. Combine first 9 ingredients in a 6-quart oval electric slow cooker. Stir in ½ teaspoon salt.
2. Rinse turkey with cold water; pat dry. Sprinkle with remaining 1 teaspoon salt and cumin. Place in cooker. Cover and cook on HIGH 1 hour. Reduce heat to LOW, and cook 4 hours. Discard cinnamon stick. Yield: 6 servings (serving size: 5 ounces turkey and about ½ cup leek mixture).

CALORIES 419 (34% from fat); FAT 16.1g (sat 4.7g, mono 5.5g, poly 4.1g); PROTEIN 32.5g; CARB 23.1g; FIBER 2.9g; CHOL 101mg; IRON 4.1mg; SODIUM 1,453mg; CALC 61mg

Tiny French Beans with Smoked Sausage

Smoked sausage and white beans simmer all day in a broth infused with shallots, garlic, and thyme. This is a hearty meal you'll be happy to come home to. Uncork a bottle of robust red wine and curl up with a bowlful of instant comfort.

  2 pounds smoked turkey sausage, cut into
     1½-inch pieces
  1 tablespoon canola oil
  ⅓ cup minced shallots
  3 garlic cloves, minced
  2 cups dried flageolets or other dried white
     beans (about 1 pound)
  2 cups water
  ¼ cup minced fresh or 1 tablespoon dried thyme
  1 teaspoon celery seeds
  ¼ teaspoon freshly ground black pepper
  2 (14-ounce) cans fat-free, less-sodium chicken
     broth
Thyme sprigs (optional)

1. Heat a large nonstick skillet over medium heat. Add sausage; sauté 5 minutes or until browned. Remove from pan; place in a 5-quart electric slow cooker. Heat oil in pan over medium heat. Add shallots and garlic; sauté 1 minute.
2. Sort and wash beans. Add beans, shallot mixture, water, and next 4 ingredients to cooker. Cover and cook on HIGH 8 hours or until beans are tender. Garnish with thyme sprigs, if desired. Yield: 8 servings (serving size: 1¼ cups).

CALORIES 366 (33% from fat); FAT 13.6g (sat 3.2g, mono 5.1g, poly 3.6g); PROTEIN 27.3g; CARB 34.9g; FIBER 0.3g; CHOL 75mg; IRON 4.4mg; SODIUM 1,362mg; CALC 92mg

salads

Salade Niçoise with Creamy Tofu
Dressing, page 273

Fresh Fig Salad with Crème Fraîche, Mint, and Prosciutto

The fresh figs' dense texture and delicate sweet flavor pair well with salty prosciutto. Look for crème fraîche—thickened cream with a nutty flavor—near the gourmet cheeses. If your supermarket doesn't carry it, substitute whole sour cream.

⅓ cup crème fraîche
1 tablespoon water
1 teaspoon grated lemon rind
2 teaspoons fresh lemon juice
¼ teaspoon salt
¼ teaspoon freshly ground black pepper
24 small dark-skinned fresh figs (such as Black Mission, Celeste, or Brown Turkey; about 2 pounds), halved
¼ cup chopped fresh mint
3 very thin slices prosciutto, cut into ½-inch strips (about ½ cup)

1. Combine first 6 ingredients, stirring well with a whisk.
2. Arrange figs on a platter. Drizzle with crème fraîche mixture. Sprinkle with chopped mint and prosciutto. Yield: 6 servings (serving size: about 1 cup).

CALORIES 169 (29% from fat); FAT 5.4g (sat 3.1g, mono 1.7g, poly 0.5g); PROTEIN 3.2g; CARB 29.8g; FIBER 5.1g; CHOL 14mg; IRON 0.7mg; SODIUM 214mg; CALC 81mg

Spicy-Sweet Melon Salad

A simple syrup and sliced jalapeño pepper enhance honeydew and cantaloupe with a subtle sweet heat. The longer this salad sits, the spicier it gets.

½ cup sugar
½ cup water
½ small jalapeño pepper, thinly sliced
2 cups cubed peeled honeydew melon
2 cups cubed peeled cantaloupe

1. Combine sugar and water in a small saucepan; bring to a boil, stirring until sugar dissolves. Remove from heat; add pepper. Chill.
2. Combine sugar mixture, honeydew, and cantaloupe in a large bowl. Cover and chill 4 hours or overnight. Serve salad with a slotted spoon. Yield: 6 servings (serving size: ⅔ cup).

CALORIES 104 (2% from fat); FAT 0.2g (sat 0.1g, mono 0g, poly 0.1g); PROTEIN 0.8g; CARB 26.5g; FIBER 0.8g; CHOL 0mg; IRON 0.2mg; SODIUM 11mg; CALC 10mg

Peach Salad with Cumin Dressing

Frozen peaches work well in this salad—just thaw them and pat them dry with paper towels to remove excess moisture. Frozen berries, however, don't have the same consistency as fresh and are better to use in a recipe where they are cooked or pureed. Pairing a small amount of fresh berries with the frozen peaches makes this salad taste like it was made using only fresh fruit.

2 cups frozen sliced peaches, thawed
1 cup thinly sliced seeded peeled cucumber
½ teaspoon grated lemon rind
1 tablespoon fresh lemon juice
2 teaspoons minced fresh mint
2 teaspoons honey
¾ teaspoon cumin seeds, toasted and crushed
½ teaspoon salt
¼ teaspoon freshly ground black pepper
½ cup raspberries

1. Combine first 6 ingredients in a large bowl; toss gently. Combine cumin, salt, and pepper; sprinkle over peach mixture. Add raspberries, and toss gently to combine. Serve immediately. Yield: 4 servings (serving size: ¾ cup).

CALORIES 144 (3% from fat); FAT 0.4g (sat 0g, mono 0.1g, poly 0.2g); PROTEIN 1.4g; CARB 36.3g; FIBER 3.7g; CHOL 0mg; IRON 1.1mg; SODIUM 307mg; CALC 21mg

How to Seed a Cucumber

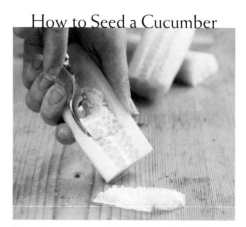

Cucumber may seem like an unusual addition to this fruit salad, but its mild flavor and crunchy texture are nice complements to the other ingredients. When purchasing cucumbers, remember that the smaller the cucumber, the smaller the seeds and the better the flavor. To seed a cucumber, simply cut it in half lengthwise and scrape out the seeds with a spoon.

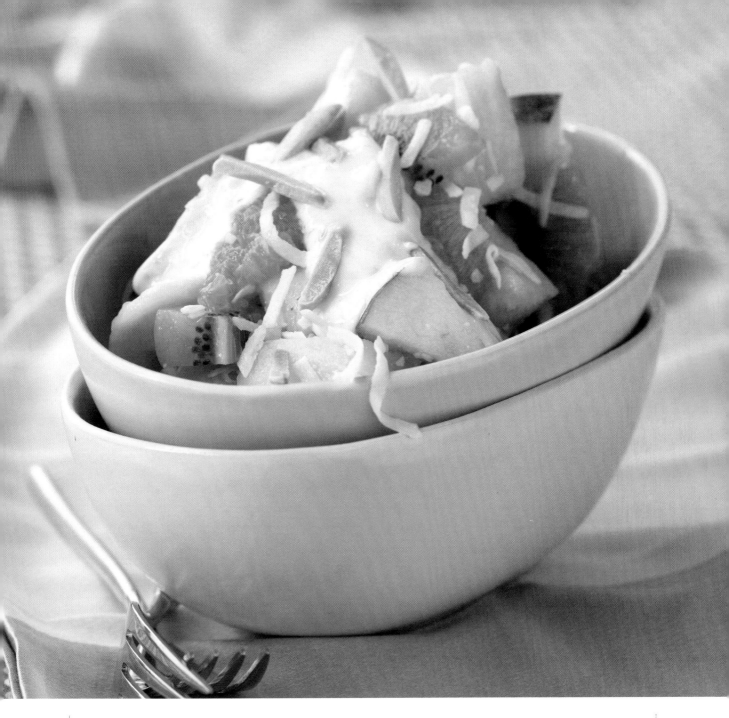

Fruit Salad with Honey-Yogurt Sauce

Prepare and refrigerate the yogurt sauce up to one day in advance. You can also combine and refrigerate the fruit mixture up to three hours ahead, but slice and stir in the banana just before serving to keep it from discoloring.

1	cup vanilla low-fat yogurt
1	tablespoon honey
1½	teaspoons grated lime rind
3	cups cubed fresh pineapple (about 1 medium)
1½	cups chopped Braeburn apple (about 1 large)
1	cup orange sections (about 2 oranges)
1	cup chopped peeled kiwifruit (about 2 large)
⅓	cup flaked sweetened coconut
1	banana, sliced
¼	cup slivered almonds, toasted

1. Combine yogurt, honey, and lime rind in a small bowl.

2. Combine pineapple and next 4 ingredients in a large bowl; toss gently. Just before serving, stir in banana. Divide fruit mixture among 6 salad bowls. Top with yogurt sauce, and sprinkle with almonds. Yield: 6 servings (serving size: 1¼ cups fruit mixture, about 2 tablespoons yogurt sauce, and 2 teaspoons almonds).

CALORIES 196 (22% from fat); FAT 4.8g (sat 1.8g, mono 1.7g, poly 0.8g); PROTEIN 4.3g; CARB 37.9g; FIBER 4.7g; CHOL 2mg; IRON 0.9mg; SODIUM 40mg; CALC 111mg

Tropical Fruit Salad

Feel free to use this recipe as a general guide, substituting your favorite tropical fruit as desired. This is a good salad to pack for lunch or to take to a potluck supper. Just be sure to store the fruit mixture and the dressing separately and toss them together just before serving.

- 2 cups (1-inch) cubed fresh pineapple
- 1 cup chopped peeled papaya or mango
- 1 cup sliced peeled kiwifruit (about 3 large)
- 1 cup red seedless grapes
- ⅔ cup (¼-inch-thick) slices carambola (star fruit; about 1)
- ¼ cup flaked sweetened coconut
- 3 tablespoons honey
- 2 tablespoons fresh lime juice

1. Combine first 6 ingredients in a medium bowl. Cover and chill at least 30 minutes.
2. Combine honey and lime juice in a small bowl; toss with fruit just before serving. Yield: 6 servings (serving size: 1 cup).

CALORIES 128 (13% from fat); FAT 1.9g (sat 1.3g, mono 0.1g, poly 0.2g); PROTEIN 1.1g; CARB 29.7g; FIBER 2.9g; CHOL 0mg; IRON 0.6mg; SODIUM 14mg; CALC 24mg

About Carambola

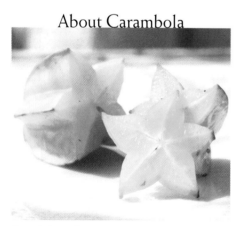

Carambola is often referred to as star fruit because its small oval body has five deep grooves running its length; when cut crosswise, it looks like a star. The tropical carambola has a waxy skin that's bright yellow and a sweet to tart yellow flesh that tastes like a combination of lemon, pineapple, and apple. When ripe, the carambola is juicy and fragrant. Choose carambola that are firm to the touch and have an even golden color. Avoid those with green on the ribs.

Iceberg Wedge with Pancetta

Pancetta—Italian bacon that has been cured but not smoked—updates this classic salad. You can use regular bacon in its place. Serve with a fork and knife to cut up the iceberg wedge.

- Cooking spray
- 1 ounce pancetta, diced (about 3 tablespoons)
- 1 head iceberg lettuce
- ½ cup Chive-Buttermilk Dressing
- 1 cup chopped tomato
- ½ cup diced English cucumber

1. Heat a nonstick skillet over medium-high heat; coat pan with cooking spray. Add pancetta to pan; cook 3 minutes or until crisp. Drain pancetta on paper towels.
2. Cut lettuce head in half; cut each half into 2 wedges. Place wedges on 4 salad plates. Drizzle with Chive-Buttermilk Dressing; top with tomato and cucumber. Sprinkle evenly with pancetta. Yield: 4 servings (serving size: 1 lettuce wedge, 2 tablespoons dressing, ¼ cup tomato, 2 tablespoons cucumber, and about 2 teaspoons pancetta).

(Totals include Chive-Buttermilk Dressing) CALORIES 80 (44% from fat); FAT 3.9g (sat 1.4g, mono 0g, poly 0.2g); PROTEIN 3.6g; CARB 9g; FIBER 2.3g; CHOL 5mg; IRON 0.7mg; SODIUM 331mg; CALC 60mg

CHIVE-BUTTERMILK DRESSING:

- ¾ cup fat-free buttermilk
- ⅓ cup light mayonnaise
- 2 to 3 teaspoons finely chopped fresh chives
- 1 teaspoon finely chopped fresh basil
- 2 teaspoons Dijon mustard
- ½ teaspoon coarsely ground black pepper
- ¼ teaspoon salt
- 1 garlic clove, minced

1. Combine all ingredients in a medium bowl, stirring with a whisk until well blended. Yield: 1 cup (serving size: 1 tablespoon).

CALORIES 13 (48% from fat); FAT 0.7g (sat 0.2g, mono 0g, poly 0g); PROTEIN 0.5g; CARB 1.4g; FIBER 0g; CHOL 0mg; IRON 0mg; SODIUM 99mg; CALC 15mg

Iceberg Wedge with Pancetta

Mixed Greens with Roasted Tomato and Goat Cheese

After roasting, the grape tomatoes will be absolutely bursting with a tart sweetness that's the focal point of this salad. Use your favorite salad greens for this tasty first course.

1 cup grape or cherry tomatoes, halved
¼ cup Maple-Balsamic Dressing, divided
Cooking spray
8 cups loosely packed baby arugula, watercress, or spinach (about 4 ounces)
¼ cup thinly vertically sliced red onion
2 tablespoons crumbled goat cheese
¼ teaspoon freshly ground black pepper

1. Preheat oven to 350°.
2. Combine tomatoes and 2 tablespoons Maple-Balsamic Dressing; toss well to coat. Arrange tomatoes, cut sides up, on a jelly-roll pan coated with cooking spray. Bake at 350° for 30 minutes or until tomatoes soften. Cool completely.
3. Combine tomatoes, arugula, and onion in a large bowl. Drizzle with remaining 2 tablespoons Maple-Balsamic Dressing; toss gently to coat. Divide salad among 6 plates. Sprinkle with cheese and pepper. Yield: 6 servings (serving size: about 1⅓ cups salad and 1 teaspoon cheese).

(Totals include Maple-Balsamic Dressing) CALORIES 47 (44% from fat); FAT 2.3g (sat 0.6g, mono 1.3g, poly 0.3g); PROTEIN 1.5g; CARB 6g; FIBER 0.9g; CHOL 1mg; IRON 0.7mg; SODIUM 97mg; CALC 54mg

MAPLE-BALSAMIC DRESSING:

½ cup tomato juice
⅓ cup balsamic vinegar
¼ cup maple syrup
1 tablespoon minced fresh rosemary
2 teaspoons Dijon mustard
½ teaspoon salt
½ teaspoon freshly ground black pepper
2 garlic cloves, minced
2½ tablespoons extravirgin olive oil

1. Combine all ingredients except oil, stirring well. Gradually add oil, stirring constantly with a whisk until mixture is well combined. Yield: about 1 cup (serving size: 1 tablespoon).
NOTE: Refrigerate dressing in an airtight container up to 5 days; stir well before using.

CALORIES 39 (53% from fat); FAT 2.3g (sat 0.3g, mono 1.7g, poly 0.2g); PROTEIN 0.2g; CARB 4.7g; FIBER 0.1g; CHOL 0mg; IRON 0.2mg; SODIUM 118mg; CALC 8mg

Caesar Salad with Crisp Croutons

Crispy croutons and Mediterranean flavors make Caesar salad hard to turn down, even if it usually comes with enough fat and cholesterol to fill a Roman coliseum. Not so with this lightened version. Tangy and tasty, it has all the zing of the classic minus the unhealthy elements. Unlike the traditional Caesar salad that sports raw egg—a real food safety no-no—our updated version uses egg substitute which is a pasteurized product.

¼ cup egg substitute
1 tablespoon fresh lemon juice
3 tablespoons extravirgin olive oil
3 tablespoons red wine vinegar
1½ teaspoons anchovy paste
1 teaspoon Worcestershire sauce
½ teaspoon freshly ground black pepper
¼ teaspoon fine sea salt
2 garlic cloves, minced
18 cups torn romaine and hearty field greens
2 cups Crisp Croutons
¼ cup (1 ounce) shredded fresh Parmesan cheese

1. Combine egg substitute and juice; gradually add oil, whisking constantly. Stir in vinegar and next 5 ingredients. Place greens, croutons, and cheese in a large bowl. Add dressing; toss well to coat. Yield: 12 servings (serving size 1½ cups).

(Totals include Crisp Croutons) CALORIES 75 (48% from fat); FAT 4.4g (sat 0.9g, mono 2.8g, poly 0.5g); PROTEIN 3g; CARB 6g; FIBER 2g; CHOL 2mg; IRON 2mg; SODIUM 210mg; CALC 63mg

CRISP CROUTONS:

1. Preheat oven to 350°.
2. Combine 6 cups (½-inch) cubed sourdough or French bread; 1 tablespoon butter, melted; 1 teaspoon paprika; and 1 teaspoon onion powder in a jelly-roll pan; toss well. Bake at 350° for 20 minutes or until toasted, turning once. Yield: 6 cups (serving size: ½ cup).

CALORIES 24 (26% from fat); FAT 0.7g (sat 0.4g, mono 0.2g, poly 0.1g); PROTEIN 0.7g; CARB 4g; FIBER 0.2g; CHOL 1mg; IRON 0.2mg; SODIUM 48mg; CALC 6mg

Roasted Squash Salad with Bacon and Pumpkin Seeds

A warm bacon-shallot vinaigrette is a savory complement to sweet roasted squash, while the pumpkin seeds are a crunchy contrast. Serve with pork chops or add grilled chicken.

 4 cups (½-inch) cubed peeled butternut squash
    (about 1 pound)
  Cooking spray
 ½ teaspoon salt, divided
 ½ teaspoon freshly ground black pepper, divided
 2 tablespoons sherry vinegar
 1 teaspoon Dijon mustard
 1 bacon slice
 1 shallot, minced
 10 cups gourmet salad greens (about 10 ounces)
 3 tablespoons unsalted pumpkin-seed kernels,
    toasted

1. Preheat oven to 400°.
2. Arrange squash in a single layer on a jelly-roll pan coated with cooking spray. Coat squash with cooking spray; sprinkle evenly with ¼ teaspoon salt and ¼ teaspoon pepper. Bake at 400° for 30 minutes or until squash is tender and lightly browned, stirring after 15 minutes. Remove squash from oven; keep warm.
3. Combine remaining ¼ teaspoon salt, remaining ¼ teaspoon pepper, vinegar, and mustard.
4. Cook bacon in a small nonstick skillet over medium-high heat until crisp. Remove bacon from pan, reserving 1 teaspoon drippings in pan. Crumble bacon; set aside. Add minced shallot to drippings in pan, and sauté 1 minute. Add shallot and bacon to vinegar mixture, stirring with a whisk.
5. Place salad greens in a large serving bowl. Drizzle vinegar mixture over greens; toss gently to coat. Top with squash and pumpkin-seed kernels. Yield: 6 servings (serving size: 1⅓ cups salad, ⅔ cup squash, and 1½ teaspoons kernels).

CALORIES 130 (25% from fat); FAT 3.6g (sat 0.9g, mono 0.9g, poly 1.2g); PROTEIN 4.8g; CARB 23.8g; FIBER 5.5g; CHOL 2mg; IRON 3.2mg; SODIUM 275mg; CALC 134mg

Jícama-Avocado Salad with Pomegranate-Lime Dressing

2 tablespoons fresh lime juice
2 tablespoons fresh pomegranate juice
1 teaspoon sugar
¾ teaspoon salt
¼ teaspoon ground cumin
1 small garlic clove, minced
1 teaspoon olive oil
2 cups arugula leaves
1½ cups (3-inch) julienne-cut peeled jícama
½ cup vertically sliced red onion
½ cup diced peeled avocado
2 tablespoons chopped fresh cilantro
¼ cup fresh pomegranate seeds
4 teaspoons pine nuts, toasted

1. Combine first 6 ingredients in a large bowl. Add oil, and stir with a whisk. Add arugula and next 4 ingredients; toss gently. Divide salad among 4 salad plates. Top with pomegranate seeds and pine nuts. Serve immediately. Yield: 4 servings (serving size: 1 cup salad, 1 tablespoon pomegranate seeds, and 1 teaspoon pine nuts).

CALORIES 126 (44% from fat); FAT 6.1g (sat 0.8g, mono 3.1g, poly 1.5g); PROTEIN 1.8g; CARB 18.7g; FIBER 4g; CHOL 0mg; IRON 1mg; SODIUM 444mg; CALC 32mg

Frisée, Baby Spinach, and Golden Beet Salad

Goat cheese and cranberries bring a bit of tartness to the mellow sweetness of roasted beets. Raspberry vinegar and walnut oil are not common pantry items, but the flavor they bring to the dressing makes them well worth buying.

¾ pound golden beets
1 cup cranberry juice cocktail
⅓ cup sweetened dried cranberries
3 tablespoons sugar
2 tablespoons raspberry vinegar
1 tablespoon minced shallots
¼ teaspoon salt
¼ teaspoon freshly ground black pepper
1 tablespoon walnut oil
4 cups frisée or radicchio
4 cups baby spinach
½ cup (2 ounces) crumbled soft (log-style) goat cheese

1. Preheat oven to 400°.
2. Wrap each beet in foil. Bake at 400° for 1½ hours or until tender. Discard foil; cool beets 30 minutes. Trim off roots, and rub off skins. Cut beets into ⅛-inch-thick slices.
3. Combine cranberry juice, cranberries, sugar, and vinegar in a small saucepan. Bring to a boil; cook 11 minutes or until thick. Remove from heat. Stir in shallots, salt, and pepper. Gradually add oil, stirring with a whisk.
4. Combine frisée and spinach in a large bowl. Add cranberry mixture, and toss to coat. Add beets; toss gently to combine. Divide salad among 6 salad plates. Top with cheese. Yield: 6 servings (serving size: about 1½ cups salad and 4 teaspoons cheese).

CALORIES 175 (28% from fat); FAT 5.4g (sat 2.2g, mono 1.2g, poly 1.6g); PROTEIN 4.2g; CARB 28.7g; FIBER 3.3g; CHOL 7mg; IRON 1.7mg; SODIUM 214mg; CALC 74mg

Fennel, Parsley, and Radicchio Salad with Pine Nuts and Raisins

⅓ cup golden raisins
4 cups thinly sliced fennel bulb (about 1 large bulb)
4 cups torn radicchio (about 1 medium head)
1½ cups loosely packed fresh flat-leaf parsley leaves
¼ cup fresh orange juice
1½ tablespoons red wine vinegar
2 teaspoons extravirgin olive oil
½ teaspoon salt
¼ teaspoon freshly ground black pepper
2 tablespoons pine nuts, toasted

1. Place raisins in a small saucepan, and cover with water. Bring to a boil; remove from heat. Cover and let stand 10 minutes. Drain well.
2. Place fennel, radicchio, and parsley in a large bowl, and toss gently to combine. Combine orange juice and next 4 ingredients, stirring well with a whisk. Stir in raisins. Drizzle orange juice mixture over fennel mixture, and toss gently to coat. Divide salad among 6 salad plates, and sprinkle with nuts. Yield: 6 servings (serving size: 1⅓ cups salad and 1 teaspoon nuts).

CALORIES 91 (38% from fat); FAT 3.8g (sat 0.4g, mono 1.7g, poly 1.2g); PROTEIN 2.3g; CARB 14.3g; FIBER 3g; CHOL 0mg; IRON 1.9mg; SODIUM 243mg; CALC 61mg

Fennel, Parsley, and Radicchio Salad
with Pine Nuts and Raisins

Watercress Salad with
Blue Cheese and Praline

Watercress Salad with Blue Cheese and Praline

A dash of tarragon imparts a delicate licorice flavor to the light lemony dressing. Peppery watercress and buttery-textured Boston lettuce make a fitting bed for the pungent cheese and sweet praline pieces.

DRESSING:
- 1 tablespoon water
- 1½ teaspoons fresh lemon juice
- 1 teaspoon Dijon mustard
- ½ teaspoon extravirgin olive oil
- ⅛ teaspoon black pepper
- Dash of salt
- Dash of dried tarragon
- 1 small garlic clove, minced

PRALINE:
- ¼ cup sugar
- 2 tablespoons chopped walnuts
- Cooking spray

SALAD:
- 1 cup trimmed watercress
- 1 cup Boston lettuce leaves
- 1 tablespoon crumbled blue cheese or feta cheese

1. To prepare dressing, combine first 8 ingredients; stir well with a whisk.

2. To prepare praline, place sugar in a small skillet over medium heat, and cook until sugar dissolves, stirring to dissolve sugar evenly. Stir in chopped walnuts, and cook over low heat 30 seconds or until golden. Remove from heat. Rapidly spread mixture onto foil coated with cooking spray. Cool completely; break into small pieces.

3. To prepare salad, combine watercress, lettuce, and blue cheese in a bowl; add dressing and praline, tossing well. Yield: 2 servings (serving size: 1½ cups).

CALORIES 180 (34% from fat); FAT 6.8g (sat 1.1g, mono 2.1g, poly 3.1g); PROTEIN 3.6g; CARB 28g; FIBER 1.4g; CHOL 3mg; IRON 0.7mg; SODIUM 280mg; CALC 58mg

Autumn Apple and Spinach Salad

Crisp sweet-tart apples are an ideal complement to the intense flavor and creamy texture of blue cheese. Try Goldrush or Braeburn apples, which both have a nice balance of sweetness and acidity.

- 2 tablespoons fresh orange juice
- 2 tablespoons fresh lime juice
- 2 teaspoons Dijon mustard
- 2 teaspoons honey
- ¼ teaspoon salt
- ⅛ teaspoon freshly ground black pepper
- 8 cups bagged prewashed baby spinach (about 8 ounces)
- ½ cup thinly vertically sliced red onion
- 1 large firm sweet-tart apple, cored and thinly sliced
- ¼ cup (1 ounce) crumbled blue cheese

1. Combine first 6 ingredients, stirring well with a whisk.

2. Combine spinach, onion, and apple in a large bowl. Drizzle with dressing; toss gently to coat. Sprinkle with cheese. Yield: 6 servings (serving size: about 1⅓ cups).

CALORIES 60 (29% from fat); FAT 1.9g (sat 1g, mono 0.5g, poly 0.1g); PROTEIN 2.7g; CARB 9.4g; FIBER 2.2g; CHOL 4mg; IRON 1.3mg; SODIUM 251mg; CALC 76mg

Stone Fruit Salad with Toasted Almonds

This salad was inspired by summer's abundance of stone fruits. A white-wine reduction marries the sweet flavors of the fruit to the vinaigrette. Fresh goat cheese adds a savory note.

    1   cup sweet riesling or other sweet white wine
    1   tablespoon white wine vinegar
    1   tablespoon almond oil
    ¼   teaspoon salt
    ⅛   teaspoon black pepper
    8   cups mixed salad greens
    3   plums, sliced
    2   peaches, peeled and sliced
    2   nectarines, peeled and sliced
    2   apricots, peeled and sliced
    ¾   cup pitted cherries, halved
    ¼   cup (1 ounce) crumbled goat cheese
    2   tablespoons sliced almonds, toasted

1. Heat wine in a medium saucepan over medium-high heat until reduced to 2 tablespoons (about 10 minutes). Remove from heat; stir in vinegar, oil, salt, and pepper.

2. To serve salad, toss salad greens and fruit with dressing. Divide salad among 6 salad bowls. Sprinkle with cheese and almonds. Serve immediately. Yield: 6 servings (serving size: 1¼ cups salad, 2 teaspoons cheese, and 1 teaspoon almonds).

CALORIES 147 (31% from fat); FAT 5.1g (sat 1.3g, mono 2.6g, poly 0.8g); PROTEIN 3.9g; CARB 24g; FIBER 4g; CHOL 4mg; IRON 1.6mg; SODIUM 141mg; CALC 64mg

Three-Pepper Slaw

For convenience, we used packaged angel hair coleslaw. If you prefer, use a very sharp chef's knife or mandoline to cut a head of cabbage into very thin strips. The sliced cabbage will resemble angel hair pasta, which explains the coleslaw's name. This quick and easy crunchy slaw goes well with grilled meats and Tex-Mex dishes.

    ½   cup thinly sliced red bell pepper strips
    ½   cup thinly sliced green bell pepper strips
    ⅓   cup chopped green onions
    ¼   cup finely chopped seeded jalapeño pepper
    1   (10-ounce) package angel hair coleslaw
         (about 6 cups)
    ¼   cup white wine vinegar
    2   tablespoons fresh lime juice
    1   teaspoon sugar
    2   teaspoons canola oil
    ½   teaspoon salt
    ¼   teaspoon white pepper

1. Place first 5 ingredients in a large bowl, tossing to combine.

2. Combine vinegar and next 5 ingredients in a small bowl, stirring with a whisk. Pour vinegar mixture over coleslaw mixture, tossing to coat. Yield: 8 servings (serving size: about ¾ cup).

CALORIES 29 (39% from fat); FAT 1.3g (sat 0.1g, mono 0.7g, poly 0.4g); PROTEIN 0.8g; CARB 4.5g; FIBER 0.2g; CHOL 0mg; IRON 0.3mg; SODIUM 153mg; CALC 21mg

About White Pepper

White pepper is ground white peppercorns, which are the mature, hulled berries of the Piper nigrum vine. (Black and green peppercorns, on the other hand, are picked while still immature.) White pepper has a pungent flavor but is milder than black pepper. Whole white peppercorns are often used in marinades and as a pickling spice. Ground white pepper is useful for seasoning light-colored foods, such as mashed potatoes or this slaw, without discoloring them.

Three-Pepper Slaw

Mixed Bean Salad with
Sun-Dried Tomatoes

Mixed Bean Salad with Sun-Dried Tomatoes

1 (8-ounce) jar oil-packed sun-dried tomato halves
½ cup chopped fresh parsley
½ cup chopped fresh basil
1 (15.8-ounce) can black-eyed peas, rinsed and drained
1 (15-ounce) can red kidney beans, rinsed and drained
1 (15-ounce) can white kidney beans, rinsed and drained
1 (15-ounce) can black beans, rinsed and drained
½ red onion, thinly sliced
⅓ cup red wine vinegar
¼ cup sugar
½ teaspoon salt
½ teaspoon dry mustard
¼ teaspoon freshly ground black pepper

1. Drain tomato halves in a sieve over a bowl, reserving oil. Place ¼ cup oil in a medium bowl. Return remaining oil to jar; refrigerate and reserve for another use.

2. Chop drained tomatoes; place in a large bowl. Add parsley and next 6 ingredients, and stir gently to combine.

3. Add vinegar and next 4 ingredients to ¼ cup reserved oil, stirring with a whisk. Drizzle over bean mixture; toss gently to coat. Cover and chill. Yield: 14 servings (serving size: ½ cup).

CALORIES 181 (28% from fat); FAT 5.7g (sat 0.7g, mono 3.6g, poly 0.9g); PROTEIN 7.2g; CARB 26.2g; FIBER 4.4g; CHOL 0mg; IRON 2.5mg; SODIUM 417mg; CALC 100mg

Peanutty Cabbage-Apple Slaw with Raisins

In this unique coleslaw, sweet raisins offer a surprising contrast to the crisp, tart Granny Smith apples.

⅓ cup white balsamic or cider vinegar
¼ cup packed brown sugar
1½ tablespoons roasted peanut oil
½ teaspoon salt
¼ teaspoon crushed red pepper
3 cups coarsely chopped Granny Smith apple
½ cup golden seedless raisins
1 (16-ounce) package cabbage-and-carrot coleslaw

1. Combine first 5 ingredients, stirring with a whisk until sugar dissolves.

2. Combine apple, raisins, and coleslaw. Drizzle with vinaigrette; toss well to combine. Cover and chill up to 3 hours. Yield: 8 servings (serving size: about 1 cup).

CALORIES 128 (20% from fat); FAT 2.9g (sat 0.5g, mono 1.2g, poly 0.9g); PROTEIN 1.2g; CARB 26.7g; FIBER 3.1g; CHOL 0mg; IRON 0.8mg; SODIUM 167mg; CALC 40mg

Multibean Salad

This updated take on three-bean salad is lower in sodium than traditional bean salads because it uses fresh beans instead of canned. Plus, edamame is a better source of protein than other beans. Try it as a flavorful side to a sandwich in lieu of chips.

2 cups (½-inch) diagonally cut haricots verts (about 8 ounces)
2 cups (½-inch) diagonally cut wax beans (about 8 ounces)
1 cup frozen shelled edamame (green soybeans)
1 cup grape or cherry tomatoes, halved
½ cup finely chopped orange bell pepper
½ cup thinly sliced red onion
2 tablespoons sherry vinegar
½ teaspoon sugar
¼ teaspoon Dijon mustard
2 teaspoons extravirgin olive oil
¼ cup chopped fresh parsley
¼ teaspoon salt
¼ teaspoon freshly ground black pepper

1. Steam first 3 ingredients, covered, 6 minutes or until haricots verts and wax beans are crisp-tender. Drain and plunge beans into ice water; drain. Combine beans, tomato halves, bell pepper, and onion in a large bowl.

2. Combine vinegar, sugar, and mustard, stirring with a whisk. Gradually add oil to vinegar mixture, stirring constantly with a whisk. Stir in parsley, salt, and black pepper. Drizzle vinaigrette over bean mixture; toss gently to coat. Yield: 6 servings (serving size: about 1 cup).

CALORIES 85 (29% from fat); FAT 2.7g (sat 0.2g, mono 1.1g, poly 0.2g); PROTEIN 4.4g; CARB 11g; FIBER 4g; CHOL 0mg; IRON 1.5mg; SODIUM 125mg; CALC 48mg

Mexican Corn Salad

For a quick make-ahead salad that tastes like it's fresh from the garden, toss thawed frozen corn with cilantro, red onion, jalapeño, and lime juice. Serve this salad alongside Tex-Mex fare or at a cookout.

- 1 (16-ounce) package frozen shoepeg white corn, thawed
- ½ cup chopped fresh cilantro
- ½ cup finely chopped red onion
- ¼ cup fresh lime juice
- 2 tablespoons minced seeded jalapeño pepper (about 1 large)
- 1 tablespoon olive oil
- ½ teaspoon salt
- ¼ teaspoon ground cumin
- ¼ teaspoon chili powder
- ¼ teaspoon black pepper
- 2 garlic cloves, minced, or 2 teaspoons bottled minced garlic

1. Combine all ingredients in a bowl; toss well. Cover and chill 8 to 24 hours. Stir well before serving. Yield: 6 servings (serving size: ½ cup).

CALORIES 112 (25% from fat); FAT 3.1g (sat 0.3g, mono 1.7g, poly 0.3g); PROTEIN 2.8g; CARB 19.1g; FIBER 2.8g; CHOL 0mg; IRON 0.2mg; SODIUM 199mg; CALC 8mg

About Cilantro

Cilantro, with its distinctive grassy flavor, is the green leaves of the coriander plant, which also gives us coriander seeds. Cilantro is part of the cuisines of Cambodia, India, Mexico, and Israel. It has gained popularity in American kitchens as a key element of Mexican fare. Cilantro has health benefits as well as taste: A tablespoon of cilantro jazzes up a dish while adding less than one calorie and offering a good bit of vitamin A. The best way to distinguish cilantro from fresh flat-leaf parsley is to press a leaf between your fingers. You should quickly detect the more pungent, distinct flavor of the cilantro.

Roasted Beet Salad with Tarragon Vinaigrette

Roasting brings out the natural sweetness of beets, which is balanced here with an herb vinaigrette. While we used rich-colored, golden beets for this flavorful salad, any color of beet will work. Beets tend to bleed, so if you're using more than one color, keep them in separate bowls until you're ready to toss together all the ingredients.

- 3 pounds golden beets
- ¼ cup olive oil, divided
- 2 tablespoons minced garlic, divided
- 1½ teaspoons chopped fresh thyme, divided
- 1½ teaspoons minced fresh tarragon, divided
- 1 teaspoon salt, divided
- 1 teaspoon black pepper, divided
- 1 cup red wine vinegar
- ¼ cup sugar
- 2 tablespoons finely chopped shallots
- ½ teaspoon chopped fresh oregano
- 2 cups vertically sliced red onion

1. Preheat oven to 350°.

2. Leave root and 1 inch of stem on beets; scrub with a brush. Place beets, 2 tablespoons oil, 1 tablespoon garlic, 1 teaspoon thyme, and 1 teaspoon tarragon in a large bowl; toss gently. Place beet mixture on a jelly-roll pan. Bake at 350° for 1 hour or until beets are tender. Drain; cool slightly. Trim off beet roots; rub off skins. Cut beets in half, and place in a large bowl. Sprinkle with ½ teaspoon salt and ½ teaspoon pepper, tossing gently.

3. Combine vinegar, sugar, shallots, oregano, 2 tablespoons oil, 1 tablespoon garlic, ½ teaspoon thyme, ½ teaspoon tarragon, ½ teaspoon salt, and ½ teaspoon pepper in a small bowl, stirring with a whisk. Add vinegar mixture and onion to beet mixture; toss gently. Yield: 8 servings (serving size: about ½ cup).

CALORIES 146 (22% from fat); FAT 3.7g (sat 0.5g, mono 2.6g, poly 0.5g); PROTEIN 3.3g; CARB 26.9g; FIBER 5.3g; CHOL 0mg; IRON 1.8mg; SODIUM 428mg; CALC 43mg

Roasted Beet Salad with
Tarragon Vinaigrette

Classic Potato Salad

There are no surprises here—just good old-fashioned comfort food. We left the skins on the potatoes for extra fiber, but you can peel them if you choose. Serve this alongside ham for Easter or with burgers for the Fourth of July. And, of course, it will be welcome on the table any other time of year, too.

1½ pounds baking potatoes, halved
½ cup finely chopped red onion
¼ cup finely chopped celery
¼ cup sweet pickle relish
2 hard-cooked large eggs, coarsely chopped
⅓ cup light mayonnaise
2 tablespoons cider vinegar
1 tablespoon Dijon mustard
¼ teaspoon salt
¼ teaspoon black pepper

1. Cook potatoes in boiling water 25 minutes or until tender; drain and cool completely.
2. Cut potatoes into ½-inch cubes. Combine potato, onion, and next 3 ingredients in a large bowl. Combine mayonnaise and next 4 ingredients in a small bowl; stir with a whisk. Pour mayonnaise mixture over potato mixture, tossing gently to coat. Cover and chill at least 8 hours. Yield: 6 servings (serving size: ¾ cup).

CALORIES 208 (25% from fat); FAT 5.7g (sat 1.1g, mono 1.7g, poly 2.2g); PROTEIN 5g; CARB 35.1g; FIBER 2.4g; CHOL 75mg; IRON 1.9mg; SODIUM 387mg; CALC 26mg

Red, White, and Blue Potato Salad

This recipe uses a trio of potatoes, but use all of one type or other varieties if you prefer. If your potatoes are larger than the ones we call for, cut them to a uniform size. Blue potatoes tend to bleed, so cook them separately. If you prepare this dish a day ahead, add the blue potatoes just before serving.

2 cups fingerling potatoes, halved lengthwise (about 10 ounces)
2 cups small red potatoes, quartered (about 10 ounces)
2 cups small blue potatoes, halved lengthwise (about 10 ounces)
¼ cup finely chopped red onion
2 tablespoons chopped fresh parsley
1 tablespoon chopped fresh dill
1 tablespoon chopped fresh chives
3 hard-cooked large eggs, finely chopped
¼ cup red wine vinegar
2 tablespoons olive oil
2 teaspoons Dijon mustard
1¼ teaspoons salt
½ teaspoon freshly ground black pepper
1 garlic clove, minced
Parsley sprig (optional)

1. Place fingerling and red potatoes in a saucepan; cover with water. Bring potatoes to a boil. Reduce heat; simmer 15 minutes or until tender. Drain; cool slightly. Place cooked potatoes in a large bowl.
2. Place blue potatoes in a saucepan; cover with water. Bring to a boil. Reduce heat; simmer 10 minutes or until tender. Drain; cool slightly. Add blue potatoes, onion, and next 4 ingredients to fingerling and red potatoes in bowl; toss gently.
3. Combine vinegar and next 5 ingredients. Pour over potato mixture; toss gently to combine. Serve warm, at room temperature, or chilled. Garnish with a parsley sprig, if desired. Yield: 6 servings (serving size: 1 cup).

CALORIES 250 (27% from fat); FAT 7.5g (sat 1.5g, mono 4.4g, poly 0.9g); PROTEIN 6.9g; CARB 39.6g; FIBER 3.9g; CHOL 106mg; IRON 2.7mg; SODIUM 576mg; CALC 36mg

Insalata Caprese

The acidity of vine-ripened tomatoes, the mellow sweetness of mozzarella cheese, and the refreshing, slightly minty flavor of fresh basil harmonize in this simple salad. For the best flavor, let the salad come to room temperature before serving. Serve with a side of crusty bread to soak up the juices that remain on the bottom of the plate. This colorful presentation from the island of Capri will add visual intrigue to your seasonal table, delighting both the eye and the palate.

2 large red tomatoes, each cut into 4 slices
2 large yellow tomatoes, each cut into 4 slices
6 (1-ounce) slices part-skim mozzarella cheese, each cut in half
12 large basil leaves
3 tablespoons fat-free balsamic vinaigrette
1 teaspoon freshly ground black pepper

1. Stack 4 tomato slices, 3 cheese slices, and 3 basil leaves in each of 4 stacks, alternating tomato, cheese, and basil. Drizzle stacks evenly with vinaigrette. Cover and chill. Sprinkle with pepper before serving. Yield: 4 servings (serving size: 1 salad).

CALORIES 172 (47% from fat); FAT 9g (sat 5.5g, mono 2.5g, poly 0.5g); PROTEIN 13g; CARB 11g; FIBER 2g; CHOL 23mg; IRON 1mg; SODIUM 404mg; CALC 336mg

Sweet-Spicy Cucumbers over Tomatoes

Make this flavorful salad when summer produce is readily available. Be sure to use pickling cucumbers, which are shorter and thinner-skinned than regular cucumbers. Though four days is the maximum time the cucumbers should marinate, the longer they soak in the vinegar mixture, the spicier and more garlicky they'll become.

2 cups thinly sliced pickling cucumber (about 2 cucumbers)
1 cup thinly sliced Vidalia or other sweet onion
½ cup cider vinegar
¼ cup sugar
½ teaspoon salt
½ teaspoon mustard seeds
4 garlic cloves, minced
2 whole dried hot red chiles
16 (¼-inch-thick) slices tomato
⅛ teaspoon salt
⅛ teaspoon freshly ground black pepper

1. Arrange half of cucumber in a 9-inch pie plate. Top with half of onion. Repeat layers with remaining cucumber and onion.

2. Combine vinegar and next 5 ingredients in a small saucepan. Bring to a boil; cook 1 minute or until sugar dissolves, stirring occasionally. Pour hot vinegar mixture over cucumber mixture. Cover; marinate in refrigerator 1 to 4 days.

3. Arrange tomato slices on a platter; sprinkle evenly with ⅛ teaspoon salt and black pepper. Remove cucumber mixture from marinade with a slotted spoon; arrange over tomato slices. Yield: 8 servings (serving size: 2 tomato slices and about ⅓ cup cucumber mixture).

CALORIES 32 (6% from fat); FAT 0.2g (sat 0g, mono 0g, poly 0.1g); PROTEIN 0.8g; CARB 7.7g; FIBER 1g; CHOL 0mg; IRON 0.4mg; SODIUM 115mg; CALC 11mg

Greek Spaghetti Squash Salad

The bold flavor components of a traditional Greek salad—feta cheese, kalamata olives, and oregano—are ideal components to mild spaghetti squash. This recipe stores well in the refrigerator for one to two days, and it's even better the second day. Serve with beef, lamb, or chicken.

    1 (3-pound) spaghetti squash
    5 cups chopped plum tomato
    1 cup (4 ounces) crumbled reduced-fat feta
       cheese
    1 cup chopped seeded cucumber
    1 cup green bell pepper strips
   ¼ cup vertically sliced red onion
   ¼ cup chopped pitted kalamata olives
    3 tablespoons sherry or red wine vinegar
    2 tablespoons chopped fresh or 2 teaspoons
       dried oregano
   ¼ teaspoon salt
   ¼ teaspoon freshly ground black pepper
    1 garlic clove, minced
   Fresh oregano leaves (optional)

1. Pierce squash with a fork; place on paper towels in microwave oven. Microwave at HIGH 15 minutes or until tender. Let stand 10 minutes. Cut squash in half lengthwise; discard seeds. Scrape inside of squash with a fork to remove spaghetti-like strands.
2. Combine cooked squash and next 6 ingredients in a large bowl, and toss well. Combine vinegar and next 4 ingredients, stirring with a whisk. Add to squash mixture, tossing to coat. Cover and chill. Garnish with fresh oregano leaves, if desired. Yield: 8 servings (serving size: 1¼ cups).

CALORIES 100 (37% from fat); FAT 4.1g (sat 1.7g, mono 0.1g, poly 0.5g); PROTEIN 4.7g; CARB 13.8g; FIBER 1.5g; CHOL 5mg; IRON 0.7mg; SODIUM 350mg; CALC 85mg

Lentil Salad

Crunchy vegetables, salty ripe olives, and tangy feta cheese are ideal companions to mellow lentils in this cool salad. If you prefer, you don't have to seed the tomato—seeding is for appearance only.

    4 cups water
    1 cup dried lentils
   ⅔ cup chopped onion
    1 cup chopped red bell pepper
    1 cup chopped green bell pepper
    1 cup chopped seeded tomato
   ⅓ cup sliced green onions
   ⅓ cup reduced-fat Italian salad dressing
    2 tablespoons fresh lemon juice
   ½ teaspoon black pepper
    1 (2¼-ounce) can sliced ripe olives, drained
    1 (4-ounce) package crumbled feta cheese with
       basil and sun-dried tomatoes

1. Combine 4 cups water, lentils, and onion in a large saucepan; bring to a boil. Cover, reduce heat, and simmer 15 minutes or just until lentils are tender; drain. Rinse under cold water; drain.
2. Combine lentil mixture, red bell pepper, and next 7 ingredients; toss well. Cover and chill at least 4 hours. Sprinkle with feta cheese. Yield: 5 servings (serving size: 1⅓ cups).

CALORIES 268 (32% from fat); FAT 9.5g (sat 3.3g, mono 1.1g, poly 0.4g); PROTEIN 15.2g; CARB 33.5g; FIBER 11.4g; CHOL 17mg; IRON 4.6mg; SODIUM 619mg; CALC 119mg

Barley "Pasta" Salad

Olive oil, tomato, bell pepper, cucumber, and cheese are common ingredients in a pasta salad, but we replaced the pasta with fiber-rich barley. This salad travels well and makes a tasty to-go lunch. Feel free to add or take out veggies to suit your taste.

 2 cups water
 ½ cup uncooked pearl barley
 2 tablespoons fresh lemon juice
 1 tablespoon olive oil
 ½ teaspoon salt
 2 cups finely chopped seeded tomato
 1 cup thinly sliced spinach
 ½ cup finely chopped green bell pepper
 ½ cup chopped peeled English cucumber
 ½ cup (2 ounces) diced part-skim mozzarella
     cheese
 ¼ cup finely chopped pepperoncini peppers
 2 teaspoons dried oregano

1. Bring 2 cups water to a boil in a large saucepan. Add barley; cover, reduce heat, and simmer 45 minutes. Drain and rinse with cold water; drain.
2. Combine lemon juice, oil, and salt in a large bowl; stir well with a whisk. Add barley, tomato, and remaining ingredients, and toss gently to coat. Yield: 5 servings (serving size: about 1 cup).

CALORIES 153 (31% from fat); FAT 5.2g (sat 1.6g, mono 2.6g, poly 0.6g); PROTEIN 6g; CARB 22.4g; FIBER 5g; CHOL 7mg; IRON 1.8mg; SODIUM 436mg; CALC 107mg

Layered Tabbouleh

 1 cup uncooked medium bulgur
 ¾ cup fresh lemon juice (about 4 large lemons)
 2 tablespoons extravirgin olive oil
 1¾ teaspoons salt, divided
 3 garlic cloves, minced
 2 cups finely chopped red onion
 5 cups chopped tomato
 ½ cup chopped fresh parsley
 ½ cup chopped fresh mint
 ¼ cup chopped fresh dill
 2 cups chopped seeded peeled cucumber
 1 cup chopped red bell pepper
 ¼ teaspoon freshly ground black pepper

1. Place bulgur in a large bowl. Combine lemon juice, oil, 1 teaspoon salt, and garlic in a small bowl; stir well with a whisk. Drizzle juice mixture over bulgur.
2. Layer onion, tomato, parsley, mint, dill, cucumber, and bell pepper evenly over bulgur mixture. Sprinkle with remaining ¾ teaspoon salt and black pepper. Cover with plastic wrap; refrigerate at least 24 hours or up to 48 hours. Toss salad well before serving. Yield: 8 servings (serving size: 1 cup).

CALORIES 148 (26% from fat); FAT 4.2g (sat 0.6g, mono 2.6g, poly 0.6g); PROTEIN 4.3g; CARB 26.9g; FIBER 6.1g; CHOL 0mg; IRON 1.6mg; SODIUM 532mg; CALC 40mg

About Bulgur

Bulgur comes from wheat berries (kernels of wheat) that have been steamed, dried, and then cracked. It comes in three types of grinds—coarse, medium, and fine. Medium-grind is an all-purpose size that's good for salads (like this tabbouleh), soups, stews, and multigrain baked goods, as well as meatless burgers and chili. You can find bulgur at most supermarkets or in Middle Eastern markets and natural-food stores.

Layered Tabbouleh

Spelt Salad with Fava Beans

Spelt Salad with Fava Beans

This hearty grain salad is full of fresh summer flavors. Once shelled, the fava beans must be removed from their tough outer skins. Blanching the beans makes the skins easier to remove. Just pinch the cooled beans, and the skins will slip off. Lima beans and edamame are good substitutes for the fava beans.

    1   cup uncooked spelt or wheat berries
    4   cups water
    2   cups shelled unpeeled fava beans (about
        2 pounds whole pods)
    ½   cup chopped drained oil-packed sun-dried
        tomato halves
    ½   cup diced celery
    ⅓   cup dried currants
    3   tablespoons balsamic vinegar
    1   tablespoon extravirgin olive oil
    ½   teaspoon salt
    ½   teaspoon freshly ground black pepper
    2   garlic cloves, crushed
    ¼   cup chopped fresh parsley

1. Place spelt in a large saucepan; cover with water to 2 inches above spelt. Bring to a boil. Cover, reduce heat, and simmer 1½ hours or until spelt is tender. Drain.

2. Bring 4 cups water to a boil in a medium saucepan. Add fava beans; cook 2 minutes. Drain and rinse beans with cold water; drain. Remove and discard tough outer skins from beans.

3. Combine spelt, fava beans, tomato, celery, and currants in a large bowl. Combine vinegar and next 4 ingredients, stirring with a whisk. Drizzle over spelt mixture, and toss well to coat. Sprinkle with parsley. Yield: 6 servings (serving size: 1 cup).

CALORIES 190 (22% from fat); FAT 4.6g (sat 0.5g, mono 2.5g, poly 0.5g); PROTEIN 6.2g; CARB 35.4g; FIBER 2.9g; CHOL 0mg; IRON 2.8mg; SODIUM 252mg; CALC 40mg

Cuban Beans and Rice Salad

This recipe can be prepared quickly and is a great side for a barbecue or picnic. Use leftover white rice if you have it.

    ½   cup diced peeled avocado
    2   tablespoons balsamic vinegar
    1   tablespoon olive oil
    1   teaspoon ground cumin
    ½   teaspoon salt
    ¼   teaspoon black pepper
    3   cups cooked white rice
    1   cup chopped seeded plum tomato (about
        3 tomatoes)
    ¼   cup minced fresh parsley
    1   (15-ounce) can black beans, rinsed and
        drained
    2   tablespoons minced fresh cilantro (optional)

1. Combine first 6 ingredients in a bowl, and toss gently. Add rice, next 3 ingredients, and cilantro, if desired; toss well. Serve chilled or at room temperature. Yield: 6 servings (serving size: 1 cup).

CALORIES 184 (23% from fat); FAT 4.6g (sat 0.7g, mono 3g, poly 0.5g); PROTEIN 4.9g; CARB 32.8g; FIBER 4g; CHOL 0mg; IRON 2.3mg; SODIUM 421mg; CALC 36mg

Greek Dinner Salad

This main-dish salad features traditional Greek ingredients, such as olive oil, lemon juice, oregano, cucumbers, tomatoes, and feta. However, it's also delicious if you try some variations—change the fresh herbs, beans, and cheese to use what you have on hand. For a heartier salad, add grilled chicken breast strips.

¼ cup coarsely chopped fresh parsley
3 tablespoons coarsely chopped fresh dill
1 tablespoon extravirgin olive oil
1 tablespoon fresh lemon juice
1 teaspoon dried oregano
6 cups shredded romaine lettuce
3 cups chopped tomato
1 cup thinly sliced red onion
¾ cup (3 ounces) crumbled feta cheese
1 tablespoon capers
1 cucumber, peeled, quartered lengthwise, and thinly sliced
1 (19-ounce) can chickpeas (garbanzo beans), rinsed and drained
6 (6-inch) whole wheat pitas, each cut into 8 wedges

1. Combine first 5 ingredients in a large bowl; stir with a whisk. Add lettuce and next 6 ingredients; toss well. Serve with pita wedges. Yield: 6 servings (serving size: 2 cups salad and 8 pita wedges).

CALORIES 388 (29% from fat); FAT 14.8g (sat 3.8g, mono 4.8g, poly 1.4g); PROTEIN 15.7g; CARB 64.9g; FIBER 11.4g; CHOL 17mg; IRON 4.8mg; SODIUM 779mg; CALC 173mg

Warm Asparagus Salad

For an outstanding springtime salad, drizzle fresh asparagus with a delicate vinaigrette made of olive oil, lemon juice, and lemon rind. Twice-baked garlicky breadcrumbs tossed in browned butter add a pleasant nuttiness that complements the garden-fresh flavor of the asparagus.

4 (½-ounce) slices day-old French bread or other firm white bread
1 garlic clove, peeled and halved
1 tablespoon unsalted butter
1 tablespoon white wine vinegar
1 teaspoon grated lemon rind
2 teaspoons fresh lemon juice
2 teaspoons extravirgin olive oil
1 shallot, peeled and minced
¼ teaspoon salt
¼ teaspoon freshly ground black pepper
1 cup water
1½ pounds asparagus
1 teaspoon grated lemon rind (optional)

1. Preheat oven to 375°.
2. Place bread in a single layer on a baking sheet. Bake at 375° for 10 minutes or until toasted. Rub cut sides of garlic over one side of each bread slice. Place bread slices in a food processor; pulse 10 times or until bread is coarsely ground. Arrange breadcrumbs in a single layer on baking sheet; bake at 375° for 5 minutes or until golden brown. Transfer breadcrumbs to a bowl.
3. Melt butter in a small saucepan over medium-high heat. Cook 1 to 2 minutes or until butter is lightly browned, shaking pan occasionally; remove from heat. Drizzle butter over toasted breadcrumbs; toss well to coat.
4. Combine vinegar and next 4 ingredients; stir well with a whisk. Stir in salt and pepper.
5. Bring water to a boil in a large skillet. Snap off tough ends of asparagus; add asparagus to pan. Cook 5 minutes or until tender, stirring constantly. Place asparagus on a serving platter; top with breadcrumb mixture. Garnish with 1 teaspoon grated lemon rind, if desired. Serve immediately with vinaigrette. Yield: 6 servings (serving size: ⅙ of asparagus salad and ½ tablespoon vinaigrette).

CALORIES 94 (36% from fat); FAT 3.8g (sat 1.3g, mono 2g, poly 0.4g); PROTEIN 4.1g; CARB 13.2g; FIBER 0.4g; CHOL 5mg; IRON 3mg; SODIUM 172mg; CALC 37mg

Greek Dinner Salad

Panzanella

Like many Italian dishes, *panzanella* (pahn-zah-NEHL-lah) was probably first made out of necessity—combining stale bread with readily available fresh garden vegetables. This classic bread salad, full of juicy tomatoes, is like summer on a plate. It's best when the toasted bread is still crisp, so serve immediately after tossing.

4   (1-ounce) slices Italian bread
Cooking spray
 1   cup torn fresh basil leaves
 ½   cup thinly sliced red onion
 ⅓   cup pitted kalamata olives, halved
 2   pounds ripe tomatoes, cored and cut into
      1-inch pieces
 1   (16-ounce) can cannellini beans or other
      white beans, rinsed and drained
 3   tablespoons red wine vinegar
 1   tablespoon water
 1   tablespoon extravirgin olive oil
 1   garlic clove, minced
 ½   teaspoon freshly ground black pepper
 ¼   teaspoon salt

1. Preheat oven to 350°.
2. Trim crusts from bread slices; discard crusts. Cut bread into 1-inch cubes. Arrange bread cubes in a single layer on a baking sheet; coat bread with cooking spray. Bake at 350° for 15 minutes or until toasted.
3. Combine basil and next 4 ingredients in a large bowl. Combine vinegar and remaining 5 ingredients in a small bowl; stir with a whisk. Pour over tomato mixture; toss to coat. Add bread cubes; toss well. Serve immediately. Yield: 4 servings (serving size: 2 cups).

CALORIES 255 (29% from fat); FAT 8.1g (sat 1g, mono 4.9g, poly 1.1g); PROTEIN 9.8g; CARB 39.9g; FIBER 8.2g; CHOL 0mg; IRON 3.4mg; SODIUM 708mg; CALC 83mg

Gazpacho Panzanella

This colorful salad combines gazpacho (the classic Spanish soup) and panzanella (the Italian bread salad). Chop the vegetables and toast the bread cubes ahead of time, but toss the salad just before serving; the bread will soak up the juices and become soggy if it sits too long. If you prefer a drier panzanella, simply add less dressing.

SALAD:
    4   (1-ounce) slices French bread, cut into
        ½-inch cubes
Cooking spray
3½ cups chopped seeded tomato (about 2 pounds)
    2   cups chopped skinless, boneless rotisserie
        chicken breast
1¾ cups chopped seeded cucumber (about
        1 pound)
    1   cup chopped green bell pepper
    ½   cup vertically sliced red onion
    ¼   cup chopped fresh flat-leaf parsley

DRESSING:
    ½   cup low-sodium vegetable juice
    ¼   cup red wine vinegar
    1   tablespoon extravirgin olive oil
    1   tablespoon water
    2   garlic cloves, minced
    ½   teaspoon salt
    ⅛   teaspoon freshly ground black pepper

1. Preheat oven to 350°.

2. To prepare salad, arrange bread cubes in a single layer on a baking sheet. Lightly coat bread cubes with cooking spray. Bake at 350° for 15 minutes or until golden brown, stirring once. Set aside.

3. Place tomato and next 5 ingredients in a large bowl; toss gently to combine.

4. To prepare dressing, combine vegetable juice and next 6 ingredients, stirring with a whisk. Drizzle over salad, tossing gently to coat. Stir in bread cubes; let salad stand 5 minutes. Serve immediately. Yield: 4 servings (serving size: 2½ cups).

CALORIES 294 (24% from fat); FAT 7.7g (sat 1.5g, mono 4.1g, poly 1.4g); PROTEIN 26.9g; CARB 29.6g; FIBER 4.4g; CHOL 60mg; IRON 3mg; SODIUM 553mg; CALC 68mg

Pork Fattoush

This traditional Middle Eastern bread salad uses toasted pita bread, which adds a dry crispness to the succulent cucumbers, tomatoes, and bell peppers. The dressing typically only includes lemon juice, olive oil, and salt, but we enjoyed the intense, sweet flavor added by balsamic vinegar. You can substitute leftover whole wheat, French, or sourdough bread cut into cubes and toasted for the pita, if desired.

1½ teaspoons bottled minced garlic
    ¾   teaspoon salt, divided
    1   pound pork tenderloin, trimmed and cut into
        ¾-inch cubes
    1   tablespoon olive oil
    2   (7-inch) pitas
    3   cups chopped tomato
    ½   cup chopped green onions
    ⅓   cup chopped fresh mint
    1   tablespoon balsamic vinegar
    1   teaspoon lemon juice
    1   cucumber, peeled, quartered lengthwise, and
        sliced into ¼-inch pieces
    1   (7-ounce) bottle roasted red bell peppers,
        drained and chopped

1. Preheat oven to 400°.

2. Combine garlic, ½ teaspoon salt, and pork, tossing well to coat. Let stand 5 minutes. Heat oil in a large nonstick skillet over medium-high heat.

3. Arrange pitas in a single layer directly on oven rack. Bake at 400° for 5 minutes or until crisp; transfer pitas to a wire rack.

4. While pitas bake, add pork to pan; cook 5 minutes or until done, stirring frequently. Place pork in a large bowl. Stir in remaining ¼ teaspoon salt, tomato, and next 6 ingredients. Break toasted pitas into bite-sized pieces. Add to pork mixture, and toss to combine. Serve immediately. Yield: 4 servings (serving size: 2 cups).

CALORIES 314 (25% from fat); FAT 8.6g (sat 2.1g, mono 4.6g, poly 1.3g); PROTEIN 28.9g; CARB 30g; FIBER 3.7g; CHOL 74mg; IRON 3.4mg; SODIUM 852mg; CALC 62mg

Curried Couscous Salad with
Dried Cranberries

Curried Couscous Salad with Dried Cranberries

With chickpeas, green peas, cranberries, and a zippy vinaigrette, this salad makes a delectable portable lunch. For heartier fare, stir in some chopped cooked turkey or chicken. Make this dish ahead because the flavors meld as it chills.

SALAD:
1½ cups uncooked couscous
    (about 1 [10-ounce] box)
  1 cup dried cranberries (about 4 ounces)
  1 cup frozen green peas, thawed
  ½ teaspoon curry powder
  2 cups boiling water
  ¼ cup thinly sliced green onions
  ¼ cup finely chopped fresh basil
  1 (15½-ounce) can chickpeas (garbanzo
    beans), rinsed and drained

DRESSING:
  ⅓ cup fresh lemon juice
  1 tablespoon grated orange rind
  2 tablespoons water
1½ tablespoons olive oil
  1 tablespoon thawed orange juice concentrate
  ½ teaspoon salt
  ¼ teaspoon black pepper
  4 garlic cloves, crushed

1. To prepare salad, combine first 4 ingredients in a large bowl. Pour 2 cups boiling water over couscous mixture; cover and let stand 5 minutes. Fluff with a fork; cool. Stir in green onions, basil, and chickpeas.
2. To prepare dressing, combine lemon juice and next 7 ingredients in a jar; cover tightly, and shake vigorously. Pour over couscous mixture; toss well to combine. Cover and chill 1 hour. Yield: 8 servings (serving size: 1 cup).

CALORIES 257 (13% from fat); FAT 3.8g (sat 0.5g, mono 2.1g, poly 0.7g); PROTEIN 8.7g; CARB 47.9g; FIBER 4.1g; CHOL 0mg; IRON 2.1mg; SODIUM 243mg; CALC 31mg

Chicken and Couscous Salad

This salad is delicious and easy to prepare, and the leftovers are tasty chilled. For an extra kick of flavor, sprinkle the salad with feta cheese before serving. If you can't find the specified box size of couscous, you can use 1 cup uncooked couscous.

SALAD:
1¼ cups fat-free, less-sodium chicken broth
  1 (5.7-ounce) box uncooked couscous
1½ cups cubed cooked chicken (about 6 ounces)
  ½ cup thinly sliced green onions
  ½ cup diced radishes (about 3 large)
  ½ cup chopped seeded peeled cucumber
  ¼ cup chopped fresh flat-leaf parsley
  2 tablespoons pine nuts, toasted

DRESSING:
  ¼ cup white wine vinegar
1½ tablespoons extravirgin olive oil
  1 teaspoon ground cumin
  ½ teaspoon salt
  ⅛ teaspoon freshly ground black pepper
  1 garlic clove, minced

1. To prepare salad, bring broth to a boil in a medium saucepan; gradually stir in couscous. Remove from heat; cover and let stand 5 minutes. Fluff with a fork. Spoon couscous into a large bowl, and cool slightly. Add chicken and next 5 ingredients; toss gently to combine.
2. To prepare dressing, combine white wine vinegar and next 5 ingredients, stirring with a whisk. Drizzle dressing over salad, and toss to combine. Yield: 4 servings (serving size: 1½ cups).
NOTE: You can toast the pine nuts quickly in a dry skillet over medium-high heat, stirring frequently. As soon as the nuts become fragrant (about 1 minute after placing them over heat), remove them from the pan.

CALORIES 334 (29% from fat); FAT 10.9g (sat 2g, mono 5.9g, poly 2.1g); PROTEIN 20.9g; CARB 35.8g; FIBER 2.9g; CHOL 39mg; IRON 1.8mg; SODIUM 484mg; CALC 23mg

Lemon-Dill Couscous with Chicken and Vegetables

When temperatures soar, this main-dish salad will cool you down with the refreshing flavors of lemon and dill. If you use the microwave instructions on the package of couscous, you won't even have to turn on your stovetop.

1½ cups water
1 cup uncooked couscous
2 cups chopped roasted skinless, boneless chicken breast (about 2 breast halves)
1½ cups diced yellow squash (about ½ pound)
1 cup diced red bell pepper
½ cup chopped fresh flat-leaf parsley
¼ cup fat-free, less-sodium chicken broth
3 tablespoons fresh lemon juice
2 tablespoons chopped fresh or 2 teaspoons dried dill
1 tablespoon extravirgin olive oil
½ teaspoon salt
⅛ teaspoon black pepper
Dill sprigs (optional)

1. Bring water to a boil in a medium saucepan, and gradually stir in couscous. Remove from heat; cover and let stand 5 minutes.
2. Fluff couscous with a fork. Spoon couscous into a large bowl. Add chicken and next 9 ingredients; toss well. Garnish with fresh dill sprigs, if desired. Yield: 4 servings (serving size: 2 cups).

CALORIES 246 (19% from fat); FAT 5.3g (sat 1.1g, mono 3g, poly 0.8g); PROTEIN 19g; CARB 31.9g; FIBER 3.2g; CHOL 35mg; IRON 2.1mg; SODIUM 624mg; CALC 43mg

Pasta Primavera

Tender asparagus and tiny fresh green peas are the quintessential ingredients in this Italian classic. When buying fresh peas, look for young, well-filled pods with a soft, velvety texture. Store unshelled peas uncovered in the refrigerator, and use them as soon as possible for the best flavor.

8 ounces uncooked fusilli (short twisted spaghetti)
2 cups (1-inch) diagonally cut thin asparagus (about ¾ pound)
½ cup shelled green peas (about ¾ pound unshelled green peas)
1 teaspoon olive oil
Cooking spray
1 small yellow bell pepper, cut into julienne strips
1 small red onion, thinly sliced
2 garlic cloves, minced
1 cup halved cherry tomatoes
⅔ cup fat-free, less-sodium chicken broth
⅓ cup whipping cream
½ teaspoon salt
½ teaspoon crushed red pepper
¼ cup (1 ounce) shredded fresh Parmesan cheese
¼ cup thinly sliced fresh basil

1. Cook pasta according to package directions, omitting salt and fat. Add asparagus and peas during last minute of cooking. Drain; place in a large bowl.
2. Heat oil in a large nonstick skillet coated with cooking spray over medium-high heat. Add bell pepper, onion, and garlic; sauté 5 minutes. Add tomatoes; sauté 1 minute. Stir in broth, whipping cream, salt, and red pepper; cook 2 minutes or until thoroughly heated.
3. Add tomato mixture to pasta mixture; toss to coat. Sprinkle with cheese and basil. Serve immediately. Yield: 4 servings (serving size: 1½ cups).

CALORIES 364 (28% from fat); FAT 11.2g (sat 6g, mono 3.4g, poly 0.6g); PROTEIN 14.1g; CARB 54g; FIBER 5.4g; CHOL 31mg; IRON 3.2mg; SODIUM 476mg; CALC 125mg

Pasta Primavera

Grilled Vegetable Pasta Salad

Pack this robust pasta salad for a family picnic or serve it for an alfresco lunch. Toss the vegetables with the pasta when they're hot off the grill or after chilling.

1 red bell pepper, halved and seeded
1 red onion, peeled and cut into 6 wedges
Cooking spray
1 (4-inch) portobello cap
¾ pound asparagus
½ tablespoon chopped serrano chile
3 garlic cloves, crushed
¼ teaspoon salt
1½ tablespoons red wine vinegar
1 tablespoon water
1 tablespoon fresh lemon juice
2 teaspoons extravirgin olive oil
2 teaspoons anchovy paste
4 cups cooked fusilli (about 8 ounces uncooked short twisted spaghetti)
¾ cup (3 ounces) crumbled feta cheese
½ cup chopped fresh basil
3 tablespoons chopped pitted kalamata olives

1. Prepare grill.
2. Coat bell pepper and onion with cooking spray; place on grill rack coated with cooking spray. Grill 15 minutes or until pepper is blackened, turning onion occasionally. Place pepper in a zip-top plastic bag; seal. Let stand 15 minutes. Coat mushroom cap and asparagus with cooking spray; place on grill rack, and grill 3 minutes on each side or until tender.
3. Chop onion into 1-inch pieces; place in a large bowl. Chop mushroom into 1-inch pieces; add to onion. Slice asparagus diagonally into 1½-inch pieces; add to onion mixture.
4. Combine chile, garlic, and salt in a mortar; mash to a paste with a pestle. Combine garlic paste, vinegar, and next 4 ingredients in a small bowl, stirring with a whisk.
5. Peel and slice pepper into ½-inch strips; add to onion mixture. Add chile mixture; toss well. Toss in pasta and remaining 3 ingredients. Yield: 4 servings (serving size: 2 cups).

CALORIES 364 (27% from fat); FAT 11.1g (sat 5g, mono 4.4g, poly 0.7g); PROTEIN 14.7g; CARB 53.1g; FIBER 4.3g; CHOL 27mg; IRON 3.2mg; SODIUM 985mg; CALC 198mg

Summer Garden Lentil and Pasta Salad

Petite green lentils are sometimes labeled "le puy lentils." Other lentils will also work, but the cook time could change, so make sure they're tender before you drain them.

VINAIGRETTE:
2½ tablespoons balsamic vinegar
1½ tablespoons olive oil
1 tablespoon minced shallots
1 tablespoon Dijon mustard
1½ teaspoons minced fresh garlic
⅛ teaspoon salt
⅛ teaspoon freshly ground black pepper
SALAD:
1 cup fat-free, less-sodium chicken broth
½ cup dried petite green lentils
1 bay leaf
2 cups uncooked orecchiette pasta ("little ears" pasta)
1 cup chopped zucchini
1 cup chopped red or yellow bell pepper
¾ cup halved cherry tomatoes
½ cup chopped red onion
2 tablespoons chopped fresh basil
2 tablespoons chopped fresh flat-leaf parsley
2 tablespoons grated Parmigiano-Reggiano cheese
1½ teaspoons chopped fresh or ½ teaspoon dried oregano
1½ teaspoons chopped fresh or ½ teaspoon dried thyme
¼ teaspoon salt
¼ teaspoon freshly ground black pepper

1. To prepare vinaigrette, place first 7 ingredients in a blender or food processor; process until well blended.
2. To prepare salad, combine broth, lentils, and bay leaf in a saucepan; bring to a boil. Reduce heat, and simmer 25 minutes or until lentils are tender. Drain; rinse with cold water. Discard bay leaf.
3. Cook pasta according to package directions, omitting salt and fat. Drain and rinse with cold water.
4. Combine lentils, pasta, zucchini, and next 10 ingredients. Drizzle with vinaigrette, and toss well. Store in an airtight container in the refrigerator. Yield: 4 servings (serving size: 1¼ cups).

CALORIES 380 (19% from fat); FAT 7.9g (sat 1.6g, mono 4.4g, poly 1.5g); PROTEIN 16.2g; CARB 63.7g; FIBER 7.6g; CHOL 3mg; IRON 3.9mg; SODIUM 447mg; CALC 97mg

Orecchiette with Tomatoes, Fresh Mozzarella, and Basil

Taking its cue from Italy's insalata caprese, this easy, make-ahead dish combines fresh mozzarella cheese with basil and tomatoes. Choose the ripest, most flavorful tomatoes for this sensational pasta salad.

2   cups uncooked orecchiette ("little ears" pasta)
3   cups chopped plum tomato
1¼ cups (5 ounces) diced fresh mozzarella cheese
1   cup loosely packed chopped fresh basil
1   tablespoon extravirgin olive oil
¾   teaspoon salt
¼   teaspoon crushed red pepper
2   garlic cloves, minced

1. Cook pasta according to package directions, omitting salt and fat; drain and rinse with cold water. Drain. Combine pasta, tomato, and remaining ingredients. Cover and chill at least 1 hour. Yield: 4 servings (serving size: 1½ cups).

CALORIES 376 (30% from fat); FAT 12.4g (sat 5.7g, mono 4.2g, poly 1.1g); PROTEIN 15.1g; CARB 50.5g; FIBER 3.4g; CHOL 28mg; IRON 3.4mg; SODIUM 361mg; CALC 239mg

Warm Tortellini and Cherry Tomato Salad

Basil, cherry tomatoes, red onion, and arugula bring fresh flavor to cheese tortellini in this satisfying main-dish salad.

2 (9-ounce) packages fresh cheese tortellini
1½ cups (1½-inch) sliced asparagus (about 1 pound)
3 tablespoons red wine vinegar
1 tablespoon balsamic vinegar
1 tablespoon extravirgin olive oil
¼ teaspoon black pepper
4 cups trimmed arugula
1½ cups halved cherry tomatoes
¾ cup (3 ounces) grated fresh Parmesan cheese
½ cup thinly sliced red onion
⅓ cup thinly sliced fresh basil
1 (14-ounce) can artichoke hearts, drained and quartered

1. Cook pasta according to package directions, omitting salt and fat. Add asparagus during last 2 minutes of cooking time. Drain.
2. While pasta cooks, combine vinegars, oil, and pepper in a large bowl, stirring with a whisk. Add pasta mixture, arugula, and remaining ingredients; toss to coat. Yield: 6 servings (serving size: 1½ cups).

CALORIES 403 (26% from fat); FAT 11.6g (sat 5.7g, mono 4.4g, poly 0.6g); PROTEIN 21.7g; CARB 52.4g; FIBER 7.9g; CHOL 50mg; IRON 1.9mg; SODIUM 725mg; CALC 415mg

Orzo Salad with Chickpeas, Dill, and Lemon

If you're not a big dill fan, use half the amount. Quick-cooking couscous can replace the orzo. When preparing the dressing, be sure your lemons are at room temperature; then, before juicing, roll them across the countertop while applying pressure with the palm of your hand. This method ensures that you get the most juice from each lemon.

1 cup uncooked orzo (rice-shaped pasta)
½ cup thinly sliced green onions
½ cup (2 ounces) crumbled feta cheese
¼ cup chopped fresh dill
1 (19-ounce) can chickpeas (garbanzo beans), rinsed and drained
3 tablespoons fresh lemon juice
1½ tablespoons extravirgin olive oil
1 tablespoon cold water
½ teaspoon salt
½ teaspoon bottled minced garlic

1. Cook pasta according to package directions, omitting salt and fat. Drain and rinse with cold water; drain.
2. Combine pasta, onions, cheese, dill, and chickpeas in a large bowl, tossing gently to combine.
3. Combine juice and remaining ingredients in a small bowl, stirring with a whisk. Drizzle over pasta mixture; toss gently to coat. Yield: 4 servings (serving size: 1¼ cups).

CALORIES 327 (29% from fat); FAT 10.4g (sat 2.9g, mono 5.1g, poly 1.8g); PROTEIN 10.8g; CARB 47.6g; FIBER 4.9g; CHOL 13mg; IRON 3mg; SODIUM 641mg; CALC 107mg

Orzo Salad with Chickpeas,
Dill, and Lemon

Summer Farfalle Salad with
Smoked Salmon

Summer Farfalle Salad with Smoked Salmon

Incorporating the best tastes of summer, this fresh salad is an ideal light supper on a hot day. Substitute leftover cooked salmon for the sliced smoked salmon, if you prefer.

8 ounces uncooked farfalle (bow tie pasta)
2 cups cherry tomatoes, halved
¼ cup chopped fresh dill
1 (6-ounce) bag baby spinach
1 teaspoon grated lemon rind
2 tablespoons fresh lemon juice
2 tablespoons cold water
1½ tablespoons extravirgin olive oil
½ teaspoon salt
¼ teaspoon black pepper
4 ounces (about 8 slices) smoked salmon, cut into thin strips

1. Cook pasta according to package directions, omitting salt and fat. Drain and rinse with cold water; drain.
2. Combine pasta, tomatoes, dill, and spinach in a large bowl, tossing gently.
3. Combine lemon rind and next 5 ingredients in a small bowl, stirring with a whisk. Drizzle over pasta mixture; toss gently to coat. Top with salmon. Yield: 6 servings (serving size: 2 cups).

CALORIES 206 (23% from fat); FAT 5.3g (sat 0.9g, mono 3.1g, poly 1.1g); PROTEIN 9.8g; CARB 31.4g; FIBER 2.7g; CHOL 4mg; IRON 2.3mg; SODIUM 603mg; CALC 43mg

Seashells with Tuscan Tuna

Tuna and red onion crostini are a favored snack on the menus of Florentine wine bars. The combination is tossed here with pasta shells. Look for tuna that's vacuum-sealed in bags—it's firmer than canned tuna and doesn't require draining.

8 ounces uncooked medium seashell pasta
½ cup chopped red onion
¼ cup thinly sliced fresh basil
2 tablespoons capers
2 tablespoons extravirgin olive oil
2 teaspoons grated lemon rind
½ teaspoon salt
¼ teaspoon freshly ground black pepper
2 (7.06-ounce) bags white albacore tuna in water

1. Cook pasta according to package directions, omitting salt and fat. Drain pasta in a colander over a bowl, reserving 2 tablespoons cooking liquid. Return pasta to pan. Add reserved cooking liquid, onion, and remaining ingredients; toss well. Yield: 4 servings (serving size: 1½ cups).

CALORIES 402 (24% from fat); FAT 10.6g (sat 1.9g, mono 5.8g, poly 1.7g); PROTEIN 31.8g; CARB 44.4g; FIBER 2.4g; CHOL 42mg; IRON 3.1mg; SODIUM 829mg; CALC 37mg

Pappardelle with Tomatoes,
Arugula, and Parmesan

Pappardelle with Tomatoes, Arugula, and Parmesan

If the cooked pasta clumps together, just rinse it under hot water, drain thoroughly, and then toss with the tomato mixture and arugula.

    9   ounces uncooked pappardelle (wide ribbon
        pasta)
    2   tablespoons extravirgin olive oil
  ¼   teaspoon crushed red pepper
    3   garlic cloves, thinly sliced
1½   cups halved yellow tear-drop cherry tomatoes
        (pear-shaped)
1½   cups halved grape tomatoes
    3   tablespoons fresh lemon juice
    1   teaspoon salt
    5   cups loosely packed trimmed arugula
  ⅓   cup (1½ ounces) shaved fresh Parmesan
        cheese
    2   bacon slices, cooked and crumbled

1. Cook pasta according to package directions, omitting salt and fat. Drain; keep warm.
2. Heat oil in a large nonstick skillet over medium heat. Add pepper and garlic to pan; cook 1 minute or until garlic is fragrant. Add tomatoes; cook 45 seconds or just until heated, stirring gently. Remove pan from heat; stir in lemon juice and salt. Combine pasta, arugula, and tomato mixture in a large bowl, tossing to coat. Top with cheese and bacon. Yield: 4 servings (serving size: 2 cups).

CALORIES 388 (29% from fat); FAT 12.5g (sat 3.5g, mono 6.6g, poly 1.1g); PROTEIN 15.2g; CARB 55.7g; FIBER 3.8g; CHOL 10mg; IRON 3.1mg; SODIUM 828mg; CALC 189mg

Pasta Salad with Shrimp, Peppers, and Olives

This Greek-style salad is perfect for casual entertaining. Serve it with a crisp wine and a side of bruschetta.

2½   cups cooked angel hair (about 5 ounces
        uncooked pasta)
  ¾   cup chopped plum tomato
  ½   cup chopped red bell pepper
  ½   cup chopped yellow bell pepper
  ⅓   cup chopped green onions
    2   tablespoons fresh lemon juice
    1   tablespoon chopped pitted kalamata olives
    1   tablespoon olive oil
1½   teaspoons chopped fresh or ½ teaspoon dried
        thyme
  ½   teaspoon white pepper
  ¼   teaspoon dried oregano
  ¾   pound cooked medium shrimp, peeled and
        deveined
    1   garlic clove, minced
  ½   cup (2 ounces) crumbled feta cheese
    1   tablespoon chopped fresh parsley

1. Combine first 13 ingredients in a large bowl. Sprinkle with cheese and parsley. Yield: 5 servings (serving size: 2 cups).

CALORIES 252 (26% from fat); FAT 7.2g (sat 2.4g, mono 2.9g, poly 1.1g); PROTEIN 19.8g; CARB 26.7g; FIBER 1.8g; CHOL 114mg; IRON 3.6mg; SODIUM 249mg; CALC 111mg

Rotini, Summer Squash, and Prosciutto Salad with Rosemary Dressing

Using white balsamic vinegar maintains the salad dressing's pure golden color. Add the yellow squash and zucchini to the pasta during the last minute of cooking.

3 cups uncooked rotini (about 8 ounces corkscrew pasta)
1½ cups coarsely chopped yellow squash
1½ cups coarsely chopped zucchini
4 ounces thinly sliced prosciutto, chopped
3 tablespoons chopped red onion
2 ounces fresh mozzarella cheese, chopped
¼ teaspoon salt
¼ teaspoon freshly ground black pepper
2 tablespoons white balsamic vinegar
1 tablespoon extravirgin olive oil
1½ teaspoons Dijon mustard
½ teaspoon finely chopped fresh rosemary

1. Cook pasta according to package directions, omitting salt and fat. Add squash and zucchini during last minute of cooking. Drain pasta mixture; rinse with cold water.
2. Heat a large nonstick skillet over medium-high heat. Add prosciutto, and cook 5 minutes or until crisp, stirring frequently.
3. Combine pasta mixture, prosciutto, onion, and cheese in a large bowl; sprinkle with salt and pepper. Combine vinegar, oil, mustard, and rosemary in a small bowl, stirring with a whisk. Add vinegar mixture to pasta mixture, tossing gently to coat. Yield: 4 servings (serving size: 2¼ cups).

CALORIES 359 (28% from fat); FAT 11.1g (sat 4g, mono 2.8g, poly 0.4g); PROTEIN 18.7g; CARB 46.3g; FIBER 2.4g; CHOL 36mg; IRON 2.5mg; SODIUM 771mg; CALC 103mg

Macaroni Salad

This classic make-ahead salad is perfect for a lunch buffet or a picnic. Remember to keep any salad with a mayonnaise-based dressing cold for food safety.

3 cups cooked medium elbow macaroni (about 1½ cups uncooked)
¾ cup (3 ounces) reduced-fat shredded sharp Cheddar cheese
½ cup frozen green peas, thawed
½ cup diced lean ham
¼ cup sliced green onions
1 cup light mayonnaise
½ teaspoon salt
¼ teaspoon black pepper

1. Combine first 5 ingredients in a bowl; toss well. Combine mayonnaise, salt, and pepper, and stir well. Add mayonnaise mixture to salad; toss well. Cover and chill. Yield: 8 servings (serving size: ⅔ cup).

CALORIES 232 (53% from fat); FAT 13.6g (sat 4g, mono 0.4g, poly 0.2g); PROTEIN 8.3g; CARB 18.8g; FIBER 1.3g; CHOL 26mg; IRON 1mg; SODIUM 399mg; CALC 90mg

About Macaroni

Cool the cooked macaroni completely before tossing the salad so that the cheese doesn't melt. A quick way to do this is to rinse the pasta in a colander under cool running water and then drain it well. This washes away some of the starch, making the pasta less sticky. Though this starch is useful for helping sauces adhere to pasta in warm dishes, chilled pasta salads benefit from having less starch.

Macaroni Salad

Peanut Chicken Soba Salad

Peanut Chicken Soba Salad

You'll only need about 15 minutes to cook the chicken and noodles for this Asian salad. If short on time, substitute rotisserie chicken or leftover cooked chicken, and purchase preshredded carrots from your supermarket's produce section.

    2 cups water
    2 (6-ounce) skinless, boneless chicken breast
       halves
    4 black peppercorns
    1 bay leaf
    2 tablespoons roasted peanut oil
    1 tablespoon rice vinegar
    2 teaspoons low-sodium soy sauce
    1 teaspoon honey
    1 teaspoon chili garlic sauce (such as Lee
       Kum Kee)
  ½ teaspoon salt
    2 cups cooked soba noodles (about 4 ounces
       uncooked)
    1 cup grated carrot
  ½ cup thinly sliced green onions
  ¼ cup minced red onion
  ¼ cup chopped fresh basil
    4 teaspoons chopped unsalted, dry-roasted
       peanuts
       Lime wedges (optional)

1. Combine first 4 ingredients in a medium saucepan; bring to a boil. Cover, remove from heat, and let stand 15 minutes or until chicken is done. Remove chicken from pan, and discard peppercorns, bay leaf, and cooking liquid. Shred chicken; place in a large bowl.

2. Combine oil and next 5 ingredients, stirring with a whisk. Pour over chicken; let stand 5 minutes. Add soba noodles and next 4 ingredients to chicken mixture, and toss well. Sprinkle with peanuts. Garnish with lime wedges, if desired. Yield: 4 servings (serving size: 1 cup salad and 1 teaspoon peanuts).

CALORIES 256 (33% from fat); FAT 9.5g (sat 1.7g, mono 4.2g, poly 2.9g); PROTEIN 23.9g; CARB 19.5g; FIBER 2.5g; CHOL 49mg; IRON 1.3mg; SODIUM 538mg; CALC 30mg

Roasted Chicken and Bow Tie Pasta Salad

This light lunch or dinner is a great alternative to the traditional mayonnaise-based chicken salad. To cut preparation time, purchase rotisserie chicken from the deli.

    3 cups uncooked farfalle (bow tie pasta; about
       8 ounces)
  ⅓ cup fresh orange juice
  ¼ cup fresh lemon juice
    2 tablespoons extravirgin olive oil
    1 tablespoon stone-ground mustard
    2 teaspoons sugar
 1¼ teaspoons salt
  ½ teaspoon freshly ground black pepper
 1½ teaspoons rice vinegar
    2 cups shredded cooked chicken breast (about
       2 breasts)
 1½ cups seedless red grapes, halved
    1 cup thin diagonally cut celery
  ⅓ cup finely chopped red onion
  ⅓ cup coarsely chopped walnuts, toasted
    3 tablespoons chopped fresh chives
    2 tablespoons chopped fresh parsley

1. Cook pasta according to package directions, omitting salt and fat; drain. Cool completely.

2. Combine orange juice and next 7 ingredients in a large bowl, stirring with a whisk. Add pasta, chicken, and remaining ingredients; toss gently to combine. Yield: 6 servings (serving size: about 1⅔ cups).

CALORIES 363 (36% from fat); FAT 14.4g (sat 2.4g, mono 5.5g, poly 4.8g); PROTEIN 18.5g; CARB 42g; FIBER 3.1g; CHOL 33mg; IRON 2.2mg; SODIUM 553mg; CALC 45mg

Salmon on Greens with Lime-Ginger Dressing

Transform a simple broiled salmon fillet into a one-dish meal by serving it over gourmet greens with fresh mango and adding a sweet, spicy dressing. Keep individually-packed frozen salmon fillets on hand so that you can put this salad together without making a trip to the fish market.

⅔ cup fresh lime juice (about 5 limes)
½ cup honey
½ teaspoon grated peeled fresh ginger
4 (6-ounce) skinless salmon fillets (about 1-inch-thick)
Cooking spray
¼ teaspoon salt
8 cups gourmet salad greens
1 cup sliced peeled mango

1. Preheat broiler.
2. Combine first 3 ingredients in a small bowl, reserving ¾ cup juice mixture for dressing. Place salmon fillets on a broiler pan coated with cooking spray, and baste with remaining juice mixture. Broil 4 minutes on each side or until desired degree of doneness, basting once after turning. Sprinkle fillets with salt.
3. Divide salad greens and mango among 4 plates; top with salmon fillets. Drizzle with reserved ¾ cup dressing. Yield: 4 servings (serving size: 2 cups salad greens, ¼ cup mango, 1 salmon fillet, and 3 tablespoons dressing).

CALORIES 462 (28% from fat); FAT 14.5g (sat 2.5g, mono 6.8g, poly 3.2g); PROTEIN 37.2g; CARB 48.3g; FIBER 2.5g; CHOL 111mg; IRON 2.2mg; SODIUM 243mg; CALC 60mg

Soba Noodle Salad with Vegetables and Tofu

This Asian-inspired pasta salad keeps well in the refrigerator, so it's excellent to make ahead. If you're short on time, substitute bagged sliced cabbage or coleslaw mix for the napa cabbage.

DRESSING:
½ cup low-sodium soy sauce
¼ cup packed brown sugar
1 tablespoon sesame seeds, toasted
2 tablespoons orange juice
1 tablespoon bottled minced or minced peeled fresh ginger
1 tablespoon rice vinegar
2 teaspoons dark sesame oil
1 teaspoon bottled minced garlic
1 teaspoon chile paste with garlic
SALAD:
4 cups hot cooked soba (about 8 ounces uncooked buckwheat noodles) or whole wheat spaghetti
3 cups very thinly sliced napa (Chinese) cabbage
2 cups fresh bean sprouts
1 cup shredded carrot
½ cup chopped fresh cilantro
1 (12.3-ounce) package firm tofu, drained and cut into 1-inch cubes

1. To prepare dressing, combine first 9 ingredients in a small bowl; stir with a whisk.
2. To prepare salad, combine noodles and remaining ingredients in a large bowl. Drizzle with dressing, tossing well to coat. Yield: 5 servings (serving size: 2 cups).

CALORIES 336 (19% from fat); FAT 7g (sat 1g, mono 1.8g, poly 3g); PROTEIN 15.1g; CARB 53.8g; FIBER 2.8g; CHOL 0mg; IRON 6.6mg; SODIUM 850mg; CALC 169mg

Soba Noodle Salad with
Vegetables and Tofu

Salade Niçoise with
Creamy Tofu Dressing

Salade Niçoise with Creamy Tofu Dressing

(pictured on page 225)

Of French origin, salade niçoise traditionally includes crisp vegetables, hard-boiled eggs, tuna, anchovies, and olive oil. We've updated it with a tofu dressing. If you're not an anchovy fan, omit them and add one tablespoon of drained capers to the dressing.

DRESSING:
- 1 tablespoon water
- 1 tablespoon red wine vinegar
- 1 tablespoon fresh lemon juice
- 1 teaspoon chopped fresh thyme
- 1/4 teaspoon salt
- 1/4 teaspoon freshly ground black pepper
- 4 ounces firm silken tofu
- 2 canned anchovy fillets
- 1 garlic clove, chopped

SALAD:
- 12 ounces small red potatoes
- 12 ounces green beans
- 1 1/2 pounds fresh tuna
- 1/2 teaspoon salt
- 1/4 teaspoon freshly ground black pepper
- Cooking spray
- 1 cup thinly sliced red onion, separated into rings
- 2 tomatoes, each cut into 12 wedges
- 1 hard-cooked large egg, cut into 6 wedges
- 2 tablespoons chopped fresh flat-leaf parsley
- 1 tablespoon capers
- 24 green picholine or niçoise olives

1. To prepare dressing, place first 9 ingredients in a food processor or blender; process 1 minute or until smooth. Cover and chill.

2. To prepare salad, place potatoes in a saucepan; cover with water. Bring to a boil. Reduce heat; simmer 10 minutes or until tender. Drain and rinse with cold water. Drain potatoes, and cut in half. Set aside.

3. Cook beans in boiling water 3 minutes or until crisp-tender. Drain and rinse with cold water; drain. Set aside.

4. Prepare grill or preheat grill pan.

5. Sprinkle fish with 1/2 teaspoon salt and 1/4 teaspoon pepper. Place fish on grill rack or grill pan coated with cooking spray; cook 4 minutes on each side or until fish is medium-rare or desired degree of doneness. Break fish into large chunks. Arrange fish, beans, and onion in center of a large serving platter; arrange potato halves, tomato, and egg around fish mixture. Sprinkle with parsley, capers, and olives. Drizzle with dressing. Yield: 6 servings (serving size: 4 ounces tuna, 1/2 cup beans, about 3 onion rings, about 5 potato halves, 4 tomato wedges, 1 egg wedge, 4 olives, 1/2 teaspoon capers, and about 2 tablespoons dressing).

CALORIES 276 (29% from fat); FAT 9g (sat 2g, mono 3.6g, poly 2.3g); PROTEIN 30.8g; CARB 18.3g; FIBER 4g; CHOL 78mg; IRON 3.1mg; SODIUM 781mg; CALC 69mg

Perfect Hard-Cooked Eggs

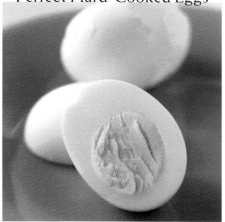

For the perfect hard-cooked eggs, place eggs in a single layer in a saucepan with just enough cool water to cover them by 1 inch. Cover the pan, and bring the water just to a boil; immediately turn off the heat. Let the eggs stand, covered, for 15 minutes. Run the eggs under cold water until completely cooled. Gently crack each shell, and peel under running water, starting with the large end. Use older eggs because eggs older than seven days are easier to peel.

Taco Rice Salad

Taco Rice Salad

Packed with classic taco fillings, this easy one-dish meal appeals to kids and adults alike. Convenience products, such as canned beans, frozen corn, preseasoned rice, and commercial picante sauce, make it supereasy to toss together this salad. Serve with light tortilla chips for an added crunch.

SALAD:
Cooking spray
1 pound ground round
1 garlic clove, minced
3 cups cooked yellow rice
1 teaspoon ground cumin
1 teaspoon chili powder
¼ teaspoon salt
¼ teaspoon black pepper
6 cups torn romaine lettuce (about 10 ounces)
3 cups chopped tomato (about 1¼ pounds)
1 cup frozen whole-kernel corn, thawed
½ cup chopped red onion
1 (15-ounce) can black beans, rinsed and drained

DRESSING:
⅔ cup fat-free sour cream
⅔ cup picante sauce
1 teaspoon chili powder
½ teaspoon ground cumin

REMAINING INGREDIENT:
½ cup (2 ounces) reduced-fat shredded sharp Cheddar cheese

1. To prepare salad, heat a large nonstick skillet over medium-high heat; coat pan with cooking spray. Add beef and garlic, and cook 9 minutes or until browned and done, stirring to crumble. Drain; return beef mixture to pan. Stir in rice and next 4 ingredients. Cool slightly.

2. Place lettuce and next 4 ingredients in a large bowl; toss to combine.

3. To prepare dressing, combine sour cream and next 3 ingredients, stirring with a whisk. Spoon dressing over lettuce mixture; toss to coat. Divide lettuce mixture among 6 plates. Top with rice mixture and cheese. Yield: 6 servings (serving size: 1⅓ cups lettuce mixture, ¾ cup rice mixture, and about 1½ tablespoons cheese).

CALORIES 360 (30% from fat); FAT 11.9g (sat 5g, mono 4.5g, poly 0.8g); PROTEIN 21.1g; CARB 46.7g; FIBER 6.7g; CHOL 48mg; IRON 4.2mg; SODIUM 994mg; CALC 177mg

Coconut, Crab, and Shrimp Salad

With the bright colors of corn, avocado, and shrimp, this fresh seafood salad is a feast for the eyes as well as the appetite. Scoop it up with baked pita wedges that are sprinkled with sesame seeds. For a spicier dish, add the jalapeño pepper seeds or use two peppers.

Cooking spray
½ pound medium shrimp, peeled and deveined
½ teaspoon salt, divided
1 cup fresh (about 2 ears) or frozen corn kernels, thawed
⅓ cup finely chopped onion
⅓ cup chopped fresh cilantro
⅓ cup diced peeled avocado
½ pound lump crabmeat, drained and shell pieces removed
1 jalapeño pepper, seeded and chopped
3 tablespoons fresh lemon juice
2 teaspoons extravirgin olive oil
6 cups torn Boston lettuce (about 3 small heads)
¼ cup flaked sweetened coconut, toasted

1. Heat a medium nonstick skillet over medium-high heat; coat pan with cooking spray. Add shrimp and ¼ teaspoon salt; cook 4 minutes or until shrimp are done, turning once. Remove from pan. Coarsely chop shrimp.

2. Combine corn and next 5 ingredients in a medium bowl. Gently stir in shrimp.

3. Combine lemon juice, oil, and remaining ¼ teaspoon salt, stirring with a whisk. Drizzle juice mixture over shrimp mixture; toss gently to coat. Divide lettuce among 4 plates; top with shrimp mixture. Sprinkle with coconut. Yield: 4 servings (serving size: 1½ cups lettuce, about 1 cup shrimp mixture, and 1 tablespoon coconut).

NOTE: To avoid using two pans, toast the coconut over medium-high heat until golden before cooking the shrimp.

CALORIES 223 (34% from fat); FAT 8.5g (sat 2.2g, mono 3.6g, poly 1.3g); PROTEIN 24g; CARB 16g; FIBER 3g; CHOL 124mg; IRON 3mg; SODIUM 613mg; CALC 94mg

Chicken Salad

Surround a scoop of our herbed chicken salad with crisp crackers and a variety of seasonal fruit for a light lunch or dinner.

1¾ cups chopped cooked chicken breast
⅓ cup diced celery
¼ cup finely chopped green onions
¼ cup light mayonnaise
3 tablespoons chopped fresh parsley
2 tablespoons plain fat-free yogurt
1 tablespoon lemon juice
½ teaspoon salt
½ teaspoon dried basil
¼ teaspoon black pepper
1 (2-ounce) jar diced pimiento, drained

1. Combine all ingredients in a bowl; stir well. Cover and chill up to 2 days. Yield: 4 servings (serving size: ½ cup).

CALORIES 168 (42% from fat); FAT 7.8g (sat 1.8g, mono 1g, poly 0.6g); PROTEIN 19.6g; CARB 3.6g; FIBER 0.8g; CHOL 57mg; IRON 1.1mg; SODIUM 476mg; CALC 36mg

About Pimientos

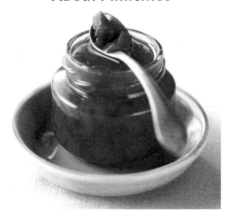

The pimiento, whose name is the Spanish word for "pepper," is a large heart-shaped pepper that's more flavorful than the red bell pepper. Pimientos are most easily found canned or jarred in whole, sliced, and diced varieties. They're a mainstay in stuffed olives, pimiento cheese, and casseroles. The pimiento's sweet flavor is a nice complement to the herbs and crunchy celery in this tasty chicken salad.

Grilled Steak Salad with Creamy Ranch Dressing

Sourdough croutons, creamy ranch dressing, and steak seasoned with a sweet-spicy rub make this down-home salad a family favorite. A grill pan imparts grilled flavor without the trouble of firing up the grill.

STEAK:
½ teaspoon garlic powder
½ teaspoon brown sugar
½ teaspoon ground red pepper
¼ teaspoon salt
¼ teaspoon black pepper
1 (1-pound) boneless sirloin steak, trimmed (about ½-inch-thick)
Cooking spray
SALAD:
4 (1-ounce) slices sourdough bread
1 garlic clove, halved
2 cups grape tomatoes
1 cup halved and sliced cucumber
1 cup sliced red onion
1 (16-ounce) bag classic iceberg salad mix (such as Dole)
½ cup fat-free ranch dressing

1. Heat a nonstick grill pan over medium-high heat.
2. Preheat broiler.
3. To prepare steak, combine first 5 ingredients, and rub evenly over both sides of steak. Coat grill pan with cooking spray. Cook steak 4 minutes on each side or until desired degree of doneness. Remove from pan; let stand 5 minutes. Cut steak diagonally across grain into thin slices.
4. While steak stands, prepare salad. Place bread slices on a baking sheet, and broil 2 minutes on each side or until lightly browned. Rub cut sides of garlic halves over bread. Cut bread into ¾-inch squares. Combine bread squares, tomatoes, cucumber, onion, and salad mix in a large bowl. Add dressing, tossing gently to coat. Divide salad among 4 plates; top with steak. Yield: 4 servings (serving size: 3 cups salad and about 3 ounces meat).

CALORIES 334 (20% from fat); FAT 7.5g (sat 2.6g, mono 3.1g, poly 0.6g); PROTEIN 29.2g; CARB 37g; FIBER 4.8g; CHOL 67mg; IRON 3.6mg; SODIUM 733mg; CALC 73mg

Grilled Steak Salad with
Creamy Ranch Dressing

Black Bean-Taco Salad with
Lime Vinaigrette

Black Bean–Taco Salad with Lime Vinaigrette

With chicken, Cheddar cheese, black beans, and veggies, this southwestern-influenced no-cook salad needs nothing on the side except some iced tea. The tart fresh lime juice and rind add an extra punch of flavor to the dressing.

VINAIGRETTE:
- ¼ cup chopped seeded tomato
- ¼ cup chopped fresh cilantro
- 2 tablespoons olive oil
- 1 tablespoon cider vinegar
- 1 teaspoon grated lime rind
- 1 tablespoon fresh lime juice
- ¼ teaspoon salt
- ¼ teaspoon ground cumin
- ¼ teaspoon chili powder
- ¼ teaspoon black pepper
- 1 garlic clove, peeled

SALAD:
- 8 cups thinly sliced iceberg lettuce
- 1½ cups chopped roasted skinless, boneless chicken breast
- 1 cup chopped tomato
- 1 cup chopped green bell pepper
- 1 cup finely diced red onion
- ½ cup (2 ounces) reduced-fat shredded sharp Cheddar cheese
- 1 (15-ounce) can black beans, rinsed and drained

REMAINING INGREDIENT:
- 4 cups fat-free baked tortilla chips (about 4 ounces)

1. To prepare vinaigrette, place first 11 ingredients in a blender or food processor; process until smooth.

2. To prepare salad, combine lettuce and next 6 ingredients in a large bowl. Add vinaigrette; toss well to coat. Serve with chips. Yield: 4 servings (serving size: about 2 cups salad and 1 cup chips).

CALORIES 402 (28% from fat); FAT 12.6g (sat 3.2g, mono 6.5g, poly 1.9g); PROTEIN 24.5g; CARB 51.6g; FIBER 8g; CHOL 35mg; IRON 3.6mg; SODIUM 861mg; CALC 236mg

White Bean and Roasted Chicken Salad

Great for picnics or lazy-day suppers, this salad stirs together in a flash. The classic red wine vinaigrette adds a nice zing to the creamy cannellini beans and roasted chicken. Red onion adds some bite, while basil imparts a subtle hint of licorice and cloves.

SALAD:
- 2 cups coarsely chopped skinless, boneless rotisserie chicken breast
- 1 cup chopped tomato
- ½ cup thinly sliced red onion
- ⅓ cup sliced fresh basil
- 2 (16-ounce) cans cannellini beans or other white beans, rinsed and drained

DRESSING:
- ¼ cup red wine vinegar
- 2 tablespoons extravirgin olive oil
- 1 tablespoon fresh lemon juice
- 2 teaspoons Dijon mustard
- ½ teaspoon salt
- ¼ teaspoon freshly ground black pepper
- 2 garlic cloves, minced

1. To prepare salad, place first 5 ingredients in a large bowl; stir gently to combine.

2. To prepare dressing, combine red wine vinegar and next 6 ingredients, stirring with a whisk. Drizzle over salad, tossing gently to coat. Yield: 5 servings (serving size: about 1¼ cups).

CALORIES 369 (25% from fat); FAT 10.1g (sat 2g, mono 5.7g, poly 1.7g); PROTEIN 29.2g; CARB 41.5g; FIBER 9.6g; CHOL 45mg; IRON 4mg; SODIUM 342mg; CALC 117mg

Cobb Salad with Green Goddess Dressing

In this healthy version of Cobb salad, we've foregone the usual bacon and decreased the amount of cheese. You won't miss these high-fat ingredients when you top this salad with our creamy, flavor-packed Green Goddess Dressing, which is named for its signature green tint.

    8   cups torn romaine lettuce
    1   cup trimmed watercress
1½   cups chopped cooked chicken breast
    2   tomatoes, each cut into 8 wedges (about
        1 pound)
    2   hard-cooked large eggs, each cut into
        4 wedges
 ½   cup diced peeled avocado
 ¼   cup plus 2 tablespoons (1½ ounces)
        crumbled blue cheese
    Green Goddess Dressing

1. Combine lettuce and watercress in a large bowl. Divide lettuce mixture among 4 plates. Arrange chicken, tomato wedges, egg wedges, avocado, and cheese over lettuce mixture. Serve with Green Goddess Dressing. Yield: 4 servings (serving size: about 2 cups lettuce mixture, 6 tablespoons chicken, 4 tomato wedges, 2 egg wedges, 2 tablespoons avocado, 1½ tablespoons cheese, and ¼ cup dressing).

(Totals include Green Goddess Dressing) CALORIES 301 (47% from fat); FAT 15.7g (sat 4.8g, mono 3.5g, poly 1.3g); PROTEIN 26g; CARB 14.4g; FIBER 3.7g; CHOL 167mg; IRON 3.2mg; SODIUM 670mg; CALC 196mg

GREEN GODDESS DRESSING:

 ½   cup plain fat-free yogurt
 ¼   cup light mayonnaise
    3   tablespoons chopped green onions
    3   tablespoons white wine vinegar
    2   tablespoons chopped fresh flat-leaf parsley
    1   tablespoon chopped fresh chives
    2   teaspoons anchovy paste
    1   teaspoon chopped fresh tarragon
 ¼   teaspoon freshly ground black pepper
 ⅛   teaspoon salt
    1   garlic clove, minced

1. Place all ingredients in a blender or food processor; process until smooth. Chill. Yield: 1 cup (serving size: 1 tablespoon).

CALORIES 18 (65% from fat); FAT 1.3g (sat 0.3g, mono 0g, poly 0g); PROTEIN 0.4g; CARB 1.2g; FIBER 0.1g; CHOL 2mg; IRON 0.3mg; SODIUM 109mg; CALC 14mg

About Watercress

Watercress, a member of the mustard family, is one of the traditional ingredients of a Cobb salad. It grows wild in cool running streams and brooks and has small, crisp dark green leaves with a sharp, peppery flavor. This green is sold year-round in small bunches in the supermarket. When buying it, look for leaves with a deep green color. If you cannot find watercress, another pungent-flavored green, such as arugula, makes a good substitute.

Cobb Salad with Green
Goddess Dressing

Grilled Chicken Salad with Feta and Orange Vinaigrette

A great way to use grilled chicken is in a fresh green salad. In this one, the sweetness of orange and bell pepper is a pleasing contrast to the tanginess of feta cheese and the orange vinaigrette.

  1 pound skinless, boneless chicken breast
Cooking spray
  8 cups torn leaf lettuce
  1 cup orange bell pepper strips
  1 cup grape or cherry tomatoes, halved
  ½ cup matchstick-cut carrots
  ½ cup (2 ounces) feta cheese, crumbled
  ¼ cup chopped green onions
  3 tablespoons thawed orange juice concentrate, undiluted
  1 tablespoon white vinegar
  1 tablespoon olive oil
  ⅛ teaspoon salt
  ⅛ teaspoon black pepper
  1 (11-ounce) can mandarin oranges in light syrup, drained
  2 tablespoons sliced almonds, toasted

1. Prepare grill.
2. Place chicken on a grill rack coated with cooking spray; grill 6 minutes on each side or until done. Cut chicken into ½-inch-thick slices. Set aside.
3. Combine lettuce and next 5 ingredients in a large bowl. Combine orange juice concentrate, vinegar, oil, salt, and black pepper; stir with a whisk. Pour juice mixture over lettuce mixture, tossing to coat. Divide lettuce mixture among 4 plates; top with chicken, oranges, and almonds. Yield: 4 servings (serving size: about 2 cups lettuce mixture, 3 ounces chicken, about 10 mandarin orange segments, and 1½ teaspoons almonds).

CALORIES 299 (28% from fat); FAT 9.3g (sat 3g, mono 4.4g, poly 1.2g); PROTEIN 25.1g; CARB 31.2g; FIBER 4.8g; CHOL 62mg; IRON 1.5mg; SODIUM 351mg; CALC 161mg

Greek Salad with Grilled Chicken

Prepare the zesty Greek dressing up to a week in advance; cover and store it in the refrigerator. Then let the dressing serve as both an enhancer for the grilled chicken and a dressing for the salad.

  ¼ cup fat-free, less-sodium chicken broth
  2 tablespoons red wine vinegar
  1 teaspoon sugar
  1 teaspoon dried oregano
  2 teaspoons olive oil
  ½ teaspoon salt
  ½ teaspoon freshly ground black pepper
  1 garlic clove, minced
  4 (6-ounce) skinless, boneless chicken breast halves
Cooking spray
  8 cups torn romaine lettuce
  1 cup sliced cucumber (about 1 small)
  8 pitted kalamata olives, halved
  4 plum tomatoes, quartered lengthwise
  2 (¼-inch-thick) slices red onion, separated into rings
  ¼ cup (1 ounce) crumbled feta cheese

1. Prepare grill or preheat broiler.
2. Combine first 8 ingredients in a small bowl. Brush chicken with 2 tablespoons dressing, and set remaining dressing aside.
3. Place chicken on grill rack or broiler pan coated with cooking spray; cook 5 minutes on each side or until done. Cut into ¼-inch-thick slices.
4. Combine romaine lettuce and next 4 ingredients in a large bowl, and toss with remaining salad dressing. Divide salad among 4 plates; top each serving with sliced chicken, and sprinkle with feta cheese. Yield: 4 servings (serving size: 2 cups salad, 3 ounces chicken, and 1 tablespoon feta cheese).

CALORIES 305 (27% from fat); FAT 9g (sat 2.6g, mono 4.2g, poly 1.3g); PROTEIN 43.3g; CARB 12.1g; FIBER 3.8g; CHOL 107mg; IRON 3.1mg; SODIUM 681mg; CALC 124mg

sandwiches

California Chicken Sandwiches,
page 300

Mediterranean Tuna Sandwiches

Traditional tuna salad is updated with the lively Mediterranean flavors of sun-dried tomatoes, olives, and capers. Serve with a cup of vegetable soup for a complete meal.

- 4 teaspoons olive oil
- 4 teaspoons red wine vinegar
- 8 slices whole-grain bread
- 2 (6-ounce) cans low-sodium tuna in water, drained and flaked
- 1/3 cup roughly chopped drained oil-packed sun-dried tomato halves
- 1/4 cup sliced ripe olives
- 1/4 cup finely chopped red onion
- 3 tablespoons light mayonnaise
- 2 teaspoons capers
- 1/4 teaspoon freshly ground black pepper
- 4 romaine lettuce leaves

1. Combine oil and vinegar in a small bowl; brush oil mixture evenly over 1 side of each bread slice.

2. Combine tuna and next 6 ingredients. Place 1 lettuce leaf on each of 4 bread slices. Top lettuce evenly with tuna mixture, and cover with remaining bread slices. Serve immediately. Yield: 4 servings (serving size: 1 sandwich).

CALORIES 314 (37% from fat); FAT 13g (sat 2.2g, mono 5.6g, poly 1.4g); PROTEIN 21.1g; CARB 29.2g; FIBER 4.5g; CHOL 21mg; IRON 3.4mg; SODIUM 683mg; CALC 72mg

Baja Fish Tacos

You can assemble these tasty tacos in less time than it takes to pick up takeout from your local taquería. A cool mixture of angel hair coleslaw, sour cream, and green onions serves as a crunchy accompaniment to the spicy fish.

- 2 tablespoons taco seasoning
- 1 tablespoon fresh lime juice
- 1 tablespoon fresh orange juice
- 1 pound mahimahi or other firm white fish fillets, cut into bite-sized pieces
- 1 tablespoon canola oil
- 2 cups angel hair coleslaw
- 1/2 cup chopped green onions
- 1/2 cup reduced-fat sour cream
- 8 (6-inch) corn tortillas
Cilantro sprigs (optional)

1. Combine first 3 ingredients in a medium bowl. Add fish; toss to coat.

2. Heat oil in a large nonstick skillet over medium-high heat. Add fish; sauté 5 minutes or until fish is done.

3. Combine coleslaw, green onions, and sour cream in a medium bowl.

4. Warm tortillas according to package directions. Spoon about 1/4 cup cabbage mixture down center of each tortilla. Divide fish evenly among tortillas, and fold in half. Garnish with cilantro, if desired. Yield: 4 servings (serving size: 2 tacos).

CALORIES 339 (26% from fat); FAT 9.9g (sat 2.7g, mono 3.2g, poly 1.4g); PROTEIN 25g; CARB 34.9g; FIBER 3.9g; CHOL 94mg; IRON 2.3mg; SODIUM 501mg; CALC 79mg

Baja Fish Tacos

Garden Tomato and Basil
Pesto Pizza

Garden Tomato and Basil Pesto Pizza

With tomatoes, mozzarella, and basil, this is similar to pizza margherita, a dish that showcases the colors of the Italian flag—red, white, and green. We added commercial pesto for more flavor. Best of all, you'll have hot pizza on your table in about 15 minutes.

    1   (12-ounce) prebaked pizza crust
        (such as Mama Mary's)
    Cooking spray
    2   tablespoons commercial pesto
    4   ounces thinly sliced fresh mozzarella cheese
    2   cups chopped tomato (about 2 large)
    ¼   teaspoon crushed red pepper
    ¼   cup thinly sliced fresh basil

1. Preheat oven to 450°.
2. Spray crust with cooking spray.
3. Place crust on a baking sheet, and bake at 450° for 10 minutes. Spread pesto evenly over crust, leaving a ½-inch border. Top with cheese slices and tomato; sprinkle with pepper. Bake at 450° for 5 minutes or until cheese melts and crust is golden. Sprinkle with basil. Cut into 8 slices. Yield: 4 servings (serving size: 2 slices).

CALORIES 377 (32% from fat); FAT 13.5g (sat 4.9g, mono 0.1g, poly 0.2g); PROTEIN 14.8g; CARB 48.1g; FIBER 3.1g; CHOL 24mg; IRON 3.2mg; SODIUM 687mg; CALC 209mg

Portobello Burgers

    ¼   cup low-sodium soy sauce
    ¼   cup balsamic vinegar
    2   tablespoons olive oil
    3   garlic cloves, minced
    4   (4-inch) portobello mushroom caps
    1   small red bell pepper
    Cooking spray
    ¼   cup low-fat mayonnaise
    ½   teaspoon olive oil
    ⅛   teaspoon ground red pepper
    4   (2-ounce) onion sandwich buns
    4   (¼-inch-thick) slices tomato
    4   curly leaf lettuce leaves

1. Combine first 4 ingredients in a large zip-top plastic bag; add mushrooms to bag. Seal; marinate at room temperature 2 hours, turning bag occasionally. Remove mushrooms from bag, and discard marinade.

2. Prepare grill.
3. Cut bell pepper in half lengthwise; discard seeds and membranes. Place pepper halves on a grill rack coated with cooking spray; grill 15 minutes or until blackened, turning occasionally. Place in a zip-top plastic bag; seal. Let stand 10 minutes. Peel. Reserve 1 pepper half for another use. Finely chop 1 pepper half; place in a small bowl. Add mayonnaise, ½ teaspoon oil, and ground red pepper; stir well.
4. Place mushrooms, gill sides down, on grill rack coated with cooking spray; grill 4 minutes on each side. Place buns, cut sides down, on grill rack coated with cooking spray; grill 30 seconds on each side or until toasted. Spread 2 tablespoons mayonnaise mixture on top half of each bun. Place 1 mushroom on bottom half of each bun. Top each mushroom with 1 tomato slice and 1 lettuce leaf; cover with top halves of buns. Yield: 4 servings (serving size: 1 burger).

CALORIES 285 (38% from fat); FAT 11.6g (sat 2.6g, mono 2.9g, poly 0.5g); PROTEIN 9g; CARB 34.7g; FIBER 2.6g; CHOL 5mg; IRON 1.9mg; SODIUM 699mg; CALC 78mg

Italian Portobello Sandwiches

    1   teaspoon olive oil
    2   cups sliced portobello mushrooms caps
    2   (¼-inch-thick) slices red onion, separated
        into rings
    ¼   cup fat-free mayonnaise
    2   tablespoons chopped fresh basil
    ¼   teaspoon freshly ground black pepper
    4   (1½-ounce) slices sourdough bread
    ⅔   cup bottled roasted red bell peppers
    2   (1-ounce) slices provolone cheese

1. Heat olive oil in a large nonstick skillet over medium heat. Add mushrooms and onion; cover and cook 7 minutes or until onion is tender, stirring occasionally. Remove from heat; cool.
2. Combine mayonnaise, basil, and black pepper. Spread 1 tablespoon mayonnaise mixture on 1 side of each bread slice; layer each of 2 bread slices with ⅓ cup bell peppers, ½ cup mushroom mixture, and 1 slice of cheese. Cover with remaining bread slices. Cut each sandwich in half. Yield: 2 servings (serving size: 1 sandwich).

CALORIES 412 (27% from fat); FAT 12.3g (sat 5.3g, mono 3.8g, poly 0.8g); PROTEIN 18.3g; CARB 60.1g; FIBER 2.6g; CHOL 20mg; IRON 5.9mg; SODIUM 1,117mg; CALC 320mg

Super Sloppy Joe Sandwiches

Kids will love the slightly sweet, saucy filling inside these sandwiches—vegetables and all. Don't be intimidated by the long ingredient list. This is quick to prepare and needs only one skillet. You can swap out the vegetables according to your taste. Eggplant, carrots, and zucchini are other options.

    1   pound ground round
    1¼ cups chopped green bell pepper
    1¼ cups chopped celery
    1   cup chopped onion
    3   garlic cloves, minced
    1   (8-ounce) package presliced mushrooms,
        chopped
    1   cup water
    1   cup ketchup
    1   tablespoon brown sugar
    1   tablespoon fresh lemon juice
    1   tablespoon red wine vinegar
    1   teaspoon paprika
    2   teaspoons Worcestershire sauce
    1   teaspoon Dijon mustard
    ¼   teaspoon fennel seeds
    ¼   teaspoon hot pepper sauce
    6   (2-ounce) Kaiser rolls or hamburger buns,
        toasted

1. Heat a large nonstick skillet over medium-high heat. Add beef; cook 3 minutes or until browned, stirring to crumble. Add bell pepper, celery, onion, garlic, and mushrooms, and cook 7 minutes or until vegetables are tender, stirring occasionally. Stir in water and next 9 ingredients; bring to a boil. Reduce heat, and simmer 25 minutes or until mixture begins to thicken, stirring occasionally.
2. Spoon ⅔ cup meat mixture onto bottom half of each roll. Cover sandwiches with top halves of rolls. Yield: 6 servings (serving size: 1 sandwich).

CALORIES 404 (31% from fat); FAT 14.2g (sat 5.1g, mono 5.5g, poly 1.8g); PROTEIN 21.3g; CARB 49.4g; FIBER 4.1g; CHOL 51mg; IRON 4.1mg; SODIUM 929mg; CALC 97mg

Roast Beef and Blue Cheese Sandwiches

Pungent blue cheese, juicy tomatoes, crunchy bell peppers, and onions come together with simple roast beef for a taste that's out of this world. This cold sandwich will satisfy even the heartiest of appetites.

    2   tablespoons fat-free mayonnaise
    1   tablespoon Dijon mustard
    ¼   teaspoon black pepper
    2   (2-ounce) onion sandwich buns, sliced
    2   romaine lettuce leaves
    4   tomato slices
    4   green bell pepper rings
    4   red onion slices
    4   ounces shaved or thinly sliced lean deli roast
        beef
    2   tablespoons crumbled blue cheese

1. Combine mayonnaise, mustard, and black pepper; stir well. Spread on cut sides of sandwich buns.
2. Line the bottom half of each bun with a lettuce leaf. Top with tomato, bell pepper, onion, roast beef, and cheese. Cover with top halves of buns. Yield: 2 servings (serving size: 1 sandwich).

CALORIES 309 (31% from fat); FAT 10.7g (sat 4.5g, mono 2.7g, poly 1.4g); PROTEIN 18.6g; CARB 35.1g; FIBER 2.5g; CHOL 5mg; IRON 2mg; SODIUM 1,133mg; CALC 53mg

How to Make a Tall Sandwich

To create a tall sandwich, ask the deli to shave the roast beef. Then loosely pile on the meat to create an authentic mile-high deli sandwich at home.

Roast Beef and Blue Cheese
Sandwiches

Classic Hamburgers

There's nothing like a good old-fashioned burger hot off the grill, and these are especially mouthwatering. Top these burgers with slices of crisp, green lettuce, juicy red-ripe tomatoes, zingy purple onion, and a whole wheat kaiser roll. It's a burger as classic as they come.

  1 pound ground round
  ½ cup quick-cooking oats
  ¼ cup minced fresh parsley
  1 tablespoon Dijon mustard
  1 tablespoon Worcestershire sauce
  ½ teaspoon freshly ground black pepper
  2 garlic cloves, minced
  1 small onion, minced (about ¾ cup)
  1 large egg white
Cooking spray
  4 lettuce leaves
  4 whole wheat kaiser rolls, split
  8 thin slices tomato
  4 slices purple onion, separated into rings

1. Prepare grill.
2. Combine first 9 ingredients in a large bowl; stir well. Shape into 4 (¼-inch-thick) patties.
3. Place patties on a grill rack coated with cooking spray; cover and grill 5 minutes on each side or until done.
4. Place 1 lettuce leaf on bottom half of each roll; place patties on rolls. Top each patty with 2 slices of tomato and 1 slice onion. Yield: 4 servings (serving size: 1 burger).

CALORIES 437 (30% from fat); FAT 14.7g (sat.5.1g, mono 5.8g, poly 1.7g); PROTEIN 31.6g; CARB 43.6g; FIBER 3.5g; CHOL 74mg; IRON 5.6mg; SODIUM 495mg; CALC 100mg

Blue Cheese-Stuffed Burgers

A traditional hamburger patty gets a makeover when you add onion, breadcrumbs, and egg white to the meat. Using English muffins, which are usually smaller than buns, allows the blue cheese and the meat to dominate the flavors in this recipe. Try stuffing these burgers with shredded Cheddar or Swiss cheese if you don't like blue cheese.

Cooking spray
  ½ cup finely chopped onion
  1 pound ground round
  3 tablespoons dry breadcrumbs
  2 tablespoons water
  1 egg white, lightly beaten
  ¼ cup (1 ounce) crumbled blue cheese
  ¼ cup fat-free sour cream
  4 (1-ounce) English muffins, toasted
  4 lettuce leaves
  4 (¼-inch-thick) slices tomato

1. Heat a small nonstick skillet over medium heat; coat pan with cooking spray. Add onion; sauté 5 minutes or until tender. Remove from heat; let cool.
2. Combine onion, beef, breadcrumbs, water, and egg white in a large bowl; stir well. Divide mixture into 8 equal portions, shaping each into a ½-inch-thick patty. Spoon 1 tablespoon cheese into center of 4 patties; top with remaining patties. Press edges together to seal.
3. Prepare grill.
4. Place patties on a grill rack coated with cooking spray; grill 4 minutes on each side or until done.
5. Spread 1 tablespoon sour cream over top half of each muffin, and set aside. Line bottom halves of muffins with lettuce leaves; top each with a tomato slice, a patty, and top half of muffin. Yield: 4 servings (serving size: 1 burger).

CALORIES 327 (28% from fat); FAT 10.3g (sat 3.9g, mono 3.7g, poly 0.7g); PROTEIN 31.4g; CARB 25.1g; FIBER 1g; CHOL 75mg; IRON 3.8mg; SODIUM 391mg; CALC 116mg

Knife-and-Fork Barbecued Brisket Sandwiches

Sink your teeth into melt-in-your mouth barbecue without the hassle of a fire pit. Beef brisket lends itself perfectly to the slow cooker, since long, slow, moist heat is the key to transforming this cut into succulent, tender barbecue.

1 (3-pound) beef brisket, trimmed
2 tablespoons all-purpose flour
2 large onions, thinly sliced and divided
1 teaspoon black pepper
¼ teaspoon salt
1 (12-ounce) bottle chili sauce
½ cup light beer
2 tablespoons brown sugar
1 tablespoon prepared horseradish
4 large garlic cloves, minced, or 1 tablespoon bottled minced garlic
12 (1-ounce) slices barbecue bread with sesame seeds, toasted

1. Cut brisket into 4 pieces. Dredge pieces in flour, reserving any remaining flour.

2. Place half of onion in a 4-quart electric slow cooker, and top with beef. Sprinkle with reserved flour, pepper, and salt. Arrange remaining half of onion over beef.

3. Combine chili sauce and next 4 ingredients; stir well. Pour over beef mixture. Cover and cook on HIGH 1 hour. Reduce heat to LOW, and cook 7 to 8 hours or until beef is tender. Remove beef with a slotted spoon. Replace cooker lid.

4. Shred beef with 2 forks; return beef to cooker, stirring well. Spoon beef mixture over toasted bread. Yield: 12 servings (serving size: ¾ cup beef mixture and 1 slice toast).

CALORIES 271 (18% from fat); FAT 5.4g (sat 1.6g, mono 1.8g, poly 0.7g); PROTEIN 27.9g; CARB 27.5g; FIBER 1.5g; CHOL 46mg; IRON 3.1mg; SODIUM 1,009mg; CALC 49mg

Garlic-Rosemary Lamb Pitas

In our superfast version of the traditional gyro, juicy seasoned lamb is tucked into a pita and drizzled with tzatziki (cucumber-yogurt sauce). Serve with a Greek salad to round out the meal.

2 teaspoons olive oil
1 tablespoon chopped fresh rosemary
1 teaspoon bottled minced garlic
½ teaspoon salt, divided
¼ teaspoon black pepper
1 pound boneless leg of lamb, cut into (¾-inch) cubes
1½ cups finely chopped seeded cucumber
1 tablespoon fresh lemon juice
⅛ teaspoon black pepper
1 (6-ounce) container plain low-fat yogurt
4 (6-inch) whole wheat pitas, halved

1. Heat oil in a large nonstick skillet over medium-high heat. Combine rosemary, garlic, ¼ teaspoon salt, ¼ teaspoon pepper, and lamb, tossing to coat. Add lamb mixture to pan; sauté 4 minutes or until done.

2. Combine remaining ¼ teaspoon salt, cucumber, lemon juice, ⅛ teaspoon pepper, and yogurt. Place lamb mixture inside pita halves, and drizzle with sauce. Yield: 4 servings (serving size: 2 pita halves and ⅔ cup sauce).

CALORIES 391 (26% from fat); FAT 11.5g (sat 3.5g, mono 4.8g, poly 1.5g); PROTEIN 32.7g; CARB 40.8g; FIBER 5.3g; CHOL 77mg; IRON 4.4mg; SODIUM 742mg; CALC 117mg

Grilled Pork Tenderloin Sandwiches

For an easy, on-the-go meal, prepare the pork and assemble the sandwiches at home. Simply wrap them in aluminum foil, and they'll stay warm while you travel. Or slice and refrigerate roasted tenderloin, and serve the sandwiches cold. Take along the dressing, and allow everyone to put together their own sandwiches.

¼ cup hot jalapeño jelly
1 teaspoon water
1 tablespoon paprika
1½ teaspoons salt
1 teaspoon granulated sugar
1 teaspoon brown sugar
1 teaspoon chili powder
1 teaspoon ground cumin
½ teaspoon freshly ground black pepper
2 (1-pound) pork tenderloins, trimmed
Cooking spray
¼ cup light ranch dressing
¼ cup sweet hickory smoke tomato-based barbecue sauce (such as Bull's-Eye)
8 (1½-ounce) hamburger buns or Kaiser rolls

1. Prepare grill.

2. Combine jelly and water; set aside.

3. Combine paprika and next 6 ingredients; rub evenly over pork. Place pork on a grill rack coated with cooking spray; cover and grill 15 minutes, turning pork occasionally. Brush pork with jelly mixture. Grill 5 minutes or until thermometer registers 160° (slightly pink).

4. Place pork on a cutting surface. Cover loosely with foil; let stand 10 minutes. Cut pork into thin slices. Combine ranch dressing and barbecue sauce. Serve pork and ranch mixture with buns. Yield: 8 servings (serving size: 1 bun, 3 ounces pork, and 1 tablespoon sauce).

CALORIES 329 (22% from fat); FAT 8g (sat 2g, mono 2.1g, poly 1.6g); PROTEIN 27.8g; CARB 34.6g; FIBER 1.8g; CHOL 76mg; IRON 3.1mg; SODIUM 920mg; CALC 73mg

Spicy Pork and Sauerkraut Sandwiches

A packaged coleslaw mix creates the base for an easy, speedy "sauerkraut" that's more colorful and less salty than jarred or canned sauerkraut. And it still adds plenty of zip when it's served over the pork. Round out this German-style sandwich with raw vegetables and a low-fat dip.

½ teaspoon dried oregano
½ teaspoon dried thyme
½ teaspoon black pepper
¼ teaspoon salt
1 pound pork tenderloin, trimmed and cut crosswise into ¼-inch-thick slices
1 tablespoon canola oil, divided
4 cups packaged cabbage-and-carrot coleslaw (about 8 ounces)
1 tablespoon prepared horseradish
1 tablespoon red wine vinegar
½ teaspoon crushed red pepper
1½ teaspoons Worcestershire sauce
⅓ cup fat-free mayonnaise
1 tablespoon Dijon mustard
4 (2-ounce) Kaiser rolls or hamburger buns
16 (⅛-inch-thick) slices cucumber

1. Combine first 4 ingredients; sprinkle pork with herb mixture. Heat 1½ teaspoons oil in a large non-stick skillet over medium-high heat. Add pork, and cook 2 minutes on each side or until done. Remove pork from pan, and keep warm.

2. Heat remaining 1½ teaspoons oil in pan over medium-high heat. Add coleslaw and next 4 ingredients; cook 2 minutes, stirring frequently. Remove from heat.

3. Combine mayonnaise and mustard; spread mixture evenly over cut sides of rolls. Divide pork, cucumber slices, and coleslaw mixture evenly among bottom halves of rolls. Cover with top halves of rolls. Yield: 4 servings (serving size: 1 sandwich).

CALORIES 368 (26% from fat); FAT 10.5g (sat 2g, mono 4.3g, poly 2.4g); PROTEIN 29.1g; CARB 37.7g; FIBER 3.6g; CHOL 65mg; IRON 3.6mg; SODIUM 754mg; CALC 73mg

Pear, Pecorino, and Prosciutto Panini

Panini (pah-NEE-nee) technically translates as "rolls" or "little bread," but in Italy, the name is synonymous with sandwiches. The key to a good panino (singular) is high-quality bread, usually ciabatta, or in this case focaccia. Thinly sliced, rust-colored prosciutto, crisp garden green arugula, perfectly ripe pears, and freshly shaved tangy pecorino Romano cheese nestle inside crunchy focaccia. If you prefer cooked prosciutto, sauté it until it's crisp. Parmigiano-Reggiano makes a good substitute for pecorino Romano cheese.

 1 firm, ripe pear, peeled, cored, and cut into
    8 wedges
 ½ teaspoon sugar
 1 (12-ounce) loaf focaccia, cut in half
    horizontally
 4 teaspoons balsamic vinegar
 1 cup trimmed arugula
 ½ cup (2 ounces) fresh pecorino Romano
    cheese, shaved
 16 very thin slices prosciutto (about 4 ounces)

1. Heat a nonstick skillet over medium-high heat. Add pear to pan, and sprinkle with sugar. Cook 2 minutes on each side or until golden.
2. Brush cut sides of bread with vinegar. Arrange pear wedges, arugula, cheese, and prosciutto evenly over bottom half of bread; cover with top half of bread.
3. Heat pan over medium heat. Add stuffed loaf to pan. Place a cast-iron or heavy skillet on top of stuffed loaf; press gently to flatten. Cook 4 minutes on each side or until bread is toasted (leave cast-iron skillet on stuffed loaf while it cooks). Cut into quarters. Yield: 4 servings (serving size: 1 sandwich quarter).

CALORIES 383 (29% from fat); FAT 12.3g (sat 5.3g, mono 2.7g, poly 1.7g); PROTEIN 18.7g; CARB 50.8g; FIBER 2.7g; CHOL 40mg; IRON 2.8mg; SODIUM 1,019mg; CALC 178mg

Chicken, Arugula, and Tomato Pizza

Even on nights when you don't feel like cooking, a gourmet meal is still in reach. Topped with chicken, arugula, and juicy tomatoes, this refreshing pizza is part salad and part open-faced sandwich. The "sauce" is a chunky combination of crunchy walnuts, tangy feta, and oregano. You can use red instead of yellow tomatoes and substitute spinach for the arugula, if desired.

 2 (7-inch) individual prebaked pizza crusts
    (such as Mama Mary's)
 2 tablespoons coarsely chopped walnuts
 ½ cup (2 ounces) reduced-fat feta cheese
 1 tablespoon fat-free milk
 1 teaspoon chopped fresh or ¼ teaspoon dried
    oregano
 ¼ teaspoon black pepper
 1 cup trimmed arugula
 1 cup shredded roasted chicken breast
 1 cup chopped yellow tomato
 ¼ cup chopped red onion
 1 teaspoon white balsamic vinegar
 ⅛ teaspoon black pepper

1. Bake pizza crusts according to package directions, omitting fat.
2. While crusts bake, heat a small skillet over medium-high heat. Add walnuts; cook 3 minutes or until lightly browned, stirring constantly. Place walnuts, feta, milk, oregano, and ¼ teaspoon pepper in a food processor; pulse to combine.
3. Combine arugula and next 5 ingredients; toss well. Divide walnut mixture evenly between pizza crusts; spread evenly. Divide arugula mixture evenly between crusts. Yield: 2 servings (serving size: 1 pizza).

CALORIES 307 (32% from fat); FAT 10.4g (sat 2.8g, mono 1.8g, poly 4.8g); PROTEIN 11.9g; CARB 37g; FIBER 4.1g; CHOL 24mg; IRON 1.4mg; SODIUM 486mg; CALC 94mg

Chicken, Arugula, and
Tomato Pizza

Balsamic-Glazed Chicken and
Bell Pepper Sandwiches

Balsamic-Glazed Chicken and Bell Pepper Sandwiches

Balsamic vinegar cooks down to a glaze that clings to the sandwich fillings, adding a hint of sweetness and a touch of acidity. Pressing the assembled sandwich traps the heat from the cooked chicken and vegetables, which melts the cheese.

4 teaspoons olive oil, divided
½ teaspoon salt, divided
1¼ pounds chicken breast tenders
½ cup balsamic vinegar, divided
2 cups red bell pepper strips (about 2 medium)
2 cups vertically sliced onion (about 1 large)
2 (8-ounce) loaves focaccia, cut in half horizontally
4 ounces provolone cheese, thinly sliced
⅛ teaspoon black pepper

1. Heat 2 teaspoons olive oil in a large nonstick skillet over medium-high heat. Sprinkle ¼ teaspoon salt over chicken. Add chicken to pan, and cook 1 minute on each side or until lightly browned. Add ¼ cup vinegar; cook 2 minutes or until chicken is done and vinegar is syrupy. Remove chicken mixture from pan; cover and keep warm. Wipe pan clean with a paper towel.
2. Return pan to medium-high heat, and add remaining 2 teaspoons oil. Add bell pepper and onion; sauté 7 minutes or until tender. Stir in remaining ¼ teaspoon salt and remaining ¼ cup vinegar; cook 1 minute or until vinegar is syrupy.
3. Arrange chicken mixture evenly over bottom halves of bread; top with bell pepper mixture. Arrange cheese over pepper mixture, and sprinkle with black pepper. Top with top halves of bread. Place a cast-iron or heavy skillet on top of sandwiches; let stand 5 minutes. Cut each sandwich into 6 wedges. Yield: 6 servings (serving size: 2 wedges).

CALORIES 433 (24% from fat); FAT 11.4g (sat 4.2g, mono 5.4g, poly 1g); PROTEIN 34g; CARB 49g; FIBER 1.9g; CHOL 68mg; IRON 3.6mg; SODIUM 709mg; CALC 170mg

Grilled Chicken Mojito Sandwiches

Chicken tenders are ideal for sandwiches because the small pieces fit nicely on rolls and buns.

DRESSING:
¼ cup light mayonnaise
¼ teaspoon finely grated lime rind
3 tablespoons minced fresh mint
1 tablespoon fresh lime juice
1 teaspoon sugar
1 teaspoon minced serrano chile (with seeds)
SANDWICHES:
1 tablespoon minced fresh mint
3 tablespoons fresh lime juice
2 tablespoons dark rum
1 teaspoon ground cumin
1 garlic clove, crushed
1 pound chicken breast tenders
4 (¼-inch-thick) slices Vidalia or other sweet onion
Cooking spray
¼ teaspoon salt
¼ teaspoon freshly ground black pepper
4 (2-ounce) French rolls, halved
8 (¼-inch-thick) slices tomato
4 red leaf lettuce leaves

1. To prepare dressing, combine first 6 ingredients in a small bowl, stirring with a whisk. Cover and chill.
2. To prepare sandwiches, combine 1 tablespoon mint and next 4 ingredients in a large zip-top plastic bag. Add chicken breast tenders; seal and marinate in refrigerator 15 minutes, turning occasionally.
3. Prepare grill.
4. Remove chicken from bag; discard marinade. Place chicken and onion on a grill rack coated with cooking spray. Grill 4 minutes on each side or until chicken is done and onion is tender. Remove chicken and onion from grill; sprinkle chicken with salt and pepper.
5. Grill roll halves, cut sides down, about 1 minute or until lightly toasted. Spread about 1 tablespoon dressing over bottom halves of rolls.
6. Top each serving with 3 ounces chicken breast tenders, 1 onion slice, 2 tomato slices, and 1 lettuce leaf; cover with top halves of rolls. Yield: 4 servings (serving size: 1 sandwich).

CALORIES 375 (22% from fat); FAT 9.1g (sat 2g, mono 1.5g, poly 0.9g); PROTEIN 32.2g; CARB 37.7g; FIBER 3.3g; CHOL 71mg; IRON 3mg; SODIUM 693mg; CALC 90mg

Chicken Soft Tacos with Sautéed
Onions and Apples

Chicken Soft Tacos with Sautéed Onions and Apples

And you thought that apples were only good in grandmother's apple pies! The unusual pairing of apples, chicken, onion, and nutmeg in this savory-sweet taco filling is divinely delicious.

1 tablespoon olive oil
1 pound skinless, boneless chicken breast, cut into bite-sized pieces
½ teaspoon salt
½ teaspoon ground nutmeg
½ teaspoon freshly ground black pepper
1 tablespoon butter
2 cups thinly sliced onion
2 cups thinly sliced peeled Granny Smith apple (about 2 apples)
2 garlic cloves, minced
8 (6-inch) flour tortillas

1. Heat oil in a large nonstick skillet over medium-high heat. Sprinkle chicken evenly with salt, nutmeg, and pepper. Add chicken to pan; sauté 7 minutes or until golden. Remove chicken from pan; keep warm.
2. Melt butter in pan over medium heat. Add onion, and cook 4 minutes or until tender, stirring frequently. Add apple; cook 6 minutes or until golden, stirring frequently. Add garlic, and sauté 30 seconds. Return chicken to pan; cook 2 minutes or until thoroughly heated, stirring frequently.
3. Heat tortillas according to package directions. Arrange ½ cup chicken mixture over each tortilla. Yield: 4 servings (serving size: 2 tacos).

CALORIES 454 (25% from fat); FAT 12.6g (sat 3.8g, mono 6.1g, poly 1.5g); PROTEIN 32.9g; CARB 51.5g; FIBER 4.8g; CHOL 73mg; IRON 3.3mg; SODIUM 705mg; CALC 116mg

Sizzling Chicken Fajitas

Sometimes the best fajitas are homemade. And these truly stack up to any local Mexican restaurant's best. Easy to prepare and packed with flavor, this recipe is one you'll turn to every time you get a craving for authentic fajita fare.

½ cup low-sodium soy sauce
⅓ cup water
⅓ cup white vinegar
¼ teaspoon garlic powder
¼ teaspoon black pepper
1½ pounds skinless, boneless chicken breast
Cooking spray
1 tablespoon canola oil
1 cup green bell pepper strips (about 1 medium)
1 cup red bell pepper strips (about 1 medium)
1 cup vertically sliced red onion
1 teaspoon seasoned salt
6 (8-inch) fat-free flour tortillas
¾ cup bottled salsa
¾ cup fat-free sour cream

1. Combine first 5 ingredients; reserve ¼ cup soy sauce mixture. Combine remaining mixture and chicken in a large zip-top plastic bag. Seal and marinate in refrigerator 3 hours, turning occasionally.
2. Prepare grill.
3. Remove chicken from marinade; discard marinade. Place chicken on a grill rack coated with cooking spray; cover and grill 10 minutes on each side or until done.
4. Heat oil in a large nonstick skillet over medium-high heat. Add bell peppers and onion; sprinkle with seasoned salt. Sauté 4 minutes or until tender. Add reserved soy sauce mixture, and cook 2 minutes. Cut chicken into thin slices; add to vegetable mixture.
5. Warm tortillas according to package directions. Keep chicken warm in skillet while preparing tortilla. Serve chicken mixture immediately with warm tortillas, salsa, and sour cream. Yield: 6 servings (serving size: 1 cup chicken mixture, 2 tablespoons salsa, 2 tablespoons sour cream, and 1 tortilla).

CALORIES 353 (11% from fat); FAT 4.4g (sat 0.6g, mono 1.7g, poly 1.1g); PROTEIN 33.9g; CARB 41.9g; FIBER 3.4g; CHOL 71mg; IRON 1.2mg; SODIUM 1,366mg; CALC 90mg

California Chicken Sandwiches

(pictured on page 283)

A citrus mayonnaise and avocado give this sandwich its West Coast appeal. Sprinkle the sandwiches with salt and freshly ground black pepper to taste.

CITRUS MAYONNAISE:
- ⅓ cup fat-free mayonnaise
- 2 tablespoons thawed orange juice concentrate
- 1 teaspoon lime juice
- ½ teaspoon ground cumin
- ⅛ teaspoon hot sauce

SANDWICHES:
- 4 (4-ounce) skinless, boneless chicken breast halves
- ¼ teaspoon salt
- ⅛ teaspoon black pepper
- Cooking spray
- 8 (1½-ounce) slices diagonally cut sourdough bread, toasted
- 4 small romaine lettuce leaves
- 2 plum tomatoes, each cut lengthwise into 4 slices
- 1 peeled avocado, cut into 8 wedges

1. To prepare citrus mayonnaise, combine first 5 ingredients in a small bowl.

2. To prepare sandwiches, sprinkle chicken with salt and pepper. Heat a large nonstick skillet over medium-high heat; coat pan with cooking spray. Add chicken. Cook 5 minutes on each side. Reduce heat to low. Cover and cook 5 minutes or until done. Remove from heat. Cut chicken diagonally across grain into thin slices.

3. Spread citrus mayonnaise evenly on each of 4 bread slices. Top each with 1 lettuce leaf, 1 sliced chicken breast half, 2 tomato slices, and 2 avocado wedges. Cover with remaining bread slices. Yield: 4 servings (serving size: 1 sandwich).

CALORIES 432 (19% from fat); FAT 8.9g (sat 1.8g, mono 4.4g, poly 1.5g); PROTEIN 35.2g; CARB 52.8g; FIBER 2.8g; CHOL 66mg; IRON 3.7mg; SODIUM 951mg; CALC 112mg

Turkey Burgers with Goat Cheese

Turkey burgers are a low-fat and delicious alternative to ground beef. Like regular hamburgers, they're shaped into patties and can be cooked on the grill or stove, or cooked in the oven.

- 3 pounds lean ground turkey
- 3 tablespoons chopped fresh parsley
- 1 tablespoon chopped fresh rosemary
- ¼ teaspoon kosher salt
- ¼ teaspoon freshly ground black pepper
- Cooking spray
- 8 (1½-ounce) hamburger buns
- 4 ounces goat cheese, cut into 8 slices
- Grilled Pepper Relish (optional)

1. Prepare grill.

2. Combine first 5 ingredients in a large bowl. Divide turkey mixture into 8 equal portions, shaping each into a ½-inch-thick patty. Place patties on a grill rack coated with cooking spray; cook 5 minutes on each side or until done. Place buns, cut sides down, on grill rack; cook 1 minute or until lightly browned. Place patties on bottom halves of buns. Top each patty with 1 slice cheese and, if desired, Grilled Pepper Relish. Cover with top halves of buns. Yield: 8 servings (serving size: 1 burger).

CALORIES 336 (19% from fat); FAT 7.1g (sat 2.5g, mono 1.1g, poly 1g); PROTEIN 48.2g; CARB 22.2g; FIBER 1.2g; CHOL 74mg; IRON 3.5mg; SODIUM 466mg; CALC 60mg

GRILLED PEPPER RELISH:

- 4 bell peppers (assorted colors, such as red, yellow, and orange)
- ¼ cup chopped fresh basil
- 2 tablespoons chopped pitted kalamata olives
- 1 tablespoon balsamic vinegar
- 1 teaspoon chopped fresh thyme
- 1½ teaspoons olive oil
- ¼ teaspoon salt
- ¼ teaspoon black pepper

1. Prepare grill.

2. Place bell peppers on grill rack. Grill, without lid, 5 to 7 minutes, turning frequently, until peppers blister. Place peppers in a zip-top plastic bag; seal. Let stand 15 minutes. Peel peppers; remove and discard seeds. Cut peppers into ½-inch pieces.

3. Combine bell peppers and remaining ingredients in a medium bowl; toss well. Yield: 8 servings (serving size: ¼ cup).

CALORIES 39 (55% from fat); FAT 2.4g (sat 0.3g, mono 1.8g, poly 0.2g); PROTEIN 0.1g; CARB 4.1g; FIBER 0.1g; CHOL 0mg; IRON 0.3mg; SODIUM 99mg; CALC 9mg

sides

Fruited Israeli Couscous,
page 308

Marinated Grilled Apples with Mint

Serve these highly flavored apple rings as a side with pork or chicken. (One serving size for this recipe is three apple slices, but you can easily double the number of slices for even larger, guilt-free portions.) We liked this recipe with Granny Smiths. For a dessert version, use Pink Lady apples, and serve with low-fat ice cream.

⅔ cup fresh orange juice
1 tablespoon chopped fresh mint
2 tablespoons honey
1 teaspoon vanilla extract
½ teaspoon ground ginger
¼ teaspoon black pepper
3 Granny Smith apples, cored and each cut
   crosswise into 4 (½-inch) slices
Cooking spray

1. Combine first 6 ingredients in a large zip-top plastic bag. Add apple slices; seal and marinate in refrigerator 1 to 2 hours, turning bag occasionally.
2. Prepare grill.
3. Remove apple from bag, reserving marinade. Place apple slices on a grill rack coated with cooking spray; grill 3 minutes on each side, turning and basting frequently with reserved marinade. Arrange apple slices on a platter; drizzle with any remaining marinade. Yield: 4 servings (serving size: 3 apple slices).

CALORIES 116 (4% from fat); FAT 0.5g (sat 0.1g, mono 0g, poly 0.1g); PROTEIN 0.6g; CARB 29.3g; FIBER 3g; CHOL 0mg; IRON 0.4mg; SODIUM 1mg; CALC 14mg

Grilled Plantains

Because the ripe plantains are so tender, they're grilled in their skins to keep them in one piece. Try with Rum-Marinated Chicken Breasts with Pineapple Relish (recipe on page 200). A ripe plantain is believed to be more easily digestible than a ripe banana and is widely known for its health benefits. Also, be careful if you want to try to peel a plantain, since the juice can stain clothing and skin, and is very difficult to remove.

  3 soft black plantains, unpeeled
      (about 1½ pounds)
  2 tablespoons butter, melted
  1 teaspoon brown sugar
 ⅛ teaspoon ground red pepper
Cooking spray
  6 lime wedges

1. Prepare grill, heating to medium.
2. Cut plantains in half lengthwise. Cut plantain halves in half crosswise. Combine butter, sugar, and pepper, and brush evenly over cut sides of plantain sections.
3. Place plantain sections, cut sides up, on a grill rack coated with cooking spray; grill 7 minutes or until flesh is soft and skins begin to pull away from flesh. Turn plantain sections over; grill 3 minutes. Serve warm with lime wedges. Yield: 6 servings (serving size: 2 plantain sections and 1 lime wedge).

CALORIES 174 (22% from fat); FAT 4.3g (sat 2.6g, mono 1.2g, poly 0.2g); PROTEIN 1.5g; CARB 36.7g; FIBER 2.6g; CHOL 10mg; IRON 0.7mg; SODIUM 44mg; CALC 5mg

Edamame-Garlic Puree

This versatile edamame puree is a perfect side dish for grilled fish or chicken. With the addition of tofu, it's creamy and packed with soy protein.

  4 cups frozen blanched shelled edamame
      (green soybeans)
 10 garlic cloves, peeled
 ¼ cup soft silken tofu
1½ teaspoons lemon juice
 ¾ teaspoon salt
 ⅛ teaspoon black pepper

1. Bring 2 quarts water to a boil in a medium saucepan over medium-high heat; add edamame and garlic. Cook 5 minutes. Drain in a colander over a bowl, reserving ½ cup liquid.

2. Place edamame, garlic, ½ cup cooking liquid, and tofu in a food processor, and process until smooth (about 3 minutes). Add lemon juice, salt, and pepper, and pulse to combine. Yield: 5 servings (serving size: ⅔ cup).

CALORIES 176 (27% from fat); FAT 5.2g (sat 0.6g, mono 0.9g, poly 3g); PROTEIN 13.8g; CARB 16.9g; FIBER 6.6g; CHOL 0mg; IRON 2.8mg; SODIUM 402mg; CALC 95mg

Roasted Sweet Onions

Serve these delicate cooked onions as an accompaniment to grilled steak or burgers or as a pizza topping. Save any liquid that remains in the slow cooker to flavor soups or stocks.

  4 medium sweet onions
  Cooking spray
  3 tablespoons extravirgin olive oil
1½ teaspoons salt
  2 teaspoons chopped fresh thyme
  2 tablespoons balsamic vinegar
 ¼ teaspoon freshly ground black pepper

1. Cut each onion into 8 wedges. Place onion in a 6-quart oval electric slow cooker coated with cooking spray; drizzle onion with olive oil. Sprinkle evenly with salt and chopped thyme. Drizzle with balsamic vinegar; sprinkle with pepper.
2. Cover and cook on HIGH 3 to 4 hours or until browned and tender. Yield: 6 servings (serving size: about 5 wedges).

CALORIES 107 (59% from fat); FAT 7g (sat 1g, mono 5.4g, poly 0.6g); PROTEIN 1.4g; CARB 10.2g; FIBER 2.1g; CHOL 0mg; IRON 0.3mg; SODIUM 586mg; CALC 30mg

Grilled Fries

Serve these fries with Grilled Porterhouse Steak (recipe on page 132). If you have a large enough grill, start grilling the potatoes with the steak so everything will be done at the same time. Otherwise, tent the beef with foil to keep it warm. This perfect combination will guarantee rave reviews from friends and family.

2 teaspoons paprika
1 teaspoon sea or kosher salt
1 teaspoon coarsely ground black pepper
½ teaspoon garlic powder
½ teaspoon onion powder
½ teaspoon chili powder
1 teaspoon olive oil
2 baking potatoes, each cut into 12 wedges (about 1½ pounds)
2 sweet potatoes, each cut into 12 wedges (about 1½ pounds)
Cooking spray

1. Combine first 6 ingredients in a small bowl. Combine oil and potatoes in a large bowl, tossing to coat. Sprinkle potatoes with paprika mixture; toss gently to coat.
2. Prepare grill.
3. Place potatoes on a grill rack coated with cooking spray over medium heat; grill 18 minutes or until sweet potatoes are tender, turning occasionally. Remove sweet potatoes; keep warm. Grill baking potatoes an additional 6 minutes or until tender. Yield: 6 servings (serving size: 8 fries).

CALORIES 171 (5% from fat); FAT 1g (sat 0.2g, mono 0.6g, poly 0.2g); PROTEIN 3.9g; CARB 37.9g; FIBER 4.3g; CHOL 0mg; IRON 1.7mg; SODIUM 441mg; CALC 43mg

Coconut-Pecan Sweet Potatoes

This sweet-potato classic is a favorite at Thanksgiving, and that's exactly when your oven is in high demand. This slow-cooker version not only saves oven space, but it also stays nice and warm in the cooker while you finish cooking the other dishes.

2 pounds sweet potatoes, peeled and cut into 1-inch pieces (about 5½ cups)
¼ cup packed brown sugar
2 tablespoons flaked sweetened coconut
2 tablespoons chopped pecans, toasted
1 tablespoon butter, melted
1 teaspoon vanilla extract
¼ teaspoon ground cinnamon
Cooking spray
½ cup miniature marshmallows

1. Place first 7 ingredients in a 3½-quart electric slow cooker coated with cooking spray; toss well. Cover and cook on LOW 6 to 8 hours or until potatoes are tender. Mash potato mixture.
2. Turn cooker off. Sprinkle marshmallows over potatoes; cover and let stand 5 minutes. Yield: 7 servings (serving size: ½ cup).

CALORIES 155 (21% from fat); FAT 3.7g (sat 1.6g, mono 1.3g, poly 0.6g); PROTEIN 1.7g; CARB 29.6g; FIBER 2.8g; CHOL 4mg; IRON 1mg; SODIUM 48mg; CALC 37mg

About Flaked Coconut

There are many types of coconut available on the market: sweetened or unsweetened; shredded or flaked; canned, frozen, or dried. Flaked sweetened coconut is the most widely used and is a useful staple ingredient to keep on hand. Look for it in bags or cans on the baking aisle. An unopened bag of flaked sweetened coconut can keep in the pantry for six months; once opened, it needs to be refrigerated and can be kept for up to one month.

Coconut-Pecan Sweet Potatoes

Root Vegetable Medley

Root Vegetable Medley

The earthy, mildly sweet flavors in this dish make this an excellent side dish to round out an autumn menu. For an elegant presentation, purchase whole baby carrots with green tops. Trim the greens and peel the carrots before adding them to the cooker. For an everyday meal, prepeeled and prewashed bagged baby carrots will do.

1	pound small red potatoes, quartered
1	pound turnips, peeled and cut into ½-inch cubes
1	pound sweet potatoes, peeled and cut into ½-inch cubes
½	pound celeriac (celery root), peeled and cut into ½-inch cubes
½	pound peeled baby carrots
2	cups thinly sliced fennel bulb
3	tablespoons extravirgin olive oil
2	tablespoons balsamic vinegar
1	teaspoon salt
1	teaspoon black pepper
1	teaspoon fennel seeds

1. Place all ingredients in a 6-quart electric slow cooker, and toss well. Cover and cook on LOW 7 to 8 hours or until vegetables are tender. Yield: 8 servings (serving size: 1 cup).

CALORIES 168 (30% from fat); FAT 5.6g (sat 0.8g, mono 4.1g, poly 0.6g); PROTEIN 3.1g; CARB 27.3g; FIBER 5.1mg; CHOL 0mg; IRON 1.3mg; SODIUM 367mg; CALC 69mg

About Turnips

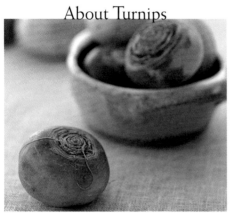

Though turnips are available year-round, their peak season is from October through February. When they're attached, fresh bright greens and a firm root are the hallmarks of a turnip's freshness. Also look for turnips that feel heavy for their size—these are the young ones. They'll be more delicately flavored and have a better texture than older turnips.

Ratatouille

Ratatouille, pronounced ra-tuh-TOO-ee, hails from the French region of Provence. Its ingredients—eggplant, onion, bell pepper, zucchini, and tomato—reflect the bounty of that area. Salting the eggplant before adding it to the slow cooker draws excess water out of the porous vegetable, firming the flesh and taking away any bitterness. Serve this side dish warm, at room temperature, or chilled.

1	(1-pound) eggplant, peeled and cut into 1-inch chunks (about 3 cups)
1½	teaspoons salt, divided
1	large onion, cut in half lengthwise and sliced (about 2½ cups)
1½	cups green bell pepper strips
1½	cups red bell pepper strips
3	medium zucchini, sliced (about 4 cups)
2	pounds plum tomatoes, cut into ½-inch wedges
3	tablespoons tomato paste
2	tablespoons extravirgin olive oil
¼	teaspoon black pepper
3	garlic cloves, minced
½	cup chopped fresh basil
¼	cup capers

Freshly ground black pepper (optional)

1. Place eggplant in a colander over a sink. Toss with ¼ teaspoon salt. Let stand 30 minutes to drain. Pat dry with paper towels.
2. Layer half each of onion, eggplant, bell pepper strips, zucchini, and tomatoes in a 6-quart electric slow cooker. Combine remaining 1¼ teaspoons salt, tomato paste, oil, black pepper, and garlic. Spoon half of oil mixture over vegetables. Repeat layers, ending with oil mixture.
3. Cover and cook on LOW 6 hours or until vegetables are tender. Stir in chopped basil and capers. Spoon ratatouille into individual bowls; sprinkle with freshly ground black pepper, if desired. Yield: 10 servings (serving size: 1 cup).

CALORIES 76 (38% from fat); FAT 3.2g (sat 0.5g, mono 2.2g, poly 0.5g); PROTEIN 2.6g; CARB 11.4g; FIBER 3.9g; CHOL 0mg; IRON 0.8mg; SODIUM 490mg; CALC 32mg

Fruited Israeli Couscous

(pictured on page 301)

The only tools this recipe requires are a saucepan, a cutting board, and a knife. Cinnamon sticks steeped in the cooking liquid lend warm spiciness to the couscous and dried fruit.

  2   teaspoons butter
  1   cup finely chopped onion
  ½   cup dried currants
  ½   cup diced dried apricots
  ½   teaspoon salt
  3   (14-ounce) cans fat-free, less-sodium chicken broth
  3   (3-inch) cinnamon sticks
2½   cups uncooked Israeli couscous
  ¼   cup chopped fresh cilantro

1. Melt butter in a large saucepan over medium-high heat. Add onion, and sauté 5 minutes. Stir in currants and next 4 ingredients; bring to a boil. Add couscous, and return to a boil. Cover, reduce heat, and simmer 15 minutes. Let couscous mixture stand 5 minutes. Discard cinnamon sticks. Stir in cilantro. Yield: 12 servings (serving size: about ⅔ cup).

CALORIES 190 (4% from fat); FAT 0.9g (sat 0.4g, mono 0.2g, poly 0.1g); PROTEIN 6.5g; CARB 38.2g; FIBER 2.8g; CHOL 2mg; IRON 1mg; SODIUM 297mg; CALC 21mg

Creamy Two-Cheese Polenta

This mildly flavored staff favorite pairs nicely with a spicy main dish such as Herb, Garlic, and Mustard-Crusted Fillet of Beef (recipe on page 140). The polenta is best served immediately, but if you have to wait a few minutes, keep it warm by covering it and placing it over very low heat. Stir occasionally.

  4   cups 1% low-fat milk
  1   cup water
1¼   teaspoons salt
  ¼   teaspoon freshly ground black pepper
1¼   cups instant dry polenta
  ⅓   cup (about 2½ ounces) mascarpone cheese
  ⅓   cup (about 1½ ounces) grated Parmigiano-Reggiano cheese
Freshly ground pepper (optional)

1. Combine first 4 ingredients in a medium saucepan over medium-high heat. Bring to a boil; gradually add polenta, stirring constantly with a whisk. Cook 2 minutes or until thick, stirring constantly. Remove from heat; stir in cheeses. Serve immediately. Yield: 8 servings (serving size: about ⅔ cup).

CALORIES 206 (28% from fat); FAT 6.4g (sat 3.7g, mono 0.7g, poly 0.1g); PROTEIN 8.5g; CARB 28.7g; FIBER 2.5g; CHOL 19mg; IRON 0.6mg; SODIUM 493mg; CALC 207mg

About Mascarpone

Mascarpone is a sweet, delicate, triple-blended cheese made from cow's milk. Originally from Italy's Lombardy region, the cheese is quite versatile and is an Italian favorite when served with fresh fruit. Here it's paired with Parmigiano-Reggiano, a dry, hard cheese, resulting in a flavorful combination that enhances both the taste and texture of this dish. While some cooks believe that cream cheese is a suitable substitution for mascarpone, our Test Kitchens prefer Fromage blanc or Quark (yogurt cheese). These cheeses are also fresh cheeses that are neither aged or ripened.

Creamy Two-Cheese Polenta

Wild Mushroom Polenta

Porcini mushrooms lend a strong, earthy, smoky flavor to this savory Italian side dish. Because porcini are some of the most sought-after wild mushrooms, finding the dried variety is often the easiest option. In this dish, the dried mushrooms reconstitute while simmering in the slow cooker with cornmeal and water, saving you a step of preparation. In the store, less flavorful varieties of mushrooms are sometimes substituted for the real thing, so look for porcini's botanical name—*Boletus edulis*—on the package.

- 1 cup yellow cornmeal
- 1 tablespoon butter
- Cooking spray
- 3 cups boiling water
- ¼ cup (1 ounce) grated fresh Parmesan cheese
- 2 tablespoons chopped dried porcini mushrooms
- ¾ teaspoon chopped fresh or ¼ teaspoon dried thyme
- ½ teaspoon salt
- ¼ teaspoon black pepper
- Thyme sprigs (optional)

1. Place cornmeal and butter in a 2-quart electric slow cooker coated with cooking spray. Gradually add 3 cups boiling water, stirring constantly with a whisk until well blended. Stir in cheese and next 4 ingredients. Cover and cook on LOW 3 hours or until thick. Stir well before serving. Spoon polenta into individual bowls; garnish with thyme sprigs, if desired. Yield: 6 servings (serving size: ½ cup).

CALORIES 126 (24% from fat); FAT 3.4g (sat 1.8g, mono 0.9g, poly 0.3g); PROTEIN 4.2g; CARB 19.6g; FIBER 2.2g; CHOL 8mg; IRON 1mg; SODIUM 260mg; CALC 40mg

Polenta with Roasted Red Peppers and Fontina Cheese

This meatless dish features just four ingredients: red bell peppers, tomatoes, polenta, and fontina cheese. Although it uses convenience items like prepared polenta and canned tomatoes, it does so in a food-savvy way by providing speed without sacrificing quality. Hands-on preparation time is less than 15 minutes.

- 3 large red bell peppers
- 1 (14.5-ounce) can whole tomatoes, undrained and chopped
- Cooking spray
- 1 (16-ounce) tube of polenta, cut crosswise into 12 slices
- 1¼ cups (5 ounces) shredded fontina cheese
- Basil sprigs (optional)

1. Preheat broiler.
2. Cut peppers in half lengthwise; discard seeds and membranes. Place pepper halves, skin sides up, on a foil-lined baking sheet; flatten with hand. Broil 10 minutes or until blackened. Place in a zip-top plastic bag; seal. Let stand 15 minutes. Peel and cut into strips.
3. Preheat oven to 350°.
4. Drain tomatoes in a sieve over a bowl; reserve liquid. Heat a large skillet over medium-low heat; add tomatoes. Cook 1 minute. Gradually add tomato liquid; simmer 1 minute. Add pepper strips, and simmer 5 minutes. Remove mixture from heat.
5. Spread ¼ cup pepper sauce in bottom of a 13 x 9-inch baking dish coated with cooking spray. Arrange polenta slices over pepper sauce, and spread remaining pepper sauce over polenta. Sprinkle with fontina cheese. Bake at 350° for 25 minutes. Garnish with basil sprigs, if desired. Yield: 6 servings (serving size: 2 slices polenta and about ¼ cup sauce).

CALORIES 187 (38% from fat); FAT 7.8g (sat 4.6g, mono 2.1g, poly 0.6g); PROTEIN 9.2g; CARB 20.2g; FIBER 3.4g; CHOL 27mg; IRON 2.4mg; SODIUM 622mg; CALC 151mg

soups

Tomato-Basil Soup,
page 325

Winter Plum Soup

This rosy puree of canned plums, wine, and Cointreau is equally good served warm, at room temperature, or chilled. It makes a wonderful first course or a refreshingly light dessert. Prepare up to one day ahead and chill in the refrigerator, allowing the flavors to meld before serving.

2 (16-ounce) cans plums in light syrup, undrained
2 cups dry red wine
1 tablespoon honey
½ teaspoon ground cinnamon
¼ teaspoon ground cloves
¼ cup Cointreau or other orange-flavored liqueur
½ teaspoon grated lemon rind
6 tablespoons vanilla low-fat yogurt
6 mint sprigs (optional)

1. Strain plums through a sieve into a bowl, reserving juice. Cut plums in half; discard pits. Combine plums, reserved juice, wine, honey, cinnamon, and cloves in a medium saucepan. Bring to a boil. Cover; reduce heat, and simmer 15 minutes. Place half of soup in a blender; process until smooth. Pour into a bowl. Repeat procedure with remaining soup. Stir in liqueur and rind. Ladle ¾ cup soup into each of 6 wine goblets. Top each serving with 1 tablespoon yogurt and 1 mint sprig, if desired. Yield: 6 servings.

CALORIES 133 (3% from fat); FAT 0.4g (sat 0.1g, mono 0.2g, poly 0.1g); PROTEIN 1.5g; CARB 32g; FIBER 1.5g; CHOL 1mg; IRON 1.7mg; SODIUM 47mg; CALC 49mg

Canadian Cheese Soup with Pumpernickel Croutons

Pair this savory soup with a green salad and a bowl of chopped fruit for a simple, satisfying meal.

3 (1-ounce) slices pumpernickel bread, cut into ½-inch cubes
1 onion, peeled and quartered
1 carrot, peeled and quartered
1 celery stalk, quartered
1 teaspoon butter
¾ cup all-purpose flour
2 (14-ounce) cans fat-free, less-sodium chicken broth
3 cups 2% reduced-fat milk
½ teaspoon salt
½ teaspoon paprika
½ teaspoon freshly ground black pepper
1½ cups (6 ounces) reduced-fat shredded sharp Cheddar cheese

1. Preheat oven to 375°.
2. Place bread cubes on a jelly-roll pan, and bake at 375° for 15 minutes or until toasted.
3. Place onion, carrot, and celery in a food processor, and pulse until chopped. Melt butter in a Dutch oven over medium-high heat. Add vegetables; sauté 5 minutes or until tender.
4. Lightly spoon flour into dry measuring cups; level with a knife. Gradually add 1 can chicken broth to flour in a medium bowl; stir well with a whisk. Add flour mixture to pan. Stir in remaining 1 can broth; bring to a boil. Reduce heat to medium; cook 10 minutes or until thick. Stir in milk, salt, paprika, and pepper; cook 10 minutes. Remove from heat. Add cheese, and stir until cheese melts. Ladle soup into individual bowls, and top with croutons. Yield: 8 servings (serving size: 1 cup soup and ¼ cup croutons).

CALORIES 203 (30% from fat); FAT 6.8g (sat 3.8g, mono 1.9g, poly 0.4g); PROTEIN 13.2g; CARB 21.9g; FIBER 1.8g; CHOL 23mg; IRON 1.1mg; SODIUM 671mg; CALC 318mg

Homestyle Potato Soup

Nothing soothes the soul on a cold day like a warm bowl of potato soup. With carrots, celery, and garlic, this chunky version is big on flavor. We've lowered the fat in this recipe while maintaining taste and texture by using reduced-fat (but not fat-free) milk and cheese.

4 cups cubed peeled baking potato
1 cup chopped onion
1 cup thinly sliced celery
¾ cup thinly sliced carrot
3 tablespoons butter, cut into small pieces
1¼ teaspoons salt
½ teaspoon freshly ground black pepper
1 (14-ounce) can vegetable broth
3 garlic cloves, minced
¼ cup all-purpose flour
1½ cups 2% reduced-fat milk
7 tablespoons shredded reduced-fat sharp Cheddar cheese
Freshly ground black pepper (optional)

1. Place first 9 ingredients in a 4½-quart electric slow cooker; stir well. Cover and cook on LOW 6 to 7 hours or until vegetables are tender. Increase heat to HIGH.

2. Lightly spoon flour into a dry measuring cup; level with a knife. Place flour in a bowl; gradually add milk, stirring with a whisk until well blended. Stir into soup. Cook, uncovered, 25 minutes or until thick, stirring frequently. Ladle soup into individual bowls, and sprinkle with cheese and additional pepper, if desired. Yield: 7 servings (serving size: 1 cup soup and 1 tablespoon cheese).

CALORIES 194 (35% from fat); FAT 7.6g (sat 4.8g, mono 1.6g, poly 0.3g); PROTEIN 5.9g; CARB 26.8g; FIBER 2.2g; CHOL 22mg; IRON 0.7mg; SODIUM 801mg; CALC 151mg

Baked Potato and Bacon Soup

You're probably familiar with this popular restaurant selection made with heavy cream and loaded with toppings. Our version has all the flavor but with far less fat and fewer calories. This recipe serves a crowd, which makes it a great choice for casual get-togethers. But it can easily be cut in half. To simplify the preparation, bake the potatoes and shred the cheese the day before making the soup. If the soup needs to simmer for a while on the stove, you may need to add more chicken broth to keep it from getting too thick.

5¼ pounds baking potatoes
7 bacon slices
4½ cups chopped onion
1 teaspoon salt
5 garlic cloves, minced
1 bay leaf
7½ cups 1% low-fat milk
¾ teaspoon black pepper
3 cups fat-free, less-sodium chicken broth
⅓ cup chopped fresh parsley (optional)
1¼ cups sliced green onions
1¼ cups (5 ounces) finely shredded reduced-fat sharp Cheddar cheese

1. Preheat oven to 400°.
2. Pierce potatoes with a fork; bake at 400° for 1 hour or until tender. Cool slightly. Partially mash potatoes, including skins, with a potato masher; set aside.
3. Cook bacon in a Dutch oven over medium heat until crisp. Remove bacon from pan; crumble, and set aside. Add onion to bacon drippings in pan; sauté 5 minutes. Add salt, garlic, and bay leaf; sauté 2 minutes. Add potato, milk, pepper, and broth; bring to a boil. Reduce heat; simmer 10 minutes. Stir in parsley, if desired. Ladle soup into individual bowls; top with bacon, green onions, and cheese. Yield: 18 servings (serving size: 1 cup soup, about 1 teaspoon bacon, about 1 tablespoon green onions, and about 1 tablespoon cheese).

CALORIES 237 (30% from fat); FAT 7.8g (sat 3.5g, mono 3.1g, poly 0.8g); PROTEIN 10.5g; CARB 31.8g; FIBER 3.1g; CHOL 15mg; IRON 2mg; SODIUM 394mg; CALC 228mg

White Velvet Soup

Celeriac and Yukon gold potatoes are the base of this deceptively rich soup. A drizzle of extravirgin olive oil at the end is a traditional method for adding subtle flavor and richness to the soup.

4 cups (¼-inch) diced peeled celeriac (celery root; about 1¼ pounds)
4 cups (¼-inch) diced peeled Yukon gold potato (about 1¼ pounds)
3 cups fat-free, less-sodium chicken broth
2 cups water
2 tablespoons fresh thyme leaves
4 large garlic cloves, chopped
⅓ cup white wine
¾ teaspoon salt
½ cup 2% reduced-fat milk
1 tablespoon extravirgin olive oil
3 tablespoons thinly sliced green onions

1. Combine first 6 ingredients in a large stockpot; bring to a boil. Partially cover, reduce heat, and simmer 30 minutes or until vegetables are tender. Place half of potato mixture in a blender; process until smooth. Repeat with remaining potato mixture. Return pureed potato mixture to pan; stir in wine and salt. Cook over medium heat 3 minutes or until thoroughly heated. Remove soup from heat, and stir in milk.
2. Ladle soup into individual bowls; drizzle oil over soup. Sprinkle with onions. Yield: 6 servings (serving size: 1⅓ cups soup, ½ teaspoon oil, and 1½ teaspoons onions).

CALORIES 161 (17% from fat); FAT 3.1g (sat 0.7g, mono 2g, poly 0.4g); PROTEIN 6.4g; CARB 28.5g; FIBER 4.4g; CHOL 2mg; IRON 2.1mg; SODIUM 625mg; CALC 97mg

White Velvet Soup

Creamy Tomato-Balsamic Soup

With summer's heat gone and winter's chill yet to come, the cool days of fall offer a welcomed opportunity for alfresco dining in your own backyard or on a roadside picnic during a leaf-viewing drive. Rosy tomato soup reflects the changing colors of the season and offers a rich taste befitting this time of year.

1   cup less-sodium beef broth, divided
1   tablespoon brown sugar
3   tablespoons balsamic vinegar
1   tablespoon low-sodium soy sauce
1   cup coarsely chopped onion
5   garlic cloves
2   (28-ounce) cans whole tomatoes, drained
Cooking spray
¾ cup half-and-half
Cracked black pepper (optional)

1. Preheat oven to 500°.
2. Combine ½ cup broth, sugar, vinegar, and soy sauce in a small bowl. Place chopped onion, garlic, and tomatoes in a 13 x 9–inch baking pan coated with cooking spray. Pour broth mixture over tomato mixture. Bake at 500° for 50 minutes or until vegetables are lightly browned.
3. Place tomato mixture in a blender. Add remaining ½ cup broth and half-and-half, and process until smooth. Strain mixture through a sieve into a bowl, and discard solids. Ladle soup into individual bowls. Garnish with cracked black pepper, if desired. Yield: 4 servings (serving size: about ½ cup).

CALORIES 120 (35% from fat); FAT 4.7g (sat 3g, mono 1.5g, poly 0.1g); PROTEIN 3.8g; CARB 14.9g; FIBER 1.7g; CHOL 23mg; IRON 1.7mg; SODIUM 452mg; CALC 120mg

Creamy Lentil Soup

Half-and-half adds creamy body and a satiny finish to this hearty soup. Serve with breadsticks and a salad for a simple, yet filling, supper. Make this a vegetarian soup by substituting 2 tablespoons canola oil for the bacon drippings and vegetable broth for the chicken broth.

3   bacon slices
2   cups chopped leek
1   cup chopped onion
3   cups water
2   cups chopped peeled baking potato
1   cup dried lentils
¾ cup chopped carrot
½ teaspoon salt
1   (14-ounce) can fat-free, less-sodium chicken broth
½ cup half-and-half
1   tablespoon dry sherry
Flat-leaf parsley sprigs (optional)

1. Cook bacon in a Dutch oven over medium heat until crisp. Remove bacon from pan, reserving drippings in pan. Crumble bacon; set aside.
2. Add leek and onion to pan; sauté 4 minutes. Add water, potato, lentils, carrot, salt, and broth; bring to a boil. Cover, reduce heat, and simmer 1 hour or until vegetables are tender.
3. Place in a blender or food processor; process until smooth. Return pureed mixture to pan; stir in half-and-half and sherry. Cook until thoroughly heated. Ladle soup into individual bowls. Sprinkle evenly with bacon. Garnish with parsley sprigs, if desired. Yield: 6 servings (serving size: 1⅓ cups).

CALORIES 287 (29% from fat); FAT 9.4g (sat 4g, mono 3.7g, poly 1.1g); PROTEIN 13.6g; CARB 37.4g; FIBER 5.8g; CHOL 15mg; IRON 4.2mg; SODIUM 465mg; CALC 72mg

Creamy Lentil Soup

Wild Rice and Mushroom Soup

Simple elegance—that's how to best describe this soup. It offers all the warmth and heartiness of a vegetable or beef soup, yet it's fancy enough to serve as a starter at a dinner party. A splash of sherry adds a little richness that will make you and your guests think there's cream in the soup, but it's actually reduced-fat milk.

2	teaspoons butter
½	cup chopped carrot (about 1 medium carrot)
1	large onion, chopped
2	celery stalks, thinly sliced (about ¾ cup)
1	(8-ounce) package presliced mushrooms
1	teaspoon chopped fresh or ¼ teaspoon dried rosemary
¼	teaspoon black pepper
3	garlic cloves, minced
2	(14-ounce) cans fat-free, less-sodium chicken broth
1	cup uncooked wild rice
⅓	cup all-purpose flour
2¾	cups 2% reduced-fat milk
2	tablespoons dry sherry
¾	teaspoon salt

1. Melt butter in a Dutch oven over medium-high heat. Add carrot and next 6 ingredients; sauté 8 minutes or until tender. Stir in broth, scraping pan to loosen browned bits. Stir in rice; bring to a boil. Cover, reduce heat, and simmer 1 hour and 15 minutes or until rice is tender.

2. Lightly spoon flour into a dry measuring cup; level with a knife. Combine flour and milk in a small bowl, stirring with a whisk. Add to soup mixture. Cook over medium heat 10 minutes or until thick, stirring frequently. Stir in sherry and salt. Yield: 8 servings (serving size: 1 cup).

CALORIES 185 (15% from fat); FAT 3g (sat 1.5g, mono 0.9g, poly 0.1g); PROTEIN 8.6g; CARB 30.1g; FIBER 1.7g; CHOL 8.8mg; IRON 0.9mg; SODIUM 557mg; CALC 119mg

Chilled Corn Bisque with Basil, Avocado, and Crab

The flavor will come through better if you take off the chill. Allow soup to stand at room temperature for about 30 minutes before serving. Chop the avocado and the basil just before serving so they don't begin to brown.

    3   cups fat-free, less-sodium chicken broth
    3   tablespoons cornstarch
    1   tablespoon butter
    1   cup finely chopped onion
    1   garlic clove, minced
    4   cups fresh corn kernels (about 8 ears)
   ¾   teaspoon salt
   ¼   teaspoon ground red pepper
   ½   cup 2% reduced-fat milk
   ½   cup half-and-half
    8   ounces lump crabmeat, shell pieces removed
        (about 1½ cups)
   ⅓   cup chopped peeled avocado
    3   tablespoons chopped fresh basil

1. Combine broth and cornstarch, stirring with a whisk.

2. Melt butter in a large saucepan over medium-high heat. Add onion; sauté 3 minutes. Add garlic; sauté 30 seconds. Stir in broth mixture, corn, salt, and pepper; bring to a simmer. Cook 7 minutes, stirring frequently (do not boil). Place half of corn mixture in a blender, and process until smooth. Pour pureed corn mixture into a large bowl. Repeat procedure with remaining corn mixture. Strain pureed corn mixture through a sieve into a large bowl; discard solids. Stir in milk and half-and-half, and chill thoroughly.

3. Stir well, and ladle ⅔ cup soup into each of 8 bowls; top each serving with 3 tablespoons crab, about 2 teaspoons avocado, and about 1 teaspoon basil. Yield: 8 servings.

CALORIES 159 (30% from fat); FAT 5.3g (sat 2.4g, mono 1.9g, poly 0.7g); PROTEIN 10.8g; CARB 18g; FIBER 2.3g; CHOL 34mg; IRON 0.6mg; SODIUM 536mg; CALC 64mg

New England Clam Chowder

There are two well-known styles of clam chowder—Manhattan and New England. New England–style is definitely the most common. Known for its creamy, white milk-base loaded with tiny, chewy clams and starchy, hearty potatoes, New England clam chowder graces the table in homes and restaurants all across the country, not just along the eastern seaboard. Manhattan-style chowder, however, is a tomato-based dish and is most popular, of course, in New York.

    2   (6½-ounce) cans minced clams, undrained
        Cooking spray
    1   cup chopped onion
    2   turkey-bacon slices, chopped
    1   garlic clove, minced
    3   cups chopped peeled red potato (about 1¼
        pounds)
   ½   teaspoon dried thyme
    2   (8-ounce) bottles clam juice
    3   tablespoons all-purpose flour
  2½   cups 2% low-fat milk
        Freshly ground black pepper
        Thyme sprigs (optional)

1. Drain clams, reserving liquid; set clams and liquid aside.

2. Heat a Dutch oven over medium heat. Coat pan with cooking spray. Add onion, bacon slices, and garlic; sauté 5 minutes. Add reserved clam liquid, potato, thyme, and clam juice; bring mixture to a boil. Cover, reduce heat, and simmer 20 minutes or until potato is tender.

3. Place 2 cups potato mixture, including bacon, in a blender, and process until smooth. Add potato puree to potato mixture in Dutch oven; stir well. Combine flour and milk, stirring with a wire whisk until blended; add to chowder. Cook over medium heat, stirring constantly, 10 minutes or until thickened. Stir in clams. Ladle soup into individual bowls; sprinkle evenly with pepper. Garnish with thyme, if desired. Yield: 6¾ cups (serving size: 1 cup).

CALORIES 163 (15% from fat); FAT 2.8g (sat 1.4g, mono 0.5g, poly 0.1g); PROTEIN 9.7g; CARB 24.9g; FIBER 1.9g; CHOL 22mg; IRON 1.8mg; SODIUM 473mg; CALC 135mg

Beet and Fennel Soup

Beet and Fennel Soup

Showcase autumn's best produce with this vermillion-hued soup, which balances sweet oven-baked beets with the sharpness of apple and lemon. Baking the beets concentrates their flavor; the onion is roasted whole. Fennel, which has become one of Italy's most important vegetables, also stars in this sensational soup. Fennel fronds make a nice green garnish atop the milky-white sour cream.

   4 beets (about 1 pound)
  ¼ cup water
   1 large onion (about 1 pound)
   4 cups organic vegetable broth (such as Swanson Certified Organic)
1¾ cups chopped fennel bulb (about 1 large)
   1 cup chopped peeled Granny Smith apple
   2 teaspoons white wine vinegar
   2 teaspoons lemon juice
  ½ teaspoon salt
  ½ teaspoon freshly ground black pepper
   8 teaspoons reduced-fat sour cream
Chopped fennel fronds

1. Preheat oven to 375°.

2. Leave root and 1 inch of stem on beets; scrub with a brush. Place beets on a large sheet of aluminum foil, and sprinkle beets with ¼ cup water. Wrap beets in foil; arrange packet of beets and onion on a baking sheet. Bake at 375° for 1 hour or until tender. Cool.

3. Combine broth, fennel, and apple in a medium saucepan. Bring to a boil; reduce heat, and simmer 15 minutes or until fennel is tender. Cool.

4. Trim off beet roots; rub off skins, and coarsely chop. Peel and quarter onion. Add beets and onion to broth mixture, stirring to combine. Place half of beet mixture in a blender; process until smooth. Pour pureed beet mixture into a large bowl. Repeat procedure with remaining beet mixture. Stir in vinegar, juice, salt, and pepper. Return beet mixture to pan.

5. Place beet mixture over medium heat, and cook 2 minutes or until thoroughly heated. Ladle soup into bowls, and top with sour cream. Sprinkle evenly with fennel fronds. Yield: 8 servings (serving size: ¾ cup soup and 1 teaspoon sour cream).

CALORIES 74 (11% from fat); FAT 0.9g (sat 0.4g, mono 0.2g, poly 0.1g); PROTEIN 2.2g; CARB 15.3g; FIBER 3.3g; CHOL 2mg; IRON 0.8mg; SODIUM 496mg; CALC 42mg

Savory Beet Soup

This rich, velvety soup is a mild version of borscht, a traditional soup made with beets, cabbage, and potatoes. We opted to omit the cabbage and to puree the soup to a smooth consistency. Ideal for autumn, this soup is ravishingly rich and comfortably creamy. For added creaminess and a lovely presentation, we swirled this vibrantly colored soup with sour cream.

  1 teaspoon olive oil
  1 cup chopped onion
  4 cups fat-free, less-sodium chicken broth
  2 cups water
 ½ teaspoon salt
 ¼ teaspoon freshly ground black pepper
  3 beets, peeled and halved
  1 medium baking potato, peeled and halved crosswise
  1 bay leaf
  1 teaspoon lemon juice
  8 teaspoons reduced-fat sour cream

1. Heat oil in a Dutch oven over medium-high heat. Add onion; sauté 3 minutes or until tender. Add broth and next 6 ingredients. Bring to a boil; reduce heat, and simmer, uncovered, 20 minutes or until beets and potato are tender. Discard bay leaf.

2. Place one-third of broth mixture in a blender or food processor; process until smooth. Place pureed mixture in a large bowl. Repeat procedure twice with remaining broth mixture. Return pureed mixture to pan. Warm soup over low heat 5 minutes or until thoroughly heated. Remove from heat, and stir in lemon juice.

3. Combine ½ cup soup and sour cream, stirring with a whisk. Ladle soup into individual bowls. Top each serving with 1 tablespoon sour cream mixture; swirl sour cream mixture using tip of a knife. Yield: 8 servings (serving size: about ¾ cup soup).

CALORIES 74 (16% from fat); FAT 1.3g (sat 0.5g, mono 0.4g, poly 0.1g); PROTEIN 3.3g; CARB 12.3g; FIBER 2.2g; CHOL 3mg; IRON 0.7mg; SODIUM 343mg; CALC 23mg

Carrot-Parsnip Soup with Parsnip Chips

Winter root vegetables lend their complementary, slightly sweet flavors to this hearty soup. Stir in more water or broth if you prefer a thinner consistency.

 2 tablespoons olive oil, divided
2½ cups chopped yellow onion
 3 cups coarsely chopped parsnip (about 1 pound)
 3 cups water
2½ cups coarsely chopped carrot (about 1 pound)
 2 (14-ounce) cans fat-free, less-sodium chicken broth
 ¼ teaspoon salt
 ¼ teaspoon freshly ground black pepper
 ½ cup (⅛-inch-thick) slices parsnip
 1 tablespoon chopped fresh chives

1. Heat 1 teaspoon oil in a Dutch oven over medium heat. Add onion; cook 10 minutes or until tender, stirring occasionally. Add chopped parsnip, water, carrot, and broth; bring to a boil. Reduce heat, and simmer 50 minutes or until vegetables are tender. Remove from heat; let stand 5 minutes.
2. Place half of carrot mixture in a blender; process until smooth. Pour pureed carrot mixture into a large bowl. Repeat procedure with remaining carrot mixture. Stir in salt and pepper.
3. Heat remaining 5 teaspoons oil in a small saucepan over medium-high heat. Add parsnip slices; cook 5 minutes or until lightly browned, turning occasionally. Drain on paper towels. Ladle soup into individual bowls. Sprinkle parsnip chips and chives over soup. Serve immediately. Yield: 6 servings (serving size: 1⅓ cups soup, about 2 teaspoons parsnip chips, and ½ teaspoon chives).

CALORIES 159 (28% from fat); FAT 4.9g (sat 0.7g, mono 3.4g, poly 0.6g); PROTEIN 3.7g; CARB 26.4g; FIBER 6.4g; CHOL 0mg; IRON 0.8mg; SODIUM 388mg; CALC 61mg

Pumpkin-Pear Soup with Maple Cream

Pumpkin deserves to be more than a once-a-year pie filling. Here, it stars with sweet, ripe pears in a silky and succulent first course for a late fall or winter evening. Serve the soup with poppy seed breadsticks made from refrigerated dough.

 1 tablespoon butter
 1 cup chopped onion
 1 tablespoon brown sugar
 ½ teaspoon ground cumin
 5 cups cubed peeled pumpkin or other winter squash (about 2½ pounds)
 3 cups fat-free, less-sodium chicken broth
 ½ teaspoon salt
 2 cups coarsely chopped peeled ripe Bartlett pear (about 2)
 ¼ cup reduced-fat sour cream
 2 tablespoons maple syrup
Thyme sprigs (optional)

1. Melt butter in a Dutch oven over medium heat. Add onion, brown sugar, and cumin; cook 5 minutes or until onions are tender, stirring occasionally.
2. Add pumpkin, broth, and salt, and bring to a boil over medium-high heat. Add pear; cover, reduce heat, and simmer 5 minutes or until pumpkin is tender.
3. Remove from heat. Cool slightly. Place half of pumpkin mixture in a blender; process until smooth. Pour into a large bowl. Repeat procedure with remaining pumpkin mixture. Return pureed mixture to pan; keep warm.
4. Combine sour cream and maple syrup. Ladle soup into individual bowls, and drizzle maple cream over each serving. Garnish soup with thyme sprigs, if desired. Yield: 8 servings (serving size: 1 cup soup and about 2 teaspoons maple cream).

CALORIES 120 (21% from fat); FAT 2.8g (sat 1.4g, mono 0.6g, poly 0.1g); PROTEIN 3.4g; CARB 23.4g; FIBER 2g; CHOL 8mg; IRON 1.3mg; SODIUM 398mg; CALC 58mg

Curry-Ginger-Butternut Squash Soup

If it's fall, then it's time for butternut squash. Straining this spicy-sweet, golden-hued soup gives the final product a velvety appearance and texture. Swirl in a dollop of yogurt, and you've got a soup that's as pretty as the colorful leaves outside your kitchen window.

2 teaspoons canola oil
3 tablespoons finely chopped peeled fresh ginger
3 garlic cloves, minced
2 teaspoons curry powder
1 cup mirin (sweet rice wine)
6 cups (½-inch) cubed peeled butternut squash (about 2½ pounds)
6 cups fat-free, less-sodium chicken broth
2½ cups (½-inch) cubed peeled celeriac (celery root; 1 to 1½ pounds)
2 teaspoons thawed orange juice concentrate
1 teaspoon Sriracha (hot chile sauce, such as Huy Fong)
½ teaspoon salt
½ cup plain low-fat yogurt
2 teaspoons chopped fresh flat-leaf parsley

1. Heat oil in a Dutch oven over medium-high heat. Add ginger and garlic; sauté 1½ minutes. Add curry, and cook 15 seconds, stirring constantly. Add mirin; cook until liquid is reduced to ½ cup (about 4 minutes). Add squash, broth, and celeriac; bring to a boil. Reduce heat; simmer 15 minutes or until tender.

2. Place one-fourth of squash mixture in a blender; process until smooth. Strain pureed squash mixture through a sieve into a large bowl; discard solids. Repeat procedure in 3 more batches with remaining squash mixture. Stir in orange juice concentrate, Sriracha, and salt. Ladle soup into individual bowls. Dollop 1 tablespoon yogurt over each serving, and sprinkle evenly with parsley. Yield: 8 servings (serving size: about 1 cup).

CALORIES 206 (8% from fat); FAT 1.8g (sat 0.3g, mono 0.8g, poly 0.5g); PROTEIN 5.8g; CARB 38.3g; FIBER 4.7g; CHOL 1mg; IRON 1.8mg; SODIUM 653mg; CALC 140mg

Fresh Tomato Soup

Fresh Tomato Soup

Tomato soup is second to chicken noodle soup in popularity. Homemade tomato stock provides the base for this soup. Prepare the soup through step 2 up to a day ahead. Reheat over medium-low heat, and add the lemon rind, butter, and basil just before serving.

```
1   teaspoon olive oil
1   cup chopped onion
4   cups chopped plum tomato (about 2 pounds)
3   (14-ounce) cans fat-free, less-sodium chicken
    broth
2   garlic cloves, crushed
7   cups chopped seeded peeled plum tomato
    (about 3 pounds)
¼   teaspoon salt
¼   teaspoon black pepper
1   teaspoon grated lemon rind
1   teaspoon butter
3   tablespoons thinly sliced fresh basil
```

1. Heat oil in a large saucepan over medium-high heat. Add onion, and sauté 4 minutes or until tender. Add 4 cups tomato; cook 2 minutes. Reduce heat to low; stir in broth and garlic. Simmer, covered, 30 minutes.

2. Uncover and simmer 45 minutes or until reduced to about 6 cups. Drain broth mixture through a sieve into a large bowl; discard solids. Return broth to pan. Stir in 7 cups tomato, salt, and pepper; bring to a boil. Reduce heat; simmer, uncovered, 10 minutes.

3. Remove soup from heat. Stir in rind and butter. Ladle soup into individual serving bowls. Sprinkle evenly with basil. Yield: 6 servings (serving size: about 1 cup).

CALORIES 100 (19% from fat); FAT 2.1g (sat 0.6g, mono 0.9g, poly 0.5g); PROTEIN 6.3g; CARB 17.1g; FIBER 4g; CHOL 2mg; IRON 1mg; SODIUM 690mg; CALC 44mg

Tomato-Basil Soup

(pictured on page 311)

No one will ever guess that the base for this soup is canned tomatoes. Basil and tomatoes are perfect partners, but in this recipe, fresh basil takes the lead. It transforms an ordinary can of tomatoes into a refreshing soup chock-full of vine-ripened tomato flavor.

```
2    teaspoons olive oil
3    garlic cloves, minced
3    cups fat-free, less-sodium chicken broth
¾    teaspoon salt
3    (14.5-ounce) cans no salt–added diced
     tomatoes, undrained
2    cups fresh basil leaves, thinly sliced
Whole basil leaves or chiffonade (optional)
```

1. Heat oil in a large saucepan over medium heat. Add garlic; cook 30 seconds, stirring constantly. Stir in broth, salt, and tomatoes; bring to a boil. Reduce heat; simmer 20 minutes. Stir in sliced basil.

2. Place half of soup in a blender; process until smooth. Pour pureed soup into a bowl; repeat procedure with remaining soup. Ladle soup into individual bowls. Garnish with whole basil leaves, if desired. Yield: 4 servings (serving size: 1½ cups).

CALORIES 103 (24% from fat); FAT 2.8g (sat 0.4g, mono 1.7g, poly 0.4g); PROTEIN 5.8g; CARB 15.9g; FIBER 4g; CHOL 0mg; IRON 2.4mg; SODIUM 809mg; CALC 129mg

How to Make a Chiffonade

Slicing into thin strips (making a chiffonade) is a good technique for herbs such as basil or for any large-leafed vegetable, such as spinach or lettuce. Start by neatly stacking four to five leaves and tightly rolling them. Use a chef's knife to slice across the roll to produce strips or ribbons.

Sun-Dried Tomato-Tortellini Soup

Fix it in a flash—this filling soup comes together in about 20 minutes. And it tastes even better the next day.

1½ teaspoons olive oil
1 cup chopped onion
1 cup (¼-inch-thick) slices carrot
⅔ cup chopped celery
2 garlic cloves, minced
5 cups fat-free, less-sodium chicken broth
2 cups water
1¼ cups sun-dried tomato halves, packed without oil, chopped (about 3 ounces)
½ teaspoon dried basil
¼ teaspoon freshly ground black pepper
1 bay leaf
3 cups (about 12 ounces) fresh cheese tortellini
1 cup chopped bok choy

1. Heat oil in a large Dutch oven over medium-high heat. Add onion, carrot, celery, and garlic; sauté 5 minutes. Add broth and next 5 ingredients; bring to a boil. Reduce heat; simmer 2 minutes. Add pasta and bok choy; simmer 7 minutes or until pasta is done. Discard bay leaf. Yield: 6 servings (serving size: about 1½ cups).

CALORIES 256 (28% from fat); FAT 8g (sat 2.6g, mono 3.9g, poly 0.7g); PROTEIN 12.1g; CARB 33.9g; FIBER 3.9g; CHOL 25mg; IRON 1.1mg; SODIUM 681mg; CALC 47mg

About Sun-Dried Tomatoes

Whether packed in oil or dry-packed, sun-dried tomatoes add vivid flavor and a healthy dose of lycopene to your cooking. To chop dry-packed tomatoes, coat a chef's knife with cooking spray; it will keep the tomatoes from sticking to the blade. There's no need to steep the tomatoes for this recipe; they rehydrate in the soup.

Golden Summer Soup

This colorful soup has a velvety texture. The garnish of fresh-from-the-garden herbs and tomatoes adds a bright burst of flavor and an appealing textural contrast.

Cooking spray
2 garlic cloves, minced
8 cups chopped yellow tomato (about 3½ pounds)
3 cups chopped Vidalia or other sweet onion
2 cups fresh corn kernels
1 cup chopped yellow bell pepper
1 teaspoon fine sea salt
1 teaspoon grated lemon rind
½ teaspoon freshly ground black pepper
½ teaspoon hot sauce
1 tablespoon coarsely chopped fresh chervil
1 tablespoon coarsely chopped fresh chives
1 tablespoon coarsely chopped fresh basil
1 tablespoon coarsely chopped fresh flat-leaf parsley
1 cup halved cherry or grape tomatoes

1. Heat a small Dutch oven over medium-high heat. Coat pan with cooking spray. Add garlic; sauté 15 seconds. Add yellow tomato, onion, corn, and bell pepper; bring to a boil. Reduce heat, and simmer 15 minutes or until onion is tender, stirring occasionally. Place half of tomato mixture in a blender; process until smooth. Press pureed tomato mixture through a large sieve into a large bowl, reserving liquid; discard solids. Repeat procedure with remaining tomato mixture. Stir in salt, lemon rind, black pepper, and hot sauce.
2. Combine chervil, chives, basil, and parsley, tossing gently. Ladle 1¼ cups soup into each of 4 bowls; top each with ¼ cup cherry tomatoes and 1 tablespoon herb mixture. Yield: 4 servings.

CALORIES 209 (12% from fat); FAT 2.7g (sat 0.4g, mono 0.5g, poly 1.2g); PROTEIN 9.2g; CARB 46.8g; FIBER 11.8g; CHOL 0mg; IRON 3.2mg; SODIUM 636mg; CALC 82mg

Split Pea Soup with Rosemary

This is a unique and tasty variation of split pea soup. Hearty enough for dinner, it also keeps well in the refrigerator. Try serving it with whole-grain bread.

1½ cups green split peas
2 teaspoons olive oil, divided
2 cups chopped onion
1 cup diced carrot
1 bay leaf
1 tablespoon minced garlic cloves, divided
1 tablespoon minced fresh rosemary, divided
1 teaspoon paprika
¼ teaspoon black pepper
1 tablespoon tomato paste
1 tablespoon low-sodium soy sauce
4 cups water
1 (14-ounce) can vegetable broth
¼ cup chopped fresh parsley, divided
¼ cup reduced-fat sour cream

1. Sort and wash peas. Place peas in a saucepan. Cover with water to 2 inches above peas; set aside. Heat 1 teaspoon oil in a Dutch oven over medium-high heat. Add onion, carrot, and bay leaf, and sauté 5 minutes, stirring frequently. Add 2 teaspoons garlic, 1 teaspoon rosemary, paprika, and pepper; cook 3 minutes. Add tomato paste and soy sauce, and cook until liquid evaporates, scraping pan to loosen browned bits.

2. Drain peas. Add peas, 4 cups water, and broth to onion mixture; bring to a boil. Cover, reduce heat to medium-low, and simmer 1 hour, stirring often. Discard bay leaf. Place half of soup in a blender or food processor; process until smooth. Pour pureed soup into a large bowl. Repeat procedure with remaining soup.

3. Combine remaining 1 teaspoon oil, remaining 1 teaspoon garlic, remaining 2 teaspoons rosemary, and 3 tablespoons parsley; stir into soup. Ladle soup into individual bowls; top each serving with sour cream and remaining 1 tablespoon parsley. Yield: 6 servings (serving size: about 1 cup soup, 2 teaspoons sour cream, and ½ teaspoon parsley).

CALORIES 249 (10% from fat); FAT 2.9g (sat 1g, mono 1.1g, poly 0.2g); PROTEIN 14.4g; CARB 42.6g; FIBER 1.8g; CHOL 5mg; IRON 2.3mg; SODIUM 299mg; CALC 43mg

Springtime Risotto Soup

If you love the flavor and creamy texture of traditional risotto but don't have the time or patience needed to gradually stir the hot broth into the rice, this soup is a must-try.

1 tablespoon olive oil
2 cups chopped onion
2 teaspoons grated lemon rind
¾ cup Arborio rice or other short-grain rice
3 (14-ounce) cans fat-free, less-sodium chicken broth
2 cups (1-inch) slices asparagus (about 1 pound)
2 cups coarsely chopped spinach
¼ teaspoon ground nutmeg
½ cup (2 ounces) grated fresh Parmesan cheese

1. Heat oil in a large saucepan over medium-high heat. Add onion; sauté 2 minutes. Add rind; sauté 2 minutes. Add rice; sauté 3 minutes.

2. Stir in chicken broth, and bring to a boil. Cover, reduce heat, and simmer 10 minutes. Stir in asparagus, spinach, and nutmeg; cook, uncovered, 2 minutes or until asparagus is crisp-tender. Ladle soup into individual bowls, and top each serving with Parmesan cheese. Serve immediately. Yield: 4 servings (serving size: 1¾ cups soup and 2 tablespoons cheese).

CALORIES 320 (21% from fat); FAT 7.5g (sat 2.9g, mono 3.6g, poly 0.5g); PROTEIN 14.9g; CARB 46.2g; FIBER 4.1g; CHOL 10mg; IRON 1.6mg; SODIUM 815mg; CALC 234mg

How to Sauté Rice

Arborio rice is an Italian-grown rice that's shorter, plumper, and higher in starch content than long-grain rice. Sautéing rice with onion in hot oil or butter infuses the rice with flavor. Gradually stirring in the broth with a wooden spoon gives the starch in the rice time to dissolve and form a creamy sauce that complements the chewy rice.

Hot and Sour Soup

A not-so-familiar Chinese proverb says to preserve the old but know the new. That's easily taken to heart with one of the great specialties of Chinese cuisine—hot and sour soup. This vegetarian version replaces the more traditional pork-based soup, helping you to eat smart and, in turn, live well.

 5 dried shiitake mushrooms (about ¼ ounce)
 5 dried wood ear mushrooms (about ¼ ounce)
 1 (32-ounce) carton fat-free, less-sodium vegetable broth
2¼ cups water, divided
 1 tablespoon minced peeled fresh ginger
 1 teaspoon minced garlic
 ¼ cup rice vinegar
 1 tablespoon low-sodium soy sauce
 ½ to 1 teaspoon freshly ground black pepper
 ½ pound reduced-fat firm or extrafirm tofu, drained and cut into ¼-inch cubes
2½ tablespoons cornstarch
 4 large egg whites, lightly beaten
 ½ cup chopped green onions
 ¼ cup minced fresh cilantro
 1 teaspoon dark sesame oil
Chili oil (optional)

1. Place mushrooms in a medium bowl; cover with boiling water. Cover and let stand 10 minutes or until tender; drain. Thinly slice mushrooms; set aside.

2. Combine broth, 2 cups water, ginger, and garlic in a large saucepan over medium-high heat; bring to a boil. Add mushrooms. Reduce heat, and simmer 5 minutes. Add vinegar, soy sauce, pepper, and tofu; bring to a boil. Reduce heat, and simmer 5 minutes.

3. Combine remaining ¼ cup water and cornstarch, stirring with a whisk. Stir cornstarch mixture into broth mixture; bring to a boil. Reduce heat, and simmer 3 minutes or until soup thickens slightly, stirring frequently. Slowly pour egg whites into broth mixture in a steady stream, stirring constantly but gently with a wooden spoon. Remove from heat, and stir in onions, cilantro, and sesame oil. Ladle soup into individual bowls. Drizzle with chili oil, if desired. Yield: 4 servings (serving size: 1¾ cups).

CALORIES 158 (22% from fat); FAT 3.8g (sat 0.2g, mono 0g, poly 0g); PROTEIN 11.1g; CARB 20.3g; FIBER 6.5g; CHOL 0mg; IRON 1.5mg; SODIUM 770mg; CALC 44mg

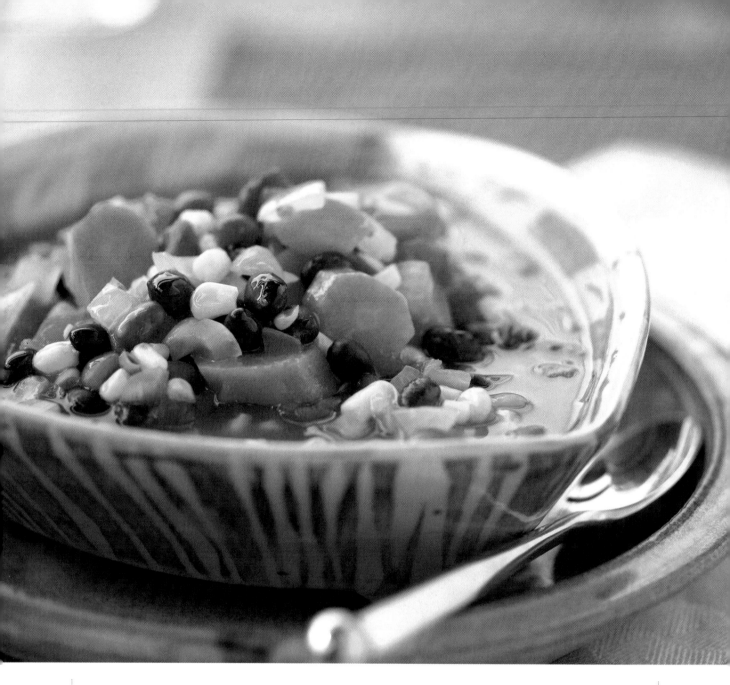

Spicy Black and Red Bean Soup

1½ cups chopped onion
1¼ cups sliced carrot
2 garlic cloves, minced
3 cups fat-free, less-sodium chicken broth
2 teaspoons sugar
1 (16-ounce) package frozen shoepeg white corn
1 (16-ounce) can red beans or kidney beans, rinsed and drained
1 (15-ounce) can black beans, rinsed and drained

1 (14.5-ounce) can Mexican-style stewed tomatoes with jalapeño peppers and spices, undrained
1 (14.5-ounce) can no salt–added diced tomatoes, undrained
1 (4.5-ounce) can chopped green chiles, undrained

1. Place all ingredients in a 5- or 6-quart electric slow cooker. Cover and cook on LOW 8 hours. Yield: 10 servings (serving size: 1 cup).

CALORIES 142 (6% from fat); FAT 0.9g (sat 0g, mono 0g, poly 0.1g); PROTEIN 6.5g; CARB 28.7g; FIBER 6.5g; CHOL 0mg; IRON 1.2mg; SODIUM 503mg; CALC 57mg

Tuscan White Bean Soup with Prosciutto

2 teaspoons olive oil
½ cup chopped prosciutto or ham (about 2 ounces)
1 cup chopped onion
¾ cup chopped celery
¾ cup chopped carrot
1 garlic clove, minced
1 cup water
2 (19-ounce) cans cannellini beans or other white beans, undrained
1 (14-ounce) can fat-free, less-sodium chicken broth
2 bay leaves
2 tablespoons minced fresh parsley
2 tablespoons sherry (optional)
¼ teaspoon black pepper

1. Heat oil in a large stockpot over medium heat. Add chopped prosciutto, and sauté 2 minutes. Add chopped onion, celery, carrot, and minced garlic; sauté 2 minutes or until soft.
2. Add 1 cup water, beans, broth, and bay leaves, and bring soup to a boil. Partially cover, reduce heat, and simmer 20 minutes.
3. Add parsley, sherry, if desired, and pepper; cook 1 minute. Discard bay leaves. Yield: 4 servings (serving size: 1½ cups).

CALORIES 292 (14% from fat); FAT 4.7g (sat 0.8g, mono 2.3g, poly 1.5g); PROTEIN 15.9g; CARB 45.3g; FIBER 12g; CHOL 8mg; IRON 4.3mg; SODIUM 1,095mg; CALC 114mg

White Bean and Sausage Ragoût with Tomatoes, Kale, and Zucchini

1 tablespoon olive oil
½ cup chopped onion
2 (4-ounce) links chicken sausage, cut into ½-inch slices
1 zucchini, quartered and cut into ½-inch slices (about 2 cups)
3 garlic cloves, peeled and crushed
6 cups chopped trimmed kale (about ½ pound)
½ cup water
¼ teaspoon salt
¼ teaspoon freshly ground black pepper
2 (16-ounce) cans cannellini beans or other white beans, rinsed and drained
1 (14.5-ounce) can diced tomatoes, undrained

1. Heat oil in a large skillet over medium-high heat. Add onion and sausage; sauté 4 minutes or until sausage is browned. Add zucchini and garlic; cook 2 minutes. Add kale and remaining ingredients; bring to a boil. Cover, reduce heat, and simmer 10 minutes or until thoroughly heated. Serve immediately. Yield: 4 servings (serving size: 1¾ cups).

CALORIES 467 (20% from fat); FAT 10.2g (sat 2.3g, mono 4.6g, poly 2.5g); PROTEIN 28.5g; CARB 71.8g; FIBER 15.4g; CHOL 42mg; IRON 8.8mg; SODIUM 764mg; CALC 370mg

How to Prepare Kale

To prepare kale, pull apart the bunch, and examine each leaf. Remove and discard any yellowed or limp portions. Wash greens in cool water, agitating with your hands. Replace water two or three times until there are no traces of dirt or grit. Lay kale flat to dry on a dish towel, or use a salad spinner to remove excess moisture. Kale leaves often have tough center veins that need to be removed. Fold the leaves in half, slice off the vein, and discard.

Hearty Vegetable–Smoked Sausage Soup

Chock-full of beans, vegetables, and smoky sausage, this recipe takes classic vegetable soup to a new level. The acid in tomatoes can prevent potatoes from getting tender in the slow cooker, so we stirred the tomatoes in at the end.

    1   (14-ounce) package low-fat smoked sausage,
        cut into ¼-inch-thick slices
 2¾   cups (½-inch) cubed peeled baking potato
    ½   (10-ounce) package angel hair slaw (about
        4 cups)
    2   cups chopped onion
    1   cup sliced carrot
 1⅓   cups diced celery
    1   cup frozen cut green beans
    1   (16-ounce) can kidney beans, rinsed and
        drained
    4   (14-ounce) cans less-sodium beef broth
    ¼   cup chopped fresh parsley
    ½   teaspoon dried thyme
    ½   teaspoon black pepper
    3   garlic cloves, minced, or 1 tablespoon bottled
        minced garlic
    1   bay leaf
    1   (14.5-ounce) can diced tomatoes with basil,
        garlic, and oregano, undrained

1. Heat a large nonstick skillet over medium-high heat. Add sausage; sauté 8 minutes or until lightly browned.
2. Layer potato and next 6 ingredients in a 6-quart electric slow cooker. Top vegetable mixture with sausage. Combine beef broth and next 5 ingredients; pour over sausage mixture. Cover and cook on LOW 10 hours or until vegetables are tender. Discard bay leaf. Stir tomatoes into soup. Yield: 10 servings (serving size: 1½ cups).

CALORIES 160 (8% from fat); FAT 1.4g (sat 0.4g, mono 0g, poly 0.1g); PROTEIN 10.7g; CARB 26.3g; FIBER 4g; CHOL 14mg; IRON 1.4mg; SODIUM 846mg; CALC 66mg

North Woods Bean Soup

You may not be a North Woods lumberjack, but you may enjoy eating like one. Pureeing some of the soup lends body to the dish. Stir in the fresh spinach after the soup is removed from the heat so it won't overcook and lose its bright color.

        Cooking spray
    1   cup baby carrots, halved
    1   cup chopped onion
    2   garlic cloves, minced
    7   ounces turkey kielbasa, halved lengthwise
        and cut into ½-inch pieces
    4   cups fat-free, less-sodium chicken broth
    ½   teaspoon dried Italian seasoning
    ½   teaspoon black pepper
    2   (15.8-ounce) cans Great Northern beans,
        rinsed and drained
    1   (6-ounce) bag fresh baby spinach

1. Heat a large saucepan over medium-high heat. Coat pan with cooking spray. Add carrots, onion, garlic, and kielbasa; sauté 3 minutes. Reduce heat to medium; cook 5 minutes. Add broth, Italian seasoning, pepper, and beans. Bring to a boil; reduce heat, and simmer 5 minutes.
2. Place 2 cups soup in a food processor or blender, and process until smooth. Return pureed mixture to pan. Simmer 5 minutes. Remove soup from heat. Add spinach, stirring until spinach wilts. Yield: 5 servings (serving size: about 1½ cups).

CALORIES 227 (15% from fat); FAT 3.9g (sat 1.2g, mono 1.3g, poly 1.2g); PROTEIN 18.1g; CARB 30.8g; FIBER 6.7g; CHOL 26mg; IRON 3.5mg; SODIUM 750mg; CALC 112mg

Sausage, Kale, and Bean Soup

Cajun sausage fires up a simple five-ingredient soup with smoky spice. Add some crusty bread, and you've got a meal on the table in no time.

    4 ounces Cajun smoked sausage, chopped (such as Conecuh)
    3 cups fat-free, less-sodium chicken broth
    1 (14.5-ounce) can no salt–added diced tomatoes, undrained
    6 cups coarsely chopped kale (about 8 ounces)
    1 (16-ounce) can navy beans, rinsed and drained

1. Heat a large saucepan over medium-high heat. Add chopped sausage; cook 2 minutes, stirring occasionally. Add broth and tomatoes; bring to a boil over high heat. Stir in kale. Reduce heat; simmer 4 minutes or until kale is tender. Stir in beans, and cook 1 minute or until thoroughly heated. Yield: 4 servings (serving size: 1¾ cups).

CALORIES 280 (29% from fat); FAT 9g (sat 3.2g, mono 3.8g, poly 1.4g); PROTEIN 17g; CARB 33.6g; FIBER 2.8g; CHOL 20mg; IRON 3.4mg; SODIUM 924mg; CALC 153mg

Black-Eyed Pea, Kale, and Ham Soup

Black-eyed peas have been a staple in the South for more than three centuries. Over the years, the peas have become part of Southern folklore, and many believe that eating black-eyes on New Year's Day will bring good luck all year long. Serve this soup with some warm, golden corn bread, and luck will be on your side.

    1 tablespoon olive oil
    4 ounces smoked ham, diced
    1 cup diced onion
  ½ cup diced celery
    2 garlic cloves, minced
    4 cups chopped kale
    1 (14.5-ounce) can petite cut diced tomatoes
    2 cups frozen black-eyed peas
  ¾ cup water
    2 (14-ounce) cans vegetable broth
    2 tablespoons tomato paste
  ¼ teaspoon freshly ground black pepper
  ⅛ teaspoon cayenne pepper

1. Heat oil in a Dutch oven over medium-high heat. Add ham, onion, celery, and garlic; sauté 5 minutes or until vegetables are tender. Stir in kale and remaining ingredients; bring to a boil. Cover, reduce heat, and simmer 45 minutes or until peas are tender. Yield: 7 servings (serving size: 1 cup).

CALORIES 155 (20% from fat); FAT 3.5g (sat 0.7g, mono 1.5g, poly 0.5g); PROTEIN 9g; CARB 23.5g; FIBER 4.7g; CHOL 8mg; IRON 2mg; SODIUM 567mg; CALC 83mg

Chunky Minestrone

In Italian, minestrone means "big soup." This filling combination of beans, fresh and frozen vegetables, and pasta lives up to the name. Vegetables lose their crunch when they're frozen, so using frozen chopped onion ensures that the onion won't still be crunchy after cooking. If you'd rather use fresh, microwave chopped fresh onion at HIGH for a minute or two to precook it a little.

    3 (14-ounce) cans fat-free, less-sodium chicken broth
    2 (14.5-ounce) cans no salt–added diced tomatoes with roasted garlic, undrained
    1 (15.5-ounce) can cannellini beans or other white beans, rinsed and drained
    1 (10-ounce) package frozen chopped spinach, thawed
    1 cup water
 1½ cups frozen chopped onion, thawed
    1 medium carrot, chopped
    1 medium zucchini, quartered and sliced
    2 teaspoons olive oil
    1 teaspoon dried Italian seasoning
  ¼ teaspoon black pepper
  ½ cup uncooked small seashell pasta
  ⅔ cup (2.5 ounces) freshly grated Parmesan cheese

1. Place first 11 ingredients in a 4-quart electric slow cooker. Cover and cook on LOW 5½ hours.
2. Add pasta; cover and cook on LOW 30 minutes. Ladle soup into individual bowls. Sprinkle with cheese. Yield: 5 servings (serving size: 2⅓ cups soup and 2 tablespoons cheese).

CALORIES 284 (27% from fat); FAT 8.4g (sat 3.6g, mono 1.4g, poly 0.6g); PROTEIN 16.4g; CARB 37.4g; FIBER 6.7g; CHOL 16mg; IRON 3.6mg; SODIUM 602mg; CALC 381mg

Minestrone Bowl

½ cup sun-dried tomatoes (packed without oil)
2 cups boiling water
1 tablespoon olive oil
2 cups chopped less-sodium ham
2 cups chopped onion
1 cup chopped carrot
1 cup chopped celery
5 garlic cloves, chopped
6 cups water
1 (14.5-ounce) can diced tomatoes, undrained
1 zucchini, halved lengthwise and sliced
1 (16-ounce) can cannellini beans or other white beans, rinsed and drained
¼ cup chopped fresh basil
¼ teaspoon salt
¾ teaspoon black pepper
3½ cups hot cooked linguine (about 7 ounces uncooked pasta)
¼ cup plus 2 teaspoons (about 1 ounce) grated fresh Parmesan cheese

1. Combine sun-dried tomatoes and boiling water in a bowl; let stand 30 minutes. Drain sun-dried tomatoes through a sieve into a bowl, reserving soaking liquid. Cut sun-dried tomatoes into julienne strips.

2. Heat olive oil in a large Dutch oven over medium-high heat. Add sun-dried tomatoes, ham, and next 4 ingredients, and sauté 5 minutes. Add reserved soaking liquid, 6 cups water, and diced tomatoes; bring to a boil. Cover, reduce heat, and simmer 30 minutes. Add zucchini and beans; cook 5 minutes. Stir in basil, salt, and pepper. Place pasta into large shallow bowls; top with broth mixture and cheese. Yield: 7 servings (serving size: ½ cup pasta, 2 cups broth mixture, and 2 teaspoons cheese).

CALORIES 319 (21% from fat); FAT 7.4g (sat 2.1g, mono 3.3g, poly 1.4g); PROTEIN 17.1g; CARB 48.1g; FIBER 5.5g; CHOL 22mg; IRON 4mg; SODIUM 822mg; CALC 139mg

Garden Minestrone

An adaptation of the classic Italian *minestra*, this recipe is full of late-summer produce: tomatoes, squash, fresh spinach, corn, and carrots. In cooler months, use peeled acorn squash and Swiss chard in place of squash and spinach. We love this minestrone for its practicality, since it's convenient for lunch or a simple dinner (just serve it with a tossed green salad and some crusty bread).

    2 teaspoons olive oil
    1 cup chopped onion
    2 teaspoons chopped fresh oregano
    4 garlic cloves, minced
    3 cups chopped yellow squash
    3 cups chopped zucchini
    1 cup chopped carrot
    1 cup fresh corn kernels (about 2 ears)
    4 cups chopped tomato, divided
    3 (14-ounce) cans fat-free, less-sodium chicken broth
    ½ cup uncooked ditalini (very short tube-shaped macaroni)
    1 (15.5-ounce) can Great Northern beans, rinsed and drained
    1 (6-ounce) package fresh baby spinach
    1 teaspoon salt
    ½ teaspoon freshly ground black pepper
    1 cup (4 ounces) grated Asiago cheese
    Coarsely ground black pepper (optional)

1. Heat oil in a Dutch oven over medium-high heat. Add chopped onion to pan, and sauté 3 minutes or until softened. Add oregano and garlic, and sauté 1 minute. Stir in squash, zucchini, carrot, and corn; sauté 5 minutes or until vegetables are tender. Remove from heat.

2. Place 3 cups tomato and 1 can broth in a blender; process until smooth. Add tomato mixture to pan; return pan to heat. Stir in remaining 1 cup tomato and 2 cans broth; bring mixture to a boil. Reduce heat, and simmer 20 minutes.

3. Add pasta and beans to pan, and cook 10 minutes or until pasta is tender, stirring occasionally. Remove from heat. Stir in spinach, salt, and ½ teaspoon freshly ground pepper. Ladle soup into individual bowls; top with cheese. Garnish with coarsely ground pepper, if desired. Yield: 8 servings (serving size: 1½ cups soup and 2 tablespoons cheese).

CALORIES 217 (25% from fat); FAT 6.1g (sat 2.7g, mono 2g, poly 0.6g); PROTEIN 12.6g; CARB 30.5g; FIBER 7.9g; CHOL 12mg; IRON 2.7mg; SODIUM 812mg; CALC 206mg

Pasta e Fagioli

Take a lesson in quick cooking from Italians with this hearty, comforting soup that's ready in less than 30 minutes. Hot turkey sausage, mellow cannellini beans, and tender seashell pasta combine to create a speedy weeknight dinner.

    1 tablespoon olive oil
    6 ounces hot turkey Italian sausage
    1½ tablespoons bottled minced garlic
    1 cup water
    1 (14-ounce) can fat-free, less-sodium chicken broth
    1 (8-ounce) can no salt–added tomato sauce
    1 cup uncooked small seashell pasta (about 4 ounces)
    ½ cup (2 ounces) shredded Romano cheese, divided
    1½ teaspoons dried oregano
    ¼ teaspoon salt
    ¼ teaspoon white pepper
    2 (15.5-ounce) cans cannellini beans or other white beans, rinsed and drained
    Minced fresh parsley (optional)

1. Heat oil in a large saucepan over medium-high heat. Add sausage and garlic; sauté 2 minutes or until browned, stirring to crumble. Add water, broth, and tomato sauce; bring to a boil. Stir in pasta, ¼ cup cheese, oregano, salt, white pepper, and beans; bring to a boil. Cover, reduce heat, and simmer 8 minutes or until pasta is done. Let stand 5 minutes; sprinkle each serving with cheese. Garnish with parsley, if desired. Yield: 6 servings (serving size: 1 cup soup and 2 teaspoons cheese).

CALORIES 244 (29% from fat); FAT 7.9g (sat 2.7g, mono 3g, poly 1.2g); PROTEIN 13g; CARB 27.7g; FIBER 4.4g; CHOL 24mg; IRON 4.9mg; SODIUM 836mg; CALC 129mg

Pinto Bean Chili with Corn and Winter Squash

The spiciness of this light yet satisfying chili is complemented by the subtle sweetness of corn and winter squash. For a heartier chili, add 1 cup of thawed frozen meatless crumbles. For a vegan version, use shredded soy Cheddar or soy mozzarella cheese.

1 tablespoon olive oil
1½ cups chopped onion
1½ cups chopped red bell pepper
1 garlic clove, minced
2 tablespoons chili powder
½ teaspoon ground cumin
4 cups (½-inch) cubed peeled butternut squash (about 1 pound)
2 (16-ounce) cans pinto beans, rinsed and drained
1½ cups water
1 cup frozen whole-kernel corn
1 teaspoon salt
1 (28-ounce) can crushed tomatoes, undrained
1 (4.5-ounce) can chopped green chiles, undrained
¾ cup (3 ounces) crumbled queso fresco
12 lime wedges

1. Heat oil in a large nonstick skillet over medium heat. Add onion, bell pepper, and garlic; cover and cook 5 minutes or until tender. Add chili powder and cumin; cook 1 minute, stirring constantly.
2. Place onion mixture in a 5-quart electric slow cooker. Add squash and next 6 ingredients. Cover and cook on LOW 8 hours or until chili is thick. Ladle chili into individual bowls. Sprinkle with cheese, and serve with lime wedges. Yield: 6 servings (serving size: 1¾ cups chili, 2 tablespoons cheese, and 2 lime wedges).

CALORIES 319 (17% from fat); FAT 6.1g (sat 2g, mono 2.5g, poly 1.3g); PROTEIN 14.3g; CARB 56g; FIBER 12.7g; CHOL 10mg; IRON 4.4mg; SODIUM 862mg; CALC 255mg

Beef and Bean Chili

Your family will love this soul-warming chili. Increase the amount of chili powder or top servings with pickled jalapeño peppers if you prefer spicier food. Serve with crackers or corn bread. You can double this chili recipe for a crowd, but make sure to use an appropriately sized slow cooker—your cooker should be between half and two-thirds full.

1 pound ground round
1 cup chopped onion
½ cup chopped green bell pepper
¼ cup dry red wine or water
1 tablespoon chili powder
1 teaspoon sugar
1 teaspoon ground cumin
¼ teaspoon salt
1 garlic clove, minced
1 (15-ounce) can kidney beans, undrained
1 (14.5-ounce) can Mexican-style stewed tomatoes with jalapeño peppers and spices, undrained

1. Cook ground round in a large nonstick skillet over medium-high heat until brown, stirring to crumble. Add onion and next 7 ingredients, and cook 7 minutes or until onion is tender. Place meat mixture in a 4-quart electric slow cooker; stir in beans and tomatoes. Cover and cook on LOW 4 hours. Yield: 6 servings (serving size: 1¼ cups).

CALORIES 233 (30% from fat); FAT 7.7g (sat 3.1g, mono 3.3g, poly 0.3g); PROTEIN 20.6g; CARB 20.5g; FIBER 5.2g; CHOL 49mg; IRON 3.2mg; SODIUM 597mg; CALC 65mg

Beef and Bean Chili

Chili con Carne with Beans

You probably have most of the ingredients for this yummy chili already in your pantry. Just pick up fresh ground sirloin and some prechopped onion from the store. Serve the chili over rice or with corn bread.

1 cup chopped onion
4 teaspoons chili powder
1 tablespoon ground cumin
1 teaspoon bottled minced garlic
¼ teaspoon ground red pepper
1 pound ground sirloin
1½ cups canned crushed tomatoes
½ teaspoon salt
1 (14.5-ounce) can diced tomatoes with green bell pepper, celery, and onion, undrained
1 (19-ounce) can kidney beans, rinsed and drained

1. Cook first 6 ingredients in a large nonstick skillet over medium-high heat until beef is browned, stirring to crumble beef.

2. Add crushed tomatoes, salt, and diced tomatoes; bring to a boil. Cook 4 minutes, stirring occasionally. Add beans, and cook 2 minutes or until thoroughly heated. Yield: 4 servings (serving size: 1½ cups).

CALORIES 403 (30% from fat); FAT 13.5g (sat 4.8g, mono 5.4g, poly 0.7g); PROTEIN 32g; CARB 38.8g; FIBER 14g; CHOL 75mg; IRON 3.9mg; SODIUM 824mg; CALC 65mg

Black Bean and Chorizo Chili

Serve with corn bread, and you've got a great meal for a casual dinner party. This chili smells so good while it's simmering that your guests will be clamoring to eat as soon as they walk in the door. The smoky chipotle chiles and Spanish chorizo combine to give this dish a kick.

   Cooking spray
- 2 canned chipotle chiles in adobo sauce, drained and finely chopped
- 1¾ cups chopped onion
- 1½ cups chopped green bell pepper
- 1½ cups chopped red bell pepper
- 5 garlic cloves, minced
- 3 links Spanish chorizo sausage, diced (about 6½ ounces)
- 1½ tablespoons chili powder
- 1 tablespoon ground cumin
- 1½ teaspoons dried oregano
- 1 tablespoon fresh lime juice
- ⅛ teaspoon ground cinnamon
- 3 (15-ounce) cans black beans, rinsed and drained
- 3 (14-ounce) cans whole peeled tomatoes, undrained and chopped
- 1 (8½-ounce) can no salt–added whole-kernel corn, drained
- 1½ ounces semisweet chocolate, chopped
- ¾ teaspoon salt
- ½ teaspoon black pepper

1. Heat a large Dutch oven over medium-high heat. Coat pan with cooking spray. Add chiles, onion, bell peppers, garlic, and chorizo, and sauté 5 minutes or until tender. Add chili powder and next 7 ingredients, stirring to combine; bring to a boil. Reduce heat; simmer, covered, 30 minutes, stirring occasionally. Remove from heat, and stir in chocolate, salt, and black pepper. Yield: 12 servings (serving size: 1 cup).

CALORIES 311 (24% from fat); FAT 8.4g (sat 3.2g, mono 3.4g, poly 1g); PROTEIN 16.5g; CARB 43.9g; FIBER 12.9g; CHOL 13mg; IRON 4.1mg; SODIUM 888mg; CALC 95mg

Mexican Black Bean Chili

Chili is one big melting pot of worldly influences. Here, we've highlighted south-of-the-border spices and the traditional use of black beans. Fast and flavorful, this chili fits the bill.

- 1 cup diced onion
- 1 cup diced green bell pepper
- 1 pound ground chuck
- 1 tablespoon chili powder
- 1½ teaspoons ground cumin
- ¾ teaspoon dried oregano
- ½ teaspoon salt
- ⅛ teaspoon black pepper
- 2 (15-ounce) cans black beans, rinsed and drained
- 2 (14.5-ounce) cans no salt–added diced tomatoes, undrained
- 1 (14-ounce) can fat-free, less-sodium beef broth
- 3 garlic cloves, crushed
- 6 tablespoons fat-free sour cream
   Cilantro sprigs (optional)

1. Cook first 3 ingredients in a large nonstick skillet over medium-high heat until browned, stirring to crumble. Drain well; return meat mixture to pan. Add chili powder and next 8 ingredients; bring to a boil. Reduce heat; simmer 20 minutes or until slightly thick, stirring occasionally.

2. Ladle chili into individual bowls; top with sour cream. Garnish with cilantro sprigs, if desired. Yield: 6 servings (serving size: 1½ cups chili and 1 tablespoon sour cream).

CALORIES 236 (15% from fat); FAT 4g (sat 1.5g, mono 1.4g, poly 0.5g); PROTEIN 23.6g; CARB 33.6g; FIBER 10.5g; CHOL 41mg; IRON 4.3mg; SODIUM 884mg; CALC 112mg

Shrimp and Spinach Soup

Vibrant green spinach leaves float in a yellow-hued mixture of sweet rice wine and vegetable broth.

½ cup water
½ cup matchstick-cut peeled fresh ginger
¼ cup mirin (sweet rice wine)
2 tablespoons low-sodium soy sauce
2 (14-ounce) cans vegetable broth
1 pound medium shrimp, peeled and deveined
2 cups bagged prewashed spinach (about 2 ounces)

1. Combine first 5 ingredients in a large saucepan, and bring to a boil. Cover, reduce heat, and simmer 10 minutes. Stir in shrimp, and cook over medium heat 2 minutes or until shrimp are almost done. Stir in spinach, and cook 1 minute, stirring occasionally. Yield: 6 servings (serving size: about ¾ cup).

CALORIES 120 (14% from fat); FAT 1.9g (sat 0.3g, mono 0.2g, poly 0.5g); PROTEIN 17.1g; CARB 6.5g; FIBER 0.3g; CHOL 115mg; IRON 2.2mg; SODIUM 861mg; CALC 52mg

Thai Shrimp and Chicken Soup

Thailand, with its irresistible combination of breathtaking natural beauty, renowned hospitality, and delicious cuisine, draws more visitors each year than any other country in southeast Asia. If a trip to Bangkok isn't in your travel plans this year, you can at least bring a bit of it to your own home tonight with this tasty recipe featuring the robust flavors of garlic, ginger, mushrooms, and snow peas.

3 cups fat-free, less-sodium chicken broth
1 cup bottled clam juice
1 tablespoon fish sauce
2 teaspoons bottled minced garlic
1½ teaspoons bottled minced ginger
¾ teaspoon red curry paste
1 (8-ounce) package presliced mushrooms
½ pound peeled and deveined large shrimp
½ pound skinless, boneless chicken breast, cut into 1-inch pieces
1 (3-ounce) package trimmed snow peas
¼ cup fresh lime juice
2 tablespoons sugar
2 tablespoons (½-inch) sliced green onion tops
2 tablespoons chopped fresh cilantro
1 (13.5-ounce) can light coconut milk

1. Combine first 6 ingredients in a large Dutch oven, stirring with a whisk. Add mushrooms, and bring to a boil. Reduce heat, and simmer 4 minutes. Add shrimp, chicken, and snow peas; bring to a boil. Cover, reduce heat, and simmer 3 minutes.
2. Stir in lime juice and remaining ingredients. Cook 2 minutes or until thoroughly heated. Yield: 4 servings (serving size: about 2 cups).

CALORIES 262 (24% from fat); FAT 7.1g (sat 3.8g, mono 0.3g, poly 0.6g); PROTEIN 30g; CARB 18.3g; FIBER 1.8g; CHOL 121mg; IRON 3.3mg; SODIUM 973mg; CALC 64mg

Spicy Chicken Soup

Comfort your soul or soothe a case of the sniffles with a bowlful of spicy chicken soup. You can keep almost all of these ingredients on hand in your pantry or fridge for a last-minute meal. Baked tortilla chips and a garden salad are excellent accompaniments.

1 chipotle chile, canned in adobo sauce
1 teaspoon olive oil
1 cup chopped green bell pepper
½ cup chopped green onions
1 tablespoon bottled minced garlic
1 teaspoon ground cumin
2 (6-ounce) packages cooked chicken breast strips, chopped (about 2 cups)
2 (14-ounce) cans fat-free, less-sodium chicken broth
1 (14½-ounce) can diced tomatoes and green chiles (such as Del Monte), undrained
1 (11-ounce) can whole-kernel corn with sweet peppers, drained

1. Mince chile. Heat oil in a large saucepan over medium-high heat. Add bell pepper, green onions, garlic, and cumin; sauté 4 minutes or until vegetables are soft. Stir in minced chile, chicken, broth, tomatoes, and corn. Bring to a boil; reduce heat, and simmer 3 minutes. Yield: 4 servings (serving size: 2 cups).

CALORIES 215 (18% from fat); FAT 4.2g (sat 0.2g, mono 0.9g, poly 0.3g); PROTEIN 25.4g; CARB 19g; FIBER 3.2g; CHOL 51mg; IRON 1mg; SODIUM 1,552mg; CALC 45mg

Spicy Chicken Soup

Roasted-Chicken Noodle Soup

Classic chicken noodle soup consists of a clear broth, often cooked with small pieces of chicken, vegetables, noodles or dumplings, or grains such as rice and barley. We kicked the flavor and richness up a couple notches by adding evaporated fat-free milk. Though we used a rotisserie chicken and canned broth to save time, this soup's health benefits remain intact.

    2   teaspoons olive oil
    1   cup chopped onion
    1   cup diced carrots
    1   cup sliced celery
    1   garlic clove, minced
  1/4   cup all-purpose flour
  1/2   teaspoon dried oregano
  1/4   teaspoon dried thyme
  1/4   teaspoon poultry seasoning
    6   cups fat-free, less-sodium chicken broth
    4   cups diced peeled baking potato
    1   teaspoon salt
    2   cups shredded cooked chicken
    1   cup evaporated fat-free milk
    4   ounces (2 cups) uncooked wide egg noodles

1. Heat olive oil in a Dutch oven over medium heat. Add onion, carrots, celery, and garlic clove; sauté 5 minutes.
2. Lightly spoon flour into a dry measuring cup; level with a knife. Sprinkle flour, oregano, thyme, and poultry seasoning over vegetables, and cook 1 minute. Stir in broth, potato, and salt; bring to a boil. Reduce heat, and simmer, partially covered, 25 minutes or until potato is tender.
3. Add chicken, milk, and noodles, and cook 10 minutes or until noodles are tender. Yield: 8 servings (serving size: 1 1/4 cups).

CALORIES 247 (16% from fat); FAT 4.5g (sat 1.1g, mono 1.8g, poly 1g); PROTEIN 18g; CARB 32.8g; FIBER 2.9g; CHOL 46mg; IRON 2mg; SODIUM 701mg; CALC 71mg

Posole

Posole (poh-SOH-leh) is a thick, hearty soup from the Pacific Coast region of Mexico. It features chicken broth, fluffy white hominy, chopped onions, zesty jalapeño peppers, and vibrant green cilantro. It's traditionally served as a main course during the Christmas season. A lime garnish adds color and a festive look to your presentation.

    1   pound tomatillos
    6   cups Brown Chicken Stock (recipe on page
        345) or fat-free, less-sodium chicken broth
    2   cups chopped onion
    3   pounds bone-in chicken breast halves,
        skinned
    4   garlic cloves, chopped
    2   jalapeño peppers, seeded and quartered
    1   (30-ounce) can white hominy, drained
    1   teaspoon salt
  1/2   cup chopped fresh cilantro
  1/4   cup reduced-fat sour cream
    8   lime wedges

1. Discard husks and stems from tomatillos. Cook tomatillos in boiling water 10 minutes or until tender; drain. Place in a blender; process until smooth.
2. Place stock and next 5 ingredients in a large stockpot; bring to a boil. Cover, reduce heat, and simmer 35 minutes or until chicken is done. Remove chicken from pot. Stir in pureed tomatillos and salt, and cook 5 minutes or until heated. Remove chicken from bones; shred. Stir in chicken. Ladle soup into individual bowls; serve with cilantro, sour cream, and lime wedges. Yield: 8 servings (serving size: 1 1/2 cups soup, 1 tablespoon cilantro, 1 1/2 teaspoons sour cream, and 1 lime wedge).

(Totals include Brown Chicken Stock) CALORIES 233 (16% from fat); FAT 4.1g (sat 1.3g, mono 0.7g, poly 0.8g); PROTEIN 31.8g; CARB 19.4g; FIBER 4g; CHOL 79mg; IRON 1.8mg; SODIUM 548mg; CALC 46mg

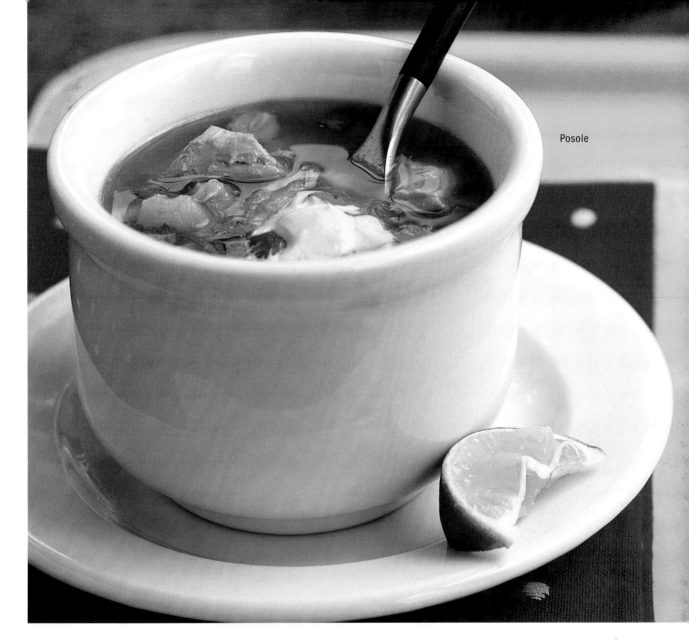

Posole

BROWN CHICKEN STOCK:

Use a pan large enough to roast the chicken and all the vegetables in a single layer. If the pan is too small, the chicken won't brown properly.

- ¼ pound fennel stalks, cut into 2-inch-thick pieces
- 3 carrots, cut into 2-inch-thick pieces
- 1 celery stalk, cut into 2-inch-thick pieces
- 1 medium onion, peeled and quartered
- 6 pounds chicken pieces
- ½ teaspoon black peppercorns
- 6 parsley sprigs
- 5 thyme sprigs
- 2 bay leaves
- 16 cups cold water, divided

1. Preheat oven to 400°.

2. Arrange first 4 ingredients in bottom of a broiler or roasting pan; top with chicken. Bake at 400° for 1½ hours; turn chicken once every 30 minutes (chicken and vegetables should be very brown).

3. Place peppercorns, parsley, thyme, and bay leaves in an 8-quart stockpot. Remove vegetables and chicken from broiler pan; place in stockpot. Discard drippings from broiler pan, leaving browned bits. Place broiler pan on stovetop; add 4 cups water. Bring to a boil over medium-high heat. Reduce heat; simmer 10 minutes, scraping pan to loosen browned bits.

4. Pour contents of pan into stockpot. Add remaining 12 cups water; bring to a boil over medium-high heat. Reduce heat; simmer 1½ hours.

5. Strain stock through a fine sieve into a large bowl. Reserve chicken for another use; discard remaining solids. Cover and chill stock 8 hours. Skim solidified fat from surface of stock; discard fat. Yield: 10 cups (serving size: 1 cup).

CALORIES 31 (32% from fat); FAT 1.1g (sat 0.3g, mono 0.4g, poly 0.2g); PROTEIN 4.7g; CARB 0.4g; FIBER 0.1g; CHOL 15mg; IRON 0.3mg; SODIUM 19mg; CALC 4mg

Tex-Mex Chicken
Tortilla Soup

Tex-Mex Chicken Tortilla Soup

Tortillas are the basis of countless Mexican dishes, such as tacos, enchiladas, and burritos, as well as for our peppy Tex-Mex soup. The crunchy texture of the tortilla chips provides the perfect contrast to this fiesta-in-a-bowl, which features bright colors, bold flavors, robust spices, and sour cream and cilantro garnishes. Don't throw away any leftover tortillas; they're also ideal toasted and sprinkled over salads or casseroles.

- 1 tablespoon olive oil
- 2 (6-ounce) skinless, boneless chicken breast halves, cut into ½-inch pieces
- 2 (4-ounce) skinless, boneless chicken thighs, cut into ½-inch pieces
- 2 cups chopped onion (about 2 medium)
- 3 garlic cloves, chopped
- 1 cup fresh corn kernels (about 2 ears) or frozen whole-kernel corn
- 1 cup water
- 1 tablespoon chopped jalapeño pepper
- 1 tablespoon chili powder
- 1½ teaspoons ground cumin
- ½ teaspoon salt
- 2 (14.5-ounce) cans no salt–added tomatoes, undrained and chopped
- 2 (14-ounce) cans fat-free, less-sodium chicken broth
- 1 (4.5-ounce) can chopped green chiles
- 2 (6-inch) corn tortillas, each cut into 8 wedges
- 5 tablespoons reduced-fat sour cream
- Cilantro sprigs (optional)

1. Heat olive oil in a large Dutch oven over medium-high heat. Add chicken pieces and chopped onion, and cook 7 minutes or until onion is tender. Add chopped garlic to pan, and sauté 30 seconds. Stir in corn and next 8 ingredients. Bring to a boil, reduce heat, and simmer 45 minutes.

2. Preheat oven to 350°.

3. Place tortilla wedges on baking sheet, and bake at 350° for 5 minutes or until crisp.

4. Ladle soup into individual bowls, and top with sour cream. Garnish with tortilla chips and cilantro sprigs, if desired. Yield: 5 servings (serving size: 1½ cups soup, 1 tablespoon sour cream, and about 3 tortilla chips).

CALORIES 331 (27% from fat); FAT 9.9g (sat 2.8g, mono 3.6g, poly 1.4g); PROTEIN 30.6g; CARB 30.9g; FIBER 6.1g; CHOL 77mg; IRON 2.3mg; SODIUM 983mg; CALC 130mg

Turkey Soup Provençal

Serve this quick-to-prepare soup with crusty French bread for a weeknight meal. Heat up your leftovers the next day for lunch.

- 1 pound ground turkey breast
- ½ teaspoon dried herbes de Provence, crushed
- 1 (15-ounce) can cannellini beans or other white beans, rinsed and drained
- 1 (14.5-ounce) can diced tomatoes with garlic and onion, undrained
- 1 (14-ounce) can fat-free, less-sodium chicken broth
- 4 cups chopped fresh spinach

1. Cook turkey in a large saucepan over medium-high heat until browned, stirring to crumble.

2. Add herbes de Provence, beans, tomatoes, and broth to pan; bring to a boil. Reduce heat; simmer 5 minutes. Stir in spinach, and simmer 5 minutes. Yield: 4 servings (serving size: 1¼ cups).

CALORIES 294 (12% from fat); FAT 3.8g (sat 1.5g, mono 0.8g, poly 0.4g); PROTEIN 40g; CARB 25.4g; FIBER 5.4g; CHOL 75mg; IRON 6.1mg; SODIUM 890mg; CALC 206mg

About Herbes de Provence

Herbes de Provence is a mixture of dried herbs native to the Provence region of southern France. It traditionally contains rosemary, basil, bay leaves, and thyme. Other herbs, including savory, lavender, fennel seeds, and dried sage, are sometimes added. The proportion of the herbs in the mixture varies depending on the manufacturer. Herbes de Provence is used to flavor grilled meat or fish; side dishes such as potatoes, rice, or pasta; and soups.

Turkey Noodle Soup

Cooking spray
1 cup (¼-inch-thick) slices carrot
¾ cup chopped onion
4 garlic cloves, minced
1 cup (¼-inch-thick) slices celery
¼ teaspoon salt
¼ teaspoon freshly ground black pepper
6 cups fat-free, less-sodium chicken broth
2 cups (3 ounces) uncooked egg noodles
1 tablespoon low-sodium soy sauce
1 bay leaf
2 cups shredded cooked turkey (about 8 ounces)
Coarsely ground black pepper (optional)

1. Heat a large saucepan over medium-high heat. Coat pan with cooking spray. Add carrot, onion, and garlic, and sauté 5 minutes or until onion is lightly browned. Add celery, salt, and ¼ teaspoon pepper, and sauté 3 minutes. Add broth and next 3 ingredients; bring to a boil. Reduce heat, and simmer 5 minutes. Add turkey; cook 3 minutes. Discard bay leaf. Ladle soup into individual bowls. Sprinkle with coarsely ground pepper, if desired. Yield: 4 servings (serving size: 2 cups).

CALORIES 280 (23% from fat); FAT 7.2g (sat 2.6g, mono 1.1g, poly 1.4g); PROTEIN 29.1g; CARB 24.3g; FIBER 2.3g; CHOL 80mg; IRON 2.6mg; SODIUM 544mg; CALC 79mg

Turkey-Pasta Soup

Holiday leftovers star in this quick and simple recipe that is excellent for a casual meal.

1 tablespoon olive oil
½ cup chopped carrot
¼ cup chopped celery
¼ cup minced onion
1 garlic clove, minced
2 cups water
⅓ cup chopped 33%-less-sodium ham (about 2 ounces)
¼ teaspoon freshly ground black pepper
4 (14-ounce) cans fat-free, less-sodium chicken broth
1 cup uncooked ditali (short tube-shaped macaroni)
3 cups chopped cooked turkey
3 cups thinly sliced napa (Chinese) cabbage

1. Heat oil in a large Dutch oven over medium-high heat. Add carrot, celery, onion, and garlic; sauté 3 minutes or until tender. Add water, ham, pepper, and broth; bring to a boil. Add pasta; cook 8 minutes or until pasta is done. Stir in turkey and cabbage, and cook 2 minutes or until cabbage wilts. Yield: 8 servings (serving size: 1½ cups).

CALORIES 194 (23% from fat); FAT 4.9g (sat 1.3g, mono 2g, poly 1g); PROTEIN 21.8g; CARB 14.2g; FIBER 1.2g; CHOL 44mg; IRON 1.6mg; SODIUM 483mg; CALC 45mg

Vegetable-Beef Soup

Convenience products eliminate most of the prep work for this easy recipe. For a classic comfort-food combo, serve this soup with half of a grilled cheese sandwich made with whole wheat bread and reduced-fat cheese.

¼ cup all-purpose flour
1½ pounds lean top round steak, cut into 1-inch cubes
Cooking spray
2 teaspoons spicy herb blend (such as Mrs. Dash Extra Spicy Seasoning Blend)
2 (16-ounce) packages frozen gumbo vegetable mix
1 (10-ounce) package frozen chopped onion
2 (14.5-ounce) cans diced tomatoes with garlic, undrained
2 (14-ounce) cans fat-free, less-sodium beef broth
1 tablespoon bottled minced garlic
1 tablespoon low-sodium Worcestershire sauce
½ teaspoon salt
½ teaspoon black pepper

1. Place flour in a large zip-top plastic bag; add steak cubes. Seal and shake to coat. Remove steak from bag, and set aside.
2. Heat a large nonstick skillet over medium-high heat; coat pan with cooking spray. Add steak, and cook until browned on all sides.
3. Place steak and remaining ingredients in a 5-quart electric slow cooker; stir well. Cover and cook on HIGH 1 hour; reduce heat to LOW, and cook 6 hours or until steak is done and vegetables are tender. Yield: 8 servings (serving size: about 1¾ cups).

CALORIES 256 (20% from fat); FAT 5.6g (sat 2g, mono 2.2g, poly 0.4g); PROTEIN 26g; CARB 26g; FIBER 6.2g; CHOL 49mg; IRON 3.4mg; SODIUM 542mg; CALC 66mg

Hanoi Beef and Rice
Noodle Soup

Hanoi Beef and Rice Noodle Soup

Traditionally a northern Vietnamese breakfast specialty, *pho bo*—a beef and noodle soup—is now eaten at any time of day. Partially freeze the eye-of-round roast to make it easier to slice. You can also use regular sweet basil in place of Thai basil.

BROTH:
- 3 pounds beef oxtail
- ¾ cup thinly sliced peeled fresh ginger (about 3 ounces)
- ⅔ cup coarsely chopped shallots (about 3 medium shallots)
- 5 quarts water
- 4 cups coarsely chopped daikon radish (about 1 pound)
- 3 tablespoons Thai fish sauce (such as Three Crabs)
- 2 tablespoons sugar
- 1 teaspoon white peppercorns
- 5 whole cloves
- 2 star anise
- 1 large yellow onion, peeled and quartered
- 1 cinnamon stick

REMAINING INGREDIENTS:
- 2 cups vertically sliced onion
- 12 ounces wide rice stick noodles (*bánh pho*)
- 2 cups fresh bean sprouts
- 12 ounces eye-of-round roast, trimmed and cut into 1/16-inch slices
- 2 cups cilantro leaves
- 1 cup Thai basil leaves
- 4 red Thai chiles, seeded and thinly sliced
- 8 lime wedges
- 1 tablespoon hoisin sauce (optional)

1. To prepare broth, heat a large stockpot over medium-high heat. Add oxtail, ginger, and shallots; sauté 8 minutes or until ginger and shallots are slightly charred. Add water and next 8 ingredients; bring to a boil. Reduce heat, and simmer 4 hours. Strain broth through a sieve into a large bowl; discard solids. Return broth to pan; bring to a boil. Reduce heat to medium, and cook until reduced to 10 cups (about 30 minutes). Skim fat from surface; discard fat. Keep warm.

2. To prepare remaining ingredients, add sliced onion to broth. Place noodles in a large bowl, and cover with boiling water. Let stand 20 minutes. Drain. Place ⅓ cup bean sprouts in each of 6 soup bowls. Top each serving with 1⅓ cups noodles and 2 ounces eye-of-round. Bring broth to a boil; carefully ladle 1⅔ cups boiling broth over each serving (boiling broth will cook meat). Serve with cilantro, basil, chiles, lime wedges, and, if desired, hoisin sauce. Yield: 6 servings.

CALORIES 404 (19% from fat); FAT 8.5g (sat 3.3g, mono 3.7g, poly 0.5g); PROTEIN 23.4g; CARB 58g; FIBER 3.5g; CHOL 57mg; IRON 3.3mg; SODIUM 751mg; CALC 69mg

Caribbean Seafood Pot

Grouper is a mild fish that takes on the flavor of the seasonings in which it cooks, so don't worry about this filling stew being too fishy. Don't add the shrimp and fish to the cooker until the last 10 minutes; they don't need to cook long.

- 2 teaspoons canola oil
- 2 cups diced peeled red potato
- 1 cup chopped onion
- ¾ cup diced red bell pepper
- ⅔ cup chopped celery
- 4 garlic cloves, minced
- 2 (14.5-ounce) cans diced tomatoes with garlic and onion, undrained
- 2 (8-ounce) bottles clam juice
- 3 tablespoons pickled jalapeño pepper slices, minced
- 1 teaspoon dried thyme
- ¼ teaspoon ground allspice
- ¾ pound grouper or other firm white fish fillet, cut into 1-inch cubes
- ¾ pound large shrimp, peeled

1. Heat oil in a large nonstick skillet over medium-high heat. Add potato and next 3 ingredients; sauté 5 minutes. Add garlic, and sauté 30 seconds. Cover, reduce heat to medium, and cook 5 minutes or until potato is tender. Place potato mixture in a 4½-quart electric slow cooker. Add tomatoes and next 4 ingredients; stir well. Cover and cook on LOW 7 hours.

2. Add grouper and shrimp; cover and cook 10 minutes or until shrimp are done and fish flakes easily when tested with a fork. Yield: 6 servings (serving size: 1¾ cups).

CALORIES 226 (18% from fat); FAT 4.4g (sat 0.5g, mono 1.2g, poly 1.1g); PROTEIN 26.8g; CARB 21g; FIBER 3.2g; CHOL 109mg; IRON 4.8mg; SODIUM 1,025mg; CALC 99mg

Gulf of Mexico Gumbo

1 cup all-purpose flour
1 teaspoon canola oil
2 cups chopped onion
1 cup chopped green bell pepper
½ cup chopped celery
4 garlic cloves, minced
1 cup sliced okra
1 cup chopped tomato
1½ cups water
1 teaspoon Cajun-Creole Seasoning
4 (8-ounce) bottles clam juice
2 bay leaves
½ pound skinless red snapper or other firm white fish fillet, cut into 1-inch pieces
¼ cup thinly sliced green onions
¾ pound crawfish, peeled
¼ pound medium shrimp, peeled and deveined
½ teaspoon hot sauce
4½ cups hot cooked long-grain rice

1. Lightly spoon flour into a dry measuring cup; level with a knife. Place flour in a 9-inch cast-iron skillet, and cook over medium heat 10 minutes or until browned, stirring constantly with a whisk. Remove from heat; set aside.

2. Heat oil in a large Dutch oven over medium heat. Add onion, bell pepper, celery, and garlic; sauté 8 minutes or until tender. Add okra and tomato. Cover; cook 5 minutes, stirring occasionally. Add water and next 3 ingredients; bring to a boil. Gradually add flour; stir with a whisk. Reduce heat. Simmer, uncovered, 45 minutes, stirring occasionally.

3. Add snapper; cook 5 minutes. Add green onions, crawfish, and shrimp; cook 10 minutes or until seafood is done. Stir in hot sauce; discard bay leaves. Serve over rice. Yield: 9 servings (serving size: 1 cup gumbo and ½ cup rice).

(Totals include Cajun-Creole Seasoning) CALORIES 251 (6% from fat); FAT 1.8g (sat 0.3g, mono 0.6g, poly 0.6g); PROTEIN 17.8g; CARB 39.8g; FIBER 2.3g; CHOL 71mg; IRON 2.8mg; SODIUM 460mg; CALC 72mg

CAJUN-CREOLE SEASONING:

1 tablespoon salt
¾ teaspoon ground red pepper
½ teaspoon garlic powder
½ teaspoon black pepper

1. Combine all ingredients. Yield: about 1½ tablespoons. Yield: 36 servings (serving size: ⅛ teaspoon).

CALORIES 0 (0% from fat); FAT 0g; PROTEIN 0g; CARB 0.1g; FIBER 0g; CHOL 0mg; IRON 0mg; SODIUM 194mg; CALC 0mg

Mother's Cioppino

Cioppino (chuh-PEE-noh) is a stew created by West Coast Italian immigrants who used readily available seafood along with homemade tomato and fish sauces. If you order cioppino in a San Francisco restaurant, be prepared for a hands-on encounter, especially if you have to wrestle with simmered seafood in shells in a thick red tomato sauce. We simplified the recipe with store-bought pasta sauce and clam juice. It's best served the same day it is made.

CROSTINI:

1 (1-pound) loaf French bread baguette, cut into 16 slices
1 tablespoon olive oil

CIOPPINO:

2 teaspoons olive oil
½ to 1 teaspoon crushed red pepper
4 garlic cloves, finely chopped
3 cups clam juice
1 cup water
½ cup finely chopped fresh parsley
½ teaspoon dried basil
¼ teaspoon dried thyme
1 (26-ounce) jar tomato-and-basil pasta sauce (such as Bertolli)
16 littleneck clams
16 small mussels, scrubbed and debearded
½ cup dry white wine
½ teaspoon salt
¼ teaspoon black pepper
1 pound cod or other lean white fish fillets, cut into 1-inch pieces
½ pound medium shrimp, peeled and deveined
2 cups torn spinach

1. Preheat oven to 350°.

2. To prepare crostini, place baguette slices on a large baking sheet; brush with 1 tablespoon oil. Bake at 350° for 15 minutes or until lightly browned.

3. To prepare cioppino, heat 2 teaspoons oil in a Dutch oven over medium-high heat. Add crushed red pepper and garlic; sauté 30 seconds. Stir in clam juice and next 5 ingredients. Add clams and mussels. Cover and cook 10 minutes or until shells open. Discard any unopened shells. Add wine and next 4 ingredients; simmer 5 minutes or until fish and shrimp are done. Stir in spinach. Serve with crostini. Yield: 8 servings (serving size: 1¼ cups stew and 2 crostini).

CALORIES 467 (24% from fat); FAT 12.4g (sat 1.7g, mono 4g, poly 3.6g); PROTEIN 31g; CARB 53g; FIBER 9.8g; CHOL 89mg; IRON 9.3mg; SODIUM 1,182mg; CALC 87mg

Chickpea Stew Scented with Lemon and Cumin

From start to finish, this hearty, one-dish meatless meal can be on the table in less than 20 minutes. The chickpeas provide plenty of protein, and the polenta gives the dish a creamy base.

 4 cups water
 1 cup instant dry polenta
 1 tablespoon butter
 1 tablespoon olive oil
 1 cup chopped onion
 1½ teaspoons bottled minced garlic
 ¼ cup lemon juice
 1 teaspoon ground cumin
 ¼ teaspoon black pepper
 2 (15-ounce) cans chickpeas (garbanzo beans), rinsed and drained
 2 (14.5-ounce) cans diced tomatoes, undrained
 ½ cup chopped green onions
 ¾ cup reduced-fat sour cream

1. Bring water to a boil in a medium saucepan. Gradually add polenta, stirring constantly with a whisk. Reduce heat, and simmer 3 minutes, stirring frequently. Remove from heat; stir in butter. Cover and set aside.

2. While polenta cooks, heat oil in a large nonstick skillet over medium-high heat. Add onion and garlic; sauté 3 minutes. Add lemon juice, cumin, pepper, chickpeas, and tomatoes; bring to a boil. Reduce heat; simmer 6 minutes. Stir in green onions. Spoon polenta into each of 6 individual bowls. Ladle stew over polenta. Top with sour cream. Yield: 6 servings (serving size: 1⅓ cups stew, ⅔ cup polenta, and 2 tablespoons sour cream).

CALORIES 400 (22% from fat); FAT 9.6g (sat 4g, mono 2.6g, poly 1g); PROTEIN 12.9g; CARB 68g; FIBER 9.8g; CHOL 21mg; IRON 2.8mg; SODIUM 838mg; CALC 180mg

Red Bean Stew with Ditalini

This hearty stew is a one-dish meal in the truest sense. Add the uncooked ditalini straight to the pot—it cooks right along with the stew.

    1   tablespoon olive oil
    1½ cups presliced mushrooms
    1   cup diced carrot
    1½ cups water
    ¼   teaspoon black pepper
    1   (15-ounce) can kidney beans, rinsed and
        drained
    1   (14.5-ounce) can diced tomatoes, undrained
    1   (14-ounce) can less-sodium beef broth
    4   ounces uncooked ditalini (short tube-shaped
        pasta)
    2   tablespoons commercial pesto (such as Alessi)
    ¼   cup (1 ounce) shredded fresh Parmesan
        cheese

1. Heat oil in a Dutch oven over medium-high heat. Add mushrooms and carrot; sauté 4 minutes. Stir in water and next 4 ingredients. Cover; bring to a boil. Stir in pasta; cook, uncovered, 11 minutes or until pasta is done. Stir in pesto; sprinkle each serving with cheese. Yield: 4 servings (serving size: 1½ cups stew and 1 tablespoon cheese).

CALORIES 324 (28% from fat); FAT 10.2g (sat 2.3g, mono 4.7g, poly 1.7g); PROTEIN 15.2g; CARB 43.7g; FIBER 10.4g; CHOL 6mg; IRON 3.1mg; SODIUM 560mg; CALC 150mg

About Pesto

Originally a sauce made from the fresh, wild basil that grows on the hills of Liguria, Italy, pesto is now a popular sauce used on more than just pasta. Made of garlic, basil, pine nuts, Parmesan or Romano cheese, and olive oil, it can be spread onto toasted bread, used in place of red sauce on pizzas, or blended into a soup, as it is here. As an added convenience, commercial pesto is available year-round from your local supermarket.

African Sweet Potato Stew with Red Beans

Vivid colors and fragrant spices are the hallmarks of this thick stew, which is garnished with crunchy peanuts. A squeeze of lime juice brightens the rich, earthy flavors.

    2   teaspoons olive oil
    1½ cups chopped onion
    1   garlic clove, minced
    4   cups (½-inch) cubed peeled sweet potato
        (about 1½ pounds)
    1½ cups cooked small red beans
    1½ cups vegetable broth
    1   cup chopped red bell pepper
    ½   cup water
    1   teaspoon grated peeled fresh ginger
    ½   teaspoon salt
    ½   teaspoon ground cumin
    ¼   teaspoon black pepper
    1   (14.5-ounce) can diced tomatoes, drained
    1   (4.5-ounce) can chopped green chiles,
        drained
    3   tablespoons creamy peanut butter
    3   tablespoons chopped dry-roasted peanuts
    6   lime wedges

1. Heat oil in a nonstick skillet over medium heat. Add onion and garlic; cover and cook 5 minutes or until tender.
2. Place onion mixture in a 5-quart electric slow cooker. Add sweet potato and next 10 ingredients. Cover and cook on LOW 8 hours or until vegetables are tender.
3. Spoon 1 cup cooking liquid into a small bowl. Add peanut butter, and stir well with a whisk. Stir peanut butter mixture into stew. Ladle stew into individual bowls. Top with peanuts; serve with lime wedges. Yield: 6 servings (serving size: 1⅓ cups stew, 1½ teaspoons peanuts, and 1 lime wedge).

CALORIES 308 (26% from fat); FAT 8.8g (sat 1.5g, mono 4.2g, poly 2.3g); PROTEIN 11.1g; CARB 49.9g; FIBER 10.2g; CHOL 0mg; IRON 2.7mg; SODIUM 574mg; CALC 64mg

African Sweet Potato Stew with Red Beans

Calabaza and Poblano Stew

Calabaza and Poblano Stew

Redolent with honey, cinnamon, and aniseed, this stew highlights the exotic flavors that are typically associated with European cuisine but are also commonly used in Mexico. Crema Mexicana, which is similar to crème fraîche but has a thinner consistency and a sweeter flavor, helps to tone down the spiciness of the stew.

    5   poblano chiles (about 1 pound)
    1   teaspoon aniseed
    1   (3-inch) cinnamon stick, broken
    1   tablespoon peanut oil
 3½   cups chopped onion
    4   garlic cloves, minced
  10   cups (2-inch) pieces peeled calabaza squash
        (about 3 pounds)
    4   cups vegetable broth
    2   cups water
    3   tablespoons honey
  ½   teaspoon salt
    6   tablespoons crema Mexicana
  ½   cup roasted pumpkinseed kernels

1. Preheat broiler.
2. Cut chiles in half; discard seeds and membranes. Place chile halves, skin sides up, on a foil-lined baking sheet; flatten with hand. Broil 5 minutes or until blackened. Place in a heavy-duty zip-top plastic bag; seal. Let stand 15 minutes. Peel chiles; discard skins. Chop chiles.
3. Place aniseed and cinnamon stick in a spice or coffee grinder; process until finely ground.
4. Heat oil in a large Dutch oven over medium-high heat. Add onion; sauté 5 minutes or until browned. Add garlic; sauté 1 minute. Add cinnamon mixture to pan; sauté 1 minute. Add chopped chiles, squash, broth, water, honey, and salt; bring to a boil. Reduce heat, and simmer 30 minutes or until squash is tender.
5. Ladle stew into individual bowls. Drizzle each serving with crema Mexicana, and sprinkle with pumpkinseeds. Yield: 8 servings (serving size: 1½ cups stew, about 2 teaspoons crema Mexicana, and 1 tablespoon pumpkinseeds).

CALORIES 266 (35% from fat); FAT 10.4g (sat 2.6g, mono 2.7g, poly 3.4g); PROTEIN 9g; CARB 40.7g; FIBER 8.4g; CHOL 8mg; IRON 4mg; SODIUM 669mg; CALC 118mg

Chicken Brunswick Stew

    5   cups chopped onion
    6   (6-ounce) skinless, boneless chicken breast
        halves
    2   (14¾-ounce) cans no salt–added cream-style
        corn
    2   (14.5-ounce) cans no salt–added diced
        tomatoes, undrained
    1   (14-ounce) can fat-free, less-sodium chicken
        broth
    1   (12-ounce) bottle chili sauce
  ¼   cup butter, cut into small pieces
    2   tablespoons Worcestershire sauce
    2   tablespoons cider vinegar
    2   teaspoons dry mustard
  ½   teaspoon freshly ground black pepper
  ½   teaspoon hot pepper sauce
Freshly ground black pepper (optional)

1. Place onion in a 5- to 6-quart electric slow cooker; top with chicken. Add corn and next 9 ingredients, and stir well. Cover and cook on HIGH 1 hour. Reduce heat to LOW, and cook 6 hours or until chicken is tender. Remove chicken; shred with 2 forks, and return to stew. Ladle stew into individual bowls; sprinkle with additional black pepper, if desired. Yield: 9 servings (serving size: 1½ cups).

CALORIES 344 (20% from fat); FAT 7.5g (sat 3.6g, mono 1.7g, poly 0.6g); PROTEIN 30.1g; CARB 39.9g; FIBER 4.3g; CHOL 79mg; IRON 1.8mg; SODIUM 1,335mg; CALC 54mg

About Hot Pepper Sauce

For this recipe, be sure to use the hot pepper sauce that contains whole peppers packed in vinegar, rather than the red-colored hot sauce. Bring the bottle to the table when serving this stew, and add more pepper sauce to suit your taste.

Brunswick Stew with Smoked Paprika

This recipe is said to have originated in Brunswick County, Virginia, in the 1800s. We spiced it up with a little Spanish smoked paprika (available at gourmet specialty stores and some supermarkets). Use rotisserie chicken to speed up preparation. This hearty stew could become a regular autumn weeknight treat.

2   cups (¾-inch) cubed Yukon gold potato
2   cups thinly sliced yellow onion
2   cups frozen corn kernels, thawed
1   cup frozen baby lima beans, thawed
½   cup tomato sauce
2   (14-ounce) cans fat-free, less-sodium chicken broth
2   bacon slices, cut crosswise into ½-inch strips
3   cups shredded cooked chicken breast
½   teaspoon sweet Spanish smoked paprika
½   teaspoon kosher salt
¼   teaspoon ground red pepper
Coarsely ground black pepper (optional)

1. Combine first 7 ingredients in a Dutch oven over medium-high heat; bring to a boil. Reduce heat to low; simmer 30 minutes or until potatoes are tender, stirring occasionally. Stir in chicken and next 3 ingredients; simmer 15 minutes. Ladle stew into individual bowls. Sprinkle with coarsely ground black pepper, if desired. Yield: 6 servings (serving size: about 1½ cups).

CALORIES 308 (22% from fat); FAT 7.5g (sat 2.4g, mono 3g, poly 1.4g); PROTEIN 29.4g; CARB 31.6g; FIBER 4.9g; CHOL 65mg; IRON 2.2mg; SODIUM 645mg; CALC 36mg

Tuscan Chicken Stew

Make your home a Tuscan villa tonight with this Italian-inspired stew. Bake biscuits from a low-fat buttermilk baking mix while the stew simmers.

½ teaspoon dried rosemary, crushed
½ teaspoon salt
¼ teaspoon black pepper
1 pound skinless, boneless chicken breast, cut into 1-inch pieces
2 teaspoons olive oil
2 teaspoons bottled minced garlic
½ cup fat-free, less-sodium chicken broth
1 (16-ounce) can cannellini beans or other white beans, rinsed and drained
1 (7-ounce) bottle roasted red bell peppers, drained and cut into ½-inch pieces
3½ cups torn spinach

1. Combine first 4 ingredients, and toss well. Heat olive oil in a large nonstick skillet over medium-high heat. Add chicken mixture, and sauté 3 minutes. Add garlic, and sauté 1 minute. Add broth, beans, and bell peppers; bring to a boil. Reduce heat, and simmer 10 minutes or until chicken is done. Stir in spinach, and simmer 1 minute. Yield: 4 servings (serving size: 1 cup).

CALORIES 290 (18% from fat); FAT 5.9g (sat 0.9g, mono 2.4g, poly 1.4g); PROTEIN 34.8g; CARB 25.1g; FIBER 5.1g; CHOL 66mg; IRON 4.5mg; SODIUM 612mg; CALC 110mg

About White Beans

"White bean" is a generic term used for a variety of ivory-white beans. We call for cannellini beans (sometimes referred to as white kidney beans) in this chicken stew, but any other white bean (such as Great Northern beans or navy beans) may be substituted.

Peasant Stew

Cumin, green chiles, and Mexican-style tomatoes give this humble stew a spicy kick. Because the chicken thighs are left whole, serve this rustic fare with a knife, fork, and spoon.

1 teaspoon ground cumin
¼ teaspoon salt
¼ teaspoon black pepper
6 chicken thighs (about 1½ pounds), skinned
Cooking spray
1 cup chopped onion
1 (14.5-ounce) can Mexican-style stewed tomatoes with jalapeño peppers and spices, undrained
1 (4.5-ounce) can chopped green chiles, undrained
1 (16-ounce) can pinto beans, rinsed and drained
1 (16-ounce) can kidney beans, rinsed and drained
¼ cup minced fresh cilantro
¼ cup reduced-fat sour cream

1. Combine cumin, salt, and black pepper; sprinkle over chicken. Heat a large skillet over medium-high heat; coat pan with cooking spray. Add chicken to pan; cook 4 to 5 minutes or until browned on all sides.
2. Place chicken in a 5-quart electric slow cooker; stir in onion, tomatoes, and chiles. Cover and cook on HIGH 3 hours. Stir in beans. Cover and cook 1 hour.
3. Ladle 1¼ cups stew into each of 6 soup bowls, and top each with 1 chicken thigh, 2 teaspoons cilantro, and 2 teaspoons sour cream. Yield: 6 servings.

CALORIES 245 (27% from fat); FAT 7.3g (sat 2.3g, mono 2.1g, poly 1.3g); PROTEIN 19.7g; CARB 24g; FIBER 6.6g; CHOL 53mg; IRON 2.7mg; SODIUM 556mg; CALC 101mg

Jamaican Chicken Stew

Jamaican Chicken Stew

This classic Jamaican stew will usher you to the island in spirit and have you saying "Yah mon!" before your second bite. Add jalapeño-style corn bread and pineapple sorbet for a simple weeknight supper.

    1   cup uncooked long-grain rice
    2   teaspoons olive oil
    1   cup chopped onion
    1   large garlic clove, minced
    1   pound skinless, boneless chicken breast, cut
        into bite-sized pieces
    1   teaspoon curry powder
    1   teaspoon dried thyme
    ½   teaspoon ground allspice
    ½   teaspoon crushed red pepper
    ½   teaspoon cracked black pepper
    ¼   cup dry red wine
    2   tablespoons capers
    1   (15-ounce) can black beans, rinsed and
        drained
    1   (14.5-ounce) can diced tomatoes, undrained
    Cilantro sprigs (optional)

1. Prepare rice according to package directions, omitting salt and fat. Keep warm.
2. Heat oil in a large nonstick skillet over medium-high heat. Add onion and garlic; sauté 3 minutes or until tender. Combine chicken and next 5 ingredients. Add chicken mixture to pan; sauté 4 minutes. Stir in wine, capers, beans, and tomatoes. Cover, reduce heat, and simmer 10 minutes or until tender. Spoon rice into individual bowls, and ladle stew over rice. Garnish with cilantro sprigs, if desired. Yield: 4 servings (serving size: 1½ cups stew and ¾ cup rice).

CALORIES 465 (10% from fat); FAT 5g (sat 1g, mono 2.2g, poly 1g); PROTEIN 38.5g; CARB 66g; FIBER 5.9g; CHOL 66mg; IRON 6mg; SODIUM 799mg; CALC 101mg

Turkey Vatapa

Vatapa is a rustic Brazilian stew, a fiery blend with beer, coconut milk, and ground peanuts as its base. Made with leftover holiday turkey or rotisserie chicken, it's a snap to prepare. Vatapa can be made up to two days in advance; keep it covered in the refrigerator. It will thicken as it sits; just add a little water. Seed the jalapeño pepper to tame its heat.

    1   teaspoon peanut or canola oil
    ½   cup finely chopped onion
    3   garlic cloves, minced
    1   tablespoon minced peeled fresh ginger
    1   jalapeño pepper, minced
    1   cup water
    1   (28-ounce) can no salt–added diced tomatoes,
        undrained
    1   (12-ounce) can light beer
    ¼   cup unsalted, dry-roasted peanuts
    3   cups chopped cooked turkey or chicken
    ½   cup light coconut milk
    ½   cup finely chopped fresh parsley
    ½   cup finely chopped fresh cilantro
    1   tablespoon fresh lime juice
    ½   teaspoon salt
    ½   teaspoon black pepper
    Cilantro sprigs (optional)

1. Heat oil in a Dutch oven over medium-high heat. Add onion and garlic; sauté 2 minutes. Add ginger and jalapeño; sauté 30 seconds. Stir in water, tomatoes, and beer; bring to a boil. Cover, reduce heat, and simmer 20 minutes.
2. Place peanuts in a spice or coffee grinder, and process until finely ground. Add ground peanuts, chopped turkey, and coconut milk to pan, stirring to combine. Increase heat to medium. Bring mixture to a simmer, and cook 5 minutes, stirring occasionally. Stir in chopped parsley, chopped cilantro, lime juice, salt, and black pepper. Ladle stew into individual bowls. Garnish with cilantro sprigs, if desired. Yield: 6 servings (serving size: 1⅓ cups).

CALORIES 195 (30% from fat); FAT 6.4g (sat 1.8g, mono 2.3g, poly 1.7g); PROTEIN 19.9g; CARB 11.8g; FIBER 3.3g; CHOL 56mg; IRON 2.3mg; SODIUM 301mg; CALC 55mg

Spicy Sausage, Barley, and Mushroom Stew

While the sausage adds spice to this stew, it's the robust flavor of the mushrooms and the chewy texture of the barley that make it so filling.

- 2 teaspoons olive oil
- 2 cups thinly sliced onion
- 8 ounces spicy Italian turkey sausage
- 1 cup chopped celery
- 1 cup sliced carrot
- 2 garlic cloves, minced
- 1 bay leaf
- 5 cups thinly sliced shiitake mushroom caps
- 1½ cups chopped portobello mushrooms
- ½ cup uncooked pearl barley
- 3 (14-ounce) cans fat-free, less-sodium chicken broth
- 2 tablespoons brandy
- 1 teaspoon salt
- ¼ teaspoon freshly ground black pepper
- 6 tablespoons chopped fresh parsley

1. Heat oil in a large Dutch oven over medium heat. Add onion; cook 5 minutes or until tender. Remove casings from sausage. Add sausage to pan; cook 8 minutes or until sausage is browned, stirring to crumble. Add celery, carrot, garlic, and bay leaf; cook 10 minutes or until onion is golden brown, stirring frequently.

2. Stir in mushrooms, and cook 10 minutes or until liquid almost evaporates. Stir in barley, broth, brandy, salt, and pepper. Bring mixture to a boil; cover, reduce heat, and simmer 1 hour or until barley is tender. Discard bay leaf. Ladle soup into individual bowls. Sprinkle with parsley. Yield: 6 servings (serving size: about 1 cup stew and 1 tablespoon parsley).

CALORIES 213 (30% from fat); FAT 7.2g (sat 2g, mono 2.5g, poly 1.8g); PROTEIN 13.3g; CARB 23.4g; FIBER 4.7g; CHOL 27mg; IRON 2.4mg; SODIUM 481mg; CALC 54mg

Beef Burgundy Stew

Perhaps the heartiest of all stews, the classic French *boeuf bourguignon* is streamlined here for calories and cooking techniques. But when it comes to flavor, this version is just as robust as the original. We added potatoes and carrots to make it a one-dish meal.

- 2 teaspoons canola oil
- Cooking spray
- 1½ pounds lean boneless round steak (½-inch-thick), trimmed and cut into 1-inch cubes
- 2 large garlic cloves, minced
- 3 cups Burgundy or other dry red wine
- ¼ cup tomato paste
- ½ teaspoon dried thyme
- 2 bay leaves
- ½ cup water
- 2 (14-ounce) cans beef broth
- 10 small red potatoes, quartered (about 1½ pounds)
- 6 medium carrots, cut into 1-inch pieces (about 1 pound)
- 2 small onions, quartered (about ½ pound)
- 1 (8-ounce) package mushrooms, halved
- 3 tablespoons water
- 3 tablespoons cornstarch
- ½ teaspoon salt
- ¼ teaspoon black pepper
- Chopped fresh parsley (optional)

1. Heat oil in a large Dutch oven coated with cooking spray over medium-high heat. Add steak, and cook 8 minutes on all sides or until browned. Add garlic; sauté 1 minute. Add wine, tomato paste, thyme, and bay leaves; bring mixture to a boil. Cover, reduce heat, and simmer 50 minutes.

2. Add ½ cup water and next 4 ingredients; bring to a boil. Cover, reduce heat, and simmer 40 minutes.

3. Stir in mushrooms; cover and cook 50 minutes or until steak is tender. Discard bay leaves.

4. Combine 3 tablespoons water and cornstarch in a small bowl; add to pan. Cook 2 minutes or until thickened, stirring constantly. Stir in salt and pepper. Ladle stew into individual bowls; sprinkle with parsley, if desired. Yield: 8 servings (serving size: about 1½ cups).

CALORIES 254 (15% from fat); FAT 4.2g (sat 1.1g, mono 1.7g, poly 0.6g); PROTEIN 23.9g; CARB 29.8g; FIBER 4g; CHOL 48mg; IRON 3.3mg; SODIUM 405mg; CALC 39mg

Beef Burgundy Stew

Beef Burgundy

Beef Burgundy (or *boeuf bourguignon* in French) is a rich beef stew flavored with, as the name suggests, Burgundy wine. It's often served as a sauce over egg noodles. A traditional version of this dish can take hours of work tending to various steps on the cooktop and in the oven. This slow-cooker version has the flavor of all-day cooking without making you spend your entire day watching over it. Serve with a mixed green salad for a complete meal.

  1 (10-ounce) package fresh pearl onions
  1 (2-pound) top round steak, trimmed and cut into 1½-inch cubes
2½ cups sliced onion (1 large)
  1 garlic clove, minced
  Cooking spray
  ⅓ cup all-purpose flour
1⅓ cups less-sodium beef broth
  ½ cup Burgundy or other dry red wine
  2 tablespoons tomato paste
  ½ teaspoon dried thyme
  ½ teaspoon salt
  ¼ teaspoon black pepper
  1 bay leaf
  1 (8-ounce) package mushrooms
  3 cups hot cooked medium egg noodles (about 4 cups uncooked pasta)
  Thyme leaves (optional)

1. Drop pearl onions in boiling water; cook 1 minute. Drain onions; peel.

2. Heat a large nonstick skillet over medium-high heat. Add steak; sauté 5 minutes or until browned. Place steak in a 3-quart electric slow cooker. Add sliced onion and garlic to pan; coat with cooking spray, and sauté over medium-high heat 5 minutes or until tender. Lightly spoon flour into a dry measuring cup; level with a knife. Sprinkle flour over onion-garlic mixture; cook 1 minute, stirring constantly. Gradually add broth, wine, and tomato paste, stirring constantly. Cook 1 minute or until thick. Add pearl onions, dried thyme, salt, pepper, bay leaf, and mushrooms.

3. Pour wine mixture over steak in cooker. Cover and cook on LOW 6 to 7 hours. Discard bay leaf. Serve over noodles. Garnish with thyme leaves, if desired. Yield: 6 servings (serving size: 1 cup steak mixture and ½ cup noodles).

CALORIES 398 (18% from fat); FAT 8.1g (sat 2.5g, mono 3.1g, poly 0.8g); PROTEIN 41.7g; CARB 38.1g; FIBER 3.3g; CHOL 106mg; IRON 5.1mg; SODIUM 392mg; CALC 67mg

Carne con Papas

This everyday meat-and-potatoes dish is best accompanied by white rice. Olives, raisins, and capers make the stew reminiscent of picadillo, a Spanish hash made from ground pork and beef or veal plus tomatoes, garlic, and onions. To streamline the preparation, chop the potatoes and olives while the beef and vegetables simmer.

  1 teaspoon canola oil
  Cooking spray
1½ pounds beef stew meat, trimmed and cut into 1-inch cubes
1½ cups chopped onion
  ½ cup chopped green bell pepper
  ½ teaspoon salt
  ½ teaspoon freshly ground black pepper
  3 garlic cloves, minced
  ¼ cup water
  1 teaspoon dried oregano
  1 teaspoon paprika
  ⅛ teaspoon ground cumin
  1 bay leaf, crumbled
  1 (14-ounce) can low-sodium beef broth
  4 cups cubed peeled baking potato (about 2 pounds)
  3 tablespoons raisins
  3 tablespoons coarsely chopped pimiento-stuffed olives
  2 tablespoons capers

1. Heat oil in a large Dutch oven coated with cooking spray over medium-high heat. Add beef; cook 2 minutes or until browned. Add onion, bell pepper, salt, black pepper, and garlic; sauté 3 minutes. Add water and next 5 ingredients; bring to a boil. Cover, reduce heat, and cook 30 minutes.

2. Stir in potato and remaining ingredients. Cook, covered, over medium heat 20 minutes or until potato is tender, stirring occasionally. Yield: 5 servings (serving size: about 1½ cups).

CALORIES 349 (29% from fat); FAT 11.2g (sat 3.7g, mono 5.1g, poly 0.7g); PROTEIN 29.8g; CARB 32.3g; FIBER 3.2g; CHOL 85mg; IRON 4.1mg; SODIUM 673mg; CALC 43mg

Carne con Papas

Veal-and-Artichoke Stew with Avgolemono

STEW:

  4 cups water, divided
 ⅔ cup fresh lemon juice (about 4 lemons), divided
  8 medium artichokes (about 10 ounces each)
  4 lemons, cut in half
2½ pounds veal round, trimmed and cut into 2-inch cubes
1½ cups coarsely chopped onion
 ½ cup dry white wine
  2 (14-ounce) cans fat-free, less-sodium chicken broth
 ½ cup chopped fresh dill
 ½ teaspoon sea salt
 ½ teaspoon freshly ground black pepper

AVGOLEMONO:

  1 large egg
  5 tablespoons water
  2 tablespoons fresh lemon juice
1½ teaspoons cornstarch
 ¼ cup chopped fresh dill
Lemon wedges (optional)

1. To prepare stew, combine 3 cups water and ⅓ cup lemon juice in a large bowl. Working with 1 artichoke at a time, cut off stem to within 1 inch of base, and peel stem. Remove bottom leaves and tough outer leaves, and trim about 2 inches from top of artichoke. Cut artichoke in half vertically. Remove fuzzy thistle from bottom with a spoon. Trim any remaining leaves and dark green layer from base. Rub edges with a lemon half, and place artichoke halves in lemon water. Repeat procedure with remaining artichokes.

2. Heat a Dutch oven over medium-high heat, and add veal, browning on all sides. Add onion, and cook 5 minutes. Add wine and 1 can of chicken broth; bring to a boil. Cover, reduce heat, and simmer 45 minutes.

3. Drain artichoke halves. Add artichoke halves, remaining 1 cup water, remaining ⅓ cup lemon juice, ½ cup dill, remaining 1 can of broth, salt, and pepper to pan; cover and simmer 30 minutes or until artichokes are tender. Remove veal and artichoke halves with a slotted spoon. Keep warm.

4. To prepare avgolemono, combine egg, 3 tablespoons water, and 2 tablespoons lemon juice in a medium bowl. Combine 2 tablespoons water and cornstarch in a small bowl; add to egg mixture. Add egg mixture to juices in pan. Bring to a boil;

cook 5 minutes, stirring constantly with a whisk. Ladle stew into individual bowls. Serve sauce over veal and artichokes, and sprinkle with ¼ cup dill. Garnish with lemon wedges, if desired. Yield: 8 servings (serving size: 4 ounces meat, 2 artichoke halves, ¼ cup sauce, and 1½ teaspoons dill).

CALORIES 256 (12% from fat); FAT 3.4g (sat 1g, mono 1.1g, poly 0.4g); PROTEIN 37.2g; CARB 22g; FIBER 7.6g; CHOL 136mg; IRON 3.1mg; SODIUM 653mg; CALC 81mg

Braised Lamb Stew with Ginger

  1 pound lamb stew meat
  2 tablespoons cornstarch
  1 tablespoon low-sodium soy sauce
  1 tablespoon dry sherry
 ¼ teaspoon freshly ground black pepper
 ½ cup boiling water
  6 dried shiitake mushrooms
  1 tablespoon canola oil
  2 tablespoons minced peeled fresh ginger
  3 garlic cloves, minced
  3 cups fat-free, less-sodium chicken broth
1⅓ cups sliced carrot
  2 tablespoons oyster sauce
 ¼ cup chopped fresh cilantro
  4 cups hot cooked rice noodles
Fresh cilantro leaves (optional)

1. Combine first 5 ingredients in a bowl.

2. Combine ½ cup boiling water and dried mushrooms in a bowl. Let stand 15 minutes; drain, reserving soaking liquid. Discard stems; thinly slice caps.

3. Heat oil in a large nonstick skillet over medium-high heat. Add ginger and garlic; sauté 30 seconds. Add lamb mixture; sauté 4 minutes. Stir in broth; bring to a boil. Cover and reduce heat; simmer 40 minutes. Uncover; bring to a boil. Add carrot, mushrooms, and reserved liquid. Cook 5 minutes or until slightly thickened. Add oyster sauce and cilantro. Ladle into bowls; serve with rice noodles. Garnish with fresh cilantro, if desired. Yield: 4 servings (serving size: 1 cup stew and 1 cup noodles).

CALORIES 451 (20% from fat); FAT 10g (sat 2g, mono 5g, poly 2g); PROTEIN 28g; CARB 59g; FIBER 4g; CHOL 74mg; IRON 3mg; SODIUM 650mg; CALC 37mg

Braised Lamb Stew with Ginger

Curry Stew with Lamb

Lamb curry is a classic dish from northern India. This version includes Thai-inspired ingredients like aromatic lemongrass, sweet coconut milk, and salty fish sauce. These additions provide an excellent backdrop to a bold blend of herbs and spices.

¼ cup firmly packed fresh basil leaves
3 tablespoons chopped peeled fresh ginger
3 tablespoons fresh lime juice
1 tablespoon Thai seasoning
2 teaspoons curry powder
1 teaspoon dried lemongrass (such as Morton & Bassett)
3 shallots, peeled and halved
1½ pounds boneless leg of lamb, trimmed and cut into 1-inch cubes
2½ cups cubed peeled Yukon Gold or red potato
2 tablespoons fish sauce
1 (14.5-ounce) can no salt–added diced tomatoes, undrained
1 (14-ounce) can light coconut milk
Freshly ground black pepper (optional)
Basil leaves (optional)

1. Place first 7 ingredients in a food processor; process until a paste forms. Spoon mixture into a 3½- to 4-quart electric slow cooker. Add lamb and next 4 ingredients; stir well. Cover and cook on HIGH 1 hour. Reduce heat to LOW, and cook 7 hours or until lamb is tender. Ladle stew into individual bowls. Sprinkle with pepper, and garnish with basil leaves, if desired. Yield: 6 servings (serving size: 1⅓ cups).

CALORIES 254 (32% from fat); FAT 9g (sat 5g, mono 2.5g, poly 0.4g); PROTEIN 23.8g; CARB 20.8g; FIBER 2.3g; CHOL 65mg; IRON 2.8mg; SODIUM 781mg; CALC 34mg

Thai-Style Pork Stew

Fragrant basmati rice, peanut butter, and classic Asian flavors meld in this thick stew with Thai flair. As with traditional Thai cuisine, the play between sweet, salty, sour, and spicy creates depth of flavor in this simple recipe that's made even easier in the slow cooker. A squeeze of fresh lime juice is a bright accent to the rich sauce.

STEW:
2 pounds boneless pork loin, cut into 4 pieces, trimmed
2 cups (1 x ¼–inch) julienne-cut red bell pepper
¼ cup teriyaki sauce
2 tablespoons rice vinegar or white wine vinegar
1 teaspoon crushed red pepper
2 garlic cloves, minced
¼ cup creamy peanut butter

REMAINING INGREDIENTS:
6 cups hot cooked basmati rice
½ cup chopped green onions
2 tablespoons chopped dry-roasted peanuts
8 lime wedges

1. Place pork, bell pepper, and next 4 ingredients in a 4-quart electric slow cooker. Cover and cook on HIGH 1 hour; reduce heat to LOW, and cook 6 hours. Remove pork from cooker, and coarsely chop. Add peanut butter to cooking liquid in cooker; stir well. Stir in pork.

2. Serve stew over rice in individual bowls, and top with onions and peanuts. Serve with lime wedges. Yield: 8 servings (serving size: about ⅓ cup stew, ¾ cup rice, about ½ teaspoon peanuts, and 1 lime wedge).

CALORIES 412 (30% from fat); FAT 13.6g (sat 3.6g, mono 6.2g, poly 2.5g); PROTEIN 28.9g; CARB 42.3g; FIBER 2.1g; CHOL 64mg; IRON 2.9mg; SODIUM 425mg; CALC 37mg

desserts

Coconut Cream Pie,
page 390

desserts

Almond-Stuffed Baked Apples with Caramel-Apple Sauce

These stuffed apples come together in minutes and bake while you enjoy dinner. When you caramelize the sugar, don't stir or move the pan until the sugar melts and begins to brown. The caramel mixture will splatter when you add the cider, so use a long-handled wooden spoon for stirring.

FILLING:
- ½ cup sliced almonds, toasted
- ¼ cup sugar
- 2 teaspoons butter, melted
- ¼ teaspoon vanilla extract
- ⅛ teaspoon salt
- Dash of ground nutmeg
- 1 large egg white, lightly beaten

APPLES:
- 4 Braeburn apples, halved
- Cooking spray
- 1 tablespoon sugar
- ¼ teaspoon ground cinnamon

SAUCE:
- ½ cup sugar
- 3 tablespoons water
- ½ cup apple cider
- 1 tablespoon brandy
- 1 tablespoon Grand Marnier (orange-flavored liqueur)
- 1 teaspoon butter
- Dash of salt

1. Preheat oven to 350°.

2. To prepare filling, place almonds in a food processor; process until finely ground. Combine ground almonds, ¼ cup sugar, and next 5 ingredients, stirring until well combined.

3. To prepare apples, core carefully, scooping out 1 tablespoon from each apple half to form a cup. Cut a thin slice off rounded side of each apple half so it will sit flat. Place apples, cup sides up, on a jelly-roll pan coated with cooking spray. Combine 1 tablespoon sugar and cinnamon; sprinkle generously over apples. Spoon about 1 tablespoon filling in cup of each apple half. Bake at 350° for 40 minutes or until apples are golden and tender.

4. To prepare sauce, combine ½ cup sugar and 3 tablespoons water in a small saucepan. Cook over medium-high heat until mixture begins to brown (do not stir); gently tilt pan, and swirl to evenly brown mixture. Reduce heat to low; slowly add cider, stirring constantly. Remove from heat; stir in brandy and next 3 ingredients. Serve over apples. Yield: 8 servings (serving size: 1 stuffed apple half and 1½ tablespoons sauce).

CALORIES 185 (22% from fat); FAT 4.5g (sat 1.1g, mono 2.3g, poly 0.8g); PROTEIN 1.7g; CARB 34.4g; FIBER 3.1g; CHOL 4mg; IRON 0.2mg; SODIUM 78mg; CALC 18mg

Saucy Apples 'n' Pears

Enhance the bounty of late fall's best pick of apples and pears with the soothing flavors of pure maple syrup, pecans, and cinnamon. Your whole house will be filled with warming aromas as the apples and pears simmer in the slow cooker. Serve the warm fruit topping with ice cream or pound cake or over pancakes.

- 3 Gala apples (about 1½ pounds), peeled and sliced
- 3 Anjou or Bartlett pears (about 1½ pounds), peeled and sliced
- 1 tablespoon fresh lemon juice
- ½ cup packed dark brown sugar
- ½ cup pure maple syrup
- ¼ cup butter, melted
- ¼ cup chopped pecans
- ¼ cup raisins
- ½ teaspoon ground cinnamon
- 2 tablespoons water
- 1 tablespoon cornstarch

1. Place apple, pear, and lemon juice in a 4½-quart electric slow cooker; toss gently.

2. Combine brown sugar, syrup, and butter. Spoon sugar mixture over fruit. Stir in pecans, raisins, and cinnamon. Cover and cook on LOW 5½ hours.

3. Combine water and cornstarch in a small bowl; stir until well blended. Stir cornstarch mixture into fruit mixture. Cover and cook 20 minutes or until slightly thickened; stir well. Yield: 4½ cups (serving size: about ⅓ cup).

CALORIES 171 (28% from fat); FAT 5.3g (sat 2.4g, mono 1.9g, poly 0.7g); PROTEIN 0.6g; CARB 32.9g; FIBER 2.5g; CHOL 9mg; IRON 0.6mg; SODIUM 30mg; CALC 27mg

Walnut-Stuffed Apples

Tart Granny Smith apples are drenched in a syrupy brown sugar glaze. Currants are a delectable addition to the classic caramelized nut topping. Serve these "baked" apples warm with low-fat frozen yogurt, if desired.

¼ cup coarsely chopped walnuts
3 tablespoons dried currants
2½ tablespoons brown sugar
¾ teaspoon ground cinnamon, divided
4 Granny Smith apples, cored
1 cup packed brown sugar
¾ cup apple cider

1. Combine first 3 ingredients in a small bowl; stir in ¼ teaspoon cinnamon. Peel top third of each apple; place apples in a 5-quart electric slow cooker.

Spoon walnut mixture evenly into cavities of apples.

2. Combine remaining ½ teaspoon cinnamon, 1 cup brown sugar, and apple cider in a small bowl. Pour over apples. Cover and cook on LOW 2 hours and 45 minutes. Remove apples with a slotted spoon. Place 1 apple on each of 4 dessert plates, and spoon ¼ cup cooking liquid over each serving. Yield: 4 servings.

CALORIES 310 (14% from fat); FAT 4.9g (sat 0.5g, mono 0.7g, poly 3.6g); PROTEIN 1.9g; CARB 70g; FIBER 3.8g; CHOL 0mg; IRON 1.6mg; SODIUM 23mg; CALC 60mg

desserts

Brennan's Bananas Foster

Bananas Foster is an exquisite dessert made of sliced bananas that are first sautéed in butter and sugar and then flambéed in rum and spooned over ice cream. First made in the 1950s in New Orleans at Brennan's Restaurant, the recipe was named after Richard Foster, one of the Brennan family's favorite customers. Even today it's one of their most requested desserts.

- 4 medium bananas
- ¼ cup butter
- 1 cup packed brown sugar
- ¼ cup crème de banane (banana liqueur)
- ½ teaspoon ground cinnamon
- ¼ cup dark rum
- 2 cups vanilla low-fat ice cream

1. Peel bananas; cut each banana in half lengthwise. Cut each half crosswise into 2 pieces.
2. Melt butter in a large nonstick skillet over medium heat. Stir in brown sugar, liqueur, and cinnamon. Bring to a simmer, and cook 2 minutes. Add bananas; cook 4 minutes or until tender. Remove from heat. Add rum to pan, and ignite rum with a long match. Stir bananas gently until flame dies down. Serve over ice cream. Yield: 8 servings (serving size: ¼ cup ice cream, 2 banana pieces, and 2 tablespoons sauce).

CALORIES 290 (21% from fat); FAT 6.9g (sat 3.4g, mono 2.4g, poly 0.3g); PROTEIN 2.2g; CARB 51.4g; FIBER 2.1g; CHOL 18mg; IRON 0.7mg; SODIUM 74mg; CALC 79mg

How to Flambé

The "flambé" cooking technique is the important final step in making Bananas Foster. The alcohol is set aflame and allowed to burn off, leaving a more intense flavor. To flambé, remove the skillet from the heated cooktop, and add rum. For safety, ignite the rum using a long match. The flames will die out naturally as you stir the bananas, creating a delicious syrup that coats the fruit.

Cherries in Spiced Wine Syrup with Pound Cake Croutons

This recipe captures the flavor of early summer. Rosemary, cinnamon, and peppercorns give the red-wine sauce a robust flavor. We served the cherry mixture with toasted pound cake, but it's equally good served over vanilla ice cream.

- ½ teaspoon grated lemon rind
- 6 black peppercorns
- 1 (3-inch) cinnamon stick
- 1 (4-inch) rosemary sprig
- 2 cups dry red wine
- ¾ cup brandy
- ½ cup water
- ⅓ cup honey
- 2 tablespoons fresh lemon juice
- 3 cups pitted sweet cherries
- ½ (10.75-ounce) loaf frozen low-fat pound cake (such as Sara Lee)
- Cooking spray
- ⅓ cup reduced-fat sour cream
- 1 tablespoon honey

1. Place first 4 ingredients on a double layer of cheesecloth. Gather edges of cheesecloth together; tie securely.
2. Combine wine and next 4 ingredients in a medium saucepan; bring to a boil. Add cheesecloth bag, and cook 5 minutes. Reduce heat, and add cherries; simmer 5 minutes, stirring occasionally. Drain cherries in a colander over a bowl, reserving cooking liquid.
3. Place cherries in a medium bowl; discard cheesecloth bag. Return cooking liquid to pan; bring to a boil. Cook 20 minutes or until reduced to 1¼ cups. Pour wine syrup over cherries, and refrigerate 1½ hours or until mixture is completely cool.
4. Preheat oven to 350°.
5. Cut cake into 24 (1-inch) cubes, and arrange cake cubes in a single layer on a nonstick baking sheet coated with cooking spray. Bake at 350° for 12 minutes or until lightly browned, turning cubes every 4 minutes.
6. Combine sour cream and 1 tablespoon honey. Spoon ½ cup cherry mixture into each of 6 bowls or parfait glasses; top each serving with 4 croutons and 1 tablespoon sour cream mixture. Yield: 6 servings.

CALORIES 283 (20% from fat); FAT 6.4g (sat 2.4g, mono 1.9g, poly 0.5g); PROTEIN 3.1g; CARB 48.5g; FIBER 1.7g; CHOL 31mg; IRON 1.3mg; SODIUM 146mg; CALC 48mg

Stuffed Figs with Marsala

Fresh figs are extremely perishable and are available only twice a year: from June through July and from September through October. We opted to use dried figs in this recipe so that you could enjoy it year-round.

1 cup sweet Marsala
¼ cup orange juice
2 tablespoons sugar
12 dried Calimyrna figs
⅓ cup (3 ounces) ⅓-less-fat cream cheese, softened
¼ cup (1 ounce) grated fresh Parmesan cheese
1 tablespoon chopped pine nuts
Orange rind curls (optional)
Mint sprigs (optional)
Pine nuts (optional)

1. Combine first 4 ingredients in a small saucepan; bring to a boil. Remove from heat; cover and let stand 15 minutes. Remove figs from pan with a slotted spoon; set aside, and keep warm. Bring Marsala mixture to a boil; cook 10 minutes or until reduced to ¼ cup.

2. Combine cheeses and chopped pine nuts in a small bowl; stir until well blended. Cut each fig to, but not through, stem end. Stuff about 1½ teaspoons cheese mixture into center of each fig. Spoon 1 tablespoon Marsala sauce onto each of 4 dessert plates; arrange 3 stuffed figs on top of sauce. Garnish with orange rind curls, mint sprigs, and pine nuts, if desired. Yield: 4 servings.

CALORIES 288 (28% from fat); FAT 9.1g (sat 4.4g, mono 2.8g, poly 1.4g); PROTEIN 6.3g; CARB 50.1g; FIBER 7.1g; CHOL 20mg; IRON 1.6mg; SODIUM 179mg; CALC 163mg

Poached Pears

Don't be deceived. As elegant as they appear, poached pears are easy to prepare. Sweet-tart Bosc pears and dried apricots simmer in a fragrant mixture of wine, honey, cloves, and vanilla.

    4 large Bosc pears
    1 cup water
    1 cup dry white wine
    2 tablespoons sugar
    2 tablespoons honey
    4 dried apricots
    2 (3 x ½–inch) strips lemon rind
    1 (3-inch) piece vanilla bean, split lengthwise,
       or 1 teaspoon vanilla extract
    1 whole clove
    4 reduced-fat vanilla wafers, crushed
    5 tablespoons coarsely chopped pistachios,
       toasted and divided

1. Peel pears. Cut each pear in half, and core, leaving stems intact. Slice about ¼ inch from base of each pear so it will sit flat.

2. Combine water and next 7 ingredients in a large saucepan; bring to a boil. Add pears; cover, reduce heat, and simmer 10 minutes or until tender. Remove pears and apricots from cooking liquid using a slotted spoon; chill pears and apricots. Bring cooking liquid to a boil; cook until reduced to 1 cup (about 15 minutes). Strain cooking liquid through a sieve over a bowl; discard solids. Chill.

3. Chop apricots. Combine apricots, wafer crumbs, and 1 tablespoon pistachios. Place 2 pear halves in each of 4 bowls. Spoon about 1 tablespoon apricot mixture into each pear cavity. Spoon ¼ cup syrup over each pear; sprinkle each with 1 tablespoon pistachios. Yield: 4 servings.

N O T E : Use a melon baller to core pears.

CALORIES 251 (22% from fat); FAT 6g (sat 0.7g, mono 3.4g, poly 0.9g); PROTEIN 3.4g; CARB 51.5g; FIBER 6g; CHOL 0mg; IRON 1.7mg; SODIUM 24mg; CALC 41mg

Warm Caramelized Pears with Clove Zabaglione

Zabaglione (zah-bahl-YOH-nay) is a Venetian dessert sauce that's known as *sabayon* in France. Made of egg yolks, sugar, and sweet Marsala, this thin, frothy, versatile sauce is worth mastering.

    1 teaspoon sugar
    ¼ teaspoon ground cloves
    ¼ teaspoon allspice
    ¼ teaspoon ground cinnamon
    ⅛ teaspoon ground nutmeg
    ½ cup sweet Marsala
    3 tablespoons honey
    1 tablespoon butter
    2 pieces lemon rind (about 1 x 3–inches long)
    4 large Bosc pears, halved and cored (about
       2 pounds)
    Cooking spray
    6 tablespoons sweet Marsala
    ¼ cup sugar
    2 tablespoons water
    ⅛ teaspoon salt
    4 large egg yolks
    1 teaspoon butter
    Lemon zest (optional)
    Ground nutmeg (optional)

1. Preheat oven to 350°.

2. Combine first 5 ingredients in a small bowl; set aside.

3. Combine ½ cup Marsala, honey, 1 tablespoon butter, rind, and 1 teaspoon spice mixture in a small saucepan. Heat over medium heat until butter is melted.

4. Place pear halves, cut sides up, in a 13 x 9–inch baking dish coated with cooking spray. Pour Marsala mixture over pears. Bake at 350° for 30 minutes or until pears are tender, basting occasionally. Remove from oven; keep warm.

5. Combine 6 tablespoons Marsala, ¼ cup sugar, water, salt, and egg yolks in a medium, heavy saucepan, stirring with a whisk. Cook over low heat, whisking constantly, until mixture is thick (about 5 minutes). Stir in remaining spice mixture and 1 teaspoon butter until blended. Place 1 pear half in each of 8 bowls. Spoon ¼ cup sauce over each pear half. Garnish with lemon zest and nutmeg, if desired. Serve immediately. Yield: 8 servings.

CALORIES 196 (19% from fat); FAT 4.2g (sat 1.8g, mono 1.8g, poly 0.5g); PROTEIN 1.8g; CARB 33.4g; FIBER 3.4g; CHOL 107mg; IRON 0.5mg; SODIUM 58mg; CALC 25mg

Strawberries and Oranges with Vanilla-Scented Wine

Late-harvest riesling is sweeter than other rieslings. If you can't find it, try an equally sweet dessert wine, such as Sauternes, Muscat, or late-harvest Gewürztraminer. Prepare and chill this refreshingly light dessert early in the day. For a nonalcoholic version, use white grape juice in place of the wine.

1 cup late-harvest riesling or other dessert wine
3 (4-inch) strips orange rind
½ cup fresh orange juice
1 tablespoon sugar
1 (3-inch) piece vanilla bean, split lengthwise
3 cups halved strawberries
1¼ cups orange sections
Mint sprigs (optional)

1. Combine first 4 ingredients in a medium saucepan. Scrape seeds from vanilla bean; add seeds and bean to wine mixture. Bring to a boil; reduce heat, and simmer 5 minutes. Strain mixture through a sieve over a large bowl; discard solids. Let cool 30 minutes. Stir in strawberries and orange sections. Cover and chill. Garnish with mint sprigs, if desired. Yield: 6 servings (serving size: ⅔ cup).

CALORIES 60 (6% from fat); FAT 0.4g (sat 0g, mono 0.1g, poly 0.2g); PROTEIN 1g; CARB 14.5g; FIBER 2.7g; CHOL 0mg; IRON 0.5mg; SODIUM 4mg; CALC 31mg

Macedonia di Frutta

A true Italian meal often ends with fruit, although occasionally Italians do like to indulge in other sweet treats. You can use any combination of fruits in this refreshing dessert. *Macedonia di Frutta* literally means "mixed marinated fruit." Substitute two additional tablespoons of orange juice for the grappa for a non-alcoholic version.

   2 cups (1-inch) cubed cantaloupe
   1 cup (½-inch) pieces peeled peaches
   1 cup sliced strawberries
   1 cup blueberries
 ⅔ cup (½-inch) pieces peeled nectarines
 ½ cup fresh orange juice (about 1 orange)
 ¼ cup sugar
   2 tablespoons grappa (Italian brandy) or brandy
1½ teaspoons grated lemon rind
   2 peeled kiwifruit, quartered and sliced

1. Place all ingredients in a large bowl; toss gently to combine. Cover and chill 2 hours. Yield: 5 servings (serving size: 1 cup).

CALORIES 154 (4% from fat); FAT 0.7g (sat 0.1g, mono 0.1g, poly 0.3g); PROTEIN 1.8g; CARB 34.8g; FIBER 4.2g; CHOL 0mg; IRON 0.5mg; SODIUM 10mg; CALC 27mg

Chocolate-Walnut Cake

CAKE:
   Cooking spray
 ½ cup chopped pitted dates
 ½ cup unsweetened cocoa
 ½ cup boiling water
  1 teaspoon instant coffee granules
  1 (1-ounce) slice firm white bread
 ½ cup walnut halves, toasted and divided
 ⅓ cup all-purpose flour
 ¼ teaspoon salt
 ⅔ cup granulated sugar, divided
  2 tablespoons canola oil
  1 teaspoon vanilla extract
  1 large egg
  3 large egg whites

GLAZE:
 ⅓ cup unsweetened cocoa
 ¼ cup semisweet chocolate chips
 ¼ cup boiling water
  1 tablespoon dark corn syrup
  1 teaspoon instant coffee granules
 ½ teaspoon vanilla extract
  1 cup powdered sugar

1. Preheat oven to 350°.

2. Coat a 9-inch round cake pan with cooking spray, and line bottom of pan with wax paper. Coat wax paper with cooking spray.

3. To prepare cake, combine dates, ½ cup cocoa, ½ cup boiling water, and 1 teaspoon coffee granules; let stand 20 minutes. Place bread in a food processor; pulse 10 times or until coarse crumbs form to measure ½ cup. Place crumbs in a large bowl. Reserve 10 walnut halves for garnish. Place remaining walnuts in a food processor. Lightly spoon flour into a dry measuring cup; level with a knife. Add flour and salt to food processor; process until walnuts are finely ground. Add to breadcrumbs. Place date mixture, ⅓ cup granulated sugar, oil, 1 teaspoon vanilla, and 1 egg in food processor; process until smooth, scraping sides of bowl once. Add date mixture to breadcrumb mixture, stirring mixture well.

4. Beat egg whites with a mixer at high speed until soft peaks form. Gradually add ⅓ cup granulated sugar, 1 tablespoon at a time, beating until stiff peaks form. Gently stir one-fourth of egg white mixture into batter; gently fold in remaining egg white mixture. Spread batter into prepared pan. Bake at 350° for 25 minutes or until cake springs back when lightly touched. Cool in pan 10 minutes on a wire rack, and remove from pan. Remove wax paper. Cool completely on wire rack.

5. To prepare glaze, combine ⅓ cup cocoa and next 4 ingredients, stirring until smooth. Stir in ½ teaspoon vanilla. Cover and chill 1 hour. Gradually add powdered sugar to cocoa mixture, beating with a mixer at medium speed until smooth and thick.

6. Place cake layer on a plate. Spread glaze evenly over top and sides of cake. Arrange reserved walnut halves on top. Yield: 10 servings (serving size: 1 wedge).

CALORIES 280 (30% from fat); FAT 9.2g (sat 2.2g, mono 3.4g, poly 3g); PROTEIN 6.1g; CARB 45.5g; FIBER 1.2g; CHOL 22mg; IRON 2mg; SODIUM 103mg; CALC 26mg

Chocolate-Walnut Cake

Pineapple-Coconut-Banana
Upside-Down Cake

Pineapple-Coconut-Banana Upside-Down Cake

This is not your typical upside-down cake—it's even better. Pineapple juice and mashed banana come together in the batter to make a most delicious and delightful dessert that's perfect for special occasions and everyday dining. This cake is excellent both warm and at room temperature.

2 tablespoons butter
¾ cup packed brown sugar
1 (15½-ounce) can pineapple slices in juice, undrained
1 cup flaked sweetened coconut
1 cup all-purpose flour
½ cup granulated sugar
1 teaspoon baking powder
½ teaspoon baking soda
½ teaspoon ground cinnamon
¼ teaspoon salt
½ cup mashed ripe banana (about 1 banana)
2 tablespoons vegetable oil
1 large egg

1. Preheat oven to 375°.
2. Melt butter in a 9-inch cast-iron skillet; sprinkle evenly with brown sugar. Drain pineapple slices over a bowl, reserving ½ cup juice. Place 1 pineapple ring in center of pan. Cut remaining pineapple rings in half, and arrange around center pineapple ring. Sprinkle evenly with coconut. Set aside.
3. Lightly spoon flour into a dry measuring cup, and level with a knife. Combine flour and next 5 ingredients in a large bowl. Combine reserved ½ cup juice, banana, oil, and egg, stirring with a whisk. Add pineapple juice mixture to flour mixture, stirring until combined. Pour flour mixture over coconut. Bake at 375° for 30 minutes or until a wooden pick inserted in center comes out clean. Invert onto a wire rack. Serve warm or at room temperature. Yield: 10 servings (serving size: 1 slice).

CALORIES 301 (27% from fat); FAT 9g (sat 4.9g, mono 1.6g, poly 1.8g); PROTEIN 2.5g; CARB 54.8g; FIBER 1.4g; CHOL 27mg; IRON 1.4mg; SODIUM 231mg; CALC 55mg

Gingerbread Squares

Surprise your friends with a homemade specialty. These moist squares, which are delicately flavored with ginger, cinnamon, and molasses, are ideal for Christmas or any other time of the year. Simply place these "can't believe they're low-fat" squares in a parchment paper–lined gift box.

1¼ cups all-purpose flour
1 teaspoon ground ginger
1 teaspoon ground cinnamon
½ teaspoon baking soda
½ cup granulated sugar
½ cup low-fat buttermilk
½ cup dark molasses
⅓ cup butter, melted
1 large egg, lightly beaten
Cooking spray
1 tablespoon powdered sugar

1. Preheat oven to 350°.
2. Lightly spoon flour into dry measuring cups; level with a knife. Combine flour, ginger, cinnamon, and baking soda, stirring with a whisk.
3. Combine granulated sugar and next 4 ingredients in a large bowl, stirring with a whisk. Stir in flour mixture. Pour batter into a 9-inch square baking pan coated with cooking spray.
4. Bake at 350° for 25 minutes or until a wooden pick inserted in center comes out clean. Cool in pan on a wire rack. Sprinkle gingerbread with powdered sugar. Yield: 25 servings (serving size: 1 [1¾-inch] square).

CALORIES 84 (30% from fat); FAT 2.8g (sat 1.6g, mono 0.8g, poly 0.2g); PROTEIN 1.1g; CARB 14g; FIBER 0.2g; CHOL 15mg; IRON 0.7mg; SODIUM 61mg; CALC 22mg

desserts

Texas Sheet Cake

CAKE:

Cooking spray
- 2 teaspoons all-purpose flour
- 2 cups all-purpose flour
- 2 cups granulated sugar
- 1 teaspoon baking soda
- 1 teaspoon ground cinnamon
- ¼ teaspoon salt
- ¾ cup water
- ½ cup butter
- ¼ cup unsweetened cocoa
- ½ cup low-fat buttermilk
- 1 teaspoon vanilla extract
- 2 large eggs

ICING:

- 6 tablespoons butter
- ⅓ cup fat-free milk
- ¼ cup unsweetened cocoa
- 3 cups powdered sugar
- ¼ cup chopped pecans, toasted
- 2 teaspoons vanilla extract

1. Preheat oven to 375°.

2. To prepare cake, coat a 15 x 10–inch jelly-roll pan with cooking spray; dust with 2 teaspoons flour.

3. Lightly spoon 2 cups flour into dry measuring cups; level with a knife. Combine 2 cups flour and next 4 ingredients in a large bowl; stir well with a whisk.

4. Combine water, ½ cup butter, and ¼ cup cocoa in a small saucepan; bring to a boil, stirring frequently. Remove from heat; pour into flour mixture. Beat with a mixer at medium speed until well blended. Add buttermilk, 1 teaspoon vanilla, and eggs; beat well.

5. Pour batter into prepared pan; bake at 375° for 17 minutes or until a wooden pick inserted in center comes out clean. Place pan on a wire rack.

6. To prepare icing, combine 6 tablespoons butter, milk, and ¼ cup cocoa in a medium saucepan; bring to a boil, stirring constantly. Remove from heat; gradually stir in powdered sugar, pecans, and 2 teaspoons vanilla. Spread over hot cake. Cool completely on wire rack. Yield: 20 servings (serving size: 1 slice).

NOTE: You can also make this recipe in a 13 x 9–inch baking pan. Bake at 375° for 22 minutes.

CALORIES 298 (30% from fat); FAT 10g (sat 5.5g, mono 3.2g, poly 0.7g); PROTEIN 3.1g; CARB 49.8g; FIBER 0.5g; CHOL 44mg; IRON 1.1mg; SODIUM 188mg; CALC 25mg

German Chocolate Cake

Cooking spray
- 1 tablespoon cake flour
- ½ cup unsweetened cocoa
- 1 ounce sweet baking chocolate
- ½ cup boiling water
- 1 cup granulated sugar
- ¾ cup packed brown sugar
- 3 tablespoons butter, softened
- 2 tablespoons vegetable oil
- ¼ cup plain fat-free yogurt
- 2½ teaspoons vanilla extract
- ½ teaspoon coconut extract
- 2 large egg whites
- 2¼ cups sifted cake flour
- 2 teaspoons baking powder
- ½ teaspoon baking soda
- ½ teaspoon salt
- 1 cup low-fat or fat-free buttermilk

Coconut-Pecan Frosting (recipe on page 381)

1. Preheat oven to 350°.

2. Coat 3 (8-inch) round cake pans with cooking spray, and dust with 1 tablespoon flour.

3. Combine cocoa and chocolate in a small bowl; add boiling water, stirring until chocolate melts. Set aside.

4. Beat sugars, butter, and oil with a mixer at medium speed until well blended (about 5 minutes). Add yogurt, extracts, and egg whites, beating well after each addition.

5. Combine 2¼ cups flour, baking powder, baking soda, and salt, stirring well with a whisk. Add flour mixture to sugar mixture alternately with buttermilk, beginning and ending with flour mixture. Beat in cocoa mixture.

6. Pour batter into prepared pans; sharply tap pans once on counter to remove air bubbles. Bake at 350° for 25 minutes or until a wooden pick inserted in center comes out clean. Cool in pans 10 minutes on wire racks, and remove from pans. Cool completely on wire racks.

7. Place 1 cake layer on a plate; spread with ⅓ cup Coconut-Pecan Frosting, and top with another cake layer. Spread with ⅓ cup frosting, and top with remaining cake layer. Spread remaining frosting over top and sides of cake. Store cake loosely covered in refrigerator. Yield: 18 servings (serving size: 1 slice).

(Totals include Coconut-Pecan Frosting) CALORIES 311 (27% from fat); FAT 9.2g (sat 4.2g, mono 2.6g, poly 1.4g); PROTEIN 4.6g; CARB 52.7g; FIBER 0.3g; CHOL 35mg; IRON 2.2mg; SODIUM 186mg; CALC 111mg

German Chocolate Cake

COCONUT-PECAN FROSTING:

- 2 tablespoons butter
- 1/3 cup finely chopped pecans
- 2/3 cup packed brown sugar
- 2 tablespoons cornstarch
- 1/4 teaspoon salt
- 1 cup fat-free sweetened condensed milk
- 1 tablespoon light-colored corn syrup
- 2 large egg yolks
- 1/2 cup flaked sweetened coconut, toasted
- 2 1/2 teaspoons vanilla extract
- 1/8 teaspoon coconut extract

1. Melt butter in a medium saucepan over medium-high heat. Add chopped pecans, and sauté until pecans are browned (about 2 1/2 minutes). Remove from heat, and stir in sugar, cornstarch, and salt. Add milk, syrup, and egg yolks; stir well. Cook over medium-high heat 2 minutes or until thick, stirring constantly. Remove from heat, and stir in flaked coconut and extracts. Pour into a bowl; cover and chill until slightly stiff (about 15 minutes). Yield: 2 cups (serving size: 1 tablespoon).

CALORIES 77 (29% from fat); FAT 2.5g (sat 1.1g, mono 0.9g, poly 0.3g); PROTEIN 1.1g; CARB 12.4g; FIBER 0.2g; CHOL 16mg; IRON 0.2mg; SODIUM 35mg; CALC 31mg

Double-Maple Cupcakes

Double-Maple Cupcakes

These easy cupcakes will bring big smiles to your family and friends. If you'd prefer a cake instead of cupcakes, bake in a 9-inch square baking pan or a 9-inch round cake pan. Spoon the batter into a pan coated with cooking spray. Bake at 350° for 25 minutes until a wooden pick inserted in center comes out clean. Cool in pan; frost top. Serves 12. The nutritional information per serving is the same as for one cupcake.

CUPCAKES:
½ cup granulated sugar
5 tablespoons butter, softened
1 teaspoon vanilla extract
½ teaspoon imitation maple flavoring
2 large eggs
1¼ cups all-purpose flour
1¼ teaspoons baking powder
¼ teaspoon salt
¼ cup 1% low-fat milk
¼ cup maple syrup

FROSTING:
3 tablespoons maple syrup
2 tablespoons butter, softened
½ teaspoon vanilla extract
½ teaspoon imitation maple flavoring
⅛ teaspoon salt
1¾ cups sifted powdered sugar

REMAINING INGREDIENT:
12 walnut halves

1. Preheat oven to 350°.
2. To prepare cupcakes, beat first 4 ingredients with a mixer at medium speed until well blended (about 5 minutes). Add eggs, 1 at a time, beating well after each addition. Lightly spoon flour into dry measuring cups; level with a knife. Combine flour, baking powder, and ¼ teaspoon salt in a bowl, stirring well with a whisk. Combine milk and ¼ cup maple syrup. Add flour mixture to sugar mixture alternately with milk mixture, beginning and ending with flour mixture; mix after each addition.
3. Spoon batter into 12 muffin cups lined with paper liners. Bake at 350° for 20 minutes or until a wooden pick inserted in center comes out clean. Cool in pan 10 minutes on a wire rack, and remove from pan. Cool completely on wire rack.
4. To prepare frosting, beat 3 tablespoons maple syrup and next 4 ingredients with a mixer at medium speed 1 minute. Gradually add powdered sugar, beating just until blended (do not overbeat). Spread frosting over cupcakes. Top each cupcake with a walnut half. Yield: 1 dozen (serving size: 1 cupcake).

CALORIES 256 (32% from fat); FAT 9g (sat 4.6g, mono 2.3g, poly 1.4g); PROTEIN 2.9g; CARB 41.5g; FIBER 0.5g; CHOL 53mg; IRON 1mg; SODIUM 186mg; CALC 53mg

Angel Food Cake

Delicate angel food cake is naturally light because it's made with egg whites, while the yolks or other fats are omitted. In addition to enjoying the sweet taste and tender texture of an unadorned piece of angel food cake, try cutting it into cubes and layering it with pudding and fruit for a trifle. Or top it with berries or sliced fruit. And if you're feeling particularly indulgent, consider spooning warm caramel or chocolate sauce over a high-volume, spongy slice.

1 cup sifted cake flour
1¼ cups sugar, divided
10 egg whites
1¼ teaspoons cream of tartar
⅛ teaspoon salt
⅛ teaspoon vanilla extract

1. Preheat oven to 350°.
2. Sift together flour and ¼ cup sugar; set aside. Beat egg whites with a mixer at high speed until foamy. Add cream of tartar and salt; beat until soft peaks form. Add remaining 1 cup sugar, 2 tablespoons at a time, beating until stiff peaks form. Sift ¼ cup flour mixture over egg white mixture, and fold in. Repeat procedure with remaining flour mixture, ¼ cup at a time. Fold in vanilla.
3. Spoon batter into an ungreased 10-inch tube pan, spreading evenly. Break air pockets by cutting through batter with a knife. Bake at 350° for 40 minutes or until cake springs back when lightly touched. Invert pan; cool 40 minutes. Loosen cake from sides of pan using a narrow metal spatula, and invert cake onto a serving plate. Yield: 12 servings (serving size: 1 slice).

CALORIES 126 (0% from fat); FAT 0.1g (sat 0g, mono 0g, poly 0g); PROTEIN 3.5g; CARB 27.6g; FIBER 0.3g; CHOL 0mg; IRON 0.6mg; SODIUM 70mg; CALC 3mg

desserts

Blueberry-Blackberry Shortcakes

SHORTCAKES:

2 cups all-purpose flour

¼ cup sugar

1 tablespoon grated lemon rind

2 teaspoons baking powder

½ teaspoon baking soda

¼ teaspoon salt

¼ cup chilled butter, cut into small pieces

½ cup fat-free buttermilk

Cooking spray

1 teaspoon water

1 large egg white, lightly beaten

2 teaspoons sugar

FILLING:

3 cups fresh blueberries, divided

½ cup sugar

2 tablespoons fresh lemon juice

2 teaspoons cornstarch

2 cups fresh blackberries

REMAINING INGREDIENTS:

1 cup frozen reduced-calorie whipped topping, thawed

Mint sprigs (optional)

1. Preheat oven to 400°.

2. To prepare shortcakes, lightly spoon flour into dry measuring cups; level with a knife. Combine flour and next 5 ingredients in a large bowl, stirring with a whisk. Cut in chilled butter with a pastry blender or 2 knives until mixture resembles coarse meal. Add buttermilk, and stir just until moist.

3. Turn dough out onto a lightly floured surface; knead lightly 4 times. Pat dough to a ½-inch thickness; cut with a 3-inch biscuit cutter to form 8 dough rounds. Place dough rounds 2 inches apart on a baking sheet coated with cooking spray. Combine water and egg white, stirring with a whisk; brush over dough rounds. Sprinkle evenly with 2 teaspoons sugar. Bake at 400° for 13 minutes or until golden. Remove shortcakes from oven, and cool on a wire rack.

4. To prepare filling, combine 1 cup blueberries, ½ cup sugar, juice, and cornstarch in a small saucepan. Bring to a boil; reduce heat, and simmer 5 minutes or until slightly thick. Place in a large bowl; add remaining 2 cups blueberries and blackberries, stirring to coat. Cover and chill.

5. Using a serrated knife, cut each shortcake in half horizontally; spoon ½ cup blueberry mixture over bottom half of each shortcake. Top each serving with 2 tablespoons whipped topping and top half of

shortcake. Garnish with a mint sprig, if desired. Yield: 8 servings (serving size: 1 filled shortcake).

CALORIES 322 (21% from fat); FAT 7.5g (sat 4.7g, mono 1.8g, poly 0.5g); PROTEIN 4.6g; CARB 60.1g; FIBER 4.3g; CHOL 16mg; IRON 1.9mg; SODIUM 354mg; CALC 108mg

Fudgy Caramel Pudding Cake

Cake in the slow cooker? You won't believe how simple it is to create moist, decadent desserts in this hands-off appliance.

1 (19.8-ounce) package fudge brownie mix

1 cup water

½ cup applesauce

3 tablespoons canola oil

1 large egg

1 large egg white

Cooking spray

½ cup fat-free caramel sundae syrup

2 tablespoons chopped walnuts or pecans

3 cups water

2¾ cups vanilla fat-free frozen yogurt

1. Combine first 5 ingredients in a large bowl; stir 50 strokes with a wooden spoon. Set aside.

2. Beat egg white with a mixer at high speed until stiff peaks form. Gently fold egg white into batter. Pour batter into a 2-quart soufflé dish or deep-sided round baking dish coated with cooking spray. Drizzle caramel syrup over batter; sprinkle with nuts (caramel will sink to bottom).

3. Place a long sheet of foil over top of dish; wrap edges under dish. Place dish on top of another long sheet of foil; press foil against sides and over top of dish, completely enclosing dish. Place a small rack, trivet, or 3 canning jar rings in a round 5-quart electric slow cooker; pour 3 cups water into cooker. Place dish on rack. Cover and cook on HIGH 4½ hours or until pudding is set. Remove dish from cooker using oven mitts, and remove foil; let pudding stand 20 minutes. Spoon into parfait glasses or dessert bowls; top with frozen yogurt. Yield: 11 servings (serving size: ½ cup pudding cake and ¼ cup frozen yogurt).

CALORIES 378 (27% from fat); FAT 11.3g (sat 1.8g, mono 5.6g, poly 2.1g); PROTEIN 5.7g; CARB 63.1g; FIBER 0.3g; CHOL 19mg; IRON 1.9mg; SODIUM 240mg; CALC 53mg

Fresh Lime Chiffon Cake

(pictured on front cover)

FILLING:

1 teaspoon finely grated lime rind

¼ cup fresh lime juice (about 2 limes)

1 (14-ounce) can sweetened condensed milk

CAKE:

Cooking spray

1 tablespoon cake flour

2 cups sifted cake flour (7½ ounces)

1¼ cups sugar, divided

2½ teaspoons baking powder

½ teaspoon salt

7 tablespoons canola oil

1 teaspoon finely grated lime rind

⅓ cup fresh lime juice (about 3 limes)

3 tablespoons water

1 teaspoon pure lemon extract

3 egg yolks

8 egg whites

1 teaspoon cream of tartar

FROSTING:

3 tablespoons sugar

2 tablespoons lime juice (about 1 lime)

2½ cups fat-free whipped topping, thawed

Mint sprigs (optional)

Fresh blueberries (optional)

Lime wedges (optional)

1. To prepare lime filling, combine first 3 ingredients in a small bowl, stirring until blended. Cover and chill 3 hours.

2. Preheat oven to 325°.

3. To prepare cake, coat bottoms of 3 (8-inch) round cake pans with cooking spray (do not coat sides of pans); line bottoms with wax paper. Coat wax paper with cooking spray; dust with 1 tablespoon flour.

4. Combine 2 cups cake flour, 1 cup sugar, baking powder, and salt in a large bowl, stirring with a whisk until well combined.

5. Combine oil and next 5 ingredients in a bowl, stirring with a whisk. Add oil mixture to flour mixture; beat with a mixer at medium speed until smooth.

6. Place egg whites in a large bowl; beat with a mixer at high speed until foamy. Add cream of tartar; beat until soft peaks form. Gradually add ¼ cup sugar, 1 tablespoon at a time, beating until stiff peaks form. Gently stir one-fourth of egg white mixture into flour mixture; gently fold in remaining egg white mixture.

7. Divide cake batter equally among prepared pans, spreading evenly. Break air pockets by cutting through batter with a knife. Bake at 325° for 20 minutes or until cake springs back when lightly touched. Cool in pans 10 minutes on a wire rack; remove from pans. Remove wax paper from cake layers. Cool completely on wire rack.

8. To prepare frosting, combine 3 tablespoons sugar and 2 tablespoons lime juice in a small microwave-safe glass bowl. Microwave at HIGH 30 seconds or until sugar dissolves. Cool completely. Fold into whipped topping.

9. To assemble cake, place 1 cake layer on a plate; spread half of filling over cake layer. Top with second layer, remaining half of filling, and third layer. Spread frosting over top and sides of cake. Garnish with mint, blueberries, and lime wedges, if desired. Store cake loosely covered in refrigerator up to 3 days. Cut cake into slices. Yield: 16 servings (serving size: 1 slice).

CALORIES 290 (29% from fat); FAT 9.3g (sat 2.1g, mono 4.6g, poly 2.1g); PROTEIN 5.3g; CARB 44.9g; FIBER 0.3g; CHOL 47mg; IRON 1.1mg; SODIUM 218mg; CALC 122mg

Triple-Chocolate Cheesecake

You won't be able to resist the combination of unsweetened cocoa, chocolate graham cracker crumbs, and semisweet chocolate.

TOPPING:

1 tablespoon sugar

2 teaspoons unsweetened cocoa

½ cup reduced-fat sour cream

CRUST:

⅔ cup chocolate graham cracker crumbs (4 cookie sheets)

1 tablespoon sugar

½ tablespoon butter

1 tablespoon water

Cooking spray

FILLING:

3 tablespoons dark rum

3 ounces semisweet chocolate, chopped

¼ cup chocolate syrup

1 (8-ounce) block fat-free cream cheese, softened

1 (8-ounce) block ⅓-less-fat cream cheese, softened

1 cup sugar

2 tablespoons unsweetened cocoa

¼ teaspoon salt

1 teaspoon vanilla extract

2 large eggs

Triple-Chocolate
Cheesecake

REMAINING INGREDIENTS:
  Chocolate shavings (optional)
  Fresh raspberries (optional)

1. Preheat oven to 350°.
2. To prepare topping, combine 1 tablespoon sugar and 2 teaspoons cocoa in a small bowl. Add sour cream, stirring until well blended; cover and chill.
3. To prepare crust, combine graham cracker crumbs and 1 tablespoon sugar. Stir in butter and water, blending well. Firmly press mixture into bottom and ½ inch up sides of a 7-inch springform pan coated with cooking spray. Bake at 350° for 8 minutes; remove from oven, and set aside. Reduce oven temperature to 325°.
4. To prepare filling, combine rum and chocolate in a small bowl. Microwave at HIGH 20 seconds; stir until smooth and glossy. Stir in chocolate syrup.
5. Place cheeses in a large bowl; beat with a mixer at low speed until smooth. Combine 1 cup sugar, 2 tablespoons cocoa, and salt; add to cheeses, beating just until smooth. Add rum mixture and vanilla; beat until blended. Add eggs, beating just until blended.
6. Pour cheese mixture into prepared pan, and bake at 325° for 50 minutes or until almost set. Remove cheesecake from oven.
7. Carefully dollop sour cream topping around edges of cheesecake, spreading over top with a small spatula. Return cheesecake to oven.
8. Turn oven off, and cool cheesecake in closed oven 1 hour. Remove cheesecake from oven; run a knife around outside edge. Cool to room temperature. Cover and chill at least 8 hours. Garnish with chocolate shavings and raspberries, if desired. Yield: 12 servings (serving size: 1 wedge).

CALORIES 252 (36% from fat); FAT 10g (sat 6g, mono 1g, poly 0.1g); PROTEIN 7.3g; CARB 33.8g; FIBER 1g; CHOL 55mg; IRON 0.5mg; SODIUM 259mg; CALC 66mg

New York Cheesecake

CRUST:

⅔ cup all-purpose flour

3 tablespoons sugar

2 tablespoons chilled butter, cut into small pieces

1 tablespoon ice water

Cooking spray

FILLING:

4 cups fat-free cottage cheese

2 cups sugar

2 (8-ounce) blocks ⅓-less-fat cream cheese, softened

¼ cup all-purpose flour

½ cup fat-free sour cream

1 tablespoon grated lemon rind

1 tablespoon vanilla extract

¼ teaspoon salt

5 large eggs

1. Preheat oven to 400°.

2. To prepare crust, lightly spoon ⅔ cup flour into dry measuring cups; level with a knife. Place ⅔ cup flour and 3 tablespoons sugar in a food processor; pulse 2 times or until combined. Add butter; pulse 6 times or until mixture resembles coarse meal. With processor on, slowly pour ice water through food chute, processing just until blended (do not allow dough to form a ball).

3. Firmly press mixture into bottom of a 9 x 3–inch springform pan coated with cooking spray. Bake at 400° for 10 minutes or until lightly browned; cool on a wire rack.

4. Reduce oven temperature to 325°.

5. To prepare filling, strain cottage cheese through a cheesecloth-lined sieve 10 minutes; discard liquid. Place cottage cheese in food processor; process until smooth.

6. Place 2 cups sugar and cream cheese in a large bowl; beat with a mixer at medium speed until smooth. Lightly spoon ¼ cup flour into a dry measuring cup; level with a knife. Add ¼ cup flour, sour cream, and next 4 ingredients to cream cheese mixture; beat well. Add cottage cheese, stirring until well blended. Pour cheese mixture into prepared crust.

7. Bake at 325° for 1½ hours or until almost set. Turn oven off. Cool cheesecake in closed oven 1 hour. Remove cheesecake from oven; run a knife around outside edge. Cool to room temperature. Cover and chill at least 8 hours. Yield: 16 servings (serving size: 1 wedge).

NOTE: You can also make cheesecake in a 10 x 2½–inch springform pan. Bake at 300° for 1½ hours or until almost set. Turn oven off. Cool cheesecake in closed oven 30 minutes.

CALORIES 291 (30% from fat); FAT 9.8g (sat 5.7g, mono 3g, poly 0.5g); PROTEIN 12.9g; CARB 37.7g; FIBER 0.2g; CHOL 98mg; IRON 0.7mg; SODIUM 410mg; CALC 93mg

Caramel Pie

This luscious pie requires only four simple ingredients. Keep them on hand, and you'll always have the makings for a winning dessert.

1 (14-ounce) can fat-free sweetened condensed milk
1 (6-ounce) reduced-fat graham cracker crust
1 (8-ounce) container frozen reduced-calorie whipped topping, thawed
1 (1.4-ounce) milk chocolate–crisp butter toffee candy bar, coarsely chopped

1. Pour milk into a 2-cup glass measure; cover with foil. Place in a 3- to 4-quart electric slow cooker. Add very hot water to cooker to reach level of milk in measure. Cover and cook on LOW 9 hours (milk should be caramel colored). Stir well with a whisk.
2. Pour caramelized milk into crust; cool. Spread whipped topping over pie; sprinkle with chopped candy bar. Yield: 8 servings (serving size: 1 wedge).

CALORIES 321 (23% from fat); FAT 8.3g (sat 4.6g, mono 0.5g, poly 0.1g); PROTEIN 5g; CARB 57.2g; FIBER 0.1g; CHOL 9mg; IRON 0.4mg; SODIUM 153mg; CALC 134mg

Chocolate Cream Pie

A thick, rich, dark brown layer of decadent chocolate filling is topped with whipped topping and a dusting of grated semisweet chocolate. Simply set it out and watch it go.

CRUST:
40 graham crackers (10 cookie sheets)
2 tablespoons sugar
2 tablespoons butter, melted
1 large egg white
Cooking spray

FILLING:
2 cups fat-free milk, divided
2/3 cup sugar
1/3 cup unsweetened cocoa
3 tablespoons cornstarch
1/8 teaspoon salt
1 large egg
2 ounces semisweet chocolate, chopped
1 teaspoon vanilla extract

REMAINING INGREDIENTS:
1 1/2 cups frozen reduced-calorie whipped topping, thawed
3/4 teaspoon grated semisweet chocolate

1. Preheat oven to 350°.
2. To prepare crust, place crackers in a food processor; process until crumbly. Add 2 tablespoons sugar, butter, and egg white; pulse 6 times or just until moist. Press crumb mixture into a 9-inch pie plate coated with cooking spray. Bake at 350° for 8 minutes; cool on a wire rack 15 minutes.
3. To prepare filling, combine 1/2 cup milk, 2/3 cup sugar, and next 4 ingredients in a bowl, stirring with a whisk.
4. Heat remaining 1 1/2 cups milk in a small, heavy saucepan over medium-high heat to 180° or until tiny bubbles form around edge (do not boil). Remove from heat. Gradually add hot milk to sugar mixture, stirring constantly with a whisk. Return milk mixture to pan. Add chopped chocolate; cook over medium heat until thick and bubbly (about 5 minutes), stirring constantly. Reduce heat to low, and cook 2 minutes, stirring constantly. Remove from heat, and stir in vanilla. Pour into prepared crust; cover surface of filling with plastic wrap. Chill 3 hours or until firm. Remove plastic wrap; spread whipped topping evenly over filling. Sprinkle with grated chocolate. Yield: 10 servings (serving size: 1 wedge).

CALORIES 242 (30% from fat); FAT 8g (sat 4.6g, mono 2.1g, poly 0.8g); PROTEIN 5g; CARB 38.5g; FIBER 0.1g; CHOL 30mg; IRON 1.4mg; SODIUM 189mg; CALC 83mg

How to Make a Graham Cracker Crust

Our homemade graham cracker crust takes a little more time to prepare than the commercial reduced-fat crust, but the flavor and texture make it worth the effort. Once you have the prepared crumb mixture ready, place about half of the mixture in the bottom of your pie plate after it's been coated with cooking spray. Using both hands, firmly press the crumb mixture against the sides of the pan, rotating the pan until the sides are completely and evenly covered. Place the remaining crumb mixture in the bottom of the pan, spreading it around to cover the pan and firmly pressing down as you go.

Coconut Cream Pie

(pictured on page 369)

The silky style of coconut cream pie suits a summer table. Though they're simple to make, cream pies need time to chill, sometimes cooling their heels in the fridge for hours on end. Their cold smoothness soothes a parched palate.

CRUST:
½ (15-ounce) package refrigerated pie dough (such as Pillsbury)

FILLING:
¼ cup all-purpose flour
½ cup sugar
⅛ teaspoon salt
2 large eggs
¾ cup 2% reduced-fat milk
¾ cup light coconut milk
¼ teaspoon coconut extract
¼ teaspoon vanilla extract

MERINGUE:
3 large egg whites
⅔ cup sugar
¼ cup water

REMAINING INGREDIENT:
1 tablespoon flaked sweetened coconut, toasted

1. Preheat oven to 400°.

2. To prepare crust, roll dough into a 13-inch circle. Fit dough into a 10-inch pie plate. Fold edges under, and flute. Pierce bottom and sides of dough with a fork; bake at 400° for 15 minutes.

3. To prepare filling, lightly spoon flour into a dry measuring cup; level with a knife. Combine flour, ½ cup sugar, salt, and eggs in a large bowl; stir well with a whisk.

4. Heat milk and coconut milk over medium-high heat in a small, heavy saucepan to 180° or until tiny bubbles form around edge (do not boil). Gradually add hot milk mixture to sugar mixture, stirring constantly with a whisk. Return milk mixture to pan; cook over medium heat until thick and bubbly (about 10 minutes), stirring constantly.

5. Remove from heat. Spoon custard into a bowl; place bowl in a large ice-filled bowl 10 minutes or until custard comes to room temperature, stirring occasionally. Remove bowl from ice. Stir in extracts; spoon mixture into prepared crust. Cover and chill 8 hours or until firm.

6. Preheat broiler.

7. To prepare meringue, place egg whites in a large bowl; beat with a mixer at high speed until soft peaks form. Combine ⅔ cup sugar and water in a saucepan; bring to a boil. Cook, without stirring, until a candy thermometer registers 250°. Pour hot sugar syrup in a thin stream over egg whites, beating at high speed until stiff peaks form.

8. Spread meringue over chilled pie; sprinkle with coconut. Broil 1 minute or until meringue is lightly browned; cool 5 minutes on a wire rack. Serve immediately. Yield: 10 servings (serving size: 1 wedge).

CALORIES 281 (30% from fat); FAT 9.3g (sat 5.6g, mono 2.6g, poly 0.4g); PROTEIN 5.3g; CARB 45.6g; FIBER 0.6g; CHOL 63mg; IRON 1.4mg; SODIUM 208mg; CALC 28mg

Key Lime Pie

Key lime pie was created by pioneer settlers of the Florida Keys; it's traditionally made with egg yolks, sweetened condensed milk, and lime juice from yellowish green Key limes. Its wonderful not-too-sweet, not-too-tart flavor; creamy texture; and ease of preparation make it one of today's classic recipes. We guarantee that this lightened version will become a family favorite.

2 large eggs
2 large egg whites
½ cup Key lime juice
1 teaspoon grated lime rind
1 (14-ounce) can fat-free sweetened condensed milk
1 (6-ounce) reduced-fat graham cracker crust
1½ cups frozen reduced-calorie whipped topping, thawed
Lime rind (optional)

1. Preheat oven to 350°.

2. Beat eggs and egg whites with a mixer at medium speed until well blended. Gradually add juice, rind, and milk to egg mixture, beating until well blended. Spoon mixture into crust, and bake at 350° for 20 minutes or until almost set (center will not be firm but will set up as it chills). Cool pie on a wire rack. Cover loosely, and chill 4 hours. Spread whipped topping evenly over filling. Garnish with lime rind, if desired. Yield: 8 servings (serving size: 1 wedge).

CALORIES 288 (18% from fat); FAT 5.9g (sat 3g, mono 1.5g, poly 1.1g); PROTEIN 7.6g; CARB 49.2g; FIBER 0.8g; CHOL 56mg; IRON 0.6mg; SODIUM 198mg; CALC 141mg

Key Lime Pie

Double-Crusted Apple Pie

PASTRY:

2½ cups all-purpose flour
½ teaspoon salt
½ cup vegetable shortening
½ cup ice water
Cooking spray

FILLING:

10 cups thinly sliced peeled Granny Smith apple (about 3 pounds)
¾ cup granulated sugar
1½ tablespoons all-purpose flour
1 teaspoon ground cinnamon
½ teaspoon salt
¼ teaspoon ground nutmeg
1 tablespoon chilled butter, cut into small pieces

TOPPING:

1 tablespoon fat-free milk
1 teaspoon turbinado sugar

1. To prepare pastry, lightly spoon 2½ cups flour into dry measuring cups; level with a knife. Combine 2½ cups flour and ½ teaspoon salt in a large bowl. Stir well with a whisk; cut in shortening with a pastry blender or 2 knives until mixture resembles coarse meal. Gradually add ice water; toss with a fork until flour mixture is moist. Divide dough into 2 equal portions. Gently press each portion into a 4-inch circle on heavy-duty plastic wrap; cover and chill 30 minutes.

2. Slightly overlap 2 sheets of plastic wrap on a slightly damp surface. Unwrap and place 1 portion of chilled dough on plastic wrap. Cover dough with 2 additional sheets of overlapping plastic wrap. Roll dough, still covered, into a 12-inch circle. Place dough in freezer 5 minutes or until plastic wrap can be easily removed. Remove top sheets of plastic wrap; fit dough, plastic wrap side up, into a 9-inch deep-dish pie plate coated with cooking spray. Remove remaining plastic wrap.

3. Preheat oven to 425°.

4. To prepare filling, combine apple and next 5 ingredients, and toss gently to coat. Spoon apple mixture into prepared pie plate; top with butter.

5. Roll remaining portion of dough into an 11-inch circle, repeating procedure from Step 2, including freezing dough. Remove top sheets of plastic wrap; fit dough, plastic wrap side up, over apple mixture. Remove remaining plastic wrap. Press edges of dough together. Fold edges under, and flute. Cut several slits in top of dough to allow steam to escape.

6. To prepare topping, brush top of dough with milk; sprinkle turbinado sugar evenly over dough. Place pie plate on a foil-lined baking sheet, and bake at 425° for 10 minutes. Reduce oven temperature to 350° (do not remove pie from oven); bake an additional 40 minutes or until browned. Cool on a wire rack. Yield: 10 servings (serving size: 1 wedge).

CALORIES 333 (30% from fat); FAT 11.2g (sat 3.1g, mono 3.7g, poly 2.6g); PROTEIN 3.7g; CARB 55.2g; FIBER 2.5g; CHOL 3mg; IRON 1.7mg; SODIUM 245mg; CALC 15mg

Plum Galette

1 cup all-purpose flour
3½ tablespoons chilled butter, cut into small pieces
¼ teaspoon salt
3 tablespoons ice water
1 tablespoon cornmeal
4 plums, each cut into 8 wedges
1 tablespoon cornstarch
¼ cup Plum Jam (recipe on page 393)
1 tablespoon Plum Jam
1 tablespoon sugar

1. Lightly spoon flour into a dry measuring cup, and level with a knife. Place flour, butter, and salt in a food processor, and process until mixture resembles coarse meal. With processor on, slowly add ice water through food chute, processing just until combined (do not form a ball). Press mixture gently into a 4-inch circle on plastic wrap. Cover and chill 30 minutes.

2. Preheat oven to 425°.

3. Line a baking sheet with parchment paper; sprinkle paper with cornmeal. Unwrap dough; roll dough into a 9-inch circle on a lightly floured surface. Place dough on prepared pan. Combine plums and cornstarch in a large bowl, tossing to coat. Add ¼ cup Plum Jam; toss well to coat. Arrange plum mixture on top of dough, leaving a 1½-inch border. Fold edges of dough over plum mixture. Bake at 425° for 20 minutes.

4. Remove galette from oven (do not turn oven off). Brush crust with 1 tablespoon Plum Jam; sprinkle galette with sugar. Bake at 425° for 20 minutes or until crust is golden brown. Cool on pan 10 minutes on a wire rack before serving. Yield: 6 servings (serving size: 1 wedge).

(Totals include Plum Jam) CALORIES 208 (32% from fat); FAT 7.3g (sat 3.4g, mono 2.8g, poly 0.3g); PROTEIN 2.8g; CARB 33.8g; FIBER 1.6g; CHOL 18mg; IRON 1mg; SODIUM 146mg; CALC 5mg

Plum Galette

PLUM JAM:

4½ cups chopped ripe red plums
(about 8 medium)
1 cup sugar
1 cup water

1. Combine all ingredients in a large saucepan; bring to a boil. Cover and reduce heat; simmer 10 minutes. Uncover and simmer 50 minutes or until mixture begins to thicken, skimming foam from surface occasionally. Cool; pour into an airtight container. Cover and chill. Yield: 2 cups (serving size: 2 tablespoons).

CALORIES 68 (4% from fat); FAT 0.3g (sat 0g, mono 0.1g, poly 0.1g); PROTEIN 0.3g; CARB 17.2g; FIBER 0.5g; CHOL 0mg; IRON 0mg; SODIUM 0mg; CALC 0mg

Classic Pecan Pie

CRUST:

  1 cup all-purpose flour

  2 tablespoons granulated sugar

 ½ teaspoon baking powder

 ¼ teaspoon salt

 ¼ cup fat-free milk

  1 tablespoon butter, melted

Cooking spray

FILLING:

  1 large egg

  4 large egg whites

  1 cup light-colored or dark corn syrup

 ⅔ cup packed dark brown sugar

 ¼ teaspoon salt

  1 cup pecan halves

  1 teaspoon vanilla extract

1. To prepare crust, lightly spoon 1 cup flour into a dry measuring cup; level with a knife. Combine 1 cup flour, granulated sugar, baking powder, and ¼ teaspoon salt. Add milk and butter; toss with a fork until moist.

2. Press mixture gently into a 4-inch circle on heavy-duty plastic wrap; cover dough with additional plastic wrap. Roll dough, still covered, into an 11-inch circle. Freeze 10 minutes or until plastic wrap can be easily removed.

3. Remove top sheet of plastic wrap; fit dough, plastic wrap side up, into a 9-inch pie plate coated with cooking spray. Remove remaining plastic wrap. Fold edges under, and flute.

4. Preheat oven to 350°.

5. To prepare filling, beat egg, egg whites, and next 3 ingredients with a mixer at medium speed until well blended. Stir in pecan halves and vanilla. Pour mixture into prepared crust. Bake at 350° for 20 minutes; then cover with foil. Bake an additional 23 minutes or until a knife inserted 1 inch from edge comes out clean (do not overbake). Cool on a wire rack. Yield: 10 servings (serving size: 1 wedge).

CALORIES 288 (29% from fat); FAT 9.2g (sat 1.5g, mono 5.1g, poly 2g); PROTEIN 4.3g; CARB 48.1g; FIBER 1g; CHOL 25mg; IRON 1.1mg; SODIUM 253mg; CALC 52mg

Pumpkin Pie

Pies speak to us so clearly of home, of hearth, and of their own indescribable goodness. And a pumpkin pie is no different. A baked single-crust custard pie with a filling of pureed pumpkin, sugar, eggs, milk, and spices, pumpkin pie is traditionally served at Thanksgiving. Refrigerated pie dough makes this recipe simple to prepare. Bake the pie in the lower third of the oven to encourage a crisp crust.

FILLING:
- ¾ cup packed brown sugar
- 1¾ teaspoons pumpkin pie spice
- ¼ teaspoon salt
- 1 (12-ounce) can evaporated low-fat milk
- 2 large egg whites
- 1 large egg
- 1 (15-ounce) can unsweetened pumpkin

CRUST:
- ½ (15-ounce) package refrigerated pie dough (such as Pillsbury)
- Cooking spray

TOPPING:
- ¼ cup whipping cream
- 1 tablespoon amaretto (almond-flavored liqueur)
- 2 teaspoons powdered sugar

1. Position oven rack to lowest setting.

2. Preheat oven to 425°.

3. To prepare filling, combine first 6 ingredients in a bowl; stir with a whisk. Add pumpkin, and stir with a whisk until smooth.

4. To prepare crust, roll dough into an 11-inch circle; fit into a 9-inch pie plate coated with cooking spray. Fold edges under, and flute.

5. Pour pumpkin mixture into prepared crust. Place pie plate on a baking sheet. Place pan on lowest oven rack. Bake at 425° for 10 minutes. Reduce oven temperature to 350° (do not remove pie from oven); bake an additional 50 minutes or until almost set. Cool completely on a wire rack.

6. To prepare topping, beat whipping cream with a mixer at high speed until stiff peaks form. Add amaretto and powdered sugar, and beat until blended. Serve with pie. Yield: 12 servings (serving size: 1 pie wedge and about 1 tablespoon topping).

CALORIES 222 (30% from fat); FAT 7.4g (sat 3.7g, mono 0.7g, poly 0.1g); PROTEIN 4.1g; CARB 35.3g; FIBER 3g; CHOL 32mg; IRON 0.8mg; SODIUM 241mg; CALC 104mg

Harvest Sweet Potato Pecan Pie Tarts

Pierce each sweet potato a few times with a fork, place in a pie plate with two tablespoons water, cover loosely with wax paper, and microwave at HIGH five minutes or until tender.

- 1 cup mashed cooked sweet potato
- 3 tablespoons granulated sugar
- ¼ teaspoon ground cinnamon
- ⅛ teaspoon salt
- ⅓ cup chopped toasted pecans
- ¼ cup firmly packed brown sugar
- 1 tablespoon dark corn syrup
- ½ teaspoon vanilla extract
- 1 egg white
- 2 (2.1-ounce) packages mini phyllo shells (such as Athens)

1. Preheat oven to 350°.

2. Combine first 4 ingredients in a small bowl, stirring well.

3. Combine pecans and next 4 ingredients in a small bowl, stirring well.

4. Spoon about 1 teaspoon sweet potato mixture into each phyllo shell, spreading to edges. Top each tart with about ½ teaspoon pecan mixture. Place filled shells on an ungreased baking sheet. Bake at 350° for 20 minutes. Cool completely on a wire rack. Yield: 15 servings (serving size: 2 tarts).

CALORIES 89 (39% from fat); FAT 3.9g (sat 0.2g, mono 2.2g, poly 0.9g); PROTEIN 0.6g; CARB 13.1g; FIBER 0.5g; CHOL 0mg; IRON 0.6mg; SODIUM 55mg; CALC 9mg

desserts

Apple Turnovers

A turnover is a round or square piece of pastry dough that's folded over a sweet or savory filling. When folded, the dough forms a semicircle, or, in this case, a triangle. Turnovers can be baked or deep-fried. They can range in size from small to large and can be served as an appetizer, an entrée, or, as we prefer, a dessert. We like the tartness a Granny Smith apple adds to these turnovers, but a Rome or Winesap apple will give you more sweetness.

    1   large cooking apple, peeled, cored, and
        quartered
    ¼   cup chopped dates
    2   tablespoons brown sugar
    ¼   teaspoon salt
    4   (14 x 9–inch) sheets frozen phyllo dough,
        thawed
    Butter-flavored cooking spray
    ¼   cup sifted powdered sugar
    ½   teaspoon water
    ⅛   teaspoon vanilla extract

1. Preheat oven to 400°.
2. Place apple in a food processor; pulse 4 times or until apple is finely chopped. Spoon apple into a bowl. Stir in dates, brown sugar, and salt.
3. Place 1 phyllo sheet on a damp towel (cover remaining dough to keep from drying). Lightly coat with cooking spray. Place second phyllo sheet over first sheet, and lightly coat with cooking spray. Cut stacked sheets lengthwise into 3 equal strips (each about 4½ inches wide).
4. Working with 1 strip at a time (cover remaining strips), place 2 tablespoons apple mixture at base of strip. Fold the right bottom corner over apple mixture to form a triangle. Continue folding triangle back and forth to end of strip. Place triangle, seam side down, on a baking sheet coated with cooking spray. Repeat Step 4 with remaining 2 phyllo strips. Repeat Steps 3 and 4 with remaining phyllo sheets and apple mixture. Coat triangles with cooking spray.
5. Bake at 400° for 12 minutes or until golden. Remove from pan; cool 5 minutes on a wire rack.
6. Combine powdered sugar, water, and vanilla, stirring until smooth. Drizzle sugar mixture evenly over turnovers. Serve warm. Yield: 6 turnovers (serving size: 1 turnover).

CALORIES 100 (7% from fat); FAT 0.8g (sat 0.2g, mono 0.4g poly 0.1g); PROTEIN 1.2g; CARB 22.9g; FIBER 1.1g; CHOL 0mg; IRON 0.6mg; SODIUM 159mg; CALC 9mg

Mocha Pudding

Humble in appearance and honest in flavor, chocolate pudding makes a simple, satisfying weeknight dessert. Add a little coffee, and the balance of flavors shifts from basic to intriguing. Spoon the pudding into your prettiest stemmed glasses, add a dollop of whipped topping, and sprinkle with grated chocolate. You'll have an elegant, grown-up dessert.

    ⅓   cup sugar
    2   tablespoons cornstarch
    1   tablespoon instant coffee granules
    ⅛   teaspoon salt
    2   cups 1% low-fat milk
    ¼   cup semisweet chocolate minichips
    1   large egg yolk, beaten
    1   teaspoon vanilla extract
    Whipped topping (optional)
    Grated chocolate (optional)

1. Combine first 4 ingredients in a medium saucepan. Gradually add milk, stirring with a whisk until blended.
2. Stir in chocolate. Cook over medium heat 7 minutes or until mixture comes to a boil, stirring constantly. Reduce heat, and simmer 1 minute, stirring constantly.
3. Gradually stir about one-fourth of hot mixture into egg yolk; add to remaining hot mixture. Cook 2 minutes, stirring constantly. Remove from heat; stir in vanilla. Pour into individual glasses; cover pudding with plastic wrap, gently pressing plastic directly onto pudding. Chill until set. Garnish with whipped topping and grated chocolate, if desired. Yield: 4 servings (serving size: ½ cup).

CALORIES 202 (25% from fat); FAT 5.6g (sat 3.1g, mono 1.9g, poly 0.3g); PROTEIN 5.3g; CARB 33.8g; FIBER 0.7g; CHOL 56mg; IRON 0.6mg; SODIUM 138mg; CALC 161mg

Vanilla-Nut Pudding

It doesn't take much longer to make this pudding than it does to make a "cook and serve" pudding from a box, and the silky, smooth texture and rich vanilla flavor will convince you that it's worth the effort. We liked the crunch of the toasted nuts, but you can serve it with fresh strawberries, peaches, or blueberries, too.

6 tablespoons sugar
2 tablespoons cornstarch
2 cups 1% low-fat milk, divided
⅛ teaspoon salt
1 large egg, lightly beaten
1 teaspoon vanilla extract
2 tablespoons finely chopped pistachios, toasted
1 tablespoon finely chopped blanched almonds, toasted
Grated whole nutmeg (optional)

1. Combine sugar and cornstarch in a medium heavy saucepan. Add ½ cup milk; stir with a whisk until well blended. Add remaining 1½ cups milk and salt; bring to a simmer over medium heat, stirring frequently. Reduce heat to medium-low; cook 9 minutes, stirring frequently.

2. Place egg in a medium bowl. Gradually add hot milk mixture, stirring constantly with a whisk. Place egg mixture in pan; cook over medium-low heat 3 minutes or until thick, stirring constantly. Remove from heat; stir in vanilla. Pour into individual bowls; cover surface of pudding with plastic wrap. Cool completely. Uncover and sprinkle with nuts. Garnish with nutmeg, if desired. Yield: 4 servings (serving size: ½ cup).

CALORIES 197 (25% from fat); FAT 5.4g (sat 1.5g, mono 2.4g, poly 1g); PROTEIN 6.9g; CARB 30.1g; FIBER 0.7g; CHOL 58mg; IRON 0.5mg; SODIUM 151mg; CALC 166mg

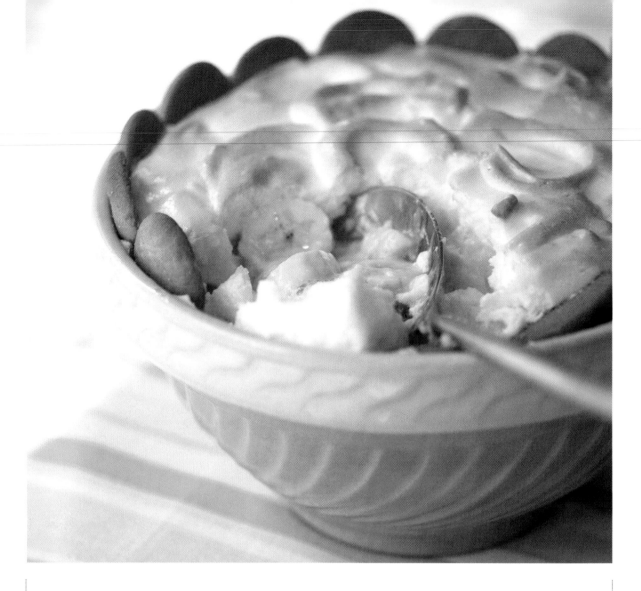

Banana Pudding

No one knows the origin of banana pudding, but it has been a favorite American dessert for decades. If you grew up in the South, chances are the recipe was a part of your grandmother's or mother's repertoire. With its creamy vanilla-banana filling, mile-high meringue peaks, and chewy cookie "crust," it just begs for you to dig in.

⅓ cup all-purpose flour
Dash of salt
2½ cups 1% low-fat milk
1 (14-ounce) can fat-free sweetened condensed milk
2 large egg yolks
2 teaspoons vanilla extract
3 cups sliced ripe banana
45 reduced-fat vanilla wafers
4 large egg whites
¼ cup sugar

1. Preheat oven to 325°.

2. Lightly spoon flour into a dry measuring cup; level with a knife. Combine flour and salt in a medium saucepan. Gradually add milks and egg yolks; stir well. Cook over medium heat, stirring constantly, until thick, about 8 to 10 minutes.

Remove from heat; stir in vanilla.

3. Arrange 1 cup banana slices in bottom of a 2-quart baking dish. Spoon one-third of pudding mixture over banana slices in dish. Arrange 15 wafers on top of pudding. Repeat layers twice, arranging the last 15 wafers around edge of dish. Push wafers into pudding.

4. Beat egg whites with a mixer at high speed until foamy. Gradually add sugar, 1 tablespoon at a time, beating until stiff peaks form. Spread meringue evenly over pudding, sealing to cookies around edge of dish. Bake at 325° for 25 minutes or until golden. Yield: 10 servings (serving size: ¾ cup).

NOTE: Banana Pudding may be a bit soupy when you first remove it from the oven. Let it cool at least 30 minutes before serving.

CALORIES 255 (10% from fat); FAT 2.9g (sat 1g, mono 0.9g, poly 0.2g); PROTEIN 7.9g; CARB 49.5g; FIBER 0.1g; CHOL 51mg; IRON 0.4mg; SODIUM 155mg; CALC 161mg

Cuban Coconut Rice Pudding

This Cuban-inspired pudding is the quintessential comfort food. It uses starchy Arborio rice, which produces a creaminess reminiscent of risotto. The coconut milk enhances the spicy flavor and contributes extra richness.

　3　cups water
　1　cup short-grain rice (such as Arborio or Valencia)
　4　whole cloves
　1　(2-inch) piece vanilla bean, split lengthwise
　1　(2-inch) cinnamon stick
　1　(14-ounce) can fat-free sweetened condensed milk
　½　cup evaporated fat-free milk
　½　cup light coconut milk
　½　cup golden raisins
　1　tablespoon chopped crystallized ginger
　1　teaspoon grated lemon rind
Pinch of salt

1. Place water and rice in a large saucepan. Place cloves, vanilla, and cinnamon stick on a double layer of cheesecloth. Gather edges of cheesecloth together; tie securely. Add to rice mixture. Bring to a simmer over medium heat, stirring frequently. Reduce heat to low; cook 20 minutes or until rice is tender and liquid is almost absorbed.
2. Stir in milks and raisins, and cook 10 minutes, stirring frequently. Stir in ginger, lemon rind, and salt; cook 5 minutes, stirring frequently. Remove cheesecloth with spices; discard. Pour rice mixture into a bowl or individual bowls; cover surface of rice mixture with plastic wrap. Chill. Yield: 8 servings (serving size: ½ cup).

CALORIES 286 (3% from fat); FAT 1g (sat 0.7g, mono 0.1g, poly 0.1g); PROTEIN 7g; CARB 61.9g; FIBER 0.8g; CHOL 7mg; IRON 1.7mg; SODIUM 95mg; CALC 184mg

Chocolate Soufflés with Pistachios

When it's time to entertain, don't skip this spectacular dessert. These chocolaty pistachio-crusted soufflés certainly fit the bill. If you're not crazy about pistachios, use your favorite chopped nut instead. Either way, you can't go wrong.

　　Cooking spray
　7　tablespoons plus 1 teaspoon sugar, divided
1½　tablespoons butter
　1　ounce semisweet chocolate
　2　tablespoons unsweetened cocoa
　2　tablespoons all-purpose flour
　⅛　teaspoon salt
　½　cup 1% low-fat milk
　3　large egg whites
　4　teaspoons chopped pistachio

1. Preheat oven to 375°.
2. Coat 4 (6-ounce) ramekins or custard cups with cooking spray, and dust each with 1 teaspoon sugar. Place on a baking sheet.
3. Combine 3 tablespoons sugar, butter, and chocolate in a small saucepan. Cook over low heat until melted. Add cocoa, flour, and salt, stirring with a whisk until blended. Gradually stir in milk, and cook over medium heat until mixture thickens (about 3 minutes), stirring constantly. Remove from heat. Cool.
4. Beat egg whites with a mixer at high speed until foamy. Add remaining 3 tablespoons sugar, 1 tablespoon at a time, beating until stiff peaks form. Gently fold one-fourth of egg white mixture into chocolate mixture; repeat procedure with remaining egg white mixture, one-fourth at a time. Spoon into prepared ramekins; sprinkle each serving with 1 teaspoon nuts. Bake at 375° for 20 minutes. Serve immediately. Yield: 4 servings.

CALORIES 221 (37% from fat); FAT 9g (sat 4.8g, mono 3.1g, poly 0.6g); PROTEIN 5.7g; CARB 33.1g; FIBER 1.5g; CHOL 13mg; IRON 1.1mg; SODIUM 174mg; CALC 52mg

desserts

Hot Maple Soufflés

These soufflés have become a holiday favorite at *Cooking Light.* The ingredients are simple, but the technique elevates the soufflés—literally and figuratively. The richness of maple syrup is added to these soufflés without weighing them down with fat and calories. By boiling syrup with bourbon, the flavors are concentrated for an intensity that memorably contrasts with the soufflés' airy texture. They taste like pancakes in maple syrup.

  1 tablespoon butter, softened
  2 tablespoons granulated sugar
  3 tablespoons bourbon
  3 tablespoons maple syrup
  1 cup maple syrup
  4 large egg whites
  ⅛ teaspoon salt
  1 teaspoon baking powder
  1 tablespoon powdered sugar

1. Preheat oven to 425°.
2. Coat 6 (10-ounce) ramekins with butter, and sprinkle evenly with granulated sugar. Combine bourbon and 3 tablespoons syrup in a small microwave-safe bowl; microwave at HIGH 1½ minutes or until mixture boils. Pour about 1 tablespoon bourbon mixture into each prepared ramekin.
3. Cook 1 cup syrup in a medium, heavy saucepan over medium-high heat 8 minutes or until a candy thermometer registers 250°.
4. Beat egg whites and salt with a mixer at medium speed until foamy. Pour hot maple syrup in a thin stream over egg whites, beating at medium speed, then at high speed, until stiff peaks form. Add baking powder; beat well.
5. Spoon evenly into ramekins; place on a jelly-roll pan. Bake at 425° for 13 minutes or until puffy and set. Sprinkle with powdered sugar. Serve immediately. Yield: 6 servings (serving size: 1 soufflé).

CALORIES 212 (8% from fat); FAT 2g (sat 0.4g, mono 0.8g, poly 0.6g); PROTEIN 2.3g; CARB 47.8g; FIBER 0g; CHOL 0mg; IRON 0.8mg; SODIUM 193mg; CALC 89mg

Instant Tiramisu

A perfect Italian meal deserves a perfect Italian dessert—tiramisu. This quick pick-me-up (that's what *tiramisu* means) is lightened by substituting ricotta and cream cheese for the super-rich mascarpone that fills most traditional versions. If you're short on time and long in the sweet tooth, then this instant indulgence is the ideal choice.

  1¼ cups part-skim ricotta cheese
  1 (8-ounce) block ⅓-less-fat cream cheese
  ½ cup sugar
  24 ladyfingers (2 [3-ounce] packages)
  ½ cup Kahlúa (coffee-flavored liqueur)
  1 tablespoon unsweetened cocoa

1. Place ricotta cheese, cream cheese, and sugar in a food processor; process until smooth.
2. Arrange 24 ladyfinger halves in a single layer in an 11 x 7–inch baking dish. Drizzle with ¼ cup Kahlúa, and let stand 5 minutes. Spread half of cheese mixture evenly over ladyfingers. Repeat procedure with remaining ladyfingers, Kahlúa, and cheese mixture. Sprinkle with cocoa. Serve immediately or chill until ready to serve. Yield: 10 servings.

CALORIES 237 (31% from fat); FAT 8.2g (sat 5.1g, mono 0.7g, poly 0.1g); PROTEIN 7.5g; CARB 28.7g; FIBER 0.4g; CHOL 56mg; IRON 0.6mg; SODIUM 263mg; CALC 121mg

Tropical-Fruit Sundaes

Some of the best desserts from around the globe come from nature in the form of sweet, juicy fruit. Tropical fruit in particular is sure to get your taste buds excited. Kiwi, mango, orange, lime, and pineapple flavors receive well-deserved attention in this fruit-filled sundae.

  1 cup chopped kiwifruit (about 2)
  1 cup chopped mango (about 1 medium)
  3 tablespoons orange juice
  1 tablespoon lime juice
  2 cups pineapple sherbet
  4 teaspoons flaked sweetened coconut, toasted

1. Combine first 4 ingredients in a small bowl; cover and chill 30 minutes. Spoon ½ cup sherbet into each of 4 dessert dishes. Top sherbet evenly with fruit mixture, and sprinkle with coconut. Serve immediately. Yield: 4 servings (serving size: ½ cup sherbet, ½ cup fruit, and 1 teaspoon coconut).

CALORIES 174 (12% from fat); FAT 2.4g (sat 1.4g, mono 0.5g, poly 0.2g); PROTEIN 1.7g; CARB 38.2g; FIBER 4.6g; CHOL 0mg; IRON 0.4mg; SODIUM 37mg; CALC 61mg

Lemon-Buttermilk Panna Cotta with Blueberry Sauce

PANNA COTTA:

Cooking spray

1½ tablespoons unflavored gelatin

1 cup whole milk

½ cup plus 2 tablespoons sugar

3 cups low-fat buttermilk

1 teaspoon grated lemon rind

SAUCE:

½ cup apple juice

¼ cup sugar

1 tablespoon fresh lemon juice

2 cups blueberries

Mint sprigs (optional)

1. To prepare panna cotta, lightly coat 8 (6-ounce) custard cups with cooking spray. Sprinkle gelatin over whole milk in a small saucepan; let stand 10 minutes. Cook milk mixture over medium-low heat 10 minutes or until gelatin dissolves, stirring constantly with a whisk. Increase heat to medium; add ½ cup plus 2 tablespoons sugar, stirring with a whisk until sugar dissolves. Remove from heat. Add buttermilk and rind, stirring well. Divide mixture evenly among prepared custard cups. Cover and chill at least 5 hours or overnight.

2. To prepare sauce, combine apple juice, ¼ cup sugar, and lemon juice in a small saucepan. Bring to a boil over medium-high heat; stir until sugar dissolves. Reduce heat to medium; stir in blueberries. Cook mixture 8 minutes or until blueberries are warm and begin to pop. Cool sauce to room temperature.

3. Place a dessert plate, upside down, on top of each custard cup; invert panna cotta onto plates. Serve with sauce. Garnish with mint sprigs, if desired. Yield: 8 servings (serving size: 1 panna cotta and about ¼ cup sauce).

CALORIES 173 (10% from fat); FAT 2g (sat 1.2g, mono 0.6g, poly 0.1g); PROTEIN 5.4g; CARB 34.8g; FIBER 1g; CHOL 8mg; IRON 0.2mg; SODIUM 117mg; CALC 148mg

Raspberry-Champagne Granita

This frozen dessert, similar to sorbet, is easy to prepare, doesn't require an ice cream maker, and is almost fat free. Much of the alcohol evaporates during cooking, but the flavor of Champagne remains.

  2   cups fresh raspberries
  2   tablespoons fresh lime juice
1½   cups water
  1   cup sugar
  ¾   cup Champagne
Lime rind (optional)

1. Place raspberries and lime juice in a blender; process until smooth.
2. Combine water, sugar, and Champagne in a medium saucepan; bring to a boil. Reduce heat; simmer 1 minute or until sugar melts. Remove from heat; stir in raspberry puree. Pour mixture into a large, shallow baking pan. Cover and freeze 8 hours.
3. Remove dish from freezer, and let stand 5 minutes. Scrape entire mixture with a fork until fluffy. Garnish with lime rind, if desired. Yield: 6 servings (serving size: 1 cup).

CALORIES 152 (1% from fat); FAT 0.2g (sat 0g, mono 0g, poly 0.1g); PROTEIN 0.5g; CARB 38.9g; FIBER 2.8g; CHOL 0mg; IRON 0.4mg; SODIUM 3mg; CALC 12mg

Cappuccino Granita

This Sicilian dessert classic starts with double-strength brewed coffee (dark roast is best) to heighten the coffee flavor when the mixture is frozen.

  ½   cup ground coffee beans
1¾   cups water
  ⅓   cup sugar
  ⅓   cup water
  1   teaspoon vanilla extract
  ¼   teaspoon ground cinnamon
  ½   cup 1% low-fat milk
Mint sprigs (optional)

1. Assemble drip coffee maker according to manufacturer's directions. Place ground coffee in coffee filter or filter basket. Add 1¾ cups water to coffee maker, and brew; set coffee aside.
2. Combine sugar and ⅓ cup water in a small saucepan. Bring to a boil, and cook 1 minute or until sugar dissolves. Stir in vanilla and cinnamon. Remove from heat, and stir in brewed coffee and milk.
3. Cool coffee mixture completely; pour into an

8-inch square baking dish. Cover; freeze at least 8 hours or until firm. Remove coffee mixture from freezer; scrape entire mixture with a fork until fluffy. Spoon into a freezer-safe container; cover and freeze up to 1 month. Garnish with mint sprigs, if desired. Yield: 6 servings (serving size: ⅔ cup).

CALORIES 56 (3% from fat); FAT 0.2g (sat 0.1g, mono 0.1g, poly 0g); PROTEIN 0.7g; CARB 12.3g; FIBER 0g; CHOL 1mg; IRON 0.1mg; SODIUM 10mg; CALC 26mg

Blueberry Gelato

  2   cups fresh or frozen blueberries
  ¼   cup blueberry preserves
  ¼   cup water
  ¼   teaspoon salt
  ⅔   cup sugar
  3   large egg yolks
  2   cups 2% reduced-fat milk
  2   tablespoons fresh lemon juice
Fresh blueberries (optional)

1. Combine first 4 ingredients in a medium non-aluminum saucepan, and bring to a boil. Reduce heat to medium; cook 10 minutes. Place mixture in a blender, and process until smooth.
2. Beat sugar and egg yolks in a large bowl with a whisk until thick and pale (about 5 minutes). Heat milk over medium-high heat in a small, heavy saucepan to 180° or until tiny bubbles form around edge of pan, stirring frequently (do not boil). Add one-third hot milk mixture to egg mixture, stirring with a whisk. Gradually add to remaining hot milk mixture, stirring constantly with a whisk. Cook over medium-low heat until mixture coats back of a spoon (about 4 minutes). Remove from heat. Stir in blueberry mixture, and cool completely. Stir in juice.
3. Pour mixture into the freezer can of an ice-cream freezer, and freeze according to manufacturer's instructions. Garnish with blueberries, if desired. Yield: 3 cups (serving size: ½ cup).

CALORIES 213 (22% from fat); FAT 4.4g (sat 1.8g, mono 1.5g, poly 0.5g); PROTEIN 4.5g; CARB 38.4g; FIBER 1.3g; CHOL 115mg; IRON 0.5mg; SODIUM 145mg; CALC 114mg

Honey Gelato

Honey is a good choice for gelato because its resistance to freezing ensures creaminess. We liked mild clover and lavender honeys in this recipe. Store the gelato in an airtight container in the freezer up to one week; it won't freeze solid but will maintain a soft texture. Purchased pirouline cookies are a delicate accompaniment to this rich dessert.

½ cup honey
⅓ cup nonfat dry milk
1 (12-ounce) can evaporated fat-free milk
⅛ teaspoon salt
4 large egg yolks
1 cup 2% reduced-fat milk
Mint sprigs (optional)

1. Combine honey, nonfat dry milk, and evaporated milk in a medium, heavy saucepan. Heat mixture over medium heat until honey dissolves, stirring frequently (do not boil). Remove from heat.
2. Combine salt and egg yolks in a large bowl; stir with a whisk. Gradually add honey mixture to egg mixture, stirring constantly with a whisk. Place honey mixture in pan; cook over medium heat until mixture reaches 180° (about 3 minutes); stir constantly (do not boil). Remove from heat; stir in 2% milk. Cool completely.
3. Pour mixture into freezer can of an ice-cream freezer; freeze according to manufacturer's instructions. Spoon gelato into a freezer-safe container. Cover and freeze 2 hours or until firm. Garnish with mint sprigs, if desired. Yield: 8 servings (serving size: ½ cup).

CALORIES 153 (19% from fat); FAT 3.3g (sat 1.2g, mono 1.2g, poly 0.4g); PROTEIN 6.7g; CARB 25.4g; FIBER 0g; CHOL 111mg; IRON 0.5mg; SODIUM 121mg; CALC 208mg

Simple Peach Ice Cream

Summer is the time for cannonball contests, grilled burgers, and lightweight novels. To add to the fun, slice some fragrant, ripe peaches, and make this homemade ice cream. With a short list of natural ingredients and a no-cook method, it's ready to freeze quickly. Use an old-fashioned ice-cream freezer, or try the newer kind that needs no ice or salt. Either way, you'll wish that summer would never end.

  6 cups sliced peeled peaches (about 3 pounds)
  ¾ cup sugar
  2 cups half-and-half
1½ teaspoons vanilla extract
  ¼ teaspoon salt

1. Combine peaches and sugar in a large bowl. Let stand 30 minutes, stirring occasionally. Place peach mixture in a food processor; pulse 10 times or until coarsely chopped. Return peach mixture to bowl, and stir in half-and-half, vanilla, and salt.

2. Pour mixture into the freezer can of an ice-cream freezer; freeze according to manufacturer's instructions. Spoon ice cream into a freezer-safe container; cover and freeze 1 hour or until firm. Yield: 12 servings (serving size: ½ cup).

CALORIES 138 (31% from fat); FAT 4.7g (sat 2.9g, mono 1.4g, poly 0.2g); PROTEIN 1.8g; CARB 23.7g; FIBER 1.7g; CHOL 15mg; IRON 0.1mg; SODIUM 65mg; CALC 46mg

Double-Chocolate Cherry Cookies

1 ¼   cups all-purpose flour
 ½   teaspoon baking powder
 ¼   teaspoon salt
 5   tablespoons butter, softened
 ½   cup granulated sugar
 ½   cup packed brown sugar
1 ½   teaspoons vanilla extract
 1   large egg white
 ⅓   cup dried tart cherries
 ¼   cup semisweet chocolate chunks
2 ½   tablespoons premium white chocolate chips
   Cooking spray

1. Preheat oven to 350°.
2. Lightly spoon flour into dry measuring cups; level with a knife. Combine flour, baking powder, and salt, stirring with a whisk.
3. Combine butter and sugars in a large bowl; beat with a mixer at medium speed until well blended. Add vanilla and egg white; beat 1 minute. Stir in flour mixture, cherries, chocolate chunks, and chocolate chips.
4. Drop by level tablespoons 2 inches apart onto baking sheets coated with cooking spray. Place pans in freezer 5 minutes. Bake at 350° for 10 minutes or until lightly browned. Cool on pans 2 minutes. Remove cookies from pans; cool completely on wire racks. Yield: 2 dozen (serving size: 1 cookie).

CALORIES 98 (30% from fat); FAT 3.3g (sat 2g, mono 1g, poly 0.1g); PROTEIN 1g; CARB 16.6g; FIBER 0.4g; CHOL 7mg; IRON 0.5mg; SODIUM 63mg; CALC 12mg

Oatmeal-Raisin Cookies

 ½   cup granulated sugar
 ½   cup packed brown sugar
 ⅓   cup butter, softened
 1   teaspoon vanilla extract
 ⅛   teaspoon salt
 1   large egg
 1   cup all-purpose flour
 1   cup regular oats
 ½   cup raisins
   Cooking spray

1. Preheat oven to 350°.
2. Beat first 6 ingredients with a mixer at medium speed until light and fluffy. Lightly spoon flour into a dry measuring cup, and level with a knife. Add flour and oats to egg mixture, and beat until blended. Stir in raisins. Drop by level tablespoons 2 inches apart onto baking sheets coated with cooking spray. Bake at 350° for 15 minutes or until golden brown. Cool on pans 3 minutes. Remove cookies from pans; cool on wire racks. Yield: 2 dozen (serving size: 1 cookie).

CALORIES 101 (28% from fat); FAT 3.1g (sat 1.7g, mono 0.9g, poly 0.2g); PROTEIN 1.5g; CARB 17.3g; FIBER 0.6g; CHOL 16mg; IRON 0.6mg; SODIUM 43mg; CALC 10mg

Gingersnaps

Crispy and flavored like gingerbread, these cookies are precisely what traditional gingersnaps should be. And you'll discover that this homemade version far outweighs the prepackaged boxed competitors in both flavor and texture. After one bite, you'll never buy commercial brands again.

 2   cups all-purpose flour
 1   tablespoon ground ginger
 2   teaspoons baking soda
 ½   teaspoon salt
 1   cup granulated sugar, divided
 7   tablespoons butter, softened
 ¼   cup packed dark brown sugar
 2   tablespoons honey
 1   teaspoon vanilla extract
 1   large egg
   Cooking spray

1. Lightly spoon flour into dry measuring cups, and level with a knife. Combine flour and next 3 ingredients in a small bowl. Place ¾ cup granulated sugar, butter, and brown sugar in a large bowl; beat with a mixer at medium speed until well blended. Add honey, vanilla, and egg; beat well. Add flour mixture, beating at low speed until well blended. Cover dough, and freeze 1 hour or until firm.
2. Preheat oven to 350°.
3. Lightly coat hands with cooking spray; shape dough into 24 (1-inch) balls. Roll balls in remaining ¼ cup granulated sugar; place balls 2 inches apart on baking sheets. Bake at 350° for 11 to 12 minutes or until lightly browned. Cool cookies 2 minutes on pans. Remove cookies from pans, and cool on wire racks. Yield: 2 dozen (serving size: 1 cookie).

CALORIES 113 (30% from fat); FAT 3.8g (sat 2.2g, mono 1.1g, poly 0.2g); PROTEIN 1.3g; CARB 18.8g; FIBER 0.3g; CHOL 18mg; IRON 0.5mg; SODIUM 155mg; CALC 5mg

Lemon-Frosted Sugar Cookies

COOKIES:

1 cup granulated sugar
½ cup butter, softened
1 large egg
1 large egg white
1 tablespoon fat-free milk
1 teaspoon grated lemon rind
1 teaspoon vanilla extract
2 cups all-purpose flour
¼ cup toasted wheat germ
1 teaspoon baking powder
½ teaspoon baking soda
⅛ teaspoon salt

FROSTING:

2 cups powdered sugar
1 tablespoon fat-free milk
1 tablespoon fresh lemon juice
¼ teaspoon vanilla extract

REMAINING INGREDIENTS:

Food coloring (optional)
Assorted sugar sprinkles (optional)

1. To prepare cookies, beat granulated sugar and butter in a large bowl with a mixer at medium speed until well blended (about 4 minutes). Add egg, egg white, and next 3 ingredients, beating well. Lightly spoon flour into dry measuring cups, and level with a knife. Combine flour and next 4 ingredients in a bowl. Add flour mixture to sugar mixture, stirring well. Spoon dough onto plastic wrap; flatten to a 1½-inch thickness. Cover tightly with plastic wrap; chill 4 hours or overnight.

2. Preheat oven to 400°.

3. Roll dough to a 15 x 12–inch rectangle on a heavily floured surface. Cut dough into 20 (3-inch) squares using a sharp knife. Place squares 2 inches apart on ungreased baking sheets. Bake at 400° for 8 minutes or until golden. Immediately remove cookies from pans using a wide spatula; cool on wire racks.

4. To prepare frosting, combine powdered sugar and next 3 ingredients. Stir in food coloring, if desired. Spread about 2 teaspoons frosting over each cookie with an offset spatula, or place frosting in a small zip-top plastic bag, snip a tiny hole in 1 corner, and drizzle frosting over cookies. Sprinkle with assorted sugar sprinkles, if desired. Yield: 20 cookies (serving size: 1 cookie).

CALORIES 183 (25% from fat); FAT 5.1g (sat 3g, mono 1.3g, poly 0.3g); PROTEIN 2.3g; CARB 32.5g; FIBER 0.7g; CHOL 23mg; IRON 0.8mg; SODIUM 110mg; CALC 21mg

Peanut Butter Icebox Cookies

    1   cup all-purpose flour
    ¼   teaspoon baking soda
    ⅛   teaspoon salt
    3   tablespoons butter, softened
    2   tablespoons chunky peanut butter
    ½   cup packed brown sugar
    ¼   cup granulated sugar
    1   teaspoon vanilla extract
    1   large egg white
Cooking spray

1. Lightly spoon flour into a dry measuring cup; level with a knife. Combine flour, baking soda, and salt in a bowl, and set aside.

2. Beat butter and peanut butter with a mixer at medium speed until light and fluffy. Gradually add sugars, beating until well blended. Add vanilla and egg white, and beat well. Add flour mixture; stir well. Turn dough out onto plastic wrap or wax paper, and shape into a 6-inch log. Wrap log in plastic wrap or wax paper, and freeze 3 hours or until firm.

3. Preheat oven to 350°.

4. Cut log into 24 (¼-inch) slices, and place slices 1 inch apart on a baking sheet coated with cooking spray. Bake at 350° for 8 to 10 minutes. Remove cookies from pan, and cool on wire racks. Yield: 2 dozen (serving size: 1 cookie).

CALORIES 66 (29% from fat); FAT 2.1g (sat 1g, mono 0.7g, poly 0.3g); PROTEIN 1g; CARB 10.9g; FIBER 0.3g; CHOL 4mg; IRON 0.4mg; SODIUM 46mg; CALC 6mg

Fudgy Mocha-Toffee Brownies

Cooking spray
    2   tablespoons instant coffee granules
    ¼   cup hot water
    ¼   cup butter
    ¼   cup semisweet chocolate chips
    1½ cups all-purpose flour
    1⅓ cups sugar
    ½   cup unsweetened cocoa
    1   teaspoon baking powder
    ½   teaspoon salt
    1   teaspoon vanilla extract
    2   large eggs, lightly beaten
    ¼   cup toffee chips

1. Preheat oven to 350°.

2. Coat bottom of a 9-inch square baking pan with cooking spray.

3. Combine coffee and hot water, stirring until coffee dissolves.

4. Combine butter and chocolate chips in a small microwave-safe bowl. Microwave at HIGH 1 minute or until butter melts; stir until chocolate is smooth.

5. Lightly spoon flour into dry measuring cups; level with a knife. Combine flour, sugar, cocoa, baking powder, and salt in a large bowl, stirring with a whisk. Combine coffee mixture, butter mixture, vanilla, and eggs in a medium bowl, stirring with a whisk. Add coffee mixture to flour mixture; stir just until combined. Spread evenly into prepared pan. Sprinkle evenly with toffee chips. Bake at 350° for 22 minutes. Cool in pan on a wire rack. Yield: 16 servings (serving size: 1 brownie).

CALORIES 179 (30% from fat); FAT 5.9g (sat 3.3g, mono 1.4g, poly 0.3g); PROTEIN 2.7g; CARB 30.7g; FIBER 1.4g; CHOL 36mg; IRON 1.2mg; SODIUM 149mg; CALC 28mg

Butterscotch Bars

    ½   cup granulated sugar
    ½   cup packed brown sugar
    ¼   cup butter, softened
    2   large egg whites
    1   teaspoon vanilla extract
    1¼ cups all-purpose flour
    ½   teaspoon baking powder
    ¼   teaspoon salt
Cooking spray
    ½   cup butterscotch morsels

1. Preheat oven to 350°.

2. Beat sugars and butter with a mixer at medium speed until well blended (about 4 minutes). Add egg whites and vanilla; beat well. Lightly spoon flour into dry measuring cups, and level with a knife. Combine flour, baking powder, and salt; stir well with a whisk. Add flour mixture to sugar mixture; beat at low speed just until blended.

3. Spread batter evenly into an 8-inch square baking pan coated with cooking spray; sprinkle evenly with morsels. Bake at 350° for 25 minutes or until a wooden pick inserted in center comes out clean. Cool in pan on a wire rack. Yield: 16 servings (serving size: 1 bar).

CALORIES 142 (27% from fat); FAT 4.3g (sat 2.6g, mono 1.3g, poly 0.2g); PROTEIN 1.6g; CARB 24g; FIBER 0.3g; CHOL 8mg; IRON 0.6mg; SODIUM 95mg; CALC 24mg

NUTRITIONAL ANALYSIS

HOW TO USE IT AND WHY Glance at the end of any *Cooking Light* recipe, and you'll see how committed we are to helping you make the best of today's light cooking. With chefs, registered dietitians, home economists, and a computer system that analyzes every ingredient we use, *Cooking Light* gives you authoritative dietary detail like no other magazine. We go to such lengths so you can see how our recipes fit into your healthful eating plan. If you're trying to lose weight, the calorie and fat figures will probably help most. But if you're keeping a close eye on the sodium, cholesterol, and saturated fat in your diet, we provide those numbers, too. And because many women don't get enough iron or calcium, we can also help there, as well. Finally, there's a fiber analysis for those of us who don't get enough roughage.

Here's a helpful guide to put our nutrition analysis numbers into perspective. Remember, one size doesn't fit all, so take your lifestyle, age, and circumstances into consideration when determining your nutrition needs. For example, pregnant or breast-feeding women need more protein, calories, and calcium. And men older than 50 need 1,200mg of calcium daily, 200mg more than the amount recommended for younger men.

IN OUR NUTRITIONAL ANALYSIS, WE USE THESE ABBREVIATIONS:

sat	saturated fat	**CHOL**	cholesterol
mono	monounsaturated fat	**CALC**	calcium
poly	polyunsaturated fat	**g**	gram
CARB	carbohydrates	**mg**	milligram

Daily Nutrition Guide

	WOMEN AGES 25 TO 50	WOMEN OVER 50	MEN OVER 24
Calories	2,000	2,000 or less	2,700
Protein	50g	50g or less	63g
Fat	65g or less	65g or less	88g or less
Saturated Fat	20g or less	20g or less	27g or less
Carbohydrates	304g	304g	410g
Fiber	25g to 35g	25g to 35g	25g to 35g
Cholesterol	300mg or less	300mg or less	300mg or less
Iron	18mg	8mg	8mg
Sodium	2,300mg or less	1,500mg or less	2,300mg or less
Calcium	1,000mg	1,200mg	1,000mg

The nutritional values used in our calculations either come from The Food Processor, Version 7.5 (ESHA Research), or are provided by food manufacturers.

METRIC EQUIVALENTS

The information in the following charts is provided to help cooks outside the United States successfully use the recipes in this book. All equivalents are approximate.

Equivalents for Different Types of Ingredients

Standard Cup	Fine Powder (ex. flour)	Grain (ex. rice)	Granular (ex. sugar)	Liquid Solids (ex. butter)	Liquid (ex. milk)
1	140 g	150 g	190 g	200 g	240 ml
¾	105 g	113 g	143 g	150 g	180 ml
⅔	93 g	100 g	125 g	133 g	160 ml
½	70 g	75 g	95 g	100 g	120 ml
⅓	47 g	50 g	63 g	67 g	80 ml
¼	35 g	38 g	48 g	50 g	60 ml
⅛	18 g	19 g	24 g	25 g	30 ml

Liquid Ingredients by Volume

¼ tsp					=	1 ml
½ tsp					=	2 ml
1 tsp					=	5 ml
3 tsp	= 1 tbl		=	½ fl oz	=	15 ml
	2 tbls	= ⅛ cup	=	1 fl oz	=	30 ml
	4 tbls	= ¼ cup	=	2 fl oz	=	60 ml
	5⅓ tbls	= ⅓ cup	=	3 fl oz	=	80 ml
	8 tbls	= ½ cup	=	4 fl oz	=	120 ml
	10⅔ tbls	= ⅔ cup	=	5 fl oz	=	160 ml
	12 tbls	= ¾ cup	=	6 fl oz	=	180 ml
	16 tbls	= 1 cup	=	8 fl oz	=	240 ml
	1 pt	= 2 cups	=	16 fl oz	=	480 ml
	1 qt	= 4 cups	=	32 fl oz	=	960 ml
				33 fl oz	= 1000 ml	= 1 l

Dry Ingredients by Weight
(To convert ounces to grams, multiply the number of ounces by 30.)

1 oz	=	1/16 lb =	30 g
4 oz	=	¼ lb =	120 g
8 oz	=	½ lb =	240 g
12 oz	=	¾ lb =	360 g
16 oz	=	1 lb =	480 g

Length
(To convert inches to centimeters, multiply the number of inches by 2.5.)

1 in =			2.5 cm
6 in =	½ ft	=	15 cm
12 in =	1 ft	=	30 cm
36 in =	3 ft =	1 yd =	90 cm
40 in =			100 cm = 1 m

Cooking/Oven Temperatures

	Fahrenheit	Celsius	Gas Mark
Freeze Water	32° F	0° C	
Room Temperature	68° F	20° C	
Boil Water	212° F	100° C	
Bake	325° F	160° C	3
	350° F	180° C	4
	375° F	190° C	5
	400° F	200° C	6
	425° F	220° C	7
	450° F	230° C	8
Broil			Grill

index

Index

Index